**Strategic Management Model**

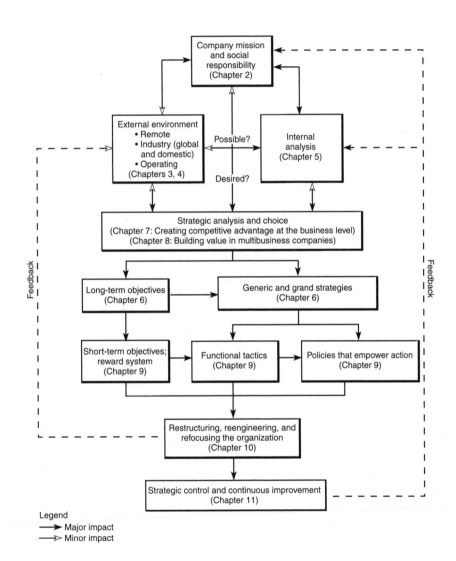

Legend
→ Major impact
⟶▷ Minor impact

# Strategic Management

# Strategic Management

**Formulation, Implementation, and Control**

Ninth Edition

John A. Pearce II

*College of Commerce and Finance*
*Villanova University*

Richard B. Robinson, Jr.

*Moore School of Business*
*University of South Carolina*

McGraw-Hill
Irwin

Boston   Burr Ridge, IL   Dubuque, IA   Madison, WI   New York   San Francisco   St. Louis
Bangkok   Bogotá   Caracas   Kuala Lumpur   Lisbon   London   Madrid   Mexico City
Milan   Montreal   New Delhi   Santiago   Seoul   Singapore   Sydney   Taipei   Toronto

The McGraw·Hill Companies

# McGraw-Hill
# Irwin

STRATEGIC MANAGEMENT: FORMULATION, IMPLEMENTATION, AND CONTROL

Published by McGraw-Hill/Irwin, a business unit of The McGraw-Hill Companies, Inc., 1221 Avenue of the Americas, New York, NY, 10020. Copyright © 2005, 2003, 2000, 1997, 1994, 1991, 1988, 1985, 1982 by The McGraw-Hill Companies, Inc. All rights reserved. No part of this publication may be reproduced or distributed in any form or by any means, or stored in a database or retrieval system, without the prior written consent of The McGraw-Hill Companies, Inc., including, but not limited to, in any network or other electronic storage or transmission, or broadcast for distance learning.

Some ancillaries, including electronic and print components, may not be available to customers outside the United States.

This book is printed on acid-free paper.

domestic       2 3 4 5 6 7 8 9 0 DOW/DOW 0 9 8 7 6 5
international   2 3 4 5 6 7 8 9 0 DOW/DOW 0 9 8 7 6 5

ISBN 0-07-289024-X

**Vice president and editor-in-chief:** *Robin J. Zwettler*
**Editorial director:** *John E. Biernat*
**Senior sponsoring editor:** *Andy Winston*
**Development editor:** *Natalie Ruffatto*
**Marketing manager:** *Lisa Nicks*
**Lead producer, Media technology:** *Victoria Parker*
**Project manager:** *Marlena Pechan*
**Senior production supervisor:** *Sesha Bolisetty*
**Freelance design coordinator:** *Kami Carter*
**Supplement producer:** *Matthew Perry*
**Senior digital content specialist:** *Brian Nacik*
**Cover design:** *Kiera Pohl*
**Typeface:** *10/12 Times New Roman*
**Compositor:** *Carlisle Communications, Ltd.*
**Printer:** *R. R. Donnelley*

**Library of Congress Cataloging-in-Publication Data**
Pearce, John A.
    Strategic management: formulation, implementation, and control/John A. Pearce II,
  Richard B. Robinson, Jr.—9th ed.
       p. cm.
    Includes access to a website; various other multimedia instructional reference tools are available to supplement the text.
    Includes bibliographical references and index.
    ISBN 0-07-289024-X (alk. paper)
    1. Strategic planning. I. Robinson, Richard B. (Richard Braden), 1947-II. Title.
HD30.28.P3395 2005
658.4'012—dc22

                                                2003065107

INTERNATIONAL EDITION ISBN 0-07-111215-4
Copyright © 2005. Exclusive rights by The McGraw-Hill Companies, Inc. for manufacture and export. This book cannot be re-exported from the country to which it is sold by McGraw-Hill. The International Edition is not available in North America.

www.mhhe.com

To Susan McCartney Pearce,
David Donham Pearce, Mark McCartney Pearce,
Katherine Elizabeth Robinson,
John Braden Robinson,
Chance Robinson—
for the love, joy, and vitality that they give to our lives.

# Preface

This ninth edition of *Strategic Management: Formulation, Implementation, and Control* is both the culmination of work by many people and a major revision designed to accommodate the needs of strategy students in the twenty-first century. These are exciting times and they are reflected on the many new developments in this book and the accompanying McGraw-Hill supplements. This preface describes what we have done to make the ninth edition uniquely effective in preparing students for strategic decisions in tomorrow's fast-paced global business arena. It also allows us the opportunity to recognize many outstanding contributors.

The ninth edition of *Strategic Management: Formulation, Implementation, and Control* is divided into 11 chapters that provide a thorough, state-of-the-art treatment of the critical business skills needed to plan and manage strategic activities. Each chapter has been filled with new, current real-world examples to illustrate concepts in companies that students recognize and regularly read about in the news around the world. Strategic ramifications of topics like executive compensation, E-commerce, the Internet, entrepreneurship, ethics, continuous improvement, virtual organization, cultural diversity, outsourcing, strategic alliances, and global competition can be found across several chapters. While the text continues a solid academic connection, students will find the text material to be practical, skills oriented, and relevant to their jobs.

We are excited and honored to be selected by *BusinessWeek* as its exclusive partner among strategic management textbooks. We were thrilled to have unlimited access to the world's best business publication to create examples, illustration modules, and various cases. The result is an extensively enhanced text and cases benefiting from hundreds of contemporary examples and illustrations provided by *BusinessWeek* writers worldwide. You will see *BusinessWeek's* impact on our discussion case feature, our Strategy in Action modules, our cases, and our website. Of course, we are also pleased with several hundred examples blended into the text material, which came from recent issues of *BusinessWeek* or www.businessweek.com.

## AN OVERVIEW OF OUR TEXT MATERIAL

The ninth edition uses a model of the strategic management process as the basis for the organization of the text material. Previous adopters have identified this model as a key distinctive competence for our text because it offers a logical flow, distinct elements, and an easy-to-understand guide to strategic management. The model has been modestly refined to reflect strategic analysis at different organizational levels as well as the importance of internal analysis in the strategic management process. The model and subsequent structure provide a student-friendly approach to the study of strategic management.

The first chapter provides an overview of the strategic management process and explains what students will find as they use this book. The remaining 10 chapters cover each part of the strategic management process and techniques that aid strategic analysis, decision making, implementation, and control. The literature and research in the strategic management area have developed at a rapid pace in recent years in both the academic and business press. This ninth edition includes several upgrades designed to incorporate major developments from both these sources. While we include cutting-edge concepts, we emphasize straight-forward, logical, and simple presentation so that students can grasp these new ideas without additional reading. The following are a few of the revisions that deserve particular note:

## Sarbanes-Oxley Act of 2002

Following the Enron bankruptcy and the wrongdoings of Worldcom executives, Washington lawmakers passed the Sarbanes-Oxley Act of 2002, which requires certifications for financial statements, new corporate regulations, disclosure requirements, and penalties for failure to comply. Chapter 2 provides in-depth coverage of the Act, including discussions of the provisions restricting the corporate control of executives, accounting firms, auditing committees, and attorneys. Also discussed is the restructuring of the governance structure of American corporations, including the heightened role of corporate internal auditors who now routinely deal directly with top corporate officials.

## Expanded Coverage of Social Responsibility

The ninth edition expands on it market-leading coverage of social responsibility. Principal perspectives are presented. A continuum of social responsibilities is discussed to help students differentiate among economic, legal, ethical, and discretionary social responsibilities. Arguments for and against social responsibility are explained. Numerous examples, drawn from recent headlines, appear in this section.

## A New Section on Management Ethics

Central to the belief that companies should be operated in a socially responsive way for the benefit of all stakeholders is the belief that managers will behave in an ethical manner. Thus planners often adopt a philosophical approach that can provide the basis for the consistency they seek. The utilitarian, moral rights, and social justice approaches are presented and explained in this new edition.

## The Value Disciplines

A new approach to generic strategy centers on delivering superior customer value through one of three value disciplines: operational excellence, customer intimacy, or product leadership. Companies that specialize in one of these disciplines, while simultaneously meeting industry standards in the other two, gain a sustainable lead in their markets. Chapter 6 provides details on these approaches with several examples of successful company experiences.

## Agency Theory

Of the recent approaches to corporate governance and strategic management, probably none has had a greater impact on managerial thinking than agency theory. While the breadth and measurement of its usefulness continue to be hotly debated, students of strategic management need to understand the role of agency in our free enterprise, capitalistic system. This edition presents agency theory in a coherent and practical manner. We believe that it arms students with a cutting-edge approach to increasing their understanding of the priorities of executive decision making and strategic control.

## Resource-Based View of the Firm

One of the most significant conceptual frameworks to systematize and "measure" a firm's strategic capabilities is the resource-based view (RBV) of the firm. The RBV has received major academic and business press attention during the last decade, helping to shape its value as a conceptual tool by adding rigor during the internal analysis and strategic analysis phases of the strategic management process. This edition provides a revised treatment of this concept in Chapter 5. We present the RBV in a logical and practical manner as a central underpinning of sound strategic analysis. Students will find several useful examples and a straightforward treatment of different types of "assets" and organizational capabilities culminating in the ability to determine when these resources create competitive advantage. They will see different ways to answer the question "what makes a resource valuable?" and be able to determine when that resource creates a competitive advantage in a systematic, disciplined, creative manner.

## Value Chain Analysis

Outsourcing is becoming a standard business practice in every facet of business operations. This trend enhances the usefulness of the value chain approach in strategic analysis. We have simplified our treatment of this useful conceptual framework and added several contemporary examples to enable students to quickly incorporate the value chain perspective into their strategic thinking process.

## Executive Compensation

While our text has led the field in providing a practice-oriented approach to strategic management, we have redoubled our efforts to treat topics with an emphasis on application. Our revised section on executive compensation in Chapter 9 is a clear example. You will find an extended discussion of executive bonus options that provides a comparison of the relative merits of the five most popular approaches, to include the current debate on the use, or overuse, of stock options and the need to accurately account for their true cost.

## Balanced Scoreboard

A recent evolution in the motivation that underpins strategic management is reflected in the adoption of the Balanced Scoreboard approach to corporate performance evaluation. While the maximization of shareholder wealth retains the top spot in executive priorities, the guideline is now widely accepted that strategic initiatives must produce favorable outcomes over a range of stakeholder objectives. We try to help our readers gain an appreciation for this perspective in our ninth edition.

## Bankruptcy

Many revisions in this book are driven by changes in business trends. Nowhere is that more evident than in our discussion of company bankruptcy. In the 1980s bankruptcy was treated as a last option that precluded any future for the firm. In the first decade of the 2000s the view has dramatically changed. Bankruptcy has been elevated to the status of a strategic option, and executives need to be well versed in its potentials and limitations, as you will see in Chapter 6.

## Strategic Analysis and Choice

We have divided the discussion of strategic analysis and choice into two chapters. Chapter 7 examines the single business setting. Chapter 8 looks at the multibusiness company and the diversification decision. We have provided extensive new coverage of the decision to diversify or not in Chapter 8. In addition to historical reviews of the portfolio and core competency approaches and their deficiencies, we include comprehensive ways to evaluate the role of the corporate parent in adding value, if any, beyond the sum of its businesses. And the concept of "patching," with its identification of "strategy as simple rules" to thrive in turbulent markets receives extensive coverage in this edition. The pages of *BusinessWeek* have helped us add numerous outstanding examples to these two chapters from business writers around the world. Samsung, Apple, Disney, Quanta, Hewlett-Packard, Delta, and Ryanair are just a few of the names students will quickly recognize in coverage that illustrates and helps them more easily understand how strategic analysis is conducted and choices made.

## Strategy Implementation

Chapter 9 focuses on reward systems, short-term objectives, and empowerment mechanisms as part of strategy implementation. Doing so allows students to move quickly into strategy implementation considerations from an executive perspective. At the same time we include in this edition an appendix containing approximately ten pages discussing various functional area tactics necessary to implement business strategy. Doing so serves as a convenient review of functional courses leading up to the capstone strategy class for instructors that prefer to do so.

## Structuring an Effective Organization

Chapter 10 provides a new perspective on the issue of organizational structure as a central mechanism for strategy implementation, particularly in larger companies. It explores three fundamental driving forces on contemporary organizational structure—globalization, the Internet, and speed. From this beginning, it covers research by academics and prominent business analysts to identify guidelines relevant to matching structure to strategy in the twenty-first century. Six contemporary guidelines to structuring an effective organization are explored in-depth providing students with useful conceptual tools to take into their postgraduation companies and contribute to specific structural challenges. A concise appendix is provided to Chapter 10 detailing the pros and cons of different basic organizational structures. It is included there rather than in the chapter to increase the readability and contemporary focus of the chapter material.

## Organizational Leadership

Chapter 10 has added coverage of outsourcing, virtual organizations, and the recruitment/development process as key contemporary considerations in building effective management teams. How to get and keep top management talent is an issue of critical importance examined in this new edition. The role that leadership and organizational culture has played in the impressive turnaround at P&G is explored in detail in the discussion case.

## Strategic Control and Continuous Improvement

Chapter 11 offers a major revision in our treatment of these topics. First, a reduced and concise treatment of four broad strategic controls used in the formulation and implementation phases of strategic management are discussed and illustrated. Second, the link between quality/continuous improvement initiatives and the strategic management process receive new, in-depth treatment in this chapter. ISO9004 and Six Sigma are examined as contemporary approaches to the continuous improvement of a company's value chain and a mechanism to guide strategic control. The experiences of several well-known companies in adopting these tools help illustrate their value in a comprehensive strategic management commitment. Finally, the increasingly popular use of the balanced scoreboard approach is explored in this chapter because of its value in supporting strategic control and continuous improvement.

# OUR STRATEGIC ALLIANCE WITH *BUSINESSWEEK*

Thanks to the leadership at McGraw-Hill and *BusinessWeek,* we have completed a strategic alliance of our own that benefits every professor and student who uses this book. Our book is *BusinessWeek*'s exclusive partner among strategic management textbooks in the collegiate market. We have long felt *BusinessWeek* to be the unquestionable leader among business periodicals for its coverage of strategic issues in businesses, industries, and economies worldwide. Personal surveys of collegiate faculty teaching strategic management confirmed our intuition: While there are many outstanding business magazines and new publications, none match the consistent quality found in *BusinessWeek* for the coverage of corporate strategies, case stories, and topics of interest to students and professors of strategic management.

Through this partnership, we get unconditional access to *BusinessWeek* material for this book and the use of their cutting-edge stories and topical coverage. From our point of view, this is a unique four-way win-win; teachers, students, authors, and *BusinessWeek* all stand to gain in many ways. The most direct way you can see the impact of the *BusinessWeek* alliance is in three book features: discussion cases, Strategy in Action modules, and *25* short cases.

## Strategy in Action Modules

Another pedagogical feature we pioneered, Strategy in Action modules, has become standard in most strategy books. Our strategic alliance with *BusinessWeek* lets us once again pioneer an innovation. We have drawn on the work of *BusinessWeek* field correspondents worldwide to fill over 60 new *BusinessWeek* Strategy in Action modules with short, hard-hitting current illustrations of key chapter topics. We are the only strategy book to have *BusinessWeek*–derived illustration modules, and we are energized by the excitement, interest, and practical illustration value our students tell us they provide.

## Short Cases

As professors of strategy management, we continually look for content or pedagogical developments or enhancements that make the strategy course more valuable. We have been concerned for some time about the length of cases typically available for classroom use. On the one hand, length often accommodates a breadth of information that in turn assures a class discussion that covers "all the bases." It even honors the professorial instruction we both experienced as students that "it is your job to extract the relevant information" from the lengthy case. The answer, we have long felt, is to have a blend of cases in terms of length. Some long cases are needed so that the professor can cover many issues within a company and allow for a truly comprehensive strategic analysis. Some shorter cases also play a role by facilitating a focus on one incident, or allow for a discussion of only 20 to 30 minutes so that the case topic can be used in concert with other materials, or provide a springboard for discussion of "real time" situations, perhaps supplemented by website and Internet-derived information. These short cases generate useful class discussions while allowing coverage of other material during the case portion of the course or as a supplement and source of variety during the text portion of the course. We think you will find it useful. We have included 25 such cases in the ninth edition while continuing to include 25 longer cases.

# CASES IN THE NINTH EDITION

We are pleased to offer 50 excellent cases in this edition. As noted above, these include 25 comprehensive cases and industry notes that adopters expect in a strategic management textbook. The remaining 25 cases are short cases built on solidly developed *BusinessWeek* articles from the most recent editions of that magazine. Both sets of cases present companies, industries, and situations that are easily recognized, current, and interesting. We have a good mixture of small and large firms, start-ups and industry leaders, global and domestically focused companies, and service, retail, manufacturing, technology, and diversified activities.

Students will feel comfortable with our cases about AOL-Time Warner, Avon, BMW, BP, Expedia, Ford, GE, Honda, Linux, Merrill Lynch, Microsoft, Mitsubishi, Motorola, NFL, Nucor, Perdue, Qualcomm, Samsung, Siebel, Southwest, VW, and Yahoo! They will also have the opportunity to learn about global aspects of strategic management by studying the Cuban Cigar Industry, Huxley Maquiladora in Mexico, Citigroup in Post-WTO China, Eli Lilly & Co in global pharmaceuticals, and IBM in the global computer services industry. We have also included smaller firms that rely on their entrepreneurial strength, including TiVo, Treo, and the LASIK eye surgery industry.

Students get to examine numerous industry situations through this 50-set case selection including the personal computer, telecom, retailing, electric vehicles, music, and global products and services industries. There are also several opportunities to incorporate the Internet's evolution and the strategic implications within several industries and implications facing specific companies.

## OUR WEBSITE

A substantial website has been designed to aid your use of this book. It includes areas accessible only to instructors and areas specifically designed to assist students. The instructor section includes downloadable supplements, which keep your work area less cluttered and let you quickly obtain information. *BusinessWeek* provides access to the article archives through the instructor website. The site offers an elaborate array of linkages to company websites and other sources that you might find useful in your course preparation. The student resources section of the website provides interactive discussion groups where students and groups using the book may interact with other students around the world doing the same thing. Students are provided company and related business periodical (and other) website linkages to aid and expedite their case research and preparation efforts. Practice quizzes and tests are provided to help students prepare for tests on the text material and attempt to lower their anxiety in that regard. Access to *BusinessWeek* articles that update the cases and key illustration modules in the book are provided. We expect students will find the website useful and interesting. Please visit us at www.mhhe.com/pearce9e.

## SUPPLEMENTS

Components of our teaching package include a revised, comprehensive instructor's manual, test bank, PowerPoint presentation, and a computerized test bank. These are all available to qualified adopters of the text.

Professors can also choose between two simulation games as a possible package with this text: The International Business Management Decision Simulation (McDonald/Neelankavil), or the Business Strategy Game (Thompson/Stappenbeck).

• The International Business Management Decision Simulation is also a Windows-based simulation that provides an international business analysis and plan simulation allowing students to create multinational business plans and compete with other student groups. Fifteen countries representing three regions of the world along with four product categories are included in the simulation. Students assess business plans by using the financial reports contained in the simulation.

- The Business Strategy Game provides an exercise to help students understand how the functional pieces of a business fit together. Students will work with the numbers, explore options, and try to unite production, marketing, finance, and human resource decisions into a coherent strategy.

# ACKNOWLEDGMENTS

We have benefited from the help of many people in the evolution of this project over nine editions. Students, adopters, colleagues, reviewers, and business contacts have provided hundreds of insightful comments, suggestions, and contributions that have progressively enhanced this book and its supplements. We are indebted to the researchers and practicing managers who have accelerated the development of the literature on strategic management.

We are particularly indebted to the talented case researchers who have produced the cases used in this book, as well as to case researchers dedicated to the revitalization of case research as an important academic endeavor. First-class case research is a major avenue through which top strategic management scholars should be recognized.

The development of this book through nine editions has benefited from the generous commitments of time, energy, and ideas from the following colleagues. The valuable ideas, recommendations, and support from these outstanding scholars, teachers, and practitioners have added quality to this book (we apologize if affiliations have changed):

Mary Ackenhusen
*INSEAD*

A. J. Almaney
*DePaul University*

James Almeida
*Fairleigh Dickinson University*

B. Alpert
*San Francisco State University*

Alan Amason
*University of Georgia*

Sonny Aries
*University of Toledo*

Katherine A. Auer
*The Pennsylvania State University*

Amy Vernberg Beekman
*University of Tampa*

Patricia Bilafer
*Bentley College*

Robert Earl Bolick
*Metropolitan State University*

Bill Boulton
*Auburn University*

Charles Boyd
*Southwest Missouri State University*

Jeff Bracker
*University of Louisville*

Dorothy Brawley
*Kennesaw State College*

James W. Bronson
*Washington State University*

Eric Brown
*George Mason University*

Robert F. Bruner
*INSEAD*

William Burr
*University of Oregon*

Gene E. Burton
*California State University–Fresno*

Edgar T. Busch
*Western Kentucky University*

Charles M. Byles
*Virginia Commonwealth University*

Jim Callahan
*University of LaVerne*

James W. Camerius
*Northern Michigan University*

Richard Castaldi
*San Francisco State University*

Gary J. Castogiovanni
*Louisiana State University*

Jafor Chowdbury
*University of Scranton*

James J. Chrisman
*University of Calgary*

Neil Churchill
*INSEAD*

J. Carl Clamp
*University of South Carolina*

Earl D. Cooper
*Florida Institute of Technology*

Louis Coraggio
*Troy State University*

Jeff Covin
*Indiana University*

John P. Cragin
*Oklahoma Baptist University*

Larry Cummings
*Northwestern University*

Peter Davis
*University of Memphis*

William Davis
*Auburn University*

Julio DeCastro
*University of Colorado*

Kim DeDee
*University of Wisconsin*

Philippe Demigne
*INSEAD*

D. Keith Denton
*Southwest Missouri State University*

F. Derakhshan
*California State University–San Bernardino*

Brook Dobni
*University of Saskatchewan*

Mark Dollinger
*Indiana University*

Jean–Christopher Donck
*INSEAD*

Max E. Douglas
*Indiana State University*

Yves Doz
*INSEAD*

Julie Driscoll
*Bentley College*

Derrick Dsouza
*University of North Texas*

Thomas J. Dudley
*Pepperdine University*

John Dunkelberg
*Wake Forest University*

Soumitra Dutta
*INSEAD*

Harold Dyck
*California State University*

Norbert Esser
*Central Wesleyan College*

Forest D. Etheredge
*Aurora University*

Liam Fahey
*Babson College*

Mary Fandel
*Bentley College*

Mark Fiegener
*University of Washington–Tacoma*

Calvin D. Fowler
*Embry-Riddle Aeronautical University*

Debbie Francis
*Jacksonville State University*

Elizabeth Freeman
*Southern Methodist University*

Mahmound A. Gaballa
*Mansfield University*

Donna M. Gallo
*Boston College*

Diane Garsombke
*Brenau University*

Betsy Gatewood
*Indiana University*

Bertrand George
*INSEAD*

Michael Geringer
*Southern Methodist University*

Manton C. Gibbs
*Indiana University of Pennsylvania*

Nicholas A. Glaskowsky, Jr.
*University of Miami*

Tom Goho
*Wake Forest University*

Jon Goodman
*University of Southern California*

Pradeep Gopalakrishna
*Hofstra University*

R. H. Gordon
*Hofstra University*

Barbara Gottfried
*Bentley College*

Peter Goulet
*University of Northern Iowa*

Walter E. Greene
*University of Texas–Pan American*

Sue Greenfeld
*California State University–San Bernardino*

David W. Grigsby
*Clemson University*

Daniel E. Hallock
*St. Edward's University*

Don Hambrick
*Pennsylvania State University*

Barry Hand
*Indiana State University*

Jean M. Hanebury
*Texas A&M University*

Karen Hare
*Bentley College*

Earl Harper
*Grand Valley State University*

Samuel Hazen
*Tarleton State University*

W. Harvey Hegarty
*Indiana University*

Edward A. Hegner
*California State University–Sacramento*

Marilyn M. Helms
*Dalton State College*

Lanny Herron
*University of Baltimore*

D. Higginbothan
*University of Missouri*

Roger Higgs
*Western Carolina University*

William H. Hinkle
*Johns Hopkins University*

Charles T. Hofer
*University of Georgia*

Alan N. Hoffman
*Bentley College*

Richard Hoffman
*Salisbury University*

Eileen Hogan
*Kutztown University*

Phyllis G. Holland
*Valdosta State University*

Gary L. Holman
*St. Martin's College*

Don Hopkins
*Temple University*

Cecil Horst
*Keller Graduate School of Management*

Mel Horwitch
*Theseus*

Henry F. House
*Auburn University–Montgomery*

William C. House
*University of Arkansas–Fayetteville*

Frank Hoy
*University of Texas–El Paso*

Warren Huckabay
*Sammamish, WA*

Eugene H. Hunt
*Virginia Commonwealth University*

Tammy G. Hunt
*University of North Carolina–Wilmington*

John W. Huonker
*University of Arizona*

Stephen R. Jenner
*California State University*

Shailendra Jha
*Wilfrid Laurier University–Ontario*

C. Boyd Johnson
*California State University–Fresno*

Troy Jones
*University of Central Florida*

Jon Kalinowski
*Mankato State University*

Al Kayloe
*Lake Erie College*

Michael J. Keefe
*Southwest Texas State University*

Kay Keels
*Brenau University*

James A. Kidney
*Southern Connecticut State University*

John D. King
*Embry-Riddle Aeronautical University*

Raymond M. Kinnunen
*Northeastern University*

John B. Knauff
*University of St. Thomas*

Rose Knotts
*University of North Texas*

Dan Kopp
*Southwest Missouri State University*

Michael Koshuta
*Valparaiso University*

Jeffrey A. Krug
*The University of Illinois*

Myroslaw Kyj
*Widener University of Pennsylvania*

Dick LaBarre
*Ferris State University*

Joseph Lampel
*City University–London*

Ryan Lancaster
*The University of Phoenix*

Sharon Ungar Lane
*Bentley College*

Roland Larose
*Bentley College*

Anne T. Lawrence
*San Jose State University*

Joseph Leonard
*Miami University–Ohio*

Robert Letovsky
*Saint Michael's College*

Michael Levy
*INSEAD*

Benjamin Litt
*Lehigh University*

Frank S. Lockwood
*Western Carolina University*

John Logan
*University of South Carolina*

Sandra Logan
*Newberry College*

Jean M. Lundin
*Lake Superior State University*

Rodney H. Mabry
*Clemson University*

Donald C. Malm
*University of Missouri–St. Louis*

Charles C. Manz
*University of Massachusetts*

John Maurer
*Wayne State University*

Denise Mazur
*Aquinas College*

Edward McClelland
*Roanoke College*

Bob McDonald
*Central Wesleyan College*

Patricia P. McDougall
*Indiana University*

S. Mehta
*San Jose State University*

Ralph Melaragno
*Pepperdine University*

Richard Merner
*University of Delaware*

Linda Merrill
*Bentley College*

Timothy Mescon
*Kennesaw State College*

Philip C. Micka
*Park College*

Bill J. Middlebrook
*Southwest Texas State University*

Robert Mockler
*St. John's University*

James F. Molly, Jr.
*Northeastern University*

Cynthia Montgomery
*Harvard University*

W. Kent Moore
*Valdosta State University*

Jaideep Motwani
*Grand Valley State University*

Karen Mullen
*Bentley College*

Gary W. Muller
*Hofstra University*

Terry Muson
*Northern Montana College*

Daniel Muzyka
*INSEAD*

Stephanie Newell
*Eastern Michigan University*

Michael E. Nix
*Trinity College of Vermont*

Kenneth Olm
*University of Texas–Austin*

Benjamin M. Oviatt
*Georgia State University*

Joseph Paolillo
*University of Mississippi*

Gerald Parker
*St. Louis University*

Paul J. Patinka
*University of Colorado*

James W. Pearce
*Western Carolina University*

Michael W. Pitts
*Virginia Commonwealth University*

Douglas Polley
*St. Cloud State University*

Carlos de Pommes
*Theseus*

Valerie J. Porciello
*Bentley College*

Mark S. Poulous
*St. Edward's University*

John B. Pratt
*Saint Joseph's College*

Oliver Ray Price
*West Coast University*

John Primus
*Golden Gate University*

Norris Rath
*Shepard College*

Paula Rechner
*California State University–Fresno*

Richard Reed
*Washington State University*

J. Bruce Regan
*University of St. Thomas*

H. Lee Remmers
*INSEAD*

F. A. Ricci
*Georgetown University*

Keith Robbins
*Winthrop University*

Gary Roberts
*Kennesaw State College*

Lloyd E. Roberts
*Mississippi College*

John K. Ross III
*Southwest Texas State University*

George C. Rubenson
*Salisbury State University*

Alison Rude
*Bentley College*

Les Rue
*Georgia State University*

Carol Rugg
*Bentley College*

J. A. Ruslyk
*Memphis State University*

Ronald J. Salazar
*Human Skills Management, LLC*

Bill Sandberg
*University of South Carolina*

Uri Savoray
*INSEAD*

Jack Scarborough
*Barry University*

Paul J. Schlachter
*Florida International University*

David Schweiger
*University of South Carolina*

John Seeger
*Bentley College*

Martin Shapiro
*Iona College*

Arthur Sharplin
*McNeese State University*

Frank M. Shipper
*Salisbury State University*

Rodney C. Shrader
*University of Illinois*

Lois Shufeldt
*Southwest Missouri State University*

Bonnie Silvieria
*Bentley College*

F. Bruce Simmons III
*The University of Akron*

Mark Simon
*Oakland University*

Michael Skipton
*Memorial University*

Fred Smith
*Western Illinois University*

Scott Snell
*Michigan State University*

Coral R. Snodgrass
*Canisius College*

Rudolph P. Snowadzky
*University of Maine*

Neil Snyder
*University of Virginia*

Melvin J. Stanford
*Mankato State University*

Romuald A. Stone
*DeVry University*

Warren S. Stone
*Virginia Commonwealth University*

Ram Subramanian
*Grand Valley State University*

Paul M. Swiercz
*George Washington University*

Robert L. Swinth
*Montana State University*

Chris Taubman
*INSEAD*

Russell Teasley
*University of South Carolina*

James Teboul
*INSEAD*

George H. Tompson
*University of Tampa*

Melanie Trevino
*University of Texas–El Paso*

Howard Tu
*University of Memphis*

Craig Tunwall
*Empire State College*

Elaine M. Tweedy
*University of Scranton*

Arieh A. Ullmann
*Binghamton University*

P. Veglahn
*James Madison University*

George Vozikis
*University of Tulsa*

William Waddell
*California State University–Los Angeles*

Bill Warren
*College of William and Mary*

Kirby Warren
*Columbia University*

Steven J. Warren
*Rutgers University*

Michael White
*University of Tulsa*

Randy White
*Auburn University*

Sam E. White
*Portland State University*

Frank Winfrey
*Lyon College*

Joseph Wolfe
*Experiential Adventures*

Robley Wood
*Virginia Commonwealth University*

Edward D. Writh, Jr.
*Florida Institute of Technology*

John Young
*University of New Mexico*

S. David Young
*INSEAD*

Jan Zahrly
*Old Dominion University*

Alan Zeiber
*Portland State University*

We are affiliated with two separate universities, both of which provide environments that deserve thanks. As the Endowed Chair of the College of Commerce and Finance at Villanova University, Jack is able to combine his scholarly and teaching activities with his coauthorship of this text. He is grateful to Villanova University and his colleagues for the support and encouragement they provide.

Richard appreciates the support provided within the Moore School of Business by Mr. Dean Kress. Mr. Kress provides multifaceted assistance on projects, classes, and research that leverages the scope of what can be accomplished each year. Moore School colleagues in the management department along with Dean Joel Smith and Program Director Brian Klass provide encouragement while staff members Cheryl Fowler, Susie Gorsage, and Carol Lucas provide logistical support for which Richard is grateful.

Leadership from Irwin/McGraw-Hill deserves our utmost thanks and appreciation. Gerald Saykes got us started and continues his support. Andy Winston's editorial leadership has enhanced our quality and success. Editorial and production assistance from Natalie Ruffatto helped this to become a much better book. The Irwin/McGraw-Hill field organization deserves particular recognition and thanks for the success of this project.

We also want to thank *BusinessWeek,* which is proving to be an excellent strategic partner.

We hope that you will find our book and ancillaries all that you expect. We welcome your ideas and recommendations about our material. Please contact us at the following addresses:

Dr. John A. Pearce II
College of Commerce and Finance
Villanova University
Villanova, PA 19085-1678
610-519-4332
john.pearce@villanova.edu

Dr. Richard Robinson
Moore School of Business
University of South Carolina
Columbia, SC 29205
803-777-5961
Robinson@sc.edu

We wish you the utmost success in teaching and studying strategic management.

*Jack Pearce and Richard Robinson*

# About the Authors

**John A. Pearce II, Ph.D.,** holds the Endowed Chair in Strategic Management and Entrepreneurship at Villanova University. In 2004, he was the Distinguished Visiting Professor at ITAM in Mexico City. Previously, Professor Pearce was the Eakin Endowed Chair in Strategic Management at George Mason University and a State of Virginia Eminent Scholar. He received the 1994 Fulbright U.S. Professional Award, which he served at INTAN in Malaysia. Dr. Pearce has taught at Penn State University, West Virginia University, the University of Malta as the Fulbright Senior Professor in International Management, and at the University of South Carolina where he was Director of Ph.D. Programs in Strategic Management. He received a Ph.D. degree in Business Administration and Strategic Management from the Pennsylvania State University.

Professor Pearce is coauthor of 36 books and has authored more than 250 articles and refereed professional papers. The articles have appeared in journals that include *Academy of Management Executive, Academy of Management Journal, Academy of Management Review, Business Horizons, California Management Review, Journal of Applied Psychology, Journal of Business Venturing, Long-Range Planning, Organizational Dynamics, Sloan Management Review,* and *Strategic Management Journal.* Several of these publications have resulted from Professor Pearce's work as a principal on research projects funded for more than $2 million. He is a widely recognized expert in the field of strategic management, with special accomplishments in the areas of strategic planning and management, including strategy formulation, implementation, and control, mission statement development, environmental assessment, industry analysis, and tools for strategy evaluation and selection.

Professor Pearce is the recipient of several awards in recognition of his accomplishments in teaching, research, scholarship, and professional service, including three Outstanding Paper Awards from the Academy of Management and the 2003 Villanova University Outstanding Faculty Research Award. A frequent leader of executive development programs and an active consultant to business and industry, Dr. Pearce's client list includes domestic and multinational firms engaged in manufacturing and service industries.

**Richard B. Robinson, Jr., Ph.D.,** is the Business Partnership Foundation Fellow in Strategic Management and Entrepreneurship in the Moore School of Business, University of South Carolina. He also serves as Director of the Faber Entrepreneurship Center at USC and Assistant Director of the Center for Manufacturing and Technology in USC's College of Engineering and Information Technology. Dr. Robinson received his Ph.D. in Business Administration from the University of Georgia. He graduated from Georgia Tech in Industrial Management.

Professor Robinson has coauthored over 30 books addressing strategic management and entrepreneurship issues that students and managers use worldwide. He has authored over 300 articles, professional papers, and case studies that have been published in major journals including the *Academy of Management Journal, Academy of Management Review, Strategic Management Journal, Academy of Entrepreneurship Journal,* and the *Journal of Business Venturing.*

Dr. Robinson has previously held executive positions with companies in the pulp and paper, hazardous waste, building products, lodging, and restaurant industries. He currently serves as a director or adviser to entrepreneurial companies that are global leaders in niche markets in the log home, building products, animation, and computer chip thermal management industries. Dr. Robinson also supervises over 50 student teams each year that undertake field consulting projects and internships with entrepreneurial companies worldwide.

# Brief Contents

# Contents

# Strategic Management

# Overview of Strategic Management

The first chapter of this book introduces strategic management, the set of decisions and actions that result in the design and activation of strategies to achieve the objectives of an organization. The chapter provides an overview of the nature, benefits, and terminology of and the need for strategic management. Subsequent chapters provide greater detail.

The first major section of Chapter 1, "The Nature and Value of Strategic Management," emphasizes the practical value and benefits of strategic management for a firm. It also distinguishes between a firm's strategic decisions and its other planning tasks.

The section stresses the key point that strategic management activities are undertaken at three levels: corporate, business, and functional. The distinctive characteristics of strategic decision making at each of these levels affect the impact of activities at these levels on company operations. Other topics dealt with in this section are the value of formality in strategic management and the alignment of strategy makers in strategy formulation and implementation. The section concludes with a review of the planning research on business, which demonstrates that the use of strategic management processes yields financial and behavioral benefits that justify their costs.

The second major section of Chapter 1 presents a model of the strategic management process. The model, which will serve as an outline for the remainder of the text, describes approaches currently used by strategic planners. Its individual components are carefully defined and explained, as is the process for integrating them into the strategic management process. The section ends with a discussion of the model's practical limitations and the advisability of tailoring the recommendations made to actual business situations.

# Chapter **One**

# Strategic Management

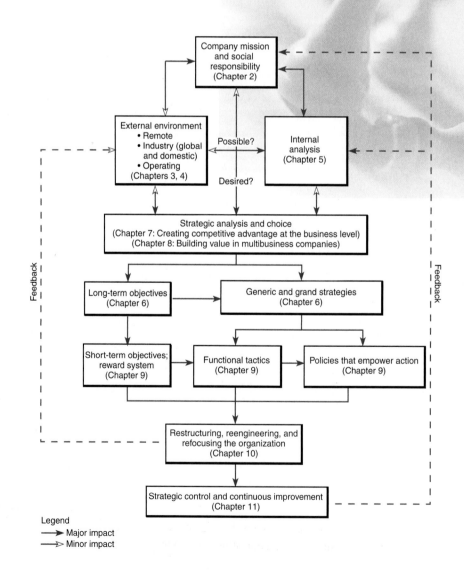

Legend
→ Major impact
⇢ Minor impact

# THE NATURE AND VALUE OF STRATEGIC MANAGEMENT

Managing activities internal to the firm is only part of the modern executive's responsibilities. The modern executive also must respond to the challenges posed by the firm's immediate and remote external environments. The immediate external environment includes competitors, suppliers, increasingly scarce resources, government agencies and their ever more numerous regulations, and customers whose preferences often shift inexplicably. The remote external environment comprises economic and social conditions, political priorities, and technological developments, all of which must be anticipated, monitored, assessed, and incorporated into the executive's decision making. However, the executive often is compelled to subordinate the demands of the firm's internal activities and external environment to the multiple and often inconsistent requirements of its stakeholders: owners, top managers, employees, communities, customers, and country. To deal effectively with everything that affects the growth and profitability of a firm, executives employ management processes that they feel will position it optimally in its competitive environment by maximizing the anticipation of environmental changes and of unexpected internal and competitive demands.

Broad-scope, large-scale management processes became dramatically more sophisticated after World War II. These processes responded to increases in the size and number of competing firms; to the expanded role of government as a buyer, seller, regulator, and competitor in the free enterprise system; and to greater business involvement in international trade. Perhaps the most significant improvement in management processes came in the 1970s, when "long-range planning," "new venture management," "planning, programming, budgeting," and "business policy" were blended. At the same time, increased emphasis was placed on environmental forecasting and external considerations in formulating and implementing plans. This all-encompassing approach is known as strategic management.

*Strategic management* is defined as the set of decisions and actions that result in the formulation and implementation of plans designed to achieve a company's objectives. It comprises nine critical tasks:

1. Formulate the company's mission, including broad statements about its purpose, philosophy, and goals.

2. Conduct an analysis that reflects the company's internal conditions and capabilities.

3. Assess the company's external environment, including both the competitive and the general contextual factors.

4. Analyze the company's options by matching its resources with the external environment.

5. Identify the most desirable options by evaluating each option in light of the company's mission.

6. Select a set of long-term objectives and grand strategies that will achieve the most desirable options.

7. Develop annual objectives and short-term strategies that are compatible with the selected set of long-term objectives and grand strategies.

8. Implement the strategic choices by means of budgeted resource allocations in which the matching of tasks, people, structures, technologies, and reward systems is emphasized.

9. Evaluate the success of the strategic process as an input for future decision making.

As these nine tasks indicate, strategic management involves the planning, directing, organizing, and controlling of a company's strategy-related decisions and actions. By *strategy,* managers mean their large-scale, future-oriented plans for interacting with the competitive environment to achieve company objectives. A strategy is a company's game plan. Although that plan does not precisely detail all future deployments (of people, finances, and material), it does provide a framework for managerial decisions. A strategy reflects a company's awareness of how, when, and where it should compete; against whom it should compete; and for what purposes it should compete.

## Dimensions of Strategic Decisions

What decisions facing a business are strategic and therefore deserve strategic management attention? Typically, strategic issues have the following dimensions.

***Strategic Issues Require Top-Management Decisions***   Since strategic decisions overarch several areas of a firm's operations, they require top-management involvement. Usually only top management has the perspective needed to understand the broad implications of such decisions and the power to authorize the necessary resource allocations. As top manager of Volvo GM Heavy Truck Corporation, Karl-Erling Trogen, president, wanted to push the company closer to the customer by overarching operations with service and customer relations empowering the workforce closest to the customer with greater knowledge and authority. This strategy called for a major commitment to the parts and service end of the business where customer relations was first priority. Trogen's philosophy was to so empower the workforce that more operating questions were handled on the line where workers worked directly with customers. He believed that the corporate headquarters should be more focused on strategic issues, such as engineering, production, quality, and marketing.

***Strategic Issues Require Large Amounts of the Firm's Resources***   Strategic decisions involve substantial allocations of people, physical assets, or moneys that either must be redirected from internal sources or secured from outside the firm. They also commit the firm to actions over an extended period. For these reasons, they require substantial resources. Whirlpool Corporation's "Quality Express" product delivery program exemplified a strategy that required a strong financial and personnel commitment from the company. The plan was to deliver products to customers when, where, and how they wanted them. This proprietary service uses contract logistics strategy to deliver Whirlpool, Kitchen Aid, Roper, and Estate brand appliances to 90 percent of the company's dealer and builder customers within 24 hours and to the other 10 percent within 48 hours. In highly competitive service-oriented businesses, achieving and maintaining customer satisfaction frequently involve a commitment from every facet of the organization.

***Strategic Issues Often Affect the Firm's Long-Term Prosperity***   Strategic decisions ostensibly commit the firm for a long time, typically five years; however, the impact of such decisions often lasts much longer. Once a firm has committed itself to a particular strategy, its image and competitive advantages usually are tied to that strategy. Firms become known in certain markets, for certain products, with certain technologies. They would jeopardize their previous gains if they shifted from these markets, products, or technologies by adopting a radically different strategy. Thus, strategic decisions have enduring effects on firms—for better or worse. Exhibit 1–1, Strategy in Action, provides an example of a problem that can arise. Commerce One created an alliance with SAP in 1999 to improve its position in the e-marketplace for B2B business. After taking three years to ready its e-portals, Commerce One and SAP were ready to take on the market in 2002. Unfortunately, the market changed. The "foolproof strategy" got to the market too late and the alliance failed.

**BusinessWeek** Commerce One's (CMRC) breakthrough came in the old-economy bastion of Detroit. In October of 1999, General Motors (GM) procurement chief Harold R. Kutner staged a bake-off between Commerce One and software giant Oracle for the right to power GM's e-marketplace. The car maker set harsh terms. It wanted stock in the tech companies, and it wouldn't pay for software or services. Oracle refused to play by those rules.

At first, Commerce One's CEO Mark Hoffman also recoiled. But while taking a shower at home in California a day after hearing GM's ultimatum, he realized that running its trading exchange could set Commerce One up for huge transaction fees. He decided it was worth the gamble, so he agreed to negotiate on those terms. They struck a deal.

The GM deal set off a business bonanza that made Commerce One the fastest-growing Nasdaq company—ever. It signed up dozens of e-marketplaces, from aerospace to wood products. And at the peak, customers even competed with one another to land it as their supplier. After logging just $33.6 million in sales in 1999, Commerce One racked up $401 million in 2000, and was on a pace to double that in 2001.

Even while Commerce One was riding high, Hoffman fretted. At a brainstorming session at the Walnut Creek Marriott in January 2000, he worried about a new alliance between Ariba, IBM, and supply-chain software maker i2 Technologies (ITWO). Commerce One needed a strong partner that would lend it credence in giant corporations that were more comfortable buying software from the likes of IBM. SAP, the king of corporate software, looked like the best choice.

Hoffman called SAP Co-CEO Hasso Plattner. By June the two companies had a deal. They would combine their engineering teams to deliver a new set of products and then unleash their sales teams on corporate America. No two technology companies had ever tried to combine forces so thoroughly—short of merging. The coupling brought Commerce One instant credibility and nearly $500 million in cash.

By the end of 2000, Commerce One's fortunes were soaring. The company boasted 567 customers and 157 e-marketplaces. Everybody there got a taste of riches. Rank-and-file employees saw their stock options grow to be worth hundreds of thousands of dollars. Top salespeople became ridiculously wealthy. And customers and partners shared in the bounty.

The problem was, it didn't get any better than that. In the first quarter of 2001, demand began to taper off. Revenues of $170 million were down 10 percent from the previous quarter. What went wrong? A bunch of things. Some of the early e-marketplaces took many months to get going, partly because of problems with the technology but mainly because the industry consortiums that formed the e-marketplaces had trouble getting coordinated.

Then the slow economy put the brakes on all kinds of technology spending. "People were buying vision in 2000. When the new products from Commerce One and SAP were ready to conquer the world in early 2001, the world had changed. E-marketplace software was no longer in demand."

The team eventually retooled the products to handle private e-marketplaces, where individual corporations would interact with their suppliers. But that fell flat too. And so did Commerce One's revenues, dropping to $101.25 million in the second quarter of 2001—roughly half of their peak.

By then, Commerce One's fate was totally entangled with SAP. The U.S. company had spent a year focusing its 400 engineers on combining its technology with SAP's e-commerce applications. Commerce One had bet everything on the SAP relationship and had let its e-procurement software slip. It wasn't competitive anymore as a stand-alone company. So when Plattner proposed merger talks during an August 10, 2001, lunch at SAP's Silicon Valley offices, Hoffman put aside his dreams of building an independent software powerhouse and said yes.

Undoing the SAP relationship practically ruined Commerce One. The deal fell through a couple of weeks after the September 11 terror attacks. Plattner, who had forged the alliance with Hoffman and was loath to give up on it, got a backchannel call from a board member. "They pre-preempted it. They asked me not to spend any more money on Commerce One," says Plattner.

Breaking up was extremely hard to do. The companies' products were thoroughly integrated with one another, and they were pushing a single e-marketplace package. Because most major corporations already had relationships with SAP, many of the new deals were written as addenda to existing SAP contracts. Now, though they maintained a marketing partnership, most of their relationship had to be unwound.

At the same time, SAP started warning corporations that they had better play it safe and buy technology from big, stable suppliers—undercutting Commerce One. Hoffman had learned the hard way to avoid intertangling alliances.

**Source:** Excerpted from Steve Hamm, Online Extra. "From Hot to Scorched at Commerce One," *BusinessWeek,* February 3, 2003.

**BusinessWeek** The hearty appetite for fancy German metal has Toyota Motor Co. (TM) spooked. "Higher-priced sedans are a traditional base of strength for Toyota," says Yasuhiko Fukatsu, managing director for domestic luxury sales. "But BMW and Mercedes-Benz are doing a better job attracting younger buyers." Toyota also is increasingly worried about a resurgent Nissan Motor Co. (NSANY), which is staging a comeback in the sedan niche.

Toyota's answer: Run its rivals off the road. To do so, it is unleashing on Japan a dozen-plus new or improved vehicles. Besides updating such midrange standbys as the Camry, Toyota is bulking up on eye-candy luxury models, most of which sell for $30,000 to $60,000. Among them: fully loaded versions of the muscular and decidedly BMW-ish Verossa, the remodeled Lexus ES 300 (known in Japan as the Windom), and a Mercedes-like sedan called the Brevis. Toyota is even debating marketing cars at home under the Lexus badge, which now exists only overseas.

Aging customers are a problem for Toyota everywhere, but nowhere more than in Japan. Most of the folks buying such luxury Toyota sedans as the best-selling Crown are graying executives who started out with entry-level Toyotas in the 1950s and 1960s. By contrast, upwardly mobile Japanese wouldn't be caught dead in a Crown, a $30,000 sedan often used as a taxi. Consider Shunsuke Kurita, a 46-year-old interior designer who drives a black 1999 BMW 318i. "It's a status symbol more than anything else, but I figure a BMW has better resale value than domestic cars," he says. "Toyota sedans have a fuddy-duddy image."

Still, why all the fuss? After all, foreign imports account for less than 10 percent of the Japanese auto market. Well, what worries Toyota is that up-and-coming Japanese drivers will develop the kind of loyalty to their German imports that their parents had to Toyota. Were that to happen, Toyota could lose out on future sales to drivers now in their late thirties and early forties.

**Source:** Extracted from C. Dawson, "Toyota: Taking on BMW," *BusinessWeek,* July 30, 2001.

Exhibit 1–2, Global Strategy in Action, is a *BusinessWeek* excerpt that provides an excellent example of a firm's strategy tied to its image and competitive advantage. For years, Toyota had a successful strategy of marketing its sedans in Japan. With this strategy came an image, a car for an older customer, and a competitive advantage, a traditional base for Toyota. The strategy was effective, but as its customer base grew older its strategy remained unchanged. A younger customer market saw the image as unattractive and began to seek out other manufacturers. Toyota's strategic task in foreign markets is to formulate and implement a strategy that will reignite interest in its image.

***Strategic Issues Are Future Oriented*** Strategic decisions are based on what managers forecast, rather than on what they know. In such decisions, emphasis is placed on the development of projections that will enable the firm to select the most promising strategic options. In the turbulent and competitive free enterprise environment, a firm will succeed only if it takes a proactive (anticipatory) stance toward change.

***Strategic Issues Usually Have Multifunctional or Multibusiness Consequences*** Strategic decisions have complex implications for most areas of the firm. Decisions about such matters as customer mix, competitive emphasis, or organizational structure necessarily involve a number of the firm's strategic business units (SBUs), divisions, or program units. All of these areas will be affected by allocations or reallocations of responsibilities and resources that result from these decisions.

***Strategic Issues Require Considering the Firm's External Environment*** All business firms exist in an open system. They affect and are affected by external conditions that are largely beyond their control. Therefore, to successfully position a firm in competitive situations, its strategic managers must look beyond its operations. They must consider what relevant others (e.g., competitors, customers, suppliers, creditors, government, and labor) are likely to do.

### Three Levels of Strategy

The decision-making hierarchy of a firm typically contains three levels. At the top of this hierarchy is the corporate level, composed principally of a board of directors and the chief executive and administrative officers. They are responsible for the firm's financial performance and for the achievement of nonfinancial goals, such as enhancing the firm's image and fulfilling its social responsibilities. To a large extent, attitudes at the corporate level reflect the concerns of stockholders and society at large. In a multibusiness firm, corporate-level executives determine the businesses in which the firm should be involved. They also set objectives and formulate strategies that span the activities and functional areas of these businesses. Corporate-level strategic managers attempt to exploit their firm's distinctive competencies by adopting a portfolio approach to the management of its businesses and by developing long-term plans, typically for a five-year period. A key corporate strategy of Airborne Express's operations involved direct sale to high-volume corporate accounts and developing an expansive network in the international arena. Instead of setting up operations overseas, Airborne's long-term strategy was to form direct associations with national companies within foreign countries to expand and diversify their operations.

Another example of the portfolio approach involved a plan by state-owned Saudi Arabian Oil to spend $1.4 billion to build and operate an oil refinery in Korea with its partner, Ssangyong. To implement their program, the Saudis embarked on a new "cut-out-the-middleman" strategy to reduce the role of international oil companies in the processing and selling of Saudi crude oil.

In the middle of the decision-making hierarchy is the business level, composed principally of business and corporate managers. These managers must translate the statements of direction and intent generated at the corporate level into concrete objectives and strategies for individual business divisions, or SBUs. In essence, business-level strategic managers determine how the firm will compete in the selected product-market arena. They strive to identify and secure the most promising market segment within that arena. This segment is the piece of the total market that the firm can claim and defend because of its competitive advantages.

At the bottom of the decision-making hierarchy is the functional level, composed principally of managers of product, geographic, and functional areas. They develop annual objectives and short-term strategies in such areas as production, operations, research and development, finance and accounting, marketing, and human relations. However, their principal responsibility is to implement or execute the firm's strategic plans. Whereas corporate- and business-level managers center their attention on "doing the right things," managers at the functional level center their attention on "doing things right." Thus, they address such issues as the efficiency and effectiveness of production and marketing systems, the quality of customer service, and the success of particular products and services in increasing the firm's market shares.

Exhibit 1–3 depicts the three levels of strategic management as structured in practice. In alternative 1, the firm is engaged in only one business and the corporate- and business-level responsibilities are concentrated in a single group of directors, officers, and managers. This is the organizational format of most small businesses.

Alternative 2, the classical corporate structure, comprises three fully operative levels: the corporate level, the business level, and the functional level. The approach taken throughout this text assumes the use of alternative 2. Moreover, whenever appropriate, topics are

**EXHIBIT 1–3**
**Alternative Strategic Management Structures**

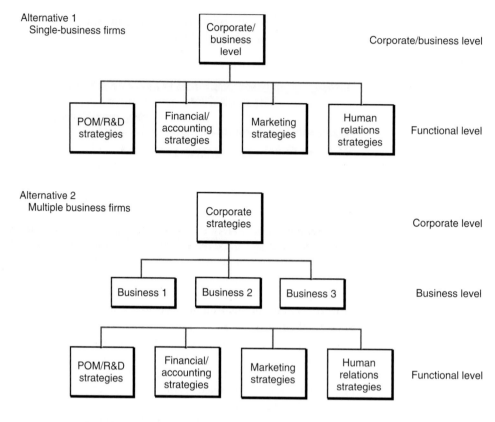

Alternative 1
Single-business firms

Corporate/business level — Corporate/business level

POM/R&D strategies | Financial/accounting strategies | Marketing strategies | Human relations strategies — Functional level

Alternative 2
Multiple business firms

Corporate strategies — Corporate level

Business 1 | Business 2 | Business 3 — Business level

POM/R&D strategies | Financial/accounting strategies | Marketing strategies | Human relations strategies — Functional level

covered from the perspective of each level of strategic management. In this way, the text presents a comprehensive discussion of the strategic management process.

### Characteristics of Strategic Management Decisions

The characteristics of strategic management decisions vary with the level of strategic activity considered. As shown in Exhibit 1–4, decisions at the corporate level tend to be more value oriented, more conceptual, and less concrete than decisions at the business or functional level. For example, at Alcoa, the world's largest aluminum maker, chairman Paul O'Neill made Alcoa one of the nation's most centralized organizations by imposing a dramatic management reorganization that wiped out two layers of management. He found that this effort not only reduced costs but also enabled him to be closer to the front-line operations managers. Corporate-level decisions are often characterized by greater risk, cost, and profit potential; greater need for flexibility; and longer time horizons. Such decisions include the choice of businesses, dividend policies, sources of long-term financing, and priorities for growth.

Functional-level decisions implement the overall strategy formulated at the corporate and business levels. They involve action-oriented operational issues and are relatively short range and low risk. Functional-level decisions incur only modest costs, because they depend on available resources. They usually are adaptable to ongoing activities and, therefore, can be implemented with minimal cooperation. For example, the corporate headquarters of Sears, Roebuck & Company spent $60 million to automate 6,900 clerical jobs by installing 28,000 computerized cash registers at its 868 stores in the United States. Though this move eliminated many functional-level jobs, top management believed that reducing annual operating expenses by at least $50 million was crucial to competitive survival.

**EXHIBIT 1–4**   Hierarchy of Objectives and Strategies

| Ends<br>(What is to be achieved?) | Means<br>(How is it to be achieved?) | Strategic Decision Makers | | | |
|---|---|---|---|---|---|
| | | Board of<br>Directors | Corporate<br>Managers | Business<br>Managers | Functional<br>Managers |
| Mission, including goals<br>and philosophy | | ✓✓ | ✓✓ | ✓ | |
| Long-term objectives | Grand strategy | ✓ | ✓✓ | ✓✓ | |
| Annual objectives | Short-term strategies and<br>policies | | ✓ | ✓✓ | ✓✓ |

Note: ✓✓ indicates a principal responsibility; ✓ indicates a secondary responsibility.

Because functional-level decisions are relatively concrete and quantifiable, they receive critical attention and analysis even though their comparative profit potential is low. Common functional-level decisions include decisions on generic versus brandname labeling, basic versus applied research and development (R&D), high versus low inventory levels, general-purpose versus specific-purpose production equipment, and close versus loose supervision.

Business-level decisions help bridge decisions at the corporate and functional levels. Such decisions are less costly, risky, and potentially profitable than corporate-level decisions, but they are more costly, risky, and potentially profitable than functional-level decisions. Common business-level decisions include decisions on plant location, marketing segmentation and geographic coverage, and distribution channels.

### Formality in Strategic Management

The formality of strategic management systems varies widely among companies. *Formality* refers to the degree to which participants, responsibilities, authority, and discretion in decision making are specified. It is an important consideration in the study of strategic management, because greater formality is usually positively correlated with the cost, comprehensiveness, accuracy, and success of planning.

A number of forces determine how much formality is needed in strategic management. The size of the organization, its predominant management styles, the complexity of its environment, its production process, its problems, and the purpose of its planning system all play a part in determining the appropriate degree of formality.

In particular, formality is associated with the size of the firm and with its stage of development. Methods of evaluating strategic success also are linked to formality. Some firms, especially smaller ones, follow an *entrepreneurial* mode. They are basically under the control of a single individual, and they produce a limited number of products or services. In such firms, strategic evaluation is informal, intuitive, and limited. Very large firms, on the other hand, make strategic evaluation part of a comprehensive, formal planning system, an approach that Henry Mintzberg called the *planning mode.* Mintzberg also identified a third mode (the *adaptive mode*), which he associated with medium-sized firms in relatively stable environments.[1] For firms that follow the adaptive mode, the identification and evaluation of alternative strategies are closely related to existing strategy. It is not unusual to find different modes within the same organization. For example, Exxon might follow an entrepreneurial mode in developing and evaluating the strategy of its solar subsidiary but follow a planning mode in the rest of the company.

---

[1] H. Mintzberg, "Strategy Making in Three Modes," *California Management Review* 16, no. 2 (1973), pp. 44–53.

### The Strategy Makers

The ideal strategic management team includes decision makers from all three company levels (the corporate, business, and functional)—for example, the chief executive officer (CEO), the product managers, and the heads of functional areas. In addition, the team obtains input from company planning staffs, when they exist, and from lower-level managers and supervisors. The latter provide data for strategic decision making and then implement strategies.

Because strategic decisions have a tremendous impact on a company and require large commitments of company resources, top managers must give final approval for strategic action. Exhibit 1.4 aligns levels of strategic decision makers with the kinds of objectives and strategies for which they are typically responsible.

Planning departments, often headed by a corporate vice president for planning, are common in large corporations. Medium-sized firms often employ at least one full-time staff member to spearhead strategic data-collection efforts. Even in small firms or less progressive larger firms, strategic planning often is spearheaded by an officer or by a group of officers designated as a planning committee.

Precisely what are managers' responsibilities in the strategic planning process at the corporate and business levels? Top management shoulders broad responsibility for all the major elements of strategic planning and management. It develops the major portions of the strategic plan and reviews, and it evaluates and counsels on all other portions. General managers at the business level typically have principal responsibilities for developing environmental analysis and forecasting, establishing business objectives, and developing business plans prepared by staff groups.

A firm's president or CEO characteristically plays a dominant role in the strategic planning process. In many ways, this situation is desirable. The CEO's principal duty often is defined as giving long-term direction to the firm, and the CEO is ultimately responsible for the firm's success and, therefore, for the success of its strategy. In addition, CEOs are typically strong-willed, company-oriented individuals with high self-esteem. They often resist delegating authority to formulate or approve strategic decisions.

However, when the dominance of the CEO approaches autocracy, the effectiveness of the firm's strategic planning and management processes is likely to be diminished. For this reason, establishing a strategic management system implies that the CEO will allow managers at all levels to participate in the strategic posture of the company.

In implementing a company's strategy, the CEO must have an appreciation for the power and responsibility of the board, while retaining the power to lead the company with the guidance of informed directors. The interaction between the CEO and board is key to any corporation's strategy. Empowerment of nonmanagerial employees has been a recent trend across major management teams. Exhibit 1–5, Strategy in Action, presents one example. In 2003, IBM replaced its 92-year-old executive board structure with three, newly created management teams: strategy, operations, and technology. Each team combined top executives, managers, and engineers going down six levels in some cases. This new team structure was responsible for guiding the creation of IBM's strategy and for helping to implement the strategies once they were authorized.

## Benefits of Strategic Management

Using the strategic management approach, managers at all levels of the firm interact in planning and implementing. As a result, the behavioral consequences of strategic management are similar to those of participative decision making. Therefore, an accurate assessment of the impact of strategy formulation on organizational performance requires not only financial evaluation criteria but also nonfinancial evaluation criteria—measures of

**BusinessWeek** IBM CEO Samuel J. Palmisano took aim at a bastion of power and privilege at Big Blue, the 92-year-old executive management committee. For generations, this 12-person body presiding over IBM's strategy and initiatives represented the inner sanctum for every aspiring Big Blue executive. The CEO hit the send button on an e-mail to 300 senior managers announcing that this venerable committee was finished. Palmisano instead would work directly, with three teams he had put in place in 2002—they comprised people from all over the company who brought the best ideas to the table. The old committee, with its monthly meetings, just slowed things down.

Palmisano asked his team to draw up a project as epochal as the mainframe. The team cobbled together a vision of systems that altered the very nature of how technology was delivered. They unveiled "e-business on demand."

In 2002 before Palmisano disbanded the executive management committee, he had put in place his management teams for the future. He created three of them: strategy, operations, and technology. Instead of picking only high-level executives for each team, Palmisano selected managers and engineers most familiar with the issues.

For IBM to come up with a broad array of on-demand technologies in a hurry, the whole company had to work smoothly from one far-flung cubicle to another. That meant bringing researchers in touch not only with product developers, but also with consultants and even customers. Only by reaching across these old boundaries did IBM find out what customers were clamoring for—and produce it fast.

**Source:** Excerpted from Ante Spencer, "The New Blue," *Business Week*, March 17, 2003, pp. 80–88.

---

behavior-based effects. In fact, promoting positive behavioral consequences also enables the firm to achieve its financial goals. However, regardless of the profitability of strategic plans, several behavioral effects of strategic management improve the firm's welfare:

1. Strategy formulation activities enhance the firm's ability to prevent problems. Managers who encourage subordinates' attention to planning are aided in their monitoring and forecasting responsibilities by subordinates who are aware of the needs of strategic planning.

2. Group-based strategic decisions are likely to be drawn from the best available alternatives. The strategic management process results in better decisions because group interaction generates a greater variety of strategies and because forecasts based on the specialized perspectives of group members improve the screening of options.

3. The involvement of employees in strategy formulation improves their understanding of the productivity-reward relationship in every strategic plan and, thus, heightens their motivation.

4. Gaps and overlaps in activities among individuals and groups are reduced as participation in strategy formulation clarifies differences in roles.

5. Resistance to change is reduced. Though the participants in strategy formulation may be no more pleased with their own decisions than they would be with authoritarian decisions, their greater awareness of the parameters that limit the available options makes them more likely to accept those decisions.

## Risks of Strategic Management

Managers must be trained to guard against three types of unintended negative consequences of involvement in strategy formulation.

First, the time that managers spend on the strategic management process may have a negative impact on operational responsibilities. Managers must be trained to minimize that impact by scheduling their duties to allow the necessary time for strategic activities.

Second, if the formulators of strategy are not intimately involved in its implementation, they may shirk their individual responsibility for the decisions reached. Thus, strategic managers must be trained to limit their promises to performance that the decision makers and their subordinates can deliver.

Third, strategic managers must be trained to anticipate and respond to the disappointment of participating subordinates over unattained expectations. Subordinates may expect their involvement in even minor phases of total strategy formulation to result in both acceptance of their proposals and an increase in their rewards, or they may expect a solicitation of their input on selected issues to extend to other areas of decision making.

Sensitizing managers to these possible negative consequences and preparing them with effective means of minimizing such consequences will greatly enhance the potential of strategic planning.

# THE STRATEGIC MANAGEMENT PROCESS

Businesses vary in the processes they use to formulate and direct their strategic management activities. Sophisticated planners, such as General Electric, Procter & Gamble, and IBM, have developed more detailed processes than less-formal planners of similar size. Small businesses that rely on the strategy formulation skills and limited time of an entrepreneur typically exhibit more basic planning concerns than those of larger firms in their industries. Understandably, firms with multiple products, markets, or technologies tend to use more complex strategic management systems. However, despite differences in detail and the degree of formalization, the basic components of the models used to analyze strategic management operations are very similar.

Because of the similarity among the general models of the strategic management process, it is possible to develop an eclectic model representative of the foremost thought in the strategic management area. This model is shown in Exhibit 1–6. It serves three major functions. First, it depicts the sequence and the relationships of the major components of the strategic management process. Second, it is the outline for this book. This chapter provides a general overview of the strategic management process, and the major components of the model will be the principal theme of subsequent chapters. Notice that the chapters of the text that discuss each of the strategic management process components are shown in each block. Finally, the model offers one approach for analyzing the case studies in this text and thus helps the analyst develop strategy formulation skills.

## Components of the Strategic Management Model

This section will define and briefly describe the key components of the strategic management model. Each of these components will receive much greater attention in a later chapter. The intention here is simply to introduce them.

### *Company Mission*

The mission of a company is the unique purpose that sets it apart from other companies of its type and identifies the scope of its operations. In short, the mission describes the company's product, market, and technological areas of emphasis in a way that reflects the values and priorities of the strategic decision makers. For example, Lee Hun-Hee, the new chairman of the Samsung Group, revamped the company mission by stamping his own

**EXHIBIT 1–6**  **Strategic Management Model**

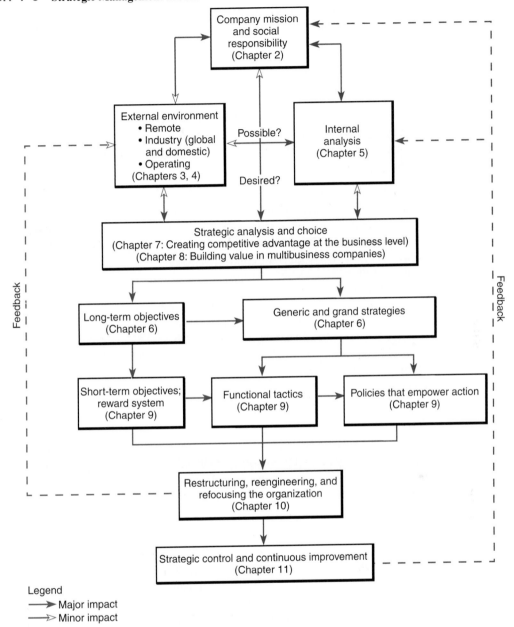

Legend
———▶ Major impact
———▷ Minor impact

brand of management on Samsung. Immediately, Samsung separated Chonju Paper Manufacturing and Shinsegae Department Store from other operations. This corporate act of downscaling reflected a revised management philosophy that favored specialization, thereby changing the direction and scope of the organization.

Social responsibility is a critical consideration for a company's strategic decision makers since the mission statement must express how the company intends to contribute to the societies that sustain it. A firm needs to set social responsibility aspirations for itself, just as it does in other areas of corporate performance.

### Internal Analysis

The company analyzes the quantity and quality of the company's financial, human, and physical resources. It also assesses the strengths and weaknesses of the company's management and organizational structure. Finally, it contrasts the company's past successes and traditional concerns with the company's current capabilities in an attempt to identify the company's future capabilities.

### External Environment

A firm's external environment consists of all the conditions and forces that affect its strategic options and define its competitive situation. The strategic management model shows the external environment as three interactive segments: the remote, industry, and operating environments.

### Strategic Analysis and Choice

Simultaneous assessment of the external environment and the company profile enables a firm to identify a range of possibly attractive interactive opportunities. These opportunities are *possible* avenues for investment. However, they must be screened through the criterion of the company mission to generate a set of possible and *desired* opportunities. This screening process results in the selection of options from which a *strategic choice* is made. The process is meant to provide the combination of long-term objectives and generic and grand strategies that optimally position the firm in its external environment to achieve the company mission.

Strategic analysis and choice in single or dominant product/service businesses center around identifying strategies that are most effective at building sustainable competitive advantage based on key value chain activities and capabilities—core competencies of the firm. Multibusiness companies find their managers focused on the question of which combination of businesses maximizes shareholder value as the guiding theme during their strategic analysis and choice.

### Long-Term Objectives

The results that an organization seeks over a multiyear period are its *long-term objectives.* Such objectives typically involve some or all of the following areas: profitability, return on investment, competitive position, technological leadership, productivity, employee relations, public responsibility, and employee development.

### Generic and Grand Strategies

Many businesses explicitly and all implicitly adopt one or more *generic strategies* characterizing their competitive orientation in the marketplace. Low cost, differentiation, or focus strategies define the three fundamental options. Enlightened managers seek to create ways their firm possesses both low cost and differentiation competitive advantages as part of their overall generic strategy. They usually combine these capabilities with a comprehensive, general plan of major actions through which their firm intends to achieve its long-term objectives in a dynamic environment. Called the *grand strategy,* this statement of means indicates how the objectives are to be achieved. Although every grand strategy is, in fact, a unique package of long-term strategies, 14 basic approaches can be identified: concentration, market development, product development, innovation, horizontal integration, vertical integration, joint venture, strategic alliances, consortia, concentric diversification, conglomerate diversification, turnaround, divestiture, and liquidation.

Each of these grand strategies will be covered in detail in Chapter 6.

### Action Plans and Short-Term Objectives

*Action plans* translate generic and grand strategies into "action" by incorporating four elements. First, they identify specific functional *tactics and actions* to be undertaken in the next week, month, or quarter as part of the business's effort to build competitive advantage. The second element is a clear time frame for completion. Third, action plans create accountability by identifying who is responsible for each "action" in the plan. Fourth, each "action" in an action plan has one or more specific, immediate objectives that are identified as outcomes that action should generate.

### Functional Tactics

Within the general framework created by the business's generic and grand strategies, each business function needs to identify and undertake activities unique to the function that help build a sustainable competitive advantage. Managers in each business function develop tactics that delineate the functional activities undertaken in their part of the business and usually include them as a core part of their action plan. *Functional tactics* are detailed statements of the "means" or activities that will be used to achieve short-term objectives and establish competitive advantage.

### Policies That Empower Action

Speed is a critical necessity for success in today's competitive, global marketplace. One way to enhance speed and responsiveness is to force/allow decisions to be made whenever possible at the lowest level in organizations. *Policies* are broad, precedent-setting decisions that guide or substitute for repetitive or time-sensitive managerial decision making. Creating policies that guide and "preauthorize" the thinking, decisions, and actions of operating managers and their subordinates in implementing the business's strategy is essential for establishing and controlling the ongoing operating process of the firm in a manner consistent with the firm's strategic objectives. Policies often increase managerial effectiveness by standardizing routine decisions and empowering or expanding the discretion of managers and subordinates in implementing business strategies.

The following are examples of the nature and diversity of company policies:

A requirement that managers have purchase requests for items costing more than $5,000 cosigned by the controller.

The minimum equity position required for all new McDonald's franchises.

The standard formula used to calculate return on investment for the 43 strategic business units of General Electric.

A decision that Sears service and repair employees have the right to waive repair charges to appliance customers they feel have been poorly served by their Sears appliance.

### Restructuring, Reengineering, and Refocusing the Organization

Until this point in the strategic management process, managers have maintained a decidedly market-oriented focus as they formulate strategies and begin implementation through action plans and functional tactics. Now the process takes an internal focus—getting the work of the business done efficiently and effectively so as to make the strategy successful. What is the best way to organize ourselves to accomplish the mission? Where should leadership come from? What values should guide our daily activities—what should the organization and its people be like? How can we shape rewards to encourage appropriate action? The intense competition in the global marketplace has made this tradition "internally focused" set of questions—how the activities within their business are conducted—recast themselves with unprecedented attentiveness to the marketplace. *Downsizing, restructuring,* and *reengineering* are terms that reflect the critical stage in strategy implementation wherein managers attempt to recast their organization. The company's structure, leadership, culture, and reward systems may all be changed to ensure cost competitiveness and quality demanded by unique requirements of its strategies.

The elements of the strategic management process are evident in the recent activities at GM, as seen in Exhibit 1–7, Strategy in Action. In 2003, GM undertook to create a strategy

# Strategy in Action
## Rick Wagoner's Game Plan

Exhibit 1–7

**BusinessWeek** A day after General Motors Corp. (GM) announced that it had lifted operating earnings 30 percent in a stagnant car market, Standard & Poor's downgraded the auto maker's debt with no warning. Surprised investors rushed to sell, and the stock dropped 8 percent. Credit analysts pointed to GM's $76 billion pension fund, which they estimated at the time to be underfunded by as much as $23 billion. GM would have had to plow in billions of dollars for years to keep the fund flush, they said.

GM finished 2002, with an operating profit of $3.9 billion, nearly double what it earned in 2001, on 5 percent higher sales of $186.2 billion. GM clearly led the rest of the U.S. big three car companies, reflecting real operational improvements. After GM lost a staggering $30 billion during a single three-year stretch in the early '90s, Wagoner and Chairman John F. "Jack" Smith Jr. forced GM back to basics. They slashed costs, cut payroll, and overhauled aging plants. Once he took over the corner office in May 2000, CEO Wagoner pulled the efficiency collar even tighter. Then GM ranked close to Honda Motor Co. (HMC) and Toyota Motor Corp. (TM) in productivity and made strides in quality. GM also recaptured leadership of the truck business from rival Ford Motor Co. (F), a coup that made the company billions. In 2000, GM increased its share of the U.S. market, to 28.3 percent from 28.1 percent.

But as good as those moves were, they paled next to the problems of GM's weak car brands and gargantuan pension payments. Even worse for GM was the buildup of lavish health and retirement benefits for workers that it agreed to in fatter days as a way to buy peace with the United Auto Workers. The company said the gap between its pension funding and future liabilities was $19.3 billion. That meant GM had to pump as much as $4 billion into the fund from 2003 to 2004. Providing health care to former and current workers would drain an additional $5 billion per year. The pension costs alone would have cut projected 2003 net income from $4.2 billion to $2.8 billion. Those huge legacy costs explained why Wagoner kept the heat on his competition with the zero percent financing deals he unleashed after September 11, 2001.

That made Wagoner's imperative clear: He had to keep up cash flow to cover those costs until they started to shrink. At the same time, he continued to rack up improvements in quality, efficiency, design, and brand appeal.

Walking around GM's sprawling headquarters complex, you realized that against all odds, Wagoner was making real progress in energizing GM's torpid culture. He broke with GM tradition by recruiting two respected outsiders for key positions—Robert A. Lutz as head of product development and John Devine as vice-chairman and chief financial officer. And he had given them extraordinary leeway to fix the company's problems. Since giving the swaggering Lutz rule over product development, Wagoner spiked the design-by-committee system and cut the time it took to develop a new car to 20 months from nearly four years. GM used to have different studios for each division working on car designs that would get passed on to marketing, then engineering, then manufacturing. Lutz had one committee to cover the entire process.

It was a testament to Wagoner's ability to cut costs that GM managed to nearly double margins in North America in 2002, to 2.6 percent of sales. Thanks to efficiency gains, GM was now one of the leanest car builders, with variable costs—labor, parts, outsourced production, and so on—amounting to 62 percent of revenues, according to UBS Warburg. That put it ahead of Ford and Chrysler (DCX) at 68 percent, and it was not far behind leaders Toyota and Honda at 60 percent.

Wagoner also streamlined GM's factories. GM became the most productive domestic auto maker, having cut the time it takes to assemble a vehicle from an average of 32 hours in 1998 to 26 hours in 2001, according to Harbour & Associates. That compared with 27 for Ford, almost 31 at DaimlerChrysler, 22.5 at Toyota, and 17.9 at Nissan. A big factor was expanding parts shared across vehicles. The new Chevy Malibu, for instance, used the same platform and many of the same parts as the Saab 9-3 sedan. . . . GM's plants were also more flexible—each of seven full-size pickup and SUV plants could make any of the vehicles designed on that platform.

The cars rolling off GM's assembly lines were undeniably better built than they used to be. Once ranked below the industry average, GM trailed only Honda and Toyota in J.D. Power & Associates Inc.'s initial quality survey.

**Source:** Excerpted from Kathleen Kenurin and David Welch, "Rick Wagoner's Game Plan," *BusinessWeek*, February 10, 2003, pp. 52–60.

to lower costs, increase efficiency, improve designs, and increase brand appeal. These improvements were needed to keep cash flows up to cover rising pension costs. For GM to accomplish this new strategy it had to improve operations. New executives were brought in to lead product development and financial controls. To break down the bureaucratic boundaries, a committee was created that included employees from the major functional areas, and it was given the assignment to reduce the time needed to develop a new-concept vehicle.

## Strategy in Action
Can Yahoo! Make the Bounce Last?

# Exhibit 1–8

**BusinessWeek** Following a $93 million loss in 2001, Terry S. Semel had led Yahoo! Inc. (YHOO) back with positive earnings in 2002. Then he predicted that in 2003 the Internet giant would best its previous records in annual sales and profits—both set in 2000, at the height of the tech boom. With Yahoo's stock still down about 20 percent, Semel convinced the market that he built a long-term growth engine that would have justified Yahoo's $10.6 billion market valuation. Semel got his chance when he presented his strategy in crucial new markets, particularly forayed into broadband access and the Internet search market.

Bulking up the broadband business, with its stable monthly subscriber fees, was Semel's most important task. True, Yahoo's five-month-old partnership with SBC Communications Inc. (SBC) to sell broadband access was by most accounts a success. The business garnered Yahoo at least $7 million in sales in the fourth quarter of 2002, with an additional $70 million expected in 2003, according to analysts.

With Yahoo capable of reaching only one-third of the country through its SBC alliance, Yahoo needed to find a way to reach the rest. Yahoo rolled out a "bring-your-own-broadband" service. Subscribers paid a monthly fee to use a souped-up Yahoo gateway, regardless of what broadband provider they used. Yahoo sold its service for about $5 a month, compared with $9.95 and $14.95 for Microsoft Corp.'s (MSFT) MSN and AOL, respectively.

Yahoo relied on blitz marketing and the low price to win customers. Yahoo needed to bolster its premium content and services. Less than 1 percent of Yahoo's visitors paid for services such as jumbo-size e-mail accounts or Yahoo's personal-ad listings. With even loyal Yahoo users reluctant to shell out for extras, it was harder to convince non-Yahoo users, who already frequent other portals.

Yahoo proved it could compete in the Internet search market, where it ranked No. 3 behind MSN and Google. In 2002, revenues from ads on its search-results pages boomed from next to nothing to over $100 million. In 2003, Yahoo tinkered with its search pages to squeeze in more ads. For that to matter, Yahoo solidified its standing as a premier search destination. The portal had long used search technology from other providers, such as Inktomi Corp. (INKT) and Google. But when Google emerged as a serious rival, Yahoo acquired Inktomi for $235 million and evicted Google as its search-technology source.

To succeed, Yahoo had to grab market share back from Google. The popular site snared 4 percent more search traffic than Yahoo in December of 2002, according to comScore Media Metrix. Proving that Inktomi's search technology rivaled Google's was more a branding challenge than a technological one.

**Source:** Excerpted from Ben Elgin, "Can Yahoo Make the Bounce Last?" *BusinessWeek*, February 17, 2003, p. 41.

### *Strategic Control and Continuous Improvement*

*Strategic control* is concerned with tracking a strategy as it is being implemented, detecting problems or changes in its underlying premises, and making necessary adjustments. In contrast to postaction control, strategic control seeks to guide action on behalf of the generic and grand strategies as they are taking place and when the end results are still several years away. The rapid, accelerating change of the global marketplace of the last 10 years has made continuous improvement another aspect of strategic control in many organizations. *Continuous improvement* provides a way for managers to provide a form of strategic control that allows their organization to respond more proactively and timely to rapid developments in hundreds of areas that influence a business's success.

In 2002–2003, Yahoo's strategy was to move into the broadband and Internet search markets, as discussed in Exhibit 1–8, Strategy in Action. However, even in its early implementation stages the strategy required revisions. Yahoo had formed an alliance with SBC to provide the broadband service, but SBC had such limited capabilities that Yahoo had to find new ways to reach users. Yahoo also needed to continuously improve its new Internet search market, given competitors' upgrades and rapidly rising customer expectations. Additionally, for Yahoo to increase its market share, it needed to continually improve its branding, rather than rely largely on its technological capabilities.

## Strategic Management as a Process

A *process* is the flow of information through interrelated stages of analysis toward the achievement of an aim. Thus, the strategic management model in Exhibit 1–6 depicts a process. In the strategic management process, the flow of information involves historical, current, and forecast data on the operations and environment of the business. Managers evaluate these data in light of the values and priorities of influential individuals and groups—often called *stakeholders*—that are vitally interested in the actions of the business. The interrelated stages of the process are the 11 components discussed in the previous section. Finally, the aim of the process is the formulation and implementation of strategies that work, achieving the company's long-term mission and near-term objectives.

Viewing strategic management as a process has several important implications. First, a change in any component will affect several or all of the other components. Most of the arrows in the model point two ways, suggesting that the flow of information usually is reciprocal. For example, forces in the external environment may influence the nature of a company's mission, and the company may in turn affect the external environment and heighten competition in its realm of operation. A specific example is a power company that is persuaded, in part by governmental incentives, to include a commitment to the development of energy alternatives in its mission statement. The company then might promise to extend its R&D efforts in the area of coal liquefaction. The external environment has affected the company's mission, and the revised mission signals a competitive condition in the environment.

A second implication of viewing strategic management as a process is that strategy formulation and implementation are sequential. The process begins with development or reevaluation of the company mission. This step is associated with, but essentially followed by, development of a company profile and assessment of the external environment. Then follow, in order, strategic choice, definition of long-term objectives, design of the grand strategy, definition of short-term objectives, design of operating strategies, institutionalization of the strategy, and review and evaluation.

The apparent rigidity of the process, however, must be qualified.

First, a firm's strategic posture may have to be reevaluated in response to changes in any of the principal factors that determine or affect its performance. Entry by a major new competitor, the death of a prominent board member, replacement of the chief executive officer, and a downturn in market responsiveness are among the thousands of changes that can prompt reassessment of a firm's strategic plan. However, no matter where the need for a reassessment originates, the strategic management process begins with the mission statement.

Second, not every component of the strategic management process deserves equal attention each time planning activity takes place. Firms in an extremely stable environment may find that an in-depth assessment is not required every five years. Companies often are satisfied with their original mission statements even after a decade of operation and spend only a minimal amount of time addressing this subject. In addition, while formal strategic planning may be undertaken only every five years, objectives and strategies usually are updated each year, and rigorous reassessment of the initial stages of strategic planning rarely is undertaken at these times.

A third implication of viewing strategic management as a process is the necessity of feedback from institutionalization, review, and evaluation to the early stages of the process. *Feedback* can be defined as the collection of postimplementation results to enhance future decision making. Therefore, as indicated in Exhibit 1–6, strategic managers should assess the impact of implemented strategies on external environments. Thus, future planning can reflect any changes precipitated by strategic actions. Strategic managers also should analyze the impact of strategies on the possible need for modifications in the company mission.

A fourth implication of viewing strategic management as a process is the need to regard it as a dynamic system. The term *dynamic* characterizes the constantly changing conditions that affect interrelated and interdependent strategic activities. Managers should recognize that the components of the strategic process are constantly evolving but that formal planning artificially freezes those components, much as an action photograph freezes the movement of a swimmer. Since change is continuous, the dynamic strategic planning process must be monitored constantly for significant shifts in any of its components as a precaution against implementing an obsolete strategy.

### Changes in the Process

The strategic management process undergoes continual assessment and subtle updating. Although the elements of the basic strategic management model rarely change, the relative emphasis that each element receives will vary with the decision makers who use the model and with the environments of their companies.

A recent study describes general trends in strategic management, summarizing the responses of over 200 corporate executives. This update shows there has been an increasing companywide emphasis on and appreciation for the value of strategic management activities. It also provides evidence that practicing managers have given increasing attention to the need for frequent and widespread involvement in the formulation and implementation phases of the strategic management process. Finally, it indicates that, as managers and their firms gain knowledge, experience, skill, and understanding in how to design and manage their planning activities, they become better able to avoid the potential negative consequences of instituting a vigorous strategic management process.

## Summary

Strategic management is the set of decisions and actions that result in the formulation and implementation of plans designed to achieve a company's objectives. Because it involves long-term, future-oriented, complex decision making and requires considerable resources, top-management participation is essential.

Strategic management is a three-tier process involving corporate-, business-, and functional-level planners, and support personnel. At each progressively lower level, strategic activities were shown to be more specific, narrow, short term, and action oriented, with lower risks but fewer opportunities for dramatic impact.

The strategic management model presented in this chapter will serve as the structure for understanding and integrating all the major phases of strategy formulation and implementation. The chapter provided a summary account of these phases, each of which is given extensive individual attention in subsequent chapters.

The chapter stressed that the strategic management process centers on the belief that a firm's mission can be best achieved through a systematic and comprehensive assessment of both its internal capabilities and its external environment. Subsequent evaluation of the firm's opportunities leads, in turn, to the choice of long-term objectives and grand strategies and, ultimately, to annual objectives and operating strategies, which must be implemented, monitored, and controlled.

## Questions for Discussion

1. Find a recent copy of *BusinessWeek* and read the "Corporate Strategies" section. Was the main decision discussed strategic? At what level in the organization was the key decision made?

2. In what ways do you think the subject matter in this strategic management–business policy course will differ from that of previous courses you have taken?

3. After graduation, you are not likely to move directly to a top-level management position. In fact, few members of your class will ever reach the top-management level. Why, then, is it important for all business majors to study the field of strategic management?

4. Do you expect outstanding performance in this course to require a great deal of memorization? Why or why not?

5. You undoubtedly have read about individuals who seemingly have given singled-handed direction to their corporations. Is a participative strategic management approach likely to stifle or suppress the contributions of such individuals?

6. Think about the courses you have taken in functional areas, such as marketing, finance, production, personnel, and accounting. What is the importance of each of these areas to the strategic planning process?

7. Discuss with practicing business managers the strategic management models used in their firms. What are the similarities and differences between these models and the one in the text?

8. In what ways do you believe the strategic planning approach of not-for-profit organizations would differ from that of profit-oriented organizations?

9. How do you explain the success of firms that do not use a formal strategic planning process?

10. Think about your postgraduation job search as a strategic decision. How would the strategic management model be helpful to you in identifying and securing the most promising position?

## Chapter 1 Discussion Case

BusinessWeek

# Kraft's Global Strategy: Can Kraft Be a Big Cheese Abroad?

1  When Aussies stroll down the aisles of their local supermarket, what catches their eyes are snacks from Unilever (UL) and Nestlé (NSRGY). Kraft Macaroni & Cheese and Oscar Mayer hot dogs, on the other hand, are hard to find and far from first choice. "They would be classified as a slow-moving line," says Terry Walters, the owner of an IGA store in Cairns, Queensland, about the classic American macaroni-and-cheese dinner. As for hot dogs: "We have the meat pie."

2  Kraft may be ubiquitous in U.S. grocery stores, but overseas it's a far different picture. Kraft isn't one of Walters' top five food suppliers, ranking below even H. J. Heinz Co. (HNZ), despite its ownership of Australia's famed Vegemite spread. Only 27 percent of its total revenues come from overseas, versus 44 percent for Heinz, more than 50 percent for McDonald's Corp. (MCD), and more than 80 percent for Coca-Cola Co. (KO)

3  That will have to change. As Kraft embarks on a giant initial public offering, expected in mid-June, its challenge is to once again become a growth company. Widely admired for the astute management of its brand lineup, Kraft's nevertheless stuck in a slow-growth industry in the United States. Smart marketing and methodical cost cutting helped it boost earnings 14.1 percent last year, but Kraft's sales actually dipped slightly, to $26.53 billion. In fact, Kraft's annual sales have dropped 16.2 percent since 1994. The company took a big step toward building revenues in December with its $19.2 billion purchase of Nabisco Group Holdings Corp. (NGH-U), whose cookie and cracker brands are growing faster than Kraft's top brands.

4  That deal should boost Kraft's sales to an expected $35.05 billion this year. But analysts say that if Kraft is to spark long-term growth, it must do a better job of tapping foreign consumers. Kraft acknowledged as much when it announced that once the IPO is completed, Betsy D. Holden, CEO of Kraft Foods North America, would share the chief executive office with Roger K. Deromedi, a 13-year Kraft veteran who has been president and CEO of Kraft Foods International Inc. for the past two years. The company declined to comment or make top executives available to *Busi-*

*nessWeek,* citing the quiet period before the IPO, as did parent Philip Morris Cos. (MO).

5  AMERICAN ICONS. The largest food company in North America by far, Kraft has dominated U.S. grocery-store shelves for decades. Its powerhouse brands are American icons: Philadelphia Cream Cheese, Oreo cookies, Tang, Jell-O, Kool-Aid, Life Savers, Planters peanuts, Lunchables prepackaged meals for kids. Its portfolio comprises a remarkable 61 brands with more than $100 million in sales last year. Supermarket consultants say it would be nearly impossible to run a U.S. grocery store without its products.

6  But these aren't the best of times, even for strong supermarket brands. Shopper loyalty has waned as the grocery chains' in-house brands compete for shelf space, and big brands such as Kraft's tend to be mature. Take salad dressing. Even though Kraft is the market leader, "there's Kraft, there's Wish-Bone, there's Hellmann's," says John P. Mahar, operations director at the Green Hills Farms supermarket in Syracuse, N.Y. "If we have Wish-Bone on sale, shoppers pick up Wish-Bone. They don't care. The majority of Kraft's brands are just another commodity."

7  TOBACCO TAINT. Boosting sales will become even more urgent once Kraft has outside shareholders to answer to. Cigarette maker Philip Morris, which has owned Kraft since 1988, is putting 16.1 percent of the company on the market in an offering that could raise as much as $8.4 billion. That would be the second-largest IPO on record, behind only AT&T Wireless Group's $10.5 billion stock market debut last year. Philip Morris will remain firmly in control, but its goal is to realize more of Kraft's value by distancing the business from the tobacco taint that has held Philip Morris' stock price down.

8  The first concern for investors might be whether Kraft's co-CEO structure can work. Deromedi, 47, and Holden, 45, who started at Kraft as an assistant product manager in 1982, will both report to Geoffrey Bible, chairman of Philip Morris. Analysts wonder how long the arrangement will last, citing a long list of prominent companies, from DaimlerChrysler to Citigroup, where co-CEO setups fizzled. "The co-CEO structure calls into question if this is truly an independent company," says Goldman, Sachs & Co. analyst Romitha

S. Mally. "At the end of the day, it will be the chairman and the board, which is controlled by Philip Morris, who will be the ultimate decision makers for Kraft."

9    In this case, though, the co-CEOs have well-defined management areas. Another plus: Their personalities seem to complement each other. James J. Drury, vice-chairman of Spencer Stuart, an executive-search firm in Chicago, describes Deromedi, who holds a math degree, as "more focused on problem solving and more likely to make tough decisions in complex situations." Holden, he says, is creative, charismatic, and more people-oriented: "She's more the one to take into consideration how a business situation may impact people."

10    A top task for the new CEOs will be figuring out how to expand outside North America. Overseas, Kraft faces a lineup of tough global competitors—Unilever, Nestlé, Groupe Danone—that were quicker to break into fast-growing markets in Asia, Latin America, and Eastern Europe. Unilever and Nestlé, for example, each get 32 percent of their sales in developing countries. Western Europe, Kraft's strongest international market, is almost as saturated as the United States. Even in Great Britain, Kraft is only the eighth-largest food company. "A truly global organization would have a quarter to one-third of their business in North America, not three-quarters," says Adrian Richardson, global consumer and retail-sector head at BT Funds Management, a large money manager in Sydney.

11    FORTRESS. One problem is that Kraft's strength, convenience products, doesn't go over well in emerging markets, where scarce shopping dollars are concentrated on necessities. Unilever, for example, sells staples in India such as rice with added protein and salt with iodine. Kraft, on the other hand, has only a tiny presence there. But Kraft plans to jump-start sales in emerging markets by introducing additional snack, beverage, cheese, and other brands in countries where it already has a presence. It also plans to enter countries where it has no operations and to make acquisitions, especially in snacks and beverages, according to its filings with the Securities & Exchange Commission. Richardson believes Kraft could make up to three significant acquisitions in the next few years to beef up its offshore operations: "If

they just build, build, build [new plants], they won't meaningfully move the dial," he says. For Kraft, "the U.S. domestic base is an absolute fortress that provides a very good cash cow" with which to go shopping. "They're not too late."

12    Close to home, Kraft is getting a much-needed shot of adrenaline from the Nabisco purchase. Last year, Kraft's sales dipped 1 percent, versus. gains of 7.3 percent at General Mills Inc. (GIS) and 6.3 percent at Hershey Foods Corp. (HSY) Many older Kraft products are in aging categories with flat or declining volumes, such as cereal and traditional store-bought coffee. But with Nabisco, Kraft picked up faster-growing product lines such as Chips Ahoy! cookies and Ritz crackers that will fuel earnings growth. Overnight, Kraft moved from a 6 percent to a 20 percent market share in crackers and cookies, a category that's expanding at more than twice the rate of the food-industry average. Goldman's Mally expects Kraft sales to rise 3.5 percent in each of the next three years, just ahead of the industry average. And with the cost savings it expects to squeeze from Nabisco, Kraft estimates that its earnings will grow at an above-average 18 percent to 22 percent annually over the same period.

13    That additional growth will be needed to cover the cost of the Nabisco deal. The newly public Kraft will carry an $18.5 billion debt load, even after using the offering proceeds to pay off a portion of the $11 billion it borrowed through Philip Morris to buy Nabisco. Next year, $7 billion of this debt comes due, and Kraft won't be able to meet that payment, according to its prospectus. But it says it plans to use its good credit rating to refinance.

14    Kraft has long been a leader in product development—in 1989 it launched the novel Lunchables line that's now a $750 million-a-year product. Innovations like that put Kraft on top of the U.S. food industry. Now investors will be counting on Deromedi and Holden to sprinkle some of that magic overseas.

**Source:** Julie Forster and Becky Gaylord, "Can Kraft Be a Big Cheese Abroad? It needs more global clout to offset a mature U.S. market," *BusinessWeek*, June 4, 2001.

# Part **Two**

# Strategy Formulation

Strategy formulation guides executives in defining the business their firm is in, the ends it seeks, and the means it will use to accomplish those ends. The approach of strategy formulation is an improvement over that of traditional long-range planning. As discussed in the next eight chapters—about developing a firm's competitive plan of action—strategy formulation combines a future-oriented perspective with concern for the firm's internal and external environments.

The strategy formulation process begins with definition of the company mission, as discussed in Chapter 2. In this chapter, the purpose of business is defined to reflect the values of a wide variety of interested parties. Social responsibility is discussed as a critical consideration for a company's strategic decision makers since the mission statement must express how the company intends to contribute to the societies that sustain it. Central to the idea that companies should be operated in socially responsible ways is the belief that managers will behave in an ethical manner. Management ethics are discussed in this chapter with special attention to the utilitarian, moral rights, and social justice approaches.

Chapter 3 deals with the principal factors in a firm's external environment that strategic managers must assess so they can anticipate and take advantage of future business conditions. It emphasizes the importance to a firm's planning activities of factors in the firm's remote, industry, and operating environments. A key theme of the chapter is the problem of deciding whether to accept environmental constraints or to maneuver around them.

Chapter 4 describes the key differences in strategic planning and implementation among domestic, multinational, and global firms. It gives special attention to the new vision that a firm must communicate in a revised company mission when it multinationalizes.

Chapter 5 shows how firms evaluate their company's strengths and weaknesses to produce an internal analysis. Strategic managers use such profiles to target competitive advantages they can emphasize and competitive disadvantages they should correct or minimize.

Chapter 6 examines the types of long-range objectives strategic managers set and specifies the qualities these objectives must have to provide a basis for direction and evaluation. The chapter also examines the generic and grand strategies that firms use to achieve long-range objectives.

Comprehensive approaches to the evaluation of strategic opportunities and to the final strategic decision are the focus of Chapter 7. The chapter shows how a firm's strategic options can be compared in a way that allows selection of the best available option. It also discusses how a company can create competitive advantages for each of its businesses.

Chapter 8 extends the attention on strategic analysis and choice by showing how managers can build value in multibusiness companies.

# Chapter **Two**

# Defining the Company's Mission and Social Responsibility

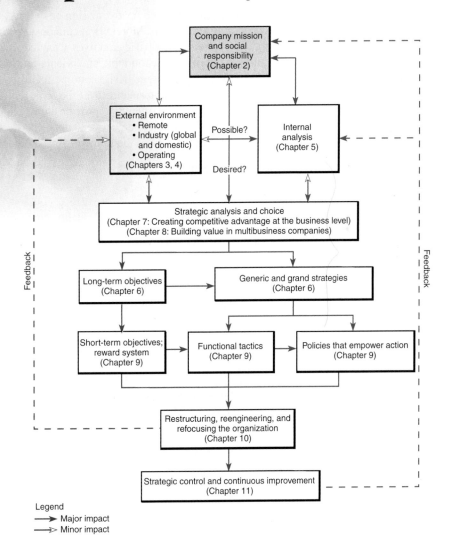

Company mission and social responsibility (Chapter 2)

External environment
• Remote
• Industry (global and domestic)
• Operating (Chapters 3, 4)

Possible?

Desired?

Internal analysis (Chapter 5)

Strategic analysis and choice
(Chapter 7: Creating competitive advantage at the business level)
(Chapter 8: Building value in multibusiness companies)

Long-term objectives (Chapter 6)

Generic and grand strategies (Chapter 6)

Short-term objectives; reward system (Chapter 9)

Functional tactics (Chapter 9)

Policies that empower action (Chapter 9)

Restructuring, reengineering, and refocusing the organization (Chapter 10)

Strategic control and continuous improvement (Chapter 11)

Feedback

Feedback

Legend
⟶ Major impact
⟶▷ Minor impact

# WHAT IS A COMPANY MISSION?

Whether a firm is developing a new business or reformulating direction for an ongoing business, it must determine the basic goals and philosophies that will shape its strategic posture. This fundamental purpose that sets a firm apart from other firms of its type and identifies the scope of its operations in product and market terms is defined as the company mission. As discussed in Chapter 1, the company mission is a broadly framed but enduring statement of a firm's intent. It embodies the business philosophy of the firm's strategic decision makers, implies the image the firm seeks to project, reflects the firm's self-concept, and indicates the firm's principal product or service areas and the primary customer needs the firm will attempt to satisfy. In short, it describes the firm's product, market, and technological areas of emphasis, and it does so in a way that reflects the values and priorities of the firm's strategic decision makers. An excellent example is the company mission statement of Nicor, Inc., shown in Exhibit 2–1, Strategy in Action.

## The Need for an Explicit Mission

No external body requires that the company mission be defined, and the process of defining it is time-consuming and tedious. Moreover, it contains broadly outlined or implied objectives and strategies rather than specific directives. Characteristically, it is a statement, not of measurable targets but of attitude, outlook, and orientation.

The mission statement is a message designed to be inclusive of the expectations of all stakeholders for the company's performance over the long run. The executives and board who prepare the mission statement attempt to provide a unifying purpose for the company that will provide a basis for strategic objective setting and decision making. In general terms, the mission statement addresses the following questions:

Why is this firm in business?

What are our economic goals?

What is our operating philosophy in terms of quality, company image, and self-concept?

What are our core competencies and competitive advantages?

What customers do and can we serve?

How do we view our responsibilities to stockholders, employees, communities, environment, social issues, and competitors?

# FORMULATING A MISSION

The process of defining the company mission for a specific business can perhaps be best understood by thinking about the business at its inception. The typical business begins with the beliefs, desires, and aspirations of a single entrepreneur. Such an owner-manager's sense of mission usually is based on the following fundamental beliefs:

1. The product or service of the business can provide benefits at least equal to its price.

2. The product or service can satisfy a customer need of specific market segments that is currently not being met adequately.

3. The technology that is to be used in production will provide a cost- and quality-competitive product or service.

## PREAMBLE

We, the management of Nicor, Inc., here set forth our belief as to the purpose for which the company is established and the principles under which it should operate. We pledge our effort to the accomplishment of these purposes within these principles.

## BASIC PURPOSE

The basic purpose of Nicor, Inc., is to perpetuate an investor-owned company engaging in various phases of the energy business, striving for balance among those phases so as to render needed satisfactory products and services and earn optimum, long-range profits.

## WHAT WE DO

The principal business of the company, through its utility subsidiary, is the provision of energy through a pipe system to meet the needs of ultimate consumers. To accomplish its basic purpose, and to ensure its strength, the company will engage in other energy-related activities, directly or through subsidiaries or in participation with other persons, corporations, firms, or entities.

All activities of the company shall be consistent with its responsibilities to investors, customers, employees, and the public and its concern for the optimum development and utilization of natural resources and for environmental needs.

## WHERE WE DO IT

The company's operations shall be primarily in the United States, but no self-imposed or regulatory geographical limitations are placed upon the acquisition, development, processing, transportation, or storage of energy resources, or upon other energy-related ventures in which the company may engage. The company will engage in such activities in any location where, after careful review, it has determined that such activity is in the best interest of its stockholders.

Utility service will be offered in the territory of the company's utility subsidiary to the best of its ability, in accordance with the requirements of regulatory agencies and pursuant to the subsidiary's purposes and principles.

---

4. With hard work and the support of others, the business can not only survive but also grow and be profitable.

5. The management philosophy of the business will result in a favorable public image and will provide financial and psychological rewards for those who are willing to invest their labor and money in helping the business to succeed.

6. The entrepreneur's self-concept of the business can be communicated to and adopted by employees and stockholders.

As the business grows or is forced by competitive pressures to alter its product, market, or technology, redefining the company mission may be necessary. If so, the revised mission statement will contain the same components as the original. It will state the basic type of product or service to be offered, the primary markets or customer groups to be served; the technology to be used in production or delivery; the firm's fundamental concern for survival through growth and profitability; the firm's managerial philosophy; the public image the firm seeks; and the self-concept those affiliated with the firm should have of it. This chapter will discuss in detail these components. The examples shown in Exhibit 2–2 provide insights into how some major corporations handle them.

## Basic Product or Service; Primary Market; Principal Technology

Three indispensable components of the mission statement are specification of the basic product or service, specification of the primary market, and specification of the principal technology for production or delivery. These components are discussed under one heading because only in combination do they describe the company's business activity. A good example of the three components is to be found in the business plan of ITT Barton, a division of ITT. Under the heading of business mission and area served, the following information is presented:

# Strategy in Action
Identifying Mission Statement Components: A Compilation
of Excerpts from Actual Corporate Mission Statements

**Exhibit 2–2**

| 1. Customer-market | We believe our first responsibility is to the doctors, nurses, and patients, to mothers and all others who use our products and services. (Johnson & Johnson) |
|---|---|
| | To anticipate and meet market needs of farmers, ranchers, and rural communities within North America. (CENEX) |
| 2. Product-service | AMAX's principal products are molybdenum, coal, iron ore, copper, lead, zinc, petroleum and natural gas, potash, phosphates, nickel, tungsten, silver, gold, and magnesium. (AMAX) |
| 3. Geographic domain | We are dedicated to total success of Corning Glass Works as a worldwide competitor. (Corning Glass) |
| 4. Technology | Control Data is in the business of applying microelectronics and computer technology in two general areas: computer-related hardware and computing-enhancing services, which include computation, information, education, and finance. (Control Data) |
| | The common technology in these areas relates to discrete particle coatings. (NASHUA) |
| 5. Concern for survival | In this respect, the company will conduct its operation prudently, and will provide the profits and growth which will assure Hoover's ultimate success. (Hoover Universal) |
| 6. Philosophy | We are committed to improve health care throughout the world. (Baxter Travenol) |
| | We believe human development to be the worthiest of the goals of civilization and independence to be the superior condition for nurturing growth in the capabilities of people. (Sun Company) |
| 7. Self-concept | Hoover Universal is a diversified, multi-industry corporation with strong manufacturing capabilities, entrepreneurial policies, and individual business unit autonomy. (Hoover Universal) |
| 8. Concern for public image | We are responsible to the communities in which we live and work and to the world community as well. (Johnson & Johnson) |
| | Also, we must be responsive to the broader concerns of the public, including especially the general desire for improvement in the quality of life, equal opportunity for all, and the constructive use of natural resources. (Sun Company) |

The unit's mission is to serve industry and government with quality instruments used for the primary measurement, analysis, and local control of fluid flow, level, pressure, temperature, and fluid properties. This instrumentation includes flow meters, electronic readouts, indicators, recorders, switches, liquid level systems, analytical instruments such as titrators, integrators, controllers, transmitters, and various instruments for the measurement of fluid properties (density, viscosity, gravity) used for processing variable sensing, data collecting, control, and transmission. The unit's mission includes fundamental loop-closing control and display devices, when economically justified, but excludes broadline central control room instrumentation, systems design, and turnkey responsibility.

Markets served include instrumentation for oil and gas production, gas transportation, chemical and petrochemical processing, cryogenics, power generation, aerospace, government, and marine, as well as other instrument and equipment manufacturers.

In only 129 words, this segment of the mission statement clearly indicates to all readers—from company employees to casual observers—the basic products, primary markets, and principal technologies of ITT Barton.

Often the most referenced public statement of a company's selected products and markets appears in "silver bullet" form in the mission statement; for example, "Dayton-Hudson Corporation is a diversified retailing company whose business is to serve the American consumer through the retailing of fashion-oriented quality merchandise." Such an abstract of company direction is particularly helpful to outsiders who value condensed overviews.

## Company Goals: Survival, Growth, Profitability

Three economic goals guide the strategic direction of almost every business organization. Whether or not the mission statement explicitly states these goals, it reflects the firm's intention to secure *survival* through *growth* and *profitability*.

A firm that is unable to survive will be incapable of satisfying the aims of any of its stakeholders. Unfortunately, the goal of survival, like the goals of growth and profitability, often is taken for granted to such an extent that it is neglected as a principal criterion in strategic decision making. When this happens, the firm may focus on short-term aims at the expense of the long run. Concerns for expediency, a quick fix, or a bargain may displace the assessment of long-term impact. Too often, the result is near-term economic failure owing to a lack of resource synergy and sound business practice. For example, Consolidated Foods, maker of Shasta soft drinks and L'eggs hosiery, sought growth through the acquisition of bargain businesses. However, the erratic sales patterns of its diverse holdings forced it to divest itself of more than four dozen companies. This process cost Consolidated Foods millions of dollars and hampered its growth.

Profitability is the mainstay goal of a business organization. No matter how profit is measured or defined, profit over the long term is the clearest indication of a firm's ability to satisfy the principal claims and desires of employees and stockholders. The key phrase here is "over the long term." Obviously, basing decisions on a short-term concern for profitability would lead to a strategic myopia. Overlooking the enduring concerns of customers, suppliers, creditors, ecologists, and regulatory agents may produce profit in the short term, but, over time, the financial consequences are likely to be detrimental.

The following excerpt from the Hewlett-Packard statement of mission ably expresses the importance of an orientation toward long-term profit:

> To achieve sufficient profit to finance our company growth and to provide the resources we need to achieve our other corporate objectives.
>
> In our economic system, the profit we generate from our operation is the ultimate source of the funds we need to prosper and grow. It is the one absolutely essential measure of our corporate performance over the long term. Only if we continue to meet our profit objective can we achieve our other corporate objectives.

A firm's growth is tied inextricably to its survival and profitability. In this context, the meaning of growth must be broadly defined. Although product impact market studies (PIMS) have shown that growth in market share is correlated with profitability, other important forms of growth do exist. Growth in the number of markets served, in the variety of products offered, and in the technologies that are used to provide goods or services frequently lead to improvements in a firm's competitive ability. Growth means change, and proactive change is essential in a dynamic business environment.

AOL's strategy provides an example, as shown in Exhibit 2–3, Strategy in Action. In 2003, some analysts believed that AOL Time Warner should change to a survival strategy because of the amount of debt that it was carrying. They believed that AOL should try to reduce debt and regain some market share that it had lost over the previous year. AOL did decide to reduce its $7 billion debt by the end of 2004, but not simply to survive. AOL was trying to position itself for the acquisition of either Adelphia or Cablevision. AOL felt that if it could acquire one of these two companies or possibly both, it could increase its footprint in the market. AOL believed that growth for its company would have to come from the Cable TV market and that the only way to grow was to serve more markets. Luckily, AOL's top competitor, Comcast, was in the same debt position as AOL and could not immediately preempt the acquisitions.

Hewlett-Packard's mission statement provides another excellent example of corporate regard for growth:

> Objective: To let our growth be limited only by our profits and our ability to develop and produce technical products that satisfy real customer needs.

AOL Time Warner Chief Executive Parsons stressed once again his goal of reducing AOL Time Warner's (AOL) total debt to $20 billion by the end of 2004, versus the $27 billion it had in January 2003. Everybody assumed that his primary aim was to adopt a more financially conservative approach to managing AOL Time Warner. That would have made sense, considering that its debt rating was lingering dangerously close to junk-bond grade, that the financial performance of its America Online division was still flagging, and that its damaged credibility with investors left its stock trading in the $10 to $12 range, far below its 52-week high of $27.44.

Parsons' debt-reduction plan was an effort to clear the decks for another AOL acquisition. While he did intend to improve the company's soundness and its stock price, industry analysts said he also wanted to make a run for the nation's number five cable operator, Adelphia Cable in Coudersport, Pa., which entered Chapter 11 bankruptcy after members of the controlling Rigas family were charged with looting their company of more than $2 billion. Alternatively, Time Warner Cable may have been interested in acquiring Cablevision (CVC), the number six operator, whose Long Island (NY) systems were contiguous with Time Warner Cable's New York City market. Both Time Warner Cable and Comcast (CMCSA), the nation's number one cable company, were salivating over Adelphia's 5.3 million subscribers. But Comcast was also too debt-laden to make an offer, and that bought Parsons a little time to clean up AOL's balance sheet and perhaps make the first move as early as a year from now.

Parsons was in the camp of media execs who believed that cable is likely, eventually, to dominate the distribution of nearly all digital media to homes. Locking up as many local cable monopolies as possible would have helped AOL distribute its TV programming, movies, music, and Internet services.

**Source:** Extracted from David Shook, "Will Cable be AOL's Lifeline?" *BusinessWeek Online,* March 10, 2003.

---

We do not believe that large size is important for its own sake; however, for at least two basic reasons, continuous growth is essential for us to achieve our other objectives.

In the first place, we serve a rapidly growing and expanding segment of our technological society. To remain static would be to lose ground. We cannot maintain a position of strength and leadership in our field without growth.

In the second place, growth is important in order to attract and hold high-caliber people. These individuals will align their future only with a company that offers them considerable opportunity for personal progress. Opportunities are greater and more challenging in a growing company.

The issue of growth raises a concern about the definition of the company mission. How can a firm's product, market, and technology be specified sufficiently to provide direction without precluding the exercise of unanticipated strategic options? How can a firm so define its mission that it can consider opportunistic diversification while maintaining the parameters that guide its growth decision? Perhaps such questions are best addressed when a firm's mission statement outlines the conditions under which the firm might depart from ongoing operations. General Electric Company's extensive global mission provided the foundation for its GE Appliances (GEA) in Louisville, Kentucky. GEA did not see consumer preferences in the world market becoming Americanized. Instead, its expansion goals allowed for flexibility in examining the unique characteristics of individual foreign markets and tailoring strategies to fit them.

The growth philosophy of Dayton-Hudson also embodies this approach:

The stability and quality of the corporation's financial performance will be developed through the profitable execution of our existing businesses, as well as through the acquisition or development of new businesses. Our growth priorities, in order, are as follows:

1. Development of the profitable market preeminence of existing companies in existing markets through new store development or new strategies within existing stores.
2. Expansion of our companies to feasible new markets.

We, the Saturn Team, in concert with the UAW and General Motors, believe that meeting the needs of customers, Saturn members, suppliers, dealers, and neighbors is fundamental to fulfilling our mission.

To meet our customer's needs . . .

- our products and services must be world leaders in value and satisfaction.

To meet our members' needs, we . . .

- will create a sense of belonging in an environment of mutual trust, respect, and dignity;

- believe that all people want to be involved in decisions that affect them, care about their jobs and each other, take pride in themselves and in their contributions, and want to share in the success of their efforts;

- will develop the tools, training, and education for each member, recognizing individual skills and knowledge;

- believe that creative, motivated, responsible team members who understand that change is critical to success are Saturn's most important asset.

To meet our suppliers' and dealers' needs, we . . .

- will strive to create real partnerships with them;

- will be open and fair in our dealings, reflecting trust, respect, and their importance to Saturn;

- want dealers and suppliers to feel ownerships in Saturn's mission and philosophy as their own.

To meet the needs of our neighbors, the communities in which we live and operate, we . . .

- will be good citizens, protect the environment, and conserve natural resources;

- will seek to cooperate with government at all levels and strive to be sensitive, open, and candid in all our public statements.

3. Acquisition of other retailing companies that are strategically and financially compatible with Dayton-Hudson.
4. Internal development of new retailing strategies.

Capital allocations to fund the expansion of existing Dayton-Hudson operating companies will be based on each company's return on investment (ROI), in relationship to its ROI objective and its consistency in earnings growth and on the ability of its management to perform up to the forecasts contained in its capital requests. Expansion via acquisition or new venture will occur when the opportunity promises an acceptable rate of long-term growth and profitability, an acceptable degree of risk, and compatibility with Dayton-Hudson's long-term strategy.

## Company Philosophy

The statement of a company's philosophy, often called the *company creed*, usually accompanies or appears within the mission statement. It reflects or specifies the basic beliefs, values, aspirations, and philosophical priorities to which strategic decision makers are committed in managing the company. Fortunately, the philosophies vary little from one firm to another. Owners and managers implicitly accept a general, unwritten, yet pervasive code of behavior that governs business actions and permits them to be largely self-regulated. Unfortunately, statements of company philosophy are often so similar and so platitudinous that they read more like public relations handouts than the commitment to values they are meant to be.

Saturn's statement of philosophy, presented in Exhibit 2–4, Strategy in Action, indicates the company's clearly defined initiatives for satisfying the needs of its customers, employees, suppliers, and dealers.

Despite the similarity of these statements, the intentions of the strategic managers in developing them do not warrant cynicism. Company executives attempt to provide a

The corporation will:

Set standards for return on investment (ROI) and earnings growth.

Approve strategic plans.

Allocate capital.

Approve goals.

Monitor, measure, and audit results.

Reward performance.

Allocate management resources.

The operating companies will be accorded the freedom and responsibility:

To manage their own business.

To develop strategic plans and goals that will optimize their growth.

To develop an organization that can ensure consistency of results and optimum growth.

To operate their businesses consistent with the corporation's statement of philosophy.

The corporate staff will provide only those services that are:

Essential to the protection of the corporation.

Needed for the growth of the corporation.

Wanted by operating companies and that provide a significant advantage in quality or cost.

The corporation will insist on:

Uniform accounting practices by type of business.

Prompt disclosure of operating results.

A systematic approach to training and developing people.

Adherence to appropriately high standards of business conduct and civic responsibility in accordance with the corporation's statement of philosophy.

distinctive and accurate picture of the firm's managerial outlook. One such statement of company philosophy is that of Dayton-Hudson Corporation. As Exhibit 2–5, Strategy in Action, shows, Dayton-Hudson's board of directors and executives have established especially clear directions for company decision making and action.

Perhaps most noteworthy in the Dayton-Hudson statement is its delineation of responsibility at both the corporate and business levels. In many ways, the statement could serve as a prototype for the three-tier approach to strategic management. This approach implies that the mission statement must address strategic concerns at the corporate, business, and functional levels of the organization. Dayton-Hudson's management philosophy does this by balancing operating autonomy and flexibility on the one hand with corporate input and direction on the other.

As seen in Exhibit 2–6, Global Strategy in Action, the philosophy of Nissan Motor Manufacturing is expressed by the company's People Principles and Key Corporate Principles. These principles form the basis of the way the company operates on a daily basis. They address the principal concepts used in meeting the company's established goals. Nissan focuses on the distinction between the role of the individual and the corporation. In this way, employees can link their productivity and success to the productivity and success of the company. Given these principles, the company is able to concentrate on the issues most important to its survival, growth, and profitability.

Strategy in Action Exhibit 2–7 provides an example of how General Motors uses a statement of company philosophy to clarify its environmental principles.

## Public Image

Both present and potential customers attribute certain qualities to particular businesses. Gerber and Johnson & Johnson make safe products; Cross Pen makes high-quality writing instruments;

# Global Strategy in Action
Principles of Nissan Motor Manufacturing (UK) Ltd.

**Exhibit 2–6**

| | **People Principles**<br>**(All Other Objectives Can Only Be Achieved by People)** |
|---|---|
| Selection | Hire the highest caliber people; look for technical capabilities and emphasize attitude. |
| Responsibility | Maximize the responsibility; staff by devolving decision making. |
| Teamwork | Recognize and encourage individual contributions, with everyone working toward the same objectives. |
| Flexibility | Expand the role of the individual: multiskilled, no job description, generic job titles. |
| Kaizen | Continuously seek 100.1 percent improvements; give "ownership of change." |
| Communications | "Every day, face to face." |
| Training | Establish individual "continuous development programs." |
| Supervisors | Regard as "the professionals at managing the production process"; give them much responsibility normally assumed by individual departments; make them the genuine leaders of their teams. |
| Single status | Treat everyone as a "first class" citizen; eliminate all illogical differences. |
| Trade unionism | Establish single union agreement with AEU emphasizing the common objective for a successful enterprise. |

| | **Key Corporate Principles** |
|---|---|
| Quality | Building profitably the highest quality car sold in Europe. |
| Customers | Achieve target of no. 1 customer satisfaction in Europe. |
| Volume | Always achieve required volume. |
| New products | Deliver on time, at required quality, within cost. |
| Suppliers | Establish long-term relationship with single-source suppliers; aim for zero defects and just-in-time delivery; apply Nissan principles to suppliers. |
| Production | Use "most appropriate" technology; develop predictable "best method" of doing job; build in quality. |
| Engineering | Design "quality" and "ease of working" into the product and facilities; establish "simultaneous engineering" to reduce development time. |

Étienne Aigner makes stylish but affordable leather products; Corvettes are power machines; and Izod Lacoste stands for the preppy look. Thus, mission statements should reflect the public's expectations, since this makes achievement of the firm's goals more likely. Gerber's mission statement should not open the possibility for diversification into pesticides, and Cross Pen's should not open the possibility for diversification into $0.59 brand-name disposables.

On the other hand, a negative public image often prompts firms to reemphasize the beneficial aspects of their mission. For example, in response to what it saw as a disturbing trend in public opinion, Dow Chemical undertook an aggressive promotional campaign to fortify its credibility, particularly among "employees and those who live and work in [their] plant communities." Dow described its approach in its annual report:

> All around the world today, Dow people are speaking up. People who care deeply about their company, what it stands for, and how it is viewed by others. People who are immensely proud of their company's performance, yet realistic enough to realize it is the public's perception of that performance that counts in the long run.

As a responsible corporate citizen, General Motors is dedicated to protecting human health, natural resources, and the global environment. This dedication reaches further than compliance with the law to encompass the integration of sound environmental practices into our business decisions.

The following environmental principles provide guidance to General Motors personnel worldwide in the conduct of their daily business practices:

1. We are committed to actions to restore and preserve the environment.

2. We are committed to reducing waste and pollutants, conserving resources, and recycling materials at every stage of the product life cycle.

3. We will continue to participate actively in educating the public regarding environmental conservation.

4. We will continue to pursue vigorously the development and implementation of technologies for minimizing pollutant emissions.

5. We will continue to work with all governmental entities for the development of technically sound and financially responsible environmental laws and regulations.

6. We will continually assess the impact of our plants and products on the environment and the communities in which we live and operate with a goal of continuous improvement.

---

Firms seldom address the question of their public image in an intermittent fashion. Although public agitation often stimulates greater attention to this question, firms are concerned about their public image even in the absence of such agitation. The following excerpt from the mission statement of Intel Corporation is an example of this attitude:

> We are sensitive to our *image with our customers and the business community.* Commitments to customers are considered sacred, and we are upset with ourselves when we do not meet our commitments. We strive to demonstrate to the business world on a continuing basis that we are credible in describing the state of the corporation, and that we are well organized and in complete control of all things that determine the numbers.

Exhibit 2–8, Strategy in Action, presents a marketing translation of the essence of the mission statements of six high-end shoe companies. The impressive feature of the exhibit is that it shows dramatically how closely competing firms can incorporate subtle, yet meaningful, differences into their mission statements.

## Company Self-Concept

A major determinant of a firm's success is the extent to which the firm can relate functionally to its external environment. To achieve its proper place in a competitive situation, the firm realistically must evaluate its competitive strengths and weaknesses. This idea—that the firm must know itself—is the essence of the company self-concept. The idea is not commonly integrated into theories of strategic management; its importance for individuals has been recognized since ancient times.

Both individuals and firms have a crucial need to know themselves. The ability of either to survive in a dynamic and highly competitive environment would be severely limited if they did not understand their impact on others or of others on them.

In some senses, then, firms take on personalities of their own. Much behavior in firms is organizationally based; that is, a firm acts on its members in other ways than their individual interactions. Thus, firms are entities whose personality transcends the personalities of their members. As such, they can set decision-making parameters based on aims different and distinct from the aims of their members. These organizational considerations have pervasive effects.

Ordinarily, descriptions of the company self-concept per se do not appear in mission statements. Yet such statements often provide strong impressions of the company self-

**Allen-Edmonds**

Allen-Edmonds provides high-quality shoes for the affluent consumer who appreciates a well-made, finely crafted, stylish dress shoe.

**Bally**

Bally shoes set you apart. They are the perfect shoe to complement your lifestyle. Bally shoes project an image of European style and elegance that ensures one is not just dressed, but well dressed.

**Bostonian**

Bostonian shoes are for those successful individuals who are well-traveled, on the "go" and want a stylish dress shoe that can keep up with their variety of needs and activities. With Bostonian, you know you will always be well dressed whatever the situation.

**Cole-Hahn**

Cole-Hahn offers a line of contemporary shoes for the man who wants to go his own way. They are shoes for the urban, upscale, stylish man who wants to project an image of being one step ahead.

**Florsheim**

Florsheim shoes are the affordable classic men's dress shoes for those who want to experience the comfort and style of a solid dress shoe.

**Johnston & Murphy**

Johnston & Murphy is the quintessential business shoe for those affluent individuals who know and demand the best.

**Source:** "Thinking on Your Feet, the Johnston & Murphy Guerrilla Marketing Competition" (Johnston & Murphy, a GENESCO Company).

concept. For example, ARCO's environment, health, and safety (EHS) managers were adamant about emphasizing the company's position on safety and environmental performance as a part of the mission statement. The challenges facing the ARCO EHS managers included dealing with concerned environmental groups and a public that has become environmentally aware. They hoped to motivate employees toward safer behavior while reducing emissions and waste. They saw this as a reflection of the company's positive self-image.

The following excerpts from the Intel Corporation mission statement describe the corporate persona that its top management seeks to foster:

Management is self-critical. The leaders must be capable of recognizing and accepting their mistakes and learning from them.

Open (constructive) confrontation is encouraged at all levels of the corporation and is viewed as a method of problem solving and conflict resolution.

Decision by consensus is the rule. Decisions once made are supported. Position in the organization is not the basis for quality of ideas.

A highly communicative, open management is part of the style.

Management must be ethical. Managing by telling the truth and treating all employees equitably has established credibility that is ethical.

We strive to provide an opportunity for rapid development.

Intel is a results-oriented company. The focus is on substance versus form, quality versus quantity.

We believe in the principle that hard work, high productivity is something to be proud of.

The concept of assumed responsibility is accepted. (If a task needs to be done, assume you have the responsibility to get it done.)

Commitments are long term. If career problems occur at some point, reassignment is a better alternative than termination.

We desire to have all employees involved and participative in their relationship with Intel.

## Newest Trends in Mission Components

Recently, three issues have become so prominent in the strategic planning for organizations that they are increasingly becoming integral parts in the development and revisions of mission statements: sensitivity to consumer wants, concern for quality, and statements of company vision.

## Customers

"The customer is our top priority" is a slogan that would be claimed by the majority of businesses in the United States and abroad. For companies including Caterpillar Tractor, General Electric, and Johnson & Johnson this means analyzing consumer needs before as well as after a sale. The bonus plan at Xerox allows for a 40 percent annual bonus, based on high customer reviews of the service that they receive, and a 20 percent penalty if the feedback is especially bad. For these firms and many others, the overriding concern for the company has become consumer satisfaction.

In addition many U.S. firms maintain extensive product safety programs to help ensure consumer satisfaction. RCA, Sears, and 3M boast of such programs. Other firms including Calgon Corporation, Amoco, Mobil Oil, Whirlpool, and Zenith provide toll-free telephone lines to answer customer concerns and complaints.

The focus on customer satisfaction is demonstrated by retailer J. C. Penney in this excerpt from its statement of philosophy: "The Penney Idea is (1) To serve the public as nearly as we can to its complete satisfaction; (2) To expect for the service we render a fair remuneration, and not all the profit the traffic will bear; (3) To do all in our power to pack the customer's dollar full of value, quality, and satisfaction."

A focus on customer satisfaction causes managers to realize the importance of providing quality customer service. Strong customer service initiatives have led some firms to gain competitive advantages in the marketplace. Hence, many corporations have made the customer service initiative a key component of their corporate mission.

## Quality

"Quality is job one!" is a rallying point not only for Ford Motor Corporation but for many resurging U.S. businesses as well. Two U.S. management experts fostered a worldwide emphasis on quality in manufacturing. W. Edwards Deming and J. M. Juran's messages were first embraced by Japanese managers, whose quality consciousness led to global dominance in several industries including automobile, TV, audio equipment, and electronic components manufacturing. Deming summarizes his approach in 14 now well-known points:

1. Create constancy of purpose.

2. Adopt the new philosophy.

3. Cease dependence on mass inspection to achieve quality.

4. End the practice of awarding business on price tag alone. Instead, minimize total cost, often accomplished by working with a single supplier.

5. Improve constantly the system of production and service.

6. Institute training on the job.

7. Institute leadership.

8. Drive out fear.

9. Break down barriers between departments.

10. Eliminate slogans, exhortations, and numerical targets.

11. Eliminate work standards (quotas) and management by objective.

12. Remove barriers that rob workers, engineers, and managers of their right to pride of workmanship.

### CADILLAC

The Mission of the Cadillac Motor Company is to engineer, produce, and market the world's finest automobiles known for uncompromised levels of distinctiveness, comfort, convenience, and refined performance. Through its people, who are its strength, Cadillac will continuously improve the quality of its products and services to meet or exceed customer expectations and succeed as a profitable business.

### MOTOROLA

Dedication to quality is a way of life at our company, so much so that it goes far beyond rhetorical slogans. Our ongoing program is one of continued improvement out for change, refinement, and even revolution in our pursuit of quality excellence.

It is the objective of Motorola, Inc., to produce and provide products and services of the highest quality. In its activities, Motorola will pursue goals aimed at the achievement of quality excellence. These results will be derived from the dedicated efforts of each employee in conjunction with supportive participation from management at all levels of the corporation.

### ZYTEC

Zytec is a company that competes on value; is market driven; provides superior quality and service, builds strong relationship with its customers; and provides technical excellence in its products.

13. Institute a vigorous program of education and self-improvement.

14. Put everyone in the company to work to accomplish the transformation.

Firms in the United States responded aggressively. The new philosophy is that quality should be the norm. For example, Motorola's production goal is 60 or fewer defects per every billion components that it manufactures.

Exhibit 2–9, Strategy in Action, presents the integration of the quality initiative into the mission statements of three corporations. The emphasis on quality has received added emphasis in many corporate philosophies since the Congress created the Malcolm Baldrige Quality Award in 1987. Each year up to two Baldrige Awards can be given in three categories of a company's operations: manufacturing, services, and small businesses.

### Vision Statement

Whereas the mission statement expresses an answer to the question "What business are we in?" a company *vision statement* is sometimes developed to express the aspirations of the executive leadership. A vision statement presents the firm's strategic intent that focuses the energies and resources of the company on achieving a desirable future. However, in actual practice, the mission and vision statement are frequently combined into a single statement. When they are separated, the vision statement is often a single sentence, designed to be memorable. For example:

Federal Express: "Our vision is to change the way we all connect with each other in the New Network Economy."

Lexmark: "Customers for Life."

Microsoft: "A computer on every desk, and in every home, running on Microsoft software."

## An Exemplary Mission Statement

When BB&T merged with Southern Bank, the Board of Directors and officers undertook the creation of a comprehensive mission statement that was designed to include most of the topics that we discussed in this chapter. In 2003, the company updated its statement and mailed the resulting booklet to its shareholders and other interested parties. The foreword to the document expresses the greatest values of such a public pronouncement and was signed by BB&T's Chairman and CEO, John A. Allison:

> In a rapidly changing and unpredictable world, individuals and organizations need a clear set of fundamental principals to guide their actions. At BB&T we know the content of our business will, and should, experience constant change. Change is necessary for progress. However, the context, our fundamental principles, is unchanging because these principles are based on basic truths.
>
> BB&T is a mission-driven organization with a clearly defined set of values. We encourage our employees to have a strong sense of purpose, a high level of self-esteem and the capacity to think clearly and logically.
>
> We believe that competitive advantage is largely in the minds of our employees as represented by their capacity to turn rational ideas into action towards the accomplishment of our mission.

Appendix 2 presents BB&T's Vision, Mission, and Purpose Statement in its entirety. It also includes detailed expressions of the company's values and views on the role of emotions, management style, the management concept, attributes of an outstanding employee, the importance of positive attitude, obligations to its employees, virtues of an outstanding credit culture, achieving the company goal, the nature of a "world standard" revenue-driven sales organization, the nature of a "world standard" client service community bank, the company's commitment to education and learning, and its passions.

# BOARDS OF DIRECTORS

Who is responsible for determining the firm's mission? Who is responsible for acquiring and allocating resources so the firm can thoughtfully develop and implement a strategic plan? Who is responsible for monitoring the firm's success in the competitive marketplace to determine whether that plan was well designed and activated? The answer to all of these questions is strategic decision makers. As you saw in Exhibit 1–3, most organizations have multiple levels of strategic decision makers; typically, the larger the firm, the more levels it will have. The strategic managers at the highest level are responsible for decisions that affect the entire firm, commit the firm and its resources for the longest periods, and declare the firm's sense of values. In other words, this group of strategic managers is responsible for overseeing the creation and accomplishment of the company mission. The term that describes the group is *board of directors.*

In overseeing the management of a firm, the board of directors operates as the representatives of the firm's stockholders. Elected by the stockholders, the board has these major responsibilities:

1. To establish and update the company mission.

2. To elect the company's top officers, the foremost of whom is the CEO.

3. To establish the compensation levels of the top officers, including their salaries and bonuses.

4. To determine the amount and timing of the dividends paid to stockholders.

5. To set broad company policy on such matters as labor–management relations, product or service lines of business, and employee benefit packages.

6. To set company objectives and to authorize managers to implement the long-term strategies that the top officers and the board have found agreeable.

7. To mandate company compliance with legal and ethical dictates.

In the current business environment, boards of directors are accepting the challenge of shareholders and other stakeholders to become active in establishing the strategic initiatives of the companies that they serve.

This chapter considers the board of directors because the board's greatest impact on the behavior of a firm results from its determination of the company mission. The philosophy espoused in the mission statement sets the tone by which the firm and all of its employees will be judged. As logical extensions of the mission statement, the firm's objectives and strategies embody the board's view of proper business demeanor. Through its appointment of top executives and its decisions about their compensation, the board reveals its priorities for organizational achievement.

# SARBANES-OXLEY ACT OF 2002

Following a string of alleged wrongdoings by corporate executives in 2000 to 2002, and the subsequent failures of their firms, Washington lawmakers proposed more than 50 policies to reassure investors. None of the resulting bills were able to pass both houses of Congress until the Banking Committee Chairman Paul Sarbanes (D-MD) proposed legislation to establish new auditing and accounting standards. The bill was called the Public Company Accounting Reform and Investor Protection Act of 2002. Later the name was changed to Sarbanes-Oxley Act of 2002.

On July 30, 2002, President George Bush signed the Sarbanes-Oxley Act into law. This revolutionary act applies to public companies with securities registered under Section 12 of the Securities Act of 1934, and those required to file reports under Section 15(d) of the Exchange Act. Sarbanes-Oxley includes required certifications for financial statements, new corporate regulations, disclosure requirements, and penalties for failure to comply.

The Sarbanes-Oxley Act states that the CEO and CFO must certify every report containing the company's financial statements. The certification acknowledges that the CEO or CFO has reviewed the report. Among the review, the officer must attest that the information does not include untrue statements or necessary omitted information. Furthermore, based on the officer's knowledge, the report is a reliable source of the company's financial condition and result of operations for the period represented. The certification also makes the officers responsible for establishing and maintaining internal controls such that they are aware of any material information relating to the company. The officers must also evaluate the effectiveness of the internal controls within 90 days of the release of the report and present their conclusions of the effectiveness of the controls. Also, the officers must disclose any fraudulent material, deficiencies in the reporting of the financial reports, or problems with the internal control to the company's auditors and auditing committee. Finally, the officers must indicate any changes to the internal controls or factors that could affect them.

The Sarbanes-Oxley Act includes provisions restricting the corporate control of executives, accounting firms, auditing committees, and attorneys. With regard to executives, the Act bans personal loans. A company can no longer directly or indirectly issue, extend, or maintain a personal loan to any director or executive officer. Executive officers and directors are not permitted to purchase, to sell, to acquire, or to transfer any equity security during any pension fund blackout period. Executives are required to notify fund participants of any blackout period and the reasons for the blackout period. The SEC will provide the company's executives with a code of ethics for the company to adopt. Failure to meet the code must be disclosed to the SEC.

The Act limits some and issues new duties of the registered public accounting firms that conduct the audits of the financial statements. Accounting firms are prohibited from performing bookkeeping or other accounting services related to the financial statements, designing or implementing financial systems, appraising, internal auditing, brokering banking services, or providing legal services unrelated to the audit. All critical accounting policies and alternative

The following outline presents the major elements of the Sarbanes-Oxley Act of 2002.

## Corporate Responsibility

- The CEO and CFO of each company are required to submit a report, based on their knowledge, to the SEC certifying the company's financial statements are fair representations of the financial condition without false statements or omissions.

- The CEO and CFO must reimburse the company for any bonuses or equity-based incentives received for the last 12-month period if the company is required to restate its financial statements due to material noncompliance with any financial reporting requirement that resulted from misconduct.

- Directors and executive officers are prohibited from trading a company's 401(k) plan, profit sharing plan, or retirement plan during any blackout period. The plan administrators are required to notify the plan participants and beneficiaries with notice of all blackout periods, reasons for the blackout period, and a statement that the participant or beneficiary should evaluate their investment even though they are unable to direct or diversify their accounts during the blackout.

- No company may make, extend, modify, or renew any personal loans to its executives or directors. Limited exceptions are for loans made in the course of the company's business, on market terms, for home improvement and home loans, consumer credit, or extension of credit.

## Increased Disclosure

- Each annual and quarterly financial report filed with the SEC must disclose all material off-balance-sheet transactions, arrangements, and obligations that may affect the current or future financial condition of the company or its operations.

- Companies must present pro forma financial information with the SEC in a manner that is not misleading and must be reconciled with the company's financial condition and with generally accepted accounting principles (GAAP).

- Each company is required to disclose whether they have adopted a code of ethics for its senior financial officers. If not, the company must explain the reasons. Any change or waiver of the code of ethics must be disclosed.

- Each annual report must contain a statement of management's responsibility for establishing and maintaining an internal control structure and procedures for financial reporting. The report must also include an assessment of the effectiveness of the internal control procedures.

- The Form 4 will be provided within two business days after the execution date of the trading of a company's securities by directors and executive officers. The SEC may extend this deadline if it determines the two-day period is not feasible.

- The company must disclose information concerning changes in financial conditions or operations "on a rapid and current basis," in plain English.

The SEC must review the financial statements of each reporting company no less than once every three years.

## Audit Committees

- The audit committee must be composed entirely of independent directors. Committee members are not permitted to accept any fees from the company, cannot control 5 percent or more of the voting of the company, nor be an officer, director, partner, or employee of the company.

treatments of financial information within GAAP, and written communication between the accounting firm and the company's management must be reported to the audit committee.

The Act defines the composition of the audit committee and specifies its responsibilities. The members of the audit committee must be members of the company's board of directors. At least one member of the committee should be classified as a "financial expert." The audit committee is directly responsible for the work of any accounting firm employed by the company, and the accounting firm must report directly to the audit committee. The audit committee must create procedures for employee complaints or concerns over accounting or auditing matters. Upon discovery of unlawful acts by the company, the audit committee must report and be supervised in its investigation by a Public Company Accounting Oversight Board.

The Act includes rules for attorney conduct. If a company's attorneys find evidence of securities violations, they are required to report the matter to the chief legal counsel or CEO. If there is not an appropriate response, the attorneys must report the information to the audit committee or the board of directors.

- The audit committee must have the authority to engage the outside auditing firm.

- The audit committee must establish procedures for the treatment of complaints regarding accounting controls or auditing matters. They are responsible for employee complaints concerning questionable accounting and auditing.

- The audit committee must disclose whether at least one of the committee members is a "financial expert." If not, the committee must explain why not.

## New Crimes and Increased Criminal Penalties

- Tampering with records with intent to impede or influence any federal investigation or bankruptcy will be punishable by a fine and/or prison sentence up to 20 years.

- Failure by an accountant to maintain all auditing papers for five years after the end of the fiscal period will be punishable by a fine and/or up to 10-year prison sentence.

- Knowingly executing, or attempting to execute, a scheme to defraud investors will be punishable by a fine and/or prison sentence of up to 25 years.

- Willfully certifying a report that does not comply with the law can be punishable with a fine up to $5,000,000 and/or a prison sentence up to 20 years.

## New Civil Cause of Action and Increased Enforcement Powers

- Protection will be provided to whistle-blowers who provide information or assist in an investigation by law enforcement, congressional committee, or employee supervisor.

- Bankruptcy cannot be used to avoid liability from securities laws violations.

- Investors are able to file a civil action for fraud up to two years after discovery of the facts and five years after the occurrence of fraud.

- The SEC can receive a restraining order prohibiting payments to insiders during an investigation.

- The SEC can prevent individuals from holding an officer's or director's position in a public company as a result of violation of the securities law.

## Auditor Independence

- All audit services must be preapproved by the audit committee and must be disclosed to investors.

- The lead audit or reviewing audit partner from the auditing accounting firm must change at least once every five fiscal years.

- The registered accounting firms must report to the audit committee all accounting policies and practices used, alternative uses of the financial information within GAAP that has been discussed with management, and written communications between the accounting firm and management.

- An auditing firm is prohibited from auditing a company if the company's CEO or CFO was employed by the auditing firm within the past year.

A Public Company Accounting Oversight Board is established by the SEC to oversee the audits of public companies. The Board will register public accounting firms, establish audit standards, inspect registered accounting firms, and discipline violators of the rules. No person can take part in an audit if not employed by a registered public accounting firm.

Other sections of the Sarbanes-Oxley Act stipulate disclosure periods for financial operations and reporting. Relevant information relating to changes in the financial condition or operations of a company must be immediately reported in plain English. Off-balance sheet transactions, correcting adjustments, and pro-forma information must be presented in the annual and quarterly financial reports. The information must not contain any untrue statements, must not omit material facts, and must meet GAAP standards.

Stricter penalties have been issued for violations of the Sarbanes-Oxley Act. If a company must restate its financial statements due to noncompliance, the CEO and CFO must relinquish any bonus or incentive-based compensation or realized profits from the sale of securities during the 12-month period following the filing with the SEC. Other securities fraud, such as destruction or falsification of records, results in fines and prison sentences up to 25 years.

More details on the Sarbanes-Oxley Act of 2002 are provided in Exhibit 2–10, Strategy in Action.

The Traditional Structure

The New Structure

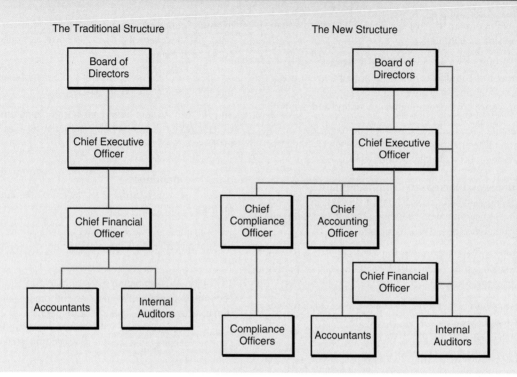

## The New Corporate Governance Structure

A major consequence of the 2000–2002 accounting scandals was the Sarbanes-Oxley Act of 2002, and a major consequence of Sarbanes-Oxley has been the restructuring of the governance structure of American corporations. The most significant change in the restructuring is the heightened role of corporate internal auditors, as depicted in Strategy in Action 2–11. Auditors have traditionally been viewed as performing a necessary but perfunctory function, namely to probe corporate financial records for unintentional or illicit misrepresentations. Although a majority of U.S. corporations have longstanding traditions of reporting that their auditors operated independently of CFO approval and that they had direct access to the board, in practice, the auditors' work usually traveled through the organization's hierarchical chain of command.

In the past, internal auditors reviewed financial reports generated by other corporate accountants. The auditors considered professional accounting and financial practices, as well as relevant aspects of corporate law, and then presented their findings to the chief financial officer (CFO). Historically, the CFO reviewed the audits and determined the financial data and information that was to be presented to top management, directors, and investors of the company.

However, because Sarbanes-Oxley requires that CEOs and audit committees sign-off on financial results, auditors now routinely deal directly with top corporate officials, as shown in the new structure in Strategy in Action 2-11. Approximately 75% of senior corporate auditors now report directly to the Board of Directors' audit committee. Additionally, to eliminate the potential for accounting problems, companies are establishing direct lines of communication between top managers and the board and auditors that inform the CFO but that are not dependent on CFO approval or authorization.

The new structure also provides the CEO information provided directly by the company's chief compliance and chief accounting officers. Consequently, the CFO, who is responsible for ultimately approving all company payments, is not empowered to be the sole provider of data for financial evaluations by the CEO and board.

# AGENCY THEORY

Whenever there is a separation of the owners (principals) and the managers (agents) of a firm, the potential exists for the wishes of the owners to be ignored. This fact, and the recognition that agents are expensive, established the basis for a set of complex but helpful ideas known as *agency theory*. Whenever owners (or managers) delegate decision-making authority to others, an agency relationship exists between the two parties. Agency relationships, such as those between stockholders and managers, can be very effective as long as managers make investment decisions in ways that are consistent with stockholders' interests. However, when the interests of managers diverge from those of owners, then managers' decisions are more likely to reflect the managers' preferences than the owners' preferences.

In general, owners seek stock value maximization. When managers hold important blocks of company stock, they too prefer strategies that result in stock appreciation. However, when managers better resemble "hired hands" than owner-partners, they often prefer strategies that increase their personal payoffs rather than those of shareholders. Such behavior can result in decreased stock performance (as when high executive bonuses reduce corporate earnings) and in strategic decisions that point the firm in the direction of outcomes that are suboptimal from a stockholder's perspective.

If, as agency theory argues, self-interested managers act in ways that increase their own welfare at the expense of the gain of corporate stockholders, then owners who delegate decision-making authority to their agents will incur both the loss of potential gain that would have resulted from owner-optimal strategies and/or the costs of monitoring and control systems that are designed to minimize the consequences of such self-centered management decisions. In combination, the cost of agency problems and the cost of actions taken to minimize agency problems, are called *agency costs*. These costs can often be identified by their direct benefit for the agents and their negative present value. Agency costs are found when there are differing self-interests between shareholders and managers, superiors and subordinates, or managers of competing departments or branch offices.

## How Agency Problems Occur

Because owners have access to only a relatively small portion of the information that is available to executives about the performance of the firm and cannot afford to monitor every executive decision or action, executives are often free to pursue their own interests.[1] This condition is known as the *moral hazard problem* or *shirking*.[2]

As a result of moral hazards, executives may design strategies that provide the greatest possible benefits for themselves, with the welfare of the organization being given only secondary consideration. For example, executives may presell products at year-end to trigger their annual bonuses even though the deep discounts that they must offer will threaten the price stability of their products for the upcoming year. Similarly, unchecked

---

[1] Substitute the terms *managers* for *owners* and *subordinates* for *executives* for another example of agency theory in operation.
[2] Shirking is described as "self-interest combined with guile."

executives may advance their own self-interests by slacking on the job, altering forecasts to maximize their performance bonuses; unrealistically assessing acquisition targets' outlooks in order to increase the probability of increasing organizational size through their acquisition; or manipulating personnel records to keep or acquire key company personnel.

The second major reason that agency costs are incurred is known as *adverse selection*. This refers to the limited ability that stockholders have to precisely determine the competencies and priorities of executives at the time that they are hired. Because principals cannot initially verify an executive's appropriateness as an agent of the owners, unanticipated problems of nonoverlapping priorities between owners and agents are likely to occur.

The most popular solution to moral dilemma and adverse selection problems is for owners to attempt to more closely align their own best interests with those of their agents through the use of executive bonus plans.[3] Foremost among these approaches are stock option plans, which enable executives to benefit directly from the appreciation of the company's stock just as other stockholders do. In most instances, executive bonus plans are unabashed attempts to align the interests of owners and executives and to thereby induce executives to support strategies that increase stockholder wealth. While such schemes are unlikely to eliminate self-interest as a major criterion in executive decision making, they help to reduce the costs associated with moral dilemmas and adverse selections.

## Problems That Can Result from Agency

From a strategic management perspective there are five different kinds of problems that can arise because of the agency relationship between corporate stockholders and their company's executives:

1. Executives pursue growth in company size rather than in earnings. Shareholders generally want to maximize earnings, because earnings growth yields stock appreciation. However, because managers are typically more heavily compensated for increases in firm size than for earnings growth, they may recommend strategies that yield company growth such as mergers and acquisitions.

In addition, managers' stature in the business community is commonly associated with company size. Managers gain prominence by directing the growth of an organization, and they benefit in the forms of career advancement and job mobility that are associated with increases in company size.

Finally, executives need an enlarging set of advancement opportunities for subordinates whom they wish to motivate with nonfinancial inducements. Acquisitions can provide the needed positions.

2. Executives attempt to diversify their corporate risk. Whereas stockholders can vary their investment risks through management of their individual stock portfolios, managers' careers and stock incentives are tied to the performance of a single corporation, albeit the one that employs them. Consequently, executives are tempted to diversify their corporation's operation, businesses, and product lines to moderate the risk incurred in any single venture. While this approach serves the executives' personal agendas, it compromises the "pure play" quality of their firm as an investment. In other words, diversifying a corporation reduces the beta associated with the firm's return, which is an undesirable outcome for many stockholders.

3. Executives avoid risk. Even when, or perhaps especially when, executives are willing to restrict the diversification of their companies, they are tempted to minimize the risk that they face. Executives are often fired for failure, but rarely for mediocre corporate per-

---

[3] An in-depth discussion of executive bonus compensation is provided in Chapter 9.

formance. Therefore, executives may avoid desirable levels of risk, if they anticipate little reward and opt for conservative strategies that minimize the risk of company failure. If they do, executives will rarely support plans for innovation, diversification, and rapid growth.

However, from an investor's perspective, risk taking is desirable when it is systematic. In other words, when investors can reasonably expect that their company will generate higher long-term returns from assuming greater risk, they may wish to pursue the greater payoff, especially when the company is positioned to perform better than its competitors that face the same nominal risks. Obviously, the agency relationship creates a problem—should executives prioritize their job security or the company's financial returns to stockholders?

4. Managers act to optimize their personal payoffs. If executives can gain more from an annual performance bonus by achieving objective 1 than from stock appreciation resulting from the achievement of objective 2, then owners must anticipate that the executives will target objective 1 as their priority, even though objective 2 is clearly in the best interest of the shareholders. Similarly, executives may pursue a range of expensive perquisites that have a net negative effect on shareholder returns. Elegant corner offices, corporate jets, large staffs, golf club memberships, extravagant retirement programs, and limousines for executive benefit are rarely good investments for stockholders.

5. Executives act to protect their status. When their companies expand, executives want to ensure that their knowledge, experience, and skills remain relevant and central to the strategic direction of the corporation. They favor doing more of what they already do well. In contrast, investors may prefer revolutionary advancement to incremental improvement. For example, when confronted with Amazon.com, competitor Barnes & Noble initiated a joint venture website with Bertelsmann. In addition, Barnes & Noble used vertical integration with the nation's largest book distributor, which supplies 60 percent of Amazon's books. This type of revolutionary strategy is most likely to occur when executives are given assurances that they will not make themselves obsolete within the changing company that they create.

## Solutions to the Agency Problem

In addition to defining an agent's responsibilities in a contract and including elements like bonus incentives that help align executives' and owners' interests, principals can take several other actions to minimize agency problems. The first is for the owners to pay executives a premium for their service. This premium helps executives to see their loyalty to the stockholders as the key to achieving their personal financial targets.

A second solution to agency problems is for executives to receive backloaded compensation. This means that executives are paid a handsome premium for superior future performance. Strategic actions taken in year one, which are to have an impact in year three, become the basis for executive bonuses in year three. This lag time between action and bonus more realistically rewards executives for the consequences of their decision making, ties the executive to the company for the long term, and properly focuses strategic management activities on the future.

Finally, creating teams of executives across different units of a corporation can help to focus performance measures on organizational rather than personal goals. Through the use of executive teams, owner interests often receive the priority that they deserve.

# THE STAKEHOLDER APPROACH TO SOCIAL RESPONSIBILITY

In defining or redefining the company mission, strategic managers must recognize the legitimate rights of the firm's claimants. These include not only stockholders and employees but also outsiders affected by the firm's actions. Such outsiders commonly include customers, suppliers, governments, unions, competitors, local communities, and the general public. Each of these interest groups has justifiable reasons for expecting (and often for demanding) that the firm satisfy their claims in a responsible manner. In general, stockholders claim appropriate returns on their investment; employees seek broadly defined job satisfactions; customers want what they pay for; suppliers seek dependable buyers; governments want adherence to legislation; unions seek benefits for their members; competitors want fair competition; local communities want the firm to be a responsible citizen; and the general public expects the firm's existence to improve the quality of life.

According to a survey of 2,361 directors in 291 of the largest southeastern U.S. companies:

1. Directors perceived the existence of distinct stakeholder groups.

2. Directors have high stakeholder orientations.

3. Directors view some stakeholders differently, depending on their occupation (CEO directors versus non-CEO directors) and type (inside versus outside directors).

The study also found that the perceived stakeholders were, in the order of their importance, customers and government, stockholders, employees, and society. The results clearly indicated that boards of directors no longer believe that the stockholder is the only constituency to whom they are responsible.

However, when a firm attempts to incorporate the interests of these groups into its mission statement, broad generalizations are insufficient. These steps need to be taken:

1. Identification of the stakeholders.

2. Understanding the stakeholders' specific claims vis-à-vis the firm.

3. Reconciliation of these claims and assignment of priorities to them.

4. Coordination of the claims with other elements of the company mission.

***Identification***    The left-hand column of Exhibit 2–12 lists the commonly encountered stakeholder groups, to which the executive officer group often is added. Obviously, though, every business faces a slightly different set of stakeholder groups, which vary in number, size, influence, and importance. In defining the company, strategic managers must identify all of the stakeholder groups and weigh their relative rights and their relative ability to affect the firm's success.

***Understanding***    The concerns of the principal stakeholder groups tend to center on the general claims listed in the right-hand column of Exhibit 2–12. However, strategic decision makers should understand the specific demands of each group. They then will be better able to initiate actions that satisfy these demands.

***Reconciliation and Priorities***    Unfortunately, the claims of various stakeholder groups often conflict. For example, the claims of governments and the general public tend to limit profitability, which is the central claim of most creditors and stockholders. Thus, claims must be reconciled in a mission statement that resolves the competing, conflicting, and contradicting claims of stakeholders. For objectives and strategies to be internally consistent and precisely focused, the statement must display a single-minded, though multidimensional, approach to the firm's aims.

There are hundreds, if not thousands, of claims on any firm—high wages, pure air, job security, product quality, community service, taxes, occupational health and safety regulations, equal employment opportunity regulations, product variety, wide markets, career opportunities, company growth, investment security, high ROI, and many, many more. Although most, perhaps all, of these claims may be desirable ends, they cannot

**EXHIBIT 2–12**

**A Stakeholder View of Company Responsibility**

Source: William R. King and David I. Cleland, *Strategic Planning and Policy.* © 1978 by Litton Educational Publishing, Inc., p. 153. Reprinted by permission of Van Nostrand Reinhold Company.

| Stakeholder | Nature of the Claim |
| --- | --- |
| Stockholders | Participation in distribution of profits, additional stock offerings, assets on liquidation; vote of stock; inspection of company books; transfer of stock; election of board of directors; and such additional rights as have been established in the contract with the corporation. |
| Creditors | Legal proportion of interest payments due and return of principal from the investment. Security of pledged assets; relative priority in event of liquidation. Management and owner prerogatives if certain conditions exist with the company (such as default of interest payments). |
| Employees | Economic, social, and psychological satisfaction in the place of employment. Freedom from arbitrary and capricious behavior on the part of company officials. Share in fringe benefits, freedom to join union and participate in collective bargaining, individual freedom in offering up their services through an employment contract. Adequate working conditions. |
| Customers | Service provided with the product; technical data to use the product; suitable warranties; spare parts to support the product during use; R&D leading to product improvement; facilitation of credit. |
| Suppliers | Continuing source of business; timely consummation of trade credit obligations; professional relationship in contracting for, purchasing, and receiving goods and services. |
| Governments | Taxes (income, property, and so on); adherence to the letter and intent of public policy dealing with the requirements of fair and free competition; discharge of legal obligations of businesspeople (and business organizations); adherence to antitrust laws. |
| Unions | Recognition as the negotiating agent for employees. Opportunity to perpetuate the union as a participant in the business organization. |
| Competitors | Observation of the norms for competitive conduct established by society and the industry. Business statesmanship on the part of peers. |
| Local communities | Place of productive and healthful employment in the community. Participation of company officials in community affairs, provision of regular employment, fair play, reasonable portion of purchases made in the local community, interest in and support of local government, support of cultural and charitable projects. |
| The general public | Participation in and contribution to society as a whole; creative communications between governmental and business units designed for reciprocal understanding; assumption of fair proportion of the burden of government and society. Fair price for products and advancement of the state-of-the-art technology that the product line involves. |

be pursued with equal emphasis. They must be assigned priorities in accordance with the relative emphasis that the firm will give them. That emphasis is reflected in the criteria that the firm uses in its strategic decision making; in the firm's allocation of its human, financial, and physical resources; and in the firm's long-term objectives and strategies.

**EXHIBIT 2–13**
**Inputs to the
Development of the
Company Mission**

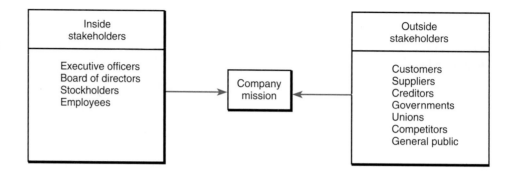

***Coordination with Other Elements***   The demands of stakeholder groups constitute only one principal set of inputs to the company mission. The other principal sets are the managerial operating philosophy and the determinants of the product-market offering. Those determinants constitute a reality test that the accepted claims must pass. The key question is: How can the firm satisfy its claimants and at the same time optimize its economic success in the marketplace?

## The Dynamics of Social Responsibility

As indicated in Exhibit 2–13, the various stakeholders of a firm can be divided into inside stakeholders and outside stakeholders. The insiders are the individuals or groups that are stockholders or employees of the firm. The outsiders are all the other individuals or groups that the firm's actions affect. The extremely large and often amorphous set of outsiders makes the general claim that the firm be socially responsible.

Perhaps the thorniest issues faced in defining a company mission are those that pertain to responsibility. The stakeholder approach offers the clearest perspective on such issues. Broadly stated, outsiders often demand that insiders' claims be subordinated to the greater good of the society; that is, to the greater good of outsiders. They believe that such issues as pollution, the disposal of solid and liquid wastes, and the conservation of natural resources should be principal considerations in strategic decision making. Also broadly stated, insiders tend to believe that the competing claims of outsiders should be balanced against one another in a way that protects the company mission. For example, they tend to believe that the need of consumers for a product should be balanced against the water pollution resulting from its production if the firm cannot eliminate that pollution entirely and still remain profitable. Some insiders also argue that the claims of society, as expressed in government regulation, provide tax money that can be used to eliminate water pollution and the like if the general public wants this to be done.

The issues are numerous, complex, and contingent on specific situations. Thus, rigid rules of business conduct cannot deal with them. Each firm *regardless of size* must decide how to meet its perceived social responsibility. While large, well-capitalized companies may have easy access to environmental consultants, this is not an affordable strategy for smaller companies. However, the experience of many small businesses demonstrates that it is feasible to accomplish significant pollution prevention and waste reduction without big expenditures and without hiring consultants. Once a problem area has been identified, a company's line employees frequently can develop a solution. Other important pollution prevention strategies include changing the materials used or redesigning how operations are bid out. Making pollution prevention a social responsibility can be beneficial to smaller companies. Publicly traded firms also can benefit directly from socially responsible strategies.

**BusinessWeek** In Colombia, Los Angeles–based Occidental Petroleum Corp. is clearing the land for an exploratory oil well to be drilled. The government believes the land holds more than half of Colombia's oil reserves and has contracted Occidental to find it. The nature-worshipping U'wa adamantly oppose the exploration. But Occidental emphatically denies that the U'wa will be affected either. The company has held dozens of meetings with community groups and says it is trying to meet all their concerns. Occidental has spent some $140,000 on educational, environmental, agricultural, and basic infrastructure projects in communities closest to the project.

The plight of indigenous groups is penetrating the boardrooms of multinationals, which are being forced to respond as never before to protect their reputations and brand names. Nowhere are the issues more contentious than in investments, such as Occidental's, that involve extracting natural resources in developing nations. Many of these projects have long been marred by corruption, military atrocities, ecological damage, and social upheaval.

Activists and environmental groups have put heavy pressure on multinationals, governments of developing nations, and the World Bank—which funds many such projects—to show there are humane, eco-friendly, and equitable ways to drill and mine in poor nations. On top of this, oil and mining companies now have to answer to institutional investors. And they must meet increasingly stringent environmental and social standards to get financial backing and political-risk guarantees from the World Bank for overseas projects.

The result is shaping up as a new era of corporate responsibility. Multinationals are hiring human-rights advisers, drafting and enforcing codes of conduct, appointing outside monitors, and improving operating practices. They are developing global standards of conduct, such as procedures for security of their installations. They are putting local people on boards of directors and urging government ministers and generals to adhere to international human-rights standards, lest their misdeeds reflect poorly on the investors, too.

**Source:** An excerpt from P. Raeburn and S. Prasso, "Whose Globe?," *BusinessWeek*, November 6, 2000.

Different approaches adopted by different firms reflect differences in competitive position, industry, country, environmental and ecological pressures, and a host of other factors. In other words, they will reflect both situational factors and differing priorities in the acknowledgment of claims. Obviously, winning the loyalty of the growing legions of consumers will require new marketing strategies and new alliances in the twenty-first century. Many marketers already have discovered these new marketing realities by adopting strategies called the "*4 E's*": (1) make it easy for the consumer to be green, (2) empower consumers with solutions, (3) enlist the support of the consumer, and (4) establish credibility with all publics and help to avoid a backlash.

As presented in Exhibit 2–14, Global Strategy in Action, Occidental Petroleum faces issues of corporate social responsibility in addressing the needs of the many stakeholders involved in the firm's oil exploration in developing countries. The article outlines the many parties that have potential to be impacted by the company's endeavors, including local inhabitants and government, environmental groups, and institutional investors. The article also describes how multinational corporations are acting to benefit the local communities, to restructure their organizations, and to implement codes of conduct to address the needs of the many stakeholders.

British Petroleum's CEO, John Browne, faces the social responsibility questions asked of all leaders of global firms. Global Strategy in Action Exhibit 2–15 presents Browne's view that for his global company to thrive, so must the communities in which his company does business.

Despite differences in their approaches, most American firms now try to assure outsiders that they attempt to conduct business in a socially responsible manner. Many firms, including Abt Associates, Dow Chemical, Eastern Gas and Fuel Associates, Exxon, and the Bank of America, conduct and publish annual social audits. Such audits attempt to evaluate a firm

**BusinessWeek** Making globalization work humanely is quickly becoming the dominant issue of our time. From Boston to Bangkok, trade, investment, and information technology are exploding across borders and overwhelming governments' ability to provide social safety nets and public services to cushion the impact on people. A political backlash is building in Asia, Europe, and Latin America. Although international corporations cannot shoulder all the *responsibility,* no challenge is more central to global management than finding a balance between the relentless pressure for short-term profits and broader social *responsibilities.*

What's a chief executive to do? To what degree should companies take on the *responsibility* heretofore shouldered by governments? To what degree can they? One chief executive, John Browne of British Petroleum Co., has a clear philosophy and strategy. Browne believes that for BP to thrive, so must the communities in which it does business. To make that happen, Browne has insisted that the economic and social health of the villages, towns, and cities in which BP does business be a matter of central concern to the company's *board* of directors. He has also made social investment for the long term an important variable in compensating BP employees around the world.

## AMBITIOUS GOALS

What to do and how to do it is left to local BP business units. But regular reviews of their activities are held by regional executives. In such areas as job training for local employees and building schools, ambitious goals are set, and performance is measured against them. Involved in the process along with BP

employees and *board* directors are local residents whose views are regularly surveyed.

BP's community investments are extensive. In Vietnam, the company is providing computer-based technology to control the damage from recurrent flooding. In Turkey, BP recently financed the replanting of a forest around the Black Sea that had been destroyed by fire. In Zambia, it has supplied 200 solar-powered refrigerators to help doctors store antimalaria vaccines. In South Africa, it has supported the development of small business in urban areas such as Soweto. In Colombia, it is turning its own waste material into bricks for local homebuilding.

In addition, accidents in the workplace, noxious emissions, and oil spills are subject to monitoring and quantification. Ernst & Young verifies company recordkeeping. There is constant pressure to eliminate accidents.

## NOT CHARITY

So far, the strategy has not impaired BP's bottom line. To the contrary. "These efforts have nothing to do with charity," says Browne, "and everything to do with our long-term self-interest. I see no trade-off between the short term and the long. Twenty years is just 80 quarters. And our shareholders want performance today, and tomorrow, and the day after."

Corporations would do well to take a page out of Browne's playbook: think long-term, invest heavily in the communities that you do business in, be obsessive about achieving profits, and fully integrate social *responsibility* into your policies on governance and compensation.

**Source:** Jeffrey E. Garten, "Globalism Doesn't Have to Be Cruel," *BusinessWeek,* February 9, 1998.

---

from the perspective of social responsibility. Private consultants often conduct them for the firm and offer minimally biased evaluations on what are inherently highly subjective issues.

# A CONTINUUM OF SOCIAL RESPONSIBILITIES

To better understand the nature and range of social responsibilities for which they must plan, strategic managers can use a continuum that encompasses four types of social commitment: economic, legal, ethical, and discretionary social responsibilities.

*Economic responsibilities* are the most basic social responsibilities of business. As we have noted, some economists see these as the only legitimate social responsibility of business. Living up to their economic responsibilities requires managers to maximize profits whenever possible. The essential responsibility of business is assumed to be providing goods and services to society at a reasonable cost. In discharging that economic responsibility, the company also emerges as socially responsible by providing productive jobs for its workforce, and tax payments for its local, state, and federal governments.

*Legal responsibilities* reflect the firm's obligations to comply with the laws that regulate business activities. The consumer and environmental movements focused increased public attention on the need for social responsibility in business by lobbying for laws that govern business in the areas of pollution control and consumer safety. The intent of consumer legislation has been to correct the "balance of power" between buyers and sellers in the marketplace. Among the most important laws are the Federal Fair Packaging and Labeling Act that regulates labeling procedures for business, the Truth in Lending Act that regulates the extension of credit to individuals, and the Consumer Product Safety Act that protects consumers against unreasonable risks of injury in the use of consumer products.

The environmental movement has had a similar impact on the regulation of business. This movement achieved stricter enforcement of existing environmental protections and it spurred the passage of new, more comprehensive laws such as the National Environmental Policy Act which is devoted to preserving the United State's ecological balance and making environmental protection a federal policy goal. It requires environmental impact studies whenever new construction may threaten an existing ecosystem, and it established the Council on Environmental Quality to guide business development. Another product of the environmental movement was the creation of the federal Environmental Protection Agency which interprets and administers the environmental protection policies of the U.S. government.

Clearly, these legal responsibilities are supplemental to the requirement that businesses and their employees comply fully with the general civil and criminal laws that apply to all individuals and institutions in the country. Yet, strangely, individual failures to adhere to the law have recently produced some of the greatest scandals in the history of American free enterprise. Strategy in Action Exhibit 2–16 presents an overview of seven of these cases that involved executives from Adelphia Communications, Arthur Andersen, Global Crossing, ImClone Systems, Merrill Lynch, WorldCom, and Xerox.

*Ethical responsibilities* reflect the company's notion of right or proper business behavior. Ethical responsibilities are obligations that transcend legal requirements. Firms are expected, but not required, to behave ethically. Some actions that are legal might be considered unethical. For example, the manufacture and distribution of cigarettes is legal. But in light of the often-lethal consequences of smoking, many consider the continued sale of cigarettes to be unethical. The topic of management ethics receives additional attention later in this chapter.

*Discretionary responsibilities* are those that are voluntarily assumed by a business organization. They include public relations activities, good citizenship, and full corporate social responsibility. Through public relations activities, managers attempt to enhance the image of their companies, products, and services by supporting worthy causes. This form of discretionary responsibility has a self-serving dimension. Companies that adopt the good citizenship approach actively support ongoing charities, public-service advertising campaigns, or issues in the public interest. A commitment to full corporate responsibility requires strategic managers to attack social problems with the same zeal in which they attack business problems. For example, teams in the National Football League provide time off for players and other employees afflicted with drug or alcohol addictions who agree to enter rehabilitation programs.

It is important to remember that the categories on the continuum of social responsibility overlap, creating gray areas where societal expectations on organizational behavior are difficult to categorize. In considering the overlaps among various demands for social responsibility, however, managers should keep in mind that in the view of the general public, economic and legal responsibilities are required, ethical responsibility is expected, and discretionary responsibility is desired.

## Adelphia Communications

On July 24, 2002, John Rigas, the 77-year-old founder of the country's sixth largest cable television operator was arrested, along with two of his sons, and accused of looting the now bankrupt company. Several other former Adelphia executives were also arrested. The SEC brought a civil suit against the company for allegedly fraudulently excluding billions of dollars in liabilities from its financial statements, falsifying statistics, inflating its earnings to meet Wall Street's expectations and concealing "rampant self-dealing by the Rigas family." The family, which founded Adelphia in 1952, gave up control of the firm in May, and on June 25 the company filed for bankruptcy protection. The company was delisted by Nasdaq in June 2002.

## Arthur Andersen

On June 15, 2002, a Texas jury found the accounting firm guilty of obstructing justice for its role in shredding financial documents related to its former client Enron. Andersen, founded in 1913, had already been largely destroyed after admitting that it sped up the shredding of Enron documents following the launch of an SEC investigation. Andersen fired David Duncan, who led its Houston office saying he was responsible for shredding the Enron documents. Duncan admitted to obstruction of justice, turned state's evidence, and testified on behalf of the government.

## Global Crossing

The SEC and the FBI are probing the five-year-old telecom company Global Crossing regarding alleged swaps of network capacity with other telecommunications firms to inflate revenue. The company ran into trouble by betting that it could borrow billions of dollars to build a fiber-optic infrastructure that would be in strong demand by corporations. Because others made the same bet, there was a glut of fiber optic and prices plunged, leaving Global Crossing with massive debts. It filed for bankruptcy on January 28, 2002. Chairman Gary Winnick, who founded Global Crossing in 1997, cashed out $734 million in stock before the company collapsed. Global Crossing was delisted from NYSE in January 2002.

## ImClone Systems

The biotech firm is being investigated by a congressional committee that is seeking to find out if ImClone correctly informed investors that the Food and Drug Administration had declined to accept for review its key experimental cancer drug, Erbitux. Former CEO Samuel Waksal pled guilty in June 2003 to insider trading charges related to Erbitux and was sentenced to seven years in prison. Also, Federal investigators filed charges against home decorating diva Martha Stewart for using insider information on the cancer drug when she sold 4,000 ImClone shares one day before the FDA initially said it would reject the drug.

## Merrill Lynch

On May 21, 2002, Merrill Lynch agreed to pay $100 million to settle New York Attorney General Eliot Spitzer's charges that the nation's largest securities firm knowingly peddled Internet stocks to investors to generate lucrative investment banking fees. Internal memos written by Merrill's feted Internet analyst Henry Blodgett revealed that company analysts thought little of the Web stocks that they urged investors to buy. Merrill agreed to strengthen firewalls between its research and investment-banking divisions, ensuring advice given to investors is not influenced by efforts to win underwriting fees.

## WorldCom

The nation's second largest telecom company filed for the nation's biggest ever bankruptcy on July 21, 2002. WorldCom's demise accelerated on June 25, 2002, when it admitted it hid $3.85 billion in expenses, allowing it to post net income of $1.38 billion in 2001, instead of a loss. The company fired its CFO Scott Sullivan and on June 28 began cutting 17,000 jobs, over 20 percent of its workforce. CEO Bernie Ebbers resigned in April amid questions about $408 million of personal loans he received from the company to cover losses he incurred in buying its shares. WorldCom was delisted from Nasdaq in July 2002.

## Xerox

Xerox said on June 28, 2002 that it would restate five years of financial results to reclassify more than $6 billion in revenues. In April, the company settled SEC charges that it used "accounting tricks" to defraud investors, agreeing to pay a $10 million fine. The firm admitted no wrongdoing. Xerox manufactures imaging products, such as copiers, printers, fax machines, and scanners.

*This section was derived in its entirety from "A guide to corporate scandals," MSNBC, www.msnbc.com/news/corpscandal front.

## Corporate Social Responsibility and Profitability

Few trends could so thoroughly undermine the very foundations of our free society as the acceptance by corporate officials of a social responsibility other than to make as much money for their stockholders as possible.

*Milton Friedman, Capitalism and Freedom, 1962*

In the four decades since Milton Friedman wrote these words, the issue of *corporate social responsibility* (CSR)—the idea that business has a duty to serve society as well as the financial interest of stockholders—has remained a highly contentious one. Yet managers recognize that deciding to what extent to embrace CSR is an important strategic decision. There are three principal reasons why managers should be concerned about the socially responsible behavior of their firms. First, a company's right to exist depends on its responsiveness to the external environment. Second, federal, state, and local governments threaten increased regulation if business does not evolve to meet changing social standards. Third, a responsive corporate social policy may enhance a firm's long-term viability. Underscoring the importance of these factors to the firm is the implicit belief that long-run profit maximization is inexorably linked to CSR.

### The Debate

Should a company behave in a socially responsible manner? Coming down on one side of the question are those who, like Friedman, believe that a business bears a responsibility only for the financial well-being of its stockholders. Implicit in this statement is the idea that corporate actions motivated by anything other than shareholder wealth maximization threatens that well-being. On the other side, proponents of CSR assert that business does not function in a vacuum; it exists to serve, depends upon its environment, cannot be separated from it, and therefore has a responsibility to ensure its well-being. The environment is represented not only by stockholders/owners and employees, but also by such external stakeholders as customers, unions, suppliers, competitors, government agencies, local communities, and society in general.

The second argument for CSR suggests that stockholders' interests may transcend the financial. Many stockholders expect more from the companies in which they invest than simple appreciation in the economic value of the firm.

The third argument in favor of CSR is that the best way for a company to maximize shareholder wealth is to act in a socially responsible manner. It suggests that when a company behaves responsibly, benefits accrue directly to the bottom line. It also implies that when a company does not behave responsibly, the company and its shareholders suffer financially.

Exhibit 2–17, Strategy in Action, presents an argument that eBay is acting in a socially irresponsible manner by allowing, and profiting from, the sale of "murderabilia" on their website. eBay's lack of prevention is perceived by some critics as "morally reprehensible" and socially irresponsible. Since there are no laws against this type of sale on the Internet, it is not illegal. However, corporate social responsibility is an element of strategic decision making that eBay cannot ignore. If websites are not responsive to society, they increase the odds that people will turn to legislation to discipline corporate behavior.

### CSR and the Bottom Line

The goal of every firm is to maintain viability through long-run profitability. Until all costs and benefits are accounted for, however, profits may not be claimed. In the case of CSR, costs and benefits are both economic and social. While economic costs and benefits are easily quantifiable, social costs and benefits are not. Managers therefore risk subordinating social consequences to other performance results that can be more straightforwardly measured.

**BusinessWeek** Serial killer Angel Resendez-Ramirez smiles as he sits behind bulletproof glass on Death Row in a maximum-security prison. He has admitted to murdering 12 women across the U.S., yet he jokes and revels in his fame. Locks of his hair and shavings from the calloused on his feet have been sold on Internet auction site eBay for $9.99 a pop. He gets a cut from dealers each time a little piece of him is sold. Tom Konvicka's mother was one of the victims. When Resendez-Ramirez was caught and locked up, Konvicka remembers feeling relief that his mom's murderer was being brought to justice. Now, he's disgusted. Serial killers shouldn't profit from their murders. Their victims are dead and gone and they're still here and making a profit on what they've done.

In Texas, as in most other states, there's nothing to prevent criminals from selling "murderabilia" on the Internet. eBay and other sites don't prevent it, either. In fact, there's little to discourage the sale of a whole range of questionable items online. As the Internet has grown in popularity, it's a ready-made market connecting individuals with a vast audience of potential buyers—all protected by a cloak of semi-anonymity and the hands-off policies of Web auction sites. That wide-open flea market has produced a cornucopia of items for sale that are in bad taste or unethical.

A growing chorus of ethicists, lawmakers, consumer groups, and Internet activists say something needs to be done—either stepped-up monitoring by auction sites themselves, or statutes that police the Netways. By refusing to take responsibility for what is sold on their site, they're cashing in on an overall lack of social accountability the Internet offers. While the sale of murderabilia is not illegal, it's morally reprehensible.

Problem is, when it comes to the Web, it's sometimes difficult to tell what's illegal, what ought to be illegal, and what's just in bad taste. It's clearly against the law to sell things such as endangered species and certain kinds of firearms. But how do you prevent minors from buying alcohol and pornography in a realm where nobody knows their age? Selling body organs online isn't necessarily a crime, but a doctor who participates could breach professional ethics. And how do you prevent the trafficking in items like neo-Nazi paraphernalia that are illegal in some places but not in others?

Given all the confusion, society's first line of defense could be auction site operators—but they're having none of it. eBay has a laissez-faire attitude about what is sold on the site. The company claims it's all part of eBay's philosophy of building a community based on trust. However, by not screening items, eBay skirts potential liability and high monitoring costs.

Now that Net auctions have become such a magnet for potentially dicey items, some states and federal agencies are stepping up their efforts to stop abuses. FBI's Internet Fraud Complaint Center gets more than 1,000 complaints of online auction fraud each month—most of them involving eBay traffic. Agents have begun turning some of these cases over to local law enforcement authorities. In October, state elections officials in Illinois and New York temporarily shut down Voteauction.com, an Internet site where Americans could sell their votes to the highest bidder. Authorities say they are keeping close watch and will nab all who accept money for their votes—and the people who pay them—charging them with violating state and federal election laws. The very nature of the Web makes the unthinkable more possible. Absent the Internet, many people might not have been exposed to the opportunity to revel in Nazi items or bloody murder photos, or be offered an easy chance to buy them without fear of social backlash. eBay is a magnet for people who previously didn't have many outlets because you're immediately linked up to millions of people.

The Web amplifies ethical dilemmas, too. Consider MedicineOnline.com, a site that connects plastic surgery doctors and patients on the Net. The site asks doctors to provide info about their education and experience—including their history of malpractice suits—but takes no responsibility for the veracity of that information. By contrast, a regular hospital is legally bound to take responsibility for the credentials and services of doctors who practice there. That's eBay's answer, too: Since it does not sell anything itself, it's not responsible for what is sold on the site. eBay asks sellers to report any breach of guidelines—in other words, to police the site themselves.

For now, eBay plans to continue to rely on its guidelines—and on its community of members—to blow the whistle on anything beyond the pale. However, with creeps and criminals like Resendez-Ramirez virtually on the loose, eBay's self-monitoring system may not be enough.

**Source:** An excerpt from Marcia Stepanek, "Making a Killing Online," *BusinessWeek,* November 20, 2000.

The dynamic between CSR and success (profit) is complex. While one concept is clearly not mutually exclusive of the other, it is also clear that neither is a prerequisite of the other. Rather than viewing these two concepts as competing, it may be better to view CSR as a component in the decision-making process of business that must determine, among other objectives, how to maximize profits.

Attempts to undertake a cost-benefit analysis of CSR have not been very successful. The process is complicated by several factors. First, some CSR activities incur no dollar costs at all. For example, Second Harvest, the largest nongovernment, charitable food distributor in the nation, accepts donations from food manufacturers and food retailers of surplus food that would otherwise be thrown out due to overruns, warehouse damage, or labeling errors. In 10 years, Second Harvest has distributed more than 2 billion pounds of food. Gifts in Kind America is an organization that enables companies to reduce unsold or obsolete inventory by matching a corporation's donated products with a charity's or other nonprofit organization's needs. In addition, a tax break is realized by the company. In the past, corporate donations have included 130,000 pairs of shoes from Nike, 10,000 pairs of gloves from Aris Isotoner, and 480 computer systems from Apple Computer.

In addition, philanthropic activities of a corporation, which have been a traditional mainstay of CSR, are undertaken at a discounted cost to the firm since they are often tax deductible. The benefits of corporate philanthropy can be enormous as is shown by the many national social welfare causes that have been spurred by corporate giving. A few of these causes are described in Exhibit 2–18. While such acts of benevolence often help establish a general perception of the involved companies within society, some philanthropic acts bring specific credit to the firm.

Second, socially responsible behavior does not come at a prohibitive cost. One needs only to look at the problems of A. H. Robbins Company (Dalkon Shield), Beech-Nut Corporation (apple juice), Drexel Burnham (insider trading), and Exxon (*Valdez*) for stark answers on the "cost" of social responsibility (or its absence) in the business environment.

Third, socially responsible practices may create savings and, as a result, increase profits. SET Laboratories uses popcorn to ship software rather than polystyrene peanuts. It is environmentally safer and costs 60 percent less to use. Corporations that offer part-time and adjustable work schedules have realized that this can lead to reduced absenteeism, greater productivity and increased morale. DuPont opted for more flexible schedules for its employees after a survey revealed 50 percent of women and 25 percent of men considered working for another employer with more flexibility for family concerns.

Proponents argue that CSR costs are more than offset in the long run by an improved company image and increased community goodwill. These intangible assets can prove valuable in a crisis, as Johnson & Johnson discovered with the Tylenol cyanide scare in 1982. Because it had established a solid reputation as a socially responsible company before the incident, the public readily accepted the company's assurances of public safety. Consequently, financial damage to Johnson & Johnson was minimized, despite the company's $100 million voluntary recall of potentially tainted capsules. CSR may also head off new regulation, preventing increased compliance costs. It may even attract investors who are themselves socially responsible. Proponents believe that for these reasons, socially responsible behavior increases the financial value of the firm in the long run. The mission statement of Johnson & Johnson is provided as Exhibit 2–19, Strategy in Action.

***Performance***   To explore the relationship between socially responsible behavior and financial performance, an important question must first be answered: How do managers measure the financial impact of corporate social performance?

Now that U.S. companies are adopting strategic philanthropy, they are assuming an activist stance on social issues. As a result, many causes, including the following, have become national movements.

## HUNGER

Before the new approach to corporate philanthropy, the foundations of food companies gave cash donations to antihunger organizations. But when the ranks of the hungry increased tenfold in the 1980s, contributions managers in companies such as General Mills, Grand Metropolitan, Kraft General Foods, and Sara Lee decided to play a larger role *and* establish a rallying point around which disparate units of their companies could come together. Marketers arranged for a portion of product sales to be donated to antihunger programs, human resources staffs deployed volunteers, operating units provided free food, and CEOs joined the board of Chicago-based Second Harvest, the food industry's antihunger voice. As a result of those efforts, a complex infrastructure of food banks and soup kitchens was developed.

## COMMUNITY AND ECONOMIC DEVELOPMENT

Major banks such as Bank of America, Chase Manhattan, Citicorp, Morgan Guaranty, and Wells Fargo explored how philanthropy could be tied to marketing, human resources, government affairs, investment, and even trust management. Their business managers were concerned about the Community Reinvestment Act, which requires lenders to be responsive to low-income communities. Philanthropy managers point out that by going beyond the CRA requirements, they develop positive relationships with regulators while scoring public relations points. For example, at least 60 banks in the United States have created community development corporations to assist run-down neighborhoods.

## LITERACY

The effort to increase literacy in the United States is the favorite cause of the communications industry. Print media companies such as McGraw-Hill, Prentice Hall, the *Los Angeles Times,* the *Washington Post,* and the *New York Times* are trying to halt the drop in readership, and broadcasters and cable companies are compensating for their role in the decline of literacy. Those companies have mobilized their marketing, human resources, and lobbying power to establish workplace literacy programs. While human resources budgets fund such programs, philanthropy dollars go mostly to volunteer organizations.

## SCHOOL REFORM

About 15 percent of the country's cash gifts go to school reform, and a recent study estimated that at least one-third of U.S. school districts have partnership programs with business. The next step toward reform, promoted by the Business Roundtable, is for companies to mobilize their lobbying power at the state level to press for the overhaul of state educational agencies.

## AIDS

AIDS is a top cause for insurance companies, who want to reduce claims; pharmaceutical companies, who want public support for the commercialization of AIDS drugs; and design-related companies, who want to support the large number of gays in their work force. Those industries put the first big money into AIDS prevention measures, and they've helped turn the American Foundation for AIDS Research into an advocate for more and better research by the National Institutes of Health.

## ENVIRONMENTALISM

Environmental support varies across industries. In high-tech companies, environmentalism is largely a human resources issue because it's the favorite cause of many employees. Among the makers of outdoor apparel, environmentalism is largely a marketing issue, so companies donate a portion of the purchase price to environmental nonprofits. In industries that pollute or extract natural resources, environmentalism is often a government affairs matter.

Critics of CSR believe that companies that behave in a socially responsible manner, and portfolios comprising these companies' securities, should perform more poorly financially than those that do not. The costs of CSR outweigh the benefits for individual firms, they suggest. In addition, traditional portfolio theory holds that investors minimize risk and maximize return by being able to choose from an infinite universe of investment opportunities. Portfolios based on social criteria should suffer, critics argue, because they are by definition restrictive in nature. This restriction should increase portfolio risk and reduce portfolio return.

"We believe our first responsibility is to the doctors, nurses and patients, to mothers and fathers and all others who use our products and services. In meeting their needs everything we do must be of high quality. We must constantly strive to reduce our costs in order to maintain reasonable prices. Customers' orders must be serviced promptly and accurately. Our suppliers and distributors must have an opportunity to make a fair profit.

We are responsible to our employees, the men and women who work with us throughout the world. Everyone must be considered as an individual. We must respect their dignity and recognize their merit. They must have a sense of security in their jobs. Compensation must be fair and adequate, and working conditions clean, orderly and safe. Employees must feel free to make suggestions and complaints. There must be equal opportunity for employment, development and advancement for those qualified. We must provide competent management, and their actions must be just and ethical.

We are responsible to the communities in which we live and work and to the world community as well. We must be good citizens—support good works and charities and bear our fair share of taxes. We must encourage civic improvements and better health and education. We must maintain in good order the property we are privileged to use, protecting the environment and natural resources.

Our final responsibility is to our stockholders. Business must make a sound profit. We must experiment with new ideas. Research must be carried on, innovative programs developed and mistakes paid for. New equipment must be purchased, new facilities provided and new products launched. Reserves must be created to provide for adverse times. When we operate according to these principles, the stockholders should realize a fair return."

Several research studies have attempted to determine the relationship between corporate social performance and financial performance. Taken together, these studies fail to establish the nature of the relationship between social and financial performance. There are a number of possible explanations for the findings. One possibility is that there is no meaningful correlation between social and financial performance. A second possibility is that the benefits of CSR are offset by its negative consequences for the firm, thus producing a nondetectable net financial effect. Other explanations include methodological weaknesses and/or insufficient conceptual models or operational definitions used in the studies. However, among experts, a sense remains that a relationship between CSR and the bottom line does exist, although the exact nature of that relationship is unclear.

### CSR Today

A survey of 2,737 senior U.S. managers revealed that 92 percent believed that business should take primary responsibility for, or an active role in, solving environmental problems; 84 percent believed business should do the same for educational concerns.[4] Despite the uncertain impact of CSR on the corporate bottom line, CSR has become a priority with American business. Why? In addition to a commonsense belief that companies should be able to "do well by doing good," at least three broad trends are driving businesses to adopt CSR frameworks: the resurgence of environmentalism, increasing buyer power, and the globalization of business.

***The Resurgence of Environmentalism***   In March 1989, the Exxon *Valdez* ran aground in Prince William Sound, spilling 11 million gallons of oil, polluting miles of ocean and shore, and helping to revive worldwide concern for the ecological environment. Six months after the *Valdez* incident, the Coalition for Environmentally Responsible Economies (CERES) was

[4] Rosabeth Moss Kanter, "Transcending Business Boundaries: 12,000 World Managers View Change," *Harvard Business Review* 69, no. 3 (May–June 1991), pp. 151–64.

formed to establish new goals for environmentally responsible corporate behavior. The group drafted the CERES Principles to "establish an environmental ethic with criteria by which investors and others can assess the environmental performance of companies. Companies that sign these Principles pledge to go voluntarily beyond the requirements of the law."

***Increasing Buyer Power*** The rise of the consumer movement has meant that buyers—consumers and investors—are increasingly flexing their economic muscle. Consumers are becoming more interested in buying products from socially responsible companies. Organizations such as the Council on Economic Priorities (CEP) help consumers make more informed buying decisions through such publications as *Shopping for a Better World,* which provides social performance information on 191 companies making more than 2,000 consumer products. CEP also sponsors the annual Corporate Conscience Awards, which recognize socially responsible companies. One example of consumer power at work is the effective outcry over the deaths of dolphins in tuna fishermen's nets.

Investors represent a second type of influential consumer. There has been a dramatic increase in the number of people interested in supporting socially responsible companies through their investments. Membership in the Social Investment Forum, a trade association serving social investing professionals, has been growing at a rate of about 50 percent annually. As baby boomers achieve their own financial success, the social investing movement has continued its rapid growth.

While social investing wields relatively low power as an individual private act (selling one's shares of Exxon does not affect the company), it can be very powerful as a collective public act. When investors vote their shares in behalf of pro-CSR issues, companies may be pressured to change their social behavior. The South African divestiture movement is one example of how effective this pressure can be.

The Vermont National Bank has added a Socially Responsible Banking Fund to its product line. Investors can designate any of their interest-bearing accounts with a $500 minimum balance to be used by the fund. This fund then lends these monies for purposes such as low-income housing, the environment, education, farming, or small business development. Although it has had a "humble" beginning of approximately 800 people investing about $11 million, the bank has attracted out-of-state depositors and is growing faster than expected.

Social investors comprise both individuals and institutions. Much of the impetus for social investing originated with religious organizations that wanted their investments to mirror their beliefs. At present, the ranks of social investors have expanded to include educational institutions and large pension funds.

Large-scale social investing can be broken down into the two broad areas of guideline portfolio investing and shareholder activism. Guideline portfolio investing is the largest and fastest-growing segment of social investing. Individual and institutional guideline portfolio investors use ethical guidelines as screens to identify possible investments in stocks, bonds, and mutual funds. The investment instruments that survive the social screens are then layered over the investor's financial screens to create the investor's universe of possible investments.

Screens may be negative (e.g., excluding all tobacco companies) or they may combine negative and positive elements (e.g., eliminating companies with bad labor records while seeking out companies with good ones). Most investors rely on screens created by investment firms such as Kinder, Lydenberg Domini & Co. or by industry groups such as the Council on Economic Priorities. In addition to ecology, employee relations, and community development, corporations may be screened on their association with "sin" products (alcohol, tobacco, gambling), defense/weapons production, and nuclear power.

In contrast to guideline portfolio investors, who passively indicate their approval or disapproval of a company's social behavior by simply including or excluding it from their portfolios, shareholder activists seek to directly influence corporate social behavior. Shareholder activists invest in a corporation hoping to improve specific aspects of the company's social performance, typically by seeking a dialogue with upper management. If this and successive actions fail to achieve the desired results, shareholder activists may introduce proxy resolutions to be voted upon at the corporation's annual meeting. The goal of these resolutions is to achieve change by gaining public exposure for the issue at hand. While the number of shareholder activists is relatively small, they are by no means small in achievement: Shareholder activists, led by such groups as the Interfaith Center on Corporate Responsibility, were the driving force behind the South African divestiture movement. Currently, there are more than 35 socially screened mutual funds available in the United States alone.

***The Globalization of Business***   Management issues, including CSR, have become more complex as companies increasingly transcend national borders: It is difficult enough to come to a consensus on what constitutes socially responsible behavior within one culture, let alone determine common ethical values across cultures. In addition to different cultural views, the high barriers facing international CSR include differing corporate disclosure practices, inconsistent financial data and reporting methods, and the lack of CSR research organizations within countries. Despite these problems, CSR is growing abroad. The United Kingdom has 30 ethical mutual funds and Canada offers 6 socially responsible funds.

## CSR's Effect on the Mission Statement

The mission statement not only identifies what product or service a company produces, how it produces it, and what market it serves, it also embodies what the company believes. As such, it is essential that the mission statement recognize the legitimate claims of its external stakeholders, which may include creditors, customers, suppliers, government, unions, competitors, local communities, and elements of the general public. This stakeholder approach has become widely accepted by U.S. business. For example, a survey of directors in 291 of the largest southeastern U.S. companies found that directors had high stakeholder orientations. Customers, government, stockholders, employees, and society, in that order, were the stakeholders these directors perceived as most important.

In developing mission statements, managers must identify all stakeholder groups and weigh their relative rights and abilities to affect the firm's success. Some companies are proactive in their approach to CSR, making it an integral part of their raison d'être (e.g., Ben & Jerry's ice cream); others are reactive, adopting socially responsible behavior only when they must (e.g., Exxon after the *Valdez* incident).

## Social Audit

A *social audit* attempts to measure a company's actual social performance against the social objectives it has set for itself. A social audit may be conducted by the company itself. However, one conducted by an outside consultant who will impose minimal biases may prove more beneficial to the firm. As with a financial audit, an outside auditor brings credibility to the evaluation. This credibility is essential if management is to take the results seriously and if the general public is to believe the company's public relations pronouncements.

Careful, accurate monitoring and evaluation of a company's CSR actions are important not only because the company wants to be sure it is implementing CSR policy as planned, but also because CSR actions by their nature are open to intense public scrutiny. To make sure it is making good on its CSR promises, a company may conduct a social audit of its performance.

Once the social audit is complete, it may be distributed internally or both internally and externally, depending on the firm's goals and situation. Some firms include a section in their annual report devoted to social responsibility activities; others publish a separate periodic report on their social responsiveness. Companies publishing separate social audits include General Motors, Bank of America, Atlantic Richfield, Control Data, and Aetna Life and Casualty Company. Nearly all Fortune 500 corporations disclose social performance information in their annual reports.

Large firms are not the only companies employing the social audit. Boutique ice cream maker Ben & Jerry's, a CSR pioneer, publishes a social audit in its annual report. The audit, conducted by an outside consultant, scores company performance in such areas as employee benefits, plant safety, ecology, community involvement, and customer service. The report is published unedited.

The social audit may be used for more than simply monitoring and evaluating firm social performance. Managers also use social audits to scan the external environment, determine firm vulnerabilities, and institutionalize CSR within the firm. In addition, companies themselves are not the only ones who conduct social audits; public interest groups and the media watch companies who claim to be socially responsible very closely to see if they practice what they preach. These organizations include consumer groups and socially responsible investing firms that construct their own guidelines for evaluating companies.

The Body Shop learned what can happen when a company's behavior falls short of its espoused mission and objectives. The 20-year-old manufacturer and retailer of naturally based hair and skin products had cultivated a socially responsible corporate image based on a reputation for socially responsible behavior. In late 1994, however, *Business Ethics* magazine published an exposé claiming that the company did not "walk the talk." It accused the Body Shop of using nonrenewable petrochemicals in its products, recycling far less than it claimed, using ingredients tested on animals, and making threats against investigative journalists. The Body Shop's contradictions were noteworthy because Anita Roddick, the company's founder, made CSR a centerpiece of the company's strategy.[5]

# MANAGEMENT ETHICS

## The Nature of Ethics in Business

Central to the belief that companies should be operated in a socially responsive way for the benefit of all stakeholders is the belief that managers will behave in an ethical manner. The term *ethics* refers to the moral principles that govern the actions of an individual or a group. Of course, the values of one individual, group, or society may be at odds with the values of another individual, group, or society. Ethical standards, therefore, reflect not a universally accepted code, but rather the end product of a process of defining and clarifying the nature and content of human interaction.

---

[5] Jon Entine, "Shattered Image," *Business Ethics* 8, no. 5 (September/October 1994), pp. 23–28.

**BusinessWeek** The fall of mighty Enron Corp. (ENE)—once one of the most valuable companies in America—was a collapse of mind-boggling proportions. In 2001, Enron had $101 billion in revenues, a stock-market capitalization of $63 billion, and a chairman who was a high-profile confidant of President Bush. Yet in a sickeningly swift spiral, the powerful energy trading company tumbled to the brink of bankruptcy in late November 2001—the victim of a botched expansion attempt, an accounting scandal, and the overweening ambition of its once widely admired top executives.

The end came quickly because Enron had overextended itself—and because investors and customers lost faith in its secretive and complex financial maneuvers. With legions of traders working out of a Houston skyscraper, the company put together trades so exotic that they mystified many Wall Street veterans. Under Chairman Kenneth L. Lay—who pressed the administration to embrace a controversial policy of electricity deregulation—and former CEO Jeffrey K. Skilling, Enron had become largely a trading operation, dubbed by some the Goldman, Sachs & Co. of the energy business.

Enron's success depended on maintaining the trust of customers that it would make good on its dealings in the market. But that trust evaporated in recent weeks as it shocked the market with changes to its nearly incomprehensible financial statements. "If you are running a trading operation, you have to be like Caesar's wife, beyond reproach. Unfortunately, the company didn't realize it," says a senior Enron employee who asked not to be identified.

The fall of Enron—to 61 cents a share on Nov. 28, 2001— has already wiped out more than 99 percent of its stock-market value. Some $3.5 billion of its bonds are trading at just a quarter of their face value. Banks that lent billions to Enron will have to fight for a share in bankruptcy court. Enron's biggest lenders are J. P. Morgan Chase & Co. and Citigroup, which together have an estimated $1.6 billion in exposure. Of that, $900 million is unsecured, according to sources. Other losers: Enron's customers, who traded everything from electricity, gas, and metals to telecom bandwidth, credit insurance, and weather derivatives.

Already the once-arrogant Enron has become vulture meat. In addition to clamoring creditors, it faces class actions by shareholders and employees, whose pensions were heavily invested in Enron stock. That raises questions about how much value is left in the company, which will probably be dismembered and sold off in parts.

Since creditors had time to shield themselves, it doesn't appear that the implosion of Enron will drag down any other big players. "The Wall Street firms have had plenty of time to unwind whatever exposure they may have had," says Richard Strauss of Goldman Sachs. "What they may still have remaining is either collateralized or hedged."

Who's to blame? Perhaps the biggest culprit was arrogance, which has caused Enron to be compared to past self-proclaimed masters of the universe such as Drexel Burnham Lambert Inc. in the 1980s and Long-Term Capital Management in the 1990s. Many fingers are pointing at Skilling, the longtime Enron financial engineer who took over as CEO in February and then resigned with little explanation in August, shortly before the company hit the skids. Also facing the music are Lay and Andrew S. Fastow, who was ousted as chief financial officer on Oct. 24, 2001. Fastow put together several partnerships that were intended to streamline Enron's balance sheet by taking on certain assets and liabilities. That created a conflict of interest for Fastow, who made over $30 million from his partnerships.

The most poignant aspect of Enron's failure is the damage to its own employees. "People have had their total savings disappear," says William Miller, business manager of the International Brotherhood of Electrical Workers union local in Portland, Ore., which represents employees of Enron's Portland General Electric Co. subsidiary. "Some lives have been pretty well destroyed." Enron flew high, but when it fell, it fell hard.

**Source:** Excerpted from Peter Coy, Emily Thornton, Stephanie Anderson Forest, and Christopher Palmeri, "Enron: Running on Empty," *BusinessWeek*, December 10, 2001, p. 80.

Unfortunately, the public's perception of the ethics of corporate executives in America is near its all-time low. A major cause is a spate of corporate scandals prompted by self-serving, and often criminal executive action that resulted in the loss of stakeholder investments and employee jobs. The most notorious of these cases was the failure of the Enron Corporation, as described in Strategy in Action Exhibit 2–20.

However, even when groups agree on what constitutes human welfare in a given case, the means they choose to achieve this welfare may differ. Therefore, ethics also involve acting to attain human goals. For example, many people would agree that health is a value worth seeking—that is, health enhances human welfare. But what if the means deemed necessary to attain this value for some include the denial or risk of health for others, as is commonly an issue faced by pharmaceutical manufacturers? During production of some drugs, employees are sometimes subjected to great risk of personal injury and infection. For example, if contacted or inhaled, the mercury used in making thermometers and blood pressure equipment can cause heavy metal poisoning. If inhaled, ethylene oxide used to sterilize medical equipment before it is shipped to doctors can cause fetal abnormalities and miscarriages. Even penicillin, if inhaled during its manufacturing process, can cause acute anaphylaxis or shock. Thus, although the goal of customer health might be widely accepted, the means (involving jeopardy to production employees) may not be.

## Approaches to Questions of Ethics

Managers report that the most critical quality of ethical decision making is consistency. Thus, they often try to adopt a philosophical approach that can provide the basis for the consistency they seek. There are three fundamental ethical approaches for executives to consider: the utilitarian approach, the moral rights approach, and the social justice approach.

Managers who adopt the *utilitarian approach* judge the effects of a particular action on the people directly involved, in terms of what provides the greatest good for the greatest number of people. The utilitarian approach focuses on actions, rather than on the motives behind the actions. Potentially positive results are weighed against potentially negative results. If the former outweigh the latter, the manager taking the utilitarian approach is likely to proceed with the action. That some people might be adversely affected by the action is accepted as inevitable. For example, the Council on Environmental Quality conducts cost-benefit analysis when selecting air pollution standards under the Clean Air Act, thereby acknowledging that some pollution must be accepted.

Managers who subscribe to the *moral rights approach* judge whether decisions and actions are in keeping with the maintenance of fundamental individual and group rights and privileges. The moral rights approach (also referred to as deontology) includes the rights of human beings to life and safety, a standard of truthfulness, privacy, freedom to express one's conscience, freedom of speech, and private property.

Managers who take the *social justice approach* judge how consistent actions are with equity, fairness, and impartiality in the distribution of rewards and costs among individuals and groups. These ideas stem from two principles known as the liberty principle and the difference principle. The liberty principle states that individuals have certain basic liberties compatible with similar liberties by other people. The difference principle holds that social and economic inequities must be addressed to achieve a more equitable distribution of goods and services.

In addition to these defining principles, three implementing principles are essential to the social justice approach. According to the distributive-justice principle, individuals should not be treated differently on the basis of arbitrary characteristics, such as race, sex, religion or national origin. This familiar principle is embodied in the Civil Rights Act. The fairness principle means that employees must be expected to engage in cooperative activities according to the rules of the company, assuming that the company rules are deemed fair. The most obvious example is that, in order to further the mutual interests of the company, themselves, and other workers, employees must accept limits on their freedom to be absent from work. The natural-duty principle points up a number of general obligations, including the duty to help others who are in need or danger, the duty not to cause unnecessary suffering, and the duty to comply with the just rules of an institution.

## Summary

Defining the company mission is one of the most often slighted tasks in strategic management. Emphasizing the operational aspects of long-range management activities comes much more easily for most executives. But the critical role of the mission statement repeatedly is demonstrated by failing firms whose short-run actions have been at odds with their long-run purposes.

The principal value of the mission statement is its specification of the firm's ultimate aims. A firm gains a heightened sense of purpose when its board of directors and its top executives address these issues: "What business are we in?" "What customers do we serve?" "Why does this organization exist?" However, the potential contribution of the company mission can be undermined if platitudes or ambiguous generalizations are accepted in response to these questions. It is not enough to say that Lever Brothers is in the business of "making anything that cleans anything" or that Polaroid is committed to businesses that deal with "the interaction of light and matter." Only if a firm clearly articulates its long-term intentions can its goals serve as a basis for shared expectations, planning, and performance evaluation.

A mission statement that is developed from this perspective provides managers with a unity of direction transcending individual, parochial, and temporary needs. It promotes a sense of shared expectations among all levels and generations of employees. It consolidates values over time and across individuals and interest groups. It projects a sense of worth and intent that can be identified and assimilated by outside stakeholders, that is, customers, suppliers, competitors, local committees, and the general public. Finally, it asserts the firm's commitment to responsible action in symbiosis with the preservation and protection of the essential claims of insider stakeholders' survival, growth, and profitability.

## Questions for Discussion

1. Reread Nicor, Inc.'s mission statement in Exhibit 2–1, Strategy in Action. List five insights into Nicor that you feel you gained from knowing its mission.

2. Locate the mission statement of a company not mentioned in the chapter. Where did you find it? Was it presented as a consolidated statement, or were you forced to assemble it yourself from various publications of the firm? How many of the mission statement elements outlined in this chapter were discussed or revealed in the statement you found?

3. Prepare a two-page typewritten mission statement for your school of business or for a firm selected by your instructor.

4. List five potentially vulnerable areas of a firm without a stated company mission.

5. Define the term *social responsibility.* Find an example of a company action that was legal but not socially responsible. Defend your example on the basis of your definition.

6. Name five potentially valuable indicators of a firm's social responsibility and describe how company performance in each could be measured.

7. Do you think a business organization in today's society benefits by defining a socially responsible role for itself? Why or why not?

8. Which of the three basic philosophies of social responsibility would you find most appealing as the chief executive of a large corporation? Explain.

9. Do you think society's expectations for corporate social responsibility will change in the next decade? Explain.

10. How much should social responsibility be considered in evaluating an organization's overall performance?

11. Is it necessary that an action be voluntary to be termed socially responsible? Explain.

12. Do you think an organization should adhere to different philosophies of corporate responsibility when confronted with different issues, or should its philosophy always remain the same? Explain.

13. After reviewing arguments for and against social responsibility, which side do you find more compelling? Why?

14. Describe yourself as a stakeholder in a company. What kind of stakeholder role do you play now? What kind of stakeholder roles do you expect to play in the future?

15. What sets the affirmative philosophy apart from the stakeholder philosophy of social responsibility? In what areas do the two philosophies overlap?

16. Cite examples of both ethical and unethical behavior drawn from your knowledge of current business events.

17. How would you describe the contemporary state of business ethics?

18. How can business self-interest also serve social interests?

## Chapter 2 Discussion Case

BusinessWeek

# Inside a Chinese Sweatshop

1  Liu Zhang (not his real name) was apprehensive about taking a job at the Chun Si Enterprise Handbag Factory in Zhongshan, a booming city in Guangdong Province in southern China, where thousands of factories churn out goods for Western companies. Chun Si, which made Kathie Lee Gifford handbags sold by Wal-Mart Stores Inc. as well as handbags sold by Kansas-based Payless ShoeSource Inc., advertised decent working conditions and a fair salary. But word among migrant workers in the area was that managers there demanded long hours of their workers and sometimes hit them. Still, Liu, a 32-year-old former farmer and construction worker from far-off Henan province, was desperate for work. A factory job would give him living quarters and the temporary-residence permit internal migrants need to avoid being locked up by police in special detention centers. So in late August 1999, he signed up.

2  Liu quickly realized that the factory was even worse than its reputation. Chun Si, owned by Chun Kwan, a Macau businessman, charged workers $15 a month for food and lodging in a crowded dorm—a crushing sum given the $22 Liu cleared his first month. What's more, the factory gave Liu an expired temporary-resident permit; and in return, Liu had to hand over his personal identification card. This left him a virtual captive. Only the local police near the factory knew that Chun Si issued expired cards, Liu says, so workers risked arrest if they ventured out of the immediate neighborhood.

3  HALF A CENT. Liu also found that Chun Si's 900 workers were locked in the walled factory compound for all but a total of 60 minutes a day for meals. Guards regularly punched and hit workers for talking back to managers or even for walking too fast, he says. And they fined them up to $1 for infractions such as taking too long in the bathroom. Liu left the factory for good in December, after he and about 60 other workers descended on the local labor office to protest Chun Si's latest offenses: requiring cash payments for dinner and a phony factory it set up to dupe Wal-Mart's auditors. In his pocket was a total of $6 for three months of 90-hour weeks—an average of about one-half cent an hour. "Workers there face a life of fines and beating," says Liu. Chun Kwan couldn't be reached, but his daughter, Selina Chun, one of the factory managers, says "this is not true,

none of this." She concedes that Chun Si did not pay overtime but says few other factories do, either. In a face-to-face interview in August, she also admitted that workers have tried to sue Chun Si.

4  Liu's Dickensian tale stands in stark contrast to the reassurances that Wal-Mart, Payless, and other U.S. companies give American consumers that their goods aren't produced under sweatshop conditions. Since 1992, Wal-Mart has required its suppliers to sign a code of basic labor standards. After exposés in the mid–1990s of abuses in factories making Kathie Lee products, which the chain carries, Wal-Mart and Kathie Lee both began hiring outside auditing firms to inspect supplier factories to ensure their compliance with the code. Many other companies that produce or sell goods made in low-wage countries do similar self-policing, from Toys 'R' Us to Nike and Gap. While no company suggests that its auditing systems are perfect, most say they catch major abuses and either force suppliers to fix them or yank production.

5  What happened at Chun Si suggests that these auditing systems can miss serious problems—and that self-policing allows companies to avoid painful public revelations about them. Allegations about Chun Si first surfaced this May in a report by the National Labor Committee (NLC), a small anti-sweatshop group in New York that in 1997 exposed Kathie Lee's connection to labor violations in Central America. For several months, Wal-Mart repeatedly denied any connection to Chun Si. Wal-Mart and Kathie Lee even went so far as to pass out a press release when the report came out dismissing it as "lies" and insisting that they never had "any relationship with a company or factory by this name anywhere in the world."

6  But in mid-September, after a three-month *BusinessWeek* investigation that involved a visit to the factory, tracking down ex-Chun Si workers, and obtaining copies of records they had smuggled out of the factory, Wal-Mart conceded that it had produced the Kathie Lee bags there until December, 1999. Wal-Mart Vice-President of Corporate Affairs Jay Allen now says that Wal-Mart denied using Chun Si because it was "defensive" about the sweatshop issue.

7  Wal-Mart Director of Corporate Compliance Denise Fenton says its auditors, Pricewaterhouse

Coopers LLP (PWC) and Cal Safety Compliance Corp., had inspected Chun Si five times in 1999 and found that the factory didn't pay the legal overtime rate and had required excessive work hours. Because the factory didn't fix the problems, she says, Wal-Mart stopped making Kathie Lee bags there. Kathie Lee, who licenses her name to Wal-Mart, which handles production, concurred with the chain's action at Chun Si, says her lawyer Richard Hofstetter. Payless also stopped production there after an investigation, a spokesman says.

8    Still, the auditors failed to uncover many of the egregious conditions in the factory despite interviews with dozens of workers, concedes Fenton. Charges NLC Executive Director Charles Kernaghan: "The real issue here is why anyone should believe their audits."

9    A SECOND LOOK. And it's not just Wal-Mart. The NLC's report, entitled Made in China, detailed labor abuses in a dozen factories producing for household-name U.S. companies (www.nlcnet.org). After it came out, bootmaker Timberland Co. asked its auditors to revisit its plant, also in Zhongshan. They found that the factory hadn't fixed most of the violations cited the first time, despite repeated assurances to Timberland that it had. Similarly, in mid-September, Social Accountability International (SAI), a New York group that started a factory monitoring system last year, revoked its certification of a Chinese factory that makes shoes for New Balance Athletic Shoe Inc. after auditors reinspected the plant following the NLC report. "The auditors found that indeed there were many violations they had not picked up the first time," says SAI President Alice Tepper Marlin.

10   Because such efforts to reassure consumers have proven so unsatisfactory, a handful of companies, including Nike Inc. and Reebok International Ltd.—so far, the companies most tarnished by anti-sweatshop activists—have concluded that self-policing isn't enough. They—along with Kathie Lee—helped form the Fair Labor Assn., created in 1998 after a White House-sponsored initiative. The FLA now has a dozen members and is setting up an independent monitoring system that includes human rights groups.

11   Wal-Mart and many other companies, though, reject such efforts, saying they don't want to tell critics or rivals where their products are made. Yet without independent inspections, such companies leave themselves open to critics' accusations that self-policing doesn't work. "The big retailers, such as Wal-Mart, drive the market today, yet . . . they're not committed to changing the way they do business," says Michael Posner, head of New York-based Lawyers Committee for Human Rights and an FLA board member. Wal-Mart's Allen says that after three years of talks, the company may soon set up independent monitoring with the Interfaith Center on Corporate Responsibility, a religious group in New York City.

12   Certainly, what happened at Chun Si illustrates the inadequacy of many labor-auditing systems in place today. Wal-Mart uses nine auditing firms, including PWC. Like other big accounting firms, PWC has a booming labor-auditing business inspecting many of the thousands of factories making toys and clothes made by Wal-Mart and other companies. After Kathie Lee's drubbing by sweatshop critics, she hired Cal Safety, a Los Angeles-based labor-auditing firm, to do separate audits of the factories that produce the clothing and accessories bearing her name. According to Wal-Mart's Fenton, Cal Safety inspected the factory four times from March to December of last year, and PWC inspected it once, in September. The auditors found that Chun Si had numerous problems, including overtime violations and excessively long hours, says Fenton.

13   But otherwise, concedes Fenton, the audits missed most of the more serious abuses listed in the NLC report and confirmed by *BusinessWeek,* including beatings and confiscated identity papers. (Wal-Mart declined to allow *BusinessWeek* to talk in detail to Cal Safety or PWC, citing confidentiality agreements. Randal H. Rankin, head of PWC's labor practices unit, insists his audit did catch many of the abuses found by the NLC, though he wouldn't provide specifics, also citing Wal-Mart's confidentiality agreement. Cal Safety President Carol Pender says her firm caught some, though not all, of the abuses.)

14   All the while, evidence was piling up at the local labor office in Zhongshan. There, officials received a constant stream of worker complaints—several a month since the factory opened 10 years ago, says Mr. Chen, the head of the local labor office, who declined to give his full name. "Since they opened their factory, the complaints never stopped," he says. Officials would call or go to the factory once a month or so to mediate disputes, but new complaints kept arising, he says. Neither Wal-Mart's nor Kathie Lee's auditors discovered this history.

15   Chun Si also tried to hoodwink the auditors, according to the workers *BusinessWeek* interviewed. After Cal Safety's initial inspection in March, 1999,

Wal-Mart (through its U.S. supplier, which placed the order with the factory) insisted that Chun Si remedy the violations or it would pull the contract. Cal Safety found little improvement when it returned in June, as did PWC in September.

16 DOUBLE STANDARD. Chun Si then took drastic steps, apparently in an effort to pass the final audit upon which its contract depended. In early November, management gave a facelift to the two attached five-story factory buildings, painting walls, cleaning workshops, even putting high-quality toilet paper in the dank bathrooms, according to Liu and Pang Yinguang (also not his real name), another worker employed there at the time whom *BusinessWeek* interviewed in mid-September. Management then split the factory into two groups. The first, with about 200 workers, was assigned to work on the fixed-up second floor, while the remaining 700 or so worked on the fourth floor, leaving the other floors largely vacant. Managers announced that those on the fourth floor were no longer working for Chun Si but for a new factory they called Yecheng. Workers signed new labor contracts with Yecheng, whose name went up outside the fourth floor.

17 The reality soon became clear. Workers on the fourth floor, including Liu and Pang, were still laboring under the old egregious conditions—illegally low pay, 14-hour days, exorbitant fees for meals—and still making the same Kathie Lee handbags. "It felt like being in prison," says Pang, 22. But those on the second floor now received the local minimum wage of $55 a month and no longer had to do mandatory overtime. A new sign went up in the cafeteria used by workers on all floors explaining that the factory was a Wal-Mart supplier and should live up to certain labor standards. Liu says there was even a phone number workers could call with problems: 1-800-WM-ETHIC. "When we saw the Wal-Mart statement, we felt very excited and happy because we thought that now there was a possibility to improve our conditions," says Liu.

18 LAST STRAW. Instead, they got worse. On Nov. 28, a second notice went up stating that starting on Dec. 10, all workers would be required to pay cash for dinner rather than just have money subtracted from their paychecks as before, say Liu and Pang. With up to 80 percent of workers already skipping breakfast to save money, the upper-floor employees were aghast, says Liu. "If we had left the factory then, we wouldn't have had even enough money for a bus ticket home," he says. "But if we stayed, we knew we wouldn't have enough money to eat."

19 A group of workers, including Liu and Pang, met around a small pond on the factory grounds on one of the following evenings. They knew that workers had fruitlessly complained before to the local labor office. So they decided on a plan to smuggle out documents to prove Chun Si's illegal fees and subminimum wages. On Dec. 1, 58 workers overcame their fears of retaliation and marched out the factory gates, down to the labor office.

20 Faced with the throng of workers, local labor officials visited Chun Si and forced the factory to immediately pay the workers and return the illegally collected fees. But the officials also told these workers they would have to give up their jobs at Chun Si. Days later, some 40 labor officials returned, ordered Chun Si to properly register or shut down the so-called Yecheng factory, and fined the company about $8,500. Shortly after the blow-up, Wal-Mart ended production at Chun Si.

21 Kernaghan and other labor activists concede that Chun Si is an extreme example of working conditions in China today. Yet many experts think most factories in China producing for Western companies routinely break China's labor laws. Some Western companies' monitoring efforts do catch and fix some of these problems. But unless companies and governments alike take more serious steps, labor watchdogs will give little credence to company claims that they're doing the best they can.

**Source:** Dexter Roberts and Aaron Bernstein, "A Life of Fines and Beating: Wal-Mart's self-policing in the Chun Si factory was a disaster. What kind of monitoring system works?" *BusinessWeek*, October 2, 2000.

# BB&T Vision, Mission, and Purpose

## BB&T VISION

**To create the best financial institution possible:** *"The Best of The Best."*

## BB&T MISSION

**To make the world a better place to live by: helping our clients achieve economic success and financial security; creating a place where our employees can learn, grow and be fulfilled in their work; making the communities in which we work better places to be; and thereby: optimizing the long-term return to our shareholders, while providing a safe and sound investment.**

## BB&T PURPOSE

**Our ultimate purpose is to create superior long-term economic rewards for our shareholders.**

This purpose is defined by the free market and is as it should be. Our shareholders provide the capital that is necessary to make our business possible. They take the risk if the business is unsuccessful. They have the right to receive economic rewards for the risk which they have undertaken.

However, our purpose, to create superior long-term economic rewards for our shareholders, can only be accomplished by providing excellent service to our clients, as our clients are our source of revenues.

To have excellent client relations, we must have outstanding employees to serve our clients. To attract and retain outstanding employees, we must reward them financially and create an environment where they can learn and grow.

Our economic results are significantly impacted by the success of our communities. The community's "quality of life" impacts its ability to attract industry for growth.

Therefore, we manage our business in a long-term context, as an integrated whole, with the ultimate objective of rewarding the shareholders for their investment, while realizing that the cause of this result is quality client service. Excellent service will be delivered by motivated employees working as an integrated team. These results will be impacted by our capacity to contribute to the growth and well-being of the communities we serve.

## VALUES

**"Excellence is an art won by training and habituation. We are what we repeatedly do. Excellence then is not an act, but a habit."—Aristotle**

The great Greek philosophers saw values as guides to excellence in thinking and action. In this context, values are standards which we strive to achieve. Values are practical habits that enable us as individuals to live, be successful and achieve happiness. For BB&T, our values enable us to achieve our mission and corporate purpose.

To be useful, values must be consciously held and be consistent (noncontradictory). Many people have conflicting values which prevent them from acting with clarity and self-confidence.

There are 10 primary values at BB&T. These values are consistent with one another and are integrated. To fully act on one of these values, you must also act consistently with the other values. Our focus on values grows from our belief that ideas matter and that an individual's character is of critical significance.

Values are important at BB&T!

# 1. REALITY (FACT-BASED)

What is, is. If we want to be better, we must act within the context of reality (the facts). Businesses and individuals often make serious mistakes by making decisions based on what they "wish was so," or based on theories which are disconnected from reality. The foundation for quality decision making is a careful understanding of the facts.

There is a fundamental difference between the laws of nature (reality), which are immutable, and the man-made. The law of gravity is the law of gravity. The existence of the law of gravity does not mean man can not create an airplane. However, an airplane must be created within the context of the law of gravity. At BB&T, we believe in being "reality grounded."

# 2. REASON (OBJECTIVITY)

Mankind has a specific means of survival, which is his ability to think, i.e., his capacity to reason logically from the facts of reality as presented to his five senses. A lion has claws to hunt. A deer has swiftness to avoid the hunter. Man has his ability to think. There is only one "natural resource"—the human mind.

Clear thinking is not automatic. It requires intellectual discipline and begins with sound premises based on observed facts. You must be able to draw general conclusions in a rational manner from specific examples (induction) and be able to apply general principles to the solution of specific problems (deduction). You must be able to think in an integrated way, thereby avoiding logical contradictions.

We cannot all be geniuses, but each of us can develop the mental habits which ensure that when making decisions we carefully examine the facts and think logically without contradiction in deriving a conclusion. We must learn to think in terms of what is essential, i.e., about what is important. Our goal is to objectively make the best decision to accomplish our purpose.

Rational thinking is a learned skill which requires mental focus and a fundamental commitment to consistently improving the clarity of our mental processes. At BB&T, we are looking for people who are committed to constantly improving their ability to reason.

# 3. INDEPENDENT THINKING

All employees are challenged to use their individual minds to their optimum to make rational decisions. In this context, each of us is *responsible* for what we do and who we are. In addition, creativity is strongly encouraged and only possible with independent thought.

We learn a great deal from each other. Teamwork is important at BB&T (as will be discussed later). However, each of us thinks alone. Our minds are not physically connected. In this regard, each of us must be willing to make an independent judgment of the facts based on our capacity to think logically. Just because the "crowd" says it is so, does not make it so.

In this context, each of us is responsible for our own actions. Each of us is responsible for our personal success or failure, i.e., it is not the bank's fault if someone does not achieve his objectives.

All human progress by definition is based on creativity, because creativity is the source of positive change. Creativity is only possible to an independent thinker. Creativity is not about just doing something different. It is about doing something better. To be better, the new method/process must be judged by its impact on the whole organization, and as to whether it contributes to the accomplishment of our mission.

There is an infinite opportunity for each of us to do whatever we do better. A significant aspect of the self-fulfillment which work can provide comes from creative thought and action.

## 4. PRODUCTIVITY

We are committed to being producers of wealth and well-being by taking the actions necessary to accomplish our mission. The tangible evidence of our productivity is that we have rationally allocated capital through our lending and investment process, and that we have provided needed services to our clients in an efficient manner resulting in superior profitability.

Profitability is a measure of the differences in the economic value of the products/services we produce and the cost of producing these products/services. In a long-term context and in a free market, the bigger the profit, the better. This is true not only from our shareholders' perspective (which would be enough justification), but also in terms of the impact of our work on society as a whole. Healthy profits represent productive work. At BB&T we are looking for people who want to create, to produce, and who are thereby committed to turning their thoughts into actions that improve economic well-being.

## 5. HONESTY

Being honest is simply being consistent with reality. To be dishonest is to be in conflict with reality, which is therefore self-defeating. A primary reason that individuals fail is because they become disconnected from reality, pretending that facts are other than they are.

To be honest does not require that we know everything. Knowledge is always contextual and man is not omniscient. However, we must be responsible for saying what we mean and meaning what we say.

## 6. INTEGRITY

Because we have developed our principles logically, based on reality, we will always act consistently with our principles. Regardless of the short-term benefits, acting inconsistently with our principles is to our long-term detriment. We do not, therefore, believe in compromising our principles in any situation.

Principles provide carefully thought-out concepts which will lead to our long-term success and happiness. Violating our principles will always lead to failure. BB&T is an organization of the highest integrity.

## 7. JUSTICE (FAIRNESS)

Individuals should be evaluated and rewarded objectively (for better or worse) based on their contributions toward accomplishing our mission and adherence to our values. Those who contribute the most should receive the most.

The single most significant way in which employees evaluate their managers is in determining whether the manager is just. Employees become extremely unhappy (and rightly so) when they perceive that a person who is not contributing is overrewarded or a strong contributor is underrewarded.

If we do not reward those who contribute the most, they will leave and our organization will be less successful. Even more important, if there is no reward for superior performance, the average person will not be motivated to maximize his productivity.

We must evaluate whether the food we eat is healthy, the clothes we wear attractive, the car we drive functional, etc., and we must also evaluate whether relationships with other people are good for us or not.

In evaluating other people, it is critical that we judge based on essentials. At BB&T we do not discriminate based on nonessentials such as race, sex, nationality, etc. We do discriminate based on competency, performance and character. We consciously reject egalitarianism and collectivism. Individuals must be judged individually based on their personal merits, not their membership in any group.

## 8. PRIDE

Pride is the psychological reward we earn from living by our values, i.e., from being just, honest, having integrity, being an independent thinker, being productive and rational.

Aristotle believed that "earned" pride (not arrogance) was the highest of virtues, because it presupposed all the others. Striving for earned pride simply reinforces the importance of having high moral values.

Each of us must perform our work in a manner as to be able to be justly proud of what we have accomplished. BB&T must be the kind of organization with which each employee and client can be proud to be associated.

## 9. SELF-ESTEEM (SELF-MOTIVATION)

We expect our employees to earn positive self-esteem from doing their work well. We expect and want our employees to act in their rational, long-term self-interest. We want employees who have strong personal goals and who expect to be able to accomplish their goals within the context of our mission.

A necessary attribute for self-esteem is self-motivation. We have a strong work ethic. We believe that you receive from your work in proportion to how much you contribute. If you do not want to work hard, work somewhere else.

While there are many trade-offs in the content of life, you need to be clear that BB&T is the best place, all things considered, for you to work to accomplish your long-term goals. When you know this, you can be more productive and happy.

## 10. TEAMWORK/MUTUAL SUPPORTIVENESS

While independent thought and strong personal goals are critically important, our work is accomplished within teams. Each of us must consistently act to achieve the agreed-upon objectives of the team, with respect for our fellow employees, while acting in a mutually supportive manner.

Our work at BB&T is so complex that it requires an integrated effort among many people to accomplish important tasks. While we are looking for self-motivated and independent thinking individuals, these individuals must recognize that almost nothing at BB&T can be accomplished without the help of their team members. One of the responsibilities of leadership in our organization is to ensure that each individual is rewarded based on their contribution to the success of the total team. We need outstanding individuals working together to create an outstanding team.

Our values are held consciously and are logically consistent. To fully execute on any one value, you must act consistently with all 10 values. At BB&T values are practical and important

## THE ROLE OF EMOTIONS

Often people believe that making logical decisions means that we should be unemotional and that emotions are thereby unimportant. In fact, emotions are important. However, the real issue is how rational are our emotions. Emotions are mental habits which are often developed as children. Emotions give us automatic responses to people and events; these responses can either be very useful or destructive indicators. Emotions as such are not means of decision or of knowledge; the issue is: How were your emotions formed? The real question is: Are we happy when we should be happy, and unhappy when we should be unhappy, or are we unhappy when we should be happy?

Emotions are learned behaviors. The goal is to "train up" our emotions so that our emotions objectively reinforce the best decisions and behaviors toward our long-term success and happiness. Just because someone is unemotional does not mean that they are logical.

## CONCEPTS THAT DESCRIBE BB&T

### 1. CLIENT-DRIVEN

"World class" client service organization.

Our clients are our partners.

Our goal is to create win/win relationships.

"You can tell we want your business."

"It is easy to do business with BB&T."

"Respect the individual, value the relationship."

We will absolutely never, ever, take advantage of anyone, nor do we want to do business with those who would take advantage of us. Our clients are long-term partners and should be treated accordingly. One of the attributes of partnerships is that both partners must keep their agreements. We keep our agreements. When our partners fail to keep their agreements, they are terminating the partnership.

There are an infinite number of opportunities where we can get better together, where we can help our clients achieve their financial goals and where our client will enable us to make a profit in doing so.

## 2. QUALITY ORIENTED

Quality must be built into the process.

In every aspect of our business we want to execute and deliver quality. It is easier and less expensive to do things correctly than to fix what has been done incorrectly.

## 3. EFFICIENT

"Waste not, want not."

Design efficiency into the system.

## 4. GROWING BOTH OUR BUSINESS AND OUR PEOPLE

Grow or die.

Life requires constant, focused thought and actions towards one's goals.

## 5. CONTINUOUS IMPROVEMENT

Everything can be done better.

Fundamental commitment to innovation.

Every employee should constantly use their reasoning ability to do whatever they do better every day. All managers of systems/processes should constantly search for better methods to solve problems and serve the client.

## 6. OBJECTIVE DECISION MAKING

Fact-Based and rational

# BB&T MANAGEMENT STYLE

Participative

Team Oriented

Fact-Based

Rational

Objective

Our management process, by intention, is designed to be participative and team oriented. We work hard to create consensus. When people are involved in the decision process, better information is available to make decisions. The participant's understanding of the decision is greater and, therefore, execution is better.

However, there is a risk in participative decision making: the decision process can become a popularity contest. Therefore, our decision process is disciplined. Our decisions will be made based on the facts using reason. The best objective decision will be the one which is enacted.

Therefore, it does not matter who you know, who your friends are, etc.; it matters whether you can offer the best objective solution to accomplishing the goal or solving the problem at hand.

## BB&T MANAGEMENT CONCEPT

Hire excellent people

Train them well

Give them an appropriate level of authority and responsibility

Expect a high level of achievement

Reward their performance

Our concept is to operate a highly autonomous, entrepreneurial organization. In order to execute this concept, we must have extremely competent individuals who are "masters" of BB&T's philosophy and who are "masters" in their field of technical expertise.

By having individuals who are "masters" in their field, we can afford to have less costly control systems and be more responsive in meeting the needs of our clients.

## ATTRIBUTES OF AN OUTSTANDING BB&T EMPLOYEE

Purpose

Rationality

Self-Esteem

Consistent with our values, successful individuals at BB&T have a sense of purpose for their lives, i.e., they believe that their lives matter and that they can accomplish something meaningful through their work. We are looking for people who are rational and have a high level of personal self-esteem. People with a strong personal self-esteem get along better with others, because they are at peace with themselves.

## BB&T POSITIVE ATTITUDE

Since we build on the facts of reality and our ability to reason, we are capable of achieving both success and happiness.

We do not believe that "realism" means pessimism. On the contrary, precisely because our goals are based on and consistent with reality, we fully expect to accomplish them.

## BB&T'S OBLIGATIONS TO ITS EMPLOYEES

We will do our best to:

Compensate employees fairly in relation to internal equity and market-comparable pay practices—performance-based compensation.

Provide a comprehensive and market-competitive benefit program.

Create a place where employees can learn and grow—to become more productive workers and better people.

Train employees so they are competent to do the work asked of them. (Never ask anyone to do anything they are not trained to do.)

Evaluate and recognize performance objectively, fairly and consistently based on the individual's contribution to the accomplishment of our mission and adherence to our values.

Treat each employee as an individual with dignity and respect.

# VIRTUES OF AN OUTSTANDING CREDIT CULTURE

Just as individuals need a set of values (virtues) to guide their actions, systems should be designed to have a set of attributes which optimize their performance towards our goals. In this regard, our credit culture has seven fundamental virtues:

1. Provides fundamental insight to help clients achieve their economic goals and solve their financial problems: We are in the high-quality financial advice business.
2. Responsive: The client deserves an answer as quickly as possible, even when the answer is no.
3. Flexible (Creative): We are committed to finding better ways to meet the client's financial needs.
4. Reliable: Our clients are selected as long-term partners and treated accordingly. BB&T must continue to earn the right to be known as the most reliable bank.
5. Manages risk within agreed-upon limits: Clients do not want to fail financially, and the bank does not want a bad loan.
6. Ensures an appropriate economic return to the bank for risk taken: The higher the risk, the higher the return. The lower the risk, the lower the return. This is an expression of justice.
7. Creates a "premium" for service delivery: The concept is to provide superior value to the client through outstanding service quality. A rational client will fairly compensate us when we provide sound financial advice, are responsive, creative and reliable, because these attributes are of economic value to the client.

# STRATEGIC OBJECTIVES

**Create a high performance financial institution that can survive and prosper in a rapidly changing, highly competitive, globally integrated environment.**

# ACHIEVING OUR GOAL

The key to maximizing our probability of being both independent and prosperous over the long term is to create a superior earnings per share (EPS) growth rate without sacrificing the fundamental quality and long-term competitiveness of our business and without taking unreasonable risk.

While being fundamentally efficient is critical, the "easy" way to rapid EPS growth is to artifically cut cost. However, not investing for the future is long-term suicide, as it destroys our capability to compete.

The intelligent process to achieve superior EPS growth is to grow revenues by providing (and selling) superior quality service while systematically enhancing our margins, improving our efficiency, expanding our profitable product offerings and creating more effective distribution channels.

# THE "WORLD STANDARD" REVENUE-DRIVEN SALES ORGANIZATION

At BB&T, selling is about identifying our clients' legitimate financial needs and finding a way to help the client achieve economic goals by providing the right products and services.

Effective selling requires a disciplined approach in which the BB&T employee asks the client about financial goals and problems and has a complete understanding of how our products can help the client achieve objectives and solve financial problems.

It also requires exceptional execution by support staffs and product managers, since service and sales are fundamentally connected and creativity is required in product design and development.

# "WORLD STANDARD" CLIENT SERVICE COMMUNITY BANKS

BB&T operates as a series of "Community Banks." The "Community Bank" concept is the foundation for local decision making and the basis for responsive, reliable and empathetic client service.

By putting decision making closer to the client, all local factors can be considered, and we can ensure that the client is being treated as an individual.

To operate in this decentralized decision-making fashion, we must have highly trained employees who understand BB&T's philosophy and are "masters" of their areas of responsibility.

# COMMITMENT TO EDUCATION/LEARNING

**Competitive advantage is in the minds of our employees.** We are committed to making substantial investments in employee education to create a "knowledge-based learning organization" founded on the premise that knowledge (understanding), properly applied, is the source of superior performance.

We believe in systematized learning founded on Aristotle's concept that "excellence is an art won by training and habituation." We attempt to train our employees with the best knowledge/methods in their fields and to habituate those behaviors through consistent management reinforcement. The goal is for each employee to be a "master" of his or her role, whether it be a computer operator, teller, lender, financial consultant or any other job responsibility.

# OUR PASSIONS

**To create the best financial institution possible.**

**To consistently provide the client with better value through rational innovation and productivity improvement.**

At BB&T we have two powerful passions. Our fundamental passion is our Vision: To Create The Best Financial Institution Possible—The "World Standard"—The "Best of the Best." We believe that the best can be objectively evaluated by rational performance standards in relation to the accomplishment of our mission.

To be the best of the best, we must constantly find ways to deliver better value to our clients in a highly profitable manner. This requires us to keep our minds focused at all times on innovative ways to enhance our productivity.

# Chapter **Three**

# The External Environment

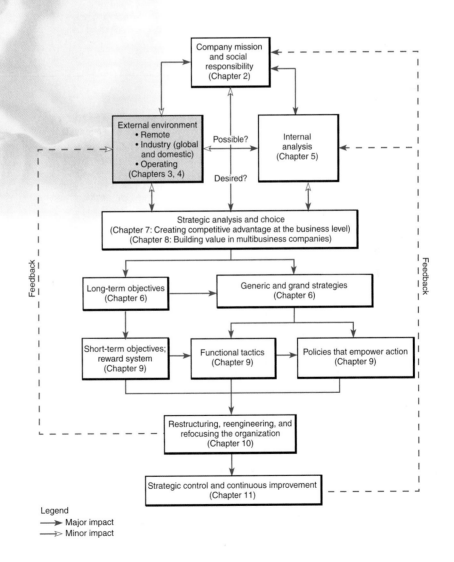

Company mission and social responsibility (Chapter 2)

External environment
• Remote
• Industry (global and domestic)
• Operating
(Chapters 3, 4)

Possible?

Desired?

Internal analysis (Chapter 5)

Strategic analysis and choice
(Chapter 7: Creating competitive advantage at the business level)
(Chapter 8: Building value in multibusiness companies)

Long-term objectives (Chapter 6)

Generic and grand strategies (Chapter 6)

Short-term objectives; reward system (Chapter 9)

Functional tactics (Chapter 9)

Policies that empower action (Chapter 9)

Restructuring, reengineering, and refocusing the organization (Chapter 10)

Strategic control and continuous improvement (Chapter 11)

Feedback

Feedback

Legend
———▶ Major impact
———▷ Minor impact

A host of external factors influence a firm's choice of direction and action and, ultimately, its organizational structure and internal processes. These factors, which constitute the *external environment,* can be divided into three interrelated subcategories: factors in the *remote* environment, factors in the *industry* environment, and factors in the *operating* environment. This chapter describes the complex necessities involved in formulating strategies that optimize a firm's market opportunities. Exhibit 3–1 suggests the interrelationship between the firm and its remote, its industry, and its operating environments. In combination, these factors form the basis of the opportunities and threats that a firm faces in its competitive environment.

**EXHIBIT 3–1**
**The Firm's External Environment**

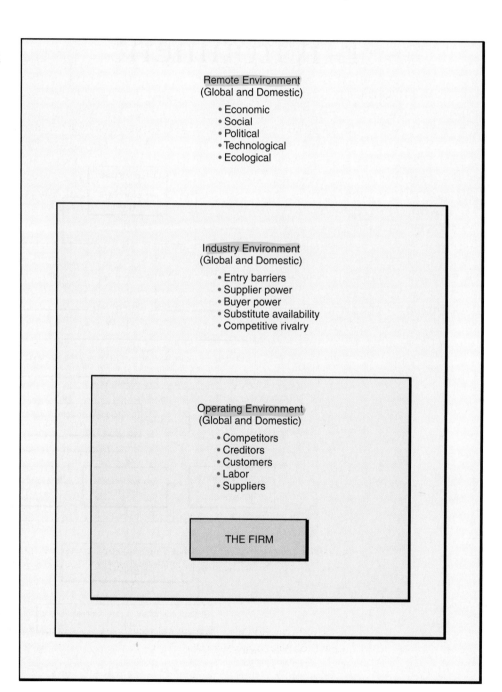

# REMOTE ENVIRONMENT

The remote environment comprises factors that originate beyond, and usually irrespective of, any single firm's operating situation: (1) economic, (2) social, (3) political, (4) technological, and (5) ecological factors. That environment presents firms with opportunities, threats, and constraints, but rarely does a single firm exert any meaningful reciprocal influence. For example, when the economy slows and construction starts to decrease, an individual contractor is likely to suffer a decline in business, but that contractor's efforts in stimulating local construction activities would be unable to reverse the overall decrease in construction starts. The trade agreements that resulted from improved relations between the United States and China and the United States and Russia are examples of political factors that impact individual firms. The agreements provided individual U.S. manufacturers with opportunities to broaden their international operations.

## Economic Factors

Economic factors concern the nature and direction of the economy in which a firm operates. Because consumption patterns are affected by the relative affluence of various market segments, each firm must consider economic trends in the segments that affect its industry. On both the national and international level, managers must consider the general availability of credit, the level of disposable income, and the propensity of people to spend. Prime interest rates, inflation rates, and trends in the growth of the gross national product are other economic factors they should monitor.

For example, in 2003, the depressed economy was hitting Crown Cork & Seal Co. especially hard because it had $2 billion in debt due in the year and no way to raise the money to pay it. The down market had caused its stock price to be too low to raise cash as it normally would. Therefore, Crown Cork managers turned to issuing bonds to refinance its debt. With the slow market, investors were taking advantage of such bonds because they could safely gain higher returns over stocks. Not only were investors getting a deal, but Crown Cork and other companies were seeing the lowest interest rates on bonds in years and by issuing bonds could reorganize their balance sheets. For more details on this example, read Exhibit 3–2, Strategy in Action

The emergence of new international power brokers has changed the focus of economic environmental forecasting. Among the most prominent of these power brokers are the European Economic Community (EEC, or Common Market), the Organization of Petroleum Exporting Countries (OPEC), and coalitions of developing countries.

The EEC, whose members include most of the West European countries, eliminated quotas and established a tariff-free trade area for industrial products among its members. By fostering intra-European economic cooperation, it has helped its member countries compete more effectively in non-European international markets.

## Social Factors

The social factors that affect a firm involve the beliefs, values, attitudes, opinions, and lifestyles of persons in the firm's external environment, as developed from cultural, ecological, demographic, religious, educational, and ethnic conditioning. As social attitudes change, so too does the demand for various types of clothing, books, leisure activities, and so on. Like other forces in the remote external environment, social forces are dynamic, with constant change resulting from the efforts of individuals to satisfy their desires and needs by controlling and adapting to environmental factors. Teresa Iglesias-Soloman hopes to benefit from social changes with *Ninos,* a children's catalog written in both English and Spanish. The catalog features books, videos, and Spanish cultural offerings for English-speaking children who

**BusinessWeek** The sluggish economy was hitting Crown Cork & Seal Co. (CCK) hard. More than half of its $4 billion in debt was coming due in the year, but its low share price ruled out raising money by issuing more stock. The Philadelphia company already had raised the prices of the aluminum cans it makes for everything from soda to aerosol, and spun off a top business, but that was far from enough. Then it found a way out.

On Feb. 11, 2003, Crown issued $2.1 billion in 8- and 10-year bonds in the country's biggest junk-bond deal in three years. Investors snapped up the debt, which carries rates from 9 1/2 percent to 10 7/8 percent, giving the company some badly needed breathing room.

Corporate America was issuing debt faster in 2003 than a tapped-out sailor on shore leave. The bond bonanza might top 2001's record $738 billion. General Electric Co. (GE) issued $5 billion in 10-year bonds on Jan. 21, 2003. Goldman Sachs Group (GS), J. P. Morgan Chase (JPM), Citigroup (C), and other investment banks have raised $38 billion in bonds for themselves, versus $23 billion in 2002.

Despite their rush to issue bonds, companies aren't digging themselves much deeper into debt. Most of the proceeds are earmarked for refinancing their old debt. And companies are seizing a chance to retool their balance sheets by locking in the lowest interest rates in years: For example, top-quality five-year bonds now pay 1.4 percentage points less than they did a year ago. Other companies are replacing short-term debt with long-term financing that may cost more—a top-rated 30-year bond will pay roughly 2.45 points more than a five-year bond—but protects them against rate increases that would jack up their future borrowing costs.

A lot more than routine refinancing is taking place. Indeed, many chief executives now consider restructuring their debt a critical mission, especially as investors increasingly scrutinize companies' credit profiles in the wake of fiascos such as Enron Corp. and WorldCom Inc. As a result, says Thomas J. Gahan, head of corporate finance in the United States for Deutsche Bank, "Debt has gone from being a commodity product to a strategic tool for management."

Many of the companies rolling over their debt would rather be reducing it, but they can't get cash any other way. Hiving off unwanted businesses won't work because buyers won't come out of hiding until the sour economic climate improves. And with stock markets still in the doldrums, most companies don't want to sell new shares at giveaway prices.

The bear market was spurring investors to look for higher returns with relative safety. That fed the huge demand for bonds, and in turn made it much easier for companies to sell them. For companies that are saddled with debt from big mergers, refinancing with longer maturities buys them time to strengthen their balance sheets.

The stubbornly high level of corporate debt means that companies may have an even tougher time paying it down if the economy doesn't pick up. Already, debt makes up 76.5 percent of the net assets of nonfarm, nonfinancial corporations, versus 70 percent in 1999. Meanwhile, ratings agency Moody's Investors Service is downgrading five investment-grade companies for every one it raises.

The strains are beginning to show as companies try to side-step a possible financing crunch by, for example, slowing down capital investments. "Corporations have little choice but to use their cash flow to pay back debt rather than increase capital expenditure," says David Bowers, chief global investment strategist at Merrill Lynch. "They are being run to generate cash instead of growth."

Many bankers, however, are optimistic. They believe that when the economy and stock market revive eventually, companies will decide it's time to clean up their balance sheets for real by issuing equity. "There will be a lot of business for investment bankers," predicts Marcel Ospel, chairman of UBS.

**Source:** Excerpted from Diane Brady and Emily Thornton, "Why Business Is Crazy for Debt," *BusinessWeek*, March 10, 2003, pp. 64–65.

want to learn Spanish and for Spanish-speaking children who want to learn English. *Ninos'* target market includes middle-to-upper-income Hispanic parents, consumers, educators, bilingual schools, libraries, and purchasing agents. Iglesias-Solomon has reason to be optimistic about the future of *Ninos,* because the Hispanic population is growing five times faster than the general U.S. population and ranks as the nation's largest minority.

One of the most profound social changes in recent years has been the entry of large numbers of women into the labor market. This has not only affected the hiring and compensation policies and the resource capabilities of their employers; it has also created or greatly expanded the demand for a wide range of products and services necessitated by their absence from the home. Firms that anticipated or reacted quickly to this social change offered such products and services as convenience foods, microwave ovens, and day care centers.

A second profound social change has been the accelerating interest of consumers and employees in quality-of-life issues. Evidence of this change is seen in recent contract negotiations. In addition to the traditional demand for increased salaries, worker demands such benefits as sabbaticals, flexible hours or four-day workweeks, lump-sum vacation plans, and opportunities for advanced training.

A third profound social change has been the shift in the age distribution of the population. Changing social values and a growing acceptance of improved birth control methods are expected to raise the mean age of the U.S. population, which was 27.9 in 1970, and 34.9 in the year 2000. This trend will have an increasingly unfavorable impact on most producers of predominantly youth-oriented goods and will necessitate a shift in their long-range marketing strategies. Producers of hair and skin care preparations already have begun to adjust their research and development to reflect anticipated changes in demand.

A consequence of the changing age distribution of the population has been a sharp increase in the demands made by a growing number of senior citizens. Constrained by fixed incomes, these citizens have demanded that arbitrary and rigid policies on retirement age be modified and have successfully lobbied for tax exemptions and increases in Social Security benefits. Such changes have significantly altered the opportunity-risk equations of many firms—often to the benefit of firms that anticipated the changes.

Cutting across these issues is concern for individual health. The fast food industry has been the target of a great deal of public concern, as discussed in Exhibit 3–3, Strategy in Action. In 2002, a great deal of popular press attention was directed toward Americans' concern over the relationship between obesity and health. McDonalds was caught in the middle of this new social concern because its menu consisted principally of high-calorie, artery clogging foods. Health experts blamed the fast food industry for the rise in obesity, claiming that companies like McDonalds created an environment that encouraged overeating and discouraged physical activity. Specifically, McDonalds had taken advantage of the fact that kids and adults were watching more TV, by targeting certain program slots to increase sales. For McDonalds and others in the industry to maintain revenues, it now appeared that they were going to have to change their strategies and successfully market new, healthier products.

Translating social change into forecasts of business effects is a difficult process, at best. Nevertheless, informed estimates of the impact of such alterations as geographic shifts in populations and changing work values, ethical standards, and religious orientation can only help a strategizing firm in its attempts to prosper.

## Political Factors

The direction and stability of political factors are a major consideration for managers on formulating company strategy. Political factors define the legal and regulatory parameters within which firms must operate. Political constraints are placed on firms through fair-trade decisions, antitrust laws, tax programs, minimum wage legislation, pollution and pricing policies, administrative jawboning, and many other actions aimed at protecting employees, consumers, the general public, and the environment. Since such laws and regulations are most commonly restrictive, they tend to reduce the potential profits of firms. However, some political actions are designed to benefit and protect firms. Such actions include patent laws, government subsidies, and product research grants. Thus, political factors either may limit or benefit the firms they influence. For example, in a pair of surprising decisions in 2003, the FCC ruled that local phone companies had to continue to lease their lines to the long-distance carriers at what the locals said was below cost. At the same time, the FCC ruled that the local companies were not required to

**BusinessWeek** McDonalds' sales were stagnant. The company's earnings had declined for six consecutive quarters. And 2001 was the company's worst year ever for profits. The company's sagging profits might have been a sign of the nation's growing concern about nutrition: Americans were getting fatter at an alarming rate, and some of them were worried enough, perhaps, to skip those trips to the Golden Arches.

Obesity was, by far, the nation's leading health problem. A growing number of health experts said this alarming rise in obesity was the consequence of an unhealthy environment that encouraged overeating and discouraged physical activity. High-calorie, artery-clogging foods were cheap and plentiful. Healthy foods could sometimes be hard to find. And children were surrounded by increasing amounts of junk-food advertising. The food industry spent an estimated $33 billion a year on ads and promotions. "When you have $33 billion of marketing aimed at you, challenging you to eat more at all times, it's difficult not to eat too much," said Marion Nestle, chair of the nutrition and food studies department at New York University and author of *Food Politics,* published in 2002.

The idea that obesity was partly the consequence of an unhealthy environment was a relatively new one—but its time had arrived. And the surest sign the antiobesity campaign was starting to work was the wave of new health programs from food makers. Many companies—from PepsiCo Inc. (PEP), with its Get Active, Stay Active program, to McDonald's, with its just-announced yogurt and sweetened-fruit menu for kids—were rushing to show their concern for the nation's health.

To understand the rise in obesity, it was useful to look at the economics of food. The U.S. food industry produced enough to supply each of us with 3,800 calories a day. That was one-third more than what most men needed and nearly doubled the needs of most women. Supply exceeded demand. Prices fell. And Americans ate more. With the exception of a spike during the oil shock in the 1970s, food prices have dropped by an average of 0.2 percent a year since World War II, according to the Bureau of Labor Statistics. At the same time, the average American's food intake, which was 1,826 calories a day in the late 1970s, rose nearly 10 percent to 2,002, by the mid-1990s.

According to the Agriculture Dept., muffins that weighed an average of 1.5 ounces in 1957 averaged half a pound each in 2002. Fast-food hamburgers had swollen from an ounce of meat to six ounces or more. An eight-ounce bottle of soda was now a monstrous one-quart tumbler. And the original order of McDonald's fries, at 200 calories, paled next to today's 610-calorie super-size fries.

Television was just as crucial a factor in the rise of obesity in children, critics said. In 1987, an average of 225 commercials was shown during Saturday morning cartoon hours. By the mid-1990s, that had jumped to 997, NYU's Nestle said. Roughly two-thirds of those commercials promoted "foods of dubious nutritional value," Nestle said—presweetened cereals, candy, and fast foods.

Solving the obesity epidemic was, on one level, quite easy. To make that happen, however, the environment in which Americans live and eat must be changed. Changing the environment could have sharply cut America's health costs. And if it was done by shifting to healthier foods, it did not have to cripple the industry. That was a lesson McDonald's, Coke, Pepsi, and others may have started to learn.

**Source:** Excerpted from Diane Brady, Dean Foust, Julie Forster, and Paul Raeburn, "Why We're So Fat," *Business Week,* October 21, 2002, pp. 112–113.

lease their broadband lines to the national carriers. These decisions were good and bad for the local companies because although they would lose money by leasing to the long-distance carriers, they could regain some of that loss with their broadband services that did not have to be leased.

As discussed in Exhibit 3–4, Strategy in Action, the decisions did not mean that the local carriers had to remove existing lines and replace them with broadband lines. Instead, the local carriers would have to run two networks to areas where they want to incorporate broadband because the long-distance carriers had a right to the conventional lines as ruled in the decision. These regulations caused the local carriers to alter their strategies. For example, they often chose to reduce capital investments on new broadband lines because they had to maintain old lines as well. The reduction in capital investments was used to offset the losses they incurred in subsidizing their current lines to the long-distance carriers.

**BusinessWeek** When the Federal Communications Commission began to debate a re-vamp of deregulation policy, the FCC ruled that local phone companies must continue to lease their networks to long-distance rivals, such as AT&T (T) and World-Com Inc., at steeply discounted rates. For local carriers, the decision was a huge setback: They complained they would have to continue selling capacity for less than their costs. The FCC had opened the door for states to weigh in with their own rules on local competition. Increased competition in the local market will benefit consumers.

Consumers should have done well, since the price of local phone service would have likely continued to fall. As carriers battle for their loyalty, customers may have also benefited from new services, such as the combination of wireless and traditional phone service under one phone number. And competition from cable and wireless rivals would have also forced the Bells to continue to invest in their networks, resulting in faster home Internet connections.

Just as no-holds-barred competition led to a debilitating price war in long distance, local carriers could have been destabilized. The economics of the local and long-distance markets were very different. The capital investment required to build a local phone system was five or six times higher than the capital costs of long-distance phone service, because local carriers must have extended their networks all the way into the homes and offices of their customers.

Rival broadband providers and consumer advocates were furious because the FCC ruled that the Bells did not have to lease their DSL lines. Still, the Bells said their victory in broadband was not as clear as it seemed. In markets where they built next-generation fiber networks, state regulators were denying the Bells permission to rip out old slow-speed copper connections to homes and offices because those wires were still serving competitors. That could have forced the Bells to operate two networks.

The FCC ruling did not help telecom-equipment makers Lucent Technologies Inc. (LU) and Nortel Networks Ltd. (NT), which were struggling to return to profitability. It did nothing to encourage new entrants in the local phone market to buy their own telephone switches, which directed traffic across the network.

**Source:** Excerpted from Roger Crockett, Charles Haddad, and Steve Rosenbush, "Telecom: What Hath the FCC Wrought?" *Business Week,* March 10, 2003, pp. 38–39.

As described in Exhibit 3–5, Global Strategy in Action, the direction and stability of political factors are a major consideration when evaluating the remote environment. Specifically, the article addresses the fact that the legal basis of piracy is political. Microsoft's performance in the Chinese market is greatly affected by the lack of legal enforcement of piracy and also by the policies of the Chinese government. Likewise, the government's actions in support of its competitor, Linux, have limited Microsoft's ability to penetrate the Chinese market.

Political activity also has a significant impact on two governmental functions that influence the remote environment of firms: the supplier function and the customer function.

### Supplier Function

Government decisions regarding the accessibility of private businesses to government-owned natural resources and national stockpiles of agricultural products will affect profoundly the viability of the strategies of some firms.

### Customer Function

Government demand for products and services can create, sustain, enhance, or eliminate many market opportunities. For example, in the same way that the Kennedy administration's emphasis on landing a man on the moon spawned a demand for thousands of new products; the Carter administration's emphasis on developing synthetic fuels created a demand for new skills, technologies, and products; the Reagan administration's strategic defense initiative (the "Star Wars" defense) sharply accelerated the development of laser technologies; Clinton's federal block grants to the states for welfare reform led to office rental and lease opportunities; and the war against terrorism during the Bush administration created enormous investment in aviation.

**BusinessWeek** One box that solves two problems. That was Microsoft's hope for Venus, a $240–$360 gadget running Windows CE software that turns Chinese TV sets into Internet appliances. Venus would solve two problems by making it both easier and cheaper for Chinese consumers to access the Web. Venus was the key to penetrating China, because it would make Windows nearly ubiquitous in living rooms from Shenzhen to Shanghai.

Fast-forward to late 2000: Venus seems more like one box containing two disasters. Of the three main Chinese companies that signed up to sell Venus boxes, two have pulled them from the market. Only Legend Computer is still selling the units in China—and it ships most of its supply to Southeast Asia. Why has Venus fizzled? Zhang blames both a lack of online content and the relatively high cost of Internet access. But others say Microsoft misjudged the willingness of Chinese to buy what is essentially low-rent technology. And with PCs selling for as little as $600, there isn't much reason to buy Venus.

The Venus project is not the only misfire in Microsoft's China strategy. Microsoft continues to battle software pirates, a poor image with Chinese authorities and consumers, and a growing threat from local rivals offering inexpensive Linux-based service. Microsoft won't release its China revenues, but analysts say they're probably under $100 million this year—less than the company makes in Hong Kong. "We are much smaller than we expected," says Microsoft General Manager Jack Gao.

Increasingly, Microsoft must contend with companies offering Linux, the open-source operating system. The threat is perhaps more political than anything else. Beijing likes to set one foreign company against another—as it has done with Boeing and Airbus. By playing up the potential of Linux, the government may be telling Microsoft that it had better play by its rules.

But Microsoft faces no greater competitor than the thieves who have elevated software piracy to a fine art. Last year, overall sales of computer hardware in China topped $18 billion. But software sales were a measly $2.1 billion. In other countries, the ratio is closer to even. Blame the shortfall on the pirates. Because of all the counterfeiting, Microsoft sold only 2 million licensed copies of its software in China during the year ending in June.

Chinese aren't ready to give up on counterfeit versions of Windows either. "We have a lot of users," says Jack Gao ruefully. "But we don't have a lot of customers." With Beijing intent on developing a local software industry, he says, cracking down on the pirates is in China's interest, too. That will take time. For now, a more humble Microsoft will have to keep trying to win friends in the emerging market it values most.

**Source:** An excerpt from B. Einhorn and A. Webb, "Microsoft Misfires in China," *BusinessWeek,* December 18, 2000.

## Technological Factors

The fourth set of factors in the remote environment involves technological change. To avoid obsolescence and promote innovation, a firm must be aware of technological changes that might influence its industry. Creative technological adaptations can suggest possibilities for new products, for improvements in existing products, or in manufacturing and marketing techniques.

A technological breakthrough can have a sudden and dramatic effect on a firm's environment. It may spawn sophisticated new markets and products or significantly shorten the anticipated life of a manufacturing facility. Thus, all firms, and most particularly those in turbulent growth industries, must strive for an understanding both of the existing technological advances and the probable future advances that can affect their products and services. This quasi-science of attempting to foresee advancements and estimate their impact on an organization's operations is known as *technological forecasting*.

Technological forecasting can help protect and improve the profitability of firms in growing industries. It alerts strategic managers to both impending challenges and promising opportunities. As examples: (1) advances in xerography were a key to Xerox's success but caused major difficulties for carbon paper manufacturers, and (2) the perfection of transistors changed the nature of competition in the radio and television industry, helping such giants as RCA while seriously weakening smaller firms whose resource commitments required that they continue to base their products on vacuum tubes.

The key to beneficial forecasting of technological advancement lies in accurately predicting future technological capabilities and their probable impacts. A comprehensive analysis of the effect of technological change involves study of the expected impact of new technologies on the remote environment, on the competitive business situation, and on the business-society interface. In recent years, forecasting in the last area has warranted particular attention. For example, as a consequence of increased concern over the environment, firms must carefully investigate the probable effect of technological advances on quality-of-life factors, such as ecology and public safety.

For example, by combining the powers of Internet technologies with the capability of downloading music in a digital format, Bertelsmann has found a creative technological adaptation for distributing music online to millions of consumers whenever or wherever they might be. Bertelsmann, AOL Time Warner, and EMI formed a joint venture called Musicnet. The ease and wide availability of Internet technologies is increasing the marketplace for online e-tailers. Bertelsmann's response to the shifts in technological factors enables it to distribute music more rapidly through Musicnet to a growing consumer base.

## Ecological Factors

The most prominent factor in the remote environment is often the reciprocal relationship between business and the ecology. The term *ecology* refers to the relationships among human beings and other living things and the air, soil, and water that support them. Threats to our life-supporting ecology caused principally by human activities in an industrial society are commonly referred to as *pollution*. Specific concerns include global warming, loss of habitat and biodiversity, as well as air, water, and land pollution.

The global climate has been changing for ages; however, it is now evident that humanity's activities are accelerating this tremendously. A change in atmospheric radiation, due in part to ozone depletion, causes global warming. Solar radiation that is normally absorbed into the atmosphere reaches the earth's surface, heating the soil, water, and air.

Another area of great importance is the loss of habitat and biodiversity. Ecologists agree that the extinction of important flora and fauna is occurring at a rapid rate and if this pace is continued, could constitute a global extinction on the scale of those found in fossil records. The earth's life forms depend on a well-functioning ecosystem. In addition, immeasurable advances in disease treatment can be attributed to research involving substances found in plants. As species become extinct, the life support system is irreparably harmed. The primary cause of extinction on this scale is a disturbance of natural habitat. For example, current data suggest that the earth's primary tropical forests, a prime source of oxygen and potential plant "cure," could be destroyed in only five decades.

Air pollution is created by dust particles and gaseous discharges that contaminate the air. Acid rain, or rain contaminated by sulfur dioxide, which can destroy aquatic and plant life, is believed to result from coal-burning factories in 70 percent of all cases. A health-threatening "thermal blanket" is created when the atmosphere traps carbon dioxide emitted from smokestacks in factories burning fossil fuels. This "greenhouse effect" can have disastrous consequences, making the climate unpredictable and raising temperatures.

Water pollution occurs principally when industrial toxic wastes are dumped or leak into the nation's waterways. Since fewer than 50 percent of all municipal sewer systems are in compliance with Environmental Protection Agency requirements for water safety, contaminated waters represent a substantial present threat to public welfare. Efforts to keep

**BusinessWeek** Outdoor clothing company Patagonia Inc. has worked hard to be one of the greenest businesses around. It was the first apparel maker to sell synthetic fleece sweaters and warm-up pants made from recycled soda bottles. Last year, it switched to organic cotton for shirts and trousers—and ate half of the 20 percent markup that organic production added to the garments' cost. Its glossy catalog, printed on recycled paper that is 50 percent chlorine-free, uses pictures of adventurers in wild places to promote environmental causes.

But Patagonia still has a troubled conscience. In a surprisingly public mea culpa, the company's fall catalog opens with a letter to customers that is a stark critique of Patagonia's reliance on waterproof coatings such as Gore-Tex, which contains chemical toxins, and bright dyes based on strip-mined metals. It is only by using such "dirty" manufacturing processes, the company confesses, that it can offer the "bombproof" outdoor gear and striking colors that customers love. As the letter laments: "The production of our clothing takes a significant toll on the earth."

Turns out it's not easy being green. Patagonia and a handful of other companies that have made protection of the environment a central tenet of their businesses are running into a new wave of polluting problems that require tougher trade-offs than those of the past. Whether it's Ben & Jerry's Home-made coping with massive amounts of high-fat dairy waste, Stonyfield Farm searching for an affordable way to convert to organic fruit for its yogurt, or Orvis, the fishing-gear maker, trying to build a new headquarters that won't threaten bear habitats, green pioneers are struggling for ways to balance *environmental principles* with profit goals.

None are backing off their commitment to the environment. Instead, the greenest companies are testing the limits of what can be done cleanly. "We want it all," Yvon Chouinard, Patagonia's president, told a meeting of the company's suppliers last year. "The best quality and the lowest environmental impact." But it's getting tougher to push the green envelope without compromising business goals. "Our whole system of commerce is not designed to be ecologically sustainable," says Matthew Arnold, director of Washington-based Management Institute for Environment & Business. "These guys are showing the limits of the system to respond."

And customers have made it clear that quality comes first, even if it means passing up the chance to have less impact on the environment. Patagonia surveys show that just 20 percent of its customers buy from the company because they believe in its environmental mission.

**Source:** Paul C. Judge in Boston, "It's Not Easy Being Green," *BusinessWeek,* November 24, 1997.

---

from contaminating the water supply are a major challenge to even the most conscientious of manufacturing firms. As described in Exhibit 3–6, Strategy in Action, highly reputed "green" supporter Patagonia has judged itself to be guilty of water pollution.

The Patagonia story is especially interesting because of the "green" fervor with which the company pursues its manufacturing objectives. It provides some details on the difficulties that Patagonia faces in its attempts to do what many ecological activists believe should be a national mandate for all corporations.

Land pollution is caused by the need to dispose of ever-increasing amounts of waste. Routine, everyday packaging is a major contributor to this problem. Land pollution is more dauntingly caused by the disposal of industrial toxic wastes in underground sites. With approximately 90 percent of the annual U.S. output of 500 million metric tons of hazardous industrial wastes being placed in underground dumps, it is evident that land pollution and its resulting endangerment of the ecology have become a major item on the political agenda.

As a major contributor to ecological pollution, business now is being held responsible for eliminating the toxic by-products of its current manufacturing processes and for cleaning up the environmental damage that it did previously. Increasingly, managers are being required by the government or are being expected by the public to incorporate ecological concerns into their decision making. For example, between 1975 and 1992, 3M cut its pollution in half by reformulating products, modifying processes, redesigning production equipment, and recycling by-products. Similarly, steel companies and public utilities have invested billions of dollars in costlier but cleaner-burning fuels and pollution control equipment. The automobile industry has been required to install expensive emission controls in cars. The gasoline industry has been forced to formulate new low-lead and no-lead products. And thousands of companies have found it necessary to direct their R&D resources into the search for ecologically superior products, such as Sears's phosphate-free laundry detergent and Pepsi-Cola's biodegradable plastic soft-drink bottle.

Environmental legislation impacts corporate strategies worldwide. Many companies fear the consequences of highly restrictive and costly environmental regulations. However, some manufacturers view these new controls as an opportunity, capturing markets with products that help customers satisfy their own regulatory standards. Other manufacturers contend that the costs of environmental spending inhibit the growth and productivity of their operations.

Despite cleanup efforts to date, the job of protecting the ecology will continue to be a top strategic priority—usually because corporate stockholders and executives choose it, increasingly because the public and the government require it. As evidenced by Exhibit 3–7, the government has made numerous interventions into the conduct of business for the purpose of bettering the ecology.

### Benefits of Eco-Efficiency

Many of the world's largest corporations are realizing that business activities must no longer ignore environmental concerns. Every activity is linked to thousands of other transactions and their environmental impact; therefore, corporate environmental responsibility must be taken seriously and environmental policy must be implemented to ensure a comprehensive organizational strategy. Because of increases in government regulations and consumer environmental concerns, the implementation of environmental policy has become a point of competitive advantage. Therefore, the rational goal of business should be to limit its impact on the environment, thus ensuring long-run benefits to both the firm and society. To neglect this responsibility is to ensure the demise of both the firm and our ecosystem.

Stephen Schmidheiny, chairman of the Business Council for Sustainable Development, has coined the term *eco-efficiency* to describe corporations that produce more-useful goods and services while continuously reducing resource consumption and pollution. He cites a number of reasons for corporations to implement environmental policy: customers demand cleaner products, environmental regulations are increasingly more stringent, employees prefer to work for environmentally conscious firms, and financing is more readily available for eco-efficient firms. In addition, the government provides incentives for environmentally responsible companies.

Setting priorities, developing corporate standards, controlling property acquisition and use to preserve habitats, implementing energy-conserving activities, and redesigning products (e.g., minimizing packaging) are a number of measures the firm can implement to enhance an eco-efficient strategy. One of the most important steps a firm can take in achieving a competitive position with regard to the eco-efficient strategy is to fully capitalize on technological developments as a method of gaining efficiency.

Four key characteristics of eco-efficient corporations are:

- Eco-efficient firms are proactive, not reactive. Policy is initiated and promoted by business because it is in their own interests and the interest of their customers, not because it is imposed by one or more external forces.

- Eco-efficiency is designed in, not added on. This characteristic implies that the optimization of eco-efficiency requires every business effort regarding the product and process to internalize the strategy.

**EXHIBIT 3–7**
**Federal Ecological Legislation**

**Centerpiece Legislation:**

**National Environmental Policy Act, 1969**   Established Environmental Protection Agency; consolidated federal environmental activities under it. Established Council on Environmental Quality to advise president on environmental policy and to review environmental impact statements.

**Air Pollution:**

**Clean Air Act, 1963**   Authorized assistance to state and local governments in formulating control programs. Authorized limited federal action in correcting specific pollution problems.

**Clean Air Act, Amendments (Motor Vehicle Air Pollution Control Act), 1965**
Authorized federal standards for auto exhaust emission. Standards first set for 1968 models.

**Air Quality Act, 1967**   Authorized federal government to establish air quality control regions and to set maximum permissible pollution levels. Required states and localities to carry out approved control programs or else give way to federal controls.

**Clean Air Act Amendments, 1970**   Authorized EPA to establish nationwide air pollution standards and to limit the discharge of six principal pollutants into the lower atmosphere. Authorized citizens to take legal action to require EPA to implement its standards against undiscovered offenders.

**Clean Air Act Amendments, 1977**   Postponed auto emission requirements. Required use of scrubbers in new coal-fired power plants. Directed EPA to establish a system to prevent deterioration of air quality in clean areas.

**Solid Waste Pollution:**

**Solid Waste Disposal Act, 1965**   Authorized research and assistance to state and local control programs.

**Resource Recovery Act, 1970**   Subsidized construction of pilot recycling plants; authorized development of nationwide control programs.

**Resource Conservation and Recovery Act, 1976**   Directed EPA to regulate hazardous waste management, from generation through disposal.

**Surface Mining and Reclamation Act, 1976**   Controlled strip mining and restoration of reclaimed land.

**Water Pollution:**

**Refuse Act, 1899**   Prohibited dumping of debris into navigable waters without a permit. Extended by court decision to industrial discharges.

**Federal Water Pollution Control Act, 1956**   Authorized grants to states for water pollution control. Gave federal government limited authority to correct specific pollution problems.

**Water Quality Act, 1965**   Provided for adoption of water quality standards by states, subject to federal approval.

**Water Quality Improvement Act, 1970**   Provided for federal cleanup of oil spills. Strengthened federal authority over water pollution control.

**Federal Water Pollution Control Act Amendments, 1972**   Authorized EPA to set water quality and effluent standards; provided for enforcement and research.

**Safe Drinking Water Act, 1974**   Set standards for drinking water quality.

**Clean Water Act, 1977**   Ordered control of toxic pollutants by 1984 with best available technology economically feasible.

- Flexibility is imperative for eco-efficient strategy implementation. Continuous attention must be paid to technological innovation and market evolution.

- Eco-efficiency is encompassing, not insular. In the modern global business environment, efforts must cross not only industrial sectors but national and cultural boundaries as well.

## ECONOMIC ENVIRONMENT

Level of economic development
Population
Gross national product
Per capita income
Literacy level
Social infrastructure
Natural resources
Climate
Membership in regional economic blocs (EU, NAFTA, LAFTA)
Monetary and fiscal policies
Wage and salary levels
Nature of competition
Currency convertibility
Inflation
Taxation system
Interest rates

## LEGAL ENVIRONMENT

Legal tradition
Effectiveness of legal system
Treaties with foreign nations
Patent trademark laws
Laws affecting business firms

## POLITICAL SYSTEM

Form of government
Political ideology
Stability of government
Strength of opposition parties and groups
Social unrest
Political strife and insurgency
Governmental attitude towards foreign firms
Foreign policy

## CULTURAL ENVIRONMENT

Customs, norms, values, beliefs
Language
Attitudes
Motivations
Social institutions
Status symbols
Religious beliefs

**Source:** Arvind V. Phatak, *International Management* (Cincinnati, OH: South-Western College Publishing, 1997), p. 6.

# INTERNATIONAL ENVIRONMENT

Monitoring the international environment, perhaps better thought of as the international dimension of the global environment, involves assessing each nondomestic market on the same factors that are used in a domestic assessment. While the importance of factors will differ, the same set of considerations can be used for each country. For example, Exhibit 3–8, Global Strategy in Action, lists economic, political, legal, and social factors used to assess international environments. However, there is one complication to this process, namely, that the interplay among international markets must be considered. For example, in recent years, conflicts in the Middle East have made collaborative business strategies among firms in traditionally antagonistic countries especially difficult to implement.

# INDUSTRY ENVIRONMENT

Harvard professor Michael E. Porter propelled the concept of industry environment into the foreground of strategic thought and business planning. The cornerstone of his work first appeared in the *Harvard Business Review,* in which Porter explains the five forces that shape competition in an industry. His well-defined analytic framework helps strategic managers to link remote factors to their effects on a firm's operating environment.

With the special permission of Professor Porter and the *Harvard Business Review,* we present in this section of the chapter the major portion of his seminal article on the industry environment and its impact on strategic management.[1]

## OVERVIEW

The nature and degree of competition in an industry hinge on five forces: the threat of new entrants, the bargaining power of customers, the bargaining power of suppliers, the threat of substitute products or services (where applicable), and the jockeying among current contestants. To establish a strategic agenda for dealing with these contending currents and to grow despite them, a company must understand how they work in its industry and how they affect the company in its particular situation. This chapter will detail how these forces operate and suggest ways of adjusting to them, and, where possible, of taking advantage of opportunities that they create.

## HOW COMPETITIVE FORCES SHAPE STRATEGY

The essence of strategy formulation is coping with competition. Yet it is easy to view competition too narrowly and too pessimistically. While one sometimes hears executives complaining to the contrary, intense competition in an industry is neither coincidence nor bad luck.

Moreover, in the fight for market share, competition is not manifested only in the other players. Rather, competition in an industry is rooted in its underlying economics, and competitive forces exist that go well beyond the established combatants in a particular industry. Customers, suppliers, potential entrants, and substitute products are all competitors that may be more or less prominent or active depending on the industry.

The state of competition in an industry depends on five basic forces, which are diagrammed in Exhibit 3–9. The collective strength of these forces determines the ultimate profit potential of an industry. It ranges from intense in industries like tires, metal cans, and steel, where no company earns spectacular returns on investment, to mild in industries like oil-field services and equipment, soft drinks, and toiletries, where there is room for quite high returns.

In the economists' "perfectly competitive" industry, jockeying for position is unbridled and entry to the industry very easy. This kind of industry structure, of course, offers the worst prospect for long-run profitability. The weaker the forces collectively, however, the greater the opportunity for superior performance.

Whatever their collective strength, the corporate strategist's goal is to find a position in the industry where his or her company can best defend itself against these forces or can influence them in its favor. The collective strength of the forces may be painfully apparent to all the antagonists; but to cope with them, the strategist must delve below the surface and analyze the sources of competition. For example, what makes the industry vulnerable to entry? What determines the bargaining power of suppliers?

Knowledge of these underlying sources of competitive pressure provides the groundwork for a strategic agenda of action. They highlight the critical strengths and weaknesses of the company, animate the positioning of the company in its industry, clarify

---

[1] M. E. Porter, "How Competitive Forces Shape Strategy," *Harvard Business Review,* March–April 1979, pp. 137–45.

**EXHIBIT 3–9   Forces Driving Industry Competition**

**Entry barriers**

Economies of scale
Proprietary product differences
Brand identity
Switching costs
Capital requirements
Access to distribution
Absolute cost advantages
   Proprietary curve
   Access to necessary inputs
   Proprietary low-cost product design
Government policy
Expected retaliation

**Rivalry Determinants**

Industry growth
Fixed (or storage) costs/value added
Intermittent overcapacity
Product differences
Brand identity
Switching costs
Concentration and balance
Informational complexity
Diversity of competitors
Corporate stakes
Exit barriers

**New Entrants**

Threat of
New Entrants

**Industry Competitors**

Intensity of Rivalry

**Suppliers**

Bargaining Power
of Suppliers

Bargaining Power
of Buyers

**Buyers**

Threat of
Substitutes

**Substitutes**

**Determinants of Supplier Power**

Differentiation of inputs
Switching costs of suppliers and firms
   in the industry
Presence of substitute inputs
Supplier concentration
Importance of volume to supplier
Cost relative to total purchases in
   the industry
Impact of inputs on cost or differentiation
Threat of forward integration relative to
   threat of backward integration by firms
   in the industry

**Determinants of
Substitution Threat**

Relative price
   performance
   of substitutes
Switching costs
Buyer propensity
   to substitute

**Determinants of Buyer Power**

| **Bargaining Leverage** | **Price Sensitivity** |
| --- | --- |
| Buyer concentration | Price/total purchases |
| versus firm concentration | Product differences |
| Buyer volume | Brand identity |
| Buyer switching costs | Impact on quality/ |
| relative to firm | performance |
| switching costs | Buyer profits |
| Buyer information | Decision makers' |
| Ability to backward | incentives |
| integrate | |
| Substitute products | |
| Pull-through | |

the areas where strategic changes may yield the greatest payoff, and highlight the places where industry trends promise to hold the greatest significance as either opportunities or threats.

Understanding these sources also proves to be of help in considering areas for diversification.

# CONTENDING FORCES

The strongest competitive force or forces determine the profitability of an industry and so are of greatest importance in strategy formulation. For example, even a company with a strong position in an industry unthreatened by potential entrants will earn low returns if it faces a superior or a lower-cost substitute product—as the leading manufacturers of vacuum tubes and coffee percolators have learned to their sorrow. In such a situation, coping with the substitute product becomes the number one strategic priority.

Different forces take on prominence, of course, in shaping competition in each industry. In the oceangoing tanker industry, the key force is probably the buyers (the major oil companies), while in tires it is powerful OEM buyers coupled with tough competitors. In the steel industry the key forces are foreign competitors and substitute materials.

Every industry has an underlying structure, or a set of fundamental economic and technical characteristics, that gives rise to these competitive forces. The strategist, wanting to position his or her company to cope best with its industry environment or to influence that environment in the company's favor, must learn what makes the environment tick.

This view of competition pertains equally to industries dealing in services and to those selling products. To avoid monotony, I refer to both products and services as *products.* The same general principles apply to all types of business.

A few characteristics are critical to the strength of each competitive force. They will be discussed in this section.

## Threat of Entry

New entrants to an industry bring new capacity, the desire to gain market share, and often substantial resources. Companies diversifying through acquisition into the industry from other markets often leverage their resources to cause a shake-up, as Philip Morris did with Miller beer.

The seriousness of the threat of entry depends on the barriers present and on the reaction from existing competitors that the entrant can expect. If barriers to entry are high and a newcomer can expect sharp retaliation from the entrenched competitors, he or she obviously will not pose a serious threat of entering.

There are six major sources of barriers to entry:

### Economies of Scale

These economies deter entry by forcing the aspirant either to come in on a large scale or to accept a cost disadvantage. Scale economies in production, research, marketing, and service are probably the key barriers to entry in the mainframe computer industry, as Xerox and GE sadly discovered. Economies of scale also can act as hurdles in distribution, utilization of the sales force, financing, and nearly any other part of a business.

### Product Differentiation

Brand identification creates a barrier by forcing entrants to spend heavily to overcome customer loyalty. Advertising, customer service, being first in the industry, and product differences are among the factors fostering brand identification. It is perhaps the most important entry barrier in soft drinks, over-the-counter drugs, cosmetics, investment banking, and public accounting. To create high fences around their business, brewers couple brand identification with economies of scale in production, distribution, and marketing.

### Capital Requirements

The need to invest large financial resources in order to compete creates a barrier to entry, particularly if the capital is required for unrecoverable expenditures in up-front advertising or R&D. Capital is necessary not only for fixed facilities but also for customer credit, inventories, and absorbing start-up losses. While major corporations have the financial resources to invade almost any industry, the huge capital requirements in certain fields, such as computer manufacturing and mineral extraction, limit the pool of likely entrants.

### Cost Disadvantages Independent of Size

Entrenched companies may have cost advantages not available to potential rivals, no matter what their size and attainable economies of scale. These advantages can stem from the effects of the learning curve (and of its first cousin, the experience curve), proprietary tech-

In recent years, the experience curve has become widely discussed as a key element of industry structure. According to this concept, unit costs in many manufacturing industries (some dogmatic adherents say in all manufacturing industries) as well as in some service industries decline with "experience," or a particular company's cumulative volume of production. (The experience curve, which encompasses many factors, is a broader concept than the better-known learning curve, which refers to the efficiency achieved over time by workers through much repetition.)

The causes of the decline in unit costs are a combination of elements, including economies of scale, the learning curve for labor, and capita-labor substitution. The cost decline creates a barrier to entry because new competitors with no "experience" face higher costs than established ones, particularly the producer with the largest market share, and have difficulty catching up with the entrenched competitors.

Adherents of the experience curve concept stress the importance of achieving market leadership to maximize this barrier to entry, and they recommend aggressive action to achieve it, such as price cutting in anticipation of falling costs in order to build volume. For the combatant that cannot achieve a healthy market share, the prescription is usually, "Get out."

Is the experience curve an entry barrier on which strategies should be built? The answer is: not in every industry. In fact, in some industries, building a strategy on the experience curve can be potentially disastrous. That costs decline with experience in some industries is not news to corporate executives. The significance of the experience curve for strategy depends on what factors are causing the decline.

A new entrant may well be more efficient than the more experienced competitors: if it has built the newest plant, it will face no disadvantage in having to catch up. The strategic prescription, "You must have the largest, most efficient plant," is a lot different from "You must produce the greatest cumulative output of the item to get your costs down."

Whether a drop in costs with cumulative (not absolute) volume erects an entry barrier also depends on the sources of the decline. If costs go down because of technical advances known generally in the industry or because of the development of improved equipment that can be copied or purchased from equipment suppliers, the experience curve is not an entry barrier at all—in fact, new or less-experienced competitors may actually enjoy a cost advantage over the leaders. Free of the legacy of heavy past investments, the newcomer or less-experienced competitor can purchase or copy the newest and lowest-cost equipment and technology.

If, however, experience can be kept proprietary, the leaders will maintain a cost advantage. But new entrants may require less experience to reduce their costs than the leaders needed. All this suggests that the experience curve can be a shaky entry barrier on which to build a strategy.

While space does not permit a complete treatment here, I want to mention a few other crucial elements in determining the appropriateness of a strategy built on the entry barrier provided by the experience curve:

The height of the barrier depends on how important costs are to competition compared with other areas like marketing, selling, and innovation.

The barrier can be nullified by product or process innovations leading to a substantially new technology and, thereby, creating an entirely new experience curve. New entrants can leapfrog the industry leaders and alight on the new experience curve, to which those leaders may be poorly positioned to jump.

If more than one strong company is building its strategy on the experience curve, the consequences can be nearly fatal. By the time only one rival is left pursuing such a strategy, industry growth may have stopped and the prospects of reaping the spoils of victory may long since have evaporated.

---

nology, access to the best raw materials sources, assets purchased at preinflation prices, government subsidies, or favorable locations. Sometimes cost advantages are enforceable legally, as they are through patents. (For analysis of the much-discussed experience curve as a barrier to entry, see Exhibit 3–10, Strategy in Action.)

### Access to Distribution Channels

The new boy or girl on the block must, of course, secure distribution of his or her product or service. A new food product, for example, must displace others from the supermarket shelf via price breaks, promotions, intense selling efforts, or some other means. The more limited the wholesale or retail channels are and the more that existing competitors have these tied up, obviously the tougher that entry into the industry will be. Sometimes this barrier is so high that, to surmount it, a new contestant must create its own distribution channels, as Timex did in the watch industry in the 1950s.

### Government Policy

The government can limit or even foreclose entry to industries, with such controls as license requirements and limits on access to raw materials. Regulated industries like trucking, liquor retailing, and freight forwarding are noticeable examples; more subtle government restrictions operate in fields like ski-area development and coal mining. The government also can play a major indirect role by affecting entry barriers through such controls as air and water pollution standards and safety regulations.

The potential rival's expectations about the reaction of existing competitors also will influence its decision on whether to enter. The company is likely to have second thoughts if incumbents have previously lashed out at new entrants, or if:

The incumbents possess substantial resources to fight back, including excess cash and unused borrowing power, productive capacity, or clout with distribution channels and customers.

The incumbents seem likely to cut prices because of a desire to keep market shares or because of industrywide excess capacity.

Industry growth is slow, affecting its ability to absorb the new arrival and probably causing the financial performance of all the parties involved to decline.

## Powerful Suppliers

Suppliers can exert bargaining power on participants in an industry by raising prices or reducing the quality of purchased goods and services. Powerful suppliers, thereby, can squeeze profitability out of an industry unable to recover cost increases in its own prices. By raising their prices, soft-drink concentrate producers have contributed to the erosion of profitability of bottling companies because the bottlers—facing intense competition from powdered mixes, fruit drinks, and other beverages—have limited freedom to raise their prices accordingly.

The power of each important supplier (or buyer) group depends on a number of characteristics of its market situation and on the relative importance of its sales or purchases to the industry compared with its overall business.

A *supplier* group is powerful if:

1. It is dominated by a few companies and is more concentrated than the industry it sells.

2. Its product is unique or at least differentiated, or if it has built-up switching costs. Switching costs are fixed costs that buyers face in changing suppliers. These arise because, among other things, a buyer's product specifications tie it to particular suppliers, it has invested heavily in specialized ancillary equipment or in learning how to operate a supplier's equipment (as in computer software), or its production lines are connected to the supplier's manufacturing facilities (as in some manufacturing of beverage containers).

3. It is not obliged to contend with other products for sale to the industry. For instance, the competition between the steel companies and the aluminum companies to sell to the can industry checks the power of each supplier.

4. It poses a credible threat of integrating forward into the industry's business. This provides a check against the industry's ability to improve the terms on which it purchases.

5. The industry is not an important customer of the supplier group. If the industry is an important customer, suppliers' fortunes will be tied closely to the industry, and they will want to protect the industry through reasonable pricing and assistance in activities like R&D and lobbying.

## Powerful Buyers

Customers likewise can force down prices, demand higher quality or more service, and play competitors off against each other—all at the expense of industry profits.

A *buyer* group is powerful if:

1. It is concentrated or purchases in large volumes. Large-volume buyers are particularly potent forces if heavy fixed costs characterize the industry—as they do in metal containers, corn refining, and bulk chemicals, for example—which raise the stakes to keep capacity filled.

2. The products it purchases from the industry are standard or undifferentiated. The buyers, sure that they always can find alternative suppliers, may play one company against another, as they do in aluminum extrusion.

3. The products it purchases from the industry form a component of its product and represent a significant fraction of its cost. The buyers are likely to shop for a favorable price and purchase selectively. Where the product sold by the industry in question is a small fraction of buyers' costs, buyers are usually much less price sensitive.

4. It earns low profits, which create great incentive to lower its purchasing costs. Highly profitable buyers, however, are generally less price sensitive (i.e., of course, if the item does not represent a large fraction of their costs).

5. The industry's product is unimportant to the quality of the buyers' products or services. Where the quality of the buyers' products is very much affected by the industry's product, buyers are generally less price sensitive. Industries in which this situation exists include oil-field equipment, where a malfunction can lead to large losses and enclosures for electronic medical and test instruments, where the quality of the enclosure can influence the user's impression about the quality of the equipment inside.

6. The industry's product does not save the buyer money. Where the industry's product or service can pay for itself many times over, the buyer is rarely price sensitive; rather, he or she is interested in quality. This is true in services like investment banking and public accounting, where errors in judgment can be costly and embarrassing, and in businesses like the mapping of oil wells, where an accurate survey can save thousands of dollars in drilling costs.

7. The buyers pose a credible threat of integrating backward to make the industry's product. The Big Three auto producers and major buyers of cars often have used the threat of self-manufacture as a bargaining lever. But sometimes an industry so engenders a threat to buyers that its members may integrate forward.

Most of these sources of buyer power can be attributed to consumers as a group as well as to industrial and commercial buyers; only a modification of the frame of reference is necessary. Consumers tend to be more price sensitive if they are purchasing products that are undifferentiated, expensive relative to their incomes, and of a sort where quality is not particularly important.

The buying power of retailers is determined by the same rules, with one important addition. Retailers can gain significant bargaining power over manufacturers when they can influence consumers' purchasing decisions, as they do in audio components, jewelry, appliances, sporting goods, and other goods.

## Substitute Products

By placing a ceiling on the prices it can charge, substitute products or services limit the potential of an industry. Unless it can upgrade the quality of the product or differentiate it somehow (as via marketing), the industry will suffer in earnings and possibly in growth.

Manifestly, the more attractive the price-performance trade-off offered by substitute products, the firmer the lid placed on the industry's profit potential. Sugar producers confronted with the large-scale commercialization of high-fructose corn syrup, a sugar substitute, learned this lesson.

Substitutes not only limit profits in normal times but also reduce the bonanza an industry can reap in boom times. The producers of fiberglass insulation enjoyed unprecedented demand as a result of high energy costs and severe winter weather. But the industry's ability to raise prices was tempered by the plethora of insulation substitutes, including cellulose, rock wool, and Styrofoam. These substitutes are bound to become an even stronger force once the current round of plant additions by fiberglass insulation producers has boosted capacity enough to meet demand (and then some).

Substitute products that deserve the most attention strategically are those that (*a*) are subject to trends improving their price-performance trade-off with the industry's product or (*b*) are produced by industries earning high profits. Substitutes often come rapidly into play if some development increases competition in their industries and causes price reduction or performance improvement.

## Jockeying for Position

Rivalry among existing competitors takes the familiar form of jockeying for position—using tactics like price competition, product introduction, and advertising slug fests. This type of intense rivalry is related to the presence of a number of factors:

1. Competitors are numerous or are roughly equal in size and power. In many U.S. industries in recent years, foreign contenders, of course, have become part of the competitive picture.

2. Industry growth is slow, precipitating fights for market share that involve expansion-minded members.

3. The product or service lacks differentiation or switching costs, which lock in buyers and protect one combatant from raids on its customers by another.

4. Fixed costs are high or the product is perishable, creating strong temptation to cut prices. Many basic materials businesses, like paper and aluminum, suffer from this problem when demand slackens.

5. Capacity normally is augmented in large increments. Such additions, as in the chlorine and vinyl chloride businesses, disrupt the industry's supply-demand balance and often lead to periods of overcapacity and price cutting.

6. Exit barriers are high. Exit barriers, like very specialized assets or management's loyalty to a particular business, keep companies competing even though they may be earning low or even negative returns on investment. Excess capacity remains functioning, and the profitability of the healthy competitors suffers as the sick ones hang on. If the entire industry suffers from overcapacity, it may seek government help—particularly if foreign competition is present.

7. The rivals are diverse in strategies, origins, and "personalities." They have different ideas about how to compete and continually run head-on into each other in the process.

As an industry matures, its growth rate changes, resulting in declining profits and (often) a shakeout. In the booming recreational vehicle industry of the early 1970s, nearly every producer did well; but slow growth since then has eliminated the high returns, except for the strongest members, not to mention many of the weaker companies. The same profit story has been played out in industry after industry—snowmobiles, aerosol packaging, and sports equipment are just a few examples.

An acquisition can introduce a very different personality to an industry, as has been the case with Black & Decker's takeover of McCullough, the producer of chain saws. Technological innovation can boost the level of fixed costs in the production process, as it did in the shift from batch to continuous-line photo finishing in the 1960s.

While a company must live with many of these factors—because they are built into the industry economics—it may have some latitude for improving matters through strategic shifts. For example, it may try to raise buyers' switching costs or increase product differentiation. A focus on selling efforts in the fastest-growing segments of the industry or on market areas with the lowest fixed costs can reduce the impact of industry rivalry. If it is feasible, a company can try to avoid confrontation with competitors having high exit barriers and, thus, can sidestep involvement in bitter price cutting.

# INDUSTRY ANALYSIS AND COMPETITIVE ANALYSIS

Designing viable strategies for a firm requires a thorough understanding of the firm's industry and competition. The firm's executives need to address four questions: (1) What are the boundaries of the industry? (2) What is the structure of the industry? (3) Which firms are our competitors? (4) What are the major determinants of competition? The answers to these questions provide a basis for thinking about the appropriate strategies that are open to the firm.

## Industry Boundaries

An industry is a collection of firms that offer similar products or services. By "similar products," we mean products that customers perceive to be substitutable for one another. Consider, for example, the brands of personal computers (PCs) that are now being marketed. The firms that produce these PCs, such as AT&T, IBM, Apple, and Compaq, form the nucleus of the microcomputer industry.

Suppose a firm competes in the microcomputer industry. Where do the boundaries of this industry begin and end? Does the industry include desktops? Laptops? These are the kinds of questions that executives face in defining industry boundaries.

Why is a definition of industry boundaries important? First, it helps executives determine the arena in which their firm is competing. A firm competing in the microcomputer industry participates in an environment very different from that of the broader electronics business. The microcomputer industry comprises several related product families, including personal computers, inexpensive computers for home use, and workstations. The unifying characteristic of these product families is the use of a central processing unit (CPU) in a microchip. On the other hand, the electronics industry is far more extensive; it includes computers, radios, supercomputers, superconductors, and many other products.

The microcomputer and electronics industries differ in their volume of sales, their scope (some would consider microcomputers a segment of the electronics industry), their rate of growth, and their competitive makeup. The dominant issues faced by the two industries also are different. Witness, for example, the raging public debate being waged on the future of the "high-definition TV." U.S. policy makers are attempting to ensure domestic control of that segment of the electronics industry. They also are considering ways to stimulate "cutting-edge" research in superconductivity. These efforts are likely to spur innovation and stimulate progress in the electronics industry.

Second, a definition of industry boundaries focuses attention on the firm's competitors. Defining industry boundaries enables the firm to identify its competitors and producers of substitute products. This is critically important to the firm's design of its competitive strategy.

Third, a definition of industry boundaries helps executives determine key factors for success. Survival in the premier segment of the microcomputer industry requires skills that are considerably different from those required in the lower end of the industry. Firms that compete in the premier segment need to be on the cutting edge of technological development and to provide extensive customer support and education. On the other hand, firms that compete in the lower end need to excel in imitating the products introduced by the premier segment, to focus on customer convenience, and to maintain operational efficiency that permits them to charge the lowest market price. Defining industry boundaries enables executives to ask these questions: Do we have the skills it takes to succeed here? If not, what must we do to develop these skills?

Finally, a definition of industry boundaries gives executives another basis on which to evaluate their firm's goals. Executives use that definition to forecast demand for their firm's products and services. Armed with that forecast, they can determine whether those goals are realistic.

### Problems in Defining Industry Boundaries

Defining industry boundaries requires both caution and imagination. Caution is necessary because there are no precise rules for this task and because a poor definition will lead to poor planning. Imagination is necessary because industries are dynamic—in every industry, important changes are under way in such key factors as competition, technology, and consumer demand.

Defining industry boundaries is a very difficult task. The difficulty stems from three sources:

1. The evolution of industries over time creates new opportunities and threats. Compare the financial services industry as we know it today with that of the 1990s, and then try to imagine how different the industry will be in the year 2020.

2. Industrial evolution creates industries within industries. The electronics industry of the 1960s has been transformed into many "industries"—TV sets, transistor radios, micro- and macrocomputers, supercomputers, superconductors, and so on. Such transformation allows some firms to specialize and others to compete in different, related industries.

3. Industries are becoming global in scope. Consider the civilian aircraft manufacturing industry. For nearly three decades, U.S. firms dominated world production in that industry. But small and large competitors were challenging their dominance by 1990. At that time, Airbus Industries (a consortium of European firms) and Brazilian, Korean, and Japanese firms were actively competing in the industry.

### Developing a Realistic Industry Definition

Given the difficulties outlined above, how do executives draw accurate boundaries for an industry? The starting point is a definition of the industry in global terms; that is, in terms that consider the industry's international components as well as its domestic components.

Having developed a preliminary concept of the industry (e.g., computers), executives flesh out its current components. This can be done by defining its product segments. Executives need to select the scope of their firm's potential market from among these related but distinct areas.

To understand the makeup of the industry, executives adopt a longitudinal perspective. They examine the emergence and evolution of product families. Why did these product families arise? How and why did they change? The answers to such questions provide executives with clues about the factors that drive competition in the industry.

Executives also examine the companies that offer different product families, the overlapping or distinctiveness of customer segments, and the rate of substitutability among product families.

To realistically define their industry, executives need to examine five issues:

1. Which part of the industry corresponds to our firm's goals?

2. What are the key ingredients of success in that part of the industry?

3. Does our firm have the skills needed to compete in that part of the industry? If not, can we build those skills?

4. Will the skills enable us to seize emerging opportunities and deal with future threats?

5. Is our definition of the industry flexible enough to allow necessary adjustments to our business concept as the industry grows?

## Industry Structure

Defining an industry's boundaries is incomplete without an understanding of its structural attributes. *Structural attributes* are the enduring characteristics that give an industry its distinctive character. Consider the cable television and financial services industries. Both industries are competitive, and both are important for our quality of life. But these industries have very different requirements for success. To succeed in the cable television industry, firms require vertical integration, which helps them lower their operating costs and ensures their access to quality programs; technological innovation, to enlarge the scope of their services and deliver them in new ways; and extensive marketing, using appropriate segmentation techniques to locate potentially viable niches. To succeed in the financial services industry, firms need to meet very different requirements, among which are extensive orientation of customers and an extensive capital base.

How can we explain such variations among industries? The answer lies in examining the four variables that industry comprises: (1) concentration, (2) economies of scale, (3) product differentiation, and (4) barriers to entry.

### *Concentration*

This variable refers to the extent to which industry sales are dominated by only a few firms. In a highly concentrated industry (i.e., an industry whose sales are dominated by a handful of companies), the intensity of competition declines over time. High concentration serves as a barrier to entry into an industry, because it enables the firms that hold large market shares to achieve significant economies of scale (e.g., savings in production costs due to increased production quantities) and, thus, to lower their prices to stymie attempts of new firms to enter the market.

The U.S. aircraft manufacturing industry is highly concentrated. Its concentration ratio—the percent of market share held by the top four firms in the industry—is 67 percent. Competition in the industry has not been vigorous. Firms in the industry have been able to deter entry through proprietary technologies and the formation of strategic alliances (e.g., joint ventures).

### Economies of Scale

This variable refers to the savings that companies within an industry achieve due to increased volume. Simply put, when the volume of production increases, the long-range average cost of a unit produced will decline.

Economies of scale result from technological and nontechnological sources. The technological sources are a higher level of mechanization or automation and a greater up-to-dateness of plant and facilities. The nontechnological sources include better managerial coordination of production functions and processes, long-term contractual agreements with suppliers, and enhanced employee performance arising from specialization.

Economies of scale are an important determinant of the intensity of competition in an industry. Firms that enjoy such economies can charge lower prices than their competitors. They also can create barriers to entry by reducing their prices temporarily or permanently to deter new firms from entering the industry.

### Product Differentiation

This variable refers to the extent to which customers perceive products or services offered by firms in the industry as different.

The differentiation of products can be real or perceived. The differentiation between Apple's Macintosh and IBM's PS/2 Personal Computer was a prime example of real differentiation. These products differed significantly in their technology and performance. Similarly, the civilian aircraft models produced by Boeing differed markedly from those produced by Airbus. The differences resulted from the use of different design principles and different construction technologies. For example, the newer Airbus planes followed the principle of "fly by wire," whereas Boeing planes utilized the laws of hydraulics. Thus, in Boeing planes, wings were activated by mechanical handling of different parts of the plane, whereas in the Airbus planes, this was done almost automatically.

Perceived differentiation results from the way in which firms position their products and from their success in persuading customers that their products differ significantly from competing products. Marketing strategies provide the vehicles through which this is done. Witness, for example, the extensive advertising campaigns of the automakers, each of which attempts to convey an image of distinctiveness. BMW ads highlight the excellent engineering of the BMW and its symbolic value as a sign of achievement. Some automakers focus on roominess and durability, which are desirable attributes for the family segment of the automobile market.

Real and perceived differentiations often intensify competition among existing firms. On the other hand, successful differentiation poses a competitive disadvantage for firms that attempt to enter an industry.

### Barriers to Entry

As Porter noted earlier in this chapter, barriers to entry are the obstacles that a firm must overcome to enter an industry. The barriers can be tangible or intangible. The tangible barriers include capital requirements, technological know-how, resources, and the laws regulating entry into an industry. The intangible barriers include the reputation of existing firms, the loyalty of consumers to existing brands, and access to the managerial skills required for successful operation in an industry.

Entry barriers both increase and reflect the level of concentration, economies of scale, and product differentiation in an industry, and such increases make it more difficult for new firms to enter the industry. Therefore, when high barriers exist in an industry, competition in that industry declines over time.

In summary, analysis of concentration, economies of scale, product differentiation, and barriers to entry in an industry enable a firm's executives to understand the forces that determine competition in an industry and set the stage for identifying the firm's competitors and how they position themselves in the marketplace.

Industry regulations are a key element of industry structure and can constitute a significant barrier to entry for corporations. Escalating regulatory standards costs have been a serious concern for corporations for years. As legislative bodies continue their stronghold on corporate activities, businesses feel the impact on their bottom line. In-house counsel departments have been perhaps the most significant additions to corporate structure in the past decade. Legal fees have skyrocketed and managers have learned the hard way about the importance of adhering to regulatory standards.

## Competitive Analysis

### How to Identify Competitors

In identifying their firm's current and potential competitors, executives consider several important variables:

1. How do other firms define the scope of their market? The more similar the definitions of firms, the more likely the firms will view each other as competitors.

2. How similar are the benefits the customers derive from the products and services that other firms offer? The more similar the benefits of products or services, the higher the level of substitutability between them. High substitutability levels force firms to compete fiercely for customers.

3. How committed are other firms to the industry? Although this question may appear to be far removed from the identification of competitors, it is in fact one of the most important questions that competitive analysis must address, because it sheds light on the long-term intentions and goals. To size up the commitment of potential competitors to the industry, reliable intelligence data are needed. Such data may relate to potential resource commitments (e.g., planned facility expansions).

### Common Mistakes in Identifying Competitors

Identifying competitors is a milestone in the development of strategy. But it is a process laden with uncertainty and risk, a process in which executives sometimes make costly mistakes. Examples of these mistakes are:

1. Overemphasizing current and known competitors while giving inadequate attention to potential entrants.

2. Overemphasizing large competitors while ignoring small competitors.

3. Overlooking potential international competitors.

4. Assuming that competitors will continue to behave in the same way they have behaved in the past.

5. Misreading signals that may indicate a shift in the focus of competitors or a refinement of their present strategies or tactics.

6. Overemphasizing competitors' financial resources, market position, and strategies while ignoring their intangible assets, such as a top-management team.

7. Assuming that all of the firms in the industry are subject to the same constraints or are open to the same opportunities.

8. Believing that the purpose of strategy is to outsmart the competition, rather than to satisfy customer needs and expectations.

# OPERATING ENVIRONMENT

The operating environment, also called the *competitive* or *task environment,* comprises factors in the competitive situation that affect a firm's success in acquiring needed resources or in profitably marketing its goods and services. Among the most important of these factors are the firm's competitive position, the composition of its customers, its reputation among suppliers and creditors, and its ability to attract capable employees. The operating environment is typically much more subject to the firm's influence or control than the remote environment. Thus, firms can be much more proactive (as opposed to reactive) in dealing with the operating environment than in dealing with the remote environment.

## Competitive Position

Assessing its competitive position improves a firm's chances of designing strategies that optimize its environmental opportunities. Development of competitor profiles enables a firm to more accurately forecast both its short- and long-term growth and its profit potentials. Although the exact criteria used in constructing a competitor's profile are largely determined by situational factors, the following criteria are often included:

1. Market share.

2. Breadth of product line.

3. Effectiveness of sales distribution.

4. Proprietary and key-account advantages.

5. Price competitiveness.

6. Advertising and promotion effectiveness.

7. Location and age of facility.

8. Capacity and productivity.

9. Experience.

10. Raw materials costs.

11. Financial position.

12. Relative product quality.

13. R&D advantages position.

14. Caliber of personnel.

15. General images.

16. Customer profile.

17. Patents and copyrights.

18. Union relations.

**EXHIBIT 3–11**
**Competitor Profile**

| Key Success Factors | Weight | Rating* | Weighted Score |
|---|---|---|---|
| Market share | 0.30 | 4 | 1.20 |
| Price competitiveness | 0.20 | 3 | 0.60 |
| Facilities location | 0.20 | 5 | 1.00 |
| Raw materials costs | 0.10 | 3 | 0.30 |
| Caliber of personnel | 0.20 | 1 | 0.20 |
|  | 1.00† |  | 3.30 |

*The rating scale suggested is as follows: very strong competitive position (5 points), strong (4), average (3), weak (2), very weak (1).
†The total of the weights must always equal 1.00.

19. Technological position.

20. Community reputation.

Once appropriate criteria have been selected, they are weighted to reflect their importance to a firm's success. Then the competitor being evaluated is rated on the criteria, the ratings are multiplied by the weight, and the weighted scores are summed to yield a numerical profile of the competitor, as shown in Exhibit 3–11.

This type of competitor profile is limited by the subjectivity of its criteria selection, weighting, and evaluation approaches. Nevertheless, the process of developing such profiles is of considerable help to a firm in defining its perception of its competitive position. Moreover, comparing the firm's profile with those of its competitors can aid its managers in identifying factors that might make the competitors vulnerable to the strategies the firm might choose to implement.

## Customer Profiles

Perhaps the most vulnerable result of analyzing the operating environment is the understanding of a firm's customers that this provides. Developing a profile of a firm's present and prospective customers improves the ability of its managers to plan strategic operations, to anticipate changes in the size of markets, and to reallocate resources so as to support forecast shifts in demand patterns. The traditional approach to segmenting customers is based on customer profiles constructed from geographic, demographic, psychographic, and buyer behavior information.

Enterprising companies have quickly learned the importance of identifying target segments. In recent years, market research has increased tremendously as companies realize the benefits of demographic and psychographic segmentation. Research by American Express showed that competitors were stealing a prime segment of the company's business, affluent business travelers. AMEX's competing companies, including Visa and Mastercard, began offering high-spending business travelers frequent flier programs and other rewards including discounts on new cars. In turn, AMEX began to invest heavily in rewards programs, while also focusing on its strongest capabilities, assets, and competitive advantage. Unlike most credit card companies, AMEX cannot rely on charging interest to make money because its customers pay in full each month. Therefore, the company charges higher transaction fees to its merchants. In this way, increases in spending by AMEX customers who pay off their balances each month are more profitable to AMEX than to competing credit card companies.

Assessing consumer behavior is a key element in the process of satisfying your target market needs. Many firms lose market share as a result of assumptions made about target segments. Market research and industry surveys can help to reduce a firm's chances of relying on illusive assumptions. Firms most vulnerable are those that have had success with one or more products in the marketplace and as a result try to base consumer behavior on past data and trends.

### Geographic

It is important to define the geographic area from which customers do or could come. Almost every product or service has some quality that makes it variably attractive to buyers from different locations. Obviously, a Wisconsin manufacturer of snow skis should think twice about investing in a wholesale distribution center in South Carolina. On the other hand, advertising in the *Milwaukee Sun-Times* could significantly expand the geographically defined customer market of a major Myrtle Beach hotel in South Carolina.

### Demographic

Demographic variables most commonly are used to differentiate groups of present or potential customers. Demographic information (e.g., information on sex, age, marital status, income, and occupation) is comparatively easy to collect, quantify, and use in strategic forecasting, and such information is the minimum basis for a customer profile.

### Psychographic

Personality and lifestyle variables often are better predictors of customer purchasing behavior than geographic or demographic variables. In such situations, a psychographic study is an important component of the customer profile. Advertising campaigns by soft-drink producers—Pepsi-Cola ("the Pepsi generation"), Coca-Cola ("the real thing"), and 7UP ("America's turning 7UP")—reflect strategic management's attention to the psychographic characteristics of their largest customer segment—physically active, group-oriented nonprofessionals.

### Buyer Behavior

Buyer behavior data also can be a component of the customer profile. Such data are used to explain or predict some aspect of customer behavior with regard to a product or service. Information on buyer behavior (e.g., usage rate, benefits sought, and brand loyalty) can provide significant aid in the design of more accurate and profitable strategies. A second approach to identifying customer groups is by segmenting industrial markets, as shown in Exhibit 3–12.

## Suppliers

Dependable relationships between a firm and its suppliers are essential to the firm's long-term survival and growth. A firm regularly relies on its suppliers for financial support, services, materials, and equipment. In addition, it occasionally is forced to make special requests for such favors as quick delivery, liberal credit terms, or broken-lot orders. Particularly at such times, it is essential for a firm to have had an ongoing relationship with its suppliers.

In the assessment of a firm's relationships with its suppliers, several factors, other than the strength of that relationship, should be considered. With regard to its competitive position with its suppliers, the firm should address the following questions:

Are the suppliers' prices competitive? Do the suppliers offer attractive quantity discounts?

How costly are their shipping charges? Are the suppliers competitive in terms of production standards?

**EXHIBIT 3–12**

**Major Segmentation Variables for Industrial Markets**

Source: Adapted from Thomas V. Bonoma and Benson P. Shapiro, *Segmenting the Industrial Market* (Lexington, MA: Lexington Books, 1983).

**Demographic**

*Industry:* Which industries that buy this product should we focus on?
*Company size:* What size companies should we focus on?
*Location:* What geographical areas should we focus on?

**Operating Variables**

*Technology:* What customer technologies should we focus on?
*User-nonuser status:* Should we focus on heavy, medium, light users or nonusers?
*Customer capabilities:* Should we focus on customers needing many services or few services?

**Purchasing Approaches**

*Purchasing-function organization:* Should we focus on companies with highly centralized or decentralized purchasing organizations?
*Power structure:* Should we focus on companies that are engineering dominated? Financially dominated? Other ways dominated?
*Nature of existing relationships:* Should we focus on companies with which we have strong existing relationships or simply go after the most desirable companies?
*General purchase policies:* Should we focus on companies that prefer leasing? Service contracts? Systems purchases? Sealed bidding?
*Purchasing criteria:* Should we focus on companies that are seeking quality? Service? Price?

**Situational Factors**

*Urgency:* Should we focus on companies that need quick and sudden delivery or service?
*Specific application:* Should we focus on certain applications of our product, rather than all applications?
*Size of order:* Should we focus on large or small orders?

**Perfect Characteristics**

*Buyer-seller similarity:* Should we focus on companies whose people and values are similar to ours?
*Attitudes toward risk:* Should we focus on risk-taking or risk-avoiding customers?
*Loyalty:* Should we focus on companies that show high loyalty to their suppliers?

In terms of deficiency rates, are the suppliers' abilities, reputations, and services competitive?

Are the suppliers reciprocally dependent on the firm?

## Creditors

Because the quantity, quality, price, and accessibility of financial, human, and material resources are rarely ideal, assessment of suppliers and creditors is critical to an accurate evaluation of a firm's operating environment. With regard to its competitive position with its creditors, among the most important questions that the firm should address are the following:

Do the creditors fairly value and willingly accept the firm's stock as collateral?

Do the creditors perceive the firm as having an acceptable record of past payment?

A strong working capital position? Little or no leverage?

Are the creditors' loan terms compatible with the firm's profitability objectives?

Are the creditors able to extend the necessary lines of credit?

The answers to these and related questions help a firm forecast the availability of the resources it will need to implement and sustain its competitive strategies.

## Human Resources: Nature of the Labor Market

A firm's ability to attract and hold capable employees is essential to its success. However, a firm's personnel recruitment and selection alternatives often are influenced by the nature of its operating environment. A firm's access to needed personnel is affected primarily by three factors: the firm's reputation as an employer, local employment rates, and the ready availability of people with the needed skills.

### Reputation

A firm's reputation within its operating environment is a major element of its ability to satisfy its personnel needs. A firm is more likely to attract and retain valuable employees if it is seen as permanent in the community, competitive in its compensation package, and concerned with the welfare of its employees, and if it is respected for its product or service and appreciated for its overall contribution to the general welfare.

### Employment Rates

The readily available supply of skilled and experienced personnel may vary considerably with the stage of a community's growth. A new manufacturing firm would find it far more difficult to obtain skilled employees in a vigorous industrialized community than in an economically depressed community in which similar firms had recently cut back operations.

### Availability

The skills of some people are so specialized that relocation may be necessary to secure the jobs and the compensation that those skills commonly command. People with such skills include oil drillers, chefs, technical specialists, and industry executives. A firm that seeks to hire such a person is said to have broad labor market boundaries; that is, the geographic area within which the firm might reasonably expect to attract qualified candidates is quite large. On the other hand, people with more common skills are less likely to relocate from a considerable distance to achieve modest economic or career advancements. Thus, the labor market boundaries are fairly limited for such occupational groups as unskilled laborers, clerical personnel, and retail clerks.

# EMPHASIS ON ENVIRONMENTAL FACTORS

This chapter has described the remote, industry, and operating environments as encompassing five components each. While that description is generally accurate, it may give the false impression that the components are easily identified, mutually exclusive, and equally applicable in all situations. In fact, the forces in the external environment are so dynamic and interactive that the impact of any single element cannot be wholly disassociated from the impact of other elements. For example, are increases in OPEC oil prices the result of economic, political, social, or technological changes? Or are a manufacturer's surprisingly good relations with suppliers a result of competitors', customers', or creditors' activities or of the supplier's own activities? The answer to both questions is probably that a number of forces in the external environment have combined to create the situation. Such is the case in most studies of the environment.

Strategic managers are frequently frustrated in their attempts to anticipate the environments changing influences. Different external elements affect different strategies at different times and with varying strengths. The only certainty is that the impact of the remote and operating environments will be uncertain until a strategy is implemented. This leads many managers, particularly in less-powerful or smaller firms to minimize long-term planning, which requires a commitment of resources. Instead, they favor allowing managers to adapt to new pressures from the environment. While such a decision has considerable merit for many firms, there is an associated trade-off, namely that absence of a strong resource and psychological commitment to a proactive strategy effectively bars a firm from assuming a leadership role in its competitive environment.

There is yet another difficulty in assessing the probable impact of remote, industry, and operating environments on the effectiveness of alternative strategies. Assessment of this kind involves collecting information that can be analyzed to disclose predictable effects. Except in rare instances, however, it is virtually impossible for any single firm to anticipate the consequences of a change in the environment; for example, what is the precise effect on alternative strategies of a 2 percent increase in the national inflation rate, a 1 percent decrease in statewide unemployment, or the entry of a new competitor in a regional market?

Still, assessing the potential impact of changes in the external environment offers a real advantage. It enables decision makers to narrow the range of the available options and to eliminate options that are clearly inconsistent with the forecast opportunities. Environmental assessment seldom identifies the best strategy, but it generally leads to the elimination of all but the most promising options.

Exhibit 3–13 provides a set of key strategic forecasting issues for each level of environmental assessment—remote, industry, and operating. While the issues that are presented are not inclusive of all of the questions that are important, they provide an excellent set of questions with which to begin. Appendix 3, Sources for Environmental Forecasting, is provided to help identify valuable sources of data and information from which answers and subsequent forecasts can be constructed. It lists governmental and private marketplace intelligence that can be used by a firm to gain a foothold in undertaking a strategic assessment of any level of the competitive environment.

## Summary

A firm's external environment consists of three interrelated sets of factors that play a principal role in determining the opportunities, threats, and constraints that the firm faces. The remote environment comprises factors originating beyond, and usually irrespective of, any single firm's operating situation—economic, social, political, technological, and ecological factors. Factors that more directly influence a firm's prospects originate in the environment of its industry, including entry barriers, competitor rivalry, the availability of substitutes, and the bargaining power of buyers and suppliers. The operating environment comprises factors that influence a firm's immediate competitive situation—competitive position, customer profiles, suppliers, creditors, and the labor market. These three sets of factors provide many of the challenges that a particular firm faces in its attempts to attract or acquire needed resources and to profitably market its goods and services. Environmental assessment is more complicated for multinational corporations (MNCs) than for domestic firms because multinationals must evaluate several environments simultaneously.

Thus, the design of business strategies is based on the conviction that a firm able to anticipate future business conditions will improve its performance and profitability. Despite the uncertainty and dynamic nature of the business environment, an assessment process that narrows, even if it does not precisely define, future expectations is of substantial value to strategic managers.

**EXHIBIT 3–13**
**Strategic Forecasting Issues**

### Key Issues in the Remote Environment Economy

What are the probable future directions of the economies in the firm's regional, national, and international market? What changes in economic growth, inflation, interest rates, capital availability, credit availability, and consumer purchasing power can be expected? What income differences can be expected between the wealthy upper middle class, the working class, and the underclass in various regions? What shifts in relative demand for different categories of goods and services can be expected?

### Society and demographics

What effects will changes in social values and attitudes regarding childbearing, marriage, lifestyle, work, ethics, sex roles, racial equality, education, retirement, pollution, and energy have on the firm's development? What effects will population changes have on major social and political expectations—at home and abroad? What constraints or opportunities will develop? What pressure groups will increase in power?

### Ecology

What natural or pollution-caused disasters threaten the firm's employees, customers, or facilities? How rigorously will existing environment legislature be enforced? What new federal, state, and local laws will affect the firm, and in what ways?

### Politics

What changes in government policy can be expected with regard to industry cooperation, antitrust activities, foreign trade, taxation, depreciation, environmental protection, deregulation, defense, foreign trade barriers, and other important parameters? What success will a new administration have in achieving its stated goals? What effect will that success have on the firm? Will specific international climates be hostile or favorable? Is there a tendency toward instability, corruption, or violence? What is the level of political risk in each foreign market? What other political or legal constraints or supports can be expected in international business (e.g., trade barriers, equity requirements, nationalism, patent protection)?

### Technology

What is the current state of the art? How will it change? What pertinent new products or services are likely to become technically feasible in the foreseeable future? What future impact can be expected from technological breakthroughs in related product areas? How will those breakthroughs interface with the other remote considerations, such as economic issues, social values, public safety, regulations, and court interpretations?

### Key Issues in the Industry Environment

### New entrants

Will new technologies or market demands enable competitors to minimize the impact of traditional economies of scale in the industry? Will consumers accept our claims of product or service differentiation? Will potential new entrants be able to match the capital requirements that currently exist? How permanent are the cost disadvantages (independent of size) in our industry? Will conditions change so that all competitors have equal access to marketing channels? Is government policy toward competition in our industry likely to change?

### Bargaining power of suppliers

How stable are the size and composition of our supplier group? Are any suppliers likely to attempt forward integration into our business level? How dependent will our suppliers be in the future? Are substitute suppliers likely to become available? Could we become our own supplier?

**Exhibit 3–13**
*(continued)*

### Substitute products or services

Are new substitutes likely? Will they be price competitive? Could we fight off substitutes by price competition? By advertising to sharpen product differentiation? What actions could we take to reduce the potential for having alternative products seen as legitimate substitutes?

### Bargaining power of buyers

Can we break free of overcommitment to a few large buyers? How would our buyers react to attempts by us to differentiate our products? What possibilities exist that our buyers might vertically integrate backward? Should we consider forward integration? How can we make the value of our components greater in the products of our buyers?

### Rivalry among existing firms

Are major competitors likely to undo the established balance of power in our industry? Is growth in our industry slowing such that competition will become fiercer? What excess capacity exists in our industry? How capable are our major competitors of withstanding intensified price competition? How unique are the objectives and strategies of our major competitors?

### Key Issues in the Operating Environment

### Competitive position

What strategic moves are expected by existing rivals—inside and outside the United States? What competitive advantage is necessary in selected foreign markets? What will be our competitors' priorities and ability to change? Is the behavior of our competitors predictable?

### Customer profiles and market changes

What will our customer regard as needed value? Is marketing research done, or do managers talk to each other to discover what the customer wants? Which customer needs are not being met by existing products? Why? Are R&D activities under way to develop means for fulfilling these needs? What is the status of these activities? What marketing and distribution channels should we use? What do demographic and population changes portend for the size and sales potential of our market? What new market segments or products might develop as a result of these changes? What will be the buying power of our customer groups?

### Supplier relationships

What is the likelihood of major cost increases because of dwindling supplies of a needed natural resource? Will sources of supply, especially of energy, be reliable? Are there reasons to expect major changes in the cost or availability of inputs as a result of money, people, or subassembly problems? Which suppliers can be expected to respond to emergency requests?

### Creditors

What lines of credit are available to help finance our growth? What changes may occur in our creditworthiness? Are creditors likely to feel comfortable with our strategic plan and performance? What is the stock market likely to feel about our firm? What flexibility would our creditors show toward us during a downturn? Do we have sufficient cash reserves to protect our creditors and our credit rating?

### Labor market

Are potential employees with desired skills and abilities available in the geographic areas in which our facilities are located? Are colleges and vocational-technical schools that can aid in meeting our training needs located near our plant or store sites? Are labor relations in our industry conductive to meeting our expanding needs for employees? Are workers whose skills we need shifting toward or away from the geographic location of our facilities?

# Questions for Discussion

1. Briefly describe two important recent changes in the remote environment of U.S. business in each of the following areas:

   a. Economic.
   b. Social.
   c. Political.
   d. Technological.
   e. Ecological.

2. Describe two major environmental changes that you expect to have a major impact on the whole-sale food industry in the next 10 years.

3. Develop a competitor profile for your college and for the college geographically closest to yours. Next, prepare a brief strategic plan to improve the competitive position of the weaker of the two colleges.

4. Assume the invention of a competitively priced synthetic fuel that could supply 25 percent of U.S. energy needs within 20 years. In what major ways might this change the external environment of U.S. business?

5. With your instructor's help, identify a local firm that has enjoyed great growth in recent years. To what degree and in what ways do you think this firm's success resulted from taking advantage of favorable conditions in its remote, industry, and operating environments?

6. Choose a specific industry and, relying solely on your impressions, evaluate the impact of the five forces that drive competition in that industry.

7. Choose an industry in which you would like to compete. Use the five-forces method of analysis to explain why you find that industry attractive.

8. Many firms neglect industry analysis. When does this hurt them? When does it not?

9. The model below depicts industry analysis as a funnel that focuses on remote-factor analysis to better understand the impact of factors in the operating environment. Do you find this model satisfactory? If not, how would you improve it?

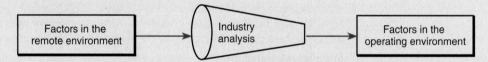

10. Who in a firm should be responsible for industry analysis? Assume that the firm does not have a strategic planning department.

## Chapter 3 Discussion Case

# McDonald's Hamburger Hell

**BusinessWeek**

**1**    Richard Steinig remembers beaming as if he had won the lottery. There he was, all of 27 when he became a junior partner with a McDonald's Corp. (MCD) franchisee in 1973, just a year after starting as a $115-a-week manager trainee in Miami. "It was an incredible feeling," says Steinig. His two stores each generated $80,000 in annual sales, and he pocketed more than 15 percent of that as profit. Not bad at a time when the minimum wage was still under $2 an hour and a McDonald's hamburger and fries set you back less than a dollar, even with a regular Coke.

**2**    Fast-forward 30 years. Franchise owner Steinig's four restaurants average annual sales of $1.56 million, but his face is creased with worry. Instead of living the American Dream, Steinig says he's barely scraping by. Sales haven't budged since 1999, but costs keep rising. So when McDonald's began advertising its $1 menu featuring the Big N' Tasty burger, Steinig rebelled. The popular item cost him $1.07 to make—so he sells it for $2.25 unless a customer asks for the $1 promotion price. No wonder profit margins are no more than half of what they were when he started out. "We have become our worst enemy," Steinig says.

**3**    Welcome to Hamburger Hell. For decades, McDonald's was a juggernaut. It gave millions of Americans their first jobs while changing the way a nation ate. It rose from a single outlet in a nondescript Chicago suburb to become an American icon. But today, McDonald's is a reeling giant that teeters from one mess to another.

**4**    Consider the events of just the past three months: On Dec. 5, after watching McDonald's stock slide 60 percent in three years, the board ousted chief executive Jack M. Greenberg, 60. His tenure was marked by the introduction of 40 new menu items, none of which caught on big, and the purchase of a handful of nonburger chains, none of which were rolled out widely enough to make much difference. Indeed, his critics say that by trying so many different things—and executing them poorly—Greenberg let the burger business deteriorate. Consumer surveys show that service and quality now lag far behind those of rivals.

**5**    The company's solution was to bring back retired vice-chairman James R. Cantalupo, 59, who had overseen McDonald's successful international expansion in the '80s and '90s. Unfortunately, seven weeks later, the company reported the first quarterly loss in its 47-year history. Then it revealed that January sales at outlets open at least a year skidded 2.4 percent, after sliding 2.1 percent in 2002.

**6**    Can Cantalupo reverse the long slide at McDonald's? When he and his new team lay out their plan to analysts in early April, they are expected to concentrate on getting the basics of service and quality right, in part by reinstituting a tough "up or out" grading system that will kick out underperforming franchises. "We have to rebuild the foundation. It's fruitless to add growth if the foundation is weak," says Cantalupo. He gives himself 18 months to do that with help from Australian-bred chief operating officer, Charles Bell, 42, whom Cantalupo has designated his successor, and Mats Lederhausen, a 39-year-old Swede in charge of global strategy.

**7**    But the problems at McDonald's go way beyond cleaning up restaurants and freshening the menu. The chain is being squeezed by long-term trends that threaten to leave it marginalized. It faces a rapidly fragmenting market, where America's recent immigrants have made once-exotic foods like sushi and burritos everyday options, and quick meals of all sorts can be found in supermarkets, convenience stores, even vending machines. One of the fastest-growing restaurant categories is the "fast-casual" segment—those places with slightly more expensive menus, such as Cosi, a sandwich shop, or Quizno's, a gourmet sub sandwich chain, where customers find the food healthier and better-tasting. As Lederhausen succinctly puts it: "We are clearly living through the death of the mass market."

**8**    If so, it may well mark the end of McDonald's long run as a growth company. Cantalupo seemed to acknowledge as much when he slashed sales growth estimates in the near term to only 2 percent annually, down from 15 percent. No one at Oak Brook (Ill.) headquarters blames the strong dollar or mad cow disease anymore for the company's problems—a big change from the Greenberg era. Perhaps most telling is that the chain plans to add only 250 new outlets in the United States this year, 40 percent fewer than in 2002. Sales in Europe rose only 1 percent, and the chain this year will add only 200 units to the 6,070 it has there—30 percent fewer new openings than last year. Meanwhile, it is closing 176 of its 2,800 stores in Japan because of the economic doldrums there.

9    Up until a few years ago, franchises clamored to jump on board. But last year, in an exodus that was unheard of in Mickey D's heyday, 126 franchises left the system, with 68, representing 169 restaurants, forced out for poor performance. The others left seeking greener pastures. The company buys back franchises if they cannot be sold, so forcing out a franchisee is not cheap. McDonald's took a pretax charge of $292 million last quarter to close 719 restaurants—200 in 2002 and the rest expected this year.

10   For their part, investors have already accepted that the growth days are over. Those who remain will happily settle for steady dividends. Last Oct. 22, when McDonald's announced a 1 cent hike in its annual dividend, to 23 1/2 cents, its stock rose 9 percent, to $18.95—even though the company said third-quarter profits would decline. It was the biggest one-day gain for McDonald's on the New York Stock Exchange in at least two years. Today, though, the stock is near an eight-year low of $13.50, off 48 percent in the past year. One of the few money managers willing to give McDonald's a chance, Wendell L. Perkins at Johnson Asset Management in Racine, Wis., says: "McDonald's needs to understand that it is a different company from 10 years ago and increase its dividend to return some of that cash flow to shareholders to reflect its mature market position."

11   The company has the cash to boost shareholder payouts. It recently canceled an expensive stock buyback program. Cantalupo won praise on Wall Street for killing an expensive revamp of the company's technology that would have cost $1 billion. But if increasing the dividend would make Wall Street happy, it would raise problems with its 2,461 franchises. That would be essentially an admission that McDonald's is giving up on the kind of growth for which they signed up.

12   Already, franchises who see the chain as stuck in a rut are jumping ship to faster-growing rivals. Paul Saber, a McDonald's franchisee for 17 years, sold his 14 restaurants back to the company in 2000 when he realized that eating habits were shifting away from McDonald's burgers to fresher, better-tasting food. So he moved to rival Panera Bread Co., a fast-growing national bakery cafe chain. "The McDonald's-type fast food isn't relevant to today's consumer," says Saber, who will open 15 Paneras in San Diego.

13   In the past, owner-operators were McDonald's evangelists. Prospective franchises were once so eager to get into the two-year training program that they would wait in line for hours when applications were handed out at the chain's offices around the country.

But there aren't any lines today, and many existing franchises feel alienated. They have seen their margins dip to a paltry 4 percent, from 15 percent at the peak. Richard Adams, a former franchisee and a food consultant, claims that as many as 20 franchises are currently leaving McDonald's every month. Why? "Because it's so hard to survive these days," he says.

14   One of the biggest sore points for franchises is the top-down manner in which Greenberg and other past CEOs attempted to fix pricing and menu problems. Many owner-operators still grumble over the $18,000 to $100,000 they had to spend in the late 1990s to install company-mandated "Made for You" kitchen upgrades in each restaurant. The new kitchens were supposed to speed up orders and accommodate new menu items. But in the end, they actually slowed service. Reggie Webb, who operates 11 McDonald's restaurants in Los Angeles, says his sales have dipped by an average of $50,000 at each of his outlets over the past 15 years. "From my perspective, I am working harder than ever and making less than I ever had on an average-store basis," says Webb. He'll have to open his wallet again if McDonald's includes his units in the next 200 restaurants it selects for refurbishing. Franchises pay 70 percent of that $150,000 cost.

15   Franchises also beef about McDonald's addiction to discounting. When McDonald's cut prices in a 1997 price war, sales fell over the next four months. The lesson should have been obvious. "Pulling hard on the price lever is dangerous. It risks cheapening the brand," says Sam Rovit, a partner at Chicago consultant Bain & Co. Yet Cantalupo is sticking with the $1 menu program introduced last year. "We like to wear out our competitors with our price," he says. Burger King and Wendy's International Inc. admit that the tactic is squeezing their sales. But in the five months since its debut, the $1 menu has done nothing to improve McDonald's results.

16   As a last resort, McDonald's is getting rid of the weakest franchises. Continuous growth can no longer bail out underperformers, so Cantalupo is enforcing a "tough love" program that Greenberg reinstated last year after the company gave it up in 1990. Owners that flunk the rating and inspection system will get a chance to clean up their act. But if they don't improve, they'll be booted.

17   The decline in McDonald's once-vaunted service and quality can be traced to its expansion of the 1990s, when headquarters stopped grading franchises for cleanliness, speed, and service. Training declined as restaurants fought for workers in a tight

labor market. That led to a falloff in kitchen and counter skills—according to a 2002 survey by Columbus (Ohio) market researcher Global Growth Group, McDonald's came in third in average service time behind Wendy's and sandwich shop Chick-fil-A Inc. Wendy's took an average 127 seconds to place and fill an order, versus 151 seconds at Chick-fil-A and 163 at McDonald's. That may not seem like much, but Greenberg has said that saving six seconds at a drive-through brings a 1 percent increase in sales.

18  Trouble is, it's tough to sell franchisees on a new quality gauge at the same time the company is asking them to do everything from offering cheap burgers to shouldering renovation costs. Franchising works best when a market is expanding and owners can be rewarded for meeting incentives. In the past, franchises who beat McDonald's national sales average were typically rewarded with the chance to open or buy more stores. The largest franchisees now operate upwards of 50 stores. But with falling sales, those incentives don't cut it. "Any company today has to be very vigilant about their business model and willing to break it, even if it's successful, to make sure they stay on top of the changing trends," says Alan Feldman, CEO of Midas Inc., who was COO for domestic operations at McDonald's until January, 2002. "You can't just go on cloning your business into the future."

19  By the late 1990s, it was clear that the system was losing traction. New menu items like the low-fat McLean Deluxe and Arch Deluxe burgers, meant to appeal to adults, bombed. Nonburger offerings did no better, often because of poor planning. Consultant Michael Seid, who manages a franchise consulting firm in West Hartford, Conn., points out that McDonald's offered a pizza that didn't fit through the drive-through window and salad shakers that were packed so tightly that dressing couldn't flow through them. By 1998, McDonald's posted its first-ever decline in annual earnings and then-CEO Michael R. Quinlan was out, replaced by Greenberg, a 16-year McDonald's veteran.

20  Greenberg won points for braking the chain's runaway U.S. expansion. He also broadened its portfolio, acquiring Chipotle Mexican Grill and Boston Market Corp. But he was unable to focus on the new ventures while also improving quality, getting the new kitchens rolled out, and developing new menu items. Says Los Angeles franchisee Webb: "We would have been better off trying fewer things and making them work." Greenberg was unable to reverse skidding sales and profits, and after last year's disastrous

fourth quarter, he offered his resignation at the Dec. 5 board meeting. There were no angry words from directors. But there were no objections, either.

21  Insiders say Cantalupo, who had retired only a year earlier, was the only candidate seriously considered to take over, despite shareholder sentiment for an outsider. The board felt that it needed someone who knew the company and could move quickly. Cantalupo has chosen to work with younger McDonald's executives, whom he feels will bring energy and fresh ideas to the table. Bell, formerly president of McDonald's Europe, became a store manager in his native Australia at 19 and rose through the ranks. There, he launched a coffeehouse concept called McCafe, which is now being introduced around the globe. He later achieved success in France, where he abandoned McDonald's cookie-cutter orange-and-yellow stores for individualized ones that offer local fare like the ham-and-cheese Croque McDo.

22  The second top executive Cantalupo has recruited is a bona fide outsider—at least by company standards. Lederhausen holds an MBA from the Stockholm School of Economics and worked with Boston Consulting Group Inc. for two years. However, he jokes that he grew up in a french-fry vat because his father introduced McDonald's to Sweden in 1973. Lederhausen is in charge of growth and menu development.

23  Getting the recipe right will be tougher now that consumers have tasted better burgers. While McDonald's says it may start toasting its buns longer to get the flavor right, rivals go even further. Industry experts point to 160-store In-N-Out, a profitable California burger chain. Its burgers are grilled when ordered—no heat lamps to warm up precooked food. Today, In-N-Out is rated No. 1 by fast-food consumers tracked by consultant Sandelman & Associates Inc. in San Diego. "The burger category has great strength," adds David C. Novak, chairman and CEO of Yum! Brands Inc. (YUM), parent of KFC and Taco Bell. "That's America's food. People love hamburgers."

24  McDonald's best hope to recapture that love might be to turn to its most innovative franchisees. Take Irwin Kruger in New York, who recently opened a 17,000-square-foot showcase unit in Times Square with video monitors showing movie trailers, brick walls, theatrical lighting—and strong profits. "We're slated to have sales of over $5 million this year and profits exceeding 10 percent," says Kruger. Rejuvenated marketing would help, too: McDonald's called its top ad agencies

together in February to draw up a plan that would go beyond the ubiquitous Disney movie tie-ins.

25    It will take nothing short of a marketing miracle, though, to return McDonald's to its youthful vigor. "They are at a critical juncture and what they do today will shape whether they just fade away or recapture some of the magic and greatness again," says Robert S. Goldin, executive vice-president at food consultant Technomic Inc. As McDonald's settles into middle age, Cantalupo and his team may have to settle for stable and reliable.

**Source:** Pallavi Gogoi and Michael Arndt, "McDonald's Hamburger Hell," *BusinessWeek Online,* March 3, 2003.

## Appendix **3**

# Sources for Environmental Forecasting

## REMOTE AND INDUSTRY ENVIRONMENTS

A. Economic considerations:
   1. *Predicasts* (most complete and up-to-date review of forecasts).
   2. National Bureau of Economic Research.
   3. *Handbook of Basic Economic Statistics.*
   4. *Statistical Abstract of the United States* (also includes industrial, social, and political statistics).
   5. Publications by Department of Commerce agencies:
      a. Office of Business Economics (e.g., *Survey of Business*).
      b. Bureau of Economic Analysis (e.g., *Business Conditions Digest*).
      c. Bureau of the Census (e.g., *Survey of Manufacturers* and various reports on population, housing, and industries).
      d. Business and Defense Services Administration (e.g., *United States Industrial Outlook*).
   6. Securities and Exchange Commission (various quarterly reports on plant and equipment, financial reports, working capital of corporations).
   7. The Conference Board.
   8. *Survey of Buying Power.*
   9. *Marketing Economic Guide.*
   10. *Industrial Arts Index.*
   11. U.S. and national chambers of commerce.
   12. American Manufacturers Association.
   13. *Federal Reserve Bulletin.*
   14. *Economic Indicators,* annual report.
   15. *Kiplinger Newsletter.*
   16. International economic sources:
      a. *Worldcasts.*
      b. Master key index for business international publications.
      c. Department of Commerce.
         (1) Overseas business reports.
         (2) Industry and Trade Administration.
         (3) Bureau of the Census—*Guide to Foreign Trade Statistics.*
   17. *Business Periodicals Index.*
B. Social considerations:
   1. Public opinion polls.
   2. Surveys such as *Social Indicators and Social Reporting,* the annals of the American Academy of Political and Social Sciences.
   3. Current controls: Social and behavioral sciences.
   4. Abstract services and indexes for articles in sociological, psychological, and political journals.
   5. Indexes for *The Wall Street Journal, New York Times,* and other newspapers.

6. Bureau of the Census reports on population, housing, manufacturers, selected services, construction, retail trade, wholesale trade, and enterprise statistics.
7. Various reports from such groups as the Brookings Institution and the Ford Foundation.
8. World Bank Atlas (population growth and GNP data).
9. World Bank–World Development Report.

C. Political considerations:
  1. *Public Affairs Information Services Bulletin.*
  2. CIS Index (Congressional Information Index).
  3. Business periodicals.
  4. Funk & Scott (regulations by product breakdown).
  5. Weekly compilation of presidential documents.
  6. *Monthly Catalog of Government Publications.*
  7. *Federal Register* (daily announcements of pending regulations).
  8. *Code of Federal Regulations* (final listing of regulations).
  9. Business International Master Key Index (regulations, tariffs).
  10. Various state publications.
  11. Various information services (Bureau of National Affairs, Commerce Clearing House, Prentice Hall).

D. Technological considerations:
  1. *Applied Science and Technology Index.*
  2. *Statistical Abstract of the United States.*
  3. Scientific and Technical Information Service.
  4. University reports, congressional reports.
  5. Department of Defense and military purchasing publishers.
  6. Trade journals and industrial reports.
  7. Industry contacts, professional meetings.
  8. Computer-assisted information searches.
  9. National Science Foundation annual report.
  10. *Research and Development Directory* patent records.

E. Industry considerations:
  1. *Concentration Ratios in Manufacturing* (Bureau of the Census).
  2. *Input-Output Survey* (productivity ratios).
  3. *Monthly Labor Review* (productivity ratios).
  4. *Quarterly Failure Report* (Dun & Bradstreet).
  5. *Federal Reserve Bulletin* (capacity utilization).
  6. *Report on Industrial Concentration and Product Diversification in the 1,000 Largest Manufacturing Companies* (Federal Trade Commission).
  7. Industry trade publications.
  8. Bureau of Economic Analysis, Department of Commerce (specialization ratios).

## INDUSTRY AND OPERATING ENVIRONMENTS

A. Competition and supplier considerations:
  1. Target Group Index.
  2. U.S. Industrial Outlook.
  3. Robert Morris annual statement studies.
  4. Troy, Leo Almanac of Business & Industrial Financial Ratios.
  5. Census of Enterprise Statistics.

6. Securities and Exchange Commission (10-K reports).
7. Annual reports of specific companies.
8. *Fortune 500 Directory, The Wall Street Journal, Barron's, Forbes, Dun's Review.*
9. Investment services and directories: Moody's, Dun & Bradstreet, Standard & Poor's, Starch Marketing, Funk & Scott Index.
10. Trade association surveys.
11. Industry surveys.
12. Market research surveys.
13. *Country Business Patterns.*
14. *Country and City Data Book.*
15. Industry contacts, professional meetings, salespeople.
16. *NFIB Quarterly Economic Report for Small Business.*

B. Customer profile:
1. *Statistical Abstract of the United States,* first source of statistics.
2. *Statistical Sources* by Paul Wasserman (a subject guide to data—both domestic and international).
3. *American Statistics Index* (Congressional Information Service Guide to statistical publications of U.S. government—monthly).
4. Office to the Department of Commerce:
    a. Bureau of the Census reports on population, housing, and industries.
    b. *U.S. Census of Manufacturers* (statistics by industry, area, and products).
    c. *Survey of Current Business* (analysis of business trends, especially February and July issues).
5. Market research studies (*A Basic Bibliography on Market Review,* compiled by Robert Ferber et al., American Marketing Association).
6. *Current Sources of Marketing Information: A Bibliography of Primary Marketing Data* by Gunther & Goldstein, AMA.
7. *Guide to Consumer Markets,* The Conference Board (provides statistical information with demographic, social, and economic data—annual).
8. *Survey of Buying Power.*
9. *Predicasts* (abstracts of publishing forecasts of all industries, detailed products, and end-use data).
10. *Predicasts Basebook* (historical data from 1960 to present, covering subjects ranging from population and GNP to specific products and services; series are coded by Standard Industrial Classifications).
11. *Market Guide* (individual market surveys of over 1,500 U.S. and Canadian cities; includes population, location, trade areas, banks, principal industries, colleges and universities, department and chain stores, newspapers, retail outlets, and sales).
12. *Country and City Data Book* (includes bank deposits, birth and death rates, business firms, education, employment, income of families, manufacturers, population, savings, and wholesale and retail trade).
13. *Yearbook of International Trade Statistics* (UN).
14. *Yearbook of National Accounts Statistics* (UN).
15. *Statistical Yearbook* (UN—covers population, national income, agricultural and industrial production, energy, external trade, and transport).
16. *Statistics of (Continents): Sources for Market Research* (includes separate books on Africa, America, Europe).

C. Key natural resources:
 1. *Minerals Yearbook, Geological Survey* (Bureau of Mines, Department of the Interior).
 2. *Agricultural Abstract* (Department of Agriculture).
 3. Statistics of electric utilities and gas pipeline companies (Federal Power Commission).
 4. Publications of various institutions: American Petroleum Institute, Atomic Energy Commission, Coal Mining Institute of America, American Steel Institute, and Brookings Institution.

# Chapter **Four**

# The Global Environment: Strategic Considerations for Multinational Firms

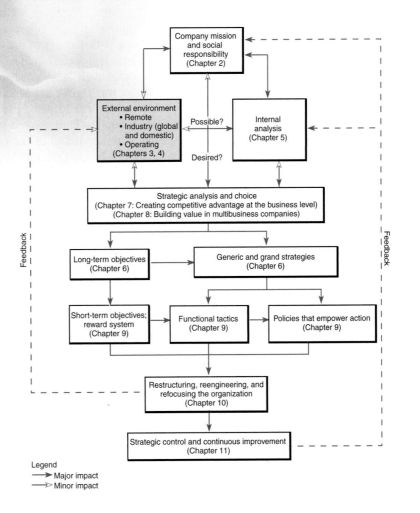

Company mission and social responsibility (Chapter 2)

External environment
- Remote
- Industry (global and domestic)
- Operating
(Chapters 3, 4)

Possible?

Internal analysis (Chapter 5)

Desired?

Strategic analysis and choice
(Chapter 7: Creating competitive advantage at the business level)
(Chapter 8: Building value in multibusiness companies)

Long-term objectives (Chapter 6)

Generic and grand strategies (Chapter 6)

Short-term objectives; reward system (Chapter 9)

Functional tactics (Chapter 9)

Policies that empower action (Chapter 9)

Restructuring, reengineering, and refocusing the organization (Chapter 10)

Strategic control and continuous improvement (Chapter 11)

Feedback

Feedback

Legend
→ Major impact
⇢ Minor impact

Special complications confront a firm involved in the globalization of its operations. *Globalization* refers to the strategy of approaching worldwide markets with standardized products. Such markets are most commonly created by end consumers that prefer lower-priced, standardized products over higher-priced, customized products and by global corporations that use their worldwide operations to compete in local markets. Global corporations headquartered in one country with subsidiaries in other countries experience difficulties that are understandably associated with operating in several distinctly different competitive arenas.

Awareness of the strategic opportunities faced by global corporations and of the threats posed to them is important to planners in almost every domestic U.S. industry. Among corporations headquartered in the United States that receive more than 50 percent of their annual profits from foreign operations are Citicorp, Coca-Cola, Exxon, Gillette, IBM, Otis Elevator, and Texas Instruments. In fact, the 100 largest U.S. globals earn an average of 37 percent of their operating profits abroad. Equally impressive is the impact of foreign-based globals that operate in the United States. Their "direct foreign investment" in the United States now exceeds $90 billion, with Japanese, German, and French firms leading the way.

Understanding the myriad and sometimes subtle nuances of competing in global markets or against global corporations is rapidly becoming a required competence of strategic managers. For example, experts in the advertising community contend that Korean companies only recently recognized the importance of making their names known abroad. In the 1980s, there was very little advertising of Korean brands, and the country had very few recognizable brands abroad. Korean companies tended to emphasize sales and production more than marketing. The opening of the Korean advertising market in the 1990s indicated that Korean firms had acquired a new appreciation for the strategic competencies that are needed to compete globally and created an influx of global firms like Saatchi and Saatchi, J. W. Thompson, Ogilvy and Mather, and Bozell. Many of them established joint ventures or partnerships with Korean agencies. An excellent example of such a strategic approach to globalization by Philip Morris's KGFI is described in Exhibit 4–1, Global Strategy in Action. The opportunities for corporate growth often seem brightest in global markets. Exhibit 4–2 reports on the growth in national shares of the world's outputs and growth in national economies to the year 2020. While the United States had a commanding lead in the size of its economy in 1992, it was caught by China in the year 2000 and will be far surpassed by 2020. Overall, in less than 20 years, rich industrial countries will be overshadowed by developing countries in their produced share of the world's output.

Because the growth in the number of global firms continues to overshadow other changes in the competitive environment, this section will focus on the nature, outlook, and operations of global corporations.

## DEVELOPMENT OF A GLOBAL CORPORATION

The evolution of a global corporation often entails progressively involved strategy levels. The first level, which often entails export-import activity, has minimal effect on the existing management orientation or on existing product lines. The second level, which can involve foreign licensing and technology transfer, requires little change in management or operation. The third level typically is characterized by direct investment in overseas operations, including manufacturing plants. This level requires large capital outlays and the development of global management skills. Although the domestic operations of a firm at this level continue to dominate its policy, such a firm is commonly categorized as a true multinational corporation (MNC). The

Outside of its core Western markets, Kraft General Foods International's (KGFI) food products have a growing presence in one of the most dynamic business environments in the world—the Asia-Pacific region. Its operations there are expanding rapidly, often aided by links with local manufacturers and distributors.

Japan and Korea are important examples. In both countries, local alliances can be crucial to market entry and success. Realizing this fact in the early 1970s, General Foods established joint ventures in both Japan and Korea. These joint ventures, combined with Kraft General Foods International's (KGFI) stand-alone operations, generate more than $1 billion in revenues. In the aggregate, their combined food operations in Japan and Korea are larger than many Fortune 500 companies.

Whereas soluble coffee accounts for just over 25 percent of the coffee consumed in U.S. homes, it fills over 70 percent of the cups consumed in the homes of convenience-minded Japan. Additionally, Japan is the origin of a unique form of packaged coffee—liquid—and a unique channel of distribution—vending machines. Japanese consumers have purchased packaged liquid coffee for years, and it amounts to a $5 billion category. Some 2 million vending machines dispense 9 billion cans of liquid coffee annually—an average of 75 cans per person.

Japan offers a culturally unique distribution channel for coffee products—the gift-set market. Many Japanese exchange specially packaged food or beverage assortments at least twice a year to commemorate holidays as well as special personal or business occasions. The gift-set business has helped Maxim products reinforce their quality image; it also will be a launching pad and support vehicle for Carte Noire coffees.

Outside the Ajinomoto General Foods joint venture, KGFI is developing a freestanding food business under the name Kraft Japan. It is building a cheese business with imported Philadelphia Brand cream cheese, the leading cream cheese in the Tokyo metropolitan market, as well as locally manufactured and licensed Kraft Milk Farm cheese slices. The cheese market is expected to grow approximately 5 percent per year. This is a rapid growth rate for a large food category. In addition to cheese, KGFI also imports Oscar Mayer prepared meats and Jacobs Suchard chocolates.

KGFI's joint venture in Korea, Doug Suh Foods Corporation, is one of the top 10 food companies in the country. Doug Suh manufactures coffees and cereals and has its own distribution network. One of Doug Suh's other businesses in Korea, Post Cereals, is also a strong number two, with a 42 percent category share.

Korea's $400 million coffee market is the fastest-growing major coffee market in the world, expanding at an average annual rate of 14 percent. Growing with the market, Maxim and Maxwell soluble coffees, in both traditional "agglomerate" and freeze-dried forms, account for more than 70 percent of the country's soluble coffee sales. The strength of these brands also brings the company a strong number one position in coffee mix, a mixture of soluble coffee, creamer, and sugar. In addition, its Frima brand leads the market in the nondairy creamer segment.

Beyond Japan and Korea, KGFI is targeting many other countries for geographic expansion. In Indonesia, for instance, KGFI has established a rapidly growing cheese business through a licensee and introduced other KGFI products. In Taiwan, the joint venture company, PremierFoods Corporation, holds a 34 percent share of the soluble coffee market and is aggressively developing a Kraft cheese and Jacobs Suchard import business. KGFI Philippines, a wholly owned subsidiary, has a leading position in the cheese and powdered soft-drink markets in its country. In the People's Republic of China, the company produces and markets Maxwell House coffees and Tang powdered soft drinks through two successful and rapidly growing joint ventures.

most involved strategy level is characterized by a substantial increase in foreign investment, with foreign assets comprising a significant portion of total assets. At this level, the firm begins to emerge as a global enterprise with global approaches to production, sales, finance, and control.

Some firms downplay their global nature (to never appear distracted from their domestic operations), whereas others highlight it. For example, General Electric's formal statement of mission and business philosophy includes the following commitment:

> To carry out a diversified, growing, and profitable worldwide manufacturing business in electrical apparatus, appliances, and supplies, and in related materials, products, systems, and services for industry, commerce, agriculture, government, the community, and the home.

A similar global orientation is evident at IBM, which operates in 125 countries, conducts business in 30 languages and more than 100 currencies, and has 23 major manufacturing facilities in 14 countries.

**EXHIBIT 4–2** **Projected Economic Growth**

Source: World Bank, *Global Economic Prospects and the Developing Countries.*

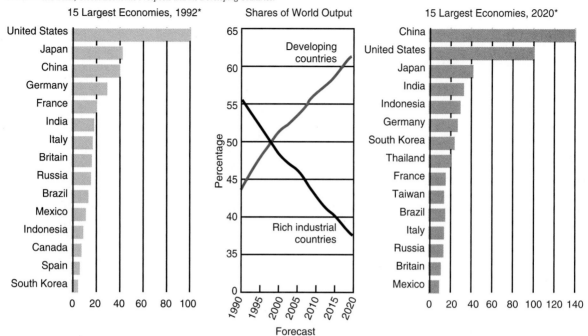

* United States = 100;
Other countries = percentage of U.S.'s GDP

# WHY FIRMS GLOBALIZE

The technological advantage once enjoyed by the United States has declined dramatically during the past 30 years. In the late 1950s, over 80 percent of the world's major technological innovations were first introduced in the United States. By 1990, the figure had declined to less than 50 percent. In contrast, France is making impressive advances in electric traction, nuclear power, and aviation. Germany leads in chemicals and pharmaceuticals, precision and heavy machinery, heavy electrical goods, metallurgy, and surface transport equipment. Japan leads in optics, solid-state physics, engineering, chemistry, and process metallurgy. Eastern Europe and the former Soviet Union, the so-called COMECON (Council for Mutual Economic Assistance) countries, generate 30 percent of annual worldwide patent applications. However, the United States has regained some of its lost technological advantage. Through globalization, U.S. firms often can reap benefits from industries and technologies developed abroad. Even a relatively small service firm that possesses a distinct competitive advantage can capitalize on large overseas operations.

As discussed in Exhibit 4–3, Global Strategy in Action, Diebold Inc. once operated solely in the United States, selling ATM machines, bank vaults, and security systems to financial institutions. However, with the U.S. market saturated, Diebold needed to expand internationally to continue its growth. The firm's globalization efforts led to both the development of new technologies in emerging markets and opportunistic entry into entirely new industries that significantly improved Diebold's sales.

In many situations, global development makes sense as a competitive weapon. Direct penetration of foreign markets can drain vital cash flows from a foreign competitor's domestic operations. The resulting lost opportunities, reduced income, and limited production can impair the competitor's ability to invade U.S. markets. A case in point is IBM's move to

**BusinessWeek** For most of its 142-year history, Diebold Inc. never worried much about global strategy. As a premier name in bank vaults—and then automated teller machines and security systems—the company focused on U.S. financial institutions, content to let partners hawk what they could abroad. But in 1998, with the U.S. ATM market saturated, Diebold decided it had to be more ambitious. Since then, Diebold has taken off. Sales of security devices, software, and services surged 38 percent in 2000, to $1.74 billion, led by a 146 percent jump in overseas sales, to $729 million. The momentum continued in 2001. International sales have gone from 22 percent of the total to 40 percent in just two years, and should soon overtake North America.

The ventures overseas have taken Diebold into whole new directions. In China, where it now has half of the fast-growing ATM market, it also is helping the giant International Commercial Bank of China design its self-service branches and data network. In Brazil, Diebold owns and manages a network of 5,000 ATMs—as well as surveillance cameras—for a state-owned bank. In Colombia, it's handling bill collection for a power utility. In Taiwan, where most consumers still prefer to pay bills in cash, Diebold is about to introduce ATMs that both accept and count stacks of up to 100 currency notes and weed out counterfeits. And in South Africa, its ATMs for the techno-illiterate scan fingerprints for identification.

Diebold found it could serve much broader needs in emerging markets than in the United States. Across Latin America, consumers use banks to pay everything from utility bills to taxes. So Diebold ATMs handle these services, 24 hours a day. In Argentina, where filing taxes is a nightmare, citizens now can fill out returns on a PC, store them on a disk, and have their disks scanned on one of 5,000 special Diebold terminals, most of them at banks. Diebold also is landing new contracts across Latin America to manage bank ATM networks.

The $240 million acquisition of Brazil's Procom also gave Diebold an entree into an entirely new line: It landed a huge contract to supply electronic voting machines for Brazil's presidential election last year. Now Diebold is getting into the voting-machine business in the United States, where it expects demand to surge in the wake of the controversial Presidential contest in Florida. Globalization, it seems, can even unveil new opportunities at home.

**Source:** Excerpt from M. Arndt, P. Engardio, and J. Goodman, "Diebold," *BusinessWeek* (3746), p. 138, August 27, 2001.

establish a position of strength in the Japanese mainframe computer industry before two key competitors, Fiyitsue and Hitachi, could dominate it. Once IBM had achieved a substantial share of the Japanese market, it worked to deny its Japanese competitors the vital cash and production experience they needed to invade the U.S. market.

Firms that operate principally in the domestic environment have an important decision to make with regard to their globalization: Should they act before being forced to do so by competitive pressures or after? Should they: (1) be proactive by entering global markets in advance of other firms and thereby enjoy the first-mover advantages often accruing to risk-taker firms that introduce new products or services; or (2) be reactive by taking the more conservative approach and following other companies into global markets once customer demand has been proven and the high costs of new-product or new-service introductions have been absorbed by competitors? Although the answers to these questions are determined by the specifics of the company and the context, the issues raised in Exhibit 4–4 are helpful to strategic decision makers faced with the dilemma.

## Strategic Orientations of Global Firms

Multinational corporations typically display one of four orientations toward their overseas activities. They have a certain set of beliefs about how the management of foreign operations should be handled. A company with an *ethnocentric orientation* believes that the values and priorities of the parent organization should guide the strategic decision making of all its operations. If a corporation has a *polycentric orientation*, then the culture of the country in which a strategy is to be implemented is allowed to dominate the decision-making process. In contrast, a *regiocentric orientation* exists when the parent attempts to blend its own predispositions with those of the region under consideration, thereby arriving at a region-sensitive compromise. Finally, a corporation with a *geocentric orientation* adopts a global systems approach to strategic decision making, thereby emphasizing global integration.

**EXHIBIT 4–4**
**Reasons for Going Global**

Source: Betty Jane Punnett and David A. Ricks, *International Business* (Boston: PWS-Kent, 1992), pp. 249–50.

| Proactive | |
|---|---|
| **Advantage/Opportunity** | **Explanation of Action** |
| Additional resources | Various inputs—including natural resources, technologies, skilled personnel, and materials—may be obtained more readily outside the home country. |
| Lowered costs | Various costs—including labor, materials, transportation, and financing—may be lower outside the home country. |
| Incentives | Various incentives may be available from the host government or the home government to encourage foreign investment in specific locations. |
| New, expanded markets | New and different markets may be available outside the home country; excess resources—including management, skills, machinery, and money—can be utilized in foreign locations. |
| Exploitation of firm-specific advantages | Technologies, brands, and recognized names can all provide opportunities in foreign locations. |
| Taxes | Differing corporate tax rates and tax systems in different locations provide opportunities for companies to maximize their after-tax worldwide profits. |
| Economies of scale | National markets may be too small to support efficient production, while sales from several combined allow for larger-scale production. |
| Synergy | Operations in more than one national environment provide opportunities to combine benefits from one location with another, which is impossible without both of them. |
| Power and prestige | The image of being international may increase a company's power and prestige and improve its domestic sales and relations with various stakeholder groups. |
| Protect home market through offense in competitor's home | A strong offense in a competitor's market can put pressure on the competitor that results in a pull-back from foreign activities to protect itself at home. |

| Reactive | |
|---|---|
| **Outside Occurrence** | **Explanation of Reaction** |
| Trade barriers | Tariffs, quotas, buy-local policies, and other restrictive trade practices can make exports to foreign markets less attractive; local operations in foreign locations thus become attractive. |
| International customers | If a company's customer base becomes international, and the company wants to continue to serve it, then local operations in foreign locations may be necessary. |
| International competition | If a company's competitors become international, and the company wants to remain competitive, foreign operations may be necessary. |
| Regulations | Regulations and restrictions imposed by the home government may increase the cost of operating at home; it may be possible to avoid these costs by establishing foreign operations. |
| Chance | Chance occurrence results in a company deciding to enter foreign locations. |

**EXHIBIT 4–5**   **Orientation of a Global Firm**

| | Orientation of the Firm | | | |
|---|---|---|---|---|
| | **Ethnocentric** | **Polycentric** | **Regiocentric** | **Geocentric** |
| Mission | Profitability (viability) | Public acceptance (legitimacy) | Both profitability and public acceptance (viability and legitimacy) | Same as regiocentric |
| Governance | Top-down | Bottom-up (each subsidiary decides on local objectives) | Mutually negotiated between region and its subsidiaries | Mutually negotiated at all levels of the corporation |
| Strategy | Global integration | National responsiveness | Regional integration and national responsiveness | Global integration and national responsiveness |
| Structure | Hierarchical product divisions | Hierarchical area divisions, with autonomous national units | Product and regional organization tied through a matrix | A network of organizations (including some stakeholders and competitor organizations) |
| Culture | Home country | Host country | Regional | Global |
| Technology | Mass production | Batch production | Flexible manufacturing | Flexible manufacturing |
| Marketing | Product development determined primarily by the needs of home-country customers | Local product development based on local needs | Standardize within region but not across regions | Global product, with local variations |
| Finance | Repatriation of profits to home country | Retention of profits in host country | Redistribution within region | Redistribution globally |
| Personnel practices | People of home country developed for key positions everywhere in the world | People of local nationality developed for key positions in their own country | Regional people developed for key positions anywhere in the region | Best people every-where in the world developed for key positions everywhere in the world |

Source: Adapted from Balaji S. Chakravarthy and Howard V. Perlmutter, "Strategic Planning for a Global Business," *Columbia Journal of World Business,* Summer 1985, pp. 5–6. Copyright 1985, Columbia Journal of World Business. Used with permission.

American firms often adopt a regiocentric orientation for pursing strategies in Europe. U.S. e-tailers have attempted to blend their own corporate structure and expertise with that of European corporations. For example, Amazon has been able to leverage its experience in the United States while developing regionally and culturally specific strategies overseas. By purchasing European franchises that have had regional success, E*Trade is pursuing a foreign strategy in which they insert their European units into corporate structure. This strategy requires the combination and use of culturally different management styles and involves major challenges for upper management.

Exhibit 4–5 shows the impacts of each of the four orientations on key activities of the firm. It is clear from the figure that the strategic orientation of a global firm plays a major role in determining the locus of control and corporate priorities of the firm's decision makers.

# AT THE START OF GLOBALIZATION

External and internal assessments are conducted before a firm enters global markets. For example, Japanese investors conduct extensive assessments and analyses before selecting a U.S. site for a Japanese-owned firm. They prefer states with strong markets, low unionization rates, and low taxes. In addition, Japanese manufacturing plants prefer counties characterized by manufacturing conglomeration; low unemployment and poverty rates; and concentrations of educated, productive workers.

External assessment involves careful examination of critical features of the global environment, particular attention being paid to the status of the host nations in such areas as economic progress, political control, and nationalism. Expansion of industrial facilities, favorable balances of payments, and improvements in technological capabilities over the past decade are gauges of the host nation's economic progress. Political status can be gauged by the host nation's power in and impact on global affairs.

Internal assessment involves identification of the basic strengths of a firm's operations. These strengths are particularly important in global operations, because they are often the characteristics of a firm that the host nation values most and, thus, offer significant bargaining leverage. The firm's resource strengths and global capabilities must be analyzed. The resources that should be analyzed include, in particular, technical and managerial skills, capital, labor, and raw materials. The global capabilities that should be analyzed include the firm's product delivery and financial management systems.

A firm that gives serious consideration to internal and external assessment is Business International Corporation, which recommends that seven broad categories of factors be considered. As shown in Exhibit 4–6, Global Strategy in Action, these categories include economic, political, geographic, labor, tax, capital source, and business factors.

# COMPLEXITY OF THE GLOBAL ENVIRONMENT

By 2003, Coke was finally achieving a goal that it had set a decade earlier when it went to India. That goal was to take the market away from Pepsi and local beverage companies. However, when it arrived, Coke found that the Indian market was extremely complex and smaller than it had estimated. As described in Exhibit 4–7, Global Strategy-in-Action, Coke also encountered cultural problems, in part because the chief of Coke India was an expatriate. The key to overcoming this cultural problem was promoting an Indian to operations chief. Coke also changed its marketing strategy by pushing their "Thums Up" products, a local brand owned by Coke. Then, they began to focus their efforts on creating new products for rural areas and lowering the prices of their existing products to increase sales. Once Coke had new products in the market, they focused on a new advertising campaign to better relate to Indian consumers.

Coke's experience highlights the fact that global strategic planning is more complex than purely domestic planning. There are at least five factors that contribute to this increase in complexity:

1. Globals face multiple political, economic, legal, social, and cultural environments as well as various rates of changes within each of them.

2. Interactions between the national and foreign environments are complex, because of national sovereignty issues and widely differing economic and social conditions.

3. Geographic separation, cultural and national differences, and variations in business practices all tend to make communication and control efforts between headquarters and the overseas affiliates difficult.

4. Globals face extreme competition, because of differences in industry structures.

The following considerations were drawn from an 88-point checklist developed by Business International Corporation.

Economic factors:

1. Size of GNP and projected rate of growth.

2. Foreign exchange position.

3. Size of market for the firm's products; rate of growth.

Political factors:

4. Form and stability of government.

5. Attitude toward private and foreign investment by government, customers, and competition.

6. Degree of antiforeign discrimination.

Geographic factors:

7. Proximity of site to export markets.

8. Availability of local raw materials.

9. Availability of power, water, gas.

Labor factors:

10. Availability of managerial, technical, and office personnel able to speak the language of the parent company.

11. Degree of skill and discipline at all levels.

12. Degree and nature of labor voice in management.

Tax factors:

13. Tax-rate trends.

14. Joint tax treaties with home country and others.

15. Availability of tariff protection.

Capital source factors:

16. Cost of local borrowing.

17. Modern banking systems.

18. Government credit aids to new businesses.

Business factors:

19. State of marketing and distribution system.

20. Normal profit margins in the firm's industry.

21. Competitive situation in the firm's industry: do cartels exist?

---

5. Globals are restricted in their selection of competitive strategies by various regional blocs and economic integrations, such as the European Economic Community, the European Free Trade Area, and the Latin American Free Trade Area.

## CONTROL PROBLEMS OF THE GLOBAL FIRM

An inherent complicating factor for many global firms is that their financial policies typically are designed to further the goals of the parent company and pay minimal attention to the goals of the host countries. This built-in bias creates conflict between the different parts of the global firm, between the whole firm and its home and host countries, and between the home country and host country themselves. The conflict is accentuated by the use of various schemes to shift earnings from one country to another in order to avoid taxes, minimize risk, or achieve other objectives.

Moreover, different financial environments make normal standards of company behavior concerning the disposition of earnings, sources of finance, and the structure of capital more problematic. Thus, it becomes increasingly difficult to measure the performance of international divisions.

In addition, important differences in measurement and control systems often exist. Fundamental to the concept of planning is a well-conceived, future-oriented approach to decision making that is based on accepted procedures and methods of analysis. Consistent

**BusinessWeek** Despite having billion-plus consumers, a growing middle class, and a hot climate, India had not been a successful market for the beverage giant Coca-Cola Co. Though various Coke products possessed more than half the market, the flagship brand, Coca Cola, remained a distant third, with an estimated market share of 16.5 percent, far behind arch rival Pepsi-Cola's 23.5 percent. Almost as embarrassing, number two was Thums Up, a sweeter local cola that Coke acquired in 1993, then proceeded to neglect.

In 1993—15 years after being thrown out by India's socialist government—Coke stormed back into the country with big plans to wrest control from Pepsi and the local beverage marketers that had risen up in its absence. Instead, the company spent years on the defensive after overestimating the size of the market, misreading consumers, and battling with the government. And Coke India has been hurt by a revolving door in the executive suite. In 10 years, it has had five expatriate heads.

Coke planned to sell 49 percent of its Indian bottler, Hindustan Coca-Cola Beverages, for $41 million. The sale was not the domestic stock listing that some in New Delhi had sought. Instead, the shares will be sold in a private placement with institutional investors and employees. But it put to rest a thorny issue that had chilled relations with the government, which wanted Indians to have a substantial ownership stake in Coke's local operation. Better yet, Indians appeared to be developing a taste for Coke products: The Company's overall sales in India jumped 24 percent, to $940 million.

India, with soft-drink consumption of just seven 8-ounce (250 milliliters) servings per capita annually, held more potential for growth than just about any other market on earth. Determined to consolidate its position and boost growth, Coke cut prices on all of its beverages by an aggressive 15 percent to 25 percent, forcing Pepsi to follow suit.

Key to Coke's battle plans was operations chief Sanjeev Gupta. Gupta's first step: revitalizing Thums Up, which led the market in 1993 with more than 60 percent of carbonated beverage sales but had slipped to just 15 percent by 1998. After Atlanta (Coca Cola's headquarters) gave the green light to pushing local brands as much as Coca-Cola, the 41-year-old Gupta spent $3.5 million to beef up advertising and distribution for Thums Up. Within a year, he built it into India's number two soda. Then Gupta—a veteran of marketing juggernaut Hindustan Lever Ltd.—persuaded Atlanta to revamp pricing and advertising for Coca-Cola. In 2001, he launched a new size, a 200-ml. bottle that sold for 10 cents and was aimed at rural areas and lower-income urban markets. Then, he dropped the price of a 300-ml. bottle to 17 cents from 24 cents. The price cuts were key to boosting sales and the little bottle was a big hit. In 2002, after years of lackluster ad campaigns, Gupta's team settled on an advertising strategy that caught the imagination of Indians. Breaking with Coke tradition, he hired a celebrity spokesman, Bollywood movie star Amir Khan.

The changes were paying Coke dividends. Execs at Coca-Cola India said the company was no longer losing money. "We have turned a corner," said N. Sridhar, Coke India's finance director. "This will release our energies to concentrate on building market share." Now, Coke planned on investing $150 million more to expand its bottling and distribution network. That would make India Coke's second-largest Asian investment after China.

**Source:** Excerpted from Manjeet Kripalani and Mark L. Clifford, "Finally Coke Gets It Right In India," *Business Week,* February 10, 2003, p. 47.

---

approaches to planning throughout a firm are needed for effective review and evaluation by corporate headquarters. In the global firm, planning is complicated by differences in national attitudes toward work measurement, and by differences in government requirements about disclosure of information.

Although such problems are an aspect of the global environment, rather than a consequence of poor management, they are often most effectively reduced through increased attention to strategic planning. Such planning will aid in coordinating and integrating the firm's direction, objectives, and policies around the world. It enables the firm to anticipate and prepare for change. It facilitates the creation of programs to deal with worldwide development. Finally, it helps the management of overseas affiliates become more actively involved in setting goals and in developing means to more effectively utilize the firm's total resources.

An example of the need for coordination in global ventures and evidence that firms can successfully plan for global collaboration (e.g., through rationalized production) is the Ford Escort (Europe), the best-selling automobile in the world, which has a component manufacturing network that consists of plants in 15 countries.

# GLOBAL STRATEGIC PLANNING

It should be evident from the previous sections that the strategic decisions of a firm competing in the global marketplace become increasingly complex. In such a firm, managers cannot view global operations as a set of independent decisions. These managers are faced with trade-off decisions in which multiple products, country environments, resource sourcing options, corporate and subsidiary capabilities, and strategic options must be considered.

A recent trend toward increased activism of stakeholders has added to the complexity of strategic planning for the global firm. *Stakeholder activism* refers to demands placed on the global firm by the foreign environments in which it operates, principally by foreign governments. This section provides a basic framework for the analysis of strategic decisions in this complex setting.

## Multidomestic Industries and Global Industries

### Multidomestic Industries

International industries can be ranked along a continuum that ranges from multidomestic to global.

A multidomestic industry is one in which competition is essentially segmented from country to country. Thus, even if global corporations are in the industry, competition in one country is independent of competition in other countries. Examples of such industries include retailing, insurance, and consumer finance.

In a multidomestic industry, a global corporation's subsidiaries should be managed as distinct entities; that is, each subsidiary should be rather autonomous, having the authority to make independent decisions in response to local market conditions. Thus, the global strategy of such an industry is the sum of the strategies developed by subsidiaries operating in different countries. The primary difference between a domestic firm and a global firm competing in a multidomestic industry is that the latter makes decisions related to the countries in which it competes and to how it conducts business abroad.

Factors that increase the degree to which an industry is multidomestic include:[1]

The need for customized products to meet the tastes or preferences of local customers.

Fragmentation of the industry, with many competitors in each national market.

A lack of economies of scale in the functional activities of firms in the industry.

Distribution channels unique to each country.

A low technological dependence of subsidiaries on R&D provided by the global firm.

### Global Industries

A global industry is one in which competition crosses national borders. In fact, it occurs on a worldwide basis. In a global industry, a firm's strategic moves in one country can be significantly affected by its competitive position in another country. The very rapidly expanding list of global industries includes commercial aircraft, automobiles, mainframe computers, and electronic consumer equipment. Many authorities are convinced that almost

---

[1] Y. Doz and C. K. Prahalad, "Patterns of Strategic Control within Multinational Corporations," *Journal of International Business Studies,* Fall1984, pp. 55–72.

all product-oriented industries soon will be global. As a result, strategic management planning must be global for at least six reasons:

1. *The increased scope of the global management task.* Growth in the size and complexity of global firms made management virtually impossible without a coordinated plan of action detailing what is expected of whom during a given period. The common practice of management by exception is impossible without such a plan.

2. *The increased globalization of firms.* Three aspects of global business make global planning necessary: (1) differences among the environmental forces in different countries, (2) greater distances, and (3) the interrelationships of global operations.

3. *The information explosion.* It has been estimated that the world's stock of knowledge is doubling every 10 years. Without the aid of a formal plan, executives can no longer know all that they must know to solve the complex problems they face. A global planning process provides an ordered means for assembling, analyzing, and distilling the information required for sound decisions.

4. *The increase in global competition.* Because of the rapid increase in global competition, firms must constantly adjust to changing conditions or lose markets to competitors. The increase in global competition also spurs managements to search for methods of increasing efficiency and economy.

5. *The rapid development of technology.* Rapid technological development has shortened product life cycles. Strategic management planning is necessary to ensure the replacement of products that are moving into the maturity stage, with fewer sales and declining profits. Planning gives management greater control of all aspects of new product introduction.

6. *Strategic management planning breeds managerial confidence.* Like the motorist with a road map, managers with a plan for reaching their objectives know where they are going. Such a plan breeds confidence, because it spells out every step along the way and assigns responsibility for every task. The plan simplifies the managerial job.

A firm in a global industry must maximize its capabilities through a worldwide strategy. Such a strategy necessitates a high degree of centralized decision making in corporate headquarters so as to permit trade-off decisions across subsidiaries.

Among the factors that make for the creation of a global industry are:

Economies of scale in the functional activities of firms in the industry.

A high level of R&D expenditures on products that require more than one market to recover development costs.

The presence in the industry of predominantly global firms that expect consistency of products and services across markets.

The presence of homogeneous product needs across markets, which reduces the requirement of customizing the product for each market. The presence of a small group of global competitors.

A low level of trade regulation and of regulation regarding foreign direction investment.[2]

---

[2] G. Harvel and C. K. Prahalad, "Managing Strategic Responsibility in the MNC," *Strategic Management Journal,* October–December 1983, pp. 341–51.

**EXHIBIT 4–8**
**Factors That Drive Global Companies**

Source: Robert N. Lussier, Robert W. Baeder, and Joel Corman, "Measuring Global Practices: Global Strategic Planning through Company Situational Analysis," p. 57. Reprinted from *Business Horizons,* September–October 1994. Copyright 1994 by the Foundation for the School of Business at Indiana University. Used with permission.

### 1. Global Management Team

Possesses global vision and culture.
Includes foreign nationals.
Leaves management of subsidiaries to foreign nationals.
Frequently travels internationally.
Has cross-cultural training.

### 2. Global Strategy

Implement strategy as opposed to independent country strategies.
Develop significant cross-country alliances.
Select country targets strategically rather than opportunistically.
Perform business functions where most efficient—no home-country bias.
Emphasize participation in the triad—North America, Europe, and Japan.

### 3. Global Operations and Products

Use common core operating processes worldwide to ensure quantity and uniformity.
Product globally to obtain best cost and market advantage.

### 4. Global Technology and R&D

Design global products but take regional differences into account.
Manage development work centrally but carry out globally.
Do not duplicate R&D and product development; gain economies of scale.

### 5. Global Financing

Finance globally to obtain lowest cost.
Hedge when necessary to protect currency risk.
Price in local currencies.
List shares on foreign exchanges.

### 6. Global Marketing

Market global products but provide regional discretion if economies of scale are not affected.
Develop global brands.
Use core global marketing practices and themes.
Simultaneously introduce new global products worldwide.

Six factors that drive the success of global companies are listed in Exhibit 4–8. They address key aspects of globalizing a business's operations and provide a framework within which companies can effectively pursue the global marketplace.

## The Global Challenge

Although industries can be characterized as global or multidomestic, few "pure" cases of either type exist. A global firm competing in a global industry must be responsive, to some degree, to local market conditions. Similarly, a global firm competing in a multidomestic industry cannot totally ignore opportunities to utilize intracorporate resources in competitive positioning. Thus, each global firm must decide which of its corporate functional activities should be performed where and what degree of coordination should exist among them.

### *Location and Coordination of functional activities*

Typical functional activities of a firm include purchases of input resources, operations, research and development, marketing and sales, and after-sales service. A multinational corporation has a wide range of possible location options for each of these activities and must

**EXHIBIT 4–9**
**Location and
Coordination Issues
of Functional
Activities**

Source: Copyright © 1986, by
The Regents of the University
of California. Reprinted from
the California Management
Review, Vol. 28, No. 2. By
permission of The Regents.

| Functional Activity | Location Issues | Coordination Issues |
|---|---|---|
| Operations | Location of production facilities for components. | Networking of international plants. |
| Marketing | Product line selection. Country (market) selection. | Commonality of brand name worldwide. |
| | | Coordination of sales to multinational accounts. |
| | | Similarity of channels and product positioning worldwide. |
| | | Coordination of pricing in different countries. |
| Service | Location of service organization. | Similarity of service standards and procedures worldwide. |
| Research and development | Number and location of R&D centers. | Interchange among dispersed R&D centers. |
| | | Developing products responsive to market needs in many countries. |
| | | Sequence of product introductions around the world. |
| Purchasing | Location of the purchasing function. | Managing suppliers located in different countries. |
| | | Transferring market knowledge. |
| | | Coordinating purchases of common items. |

decide which sets of activities will be performed in how many and which locations. A multinational corporation may have each location perform each activity, or it may center an activity in one location to serve the organization worldwide. For example, research and development centered in one facility may serve the entire organization.

A multinational corporation also must determine the degree to which functional activities are to be coordinated across locations. Such coordination can be extremely low, allowing each location to perform each activity autonomously, or extremely high, tightly linking the functional activities of different locations. Coca-Cola tightly links its R&D and marketing functions worldwide to offer a standardized brand name, concentrate formula, market positioning, and advertising theme. However, its operations function is more autonomous, with the artificial sweetener and packaging differing across locations.

### Location and Coordination Issues

Exhibit 4–9 presents some of the issues related to the critical dimensions of location and coordination in multinational strategic planning. It also shows the functional activities that the firm performs with regard to each of these dimensions. For example, in connection with the service function, a firm must decide where to perform after-sale service and whether to standardize such service.

How a particular firm should address location and coordination issues depends on the nature of its industry and on the type of international strategy that the firm is pursuing. As discussed earlier, an industry can be ranked along a continuum that ranges between multidomestic at one extreme and global at the other. Little coordination of functional

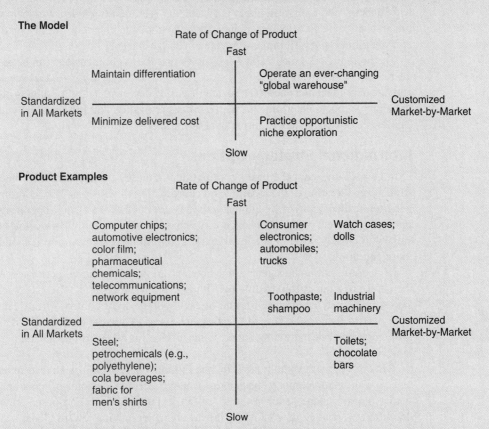

**The Model**

Rate of Change of Product

Fast

Maintain differentiation | Operate an ever-changing "global warehouse"

Standardized in All Markets ——————————————————— Customized Market-by-Market

Minimize delivered cost | Practice opportunistic niche exploration

Slow

**Product Examples**

Rate of Change of Product

Fast

Computer chips; automotive electronics; color film; pharmaceutical chemicals; telecommunications; network equipment | Consumer electronics; automobiles; trucks | Watch cases; dolls

Toothpaste; shampoo | Industrial machinery

Standardized in All Markets ——————————————————— Customized Market-by-Market

Steel; petrochemicals (e.g., polyethylene); cola beverages; fabric for men's shirts | Toilets; chocolate bars

Slow

**Source:** Lawrence H. Wortzel, *1989 International Business Resource Book* (Strategic Direction Publishers, 1989).

activities across countries may be necessary in a multidomestic industry, since competition occurs within each country in such an industry. However, as its industry becomes increasingly global, a firm must begin to coordinate an increasing number of functional activities to effectively compete across countries.

Going global impacts every aspect of a company's operations and structure. As firms redefine themselves as global competitors, workforces are becoming increasingly diversified. The most significant challenge for firms, therefore, is the ability to adjust to a workforce of varied cultures and lifestyles and the capacity to incorporate cultural differences to the benefit of the company's mission.

## Market Requirements and Product Characteristics

Businesses have discovered that being successful in foreign markets often demands much more than simply shipping their well-received domestic products overseas. Firms must assess two key dimensions of customer demand: customers' acceptance of standardized products and the rate of product innovation desired. As shown in the top figure of Exhibit 4–10, Global Strategy in Action, all markets can be arrayed along a continuum from markets in which products are standardized to markets in which products must be customized for customers from market to market. Standardized products in all markets include color film and petrochemicals, while dolls and toilets are good examples of customized products.

Similarly, products can be arrayed along a continuum from products that are not subject to frequent product innovations to products that are often upgraded. Products with a fast rate of change include computer chips and industrial machinery, while steel and chocolate bars are products that fit in the slow rate of change category.

The bottom figure of Exhibit 4–10 shows that the two dimensions can be combined to enable companies to simultaneously assess both customer need for product standardization and rate of product innovation. The examples listed demonstrate the usefulness of the model in helping firms to determine the degree of customization that they must be willing to accept to become engaged in transnational operations.

## International Strategy Options

Exhibit 4–11 presents the basic multinational strategy options that have been derived from a consideration of the location and coordination dimensions. Low coordination and geographic dispersion of functional activities are implied if a firm is operating in a multidomestic industry and has chosen a country-centered strategy. This allows each subsidiary to closely monitor the local market conditions it faces and to respond freely to these conditions.

High coordination and geographic concentration of functional activities result from the choice of a pure global strategy. Although some functional activities, such as after-sale service, may need to be located in each market, tight control of those activities is necessary to ensure standardized performance worldwide. For example, IBM expects the same high level of marketing support and service for all of its customers, regardless of their location.

Two other strategy options are shown in Exhibit 4–11. High foreign investment with extensive coordination among subsidiaries would describe the choice of remaining at a particular growth stage, such as that of an exporter. An export-based strategy with decentralized marketing would describe the choice of moving toward globalization, which a multinational firm might make.

**EXHIBIT 4–11**
**International Strategy Options**

Source: Copyright © 1986, by The Regents of the University of California. Reprinted from the California Management Review, Vol. 28, No. 2. By permission of The Regents.

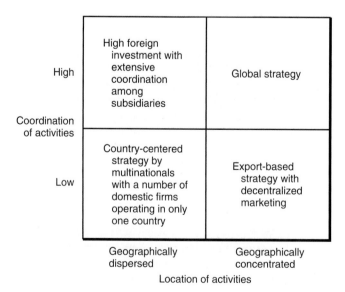

# COMPETITIVE STRATEGIES FOR FIRMS IN FOREIGN MARKETS

Strategies for firms that are attempting to move toward globalization can be categorized by the degree of complexity of each foreign market being considered and by the diversity in a company's product line (see Exhibit 4–12). *Complexity* refers to the number of critical success factors that are required to prosper in a given competitive arena. When a firm must consider many such factors, the requirements of success increase in complexity. *Diversity,* the second variable, refers to the breadth of a firm's business lines. When a company offers many product lines, diversity is high.

Together, the complexity and diversity dimensions form a continuum of possible strategic choices. Combining these two dimensions highlights many possible actions.

## Niche Market Exporting

The primary niche market approach for the company that wants to export is to modify select product performance or measurement characteristics to meet special foreign demands. Combining product criteria from both the U.S. and the foreign markets can be slow and tedious. There are, however, a number of expansion techniques that provide the U.S. firm with the know-how to exploit opportunities in the new environment. For example, copying product innovations in countries where patent protection is not emphasized and utilizing nonequity contractual arrangements with a foreign partner can assist in rapid product innovation. N. V. Philips and various Japanese competitors, such as Sony and Matsushita, now are working together for common global product standards within their markets. Siemens, with a centralized R&D in electronics, also has been very successful with this approach.

As described in Exhibit 4–13, Global Strategy in Action, the Taiwanese company, Gigabyte, researched the U.S. market and found that a sizable number of computer buyers wanted a PC that could complete the basic tasks provided by domestic desktops, but that would be considerably smaller. Gigabyte decided to serve this niche market by exporting their mini-PCs into the United States with a price tag of $200 to $300. This price was considerably less than the closest U.S. manufacturer, Dell, whose minicomputer was still larger and cost $766.

**EXHIBIT 4–12**
**International
Strategy Options**

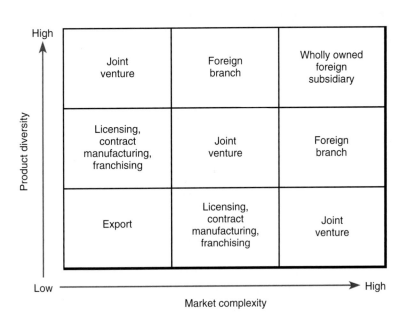

**BusinessWeek** Gigabyte rolled out its first mini-PC, a no-frills computer for word processing, accessing the Web, and playing CD-ROMs and DVDs. It could not be upgraded, but the price was right. Depending on features, the mini-PC sold for between $200 and $300, said Alonzo Cardenas, vice-president for marketing and business development at Gigabyte-USA. That was a lot less than the $1,100 for a typical consumer desktop, and it came at a time when many buyers were no longer entranced by fancy bells and whistles.

What lots of customers wanted was a smaller box. As the mini-PC name suggested, the box containing the processor occupied 30 percent less space than a standard desktop. Saving space also appealed to consumers, who have shown a willingness to pay extra for smaller PCs that boasted all the features of high-end models but could fit on the VCR shelf of their entertainment centers. That was an opportunity for Gigabyte and other newcomers.

By some accounts, the market for smaller PCs exploded. In the United States alone, sales growth had been up as much as 50 percent a month. It had been estimated that by 2008, mini-models should account for more than 50 percent of all desktops sold. That would be a huge market considering that 75 percent of the 128 million PCs shipped worldwide in 2001 were desktops, according to market consultancy Gartner Dataquest.

Major manufacturers started to notice. Dell, which held 25 percent of the corporate desktop market, introduced its most diminutive desktop, the OptiPlex SX260. About 50 percent smaller than its predecessor (but still bigger than Gigabyte's model), it weighed eight pounds and could be mounted vertically or horizontally. Unlike the Taiwanese makers, Dell had retained PC-level power. The downside was that Dell's cheapest mini-PC still cost a not-so-mini $766. Still, prices on the biggest players' mini-PCs and Media Centers remained high compared with what newcomers like Gigabyte were charging.

**Source:** Extracted from Olga Kharif, "Can Mini-PC's Mean Maxi Profits?" *BusinessWeek Online,* January 23, 2003.

Exporting usually requires minimal capital investment. The organization maintains its quality control standards over production processes and finished goods inventory, and risk to the survival of the firm is typically minimal. Additionally, the U.S. Commerce Department through its Export Now Program and related government agencies lowers the risks to smaller companies by providing export information and marketing advice.

## Licensing/Contract Manufacturing

Establishing a contractual arrangement is the next step for U.S. companies that want to venture beyond exporting but are not ready for an equity position on foreign soil. Licensing involves the transfer of some industrial property right from the U.S. licensor to a motivated licensee. Most tend to be patents, trademarks, or technical know-how that are granted to the licensee for a specified time in return for a royalty and for avoiding tariffs or import quotas. Bell South and U.S. West, with various marketing and service competitive advantages valuable to Europe, have extended a number of licenses to create personal computer networks in the United Kingdom.

Another licensing strategy open to U.S. firms is to contract the manufacturing of its product line to a foreign company to exploit local comparative advantages in technology, materials, or labor.

U.S. firms that use either licensing option will benefit from lowering the risk of entry into the foreign markets. Clearly, alliances of this type are not for everyone. They are used best in companies large enough to have a combination of international strategic activities and for firms with standardized products in narrow margin industries.

Two major problems exist with licensing. One is the possibility that the foreign partner will gain the experience and evolve into a major competitor after the contract expires. The experience of some U.S. electronics firms with Japanese companies shows that licensees gain the potential to become powerful rivals. The other potential problem stems from the control that the licensor forfeits on production, marketing, and general distribution of its products. This loss of control minimizes a company's degrees of freedom as it reevaluates its future options.

## Franchising

A special form of licensing is franchising, which allows the franchisee to sell a highly publicized product or service, using the parent's brand name or trademark, carefully developed procedures, and marketing strategies. In exchange, the franchisee pays a fee to the parent company, typically based on the volume of sales of the franchisor in its defined market area. The franchise is operated by the local investor who must adhere to the strict policies of the parent.

Franchising is so popular that an estimated 500 U.S. businesses now franchise to over 50,000 local owners in foreign countries. Among the most active franchisees are Avis, Burger King, Canada Dry, Coca-Cola, Hilton, Kentucky Fried Chicken, Manpower, Marriott, Midas, Muzak, Pepsi, and Service Master. However, the acknowledged global champion of franchising is McDonald's, which has 70 percent of its company-owned stores as franchisees in foreign nations.

## Joint Ventures

As the multinational strategies of U.S. firms mature, most will include some form of joint venture (JV) with a target nation firm. AT&T followed this option in its strategy to produce its own personal computer by entering into several joint ventures with European producers to acquire the required technology and position itself for European expansion. Because JVs begin with a mutually agreeable pooling of capital, production or marketing equipment, patents, trademarks, or management expertise, they offer more permanent cooperative relationships than export or contract manufacturing.

Compared with full ownership of the foreign entity, JVs provide a variety of benefits to each partner. U.S. firms without the managerial or financial assets to make a profitable independent impact on the integrated foreign markets can share management tasks and cash requirements often at exchange rates that favor the dollar. The coordination of manufacturing and marketing allows ready access to new markets, intelligence data, and reciprocal flows of technical information.

For example, Siemens, the German electronics firm, has a wide range of strategic alliances throughout Europe to share technology and research developments. For years, Siemens grew by acquisitions, but now, to support its horizontal expansion objectives, it is engaged in joint ventures with companies like Groupe Bull of France, International Computers of Britain, General Electric Company of Britain, IBM, Intell, Philips, and Rolm. Another example is Airbus Industries, which produces wide-body passenger planes for the world market as a direct result of JVs among many companies in Britain, France, Spain, and Germany.

JVs speed up the efforts of U.S. firms to integrate into the political, corporate, and cultural infrastructure of the foreign environment, often with a lower financial commitment than acquiring a foreign subsidiary. General Electric's (GE) 3 percent share in the European lighting market was very weak and below expectations. Significant increases in competition throughout many of their American markets by the European giant, Philips Lighting, forced GE to retaliate by expanding in Europe. GE's first strategy was an attempted joint venture with the Siemens lighting subsidiary, Osram, and with the British electronics firm, Thorn EMI. Negotiations failed over control issues. When recent events in Eastern Europe opened the opportunity for a JV with the Hungarian lighting manufacturer, Tungsram, which was receiving 70 percent of revenues from the West, GE capitalized on it.

Although joint ventures can address many of the requirements of complex markets and diverse product lines, U.S. firms considering either equity- or nonequity-based JVs face many challenges. For example, making full use of the native firm's comparative advantage may involve managerial relationships where no single authority exists to make strategic decisions or solve conflicts. Additionally, dealing with host-company management requires the disclosure of proprietary information and the potential loss of control over production and marketing quality standards. Addressing such challenges with well-defined covenants agreeable to all parties is difficult. Equally important is the compatibility of partners and their enduring commitments to mutually supportive goals. Without this compatibility and commitment, a joint venture is critically endangered.

## Foreign Branching

A foreign branch is an extension of the company in its foreign market—a separately located strategic business unit directly responsible for fulfilling the operational duties assigned to it by corporate management, including sales, customer service, and physical distribution. Host countries may require that the branch be "domesticated", that is, have some local managers in middle and upper-level positions. The branch most likely will be outside any U.S. legal jurisdiction, liabilities may not be restricted to the assets of the given branch, and business licenses for operations may be of short duration, requiring the company to renew them during changing business regulations.

## Wholly Owned Subsidiaries

Wholly owned foreign subsidiaries are considered by companies that are willing and able to make the highest investment commitment to the foreign market. These companies insist on full ownership for reasons of control and managerial efficiency. Policy decisions about local product lines, expansion, profits, and dividends typically remain with the U.S. senior managers.

Fully owned subsidiaries can be started either from scratch or by acquiring established firms in the host country. U.S. firms can benefit significantly if the acquired company has complementary product lines or an established distribution or service network.

U.S. firms seeking to improve their competitive postures through a foreign subsidiary face a number of risks to their normal mode of operations. First, if the high capital investment is to be rewarded, managers must attain extensive knowledge of the market, the host nation's language, and its business culture. Second, the host country expects both a long-term commitment from the U.S. enterprise and a portion of their nationals to be employed in positions of management or operations. Fortunately, hiring or training foreign managers for leadership positions is commonly a good policy, since they are close to both the market and contacts. This is especially important for smaller firms when markets are regional. Third, changing standards mandated by foreign regulations may eliminate a company's protected market niche. Product design and worker protection liabilities also may extend back to the home office.

The strategies shown in Exhibit 4–12 are not exhaustive. For example, a firm may engage in any number of joint ventures while maintaining an export business. Additionally, there are a number of other strategies that a firm should consider before deciding on its long-term approach to foreign markets. These will be discussed in detail in Chapter 6 under the topic of grand strategies. However, the strategies discussed in this chapter provide the most popular starting points for planning the globalization of a firm.

## Summary

To understand the strategic planning options available to a corporation, its managers need to recognize that different types of industry-based competition exist. Specifically, they must identify the position of their industry along the global versus multidomestic continuum and then consider the implications of that position for their firm.

The differences between global and multidomestic industries about the location and coordination of functional corporate activities necessitate differences in strategic emphasis. As an industry becomes global, managers of firms within that industry must increase the coordination and concentration of functional activities.

Appendix 4 at the end of this chapter lists many components of the environment with which global corporations must contend. This list is useful in understanding the issues that confront global corporations and in evaluating the thoroughness of global corporation strategies.

As a starting point for global expansion, the firm's mission statement needs to be reviewed and revised. As global operations fundamentally alter the direction and strategic capabilities of a firm, its mission statement, if originally developed from a domestic perspective, must be globalized.

The globalized mission statement provides the firm with a unity of direction that transcends the divergent perspectives of geographically dispersed managers. It provides a basis for strategic decisions in situations where strategic alternatives may appear to conflict. It promotes corporate values and commitments that extend beyond single cultures and satisfies the demands of the firm's internal and external claimants in different countries. Finally, it ensures the survival of the global corporation by asserting the global corporation's legitimacy with respect to support coalitions in a variety of operating environments.

Movement of a firm toward globalization often follows a systematic pattern of development. Commonly, businesses begin their foreign nation involvements progressively through niche market exporting, license-contract manufacturing, franchising, joint ventures, foreign branching, and foreign subsidiaries.

## Questions for Discussion

1. How does environmental analysis at the domestic level differ from global analysis?

2. Which factors complicate environmental analysis at the global level? Which factors are making such analysis easier?

3. Do you agree with the suggestion that soon all industries will need to evaluate global environments?

4. Which industries operate almost devoid of global competition? Which inherent immunities do they enjoy?

## Chapter 4 Discussion Case

BusinessWeek

# Planet Starbucks:
# To Keep up the Growth, It Must Go Global Quickly

1   The Starbucks coffee shop on Sixth Avenue and Pine Street in downtown Seattle sits serene and orderly, as unremarkable as any other in the chain bought 15 years ago by entrepreneur Howard Schultz. A little less than three years ago, however, the quiet storefront made front pages around the world. During the World Trade Organization talks in November, 1999, protesters flooded Seattle's streets, and among their targets was Starbucks, a symbol, to them, of free-market capitalism run amok, another multinational out to blanket the earth. Amid the crowds of protesters and riot police were black-masked anarchists who trashed the store, leaving its windows smashed and its tasteful green-and-white decor smelling of tear gas instead of espresso. Says an angry Schultz: "It's hurtful. I think people are ill-informed. It's very difficult to protest against a can of Coke, a bottle of Pepsi, or a can of Folgers. Starbucks is both this ubiquitous brand and a place where you can go and break a window. You can't break a can of Coke."

2   The store was quickly repaired, and the protesters have scattered to other cities. Yet cup by cup, Starbucks really is caffeinating the world, its green-and-white emblem beckoning to consumers on three continents. In 1999, Starbucks Corp. had 281 stores abroad. Today, it has about 1,200—and it's still in the early stages of a plan to colonize the globe. If the protesters were wrong in their tactics, they weren't wrong about Starbucks' ambitions. They were just early.

3   The story of how Schultz & Co. transformed a pedestrian commodity into an up-scale consumer accessory has a fairy-tale quality. Starbucks has grown from 17 coffee shops in Seattle 15 years ago to 5,689 outlets in 28 countries. Sales have climbed an average of 20 percent annually since the company went public 10 years ago, to $2.6 billion in 2001, while profits bounded ahead an average of 30 percent per year, hitting $181.2 million last year. And the momentum continues. In the first three quarters of this fiscal year, sales climbed 24 percent, year to year, to $2.4 billion, while profits, excluding onetime charges and capital gains, rose 25 percent, to $159.5 million.

4   Moreover, the Starbucks name and image connect with millions of consumers around the globe. It was one of the fastest-growing brands in a *BusinessWeek* survey of the to100 global brands published Aug. 5. At a time when one corporate star after another has crashed to earth, brought down by revelations of earnings misstatements, executive greed, or worse, Starbucks hasn't faltered: The company confidently predicts up to 25 percent annual sales and earnings growth this year. On Wall Street, Starbucks is the last great growth story. Its stock, including four splits, has soared more than 2,200 percent over the past decade, surpassing Wal-Mart, General Electric, PepsiCo, Coca-Cola, Microsoft, and IBM in total return. Now at $21, it is hovering near its all-time high of $23 in July, before the overall market drop.

5   And after a slowdown last fall and winter, when consumers seemed to draw inward after September 11, Starbucks is rocketing ahead once again. Sales in stores open at least 13 months grew by 6 percent in the 43 weeks through July 28, and the company predicts monthly same-store sales gains as high as 7 percent through the end of this fiscal year. That's below the 9 percent growth rate in 2000, but investors seem encouraged. "We're going to see a lot more growth," says Jerome A. Castellini, president of Chicago-based CastleArk Management, which controls about 300,000 Starbucks shares. "The stock is on a run."

6   But how long can that run last? Already, Schultz's team is hard-pressed to grind out new profits in a home market that is quickly becoming saturated. Amazingly, with 4,247 stores scattered across the U.S. and Canada, there are still eight states in the U.S. with no Starbucks stores. Frappuccino-free cities include Butte, Mont., and Fargo, N. D. But big cities, affluent suburbs, and shopping malls are full to the brim. In coffee-crazed Seattle, there is a Starbucks outlet for every 9,400 people, and the company considers that the upper limit of coffee-shop saturation. In Manhattan's 24 square miles, Starbucks has 124 cafés, with four more on the way this year. That's one for every 12,000 people— meaning that there could be room for even more stores. Given such concentration, it is likely to take annual

same-store sales increases of 10 percent or more if the company is going to match its historic overall sales growth. That, as they might say at Starbucks, is a tall order to fill.

7   Indeed, the crowding of so many stores so close together has become a national joke, eliciting quips such as this headline in *The Onion,* a satirical publication: "A New Starbucks Opens in Rest-room of Existing Starbucks." And even the company admits that while its practice of blanketing an area with stores helps achieve market dominance, it can cut sales at existing outlets. "We probably self-cannibalize our stores at a rate of 30 percent a year," Schultz says: Adds Lehman Brothers Inc. analyst Mitchell Speiser. "Starbucks is at a defining point in its growth. It's reaching a level that makes it harder and harder to grow, just due to the law of large numbers."

8   To duplicate the staggering returns of its first decade, Starbucks has no choice but to export its concept aggressively. Indeed, some analysts give Starbucks only two years at most before it saturates the U.S. market. The chain now operates 1,200 international outlets, from Beijing to Bristol. That leaves plenty of room to grow. Indeed, about 400 of its planned 1,200 new stores this year will be built overseas, representing a 35 percent increase in its foreign base. Starbucks expects to double the number of its stores worldwide, to 10,000 in three years. During the past 12 months, the chain has opened stores in Vienna, Zurich, Madrid, Berlin, and even in far-off Jakarta. Athens comes next. And within the next year, Starbucks plans to move into Mexico and Puerto Rico. But global expansion poses huge risks for Starbucks. For one thing, it makes less money on each overseas store because most of them are operated with local partners. While that makes it easier to start up on foreign turf, it reduces the company's share of the profits to only 20 percent to 50 percent.

9   Moreover Starbucks must cope with some predictable challenges of becoming a mature company in the U.S. After riding the wave of successful baby boomers through the '90s, the company faces an ominously hostile reception from its future consumers, the twenty- or thirtysomethings of Generation X. Not only are the activists among them turned off by the power and image of the well-known brand, but many others say that Starbucks' latte-sipping sophisticates and piped-in Kenny G music are a real turn-off. They don't feel wanted in a place that sells designer coffee at $3 a cup.

10   Even the thirst of loyalists for high-price coffee can't be taken for granted. Starbucks' growth over the past decade coincided with a remarkable surge in the economy. Consumer spending has continued strong in the downturn, but if that changes, those $3 lattes might be an easy place for people on a budget to cut back. Starbucks executives insist that won't happen, pointing out that even in the weeks following the terrorist attacks, same-store comparisons stayed positive while those of other retailers skidded.

11   Starbucks also faces slumping morale and employee burnout among its store managers and its once cheery army of *baristas.* Stock options for part-timers in the restaurant business was a Starbucks innovation that once commanded awe and respect from its employees. But now, though employees are still paid better than comparable workers elsewhere— about $7 per hour—many regard the job as just another fast-food gig. Dissatisfaction over odd hours and low pay is affecting the quality of the normally sterling service and even the coffee itself, say some customers and employees. Frustrated store managers among the company's roughly 470 California stores sued Starbucks in 2001 for allegedly refusing to pay legally mandated overtime. Starbucks settled the suit for $18 million this past April, shaving $0.03 per share off an otherwise strong second quarter.

12   However, the heart of the complaint—feeling overworked and underappreciated—doesn't seem to be going away.

To be sure, Starbucks has a lot going for it as it confronts the challenge of maintaining its growth. Nearly free of debt, it fuels expansion with internal cash flow. And Starbucks can maintain a tight grip on its image because stores are company-owned: There are no franchisees to get sloppy about running things. By relying on mystique and word-of-mouth, whether here or overseas, the company saves a bundle on marketing costs. Starbucks spends just $30 million annually on advertising, or roughly 1 percent of revenues, usually just for new flavors of coffee drinks in the summer and product launches, such as its new in-store Web service. Most consumer companies its size shell out upwards of $300 million per year. Moreover, unlike a McDonald's or a Gap Inc., two other retailers that rapidly grew in the U.S., Starbucks has no nationwide competitor.

Starbucks also has a well-seasoned management team. Schultz, 49, stepped down as chief executive in 2000 to become chairman and chief global strategist. Orin Smith, 60, the company's numbers-cruncher, is now CEO and in charge of day-to-day operations. The head of North American operations is Howard Behar, 57, a retailing expert who returned last September, two years after retiring. The management trio is known as H$_2$O, for Howard, Howard, and Orin.

13   Schultz remains the heart and soul of the operation. Raised in a Brooklyn public-housing project, he found his way to Starbucks, a tiny chain of Seattle coffee shops, as a marketing executive in the early '80s. The name came about when the original owners looked to Seattle history for inspiration and chose the moniker of an old mining camp: Starbo. Further refinement led to Starbucks, after the first mate in *Moby-Dick,* which they felt evoked the seafaring romance of the early coffee traders (hence the mermaid logo). Schultz got the idea for the modern Starbucks format while visiting a Milan coffee bar. He bought out his bosses in 1987 and began expanding. Today, Schultz has a net worth of about $700 million, including $400 million of company stock.

14   Starbucks has come light years from those humble beginnings, but Schultz and his team still think there's room to grow in the U.S.—even in communities where the chain already has dozens of stores. Clustering stores increases total revenue and market share, Smith argues, even when individual stores poach on each other's sales. The strategy works, he says, because of Starbucks' size. It is large enough to absorb losses at existing stores as new ones open up, and soon overall sales grow beyond what they would have with just one store. Meanwhile, it's cheaper to deliver to and manage stores located close together. And by clustering, Starbucks can quickly dominate a local market.

15   The company is still capable of designing and opening a store in 16 weeks or less and recouping the initial investment in three years. The stores may be oases of tranquility, but management's expansion tactics are something else. Take what critics call its "predatory real estate" strategy—paying more than market-rate rents to keep competitors out of a location. David C. Schomer, owner of Espresso Vivace in Seattle's hip Capitol Hill neighborhood, says Starbucks approached his landlord and offered to pay nearly double the rate to put a coffee shop in the same building. The landlord stuck with Schomer, who says: "It's a little disconcerting to know that someone is willing to pay twice the going rate." Another time, Starbucks and Tully's Coffee Corp., a Seattle-based coffee chain, were competing for a space in the city. Starbucks got the lease but vacated the premises before the term was up. Still, rather than let Tully's

get the space, Starbucks decided to pay the rent on the empty store so its competitor could not move in. Schultz makes no apologies for the hardball tactics. "The real estate business in America is a very, very tough game," he says. "It's not for the faint of heart."

16   Still, the company's strategy could backfire. Not only will neighborhood activists and local businesses increasingly resent the tactics, but customers could also grow annoyed over having fewer choices. Moreover, analysts contend that Starbucks can maintain about 15 percent square-footage growth in the U.S.— equivalent to 550 new stores—for only about two more years. After that, it will have to depend on overseas growth to maintain annual 20 percent revenue growth.

17   Starbucks was hoping to make up much of that growth with more sales of food and other noncoffee items, but has stumbled somewhat. In the late '90s, Schultz thought that offering $8 sandwiches, desserts, and CDS in his stores and selling packaged coffee in supermarkets would significantly boost sales. The specialty business now accounts for about 16 percent of sales, but growth has been less than expected. A healthy 19 percent this year, it's still far below the 38 percent growth rate of fiscal 2000. That suggests that while coffee can command high prices in a slump, food—at least at Starbucks—cannot. One of Behar's most important goals is to improve that record. For instance, the company now has a test program of serving hot breakfasts in 20 Seattle stores and may move to expand supermarket sales of whole beans.

18   What's more important for the bottom line, though, is that Starbucks has proven to be highly innovative in the way it sells its main course: coffee. In 800 locations it has installed automatic espresso machines to speed up service. And in November, it began offering prepaid Starbucks cards, priced from $5 to $500, which clerks swipe through a reader to deduct a sale. That, says the company, cuts transaction times in half. Starbucks has sold $70 million of the cards.

19   In early August, Starbucks launched Starbucks Express, its boldest experiment yet, which blends java, Web technology, and faster service. At about 60 stores in the Denver area, customers can pre-order and prepay for beverages and pastries via phone or on the Starbucks Express Web site. They just make the call or click the mouse before arriving at the store, and their beverage will be waiting—with their name printed on the cup. The company will decide in January on a national launch.

20    And Starbucks is bent on even more fundamental store changes. On Aug. 21, it announced expansion of a high-speed wireless Internet service to about 1,200 Starbucks locations in North America and Europe. Partners in the project—which Starbucks calls the world's largest Wi-Fi network—include Mobile International, a wireless subsidiary of Deutsche Telekom, and Hewlett-Packard. Customers sit in a store and check e-mail, surf the Web, or download multimedia presentations without looking for connections or tripping over cords. They start with 24 hours of free wireless broadband before choosing from a variety of monthly subscription plans.

21    Starbucks executives hope such innovations will help surmount their toughest challenge in the home market: attracting the next generation of customers. Younger coffee drinkers already feel uncomfortable in the stores. The company knows that because it once had a group of twentysomethings hypnotized for a market study. When their defenses were down, out came the bad news. "They either can't afford to buy coffee at Starbucks, or the only peers they see are those working behind the counter," says Mark Barden, who conducted the research for the Hal Riney & Partners ad agency (now part of Publicis Worldwide) in San Francisco. One of the recurring themes the hypnosis brought out was a sense that "people like me aren't welcome here except to serve the yuppies," he says. Then there are those who just find the whole Starbucks scene a bit pretentious. Katie Kelleher, 22, a Chicago paralegal, is put off by Starbucks' Italian terminology of *grande* and *venti* for coffee sizes. She goes to Dunkin' Donuts, saying: "Small, medium, and large is fine for me."

22    As it expands, Starbucks faces another big risk: that of becoming a far less special place for its employees. For a company modeled around enthusiastic service, that could have dire consequences for both image and sales. During its growth spurt of the mid- to late 1990s, Starbucks had the lowest employee turnover rate of any restaurant or fast-food company, largely thanks to its then unheard-of policy of giving health insurance and modest stock options to part-timers making barely more than minimum wage.

23    Such perks are no longer enough to keep all the workers happy. Starbucks' pay doesn't come close to matching the workload it requires, complain some staff. Says Carrie Shay, a former store manager in West Hollywood, Calif.: "If I were making a decent living, I'd still be there." Shay, one of the plaintiffs in the suit against the company says she earned $32,000 a year to run a store with 10 to 15 part-time employees. She hired employees, managed their schedules, and monitored the store's weekly profit-and-loss statement. But she was also expected to put in significant time behind the counter and had to sign an affidavit pledging to work up to 20 hours of overtime a week without extra, pay—a requirement the company has dropped since the settlement. Smith says that Starbucks offers better pay, benefits, and training than comparable companies, while it encourages promotions from within.

24    For sure, employee discontent is far from the image Starbucks wants to project of relaxed workers cheerfully making cappuccinos. But perhaps it is inevitable. The business model calls for lots of low-wage workers. And the more people who are hired as Starbucks expands, the less they are apt to feel connected to the original mission of high service—bantering with customers and treating them like family. Robert J. Thompson, a professor of popular culture at Syracuse University, says of Starbucks: "It's turning out to be one of the great twenty-first century American success stories—complete with all the ambiguities."

25    Overseas, though, the whole Starbucks package seems new and, to many young people, still very cool. In Vienna, where Starbucks had a gala opening for its first Austrian store last December, Helmut Spudich, a business editor for the paper *Der Standard,* predicted that Starbucks would attract a younger crowd than the established cafés. "The coffeehouses in Vienna are nice, but they are old. Starbucks is considered hip," he says.

26    But if Starbucks can count on its youth appeal to win a welcome in new markets, such enthusiasm cannot be counted on indefinitely. In Japan, the company beat even its own bullish expectations, growing to 368 stores after opening its first in Tokyo in 1996. Affluent young Japanese women like Anna Kato, a 22-year-old Toyota Motor Corp. worker, loved the place. "I don't care if it costs more, as long as it tastes sweet," she says, sitting in the world's busiest Starbucks, in Tokyo's Shibuya district. Yet same-store sales growth has fallen in the past 10 months in Japan, Starbucks' top foreign market, as rivals offer similar fare. Add to that the depressed economy, and Starbucks Japan seems to be losing steam. Although it forecasts a 30 percent gain in net profit, to $8 million, for the year started in April, on record sales of $516 million, same-store sales are down 14 percent for the year ended in June. Meanwhile in England, Starbucks' second-biggest overseas market, with 310

stores, imitators are popping up left and right to steal market share.

27    Entering other big markets may be tougher yet. The French seem to be ready for Starbucks' sweeter taste, says Philippe Bloch, cofounder of Columbus Café, a Starbucks-like chain. But he wonders if the company can profitably cope with France's arcane regulations and generous labor benefits. And in Italy, the epicenter of European coffee culture, the notion that the locals will abandon their own 200,000 coffee bars en masse for Starbucks strikes many as ludicrous. For one, Italian coffee bars prosper by serving food as well as coffee, an area where Starbucks still struggles. Also, Italian coffee is cheaper than U.S. java and, say Italian purists, much better. Americans pay about $1.50 for an espresso. In northern Italy, the price is 67¢; in the south, just 55¢. Schultz insists that Starbucks will eventually come to Italy. It'll have a lot to prove when it does. Carlo Petrini, founder of the antiglobalization movement Slow Food, sniffs that Starbucks' "substances served in styrofoam" won't cut it. The cups are paper, of course. But the skepticism is real.

28    As Starbucks spreads out, Schultz will have to be increasingly sensitive to those cultural challenges. In December, for instance, he flew to Israel to meet with Foreign Secretary Shimon Peres and other Israeli officials to discuss the Middle East crisis. He won't divulge the nature of his discussions. But subsequently, at a Seattle synagogue, Schultz let the Palestinians have it. With Starbucks outlets already in Kuwait, Lebanon, Oman, Qatar, and Saudi Arabia, he created a mild uproar among Palestinian supporters. Schultz quickly backpedaled, saying that his words were taken out of context and asserting that he is "pro-peace" for both sides.

29    There are plenty more minefields ahead. So far, the Seattle coffee company has compiled an envious record of growth. But the giddy buzz of that initial expansion is wearing off. Now, Starbucks is waking up to the grande challenges faced by any corporation bent on becoming a global powerhouse.

*By Stanley Holmes in Seattle, with Drake Bennett in Paris, Kate Carlisle in Rome, and Chester Dawson in Tokyo, with bureau reports.*

**Source:** Drake Bennett, Kate Carlisle, Chester Dawson, and Stanley Holmes, "Planet Starbucks; To Keep Up Growth it Must Go Global Quickly," *BusinessWeek*, September 9, 2002.

# Components of the Multinational Environment

Multinational firms must operate within an environment that has numerous components. These components include:

1. Government, laws, regulations, and policies of home country (United States, for example).
   a. Monetary and fiscal policies and their effect on price trends, interest rates, economic growth, and stability.
   b. Balance-of-payments policies.
      1. Mandatory controls on direct investment.
      2. Interest equalization tax and other policies.
   c. Commercial policies, especially tariffs, quantitative import restrictions, and voluntary import controls.
   d. Export controls and other restrictions on trade.
   e. Tax policies and their impact on overseas business.
   f. Antitrust regulations, their administration, and their impact on international business.
   g. Investment guarantees, investment surveys, and other programs to encourage private investments in less-developed countries.
   h. Export-import and government export expansion programs.
   i. Other changes in government policy that affect international business.
2. Key political and legal parameters in foreign countries and their projection.
   a. Type of political and economic system, political philosophy, national ideology.
   b. Major political parties, their philosophies, and their policies.
   c. Stability of the government.
      1. Changes in political parties.
      2. Changes in governments.
   d. Assessment of nationalism and its possible impact on political environment and legislation.
   e. Assessment of political vulnerability.
      1. Possibilities of expropriation.
      2. Unfavorable and discriminatory national legislation and tax laws.
      3. Labor laws and problems.
   f. Favorable political aspects.
      1. Tax and other concessions to encourage foreign investments.
      2. Credit and other guarantees.
   g. Differences in legal system and commercial law.
   h. Jurisdiction in legal disputes.
   i. Antitrust laws and rules of competition.
   j. Arbitration clauses and their enforcement.
   k. Protection of patents, trademarks, brand names, and other industrial property rights.
3. Key economic parameters and their projection.
   a. Population and its distribution by age groups, density, annual percentage increase, percentage of working age, percentage of total in agriculture, and percentage in urban centers.
   b. Level of economic development and industrialization.
   c. Gross national product, gross domestic product, or national income in real terms and also on a per capita basis in recent years and projections over future planning period.

    *d.* Distribution of personal income.

    *e.* Measures of price stability and inflation, wholesale price index, consumer price index, other price indexes.

    *f.* Supply of labor, wage rates.

    *g.* Balance-of-payments equilibrium or disequilibrium, level of international monetary reserves, and balance-of-payments policies.

    *h.* Trends in exchange rates, currency stability, evaluation of possibility of depreciation of currency.

    *i.* Tariffs, quantitative restrictions, export controls, border taxes, exchange controls, state trading, and other entry barriers to foreign trade.

    *j.* Monetary, fiscal, and tax policies.

    *k.* Exchange controls and other restrictions on capital movements, repatriation of capital, and remission of earnings.

4. Business system and structure.

    *a.* Prevailing business philosophy: mixed capitalism, planned economy, state socialism.

    *b.* Major types of industry and economic activities.

    *c.* Numbers, size, and types of firms, including legal forms of business.

    *d.* Organization: proprietorships, partnerships, limited companies, corporations, cooperatives, state enterprises.

    *e.* Local ownership patterns: public and privately held corporations, family-owned enterprises.

    *f.* Domestic and foreign patterns of ownership in major industries.

    *g.* Business managers available: their education, training, experience, career patterns, attitudes, and reputations.

    *h.* Business associations and chambers of commerce and their influence.

    *i.* Business codes, both formal and informal.

    *j.* Marketing institutions: distributors, agents, wholesalers, retailers, advertising agencies, advertising media, marketing research, and other consultants.

    *k.* Financial and other business institutions: commercial and investment banks, other financial institutions, capital markets, money markets, foreign exchange dealers, insurance firms, engineering companies.

    *l.* Managerial processes and practices with respect to planning, administration, operations, accounting, budgeting, and control.

5. Social and cultural parameters and their projections.

    *a.* Literacy and educational levels.

    *b.* Business, economic, technical, and other specialized education available.

    *c.* Language and cultural characteristics.

    *d.* Class structure and mobility.

    *e.* Religious, racial, and national characteristics.

    *f.* Degree of urbanization and rural-urban shifts.

    *g.* Strength of nationalistic sentiment.

    *h.* Rate of social change.

    *i.* Impact of nationalism on social and institutional change.

# Chapter **Five**

# Internal Analysis

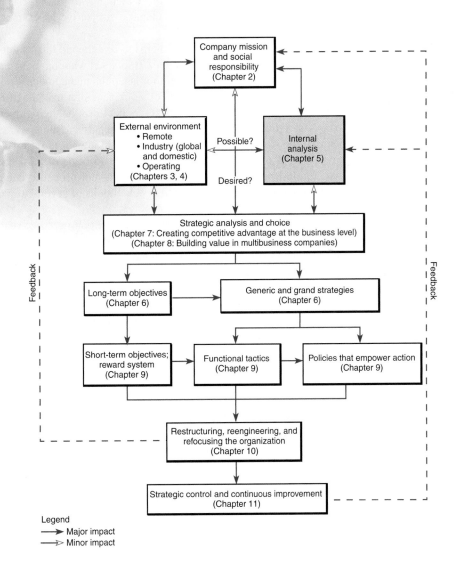

Company mission and social responsibility (Chapter 2)

External environment
• Remote
• Industry (global and domestic)
• Operating
(Chapters 3, 4)

Possible?

Desired?

Internal analysis (Chapter 5)

Strategic analysis and choice
(Chapter 7: Creating competitive advantage at the business level)
(Chapter 8: Building value in multibusiness companies)

Long-term objectives (Chapter 6)

Generic and grand strategies (Chapter 6)

Short-term objectives; reward system (Chapter 9)

Functional tactics (Chapter 9)

Policies that empower action (Chapter 9)

Restructuring, reengineering, and refocusing the organization (Chapter 10)

Strategic control and continuous improvement (Chapter 11)

Feedback

Feedback

Legend
⟶ Major impact
⟶ Minor impact

Three ingredients are critical to the success of a strategy. First, the strategy must be *consistent* with conditions in the competitive environment. Specifically, it must take advantage of existing or projected opportunities and minimize the impact of major threats. Second, the strategy must place *realistic* requirements on the firm's resources. In other words, the firm's pursuit of market opportunities must be based not only on the existence of external opportunities but also on competitive advantages that arise from the firm's key resources. Finally, the strategy must be *carefully executed.* The focus of this chapter is on the second ingredient: *realistic analysis of the firm's resources.*

Managers often do this subjectively, based on intuition and "gut feel." Years of seasoned industry experience positions managers to make sound subjective judgments. But just as often, or more often, this may not be the case. In fast-changing environments, reliance on past experiences can cause management myopia or a tendency to accept the status quo and disregard signals that change is needed. And with managers new to strategic decision making, subjective decisions are particularly suspect. A lack of experience is easily replaced by emotion, narrow functional expertise, and the opinions of others creating the foundation on which newer managers build strategic recommendations. So it is that new managers' subjective assessments often come back to haunt them.

Strategy in Action Exhibit 5–1 helps us understand this "subjective" tendency among both new and experienced managers. It looks at what happened a few years ago at Navistar when CEO John R. Horne admonished his management team to join him in buying their rapidly deteriorating (in price) stock as a sign to Wall Street that they had confidence in their company. Most managers declined, as their subjective sense of the company's situation and resources was quite negative. Some were reported to have even shorted the stock. The CEO acted virtually alone based on his view that several Navistar resources provided potential competitive advantages. Two years later, Navistar stock was up 400 percent. Subjective assessment had probably been holding the company back. It undoubtedly hit hard in the pocketbooks of several key managers that saw their own stock as an unwise investment.

Internal analysis has received increased attention in recent years as being a critical underpinning to effective strategic management. Indeed many managers and writers have adopted a new perspective on understanding firm success based on how well the firm uses its internal resources—the *resource-based view* (RBV) of the firm. This chapter will start with a look at the RBV to provide a useful vocabulary for identifying and examining internal *resources.* The recent recession has seen insightful managers return to the notion of examining their business as a chain of activities that add value by creating the products or services they sell. Associated with this perspective is a powerful concept for introducing rigor and objectivity into internal analysis, the *value chain,* which this chapter will examine in great detail.

Next the chapter looks at ways managers achieve greater objectivity and rigor as they analyze their company's resources and value chain activities. Managers often start their internal analysis with questions like: "How well is the current strategy working? What is our current situation? Or what are our strengths and weaknesses?" Traditional *SWOT analysis* is then presented because it remains an approach that managers frequently use to answer these questions. Finally, objectivity and realism are enhanced when managers use meaningful standards for comparison regardless of the particular analytical framework they employ in internal analysis. We conclude this chapter by examining how managers do this using *past performance, stages of industry evolution, comparison with competitors* or other *"benchmarks," industry norms,* and traditional *financial analysis.*

**BusinessWeek** As it moved toward a new century, things looked bleak for Navistar International Corp. After decades of crippling labor problems and manufacturing snafus, the $6.4 billion Chicago truck and engine maker had suffered another steep earnings slide last year. Then, in a showdown with United Auto Workers members over costs, CEO John R. Horne had been forced to scrap the company's latest truck introduction. Disheartened investors let the stock drop to $9 a share, just 50¢ above its low.

That's when Horne called his 30 top executives into his office to make a personal plea. Looking for a show of faith in the company, he implored all of them to spend their own money to buy as many shares of Navistar stock as they could. Horne knew it was a lot to ask. Over the previous 10 years, the company—once known as International Harvester—had tallied the worst total return to shareholders of all publicly traded U.S. companies. But he was convinced that if his managers bought, Wall Street would see that as a sign that Navistar's fortunes were turning.

Management's reply was a unanimous no. Many felt that Navistar's shares might drop as low as 6, and all 30 backed away. So Horne bit the bullet alone, buying as much as he could for cash and also turning his 401(k) account entirely into Navistar stock. "I couldn't force them because it was their money," he says. "I laugh at them some now."

All the way to the bank, he might add. By late 2001, Navistar's stock hit 40, a blazing 350 percent return to shareholders.

What Horne—a 34-year veteran who became president in 1991 and CEO in 1995—convinced himself about was the presence of key resources that were on the verge of becoming distinctive competencies, and key strengths, at Navistar.

## TANGIBLE ASSET: CLEANEST BURNING DIESEL ENGINE

Navistar's diesel engine business was the first to be worked over. Horne immediately cut the number of engines in production to two, down from 70 in the mid-80s, for example. And by 1994, with Navistar's balance sheet improving, he introduced a new engine.

Navistar's offering, still the cleanest burning model on the market, quickly attracted major truck manufacturers such as Ford Motor Co. Ford puts the engine in vans and pickups and recently on its hot Expedition sport utility vehicle. Thanks largely to this model, Navistar's share of the diesel engine market rose from 25 percent in 1990 to 44 percent in 1998. That's one big reason operating results climbed from a $355 million loss in 1993 to a $349 million profit for the fiscal year ended October 2000.

## TANGIBLE ASSET: EXCESS TRUCK AND ENGINE MANUFACTURING CAPACITY

Horne began a wide-ranging overhaul of Navistar's remaining truck and engine manufacturing lines. He started by drastically slicing the number of products Navistar made. Assembly was rationalized too. While Navistar plants used to build multiple trucks for several different markets, today each one specializes in one type of truck with fewer models.

Tackling problems in Navistar's truck and tractor division proved far tougher. Two years ago, for example, Horne laid out a plan to introduce a new generation of trucks. By simplifying the design of components, Horne hoped to bring out a series of truck and trailer models with interchangeable designs and standardized parts, thus cutting costs while reducing errors on the assembly line. Horne's goal: to reduce the 19 heavy-duty and medium truck designs in his main Springfield (Illinois) plant to one or two.

## ORGANIZATIONAL CAPABILITY: IMPROVED UNION RELATIONS

Before he got that far, Horne ran smack into the problem that has dogged Navistar for more than a decade: He needed significant concessions from the UAW, which represents almost 80 percent of Navistar's truck workers. Horne demanded a wage freeze until 2002 and the flexibility to consolidate production. He took a direct approach. "I showed them the books," he says. "They knew survival of the plants depended on the changes."

Union leaders may have known it, but U.S. union members weren't convinced. They rejected the contract outright. Convinced that he could never achieve his profitability goals without the changes, Horne cancelled the new trucks. He took a $35 million charge and made clear his next step would be to look abroad for lower labor costs. By August 1997, the workers folded their cards and approved the plan. Horne's tough stance has paid off. He quickly revived plans for the new truck. And since the new labor contract and other manufacturing changes went into effect last fall, productivity at U.S. plants has already risen 15 percent.

## ORGANIZATIONAL CAPABILITY: NEW PRODUCT DEVELOPMENT PROCESS

Just as important, Horne got Navistar working on new models again for the first time in years. Having brought out few new products during Navistar's long slide, most of the company's models were aging. But to make sure the new products pay off, Horne also introduced tight financial discipline: Today, new projects only win the nod if they can earn a 17.5 percent return on equity and a 15 percent return on assets through a

*(continued)*

business cycle and be available in 2 years or less. *Popular Science* recognized Navistar's revolutionary camless engine technology as "Best of What's New in 2002."

**INTANGIBLE ASSET: A VISIONARY LEADER WITH STRONG LEADERSHIP SKILLS**

"Horne did a magnificent job," said David Pedowitz, director of research at New York's David J. Greene & Co. brokerage firm, the largest outside investor with a 5 percent stake. "For the first time since the breakup of International Harvester, they're in a position to be a world-class competitor."

In the meantime, Horne continued to spread his penny-pinching gospel. Indeed, though a big basketball fan, he would not buy courtside seats to see his favorite competitor, Washington Wizards' Michael Jordan, in Jordan's final season. When Horne went to a home game, it was always as a guest. He had other things to do with the fortune he's made in Navistar stock. Like reinvest.

**Source:** "Navistar: Gunning the Engines," *BusinessWeek*, February 2, 1998; "Diesels Are the New Thing—Again," *BusinessWeek*, November 13, 2000, and "Up from the Scrap Heap," *Business Week*, July 21, 2003.

# RESOURCE-BASED VIEW OF THE FIRM

Coca-Cola versus Pepsi is a competitive situation virtually all of us recognize. Stock analysts look at the two and frequently conclude that Coke is the clear leader. They cite Coke's superiority in tangible assets (warehouses, bottling facilities, computerization, cash, etc.) and intangible assets (reputation, brand name awareness, tight competitive culture, global business system, etc.). They also mention that Coke leads Pepsi in several capabilities to make use of these assets effectively—managing distribution globally, influencing retailer shelf space allocation, managing franchise bottler relations, marketing savvy, investing in bottling infrastructure, and speed of decision making to take quick advantage of changing global conditions are just a few that are frequently mentioned. The combination of capabilities and assets, most analysts conclude, creates several competencies that give Coke several competitive advantages over Pepsi that are durable and not easily imitated.

The Coke-Pepsi situation provides a useful illustration for understanding several concepts central to the resource-based view (RBV) of the firm. The RBV's underlying premise is that firms differ in fundamental ways because each firm possesses a unique "bundle" of resources—tangible and intangible assets and organizational capabilities to make use of those assets. Each firm develops competencies from these resources and, when developed especially well, these become the source of the firm's competitive advantages. Coke's decision to buy out weak bottling franchisees and regularly invest in or own newer bottling locations worldwide has given Coke a competitive advantage analysts estimate Pepsi will take at least 10 years or longer to match. Coke's strategy for the last 15 years was based in part on the identification of this resource and the development of it into a distinctive competence—a sustained competitive advantage. The RBV is a useful starting point for understanding internal analysis. Let's look at the basic concepts underlying the RBV.

## Three Basic Resources: Tangible Assets, Intangible Assets, and Organizational Capabilities

Executives charting the strategy of their businesses historically concentrated their thinking on the notion of a "core competence." Basically, a core competence was seen as a capability or skill running through a firm's businesses that once identified, nurtured, and deployed throughout the firm became the basis for lasting competitive advantage. Executives, enthusiastic about the notion that their job as strategists was to identify and leverage core competencies, encountered difficulty applying the concept because of the generality of its level of analysis. The RBV emerged as a way to make the core competency concept more focused and measurable—creating a more meaningful internal analysis. Central to the RBV's ability to do this is its notion of three basic types of resources that together create the building blocks for distinctive competencies. They are defined below and illustrated in Exhibit 5–2.

*Tangible assets* are the easiest to identify and are often found on a firm's balance sheet. They include production facilities, raw materials, financial resources, real estate, and computers. Tangible assets are the physical and financial means a company uses to provide value to its customers.

*Intangible assets* are things like brand names, company reputation, organizational morale, technical knowledge, patents and trademarks, and accumulated experience within an organization. While they are not assets that you can touch or see, they are very often critical in creating competitive advantage.

*Organizational capabilities* are not specific "inputs" like tangible or intangible assets; rather, they are the skills—the ability and ways of combining assets, people, and processes—that a company uses to transform inputs into outputs. Dell Computer built its first 10 years of unprecedented growth by creating an organization capable of the speedy and inexpensive manufacture and delivery of custom-built PCs. Gateway and Micron have attempted to copy Dell for most of that time but remain far behind Dell's diverse organizational capabilities. Dell subsequently revolutionized its own "system" using the Internet to automate and customize service, creating a whole new level of organizational capability that combines assets, people, and processes throughout and beyond their organization. Concerning this organizational capability, Michael Dell recently said: "Anyone who tries to go direct now will find it very difficult—like trying to jump over the Grand Canyon." Finely developed capabilities, such as Dell's Internet-based customer-friendly system, can be a source of sustained competitive advantage. They enable a firm to take the same input factors as rivals (like Gateway and Micron) and convert them into products and services, either with greater efficiency in the process or greater quality in the output or both.

## What Makes a Resource Valuable?

Once managers begin to identify their firm's resources, they face the challenge of determining which of those resources represent strengths or weaknesses—which resources generate core competencies that are sources of sustained competitive advantage. This has been a complex task for managers attempting to conduct a meaningful internal analysis. The RBV has addressed this by setting forth some key guidelines that help determine what constitutes a valuable asset, capability, or competence—that is, what makes a resource valuable.

1. **Competitive superiority: Does the resource help fulfill a customer's need better than those of the firm's competitors?** Two restaurants offer similar food, at similar prices, but one has a location much more convenient to downtown offices than the other. The tangible asset, location, helps fulfill daytime workers' lunch eating needs better than its competitor, resulting in greater profitability and sales volume for the conveniently located restaurant. Wal-Mart redefined discount retailing and outperformed the industry in profitability by 4.5 percent of sales—a 200 percent improvement. Four resources—store locations, brand recognition, employee loyalty, and sophisticated

**EXHIBIT 5–2**
**Examples of Different Resources**

Source: R. M. Grant, *Contemporary Strategy Analysis* (Oxford: Blackwell, 2001), p. 140.

| Tangible Assets | Intangible Assets | Organizational Capabilities |
|---|---|---|
| Hampton Inn's reservation system | Budweiser's brand name | Dell Computer's customer service<br>P & G's management training program |
| Ford Motor Company's cash reserves | Dell Computer's reputation | Wal-Mart's purchasing and inbound logistics |
| Georgia Pacific's land holdings | Nike's advertising with LeBron James | Sony's product-development processes |
| Virgin Airlines' plane fleet | Katie Couric as NBC's "Today" host | Coke's global distribution coordination |
| Coca-Cola's Coke formula | IBM's management team<br>Wal-Mart's culture | 3M's innovation process |

**Classifying and Assessing the Firm's Resources**

| Resource | Relevant Characteristics | Key Indicators |
|---|---|---|
| *Tangible Resources*<br>Financial Resources | The firm's borrowing capacity and its internal funds generation determine its resilience and capacity for investment. | • Debt/equity ratio<br>• Operating cash flow/free cash flow<br>• Credit rating |
| Physical Resources | Physical resources constrain the firm's set of production possibilities and impact its cost position. Key characteristics include:<br>• The size, location, technical sophistication, and flexibility of plant and equipment<br>• Location and alternative uses for land and buildings<br>• Reserves of raw materials | • Market values of fixed assets<br>• Vintage of capital equipment<br>• Scale of plants<br>• Flexibility of fixed assets |
| *Intangible Resources*<br>Technological Resources | Intellectual property: patent portfolio, copyright, trade secrets<br>Resources for innovation: research facilities, technical and scientific employees | • Number and significance of patents<br>• Revenue from licensing patents and copyrights<br>• R&D staff as a percent of total employment<br>• Number and location of research facilities |
| Reputation | Reputation with customers through the ownership of brands and trademarks; established relationships with customers; the reputation of the firm's products and services for quality and reliability. The reputation of the company with suppliers (including component suppliers, banks and financiers, employees and potential employees), with government and government agencies, and with the community. | • Brand recognition<br>• Brand equity<br>• Percent of repeat buying<br>• Objective measures of comparative product performance (e.g., Consumers' Association ratings, J. D. Power ratings)<br>• Surveys of corporate reputation (e.g., *BusinessWeek*) |

**EXHIBIT 5–3**
**Wal-Mart's Resource-Based Competitive Advantage**

Source: Pankaj Ghemawat, "Wal-Mart Stores' Discount Operations," Harvard Business School case number 9–387–018.

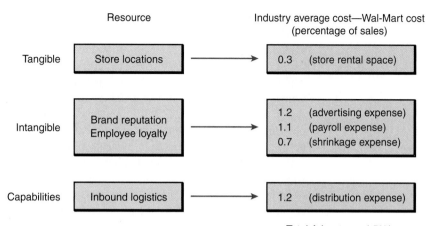

*Wal-Mart's cost advantage as a percent of sales. Each percentage point advantage is worth $500 million in net income to Wal-Mart.

inbound logistics—allowed Wal-Mart to fulfill customer needs much better and more cost effectively than Kmart and other discount retailers, as shown in Exhibit 5–3. In both of these examples, *it is important to recognize that only resources that contributed to competitive superiority were valuable.* At the same time, other resources such as the restaurant's menu and specific products or parking space at Wal-Mart were essential to doing business but contributed little to competitive advantage because they did not distinguish how the firm fulfilled customer needs.

2. **Resource scarcity: Is the resource in short supply?** When it is, it is more valuable. When a firm possesses a resource and few if any others do, and it is central to fulfilling customers' needs, then it becomes a distinctive competence for the firm. The real way resource scarcity contributes value is when it can be sustained over time. To really answer this very basic question we must explore the following questions.

3. **Inimitability: Is the resource easily copied or acquired?** A resource that competitors can readily copy can only generate temporary value. It cannot generate a long-term competitive advantage. When Wendy's first emerged, it was the only major hamburger chain with a drive-through window. This unique organizational capability was part of a "bundle" of resources that allowed Wendy's to provide unique value to its target customers, young adults seeking convenient food service. But once this resource, or organizational capability, proved valuable to fast-food customers, every fast-food chain copied the feature. Then Wendy's continued success was built on other resources that generated other distinctive competencies.

Inimitability doesn't last forever, as the Wendy's example illustrates. Competitors will match or better any resource as soon as they can. It should be obvious, then, that the firm's ability to forestall this eventuality is very important. The RBV identifies four characteristics, called *isolating mechanisms,* that make resources difficult to imitate:

• **Physically unique resources** are virtually impossible to imitate. A one-of-a-kind real estate location, mineral rights, and patents are examples of resources that cannot be imitated. Disney's Mickey Mouse copyright or Winter Park, Colorado's Iron Horse resort possess physical uniqueness. While many strategists claim that resources are physically unique, this is seldom true. Rather, other characteristics are typically what make most resources difficult to imitate.

- **Path-dependent resources** are very difficult to imitate because of the difficult "path" another firm must follow to create the resource. These are resources that cannot be instantaneously acquired but rather must be created over time in a manner that is frequently very expensive and always difficult to accelerate. When Michael Dell said that "anyone who tries to go direct now will find it very difficult—like trying to jump over the Grand Canyon" (see page 151), he was asserting that Dell's system of selling customized PCs direct via the Internet and Dell's unmatched customer service is in effect a path-dependent organizational capability. It would take any competitor years to develop the expertise, infrastructure, reputation, and capabilities necessary to compete effectively with Dell. Coca-Cola's brand name, Gerber Baby Food's reputation for quality, and Steinway's expertise in piano manufacture would take competitors many years and millions of dollars to match. Consumers' many years of experience drinking Coke or using Gerber or playing a Steinway would also need to be matched.

- **Causal ambiguity** is a third way resources can be very difficult to imitate. This refers to situations where it is difficult for competitors to understand exactly how a firm has created the advantage it enjoys. Competitors can't figure out exactly what the uniquely valuable resource is, or how resources are combined to create the competitive advantage. Causally ambiguous resources are often organizational capabilities that arise from subtle combinations of tangible and intangible assets and culture, processes, and organizational attributes the firm possesses. Southwest Airlines has regularly faced competition from major and regional airlines, with some like United and Continental eschewing their traditional approach and attempting to compete by using their own version of the Southwest approach—same planes, routes, gate procedures, number of attendants, and so on. They have yet to succeed. The most difficult thing to replicate is Southwest's "personality," or culture of fun, family, and frugal yet focused services and attitude. Just how that works is hard for United and Continental to figure out.

- **Economic deterrence** is a fourth source of inimitability. This usually involves large capital investments in capacity to provide products or services in a given market that are scale sensitive. It occurs when a competitor understands the resource that provides a competitive advantage and may even have the capacity to imitate, but chooses not to because of the limited market size that realistically would not support two players the size of the first mover.

While we may be inclined to think of a resource's inimitability as a yes-or-no situation, inimitability is more accurately measured on a continuum that reflects difficulty and time. Exhibit 5–4 illustrates such a continuum. Some resources may have multiple imitation deterrents. For example, 3M's reputation for innovativeness may involve path dependencies and causal ambiguity.

    4. **Appropriability: Who actually gets the profit created by a resource?** Warren Buffet is known worldwide as one of the most successful investors of the last 25 years. One of his legendary investments was the Walt Disney Company, which he once said he liked "because the Mouse does not have an agent."[1] What he was really saying was that Disney owned the Mickey Mouse copyright, and all profits from that valuable resource went directly to Disney. Other competitors in the "entertainment" industry generated similar profits from their competing offerings, for example, movies, but they often "captured" substantially less of those profits because of the amounts that had to be paid to well-known actors or directors or other entertainment contributors seen as the real creators of the movie's value.

[1]*The Harbus,* March 25, 1996, p. 12.

**EXHIBIT 5–4**
**Resource Inimitability**

Source: Cynthia A. Montgomery, "Resources: The Essence of Corporate Advantage," Harvard Business School Case N1–792–064.

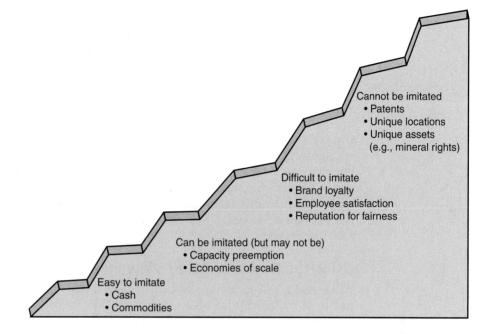

Cannot be imitated
• Patents
• Unique locations
• Unique assets
  (e.g., mineral rights)

Difficult to imitate
• Brand loyalty
• Employee satisfaction
• Reputation for fairness

Can be imitated (but may not be)
• Capacity preemption
• Economies of scale

Easy to imitate
• Cash
• Commodities

Sports teams, investment services, and consulting businesses are other examples of companies that generate sizable profits based on resources (key people, skills, contacts, for example) that are not inextricably linked to the company and therefore do not allow the company to easily capture the profits. Superstar sports players can move from one team to another, or command excessively high salaries, and this circumstance could arise in other personal services business situations. It could also occur when one firm joint ventures with another, sharing resources and capabilities and the profits that result. Sometimes restaurants or lodging facilities that are franchisees of a national organization are frustrated by the fees they pay the franchisor each month and decide to leave the organization and go "independent." They often find, to their dismay, that the business declines significantly. The value of the franchise name, reservation system, and brand recognition is critical in generating the profits of the business.

Bottom line: resources that one develops and controls—where ownership of the resource and its role in value creation is obvious—are more valuable than resources that can be easily bought, sold, or moved from one firm to another. And it is the presence of resources and capabilities that are not easily sold, bought, or moved that create sustained competitive advantage.

5. **Durability: How rapidly will the resource depreciate?** The slower a resource depreciates, the more valuable it is. Tangible assets, like commodities or capital, can have their depletion measured. Intangible resources, like brand names or organizational capabilities, present a much more difficult depreciation challenge. The Coca-Cola brand has continued to appreciate, whereas technical know-how in various computer technologies depreciates rapidly. In the increasingly hypercompetitive global economy of the twenty-first century, distinctive competencies and competitive advantages can fade quickly, making the notion of durability a critical test of the value of key resources and capabilities. Some believe that this reality makes well-articulated visions and associated cultures within organizations potentially the most important contributor to long-term survival.[2]

[2]James C. Collins, *Good to Great: Why Some Companies Make the Leap . . . and Others Don't* (New York: HarperCollins, 2001).

6. **Substitutability: Are other alternatives available?** We discussed the threat of substitute products in Chapter 3 as part of the five forces model for examining industry profitability. This basic idea can be taken further and used to gauge the value of particular resources. DeLite's of America was once a hot IPO as a new fast-food restaurant chain focused exclusively on selling lite food—salads, lean sandwiches, and so on. The basic idea was to offer, in a fast-food format, food low in calories and saturated fat. Investors were very excited about this concept because of the high-calorie, high-fat content of the foods offered by virtually every existing chain. Unfortunately for these investors, several key fast-food players, like Wendy's and later McDonald's, Burger King, and Hardees, adapted their operations to offer salad bars or premade salads and other "lean" sandwich offerings without disrupting their more well known fare. With little change and adaptation of their existing facility and operational resources, these chains quickly created alternatives to DeLite's offerings and the initial excitement about those offerings faded. DeLite's was driven out of business by substitute resources and capabilities rather than substitute products.

## Using the Resource-Based View in Internal Analysis

To use the RBV in internal analysis, a firm must first identify and evaluate its resources to find those that provide the basis for future competitive advantage. This process involves defining the various resources the firm possesses, and examining them based on the above discussion to gauge which resources truly have strategic value. Four final guidelines have proven helpful in this undertaking:

- *Disaggregate resources*—break them down into more specific competencies—rather than stay with broad categorizations. Saying that Domino's Pizza has better marketing skills than Pizza Hut conveys little information. But dividing that into subcategories such as advertising that, in turn, can be divided into national advertising, local promotions, and couponing allows for a more measurable assessment. Exhibit 5–5 provides a useful illustration of this at Whitbread's Restaurant.

- *Utilize a functional perspective.* Looking at different functional areas of the firm, disaggregating tangible and intangible assets as well as organizational capabilities that are present, can begin to uncover important value-building resources and activities that deserve further analysis. Exhibit 5–6 lists a variety of functional area resources and activities that deserve consideration.

- *Look at organizational processes* and combinations of resources and not only at isolated assets or capabilities. While disaggregation is critical, you must also take a creative, gestalt look at what competencies the firm possesses or has the potential to possess that might generate competitive advantage.

- *Use the value chain approach* to uncover organizational capabilities, activities, and processes that are valuable potential sources of competitive advantage. Value chain analysis is discussed starting on page 159.

Although the RBV enables a systematic assessment of internal resources, it is important to stress that a meaningful analysis of those resources best takes place in the context of the firm's competitive environment. Possessing valuable resources will not generate commensurate profits unless resources are applied in an effective product market strategy; they must be deployed in an optimum way and align related activities for the firm to pursue its chosen sources of competitive advantage. Traditional strategy formulation—externally positioning a firm to capitalize on its strengths and opportuni-

**EXHIBIT 5–5**
**Disaggregating Whitbread Restaurant's Customer Service Resource**

Source: Andrew Campbell and Kathleen Sommers-Luchs, *Core Competency-Based Strategy* (London: International Thomson, 1997).

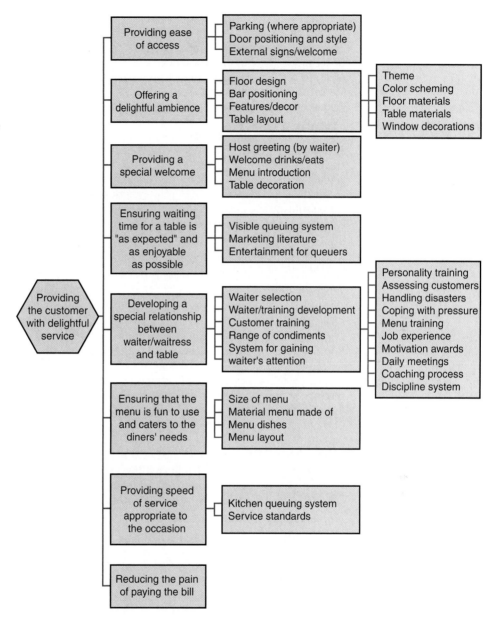

ties and to minimize its threats and weaknesses—remains essential to realizing the competitive advantage envisioned from an RBV of the firm.[3] A subsequent section examines this traditional approach, often called *SWOT analysis,* as a conceptual framework that applies input from the RBV in conducting a sound internal analysis. Before doing so, it is important to understand a second way to look at a firm's capabilities—as components in a value chain of activities.

[3]Jay B. Barney and Asli M. Arikan, "The Resource-Based View: Origins and Implications," in *Handbook of Strategic Management,* Michael A. Hitt, R. Edward Freeman, and Jeffrey S. Harrison, editors (Oxford, UK: Blackwell Publishers, 2001).

**EXHIBIT 5–6**
**Key Resources across Functional Areas**

### Marketing

Firm's products-services: breadth of product line.
Concentration of sales in a few products or to a few customers.
Ability to gather needed information about markets.
Market share or submarket shares.
Product-service mix and expansion potential: life cycle of key products; profit-sales balance in product-service.
Channels of distribution: number, coverage, and control.
Effective sales organization: knowledge of customer needs.
Internet usage.
Product-service image, reputation, and quality.
Imaginativeness, efficiency, and effectiveness of sales promotion and advertising.
Pricing strategy and pricing flexibility.
Procedures for digesting market feedback and developing new products, services, or markets.
After-sale service and follow-up.
Goodwill—brand loyalty.

### Financial and Accounting

Ability to raise short-term capital.
Ability to raise long-term capital; debt-equity.
Corporate-level resources (multibusiness firm).
Cost of capital relative to that of industry and competitors.
Tax considerations.
Relations with owners, investors, and stockholders.
Leverage position; capacity to utilize alternative financial strategies, such as lease or sale and leaseback.
Cost of entry and barriers to entry.
Price-earnings ratio.
Working capital; flexibility of capital structure.
Effective cost control; ability to reduce cost.
Financial size.
Efficiency and effectiveness of accounting system for cost, budget, and profit planning.

### Production, Operations, Technical

Raw materials' cost and availability, supplier relationships.
Inventory control systems; inventory turnover.
Location of facilities; layout and utilization of facilities.
Economies of scale.
Technical efficiency of facilities and utilization of capacity.
Effectiveness of subcontracting use.
Degree of vertical integration; value added and profit margin.
Efficiency and cost-benefit of equipment.
Effectiveness of operation control procedures: design, scheduling, purchasing, quality control, and efficiency.
Costs and technological competencies relative to those of industry and competitors.
Research and development—technology—innovation.
Patents, trademarks, and similar legal protection.

### Personnel

Management personnel.
Employees' skill and morale.
Labor relations costs compared with those of industry and competitors.
Efficiency and effectiveness of personnel policies.

**EXHIBIT 5–6**
*(continued)*

Personnel *(continued)*

Effectiveness of incentives used to motivate performance.
Ability to level peaks and valleys of employment.
Employee turnover and absenteeism.
Specialized skills.
Experience.

**Quality Management**

Relationship with suppliers, customers.
Internal practices to enhance quality of products and services.
Procedures for monitoring quality.

**Information Systems**

Timeliness and accuracy of information about sales, operations, cash, and suppliers.
Relevance of information for tactical decisions.
Information to manage quality issues: customer service.
Ability of people to use the information that is provided.
Linkages to suppliers and customers.

**Organization and General Management**

Organizational structure.
Firm's image and prestige.
Firm's record in achieving objectives.
Organization of communication system.
Overall organizational control system (effectiveness and utilization).
Organizational climate; organizational culture.
Use of systematic procedures and techniques in decision making.
Top-management skill, capabilities, and interest.
Strategic planning system.
Intraorganizational synergy (multibusiness firms).

# VALUE CHAIN ANALYSIS

The term *value chain* describes a way of looking at a business as a chain of activities that transform inputs into outputs that customers value. Customer value derives from three basic sources: activities that differentiate the product, activities that lower its cost, and activities that meet the customer's need quickly. *Value chain analysis* (VCA) attempts to understand how a business creates customer value by examining the contributions of different activities within the business to that value.

VCA takes a process point of view: It divides (sometimes called disaggregates) the business into sets of activities that occur *within the business,* starting with the inputs a firm receives and finishing with the firm's products (or services) and after-sales service to customers. VCA attempts to look at its costs across the series of activities the business performs to determine where low-cost advantages or cost disadvantages exist. It looks at the attributes of each of these different activities to determine in what ways each activity that occurs between purchasing inputs and after-sales service helps differentiate the company's products and services. Proponents of VCA believe it allows managers to better identify their firm's strengths and weaknesses by looking at the business as a process—a chain of activities—of what actually happens in the business rather than simply looking at it based on arbitrary organizational dividing lines or historical accounting protocol.

Exhibit 5–7 shows a typical value chain framework. It divides activities within the firm into two broad categories: primary activities and support activities. *Primary activities*

**EXHIBIT 5–7**

**The Value Chain**

Source: Based on Michael
Porter, On Competition, 1998,
Harvard Business School Press.

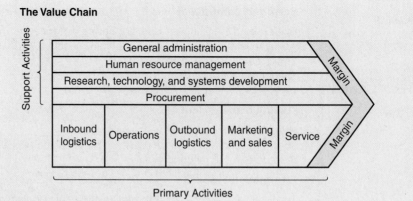

**The Value Chain**

## Primary Activities

- **Inbound Logistics**—Activities, costs, and assets associated with obtaining fuel, energy, raw materials, parts components, merchandise, and consumable items from vendors; receiving, storing, and disseminating inputs from suppliers; inspection; and inventory management.
- **Operations**—Activities, costs, and assets associated with converting inputs into final product form (production, assembly, packaging, equipment maintenance, facilities, operations, quality assurance, environmental protection).
- **Outbound Logistics**—Activities, costs, and assets dealing with physically distributing the product to buyers (finished goods warehousing, order processing, order picking and packing, shipping, delivery vehicle operations).
- **Marketing and Sales**—Activities, costs, and assets related to sales force efforts, advertising and promotion, market research and planning, and dealer/distributor support.
- **Service**—Activities, costs, and assets associated with providing assistance to buyers, such as installation, spare parts delivery, maintenance and repair, technical assistance, buyer inquiries, and complaints.

## Support Activities

- **General Administration**—Activities, costs, and assets relating to general management, accounting and finance, legal and regulatory affairs, safety and security, management information systems, and other "overhead" functions.
- **Human Resources Management**—Activities, costs, and assets associated with the recruitment, hiring, training, development, and compensation of all types of personnel; labor relations activities; development of knowledge-based skills.
- **Research, Technology, and Systems Development**—Activities, costs, and assets relating to product R&D, process R&D, process design improvement, equipment design, computer software development, telecommunications systems, computer-assisted design and engineering, new database capabilities, and development of computerized support systems.
- **Procurement**—Activities, costs, and assets associated with purchasing and providing raw materials, supplies, services, and outsourcing necessary to support the firm and its activities. Sometimes this activity is assigned as part of a firm's inbound logistic purchasing activities.

(sometimes called *line* functions) are those involved in the physical creation of the product, marketing and transfer to the buyer, and after-sale support. *Support activities* (sometimes called *staff* or *overhead* functions) assist the firm as a whole by providing infrastructure or inputs that allow the primary activities to take place on an ongoing basis. The value chain includes a *profit margin* since a markup above the cost of providing a firm's value-adding

**BusinessWeek**

Founder Fred Smith and executives running companies controlled by FedEx say they are planning a monumental shift in the FedEx mission. They are accelerating plans to focus on information systems that track and coordinate packages. They are seeking to "morph" themselves from being a transportation company into an information company.

FedEx already has one of the most heavily used websites on the Internet. Company management claims to have 1,500 in-house programmers writing more software code than almost any other non-software company. To complement package delivery, FedEx designs and operates high-tech warehouses and distribution systems for big manufacturers and retailers around the world. For almost two decades, FedEx has been investing massive amounts to develop software and create a giant digital network. FedEx has built corporate technology campuses around the world, and its electronic systems are directly linked via the Internet or otherwise to over 1 million customers worldwide. That system now allows FedEx to track packages on an hourly basis, but it also allows FedEx to predict future flow of goods and then rapidly refigure the information and logistical network to handle those flows.

"Moving an item from point A to point B is no longer a big deal," say James Barksdale, CEO of Netscape and early architect of FedEx's information strategies. "Having the information about that item, and where it is, and the best way to use it. . . . That is value. The companies that will be big winners will be the ones who can best maximize the value of these information systems." Where FedEx's value has long been built on giant airplanes and big trucks, founder Smith sees a time when it will be built on information, computers, and the allure of the FedEx brand name.

If it works, FedEx's value chain will shrink in areas involved with inbound and outbound operations—taking off and landing on the tarmac—and will expand in areas involved with zapping around the pristine and pilot-free world of cyberspace to manage a client's supply chain and its distribution network.

**Source:** "UPS vs. FedEx: Ground Wars," *BusinessWeek*, May 21, 2001.

---

activities is normally part of the price paid by the buyer—creating value that exceeds cost so as to generate a return for the effort.[4]

Judgment is required across individual firms and different industries because what may be seen as a support activity in one firm or industry may be a primary activity in another. Computer operations might typically be seen as infrastructure support, for example, but may be seen as a primary activity in airlines, newspapers, or banks. Exhibit 5–8, Strategy in Action, describes how Federal Express reconceptualized its company using a value chain analysis that ultimately saw its information support become its primary activity and source of customer value.

## Conducting a Value Chain Analysis

### Identify Activities

The initial step in value chain analysis is to divide a company's operations into specific activities or business processes, usually grouping them similarly to the primary and support activity categories shown in Exhibit 5–7. Within each category, a firm typically performs a number of discrete activities that may represent key strengths or weaknesses. Service activities, for example, may include such discrete activities as installation, repair, parts distribution, and upgrading—any of which could be a major source of competitive advantage or disadvantage. The manager's challenge at this point is to be very detailed attempting to "disaggregate" what actually goes on into numerous distinct, analyzable activities rather than settling for a broad, general categorization.

### Allocate Costs

The next step is to attempt to attach costs to each discrete activity. Each activity in the value chain incurs costs and ties up time and assets. Value chain analysis requires managers to

---

[4]Different "value chain" or value activities may become the focus of value chain analysis. For example, companies using Hammer's *Reengineering the Corporation* might use (1) order procurement, (2) order fulfillment, (3) customer service, (4) product design, and (5) strategic planning plus support activities.

## EXHIBIT 5–9
**The Difference between Traditional Cost Accounting and Activity-Based Cost Accounting**

| Traditional Cost Accounting in a Purchasing Department | | Activity-Based Cost Accounting in the Same Purchasing Department for its "Procurement" Activities | |
| --- | --- | --- | --- |
| Wages and salaries | $175,000 | Evaluate supplier capabilities | $ 67,875 |
| Employee benefits | 57,500 | Process purchase orders | 41,050 |
| Supplies | 3,250 | Expedite supplier deliveries | 11,750 |
| Travel | 1,200 | Expedite internal processing | 7,920 |
| Depreciation | 8,500 | Check quality of items purchased | 47,150 |
| Other fixed charges | 62,000 | Check incoming deliveries against purchase orders | 24,225 |
| Miscellaneous operating expenses | 12,625 | Resolve problems | 55,000 |
| | $320,075 | Internal administration | 65,105 |
| | | | $320,075 |

assign costs and assets to each activity, thereby providing a very different way of viewing costs than traditional cost accounting methods would produce. Exhibit 5–9 helps illustrate this distinction. Both approaches in Exhibit 5–9 tell us that the purchasing department (procurement activities) cost $320,075. The traditional method lets us see that payroll expenses are 73 percent [(175 + 57.5)/320] of our costs with "other fixed charges" the second largest cost, 19 percent [62/320] of the total procurement costs. VCA proponents would argue that the benefit of this information is limited. Their argument might be the following:

> With this information we could compare our procurement costs to key competitors, budgets, or industry averages, and conclude that we are better, worse, or equal. We could then ascertain that our "people" costs and "other fixed charges" cost are advantages, disadvantages, or "in line" with competitors. Managers could then argue to cut people, add people, or debate fixed overhead charges. However, they would get lost in what is really a budgetary debate without ever examining what it is those people do in accomplishing the procurement function, what value that provides, and how cost effective each activity is.

VCA proponents hold that the activity-based VCA approach would provide a more meaningful analysis of the procurement function's costs and consequent value-added. The activity-based side of Exhibit 5–9 shows that approximately 21 percent of the procurement cost or value-added involves evaluating supplier capabilities. A rather sizable cost, 20 percent, involves internal administration, with an additional 17 percent spent resolving problems and almost 15 percent spent on quality control efforts. VCA advocates see this information as being much more useful than traditional cost accounting information, especially when compared to the cost information of key competitors or other "benchmark" companies. VCA supporters might assert the following argument that the benefit of this activity-based information is substantial:

> Rather than analyzing just "people" and "other charges," we are now looking at meaningful categorizations of the work that procurement actually does. We see, for example, that a key value-added activity (and cost) involves "evaluating supplier capabilities." The amount spent on "internal administration" and "resolving problems" seems high, and may indicate a weakness or area for improvement if the other activities' costs are in line and outcomes favorable. The bottom line is that this approach lets us look at what we actually "do" in the business— the specific activities—to create customer value, and that in turn allows more specific internal analysis than traditional, accounting-based cost categories.

***Recognize the Difficulty in Activity-Based Cost Accounting*** It is important to note that existing financial management and accounting systems in many firms are not set up to easily provide activity-based cost breakdowns. Likewise, in virtually all firms, the information requirements to support activity-based cost accounting can create redundant work because of the financial reporting requirements that may force firms to retain the traditional approach for financial statement purposes. The time and energy to change to an activity-based approach can be formidable, and still typically involves arbitrary cost allocation decisions trying to allocate selected asset or people costs across multiple activities in which they are involved. Challenges dealing with a cost-based use of VCA have not deterred use of the framework to identify sources of differentiation. Indeed, conducting a VCA to analyze competitive advantages that differentiate the firm is compatible with the RBV's examination of intangible assets and capabilities as sources of distinctive competence.

### Identify the Activities That Differentiate the Firm

Scrutinizing a firm's value chain may not only reveal cost advantages or disadvantages, it may also bring attention to several sources of differentiation advantage relative to competitors. Dell Computer considers its Internet-based after-sales service (activities) to be far superior to any competitor's. Dell knows it has cost advantage because of the time and expense replicating this activity would take. But Dell considers it an even more important source of value to the customer because of the importance customers place on this activity, which differentiates Dell from many similarly priced competitors. Likewise Federal Express, as we noted earlier, considers its information management skills to have become the core competence and essence of the company because of the value these skills allow FedEx to provide its customers and the importance they in turn place on such skills. Exhibit 5–10 suggests some factors for assessing primary and support activities' differentiation and contribution.

### Examine the Value Chain

Once the value chain has been documented, managers need to identify the activities that are critical to buyer satisfaction and market success. It is those activities that deserve major scrutiny in an internal analysis. Three considerations are essential at this stage in the value chain analysis. First, the company's basic mission needs to influence managers' choice of the activities they examine in detail. If the company is focused on being a low-cost provider, then management attention to lower costs should be very visible; and missions built around commitment to differentiation should find managers spending more on activities that are differentiation cornerstones. Retailer Wal-Mart focuses intensely on costs related to inbound logistics, advertising, and loyalty to build its competitive advantage (see Exhibit 5–3), while Nordstrom builds its distinct position in retailing by emphasizing sales and support activities on which they spend twice the retail industry average. The application of value chain analysis to explore Volkswagen's strategic situation in 2003–2004 is described in Exhibit 5–11, Strategy in Action.

Second, the nature of value chains and the relative importance of the activities within them vary by industry. Lodging firms like Holiday Inn's major costs and concerns involve operational activities—it provides its service instantaneously at each location—and marketing activities, while having minimal concern for outbound logistics. Yet for a distributor, such as the food distributor PYA, inbound and outbound logistics are the most critical area. Major retailers like Wal-Mart have built value advantages focusing on purchasing and inbound logistics while the most successful personal computer companies have built via sales, outbound logistics, and service through the mail order process.

Third, the relative importance of value activities can vary by a company's position in a broader value system that includes the value chains of its upstream suppliers and downstream customers or partners involved in providing products or services to end users. A producer of roofing shingles depends heavily on the downstream activities of wholesale distributors and building supply retailers to reach roofing contractors and do-it-yourselfers.

**EXHIBIT 5–10** Possible Factors for Assessing Sources of Differentiation in Primary and Support Activities

Source: Based on Michael Porter, On Competition, 1998, Harvard Business School Press.

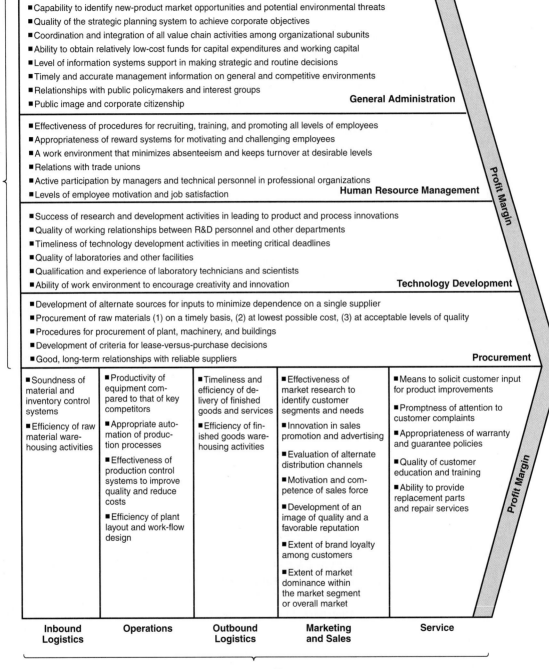

**Support Activities**

■ Capability to identify new-product market opportunities and potential environmental threats
■ Quality of the strategic planning system to achieve corporate objectives
■ Coordination and integration of all value chain activities among organizational subunits
■ Ability to obtain relatively low-cost funds for capital expenditures and working capital
■ Level of information systems support in making strategic and routine decisions
■ Timely and accurate management information on general and competitive environments
■ Relationships with public policymakers and interest groups
■ Public image and corporate citizenship

**General Administration**

■ Effectiveness of procedures for recruiting, training, and promoting all levels of employees
■ Appropriateness of reward systems for motivating and challenging employees
■ A work environment that minimizes absenteeism and keeps turnover at desirable levels
■ Relations with trade unions
■ Active participation by managers and technical personnel in professional organizations
■ Levels of employee motivation and job satisfaction

**Human Resource Management**

■ Success of research and development activities in leading to product and process innovations
■ Quality of working relationships between R&D personnel and other departments
■ Timeliness of technology development activities in meeting critical deadlines
■ Quality of laboratories and other facilities
■ Qualification and experience of laboratory technicians and scientists
■ Ability of work environment to encourage creativity and innovation

**Technology Development**

■ Development of alternate sources for inputs to minimize dependence on a single supplier
■ Procurement of raw materials (1) on a timely basis, (2) at lowest possible cost, (3) at acceptable levels of quality
■ Procedures for procurement of plant, machinery, and buildings
■ Development of criteria for lease-versus-purchase decisions
■ Good, long-term relationships with reliable suppliers

**Procurement**

*Profit Margin*

| Inbound Logistics | Operations | Outbound Logistics | Marketing and Sales | Service |
|---|---|---|---|---|
| ■ Soundness of material and inventory control systems<br><br>■ Efficiency of raw material warehousing activities | ■ Productivity of equipment compared to that of key competitors<br><br>■ Appropriate automation of production processes<br><br>■ Effectiveness of production control systems to improve quality and reduce costs<br><br>■ Efficiency of plant layout and work-flow design | ■ Timeliness and efficiency of delivery of finished goods and services<br><br>■ Efficiency of finished goods warehousing activities | ■ Effectiveness of market research to identify customer segments and needs<br><br>■ Innovation in sales promotion and advertising<br><br>■ Evaluation of alternate distribution channels<br><br>■ Motivation and competence of sales force<br><br>■ Development of an image of quality and a favorable reputation<br><br>■ Extent of brand loyalty among customers<br><br>■ Extent of market dominance within the market segment or overall market | ■ Means to solicit customer input for product improvements<br><br>■ Promptness of attention to customer complaints<br><br>■ Appropriateness of warranty and guarantee policies<br><br>■ Quality of customer education and training<br><br>■ Ability to provide replacement parts and repair services |

*Profit Margin*

**Primary Activities**

# Strategy in Action

## Value Chain Analysis Explains Volkswagen's Reasons for Success and Concern

**Exhibit 5–11**

BusinessWeek Volkswagen CEO Ferdinand Piëch had every reason to feel satisfied. The Austrian engineer and scion of one of Europe's most noted automotive dynasties was less than a year from retirement as chief of the German carmaker. As he looked back, Piëch could boast of one of the great turnarounds in automotive history. Since taking the top job at the Wolfsburg headquarters in 1993, his engineering brilliance had helped resurrect Volkswagen quality and turn models such as the Golf and Passat into all-time best-sellers. Piëch's relaunch of the Beetle cemented VW's hold in the U.S. market. Only VW had successfully revived a communist-era carmaker, Skoda of the Czech Republic. In 2001, as the global car industry lurched through a stressful year, VW saw profits grow above 2000 levels, when they more than doubled, to $1.8 billion, on sales of $76 billion.

Yet Piëch was stressed. Value chain analysis suggested two key value activities had driven his success—product development and operations. It also suggested that two other activities were becoming serious potential drains on the value chain and value he had so meticulously driven—human resource management and marketing and sales.

### PRODUCT DEVELOPMENT

Piëch was driven. Unlike many other auto chiefs, he called the shots on product design and engineering. And if you worked for Dr. Piëch, you had better get it right. In Wolfsburg, executives joked that PEP, the acronym for the product development process *(Produktentwicklungsprozess)* really stands for *Piëch entscheidet persönlich—Piëch* decides himself. And he did so fast. He is said to have sketched out the Audi's all-wheel-drive system on the back of an envelope.

Without question, those achievements have been considerable. Volkswagen's four main brands—VW, Audi, Seat, and Skoda—have taken 19 percent of the European auto market, a gain of some three points in eight years, mostly at the expense of General Motors Corp. and Ford. Not bad for a company that eight years ago suffered from quality problems and a paucity of hit models. In South America, VW vehicles account for one-quarter of car sales, and in China, one-half. The top VW brands in the United States are the Jetta, Passat, and the new Beetle, a remake of the humble bug so beloved of 60s youth. Part of VW success lies in its quirky features. At night, the dashboard instruments the driver looks at, such as the speedometer and clock, light up in red, while those the driver touches, such as the radio, are backlit in blue. "It gives the vehicle some soul, which many of VW's competitors lack horribly," says Wes Brown, a consultant at Nextrend Inc., a Thousand Oaks (Calif.) auto-research firm.

### OPERATIONS

When Piëch wasn't drawing up the plans, he was examining them with a gimlet eye. No screaming, of course: That was not the way for Piëch, an Austrian blueblood. One former transmission-plant manager said Piëch would tour the factory quietly, reviewing production data sheets and zeroing in instantly on any numbers suggesting something was amiss in the manufacturing process. "He's the only person whose very presence on the floor would make my stomach begin to hurt," says this manager.

Terrifying, yet inspiring. Under Piëch's tutelage, VW sweated the small stuff. Check this out, says one rival exec: On VW models, the gap between body panels—say between the front fender and wheel panel—had been cut to 1 millimeter. That puts them in a league with the industry's best.

### HUMAN RESOURCE MANAGEMENT

In 1993, to buy labor peace, Piëch cut the workweek at VW's German plants from 35 hours to 28.8. That saved 30,000 jobs. But now VW workers can make upwards of $34 an hour. Piëch tried to push through a plan to lower the base wages of new German workers and link them to output instead of hours as this story was published. If this doesn't succeed, VW threatens to put new projects in places such as the Czech Republic, where wages are less than one-third German levels. Cutting such a deal is turning into a hard slog. The unions concede they need to be more flexible. But they are resisting management's demands to increase the workweek to more than 40 hours during peak production without paying overtime.

And investors frustrated with a low stock-PE ratio cannot expect a swift boost to the stock price. The government of Lower Saxony, the biggest investor, worries more about jobs than shareholder value. Five of VW's seven German factories are located in Lower Saxony, and they're among the least productive in Europe. According to World Markets Research Center in London, production at the Wolfsburg plant runs at 46 cars per worker per year, compared with 101 at Nissan Motor Co.'s British factory in Sunderland.

### MARKETING AND SALES

VW also had gaps in its product lineup. It had nothing to offer in the category of compact minivans—the scaled-down versions of minivans that are popular in Europe. A sport utility vehicle was not scheduled to come out until 2003. "We're [also] missing some niche models—sports car, roadster, another convertible," said Jürgen Lehmann, manager of the Autohaus Moltke dealership in Stuttgart. VW had to sort out these issues while the competition gets tougher.

Bottomline, VW's value chain presents interesting challenges for Piëch's successor, Bernd Pischetsrieder. He inherited extraordinary strengths in product development and manufacturing operations. But for all of the success of the last decade, and an impressive market presence worldwide, he faces emerging value chain weaknesses in human resource management cost considerations and product line gaps in marketing and sales.

**Source:** "Volkswagen," *BusinessWeek,* July 23, 2001; "VW Needs a Jump," *BusinessWeek;* May 12, 2003.

Maytag manufactures its own appliances, sells them through independent distributors, and provides warranty service to the buyer. Sears outsources the manufacture of its appliances while it promotes its brand name—Kenmore—and handles all sales and service.

As these examples suggest, it is important that managers take into account their level of vertical integration when comparing their cost structure for activities on their value chain to those of key competitors. Comparing a fully integrated rival with a partially integrated one requires adjusting for the scope of activities performed to achieve meaningful comparison. It also suggests the need for examining costs associated with activities provided by upstream or downstream companies; these activities ultimately determine comparable, final costs to end users. Said another way, one company's comparative cost disadvantage (or advantage) may emanate more from activities undertaken by upstream or downstream "partners" than from activities under the direct control of that company—therefore suggesting less of a relative advantage or disadvantage within the company's direct value chain.

### Value Chain Activities as Strengths or Weaknesses

The final basic consideration when applying value chain analysis is the need to have a meaningful comparison to use when evaluating a value activity as a strength or weakness. Similarly, the RBV identifies resources and competencies that become the basis for a sustained competitive advantage based on whether they provide the company with key strengths or weaknesses to shape strategic action. To do so requires a SWOT analysis which we now explore.

# SWOT ANALYSIS

SWOT is an acronym for the internal Strengths and Weaknesses of a firm and the environmental Opportunities and Threats facing that firm. SWOT analysis is a widely used technique through which managers create a quick overview of a company's strategic situation. It is based on the assumption that an effective strategy derives from a sound "fit" between a firm's internal resources (strengths and weaknesses) and its external situation (opportunities and threats). A good fit maximizes a firm's strengths and opportunities and minimizes its weaknesses and threats. Accurately applied, this simple assumption has powerful implications for the design of a successful strategy.

Environmental and industry analysis in Chapters 3 and 4 provides the information needed to identify opportunities and threats in a firm's environment, the first fundamental focus in SWOT analysis.

## Opportunities

An *opportunity* is a major favorable situation in a firm's environment. Key trends are one source of opportunities. Identification of a previously overlooked market segment, changes in competitive or regulatory circumstances, technological changes, and improved buyer or supplier relationships could represent opportunities for the firm.

## Threats

A *threat* is a major unfavorable situation in a firm's environment. Threats are key impediments to the firm's current or desired position. The entrance of new competitors, slow market growth, increased bargaining power of key buyers or suppliers, technological changes, and new or revised regulations could represent threats to a firm's success.

Understanding the key opportunities and threats facing a firm helps its managers identify realistic options from which to choose an appropriate strategy and clarifies the most effective niche for the firm. The second fundamental focus in SWOT analysis is the identification of internal strengths and weaknesses.

## Strengths

A *strength* is a resource advantage relative to competitors and the needs of the markets a firm serves or expects to serve. It is a *distinctive competence* when it gives the firm a comparative advantage in the marketplace. Strengths arise from the resources and competencies available to the firm.

## Weaknesses

A *weakness* is a limitation or deficiency in one or more resources or competencies relative to competitors that impedes a firm's effective performance.

The sheer size and level of Microsoft's user base have proven to be a key strength on which it built its aggressive entry into Internet services. Limited financial capacity was a weakness recognized by Southwest Airlines, which charted a selective route expansion strategy to build the best profit record in a deregulated airline industry.

SWOT analysis can be used in many ways to aid strategic analysis. The most common way is to use it as a logical framework guiding systematic discussion of a firm's resources and the basic alternatives that emerge from this resource-based view. What one manager sees as an opportunity, another may see as a potential threat. Likewise, a strength to one manager may be a weakness to another. Different assessments may reflect underlying power considerations within the firm or differing factual perspectives. Systematic analysis of these issues facilitates objective internal analysis.

The diagram in Exhibit 5–12 illustrates how SWOT analysis builds on the results of an RBV of a firm to aid strategic analysis. Key external opportunities and threats are systematically

**EXHIBIT 5–12**
**SWOT Analysis Diagram**

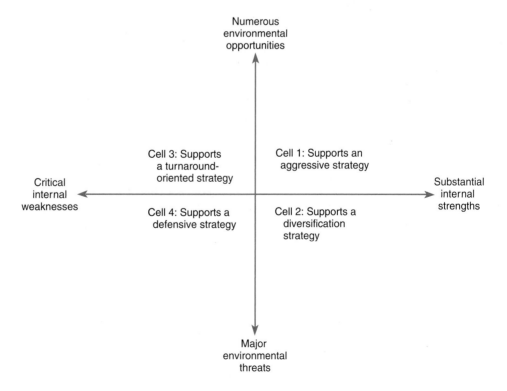

compared with internal resources and competencies—that is, strengths and weaknesses—in a structured approach. The objective is identification of one of four distinct patterns in the match between a firm's internal resources and external situation. Cell 1 is the most favorable situation; the firm faces several environmental opportunities and has numerous strengths that encourage pursuit of those opportunities. This situation suggests growth-oriented strategies to exploit the favorable match. America OnLine's intensive market development strategy in the online services market is the result of a favorable match of its strong technical expertise, early entry, and reputation resources with an opportunity for impressive market growth as millions of people joined the information highway in the last decade. Its continued strength in interactivity with Net-delivered media is currently a key component of AOL-Time Warner's new growth-oriented strategy in 2004.

Cell 4 is the least favorable situation, with the firm facing major environmental threats from a weak resource position. This situation clearly calls for strategies that reduce or redirect involvement in the products or markets examined by means of SWOT analysis. Texas Instruments offers a good example of a Cell 4 firm. It was a sprawling maker of chips, calculators, laptop PCs, military electronics, and engineering software on a sickening slid toward oblivion just ten years ago. Its young CEO, Tom Engibous, reinvigorated the ailing electronics giant and turned it into one of the hottest plays in semiconductors by betting the company on an emerging class of chips known as digital signal processors (DSPs). The chips crunch vast streams of data for an array of digital gadgets, including modems and cellular phones. Engibous shed billions of dollars worth of assets to focus on DSPs, which he calls "the most important silicon technology of the next decade." TI now commands nearly half of the $4.4 billion global market for the most advanced DSPs, and it's the No. 1 chip supplier to the sizzling digital wireless phone market.

In Cell 2, a firm whose RBV has identified several key strengths faces an unfavorable environment. In this situation, strategies would seek to redeploy those strong resources and competencies to build long-term opportunities in more opportunistic product markets. IBM, a dominant manufacturer of mainframes, servers, and PCs worldwide, has nurtured many strengths in computer-related and software-related markets for many years. Increasingly, however, it has had to address major threats that include product commoditization, pricing pressures, accelerated pace of innovation, and the like. Fortunately, Sam Palmisano's determined development of ISSC, better known now as IBM Global Services, has allowed IBM to build a long-term opportunity in more profitable growing markets of the next decade. In the last ten years since Palmisano ran it, Global Services has become the fastest-growing division of the company, its largest employer, and the keystone of IBM's strategic future. The group does everything from running a customer's IT department to consulting on legacy system upgrades to building custom supply-chain management applications. As IBM's hardware divisions struggle against price wars and commoditization and its software units fight to gain share beyond mainframes, it is Global Services that drives the company's growth.

A firm in Cell 3 faces impressive market opportunity but is constrained by weak internal resources. The focus of strategy for such a firm is eliminating the internal weaknesses so as to more effectively pursue the market opportunity. The AOL-Time Warner merger may well have afforded both companies a way to overcome key weaknesses, keeping them from pursuing vast twenty-first-century, Internet-based opportunities. AOL lacks programming content and the ability to sell programming profitably over time. Time Warner is at a loss in managing the complexities of interactive media services.

SWOT analysis has been a framework of choice among many managers for a long time because of its simplicity and its portrayal of the essence of sound strategy formulation—matching a firm's opportunities and threats with its strengths and weaknesses. Central to making SWOT analysis effective is accurate internal analysis—the identification of specific strengths and weaknesses around which sound strategy can be built. One of the historical deficiencies of SWOT analysis was the tendency to rely on a very general, categorical assessment of internal capabilities. The resource-based view came to exist in part as a remedy to this void in the strategic management field. It is an excellent way to identify internal strengths and weaknesses and use that information to enhance the quality of a SWOT analysis. Similarly, value chain analysis identifies elements of a company's capabilities and operations that are useful in conducting a SWOT analysis.

Using RBV, value chain analysis, and SWOT analysis improves the quality of internal analysis. This is particularly the case when managers make meaningful comparisons. The next section examines how meaningful comparisons are accomplished.

# INTERNAL ANALYSIS: MAKING MEANINGFUL COMPARISONS

Managers need objective standards to use when examining internal resources and value-building activities. Whether applying the RBV, value chain analysis, or the SWOT approach, strategists rely on four basic perspectives to evaluate where their firm stacks up on its internal capabilities. These four perspectives are discussed in this section.

## Comparison with Past Performance

Strategists use the firm's historical experience as a basis for evaluating internal factors. Managers are most familiar with the internal capabilities and problems of their firm because they have been immersed in its financial, marketing, production, and R&D activities. Not surprisingly, a manager's assessment of whether a certain internal factor—such as production facilities, sales organization, financial capacity, control systems, or key personnel—is a strength or a weakness will be strongly influenced by his or her experience in connection with that factor. In the capital-intensive airline industry, for example, debt capacity is a strategic internal factor. Delta Airlines managers view Delta's debt-equity ratio of less than 1.9 brought on by its acquisition of PanAm's international operations as a real weakness limiting its flexibility to invest in facilities because it maintained a ratio less than 0.6 for over 20 years. Continental Airlines managers, on the other hand, view Continental's much higher 3.5 debt-equity ratio as a growing strength, because it is down 50 percent from its 7.0 level five years earlier.

Although historical experience can provide a relevant evaluation framework, strategists must avoid tunnel vision in making use of it. NEC, Japan's IBM, initially dominated Japan's PC market with a 70 percent market share using a proprietary hardware system, much higher screen resolution, powerful distribution channels, and a large software library from third-party vendors. Far from worried, Hajime Ikeda, manager of NEC's planning division at the time, was quoted as saying: "We don't hear complaints from our users." By 2001, IBM, Apple, and Compaq filled the shelves in Japan's famous consumer electronics district, Akihabara. Hiroki Kamata, president of a Japanese computer research firm, reported that Japan's PC market, worth over $25 billion in 2001, saw Apple and IBM compatibles each having more market share than NEC because of better technology, software, and the restrictions created by NEC's proprietary technology. Clearly, using only historical experience as a basis for identifying strengths and weaknesses can prove dangerously inaccurate.

## Stages of Industry Evolution

The requirements for success in industry segments change over time. Strategists can use these changing requirements, which are associated with different stages of industry evolution, as a framework for identifying and evaluating the firm's strengths and weaknesses.

Exhibit 5–13 depicts four stages of industry evolution and the typical changes in functional capabilities that are often associated with business success at each of these stages. The early development of a product market, for example, entails minimal growth in sales,

## EXHIBIT 5–13
**Sources of Distinctive Competence at Different Stages of Industry Evolution**

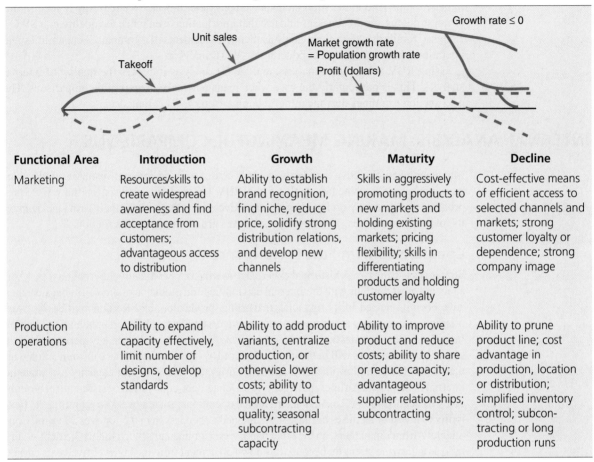

| Functional Area | Introduction | Growth | Maturity | Decline |
|---|---|---|---|---|
| Marketing | Resources/skills to create widespread awareness and find acceptance from customers; advantageous access to distribution | Ability to establish brand recognition, find niche, reduce price, solidify strong distribution relations, and develop new channels | Skills in aggressively promoting products to new markets and holding existing markets; pricing flexibility; skills in differentiating products and holding customer loyalty | Cost-effective means of efficient access to selected channels and markets; strong customer loyalty or dependence; strong company image |
| Production operations | Ability to expand capacity effectively, limit number of designs, develop standards | Ability to add product variants, centralize production, or otherwise lower costs; ability to improve product quality; seasonal subcontracting capacity | Ability to improve product and reduce costs; ability to share or reduce capacity; advantageous supplier relationships; subcontracting | Ability to prune product line; cost advantage in production, location or distribution; simplified inventory control; subcontracting or long production runs |

major R&D emphasis, rapid technological change in the product, operating losses, and a need for sufficient resources or slack to support a temporarily unprofitable operation. Success at this introduction stage may be associated with technical skill, with being first in new markets, or with having a marketing advantage that creates widespread awareness. Radio Shack's initial success with its TRS–80 home computer was based in part on its ability to gain widespread exposure and acceptance in the ill-defined home computer market via the large number of existing Radio Shack outlets throughout the country.

The strengths necessary for success change in the growth stage. Rapid growth brings new competitors into the product market. At this stage, such factors as brand recognition, product differentiation, and the financial resources to support both heavy marketing expenses and the effect of price competition on cash flow can be key strengths. IBM entered the personal computer market in the growth stage and was able to rapidly become the market leader with a strategy based on its key strengths in brand awareness and possession of the financial resources needed to support consumer advertising. Radio Shack discontinued its TRS–80 due to IBM's strength. Within a few years, however, IBM lost that lead in the next stage as speed in distribution and cost structures became the key success factors—strengths for Dell and several mail order–oriented computer assemblers.

**EXHIBIT 5–13**
*(continued)*

| Functional Area | Introduction | Growth | Maturity | Decline |
|---|---|---|---|---|
| Finance | Resources to support high net cash overflow and initial losses; ability to use leverage effectively | Ability to finance rapid expansion, to have net cash outflows but increasing profits; resources to support product improvements | Ability to generate and redistribute increasing net cash inflows; effective cost control systems | Ability to reuse or liquidate unneeded equipment; advantage in cost of facilities; control system accuracy; streamlined management control |
| Personnel | Flexibility in staffing and training new management; existence of employees with key skills in new products or markets | Existence of an ability to add skilled personnel; motivated and loyal workforce | Ability to cost effectively, reduce workforce, increase efficiency | Capacity to reduce and reallocate personnel; cost advantage |
| Engineering and research and development | Ability to make engineering changes, have technical bugs in product and process resolved | Skill in quality and new feature development; ability to start developing successor product | Ability to reduce costs, develop variants, differentiate products | Ability to support other grown areas or to apply product to unique customer needs |
| Key functional area and strategy focus | Engineering: market penetration | Sales: consumer loyalty; market share | Production efficiency; successor products | Finance; maximum investment recovery |

As the industry moves through a shakeout phase and into the maturity stage, industry growth continues, but at a decreasing rate. The number of industry segments expands, but technological change in product design slows considerably. As a result, competition usually becomes more intense, and promotional or pricing advantages and differentiation become key internal strengths. Technological change in process design becomes intense as the many competitors seek to provide the product in the most efficient manner. Where R&D was critical in the introduction stage, efficient production is now crucial to continued success in the broader industry segments. Ford's emphasis on quality control and modern, efficient production has helped it prosper in the maturing U.S. auto industry, while General Motors, which pays almost 50 percent more than Ford to produce a comparable car, continues to decline.

When the industry moves into the decline stage, strengths and weaknesses center on cost advantages, superior supplier or customer relationships, and financial control. Competitive advantage can exist at this stage, at least temporarily, if a firm serves gradually shrinking markets that competitors are choosing to leave.

Exhibit 5–13 is a rather simple model of the stages of industry evolution. These stages can and do vary from the model. What should be borne in mind is that the relative importance of various determinants of success differs across the stages of industry evolution. Thus, the state of that evolution must be considered in internal analysis. Exhibit 5–13 suggests dimensions that are particularly deserving of in-depth consideration when a company profile is being developed.

## Benchmarking—Comparison with Competitors

A major focus in determining a firm's resources and competencies is comparison with existing (and potential) competitors. Firms in the same industry often have different marketing skills, financial resources, operating facilities and locations, technical know-how, brand images, levels of integration, managerial talent, and so on. These different internal resources can become relative strengths (or weaknesses) depending on the strategy a firm chooses. In choosing a strategy, managers should compare the firm's key internal capabilities with those of its rivals, thereby isolating its key strengths and weaknesses.

In the home appliance industry, for example, Sears and General Electric are major rivals. Sears's principal strength is its retail network. For GE, distribution—through independent franchised dealers—has traditionally been a relative weakness. GE's possession of the financial resources needed to support modernized mass production has enabled it to maintain both cost and technological advantages over its rivals, particularly Sears. This major strength for GE is a relative weakness for Sears, which depends solely on subcontracting to produce its Kenmore appliances. On the other hand, maintenance and repair service are important in the appliance industry. Historically, Sears has had strength in this area because it maintains fully staffed service components and spreads the costs of components over numerous departments at each retail location. GE, on the other hand, has had to depend on regional service centers and on local contracting with independent service firms by its independent local dealers. Among the internal factors that Sears and GE must consider in developing a strategy are distribution networks, technological capabilities, operating costs, and service facilities. Managers in both organizations have built successful strategies yet those strategies are quite different. Benchmarking each other, they have identified ways to build on relative strengths while avoiding dependence on capabilities at which the other firm excels.

Benchmarking, comparing the way "our" company performs a specific activity with a competitor or other company doing the same thing, has become a central concern of managers in quality commitment companies worldwide. Particularly as the value chain framework has taken hold in structuring internal analysis, managers seek to systematically benchmark the costs and results of the smallest value activities against relevant competitors or other useful standards because it has proven to be an effective way to continuously improve that activity. The ultimate objective in benchmarking is to identify the "best practices" in performing an activity, to learn how lower costs, fewer defects, or other outcomes linked to excellence are achieved. Companies committed to benchmarking attempt to isolate and identify where their costs or outcomes are out of line with what the best practicers of a particular activity experience (competitors and noncompetitors) and then attempt to change their activities to achieve the new best practices standard.

Comparison with key competitors can prove useful in ascertaining whether their internal capabilities on these and other factors are strengths or weaknesses. Significant favorable differences (existing or expected) from competitors are potential cornerstones of a firm's strategy. Moreover, through comparison with major competitors, a firm may avoid strategic commitments that it cannot competitively support. Exhibit 5–14, Strategy in Action, shows how UPS used competitor comparison to assess its strengths and weaknesses in the package transportation industry.

## Comparison with Success Factors in the Industry

Industry analysis (see Chapter 3) involves identifying the factors associated with successful participation in a given industry. As was true for the evaluation methods discussed above,

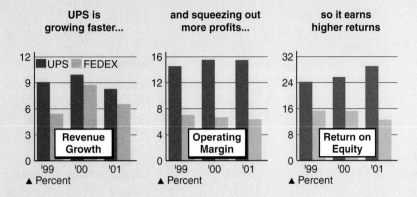

**Success Begets Success**
Stacking UPS up against FedEx

Data: Banc of America Securities ©BW

Over the past two years, the company has quietly shed its image as the slowpoke of shipping. Be it e-tailing frenzy or dot-com crash, UPS has captured customers by bombarding them with choices: fast flights versus cheap ground delivery, simple shipping or a panoply of manufacturing, warehousing, and supply-chain services. In the United States and several foreign markets, UPS has grabbed a commanding lead over FedEx—and not just in everyday package delivery but in the New Economy services such as logistics. In North America, UPS has even snagged the distinction of preferred carrier to the Web generation: The company handles 36 percent of all online purchases, versus 13 percent for FedEx. "UPS is doing things in e-commerce that other companies are just starting to talk about," says Jack R. Staff, chief economist at Zona Research in Redwood City, Calif.

The ascent of UPS charts a reversal of fortune in one of the fiercest rivalries in Corporate America. It was FedEx, after all, that pioneered both overnight delivery of packages and the ability to track their journey using computers. These 1970s' era innovations rocked the shipping industry and helped set the stage for the Internet Revolution of the 1990s. Even now, FedEx rules in certain areas of air freight. Its carefully burnished brand still says "absolutely, positively" to thousands of loyal customers—and not without reason. FedEx is one of America's great success stories, extolled for its customer service.

In the view of many analysts and industry execs, however, UPS now has a pronounced advantage in several hotly contested areas. In addition to its overwhelming lead in ground shipping and its online triumphs, UPS can point to a logistics business that is growing by 40 percent a year. FedEx is struggling to reverse a decline in this area.

Even in sectors where FedEx still rules, UPS is catching up quickly. FedEx has a commanding lead in the profitable overnight service, for example, delivering more than 3 million such packages daily in 200-plus countries and accounting for 39 percent of the market. UPS is No. 2, with 2.2 million overnight packages—but its volume has been growing faster than FedEx's for at least three years. In 2000, UPS's overnight business grew at 8 percent, compared with FedEx's 3.6 percent. And UPS's operating margin on its domestic air-express service is higher—24 percent versus 6 percent—according to Gary H. Yablon, a transportation analyst at Credit Suisse First Boston.

So what accounts for UPS's growth in overnight? The company trumpets its decision in 1999 to integrate overnight delivery into its vast ground-transportation network. UPS, like FedEx, still uses planes to make most such deliveries. But in the past two years, its logisticians have also figured out how to make quick mid-distance deliveries—as far as 500 miles in one night—by truck, which is much less expensive than by air. As a result, UPS's overall cost per package is $6.65, compared with FedEx's $11.89, according to CSFB. Even though FedEx also uses trucks for short hauls, "UPS has a real cost advantage," says John D. Kasarda, director of the University of North Carolina's Frank Hawkins Kenan Institute of Private Enterprise and a former FedEx consultant.

UPS's core strength is its fleet of 152,000 brown trucks, which reach virtually every address in the United States—and increasingly, the world. FedEx has belatedly begun to build its own home-delivery system. But the cost of duplicating a system UPS has spent nearly 100 years building could prove prohibitive. And with $3 billion in cash on hand, UPS could easily wage a price war against FedEx, which isn't generating any spare cash. "This is a game FedEx can't win,"

*(continued)*

says Peter V. Coleman, a transportation analyst at Bank of America Securities. That leaves FedEx dependent on an air-delivery system that is increasingly expensive to operate.

|  | UPS | FedEx |
|---|---|---|
| Founded | 1907 | 1971 |
| Chairman | James P. Kelly | Frederick W. Smith |
| Headquarters | Atlanta, Ga. | Memphis, Tenn. |
| 2000 Revenue | $29.77 billion | $18.3 billion |
| Net Income | $2.93 billion | $688 million |
| Employees | 359,000 | 215,000 |
| Daily Package Volume | 13.2 million | 5 million |
| Fleet | 152,500 trucks, 560 planes | 43,500 trucks, 662 planes |

| | Unit Cost | Unit Profit | Operating Margin | Avg Daily Volume |
|---|---|---|---|---|
| **Air Deliveries, U.S.** | | | | |
| FedEx | $15.27 | $0.93 | 6% | 2,924,000 |
| UPS | $14.60 | $3.76 | 22% | 2,162,000 |
| **Ground Deliveries, U.S.** | | | | |
| FedEx | $4.77 | $0.68 | 13% | 1,541,000 |
| UPS | $4.95 | $0.61 | 11% | 10,945,000 |
| **Overall Average, including International** | | | | |
| FedEx | $11.89 | $0.85 | 7% | 4,788,000 |
| UPS | $6.65 | $1.17 | 15% | 14,236,000 |

Data: Credit Suisse First Boston

**Source:** "UPS: Can It Keep Delivering?" *BusinessWeek*, 3/24/03.

the key determinants of success in an industry may be used to identify a firm's internal strengths and weaknesses. By scrutinizing industry competitors, as well as customer needs, vertical industry structure, channels of distribution, costs, barriers to entry, availability of substitutes, and suppliers, a strategist seeks to determine whether a firm's current internal capabilities represent strengths or weaknesses in new competitive arenas. The discussion in Chapter 3 provides a useful framework—five industry forces—against which to examine a firm's potential strengths and weaknesses. General Cinema Corporation, the largest U.S. movie theater operator, determined that its internal skills in marketing, site analysis, creative financing, and management of geographically dispersed operations were key strengths relative to major success factors in the soft-drink bottling industry. This assessment proved accurate. Within 10 years after it entered the soft-drink bottling industry, General Cinema became the largest franchised bottler of soft drinks in the United States, handling Pepsi, 7UP, Dr Pepper, and Sunkist. Exhibit 5–15, Strategy in Action, describes how Avery Dennison used industry evolution benchmarking versus 3M to create a new, successful strategy.

# Summary

This chapter looked at several ways managers achieve greater objectivity and rigor as they analyze their company's internal capabilities. Managers often start their internal analysis with questions like: "How well is the current strategy working? What is our current situation? Or what are our strengths and weaknesses?" The resource-based view provides a key, fundamental framework for analyzing firm success based on the firm's internal resources and competencies. This chapter described how insightful managers look at their business as a chain of activities that add value creating the products or services they sell—this is called *value chain analysis.* Managers who use value chain analysis to understand the value structure within their firm's activities and look at the value system, which also includes upstream suppliers and downstream partners and buyers, often gain very meaningful insights into their company's strategic resources, competencies, and options. *SWOT analysis,* a widely used approach to internal analysis, provides a logical way to apply the results of an RBV and a value chain analysis. Managers frequently use RBV, value chain, and SWOT analysis to introduce realism and greater objectivity into their internal analysis.

**BusinessWeek**

Avery Dennison has long made adhesives and what it calls "sticky papers" for business customers. Ten years ago, AD decided to take on 3M with its own version of 3M's highly successful Post-It notes and Scotch transparent tape.

How frequently did you buy Avery Notes and Avery Tape? You probably have never heard of them, right? That is because Avery was beat up in that market by 3M and AD exited the business after just a few years. Key strengths, distribution and brand name, that 3M used to build those products were major weaknesses at AD. Plus, in President Charles Miller's way of viewing it, 3M remained aggressive and true to an innovative culture to back its products while AD had grown rusty and "me too" rather than being the innovator it had traditionally been with pressure-sensitive papers. So faced with considerable weakness competing against a major threat, Miller refocused AD on getting innovative in areas of traditional technical strength.

Today, AD has 30 percent of its sales from products introduced in the past five years. It has half the market for adhesive paper stock and 40 percent of the market for coated paper films for package labels. Says Miller, "We believe in market evolution. The best way to control a market is to invent it. With innovative products, superstores aren't able to squeeze margins, as they can in commodity products." New products now pour out of AD labs to position AD strengths against early life cycle stage opportunities.

**Source:** "The Business Week 50," *BusinessWeek,* March 23, 2001.

Finally, this chapter covered four ways objectivity and realism are enhanced when managers use meaningful standards for comparison regardless of the particular analytical framework they employ in internal analysis. This chapter is followed by an appendix covering traditional financial analysis to serve as a refresher and reminder about this basic internal analysis tool.

When matched with management's environmental analyses and mission priorities, the process of internal analysis provides the critical foundation for strategy formulation. Armed with an accurate, thorough, and timely internal analysis, managers are in a better position to formulate effective strategies. The next chapter describes basic strategy alternatives that any firm may consider.

## Questions for Discussion

1. Describe SWOT analysis as a way to guide internal analysis. How does this approach reflect the basic strategic management process?

2. What is the resource-based view of the firm? Give examples of three different types of resources.

3. What are three characteristics that make resources more, or less, valuable? Provide an example of each.

4. Why do you think value chain analysis has become a preferred approach to guide internal analysis? What are its strengths? Its weaknesses?

5. Apply SWOT analysis to yourself and your career aspirations. What are your major strengths and weaknesses? How might you use your knowledge of these strengths and weaknesses to develop your future career plans?

## Chapter 5 Discussion Case

# Can Dunkin' KO Krispy?

**BusinessWeek**

1 In the war of the doughnuts, the reigning champ has been getting hopped by the upstart. Now, Dunkin' Donuts is plotting a new offensive. For half a century, Krispy Kreme and Dunkin' Donuts have warily eyed each other from different sides of the Mason-Dixon line, Krispy Kreme Doughnuts ruled the Southeast with its hot, gooey glazed doughnuts, and Dunkin' blanketed New England with boxy outlets that served more cups of coffee than they did crullers.

2 Each chain built a cult following: Krispy Kreme combined a wholesome, 1950s image with an airy, sweet-beyond-imagination doughnut. Dunkin' was the dependable delight at the strip mall, a blue-collar joint that supplied cops and construction workers but also drew regular folks who shunned $3 lattes from Starbucks.

## SUNKEN REPUTATION

3 Yet the doughnut détente is about to end as both chains race to expand nationwide. Krispy Kreme took a major step in June when it opened its first store in Massachusetts—Dunkin' Donuts' home turf. But the impact of KK's lone Bay State outlet on DD will be more symbolic than financial in the near term, Dunkin', a division of Allied Domecq based in Randolph, Mass., boasts 600 stores in the Boston area and 3,800 stores nationwide, versus Krispy Kreme's 292. Its $2.8 billion in annual revenue dwarfs Krispy Kreme's sales of $492 million in the year ending Feb. 2.

4 So why does Dunkin' Donuts seem like the underdog in this battle? Partly because Krispy Kreme has come on so strong since it went public in April, 2000. Since then, it has opened about 150 stores—more than it estimated in half the time it allotted. Krispy's stock price has quadrupled to more than $40, and same-store sales grew 11 percent last year, versus 6 percent for Dunkin' Donuts. Krispy Kreme spends nothing on advertising (except for handing out free doughnuts to local media outlets when it opens a new store), yet it boasts nearly as much brand buzz as megamarketing wonders like Nike or Coke.

5 For investors, the question is whether Krispy Kreme's run in the sun on Wall Street is threatened. Dunkin' Donuts is gearing up big-time to fight back even as it has had to combat negative images about its brand. Outlets that weren't doing enough housekeeping to meet the chain's standards became the butt of late-night jokes. Some franchisees were convicted of underreporting income and evading income taxes. Dunkin' sued hundreds of franchisees to help clean up the chain's reputation.

## COFFEE AND KREME

6 Unlike Krispy Kreme, investors can't bet on just Dunkin' Donuts. It's just one part of the Quick Service Restaurant (QSR) division of the British-based Allied Domecq. Baskin Robbins and Togo's are the other two. QSR makes up 9.5 percent of sales and 13 percent of the parent's profit.

7 Still, Dunkin' has its work cut out for it. After 53 years of making doughnuts, the chain has yet to match its well-known brand name with a nationwide presence. "Dunkin' Donuts is the 800-pound gorilla that is only living in 40 percent of the forest," says Christopher Muller, an associate professor at the University of Florida's Rosen School of Hospitality. Nearly two-thirds of its stores are located in the Northeast and mid-Atlantic states, with very few west of the Mississippi.

8 Meanwhile, Krispy Kreme's blistering expansion has helped it pick up market share. In 2002, it owned 13.1 percent of the U.S. doughnut market, up from 4.8 percent in 1999. In the same period, Dunkin' Donuts' share has dropped 20 points, to 57 percent. Some of that has gone to mom-and-pop operations, but a huge chunk has gone to its main rival, according to Technomic Information Services.

## MORNING RITUAL

9 Dunkin's numbers could erode further as Krispy Kreme borrows a move from its competitor's playbook. First, it's not stopping at doughnuts. It'll be building a bread business, and it's heating up its coffee offerings—just like Dunkin' Doughnuts. And Krispy plans to open smaller, cheaper satellite stores.

"They'll make Krispy Kreme much more convenient for customers," says Scott Livengood, the Southern chain's CEO.

10  Convenience is exactly what has made Dunkin' Donuts thrive. In the densest parts of its core New England market, it boasts one store per 6,750 people (Krispy Kreme until now has aimed for one store to serve 100,000). In some places, four or five Dunkin' outlets can be found within a half mile of each other, each with cars lined up through the parking lot and out onto the highway shoulder during morning rush hour. For Boston-area commuters, stopping at a Dunkin' Donuts outlet for coffee in the morning is about as routine as getting dressed.

11  "We're talking massive customer loyalty," says Nancy Koehn, professor of business administration at Harvard Business School. Even a Krispy Kreme manager at the Medford (Mass.) construction site had an orange-and-purple Dunkin' cup and bag on his desk.

## MASSIVE BUILDOUT

12  Yet spreading that customer loyalty beyond the Northeast and getting existing customers to spend more each time they come in is a tall order. Jon Luther, who heads the chain as CEO of Allied Domecq's QSR unit, is trying to serve up solutions. To get more franchisees in new areas to sign on, he has offered to build doughnut-production facilities for them and run them for up to five years. In the past, franchisees in an area formed a co-op and shared the burden.

13  "Dunkin' Donuts' weakness is that it isn't national, but it will be," says Luther, the first outsider to run the company since founder Bill Rosenberg sold his first Dunkin' doughnut in 1950. The chain plans to open 342 new stores this year in the United States and 630 more in 2004—the equivalent of more than three entire Krispy Kreme chains.

14  Next, Luther will try to convince customers used to a regular cuppa joe to switch to pricier espresso and latte. But doesn't the upscale coffee clash with the chain's Joe Doughnut image? Not necessarily, say some marketing experts. The popularity of Starbucks and other specialty coffee stores has started to move once-elite espresso and cappuccino into the mainstream—where Dunkin' Donuts rules.

## DUNKINIZATION

15  "Small luxuries [like premium coffee] have become more mass market," says Koehn of Harvard. "Core customers are considering trying a latte or cappuccino. It may seem more palatable or trustworthy in a Dunkin' Donuts cup." The trick for Dunkin' will be to serve them fast. The chain promises to deliver a cappuccino in less than a minute.

16  Dunkin' has never claimed to be a trendsetter. Quite the opposite, in fact. After Starbucks introduced frappuccino, Dunkin' came out with its Coolatta and saw beverage sales soar. When bagels took off in the mid '90s, Dunkin' jumped on that trend, too. Now it's the largest bagel retailer in the country. "We watch trends and then Dunkinize them," says Ken Kimmel, a vice-president of Dunkin' Donuts Concepts, the chain's marketing arm.

17  And at the pace Dunkin is going now, the pressure on Krispy Kreme to execute its strategy perfectly increases. It's something for investors to think about the next time they bite into a nice sugary donut.

**Source:** Faith Arner, "Can Dunkin' KO Krispy?" *Business Week*, July 3, 2003.

## Appendix 5

# Using Financial Analysis

One of the most important tools for assessing the strength of an organization within its industry is financial analysis. Managers, investors, and creditors all employ some form of this analysis as the beginning point for their financial decision making. Investors use financial analyses in making decisions about whether to buy or sell stock, and creditors use them in deciding whether or not to lend. They provide managers with a measurement of how the company is doing in comparison with its performance in past years and with the performance of competitors in the industry.

Although financial analysis is useful for decision making, some weaknesses should be noted. Any picture that it provides of the company is based on past data. Although trends may be noteworthy, this picture should not automatically be assumed to be applicable to the future. In addition, the analysis is only as good as the accounting procedures that have provided the information. When making comparisons between companies, one should keep in mind the variability of accounting procedures from firm to firm.

There are four basic groups of financial ratios: liquidity, leverage, activity, and profitability.

Depicted in Exhibit 5–A are the specific ratios calculated for each of the basic groups. Liquidity and leverage ratios represent an assessment of the risk of the firm. Activity and profitability ratios are measures of the return generated by the assets of the firm. The interaction between certain groups of ratios is indicated by arrows.

Typically, two common financial statements are used in financial analyses: the balance sheet and the income statement. Exhibit 5–B is a balance sheet and Exhibit 5–C an income statement for the ABC Company. These statements will be used to illustrate the financial analyses.

## LIQUIDITY RATIOS

Liquidity ratios are used as indicators of a firm's ability to meet its short-term obligations. These obligations include any current liabilities, including currently maturing long-term debt. Current assets move through a normal cash cycle of inventories—sales—accounts receivable—cash. The firm then uses cash to pay off or reduce its current liabilities. The best-known liquidity ratio is the current ratio: current assets divided by current liabilities. For the ABC Company, the current ratio is calculated as follows:

$$\frac{\text{Current assets}}{\text{Current liabilities}} = \frac{\$4,125,000}{\$2,512,500} = 1.64 \ (2005)$$

$$= \frac{\$3,618,000}{\$2,242,250} = 1.161 \ (2004)$$

Most analysts suggest a current ratio of 2 to 3. A large current ratio is not necessarily a good sign; it may mean that an organization is not making the most efficient use of its assets. The optimum current ratio will vary from industry to industry, with the more volatile industries requiring higher ratios.

**Source:** Prepared by Elizabeth Gatewood, Indiana University. ©Elizabeth Gatewood, 2004. Reprinted by permission of Elizabeth Gatewood.

**EXHIBIT 5–A**  **Financial Ratios**

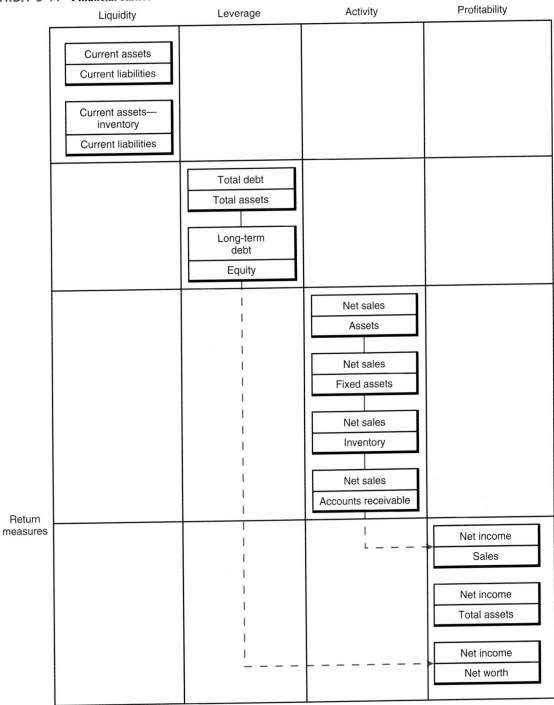

## EXHIBIT 5–B

**ABC Company Balance Sheet As of December 31, 2004, and 2005**

|  | | 2005 | | 2004 |
|---|---|---|---|---|
| **Assets** | | | | |
| Current assets: | | | | |
| Cash | | $ 140,000 | | $ 115,000 |
| Accounts receivable | | 1,760,000 | | 1,440,000 |
| Inventory | | 2,175,000 | | 2,000,000 |
| Prepaid expenses | | 50,000 | | 63,000 |
| Total current assets | | 4,125,000 | | 3,618,000 |
| Fixed assets: | | | | |
| Long-term receivable | | 1,255,000 | | 1,090,000 |
| Property and plant | $2,037,000 | | $2,015,000 | |
| Less: Accumulated depreciation | 862,000 | | 860,000 | |
| Net property and plant | | 1,175,000 | | 1,155,000 |
| Other fixed assets | | 550,000 | | 530,000 |
| Total fixed assets | | 2,980,000 | | 2,775,000 |
| Total assets | | $7,105,000 | | $6,393,000 |
| **Liabilities and Stockholders' Equity** | | | | |
| Current liabilities: | | | | |
| Accounts payable | | $1,325,000 | | $1,225,000 |
| Bank loans payable | | 475,000 | | 550,000 |
| Accrued federal taxes | | 675,000 | | 425,000 |
| Current maturities (long-term debt) | | 17,500 | | 26,000 |
| Dividends payable | | 20,000 | | 16,250 |
| Total current liabilities | | 2,512,500 | | 2,242,250 |
| Long-term liabilities | | 1,350,000 | | 1,425,000 |
| Total liabilities | | 3,862,000 | | 3,667,250 |
| Stockholders' equity: | | | | |
| Common stock | | | | |
| (104,046 shares outstanding in 1995; | | | | |
| 101,204 shares outstanding in 1994) | | 44,500 | | 43,300 |
| Additional paid-in-capital | | 568,000 | | 372,450 |
| Retained earnings | | 2,630,000 | | 2,310,000 |
| Total stockholders' equity | | 3,242,500 | | 2,725,750 |
| Total liabilities and stockholders' equity | | $7,105,000 | | $6,393,000 |

Since slow-moving or obsolescent inventories could overstate a firm's ability to meet short-term demands, the quick ratio is sometimes preferred to assess a firm's liquidity. The quick ratio is current assets minus inventories, divided by current liabilities. The quick ratio for the ABC Company is calculated as follows:

$$\frac{\text{Current assets} - \text{Inventories}}{\text{Current liabilities}} = \frac{\$1,950,000}{\$2,512,500} = 0.78 \ (2005)$$

$$= \frac{\$1,618,000}{\$2,242,250} = 0.72 \ (2004)$$

**EXHIBIT 5–C**
**ABC Company Income Statement For the Years Ending December 31, 2004, and 2005**

|                                      |            | **2005**   |            | **2004**   |
|--------------------------------------|-----------:|-----------:|-----------:|-----------:|
| Net sales                            |            | $8,250,000 |            | $8,000,000 |
| Cost of goods sold                   | $5,100,000 |            | $5,000,000 |            |
| Administrative expenses              | 1,750,000  |            | 1,680,000  |            |
| Other expenses                       | 420,000    |            | 390,000    |            |
| Total                                |            | 7,270,000  |            | 7,070,000  |
| Earnings before interest and taxes   |            | 980,000    |            | 930,000    |
| Less: Interest expense               |            | 210,000    |            | 210,000    |
| Earnings before taxes                |            | 770,000    |            | 720,000    |
| Less: Federal income taxes           |            | 360,000    |            | 325,000    |
| Earnings after taxes (net income)    |            | $  410,000 |            | $  395,000 |
| Common stock cash dividends          |            | $   90,000 |            | $   84,000 |
| Addition to retained earnings        |            | $  320,000 |            | $  311,000 |
| Earnings per common share            |            | $    3.940 |            | $     3.90 |
| Dividends per common share           |            | $    0.865 |            | $     0.83 |

A quick ratio of approximately 1 would be typical for American industries. Although there is less variability in the quick ratio than in the current ratio, stable industries would be able to operate safely with a lower ratio.

## LEVERAGE RATIOS

Leverage ratios identify the source of a firm's capital—owners or outside creditors. The term *leverage* refers to the fact that using capital with a fixed interest charge will "amplify" either profits or losses in relation to the equity of holders of common stock. The most commonly used ratio is total debt divided by total assets. Total debt includes current liabilities and long-term liabilities. This ratio is a measure of the percentage of total funds provided by debt. A total debt–total assets ratio higher than 0.5 is usually considered safe only for firms in stable industries.

$$\frac{\text{Total debt}}{\text{Total assets}} = \frac{\$3,862,500}{\$7,105,000} = 0.54 \, (2005)$$

$$= \frac{\$3,667,250}{\$6,393,000} = 0.57 \, (2004)$$

The ratio of long-term debt to equity is a measure of the extent to which sources of long-term financing are provided by creditors. It is computed by dividing long-term debt by the stockholders' equity.

$$\frac{\text{Long-term debt}}{\text{Equity}} = \frac{\$1,350,000}{\$3,242,500} = 0.42 \, (2005)$$

$$= \frac{\$1,425,000}{\$2,725,750} = 0.52 \, (2004)$$

# ACTIVITY RATIOS

Activity ratios indicate how effectively a firm is using its resources. By comparing revenues with the resources used to generate them, it is possible to establish an efficiency of operation. The asset turnover ratio indicates how efficiently management is employing total assets. Asset turnover is calculated by dividing sales by total assets. For the ABC Company, asset turnover is calculated as follows:

$$\text{Asset turnover} = \frac{\text{Sales}}{\text{Total assets}} = \frac{\$8,250,000}{\$7,105,000} = 1.16 \ (2005)$$

$$= \frac{\$8,000,000}{\$6,393,000} = 1.25 \ (2004)$$

The ratio of sales to fixed assets is a measure of the turnover on plant and equipment. It is calculated by dividing sales by net fixed assets.

$$\text{Fixed asset turnover} = \frac{\text{Sales}}{\text{Net fixed assets}} = \frac{\$8,250,000}{\$2,980,000} = 2.77 \ (2005)$$

$$= \frac{\$8,000,000}{\$2,775,000} = 2.88 \ (2004)$$

Industry figures for asset turnover will vary with capital-intensive industries, and those requiring large inventories will have much smaller ratios.

Another activity ratio is inventory turnover, estimated by dividing sales by average inventory. The norm for U.S. industries is 9, but whether the ratio for a particular firm is higher or lower normally depends on the product sold. Small, inexpensive items usually turn over at a much higher rate than larger, expensive ones. Since inventories normally are carried at cost, it would be more accurate to use the cost of goods sold in place of sales in the numerator of this ratio. Established compilers of industry ratios, such as Dun & Bradstreet, however, use the ratio of sales to inventory.

$$\text{Inventory turnover} = \frac{\text{Sales}}{\text{Inventory}} = \frac{\$8,250,000}{\$2,175,000} = 3.79 \ (2005)$$

$$= \frac{\$8,000,000}{\$2,000,000} = 4 \ (2004)$$

The accounts receivable turnover is a measure of the average collection period on sales. If the average number of days varies widely from the industry norm, it may be an indication of poor management. A too-low ratio could indicate the loss of sales because of a too restrictive credit policy. If the ratio is too high, too much capital is being tied up in accounts receivable, and management may be increasing the chance of bad debts. Because of varying industry credit policies, a comparison for the firm over time or within an industry is the only useful analysis. Because information on credit sales for other firms generally is unavailable, total sales must be used. Since not all firms have the same percentage of credit sales, there is only approximate comparability among firms.

$$\begin{array}{c}\text{Accounts receivable}\\\text{turnover}\end{array} = \frac{\text{Sales}}{\text{Accounts receivable}} = \frac{\$8,250,000}{\$1,760,000} = 4.69 \ (2005)$$

$$= \frac{\$8,000,000}{\$1,440,000} = 5.56 \ (2004)$$

$$\text{Average collection period} = \frac{360}{\text{Accounts receivable turnover}}$$

$$= \frac{360}{4.69} = 77 \text{ days } (2005)$$

$$= \frac{360}{5.56} = 65 \text{ days } (2004)$$

# PROFITABILITY RATIOS

Profitability is the net result of a large number of policies and decisions chosen by an organization's management. Profitability ratios indicate how effectively the total firm is being managed. The profit margin for a firm is calculated by dividing net earnings by sales. This ratio is often called *return on sales* (ROS). There is wide variation among industries, but the average for U.S. firms is approximately 5 percent.

$$\frac{\text{Net earnings}}{\text{Sales}} = \frac{\$410,000}{\$8,250,000} = 0.0497 \text{ (2005)}$$

$$= \frac{\$395,000}{\$8,000,000} = 0.0494 \text{ (2004)}$$

A second useful ratio for evaluating profitability is the return on investment—or *ROI,* as it is frequently called—found by dividing net earnings by total assets. The ABC Company's ROI is calculated as follows:

$$\frac{\text{Net earnings}}{\text{Total assets}} = \frac{\$410,000}{\$7,105,000} = 0.0577 \text{ (2005)}$$

$$= \frac{\$395,000}{\$6,393,000} = 0.0618 \text{ (2004)}$$

The ratio of net earnings to net worth is a measure of the rate of return or profitability of the stockholders' investment. It is calculated by dividing net earnings by net worth, the common stock equity and retained earnings account. ABC Company's return on net worth, also called ROE, is calculated as follows:

$$\frac{\text{Net earnings}}{\text{Net worth}} = \frac{\$410,000}{\$3,242,500} = 0.1264 \text{ (2005)}$$

$$= \frac{\$395,000}{\$2,725,750} = 0.1449 \text{ (2004)}$$

It is often difficult to determine causes for lack of profitability. The Du Pont system of financial analysis provides management with clues to the lack of success of a firm. This financial tool brings together activity, profitability, and leverage measures and shows how these ratios interact to determine the overall profitability of the firm. A depiction of the system is set forth in Exhibit 5–D.

The right side of the exhibit develops the turnover ratio. This section breaks down total assets into current assets (cash, marketable securities, accounts receivable, and inventories) and fixed assets. Sales divided by these total assets gives the turnover on assets.

**EXHIBIT 5–D**   **Du Pont's Financial Analysis**

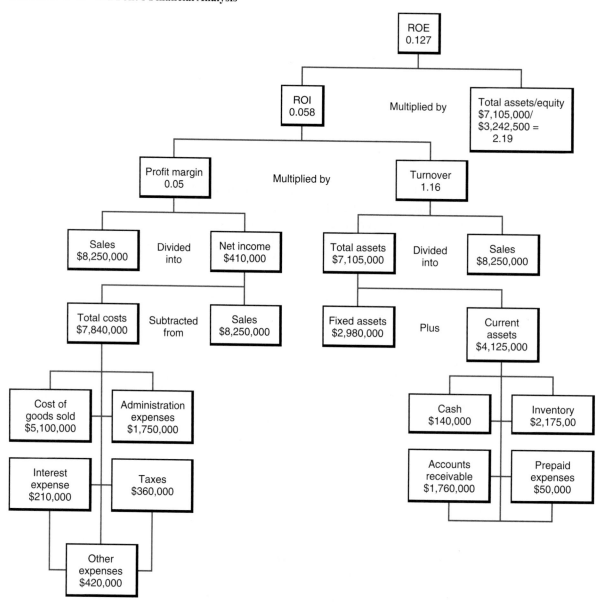

The left side of the exhibit develops the profit margin on sales. The individual expense items plus income taxes are subtracted from sales to produce net profits after taxes. Net profits divided by sales gives the profit margin on sales. When the asset turnover ratio on the right side of Exhibit 5–D is multiplied by the profit margin on sales developed on the left side of the exhibit, the product is the return on assets (ROI) for the firm. This can be shown by the following formula:

$$\frac{\text{Sales}}{\text{Total assets}} \times \frac{\text{Net earnings}}{\text{Sales}} = \frac{\text{Net earnings}}{\text{Total assets}} = \text{ROI}$$

The last step in the Du Pont analysis is to multiply the rate of return on assets (ROI) by the equity multiplier, which is the ratio of assets to common equity, to obtain the rate of return on equity (ROE). This percentage rate of return, of course, could be calculated directly by dividing net income by common equity. However, the Du Pont analysis demonstrates how the return on assets and the use of debt interact to determine the return on equity.

The Du Pont system can be used to analyze and improve the performance of a firm. On the left, or profit, side of the exhibit, attempts to increase profits and sales could be investigated. The possibilities of raising prices to improve profits (or lowering prices to improve volume) or seeking new products or markets, for example, could be studied. Cost accountants and production engineers could investigate ways to reduce costs. On the right, or turnover, side, financial officers could analyze the effect of reducing investment in various assets as well as the effect of using alternative financial structures.

There are two basic approaches to using financial ratios. One approach is to evaluate the corporation's performance over several years. Financial ratios are computed for different years, and then an assessment is made about whether there has been an improvement or deterioration over time. Financial ratios also can be computed for projected, pro forma, statements and compared with present and past ratios.

The other approach is to evaluate a firm's financial condition and compare it with the financial conditions of similar firms or with industry averages in the same period. Such a comparison gives insight into the firm's relative financial condition and performance. Financial ratios for industries are provided by Robert Morris Associates, Dun & Bradstreet, and various trade association publications. (Associations and their addresses are listed in the *Encyclopedia of Associations* and in the *Directory of National Trade Associations.*) Information about individual firms is available through *Moody's Manual,* Standard & Poor's manuals and surveys, annual reports to stockholders, and the major brokerage houses.

To the extent possible, accounting data from different companies must be so standardized that companies can be compared or so a specific company can be compared with an industry average. It is important to read any footnotes of financial statements, since various accounting or management practices can have an effect on the financial picture of the company. For example, firms using sale-leaseback methods may have leverage pictures quite different from what is shown as debts or assets on the balance sheet.

## ANALYSIS OF THE SOURCES AND USES OF FUNDS

The purpose of this analysis is to determine how the company is using its financial resources from year to year. By comparing balance sheets from one year to the next, one may determine how funds were obtained and how these funds were employed during the year.

To prepare a statement of the sources and uses of funds, it is necessary to (1) classify balance sheet changes that increase and decrease cash, (2) classify from the income statement those factors that increase or decrease cash, and (3) consolidate this information on a sources and uses of funds statement form.

Sources of funds that increase cash are:

1. A net decrease in any other asset than a depreciable fixed asset.
2. A gross decrease in a depreciable fixed asset.
3. A net increase in any liability.
4. Proceeds from the sale of stock.
5. The operation of the company (net income, and depreciation if the company is profitable).

Uses of funds include:

1. A net increase in any other asset than a depreciable fixed asset.
2. A gross increase in depreciable fixed assets.

3. A net decrease in any liability.
4. A retirement or purchase of stock.
5. Payment of cash dividends.

We compute gross changes to depreciable fixed assets by adding depreciation from the income statement for the period to net fixed assets at the end of the period and then subtracting from the total net fixed assets at the beginning of the period. The residual represents the change in depreciable fixed assets for the period.

For the ABC Company, the following change would be calculated:

| | |
|---|---|
| Net property and plant (2005) | $1,175,000 |
| Depreciation for 2005 | + 80,000 |
| | $1,255,000 |
| Net property and plant (2004) | −1,155,000 |
| | $ 100,000 |

To avoid double counting, the change in retained earnings is not shown directly in the funds statement. When the funds statement is prepared, this account is replaced by the earnings after taxes, or net income, as a source of funds, and dividends paid during the year as a use of funds. The difference between net income and the change in the retained earnings account will equal the amount of dividends paid during the year. The accompanying sources and uses of funds statement was prepared for the ABC Company.

A funds analysis is useful for determining trends in working-capital positions and for demonstrating how the firm has acquired and employed its funds during some period.

---

**ABC Company**
**Sources and Uses of Funds Statement**
**for 2005**

**Sources**

| | |
|---|---|
| Prepaid expenses | $ 13,000 |
| Accounts payable | 100,000 |
| Accrued federal taxes | 250,000 |
| Dividends payable | 3,750 |
| Common stock | 1,200 |
| Additional paid-in capital | 195,000 |
| Earnings after taxes (net income) | 410,000 |
| Depreciation | 80,000 |
| Total sources | $1,053,500 |

**Uses**

| | |
|---|---|
| Cash | $ 25,000 |
| Accounts receivable | 320,000 |
| Inventory | 175,000 |
| Long-term receivables | 165,000 |
| Property and plant | 100,000 |
| Other fixed assets | 20,000 |
| Bank loans payable | 75,000 |
| Current maturities of long-term debt | 8,500 |
| Long-term liabilities | 75,000 |
| Dividents paid | 90,000 |
| Total uses | $1,053,500 |

---

**EXHIBIT 5–E**
**A Summary of the Financial Position of a Firm**

| Ratios and Working Capital | 2001 | 2002 | 2003 | 2004 | 2005 | Trend | Industry Average | Interpre-tation |
|---|---|---|---|---|---|---|---|---|
| *Liquidity:* Current | | | | | | | | |
| Quick | | | | | | | | |
| *Leverage:* Debt-assets | | | | | | | | |
| Debt-equity | | | | | | | | |
| *Activity:* Asset turnover | | | | | | | | |
| Fixed asset ratio | | | | | | | | |
| Inventory turnover | | | | | | | | |
| Accounts receivable turnover | | | | | | | | |
| Average collection period | | | | | | | | |
| *Profitability:* ROS | | | | | | | | |
| ROI | | | | | | | | |
| ROE | | | | | | | | |
| Working-capital position | | | | | | | | |

# CONCLUSION

It is recommended that you prepare a chart, such as that shown in Exhibit 5–E, so you can develop a useful portrayal of these financial analyses. The chart allows a display of the ratios over time. The "Trend" column could be used to indicate your evaluation of the ratios over time (e.g., "favorable," "neutral," or "unfavorable"). The "Industry Average" column could include recent industry averages on these ratios or those of key competitors. These would provide information to aid interpretation of the analyses. The "Interpretation" column could be used to describe your interpretation of the ratios for this firm. Overall, this chart gives a basic display of the ratios that provides a convenient format for examining the firm's financial condition.

Finally, Exhibit 5–F is included to provide a quick reference summary of the calculations and meanings of the ratios discussed earlier.

**EXHIBIT 5–F**

**A Summary of Key Financial Ratios**

| Ratio | Calculation | Meaning |
|---|---|---|
| **Liquidity Ratios:** | | |
| Current ratio | $\dfrac{\text{Current assets}}{\text{Current liabilities}}$ | The extent to which a firm can meet its short-term obligations. |
| Quick ratio | $\dfrac{\text{Current assets–Inventory}}{\text{Current liabilities}}$ | The extent to which a firm can meet its short-term obligations without relying on the sale of inventories. |
| **Leverage Ratios:** | | |
| Debt-to-total-assets ratio | $\dfrac{\text{Total debt}}{\text{Total assets}}$ | The percentage of total funds that are provided by creditors. |
| Debt-to-equity ratio | $\dfrac{\text{Total debt}}{\text{Total stockholders' equity}}$ | The percentage of total funds provided by creditors versus the percentage provided by owners. |
| Long-term-debt-to-equity ratio | $\dfrac{\text{Long-term debt}}{\text{Total stockholders' equity}}$ | The balance between debt and equity in a firm's long-term capital structure. |
| Times-interest-earned ratio | $\dfrac{\text{Profits before interest and taxes}}{\text{Total interest charges}}$ | The extent to which earnings can decline without the firm becoming unable to meet its annual interest costs. |
| **Activity Ratios:** | | |
| Inventory turnover | $\dfrac{\text{Sales}}{\text{Inventory of finished goods}}$ | Whether a firm holds excessive stocks of inventories and whether a firm is selling its inventories slowly compared to the industry average. |
| Fixed assets turnover | $\dfrac{\text{Sales}}{\text{Fixed assets}}$ | Sales productivity and plant equipment utilization. |
| Total assets turnover | $\dfrac{\text{Sales}}{\text{Total assets}}$ | Whether a firm is generating a sufficient volume of business for the size of its assets investment. |
| Accounts receivable turnover | $\dfrac{\text{Annual credit sales}}{\text{Account receivable}}$ | In percentage terms, the average length of time it takes a firm to collect on credit sales. |
| Average collection period | $\dfrac{\text{Account receivable}}{\text{Total sales/365 days}}$ | In days, the average length of time it takes a firm to collect on credit sales. |

**EXHIBIT 5–F**
*(continued)*

| Ratio | Calculation | Meaning |
|---|---|---|
| **Profitability Ratios:** | | |
| Gross profit margin | $\dfrac{\text{Sales} - \text{Cost of goods sold}}{\text{Sales}}$ | The total margin available to cover operating expenses and yield a profit. |
| Operating profit margin | $\dfrac{\text{Earning before interest and taxes (EBIT)}}{\text{Sales}}$ | Profitability without concern for taxes and interest. |
| Net profit margin | $\dfrac{\text{Net income}}{\text{Sales}}$ | After-tax profits per dollar of sales. |
| Return on total assets (ROA) | $\dfrac{\text{Net income}}{\text{Total assets}}$ | After-tax profits per dollar of assets; this ratio is also called *return on investment* (ROI). |
| Return on stockholders' equity (ROE) | $\dfrac{\text{Net income}}{\text{Total stockholders' equity}}$ | After-tax profits per dollar of stockholders investment in the firm. |
| Earnings per share (EPS) | $\dfrac{\text{Net income}}{\text{Number of shares of common stock outstanding}}$ | Earnings available to the owners of common stock. |
| **Growth Ratio:** | | |
| Sales | Annual percentage growth in total sales | Firm's growth rate in sales. |
| Income | Annual percentage growth in profits | Firm's growth rate in profits. |
| Earnings per share | Annual percentage growth in EPS | Firm's growth rate in EPS. |
| Dividends per share | Annual percentage growth in dividends per share | Firm's growth rate in dividends per share. |
| Price-earnings ratio | $\dfrac{\text{Market price per share}}{\text{Earnings per share}}$ | Faster-growing and less risky firms tend to have higher price-earnings ratios. |

# Chapter **Six**

# Formulating Long-Term Objectives and Grand Strategies

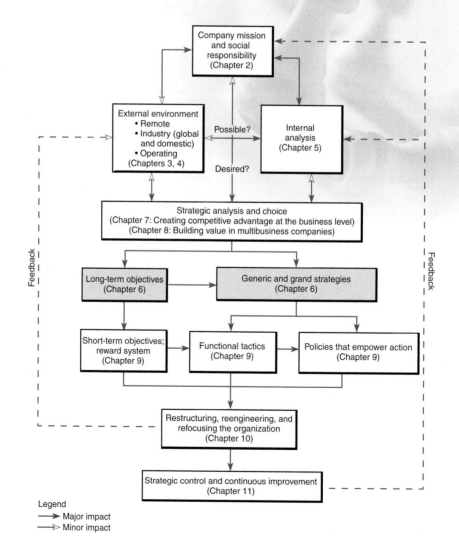

Company mission and social responsibility (Chapter 2)

External environment
- Remote
- Industry (global and domestic)
- Operating
(Chapters 3, 4)

Possible?

Desired?

Internal analysis (Chapter 5)

Strategic analysis and choice
(Chapter 7: Creating competitive advantage at the business level)
(Chapter 8: Building value in multibusiness companies)

Long-term objectives (Chapter 6)

Generic and grand strategies (Chapter 6)

Short-term objectives; reward system (Chapter 9)

Functional tactics (Chapter 9)

Policies that empower action (Chapter 9)

Restructuring, reengineering, and refocusing the organization (Chapter 10)

Strategic control and continuous improvement (Chapter 11)

Feedback

Feedback

Legend
→ Major impact
⇢ Minor impact

The company mission was described in Chapter 2 as encompassing the broad aims of the firm. The most specific statement of aims presented in that chapter appeared as the goals of the firm. However, these goals, which commonly dealt with profitability, growth, and survival, were stated without specific targets or time frames. They were always to be pursued but could never be fully attained. They gave a general sense of direction but were not intended to provide specific benchmarks for evaluating the firm's progress in achieving its aims. Providing such benchmarks is the function of objectives.[1]

The first part of this chapter will focus on long-term objectives. These are statements of the results a firm seeks to achieve over a specified period, typically three to five years. The second part will focus on the formulation of grand strategies. These provide a comprehensive general approach in guiding major actions designed to accomplish the firm's long-term objectives.

The chapter has two major aims: (1) to discuss in detail the concept of long-term objectives, the topics they cover, and the qualities they should exhibit; and (2) to discuss the concept of grand strategies and to describe the 15 principal grand strategy options that are available to firms singly or in combination, including three newly popularized options that are being used to provide the basis for global competitiveness.

# LONG-TERM OBJECTIVES

Strategic managers recognize that short-run profit maximization is rarely the best approach to achieving sustained corporate growth and profitability. An often repeated adage states that if impoverished people are given food, they will eat it and remain impoverished; however, if they are given seeds and tools and shown how to grow crops, they will be able to improve their condition permanently. A parallel choice confronts strategic decision makers:

1. Should they eat the seeds to improve the near-term profit picture and make large dividend payments through cost-saving measures such as laying off workers during periods of slack demand, selling off inventories, or cutting back on research and development?

2. Or should they sow the seeds in the effort to reap long-term rewards by reinvesting profits in growth opportunities, committing resources to employee training, or increasing advertising expenditures?

For most strategic managers, the solution is clear—distribute a small amount of profit now but sow most of it to increase the likelihood of a long-term supply. This is the most frequently used rationale in selecting objectives.

To achieve long-term prosperity, strategic planners commonly establish long-term objectives in seven areas:

*Profitability*   The ability of any firm to operate in the long run depends on attaining an acceptable level of profits. Strategically managed firms characteristically have a profit objective, usually expressed in earnings per share or return on equity.

*Productivity*   Strategic managers constantly try to increase the productivity of their systems. Firms that can improve the input-output relationship normally increase profitability. Thus, firms almost always state an objective for productivity. Commonly used productivity objectives are the number of items produced or the number of services rendered per unit of

---

[1]The terms *goals* and *objectives* are each used to convey a special meaning, with goals being the less specific and more encompassing concept. Most authors follow this usage; however, some use the two words interchangeably, while others reverse the usage.

input. However, productivity objectives sometimes are stated in terms of desired cost decreases. For example, objectives may be set for reducing defective items, customer complaints leading to litigation, or overtime. Achieving such objectives increases profitability if unit output is maintained.

***Competitive Position***    One measure of corporate success is relative dominance in the marketplace. Larger firms commonly establish an objective in terms of competitive position, often using total sales or market share as measures of their competitive position. An objective with regard to competitive position may indicate a firm's long-term priorities. For example, Gulf Oil set a five-year objective of moving from third to second place as a producer of high-density polypropylene. Total sales were the measure.

***Employee Development***    Employees value education and training, in part because they lead to increased compensation and job security. Providing such opportunities often increases productivity and decreases turnover. Therefore, strategic decision makers frequently include an employee development objective in their long-range plans. For example, PPG has declared an objective of developing highly skilled and flexible employees and, thus, providing steady employment for a reduced number of workers.

***Employee Relations***    Whether or not they are bound by union contracts, firms actively seek good employee relations. In fact, proactive steps in anticipation of employee needs and expectations are characteristic of strategic managers. Strategic managers believe that productivity is linked to employee loyalty and to appreciation of managers' interest in employee welfare. They, therefore, set objectives to improve employee relations. Among the outgrowths of such objectives are safety programs, worker representation on management committees, and employee stock option plans.

***Technological Leadership***    Firms must decide whether to lead or follow in the marketplace. Either approach can be successful, but each requires a different strategic posture. Therefore, many firms state an objective with regard to technological leadership. For example, Caterpillar Tractor Company established its early reputation and dominant position in its industry by being in the forefront of technological innovation in the manufacture of large earthmovers. E-commerce technology officers will have more of a strategic role in the management hierarchy of the future, demonstrating that the Internet has become an integral aspect of corporate long-term objective setting. In offering an e-technology manager higher-level responsibilities, a firm is pursuing a leadership position in terms of innovation in computer networks and systems. Officers of e-commerce technology at GE and Delta Air have shown their ability to increase profits by driving down transaction-related costs with Web-based technologies that seamlessly integrate their firms' supply chains. These technologies have the potential to "lock in" certain suppliers and customers and heighten competitive position through supply chain efficiency.

***Public Responsibility***    Managers recognize their responsibilities to their customers and to society at large. In fact, many firms seek to exceed government requirements. They work not only to develop reputations for fairly priced products and services but also to establish themselves as responsible corporate citizens. For example, they may establish objectives for charitable and educational contributions, minority training, public or political activity, community welfare, or urban revitalization. In an attempt to exhibit their public responsibility in the United States, Japanese companies, such as Toyota, Hitachi, and Matsushita, contribute more than $500 million annually to American educational projects, charities, and nonprofit organizations.

## Qualities of Long-Term Objectives

What distinguishes a good objective from a bad one? What qualities of an objective improve its chances of being attained? These questions are best answered in relation to seven criteria that should be used in preparing long-term objectives: acceptable, flexible, measurable over time, motivating, suitable, understandable, and achievable.

*Acceptable*  Managers are most likely to pursue objectives that are consistent with their preferences. They may ignore or even obstruct the achievement of objectives that offend them (e.g., promoting a high-sodium food product) or that they believe to be inappropriate or unfair (e.g., reducing spoilage to offset a disproportionate allocation of fixed overhead). In addition, long-term corporate objectives frequently are designed to be acceptable to groups external to the firm. An example is efforts to abate air pollution that are undertaken at the insistence of the Environmental Protection Agency.

*Flexible*  Objectives should be adaptable to unforeseen or extraordinary changes in the firm's competitive or environmental forecasts. Unfortunately, such flexibility usually is increased at the expense of specificity. One way of providing flexibility while minimizing its negative effects is to allow for adjustments in the level, rather than in the nature, of objectives. For example, the personnel department objective of providing managerial development training for 15 supervisors per year over the next five-year period might be adjusted by changing the number of people to be trained. In contrast, changing the personnel department's objective of "assisting production supervisors in reducing job-related injuries by 10 percent per year" after three months had gone by would understandably create dissatisfaction.

*Measurable*  Objectives must clearly and concretely state what will be achieved and when it will be achieved. Thus, objectives should be measurable over time. For example, the objective of "substantially improving our return on investment" would be better stated as "increasing the return on investment on our line of paper products by a minimum of 1 percent a year and a total of 5 percent over the next three years."

*Motivating*  People are most productive when objectives are set at a motivating level—one high enough to challenge but not so high as to frustrate or so low as to be easily attained. The problem is that individuals and groups differ in their perceptions of what is high enough. A broad objective that challenges one group frustrates another and minimally interests a third. One valuable recommendation is that objectives be tailored to specific groups. Developing such objectives requires time and effort, but objectives of this kind are more likely to motivate.

*Suitable*  Objectives must be suited to the broad aims of the firm, which are expressed in its mission statement. Each objective should be a step toward the attainment of overall goals. In fact, objectives that are inconsistent with the company mission can subvert the firm's aims. For example, if the mission is growth oriented, the objective of reducing the debt-to-equity ratio to 1.00 would probably be unsuitable and counterproductive.

*Understandable*  Strategic managers at all levels must understand what is to be achieved. They also must understand the major criteria by which their performance will be evaluated. Thus, objectives must be so stated that they are as understandable to the recipient as they are to the giver. Consider the misunderstandings that might arise over the objective of "increasing the productivity of the credit card department by 20 percent within two years." What does this objective mean? Increase the number of outstanding cards? Increase the use of outstanding cards? Increase the employee workload? Make productivity gains each year? Or hope that the new computer-assisted system, which should improve productivity, is approved by year 2? As this simple example illustrates, objectives must be clear, meaningful, and unambiguous.

***Achievable*** Finally, objectives must be possible to achieve. This is easier said than done. Turbulence in the remote and operating environments affects a firm's internal operations, creating uncertainty and limiting the accuracy of the objectives set by strategic management. To illustrate, the rapidly declining U.S. economy in 2000–2003 made objective setting extremely difficult, particularly in such areas as sales projections.

## The Balanced Scorecard

The Balanced Scorecard is a set of measures that are directly linked to the company's strategy. Developed by Robert S. Kaplan and David P. Norton, it directs a company to link its own long-term strategy with tangible goals and actions. The scorecard allows managers to evaluate the company from four perspectives: financial performance, customer knowledge, internal business processes, and learning and growth.

The Balanced Scorecard, as shown in Exhibit 6–1, contains a concise definition of the company's vision and strategy. Surrounding the vision and strategy are four additional boxes; each box contains the objectives, measures, targets, and initiatives for one of the four perspectives:

- The box at the top of Exhibit 6–1 represents the financial perspective, and answers the question "To succeed financially, how should we appear to our shareholders?"

- The box to the right represents the internal business process perspective and addresses the question "To satisfy our shareholders and customers, what business processes must we excel at?"

- The learning and growth box at the bottom of Exhibit 6–1 answers the question "To achieve our vision, how will we sustain our ability to change and improve?"

- The box at the left reflects the customer perspective, and responds to the question "To achieve our vision, how should we appear to our customers?"

**EXHIBIT 6–1** **The Balanced Scorecard**

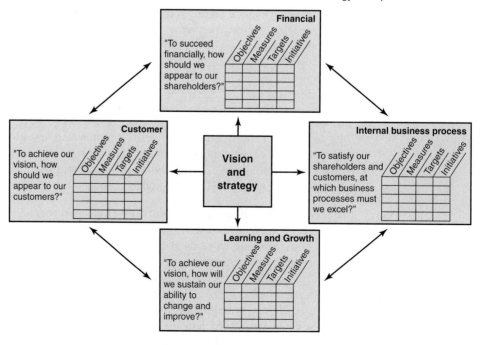

The balanced scorecard provides a framework to translate a strategy into operational terms

All of the boxes are connected by arrows to illustrate that the objectives and measures of the four perspectives are linked by cause-and-effect relationships that lead to the successful implementation of the strategy. Achieving one perspective's targets should lead to desired improvements in the next perspective, and so on, until the company's performance increases overall.

A properly constructed scorecard is balanced between short- and long-term measures; financial and nonfinancial measures; and internal and external performance perspectives.

The Balanced Scorecard is a management system that can be used as the central organizing framework for key managerial processes. Chemical Bank, Mobil Corporation's US Marketing and Refining Division, and CIGNA Property and Casualty Insurance have used the Balanced Scorecard approach to assist in individual and team goal setting, compensation, resource allocation, budgeting and planning, and strategic feedback and learning.

# GENERIC STRATEGIES

Many planning experts believe that the general philosophy of doing business declared by the firm in the mission statement must be translated into a holistic statement of the firm's strategic orientation before it can be further defined in terms of a specific long-term strategy. In other words, a long-term or grand strategy must be based on a core idea about how the firm can best compete in the marketplace.

The popular term for this core idea is *generic strategy*. From a scheme developed by Michael Porter, many planners believe that any long-term strategy should derive from a firm's attempt to seek a competitive advantage based on one of three generic strategies:

1. Striving for overall low-cost leadership in the industry.

2. Striving to create and market unique products for varied customer groups through *differentiation*.

3. Striving to have special appeal to one or more groups of consumer or industrial buyers, *focusing* on their cost or differentiation concerns.

Advocates of generic strategies believe that each of these options can produce above-average returns for a firm in an industry. However, they are successful for very different reasons.

Low-cost leaders depend on some fairly unique capabilities to achieve and sustain their low-cost position. Examples of such capabilities are: having secured suppliers of scarce raw materials, being in a dominant market share position, or having a high degree of capitalization. Low-cost producers usually excel at cost reductions and efficiencies. They maximize economies of scale, implement cost-cutting technologies, stress reductions in overhead and in administrative expenses, and use volume sales techniques to propel themselves up the earning curve. The commonly accepted requirements for successful implementation of the low-cost and the other two generic strategies are overviewed in Exhibit 6–2.

A low-cost leader is able to use its cost advantage to charge lower prices or to enjoy higher profit margins. By so doing, the firm effectively can defend itself in price wars, attack competitors on price to gain market share, or, if already dominant in the industry, simply benefit from exceptional returns. As an extreme case, it has been argued that National Can Company, a corporation in an essentially stagnant industry, is able to generate attractive and improving profits by being the low-cost producer.

Strategies dependent on differentiation are designed to appeal to customers with a special sensitivity for a particular product attribute. By stressing the attribute above other product qualities, the firm attempts to build customer loyalty. Often such loyalty translates into

**EXHIBIT 6–2**
**Requirements for Generic Competitive Strategies**

Source: Free Press *Competitive Strategy: Techniques for Analyzing Industries and Competitors,* pp. 40–41. Reprinted with permission of the Free Press, a division of Simon & Schuster, from *Competitive Strategy: Techniques for Analyzing Industries and Competitors,* by Michael E. Porter. Copyright © 1980 by Michael E. Porter.

| Generic Strategy | Commonly Required Skills and Resources | Common Organizational Requirements |
|---|---|---|
| Overall cost leadership | Sustained capital investment and access to capital. Process engineering skills. Intense supervision of labor. Products designed for ease in manufacture. Low-cost distribution system. | Tight cost control. Frequent, detailed control reports. Structured organization and responsibilities. Incentives based on meeting strict quantitative targets. |
| Differentiation | Strong marketing abilities. Product engineering. Creative flare. Strong capability in basic research. Corporate reputation for quality or technological leadership. Long tradition in the industry or unique combination of skills drawn from other businesses. Strong cooperation from channels. | Strong coordination among functions in R&D, product development, and marketing. Subjective measurement and incentives instead of quantitative measures. Amenities to attract highly skilled labor scientists, or creative people. |
| Focus | Combination of the above policies directed at the particular strategic target. | Combination of the above policies directed at the regular strategic target. |

a firm's ability to charge a premium price for its product. Cross-brand pens, Brooks Brothers suits, Porsche automobiles, and Chivas Regal Scotch whiskey are all examples.

The product attribute also can be the marketing channels through which it is delivered, its image for excellence, the features it includes, and the service network that supports it. As a result of the importance of these attributes, competitors often face "perceptual" barriers to entry when customers of a successfully differentiated firm fail to see largely identical products as being interchangeable. For example, General Motors hopes that customers will accept "only genuine GM replacement parts."

A focus strategy, whether anchored in a low-cost base or a differentiation base, attempts to attend to the needs of a particular market segment. Likely segments are those that are ignored by marketing appeals to easily accessible markets, to the "typical" customer, or to customers with common applications for the product. A firm pursuing a focus strategy is willing to service isolated geographic areas; to satisfy the needs of customers with special financing, inventory, or servicing problems; or to tailor the product to the somewhat unique demands of the small- to medium-sized customer. The focusing firms profit from their willingness to serve otherwise ignored or underappreciated customer segments. The classic example is cable television. An entire industry was born because of a willingness of cable firms to serve isolated rural locations that were ignored by traditional television services. Brick producers that typically service a radius of less than 100 miles and commuter airlines that serve regional geographic areas are other examples of industries where a focus strategy frequently yields above-average industry profits.

While each of the generic strategies enables a firm to maximize certain competitive advantages, each one also exposes the firm to a number of competitive risks. For example, a low-cost leader fears a new low-cost technology that is being developed by a competitor; a differentiating firm fears imitators; and a focused firm fears invasion by a firm that largely targets customers. As Exhibit 6–3 suggests, each generic strategy presents the firm with a number of risks.

**EXHIBIT 6–3**
**Risks of the Generic Strategies**

Source: Free Press *Competitive Advantage: Creating and Sustaining Superior Performance*, p. 21. Adapted with the permission of the Free Press, a division of Simon & Schuster, from *Competitive Strategy: Creating and Sustaining Superior Performance*, by Michael E. Porter. Copyright © 1985 by Michael E. Porter.

| Risks of Cost Leadership | Risks of Differentiation | Risks of Focus |
|---|---|---|
| Cost of leadership is not sustained:<br>• Competitors imitate.<br>• Technology changes.<br>• Other bases for cost leadership erode. | Differentiation is not sustained:<br>• Competitors imitate.<br>• Bases for differentiation become less important to buyers. | The focus strategy is imitated.<br>The target segment becomes structurally unattractive:<br>• Structure erodes.<br>• Demand disappears. |
| Proximity in differentiation is lost. | Cost proximity is lost. | Broadly targeted competitors overwhelm the segment:<br>• The segment's differences from other segments narrow.<br>• The advantages of a broad line increase. |
| Cost focusers achieve even lower cost in segments. | Differentiation focusers achieve even greater differentiation in segments. | New focusers subsegment the industry. |

# THE VALUE DISCIPLINES

International management consultants Michael Treacy and Fred Wiersema propose an alternative approach to generic strategy that they call the value disciplines.[2] They believe that strategies must center on delivering superior customer value through one of three value disciplines: operational excellence, customer intimacy, or product leadership.

Operational excellence refers to providing customers with convenient and reliable products or services at competitive prices. Customer intimacy involves offerings tailored to match the demands of identified niches. Product leadership, the third discipline, involves offering customers leading-edge products and services that make rivals' goods obsolete.

Companies that specialize in one of these disciplines, while simultaneously meeting industry standards in the other two, gain a sustainable lead in their markets. This lead is derived from the firm's focus on one discipline, aligning all aspects of operations with it. Having decided on the value that must be conveyed to customers, firms understand more clearly what must be done to attain the desired results. After transforming their organizations to focus on one discipline, companies can concentrate on smaller adjustments to produce incremental value. To match this advantage, less focused companies require larger changes than the tweaking that discipline leaders need.

## Operational Excellence

Operational excellence is a specific strategic approach to the production and delivery of products and services. A company that follows this strategy attempts to lead its industry in price and convenience by pursuing a focus on lean and efficient operations. Companies that employ operational excellence work to minimize costs by reducing overhead, eliminating intermediate production steps, reducing transaction costs, and optimizing business

---

[2]The ideas and examples in this section are drawn from Michael Treacy and Fred Wiersema, "Customer Intimacy and Other Value Disciplines," *Harvard Business Review,* 71(1): 84–94, 1993.

processes across functional and organizational boundaries. The focus is on delivering products or services to customers at competitive prices with minimal inconvenience.

Through its focus on operational excellence, Dell Computer has shown PC buyers that they do not have to sacrifice quality of state-of-the art technology in order to buy personal computers easily and inexpensively. Dell recognized the opportunity to cut retail dealers out of the industry's traditional distribution process. Through this approach—which includes direct sales, building to order, and creating a disciplined, extremely low-cost culture—Dell has been able to undercut other PC makers in price yet provide high-quality products and service.

Operational excellence is also the strategic focus of General Electric's large appliance business. Historically, the distribution strategy for large appliances was based on requiring that dealers maintain large inventories. Price breaks for dealers were based on order quantities. However, as the marketplace became more competitive, principally as a result of competition for multibrand dealers like Sears, GE recognized the need to adjust its production and distribution plans.

The GE system addresses the delivery of products. As a step toward organizational excellence, GE created a computer-based logistics system to replace its in-store inventories model. Retailers use this software to access a 24-hour on-line order processing system that guarantees GE's best price. This system allows dealers to better meet customer needs, with instantaneous access to a warehouse of goods and accurate shipping and production information. GE benefits from the deal as well. Efficiency is increased since manufacturing now occurs in response to customer sales. Additionally, warehousing and distribution systems have been streamlined to create the capability of delivering to 90 percent of destinations in the continental United States within one business day.

Firms that implement the strategy of operational excellence typically restructure their delivery processes to focus on efficiency and reliability, and use state-of-the art information systems that emphasize integration and low-cost transactions.

## Customer Intimacy

Companies that implement a strategy of customer intimacy continually tailor and shape products and services to fit an increasingly refined definition of the customer. Companies excelling in customer intimacy combine detailed customer knowledge with operational flexibility. They respond quickly to almost any need, from customizing a product to fulfilling special requests to create customer loyalty.

Customer-intimate companies are willing to spend money now to build customer loyalty for the long term, considering each customer's lifetime value to the company, not the profit of any single transaction. Consequently, employees in customer-intimate companies go to great lengths to ensure customer satisfaction with low regard for initial cost.

Home Depot implements the discipline of customer intimacy. Home Depot clerks spend the necessary time with customers to determine the product that best suits their needs, because the company's business strategy is built around selling information and service in addition to home-repair and improvement items. Consequently, consumers concerned solely with price fall outside Home Depot's core market.

Companies engaged in customer intimacy understand the difference between the profitability of a single transaction and the profitability of a lifetime relationship with a single customer. The company's profitability depends in part on its maintaining a system that differentiates quickly and accurately the degree of service that customers require and the revenues their patronage is likely to generate. Firms using this approach recognize that not every customer is equally profitable. For example, a financial services company installed a telephone-computer system capable of recognizing individual clients by their telephone numbers when they call. The system routes customers with large accounts and frequent transactions to their own senior account representative. Other customers may be routed to a trainee or junior representative. In any case, the customer's file appears on the representative's screen before the phone is answered.

The new system allows the firm to segment its services with great efficiency. If the company has clients who are interested in trading in a particular financial instrument, it can group them under the one account representative who specializes in that instrument. This saves the firm the expense of training every representative in every facet of financial services. Additionally, the company can direct certain value-added services or products to a specific group of clients that would have interest in them.

Businesses that select a customer intimacy strategy have decided to stress flexibility and responsiveness. They collect and analyze data from many sources. Their organizational structure emphasizes empowerment of employees close to customers. Additionally, hiring and training programs stress the creative decision-making skills required to meet individual customer needs. Management systems recognize and utilize such concepts as customer lifetime value, and norms among employees are consistent with a "have it your way" mind set.

## Product Leadership

Companies that pursue the discipline of product leadership strive to produce a continuous stream of state-of-the-art products and services. Three challenges must be met to attain that goal. Creativity is the first challenge. Creativity is recognizing and embracing ideas usually originating outside the company. Second, innovative companies must commercialize ideas quickly. Thus, their business and management processes need to be engineered for speed. Product leaders relentlessly pursue new solutions to problems. Finally, firms utilizing this discipline prefer to release their own improvements rather than wait for competitors to enter. Consequently, product leaders do not stop for self-congratulation; they focus on continual improvement.

For example, Johnson & Johnson's organizational design brings good ideas in, develops them quickly, and looks for ways to improve them. In 1983, the president of J&J's Vistakon, Inc., a maker of specialty contact lenses, received a tip concerning an ophthalmologist who had conceived of a method to manufacture disposable contact lenses inexpensively. Vistakon's president received this tip from a J&J employee from a different subsidiary whom he had never met. Rather than dismiss the tip, the executives purchased the rights to the technology, assembled a management team to oversee the product's development team to oversee the product's development, and built a state-of-the-art facility in Florida to manufacture disposable contact lenses called Acuvue. Vistakon and its parent, J&J, were willing to incur high manufacturing and inventory costs before a single lens was sold. A high-speed production facility helped give Vistakon a six-month head start over the competition that, taken off guard, never caught up.

Like other product leaders, J&J creates and maintains an environment that encourages employees to share ideas. Additionally, product leaders continually scan the environment for new product or service possibilities and rush to capitalize them. Product leaders also avoid bureaucracy because it slows commercialization of their ideas. In a product leadership company, a wrong decision often is less damaging than one made late. As a result, managers make decisions quickly, their companies encouraging them to decide today and implement tomorrow. Product leaders continually look for new methods to shorten their cycle times.

The strength of product leaders lies in reacting to situations as they occur. Shorter reaction times serve as an advantage in dealings with the unknown. For example, when competitors challenged the safety of Acuvue lenses, the firm responded quickly and distributed data combating the charges to eye-care professionals. This reaction created goodwill in the marketplace.

Product leaders act as their own competition. These firms continually make the products and services they have created obsolete. Product leaders believe that if they do not develop a successor, a competitor will. So, although Acuvue is successful in the marketplace, Vistakon continues to investigate new material that will extend the wearability of contact lenses and technologies that will make current lenses obsolete. J&J and other innovators recognize that the long-run profitability of an existing product or service is less important to the company's future than maintaining its product leadership edge and momentum.

# GRAND STRATEGIES

While the need for firms to develop generic strategies remains an unresolved debate, designers of planning systems agree about the critical role of grand strategies. *Grand strategies,* often called master or business strategies, provide basic direction for strategic actions. They are the basis of coordinated and sustained efforts directed toward achieving long-term business objectives.

The purpose of this section is twofold: (1) to list, describe, and discuss 15 grand strategies that strategic managers should consider and (2) to present approaches to the selection of an optimal grand strategy from the available alternatives.

Grand strategies indicate the time period over which long-range objectives are to be achieved. Thus, a grand strategy can be defined as a comprehensive general approach that guides a firm's major actions.

The 15 principal grand strategies are: concentrated growth, market development, product development, innovation, horizontal integration, vertical integration, concentric diversification, conglomerate diversification, turnaround, divestiture, liquidation, bankruptcy, joint ventures, strategic alliances, and consortia. Any one of these strategies could serve as the basis for achieving the major long-term objectives of a single firm. But a firm involved with multiple industries, businesses, product lines, or customer groups—as many firms are—usually combines several grand strategies. For clarity, however, each of the principal grand strategies is described independently in this section, with examples to indicate some of its relative strengths and weaknesses.

## Concentrated Growth

Many of the firms that fell victim to merger mania were once mistakenly convinced that the best way to achieve their objectives was to pursue unrelated diversification in the search for financial opportunity and synergy. By rejecting that "conventional wisdom," such firms as Martin-Marietta, KFC, Compaq, Avon, Hyatt Legal Services, and Tenant have demonstrated the advantages of what is increasingly proving to be sound business strategy. A firm that has enjoyed special success through a strategic emphasis on increasing market share through concentration is Chemlawn. With headquarters in Columbus, Ohio, Chemlawn is the North American leader in professional lawn care. Like others in the lawn-care industry, Chemlawn is experiencing a steadily declining customer base. Market analysis shows that the decline is fueled by negative environmental publicity, perceptions of poor customer service, and concern about the price versus the value of the company's services, given the wide array of do-it-yourself alternatives. Chemlawn's approach to increasing market share hinges on addressing quality, price, and value issues; discontinuing products that the public or environmental authorities perceive as unsafe; and improving the quality of its workforce.

These firms are just a few of the majority of American firms that pursue a concentrated growth strategy by focusing on a specific product and market combination. *Concentrated growth* is the strategy of the firm that directs its resources to the profitable growth of a single product, in a single market, with a single dominant technology. The main rationale for this approach, sometimes called a market penetration or concentration strategy, is that the firm thoroughly develops and exploits its expertise in a delimited competitive arena.

### Rationale for Superior Performance

Concentrated growth strategies lead to enhanced performance. The ability to assess market needs, knowledge of buyer behavior, customer price sensitivity, and effectiveness of promotion are characteristics of a concentrated growth strategy. Such core capabilities are a more important determinant of competitive market success than are the environmental forces faced by the firm. The high success rates of new products also are tied to avoiding situations that require undeveloped skills, such as serving new customers and markets, acquiring new technology, building new channels, developing new promotional abilities, and facing new competition.

A major misconception about the concentrated growth strategy is that the firm practicing it will settle for little or no growth. This is certainly not true for a firm that correctly utilizes the strategy. A firm employing concentrated growth grows by building on its competences, and it achieves a competitive edge by concentrating in the product-market segment it knows best. A firm employing this strategy is aiming for the growth that results from increased productivity, better coverage of its actual product-market segment, and more efficient use of its technology.

### Conditions That Favor Concentrated Growth

Specific conditions in the firm's environment are favorable to the concentrated growth strategy. The first is a condition in which the firm's industry is resistant to major technological advancements. This is usually the case in the late growth and maturity stages of the product life cycle and in product markets where product demand is stable and industry barriers, such as capitalization, are high. Machinery for the paper manufacturing industry, in which the basic technology has not changed for more than a century, is a good example.

An especially favorable condition is one in which the firm's targeted markets are not product saturated. Markets with competitive gaps leave the firm with alternatives for growth, other than taking market share away from competitors. The successful introduction of traveler services by Allstate and Amoco demonstrates that even an organization as entrenched and powerful as the AAA could not build a defensible presence in all segments of the automobile club market.

A third condition that favors concentrated growth exists when the firm's product markets are sufficiently distinctive to dissuade competitors in adjacent product markets from trying to invade the firm's segment. John Deere scrapped its plans for growth in the construction machinery business when mighty Caterpillar threatened to enter Deere's mainstay, the farm machinery business, in retaliation. Rather than risk a costly price war on its own turf, Deere scrapped these plans.

A fourth favorable condition exists when the firm's inputs are stable in price and quantity and are available in the amounts and at the times needed. Maryland-based Giant Foods is able to concentrate in the grocery business largely due to its stable long-term arrangements with suppliers of its private-label products. Most of these suppliers are makers of the national brands that compete against the Giant labels. With a high market share and aggressive retail distribution, Giant controls the access of these brands to the consumer. Consequently, its suppliers have considerable incentive to honor verbal agreements, called *bookings,* in which they commit themselves for a one-year period with regard to the price, quality, and timing of their shipments to Giant.

The pursuit of concentrated growth also is favored by a stable market—a market without the seasonal or cyclical swings that would encourage a firm to diversify. Night Owl Security, the District of Columbia market leader in home security services, commits its customers to initial four-year contracts. In a city where affluent consumers tend to be quite transient, the length of this relationship is remarkable. Night Owl's concentrated growth strategy has been reinforced by its success in getting subsequent owners of its customers' homes to extend and renew the security service contracts. In a similar way, Lands' End reinforced its growth strategy by asking customers for names and addresses of friends and relatives living overseas who would like to receive Lands' End catalogs.

A firm also can grow while concentrating, if it enjoys competitive advantages based on efficient production or distribution channels. These advantages enable the firm to formulate advantageous pricing policies. More efficient production methods and better handling of distribution also enable the firm to achieve greater economies of scale or, in conjunction with marketing, result in a product that is differentiated in the mind of the consumer. Graniteville Company, a large South Carolina textile manufacturer, enjoyed decades of growth and profitability by adopting a "follower" tactic as part of its concentrated growth strategy. By producing fabrics only after market demand had been well established, and by featuring products that reflected its expertise in adopting manufacturing innovations and in maintaining highly efficient long production runs, Graniteville prospered through concentrated growth.

Finally, the success of market generalists creates conditions favorable to concentrated growth. When generalists succeed by using universal appeals, they avoid making special appeals to particular groups of customers. The net result is that many small pockets are left open in the markets dominated by generalists, and that specialists emerge and thrive in these pockets. For example, hardware store chains, such as Home Depot, focus primarily on routine household repair problems and offer solutions that can be easily sold on a self-service, do-it-yourself basis. This approach leaves gaps at both the "semiprofessional" and "neophyte" ends of the market—in terms of the purchaser's skill at household repairs and the extent to which available merchandise matches the requirements of individual homeowners.

### Risk and Rewards of Concentrated Growth

Under stable conditions, concentrated growth poses lower risk than any other grand strategy; but, in a changing environment, a firm committed to concentrated growth faces high risks. The greatest risk is that concentrating in a single product market makes a firm particularly vulnerable to changes in that segment. Slowed growth in the segment would jeopardize the firm because its investment, competitive edge, and technology are deeply entrenched in a specific offering. It is difficult for the firm to attempt sudden changes if its product is threatened by near-term obsolescence, a faltering market, new substitutes, or changes in technology or customer needs. For example, the manufacturers of IBM clones faced such a problem when IBM adopted the OS/2 operating system for its personal computer line. That change made existing clones out of date.

The concentrating firm's entrenchment in a specific industry makes it particularly susceptible to changes in the economic environment of that industry. For example, Mack Truck, the second-largest truck maker in America, lost $20 million as a result of an 18-month slump in the truck industry.

Entrenchment in a specific product market tends to make a concentrating firm more adept than competitors at detecting new trends. However, any failure of such a firm to properly forecast major changes in its industry can result in extraordinary losses. Numerous makers of inexpensive digital watches were forced to declare bankruptcy because they failed to anticipate the competition posed by Swatch, Guess, and other trendy watches that emerged from the fashion industry.

A firm pursuing a concentrated growth strategy is vulnerable also to the high opportunity costs that result from remaining in a specific product market and ignoring other options that could employ the firm's resources more profitably. Overcommitment to a specific technology and product market can hinder a firm's ability to enter a new or growing product market that offers more attractive cost-benefit trade-offs. Had Apple Computers maintained its policy of making equipment that did not interface with IBM equipment, it would have missed out on what have proved to be its most profitable strategic options.

### Concentrated Growth Is Often the Most Viable Option

Examples abound of firms that have enjoyed exceptional returns on the concentrated growth strategy. Such firms as McDonald's, Goodyear, and Apple Computers have used firsthand knowledge and deep involvement with specific product segments to become powerful competitors in their markets. The strategy is associated even more often with successful smaller firms that have steadily and doggedly improved their market position.

The limited additional resources necessary to implement concentrated growth, coupled with the limited risk involved, also make this strategy desirable for a firm with limited funds. For example, through a carefully devised concentrated growth strategy, medium-sized John Deere & Company was able to become a major force in the agricultural machinery business even when competing with such firms as Ford Motor Company. While other firms were trying to exit or diversify from the farm machinery business, Deere spent $2 billion in upgrading its machinery, boosting its efficiency, and engaging in a program to strengthen its dealership system. This concentrated growth strategy enabled it to become the leader in the farm machinery business despite the fact that Ford was more than 10 times its size.

The firm that chooses a concentrated growth strategy directs its resources to the profitable growth of a narrowly defined product and market, focusing on a dominant technology. Firms that remain within their chosen product market are able to extract the most from their technology and market knowledge and, thus, are able to minimize the risk associated with unrelated diversification. The success of a concentration strategy is founded on the firm's use of superior insights into its technology, product, and customer to obtain a sustainable competitive advantage. Superior performance on these aspects of corporate strategy has been shown to have a substantial positive effect on market success.

A grand strategy of concentrated growth allows for a considerable range of action. Broadly speaking, the firm can attempt to capture a larger market share by increasing the usage rates of present customers, by attracting competitors' customers, or by selling to nonusers. In turn, each of these options suggests more specific options, some of which are listed in the top section of Exhibit 6–4.

When strategic managers forecast that their current products and their markets will not provide the basis for achieving the company mission, they have two options that involve moderate costs and risk: market development and product development.

## Market Development

*Market development* commonly ranks second only to concentration as the least costly and least risky of the 15 grand strategies. It consists of marketing present products, often with only cosmetic modifications, to customers in related market areas by adding channels of distribution or by changing the content of advertising or promotion. Several specific market development approaches are listed in Exhibit 6–4. Thus, as suggested by the figure,

**EXHIBIT 6–4**

**Specific Options under the Grand Strategies of Concentration, Market Development, and Product Development**

Source: Adapted from Philip Kotler, *Marketing Management Analysis, Planning, and Control,* 11th ed., 2002. Reprinted by permission of Prentice Hall, Inc., Upper Saddle River, NJ.

**Concentration (increasing use of present products in present markets):**

1. Increasing present customers' rate of use:
   a. Increasing the size of purchase.
   b. Increasing the rate of product obsolescence.
   c. Advertising other uses.
   d. Giving price incentives for increased use.
2. Attracting competitors' customers:
   a. Establishing sharper brand differentiation.
   b. Increasing promotional effort.
   c. Initiating price cuts.
3. Attracting nonusers to buy the product:
   a. Inducing trial use through sampling, price incentives, and so on.
   b. Pricing up or down.
   c. Advertising new uses.

**Market development (selling present products in new markets):**

1. Opening additional geographic markets:
   a. Regional expansion.
   b. National expansion.
   c. International expansion.
2. Attracting other market segments:
   a. Developing product versions to appeal to other segments.
   b. Entering other channels of distribution.
   c. Advertising in other media.

**Product development (developing new products for present markets):**

1. Developing new product features:
   a. Adapt (to other ideas, developments).
   b. Modify (change color, motion, sound, odor, form, shape).
   c. Magnify (stronger, longer, thicker, extra value).
   d. Minify (smaller, shorter, lighter).
   e. Substitute (other ingredients, process, power).
   f. Rearrange (other patterns, layout, sequence, components).
   g. Reverse (inside out).
   h. Combine (blend, alloy, assortment, ensemble; combine units, purposes, appeals, ideas).
2. Developing quality variations.
3. Developing additional models and sizes (product proliferation).

firms that open branch offices in new cities, states, or countries are practicing market development. Likewise, firms are practicing market development if they switch from advertising in trade publications to advertising in newspapers or if they add jobbers to supplement their mail-order sales efforts. Kmart pursued market development with its recent emphasis on increasing market share among Hispanics as described in Strategy in Action Exhibit 6–5.

Market development allows firms to practice a form of concentrated growth by identifying new uses for existing products and new demographically, psychographically, or geographically defined markets. Frequently, changes in media selection, promotional appeals, and distribution are used to initiate this approach. Du Pont used market development when it found a new application for Kevlar, an organic material that police, security, and military personnel had used primarily for bulletproofing. Kevlar now is being used to

**BusinessWeek** Move over, Martha. Here comes Thalia. The sexy Mexico-born pop star is about to add some sizzle to Kmart Corp.'s tired image. Industry sources say the queen of Latin pop will lend her name to a new line of clothing, shoes, and cosmetics for Kmart. Although unknown to many English-speaking Americans, Thalia (pronounced Tah-lee-ah) has a big following among Hispanics in the United States. The exclusive apparel line is part of a new strategy to woo Hispanic shoppers that may be Kmart's best hope for reviving its flagging business.

For years, Kmart has struggled to find a niche between Wal-Mart's low prices and Target's cheap chic. Kmart's biggest failure, last year's price war with Wal-Mart, helped land the company in bankruptcy court. Now, in its bid to survive, Kmart is latching on to the one advantage it has over its discount rivals: stores in heavily populated urban areas. That means catering more to multicultural consumers, who already make up nearly 40 percent of Kmart's sales.

Thalia's line is just the start. Kmart says it hopes to announce a similar deal with an African American celebrity by year-end. Meanwhile, it is adding more Hispanic merchandise to its stores and reaching out to Hispanics with new Spanish-language ads and publications. "It's a very strong step Kmart is taking," says Kurt Barnard, publisher of *Barnard's Retail Trend Report.* "It's going to pay big dividends."

The strategy isn't risk-free. Kmart could alienate its existing customers if it swings too far toward the Hispanic market. And Wal-Mart, already targeting Hispanics, plans to open more urban stores. "There's a window of opportunity for Kmart," says Ira Kalish, chief economist at Columbus (Ohio) consultant Retail Forward, Inc., "But it's going to close quickly."

Kmart is coming late to this party. Wal-Mart and Sears, Roebuck & Co. several years ago began letting local managers buy products suited to their communities. Kmart's previous management thought it more efficient for buyers at headquarters to purchase for stores nationwide. But, says CEO James B. Adamson, who took over in March, "people sitting in Troy, Mich., can't understand the difference between stores in Los Angeles, New York, Texas, or Miami."

That's why Adamson is giving store managers more say over what goes on their shelves. For Frank Gonzales, manager of a San Jose (Calif.) Kmart, that means selling tortilla warmers, tamale pots, and such produce as avocados, mangoes, and cilantro. "We were missing a lot of those sales," says Gonzales.

Kmart knows its Hispanic focus must not be seen as pandering. "They've got to know you're not giving them lip service," says Adamson, who is credited with turning around the Denny's restaurant chain after complaints of racial discrimination tarnished its image. In an effort to build loyalty, Kmart is launching on Sept. 15 *La Vida,* a four-page weekly magazine in Spanish to go out with a new Spanish ad circular. It will feature celebrities and lifestyle articles.

With Hispanics expected to outnumber African Americans by 2009, this may be Kmart's best chance. But it will take more than Hispanic shoppers to save the company. Its problems—ranging from poor inventory controls to lousy distribution—are deep-seated and can't be fixed overnight. But getting shoppers back is a start. And Thalia may help.

**Source:** *By Joann Muller in Troy, Mich., with Wendy Zellner in Dallas. BusinessWeek, September 9, 2002, p. 46.*

refit and maintain wooden-hulled boats, since it is lighter and stronger than glass fibers and has 11 times the strength of steel.

The medical industry provides other examples of new markets for existing products. The National Institutes of Health's report of a study showing that the use of aspirin may lower the incidence of heart attacks was expected to boost sales in the $2.2 billion analgesic market. It was predicted that the expansion of this market would lower the market share of nonaspirin brands, such as industry leaders Tylenol and Advil. Product extensions currently planned include Bayer Calendar Pack, 28-day packaging to fit the once-a-day prescription for the prevention of a second heart attack.

Another example is Chesebrough-Ponds, a major producer of health and beauty aids, which decided several years ago to expand its market by repacking its Vaseline Petroleum Jelly in pocket-size squeeze tubes as Vaseline "Lip Therapy." The corporation decided to place a strategic emphasis on market development, because it knew from market studies that its petroleum-jelly customers already were using the product to prevent chapped lips. Company leaders reasoned that their market could be expanded significantly if the product were repackaged to fit conveniently in consumers' pockets and purses.

**BusinessWeek** PepsiCo Corp. diverted some of its advertising attention away from its flagship cola toward newer and narrower brands like Sierra Mist and Pepsi Twist. It was the latest sign of how the soft-drink giant had reformulated its mission from bolstering core brands like Pepsi-Cola and Mountain Dew to peppering the market with niche products and brand extensions. Pepsi's market had splintered and big brands no longer had universal appeal. To attract a younger, less cohesive generation, Purchase (N.Y.)-based Pepsi had to rethink the way it developed and marketed its wares. "The era of the mass brand has been over for a long time," said David Burwick, chief marketing officer of Pepsi-Cola North America.

Pepsi's response had been a raft of new products, most bearing the Pepsi or Mountain Dew names. Its biggest hit had been cherry-flavored, caffeine-loaded Mountain Dew Code Red. Pepsi Twist and berry-flavored Pepsi Blue had developed more modest followings. Sierra Mist was a youth-skewed challenger to Cadbury Schweppes PLC's 7 Up.

Code Red, Twist, Blue, and Mist accounted for barely 5 percent of Pepsi's soft-drink sales. In the past, Pepsi might not have bothered with such small fry. In 2003, though, it was looking for products that could crack a hard-to-reach demographic group. Code Red, for example, had reeled in urbanites, women, and African Americans who had not previously shown any impulse to do the Dew. That could have helped offset flagship Pepsi's 2 percent volume sales decline in 2002.

Because these new drinks were more narrowly targeted, Pepsi had to refine its marketing techniques. To launch Code Red in 2001, the company handed out a million samples at youth magnets like the Winter X Games and the NCAA Final Four basketball tourney before the brand was available in stores. That helped create a buzz that got Code Red off to a brisk start. For teen-oriented Pepsi Blue last fall, Pepsi went beyond hiring rock stars to appear in ads. Instead, it worked out an innovative deal with Universal Music Group.

**Source:** Excerpted from Gerry Khermouch, "Call It the Pepsi Blue Generation." *BusinessWeek,* February 3, 2003, p. 96.

## Product Development

*Product development* involves the substantial modification of existing products or the creation of new but related products that can be marketed to current customers through established channels. The product development strategy often is adopted either to prolong the life cycle of current products or to take advantage of a favorite reputation or brand name. The idea is to attract satisfied customers to new products as a result of their positive experience with the firm's initial offering. The bottom section in Exhibit 6–4 lists some of the options available to firms undertaking product development. A revised edition of a college textbook, a new car style, and a second formula of shampoo for oily hair are examples of the product development strategy.

A detailed example of Pepsi's product development activities is provided in Exhibit 6–6, Strategy in Action. In 2001, Pepsi changed its strategy on beverage products by creating new products to follow the industry movement away from mass branding. This new movement was designed to attract a younger, hipper customer segment. Pepsi's new products include a version of Mountain Dew, called Code Red, and new Pepsi brands, called Pepsi Twist and Pepsi Blue.

The product development strategy is based on the penetration of existing markets by incorporating product modifications into existing items or by developing new products with a clear connection to the existing product line. The telecommunications industry provides an example of product extension based on product modification. To increase its estimated 8 to 10 percent share of the $5 to $6 billion corporate user market, MCI Communication Corporation extended its direct-dial service to 146 countries, the same as those serviced by AT&T, at lower average rates than those of AT&T. MCI's addition of 79 countries to its network underscores its belief in this market, which it expects to grow 15 to 20 percent annually. Another example of expansions linked to existing lines is Gerber's decision to engage in general merchandise marketing. Gerber's recent introduction included 52 items that ranged from feeding accessories to toys and children's wear. Likewise, Nabisco Brands seeks competitive advantage by placing its strategic emphasis on product development.

With headquarters in Parsippany, New Jersey, the company is one of three operating units of RJR Nabisco. It is the leading producer of biscuits, confections, snacks, shredded cereals, and processed fruits and vegetables. To maintain its position as leader, Nabisco pursues a strategy of developing and introducing new products and expanding its existing product line. Spoon Size Shredded Wheat and Ritz Bits crackers are two examples of new products that are variations on existing products.

## Innovation

In many industries, it has become increasingly risky not to innovate. Both consumer and industrial markets have come to expect periodic changes and improvements in the products offered. As a result, some firms find it profitable to make *innovation* their grand strategy. They seek to reap the initially high profits associated with customer acceptance of a new or greatly improved product. Then, rather than face stiffening competition as the basis of profitability shifts from innovation to production or marketing competence, they search for other original or novel ideas. The underlying rationale of the grand strategy of innovation is to create a new product life cycle and thereby make similar existing products obsolete. Thus, this strategy differs from the product development strategy of extending an existing product's life cycle. For example, Intel, a leader in the semiconductor industry, pursues expansion through a strategic emphasis on innovation. With headquarters in California, the company is a designer and manufacturer of semiconductor components and related computers, of microcomputer systems, and of software. Its Pentium microprocessor gives a desktop computer the capability of a mainframe.

While most growth-oriented firms appreciate the need to be innovative occasionally, a few firms use it as their fundamental way of relating to their markets. An outstanding example is Polaroid, which heavily promotes each of its new cameras until competitors are able to match its technological innovation; by this time, Polaroid normally is prepared to introduce a dramatically new or improved product. For example, it introduced consumers in quick succession to the Swinger, the SX-70, the One Step, and the Sun Camera 660.

Few innovative ideas prove profitable because the research, development, and premarketing costs of converting a promising idea into a profitable product are extremely high. A study by the Booz Allen & Hamilton management research department provides some understanding of the risks. As shown in Exhibit 6–7, Booz Allen & Hamilton found that less

**EXHIBIT 6–7**
**Decay of New Product Ideas (51 Companies)**

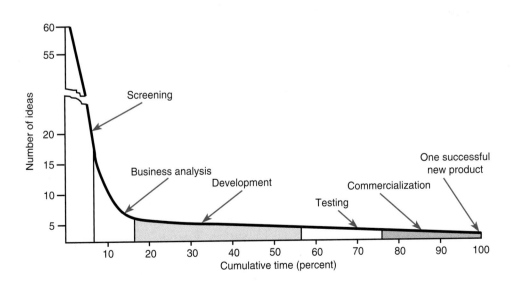

**BusinessWeek** Measured against the nation's wireless giants, VoiceStream Wireless Corp. has been a bit of a pipsqueak. So why would Germany's Deutsche Telekom pay an eye-popping $21,639 per subscriber for the little Bellevue, Washington, cell phone company? Simply put, Deutsche Telekom is not buying subscribers in the United States. It's buying potential—in this case, the potential to become a dominant player—not just in the United States, but globally. By the end of 2000, only about 32.5 percent of the U.S. population was using some form of wireless compared with 52 percent in Europe and 60 percent in Japan. Growth prospects in such a relatively undeveloped market, the German executives reckon, are so high that their company will emerge almost immediately as a formidable rival. U.S. telecom execs say a DT-VoiceStream link will force U.S. players to step up efforts to provide wireless Net service to a broader market, including overseas.

To gain this kind of sway over the lucrative U.S. market and the global market, Deutsche Telekom felt it was worth significantly besting the $4,390 per subscriber Britain's Vodafone paid for AirTouch in 1999 or the estimated $12,400 that the combined Vodafone-AirTouch paid for Mannesmann earlier

this year. That has set off a torrent of criticism that it has wildly overpaid for its position. However, Deutsche Telekom's CEO Sommer is confident. Here's what he considered when he agreed to the price: VoiceStream owns licenses in 23 of the top 25 U.S. markets. In wireless lingo, its licenses cover areas with a 220 million subscriber base. Though it has relatively few subscribers signed up and currently does not actually provide service to many of the locales where it holds licenses, it is adding subscribers at a sizzling pace—an 18.5 percent growth rate that is among the top in the industry.

Wireless companies across the country are taking note, given DT's deep pockets and promise to make a starting investment of at least $5 billion in VoiceStream. With the $5 billion, VoiceStream can accelerate construction of wireless systems in places like California and Ohio. Stanton estimates that the cash infusion will help him push up the roll-out of his service by 6 to 18 months. Also, Deutsche Telekom's cash is expected to allow VoiceStream to participate in a major way in the upcoming auction of more spectrum licenses by the FCC.

**Source:** Excerpted from R. O. Crockett and D. Fairlamb, August 7, 2000, "Deutsche Telekom's Wireless Wager," *BusinessWeek* (3693), pp. 30–32.

than 2 percent of the innovative projects initially considered by 51 companies eventually reached the marketplace. Specifically, out of every 58 new product ideas, only 12 pass an initial screening test that finds them compatible with the firm's mission and long-term objectives, only 7 remain after an evaluation of their potential, and only 3 survive development attempts. Of the three survivors, two appear to have profit potential after test marketing and only one is commercially successful.

## Horizontal Integration

When a firm's long-term strategy is based on growth through the acquisition of one or more similar firms operating at the same stage of the production-marketing chain, its grand strategy is called *horizontal integration*. Such acquisitions eliminate competitors and provide the acquiring firm with access to new markets. One example is Warner-Lambert's acquisition of Parke Davis, which reduced competition in the ethical drugs field for Chilcott Laboratories, a firm that Warner-Lambert previously had acquired. Another example is the long-range acquisition pattern of White Consolidated Industries, which expanded in the refrigerator and freezer market through a grand strategy of horizontal integration, by acquiring Kelvinator Appliance, the Refrigerator Products Division of Bendix Westinghouse Automotive Air Brake, and Frigidaire Appliance from General Motors. Nike's acquisition in the dress shoes business and N. V. Homes's purchase of Ryan Homes have vividly exemplified the success that horizontal integration strategies can bring.

Exhibit 6–8, Global Strategy in Action, describes Deutsche Telekom growth strategy of horizontal acquisition. Deutsche Telekom was a dominant player in the European wireless services market, but without a presence in the fast-growing U.S. market. To correct this limitation, Deutsche Telekom horizontally integrated by purchasing the American firm Voice-Stream Wireless, a company that was growing faster than most domestic rivals and that owned spectrum licenses providing access to 220 million potential customers.

## Vertical Integration

When a firm's grand strategy is to acquire firms that supply it with inputs (such as raw materials) or are customers for its outputs (such as warehousers for finished products), *vertical integration* is involved. To illustrate, if a shirt manufacturer acquires a textile producer—by purchasing its common stock, buying its assets, or exchanging ownership interests—the strategy is vertical integration. In this case, it is *backward* vertical integration, since the acquired firm operates at an earlier stage of the production-marketing process. If the shirt manufacturer had merged with a clothing store, it would have been *forward* vertical integration—the acquisition of a firm nearer to the ultimate consumer.

Amoco emerged as North America's leader in natural gas reserves and products as a result of its acquisition of Dome Petroleum. This backward integration by Amoco was made in support of its downstream businesses in refining and in gas stations, whose profits made the acquisition possible.

Exhibit 6–9 depicts both horizontal and vertical integration. The principal attractions of a horizontal integration grand strategy are readily apparent. The acquiring firm is able to greatly expand its operations, thereby achieving greater market share, improving economies of scale, and increasing the efficiency of capital use. In addition, these benefits are achieved with only moderately increased risk, since the success of the expansion is principally dependent on proven abilities.

The reasons for choosing a vertical integration grand strategy are more varied and sometimes less obvious. The main reason for backward integration is the desire to increase the dependability of the supply or quality of the raw materials used as production inputs. That desire is particularly great when the number of suppliers is small and the number of competitors is large. In this situation, the vertically integrating firm can better control its costs and, thereby, improve the profit margin of the expanded production-marketing system. Forward integration is a preferred grand strategy if great advantages accrue to stable production. A firm can increase the predictability of demand for its output through forward integration; that is, through ownership of the next stage of its production-marketing chain.

**EXHIBIT 6–9**
**Vertical and Horizontal Integrations**

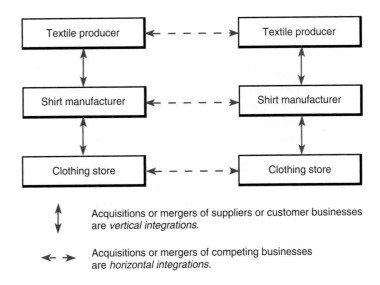

Some increased risks are associated with both types of integration. For horizontally integrated firms, the risks stem from increased commitment to one type of business. For vertically integrated firms, the risks result from the firm's expansion into areas requiring strategic managers to broaden the base of their competences and to assume additional responsibilities.

## Concentric Diversification

Grand strategies involving diversification represent distinctive departures from a firm's existing base of operations, typically the acquisition or internal generation (spin-off) of a separate business with synergistic possibilities counterbalancing the strengths and weaknesses of the two businesses. For example, Head Ski initially sought to diversify into summer sporting goods and clothing to offset the seasonality of its "snow" business. However, diversifications occasionally are undertaken as unrelated investments, because of their high profit potential and their otherwise minimal resource demands.

Regardless of the approach taken, the motivations of the acquiring firms are the same:

- Increase the firm's stock value. In the past, mergers often have led to increases in the stock price or the price-earnings ratio.

- Increase the growth rate of the firm.

- Make an investment that represents better use of funds than plowing them into internal growth.

- Improve the stability of earnings and sales by acquiring firms whose earnings and sales complement the firm's peaks and valleys.

- Balance or fill out the product line.

- Diversify the product line when the life cycle of current products has peaked.

- Acquire a needed resource quickly (e.g., high-quality technology or highly innovative management).

- Achieve tax savings by purchasing a firm whose tax losses will offset current or future earnings.

- Increase efficiency and profitability, especially if there is synergy between the acquiring firm and the acquired firm.[3]

*Concentric diversification* involves the acquisition of businesses that are related to the acquiring firm in terms of technology, markets, or products. With this grand strategy, the selected new businesses possess a high degree of compatibility with the firm's current businesses. The ideal concentric diversification occurs when the combined company profits increase the strengths and opportunities and decrease the weaknesses and exposure to risk. Thus, the acquiring firm searches for new businesses whose products, markets, distribution channels, technologies, and resource requirements are similar to but not identical with its own, whose acquisition results in synergies but not complete interdependence.

## Conglomerate Diversification

Occasionally a firm, particularly a very large one, plans to acquire a business because it represents the most promising investment opportunity available. This grand strategy is commonly known as *conglomerate diversification.* The principal concern, and often the sole

---

[3]Godfrey Devlin and Mark Bleackley, "Strategic Alliances—Guidelines for Success," *Long Range Planning,* October 1988, pp. 18–23.

**EXHIBIT 6–11   A Model of the Turnaround Process**

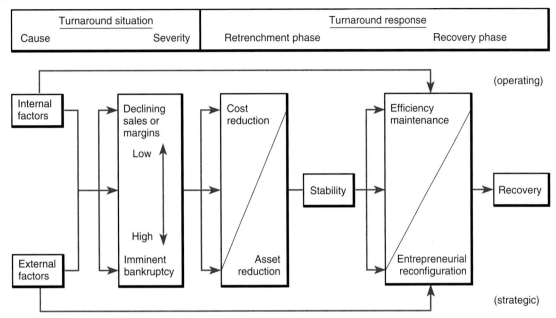

asset reduction measures. Assets targeted for divestiture are those determined to be under-productive. In contrast, more productive resources are protected from cuts and represent critical elements of the future core business plan of the company (i.e., the intended recovery response).

*Turnaround responses* among successful firms typically include two stages of strategic activities: retrenchment and the recovery response. *Retrenchment* consists of cost-cutting and asset-reducing activities. The primary objective of the retrenchment phase is to stabilize the firm's financial condition. Situation severity has been associated with retrenchment responses among successful turnaround firms. Firms in danger of bankruptcy or failure (i.e., severe situations) attempt to halt decline through cost and asset reductions. Firms in less severe situations have achieved stability merely through cost retrenchment. However, in either case, for firms facing declining financial performance, the key to successful turnaround rests in the effective and efficient management of the retrenchment process.

The primary causes of the turnaround situation have been associated with the second phase of the turnaround process, the *recovery response.* For firms that declined primarily as a result of external problems, turnaround most often has been achieved through creative new entrepreneurial strategies. For firms that declined primarily as a result of internal problems, turnaround has been most frequently achieved through efficiency strategies. *Recovery* is achieved when economic measures indicate that the firm has regained its predownturn levels of performance.

## Divestiture

A *divestiture strategy* involves the sale of a firm or a major component of a firm. Sara Lee Corp. (SLE) provides a good example. It sells everything from Wonderbras and Kiwi shoe polish to Endust furniture polish and Chock full o'Nuts coffee. The company used a conglomerate diversification strategy to build Sara Lee into a huge portfolio of disparate brands. A new president, C. Steven McMillan, faced stagnant revenues and earnings. So he consolidated, streamlined, and focused the company on its core categories—food, underwear, and household products. He divested 15 businesses, including Coach leather goods, which together equaled over 20 percent of the company's revenue, and laid off 13,200 employees, nearly 10 percent of the workforce. McMillan used the cash from asset sales to snap up brands that enhanced Sara Lee's clout in key categories, like the $2.8 billion purchase of St. Louis-based breadmaker Earthgrains Co. to quadruple Sara Lee's bakery operations.

When retrenchment fails to accomplish the desired turnaround, as in the Goodyear situation, or when a nonintegrated business activity achieves an unusually high market value, strategic managers often decide to sell the firm. However, because the intent is to find a buyer willing to pay a premium above the value of a going concern's fixed assets, the term *marketing for sale* is often more appropriate. Prospective buyers must be convinced that because of their skills and resources or because of the firm's synergy with their existing businesses, they will be able to profit from the acquisition.

As discussed in Exhibit 6–12, Strategy in Action, Corning undertook a turnaround that followed retrenchment with divestitures. In 2001, Corning found itself in a declining market for its core product of fiber optic cable. The company needed to develop a strategy that would allow it to turnaround its falling sales and begin to grow once more. It began with retrenchment. Corning laid off 12,000 workers in 2001 and another 4,000 in 2002. Corning also began the divestiture of its non-core assets, such as its non-telecom businesses, and its money-losing photonics operation to stabilize its financial situation so that it could begin its recovery.

The reasons for divestiture vary. They often arise because of partial mismatches between the acquired firm and the parent corporation. Some of the mismatched parts cannot be integrated into the corporation's mainstream activities and, thus, must be spun off. A second reason is corporate financial needs. Sometimes the cash flow or financial stability of the corporation as a whole can be greatly improved if businesses with high market value can be sacrificed. The result can be a balancing of equity with long-term risks or of long-term debt payments to optimize the cost of capital. A third, less frequent reason for divestiture is government antitrust action when a firm is believed to monopolize or unfairly dominate a particular market.

Although examples of the divestiture grand strategy are numerous, CBS, Inc., provides an outstanding example. In a two-year period, the once diverse entertainment and publishing giant sold its Records Division to Sony, its magazine publishing business to Diamandis Communications, its book publishing operations to Harcourt Brace Jovanovich, and its music publishing operations to SBK Entertainment World. Other firms that have pursued this type of grand strategy include Esmark, which divested Swift & Company, and White Motors, which divested White Farm.

## Liquidation

When liquidation is the grand strategy, the firm typically is sold in parts, only occasionally as a whole—but for its tangible asset value and not as a going concern. In selecting liquidation, the owners and strategic managers of a firm are admitting failure and recognize that this action is likely to result in great hardships to themselves and their employees. For these reasons, liquidation usually is seen as the least attractive of the grand strategies. As a long-term strategy, however, it minimizes the losses of all the firm's stockholders. Faced with bankruptcy, the liquidating firm usually tries to develop a planned and orderly system that will result in the greatest possible return and cash conversion as the firm slowly relinquishes its market share.

Planned liquidation can be worthwhile. For example, Columbia Corporation, a $130 million diversified firm, liquidated its assets for more cash per share than the market value of its stock.

**BusinessWeek** The year is 2002. Corning, the deeply weakened fiber-optic powerhouse, is trying to navigate between the telecom meltdown and a looming liquidity squeeze.

When James Houghton left retirement to retake the reins at Corning (GLW) in June, 2001, the world's largest fiber-optic cable maker clearly had lost its footing. Its customers were cutting their capital budgets as their own customers demanded lower prices. Corning's revenues were beginning to drop precipitously. Houghton, who joined Corning in 1962 and became its chairman and CEO before retiring in 1996, was returning just as his glass empire was starting to crack.

Things haven't improved much so far in 2002. Corning's sales, at $2 billion in the fourth quarter of 2000, reached only $896 million in the second quarter of 2002. That's down 52 percent from year-ago levels and slightly down from the first quarter. Corning had already laid off 12,000 workers in 2001 at its Corning (N.Y.) headquarters. But on July 23, it announced an additional 4,000 layoffs, bringing its workforce down to 28,000. Its stock, trading at $340 per share in 2000, before a split, hit a new low of $1.50 on Aug. 1. Analysts say a $2 billion credit line could be in jeopardy. And Corning might not reach profitability in 2003, as promised. It might even have difficulty paying off $2.1 billion zero-coupon, convertible bonds due in 2005. Ironically, no one is saying that Corning's products are substandard. Just the opposite, in fact. But that might not be enough to get it over a very tough financial patch.

Liquidity remains a key concern. At the end of its most recent quarter, Corning had $940 million in cash and $383 million in short-term investments. But the funds are needed for day-to-day operations, restructuring, and debt payments, so by the end of 2003, Corning will go through most of that stash. Standard & Poor's has downgraded Corning's credit rating to below investment grade, meaning the company could have trouble raising additional funds—which are exactly what Corning might need for operations if some of its short-term investments aren't sellable, says Kingston. As of June 30, Corning had $4.76 billion in property, plants, and equipment. Its four fiber plants—two in North Carolina, one in Germany, and one in Australia—are running at 40 percent capacity. The larger, U.S.-based plants cost about $450 million each to build, and Corning could, potentially, write off half of the capacity, or about $1 billion.

Goodwill write-offs could be massive as well. Most of the value in the $2 billion goodwill account comes from Corning's optical-components business. Considering that several companies currently trying to sell similar businesses are having a hard time getting even a few cents on the dollar, the write-off could be huge.

Corning could raise money by issuing more equity—and diluting the interests of existing shareholders. Recently, it sold $575 million of three-year mandatory convertible preferred stock, with a coupon rate of 7 percent. Of course, Corning could sell some of its businesses for cash. Though it's known mainly for its optical cable, Corning also makes glass for flat-panel monitors, funnels for large-screen TVs, and frequency controls for electronics. These businesses account for half of its revenues, and many are growing and are profitable.

Barring some unprecedented telecom turnaround, without more cost cuts Corning is unlikely to reach profitability in 2003. That's a long time to ask investors to hang tough in this kind of market. And demand for fiber could remain weak for three more years, says Russ McGuire, chief strategist at telecom consultancy TeleChoice. Even when it does turn up, demand likely won't soar. All of the major telecom networks are already built out, and the stretches that remain will require less capacity—and less fiber, says Patrick Fay, an analyst at fiber-consultancy KMI.

**Source:** Excerpted from Olga Kharif, "Corning's 'Very Narrow Straits.'" *BusinessWeek Online,* August 30, 2002.

## Bankruptcy

Business failures are playing an increasingly important role in the American economy. In an average week, more than 300 companies fail. More than 75 percent of these financially desperate firms file for a *liquidation bankruptcy*—they agree to a complete distribution of their assets to creditors, most of whom receive a small fraction of the amount they are owed. Liquidation is what the layperson views as bankruptcy: The business cannot pay its debts, so it must close its doors. Investors lose their money, employees lose their jobs, and managers lose their credibility. In owner-managed firms, company and personal bankruptcy commonly go hand in hand.

The other 25 percent of these firms refuse to surrender until one final option is exhausted. Choosing a strategy to recapture its viability, such a company asks the courts for a *reorganization bankruptcy.* The firm attempts to persuade its creditors to temporarily freeze their claims while it undertakes to reorganize and rebuild the company's operations more profitably. The appeal of a reorganization bankruptcy is based on the company's ability to convince creditors that it can succeed in the marketplace by implementing a new strategic plan, and that when the plan produces profits, the firm will be able to repay its creditors, perhaps in full. In other words, the company offers its creditors a carefully designed alternative to forcing an immediate, but fractional, repayment of its financial obligations. The option of reorganization bankruptcy offers maximum repayment of debt at some specified future time if a new strategic plan is successful.

### The Bankruptcy Situation

Imagine that your firm's financial reports have shown an unabated decline in revenue for seven quarters. Expenses have increased rapidly, and it is becoming difficult, and at times not possible, to pay bills as they become due. Suppliers are concerned about shipping goods without first receiving payment, and some have refused to ship without advanced payment in cash. Customers are requiring assurances that future orders will be delivered and some are beginning to buy from competitors. Employees are listening seriously to rumors of financial problems and a higher than normal number have accepted other employment. What can be done? What strategy can be initiated to protect the company and resolve the financial problems in the short term?

### The Harshest Resolution

If the judgment of the owners of a business is that its decline cannot be reversed, and the business cannot be sold as a going concern, then the alternative that is in the best interest of all may be a liquidation bankruptcy, also known as Chapter 7 of the Bankruptcy Code. The court appoints a trustee, who collects the property of the company, reduces it to cash, and distributes the proceeds proportionally to creditors on a pro rata basis as expeditiously as possible. Since all assets are sold to pay outstanding debt, a liquidation bankruptcy terminates a business. This type of filing is critically important to sole proprietors or partnerships. Their owners are personally liable for all business debts not covered by the sale of the business assets unless they can secure a Chapter 7 bankruptcy, which will allow them to cancel any debt in excess of exempt assets. Although they will be left with little personal property, the liquidated debtor is discharged from paying the remaining debt.

The shareholders of corporations are not liable for corporate debt and any debt existing after corporate assets are liquidated is absorbed by creditors. Corporate shareholders may simply terminate operations and walk away without liability to remaining creditors. However, filing a Chapter 7 proceeding will provide for an orderly and fair distribution of assets to creditors and thereby may reduce the negative impact of the business failure.

### A Conditional Second Chance

A proactive alternative for the endangered company is reorganization bankruptcy. Chosen for the right reasons, and implemented in the right way, reorganization bankruptcy can provide a financially, strategically, and ethically sound basis on which to advance the interests of all of the firm's stakeholders.

A thorough and objective analysis of the company may support the idea of its continuing operations if excessive debt can be reduced and new strategic initiatives can be undertaken. If the realistic possibility of long-term survival exists, a reorganization under Chapter 11 of the Bankruptcy Code can provide the opportunity. Reorganization allows a business debtor to restructure its debts and, with the agreement of creditors and approval of the court, to continue as a viable business. Creditors involved in Chapter 11 actions often receive less than the total debt due to them but far more than would be available from liquidation.

A Chapter 11 bankruptcy can provide time and protection to the debtor firm (which we will call the *Company*) to reorganize and use future earnings to pay creditors. The Company may restructure debts, close unprofitable divisions or stores, renegotiate labor contracts, reduce its workforce, or propose other actions that could create a profitable business. If the plan is accepted by creditors, the Company will be given another chance to avoid liquidation and emerge from the bankruptcy proceedings rehabilitated.

### Seeking Protection of the Bankruptcy Court

If creditors file lawsuits or schedule judicial sales to enforce liens, the Company will need to seek the protection of the Bankruptcy Court. Filing a bankruptcy petition will invoke the protection of the court to provide sufficient time to work out a reorganization that was not achievable voluntarily. If reorganization is not possible, a Chapter 7 proceeding will allow for the fair and orderly dissolution of the business.

If a Chapter 11 proceeding is the required course of action, the Company must determine what the reorganized business will look like, if such a structure can be achieved, and how it will be accomplished while maintaining operations during the bankruptcy proceeding. Will sufficient cash be available to pay for the proceedings and reorganization? Will customers continue to do business with the Company or seek other more secure businesses with which to deal? Will key personnel stay on or look for more secure employment? Which operations should be discontinued or reduced?

### Emerging from Bankruptcy

Bankruptcy is only the first step toward recovery for a firm. Many questions should be answered: How did the business get to the point at which the extreme action of bankruptcy was necessary? Were warning signs overlooked? Was the competitive environment understood? Did pride or fear prevent objective analysis? Did the business have the people and resources to succeed? Was the strategic plan well designed and implemented? Did financial problems result from unforeseen and unforeseeable problems or from bad management decisions?

Commitments to "try harder," "listen more carefully to the customer," and "be more efficient" are important but insufficient grounds to inspire stakeholder confidence. A recovery strategy must be developed to delineate how the company will compete more successfully in the future.

An assessment of the bankruptcy situation requires executives to consider the causes of the Company's decline and the severity of the problem it now faces. Investors must decide whether the management team that governed the company's operations during the downturn can return the firm to a position of success. Creditors must believe that the company's managers have learned how to prevent a recurrence of the observed and similar problems. Alternatively, they must have faith that the company's competencies can be sufficiently augmented by key substitutions to the management team, with strong support in decision making from a board of directors and consultants, to restore the firm's competitive strength.

# CORPORATE COMBINATIONS

The 15 grand strategies discussed above, used singly and much more often in combinations, represent the traditional alternatives used by firms in the United States. Recently, three new grand types have gained in popularity; all fit under the broad category of corporate combinations. Although they do not fit the criterion by which executives retain a high degree of control over their operations, these grand strategies deserve special attention and consideration especially by companies that operate in global, dynamic, and technologically driven industries. These three newly popularized grand strategies are joint ventures, strategic alliances, and consortia.

## Joint Ventures

Occasionally two or more capable firms lack a necessary component for success in a particular competitive environment. For example, no single petroleum firm controlled sufficient resources to construct the Alaskan pipeline. Nor was any single firm capable of processing and marketing all of the oil that would flow through the pipeline. The solution was a set of *joint ventures,* which are commercial companies (children) created and operated for the benefit of the co-owners (parents). These cooperative arrangements provided both the funds needed to build the pipeline and the processing and marketing capacities needed to profitably handle the oil flow.

The particular form of joint ventures discussed above is *joint ownership.* In recent years, it has become increasingly appealing for domestic firms to join foreign firms by means of this form. For example, Diamond-Star Motors is the result of a joint venture between a U.S. company, Chrysler Corporation, and Japan's Mitsubishi Motors corporation. Located in Normal, Illinois, Diamond-Star was launched because it offered Chrysler and Mitsubishi a chance to expand on their long-standing relationship in which subcompact cars (as well as Mitsubishi engines and other automotive parts) are imported to the United States and sold under the Dodge and Plymouth names.

The joint venture extends the supplier-consumer relationship and has strategic advantages for both partners. For Chrysler, it presents an opportunity to produce a high-quality car using expertise brought to the venture by Mitsubishi. It also gives Chrysler the chance to try new production techniques and to realize efficiencies by using the workforce that was not included under Chrysler's collective bargaining agreement with the United Auto Workers. The agreement offers Mitsubishi the opportunity to produce cars for sale in the United States without being subjected to the tariffs and restrictions placed on Japanese imports.

As a second example, Bethlehem Steel acquired an interest in a Brazilian mining venture to secure a raw material source. The stimulus for this joint ownership venture was grand strategy, but such is not always the case. Certain countries virtually mandate that foreign firms entering their markets do so on a joint ownership basis. India and Mexico are good examples. The rationale of these countries is that joint ventures minimize the threat of foreign domination and enhance the skills, employment, growth, and profits of local firms.

It should be noted that strategic managers understandably are wary of joint ventures. Admittedly, joint ventures present new opportunities with risks that can be shared. On the other hand, joint ventures often limit the discretion, control, and profit potential of partners, while demanding managerial attention and other resources that might be directed toward the firm's mainstream activities. Nevertheless, increasing globalization in many industries may require greater consideration of the joint venture approach, if historically national firms are to remain viable.

## Strategic Alliances

*Strategic alliances* are distinguished from joint ventures because the companies involved do not take an equity position in one another. In many instances, strategic alliances are partnerships that exist for a defined period during which partners contribute their skills and expertise to a cooperative project. For example, one partner provides manufacturing capabilities while a second partner provides marketing expertise. Many times, such alliances are undertaken because the partners want to learn from one another with the intention to be able to develop in-house capabilities to supplant the partner when the contractual arrangement between them reaches its termination date. Such relationships are tricky since in a sense the partners are attempting to "steal" each other's know-how. Exhibit 6–13, Global Strategy in Action, lists many important

| Objective | Major Questions |
|---|---|
| 1. Assess and value partner knowledge. | • What were the strategic objectives in forming the alliance?<br>• What are the core competencies of our alliance partner?<br>• What specific knowledge does the partner have that could enhance our competitive strategy?<br>• What are the core partner skills relevant for our product/markets? |
| 2. Determine knowledge accessibility. | • How have key alliance responsibilities been allocated to the partners?<br>• Which partner controls key managerial responsibilities?<br>• Does the alliance agreement specify restrictions on our access to the alliance operations? |
| 3. Evaluate knowledge tacitness and ease of transfer. | • Is our learning objective focused on explicit operational knowledge?<br>• Where in the alliance does the knowledge reside?<br>• Is the knowledge strategic or operational?<br>• Do we understand what we are trying to learn and how we can use the knowledge? |
| 4. Establish knowledge connections between the alliance and the partner. | • Are parent managers in regular contact with senior alliance managers?<br>• Has the alliance been incorporated into parent strategic plans and do alliance managers participate in parent strategic planning discussions?<br>• What is the level of trust between parent and alliance managers?<br>• Do alliance financial issues dominate meetings between alliance and parent managers? |
| 5. Draw on existing knowledge to facilitate learning. | • In the learning process, have efforts been made to involve managers with prior experience in either/both alliance management and partner ties?<br>• Are experiences with other alliances being used as the basis for managing the current alliance?<br>• Are we realistic about our partner's learning objectives?<br>• Are we open-minded about knowledge without immediate short-term applicability? |
| 6. Ensure that partner and alliance managerial cultures are in alignment. | • Is the alliance viewed as a threat or an asset by parent managers?<br>• In the parent, is there agreement on the strategic rationale for the alliance?<br>• In the alliance, do managers understand the importance of the parent's learning objective? |

questions about their learning intentions that prospective partners should ask themselves before entering into a strategic alliance.

In other instances, strategic alliances are synonymous with licensing agreements. Licensing involves the transfer of some industrial property right from the U.S. licensor to a motivated licensee in a foreign country. Most tend to be patents, trademarks, or technical know-how that are granted to the licensee for a specified time in return for a royalty and for avoiding tariffs or import quotas. Bell South and U.S. West, with various marketing and service competitive advantages valuable to Europe, have extended a number of licenses to create personal computer networks in the United Kingdom (U.K.).

Another licensing strategy open to U.S. firms is to contract the manufacturing of its product line to a foreign company to exploit local comparative advantages in technology, materials, or labor. For example, MIPS Computer Systems has licensed Digital Equipment Corporation, Texas Instruments, Cypress Semiconductor, and Bipolar Integrated Technology in the United States, and Fujitsu, NEC, and Kubota in Japan to market computers based on its designs in the partner's country.

Service and franchise-based firms—including Anheuser-Busch, Avis, Coca-Cola, Hilton, Hyatt, Holiday Inns, Kentucky Fried Chicken, McDonald's, and Pepsi—have long engaged in licensing arrangements with foreign distributors as a way to enter new markets with standardized products that can benefit from marketing economies.

Outsourcing is a rudimentary approach to strategic alliances that enables firms to gain a competitive advantage. Significant changes within many segments of American business continue to encourage the use of outsourcing practices. Within the health care arena, an industry survey recorded 67 percent of hospitals using provider outsourcing for at least one department within their organization. Services such as information systems, reimbursement, and risk and physician practice management are outsourced by 51 percent of the hospitals that use outsourcing.

Another successful application of outsourcing is found in human resources. A survey of human resource executives revealed 85 percent have personal experience leading an outsourcing effort within their organization. In addition, it was found that two-thirds of pension departments have outsourced at least one human resource function.

Within customer service and sales departments, outsourcing increased productivity in such areas as product information, sales and order taking, sample fulfillment, and complaint handling. Exhibit 6–14 presents the top five strategic and tactical reasons for exploiting the benefits of outsourcing.

---

**EXHIBIT 6–14**
**The Top Five Strategic Reasons for Outsourcing**

1. **Improve Business Focus.**
   For many companies, the single most compelling reason for outsourcing is that several "how" issues are siphoning off huge amounts of management's resources and attention.
2. **Access to World-Class Capabilities.**
   By the very nature of their specialization, outsourcing providers bring extensive worldwide, world-class resources to meeting the needs of their customers. Partnering with an organization with world-class capabilities can offer access to new technology, tools, and techniques that the organization may not currently possess; better career opportunities for personnel who transition to the outsourcing provider; more structured methodologies, procedures, and documentation; and competitive advantage through expanded skills.
3. **Accelerated Reengineering Benefits.**
   Outsourcing is often a byproduct of another powerful management tool—business process reengineering. It allows an organization to immediately realize the anticipated benefits of reengineering by having an outside organization—one that is already reengineered to world-class standards—take over the process.
4. **Shared Risks.**
   When companies outsource they become more flexible, more dynamic, and better able to adapt to changing opportunities.
5. **Free Resources for Other Purposes.**
   Outsourcing permits an organization to redirect its resources from noncore activities toward activities that have the greater return in serving the customer.

## Consortia, Keiretsus, and Chaebols

*Consortia* are defined as large interlocking relationships between businesses of an industry. In Japan such consortia are known as *keiretsus,* in South Korea as *chaebols.*

In Europe, consortia projects are increasing in number and in success rates. Examples include the Junior Engineers' and Scientists' Summer Institute, which underwrites cooperative learning and research; the European Strategic Program for Research and Development in Information Technologies, which seeks to enhance European competitiveness in fields related to computer electronics and component manufacturing; and EUREKA, which is a joint program involving scientists and engineers from several European countries to coordinate joint research projects.

A Japanese *keiretsu* is an undertaking involving up to 50 different firms that are joined around a large trading company or bank and are coordinated through interlocking directories and stock exchanges. It is designed to use industry coordination to minimize risks of competition, in part through cost sharing and increased economies of scale. Examples include Sumitomo, Mitsubishi, Mitsui, and Sanwa. Exhibit 6–15, Global Strategy in Action, presents a new side to *keiretsus,* namely, that they are adding global partners, including several from the United States. Their cooperative nature is growing in evidence as is their market success.

A South Korean chaebol resembles a consortium or keiretsu except that they are typically financed through government banking groups and largely are run by professional managers trained by participating firms expressly for the job.

# SELECTION OF LONG-TERM OBJECTIVES AND GRAND STRATEGY SETS

At first glance, the strategic management model, which provides the framework for study throughout this book, seems to suggest that strategic choice decision making leads to the sequential selection of long-term objectives and grand strategies. In fact, however, strategic choice is the simultaneous selection of long-range objectives and grand strategies. When strategic planners study their opportunities, they try to determine which are most likely to result in achieving various long-range objectives. Almost simultaneously, they try to forecast whether an available grand strategy can take advantage of preferred opportunities so the tentative objectives can be met. In essence, then, three distinct but highly interdependent choices are being made at one time. Several triads, or sets, of possible decisions are usually considered.

A simplified example of this process is shown in Exhibit 6–16. In this example, the firm has determined that six strategic choice options are available. These options stem from three interactive opportunities (e.g., West Coast markets that present little competition). Because each of these interactive opportunities can be approached through different grand strategies—for options 1 and 2, the grand strategies are horizontal integration and market development—each offers the potential for achieving long-range objectives to varying degrees. Thus, a firm rarely can make a strategic choice only on the basis of its preferred opportunities, long-range objectives, or grand strategy. Instead, these three elements must be considered simultaneously, because only in combination do they constitute a strategic choice.

In an actual decision situation, the strategic choice would be complicated by a wider variety of interactive opportunities, feasible company objectives, promising grand strategy options, and evaluative criteria. Nevertheless, Exhibit 6–16 does partially reflect the nature and complexity of the process by which long-term objectives and grand strategies are selected.

In the next chapter, the strategic choice process will be fully explained. However, knowledge of long-term objectives and grand strategies is essential to understanding that process.

**BusinessWeek** Amid rolling hills outside Nagoya, Toshiba Corp. recently took the wraps off a new $1 billion chipmaking facility that uses ultraviolet lithography to etch circuits less than one micron wide—a tiny fraction of the width of a human hair.

The Toshiba chip site owes much to a strategic alliance with IBM and Siemens of Germany. In fact, IBM's know-how in chemical mechanical polishing, essential to smoothing the tiny surfaces of multilayered chips, played a critical role. "We had little expertise here," concedes Toshiba's Koichi Suzuki.

## QUIET CHANGE

What's more, about 20 IBM engineers will show up shortly to transfer the technology back to an IBM-Toshiba facility in Manassas, Virginia. In addition to the semiconductor cooperation, IBM and Toshiba jointly make liquid-crystal display panels—even though they use the LCDs in their fiercely competitive lines of laptop computers. "It's no longer considered a loss of corporate manhood to let others help out," says IBM Asia Pacific President Robert C. Timpson.

For years, many U.S. tie-ups with Japanese companies tended to be defensive in nature, poorly managed, and far removed from core businesses. Now, the alliances are deepening, taking on increasingly important products, and expanding their geographic reach in terms of sales. U.S.-Japanese partnerships are, for example, popping up in Asia's emerging but tricky markets, reducing the risks each company faces.

This deepening web of relationships reflects a quiet change in thinking by Japanese and U.S. multinationals in an era when keeping pace with technological change and competing globally have stretched the resources of even the richest companies. "The scale and technology are so great that neither can do it alone," says Jordan D. Lewis, author of *The Connected Corporation*.

Overall, instances of joint investments in research, products, and distribution by Japanese companies and foreign counterparts, mostly American, jumped 26 percent, to 155, in the first quarter of 1996—on top of a 33 percent increase between 1993 and 1995—according to the Sakura Institute of Research.

## ENVY

And while Uncle Sam and U.S. companies with grievances have attacked Japan's system of big industrial groups, called keiretsu, as exclusionary, other chieftains of Corporate America have quietly become *stakeholders* of sorts. The list includes companies as diverse as IBM, General Motors, TRW, Boeing, and Caterpillar.

Many American executives who established these alliances say they appreciate the attributes of Japan's big industrial groups. U.S. managers have always envied the keiretsu edge in spreading risk over a cluster of companies when betting on a new technology or blitzing emerging markets.

In one industry after another, U.S. and Japanese partners are breaking new ground in their level of cooperation. The impact is felt far beyond the U.S. and Japanese home markets. Take the 50–50 venture between Caterpillar Inc. and Mitsubishi Heavy Industries LTD., part of Japan's $200 billion keiretsu of the same name. Early on, Cat wanted a way to sell its construction equipment in Japan and compete with rival Komatsu Ltd. on its home turf. Mitsubishi wanted to play catch-up with Komatsu, too, and expand its export markets.

Their alliance played a key role in taming Komatsu. But the partners have broader ambitions. Since Cat shifted all design work for its "300" series of excavators to the partnership back in 1987, the venture's two Japanese factories have emerged as Cat's primary source of production for sales to fast-growing Asia. The alliance's products reach the world market through Cat's network of 186 independent dealers in 197 countries.

**Source:** Brian Bemner in Tokyo, with Zachary Schiller in Cleveland, Tim Smart in Fairfield, William J. Holstein in New York, and bureau reports, "Keiretsu Connections," *BusinessWeek*, July 22, 1996.

# SEQUENCE OF OBJECTIVES AND STRATEGY SELECTION

The selection of long-range objectives and grand strategies involves simultaneous, rather than sequential, decisions. While it is true that objectives are needed to prevent the firm's direction and progress from being determined by random forces, it is equally true that objectives can be achieved only if strategies are implemented. In fact, long-term objectives and grand strategies are so interdependent that some business consultants do not distinguish between them. Long-term objectives and grand strategies are still combined under the heading of company strategy in most of the popular business literature and in the thinking of most practicing executives.

**EXHIBIT 6–16**

**A Profile of Strategic Choice Options**

| | Six Strategic Choice Options | | | | | |
|---|---|---|---|---|---|---|
| | **1** | **2** | **3** | **4** | **5** | **6** |
| Interactive opportunities | West Coast markets present little competition | | Current markets sensitive to price competition | | Current industry product lines offer too narrow a range of markets | |
| Appropriate long-range objectives (limited sample): Average 5-year ROI. Company sales by year 5. Risk of negative profits. | 15% +50% .30 | 19% +40% .25 | 13% +20% .10 | 17% +0% .15 | 23% +35% .20 | 15% +25% .05 |
| Grand strategies | Horizontal integration | Market development | Concentration | Selective retrenchment | Product development | Concentration |

However, the distinction has merit. Objectives indicate what strategic managers want but provide few insights about how they will be achieved. Conversely, strategies indicate what types of actions will be taken but do not define what ends will be pursued or what criteria will serve as constraints in refining the strategic plan.

Does it matter whether strategic decisions are made to achieve objectives or to satisfy constraints? No, because constraints are themselves objectives. The constraint of increased inventory capacity is a desire (an objective), not a certainty. Likewise, the constraint of an increase in the sales force does not ensure that the increase will be achieved, given such factors as other company priorities, labor market conditions, and the firm's profit performance.

## Summary

Before we learn how strategic decisions are made, it is important to understand the two principal components of any strategic choice; namely, long-term objectives and the grand strategy. The purpose of this chapter was to convey that understanding.

Long-term objectives were defined as the results a firm seeks to achieve over a specified period, typically five years. Seven common long-term objectives were discussed: profitability, productivity, competitive position, employee development, employee relations, technological leadership, and public responsibility. These, or any other long-term objectives, should be acceptable, flexible, measurable over time, motivating, suitable, understandable, and achievable.

Grand strategies were defined as comprehensive approaches guiding the major actions designed to achieve long-term objectives. Fifteen grand strategy options were discussed: concentrated growth, market development, product development, innovation, horizontal integration, vertical integration, concentric diversification, conglomerate diversification, turnaround, divestiture, liquidation, bankruptcy, joint ventures, strategic alliances, and consortia.

# Questions for Discussion

1. Identify firms in the business community nearest to your college or university that you believe are using each of the 15 grand strategies discussed in this chapter.

2. Identify firms in your business community that appear to rely principally on 1 of the 15 grand strategies. What kind of information did you use to classify the firms?

3. Write a long-term objective for your school of business that exhibits the seven qualities of long-term objectives described in this chapter.

4. Distinguish between the following pairs of grand strategies:

   a. Horizontal and vertical integration.
   b. Conglomerate and concentric diversification.
   c. Product development and innovation.
   d. Joint venture and strategic alliance.

5. Rank each of the 15 grand strategy options discussed in this chapter on the following three scales:

   High                          Low

   Cost

   High                          Low

   Risk of failure

   High                          Low

   Potential for exceptional growth

6. Identify firms that use one of the eight specific options shown in Exhibit 6–4 under the grand strategies of concentration, market development, and product development.

## Chapter 6 Discussion Case

# Novartis

**BusinessWeek**

1   Novartis (NVS) Chairman and CEO Daniel L. Vasella doesn't take no for an answer. The head of the world's sixth-largest drugmaker (by sales) goes after what he wants and, more often than not, gets it. When the Swiss company began work on a $4 billion research facility in Cambridge, Mass., last year, Vasella decided to draft a world-famous scientist to run it. But his candidate, Dr. Mark C. Fishman, a renowned geneticist and cardiologist at Harvard Medical School, flatly refused, saying he was happy in his current job. "It has been years since that happened to me," Vasella recalls with a laugh. But Vasella wore him down. After six months of persistent wooing on two continents, the Cambridge center was up and running by the end of March with Fishman in charge.

2   Hiring Fishman—and turning the Cambridge center into a leader in the discovery of cardiovascular, cancer, antiviral, and diabetes drugs—are the latest elements of a grand plan that the courteous, soft-spoken Swiss has developed with a mixture of patience and quiet ferocity. The first stage was to generate some respect for Novartis, a product of the 1996 merger of two Swiss companies, Sandoz Ltd. and Ciba-Geigy. That was the hard part. Until two years ago, the industry dismissed Novartis as a sleepy European giant without the marketing and sales firepower to compete in the United States, the world's most lucrative market for prescription drugs. There, Novartis was a midtier player—certainly no match for Merck (MRK) & Co. or Pfizer (PFE) Inc. But Vasella, a physician himself, devoted every penny he could find to marketing and research and took the world by surprise in May 2001 with Glivec, one of the most effective new cancer therapies going. "Novartis is emerging as one of the premier powerhouses in the global pharmaceuticals industry," says Richard R. Stover, senior analyst with brokerage Natexis Bleichroeder Inc. in New York.

3   Glivec's success set the stage for the next phase of the plan: creating a profit machine. On April 15, Novartis reported a 24 percent jump in first-quarter operating earnings, to $1.4 billion, on sales of $5.7 billion. That news was better than expected, thanks partially to Novartis' decision to begin reporting results in dollars rather than in Swiss francs. A currency switch isn't the whole story, though. Despite higher spending on research and development, pharmaceutical margins at the Swiss drugmaker powered ahead, to 30.5 percent from 28.1 percent year on year. The stock has climbed 15 percent since mid-March and continues to outperform the industry (charts).

4   Now for stage three, elevating Novartis to the pantheon of the truly great global pharmaceutical giants. Novartis' No. 6 ranking is good, but more blockbusters such as Glivec would make it better. That's where hugely ambitious projects like the Cambridge research center come in. "Personally, I'd simply like to beat the competition," says Vasella.

5   That means building a portfolio of superior drugs. Making them in your own labs is one way to do that; buying them from rivals is another. Novartis certainly has money to spend. The Swiss company is sitting on $7 billion in net cash, more than any other drugmaker in Europe—more even than the money-spinning GlaxoSmithKline (GSK) PLC. And that figure is set to rise to $10 billion by yearend, estimates Marc Booty, European pharmaceuticals analyst at Commerzbank Securities in London.

6   Vasella has been carefully laying the groundwork for acquisitions. That's one reason he switched the company's financial reporting to dollars. It makes a deal with a U.S. company much easier for American investors to figure out (and signals to Pfizer and Merck that Novartis thinks it's in the same league). Takeover candidates? Schering-Plough (SGP) Corp., for one. Vasella and Schering's newly appointed CEO, Fred Hassan, go way back, plus Schering has the exclusive rights to sell Novartis' Foradil for asthma in the United States. Another possibility is Wyeth, whose pipeline would complement Novartis' own.

7   Big transatlantic deals are notoriously tough due to regulatory hurdles, so Vasella is not waiting around. In March, Novartis paid $225 million in cash for a majority stake in Cambridge (Mass.)–based Idenix Pharmaceuticals Inc. The acquisition gives Novartis access to a promising line of new drugs to treat hepatitis B and C.

8   Certainly, a play for a top American drugmaker would vastly strengthen Novartis' hand in the United States, where all of the European pharmaceuticals get the bulk of their profits, thanks to higher prices for prescription drugs and doctors' willingness to prescribe innovative treatments, regardless of the cost. But Vasella is already working on a deal closer to home

that could, in a stroke, turn Novartis into the second-biggest pharmaceutical company on the planet, behind Pfizer. This is a target Vasella can practically see from his office window: Roche Group, also based in Basel.

9   A union between the crosstown rivals would have repercussions far beyond this picturesque city on the Rhine. The merged company would have sales of more than $45 billion, a nearly 7 percent share of the global market, a powerful cancer franchise, and one of the best biotech research facilities around, thanks to Roche's ownership of U.S. biotech Genentech (DNA) Inc. Novartis already owns 32.7 percent of Roche, just under the one-third stake that would require the company to make a formal bid under Swiss stock exchange rules.

10   There's just one hitch: Roche CEO Franz B. Humer is staunchly opposed to any deal. "We are better off as an independent company, and a megamerger with Novartis or anyone else is not an answer," he says. And for now, at least, Humer has the backing of the descendants of founder Fritz Hoffman-La Roche, who control the majority of the company's voting rights despite owning less than 10 percent of the equity. André Hoffman, the family spokesman, vows Roche will elude takeover.

11   Vasella is equally determined to make it happen. "There has been value destruction [at Roche], and as a shareholder, one can't be happy with that," he says. "Roche's management and board need to do the right thing for all [of] their shareholders." Roche shares have declined 16 percent in the last 12 months. The company posted a $3 billion loss in 2002 due mainly to the poor performance of its investment portfolio.

12   Vasella can afford to bide his time. Novartis' pipeline is full, a rarity in the industry. The company has launched 10 drugs since 2000, three times more than its nearest rival. Another 15 are expected to debut by 2006. Among the current crop are Zelmac, a drug for irritable-bowel syndrome; eczema treatment Elidel; and Zometa, a treatment for bone metastases. What's more, none of Novartis' major moneymakers is set to go off-patent soon. Earnings should rise almost 10 percent this year; they would go higher were it not for Vasella's insistence on ramping up the research budget to $3.5 billion in 2003, equal to 17.5 percent of sales, well above the industry average.

13   Then there's Glivec, the first treatment ever proven to cause certain types of tumors to disappear. While other cancer drugs work indiscriminately, killing off healthy cells along with sick ones, Glivec is part of a new class of drugs that interfere with the proteins that cause tumors to grow. Initially approved for the treatment of chronic myeloid leukemia, Glivec also is used to treat other rare types of cancer such as gastrointestinal stromal tumors (GIST) and is now being tested in combination with other drugs in fighting prostate cancer. "Novartis shows other drugmakers that these little niches can be extraordinarily valuable scientifically, as well as commercially feasible," says Dr. George D. Demetri, director of the sarcoma center at Harvard Medical School's Dana-Farber Cancer Institute in Boston. Other drugmakers already are developing targeted drugs, such as AstraZenecas (AZN) Iressa for lung cancer, and ImClone (IMCLE) Erbitux, for colorectal cancer.

14   Glivec, introduced in the United States in 2001 under the brand name Gleevec, was worth every penny that Novartis invested. Sales rose more than 300 percent in 2002, and could hit the $1 billion mark by the end of this year, according to Commerzbank's Booty. Although an annual course of Glivec can cost as much as $25,000, demand for the drug took off so quickly that Novartis was forced to run its production line around the clock. One of the first patients to have access to the medicine was Anita Scherzer of Little Falls, N.J. In 1994, the then 52-year-old Scherzer was diagnosed with gastrointestinal stromal tumors. She underwent countless surgeries to remove tumors in her stomach and liver, followed by chemotherapy, but the cancer kept spreading. She enrolled in a small clinical trial for Glivec in August 2000. Just 10 days after taking her first dose of the drug, doctors were astonished to discover that a tumor in Anita's liver had shrunk. Just a month after starting treatment, she was in remission. "I knew I was getting better when I went for a biopsy and the doctor couldn't find the tumor," Scherzer says. Glivec is not a magic bullet, though. Some patients have developed resistance to the drug.

15   Glivec's success stems from Novartis' stress on science. Under the leadership of Joerg Reinhardt, a 20-year company veteran who heads global development, the company has shaved nearly two years off the time it takes to bring a drug from clinic to market. Novartis now needs just over 7 years—18 months less than the industry average.

16   He did it partly by running discovery-and-development projects in parallel instead of sequentially. That means a potential drug being tested for colon cancer might simultaneously be screened for effectiveness against lung cancer or even schizophrenia. Before the mapping of the human genome, scientists made such discoveries by chance. Today, technologies such as functional genomics, in which Novartis invests approximately $150 million a year, have given scientists a bet-

ter understanding of the molecular causes of some diseases. Vasella wants the Cambridge center to be at the forefront of this type of research.

17    Reinhardt's breakthrough is due in part to the constant pressure Vasella puts on employees to beat industry benchmarks. Employees describe him as a demanding boss with exceptionally high standards. When Vasella saw the early clinical results on Glivec, he gave the development team just two years to bring the drug to market. "When I think something needs to be done," says Vasella, "I generally think it needs to be done quickly."

18    Novartis' boss is an unusual mix, an aggressive manager who still keeps something of the gentle bedside manner he developed as a general practitioner. Although Vasella recognizes his first loyalty is to his shareholders, he never loses sight of the patients. It's an attitude that grows out of his own admiration for the doctors who treated him as a child, when he contracted tuberculosis and meningitis. Vasella is also an unbuttoned type who likes roaring around the Swiss countryside on his BMW bike.

19    Vasella's rivals underestimated him at first, especially when he embarked on the merger of Sandoz and Ciba. The companies were old-style conglomerates with roots in the agrichemicals industry, but with very different corporate cultures. Sandoz was autocratic and hierarchical, while at Ciba a collegial and informal atmosphere bred better morale but little accountability among the staff. "It was a difficult marriage to make work," says Natexis' Stover. Vasella's appointment to the top job at the newly merged company in March, 1996, fueled accusations of nepotism (his high-school sweetheart and wife of 25 years, Anne-Laurence, is the niece of Sandoz' former chairman) and grumblings that he was in over his head.

20    Determined to prove critics wrong, the new boss promptly set about cleaning house. After much-touted synergies failed to materialize, he dumped the company's ailing agrochemicals unit to focus on higher-margin pharmaceuticals. He also rapidly boosted R&D spending.

21    But one of Vasella's shrewdest moves was to sharpen marketing in the United States, one of Novartis' big weaknesses. So in 1999 he hired Paulo Costa, a former Johnson & Johnson (JNJ) exec, to head Novartis' stateside pharmaceutical business. Costa doubled the size of the U.S. sales force to 6,200 and this year tripled spending on direct-to-consumer advertising to $120 million. So far, it seems to be working: Launched in March 2002 with massive marketing support, Elidel became the No. 1 branded eczema product in the United States after just four months on the market. "They've changed the market's perception about how well a European company can compete in the United States," says Commerzbank's Booty. Today, U.S. sales account for 43 percent of overall revenues. Credit also goes to Thomas Ebeling, a marketing whiz from PepsiCo (PEP) Inc., who was promoted in July, 2001, to head Novartis global pharmaceutical business. In a quest to create global brands, Ebeling decided to devote more than 50 percent of the Novartis' marketing budget to a handful of drugs, such as hypertension medicine Diovan, Lotrel, Glivec, and Zometa.

22    Vasella increasingly sees the United States as vital to the company's destiny (a merger with Roche, which relies so much on California-based Genentech for its pipeline and profits, would reinforce Novartis' American position). That's why he has been shifting more and more of the company's R&D to the United States, a country which he says has a much better regulatory and scientific environment for drugmakers than Europe. This year alone, spending on R&D is set to rise by 20 percent, to $3.5 billion, to cover the development of new drugs such as Prexige, a treatment for osteoarthritis and acute pain, and Xolair, for severe asthma.

23    Still, there are considerable risks. Vasella concedes that the big boost in R&D spending will put pressure on margins and earnings. But he contends that this is inevitable if Novartis wants to keep innovating. "It's not an option to stand still," he says. His biggest challenge will be revving up sales of new drugs to offset the large increases in investment. It won't be easy. Many of Novartis' newer drugs are in either crowded or immature markets. Prexige, slated for launch in mid-2004, will be the fifth entrant into a large field dominated by Pharmacia's Celebrex. To make a dent, analysts estimate Novartis may have to spend as much as $1 billion in the first three years after launch.

24    Costly stuff. But Vasella has deep pockets. In March, Novartis acquired the rights to Pfizer's incontinence drug Enablex for $255 million, beating out bigger players such as GlaxoSmithKline. The drug, which Pfizer was forced to sell as part of an antitrust agreement before it could take over Pharmacia, is considered a potential billion-dollar blockbuster. One way or another, the doctor is determined to build his powerhouse.

**Source:** Kerry Capell, "Novartis," *BusinessWeek*, May 26, 2003

# Chapter **Seven**

# Strategic Analysis and Choice in Single- or Dominant-Product Businesses: Building Sustainable Competitive Advantages

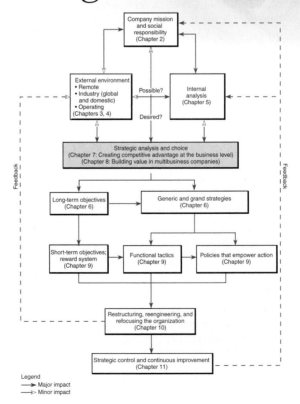

Company mission and social responsibility (Chapter 2)

External environment
• Remote
• Industry (global and domestic)
• Operating
(Chapters 3, 4)

Possible?

Desired?

Internal analysis (Chapter 5)

Strategic analysis and choice
(Chapter 7: Creating competitive advantage at the business level)
(Chapter 8: Building value in multibusiness companies)

Long-term objectives (Chapter 6)

Generic and grand strategies (Chapter 6)

Short-term objectives; reward system (Chapter 9)

Functional tactics (Chapter 9)

Policies that empower action (Chapter 9)

Restructuring, reengineering, and refocusing the organization (Chapter 10)

Strategic control and continuous improvement (Chapter 11)

Feedback

Feedback

Legend
——→ Major impact
——▷ Minor impact

Strategic analysis and choice is the phase of the strategic management process when business managers examine and choose a business strategy that allows their business to maintain or create a sustainable competitive advantage. Their starting point is to evaluate and determine which value chain activities provide the basis for distinguishing the firm in the customer's mind from other reasonable alternatives. Businesses with a dominant product or service line must also choose among alternate grand strategies to guide the firm's activities, particularly when they are trying to decide about broadening the scope of the firm's activities beyond its core business.

This chapter examines strategic analysis and choice in single- or dominant-product/service businesses by addressing two basic issues:

1. **What strategies are most effective at building sustainable competitive advantages for single business units?** What competitive strategy positions a business most effectively in its industry? For example, Scania, the most productive truck manufacturer in the world, joins its major rival Volvo as two anchors of Sweden's economy. Scania's return on sales of 9.9 percent far exceeds Mercedes (2.6 percent) and Volvo (2.5 percent), a level it has achieved most of the last 60 years. Scania has built a sustainable competitive advantage with a strategy of focusing solely on heavy trucks, in a limited geographic area—Europe—and by providing customized trucks with standardized components (20,000 components per truck versus 25,000 for Volvo and 40,000 for Mercedes). Scania is a low-cost producer of a differentiated truck that can be custom-manufactured quickly and sold to a regionally focused market.

2. **Should dominant-product/service businesses diversify** to build value and competitive advantage? What grand strategies are most appropriate? For example, Compaq Computers and Coca-Cola managers have examined the question of diversification and apparently concluded that continued concentration on their core products and services and development of new markets for those same core products and services are best. IBM and Pepsi examined the same question and concluded that concentric diversification and vertical integration were best. Why?

# EVALUATING AND CHOOSING BUSINESS STRATEGIES: SEEKING SUSTAINED COMPETITIVE ADVANTAGE

Business managers evaluate and choose strategies that they think will make their business successful. Businesses become successful because they possess some advantage relative to their competitors. The two most prominent sources of competitive advantage can be found in the business's cost structure and its ability to differentiate the business from competitors. Disney World in Orlando offers theme park patrons several unique, distinct features that differentiate it from other entertainment options. Wal-Mart offers retail customers the lowest prices on popular consumer items because they have created a low-cost structure resulting in a competitive advantage over most competitors.

Businesses that create competitive advantages from one or both of these sources usually experience above-average profitability within their industry. Businesses that lack a cost or differentiation advantage usually experience average or below-average profitability. Two recent studies found that businesses that do not have either form of competitive advantage perform the poorest among their peers while businesses that possess both forms of competitive advantage enjoy the highest levels of profitability within their industry.[1]

---

[1] R. B. Robinson and J. A. Pearce, "Planned Patterns of Strategic Behavior and Their Relationship to Business Unit Performance," *Strategic Management Journal* 9, no. 1 (1988), pp. 43–60; G. G. Dess and G. T. Lumpkin, "Emerging Issues in Strategy Process Research," in *Handbook of Strategic Management*, Hitt et al., 2002.

The average return on investment for over 2,500 businesses across seven industries looked as follows:

| Differentiation Advantage | Cost Advantage | Overall Average ROI across Seven Industries |
|---|---|---|
| High | High | 35.0% |
| Low | High | 26.0 |
| High | Low | 22.0 |
| Low | Low | 9.5 |

Initially, managers were advised to evaluate and choose strategies that emphasized one type of competitive advantage. Often referred to as *generic strategies,* firms were encouraged to become either a differentiation-oriented or low-cost–oriented company. In so doing, it was logical that organizational members would develop a clear understanding of company priorities and, as these studies suggest, likely experience profitability superior to competitors without either a differentiation or low-cost orientation.

The studies mentioned above, and the experience of many other businesses, indicate that the highest profitability levels are found in businesses that possess both types of competitive advantage at the same time. In other words, businesses that have one or more value chain activities that truly differentiate them from key competitors and also have value chain activities that let them operate at a lower cost will consistently outperform their rivals that don't. So the challenge for today's business managers is to evaluate and choose business strategies based on core competencies and value chain activities that sustain both types of competitive advantage simultaneously. Exhibit 7–1, Global Strategy in Action, shows Honda Motor Company attempting to do just this in Europe.

## Evaluating Cost Leadership Opportunities

Business success built on cost leadership requires the business to be able to provide its product or service at a cost below what its competitors can achieve. And it must be a sustainable cost advantage. Through the skills and resources identified in Exhibit 7–2, a business must be able to accomplish one or more activities in its value chain activities—procuring materials, processing them into products, marketing the products, and distributing the products or support activities—in a more cost-effective manner than that of its competitors or it must be able to reconfigure its value chain so as to achieve a cost advantage. Exhibit 7–2 provides examples of ways this might be done.

Strategists examining their business's value chain for low-cost leadership advantages evaluate the sustainability of those advantages by *benchmarking* (refer to Chapter 5 for a discussion of this comparison technique) their business against key competitors and by considering the impact of any cost advantage on the five forces in their business's competitive environment. Low-cost activities that are sustainable and that provide one or more of these advantages relative to key industry forces should become the basis for the business's competitive strategy.

***Low-Cost Advantages That Reduce the Likelihood of Pricing Pressure from Buyers***
When key competitors cannot match prices from the low-cost leader, customers pressuring the leader risk establishing a price level that drives alternate sources out of business.

***Truly Sustained Low-Cost Advantages May Push Rivals into Other Areas, Lessening Price Competition***   Intense, continued price competition may be ruinous for all rivals, as seen occasionally in the airline industry.

**BusinessWeek** Honda is hot. In the United States, the Tokyo company can barely keep up with demand for models like the Acura MDX sport utility vehicle and the Odyssey minivan. North American sales have grown 60 percent in the last decade and its cost leadership is legendary: Honda earned $1,581 on every car sold in North America last year, versus $701 for General Motors.

But the road is not entirely smooth for the Japanese carmaker. Honda Motor Co. has suffered a serious breakdown in Europe. Honda's operations in the Old World reported a loss of nearly a billion dollars in Britain and the Continent for 2002. "A big worry for us is weak sales in Europe," says CEO Takeo Fukui.

So Honda managers have gone into overdrive to repair the European business. Their game plan includes cost leadership initiatives: boosting capacity at two plants in Britain, heeding European calls for cars with diesel engines, and implementing a hard-nosed cost-cutting program that targets parts suppliers . . . and differentiation opportunities: launching an all-new car for the subcompact market.

Honda has a reputation for tackling all of its challenges head-on. But the European problem, even against the background of record results in the United States, underscores Honda's fragility. Although less than 10 percent of Honda's global volume—and far less revenue—comes from Europe, the region has outsized importance to Fukui and his deputies. Why? Because Honda has no safe harbor if its sales in the United States begin to flag, as some analysts expect. The company earns some 90 percent of its profits in America, a far higher percentage than other Japanese carmakers. "Honda is the least globally diverse Japanese automobile manufacturer," says Chris Redl, director of equity research at UBS Warburg's office in Tokyo. "It's a minor problem for now, but with the U.S. market heading down, it could become a major problem." So a closer look at the cost leadership and differentiation approach at Honda Europe, their confident answer, is as follows:

## COST LEADERSHIP

Honda's struggles in Europe today are partly the result of a key strategic error it made when it started making cars in Britain 10 years ago. Company officials didn't foresee the huge runup in the value of the British pound against Europe's single currency, the euro, which made its cars more expensive than competing models manufactured on the Continent. Subpar sales cut output in Britain last year to levels near 50 percent of capacity: It's impossible to make money at that production level. "Europe is definitely an Achilles' heel for Honda," says Toru Shimano, an analyst at Okasan Securities Co. in Tokyo.

So Honda is increasing purchases of cheaper parts from suppliers outside Britain and moving swiftly to freshen its lineup. Earlier this year, a remodeled and roomier five-door Civic hatchback with improved fuel efficiency rolled off production lines in Britain. To goose output at its British operations, Honda will start exporting perky three-door Civic sedans built at its newest plant to the United States and Japan this year. It also plans to export its British-made CR-V compact SUV to America to augment the Japan-made CR-Vs now being sold there.

## DIFFERENTIATION

All of that will help, but Honda's big issue is the hole in its lineup: subcompacts. While 1-liter-engine cars sell poorly in the United States, Europeans and Japanese can't get enough of them. "Honda does not have a product for Europe yet," says UBS Warburg's Redl. It missed out with its 1-liter Logo. "It didn't stand out from the crowd," Yoshino admits.

So the Logo is history, and Honda's new salvation in Europe is a five-door hatchback called the Fit. At 1.3 liters, its engine outpowers Toyota's competing Vitz-class line of cars. Honda says the sporty Fit also boasts a number of nifty features. The only one it would confirm, however, is that owners will be able to flatten all four seats, including the driver's, at the flick of a switch—a selling point for youths keen to load bikes or sleep in it on long road trips.

**Source:** "Honda is Ready for a Tune Up," *BusinessWeek,* July 7, 2003; and "Honda's Weak Spot: Europe," *BusinessWeek,* June 11, 2001.

*New Entrants Competing on Price Must Face an Entrenched Cost Leader without the Experience to Replicate Every Cost Advantage* EasyJet, a British startup with a Southwest Airlines copycat strategy, entered the European airline market with much fanfare and low priced, city-to-city, no-frills flights.

Analysts caution that by the time you read this, British Airways, KLM's no-frills offshoot, Buzz, and Virgin Express will simply match fares on EasyJet's key routes and let high landing fees and flight delays take their toll on the British upstart.

## EXHIBIT 7–2
**Evaluating a Business's Cost Leadership Opportunities**

Source: Based on Michael Porter, On Competition, 1998, Harvard Business School Press.

### A. Skills and Resources That Foster Cost Leadership

Sustained capital investment and access to capital.
Process engineering skills.
Intense supervision of labor or core technical operations.
Products or services designed for ease of manufacture or delivery.
Low-cost distribution system.

### B. Organizational Requirements to Support and Sustain Cost Leadership Activities

Tight cost control.
Frequent, detailed control reports.
Continuous improvement and benchmarking orientation.
Structured organization and responsibilities.
Incentives based on meeting strict, usually quantitative targets.

### C. Examples of Ways Businesses Achieve Competitive Advantage via Cost Leadership

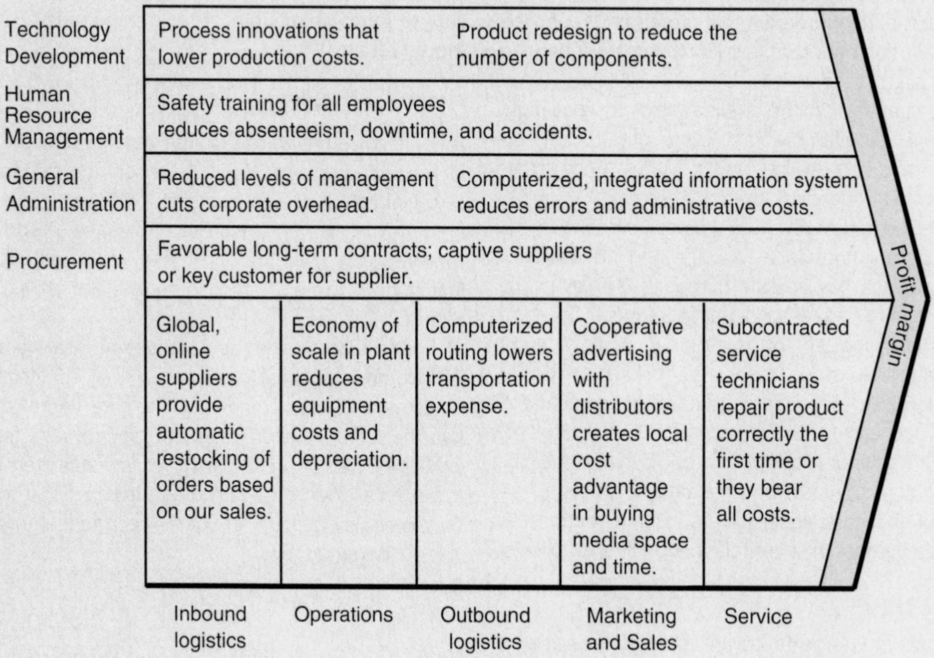

| | | | | | | |
|---|---|---|---|---|---|---|
| Technology Development | Process innovations that lower production costs. | | Product redesign to reduce the number of components. | | | |
| Human Resource Management | Safety training for all employees reduces absenteeism, downtime, and accidents. | | | | | |
| General Administration | Reduced levels of management cuts corporate overhead. | | Computerized, integrated information system reduces errors and administrative costs. | | | |
| Procurement | Favorable long-term contracts; captive suppliers or key customer for supplier. | | | | | |
| | Global, online suppliers provide automatic restocking of orders based on our sales. | Economy of scale in plant reduces equipment costs and depreciation. | Computerized routing lowers transportation expense. | Cooperative advertising with distributors creates local cost advantage in buying media space and time. | Subcontracted service technicians repair product correctly the first time or they bear all costs. | *Profit margin* |
| | Inbound logistics | Operations | Outbound logistics | Marketing and Sales | Service | |

***Low-Cost Advantages Should Lessen the Attractiveness of Substitute Products*** A serious concern of any business is the threat of a substitute product in which buyers can meet their original need. Low-cost advantages allow the holder to resist this happening because it allows them to remain competitive even against desirable substitutes and it allows them to lessen concerns about price facing an inferior, lower-priced substitute.

***Higher Margins Allow Low-Cost Producers to Withstand Supplier Cost Increases and Often Gain Supplier Loyalty over Time*** Sudden, particularly uncontrollable increases in the costs suppliers face can be more easily absorbed by low-cost, higher-margin producers. Severe droughts in California quadrupled the price of lettuce—a key restaurant demand. Some chains absorbed the cost; others had to confuse customers with a "lettuce tax." Furthermore, chains that worked well with produce suppliers gained a loyal, cooperative "partner" for possible assistance in a future, competitive situation.

Once managers identify opportunities to create cost advantage–based strategies, they must consider whether key risks inherent in cost leadership are present in a way that may mediate sustained success. The key risks with which they must be concerned are discussed next.

***Many Cost-Saving Activities Are Easily Duplicated***   Computerizing certain order entry functions among hazardous waste companies gave early adopters lower sales costs and better customer service for a brief time. Rivals quickly adapted, adding similar capabilities with similar impacts on their costs.

***Exclusive Cost Leadership Can Become a Trap***   Firms that emphasize lowest price and can offer it via cost advantages where product differentiation is increasingly not considered must truly be convinced of the sustainability of those advantages. Particularly with commodity-type products, the low-cost leader seeking to sustain a margin superior to lesser rivals may encounter increasing customer pressure for lower prices with great damage to both leader and lesser players.

***Obsessive Cost Cutting Can Shrink Other Competitive Advantages Involving Key Product Attributes***   Intense cost scrutiny can build margin, but it can reduce opportunities for or investment in innovation, processes, and products. Similarly, such scrutiny can lead to the use of inferior raw materials, processes, or activities that were previously viewed by customers as a key attribute of the original products. Some mail-order computer companies that sought to maintain or enhance cost advantages found reductions in telephone service personnel and automation of that function backfiring with a drop in demand for their products even though their low prices were maintained.

***Cost Differences Often Decline over Time***   As products age, competitors learn how to match cost advantages. Absolute volumes sold often decline. Market channels and suppliers mature. Buyers become more knowledgeable. All of these factors present opportunities to lessen the value or presence of earlier cost advantages. Said another way, cost advantages that are not sustainable over a period of time are risky.

Once business managers have evaluated the cost structure of their value chain, determined activities that provide competitive cost advantages, and considered their inherent risks, they start choosing the business's strategy. Those managers concerned with differentiation-based strategies, or those seeking optimum performance incorporating both sources of competitive advantage, move to evaluating their business's sources of differentiation.

## Evaluating Differentiation Opportunities

Differentiation requires that the business have sustainable advantages that allow it to provide buyers with something uniquely valuable to them. A successful differentiation strategy allows the business to provide a product or service of perceived higher value to buyers at a "differentiation cost" below the "value premium" to the buyers. In other words, the buyer feels the additional cost to buy the product or service is well below what the product or service is worth compared to other available alternatives.

Differentiation usually arises from one or more activities in the value chain that create a unique value important to buyers. Perrier's control of a carbonated water spring in France, Stouffer's frozen food packaging and sauce technology, Apple's highly integrated chip designs in its Mac computers, American Greeting Card's automated inventory system for retailers, and Federal Express's customer service capabilities are all examples of sustainable advantages around which successful differentiation strategies have been built. A business

**EXHIBIT 7–3**
**Evaluating a Business's Differentiation Opportunities**

Source: Based on Michael Porter, On Competition, 1998, Harvard Business School Press.

## A. Skills and Resources That Foster Differentiation

Strong marketing abilities.
Product engineering.
Creative talent and flair.
Strong capabilities in basic research.
Corporate reputation for quality or technical leadership.
Long tradition in an industry or unique combination of skills drawn from other businesses.
Strong cooperation from channels.
Strong cooperation from suppliers of major components of the product or service.

## B. Organizational Requirements to Support and Sustain Differentiation Activities

Strong coordination among functions in R&D, product development, and marketing.
Subjective measurement and incentives instead of quantitative measures.
Amenities to attract highly skilled labor, scientists, and creative people.
Tradition of closeness to key customers.
Some personnel skilled in sales and operations—technical and marketing.

## C. Examples of Ways Businesses Achieve Competitive Advantage via Differentiation

| | |
|---|---|
| Technology Development | Cutting-edge production technology and product features to maintain a "distinct" image and actual product. |
| Human Resource Management | Programs to ensure technical competence of sales staff and a marketing orientation of service personnel. |
| General Administration | Comprehensive, personalized database to build knowledge of groups of customers and individual buyers to be used in "customizing" how products are sold, serviced, and replaced. |
| Procurement | Quality control presence at key supplier facilities; work with suppliers' new product development activities |

| Inbound logistics | Operations | Outbound logistics | Marketing and Sales | Service |
|---|---|---|---|---|
| Purchase superior quality, well-known components, raising the quality and image of final products. | Careful inspection of products at each step in production to improve product performance and lower defect rate. | JIT coordination with buyers; use of own or captive transportation service to ensure timeliness. | Expensive, informative advertising and promotion to build brand image. | Allowing service personnel considerable discretion to credit customers for repairs. |

*Profit margin*

can achieve differentiation by performing its existing value activities or reconfiguring in some unique way. And the sustainability of that differentiation will depend on two things—a continuation of its high perceived value to buyers and a lack of imitation by competitors.

Exhibit 7–3 suggests key skills that managers should ensure are present to support an emphasis on differentiation. Examples of value chain activities that provide a differentiation advantage are also provided.

Strategists examining their business's value chain for differentiation advantages evaluate the sustainability of those advantages by *benchmarking* (refer to Chapter 5 for a discussion of this comparison technique) their business against key competitors and by considering the impact of any differentiation advantage on the five forces in their business's competitive environment. Sustainable activities that provide one or more of the following opportunities relative to key industry forces should become the basis for differentiation aspects of the business's competitive strategy:

***Rivalry Is Reduced When a Business Successfully Differentiates Itself***  BMW's new Z23, made in Greer, South Carolina, does not compete with Saturns made in central Tennessee. A Harvard education does not compete with an education from a local technical school. Both situations involve the same basic needs, transportation or education. However, one rival has clearly differentiated itself from others in the minds of certain buyers. In so doing, they do not have to respond competitively to that competitor.

***Buyers Are Less Sensitive to Prices for Effectively Differentiated Products***  The Highlands Inn in Carmel, California, and the Ventana Inn along the Big Sur charge a minimum of $600 and $900, respectively, per night for a room with a kitchen, fireplace, hot tub, and view. Other places are available along this beautiful stretch of California's spectacular coastline, but occupancy rates at these two locations remain over 90 percent. Why? You can't get a better view and a more relaxed, spectacular setting to spend a few days on the Pacific Coast. Similarly, buyers of differentiated products tolerate price increases low-cost–oriented buyers would not accept. The former become very loyal to certain brands.

***Brand Loyalty Is Hard for New Entrants to Overcome***  Many new beers are brought to market in the United States, but Budweiser continues to gain market share. Why? Brand loyalty is hard to overcome! And Anheuser-Busch has been clever to extend its brand loyalty from its core brand into newer niches, like nonalcohol brews, that other potential entrants have pioneered.

Managers examining differentiation-based advantages must take potential risks into account as they commit their business to these advantages. Some of the more common ways risks arise are discussed next.

***Imitation Narrows Perceived Differentiation, Rendering Differentiation Meaningless***  AMC pioneered the Jeep passenger version of a truck 40 years ago. Ford created the Explorer, or luxury utility vehicle, in 1990. It took luxury car features and put them inside a jeep. Ford's payoff was substantial. The Explorer has become Ford's most popular domestic vehicle. However, virtually every vehicle manufacturer offered a luxury utility in 2003, with customers beginning to be hard pressed to identify clear distinctions between lead models. Ford's Explorer managers were looking for a new business strategy for the next decade that relied on new sources of differentiation and placed greater emphasis on low-cost components in their value chain.

***Technological Changes That Nullify Past Investments or Learning***  The Swiss controlled over 95 percent of the world's watch market into the 1970s. The bulk of the craftspeople, technology, and infrastructure resided in Switzerland. U.S.-based Texas Instruments decided to experiment with the use of its digital technology in watches. Swiss producers were not interested, but Japan's SEIKO and others were. In 2005, the Swiss will make less than 5 percent of the world's watches.

***The Cost Difference between Low-Cost Competitors and the Differentiated Business Becomes Too Great for Differentiation to Hold Brand Loyalty***  Buyers may begin to choose to sacrifice some of the features, services, or image possessed by the differentiated business for large cost savings. The rising cost of a college education, particularly at several "premier" institutions, has caused many students to opt for lower-cost destinations that offer very similar courses without image, frills, and professors that seldom teach undergraduate students anyway.

## Evaluating Speed as a Competitive Advantage

While most telecommunication companies have used the last decade to leap aboard the information superhighway, GTE continued its impressive turnaround focusing on its core business—providing local telephone services. Long lagging behind the Baby Bells in profitability and efficiency, GTE has emphasized improving its poor customer service throughout the decade. The service was so bad in Santa Monica, California, that officials once tried to remove GTE as the local phone company. Candidly saying "we were the pits," new CEO Chuck Lee largely did away with its old system of taking customer service requests by writing them down and passing them along for resolution. Now, using personal communication services and specially designed software, service reps can solve 70 percent of all problems on the initial call—triple the success rate at the beginning of the last decade. Repair workers meanwhile plan their schedules on laptops, cutting down-time and speeding responses. CEO Lee has spent $1.5 billion on reengineering that slashed 17,000 jobs, replaced people with technology, and prioritized *speed* as the defining feature of GTE's business practices.

Speed, or rapid response to customer requests or market and technological changes, has become a major source of competitive advantage for numerous firms in today's intensely competitive global economy. Speed is certainly a form of differentiation, but it is more than that. Speed involves the *availability of a rapid response* to a customer by providing current products quicker, accelerating new product development or improvement, quickly adjusting production processes, and making decisions quickly. While low cost and differentiation may provide important competitive advantages, managers in tomorrow's successful companies will base their strategies on creating speed-based competitive advantages. Exhibit 7–4 describes and illustrates key skills and organizational requirements that are associated with speed-based competitive advantage. Jack Welch, now retired, the CEO who transformed General Electric from a fading company into one of Wall Street's best performers over the last 20 years, had this to say about speed:

> Speed is really the driving force that everyone is after. Faster products, faster product cycles to market. Better response time to customers. . . . Satisfying customers, getting faster communications, moving with more agility, all these things are easier when one is small. And these are all characteristics one needs in a fast-moving global environment.[2]

Speed-based competitive advantages can be created around several activities:

***Customer Responsiveness*** All consumers have encountered hassles, delays, and frustration dealing with various businesses from time to time. The same holds true when dealing business to business. Quick response with answers, information, and solutions to mistakes can become the basis for competitive advantage . . . one that builds customer loyalty quickly.

***Product Development Cycles*** Japanese car makers have focused intensely on the time it takes to create a new model because several experienced disappointing sales growth in the last decade in Europe and North America competing against new vehicles like Ford's Explorer and Renault's Megane. VW had recently conceived, prototyped, produced, and marketed a totally new 4-wheel-drive car in Europe within 12 months. Honda, Toyota, and Nissan lowered their product development cycle from 24 months to 9 months from con-

---

[2] "Jack Welch: A CEO Who Can't Be Cloned," *BusinessWeek,* September 17, 2001.

## EXHIBIT 7–4
**Evaluating a Business's Rapid Response (Speed) Opportunities**

### A. Skills and Resources That Foster Speed

Process engineering skills.
Excellent inbound and outbound logistics.
Technical people in sales and customer service.
High levels of automation.
Corporate reputation for quality or technical leadership.
Flexible manufacturing capabilities.
Strong downstream partners.
Strong cooperation from suppliers of major components of the product or service.

### B. Organizational Requirements to Support and Sustain Rapid Response Activities

Strong coordination among functions in R&D, product development, and marketing.
Major emphasis on customer satisfaction in incentive programs.
Strong delegation to operating personnel.
Tradition of closeness to key customers.
Some personnel skilled in sales and operations—technical and marketing.
Empowered customer service personnel.

### C. Examples of Ways Businesses Achieve Competitive Advantage via Speed

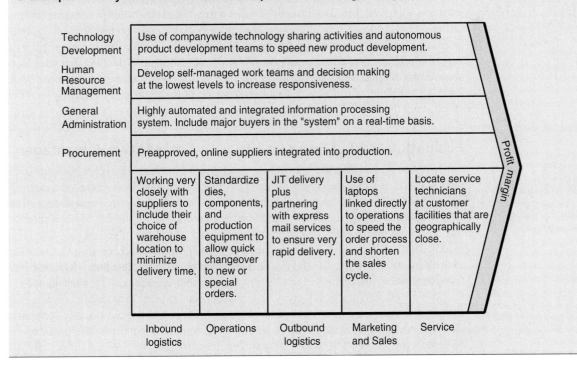

ception to production. This capability is old hat to 3M Corporation, which is so successful at speedy product development that one-fourth of its sales and profits each year are from products that didn't exist five years earlier.

***Product or Service Improvements***   Like development time, companies that can rapidly adapt their products or services and do so in a way that benefits their customers or creates new customers have a major competitive advantage over rivals that cannot do this.

***Speed in Delivery or Distribution*** Firms that can get you what you need when you need it, even when that is tomorrow, realize that buyers have come to expect that level of responsiveness. Federal Express's success reflects the importance customers place on speed in inbound and outbound logistics.

***Information Sharing and Technology*** Speed in sharing information that becomes the basis for decisions, actions, or other important activities taken by a customer, supplier, or partner has become a major source of competitive advantage for many businesses. Telecommunications, the Internet, and networks are but a part of a vast infrastructure that is being used by knowledgeable managers to rebuild or create value in their businesses via information sharing.

These rapid response capabilities create competitive advantages in several ways. They create a way to lessen rivalry because they have *availability* of something that a rival may not have. It can allow the business to charge buyers more, engender loyalty, or otherwise enhance the business's position relative to its buyers. Particularly where impressive customer response is involved, businesses can generate supplier cooperation and concessions since their business ultimately benefits from increased revenue. Finally, substitute products and new entrants find themselves trying to keep up with the rapid changes rather than introducing them. Exhibit 7–5, Strategy in Action, provides examples of how "speed" has become a source of competitive advantage for several well-known companies around the world.

While the notion of speed-based competitive advantage is exciting, it has risks managers must consider. First, speeding up activities that haven't been conducted in a fashion that prioritizes rapid response should only be done after considerable attention to training, reorganization, and/or reengineering. Second, some industries—stable, mature ones that have very minimal levels of change—may not offer much advantage to the firm that introduces some forms of rapid response. Customers in such settings may prefer the slower pace or the lower costs currently available or they may have long time frames in purchasing such that speed is not that important to them.

## Evaluating Market Focus as a Way to Competitive Advantage

Small companies, at least the better ones, usually thrive because they serve narrow market niches. This is usually called *focus,* the extent to which a business concentrates on a narrowly defined market. Take the example of Soho Beverages, a business former Pepsi manager Tom Cox bought from Seagram after Seagram had acquired it and was unable to make it thrive. The tiny brand, once a healthy niche product in New York and a few other east coast locations, muddled within Seagrams because its sales force was unused to selling in delis. Cox was able to double sales in one year. He did this on a lean marketing budget that didn't include advertising or database marketing. He hired Korean- and Arabic-speaking college students and had his people walk into practically every deli in Manhattan in order to reacquaint owners with the brand, spot consumption trends, and take orders. He provided rapid stocking services to all Manhattan-area delis, regardless of size. The business has continued sales growth at over 50 percent per year. Why? Cox says "It is attributable to focusing on a niche market, delis; differentiating the product and its sales force; achieving low costs in promotion and delivery; and making rapid, immediate response to any deli owner request its normal practice."

Two things are important in this example. First, this business focused on a narrow niche market in which to build a strong competitive advantage. But focus alone was not enough to build competitive advantage. Rather, Cox created several value chain activities that achieved differentiation, low-cost, and rapid response competitive advantages within this niche market that would be hard for other firms, particularly mass market-oriented firms, to replicate.

**BusinessWeek**

## SPEED IN DISTRIBUTION AND DELIVERY

Clad in a blue lab coat, a technician in Singapore waves a scanner like a wand over a box of newly minted computer chips. With that simple act, he sets in motion a delivery process that is efficient and automated, almost to the point of magic. This cavernous National Semiconductor Corp. (NSM) warehouse was designed and built by shipping wizards at United Parcel Service Inc. (UPS). It is UPS's computers that speed the box of chips to a loading dock, then to truck, to plane, and to truck once again. In just 12 hours, the chips will reach one of National's customers, a PC maker half a world away in Silicon Valley. Throughout the journey, electronic tags embedded in the chips will let the customer track the order with accuracy down to about three feet. In the two years since UPS and National starting this relationship, the team in brown has slashed National Semiconductor's inventory and shipment costs by 15 percent while reducing the time from factory floor to customer site by 60 percent.

## INFORMATION SHARING AND TECHNOLOGY

Meanwhile, in the Old Economy, UPS is winning giant customers such as Ford Motor Co., which uses UPS's computerized logistics to route cars more efficiently to its dealerships. In a year, Ford has reduced delivery times by 26 percent and saved $240 million, says Frank M. Taylor, Ford's vice president for material planning and logistics. "Speed is the mindset at UPS. They'll meet a deadline at any cost," Taylor says. UPS Chairman James P. Kelly chalks it up to the company's slow-and-steady work ethic. "We've spent the past seven years studying where we should be long-term," he says.

While FedEx backpedals in logistics, UPS is in growth mode. And it has figured out how to manage distribution for many companies at one central location—a massive warehouse in Louisville, Ky. Here, UPS handles storage, tracking, repair, and shipping for clients such as Sprint, Hewlett-Packard (HWP), and Nike (NKE) using a mix of high- and low-tech methods. Computerized forklifts scan in new inventory while people in sneakers dash across the vast warehouse to pluck products, box them, and ship them out. In short, UPS uses expensive technology only where it cuts costs.

## SPEED IN NEW PRODUCT DEVELOPMENT AND MANAGEMENT DECISION MAKING

Recently retired Volkswagen CEO Ferdinand Piëch has every reason to feel satisfied. The Austrian engineer and scion of one of Europe's most noted automotive dynasties can boast of one of the great turnarounds in automotive history, based on his attention to new product development combined with speed of decision making. Unlike many other auto chiefs, he called the shots on product design and engineering. And if you worked for Dr. Piëch, you had better get it right. In Wolfsburg, executives used to joke that PEP, the acronym for the product development process (Produkt entwicklungsprozess) really stood for Piëch entscheidet persönlich—Piëch decides himself. And he did it fast. He is said to have sketched out the Audi's all-wheel-drive system on the back of an envelope.

Obsession with detail and speed are key reasons VW has succeeded so brilliantly reviving its fortunes in the United States, where the VW brand was road kill a decade ago. Last year, VW and Audi sales in the United States jumped 14 percent, to 437,000 units, for a combined 2.5 percent market share. That's up from a microscopic 0.5 percent five years earlier. Although VW trails its Japanese rivals, it's the only European mass-market carmaker in the United States. Volkswagen's four main brands—VW (VLKAY), Audi, Seat, and Skoda—have taken 19 percent of the European auto market, a gain of some three points in eight years, mostly at the expense of General Motors Corp. (GM) and Ford. Not bad for a company that eight years ago suffered from quality problems and a paucity of hit models. In South America, VW vehicles account for one-quarter of car sales, and in China, one-half.

## SPEED IN CUSTOMER RESPONSIVENESS

Stuart Klaskin's flight on Delta Air Lines was leaving in just 20 minutes. Although he raced through New York's LaGuardia Airport, the behind-schedule aviation consultant suspected he would make it. Why? He bypassed the long check-in lines, stopping instead at one of Delta's 670 self-service kiosks, where all he did was insert his frequent-flier card to get a boarding pass. Not only did Klaskin make his flight but, he says, "I even had time to grab a cup of coffee."

Kiosks are just the start. Delta is using everything from high-definition screens providing real-time info to direct phone access to reservation agents to speed up travel. While its rivals use similar technologies, Delta is the first airline to package it all as a comprehensive, hassle-free system. "We are pioneering significant changes in the way passengers will move through airports," says Richard W. Cordell, Delta's senior vice-president for airport customer service. "In two years, 80 percent of our passengers will check in somewhere other than the old counter."

**Source:** "Delta's Flight to Self-Service," *BusinessWeek,* July 7, 2003; "UPS: Can It Keep Delivering," *BusinessWeek,* March 24 2003; "VW Needs a Jump," *BusinessWeek,* May 12, 2003.

Focus allows some businesses to compete on the basis of low cost, differentiation, and rapid response against much larger businesses with greater resources. Focus lets a business "learn" its target customers—their needs, special considerations they want accommodated—and establish personal relationships in ways that "differentiate" the smaller firm or make it more valuable to the target customer. Low costs can also be achieved filling niche needs in a buyer's operations that larger rivals either do not want to bother with or cannot do as cost effectively. Cost advantage often centers around the high level of customized service the focused, smaller business can provide. And perhaps the greatest competitive weapon that can arise is rapid response. With enhanced knowledge of its customers and intricacies of their operations, the small, focused company builds up organizational knowledge about timing sensitive ways to work with a customer. Often the needs of that narrow set of customers represent a large part of the small, focused business's revenues. Exhibit 7–6, Global Strategy in Action, illustrates how Ireland's Ryanair has become the European leader in discount air travel via the focused application of low cost, differentiation, and speed.

The risk of focus is that you attract major competitors that have waited for your business to "prove" the market. Domino's proved that a huge market for pizza delivery existed and now faces serious challenges. Likewise, publicly traded focused companies become takeover targets for large firms seeking to fill out a product portfolio. And perhaps the greatest risk of all is slipping into the illusion that it is focus itself, and not some special form of low cost, differentiation, or rapid response, that is creating the business's success.

Managers evaluating opportunities to build competitive advantage should link strategies to value chain activities that exploit low cost, differentiation, and rapid response competitive advantages. When advantageous, they should consider ways to use focus to leverage these advantages. One way business managers can enhance their likelihood of identifying these opportunities is to consider several different "generic" industry environments from the perspective of the typical value chain activities most often linked to sustained competitive advantages in those unique industry situations. The next section discusses five key generic industry environments and the value chain activities most associated with success.

# SELECTED INDUSTRY ENVIRONMENTS AND BUSINESS STRATEGY CHOICES

The analysis and choice of the ways a business will seek to build competitive advantage can be enhanced when managers take industry conditions into account. Chapter 3 discussed ways to examine industry conditions, so we do not repeat that here. Likewise, Chapter 5 showed how the market life cycle concept can be used to examine business strengths. What is important to recognize as managers evaluate opportunities to emphasize a narrow set of core competencies and potential competitive advantages is that different sets appear to be more useful in different, unique industry environments. We examine five "typical" industry settings and opportunities for generating competitive advantages that strategists should look for in their deliberations. Three of these five settings relate to industry life cycle. Managers use these as ways to evaluate their value chain activities and then select the ones around which it is most critical to build competitive advantage.[3]

---

[3] These industry characterizations draw heavily on the work of Michael E. Porter, *Competitive Advantage: Creating and Sustaining Superior Performance* (New York: Free Press, 1985).

**BusinessWeek** It was vintage Michael O'Leary. The 42-year-old CEO of Dublin-based discount airline Ryanair outfitted his staff in full combat gear, drove an old World War II tank to England's Luton airport, an hour north of London, then demanded access to the base of archrival easy Jet Airline Co. With the theme to the old television series *The A-Team* blaring, O'Leary declared he was "liberating the public from easy Jet's high fares." When security—surprise!—refused to let the Ryanair armor roll in, O'Leary led the troops in his own rendition of a platoon march song: "I've been told and it's no lie. easy Jet's fares are way too high!"

Buffoonery? Of course. But O'Leary can get away with it. Ryanair's 31 percent operating margin dwarfs British Airways 3.8 percent, easy Jet's 8.7 percent, and the 8.6 percent of the granddaddy of discount carriers, Dallas-based Southwest Airlines. Ryanair has built up $1 billion in cash. Its $5 billion market capitalization exceeds that of British Air, Lufthansa, and Air France. Ryanair, meanwhile, is expected to post pretax profits of $308 million for the year ended Mar. 31, up 53 percent from 2002 on sales of close to $1 billion. "O'Leary and his management team are absolutely the best at adopting a focus strategy and sticking to it relentlessly," says Ryanair's Chairman David Bonderman.

Ryanair's Focus Strategy has key differentiation, low cost, and speed elements allowing it to far outpace direct and indirect European airline competitors. They are as follows:

## DIFFERENTIATION

Ryanair flies to small, secondary airports outside major European cities. Often former military bases are attractive access points to European tourists, which the airports and small towns encourage. Virtually all of its rivals, including discount rival easy Jet, focus on business travelers and major international airports in Europe's largest cities. Its fares average 30 percent less than rival easy Jet, and are far lower than major European airlines. And Ryanair vows to lower its fares 5 percent a year for the foreseeable future, further differentiating itself from others, much like Southwest in the United States. It also offers one of Europe's leading e-tailers, Ryanair.com which sells more than 90 percent of its tickets online, and has hooked up with hotel chains, car rentals, life insurers and mobile phone companies to offer one-stop shopping to the European leisure traveler.

## LOW COST

Ryanair ordered 100 new Boeing 737-800s to facilitate the company's rapid European growth plans, less than a year after placing an order for 150 next-generation 737s. Analysts estimate Boeing offered Ryanair 40 percent off list price, significantly lowering Ryanair's cost of capital, maintenance costs, and operating expenses. Ryanair's differentiation choice of flying mainly to small, secondary airports outside major European cities has led to sweetheart deals on everything from landing and handling fees to marketing support. Less congestion lets Ryanair significantly lower personnel costs and the time a plane stays on the ground compared with rivals. Ryanair grows by acquiring small, recent entrants into the discount segment that are losing money at bargain basement prices—like Buzz, the loss-making discount carrier of KLM Royal Dutch Airlines—and then reducing routes, personnel, and bloated costs by 80 percent or more. Ryanair sells snacks and rents the back of seats and overhead storage to advertisers. Its use of less congested airports allows Ryanair to get its planes back in the air in 25 minutes—half the time it takes competitors at major airports.

## SPEED

Ryanair's Ryanair.com sells over 90 percent of its tickets quickly and conveniently for customers seeking simplicity, speed, and convenience. Its large purchases from Boeing allow it to grow to additional airports at a rate of about 30 percent annually. Airport turnaround time that is half the industry average allows Ryanair to provide significantly more frequent flights which simplifies and adds time-saving convenience for the leisure traveler and business traveler.

## FOCUS

O'Leary continues to focus like a light beam on small outlying airports and leisure travelers with speedy, low-cost services.

O'Leary's currently talking to 40 new European airports and scouting out future options in Eastern Europe. When he's not travelling in Europe, he's back at headquarters at Dublin Airport, where he joins in the company's Thursday football match. He recently acquired a Mercedes taxi and driver, enabling him to speed through Dublin's notorious traffic in the bus and taxi lane. "I've always been a transport innovator," he jokes. Millions of Europeans flying Ryanair planes would agree.

**Source:** "Ryanair Rising," *BusinessWeek,* June 2, 2003.

## Competitive Advantage in Emerging Industries

Emerging industries are newly formed or re-formed industries that typically are created by technological innovation, newly emerging customer needs, or other economic or sociological changes. Emerging industries of the last decade have been the Internet browser, fiber optics, solar heating, cellular telephone, and on-line services industries.

From the standpoint of strategy formulation, the essential characteristic of an emerging industry is that there are no "rules of the game." The absence of rules presents both a risk and an opportunity—a wise strategy positions the firm to favorably shape the emerging industry's rules.

Business strategies must be shaped to accommodate the following characteristics of markets in emerging industries.

Technologies that are mostly proprietary to the pioneering firms and technological uncertainty about how product standardization will unfold.

Competitor uncertainty because of inadequate information about competitors, buyers, and the timing of demand.

High initial costs but steep cost declines as the experience curve takes effect.

Few entry barriers, which often spurs the formation of many new firms.

First-time buyers requiring initial inducement to purchase and customers confused by the availability of a number of nonstandard products.

Inability to obtain raw materials and components until suppliers gear up to meet the industry's needs.

Need for high-risk capital because of the industry's uncertainty prospects.

For success in this industry setting, business strategies require one or more of these features:

1. The ability to *shape the industry's structure* based on the timing of entry, reputation, success in related industries or technologies, and role in industry associations.

2. The ability to *rapidly improve product quality* and performance features.

3. *Advantageous relationships* with key suppliers and promising distribution channels.

4. The ability to *establish the firm's technology as the dominant one* before technological uncertainty decreases.

5. The early acquisition of *a core group of loyal customers* and then the expansion of that customer base through model changes, alternative pricing, and advertising.

6. The ability to *forecast future competitors* and the strategies they are likely to employ.

A firm that has had repeated successes with business in emerging industries is 3M Corporation. In each of the last 20 years, over 25 percent of 3M's annual sales have come from products that did not exist 5 years earlier. Start-up companies enhance their success by having experienced entrepreneurs at the helm, a knowledgeable management team and board of directors, and patient sources of venture capital. Steven Jobs' dramatic unveiling of Apple's iChat technology in 2003 was seen by some as the catalyst for a revolution in long-distance telephone service—perhaps an emerging niche industry. Jobs is certainly an experienced entrepreneur. So read  Exhibit 7–7 and see if an emerging industry was born and if Apple's strategy foretells success.

# Strategy in Action
Has Steven Jobs Done It Again?

Exhibit 7–7

**BusinessWeek** Read this *BusinessWeek* account of Apple's iChat innovation and see if it spawned a new industry niche along with positioning Apple with a strategy to succeed in that emerging industry niche.

Give Steve Jobs credit. For a man who heads a comparatively small technology company, he sure knows how to alter the tech landscape. The exuberant and often exasperating CEO of Apple Computer gave the music industry its groove back in April when he introduced a powerful one-two punch of iTunes and the online Apple Music Store. With 99-cent downloads, Jobs also handed music lovers what they wanted: high-quality downloads, a fair price, a good selection, and the right to do what they see fit with their music. With 5 million paid downloads in two months and a version for Microsoft Windows users on the way, it's easy to see why music industry execs are dancing in their boardrooms. While the record labels have been a lucky benefactor of Jobsian innovation, the phone companies are about to get whacked by Jobs's quest to give Apple users something else they want. All you need is a Mac running OS X, a decent external microphone, and a connection of 28 kilobits per second or so.

Best of all, iChat lets me bypass the phone company. For the few people on my instant-messaging buddy list who have iChat, I don't pick up the phone anymore to talk to them. I simply look to see if they're available and, if they are, I click on the voice connection button in iChat. A few seconds later, I have the equivalent of a phone line. If everyone on my IM list had the new version of iChat, I would think very seriously about dumping my wireline phone service. Just give me a cordless headset to connect to my Mac, and my IM will supplant the phone almost entirely.

Take this one step further, and it's not so farfetched to imagine that the various IM systems from America Online (AOL), Microsoft (MSET) and Yahoo! (YHOO), among others, will quickly morph into major competitors against the lumbering telecoms. And it will hasten the day when Internet users can set up their own phone service, or at least something that functions as phone service does today. All they'll need is a dumb pipe connected to the Internet with no costly bells and whistles attached.

Everyone agrees that communications using packets of data typified by the Internet will ultimately replace the circuit-based system used by the legacy phone network. All the big telecom providers are busily switching from networks built largely to handle dedicated circuits for voice calls to vastly more efficient and flexible networks that handle voice traffic in bits and bytes, just like data. But their efforts presuppose a paradigm where they'll continue their role as the middlemen who route all calls.

Already the Baby Bells and long-distance companies are seeking to consolidate their hold on that role with fierce lobbying efforts aimed at regulating so-called voice-over-IP communications, like iChart. Upstart companies, such as New Jersey–based Vonage, have the audacity to tap into the phone system the cheap way. Rather than pay stiff interconnection fees to complete long-distance calls or costly tariffs to rent high-capacity local circuits, Vonage and others sell specially equipped phones that can turn any home broadband connection into a phone hook-up. The voice traffic flowing over these users' broadband connections is virtually indistinguishable from data traffic. On the Net, surfing to Amazon.com and phoning Grandma can be one and the same.

Still, all of this presupposes a phone network and a system designed specifically to move voice traffic. Now, though, there's no longer any need for someone to sell voice service. Consumers can piece together their own phone networks over the Internet, thanks to the rising tide of iChat-like technology. Since most Internet traffic still travels over dial-up connections, that part of the phone network will still be necessary, and users will continue paying for connections to the Net. But there would be no reason to pay special fees, such as long-distance charges, for antiquated, dedicated voice phone service.

Let's do the numbers. America Online (AOL) alone has 350 million users on its two IM services, AOL Instant Messenger and ICQ. Several technologists have told me that what Apple has done, while technologically sophisticated, wouldn't be hard for other IM services to replicate. In fact, iChat and AOL IM are already compatible. iChat users show up on the buddy lists of AOL IM users and vice versa. Give all those users an iChat-like voice capability, and all of a sudden you have a phone network with more than 350 million users.

These number don't include Yahoo and MSN's IM customers. If at some point those two interconnect with AOL's dominant IM network, the tally would likely eclipse 500 million. And once word gets out that you can have free phone service simply by signing up for IM, I guarantee millions more people will come aboard.

## AN INDUSTRY REBIRTH?

The net effect on the telecoms would be nothing short of catastrophic. The rise of IM as a viable mechanism for voice communication would undermine the pricing power of flat-rate voice plans by virtue of being even cheaper than Vonage, which mails out phones that it sells below cost. A desktop microphone suitable for iChat costs $15.

It will also eliminate the need for a middleman to mind the huge chunk of the phone networks used for interconnecting

*(continued)*

dedicated voice calls and the services associated with those calls. Everyone will be able to connect directly. That would hasten the decrease in the value and utility of legacy phone networks, which rely on massive penetration and use to make money.

Granted, none of this could happen overnight. Big shifts in technology take shape over years, not months. Although Apple is making a big splash, it remains a bit player in the grand scheme, without enough users to shift markets.

Further, traditional phone service carries all sorts of regulatory baggage that makes replacing it with IM tricky. For example, voice-over-IP won't work if someone can't afford to buy a computer. Likewise, the phone goes down if power or the Internet connection goes down. That would be a serious problem because the legacy phone system remains a lifeline, although cell phones are a potential replacement here, too. After all, most users find their cell phones as reliable as local phone connections because no one buys a cell with a coverage plan that doesn't work in their own home and neighborhood. Further, cell networks have proven more resilient. Witness the aftermath of September 11, when mobile networks held up while Lower Manhattan's wireline circuits remained dark for days.

In the past, Apple has contributed to big technological shifts such as introducing the graphical user interface to consumers and, more recently, creating a viable platform for digital music sales online. If past is prologue, then Jobs's latest innovation could hasten a coming age when anyone who wants to can use their PC to bypass traditional phone services and spawn a new industry in the process . . . like dropping a phone book on the Baby Bells' heads.

**Source:** "With iChat, Who Needs A Phone?" *BusinessWeek,* July 9, 2003.

## Competitive Advantage in the Transition to Industry Maturity

As an industry evolves, its rate of growth eventually declines. This "transition to maturity" is accompanied by several changes in its competitive environment:

Competition for market share becomes more intense as firms in the industry are forced to achieve sales growth at one another's expense.

Firms in the industry sell increasingly to experienced, repeat buyers that are now making choices among known alternatives.

Competition becomes more oriented to cost and service as knowledgeable buyers expect similar price and product features.

Industry capacity "tops out" as sales growth ceases to cover up poorly planned expansions.

New products and new applications are harder to come by.

International competition increases as cost pressures lead to overseas production advantages.

Profitability falls, often permanently, as a result of pressure to lower prices and the increased costs of holding or building market share.

These changes necessitate a fundamental strategic reassessment. Strategy elements of successful firms in maturing industries often include:

1. *Pruning the product line* by dropping unprofitable product models, sizes, and options from the firm's product mix.

2. *Emphasis on process innovation* that permits low-cost product design, manufacturing methods, and distribution synergy.

3. *Emphasis on cost reduction* through exerting pressure on suppliers for lower prices, switching to cheaper components, introducing operational efficiencies, and lowering administrative and sales overhead.

4. *Careful buyer selection* to focus on buyers that are less aggressive, more closely tied to the firm, and able to buy more from the firm.

5. *Horizontal integration* to acquire rival firms whose weaknesses can be used to gain a bargain price and are correctable by the acquiring firms.

6. *International expansion* to markets where attractive growth and limited competition still exist and the opportunity for lower-cost manufacturing can influence both domestic and international costs.

Business strategists in maturing industries must avoid several pitfalls. First, they must make a clear choice among the three generic strategies and avoid a middle-ground approach, which would confuse both knowledgeable buyers and the firm's personnel. Second, they must avoid sacrificing market share too quickly for short-term profit. Finally, they must avoid waiting too long to respond to price reductions, retaining unneeded excess capacity, engaging in sporadic or irrational efforts to boost sales, and placing their hopes on "new" products, rather than aggressively selling existing products.

## Competitive Advantage in Mature and Declining Industries

Declining industries are those that make products or services for which demand is growing slower than demand in the economy as a whole or is actually declining. This slow growth or decline in demand is caused by technological substitution (such as the substitution of electronic calculators for slide rules), demographic shifts (such as the increase in the number of older people and the decrease in the number of children), and shifts in needs (such as the decreased need for red meat).

Firms in a declining industry should choose strategies that emphasize one or more of the following themes:

1. *Focus* on segments within the industry that offer a chance for higher growth or a higher return.

2. *Emphasize product innovation and quality improvement,* where this can be done cost effectively, to differentiate the firm from rivals and to spur growth.

3. *Emphasize production and distribution efficiency* by streamlining production, closing marginal productions facilities and costly distribution outlets, and adding effective new facilities and outlets.

4. *Gradually harvest the business*—generate cash by cutting down on maintenance, reducing models, and shrinking channels and make no new investment.

Strategists who incorporate one or more of these themes into the strategy of their business can anticipate relative success, particularly where the industry's decline is slow and smooth and some profitable niches remain. Penn Tennis, the nations' number one maker of tennis balls, watched industrywide sales steadily decline the last decade. In response it started marketing tennis balls as "dog toys" in the rapidly growing pet products industry. It secondly made Penn balls the official ball at major tournaments. Third, it created three different quality levels, then, as sales revived, Penn Sports sold its tennis ball business to Head Sports.

# Competitive Advantage in Fragmented Industries

A fragmented industry is one in which no firm has a significant market share and can strongly influence industry outcomes. Fragmented industries are found in many areas of the economy and are common in such areas as professional services, retailing, distribution, wood and metal fabrication, and agricultural products. The funeral industry is an example of a highly fragmented industry. Business strategists in fragmented industries pursue low-cost, differentiation, or focus competitive advantages in one of five ways.

### *Tightly Managed Decentralization*

Fragmented industries are characterized by a need for intense local coordination, a local management orientation, high personal service, and local autonomy. Recently, however, successful firms in such industries have introduced a high degree of professionalism into the operations of local managers.

### *"Formula" Facilities*

This alternative, related to the previous one, introduces standardized, efficient, low-cost facilities at multiple locations. Thus, the firm gradually builds a low-cost advantage over localized competitors. Fast-food and motel chains have applied this approach with considerable success.

### *Increased Value-Added*

The products or services of some fragmented industries are difficult to differentiate. In this case, an effective strategy may be to add value by providing more service with the sale or by engaging in some product assembly that is of additional value to the customer.

### *Specialization*

Focus strategies that creatively segment the market can enable firms to cope with fragmentation. Specialization can be pursued by:

1. *Product type.* The firm builds expertise focusing on a narrow range of products or services.

2. *Customer type.* The firm becomes intimately familiar with and serves the needs of a narrow customer segment.

3. *Type of order.* The firm handles only certain kinds of orders, such as small orders, custom orders, or quick turnaround orders.

4. *Geographic area.* The firm blankets or concentrates on a single area.

Although specialization in one or more of these ways can be the basis for a sound focus strategy in a fragmented industry, each of these types of specialization risks limiting the firm's potential sales volume.

### *Bare Bones/No Frills*

Given the intense competition and low margins in fragmented industries, a "bare bones" posture—low overhead, minimum wage employees, tight cost control—may build a sustainable cost advantage in such industries.

## Competitive Advantage in Global Industries

A global industry is one that comprises firms whose competitive positions in major geographic or national markets are fundamentally affected by their overall global competitive positions. To avoid strategic disadvantages, firms in global industries are virtually required to compete on a worldwide basis. Oil, steel, automobiles, apparel, motorcycles, televisions, and computers are examples of global industries.

Global industries have four unique strategy-shaping features:

Differences in prices and costs from country to country due to currency exchange fluctuations, differences in wage and inflation rates, and other economic factors.

Differences in buyer needs across different countries.

Differences in competitors and ways of competing from country to country.

Differences in trade rules and governmental regulations across different countries.

These unique features and the global competition of global industries require that two fundamental components be addressed in the business strategy: (1) the approach used to gain global market coverage and (2) the generic competitive strategy.

Three basic options can be used to pursue global market coverage:

1. *License* foreign firms to produce and distribute the firm's products.

2. *Maintain a domestic production base* and export products to foreign countries.

3. *Establish foreign-based plants and distribution* to compete directly in the markets of one or more foreign countries.

Along with the market coverage decision, strategists must scrutinize the condition of the global industry features identified earlier to choose among four generic global competitive strategies:

1. *Broad-line global competition*—directed at competing worldwide in the full product line of the industry, often with plants in many countries, to achieve differentiation or an overall low-cost position.

2. *Global focus* strategy—targeting a particular segment of the industry for competition on a worldwide basis.

3. *National focus* strategy—taking advantage of differences in national markets that give the firm an edge over global competitors on a nation-by-nation basis.

4. *Protected niche* strategy—seeking out countries in which governmental restraints exclude or inhibit global competitors or allow concessions, or both, that are advantageous to localized firms.

Competing in global industries is an increasing reality for many U.S. firms. Strategists must carefully match their skills and resources with global industry structure and conditions in selecting the most appropriate strategy option.

In conclusion, the analysis and choice of business strategy involves three basic considerations. First, strategists must recognize that their overall choice revolves around three sources of competitive advantage that require total, consistent commitment. Second, strategists must carefully weigh the skills, resources, organizational requirements, and risks associated with each source of competitive advantage. Finally, strategists must consider the unique influence that the generic industry environment most similar to the firm's situation will have on the set of value chain activities they choose to build competitive advantage.

# DOMINANT PRODUCT/SERVICE BUSINESSES: EVALUATING AND CHOOSING TO DIVERSIFY TO BUILD VALUE

McDonald's has frequently looked at numerous opportunities to diversify into related businesses or to acquire key suppliers. Its decision has consistently been to focus on its core business using the grand strategies of concentration, market development, and product development. Rival Pepsi, on the other hand, has chosen to diversify into related businesses and vertical integration as the best grand strategies for it to build long-term value. Both firms experienced unprecedented success during the last 20 years.

Many dominant product businesses face this question as their core business proves successful: What grand strategies are best suited to continue to build value? Under what circumstances should they choose an expanded focus (diversification, vertical integration); steady continued focus (concentration, market or product development); or a narrowed focus (turnaround or divestiture)? This section examines two ways you can analyze a dominant product company's situation and choose among the 15 grand strategies identified in Chapter 6.

## Grand Strategy Selection Matrix

One valuable guide to the selection of a promising grand strategy is the matrix shown in Exhibit 7–8. The basic idea underlying the matrix is that two variables are of central concern in the selection process: (1) the principal purpose of the grand strategy and (2) the choice of an internal or external emphasis for growth or profitability.

In the past, planners were advised to follow certain rules or prescriptions in their choice of strategies. Now, most experts agree that strategy selection is better guided by the conditions of the planning period and by the company strengths and weaknesses. It should be noted, however, that even the early approaches to strategy selection sought to match a concern over internal versus external growth with a desire to overcome weaknesses or maximize strengths.

**EXHIBIT 7–8**
**Grand Strategy
Selection Matrix**

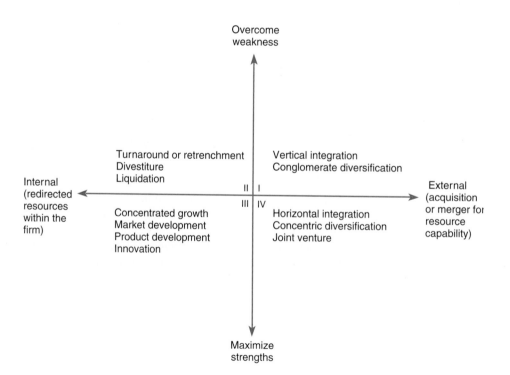

The same considerations led to the development of the grand strategy selection matrix. A firm in quadrant I, with "all its eggs in one basket," often views itself as over-committed to a particular business with limited growth opportunities or high risks. One reasonable solution is *vertical integration,* which enables the firm to reduce risk by reducing uncertainty about inputs or access to customers. Another is *conglomerate diversification,* which provides a profitable investment alternative with diverting management attention from the original business. However, the external approaches to overcoming weaknesses usually result in the most costly grand strategies. Acquiring a second business demands large investments of time and sizable financial resources. Thus, strategic managers considering these approaches must guard against exchanging one set of weaknesses for another.

More conservative approaches to overcoming weaknesses are found in quadrant II. Firms often choose to redirect resources from one internal business activity to another. This approach maintains the firm's commitment to its basic mission, rewards success, and enables further development of proven competitive advantages. The least disruptive of the quadrant II strategies is *retrenchment,* pruning the current activities of a business. If the weaknesses of the business arose from inefficiencies, retrenchment can actually serve as a *turnaround* strategy—that is, the business gains new strength from the streamlining of its operations and the elimination of waste. However, if those weaknesses are a major obstruction to success in the industry and the costs of overcoming them are unaffordable or are not justified by a cost-benefit analysis, then eliminating the business must be considered. *Divestiture* offers the best possibility for recouping the firm's investment, but even *liquidation* can be an attractive option if the alternatives are bankruptcy or an unwarranted drain on the firm's resources.

A common business adage states that a firm should build from strength. The premise of this adage is that growth and survival depend on an ability to capture a market share that is large enough for essential economies of scale. If a firm believes that this approach will be profitable and prefers an internal emphasis for maximizing strengths, four grand strategies hold considerable promise. As shown in quadrant III, the most common approach is *concentrated growth,* that is, market penetration. The firm that selects this strategy is strongly committed to its current products and markets. It strives to solidify its position by reinvesting resources to fortify its strengths.

Two alternative approaches are *market development* and *product development.* With these strategies, the firm attempts to broaden its operations. Market development is chosen if the firm's strategic managers feel that its existing products would be well received by new customer groups. Product development is chosen if they feel that the firm's existing customers would be interested in products related to its current lines. Product development also may be based on technological or other competitive advantages. The final alternative for quadrant III firms is *innovation.* When the firm's strengths are in creative product design or unique production technologies, sales can be stimulated by accelerating perceived obsolescence. This is the principle underlying the innovative grand strategy.

Maximizing a firm's strengths by aggressively expanding its base of operations usually requires an external emphasis. The preferred options in such cases are shown in quadrant IV. *Horizontal integration* is attractive because it makes possible a quick increase in output capability. Moreover, in horizontal integration, the skills of the managers of the original business often are critical in converting newly acquired facilities into profitable contributors to the parent firm; this expands a fundamental competitive advantage of the firm—its management.

*Concentric diversification* is a good second choice for similar reasons. Because the original and newly acquired businesses are related, the distinctive competencies of the diversifying firm are likely to facilitate a smooth, synergistic, and profitable expansion.

The final alternative for increasing resource capability through external emphasis is a *joint venture* or *strategic alliance.* This alternative allows a firm to extend its strengths into

**EXHIBIT 7–9**
**Model of Grand
Strategy Clusters**

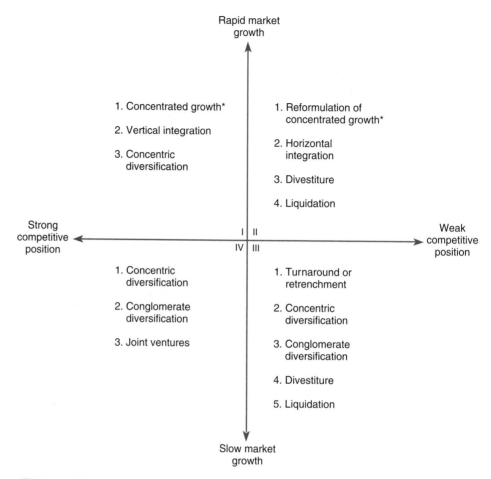

Rapid market
growth

1. Concentrated growth*

2. Vertical integration

3. Concentric
   diversification

1. Reformulation of
   concentrated growth*

2. Horizontal
   integration

3. Divestiture

4. Liquidation

Strong
competitive
position

Weak
competitive
position

I | II
IV | III

1. Concentric
   diversification

2. Conglomerate
   diversification

3. Joint ventures

1. Turnaround or
   retrenchment

2. Concentric
   diversification

3. Conglomerate
   diversification

4. Divestiture

5. Liquidation

Slow market
growth

*This is usually via market development, product development, or a combination of both.

competitive arenas that it would be hesitant to enter alone. A partner's production, technological, financial, or marketing capabilities can reduce the firm's financial investment significantly and increase its probability of success.

## Model of Grand Strategy Clusters

A second guide to selecting a promising grand strategy is shown in Exhibit 7–9. The figure
is based on the idea that the situation of a business is defined in terms of the growth rate of
the general market and the firm's competitive position in that market. When these factors
are considered simultaneously, a business can be broadly categorized in one of four quadrants: (I) strong competitive position in a rapidly growing market, (II) weak position in a
rapidly growing market, (III) weak position in a slow-growth market, or (IV) strong position in a slow-growth market. Each of these quadrants suggests a set of promising possibilities for the selection of a grand strategy.

Firms in quadrant I are in an excellent strategic position. One obvious grand strategy for
such firms is continued concentration on their current business as it is currently defined. Because consumers seem satisfied with the firm's current strategy, shifting notably from it would
endanger the firm's established competitive advantages. McDonald's Corporation has followed

this approach for 25 years. However, if the firm has resources that exceed the demands of a concentrated growth strategy, it should consider vertical integration. Either forward or backward integration helps a firm protect its profit margins and market share by ensuring better access to consumers or material inputs. Finally, to diminish the risks associated with a narrow product or service line, a quadrant I firm might be wise to consider concentric diversification; with this strategy, the firm continues to invest heavily in its basic area of proven ability.

Firms in quadrant II must seriously evaluate their present approach to the marketplace. If a firm has competed long enough to accurately assess the merits of its current grand strategy, it must determine (1) why that strategy is ineffectual and (2) whether it is capable of competing effectively. Depending on the answers to these questions, the firm should choose one of four grand strategy options: formulation or reformulation of a concentrated growth strategy, horizontal integration, divestiture, or liquidation.

In a rapidly growing market, even a small or relatively weak business often is able to find a profitable niche. Thus, formulation or reformulation of a concentrated growth strategy is usually the first option that should be considered. However, if the firm lacks either a critical competitive element or sufficient economies of scale to achieve competitive cost efficiencies, then a grand strategy that directs its efforts toward horizontal integration is often a desirable alternative. A final pair of options involve deciding to stop competing in the market or product area of the business. A multiproduct firm may conclude that it is most likely to achieve the goals of its mission if the business is dropped through divestiture. This grand strategy not only eliminates a drain on resources but also may provide funds to promote other business activities. As an option of last resort, a firm may decide to liquidate the business. This means that the business cannot be sold as a going concern and is at best worth only the value of its tangible assets. The decision to liquidate is an undeniable admission of failure by a firm's strategic management and, thus, often is delayed—to the further detriment of the firm.

Strategic managers tend to resist divestiture because it is likely to jeopardize their control of the firm and perhaps even their jobs. Thus, by the time the desirability of divestiture is acknowledged, businesses often deteriorate to the point of failing to attract potential buyers. The consequences of such delays are financially disastrous for firm owners because the value of a going concern is many times greater than the value of its assets.

Strategic managers who have a business in quadrant III and expect a continuation of slow market growth and a relatively weak competitive position will usually attempt to decrease their resource commitment to that business. Minimal withdrawal is accomplished through retrenchment; this strategy has the side benefits of making resources available for other investments and of motivating employees to increase their operating efficiency. An alternative approach is to divert resources for expansion through investment in other businesses. This approach typically involves either concentric or conglomerate diversification because the firm usually wants to enter more promising arenas of competition than integration or concentrated growth strategies would allow. The final options for quadrant III businesses are divestiture, if an optimistic buyer can be found, and liquidation.

Quadrant IV businesses (strong competitive position in a slow-growth market) have a basis of strength from which to diversify into more promising growth areas. These businesses have characteristically high cash flow levels and limited internal growth needs. Thus, they are in an excellent position for concentric diversification into ventures that utilize their proven acumen. A previous example in this chapter described how the number-one tennis ball maker, Penn Racquet Sports, chose concentric diversification from humans to dogs as their best option. A second option is conglomerate diversification, which spreads investment risk and does not divert managerial attention from the present business. The final option is joint ventures, which are especially attractive to multinational firms. Through joint ventures, a domestic business can gain competitive advantages in promising new fields while exposing itself to limited risks.

## Opportunities for Building Value as a Basis for Choosing Diversification or Integration

The grand strategy selection matrix and model of grand strategy clusters are useful tools to help dominant product company managers evaluate and narrow their choices among alternative grand strategies. When considering grand strategies that would broaden the scope of their company's business activities through integration, diversification, or joint venture strategies, managers must examine whether opportunities to build value are present. Opportunities to build value via diversification, integration, or joint venture strategies are usually found in market-related, operating-related, and management activities. Such opportunities center around reducing costs, improving margins, or providing access to new revenue sources more cost effectively than traditional internal growth options via concentration, market development, or product development. Major opportunities for sharing and value building as well as ways to capitalize on core competencies are outlined in the next chapter, which covers strategic analysis and choice in diversified companies.

Dominant product company managers who choose diversification or integration eventually create another management challenge. That challenge is charting the future of a company that becomes a collection of several distinct businesses. These distinct businesses often encounter different competitive environments, challenges, and opportunities. The next chapter examines ways managers of such diversified companies attempt to evaluate and choose corporate strategy. Central to their challenge is the continued desire to build value, particularly shareholder value.

## Summary

This chapter examined how managers in businesses that have a single or dominant product or service evaluate and choose their company's strategy. Two critical areas deserve their attention: first, their business's value chain; second, the appropriateness of 12 different grand strategies based on matching environmental factors with internal capabilities.

Managers in single-product-line business units examine their business's value chain to identify existing or potential activities around which they can create sustainable competitive advantages. As managers scrutinize their value chain activities, they are looking for three sources of competitive advantage: low cost, differentiation, and rapid response capabilities. They also examine whether focusing on a narrow market niche provides a more effective, sustainable way to build or leverage these three sources of competitive advantage.

Managers in single or dominant product/service businesses face two interrelated issues. First, they must choose which grand strategies make best use of their competitive advantages. Second, they must ultimately decide whether to diversify their business activity. Twelve grand strategies were identified in this chapter along with three frameworks that aid managers in choosing which grand strategies should work best and when diversification or integration should be the best strategy for the business. The next chapter expands the coverage of diversification to look at how multibusiness companies evaluate continued diversification and how they construct corporate strategy.

## Questions for Discussion

1. What are three activities or capabilities a firm should possess to support a low-cost leadership strategy? Use Exhibit 7–2 to help you answer this question. Can you give an example of a company that has done this?

2. What are three activities or capabilities a firm should possess to support a differentiation-based strategy? Use Exhibit 7–3 to help you answer this question. Can you give an example of a company that has done this?

3. What are three ways a firm can incorporate the advantage of speed in its business? Use Exhibit 7–4 to help you answer this question. Can you give an example of a company that has done this?

4. Do you think is it better to concentrate on one source of competitive advantage (cost versus differentiation versus speed) or to nurture all three in a firm's operation?

5. How does market focus help a business create competitive advantage? What risks accompany such a posture?

6. Using Exhibits 7–8 and 7–9, describe situations or conditions under which horizontal integration and concentric diversification would be preferred strategic choices.

## Chapter 7 Discussion Case

# Strategic Analysis and Choice at Korea's Samsung Electronics

*The Samsung Way*

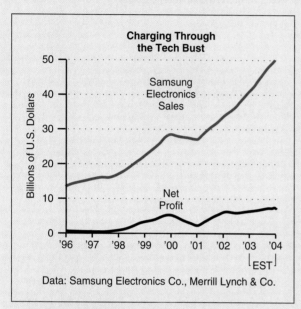

**Charging Through the Tech Bust**

Billions of U.S. Dollars

Samsung Electronics Sales

Net Profit

'96 '97 '98 '99 '00 '01 '02 '03 '04 ⌊EST⌋

Data: Samsung Electronics Co., Merrill Lynch & Co.

**It thrives in low-margin consumer electronics. It favors hardware over software. It's still a conglomerate that makes everything itself. Can Samsung keep defying conventional wisdom?**

1   A black-suited Agent Smith sprints down a city street. As he is felled by an acrobatic kung fu kick from Trinity, the camera pulls back to show the action taking place inside a giant, floating Samsung TV. The screen rotates, revealing that the set is just three inches thick. "You cannot escape the Samsung 40-inch LCD flat-panel TV," intones the baritone voice of actor Laurence Fishburne. "Welcome to the new dimension."

2   The ad, which appeared in many U.S. theaters showing *The Matrix: Reloaded,* had an element of truth: Whether you're a consumer in America, Europe, or Asia, it's getting pretty darn hard to escape anything made by Samsung Electronics Co. Take the United States alone. Stroll the aisles of Best Buy Co. (BBY) electronics stores, and stylish Samsung high-definition TVs, phones, plasma displays, and digital music and video players are everywhere. Log on to the home pages of *USA Today* (GCI) CNN (AOL) and other heavily trafficked sites, and Samsung's ads are first to pop out. You see its blue elliptical logo emblazoned on Olympic scoreboards. And expect more Matrix tie-ins: Samsung is selling a wireless phone just like the one Keanu Reeves uses to transport himself in the movie. Samsung was even more visible in the fall 2003 sequel, *The Matrix: Revolutions.*

## STRATEGIC ANALYSIS AT SAMSUNG

3   Samsung's Matrix moment was just one of its latest steps in its reincarnation as one of the world's coolest brands. Its success in a blizzard of digital gadgets and in chips has wowed consumers and scared rivals around the world. The achievement is all the more remarkable considering that just six years earlier, Samsung was financially crippled, its brand associated with cheap, me-too TVs and microwaves.

4   Samsung Electronics' ascent is an unlikely tale. The company was left with huge debt following the 1997 Korean financial crisis, a crash in memory-chip prices, and a $700 million write-off after an ill-advised takeover of AST Technologies, a U.S. maker of PCs. Its subsidiaries paid little heed to profits and focused on breaking production and sales records—even if much of the output ended up unsold in warehouses.

5   A jovial toastmaster at company dinners but a tough-as-nails boss when he wants results, CEO Yun Jong Yong shuttered Samsung's TV factories for two months until old inventory cleared. Yun also decreed Samsung would sell only high-end goods. Many cellular operators resisted. "Carriers didn't buy our story," says telecom exec Park. "They wanted lower prices all the time. At some point, we had to say no to them."

6   A top priority was straightening out the business in the United States, where "we were in a desperate position," recalls Samsung America chief Oh, appointed in early 2001. "We had a lot of gadgets. But they had nowhere to go." Samsung lured Peter

Skaryznski from AT&T (T) to run handset sales, and Peter Weedfald, who worked at ViewSonic Corp. and *Computer World* magazine, to head marketing.

**7**  Yun brought new blood to Seoul, too. One recruit was Eric B. Kim, 48, who moved to the United States from Korea at age 13 and worked at various tech companies. Kim was named executive vice-president of global marketing in 2000. With his Korean rusty, Kim made his first big presentation to 400 managers in English. Sensing Kim would be resented, Yun declared: "Some of you may want to put Mr. Kim on top of a tree and then shake him down. If anybody tries that, I will kill you!"

**8**  The first coup in the United States came in 1997 when Sprint PCS Group began selling Samsung handsets. Sprint's service was based on CDMA, and Samsung had an early lead in the standard due to an alliance in Korea with Qualcomm (QCOM) Inc. Samsung's SCH-3500, a silver, clamshell-shaped model priced at $149, was an instant hit. Soon, Samsung was world leader in CDMA phones. Under Weedfald, Samsung also pulled its appliances off the shelves of Wal-Mart and Target and negotiated deals with higher-end chains like Best Buy and Circuit City.

**9**  Samsung's status in chips and displays, which can make up 90 percent of the cost of most digital devices, gives it an edge in handsets and other products. Besides dominating DRAM chips, Samsung leads in static random access memory and controls 55 percent of the $2 billion market for NAND flash memory, a technology mainly used in removable cards that store large music and color-image files. With portable digital appliances expected to skyrocket, analysts predict NAND flash sales will soar to $7 billion by 2005, overtaking the more established market for NOR flash, which is embedded onto PCs, dominated by Intel and Advanced Micro Devices (AMD).

**10**  The company's breadth in displays gives it a similar advantage. It leads in thin-film LCDs, which are becoming the favored format for PCs, normal-size TVs, and all mobile devices. Samsung predicts a factory being built in Tangjung, Korea, that will produce LCD sheets as big as a queen-size mattress and will help to halve prices of large-screen LCD TVs by 2005. Samsung also aims to be No. 1 in plasma and projection displays.

**11**  If Samsung has a major flaw, it may be its lack of software and content. Samsung has no plans to branch out into music, movies, and games, as Sony and Apple have done. Sony figures that subscription-to-content will provide a more lucrative source of revenue. Samsung's execs remain convinced they're better off collaborating with content and software providers. They say this strategy offers customers more choices than Nokia, which uses its own software.

**12**  Can the good times last? That's a serious question, since Samsung is challenging basic New Economy dogma. In high tech, the assumption is that developing proprietary software and content gives you higher margins and a long lead time over rivals. Yet Samsung defiantly refuses to enter the software business. It's wedded to hardware and betting it can thrive in a period of relentless deflation for the industry. Rather than outsource manufacturing, the company sinks billions into huge new factories. Instead of bearing down on a few "core competencies," Samsung remains diversified and vertically integrated—Samsung chips and displays go into its own digital products. "If we get out of manufacturing," says CEO and Vice Chairman Yun Jong Yong, "we will lose."

**13**  Yet the industrial history of the past two decades suggests that this model does not work in the long run. The hazard—as many Japanese, U.S., and European companies learned in the 1980s and '90s—is that Samsung must keep investing heavily in R&D and new factories across numerous product lines. Samsung has sunk $19 billion over five years into new chip facilities. Rivals can buy similar technologies from other vendors without tying up capital or making long-term commitments. What's more, the life cycle of much hardware is brutally short and subject to relentless commoditization. The average price of a TV set has dropped 30 percent in five years; a DVD player goes for less than a quarter. The Chinese keep driving prices ever lower, leveraging supercheap wages and engineering talent. Meanwhile, the Japanese are building their own Chinese factories to lower costs. No wonder Samsung exited the low-margin market for TV sets 27 inches and under.

**14**  Faced with these perils, Samsung needs a constant stream of well-timed hits to stay on top. Even Sony has stumbled in this race: It now depends on PlayStation to support a consumer-electronics business whose glory days seem behind it. Other legendary hardware makers—Apple, Motorola, Ericsson (ERICY)—have learned the perils of the hardware way.

**15**  Investors got a sharp reminder of the risks Samsung is running when the company announced first-quarter results. In a tough environment, Samsung racked up the biggest market-share gain of any company in handsets, from 9.3 percent to 10.5 percent. Yet it had to lower prices to get there, and memory-chip prices also hit the bottom line. The result was a drop in first-quarter profits of 41 percent, to $942 million, on sales of $8 billion. Second-quarter profits could drop further, analysts say, hurt by lower sales in Korea's slumping economy—and in China and other Asian countries struck by the 2003 SARS epidemic. Controversy also flared in 2003 when Samsung Electronics agreed to invest a further $93 million in a troubled credit-card affiliate. Many critics believe Samsung should divest the unit but that it is propping it up under orders of its parent, Samsung Group. Concern over corporate governance is the big reason Samsung continues to trade at a discount to its global peers. Even though it's regarded as one of the most transparent emerging-market companies anywhere, Korea's history of corporate scandals means many foreigners will always suspect its numbers.

16    If the earnings continue to soften, plenty of investors around the world will stand to lose. Samsung is the most widely held emerging-market stock, with $41 billion in market capitalization, and foreigners hold more than half its shares. Over the past five years, the shares have risen more than tenfold, to a recent $273. But concerns over recent earnings have driven the shares off their recent high this year.

17    The challenges are huge, but so are Samsung's strengths. It is used to big swings: Nearly half its profits come from memory chips, a notoriously cyclical business. Even in the weak first quarter, Samsung earned more than any U.S. tech company other than Microsoft, IBM, and Cisco. Meanwhile, Sony lost $940 million in this year's first three months and chip rivals Micron, Infineon, and Hynix lost a combined $1.88 billion. In cell phones, Samsung has kept its average selling price at $191, compared with $154 for Nokia (NOK) and $147 for Motorola, according to Technology Business Research. What's more, since 1997 its debt has shrunk from an unsustainable $10.8 billion to $1.4 billion, leaving Samsung in a healthy net cash position. And its net margins have risen from 0.4 percent to 12 percent.

18    Driving this success is CEO Yun, a career company man who took over in the dark days of 1997. Yun and his boss, Samsung Group Chairman Lee Kun Hee, grasped that the electronics industry's shift from analog to digital, making many technologies accessible, would leave industry leadership up for

grabs. "In the analog era, it was difficult for a latecomer to catch up," Yun says. But in the digital era, "if you are two months late, you're dead. So speed and intelligence are what matter, and the winners haven't yet been determined."

## SAMSUNG'S STRATEGIC CHOICE: FOCUSED DIFFERENTIATION, LOW COST, AND SPEED

### DIFFERENTIATION: FOCUS ON HIGH-END CONSUMER ELECTRONIC ITEMS

19    Now the company seems to be entering a new dimension. Its feature-jammed gadgets are racking up design awards, and the company is rapidly muscling its way to the top of consumer-brand awareness surveys. Samsung thinks the moment is fast arriving when it can unseat Sony Corp. as the most valuable electronics brand and the most important shaper of digital trends. "We believe we can be No. 1," says Samsung America Chief Executive Oh Dong Jin. Its rivals are taking the challenge seriously. "I ask for a report on what Samsung is doing every week," says Sony President Kunitake Ando.

20    The next step is to customize as much as possible. Even in memory chips, the ultimate commodity, Samsung commands prices that are 17 percent above the industry average. A key reason is that 60 percent of its memory devices are custom-made for products like Dell servers, Microsoft Xbox game consoles, and even Nokia's cell phones. "Samsung is one of a handful of companies you can count on to bridge the technical and consumer experiences and bring them successfully to market," says Will Poole, Senior Vice President at Microsoft's Windows Client Business, which works with the Koreans.

21    A few measures of Samsung's progress: It has become the biggest maker of digital mobile phones using code division multiple access (CDMA) technology—and while it still lags No. 2 Motorola (MOT) Inc. in handsets sold, it has just passed it in overall global revenues. A year ago, you'd have been hard pressed to find a Samsung high-definition TV in the United States. Now, Samsung is the best-selling brand in TVs priced at $3,000 and above—a mantle long held by Sony and Mitsubishi Corp. In the new market for digital music players, Samsung's three-year-old Yepp is behind only the Rio of Japan's D&M Holdings Inc. and Apple Computer (AAPI) Inc.'s

iPod. Samsung has blown past Micron Technology (MU), Infineon Technologies (IFX), and Hynix Semiconductor in dynamic random-access memory (DRAM) chips—used in all PCs—and is gaining on Intel (INTC) in the market for flash memory, used in digital cameras, music players, and handsets. In 2002, with most of techdom reeling, Samsung earned $5.9 billion on sales of $33.8 billion.

## LOWER COSTS

22  Samsung's strategy to win is pretty basic, but it's executing it with ferocious drive over a remarkably broad conglomerate. To streamline, Yun cut 24,000 workers and sold $2 billion in noncore businesses when he took over. Second, Samsung often forces its own units to compete with outsiders to get the best solution. In the liquid-crystal-display business, Samsung buys half of its color filters from Sumitomo Chemical Co. of Japan and sources the other half internally, pitting the two teams against each other. "They really press these departments to compete," says Sumitomo President Hiromasa Yonekura. Third, Samsung makes its own semiconductors, thereby internalizing limited margins plus, perhaps more importantly, customizing their semiconductors in a way that cost-effectively enhances Samsung's end products as well as the products of customers Dell, Microsoft, and Nokia.

## SPEED

23  The final ingredient is speed. Samsung says it takes an average of five months to go from new product concept to rollout, compared with 14 months six years ago. After Samsung persuaded T-Mobile, the German–U.S. cell-phone carrier, to market a new camera-phone last April, for example, it quickly assembled 80 designers and engineers from its chip, telecom, display, computing, and manufacturing operations. In four months, they had a prototype for the V205, which has an innovative lens that swivels 270 degrees and transmits photos wirelessly. Then Samsung flew 30 engineers to Seattle to field-test the phone on T-Mobile's servers and networks. By November, the phones were rolling out of the Korean plant. Since then, Samsung has sold 300,000 V205s a month at $350 each. Park Sang Jin, executive vice-president for mobile communications, estimates the turnaround time is half what Japanese rivals would require. "Samsung has managed to get all its best companies globally to pull in the same direction, something Toshiba, Motorola, and Sony have faced

big challenges in doing," says Allen Delattre, director of Accenture Ltd. (ACN) high-tech practice.

24  Samsung can also use South Korea as a test market. Some 70 percent of the country's homes are wired for broadband. Twenty percent of the population buys a new cell phone every seven months. Samsung already sells a phone in Korea that allows users to download and view up to 30 minutes of video and watch live TV for a fixed monthly fee. Samsung is selling 100,000 video-on-demand phones a month in Korea at $583 each. Verizon plans to introduce them in three U.S. cities this fall.

25  Samsung managers who have worked for big competitors say they go through far fewer layers of bureaucracy to win approval for new products, budgets, and marketing plans, speeding up their ability to seize opportunities. In a recent speech, Sony Chairman Nobuyuki Idei noted Samsung's "aggressive restructuring" and said: "To survive as a global player, we too have to change."

26  This year alone, Samsung will launch 95 new products in the United States, including 42 new TVs. Motorola plans to introduce a dozen new cell-phone models, says Technology Business Research Inc. analyst Chris Foster. Samsung will launch 20. Nokia also is a whiz at snapping out new models. But most are based on two or three platforms, or basic designs. The 130 models Samsung will introduce globally this year are based on 78 platforms. Whereas Motorola completely changes its product line every 12 to 18 months, Foster says, Samsung refreshes its lineup every nine months. Samsung has already introduced the first voice-activated phones, handsets with MP3 players, and digital camera phones that send photos over global system for mobile (GSM) communications networks.

27  Samsung has been just as fast in digital TVs. It became the first to market projection TVs using new chips from Texas Instruments Inc. (TXN) that employed digital-light processing (DLP). DLP chips contain 1.3 million micromirrors that flip at high speeds to create a sharper picture. TI had given Japanese companies the technology early in 1999, but they never figured out how to make the sets economically. Samsung entered the scene in late 2001, and already has seven DLP projection sets starting at $3,400 that have become the hottest-selling sets in their price range. "They'll get a product to market a lot faster than their counterparts," says George Danko, Best Buy's senior vice-president for consumer electronics.

28  Samsung hopes all this is just a warm-up for its bid to dominate the digital home. For years, Philips,

Sony, and Apple have been developing home appliances, from handheld computers to intelligent refrigerators, that talk to each other and adapt to consumers' personal needs. Infrastructure bottlenecks and a lack of uniform standards got in the way.

29    Now, many analysts predict that digital appliances will take off within five years. By then, as many as 40 percent of U.S. households should be wired for high-speed Internet access, and digital TVs, home appliances, and networking devices will be much more affordable. Samsung is showing a version of its networked home in Seoul's Tower Palace apartment complex, where 2,400 families can operate appliances from washing machines to air conditioners by tapping on a wireless "Web pad" device, which doubles as a portable flat-screen TV.

30    It's a grandiose dream. But if the digital home becomes reality, Samsung has a chance. "They've got the products, a growing reputation as the innovator,

and production lines to back that up," says In-Stat/MDR consumer-electronics analyst Cindy Wolf. With nearly $7 billion in cash, Samsung has plenty to spend on R&D, factories, and marketing.

31    Yun has heard tech gurus, publications, and even Samsung execs warn him to forsake the vertical model. His response: Samsung needs it all. "Everyone can get the same technology now," he says. "But that doesn't mean they can make an advanced product." Stay at the forefront of core technologies and master the manufacturing, Yun believes, and you control your future. Many tech companies have tried that strategy and failed. Samsung is betting billions it can overcome the odds.

**Source:** Cliff Edwards in Ridgefield Park, NJ, Moon Ihlwan in Seoul, and Pete Engardio in Suwon. "The Samsung Way," *BusinessWeek,* June 16, 2003.

# Chapter **Eight**

# Strategic Analysis and Choice in the Multibusiness Company: Rationalizing Diversification and Building Shareholder Value

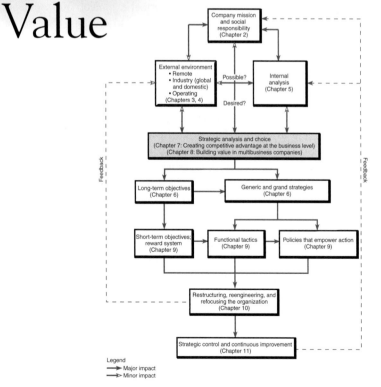

Company mission and social responsibility (Chapter 2)

External environment
• Remote
• Industry (global and domestic)
• Operating (Chapters 3, 4)

Possible?

Desired?

Internal analysis (Chapter 5)

Strategic analysis and choice
(Chapter 7: Creating competitive advantage at the business level)
(Chapter 8: Building value in multibusiness companies)

Long-term objectives (Chapter 6)

Generic and grand strategies (Chapter 6)

Short-term objectives; reward system (Chapter 9)

Functional tactics (Chapter 9)

Policies that empower action (Chapter 9)

Restructuring, reengineering, and refocusing the organization (Chapter 10)

Strategic control and continuous improvement (Chapter 11)

Feedback

Feedback

Legend
→ Major impact
⇢ Minor impact

Strategic analysis and choice is more complicated for corporate-level managers because they must create a strategy to guide a company that contains numerous businesses. They must examine and choose which businesses to own and which ones to forgo or divest. They must consider business managers' plans to capture and exploit competitive advantage in each business, and then decide how to allocate resources among those businesses. This chapter covers ways managers in multibusiness companies analyze and choose what businesses to be in and how to allocate resources across those businesses.

The portfolio approach was one of the early approaches to chart strategy and allocate resources in multibusiness companies. While many companies have moved on to use other approaches, the portfolio approach remains a useful technique for many as well. At the heart of effective diversification is the identification of core competencies in a business or set of businesses to then leverage as the basis for competitive advantage in the growth of those businesses and the entry in or divestiture of other businesses. This notion of leveraging core competencies as a basis for strategic choice in multibusiness companies has been a popular one for the last 20 years.

Recent evolution of strategic analysis and choice in this setting has expanded on the core competency notion to focus on a series of fundamental questions that multibusiness companies should address in order to make diversification work. With both the accelerated rates of change in most global markets and trying economic conditions, multibusiness companies have adapted the fundamental questions into an approach called "patching" to map and remap their business units swiftly against changing market opportunities. Finally, as companies have embraced lean organizational structures, strategic analysis in multibusiness companies has included careful assessment of the corporate parent, its role, and value or lack thereof in contributing to the stand-alone performance of their business units.

# THE PORTFOLIO APPROACH

The last 30 years we have seen a virtual explosion in the extent to which businesses seek to acquire other businesses to grow and to diversify. Several rationales gave rise to this trend years ago—to enter businesses with greater growth potential, businesses with different cyclical considerations, to diversify inherent risks, to increase vertical integration, to capture value added, to instantly have a market presence rather than slower internal growth—to name just a few. As corporate strategists jumped on the diversification bandwagon, they soon found a challenge in managing the resource needs of diverse businesses and their respective strategic missions, particularly in times of limited resources. Responding to this challenge, the Boston Consulting Group pioneered an approach called *portfolio techniques* that attempted to help managers "balance" the flow of cash resources among their various businesses while also identifying their basic strategic purpose within the overall portfolio. Three of these techniques are reviewed here. Once reviewed, we will identify some of the problems with the portfolio approach that you should keep in mind when considering its use.

## The BCG Growth-Share Matrix

Managers using the BCG matrix plotted each of the company's businesses according to market growth rate and relative competitive position. *Market growth rate* is the projected rate of sales growth for the market being served by a particular business. Usually measured as the percentage increase in a market's sales or unit volume over the two most recent years, this rate serves as an indicator of the relative attractiveness of the markets served by each

**EXHIBIT 8–1**  The BCG Growth-Share Matrix

Source: The growth-share matrix was originally developed by the Boston Consulting Group.

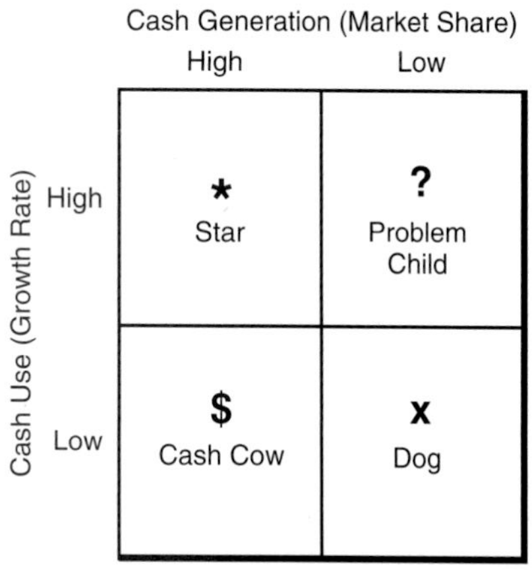

Cash Generation (Market Share)

| | High | Low |
|---|---|---|
| **High** (Cash Use / Growth Rate) | ★ Star | ? Problem Child |
| **Low** | $ Cash Cow | ✗ Dog |

---

**Description of Dimensions**

*Market Share:* Sales relative to those of other competitors in the market (dividing point is usually selected to have only the two–three largest competitors in any market fall into the high market share region)

*Growth Rate:* Industry growth rate in constant dollars (dividing point is typically the GNP's growth rate)

---

business in the firm's portfolio of businesses. *Relative competitive position* usually is expressed as the market share of a business divided by the market share of its largest competitor. Thus, relative competitive position provides a basis for comparing the relative strengths of the businesses in the firm's portfolio in terms of their positions in their respective markets. Exhibit 8–1 illustrates the growth-share matrix.

The *stars* are businesses in rapidly growing markets with large market shares. These businesses represent the best long-run opportunities (growth and profitability) in the firm's portfolio. They require substantial investment to maintain (and expand) their dominant position in a growing market. This investment requirement is often in excess of the funds that they can generate internally. Therefore, these businesses are often short-term, priority consumers of corporate resources.

*Cash cows* are businesses with a high market share in low-growth markets or industries. Because of their strong positions and their minimal reinvestment requirements, these businesses often generate cash in excess of their needs. Therefore, they are selectively "milked" as a source of corporate resources for deployment elsewhere (to stars and question marks). Cash cows are yesterday's stars and the current foundation of corporate portfolios. They provide the cash needed to pay corporate overhead and dividends and provide debt capacity. They are managed to maintain their strong market share while generating excess resources for corporatewide use. Strategy in Action Exhibit 8–2 summarizes *BusinessWeek's* 2003 assessment of Hewlett-Packard's "cash cow," its printer business.

Low market share and low market growth businesses are the *dogs* in the firm's portfolio. Facing mature markets with intense competition and low profit margins, they are managed for short-term cash flow (through ruthless cost cutting, for example) to supplement corporate-level resource needs. According to the original BCG prescription, they are divested or liquidated once this short-term harvesting has been maximized.

**BusinessWeek** HP's $20 billion printing division contributed 28% of 2002 sales and 105% of operating profits. The company boasts nearly 40% of the worldwide printer market and over half of the lucrative U.S. ink market. But it faces a growing number of challenges.

| Challenge | Response | Bottom Line |
|---|---|---|
| **THE DELL FACTOR** Last September, Dell Computer began selling printers, suggesting that one day it will apply its margin-busting business model to this market. | **INNOVATION MATTERS** By spending $1 billion in annual printer R&D (more than Dell's entire R&D budget), HP is betting it can prevent printers from becoming commodities. | **NOT A BIG THREAT** Dell's direct-sales model doesn't fit the printer biz well: Consumers are used to buying ink in stores, and printer components aren't as standardized as PC components. |
| **NEW MARKETS** Customers are migrating away from black-and-white printers, where HP is most dominant, to color printers and all-in-one print, copy, fax, and scan units. | **NEW-PRODUCT BLITZ** HP is uncorking 100 new printer products this fall, in a move internally dubbed "Big Bang II," The idea: Offer the most complete range of products in these growth markets. | **NOT TO WORRY** Already a leader in many of these strengthening printer markets, HP should solidify its standing by the end of this year. |
| **INK SPILL** The EU's Parliament has passed legislation that could force printer makers to eliminate by 2006 chips embedded in ink cartridges that make them hard to refill and reuse. | **DEFUSE THE ISSUE** Increasingly, HP and its competitors are marketing cartridges for which only the ink needs to be replaced when it runs out–not the entire cartridge. | **A FUTURE THREAT** While not an imminent concern, the EU ruling is a symptom of a growing backlash over the cost and environmental Impact of printer supplies that could one day hurt HP. |

**Source:** "What's Ahead for HP's Cash Cow," *BusinessWeek*, July 19, 2003.

*Question marks* are businesses whose high growth rate gives them considerable appeal but whose low market share makes their profit potential uncertain. Question marks are cash guzzlers because their rapid growth results in high cash needs, while their small market share results in low cash generation. At the corporate level, the concern is to identify the question marks that would increase their market share and move into the star group if extra corporate resources were devoted to them. Where this long-run shift from question mark to star is unlikely, the BCG matrix suggests divesting the question mark and repositioning its resources more effectively in the remainder of the corporate portfolio.

## The Industry Attractiveness–Business Strength Matrix

Corporate strategists found the growth-share matrix's singular axes limiting in their ability to reflect the complexity of a business's situation. Therefore, some companies adopted a matrix with a much broader focus. This matrix, developed by McKinsey & Company at General Electric, is called the Industry Attractiveness–Business Strength Matrix. This matrix uses multiple factors to assess industry attractiveness and business strength rather than the single measures (market share and market growth, respectively) employed in the BCG matrix. It also has nine cells as opposed to four—replacing the high/low axes with high/medium/low axes to make finer distinctions among business portfolio positions.

**EXHIBIT 8–3**
**Factors Considered in Constructing an Industry Attractiveness–Business Strength Matrix**

### Industry Attractiveness

#### Nature of Competitive Rivalry
Number of competitors
Size of competitors
Strength of competitors' corporate parents
Price wars
Competition on multiple dimensions

#### Bargaining Power of Suppliers/Customers
Relative size of typical players
Numbers of each
Importance of purchases from or sales to
Ability to vertically integrate

#### Threat of Substitute Products/ New Entrants
Technological maturity/stability
Diversity of the market
Barriers to entry
Flexibility of distribution system

#### Economic Factors
Sales volatility
Cyclicality of demand
Market growth
Capital intensity

#### Financial Norms
Average profitability
Typical leverage
Credit practices

#### Sociopolitical Considerations
Government regulation
Community support
Ethical standards

### Business Strength

#### Cost Position
Economies of scale
Manufacturing costs
Overhead
Scrap/waste/rework
Experience effects
Labor rates
Proprietary processes

#### Level of Differentiation
Promotion effectiveness
Product quality
Company image
Patented products
Brand awareness

#### Response Time
Manufacturing flexibility
Time needed to introduce new products
Delivery times
Organizational flexibility

#### Financial Strength
Solvency
Liquidity
Break-even point
Cash flows
Profitability
Growth in revenues

#### Human Assets
Turnover
Skill level
Relative wage/salary
Morale
Managerial commitment
Unionization

#### Public Approval
Goodwill
Reputation
Image

The company's businesses are rated on multiple strategic factors within each axis, such as the factors described in Exhibit 8–3. The position of a business is then calculated by "subjectively" quantifying its rating along the two dimensions of the matrix. Depending on the location of a business within the matrix as shown in Exhibit 8–4, one of the following strategic approaches is suggested: (1) invest to grow, (2) invest selectively and manage for earnings, or (3) harvest or divest for resources. The resource allocation decisions remain quite similar to those of the BCG approach.

**EXHIBIT 8–4**

**The Industry Attractiveness–Business Strength Matrix**

Source: McKinsey & Company and General Electric.

**Industry Attractiveness**

| | High | Medium | Low |
|---|---|---|---|
| **High** | Invest | Selective Growth | Grow or Let Go |
| **Medium** | Selective Growth | Grow or Let Go | Harvest |
| **Low** | Grow or Let Go | Harvest | Divest |

Business Strength

**Description of Dimensions**

*Industry Attractiveness:* Subjective assessment based on broadest possible range of external opportunities and threats beyond the strict control of management

*Business Strength:* Subjective assessment of how strong a competitive advantage is created by a broad range of the firm's internal strengths and weaknesses

Although the strategic recommendations generated by the Industry Attractiveness–Business Strength Matrix are similar to those generated by the BCG matrix, the Industry Attractiveness–Business Strength Matrix improves on the BCG matrix in three fundamental ways. First, the terminology associated with the Industry Attractiveness–Business Strength Matrix is preferable because it is less offensive and more understandable. Second, the multiple measures associated with each dimension of the business strength matrix tap many factors relevant to business strength and market attractiveness besides market share and market growth. And this, in turn, makes for broader assessment during the planning process, bringing to light considerations of importance in both strategy formulation and strategy implementation.

## The Life Cycle–Competitive Strength Matrix

One criticism of the first two portfolio methods was their static quality—their portrayal of businesses as they exist at one point in time, rather than as they evolve over time. A third portfolio approach was introduced that attempted to overcome these deficiencies and better identify "developing winners" or potential "losers."[1] This approach uses the multiple-

---

[1]Attributed to Arthur D. Little, a consulting firm, and to Charles W. Hofer in "Conceptual Constructs for Formulating Corporate and Business Strategies" (Boston: Harvard Case Services, #9-378-754, 1977).

**EXHIBIT 8–5**

**The Market Life Cycle–Competitive Strength Matrix**

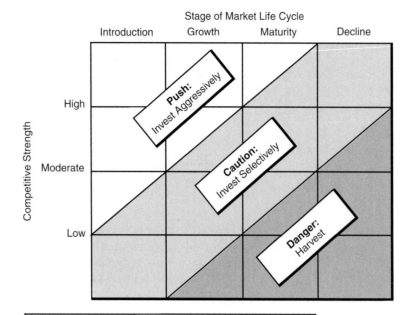

**Description of Dimensions**

*Stage of Market Life Cycle:* See Exhibit 5–13 on pages 170–171 for a description of each stage of the market life cycle.

*Competitive Strength:* Overall subjective rating, based on a wide range of factors regarding the likelihood of gaining and maintaining a competitive advantage

factor approach to assess competitive strength as one dimension and stage of the market life cycle as the other dimension.

The life cycle dimension allows users to consider multiple strategic issues associated with each life cycle stage (refer to the discussion in Chapter 5), thereby enriching the discussion of strategic options. It also gives a "moving indication" of both issues—those strategy needs to address currently and those that could arise next. Exhibit 8–5 provides an illustration of this matrix. It includes basic strategic investment parameters recommended for different positions in the matrix. While this approach seems valuable, its recommendations are virtually identical to the previous two portfolio matrices.

## BCG's Strategic Environments Matrix

BCG's latest matrix offering (see Exhibit 8–6) took a different approach using the idea that it was the nature of competitive advantage in an industry that determined the strategies available to a companies businesses, which in turn determined the structure of the industry. Their idea was that such a framework could help ensure that individual business' strategies were consistent with strategies appropriate to their strategic environment. Furthermore, for corporate managers in multiple business companies, this matrix offered one way to rationalize which businesses they are in—businesses that share core competencies and associated competitive advantages because of similar strategic environments.

The matrix has two dimensions. The number of sources of competitive advantage could be many with complex products and services (e.g. automobiles, financial services) and few with commodities (chemicals, microprocessors). Complex products offer

**EXHIBIT 8–6**

**BCG's Strategic Environments Matrix**

Source: R. M. Grant, *Contemporary Strategy Analysis* (Oxford: Blackwell, 2002), p. 327.

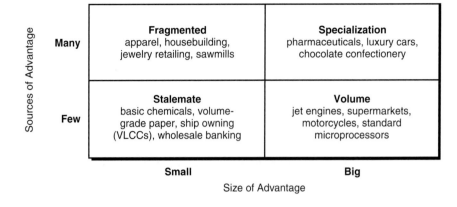

| | Small | Big |
|---|---|---|
| **Many** | **Fragmented** apparel, housebuilding, jewelry retailing, sawmills | **Specialization** pharmaceuticals, luxury cars, chocolate confectionery |
| **Few** | **Stalemate** basic chemicals, volume-grade paper, ship owning (VLCCs), wholesale banking | **Volume** jet engines, supermarkets, motorcycles, standard microprocessors |

*(Vertical axis: Sources of Advantage; Horizontal axis: Size of Advantage)*

multiple opportunities for differentiation as well as cost, while commodities must seek opportunities for cost advantages to survive.

The second dimension is size of competitive advantage. How big is the advantage available to the industry leader? The two dimensions then define four industry environments as follows:

*Volume businesses* are those that have few sources of advantage, but the size is large—typically the result of scale economies. Advantages established in one such business may be transferable to another as Honda has done with its scale and expertise with small gasoline engines.

*Stalemate businesses* have few sources of advantage, with most of those small. This results in very competitive situations. Skills in operational efficiency, low overhead, and cost management are critical to profitability.

*Fragmented businesses* have many sources of advantage, but they are all small. This typically involves differentiated products with low brand loyalty, easily replicated technology, and minimal scale economies. Skills in focused market segments, typically geographic, the ability to respond quickly to changes, and low costs are critical in this environment.

*Specialization businesses* have many sources of advantage, and find those advantages potentially sizable. Skills in achieving differentiation—product design, branding expertise, innovation, first-mover, and perhaps scale—characterize winners here.

BCG viewed this matrix as providing guidance to multibusiness managers to determine whether they possessed the sources and size of advantage associated with the type of industry facing each business; and allow them a framework to realistically explore the nature of the strategic environments in which they competed or were interested in entering.

## Limitations of Portfolio Approaches

Portfolio approaches made several contributions to strategic analysis by corporate managers convinced of their ability to transfer the competitive advantage of professional management across a broad array of businesses. They helped convey large amounts of information about diverse business units and corporate plans in a greatly simplified format. They illuminated similarities and differences between business units and helped convey the logic behind corporate strategies for each business with a common vocabulary. They simplified priorities for sharing corporate resources across diverse business units that generated and used those resources. They provided a simple prescription that gave corporate managers a sense of what they should accomplish—a balanced portfolio of businesses—and a way to control and allocate resources among them. While these approaches offered meaningful contributions, they had several critical limitations and shortcomings:

- A key problem with the portfolio matrix was that it did not address how value was being created across business units—the only relationship between them was cash. Addressing each business unit as a stand-alone entity ignores common core competencies and internal synergies among operating units.

- Truly accurate measurement for matrix classification was not as easy as the matrices portrayed. Identifying individual businesses, or distinct markets, was not often as precise as underlying assumptions required. Comparing business units on only two fundamental dimensions can lead to the conclusion that these are the only factors that really matter, and that every unit can be compared fairly on those bases.

- The underlying assumption about the relationship between market share and profitability—the experience curve effect—varied across different industries and market segments. Some have no such link. Some find that firms with low market share can generate superior profitability with differentiation advantages.

- The limited strategic options, intended to describe the flow of resources in a company, came to be seen more as basic strategic missions. Doing this creates a false sense of what strategies were when none really existed. This becomes more acute when attempting to use the matrices to conceive strategies for average businesses in average growth markets.

- The portfolio approach portrayed the notion that firms needed to be self-sufficient in capital. This ignored capital raised in capital markets.

- The portfolio approach typically failed to compare the competitive advantage a business received from being owned by a particular company with the costs of owning it. The 1980s saw many companies build enormous corporate infrastructures that created only small gains at the business level. The reengineering and deconstruction of numerous global conglomerates in the last ten years reflects this important omission. We will examine this consideration in greater detail later in this chapter.

Constructing business portfolio matrices must be undertaken with these limitations in mind. Perhaps it is best to say that they provide one form of input to corporate managers seeking to balance financial resources and to provide a basis for further discussion of corporate strategy and the allocation of corporate resources, and to provide a picture of the "balance" of resource generators and users to test underlying assumptions about these issues in more involved corporate planning efforts to leverage core competencies to build sustained competitive advantages. Indeed the next major approach in the evolution of multibusiness strategic analysis was to leverage shared capabilities and core competencies.

# THE SYNERGY APPROACH: LEVERAGING CAPABILITIES AND CORE COMPETENCIES

Opportunities to build value via diversification, integration, or joint venture strategies are usually found in market-related, operating-related, and management activities. Each business's basic value chain activities or infrastructure becomes a source of potential synergy and competitive advantage for another business in the corporate portfolio. Morrison's Cafeteria, long a mainstay in U.S. food services markets, rapidly accelerated its diversification into other restaurant concepts like Ruby Tuesdays. Numerous opportunities for shared operating capabilities and management capabilities drove this decision and, upon repeated strategic analysis, accelerated corporate managers' decision to move Morrison's totally out of the cafeteria segment by 2000. Some of the more common opportunities to share value chain activities and build value are identified in Exhibit 8–7.

**EXHIBIT 8–7**   **Value Building in Multibusiness Companies**

Source: Based on Michael Porter, On Competition, 1998, Harvard Business School Press.

| Opportunities to Build Value or Sharing | Potential Competitive Advantage | Impediments to Achieving Enhanced Value |
|---|---|---|
| **Market-Related Opportunities:** | | |
| Shared sales force activities or shared sales office, or both. | Lower selling costs. Better market coverage. Stronger technical advice to buyers. Enhanced convenience for buyers (can buy from single source). Improved access to buyers (have more products to sell). | • Buyers have different purchasing habits toward the products. • Different salespersons are more effective in representing the product. • Some products get more attention than others. • Buyers prefer to multiple-source rather than single-source their purchases. |
| Shared after-sale service and repair work. | Lower servicing costs. Better utilization of service personnel (less idle time). Faster servicing of customer calls. | • Different equipment or different labor skills, or both, are needed to handle repairs. • Buyers may do some in-house repairs. |
| Shared brand name. | Stronger brand image and company reputation. Increased buyer confidence in the brand. | • Company reputation is hurt if quality of one product is lower. |
| Shared advertising and promotional activities. | Lower costs. Greater clout in purchasing ads. | • Appropriate forms of messages are different. • Appropriate timing of promotions is different. |
| Common distribution channels. | Lower distribution costs. Enhanced bargaining power with distributors and retailers to gain shelf space, shelf positioning, stronger push and more dealer attention, and better profit margins. | • Dealers resist being dominated by a single supplier and turn to multiple sources and lines. • Heavy use of the shared channel erodes willingness of other channels to carry or push the firm's products. |
| Shared order processing. | Lower order processing costs. One-stop shopping for buyer enhances service and, thus, differentiation. | • Differences in ordering cycles disrupt order processing economies. |
| **Operating Opportunities:** | | |
| Joint procurement of purchased inputs. | Lower input costs. Improved input quality. Improved service from suppliers. | • Input needs are different in terms of quality or other specifications. • Inputs are needed at different plant locations, and centralized purchasing is not responsive to separate needs of each plant. |

**EXHIBIT 8–7**
*continued*

| Opportunities to Build Value or Sharing | Potential Competitive Advantage | Impediments to Achieving Enhanced Value |
|---|---|---|
| **Operating Opportunities: (continued)** | | |
| Shared manufacturing and assembly facilities. | Lower manufacturing/assembly costs. Better capacity utilization, because peak demand for one product correlates with valley demand for other. Bigger scale of operation improves access to better technology and results in better quality. | • Higher changeover costs in shifting from one product to another. • High-cost special tooling or equipment is required to accommodate quality differences or design differences. |
| Shared inbound or outbound shipping and materials handling. | Lower freight and handling costs. Better delivery reliability. More frequent deliveries, such that inventory costs are reduced. | • Input sources or plant locations, or both, are in different geographic areas. • Needs for frequency and reliability of inbound/outbound delivery differ among the business units. |
| Shared product and process technologies or technology development or both. | Lower product or process design costs, or both, because of shorter design times and transfers of knowledge from area to area. More innovative ability, owing to scale of effort and attraction of better R&D personnel. | • Technologies are the same, but the applications in different business units are different enough to prevent much sharing of real value. |
| Shared administrative support activities. | Lower administrative and operating overhead costs. | • Support activities are not a large proportion of cost, and sharing has little cost impact (and virtually no differentiation impact). |
| **Management Opportunities:** | | |
| Shared management know-how, operating skills, and proprietary information. | Efficient transfer of a distinctive competence—can create cost savings or enhance differentiation. More effective management as concerns strategy formulation, strategy implementation, and understanding of key success factors. | • Actual transfer of know-how is costly or stretches the key skill personnel too thinly, or both. • Increased risks that proprietary information will leak out. |

Strategic analysis is concerned with whether or not the potential competitive advantages expected to arise from each value opportunity have materialized. Where advantage has not materialized, corporate strategists must take care to scrutinize possible impediments to achieving the synergy or competitive advantage. We have identified in Exhibit 8–7 several impediments associated with each opportunity, which strategists are well advised to examine. Good strategists assure themselves that their organization has ways to avoid or minimize the impact of any impediments or they recommend against further integration or diversification and consider divestiture options.

Two elements are critical in meaningful shared opportunities. First, the shared opportunities must be a significant portion of the value chain of the businesses involved. Returning to Morrison's Cafeteria, its purchasing and inbound logistics infrastructure give Ruby Tuesday's operators an immediate cost-effective purchasing and inventory management capability that lowered its cost in a significant cost activity. Second, the businesses involved must truly have shared needs—need for the same activity—or there is no basis for synergy in the first place. Novell, the U.S.-based networking software giant, paid $900 million for Word-Perfect, envisioning numerous synergies serving offices globally not to mention 15 million WordPerfect users. Little more than a year later, Novell would sell WordPerfect for less than $300 million, because, as CEO Bob Frankenberg said, "It is not because WordPerfect is not a business without a future, but for Novell it represented a distraction from our strategy." Corporate strategies have repeatedly rushed into diversification only to find perceived opportunities for sharing were nonexistent because the businesses did not really have shared needs.

## Capitalize on Core Competencies

Perhaps the most compelling reason companies should diversify can be found in situations where core competencies—key value-building skills—can be leveraged with other products or into markets that are not a part of where they were created. Where this works well, extraordinary value can be built. Managers undertaking diversification strategies should dedicate a significant portion of their strategic analysis to this question.

General Cinema was a company that grew from drive-in theaters to eventually dominate the multicinema, movie exhibition industry. Next, they entered soft-drink bottling and became the largest bottler of soft drinks (Pepsi) in North America. Their stock value rose 2,000 percent in 10 years. They found that core competencies in movie exhibition—managing many small, localized businesses; dealing with a few large suppliers; applying central marketing skills locally; and acquiring or crafting a "franchise"—were virtually the same in soft-drink bottling. On the other hand, Disney and ABC are still searching for the shared core competencies they thought would be central to their success in today's global entertainment industry (see Strategy in Action Exhibit 8–8). These and many more companies look to three basic considerations to evaluate whether they are capitalizing on core competencies.

## Each Core Competency Should Provide a Relevant Competitive Advantage to the Intended Businesses

The core competency must assist the intended business in creating strength relative to key competition. This could occur at any step in the business's value chain. But it must represent a major source of value to be a basis for competitive advantage—and the core competence must be transferrable. Honda of Japan viewed itself as having a core competence in manufacturing small, internal combustion engines. It diversified into small garden tools, perceiving that traditional electric tools would be much more attractive if powered by a lightweight, mobile, gas combustion motor. Their core competency created a major competitive advantage in a market void of gas-driven hand tools. When Coca-Cola added bottled water to its portfolio of products, it expected its extraordinary core competencies in marketing and distribution to rapidly build value in this business. Ten years later, Coke sold its water assets, concluding that the product did not have enough margin to interest its franchised bottlers and that marketing was not a significant value-building activity among many small suppliers competing primarily on the cost of "producing" and shipping water. In the last few years, however, Coke has reversed its decision and added the Dasani water

**BusinessWeek** Hit movies have boosted earnings. However, from the theme parks to ABC to Pixar, Mouse House problems are stifling. Shared infrastructure, core competencies, and overall synergies expected in the ABC merger remain elusive or nonexistent.

In *Finding Nemo,* 2003's animated blockbuster from Walt Disney, a timid clownfish searching for his son struggles against all odds. Disney can relate. Hammered by falling ratings at its ABC network, a prolonged travel slump that savaged its theme-park business, and an economic slowdown that crimped sales of Mickey and Minnie merchandise, Disney has been looking to sprinkle some magic on its balance sheet. Virtually a decade after its merger with ABC, Disney is still in search of synergies in TV and movie production, advertising, and shared broad media access that diversification was supposed to bring.

Disney's movie studio is hitting on all cylinders, with *Finding Nemo* swimming past $320 million at the box office and the Jerry Bruckheimer–produced action film *Pirates of the Caribbean* closing in on $220 million. But Disney is still hampered by lackluster performance at its giant theme-park unit, which, in better times, contributed about half of operating income. Theme-park earnings were down 22 percent in 2003.

## VANISHED VISITORS

Analysts would like to see the return of free-spending international travelers to Walt Disney World in Orlando, which gets nearly one-third of its visitors from overseas, or to the trio of Disneyland Resort hotels in Anaheim, Calif. Instead, attendance at Disney World this summer has been off by 8 percent. And while Disneyland—which relies less heavily on foreign tourists—saw attendance rise by 7 percent, many of those visitors hailed from close by. Such patrons tend to spend less on food and lengthy hotel stays, further cutting into the parks' operating earnings.

When will they come back? Disney executives don't sound terribly optimistic. "A dramatic uptick in visitation is unlikely in the near term," admits President Robert Iger. Indeed, SG Cowen analyst Lowell Singer figures it may take until mid-2004 before European travelers return to the United States in sufficient numbers to help Disney.

In the meantime, the Mouse House is heavily discounting travel packages and ticket prices to generate what business it can from those markets. Travelers can get seven-day Disney World packages for the price of a four-day trip. And in California, a four-day pass to Disneyland and the adjacent Disney California Adventure in Anaheim is going for 50 percent off the daily ticket price.

## STUCK IN PARK

Result? The promotional cost has taken its toll. Theme-park earnings will likely decline to $166 million in the fourth quarter, down 29 percent from the $235 million in for the year-ago quarter. While Disney awaits the tourists' return, it's struggling on other fronts. Ratings at ABC stubbornly refuse to rise. So, Disney is slashing program costs by relying less on expensive, one-hour dramas and leaning more toward sitcoms, which bring the added benefit of selling better as reruns. Also, the network has reduced what it pays to buy shows from other studios. ABC was expected to reduce losses to $420 million in 2004, down from the $540 million in 2003. An advertising upturn will help ABC, its wholly owned and network-affiliated TV stations, and Disney's ESPN cable sports channel, all of which are writing contracts with double-digit price hikes. Overall, analysts see earnings at Disney's TV operations rising by 30 percent in 2004.

## THE PIXAR WRANGLE

Disney is also overhauling some of its less profitable units. It has hired investment bankers to sell off its 500-outlet Disney Store chain, which loses about $100 million a year. Also, it has trimmed the number of products it licenses, focusing on higher-end wares and reducing its reliance on movie-driven products that don't sell as well.

Another gambit is beefing up products based on Disney Channel TV shows like *Kim Possible* and *Lizzie McGuire.* To improve earnings at its studio operation, CEO Michael Eisner says Disney has cut back on the number of expensive films it produces and is churning out more lower-budget films like the Queen Latifah comedy *Bringing Down the House* and remakes like the recently opened *Freaky Friday.*

Disney is locked in negotiations to extend its contract with Pixar Animation Studios, which made such Disney blockbusters as *Monsters, Inc.,* the *Toy Story* movies, and *Nemo.* Pixar, controlled by Apple Chairman Steve Jobs, wants to reduce Disney's 50 percent stake in films Pixar makes, starting in 2006. The studio wants to finance its own films and give Disney a much lower percentage, perhaps as little as 6 percent to distribute its films.

## FRENCH CONNECTION

"During a recent conference call with analysts, Eisner refused to answer questions on the talks, saying that Disney would sign a contract with Pixar only "if there is a deal that makes sense for both Disney and Pixar shareholders." Pixar remains under contract to deliver two more films to Disney, *The Incredibles* next year, and *Cars* in 2005 or 2006, Eisner added.

*(continued)*

Another hot spot: Disney may have to provide funding to its 39 percent-owned Euro Disney theme park in France. Staggered by a slowdown in European travel, Disney says it has already agreed not to charge royalties and management fees to the separately traded company. On top of that, Disney may be required to take a noncash writedown of its $522 million loan to the park if its management can't restructure debt and violates covenant agreements. Disney CFO Tom Staggs says he's confident Euro Disney can restructure, as its executives have done in the past.

Disney, which long relished its reputation as the Happiest Place on Earth for shareholders, still has plenty of remodeling to do. It could use a lift in worldwide travel, some hits at ABC, and a diplomatic coup that would keep Jobs's Pixar in the family. A turnaround could have more twists and curves than Disneyland's Matterhorn ride—but it sure won't be as fast. So, it seems, Disney's search for multiple synergies in its blockbuster merger with ABC and other entertainment diversification remain where it all started—an intriguing yet elusive strategic assumption.

**Source:** "Disney's Hunt for a Happy Ending," *BusinessWeek,* August 8, 2003.

brand because a rapidly increasing consumer demand has made the value of its extensive distribution network a relevant competitive advantage to the Dasani water product line.

### Businesses in the Portfolio Should be Related in Ways That Make the Company's Core Competencies Beneficial

Related versus unrelated diversification is an important distinction to understand as you evaluate the diversification question. "Related" businesses are those that rely on the same or similar capabilities to be successful and attain competitive advantage in their respective product markets. Earlier, we described General Cinema's spectacular success in both movie exhibition and soft-drink bottling. Seemingly unrelated, they were actually very related businesses in terms of key core competencies that shaped success—managing a network of diverse business locations, localized competition, reliance on a few large suppliers, and centralized marketing advantages. Thus, the products of various businesses do not necessarily have to be similar to leverage core competencies. While their products may not be related, it is essential that some activities in their value chains require similar skills to create competitive advantage if the company is going to leverage its core competence(s) in a value-creating way.

Situations that involve "unrelated" diversification occur when no real overlapping capabilities or products exist other than financial resources. We refer to this as *conglomerate diversification* in Chapter 6. Recent research indicates that the most profitable firms are those that have diversified around a set of resources and capabilities that are specialized enough to confer a meaningful competitive advantage in an attractive industry, yet adaptable enough to be advantageously applied across several others. The least profitable are broadly diversified firms whose strategies are built around very general resources (e.g., money) that are applied in a wide variety of industries, but are seldom instrumental to competitive advantage in those settings.[2]

### Any Combination of Competencies Must be Unique or Difficult to Re-create

Skills that corporate strategists expect to transfer from one business to another, or from corporate to various businesses, may be transferrable. They may also be easily replicated by competitors. When this is the case, no sustainable competitive advantage is created. Sometimes

[2]David J. Collis and Cynthia A. Montgomery, *Corporate Strategy* (Chicago: Irwin), 1997, p. 88. "Why Mergers Fail," *McKinsey Quarterly Report,* 2001, vol. 4. "Deals That Create Value," *McKinsey Quarterly Report,* 2001, vol. 1.

## WHAT CAN OUR COMPANY DO BETTER THAN ANY OF ITS COMPETITORS IN ITS CURRENT MARKET(S)?

Managers often diversify on the basis of vague definitions of their business rather than on a systematic analysis of what sets their company apart from its competitors. By determining what they can do better than their existing competitors, companies will have a better chance of succeeding in new markets.

## WHAT CORE COMPETENCIES DO WE NEED IN ORDER TO SUCCEED IN THE NEW MARKET?

Excelling in one market does not guarantee success in a new and related one. Managers considering diversification must ask whether their company has every core competency necessary to establish a competitive advantage in the territory it hopes to conquer.

## CAN WE CATCH UP TO OR LEAPFROG COMPETITORS AT THEIR OWN GAME?

All is not necessarily lost if managers find that they lack a critical core competency. There is always the potential to buy what is missing, develop it in-house, or render it unnecessary by changing the competitive rules of the game.

## WILL DIVERSIFICATION BREAK UP CORE COMPETENCIES THAT NEED TO BE KEPT TOGETHER?

Many companies introduce their time-tested core competencies and capabilities in a new market and still fail. That is because they have separated core competencies and capabilities that rely on one another for their effectiveness and hence are not able to function alone.

## WILL WE BE SIMPLY A PLAYER IN THE NEW MARKET OR WILL WE EMERGE A WINNER?

Diversifying companies are often quickly outmaneuvered by their new competitors. Why? In many cases, they have failed to consider whether their strategic assets can be easily imitated, purchased on the open market, or replaced.

## WHAT CAN OUR COMPANY LEARN BY DIVERSIFYING, AND ARE WE SUFFICIENTLY ORGANIZED TO LEARN IT?

Savvy companies know how to make diversification a learning experience. They see how new businesses can help improve existing ones, act as stepping-stones to industries previously out of reach, or improve organizational efficiency.

**Source:** Reprinted by permission of Harvard Business Review. Exhibit from "To Diversify or Not to Diversify," by C. C. Markides, Nov.–Dec. 1997. Copyright © 1997 by the Harvard Business School Publishing Corporation, all rights reserved.

strategists look for a combination of competencies, a package of various interrelated skills, as another way to create a situation where seemingly easily replicated competencies become unique, sustainable competitive advantages. 3M Corporation has the enviable record of having 25 percent of its earnings always coming from products introduced within the last five years. 3M has been able to "bundle" the skills necessary to accelerate the introduction of new products so that it consistently extracts early life cycle value from adhesive-related products that hundreds of competitors with similar technical or marketing competencies cannot touch.

All too often companies envision a combination of competencies that make sense conceptually. This vision of synergy develops an energy of its own leading CEOs to relentlessly push the merger of the firms involved. But what makes sense conceptually and is seen as difficult for competitors to re-create often proves difficult if not impossible to create in the first place. Exhibit 8–9, Strategy in Action, summaries six key questions managers should answer in order to identify the strategic risks and opportunities that diversification presents.

# STRATEGIC ANALYSIS AND CHOICE IN MULTIBUSINESS COMPANIES: THE CORPORATE PARENT ROLE

Realizing synergies from shared capabilities and core competencies is a key way value is added in multibusiness companies. Research suggests that figuring out if the synergies are real and, if so, how to capture those synergies is most effectively accomplished by business unit managers, not the corporate parent.[3] How then can the corporate parent add value to its businesses in a multibusiness company? We want to acquaint you with two perspectives to use in attempting to answer this question: the parenting framework, and the patching approach.

## The Parenting Framework

This perspective sees multibusiness companies as creating value by influencing—or parenting—the businesses they own. The best parent companies create more value than any of their rivals do or would if they owned the same businesses. To add value, a parent must improve its businesses. Obviously there must be room for improvement. Advocates of this perspective call the potential for improvement within a business "a parenting opportunity." They identify ten places to look for parenting opportunities which become the focus of strategic analysis and choice across multiple businesses and their interface with the parent organization.[4] Let's look at each briefly.

***Size and Age***   Old, large, successful businesses frequently engender entrenched bureaucracies and overhead structures that are hard to dismantle from inside the business. Doing so may add value, and getting it done may be best done by an external catalyst, the parent. Small, young businesses may lack some key functional skills, or outgrow their top managers' capabilities, or lack capital to deal with a temporary downturn or accelerated growth opportunity. Where these are relevant issues within one or more businesses, a parenting opportunity to add value may exist.

***Management***   Does the business employ managers superior in comparison with its competitors? Is the business' success dependent on attracting and keeping people with specialized skills? Are key managers focused on the right objectives? Ensuring that these issues are addressed, objectively assessed, and assisting in any resolution may be a parenting opportunity that could add value.

***Business Definition***   Business unit managers may have a myopic or erroneous vision of what their business should be, which, in turn, has them targeting a market that is too narrow or broad. They may employ too much vertical integration, or not enough. Accelerated trends toward outsourcing and strategic alliances are changing the definitions of many businesses. All of this creates a parenting opportunity to help redefine a business unit in a way that creates greater value.

***Predictable Errors***   The nature of a business and its unique situation can lead managers to make predictable mistakes. Managers responsible for previous strategic decisions are vested in the success of those decisions, which may prevent openness to new alternatives. Older, mature businesses often accumulate a variety of products and markets, which becomes excessive diversification within a particular business. Cyclical markets can lead to underinvestment during downturns and overinvestment during the upswing. Lengthy product life cycles can lead to overreliance on old products. All of these are predictable errors a parent can monitor and attempt to avoid creating, in turn, adding value.

---

[3]Michael Goold, Andrew Campbell, and Marcus Alexander, "The Quest For Parenting Advantage," *Harvard Business Review,* March–April, 1995; Michael Goold, Andrew Campbell, and Marcus Alexander, "How Corporate Parents Add Value to the Stand-Alone Performance of Their Businesses," *Business Strategy Review,* Winter, 1994.

[4]*Ibid,* page 126. These ten areas of opportunity are taken from an insert entitled "Ten places to look for parenting opportunities" on this page of the *Harvard Business Review* article.

***Linkages***   Business units may be able to improve market position or efficiency by linking with other businesses that are not readily apparent to the management of the business unit in question. Whether apparent or not, linkages among business units within or outside the parent company may be complex or difficult to establish without parent company help. In either case, an opportunity to add value may exist.

***Common Capabilities***   Fundamental to successful diversification, as we have discussed earlier, is the notion of sharing capabilities and competencies needed by multiple business units. Parenting opportunities to add value may arise from time-to-time through regular scrutiny of opportunities to share capabilities or add shared capabilities that would otherwise go unnoticed by business unit managers closer to daily business operations.

***Specialized Expertise***   There may be situations where the parent company possesses specialized or rare expertise that may benefit a business unit and add value in the process. Unique legal, technical, or administrative expertise critical in a particular situation or decision point, which is quickly and easily available, can prove very valuable.

***External Relations***   Does the business have external stakeholders—governments, regulators, unions, suppliers, shareholders—which the parent company could manage more effectively than individual business units? If so, a natural parenting opportunity exists that should add value.

***Major Decisions***   A business unit may face difficult decisions in areas which it lacks expertise—for example, making an acquisition, entering China, a major capacity expansion, divesting and outsourcing a major part of the business' operations. Obtaining capital externally to fund a major investment may be much more difficult than doing so through the parent company—GE proved this could be a major parenting advantage in the way it developed GE Capital into a major source of capital for its other business units as well as to finance major capital purchases by customers of its own business units.

***Major Changes***   Sometimes a business needs to make major changes in ways critical to the business' future success yet which involve areas or considerations in which the business unit's management has little or no experience. A complete revamping of a business unit's information management process, outsourcing all that capability to India, or shifting all of a business units' production operations to another business unit in another part of the world—these are just a few examples of major changes in which the parent may have extensive experience with that feels like unknown territory to the business' management team.

Overlap in some of these ten sources of parenting opportunities may exist. For example, specialized expertise in China and a major decision to locate or outsource operations there may be the same source of added value. And that decision would involve a major change. The fact that overlap, or redundancy may exist in classifying sources of parenting opportunity is a minor consideration, however, relative to the value of the parenting framework for strategic analysis in multibusiness companies. The portfolio approaches focus on how businesses' cash, profit, and growth potential create a balance within the portfolio. The core competence approach concentrates on how business units are related and can share technical and operating know-how and capacity. The parenting framework adds to these approaches and the strategic analysis in a multibusiness company because it focuses on competencies of the parent organization and on the value created from the relationship between the parent and its businesses.

## The Patching Approach

Another approach that focuses on the role and ability of corporate managers to create value in the management of multibusiness companies is called "patching."[5] *Patching* is the process by which corporate executives routinely remap businesses to match rapidly changing market opportunities. It can take the form of adding, splitting, transferring, exiting, or combining chunks of businesses. Patching is not seen as critical in stable, unchanging markets. When markets are turbulent and rapidly changing, patching is seen as critical to the creation of economic value in a multibusiness company.

Proponents of this perspective on the strategic decision-making function of corporate executives say it is the critical and arguably only way corporate executives can add value beyond the sum of the businesses within the company. They view traditional corporate strategy as creating defensible strategic positions for business units by acquiring or building valuable assets, wisely allocating resources to them, and weaving synergies among them. In volatile markets, they argue, this traditional approach results in business units with strategies that are quickly outdated and competitive advantages rarely sustained beyond a few years.[6] As a result, they say, strategic analysis should center on *strategic processes* more than *strategic positioning.* In these volatile markets, patchers' strategic analysis focuses on making quick, small frequent changes in parts of businesses and organizational processes that enable dynamic strategic repositioning rather than building long-term defensible positions. Exhibit 8–10 compares differences between traditional approaches to shaping corporate strategy with the patching approach.

To be successful with a patching approach to corporate strategic analysis and choice in turbulent markets, Eisenhardt and Sull suggest that managers should flexibly seize opportunities—as long as that flexibility is disciplined. Effective corporate strategists, they argue, focus on key processes and *simple rules.* The following example at Miramax helps illustrate the notion of strategy as simple rules:

> Miramax—well known for artistically innovative movies such as *The Crying Game, Life is Beautiful,* and *Pulp Fiction*—has boundary rules that guide the all-important movie-picking process: first, every movie must revolve around a central human condition, such as love (*The Crying Game*) or envy (*The Talented Mr. Ripley*). Second, a movie's main character must be appealing but deeply flawed—the hero of *Shakespeare in Love* is gifted and charming but steals ideas from friends and betrays his wife. Third, movies must have a very clear story line with a beginning, middle, and end (although in *Pulp Fiction* the end comes first). Finally, there is a firm cap on production costs. Within the rules, there is flexibility to move quickly when a writer or director shows up with a great script. The result is an enormously creative and even surprising flow of movies and enough discipline to produce superior, consistent financial results. *The English Patient,* for example, cost $27 million to make, grossed more than $200 million, and grabbed nine Oscars.[7]

Different types of rules help managers and strategists manage different aspects of seizing opportunities. Exhibit 8–11 explains and illustrates five such types of rules. These rules are called "simple" rules because they need to be brief, axiomatic, and convey fundamental guidelines to decisions or actions. They need to provide just enough structure to allow managers to move quickly to capture opportunities with confidence that the judgments and

---

[5]Kathleen M. Eisenhardt and Shona L. Brown, "Patching: Restitching Business Portfolios in Dynamic Markets," *Harvard Business Review,* May–June, 1999, pp. 72–82.

[6]*Ibid,* p. 76; K. M. Eisenhardt and D. N. Sull, "Strategy as Simple Rules," *Harvard Business Review,* January, 2001.

[7]*Ibid,* Eisenhardt and Sull, 2001, p. 111.

## EXHIBIT 8–10
### Three Approaches to Strategy

Source: Reprinted by permission of Harvard Business Review. Exhibit from "Strategy as Simple Rules," by K. M. Eisenhardt and D. N. Sull, January 2001. Copyright © 2001 by the Harvard Business School Publishing Corporation; all rights reserved.

Managers competing in business can choose among three distinct ways to fight. They can build a fortress and defend it; they can nurture and leverage unique resources; or they can flexibly pursue fleeting opportunities within simple rules. Each approach requires different skill sets and works best under different circumstances.

| | Position | Resources | Simple Rules |
|---|---|---|---|
| **Strategic logic** | Establish position | Leverage resources | Pursue opportunities |
| **Strategic steps** | Identify an attractive market<br>Locate a defensible position<br>Fortify and defend | Establish a vision<br>Build resources<br>Leverage across markets | Jump into the confusion<br>Keep moving<br>Seize opportunities<br>Finish strong |
| **Strategic question** | Where should we be? | What should we be? | How should we proceed? |
| **Source of advantage** | Unique, valuable position with tightly integrated activity system | Unique, valuable, inimitable resources | Key processes and unique simple rules |
| **Works best in** | Slowly changing, well-structured markets | Moderately changing, well-structured markets | Rapidly changing, ambiguous markets |
| **Duration of advantage** | Sustained | Sustained | Unpredictable |
| **Risk** | It will be too difficult to alter position as conditions change | Company will be too slow to build new resources as conditions change | Managers will be too tentative in executing on promising opportunities |
| **Performance goal** | Profitability | Long-term dominance | Growth |

commitments they make are consistent with corporate intent. At the same time, while they set parameters on actions and decisions, they are not thick manuals or rules and policies which managers in turbulent environments may find paralyze any efforts to quickly capitalize on opportunities. Strategy in Action Exhibit 8–12 helps explain the simple rules idea behind the patching approach to corporate strategic decision making by explaining what simple rules are not.

The patching approach then relies on simple rules unique to a particular parent company that exist to guide managers in the corporate organization and its business units in making rapid decisions about quickly reshaping parts of the company and allocating time as well as money to capitalize on rapidly shifting market opportunities. The fundamental argument of this approach is that no one can predict how long a competitive advantage will last, particularly in turbulent, rapidly changing markets. While managers in stable markets may be able to rely on complex strategies built on detailed predictions of future trends, managers in complex, fast-moving markets where significant growth and wealth creation may occur face constant unpredictability; hence, strategy must be simple, responsive, and dynamic to encourage success.

## EXHIBIT 8–11
### Simple Rules, Summarized

Source: Reprinted by permission of Harvard Business Review. Exhibit from "Strategy as Simple Rules," by K. M. Eisenhardt and D. N. Sull, January 2001. Copyright © 2001 by the Harvard Business School Publishing Corporation; all rights reserved.

In turbulent markets, managers should flexibly seize opportunities—but flexibility must be disciplined. Smart companies focus on key processes and simple rules. Different types of rules help executives manage different aspects of seizing opportunities.

| Type | Purpose | Example |
|---|---|---|
| How-to rules | They spell out key features of how a process is executed—"What makes our process unique?" | Akamai's rules for the customer service process: staff must consist of technical gurus, every question must be answered on the first call or e-mail, and R&D staff must rotate through customer service. |
| Boundary rules | They focus managers on which opportunities can be pursued and which are outside the pale. | Cisco's early acquisitions rule: companies to be acquired must have no more than 75 employees, 75 percent of whom are engineers. |
| Priority rules | They help managers rank the accepted opportunities. | Intel's rule for allocating manufacturing capacity: allocation is based on a product's gross margin. |
| Timing rules | They synchronize managers with the pace of emerging opportunities and other parts of the company. | Nortel's rules for product development: project teams must know when a product has to be delivered to the leading customer to win, and product development time must be less than 18 months. |
| Exit rules | They help managers decide when to pull out of yesterday's opportunities. | Oticon's rule for pulling the plug on projects in development: if a key team member—manager or not—chooses to leave the project for another within the company, the project is killed. |

## Summary

This chapter examined how managers make strategic decisions in multibusiness companies. One of the earliest approaches was to look at the company as a portfolio of businesses. This portfolio was then examined and evaluated based on each business' growth potential, market position, and need for and ability to generate cash. Corporate strategists then allocated resources, divested, and acquired businesses based on the balance across this portfolio of businesses or possible businesses.

The notion of synergy across business units, sharing capabilities, and leveraging core competencies, has been another very widely adopted approach to making strategic decisions in multibusiness companies. Sharing capabilities allows for greater efficiencies, enhanced expertise, and competitive advantage. Core competencies that generate competitive advantage can often be leveraged across multiple businesses, thereby expanding the impact and value added from that competitive advantage.

Globalization, rapid change, outsourcing, and other major forces shaping today's economic landscape have ushered in multibusiness strategic decision making that also focuses on the role and value-added contributions, if any, of the parent company itself. Does the parent company add or could it add value beyond the sum of the businesses it owns? Two perspectives that have gained popularity in multibusiness companies' strategic decision making are the *parenting framework* and the *patching approach*. The parenting framework focuses on ten areas of opportunity managers should carefully explore to find ways the parent organization might add value to one or more businesses and the overall company. The patching approach concentrates on multibusiness companies in turbulent markets of the twenty-first century where managers need to make quick, small shifts and adjustments in processes, markets, and products and offers five types of "simple rules" which managers use as guidelines to structure quick decisions throughout a multibusiness company on a continuous basis.

It is impossible to dictate exactly what a company's simple rules should be. It is possible, however, to say what they should *not* be.

## BROAD

Managers often confuse a company's guiding principles with simple rules. The celebrated "HP way," for example, consists of principles like "we focus on a high level of achievement and contribution" and "we encourage flexibility and innovation." The principles are designed to apply to every activity within the company, from purchasing to product innovation. They may create a productive culture, but they provide little concrete guidance for employees trying to evaluate a partner or decide whether to enter a new market. The most effective simple rules, in contrast, are tailored to a single process.

## VAGUE

Some rules cover a single process but are too vague to provide real guidance. One Western bank operating in Russia, for example, provided the following guideline for screening investment proposals: all investments must be currently undervalued and have potential for long-term capital appreciation. Imagine the plight of a newly hired associate who turns to that rule for guidance!

A simple screen can help managers test whether their rules are too vague. Ask: could any reasonable person argue the exact opposite of the rule? In the case of the bank in Russia, it is hard to imagine anyone suggesting that the company target overvalued companies with no potential for long-term capital appreciation. If your rules flunk this test, they are not effective.

## MINDLESS

Companies whose simple rules have remained implicit may find upon examining them that these rules destroy rather than create value. In one company, managers listed their recent partnership relationships and then tried to figure out what rules could have produced the list. To their chagrin, they found that one rule seemed to be: always form partnerships with small, weak companies that we can control. Another was: always form partnerships with companies that are not as successful as they once were. Again, use a simple test—reverse-engineer your processes to determine your implicit simple rules. Throw out the ones that are embarrassing.

## STALE

In high-velocity markets, rules can linger beyond their sell-by dates. Consider Banc One. The Columbus, Ohio-based bank grew to be the seventh-largest bank in the United States by acquiring more than 100 regional banks. Banc One's acquisitions followed a set of simple rules that were based on experience: Banc One must never pay so much that earnings are diluted, it must only buy successful banks with established management teams, it must never acquire a bank with assets greater than one-third of Banc One's, and it must allow acquired banks to run as autonomous affiliates. The rules worked well until others in the banking industry consolidated operations to lower their costs substantially. Then Banc One's loose confederation of banks was burdened with redundant operations, and it got clobbered by efficient competitors.

How do you figure out if your rules are stale? Slowing growth is a good indicator. Stock price is even better. Investors obsess about the future, while your own financials report the past. So if your share price is dropping relative to your competitors' share prices, or if your percentage of the industry's market value is declining, or if growth is slipping, your rules may need to be refreshed.

## Questions for Discussion

1. How does strategic analysis at the corporate level differ from strategic analysis at the business unit level? How are they related?

2. When would multi-industry companies find the portfolio approach to strategic analysis and choice useful?

3. What are three types of opportunities for sharing that form a sound basis for diversification or vertical integration? Give an example of each from companies you have read about.

4. Describe three types of opportunities through which a corporate parent could add value beyond the sum of its separate businesses.

5. What does "patching" refer to and describe and illustrate two rules that might guide managers to build value in their businesses.

## Chapter 8    Discussion Case

BusinessWeek

# Quanta Group—Is Diversification Wise?

One of the exciting entrepreneurial success stories in the computer industry over the last ten years has been Taiwan's Quanta Computer, recently renamed Quanta Group. Started just 15 years ago by a former calculator salesman, Quanta became the largest maker of notebook computers in the world in 2003. It became number two on *BusinessWeek's* list of the top IT companies worldwide in 2003.

What follows is a short *BusinessWeek* article about Quanta's founder and CEO making the decision to pursue a diversification strategy at Quanta. Since it is occurring just as we write this chapter, we are also including some additional articles about two Asian companies that are focused competitors of Quanta. Once you read these articles, discuss whether CEO Lam appears to be making a sound decision diversifying Quanta. Then conduct current research through www.BusinessWeek.com and other sources to see where Quanta stands on its diversification strategy as you read this discussion case.

## ONLINE EXTRA: QUANTA'S NEW LEAP

### THE TAIWANESE PRIVATE-LABEL COMPUTER MAKER PLANS TO EXPAND BEYOND NOTEBOOKS AND INTO HIGHER-MARGIN DISPLAYS AND SERVERS

1    If you want to see where Barry Lam is taking his business, consider the new name that he uses for it. Today, he calls his suburban Taipei-based company Quanta Group (2382 TW). It's a slight but significant change from the name he had been using since founding the company back in 1988: Quanta Computer. (The Quanta name in Chinese translates into "vast, wide, extensive.")

2    As its original moniker suggests, Quanta focused zealously on computers, in particular notebook PCs. Like many other Taiwanese computer makers, it was an anonymous producer of notebooks on a contract basis for some of the world's biggest brand-name players.

3    There's no question that former calculator salesman Lam has succeeded as a computer maker. Quanta last year produced 16 percent of the world's note-

books, designing and manufacturing machines for the likes of Hewlett-Packard (HPO) and Gateway (GTW).

### BIG BACKING

4    This year, Lam is likely to see his company's market share increase to 20 percent, thanks to the addition of several new customers such as NEC (NIPNY) and Acer and increases in orders from old ones like Dell (DELL) and Apple (AAPL). Such results helped catapult Quanta near the top of the world's information-technology mountain, landing at number two in this year's *BusinessWeek* IT 100.

5    Lam isn't content to be the number one producer of outsourced notebook PCs, though. He wants to make the company as synonymous with products like servers and flat-panel displays as it is now with laptops. So Quanta has diversified, with one subsidiary—Quanta Display—making TFT-LCDs (the thin liquid crystal display screens used in notebook PCs and, increasingly, desktops). A joint venture with Sharp and several Taiwanese investors, Quanta Display has already received $1 billion in investment from Quanta and is due to receive another $1 billion in the coming 18 months, Lam says.

6    Another subsidiary—Quanta Storage—will have an initial public offering this year in Taiwan, Lam says. A few other subsidiaries are less capital-intensive. For instance, Quanta Network Systems develops set-top boxes. And Quanta has also developed a venture-capital arm to help fund startups that can provide technology to support these businesses.

7    Why branch out like this? "This strategy will make Quanta grow bigger," says Lam. "It's a big market with much bigger value and a much bigger product range. This is something that makes Quanta valuable to customers."

### "SWEET SPOT"

8    Lam figures this diversification can help Quanta escape becoming a victim of its own success. As it wins more outsourcing customers thanks to the need for multinationals to reduce costs, the ability to grow becomes more limited. After all, Taiwanese notebook makers already control 60 percent of the market. It won't be long before there are no new outsourcing orders to win.

9     Moreover, the merger of Hewlett Packard with Compaq means that Taiwanese are feeling even more pressure to lower prices. So Quanta needs to find businesses with fatter margins.

10     "The notebook PC is continuously replacing the desktop, so the market will further expand," says Lam. But when it comes to flat panels, servers, and storage devices, "the margins are much higher," he adds. "More than two times higher." Hence Quanta's move into new products that are "value-added and involve a lot of R&D," he says. "This kind of business is really a sweet spot for Quanta."

11     This strategy isn't unique to Quanta. At the big Computex electronics trade show in Taipei in early June, most of the big Taiwanese players were touting their ability to diversify. Analysts say their chances are good, as Taiwanese manufacturers relying on outsourcing orders have a big advantage as they pursue these new businesses. Unlike North American-based contract manufacturers like Celestica (CLS) or Flextronics (FLEX), which stick largely to manufacturing, many Taiwanese have engineers who do much of the design work for their customers.

## BARGAIN TIME?

12     That should help Taiwan's outsourcers as they seek to expand into new types of products, says Sean Debow, Asia tech strategist at UBS Warburg in Hong Kong. Design experience means "they bring more to the table," he says. "That's a big value-added. It's the right place to be in a difficult tech market—being able to cut costs and increase design innovation."

13     Investors focused on the short term, though, might want to be wary about the Taiwanese players such as Quanta. While most of the island's electronics stocks soared in the months after September 11, they have been struggling recently. Quanta's stock closed June 12 at T$90 (that's $2.65), down from a high of T$146 ($4.29) on Jan. 11. That's partially because of growing doubts about when U.S. demand will recover. Indeed, citing worries about weakness in the PC industry, Salomon Smith Barney on June 12 downgraded Quanta shares from a buy to a hold.

14     Taiwan's computer makers are now trading at an average price-earnings ratio of 16 times next year's earnings, at the low end of the long-term range. That's because many investors are downbeat about the chances of American corporate buyers splurging for new computers in the months ahead. On the other hand, that also means the stocks are now relatively

cheap. That could be good news for investors who believe in Quanta's diversification strategy.

# MEET THE LATEST TECH ALL-STAR FROM TAIWAN

## HTC IS GROWING FAST, THANKS TO PDAs AND SMART PHONES

15     For years, big U.S. tech companies such as Dell Computer (DELL), Motorola (MOT), and Hewlett-Packard (HPO) have relied on nimble Taiwanese manufacturers to make PCs, cell phones, and chips for them. This outsourcing has turned the likes of Quanta Computer, Compal Electronics, and Taiwan Semiconductor Manufacturing (TSM) into billion-dollar players in the global electronics industry. Now, it may be time to add a new name to this all-star list: High Tech Computer Corp., based near Taipei. "HTC knocks the leather off the ball," raves Brian Burns, vice-president of Asia Pacific Ventures, a venture-capital and consulting firm in Palo Alto, Calif.

16     Part of HTC's success can be attributed to heavyweight friends. HTC produces the successful iPAQ handheld PC for Hewlett-Packard. Taiwanese chip-design house Via Technologies is the biggest shareholder. HTC's chairwoman is Cher Wang, daughter of one of Taiwan's richest men, petrochemicals billionaire Y. C. Wang. Cellular-technology giant Qualcomm (QCOM) is an investor, and Texas Instruments and Intel help HTC design new products.

17     Oh—and then there's Microsoft Corp. (MSFT). Two years ago, when HTC was showing off its first "smart phone"—a cellular handset that can double as a personal digital assistant—the little-known Taiwanese manufacturer got a boost when Microsoft Chief Executive Steven A. Ballmer demonstrated the gizmo at a big trade show in Orlando. After that high-profile debut, HTC worked with the U.S. software giant on a Windows-based handset that would go far beyond simple voice calls and allow users to view photos, listen to music, watch videos, manage appointments, and more.

18     Those devices are now hitting the streets. Last year, British cellular carrier Orange started selling HTC's $300 SPV phone, one of the first to use Microsoft's new Smartphone 2002 software. This year, German operator T-Mobile, Smart Communications of the Philippines, and U.S. carrier AT&T Wireless (AWE) all plan to introduce HTC-made phones. That's helping HTC reduce its dangerous dependence on sales of the iPAQ, which accounted for 85 percent of HTC's revenues in

2001. This year, brokerage Morgan Stanley estimates the iPAQ will represent just a third of HTC's sales.

19 All the new business is firing up HTC's results. Revenues last year grew by 32 percent, to $592 million, while profits jumped by 45 percent, to $40 million, according to the company's unaudited results. For 2003, Morgan Stanley expects sales to grow by 27 percent and earnings to soar by 83 percent. HTC's share price has shot up by 50 percent since September. "No one expected this little Taiwanese company to come along so fast," says Julian Snelder, a Morgan Stanley banker.

20 So is this Taiwan's answer to Nokia (NOK)? Well, not yet. HTC's bright light is attracting some unwanted attention. On the Internet, message boards are hopping with comments from British consumers who have purchased the SPV from Orange. Some are rapturous, but others gripe about bugs and slow performance. On Feb. 24, the companies released new software that's intended to address the problems. Perhaps even more worrisome for HTC, British phonemaker Sendo has sued Microsoft, claiming that the U.S. giant gave Sendo's intellectual property to HTC. Microsoft denies the claim. It's possible that HTC will be the next target for Sendo's lawyers, but neither company would comment.

21 HTC faces growing competition at home, too. Computer maker Wistron, a subsidiary of Acer, is branching out from the slumping PC business last year with contracts to make handhelds for Dell and a smart phone with Microsoft and Intel (INTC). Compal Electronics in late December unveiled its own Microsoft-powered phone. And on Feb. 12, Symbian Ltd., the British rival to Microsoft, announced it would help Taipei-based BenQ Corp. launch a similar device this year.

22 HTC CEO H. T. Cho says he won't get burned by rivals. He plans to trim costs by moving some production to China as early as next year. More important, he'll concentrate on "slimmer and lighter and more attractive" machines with wireless links. He says Taiwanese newcomers to the handheld industry are more accustomed to operating in the high-volume, low-innovation PC business. Cho figures these would-be rivals aren't up to the complicated work of producing wireless devices. "We are only working on PDAs and smart phones, and the whole company's engineering and manufacturing is focused on this area," Cho says. If Cho's confidence is justified, then the world will be hearing a lot more from this Taiwan hotshot.

# THE UNDERDOG NIPPING AT QUANTA'S HEELS

## NOTEBOOK MAKER COMPAL IS CLOSING THE SALES GAP WITH ITS ARCHRIVAL

23 In the ultracompetitive Taiwanese tech industry, few rivalries match that of Quanta Computer Inc. and Compal Electronics Inc. Both have the same focus: designing and manufacturing notebook PCs for other companies. The two compete for business from major laptop makers and count Dell Computer Corp. (DELL) as their leading customer. And they're both diversifying into new markets such as cell phones and handhelds. To top it off, Quanta Chairman Barry Lam used to run Compal: He quit to launch Quanta in 1988, when Compal was reeling from a factory fire. "The company almost collapsed—and he left," says Compal President Ray Chen, still angry at the departure of his old boss.

24 The competition is about to get even fiercer. Since founding Quanta, Lam has built it into Taiwan's biggest producer of notebook PCs, while Compal has had to settle for second place. But now, Compal is coming on strong: Taipei brokerage KGI Securities PLC expects Compal to boost laptop sales by 70 percent this year, to 3.9 million units, compared with a 20 percent increase, to 5.2 million, for Quanta. KGI says Compal will see overall sales of $2.8 billion for 2002, up 30 percent, while it expects Quanta's sales to grow by 27 percent, to $4.1 billion.

25 Better yet, Compal's share price is surging. It's up by 10.4 percent since July, compared with a 24.9 percent fall for Quanta. Now, Chen isn't going to settle for also-ran status anymore. "We believe we are the best," he boasts. Lam isn't losing sleep. "Compal makes a lot of noise," he says. "It doesn't mean a lot."

26 The biggest driver of Compal's success has been Dell. In early October, the Texas dynamo announced its third-quarter revenue would grow 22 percent from last year. While that's good news for both Taiwanese rivals—Dell accounts for about half of sales at each—Compal has benefited more, says UBS Warburg analyst Sharon Su. The reason: Dell has made a strong push into consumer PCs this year, and the bulk of Compal's sales to Dell are consumer machines. Quanta concentrates on corporate laptops, a sector that remains weak.

27 Another competitive edge for Compal is its expansion into China. Since early last year, Compal has been making computers on the mainland, where costs

are about one-third what they are in Taiwan. Now, Compal makes 60 percent of its notebooks in China. Quanta, meanwhile, leased a small Chinese plant last year but didn't open a big factory until July.

28    Still, Compal has a way to go before it can topple Quanta. KGI analyst Angela Hsiang points out that Quanta serves 9 of the 10 biggest notebook makers. Compal, in comparison, focuses largely on Dell, Toshiba, Hewlett-Packard, and Apple. And, she says, with Quanta's new plant coming on line, Compal can't rely on its head start on the mainland much longer. "Quanta will catch up in China," she says.

29    The Quanta-Compal competition now extends beyond laptops. Compal makes handsets for Motorola Inc. (MOT) as well as up-and-coming Chinese players such as Eastcom Corp. and Haier Corp. By next year, Chen says, phones will account for 25 percent of sales, up from 10 percent today. And like Quanta, Compal has diversified into liquid crystal displays. It has a $1.1 billion venture with Taiwanese foodmaker Uni-President Enterprises Corp. to produce the tiny screens used in next-generation cell phones and handheld computers.

30    It's a risky move, given the volatility of the phone business, but Chen is convinced the bet will pay off once the industry's funk lifts. "Next year, when there's a shortage in the market, [LCDs] will be a very strong advantage," he says. And nothing gives Chen more pleasure than gaining an advantage over Barry Lam.

**Source:** "Meet the Latest Tech All-Star From Taiwan," *BusinessWeek,* March 10, 2003; "The Underdog Nipping at Quanta's Heels," *BusinessWeek,* October 21, 2002; "Quanta's New Leap," *BusinessWeek,* June 24, 2002.

# Strategy Implementation

The last section of this book examines what is often called the action phase of the strategic management process: implementation of the chosen strategy. Up to this point, three phases of that process have been covered—strategy formulation, analysis of alternative strategies, and strategic choice. Although important, these phases alone cannot ensure success. To ensure success, the strategy must be translated into carefully implemented action. This means that:

1. The strategy must be translated into guidelines for the daily activities of the firm's members.

2. The strategy and the firm must become one—that is, the strategy must be reflected in the way the firm organizes its activities and in the firm's values, beliefs, and tone.

3. In implementing the strategy, the firm's managers must direct and control actions and outcomes and adjust to change.

Chapter 9 explains how organizational action is successfully initiated in four interrelated steps:

1. Creation of clear *short-term objectives* and *action plans*.

2. Development of specific *functional tactics* that create competitive advantage.

3. Empowerment of operating personnel through *policies* to guide decisions.

4. Implementation of effective *reward system*.

Short-term objectives and action plans guide implementation by converting long-term objectives into short-term actions and targets. Functional tactics translate the business strategy into activities that build advantage. Policies empower operating personnel by defining guidelines for making decisions. Reward systems encourage effective results.

Today's competitive environment often necessitates restructuring and reengineering the organization to sustain competitive advantage. Chapter 10 examines how restructuring and reengineering are pursued in three organizational elements that provide fundamental, long-term means for institutionalizing the firm's strategy:

1. The firm's *structure.*

2. The *leadership* provided by the firm's CEO and key managers.

3. The fit between the strategy and the firm's *culture.*

Since the firm's strategy is implemented in a changing environment, successful implementation requires that execution be controlled and continuously improved. The control and improvement process must include at least these dimensions:

1. *Strategic controls* that "steer" execution of the strategy.

2. *Operations control systems* that monitor performance, evaluate deviations, and initiate corrective action.

3. *Continuous improvement* through total quality initiatives of a balanced scorecard perspective.

Chapter 11 examines the dimensions of the control and improvement process. It explains the essence of change as an ever-present force driving the need for strategic control. The chapter concludes with a look at the global "quality imperative," which is redefining the essence of control into the twenty-first century.

Implementation is "where the action is." It is the arena that most students enter at the start of their business careers. It is the strategic phase in which staying close to the customer, achieving competitive advantage, and pursuing excellence become realities. The chapters in this part will help you understand how this is done.

# Chapter **Nine**

# Implementing Strategy through Short-Term Objectives, Functional Tactics, Reward System, and Employee Empowerment

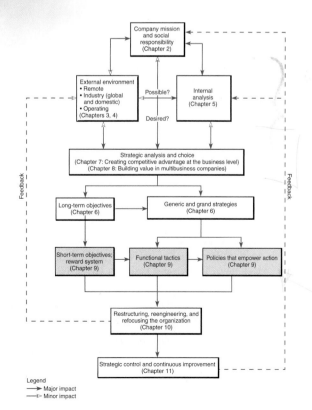

Company mission and social responsibility (Chapter 2)

External environment
• Remote
• Industry (global and domestic)
• Operating
(Chapters 3, 4)

Possible?

Desired?

Internal analysis (Chapter 5)

Strategic analysis and choice
(Chapter 7: Creating competitive advantage at the business level)
(Chapter 8: Building value in multibusiness companies)

Long-term objectives (Chapter 6)

Generic and grand strategies (Chapter 6)

Short-term objectives; reward system (Chapter 9)

Functional tactics (Chapter 9)

Policies that empower action (Chapter 9)

Restructuring, reengineering, and refocusing the organization (Chapter 10)

Strategic control and continuous improvement (Chapter 11)

Feedback

Feedback

Legend
→ Major impact
⇢ Minor impact

Once corporate and business strategies have been agreed upon and long-term objectives set, the strategic management process moves into a critical new phase—translating strategic thought into organizational action. In the words of two well-worn phrases, they move from "planning their work" to "working their plan" as they shift their focus from strategy formulation to strategy implementation. Managers successfully make this shift when they do four things well:

1. Identify short-term objectives.

2. Initiate specific functional tactics.

3. Communicate policies that empower people in the organization.

4. Design effective rewards.

Short-term objectives translate long-range aspirations into this year's targets for action. If well developed, these objectives provide clarity, a powerful motivator and facilitator of effective strategy implementation.

Functional tactics translate business strategy into daily activities people need to execute. Functional managers participate in the development of these tactics, and their participation, in turn, helps clarify what their units are expected to do in implementing the business's strategy.

Policies are empowerment tools that simplify decision making by empowering operating managers and their subordinates. Policies can empower the "doers" in an organization by reducing the time required to decide and act.

A powerful part of getting things done in any organization can be found in the way its reward system rewards desired action and results. Rewards that align manager and employee priorities with organizational objectives and shareholder value provide very effective direction in strategy implementation.

## SHORT-TERM OBJECTIVES

Chapter 6 described business strategies, grand strategies, and long-term objectives that are critically important in crafting a successful future. To make them become a reality, however, the people in an organization that actually "do the work" of the business need guidance in exactly what needs to be done today and tomorrow to make those long-term strategies become reality. Short-term objectives help do this. They provide much more specific guidance for what is to be done, a clear delineation of impending actions needed, which helps translate vision into action.

Short-term objectives help implement strategy in at least three ways. First, short-term objectives "operationalize" long-term objectives. If we commit to a 20 percent gain in revenue over five years, what is our specific target or objective in revenue during the current year, month, or week to indicate we are making appropriate progress? Second, discussion about and agreement on short-term objectives help raise issues and potential conflicts within an organization that usually require coordination to avoid otherwise dysfunctional consequences. Exhibit 9–1 illustrates how objectives within marketing, manufacturing, and accounting units within the same firm can be very different even when created to pursue the same firm objective (e.g., increased sales, lower costs). The third way short-term objectives assist strategy implementation is to identify measurable outcomes of action plans or functional activities, which can be used to make feedback, correction, and evaluation more relevant and acceptable.

Short-term objectives are usually accompanied by action plans, which enhance these objectives in three ways. First, action plans usually identify functional tactics and activities

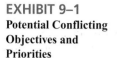

**EXHIBIT 9–1**
**Potential Conflicting Objectives and Priorities**

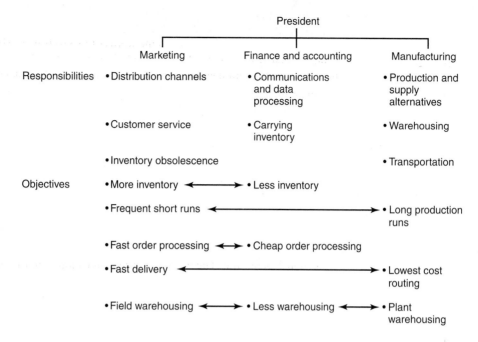

that will be undertaken in the next week, month, or quarter as part of the business's effort to build competitive advantage. The important point here is *specificity*—what exactly is to be done. We will examine functional tactics in a subsequent section of this chapter. The second element of an action plan is a clear *time frame for completion*—when the effort will begin and when its results will be accomplished. A third element action plans contain is identification of *who is responsible* for each action in the plan. This accountability is very important to ensure action plans are acted upon.

Because of the particular importance of short-term objectives in strategy implementation, the next section addresses how to develop meaningful short-term objectives. Exhibit 9–2 provides a *BusinessWeek* interview with Symantec CEO John Thompson about the nature and importance of short-term objectives to Symantec's success.

## Qualities of Effective Short-Term Objectives

### Measurable

Short-term objectives are more consistent when they clearly state *what* is to be accomplished, *when* it will be accomplished, and *how* its accomplishment will be *measured.* Such objectives can be used to monitor both the effectiveness of each activity and the collective progress across several interrelated activities. Exhibit 9–3 illustrates several effective and ineffective short-term objectives. Measurable objectives make misunderstanding less likely among interdependent managers who must implement action plans. It is far easier to quantify the objectives of *line* units (e.g., production) than of certain *staff* areas (e.g., personnel). Difficulties in quantifying objectives often can be overcome by initially focusing on *measurable activity* and then identifying *measurable outcomes.*

### Priorities

Although all annual objectives are important, some deserve priority because of a timing consideration or their particular impact on a strategy's success. If such priorities are not established, conflicting assumptions about the relative importance of annual objectives may inhibit progress toward strategic effectiveness. Facing the most rapid, dramatic decline in

**BusinessWeek** "You can't manage what you don't measure," says Symantec CEO John Thompson, who explains why objectives are vital in implementing strategy.

"If you could only monitor five objectives to run/steer your business, what would they be and why?" is a question *BusinessWeek* posed Thompson, chairman and CEO of Symantec, a Cupertino (Calif)-based Internet security outfit that makes antivirus and firewall technology. In the four years since Thompson joined Symantec as top exec, revenues have more than doubled, from $632 million $1,407 billion in 2003. The company has not missed an earnings projection in the last two years.

**Q:** So what would be your critical objectives, and why?

**A:** Let's define what objectives are: They are vectors for how you are performing now, but also indicators for how you will do in the future. Here are five critical objectives I use to manage Symantec. Our most critical objectives are customer satisfaction and market share.

**Customer satisfaction**

We use an outside firm to poll customers on a continuous basis to determine their satisfaction with our products and services. This needs to be an anonymous relationship—a conversation between our pollster and our customers. Polling is done by product area: firewall, antivirus, services, and other product lines.

**Market share**

There are a couple of ways we look at this. We have our own views based on relevant markets. Then we use industry analysts such as Gartner, IDC, and Giga as benchmarks for annualized results on market share. On a quarterly basis, we look at our revenue performance and growth rates, and that of our competitors. We compare against actual realized growth rates, as compared to growth rates of relevant competitors in similar segments.

The purpose is to get trending data. That gives us a sense of market changes and market growth. We also use a blended (rating) of analyst companies in the same space. Each industry-analyst firm counts things a bit differently, based on its methodology. The numbers don't have to be spot on or Six Sigma precise.

**Revenue growth**

You have to consider if revenue is growing at a rate equal to or greater than the market rate. If you look at the antivirus market, for example, industry analysts projected growth in the high teens while our enterprise antivirus sector grew at a rate of 32 percent. This indicates that we are gaining market share faster than the market growth rate for the industry.

We can then assess how we had planned to grow. Did we plan to grow at 32 percent or less—or more? You have to gauge your growth relative to the market for your product or service and your own internal expectations of your performance.

**Expenses**

It is important to always plan for how much money will have to be spent to generate a certain level of revenue. This enables you to monitor funds flow in the company. Did I plan to spend $10 or $12, and what did I get for that expense in return? The purpose is to keep expenses in equilibrium to revenue generation.

**Earnings**

Two keys to watch here—operating margins and earnings per share (EPS). A business running efficiently is improving its operating margins. If you are efficient in your operating margins, this should produce a strong EPS, which is a strong objective that Wall Street looks at all the time.

**Q:** What problems do tracking objectives solve for a corporation? How does maintaining objectives help you manage and steer the direction of the corporation?

**A:** I am a little old-fashioned—I don't believe you can manage what you don't measure. The importance of objectives becomes more important as the enterprise grows in size and scale. Objectives also serve as an indication for the team about what you are paying attention

---

profitability of any major computer manufacturer as it confronted relentless lower pricing by Dell Computer and AST, Compaq Computer formulated a retrenchment strategy with several important annual objectives in pricing, product design, distribution, and financial condition. But its highest priority was to dramatically lower overhead and production costs so as to satisfy the difficult challenge of dramatically lowering prices while also restoring profitability.

Priorities are established in various ways. A simple *ranking* may be based on discussion and negotiation during the planning process. However, this does not necessarily communicate the real difference in the importance of objectives, so such terms as *primary, top,* and *secondary* may be used to indicate priority. Some firms assign *weights* (e.g., 0 to 100 per-to. If employees know you are measuring market growth and customer satisfaction, they will pay attention to those considerations and will behave based on indicators that you, as the leader, provide to the organization. Objectives helps the team focus on what's important for an organization.

**Q:** To what degree is maintaining objectives also about managing expectations of different audiences: investors, Wall Street analysts, and other parties? How do you manage the expectations of these third parties and other constituent groups?

**A:** The one that is the most interesting group to try to manage today is the expectation that investors have in our company and its performance. Our chief financial officer and I spend a lot of time on that topic. The ones investors watch most closely are revenue growth and EPS. We set expectations realistically and deliver against those expectations consistently. These considerations are at the core of how Wall Street fundamentally values a company. You have to properly set expectations and cascade those objectives down through the organization.

I wouldn't want to say to Wall Street that we have revenue growth rate projections of 18 percent and not internalize communication of that objective to the 4,500 people that are part of the company. It would be a huge mistake if you set up different expectations for what you communicate externally and how you manage internally. You can't have a disconnect between the two.

**Q:** How should companies consider industry-specific objectives versus broad financial objectives: P/E ratio, etc?

**A:** This is an issue for all of us. I am on the board of a utility company. The company has achieved modest single-digit revenue growth. They are quite proud of that, while I would be quite concerned if that were to be the growth rate for a software firm. For example: An important

consideration may be what you are spending in R&D in comparison to your peer group. Or, for a software firm, what is the license revenue mix?

I couldn't care less about the performance of Symantec relative to that of a financial-services company. But I would care about the performance of Symantec in comparison with an enterprise software company or with another securities software firm. Whatever measures you choose should give you the ability to measure your performance against like-industry companies.

**Q:** What do other CEOs need to keep in mind as they consider/reevaluate the use of objectives for their companies?

**A:** Live by the adage that you can't manage what you can't measure. The best objectives are simple to understand, simple to communicate, and relatively easy for everyone to get access to the data that represents the results. That makes your objectives an effective management tool. If you make your objectives difficult to gather, manage, or communicate, they won't be effective. Simplicity is key.

My experience has proven to me the importance of picking the few objectives that are the most critical for the running of the business. Stick with them—and communicate them to both internal and external audiences.

You don't change these objectives regardless of the whimsical views of Wall Street or the problem du jour. You have to pick the most important objectives and manage to this set standard. At the same time, you have to continually evaluate as the business changes over time to ensure that your objectives remain relevant. I would argue that all good leaders do this.

**Source:** "The Key to Success? Go Figure," *BusinessWeek,* July 21, 2003.

---

cent) to establish and communicate the relative priority of objectives. Whatever the method, recognizing priorities is an important dimension in the implementation value of short-term objectives.

### Linked to Long-Term Objectives

Short-term objectives can add breadth and specificity in identifying *what* must be accomplished to achieve long-term objectives. For example, Wal-Mart's top management recently set out "to obtain 45 percent market share in five years" as a long-term objective. Achieving that objective can be greatly enhanced if a series of specific short-term objectives identify what must be accomplished each year in order to do so. If Wal-Mart's market share is

**EXHIBIT 9–3**
**Creating Measurable Objectives**

| Examples of Deficient Objectives | Examples of Objectives with Measurable Criteria for Performance |
|---|---|
| To improve morale in the division (plant, department, etc.) | To reduce turnover (absenteeism, number of rejects, etc.) among sales managers by 10 percent by January 1, 2004.<br><br>*Assumption:* Morale is related to measurable outcomes (i.e., high and low morale are associated with different results). |
| To improve support of the sales effort | To reduce the time lapse between order data and delivery by 8 percent (two days) by June 1, 2004.<br><br>To reduce the cost of goods produced by 6 percent to support a product price decrease of 2 percent by December 1, 2004.<br><br>To increase the rate of before- or on-schedule delivery by 5 percent by June 1, 2004. |
| To improve the firm's image | To conduct a public opinion poll using random samples in the five largest U.S. metropolitan markets to determine average scores on 10 dimensions of corporate responsibility by May 15, 2004. To increase our score on those dimensions by an average of 7.5 percent by May 1, 2005. |

now 25 percent, then one likely annual objective might be "to have each regional office achieve a minimum 4 percent increase in market share in the next year." "Open two regional distribution centers in the Southwest in 2005" might be an annual objective that Wal-Mart's marketing and distribution managers consider essential if the firm is to achieve a 45 percent market share in five years. "Conclude arrangements for a $1 billion line of credit at 0.25 percent above prime in 2004" might be an annual objective of Wal-Mart's financial managers to support the operation of new distribution centers and the purchase of increased inventory in reaching the firm's long-term objective.

The link between short-term and long-term objectives should resemble cascades through the firm from basic long-term objectives to specific short-term objectives in key operation areas. The cascading effect has the added advantage of providing a clear reference for communication and negotiation, which may be necessary to integrate and coordinate objectives and activities at the operating level.

The qualities of good objectives discussed in Chapter 6—acceptable, flexible, suitable, motivating, understandable, and achievable—also apply to short-term objectives. They will not be discussed again here, but you should review the discussion in Chapter 6 to appreciate these qualities, common to all good objectives.

## The Value-Added Benefits of Short-Term Objectives and Action Plans

One benefit of short-term objectives and action plans is that they give operating personnel a better understanding of their role in the firm's mission. "Achieve $2.5 million in 2005 sales in the Chicago territory," "Develop an OSHA-approved safety program for handling acids at all Georgia Pacific plants in 2005," and "Reduce Ryder Truck's average age of accounts receivable to 31 days by the end of 2005" are examples of how short-term objectives clarify the role of particular personnel in their firm's broader mission. Such *clarity of purpose* can be a major force in helping use a firm's "people assets" more effectively, which may add tangible value.

A second benefit of short-term objectives and action plans comes from the process of developing them. If the managers responsible for this accomplishment have participated in their development, short-term objectives and action plans provide valid bases for addressing and accommodating conflicting concerns that might interfere with strategic effectiveness (see Exhibit 9–1). Meetings to set short-term objectives and action plans become the forum for raising and resolving conflicts between strategic intentions and operating realities.

A third benefit of short-term objectives and action plans is that they provide a *basis for strategic control.* The control of strategy will be examined in detail in Chapter 11. However, it is important to recognize here that short-term objectives and action plans provide a clear, measurable basis for developing budgets, schedules, trigger points, and other mechanisms for controlling the implementation of strategy. Exhibit 9–2, Strategy in Action, describes how new Symantec CEO John Thompson used short-term objectives as a key basis for strategic control.

A fourth benefit is often a *motivational payoff.* Short-term objectives and action plans that clarify personal and group roles in a firm's strategies and are also measurable, realistic, and challenging can be powerful motivators of managerial performance—particularly when these objectives are linked to the firm's reward structure.

# FUNCTIONAL TACTICS THAT IMPLEMENT BUSINESS STRATEGIES

Functional tactics are the key, routine activities that must be undertaken in each functional area—marketing, finance, production/operations, R&D, and human resource management—to provide the business's products and services. In a sense, functional tactics translate thought (grand strategy) into action designed to accomplish specific short-term objectives. Every value chain activity in a company executes functional tactics that support the business's strategy and help accomplish strategic objectives.

Exhibit 9–4 illustrates the difference between functional tactics and corporate and business strategy. It also shows that functional tactics are essential to implement business strategy. The corporate strategy defined General Cinema Corporation's general posture in the broad economy. The business strategy outlined the competitive posture of its operations in the movie theater industry. To increase the likelihood that these strategies would be successful, specific functional tactics were needed for the firm's operating components. These functional tactics clarified the business strategy, giving specific, short-term guidance to operating managers in the areas of marketing, operations, and finance.

## Differences between Business Strategies and Functional Tactics

Functional tactics are different from business or corporate strategies in three fundamental ways:

1. Time horizon.

2. Specificity.

3. Participants who develop them.

### *Time Horizon*

Functional tactics identify activities to be undertaken "now" or in the immediate future. Business strategies focus on the firm's posture three to five years out. Delta Air lines is committed to a concentration/market development business strategy that seeks competitive advantage via differentiation in its level of service and focus on the business traveler. Its pricing tactics are often to price above industry averages, but it often lowers fares on selected routes to thwart low-cost competition. Its business strategy is focused 10 years out; its pricing tactics change weekly.

**EXHIBIT 9–4**
**Functional Tactics at General Cinema Corporation**

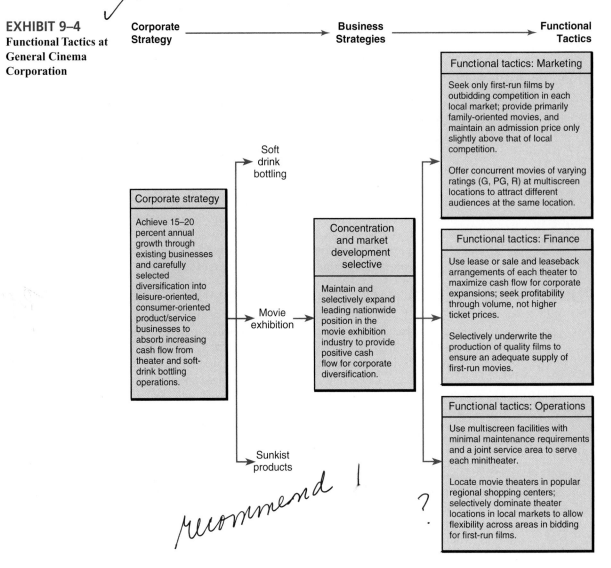

Corporate Strategy ⟶ Business Strategies ⟶ Functional Tactics

**Corporate strategy**

Achieve 15–20 percent annual growth through existing businesses and carefully selected diversification into leisure-oriented, consumer-oriented product/service businesses to absorb increasing cash flow from theater and soft-drink bottling operations.

Soft drink bottling

Movie exhibition

Sunkist products

*recommend 1*

**Concentration and market development selective**

Maintain and selectively expand leading nationwide position in the movie exhibition industry to provide positive cash flow for corporate diversification.

**Functional tactics: Marketing**

Seek only first-run films by outbidding competition in each local market; provide primarily family-oriented movies, and maintain an admission price only slightly above that of local competition.

Offer concurrent movies of varying ratings (G, PG, R) at multiscreen locations to attract different audiences at the same location.

**Functional tactics: Finance**

Use lease or sale and leaseback arrangements of each theater to maximize cash flow for corporate expansions; seek profitability through volume, not higher ticket prices.

Selectively underwrite the production of quality films to ensure an adequate supply of first-run movies.

**Functional tactics: Operations**

Use multiscreen facilities with minimal maintenance requirements and a joint service area to serve each minitheater.

Locate movie theaters in popular regional shopping centers; selectively dominate theater locations in local markets to allow flexibility across areas in bidding for first-run films.

*?*

The shorter time horizon of functional tactics is critical to the successful implementation of a business strategy for two reasons. First, it focuses the attention of functional managers on what needs to be done *now* to make the business strategy work. Second, it allows functional managers like those at Delta to adjust to changing current conditions.

### Specificity

Functional tactics are more specific than business strategies. Business strategies provide general direction. Functional tactics identify the specific activities that are to be undertaken in each functional area and thus allow operating managers to work out *how* their unit is expected to pursue short-term objectives. General Cinema's business strategy gave its movie theater division broad direction on how to pursue a concentration and selective market development strategy. Two functional tactics in the marketing area gave managers specific direction on what types of movies (first-run, primarily family-oriented, G, PG, R) should be shown and what pricing strategy (competitive in the local area) should be followed.

Specificity in functional tactics contributes to successful implementation by:

- Helping ensure that functional managers know what needs to be done and can focus on accomplishing results.

- Clarifying for top management how functional managers intend to accomplish the business strategy, which increases top management's confidence in and sense of control over the business strategy.

- Facilitating coordination among operating units *within* the firm by clarifying areas of interdependence and potential conflict.

Exhibit 9–5, Strategy in Action, illustrates the nature and value of specificity in functional tactics versus business strategy in an upscale pizza restaurant chain.

### Participants

Different people participate in strategy development at the functional and business levels. Business strategy is the responsibility of the general manager of a business unit. That manager typically delegates the development of functional tactics to subordinates charged with running the operating areas of the business. The manager of a business unit must establish long-term objectives and a strategy that corporate management feels contributes to corporate-level goals. Similarly, key operating managers must establish short-term objectives and operating strategies that contribute to business-level goals. Just as business strategies and objectives are approved through negotiation between corporate managers and business managers, so, too, are short-term objectives and functional tactics approved through negotiation between business managers and operating managers.

Involving operating managers in the development of functional tactics improves their understanding of what must be done to achieve long-term objectives and, thus, contributes to successful implementation. It also helps ensure that functional tactics reflect the reality of the day-to-day operating situation. And perhaps most important, it can increase the commitment of operating managers to the strategies developed.

## EMPOWERING OPERATING PERSONNEL: THE ROLE OF POLICIES

Specific functional tactics provide guidance and initiate action implementing a business's strategy, but more is needed. Supervisors and personnel in the field have been charged in today's competitive environment with being responsible for customer value—for being the "front line" of the company's effort to truly meet customers' needs. Meeting customer needs, becoming obsessed with quality service, was the buzzword that started organizational revolutions in the 1980s. Efforts to do so often failed because employees that were the real contact point between the business and its customers were not *empowered* to make decisions or act to fulfill customer needs. One solution has been to empower operating personnel by pushing down decision making to their level. General Electric allows appliance repair personnel to decide about warranty credits on the spot, a decision that used to take several days and multiple organizational levels. Delta Air Lines allows customer service personnel and their supervisors wide range in resolving customer ticket pricing decisions. Federal Express couriers make decisions and handle package routing information that involves five management levels in the U.S. Postal Service.

Empowerment is being created in many ways. Training, self-managed work groups, eliminating whole levels of management in organizations, and aggressive use of automation are some of the ways and ramifications of this fundamental change in the way business organizations function. At the heart of the effort is the need to ensure that decision making

# Strategy in Action
## The Nature and Value of Specificity in Functional Tactics versus Business Strategy

# Exhibit 9–5

A restaurant business was encountering problems. Although its management had agreed unanimously that it was committed to a business strategy to differentiate itself from other competitors based on concept and customer service rather than price, it continued to encounter inconsistencies across different store locations in how well it did this. Consultants indicated that the customer experience varied greatly from store to store. The conclusion was that while the management understood the "business strategy," and the employees did too in general terms, the implementation was inadequate because of a lack of specificity in the functional tactics—what everyone should do every day in the restaurant—to make the vision a reality in terms of the customers' dining experience. The following breakdown of part of their business strategy into specific functional tactics just in the area of customer service helps illustrate the value specificity in functional tactics brings to strategy implementation.

**Source:** Adapted from "California Pizza Kitchen: Say Cheese!," *BusinessWeek,* July 15, 2003; and A. Campbell and K. Luchs, *Strategic Synergy* (London: Butterworth-Heineman, 1992).

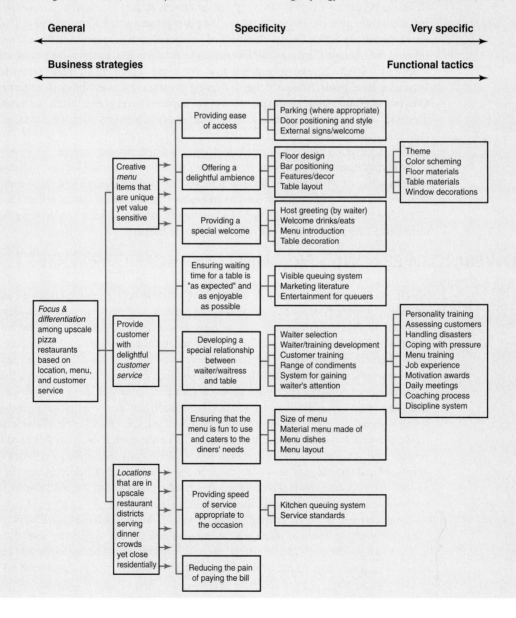

is consistent with the mission, strategy, and tactics of the business while at the same time allowing considerable latitude to operating personnel. One way operating managers do this is through the use of policies.

*Policies* are directives designed to guide the thinking, decisions, and actions of managers and their subordinates in implementing a firm's strategy. Previously referred to as *standard operating procedures,* policies increase managerial effectiveness by standardizing many routine decisions and clarifying the discretion managers and subordinates can exercise in implementing functional tactics. Logically, policies should be derived from functional tactics (and, in some instances, from corporate or business strategies) with the key purpose of aiding strategy execution.[1] Exhibit 9–6, Strategy in Action, illustrates selected policies of several well-known firms.

## Creating Policies That Empower

Policies communicate guidelines to decisions. They are designed to control decisions while defining allowable discretion within which operational personnel can execute business activities. They do this in several ways:

1. *Policies establish indirect control over independent action* by clearly stating how things are to be done *now.* By defining discretion, policies in effect control decisions yet empower employees to conduct activities without direct intervention by top management.

2. *Policies promote uniform handling of similar activities.* This facilitates the coordination of work tasks and helps reduce friction arising from favoritism, discrimination, and the disparate handling of common functions—something that often hampers operating personnel.

3. *Policies ensure quicker decisions* by standardizing answers to previously answered questions that otherwise would recur and be pushed up the management hierarchy again and again—something that required unnecessary levels of management between senior decision makers and field personnel.

4. *Policies institutionalize basic aspects of organization behavior.* This minimizes conflicting practices and establishes consistent patterns of action in attempts to make the strategy work—again, freeing operating personnel to act.

5. *Policies reduce uncertainty in repetitive and day-to-day decision making,* thereby providing a necessary foundation for coordinated, efficient efforts and freeing operating personnel to act.

6. *Policies counteract resistance to or rejection of chosen strategies by organization members.* When major strategic change is undertaken, unambiguous operating policies clarify what is expected and facilitate acceptance, particularly when operating managers participate in policy development.

---

[1] The term *policy* has various definitions in management literature. Some authors and practitioners equate policy with strategy. Others do this inadvertently by using *policy* as a synonym for company mission, purpose, or culture. Still other authors and practitioners differentiate policy in terms of "levels" associated respectively with purpose, mission, and strategy. "Our policy is to make a positive contribution to the communities and societies we live in" and "our policy is not to diversify out of the hamburger business" are two examples of the breadth of what some call policies. This book defines *policy* much more narrowly as specific guides to managerial action and decisions in the implementation of strategy. This definition permits a sharper distinction between the formulation and implementation of functional strategies. And, of even greater importance, it focuses the tangible value of the policy concept where it can be most useful—as a key administrative tool to enhance effective implementation and execution of strategy.

3M Corporation has a *personnel policy,* called the *15 percent rule,* that allows virtually any employee to spend up to 15 percent of the workweek on anything that he or she wants to, as long as it's product related.

(This policy supports 3M's corporate strategy of being a highly innovative manufacturer, with each division required to have a quarter of its annual sales come from products introduced within the past five years.)

Wendy's has a *purchasing policy* that gives local store managers the authority to buy fresh meat and produce locally, rather than from regionally designated or company-owned sources.

(This policy supports Wendy's functional strategy of having fresh, unfrozen hamburgers daily.)

General Cinema has a *financial policy* that requires annual capital investment in movie theaters not to exceed annual depreciation.

(By seeing that capital investment is no greater than depreciation, this policy supports General Cinema's financial strategy of maximizing cash flow—in this case, all profit—to its growth areas. The policy also reinforces General Cinema's financial strategy of leasing as much as possible.)

IBM had a *marketing policy* of not giving free IBM personal computers (PCs) to any person or organization.

(This policy attempted to support IBM's image strategy by maintaining its image as a professional, high-value, service business as it sought to dominate the PC market.)

Crown, Cork, and Seal Company has an *R&D policy* of not investing any financial or people resources in basic research.

(This policy supports Crown, Cork, and Seal's functional strategy, which emphasizes customer services, not technical leadership.)

Bank of America has an *operating policy* that requires annual renewal of the financial statement of all personal borrowers.

(This policy supports Bank of America's financial strategy, which seeks to maintain a loan-to-loss ratio below the industry norm.)

7. *Policies offer predetermined answers to routine problems.* This greatly expedites dealing with both ordinary and extraordinary problems—with the former, by referring to these answers; with the latter, by giving operating personnel more time to cope with them.

8. *Policies afford managers a mechanism for avoiding hasty and ill-conceived decisions in changing operations.* Prevailing policy can always be used as a reason for not yielding to emotion-based, expedient, or temporarily valid arguments for altering procedures and practices.

Policies may be written and formal or unwritten and informal. Informal, unwritten policies are usually associated with a strategic need for competitive secrecy. Some policies of this kind, such as promotion from within, are widely known (or expected) by employees and implicitly sanctioned by management. Managers and employees often like the latitude granted by unwritten and informal policies. However, such policies may detract from the long-term success of a strategy. Formal, written policies have at least seven advantages:

1. They require managers to think through the policy's meaning, content, and intended use.

2. They reduce misunderstanding.

3. They make equitable and consistent treatment of problems more likely.

4. They ensure unalterable transmission of policies.

5. They communicate the authorization or sanction of policies more clearly.

6. They supply a convenient and authoritative reference.

7. They systematically enhance indirect control and organizationwide coordination of the key purposes of policies.

**EXHIBIT 9–7**
**Make Sure Policies Aren't Used To Drive Away Customers**

Every Year *Inc. Magazine* sponsors a conference for the 500 fastest growing companies in the United States to share ideas, hear speakers, and network. A recent conference included a talk by Martha Rogers, coauther of *The One to One Future*. Here is an interesting anecdote about policies she used in her talk:

*"The story was about a distinguished-looking gentleman in blue jeans who walked into a bank and asked a teller to complete a transaction. The teller said she was sorry, but the person responsible was out for the day. The man would have to come back. He then asked to have his parking receipt validated. Again, she said she was sorry, but under bank policy she could not validate a parking receipt unless the customer completed a transaction. The man pressed her. She did not waver. "That's our policy," she said.*

*So the man completed a transaction. He withdrew all $1.5 million from his account. It turned out he was John Akers, then chairman of IBM.*

*The moral: Give employees information about the value of customers, not mindless policies."*

The strategic significance of policies can vary. At one extreme are such policies as travel reimbursement procedures, which are really work rules and may not have an obvious link to the implementation of a strategy. Exhibit 9–7 provides an interesting example of how the link between a simple policy and strategy implementation regarding customer service can have serious negative consequences when it is neither obvious to operating personnel nor well thought out by bank managers. At the other extreme are organizationwide policies that are virtually functional strategies, such as Wendy's requirement that every location invest 1 percent of its gross revenue in local advertising.

Policies can be externally imposed or internally derived. Policies regarding equal employment practices are often developed in compliance with external (government) requirements, and policies regarding leasing or depreciation may be strongly influenced by current tax regulations.

Regardless of the origin, formality, and nature of policies, the key point to bear in mind is that they can play an important role in strategy implementation. Communicating specific policies will help overcome resistance to strategic change, empower people to act, and foster commitment to successful strategy implementation.

Policies empower people to act. Compensation, at least theoretically, rewards their action. The last decade has seen many firms realize that the link between compensation, particularly executive management compensation, and value-building strategic outcomes within their firms was uncertain. The recognition of this uncertainty has brought about increased recognition of the need to link management compensation with the successful implementation of strategies that build long-term shareholder value. The next section examines this development and major types of executive bonus compensation plans.

# EXECUTIVE BONUS COMPENSATION PLANS[2]

## Major Plan Types

The goal of an executive bonus compensation plan is to motivate executives to achieve maximization of shareholder wealth—the underlying goal of most firms. Since shareholders are both owners and investors of the firm, they desire a reasonable return on their investment. Because they are absentee landlords, shareholders want the decision-making logic of their firm's executives to be concurrent with their own primary motivation.

---

[2] We wish to thank Roy Hossler for his assistance on this section.

However, agency theory instructs us that the goal of shareholder wealth maximization is not the only goal that executives may pursue. Alternatively, executives may choose actions that increase their personal compensation, power, and control. Therefore, an executive compensation plan that contains a bonus component can be used to orient management's decision making toward the owners' goals. The success of bonus compensation as an incentive hinges on a proper match between an executive bonus plan and the firm's strategic objectives. As one author has written: "Companies can succeed by clarifying their business vision or strategy and aligning company pay programs with its strategic direction."[3]

### Stock Options

A common measure of shareholder wealth creation is appreciation of company stock price. Therefore, a popular form of bonus compensation is stock options. Stock options have typically represented over 50 percent of a chief executive officer's average pay package.[4] Stock options provide the executive with the right to purchase company stock at a fixed price in the future. The precise amount of compensation is based on the difference, or "spread," between the option's initial price and its selling, or exercised, price. As a result, the executive receives a bonus only if the firm's share price appreciates. If the share price drops below the option price, the options become worthless. The largest single option sale of all time occurred on December 3, 1997. Disney Chief Executive Officer Michael D. Eisner exercised more than 7 million options on Disney stock that he had been given in 1989 as part of his bonus plan. Eisner sold his shares for more than $400 million.

Stock options were the source of extraordinary wealth creation for executives, managers, and rank-and-file employees in the technology boom of the last decade. Behind using options as compensation incentives was the notion that they were essentially free. Although they dilute shareholders' equity when they're exercised, taking the cost of stock options as an expense against earnings was not required. That, in turn, helped keep earnings higher than actual costs to the company and its shareholders. The bear market and corporate scandals of the last few years brought increased scrutiny on the use of and accounting for stock options. As of this writing there is increased pressure to begin expensing stock options to more accurately reflect company performance. The table below shows the effect expensing stocks options would have on the net earnings of the S&P 500 firms in recent years. "Stock options were a free resource, and because of that, they were used freely," said BankOne CEO James Dimon, who voluntarily began to expense stock options in 2003. "But now," he said, "when you have to expense options, you start to think" 'Is it an effective cost?' Is there a better way?" The Financial Accounting Standards Board was preparing a new ruling in 2004 that would require expensing of stock options.

---

**A Big Hit To Earnings**

If options had been expensed, earnings would have been whacked as their popularity grew

Options Expense As a Percent of Net Earnings for S&P 500 Companies

| 1996 | 1998 | 2000 | 2002 |
| --- | --- | --- | --- |
| 2% | 5% | 8% | 23% |

Data: The Analysis Accounting Observer R. G. Associates Inc.

---

[3] James E. Nelson, "Linking Compensation to Business Strategy," *The Journal of Business Strategy* 19, no. 2 (1998), pp. 25–27.
[4] Louis Lavelle, Frederick Jespersen, and Spencer Ante, "Executive Pay," *BusinessWeek,* April 21, 2003.

Microsoft shocked the business world in 2003 by announcing it would discontinue stock options, eliminating a form of pay that made thousands of Microsoft employees millionaires and helped define the culture of the tech industry. Starting in September, 2003, the company began paying its 54,000 employees with restricted stock, a move that will let employees make money even if the company's share price declines. Like options, the restricted stock will vest gradually over a five-year period and grants of restricted stock counted as expenses and charged against earnings. Said CEO Steven Ballmer, "We asked: Is there a smarter way to compensate our people, a way that would make them feel even more excited about their financial deal at Microsoft and at the same time be something that was at least as good for the shareholders as today's compensation package?" At the time of Ballmer's announcement, over 20,000 employees that had joined Microsoft in the past three years held millions of stock options that were "under water," meaning the market value of Microsoft stock was far below the stock price of their stock options.

Restricted stock has the advantage of offering employees more certainty, even if there is less potential for a big win. It also means shareholders don't have to worry about massive dilution after employees exercise big stock gains, as happened in the 1990s. Another advantage is that grants of restricted stock are much easier to value than options since restricted stock is equivalent to a stock transfer at the market price. That improves the transparency of corporate accounting.[5] At the same time, while several tech companies started downsizing their options programs in recent years, several old-line companies have been beefing their options programs up as shown in the box below.

**Late to The Party**
**As many technology companies have downsized their options programs, old-line companies have been beefing theirs up.**

| | 2002 Options Grant Millions | Change In Shares From 2001 | | 2002 Options Grant Millions | Change In Shares From 2001 |
|---|---|---|---|---|---|
| Lucent | 14 | −96% | Conoco Philips | 29 | +600% |
| Siebel Systems | 6 | −95 | Sysco | 31 | +560 |
| Aplied Materials | 9 | −91 | Southwest Airlines | 53 | +435 |
| Microsoft | 41 | −82 | Safeco | 3 | +326 |
| AOL Time Warner | 115 | −41 | Campbell Soup | 15 | +301 |

Data: The Analyst's Accounting Observer, R.G. Associates Inc.

Research suggests that stock option plans lack the benefits of plans that include true stock ownership. Stock option plans provide unlimited upside potential for executives, but limited downside risk since executives incur only opportunity costs. Because of the tremendous advantages to the executive of stock price appreciation, there is an incentive for the executive to take undue risk. Thus, supporters of stock ownership plans argue that direct ownership instills a much stronger behavioral commitment, even when the stock price falls, since it binds

[5] Many argue that stock options are critical to start-up firms as a way to motivate and retain talented employees with the promise of getting rich should the new venture succeed. Among them appear to be FASB chairman Robert Herz, who favors sentiment to make special exceptions in the expensing of options in pre-IPO firms.

executives to their firms more than do options.[6] Additionally, "Executive stock options may be an efficient means to induce management to undertake more risky projects."[7]

Options may have been overused in the last bull market, but evidence suggests that the smart use of options and other incentive compensation does boost performance. Companies that spread ownership throughout a large portion of their workforce deliver higher returns than similar companies with more concentrated ownership. If options seemed for a time to be the route that enriched CEOs, employees, and investors alike, it still appears they will be used although with less emphasis than a mix of options, restricted stock, and cash bonuses. Whatever the exact mix, they are likely to be more closely tied to achieving specific operating goals. The next section examines restricted stock and cash bonuses in greater detail.

### Restricted Stock

A restricted stock plan is designed to provide benefits of direct executive stock ownership. In a typical restricted stock plan, an executive is given a specific number of company stock shares. The executive is prohibited from selling the shares for a specified time period. Should the executive leave the firm voluntarily before the restricted period ends, the shares are forfeited. Therefore, restricted stock plans are a form of deferred compensation that promotes longer executive tenure than other types of plans.

In addition to being contingent on a vesting period, restricted stock plans may also require the achievement of predetermined performance goals. Price-vesting restricted stock plans tie vesting to the firm's stock price in comparison to an index, or to reaching a predetermined goal or annual growth rate. If the executive falls short on some of the restrictions, a certain amount of shares are forfeited. The design of these plans motivates the executive to increase shareholder wealth while promoting a long-term commitment to stay with the firm.

If the restricted stock plan lacks performance goal provisions, the executive needs only to remain employed with the firm over the vesting period to cash in on the stock. Performance provisions make sure executives are not compensated without achieving some level of shareholder wealth creation. Like stock options, restricted stock plans offer no downside risk to executives, since the shares were initially gifted to the executive. Unlike options, the stock retains value tied to its market value once ownership is fully vested. Shareholders, on the other hand, do suffer a loss in personal wealth resulting from a share price drop.

Investment bank Lehman Brothers has a restricted stock plan in place for hundreds of managing directors and senior vice presidents. The plan vests with time and does not include stock price performance provisions. It is a two-tiered plan consisting of a principal stock grant and a discounted share plan. For managing directors, the discount is 30 percent. For senior vice presidents, the discount is 25 percent. The principal stock grant is a block of shares given to the executive. The discounted share plan allows executives to purchase shares with their own money at a discount to current market prices.

Managing directors at Lehman are able to cash in on one-half the principal portion of their stock grant three years after the grant is awarded. The rest of the principal and any shares bought at a discount must vest for five years. Senior vice presidents receive the entire principal after two years and any discounted shares after five years. Provisions also exist for resignation. If managing directors leave Lehman for a competitor within three years

---

[6] Jeffrey Pfeffer, "Seven Practices of Successful Organizations," *California Management Review,* Winter 1998.

[7] Richard A. DeFusco, Robert R. Johnson, and Thomas S. Zorn, "The Effect of Executive Stock Option Plans on Stockholders and Bondholders," *Journal of Finance* 45, no. 2 (1990), pp. 617–35.

of the award, all stock compensation is forfeited. For senior vice presidents, the period is two years, and the penalties for jumping to a noncompetitor of Lehman's are not as severe.

### Golden Handcuffs

The rationale behind plans that defer compensation forms the basis for another type of executive compensation called *golden handcuffs*. Golden handcuffs refer to either a restricted stock plan, where the stock compensation is deferred until vesting time provisions are met, or to bonus income deferred in a series of annual installments. This type of plan may also involve compensating an executive a significant amount upon retirement or at some predetermined age. In most cases, compensation is forfeited if the executive voluntarily resigns or is discharged before certain time restrictions.

Many boards consider their executives' skills and talents to be their firm's most valuable assets. These "assets" create and sustain the professional relationships that generate revenue and control expenses for the firm. Research suggests that the departure of key executives is unsettling for companies and often disrupts long-range plans when new key executives adopt a different management strategy.[8] Thus, the golden handcuffs approach to executive compensation is more congruent with long-term strategies than short-term performance plans, which offer little staying-power incentive.

Firms may turn to golden handcuffs if they believe stability of management is critical to sustain growth. Jupiter Asset Management recently tied 10 fund managers to the firm with golden handcuffs. The compensation scheme calls for a cash payment in addition to base salaries if the managers remain at the firm for five years. In the first year of the plan, the firm's pretax profits more than doubled, and their assets under management increased 85 percent. The firm's chairman has also signed a new incentive deal that will keep him at Jupiter for four years.

Deferred compensation is worrisome to some executives. In cases where the compensation is payable when the executives are retired and no longer in control, as when the firm is acquired by another firm or a new management hierarchy is installed, the golden handcuff plans are considerably less attractive to executives.

Golden handcuffs may promote risk averseness in executive decision making due to the huge downside risk borne by executives. This risk averseness could lead to mediocre performance results from executives' decisions. When executives lose deferred compensation if the firm discharges them voluntarily or involuntarily, the executive is less likely to make bold and aggressive decisions. Rather, the executive will choose safe, conservative decisions to reduce the downside risk of bold decision making.

### Golden Parachutes

Golden parachutes are a form of bonus compensation that is designed to retain talented executives. A *golden parachute* is an executive perquisite that calls for a substantial cash payment if the executive quits, is fired, or simply retires. In addition, the golden parachute may also contain covenants that allow the executive to cash in on noninvested stock compensation.

The popularity of golden parachutes grew during the last decade, when abundant hostile takeovers would often oust the acquired firm's top executives. In these cases, the golden parachutes encouraged executives to take an objective look at takeover offers. The executives could decide which move was in the best interests of the shareholders, having been

---

[8] William E. Hall, Brian J. Lake, Charles T. Morse, and Charles T. Morse, Jr., "More Than Golden Handcuffs," *Journal of Accountancy* 184, no. 5 (1997), pp. 37–42.

personally protected in the event of a merger. The "parachute" helps soften the fall of the ousted executive. It is "golden" because the size of the cash payment often varies from several to tens of millions of dollars.

AMP Incorporated, the world's largest producer of electronic connectors, had golden parachutes for several executives. When Allied Signal proclaimed itself an unsolicited suitor for AMP, the action focused attention on the AMP parachutes for its three top executives. Robert Ripp became AMP's chief executive officer during this time. If Allied Signal ousted him, he stood to receive a cash payment of three times the amount of his salary as well as his highest annual bonus from the previous three years. His salary at the time was $600,000 and his previous year's bonus was $200,000. The cash payment to Ripp would therefore exceed $2 million. Parachutes would also open for the former chief executive officer and the former chairman who were slated to officially retire a year later. They stood to receive their parachutes if they were ousted before their respective retirement dates with each parachute valued at more than $1 million.

In addition to cash payments, these three executives' parachutes also protect existing blocks of restricted stock grants and nonvested stock options. The restricted stock grants were scheduled to become available within three years. Should the takeover come to fruition, the executives would receive the total value of the restricted stock even if it was not yet vested. The stock options would also become available immediately. Some of the restricted stock was performance restricted. Under normal conditions this stock would not be available without the firm reaching certain performance levels. However, the golden parachutes allow the executives to receive double the value of the performance-restricted stock.

Golden parachutes are designed in part to anticipate hostile takeovers like this. In AMP's case, Ripp's position is to lead the firm's board of directors in deciding if Allied Signal's offer is in the long-term interests of shareholders. Since Ripp is compensated heavily whether AMP is taken over or not, the golden parachute has helped remove the temptation that Ripp could have of not acting in the best interests of shareholders.

By design, golden parachutes benefit top executives whether or not there is evidence that value is created for shareholders. In fact, research has suggested that since high-performing firms are rarely taken over, golden parachutes often compensate top executives for abysmal performance.[9] Recent stockholder reactions to excessive executive compensation regardless of company performance are seen in Exhibit 9–8.

### Cash

Executive bonus compensation plans that focus on accounting measures of performance are designed to offset the limitations of market-based measures of performance. This type of plan is most usually associated with the payment of periodic (quarterly or annual) cash bonuses. Market factors beyond the control of management, such as pending legislation, can keep a firm's share price repressed even though a top executive is exceeding the performance expectations of the board. In this situation, a highly performing executive loses bonus compensation due to the undervalued stock. However, accounting measures of performance correct for this problem by tying executive bonuses to improvements in internally measured performance.

Traditional accounting measures, such as net income, earnings per share, return on equity, and return on assets, are used because they are easily understood, are familiar to senior management, and are already tracked by firm data systems.[10] Sears bases annual bonus

---

[9] Graef S. Crystal, *In Search of Excess* (New York: W. W. Norton & Company, 1991).
[10] Francine C. McKenzie and Matthew D. Shilling, "Avoiding Performance Measurement Traps: Ensuring Effective Incentive Design and Implementation," *Compensation and Benefits Review,* July–August 1998, pp. 57–65.

## FED-UP SHAREHOLDERS

*Unions and public pension funds have racked up more than two dozen majority votes for shareholder resolutions opposing high executive pay*

**GOLDEN PARACHUTES**
At Alcoa, 65% of shareholders voted for a union resolution calling for stockholder approval of lavish executive severance packages. Similar proposals won majorities at Delta and Raytheon.

**CUSHY RETIREMENT DEALS**
A proposal at U.S. Bancorp seeking shareholder votes on special executive pension benefits passed by 52%. Labor pulled resolutions at GE, Coke, and Exelon after they agreed to reforms.

**EXPENSING STOCK OPTIONS**
Labor resolutions demanding that companies deduct option costs from earnings have garnered majorities at 15 companies, including Apple and Capital One.

Source: "Executive Pay: Labor Strikes Back," *BusinessWeek,* May 26, 2003.

payments on such performance criteria, given an executive's business unit and level with the firm. The measures used by Sears include return on equity, revenue growth, net sales growth, and profit growth.

Critics argue that due to inherent flaws in accounting systems, basing compensation on these figures may not result in an accurate gauge of managerial performance. Return on equity estimates, for example, are skewed by inflation distortions and arbitrary cost allocations. Accounting measures are also subject to manipulation by firm personnel to artificially inflate key performance figures. Firm performance schemes, critics believe, need to be based on a financial measure that has a true link to shareholder value creation.[11] This issue led to the creation of the Balanced Scorecard, which emphasizes not only financial measures, but also such measures as new product development, market share, and safety as discussed in Chapters 6 and 11 of this book.

## Matching Bonus Plans and Corporate Goals

Exhibit 9–9 provides a summary of the five types of executive bonus compensation plans. The figure includes a brief description, a rationale for implementation, and the identification of possible shortcomings for each of the compensation plans. Not only do compensation plans differ in the method through which compensation is rewarded to the executive, but they also provide the executive with different incentives.

[11] William Franklin, "Making the Fat Cats Earn Their Cream," *Accountancy,* July 1998, pp. 38–39.

## EXHIBIT 9–9
**Types of Executive Bonus Compensation**

| Bonus Type | Description | Rationale | Shortcomings |
|---|---|---|---|
| Stock option grants | Right to purchase stock in the future at a price set now. Compensation is determined by "spread" between option price and exercise price. | Provides incentive for executive to create wealth for shareholders as measured by increase in firm's share price. | Movement in share price does not explain all dimensions of managerial performance. |
| Restricted stock plan | Shares given to executive who is prohibited from selling them for a specific time period. May also include performance restrictions. | Promotes longer executive tenure than other forms of compensation. | No downside risk to executive, who always profits unlike other shareholders. |
| Golden handcuffs | Bonus income deferred in a series of annual installments. Deferred amounts not yet paid are forfeited with executive resignation. | Offers an incentive for executive to remain with the firm. | May promote risk-averse decision making due to downside risk borne by executive. |
| Golden parachute | Executives have right to collect the bonus if they lose position due to takeover, firing, retirement, or resignation. | Offers an incentive for executive to remain with the firm. | Compensation is achieved whether or not wealth is created for shareholders. Rewards either success or failure. |
| Cash based on internal business performance using financial measures | Bonus compensation based on accounting performance measures such as return on equity. | Offsets the limitations of focusing on market-based measures of performance. | Weak correlation between earnings measures and shareholder wealth creation. Annual earnings do not capture future impact of current decisions. |

Exhibit 9–10 matches a company's strategic goal with the most likely compensation plan. On the vertical axis are common strategic goals. The horizontal axis lists the main compensation types that serve as incentives for executives to reach the firm's goals. A rationale is provided to explain the logic behind the connection between the firm's goal and the suggested method of executive compensation.

Researchers emphasize that fundamental to these relationships is the importance of incorporating the level of strategic risk of the firm into the design of the executive's compensation plan. Incorporating an appropriate level of executive risk can create a desired behavioral change commensurate with the risk level of strategies shareholders and their firms want.[12] To help motivate an executive to pursue goals of a certain risk-return level, the compensation plan can quantify that risk-return level and reward the executive accordingly.

The links we show between bonus compensation plans and strategic goals were derived from the results of prior research. The basic principle underlying Exhibit 9–10 is that different types of bonus compensation plans are intended to accomplish different purposes; one element

---

[12] "Executive Pay," *Business Week,* April 21, 2003.

**EXHIBIT 9–10**
**Compensation Plan Selection Matrix**

| | Type of Bonus Compensation | | | | | |
|---|---|---|---|---|---|---|
| **Strategic Goal** | **Cash** | **Golden Handcuffs** | **Golden Parachutes** | **Restricted Stock Plans** | **Stock Options** | **Rationale** |
| Achieve corporate turnaround | | | | | X | Executive profits only if turnaround is successful in returning wealth to shareholders. |
| Create and support growth opportunities | | | | | X | Risk associated with growth strategies warrants the use of this high-reward incentive. |
| Defend against unfriendly takeover | | | X | | | Parachute helps remove temptation for executive to evaluate takeover based on personal benefits. |
| Evaluate suitors objectively | | | X | | | Parachute compensates executive if job is lost due to a merger favorable to the firm. |
| Globalize operations | | | | | X | Risk of expanding overseas requires a plan that compensates only for achieved success. |
| Grow share price incrementally | X | | | | | Accounting measures can identify periodic performance benchmarks. |
| Improve operational efficiency | X | | | | | Accounting measures represent observable and agreed-upon measures of performance. |
| Increase assets under management | | | | X | | Executive profits proportionally as asset growth leads to long-term growth in share price. |
| Reduce executive turnover | | X | | | | Handcuffs provide executive tenure incentive. |
| Restructure organization | | | | | X | Risk associated with major change in firm's assets warrant the use of this high-reward incentive. |
| Streamline operations | | | | X | | Rewards long-term focus on efficiency and cost control. |

may serve to attract and retain executives, another may serve as an incentive to encourage behavior that accomplishes firm goals.[13] Although every strategy option has probably been linked to each compensation plan at some time, experience shows that there may be scenarios where a plan type best fits a strategy option. Exhibit 9–10 attempts to display the "best matches."

Once the firm has identified strategic goals that will best serve shareholders' interests, an executive bonus compensation plan can be structured in such a way as to provide the executive with an incentive to work toward achieving these goals.

## Summary

The first concern in the implementation of business strategy is to translate that strategy into action throughout the organization. This chapter discussed four important tools for accomplishing this.

Short-term objectives are derived from long-term objectives, which are then translated into current actions and targets. They differ from long-term objectives in time frame, specificity, and measurement. To be effective in strategy implementation, they must be integrated and coordinated. They also must be consistent, measurable, and prioritized.

Functional tactics are derived from the business strategy. They identify the specific, immediate actions that must be taken in key functional areas to implement the business strategy.

Employee empowerment through policies provides another means for guiding behavior, decisions, and actions at the firm's operating levels in a manner consistent with its business and functional strategies. Policies empower operating personnel to make decisions and take action quickly.

Compensation rewards action and results. Once the firm has identified strategic objectives that will best serve stockholder interests, there are five bonus compensation plans that can be structured to provide the executive with an incentive to work toward achieving those goals.

Objectives, functional tactics, policies, and compensation represent only the start of the strategy implementation. The strategy must be institutionalized—it must permeate the firm. The next chapter examines this phase of strategy implementation.

## Questions for Discussion

1. How does the concept "translate thought into action" bear on the relationship between business strategy and operating strategy? Between long-term and short-term objectives?

2. How do functional tactics differ from corporate and business strategies?

3. What key concerns must functional tactics address in marketing? Finance? POM? Personnel?

4. How do policies aid strategy implementation? Illustrate your answer.

5. Use Exhibits 9–9 and 9–10 to explain five executive bonus compensation plans.

6. Illustrate a policy, an objective, and a functional tactic in your personal career strategy.

7. Why are short-term objectives needed when long-term objectives are already available?

[13] James E. Nelson, "Linking Compensation to Business Strategy," *The Journal of Business Strategy* 19, no. 2 (1998), pp. 25–27.

## Chapter 9 Discussion Case A

# Thinking outside the Cereal Box

*General Mills' Far-flung Search for Efficiency Ideas*

BusinessWeek

General Mills' CEO searches for short-term objectives, functional tactics, and operating policies in unusual ways and places so he can translate a 10-year goal into tactical actions and results. Read this story about what he is doing and then see if you detect ways he is doing so!

1  As the economy has unraveled over the past three years, managers desperate to prop up profits have been beating the bushes for new ways to cut costs. Few, however, have wandered further afield in pursuit of smart ideas than General Mills (GIS), Inc. chief technical officer Randy G. Darcy. He has participated in predawn raids with a U.S. Marshals Service SWAT team, hung out with a NASCAR pit crew, and watched Air Force mechanics fix Stealth bombers. Darcy's unlikely goal: to make his operation "the best supply chain in the world."

2  It's more than just a theoretical ambition. CEO Stephen W. Sanger has given Darcy an epic challenge: cut $1 billion out of General Mills' supply chain in 10 years. By getting the company into fighting trim, Sanger hopes he'll be able to dig out from under a staggering $8.9 billion in debt from his $10.1 billion acquisition of Pillsbury from Diageo PLC in 2001. That's no small task for a company with $10.5 billion in sales that has already cut hundreds of millions of dollars over the last decade.

3  Slashing costs is just one of many challenges General Mills faces. It needs to regain market share that it ceded to archrival Kellogg Co., which became the number one U.S. cereal maker last year. And it's fighting off fierce competition from Campbell Soup Co. and ConAgra Foods Inc. in canned soups and ready-to-eat meals. Says Sanger: "We can't get by doing what we did yesterday."

4  Darcy is confident that he can save $800 million of the $1 billion target by adapting lessons in efficiency learned elsewhere. But money-saving ideas from pit crews and SWAT teams? Don't laugh: He has already made considerable progress. Darcy targets groups that routinely take performance to the extreme, studying them for efficiency secrets that might benefit General Mills—either by applying those secrets directly or by jolting employees into thinking of new ways of doing their jobs. By observing how a NASCAR pit crew was able to work with blinding speed simply through better organization, General Mills was able to cut the time it took workers to change a production line at a Lodi (Calif.) factory from one Betty Crocker product to another from 4.5 hours to just 12 minutes. And by watching the way that Stealth bomber pilots and maintenance crews cooperated, the company was able to improve its own teamwork, helping to cut cereal production costs by 25 percent at a plant in Buffalo.

5  Such gains, while impressive, may represent only a fraction of what's possible for General Mills, the maker of Cheerios cereal, Betty Crocker cake mixes, and Hamburger Helper. Anand Sharma, the CEO of TBM Consulting Group Inc. in Durham, N.C., who specializes in efficiency, says the company should be able to triple its cost-cutting goals—aiming for annual productivity improvements of 15 percent and profit gains of an additional 4 percent by aggressively applying what it learns. Moreover, experts say that seeking inspiration outside one's industry, as General Mills is doing, is the only way to leapfrog ahead of rivals. "Given how efficient many organizations have become, the next big idea won't come from internal thinking," says Ravin Jesuthasan, principal at Towers Perrin's reward and performance management consulting practice in Chicago. "It has got to come from revolutionary, outside-the-box thinking."

6  But even with all of General Mills' efforts to borrow management ideas from the unlikeliest of places, reaching the $1 billion savings goal won't be easy. Companies like General Mills, which has been cutting costs for years, may find future efficiency gains harder to come by.

7  And while Darcy believes the benefits from his excursions outside the cereal biz are real, some are impossible to measure. For example, the SWAT team's cooperative approach to nabbing fugitives inspired General Mills to replace separate performance goals for engineering, purchasing, and production with a single set of goals for all departments, eliminating the incentive for one department to cut corners at another's expense. Darcy cites a purchasing manager who met

cost-cutting goals under the old system by buying thinner cartons—even though they jammed up the production lines, raising manufacturing costs. Gross margins have improved in the four years since the new incentives were implemented—from 44 percent to 47 percent—but it's unclear how much of the improvement can be attributed to the change.

8    Finally, not all the efficiency lessons that Darcy brings back from the field can be adapted throughout General Mills. While the company was able to use the NASCAR lessons to transform the Betty Crocker plant—by replacing standard bolts with those requiring only a quarter turn and stocking toolboxes with the specific gear needed to switch product lines—efforts to duplicate much of that success elsewhere failed because many plant functions were unique.

9    Darcy isn't giving up, though. Lately, he's been working with Erik Weihenmayer, a blind mountaineer who has scaled the seven greatest summits. The goal: to understand his method for assembling expedition teams based on personality traits, instead of climbing skill, insights that Darcy says will prove critical to the success of the Pillsbury integration. "The only way to cross a glacier is on a rope to which your entire team is tied," says Weihenmayer. "You either all plunge together or succeed together." Darcy and his team are betting they won't be falling into the abyss any time soon.

**Source:** "Thinking Outside the Box," *BusinessWeek,* July 28, 2003.

## Chapter 9 Discussion Case B

BusinessWeek

# Is Kohl's Coming Unbuttoned?

*Slovenly Stores and Shrewd Competition Have Hurt Sales*

1  Shopping recently at a Kohl's (KSS) store in Niles, Ill., Kimberly Rellinger can't find any boys' shorts as she digs through a jumble of misplaced items. And she gives up on the shorts idea altogether when she sees the five-person checkout line. Instead, she heads to a nearby Old Navy (GPS) where she finds what she wants with no wait. "Now I will go there first," says the 36-year-old mother of two boys.

2  Plenty of Kohl's shoppers seem to be making the same call these days. On July 10, the apparel discounter reported a 2.4 percent decline in June sales at stores open at least a year. Worse, it warned that for the first time since going public in 1992, second-quarter earnings would decline. In part, the disappointing numbers reflect growing competition from department and specialty-apparel stores. But Kohl's Corp. execs may also have lost their Midas touch: Distracted by a big expansion into California, they have misjudged inventories and relaxed once-tight control of existing operations.

3  It's quite a reversal for this '90s retail star. Until recently, it seemed the Menomonee Falls (Wis,) chain could do no wrong. Kohl's has posted 35 percent compounded annual earnings growth over the past five years. It did so with the simplest of strategies: selling casual brands at low prices. By locating its stores in strip centers, Kohl's draws shoppers who find malls inconvenient. Now, having missed sales targets for 7 of the past 9 months, Kohl's heady days may be over. "It's the first crack in the growth story," says Deutsche Bank Securities Inc. analyst Bill Dreher.

4  Nonsense, says Kohl's CEO R. Lawrence Montgomery. He attributes the weak sales to a sluggish market for apparel, which affects Kohl's more than department-store rivals because clothing makes up a higher percentage of its sales. But, he admits, the competition has "narrowed a little bit."

5  Indeed, rivals ranging from JCPenney (JCP) and Sears, Roebuck to Federated Department Stores (FD) Macy's unit have borrowed from Kohl's playbook. Like Kohl's, they made their stores easier to navigate and beefed up casual brands. Most of all, they have cut prices to counter the advantage of Kohl's locations, says Marshall Cohen, chief analyst at market-research firm NPD Group Inc. As a result, Penney, Sears, and Federated all posted better sales results than Kohl's in June. "The consumer is going back to the mail because they can get a better price with a wider variety," Cohen says.

6  Department stores aren't the only ones playing better defense. Gap (GPS) Inc.'s Old Navy unit, whose shops are often based in strip centers with Kohl's, has recently shifted from trendy teenage fashion toward clothing that appeals to mothers with children, one of Kohl's targets. On the low end, Kohl's is facing more pressure from Wal-Mart (WMT) Stores Inc., which is upping the quality of its apparel and adding national brands like Levi's. "Wal-Mart is also after the same middle-level shopper," says Patrick McKeever, an analyst at Sun Trust Robinson Humphrey Capital Markets.

7  Meanwhile, Kohl's expansion into California seems to be distracting management. The chain has opened 28 stores this year in the greater Los Angeles area, where it is encountering fierce resistance from entrenched players such as Mervyn's and Macy's West. Some analysts say the challenging expansion helps explain recent stumbles at Kohl's existing stores. While the retailer has always loaded up on inventory, this year it misjudged demand and wound up having to discount heavily, which dented profits. Shoppers also complain that stores are less well-kept and check-out lines longer than they were.

8  Most troubling, perhaps, is that sales have slipped at Kohl's most mature outlets. That raises questions about the chain's growth prospects as older stores become a larger percentage of Kohl's locations. Deutsche Bank estimates that same-store sales at outlets five years old or more have declined for the past three years. In June, Kohl's worst-performing stores were in the Midwest, home to the bulk of its older shops. Montgomery blames a weak Midwest economy and lousy weather. If he's wrong, Kohl's days of rapid growth may be behind it.

**Source:** "Is Kohl's Coming Unbuttoned?" *BusinessWeek,* July 28, 2003.

## Appendix 9

# Functional Tactics

## FUNCTIONAL TACTICS THAT IMPLEMENT BUSINESS STRATEGIES

Functional tactics are the key, routine activities that must be undertaken in each functional area—marketing, finance, production/operations, R&D, and human resource management—to provide the business's products and services. In a sense, functional tactics translate thought (grand strategy) into action designed to accomplish specific short-term objectives. Every value chain activity in a company executes functional tactics that support the business's strategy and help accomplish strategic objectives.

The next several sections will highlight key tactics around which managers can build competitive advantage and add value in each of the various functional areas.

## FUNCTIONAL TACTICS IN PRODUCTION/OPERATIONS

### Basic Issues

Production/operations management (POM) is the core function of any organization. That function converts inputs (raw materials, supplies, machines, and people) into value-enhanced output. The POM function is most easily associated with manufacturing firms, but it also applies to all other types of businesses (service and retail firms, for example). POM tactics must guide decisions regarding (1) the basic nature of the firm's POM system, seeking an optimum balance between investment input and production/operations output and (2) location, facilities design, and process planning on a short-term basis. Exhibit 9–A highlights key decision areas in which the POM tactics should provide guidance to functional personnel.

POM facility and equipment tactics involve decisions regarding plant location, size, equipment replacement, and facilities utilization that should be consistent with grand strategy and other operating strategies. In the mobile home industry, for example, the facilities and equipment tactic of Winnebago was to locate one large centralized, highly integrated production center (in Iowa) near its raw materials. On the other extreme, Fleetwood, Inc., a California-based competitor, located dispersed, decentralized production facilities near markets and emphasized maximum equipment life and less-integrated, labor-intensive production processes. Both firms are leaders in the mobile home industry, but have taken very different tactical approaches.

The interplay between computers and rapid technological advancement has made flexible manufacturing systems (FMS) a major consideration for today's POM tacticians. FMS allows managers to automatically and rapidly shift production systems to retool for different products or other steps in a manufacturing process. Changes that previously took hours or days can be done in minutes. The result is decreased labor cost, greater efficiency, and increased quality associated with computer-based precision.

Sourcing has become an increasingly important component in the POM area. Many companies now accord sourcing a separate status like any other functional area. Sourcing tactics provide guidelines about questions such as: Are the cost advantages of using only a few suppliers outweighed by the risk of overdependence? What criteria (e.g., payment requirements) should be used in selecting vendors? Which vendors can provide "just-in-time" inventory and how can the business provide it to our customers? How can operations be supported by the volume and delivery requirements of purchases?

**EXHIBIT 9–A**
**Key Functional Tactics in POM**

| Functional Tactic | Typical Questions That the Functional Tactic Should Answer |
| --- | --- |
| Facilities and equipment | How centralized should the facilities be? (One big facility or several small facilities?) |
| | How integrated should the separate processes be? |
| | To what extent should further mechanization or automation be pursued? |
| | Should size and capacity be oriented toward peak or normal operating levels? |
| Sourcing | How many sources are needed? |
| | How should suppliers be selected, and how should relationships with suppliers be managed over time? |
| | What level of forward buying (hedging) is appropriate? |
| Operations planning and control | Should work be scheduled to order or to stock? |
| | What level of inventory is appropriate? |
| | How should inventory be used (FIFO/LIFO), controlled, and replenished? |
| | What are the key foci for control efforts (quality, labor cost, downtime, product use, other)? |
| | Should maintenance efforts be oriented to prevention or to breakdown? |
| | What emphasis should be placed on job specialization? Plant safety? The use of standards? |

POM planning and control tactics involve approaches to the management of ongoing production operations and are intended to match production/operations resources with longer range, overall demand. These tactical decisions usually determine whether production/operations will be demand oriented, inventory oriented, or outsourcing oriented to seek a balance between the two extremes. Tactics in this component also address how issues like maintenance, safety, and work organization are handled. Quality control procedures are yet another focus of tactical priorities in this area.

Just-in-time (JIT) delivery, outsourcing, and statistical process control (SPC) have become prominent aspects of the way today's POM managers create tactics that build greater value and quality in their POM system. JIT delivery was initially a way to coordinate with suppliers to reduce inventory carrying costs of items needed to make products. It also became a quality control tactic because smaller inventories made quality checking easier on smaller, frequent deliveries. It has become an important aspect of supplier-customer relationships in today's best businesses.

Outsourcing, or the use of a source other than internal capacity to accomplish some task or process, has become a major operational tactic in today's downsizing-oriented firms. Outsourcing is based on the notion that strategies should be built around core competencies that add the most value in the value chain, and functions or activities that add little value or that cannot be done cost effectively should be done outside the firm—outsourced. When done well, the firm gains a supplier that provides superior quality at lower cost than it could provide itself. JIT and outsourcing have increased the strategic importance of the purchasing function. Outsourcing must include intense quality control by the buyer. ValuJet's tragic 1996 crash in the Everglades was caused by poor quality control over its outsourced maintenance providers.

The Internet and "E-commerce" have begun to revolutionize functional tactics in operations and marketing. How we sell, where we make things, how we logistically coordinate what we do, all of these basic business functions and questions have new perspectives and

ways of being addressed because of the technological impact of the globally emerging ways we link together electronically, quickly, and accurately.

## FUNCTIONAL TACTICS IN MARKETING

The role of the marketing function is to achieve the firm's objectives by bringing about the profitable sale of the business's products/services in target markets. Marketing tactics should guide sales and marketing managers in determining who will sell what, where, to whom, in what quantity, and how. Marketing tactics at a minimum should address four fundamental areas: products, price, place, and promotion. Exhibit 9–B highlights typical questions marketing tactics should address.

In addition to the basic issues raised in Exhibit 9–B, marketing tactics today must guide managers addressing the impact of the *communication revolution* and the *increased diversity* among market niches worldwide. The Internet and the accelerating blend of computers and telecommunications has facilitated instantaneous access to several places around the world. A producer of plastic kayaks in Easley, South Carolina, receives orders from somewhere in the world about every 30 minutes over the Internet without any traditional distribution structure or global advertising. It fills the order within five days without any transportation capability. Speed linked to the ability to communicate instantaneously is causing marketing tacticians to radically rethink what they need to do to remain competitive and maximize value.

Diversity has accelerated because of communication technology, logistical capability worldwide, and advancements in flexible manufacturing systems. The diversity that has resulted is a

**EXHIBIT 9–B**
**Key Functional Tactics in Marketing**

| Functional Tactic | Typical Questions That the Functional Tactic Should Answer |
| --- | --- |
| Product (or service) | Which products do we emphasize?<br>Which products/services contribute most to profitability?<br>What product/service image do we seek to project?<br>What consumer needs does the product/service seek to meet?<br>What changes should be influencing our customer orientation? |
| Price | Are we competing primarily on price?<br>Can we offer discounts or other pricing modifications?<br>Are our pricing policies standard nationally, or is there regional control?<br>What price segments are we targeting (high, medium, low, and so on)?<br>What is the gross profit margin?<br>Do we emphasize cost/demand or competition-oriented pricing? |
| Place | What level of market coverage is necessary?<br>Are there priority geographic areas?<br>What are the key channels of distribution?<br>What are the channel objectives, structure, and management?<br>Should the marketing managers change their degree of reliance on distributors, sales reps, and direct selling?<br>What sales organization do we want?<br>Is the sales force organized around territory, market, or product? |
| Promotion | What are the key promotion priorities and approaches?<br>Which advertising/communication priorities and approaches are linked to different products, markets, and territories?<br>Which media would be most consistent with the total marketing strategy? |

virtual explosion of market niches, adaptations of products to serve hundreds of distinct and diverse customer segments that would previously have been served with more mass-market, generic products or services. Where firms used to rely on volume associated with mass markets to lower costs, they now encounter smaller niche players carving out subsegments they can serve more timely *and* more cost effectively. These new, smaller players lack the bureaucracy and committee approach that burdens the larger firms. They make decisions, outsource, incorporate product modifications, and make other agile adjustments to niche market needs before their larger competitors get through the first phase of committee-based decision making. Jack Welch, the CEO of General Electric, commented on this recently with the editors of *BusinessWeek:*

> Size is no longer the trump card it once was in today's brutally competitive world marketplace— a marketplace that is unimpressed with logos and sales numbers but demands, instead, value and performance. At GE we're trying to get that small-company soul—and small-company speed— inside our big-company body. Faster products, faster product cycles to market. Better response time. New niches, Satisfying customers, getting faster communications, moving with more agility, all these are easier when one is small. All these are essential to succeed in the diverse, fast-moving global environment.

## FUNCTIONAL TACTICS IN ACCOUNTING AND FINANCE

While most functional tactics guide implementation in the immediate future, the time frame for functional tactics in the area of finance varies, because these tactics direct the use of financial resources in support of the business strategy, long-term goals, and annual objectives. Financial tactics with longer time perspectives guide financial managers in long-term capital investment, debt financing, dividend allocation, and leveraging. Financial tactics designed to manage working capital and short-term assets have a more immediate focus. Exhibit 9–C highlights some key questions that financial tactics must answer.

## EXHIBIT 9–C
**Key Functional Tactics in Finance and Accounting**

Source: From Terence P. Pare, "A New Tool for Managing Costs," Fortune, June 14, 1993, pp. 124–129. Copyright © 1993 Time Inc. All rights reserved.

| Functional Tactic | Typical Questions That the Functional Tactics Should Answer |
|---|---|
| Capital acquisition | What is an acceptable cost of capital? |
| | What is the desired proportion of short- and long-term debt? Preferred and common equity? |
| | What balance is desired between internal and external funding? |
| | What risk and ownership restrictions are appropriate? |
| | What level and forms of leasing should be used? |
| Capital allocation | What are the priorities for capital allocation projects? |
| | On what basis should the final selection of projects be made? |
| | What level of capital allocation can be made by operating managers without higher approval? |
| Dividend and working capital management | What portion of earnings should be paid out as dividends? |
| | How important is dividend stability? |
| | Are things other than cash appropriate as dividends? |
| | What are the cash flow requirements? The minimum and maximum cash balances? |
| | How liberal/conservative should the credit policies be? |
| | What limits, payment terms, and collection procedures are necessary? |
| | What payment timing and procedure should be followed? |

Accounting managers have seen their need to contribute value increasingly scrutinized. Traditional expectations centered around financial accounting; reporting requirements from bank and SEC entities and tax law compliance remain areas in which actions are dictated by outside governance. Managerial accounting, where managers are responsible for keeping records of costs and the use of funds within their company, has taken on increased strategic significance in the last decade. This change has involved two tactical areas: (1) how to account for costs of creating and providing their business's products and services, and (2) valuing the business, particularly among publicly traded companies.

Managerial cost accounting has traditionally provided information for managers using cost categories like those shown on the left side below. However, value chain advocates have been increasingly successful getting managers to seek activity-based cost accounting information like that shown on the right side below. In so doing, accounting is becoming a more critical, relevant source of information that truly benefits strategic management.

| Traditional Cost Accounting In a Purchasing Department | | Activity-Based Cost Accounting in the Same Purchasing Department | |
|---|---|---|---|
| Wages and salaries | $350,000 | Evaluate supplier capabilities | $135,750 |
| Employee benefits | 115,000 | Process purchase orders | 82,100 |
| Supplies | 6,500 | Expedite supplier deliveries | 23,500 |
| Travel | 2,400 | Expedite internal processing | 15,840 |
| Depreciation | 17,000 | Check quality of items purchased | 94,300 |
| Other fixed charges | 124,000 | Check incoming deliveries against purchase orders | 48,450 |
| Miscellaneous operating expenses | 25,250 | Resolve problems | 110,000 |
| | | Internal administration | 130,210 |
| | $640,150 | | $640,150 |

Source: Adapted from information in Terence P. Paré, "A New Tool for Managing Costs," *Fortune*, June 14, 1993, pp. 124–29. *Fortune*, © 1993, Time, Inc. All rights reserved.

## FUNCTIONAL TACTICS IN RESEARCH AND DEVELOPMENT

With the increasing rate of technological change in most competitive industries, research and development (R&D) has assumed a key strategic role in many firms. In the technology-intensive computer and pharmaceutical industries, for example, firms typically spend between 4 and 6 percent of their sales dollars on R&D. In other industries, such as the hotel/motel and construction industries, R&D spending is less than 1 percent of sales. Thus, functional R&D tactics may be more critical instruments of the business strategy in some industries than in others.

Exhibit 9–D illustrates the types of questions addressed by R&D tactics. First, R&D tactics should clarify whether basic research or product development research will be emphasized. Several major oil companies now have solar energy subsidiaries in which basic research is emphasized, while the smaller oil companies emphasize product development research.

The choice of emphasis between basic research and product development also involves the time horizon for R&D efforts. Should these efforts be focused on the near term or the long term? The solar energy subsidiaries of the major oil companies have long-term per-

**EXHIBIT 9–D**
**Key Functional Tactics in R&D**

| R&D Decision Area | Typical Questions That the Functional Tactics Should Answer |
| --- | --- |
| Basic research versus product and process development | To what extent should innovation and breakthrough research be emphasized? In relation to the emphasis on product development, refinement, and modification? |
| | What critical operating processes need R&D attention? |
| | What new projects are necessary to support growth? |
| Time horizon | Is the emphasis short term or long term? |
| | Which orientation best supports the business strategy? The marketing and production strategy? |
| Organizational fit | Should R&D be done in-house or contracted out? |
| | Should R&D be centralized or decentralized? |
| | What should be the relationship between the R&D units and product managers? Marketing managers? Production managers? |
| Basic R&D posture | Should the firm maintain an offensive posture, seeking to lead innovation in its industry? |
| | Should the firm adopt a defensive posture, responding to the innovations of its competitors? |

spectives, while the smaller oil companies focus on creating products now in order to establish a competitive niche in the growing solar industry.

R&D tactics also involve organization of the R&D function. For example, should R&D work be conducted solely within the firm, or should portions of that work be contracted out? A closely related issue is whether R&D should be centralized or decentralized. What emphasis should be placed on process R&D versus product R&D?

Decisions on all of the above questions are influenced by the firm's R&D posture, which can be offensive or defensive, or both. If that posture is offensive, as is true for small high-technology firms, the firm will emphasize technological innovation and new product development as the basis for its future success. This orientation entails high risks (and high payoffs) and demands considerable technological skill, forecasting expertise, and the ability to quickly transform innovations into commercial products.

A defensive R&D posture emphasizes product modification and the ability to copy or acquire new technology. Converse Shoes is a good example of a firm with such an R&D posture. Faced with the massive R&D budgets of Nike and Reebok, Converse placed R&D emphasis on bolstering the product life cycle of its prime products (particularly canvas shoes).

Large companies with some degree of technological leadership often use a combination of offensive and defensive R&D strategy. GE in the electrical industry, IBM in the computer industry, and Du Pont in the chemical industry all have a defensive R&D posture for currently available products *and* an offensive R&D posture in basic, long-term research.

## FUNCTIONAL TACTICS IN HUMAN RESOURCE MANAGEMENT (HRM)

The strategic importance of HRM tactics received widespread endorsement in the 1990s. HRM tactics aid long-term success in the development of managerial talent and competent employees; the creation of systems to manage compensation or regulatory concerns; and

**EXHIBIT 9–E**
**Key Functional Tactics in HRM**

| Functional Tactic | Typical Questions That HRM Tactics Should Answer |
|---|---|
| Recruitment, selection, and orientation | What key human resources are needed to support the chosen strategy? |
| | How do we recruit these human resources? |
| | How sophisticated should our selection process be? |
| | How should we introduce new employees to the organization? |
| Career development and training | What are our future human resource needs? |
| | How can we prepare our people to meet these needs? |
| | How can we help our people develop? |
| Compensation | What levels of pay are appropriate for the tasks we require? |
| | How can we motivate and retain good people? |
| | How should we interpret our payment, incentive, benefit, and seniority policies? |
| Evaluation, discipline, and control | How often should we evaluate our people? Formally or informally? |
| | What disciplinary steps should we take to deal with poor performance or inappropriate behavior? |
| | In what ways should we "control" individual and group performance? |
| Labor relations and equal opportunity requirements | How can we maximize labor-management cooperation? |
| | How do our personnel practices affect women/minorities? Should we have hiring policies? |

guiding the effective utilization of human resources to achieve both the firm's short-term objectives and employees' satisfaction and development. HRM tactics are helpful in the areas shown in Exhibit 9–E. The recruitment, selection, and orientation should establish the basic parameters for bringing new people into a firm and adapting them to "the way things are done" in the firm. The career development and training component should guide the action that personnel takes to meet the future human resources needs of the overall business strategy. Merrill Lynch, a major brokerage firm whose long-term corporate strategy is to become a diversified financial service institution, has moved into such areas as investment banking, consumer credit, and venture capital. In support of its long-term objectives, it has incorporated extensive early-career training and ongoing career development programs to meet its expanding need for personnel with multiple competencies. Larger organizations need HRM tactics that guide decisions regarding labor relations; EEOC requirements; and employee compensation, discipline, and control.

Current trends in HRM parallel the reorientation of managerial accounting by looking at their cost structure anew. HRM's "paradigm shift" involves looking at people expense as an investment in human capital. This involves looking at the business's value chain and the "value" of human resource components along the various links in that chain. One of the results of this shift in perspective has been the downsizing and outsourcing phenomena of the last quarter century. While this has been traumatic for millions of employees in companies worldwide, its underlying basis involves an effort to examine the use of "human capital" to create value in ways that maximize the human contribution. This scrutiny continues to challenge the HRM area to include recent major trends to outsource some or all HRM activities not regarded as part of a firm's core competence. The emerging implications for human re-

source management tactics may be a value-oriented perspective on the role of human re-sources in a business's value chain as suggested below.

| Traditional HRM Ideas | Emerging HRM Ideas |
| --- | --- |
| Emphasis solely on physical skills | Emphasis on total contribution to the firm |
| Expectation of predictable, repetitious behavior | Expectation of innovative and creative behavior |
| Comfort with stability and conformity | Tolerance of ambiguity and change |
| Avoidance of responsibility and decision making | Accepting responsibility for making decisions |
| Training covering only specific tasks | Open-ended commitment; broad continuous development |
| Emphasis placed on outcomes and results | Emphasis placed on processes and means |
| High concern for quantity and throughput | High concern for total customer value |
| Concern for individual efficiency | Concern for overall effectiveness |
| Functional and subfunctional specialization | Cross-functional integration |
| Labor force seen as unnecessary expense | Labor force seen as critical investment |
| Workforce is management's adversary | Management and workforce are partners |

**Source:** A. Miller, *Strategic Management*, p. 400. © 2002 by McGraw-Hill, Inc. Reproduced with the permission of The McGraw-Hill Companies.

To summarize, functional tactics reflect how each major activity of a firm contributes to the implementation of the business strategy. The specificity of functional tactics and the in-volvement of operating managers in their development help ensure understanding of and commitment to the chosen strategy. A related step in implementation is the development of policies that empower operating managers and their subordinates to make decisions and to act autonomously.

# Chapter **Ten**

# Implementing Strategy: Structure, Leadership, and Culture

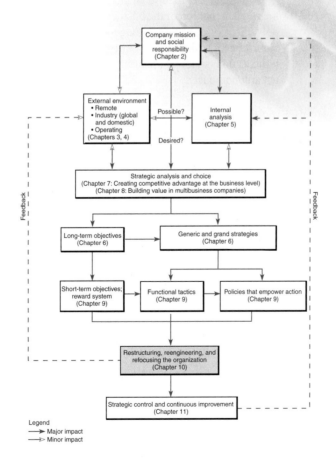

Company mission and social responsibility (Chapter 2)

External environment
• Remote
• Industry (global and domestic)
• Operating
(Chapters 3, 4)

Possible?

Internal analysis (Chapter 5)

Desired?

Strategic analysis and choice
(Chapter 7: Creating competitive advantage at the business level)
(Chapter 8: Building value in multibusiness companies)

Long-term objectives (Chapter 6)

Generic and grand strategies (Chapter 6)

Short-term objectives; reward system (Chapter 9)

Functional tactics (Chapter 9)

Policies that empower action (Chapter 9)

Restructuring, reengineering, and refocusing the organization (Chapter 10)

Strategic control and continuous improvement (Chapter 11)

Feedback

Feedback

Legend
→ Major impact
⇢ Minor impact

Until this point in the strategic management process, managers have maintained a decidedly market-oriented focus as they formulate strategies and begin implementation through action plans detailing the tactics and actions that will be taken in each functional activity. Now the process takes an organizational focus—getting the work of the business done efficiently and effectively so as to make the strategy work. What is the best way to organize ourselves to accomplish the mission? Where should leadership come from? What values should guide our activities each day? What should this organization and its people be like? These are some of the fundamental issues managers face as they turn to the heart of strategy implementation.

While the focus is internal, the firm must still consider external factors as well. The intense competition in today's global marketplace has led most companies to consider their structure, or how the activities within their business are conducted, with an unprecedented attentiveness to what that marketplace—customers, competitors, suppliers, distribution partners—suggests or needs from the "internal" organization. This chapter explores three basic "levers" through which managers can implement strategy. The first lever is structure—the basic way the firm's different activities are organized. Second is leadership, encompassing the need to establish direction, embrace change and build a team to execute the strategy. The third lever is culture—the shared values that create the norms of individual behavior and the tone of the organization.

Consider the situation new CEO Carly Fiorina faced at Hewlett Packard in the midst of a global recession. The unfortunate reality for her: HP's lumbering organization was losing touch with its global customers. Her response: As illustrated in Exhibit 10–1, Strategy in Action, Fiorina immediately dismantled the decentralized structure honed throughout HP's 64-year history. Pre-Fiorina, HP was a collection of 83 independently run units, each focused on a product such as scanners or security software. Fiorina collapsed those into four sprawling organizations. One so-called back-end unit develops and builds computers, and another focuses on printers and imaging equipment. The back-end divisions hand products off to two "front-end" sales and marketing groups that peddle the wares—one to consumers, the other to corporations. The theory: The new structure would boost collaboration, giving sales and marketing execs a direct pipeline to engineers so products are developed from the ground up to solve customer problems. This was the first time a company with thousands of product lines and scores of businesses attempted a front-back approach, a structure that requires laser focus and superb coordination.

Fiorina believed she had little choice lest the company experience a near-death experience like Xerox or, ten years earlier, IBM. The conundrum: how to put the full force of the company behind winning in its immediate fiercely competitive technology business when they must also cook up brand-new megamarkets? It's a riddle Fiorina said she could solve only by sweeping structural change that would ready HP for the next stage of the technology revolution, when companies latch on to the Internet to transform their operations. At its core lay a conviction that HP must become "ambidextrous" excelling at short-term execution while pursuing long-term visions that create new markets. In addition to changing HP's structure, Fiorina also sought to revamp its culture of creativity. Her plan for unleashing a new culture of creativity was what she called "inventing at the intersection." Until 2001, HP made stand-alone products and innovations from $20 ink cartridges to $3 million servers. To revolutionize HP's culture and approach, she launched three "cross-company initiatives"—wireless services, digital imaging, and printing—the first formal effort to get all of HP's separate and sometimes warring "tribes" working together.

Will it work? You are in the position of using hindsight to find out. Regardless, she earned high marks for zeroing in on HP's core problems and for having the courage to tackle them head-on. And, if it did, the then 46-year-old CEO would become a twenty-first century management hero for a reinvigorated HP becoming a blueprint for others trying to transform major technology companies into twenty-first century dynamos. Said Stanford

## The New HP

When Fiorina arrived at HP, the company was a confederation of 83 autonomous product units reporting through four groups. She radically revamped the structure into two "back-end" divisions—one developing printers, scanners, and the like, and the other computers. These report to "front-end" groups that market and sell HP's wares. Here's how the overhaul stacks up:

## The Old HP
Each product unit was responsible for its own profit/loss performance

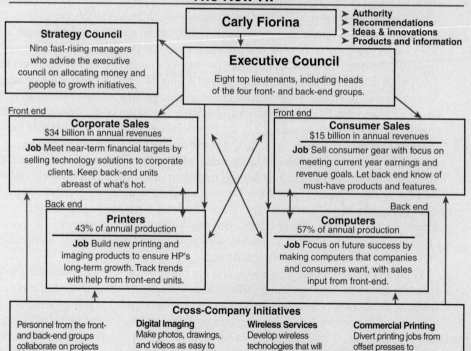

**The New HP**

Carly Fiorina

➤ Authority
➤ Recommendations
➤ Ideas & innovations
➤ Products and information

**Strategy Council**
Nine fast-rising managers who advise the executive council on allocating money and people to growth initiatives.

**Executive Council**
Eight top lieutenants, including heads of the four front- and back-end groups.

**Front end**
**Corporate Sales**
$34 billion in annual revenues
**Job** Meet near-term financial targets by selling technology solutions to corporate clients. Keep back-end units abreast of what's hot.

**Front end**
**Consumer Sales**
$15 billion in annual revenues
**Job** Sell consumer gear with focus on meeting current year earnings and revenue goals. Let back end know of must-have products and features.

**Back end**
**Printers**
43% of annual production
**Job** Build new printing and imaging products to ensure HP's long-term growth. Track trends with help from front-end units.

**Back end**
**Computers**
57% of annual production
**Job** Focus on future success by making computers that companies and consumers want, with sales input from front-end.

**Cross-Company Initiatives**

Personnel from the front- and back-end groups collaborate on projects aimed at sniffing out new markets that will create growth.

**Digital Imaging**
Make photos, drawings, and videos as easy to create, store, and send as e-mail.

**Wireless Services**
Develop wireless technologies that will fuel sales of HP-made devices, ranging from handhelds to servers.

**Commercial Printing**
Divert printing jobs from offset presses to Net-linked HP printers.

## The Assessment

### Benefits

**Happier Customers** Clients should find HP easier to deal with, since they'll work with just one account team.

**Sales Boost** HP should maximize its selling opportunities because account reps will sell all HP products, not just those from one division.

**Real Solutions** HP can sell its products in combination as "solutions"—instead of just PCs or printers—to companies facing e-business problems.

**Financial Flexibility** With all corporate sales under one roof, HP can measure the total value of a customer, allowing reps to discount some products and still maximize profits on the overall contract.

### Risks

**Overwhelmed with duties** With so many products being made and sold by just four units, HP execs have more on their plates and could miss the details that keep products competitive

**Poorer Execution** When product managers oversaw everything from manufacturing to sales, they could respond quickly to changes. That will be harder with front- and back-end groups synching their plans only every few weeks.

**Less Accountability** Profit-and-loss responsibility is shared between the front- and back-end groups so no one person is on the hot seat. Finger-pointing and foot-dragging could replace HP's collegial cooperation.

**Fewer Spending Controls** With powerful division chiefs keeping a tight rein on the purse strings, spending rarely got out of hand in the old HP. In the fourth quarter, expenses soared as those lines of command broke down.

**EXHIBIT 10–2**
**What a Difference a Century Can Make**

Source: "21st Century Corporation," *BusinessWeek*, August 28, 2000.

**Contrasting views of the corporation:**

| Characteristic | 20th Century | 21st Century |
|---|---|---|
| ORGANIZATION | The Pyramid | The Web or Network |
| FOCUS | Internal | External |
| STYLE | Structured | Flexible |
| SOURCE OF STRENGTH | Stability | Change |
| STRUCTURE | Self-sufficiency | Interdependencies |
| RESOURCES | Atoms—physical assets | Bits—information |
| OPERATIONS | Vertical integration | Virtual integration |
| PRODUCTS | Mass production | Mass customization |
| REACH | Domestic | Global |
| FINANCIALS | Quarterly | Real-time |
| INVENTORIES | Months | Hours |
| STRATEGY | Top-down | Bottom-up |
| LEADERSHIP | Dogmatic | Inspirational |
| WORKERS | Employees | Employees and free agents |
| JOB EXPECTATIONS | Security | Personal growth |
| MOTIVATION | To compete | To build |
| IMPROVEMENTS | Incremental | Revolutionary |
| QUALITY | Affordable best | No compromise |

professor Robert Burgelman at the time, "there isn't a major technology company in the world that has solved the problem she's trying to address, and we're all going to learn from her experience."[1]

What CEO Fiorina faced, and Professor Burgelman recognizes, is the vast difference between business organizations of the twentieth century and those of today. Exhibit 10–2 compares both on 18 different characteristics. The contrasts are striking, perhaps most so for leaders and managers faced with implementing strategies within them.

Fiorina offers a courageous example of a leader who recognized these compelling differences in the HP of the twentieth century and what the HP of the twenty-first century needed to be. And her decision to adopt a laserlike focus on three key "levers" within HP to attempt to make HP's strategy successful are reflected in the focus of this chapter. Her first lever was HP's *organizational structure,* which was so important from her point of view that, without major change, would mean a partial or complete failure of HP. Her second concern was *leadership,* both from herself and key managers throughout HP. Finally, she knew that the HP *culture,* in this case birth of a new one, was the third critical lever with which to make the new HP vision and strategy have a chance for success.

# STRUCTURING AN EFFECTIVE ORGANIZATION

Exhibit 10–2 offers a useful starting point in examining effective organizational structure. In contrasting twentieth century and twenty-first century corporations on different characteristics, it offers a historical or evolutionary perspective on organizational attributes associated with successful strategy execution today and just a few years ago. Successful organization once required an internal focus, structured interaction, self-sufficiency, a top-down approach. Today and tomorrow, organizational structure reflects an external focus,

---

[1] "The Radical," *BusinessWeek,* February 19, 2001.

flexible interaction, interdependency, and a bottom-up approach, just to mention a few characteristics associated with strategy execution and success. Three fundamental trends are driving decisions about effective organizational structures in the twenty-first century: globalization, the Internet, and speed of decision making.

***Globalization*** The earlier example at Hewlett-Packard showed CEO Fiorina facing a desperate truth: HP's cumbersome organization was losing touch with its global customers. So she radically reorganized HP in part so multinational clients could go to just one sales and marketing group to buy everything from ink cartridges to supercomputers, in Buffalo or Bangkok. Over two-thirds of all industry either operates globally (e.g., computers, aerospace) or will soon do so. In the last ten years, the percentage of sales from outside the home market for these five companies grew dramatically:

|                  | 1995  | 2000  | 2005  |
|------------------|-------|-------|-------|
| General Electric | 16.5% | 35.1% | 41.7% |
| Wal-Mart         | 0.0   | 18.8  | 32.2  |
| McDonald's       | 46.9  | 65.5  | 71.8  |
| Nokia            | 85.0  | 98.6  | 99.1  |
| Toyota           | 44.6  | 53.5  | 61.2  |

The need for global coordination and innovation is forcing constant experimentation and adjustment to get the right mix of local initiative, information flow, leadership, and corporate culture. At Swedish-based Ericsson, top managers scrutinize compensation schemes to make managers pay attention to global performance and avoid turf battles, while also attending to their local operations. Companies like Dutch electronics giant Philips regularly move headquarters for different businesses to the hottest regions for new trends—the "high voltage" markets. Its digital set-top box is now in California, its audio business moved from Europe to Hong Kong.[2]

Global once meant selling goods in overseas markets. Next was locating operations in numerous countries. Today it will call on talents and resources wherever they can be found around the globe, just as it now sells worldwide. It may be based in the United States, do its software programming in New Delhi, its engineering in Germany, and its manufacturing in Indonesia. The ramifications for organizational structures are revolutionary.

***The Internet*** The Net gives everyone in the organization, or working with it, from the lowest clerk to the CEO to any supplier or customer, the ability to access a vast array of information—instantaneously, from anywhere. Ideas, requests, instructions zap around the globe in the blink of an eye. It allows the global enterprise with different functions, offices, and activities dispersed around the world to be seamlessly connected so that far-flung customers, employees, and suppliers can work together in real time. The result—coordination, communication and decision-making functions accomplished through and the purpose for traditional organizational structures become slow, inefficient, noncompetitive weights on today's organization.

***Speed*** Technology, or digitization, means removing human minds and hands from an organization's most routine tasks and replacing them with computers and networks. Digitizing everything from employee benefits to accounts receivable to product design cuts cost,

---

[2] "See the World, Erase Its Borders," *BusinessWeek*, August 28, 2000.

time, and payroll resulting in cost savings and vast improvements in speed. "Combined with the Internet, the speed of actions, deliberations, and information will increase dramatically," says Intel's Andy Grove. "You are going to see unbelievable speed and efficiencies," says Cisco's John Chambers, "with many companies about to increase productivity 20 percent to 40 percent per year." Leading-edge technologies will enable employees throughout the organization to seize opportunity as it arises. These technologies will allow employees, suppliers, and freelancers anywhere in the world to converse in numerous languages online without need for a translator to develop markets, new products, new processes. Again, the ramifications for organizational structures are revolutionary.

Whether technology assisted or not, globalization of business activity creates a potential sheer velocity of decisions that must be made which challenges traditional hierarchial organizational structures. A company like Cisco, for example, may be negotiating 50–60 alliances at one time due to the nature of its diverse operations. The speed at which these negotiations must be conducted and decisions made require a simple and accommodating organizational structure lest the opportunities may be lost.

Faced with these and other major trends, how should managers structure effective organizations? Consider these recent observations by *BusinessWeek* editors at the end of a year-long research effort asking just the same question:

> The management of multinationals used to be a neat discipline with comforting rules and knowable best practices. But globalization and the arrival of the information economy have rapidly demolished all the old precepts. The management of global companies, which must innovate simultaneously and speed information through horizontal, global-spanning networks, has become a daunting challenge. Old, rigid hierarchies are out—and flat, speedy, virtual organizations are in. Teamwork is a must and compensation schemes have to be redesigned to reward team players. But aside from that bit of wisdom, you can throw out the textbooks.
>
> CEOs will have to custom-design their organizations based on their industry, their own corporate legacy, and their key global customers—and they may have to revamp more than once to get it right. Highly admired companies such as General Electric, Hewlett-Packard, ABB Ltd., and Ericsson have already been through several organizational reincarnations in the past decade to boost global competitiveness.[3]

Our research concurs with these findings by *BusinessWeek* editors—there is no one best organizational structure. At the same time, there are several useful guidelines and approaches that help answer this question which we will now cover in the next several sections.

### Match Structure to Strategy

The recent changes at Hewlett-Packard in Exhibit 10–1, Strategy in Action, illustrate this fundamental guideline. CEO Fiorina adopted the difficult, career-risking path of creating a major new structure at HP because that new structure reflected the needs of HP's strategy for the twenty-first century. An easier alternative would have been to create a strategy compatible with the existing decentralized structure of 83 semiautonomous business units that had been in place for over half a century. While easier, however, the result would have been damaging to HP in the long run, perhaps even fatal, because strategic priorities and initiatives would have been guided by structural considerations, rather than the other way around.

---

[3] "The 21st Century Corporation," *BusinessWeek,* August 28, 2000.

The origins of this maxim come from a historical body of strategic management research[4] that examined how the evolution of a business over time and the degree of diversification from a firm's core business affected its choice of organizational structure. The primary organizational structures associated with this important research are still prevalent today—simple functional structures, geographical structures, multidivisional structures, and strategic business units.[5] Four basic conclusions were derived from this research:

1. *A single-product firm or single dominant business firm should employ a functional structure.* This structure allows for strong task focus through an emphasis on specialization and efficiency, while providing opportunity for adequate controls through centralized review and decision making.

2. *A firm in several lines of business that are somehow related should employ a multidivisional structure.* Closely related divisions should be combined into groups within this structure. When synergies (i.e., shared or linked activities) are possible within such a group, the appropriate location for staff influence and decision making is at the group level, with a lesser role for corporate-level staff. The greater the degree of diversity across the firm's businesses, the greater should be the extent to which the power of staff and decision-making authority is lodged within the divisions.

3. *A firm in several unrelated lines of business should be organized into strategic business units.* Although the strategic business unit structure resembles the multidivisional structure, there are significant differences between the two. With a strategic business unit structure, finance, accounting, planning, legal, and related activities should be centralized at the corporate office. Since there are no synergies across the firm's businesses, the corporate office serves largely as a capital allocation and control mechanism. Otherwise, its major decisions involve acquisitions and diverstitures. All operational and business-level strategic plans are delegated to the strategic business units.

4. *Early achievement of a strategy-structure fit can be a competitive advantage.* A competitive advantage is obtained by the first firm among competitors to achieve appropriate strategy-structure fit. That advantage will disappear as the firm's competitors also attain such a fit. Moreover, if the firm alters its strategy, its structure must obviously change as well. Otherwise, a loss of fit will lead to a competitive disadvantage for the firm.

These research-based guidelines were derived from twentieth century companies not yet facing the complex, dynamically changing environments we see today. So an easy conclusion would be to consider them of little use. That is not the case, however. First, the admonition to let strategy guide structure rather than the other way around is very im-

---

[4] Alfred D. Chandler, *Strategy and Structure* (Cambridge: MIT Press, 1962); Larry Wrigley, *Divisional Autonomy and Diversification,* doctoral dissertation, Harvard Business School, 1970; Richard Rumelt, "Diversification Strategy and Performance," *Strategic Management Journal* 3 (January–February 1982), pp. 359–69; Richard Rumelt, *Strategy, Structure and Economic Performance* (Boston: HBS Press, 1986). Rumelt used a similar, but more detailed classification scheme; D. A. Nathanson and J. S. Cassano, "Organization, Diversity, and Performance," *Wharton's Magazine* 6 (1982), pp. 19–26; and Christopher A. Bartlett and Sumantra Ghoshal, "Matrix Management: Not a Structure, a Frame of Mind," *Harvard Business Review* 68, no. 4 (1990), pp. 138–45; V. R. Galbraith and R. K. Kazanjian, *Strategy Implementation: Structure, Systems & Processes* (St. Paul, MN: West Publishing, 1986).
[5] Each primary structure is diagrammed and described in detail along with the advantages and disadvantages historically associated with each in an appendix to this chapter.

portant today. While seemingly simple and obvious, resistance to changing existing structures—"the way we do things around here"—continues to be a major challenge to new strategies in many organizations even today as HP again illustrates. Second, the notion that firms evolve over time from a single product/service focus to multiple products/services and markets requiring different structures is an important reality to accommodate when implementing growth strategies. Finally, many firms today have found value in multiple structures operating simultaneously in their company. People may be assigned within the company as part of a functional structure, but they work on teams or other groupings that operate outside the primary functional structure. We will explore this practice in a subsequent section, but the important point here is that while new and important hybrid organizational structures have proven essential to strategy implementation in the twenty-first century, these same "innovative" firms incorporate these "older" primary organizational structures in the fabric of their contemporary organizational structure.

### Balance the Demands for Control/Differentiation with the Need for Coordination/Integration

Specialization of work and effort allows a unit to develop greater expertise, focus, and efficiency. So it is that some organizations adopt functional, or similar structures. Their strategy depends on dividing different activities within the firm into logical, common groupings—sales, operations, administration, or geography—so that each set of activity can be done most efficiently. Control of sets of activities is at a premium. Dividing activities in this manner, sometimes called "differentiation," is an important structural decision. At the same time, these separate activities, however they are differentiated, need to be coordinated and integrated back together as a whole so the business functions effectively. Demands for control and the coordination needs differ across different types of businesses and strategic situations.

The rise of a consumer culture around the world has led brand marketers to realize they need to take a multidomestic approach to be more responsive to local preferences. Coca-Cola, for example, used to control its products rigidly from its Atlanta headquarters. But managers have found in some markets consumers thirst for more than Coke, Diet Coke, and Sprite. So Coke has altered its structure to reduce the need for control in favor of greater coordination/integration in local markets where local managers independently launch new flavored drinks. At the same time, GE, the paragon of new age organization, had altered its GE Medical Systems organization structure to allow local product managers to handle everything from product design to marketing. This emphasis on local coordination and reduced central control of product design led managers obsessed with local rivalries to design and manufacture similar products for different markets—a costly and wasteful duplication of effort. So GE reintroduced centralized control of product design, with input from a worldwide base of global managers, and their customers, resulting in the design of several single global products produced quite cost competitively to sell worldwide. GE's need for control of product design outweighed the coordination needs of locally focused product managers.[6] At the same time, GE obtained input from virtually every customer or potential customer worldwide before finalizing the product design of several initial products, suggesting that it rebalanced in favor of more control, but organizationally coordinated input from global managers and customers so as to ensure a better potential series of medical scanner for hospitals worldwide.

---

[6] See the World, Erase Its Borders," *BusinessWeek,* August 28, 2000.

### Restructure to Emphasize and Support Strategically Critical Activities

*Restructuring* has been the buzzword of global enterprise for the last 10 years. Its contemporary meaning is multifaceted. At the heart of the restructuring trend is the notion that some activities within a business's value chain are more critical to the success of the business's strategy than others. Wal-Mart's organizational structure is designed to ensure that its impressive logistics and purchasing competitive advantages operate flawlessly. Coordinating daily logistical and purchasing efficiencies among separate stores lets Wal-Mart lead the industry in profitability yet sell retail for less than many competitors buy the same merchandise at wholesale. Motorola's organizational structure is designed to protect and nurture its legendary R&D and new product development capabilities—spending over twice the industry average in R&D alone each year. Motorola's R&D emphasis continually spawns proprietary technologies that support its technology-based competitive advantage. Coca-Cola emphasizes the importance of distribution activities, advertising, and retail support to its bottlers in its organizational structure. All three of these companies emphasize very different parts of the value chain process, but they are extraordinarily successful in part because they have designed their organizational structures to emphasize and support strategically critical activities. Exhibit 10–3, Strategy in Action, provides some guidelines that should influence how an organization is structured, depending on which among five different sources of competitive advantage are emphasized in its strategy.

Two critical considerations arise when restructuring the organization to emphasize and support strategically critical activities. First, managers need to make the strategically critical activities the central building blocks for designing organization structure. Those activities should be identified and separated as much as possible into self-contained parts of the organization. Then the remaining structure must be designed so as to ensure timely integration with other parts of the organization.

While this is easily proposed, managers need to recognize that strategically relevant activities may still reside in different parts of the organization, particularly in functionally organized structures. Support activities like finance, engineering, or information processing are usually self-contained units, often outside the unit around which core competencies are built. This often results in an emphasis on departments obsessed with performing their own tasks more than emphasizing the key results (customer satisfaction, differentiation, low costs, speed) the business as a whole seeks. So the second consideration is to design the organizational structure so that it helps coordinate and integrate these support activities to (1) maximize their support of strategy-critical primary activities in the firm's value chain and (2) does so in a way to minimize the costs for support activities and the time spent on internal coordination. Managerial efforts to do this in the 1990s have placed reengineering, downsizing, and outsourcing as prominent tools for strategists restructuring their organizations.

### Reengineer Strategic Business Processes

Business process reengineering (BPR), popularized by consultants Michael Hammer and James Champy,[7] is one of the more popular methods by which organizations worldwide are undergoing restructuring efforts to remain competitive in the twenty-first century. BPR is intended to place the decision-making authority that is most relevant to the customer closer to the customer, in order to make the firm more responsive to the needs of the customer. This is accomplished through a form of empowerment, facilitated revamping organizational structure.

Business reengineering reduces fragmentation by crossing traditional departmental lines and reducing overhead to compress formerly separate steps and tasks that are strategically intertwined in the process of meeting customer needs. This "process orientation," rather than a traditional functional orientation, becomes the perspective around which various activities

---

[7] Michael Hammer and James Champy, *Reengineering the Corporation* (New York: HarperBusiness, 1993).

One of the key things business managers should keep in mind when restructuring their organizations is to devise the new structure so that it emphasizes strategically critical activities within the business's value chain. This means that the structure should allow those activities to have considerable autonomy over issues that influence their operating excellence and time-liness; they should be in a position to easily coordinate with other parts of the business—to get decisions made fast.

Below are five different types of critical activities that may be at the heart of a business's effort to build and sustain competitive advantage. Beside each one are typical conditions that will affect and shape the nature of the organization's structure:

| Potential Strategic Priority and Critical Activities | Concomitant Conditions That May Affect or Place Demands on the Organizational Structure and Operating Activities to Build Competitive Advantage |
|---|---|
| 1. Compete as low-cost provider of goods or services. | Broadens market.<br>Requires longer production runs and fewer product changes.<br>Requires special-purpose equipment and facilities. |
| 2. Compete as high-quality provider. | Often possible to obtain more profit per unit, and perhaps more total profit from a smaller volume of sales.<br>Requires more quality-assurance effort and higher operating cost.<br>Requires more precise equipment, which is more expensive.<br>Requires highly skilled workers, necessitating higher wages and greater training efforts. |
| 3. Stress customer service. | Requires broader development of servicepeople and service parts and equipment.<br>Requires rapid response to customer needs or changes in customer tastes, rapid and accurate information system, careful coordination.<br>Requires a higher inventory investment. |
| 4. Provide rapid and frequent introduction of new products. | Requires versatile equipment and people.<br>Has higher research and development costs.<br>Has high retraining costs and high tooling and changeover costs.<br>Provides lower volumes for each product and fewer opportunities for improvements due to the learning curve. |
| 5. Seek vertical integration. | Enables firm to control more of the process.<br>May not have economies of scale at some stages of process.<br>May require high capital investment as well as technology and skills beyond those currently available within the firm. |

and tasks are then grouped to create the building blocks of the organization's structure. This is usually accomplished by assembling a multifunctional, multilevel team that begins by identifying customer needs and how the customer wants to deal with the firm. Customer focus must permeate all phases. Companies that have successfully reengineered their operations around strategically critical business processes have pursued the following steps:[8]

- Develop a flowchart of the total business process, including its interfaces with other value chain activities.

[8] Judy Wade, "How to Make Reengineering Really Work," *Harvard Business Review* 71, no. 6 (November–December 1993), pp. 119–31.

- Try to simplify the process first, eliminating tasks and steps where possible and analyzing how to streamline the performance of what remains.

- Determine which parts of the process can be automated (usually those that are repetitive, time-consuming, and require little thought or decision); consider introducing advanced technologies that can be upgraded to achieve next-generation capability and provide a basis for further productivity gains down the road.

- Evaluate each activity in the process to determine whether it is strategy-critical or not. Strategy-critical activities are candidates for benchmarking to achieve best-in-industry or best-in-world performance status.

- Weigh the pros and cons of outsourcing activities that are noncritical or that contribute little to organizational capabilities and core competencies.

- Design a structure for performing the activities that remain; reorganize the personnel and groups who perform these activities into the new structure.

When asked about his networking-oriented structure that helped revitalize IBM, former IBM CEO Gerstner responded: "It's called *reengineering.* It's called *getting competitive.* It's called *reducing cycle time and cost, flattening organizations, increasing customer responsiveness.* All of these require a collaboration with the customer and with suppliers and with vendors."

### Downsize and Self-Manage: Force Decisions to Operating Level

Reengineering and a value orientation have led managers to scrutinize even further the way their organizational structures are crucial to strategy implementation. That scrutiny has led to downsizing, outsourcing, and self-management as three important themes influencing the organizational structures into the twenty-first century. *Downsizing* is eliminating the number of employees, particularly middle management, in a company. The arrival of a global marketplace, information technology, and intense competition caused many companies to reevaluate middle management activities to determine just what value was really being added to the company's products and services. The result of this scrutiny, along with continuous improvements in information processing technology, has been widespread downsizing in the number of management personnel in thousands of companies worldwide. These companies often eliminate whole levels of management. General Electric went from 400,000 to 280,000 employees in the last decade while its sales tripled and its profit rose fivefold. Former CEO Jack Welch's observations about GE's downsizing and the results of *BusinessWeek*'s survey of companies worldwide that have been actively downsizing (which attempts to extract guidelines for downsizing) are shown in Strategy in Action Exhibit 10–4.

One of the outcomes of downsizing was increased *self-management* at operating levels of the company. Cutbacks in the number of management people left those that remained with more work to do. The result was that they had to give up a good measure of control to workers, and they had to rely on those workers to help out. Spans of control, traditionally thought to maximize under 10 people, have become much larger due to information technology, running "lean and mean," and delegation to lower levels. Ameritech, one of the Baby Bells, has seen its spans of control rise to as much as 30 to 1 in some divisions because most of the people that did staff work—financial analysts, assistant managers, and so on—have disappeared. This delegation, also known as empowerment, is accomplished through concepts like self-managed work groups, reengineering, and automation. It is also seen through efforts to create distinct businesses within a business—conceiving a business

**BusinessWeek** GE used to have things like department managers, subsection managers, unit managers, supervisors. We're driving those titles out . . . We used to go from the CEO to sectors, to groups, to businesses. We now go from the CEO to businesses. Nothing else.

—Jack Welch

It's hard to find a major corporation that hasn't downsized in recent years. But simple reductions in staffing don't make for lean management. Here's a checklist, developed by *BusinessWeek* from interviews with executives and consultants, that may tell you if your company needs a diet.

| Company Characteristic | Analysis |
|---|---|
| 1. Layers of management between CEO and the shop floor. | Some companies, such as Ameritech, now have as few as four or five where as many as 12 had been common. More than six is most likely too many. |
| 2. Number of employees managed by the typical executive. | At lean companies, spans of control range up to one manager to 30 staffers. A ratio of lower than 1:10 is a warning of arterial sclerosis. |
| 3. Amount of work cut out by your downsizing. | Eliminating jobs without cutting out work can bring disaster. A downsizing should be accompanied by at least a 25 percent reduction in the number of tasks performed. Some lean companies have hit 50 percent. |
| 4. Skill levels of the surviving management group. | Managers must learn to accept more responsibility and to eliminate unneeded work. Have you taught them how? |
| 5. Size of your largest profit center by number of employees. | Break down large operating units into smaller profit centers—less than 500 employees is a popular cutoff—to gain the economies of entrepreneurship and offset the burdens of scale. |
| 6. Post-downsizing size of staff at corporate headquarters. | The largest layoffs, on a percentage basis, should be at corporate headquarters. It is often the most overstaffed—and the most removed from customers. |

**Source:** "The 21st Century Corporation," *BusinessWeek*, August 28, 2000.

as a confederation of many "small" businesses, rather than one large, interconnected business. Whatever the terminology, the idea is to push decision making down in the organization by allowing major management decisions to be made at operating levels. The result is often the elimination of up to half the levels of management previously existing in an organizational structure.

### Allow Multiple Structures to Operate Simultaneously within the Organization to Accommodate Products, Geography, Innovation and Customers

The *matrix organization* described in this chapter's Appendix was one of the early structural attempts to do this so that skills and resources could be better assigned and used within a large company. People typically had a permanent assignment to a certain organizational unit, usually a functional or staff department, yet they were also frequently assigned to work in another project or activity at the same time. For example, a product development project

**EXHIBIT 10–5**
**The Product-Team Structure**

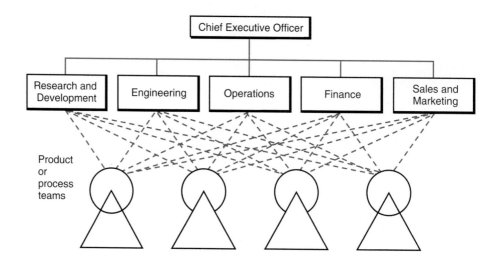

may need a market research specialist for several months and a financial analyst for a week. It was tried by many companies, and is still in use today. The dual chains of command, particularly given a temporary assignment approach, proved problematic for some organizations, particularly in an international context complicated by distance, language, time, and culture.

The *product-team structure* emerged as an alternative to the matrix approach to simplify and amplify the focus of resources on a narrow but strategically important product, project, market, customer or innovation. Exhibit 10–5 illustrates how the product-team structure looks.

The product-team structure assigns functional managers and specialists (e.g., engineering, marketing, financial, R&D, operations) to a new product, project, or process team that is empowered to make major decisions about their product. The team is usually created at the inception of the new product idea, and they stay with it indefinitely if it becomes a viable business. Instead of being assigned on a temporary basis, as in the matrix structure, team members are assigned permanently to that team in most cases. This results in much lower coordination costs and, since every function is represented, usually reduces the number of management levels above the team level needed to approve team decisions.

It appears that product teams formed at the beginning of product-development processes generate cross-functional understanding that irons out early product or process design problems. They also reduce costs associated with design, manufacturing, and marketing, while typically speeding up innovation and customer responsiveness because authority rests with the team allowing decisions to be made more quickly. That ability to make speedier, cost-saving decisions has the added advantage of eliminating the need for one or more management layers above the team level, which would traditionally have been in place to review and control these types of decisions. While seemingly obvious, it has only recently become apparent that those additional management layers were also making these decisions with less firsthand understanding of the issues involved than the cross-functional team members brought to the product or process in the first place. Exhibit 10–6, Strategy in Action, gives examples of a product-team approach at several well-known companies and some of the advantages that appear to have accrued.

### Take Advantage of Being a Virtual Organization

True twenty-first century corporations will increasingly see their structure become an elaborate network of external and internal relationships. This organizational phenomenon has been termed the *virtual organization,* which is defined as a temporary network of inde-

**BusinessWeek** Building teams is a new organization art form for Corporate America. Getting people to work together successfully has become a critical managerial skill. Those companies that learn the secrets of creating cross-functional teams are winning the battle for global market share and profits. Those that don't are losing out.

One of the most effective uses of the cross-functional teams is in the area of product development—everything from designing cars to developing new prescription drugs. This kind of teamwork not only increases efficiency but boosts innovation—the holy grail of companies hoping to produce the Next Big Thing in their industry. General Motors, for one, chalked up big wins since setting up a collaborative engineering system in 2000 that allows GM employees and external auto parts suppliers to share product design information. Previously, GM had no way of coordinating its complex designs across its 14 engineering sites scattered across the world, plus the dozens of partners who design subsystems. Now, GM's collaboration system serves as a centralized clearinghouse for all the design data. More than 16,000 designers and other workers use the new Web system from Electronic Data Systems Corp. to share 3-D designs and keep track of parts and subassemblies. The system automatically updates the master design when changes are finalized so everyone is on the same page. The result: GM has slashed the time it takes to complete a full mock-up of a car from 12 weeks to two. The time saved by online collaboration frees up workers to think more creatively—mocking up three or four more alternative designs per car.

Consider Modicon Inc., a North Andover (Massachusetts) maker of automation-control equipment with annual revenues of $300 million. Instead of viewing product development as a task of the engineering function, President Paul White defined it more broadly as a process that would involve a team of 15 managers from engineering, manufacturing, marketing, sales, and finance. By working together, Modicon's team avoided costly delays from disagreements and misunderstandings. "In the past," says White, "an engineering team would have worked on this alone with some dialogue from marketing. Manufacturing wouldn't get involved until the design was brought into the factory. Now, all the business issues are right on the table from the beginning." The change allowed Modicon to bring six software products to market in one-third the time it would normally take. The company still has a management structure organized by function. But many of the company's 900 employees are involved in up to 30 teams that span several functions and departments. Predicts White: "In five years, we'll still have some formal functional structure, but people will probably feel free enough to spend the majority of their time outside their functions."

Eastman Chemical Co., the $3.5 billion unit of Eastman Kodak Co. recently spun off as a stand-alone company, replaced several of its senior vice-presidents in charge of the key functions with "self-directed work teams." Instead of having a head of manufacturing, for example, the company uses a team consisting of all its plant managers. "It was the most dramatic change in the company's 70-year history," maintains Ernest W. Deavenport Jr., president of Eastman Chemical. "It makes people take off their organizational hats and put on their team hats. It gives people a much broader perspective and forces decision-making down at least another level." In creating the new organization, the 500 senior managers agreed that the primary role of the functions was to support Eastman's business in chemicals, plastics, fibers, and polymers. "A function does not and should not have a mission of its own," insists Deavenport. Common sense? Of course. But over the years, the functional departments had grown strong and powerful, as they have in many organizations, often at the expense of the overall company as they fought to protect and build turf. Now, virtually all of the company's managers work on at least one cross-functional team, and most work on two or more on a daily basis. For example, Tom O. Nethery, a group vice-president, runs an industrial-business group. But he also serves on three other teams that deal with such diverse issues as human resources, cellulose technology, and product-support services.

**Source:** "The New Teamwork," *BusinessWeek*, Feb. 18, 2002.

---

pendent companies—suppliers, customers, subcontractors, even competitors—linked primarily by information technology to share skills, access to markets, and costs.[9] Outsourcing along with strategic alliances are integral in making a virtual organization work. Globalization has accelerated the use of and need for the virtual organization.

*Outsourcing* was an early driving force for the virtual organization trend. Dell does not make PCs. Cisco doesn't make its world renowned routers. Motorola doesn't make cell phones. Sony makes Apple's low-end PowerBook computers. *Outsourcing* is simply obtaining

[9] W. H. Davidow and M. S. Malone, *The Virtual Corporation* (New York: Harper, 1992).

**EXHIBIT 10–7**
**General Motors: Alliances with Competitors**

**Source:** General Motors Corporation Annual Reports; "Carmakers Take Two Routes to Global Growth," *Financial Times* (July 11, 2000), p. 19.

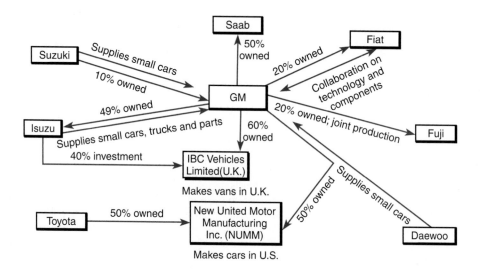

work previously done by employees inside the companies from sources outside the company. Managers have found that as they attempt to restructure their organizations, particularly if they do so from a business process orientation, numerous activities can often be found in their company that are not "strategically critical activities." This has particularly been the case of numerous staff activities and administrative control processes previously the domain of various middle management levels in an organization. But it can also refer to primary activities that are steps in their business's value chain—purchasing, shipping, making certain parts, and so on. Further scrutiny has led managers to conclude that these activities not only add little or no value to the product or services, but that they can be done much more cost effectively (and competently) by other businesses specializing in these activities. If this is so, then the business can enhance its competitive advantage by outsourcing the activities. Many organizations have outsourced information processing, various personnel activities, and production of parts that can be done better outside the company. Outsourcing, then, can be a source of competitive advantage and result in a leaner, flatter organizational structure.

*Strategic alliances,* some long-term and others for very short periods, with suppliers, partners, contractors, and other providers of world class capabilities allow partners to the alliance to focus on what they do best, farm out everything else, and quickly provide value to the customer. Engaging in alliances, whether long term or one time, lets each participant take advantage of fleeting opportunities quickly, usually without tying up vast amounts of capital. FedEx and the U.S. Postal Service have formed an alliance—FedEx planes carry USPS next-day letters and USPS delivers FedEx ground packages—to allow both to challenge their common rival, UPS. Exhibit 10–7 shows how General Motors, in its effort to become more competitive globally, has entered into numerous alliances with competitors. Cisco owns only two of 34 plants that produce its routers, and over 50 percent of all orders fulfilled by Cisco are done without a Cisco employee being involved.

***Web-Based Organizations*** As we noted at the beginning of this section, globalization has accelerated many changes in the way organizations are structured, and that is certainly the case in driving the need to become part of a virtual organization or make use of one. Technology, particularly driven by the Internet, has and will be a major driver of the virtual organization. Commenting on technology's impact on Cisco, John Chambers observed that with all its outsourcing and strategic alliances, roughly 90 percent of all orders come into Cisco without ever being touched by human hands. "To my customers, it looks like one big virtual plant where my suppliers and inventory systems are directly tied into our virtual or-

**EXHIBIT 10–8**
**From Traditional Structure to B-Web Structure**

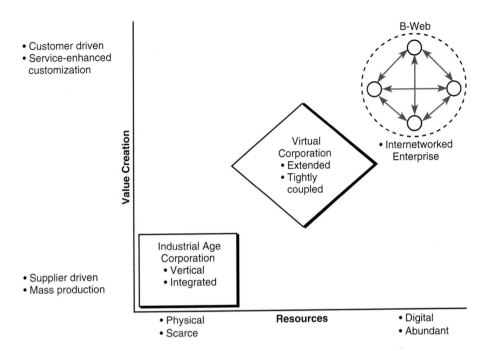

ganization," he said. "That will be the norm in the future. Everything will be completely connected, both within a company and between companies. The people who get that will have a huge competitive advantage."

The Web's contribution electronically has simultaneously become the best analogy in explaining the future virtual organization. So it is not just the Web as in the Internet, but a weblike shape of successful organizational structures in the future. If there are a pair of images that symbolize the vast changes at work, they are the pyramid and the web. The organizational chart of large-scale enterprise had long been defined as a pyramid of ever-shrinking layers leading to an omnipotent CEO at its apex. The twenty-first century corporation, in contrast, is far more likely to look like a web: a flat, intricately woven form that links partners, employees, external contractors, suppliers, and customers in various collaborations. The players will grow more and more interdependent. Fewer companies will try to master all the disciplines necessary to produce and market their goods but will instead outsource skills—from research and development to manufacturing—to outsiders who can perform those functions with greater efficiency.[10] Exhibit 10–8 illustrates this evolution in organization structure to what it calls the B-Web, a truly Internet-driven form of organization designed to deliver speed, customized service-enhanced products to savvy customers from an integrated virtual B-Web organization pulling together abundant, world-class resources digitally.

Managing this intricate network of partners, spin-off enterprises, contractors, and freelancers will be as important as managing internal operations. Indeed, it will be hard to tell the difference. All of these constituents will be directly linked in ways that will make it nearly impossible for outsiders to know where an individual firm begins and where it ends. "Companies will be much more molecular and fluid," predicts Don Tapscott, co-author of *Digital Capital*. "They will be autonomous business units connected not necessarily by a big building but across geographies all based on networks. The boundaries of the firm will be not only fluid or blurred but in some cases hard to define."[11]

[10] "The 21st Century Organization," *BusinessWeek*, August 28, 2000.
[11] Ibid.

### Remove Structural Barriers and Create a Boundaryless, Ambidextrous Learning Organization

The evolution of the virtual organizational structure as an integral mechanism managers use to implement strategy has brought with it recognition of the central role knowledge plays in this process. *Knowledge* may be in terms of operating know-how, relationships with and knowledge of customer networks, technical knowledge upon which products or processes are based or will be, relationships with key people or a certain person than can get things done quickly, and so forth. Exhibit 10–9, Strategy in Action, shares how McKinsey organizational expert Lowell Bryan sees this shaping future organizational structure with managers becoming knowledge "nodes" through which intricate networks of personal relationships—inside and outside the formal organization—are constantly coordinated to bring together relevant know-how and successful action.

Management icon Jack Welch coined the term *boundaryless* organization, to characterize what he attempted to make GE become in order for it to be able to generate knowledge, share knowledge and get knowledge to the places it could be best used to provide superior value. A key component of this concept was erasing internal divisions so the people in GE could work across functional, business, and geographic boundaries to achieve an integrated diversity—the ability to transfer the best ideas, the most developed knowledge, and the most valuable people quickly, easily, and freely throughout GE. Here is his description:

> Boundaryless behavior is the soul of today's GE . . . Simply put, people seem compelled to build layers and walls between themselves and others, and that human tendency tends to be magnified in large, old institutions like ours. These walls cramp people, inhibit creativity, waste time, restrict vision, smother dreams and above all, slow things down . . . Boundaryless behavior shows up in actions of a woman from our Appliances Business in Hong Kong helping NBC with contacts needed to develop satellite television service in Asia . . . And finally, boundaryless behavior means exploiting one of the unmatchable advantages a multibusiness GE has over almost any other company in the world. Boundaryless behavior combines 12 huge global businesses—each number one or number two in its markets—into a vast laboratory whose principal product is new ideas, coupled with a common commitment to spread them throughout the Company.
>
> —Letter to Shareholders, Jack Welch
> Chairman, General Electric Company, 1981–2001

A shift from what Subramanian Rangan calls *exploitation to exploration* indicates the growing importance of organizational structures that enable a *learning organization* to allow global companies the chance to build competitive advantage.[12] Rather than going to markets to exploit brands or for inexpensive resources, in Rangan's view, the smart ones are going global to learn. This shift in the intent of the structure, then, is to seek information, to create new competences. Demand in another part of the world could be a new product trend-setter at home. So a firm's structure needs to be organized to enable learning, to share knowledge, to create opportunities to create it. Others look to companies like 3M or Procter & Gamble that allow slack time, new product champions, manager mentors—all put in place in the structure to provide resources, support, and advocacy for cross-functional collaboration leading to innovation in new product development, the generation and use of new ideas. This perspective is similar to the boundaryless notion—accommodate the speed of change and therefore opportunity by freeing up historical constraints found in traditional organizational approaches. So having structures that emphasize coordination over control, that allow flexibility (are *ambidextrous*), that emphasize the value and importance of informal relationships

---

[12] Subramanian Rangan, *A Prism on Globalization* (Fountainebleau, FR.: INSEAD, 1999).

**BusinessWeek** Lowell Bryan, a senior partner and director at consultancy McKinsey & Co., leads McKinsey's global industries practice and is the author of *Race for the World: Strategies to Build a Great Global Firm* and *Market Unbound: Unleashing Global Capitalism.*

**Q:** How will global companies be managed in the twenty-first century?

**A:** Describing it is hard because the language of management is based on command-and-control structures and "who reports to whom." Now, the manager is more of a network operator. He is part of a country team and part of a business unit. Some companies don't even have country managers anymore.

**Q:** What is the toughest challenge in managing global companies today?

**A:** Management structures are now three-dimensional. You have to manage by geography, products, and global customers. The real issue is building networked structures between those three dimensions. That is the state of the art. It's getting away from classic power issues. Managers are becoming nodes, which are part of geographical structures and part of a business unit.

**Q:** What are the telltale questions that reflect whether a company is truly global?

**A:** CEOs should ask themselves four questions: First, how do people interact with each other: Do employees around the world know each other and communicate regularly? Second, do management processes reflect a network or an old-style hierarchy? Third, is information provided to everyone simultaneously? And fourth, is the company led from the bottom up, not the top down?

**Q:** Why do multinationals that have operated for decades in foreign markets need to overhaul their management structures?

**A:** The sheer velocity of decisions that must be made is impossible in a company depending on an old-style vertical hierarchy. Think of a company [like] Cisco that is negotiating 50 to 60 alliances at one time. The old corporate structures [can't] integrate these decisions fast enough. The CEO used to be involved in every acquisition, every alliance. Now, the role of the corporate center is different. Real business decisions move down to the level of business units.

**Q:** If there is not clear hierarchy, and managers have conflicting opinions, how does top management know when to take a decision? Doesn't that raise the risk of delay and inaction?

**A:** In the old centralized model, there was no communication. If you have multiple minds at work on a problem, the feedback is much quicker. If five managers or "nodes" in the network say something is not working right, management better sit up and take notice.

**Q:** Are there any secrets to designing a new management architecture?

**A:** Many structures will work. [H]aving the talent and capabilities you need to make a more fluid structure work [is key]. [But] it's much harder to do. The key is to create horizontal flow across silos to meet customers needs. The question is how you network across these silos. [G]etting people to work together [is paramount]. That's the revolution that is going on now.

**Q:** What is the role of the CEO?

**A:** The CEO is the architect. He puts in place the conditions to let the organization innovate. No one is smart enough to do it alone anymore. Corporate restructuring should liberate the company from the past. As you break down old formal structures, knowledge workers are the nodes or the glue that hold different parts of the company together. They are the network. Nodes are what it is all about.

**Q:** How do you evaluate performance in such a squishy system?

**A:** The role of the corporate center is to worry about talent and how people do relative to each other. Workers build a set of intangibles around who they are. If they are not compensated for their value-added, they will go somewhere else.

**Source:** *BusinessWeek*, August 28, 2000.

and interaction over formal systems, techniques, and controls are all characteristics associated with what are seen as effective structures for the twenty-first century.

### *Redefine the Role of Corporate Headquarters from Control to Support and Coordination*

The role of corporate management is multibusiness, and multinational companies increasingly face a common dilemma—how can the resource advantages of a large company be exploited, while ensuring the responsiveness and creativity found in the small companies against which each of their businesses compete? This dilemma constantly presents managers with conflicting priorities or adjustments as corporate managers:[13]

- Rigorous financial controls and reporting enable cost efficiency, resource deployment, and autonomy across different units; flexible controls are conductive to responsiveness, innovation and "boundary spanning."

- Multibusiness companies historically gain advantage by exploiting resources and capabilities across different business and markets, yet competitive advantage in the future increasingly depends on the creation of new resources and capabilities.

- Aggressive portfolio management seeking maximum shareholder value is often best achieved through independent businesses; the creation of competitive advantage increasingly requires the management—recognition and coordination—of business interdependencies.

Increasingly, globally engaged multibusiness companies are changing the role of corporate headquarters from one of control, resource allocation, and performance monitoring to one of coordinator of linkages across multiple business, supporter and enabler of innovation and synergy. One way this has been done is to create an executive council comprised of top managers from each business, usually including four to five of their key managers, with the council then serving as the critical forum for corporate decision, discussions, and analysis. Exhibit 10–1, Strategy in Action, at the beginning of this chapter showed this type of forum as central to HP's radical restructuring. GE created this approach over 20 years ago in its rise to top corporate success. These councils replace the traditional corporate staff function of overseeing and evaluating various business units, replacing it instead with a forum to share business unit plans, to discuss problems and issues, to seek assistance and expertise, and to foster cooperation and innovation.

Welch's experience at GE provides a useful example. Upon becoming chairman, he viewed GE headquarters as interfering too much in GE's various businesses, generating too much paperwork, and offering minimal value added. He sought to "turn their role 180 degrees from checker, inquisitor, and authority figure to facilitator, helper, and supporter of GE's 13 businesses." He said, "What we do here at headquarters . . . is to multiply the resources we have, the human resources, the financial resources, and the best practices . . . Our job is to help, it's to assist, it's to make these businesses stronger, to help them grow and be more powerful." GE's Corporate Executive Council was reconstituted from predominantly a corporate level group of sector managers (which was eliminated) into a group comprised of the leaders of GE's 13 businesses and a few corporate executives. They met formally two days each quarter to discuss problems and issues and to enable cooperation and resource sharing. This has expanded to other councils throughout GE intent on greater coordination, synergy, and idea sharing.

---

[13] Robert M. Grant, *Contemporary Strategy Analysis* (Oxford: Blackwell, 2001), p. 503.

# ORGANIZATIONAL LEADERSHIP

The job of leading a company has never been more demanding, and it will only get tougher in the twenty-first century. The CEO will retain ultimate authority, but the corporation will depend increasingly on the skills of the CEO and a host of subordinate leaders. The accelerated pace and complexity of business will continue to force corporations to push authority down through increasingly horizontal management structures. In the future, every line manager will have to exercise leadership's prerogatives—and bear its burdens—to an extent unthinkable 20 years ago.[14]

John Kotter, a widely recognized leadership expert, predicted this evolving role of leadership in an organization when he distinguished between management and leadership:[15]

> Management is about coping with complexity. Its practices and procedures are largely a response to one of the most significant developments of the twentieth century: the emergence of large organizations. Without good management, complex enterprises tend to become chaotic in ways that threaten their very existence. Good management brings a degree of order and consistency to key dimensions like the quality and profitability of products.
>
> Leadership, by contrast, is about coping with change. Part of the reason it has become so important in recent years is that the business world has become more competitive and more volatile. . . . The net result is that doing what was done yesterday, or doing it 5 percent better, is no longer a formula for success. Major changes are more and more necessary to survive and compete effectively in this new environment. More change always demands more leadership.

Organizational leadership, then, involves action on two fronts. The first is in guiding the organization to deal with constant change. This requires CEOs that embrace change, and that do so by clarifying strategic intent, that build their organization and shape their culture to fit with opportunities and challenges change affords. *BusinessWeek* Strategy in Action, Exhibit 10–10, provides an interview with P&G CEO Alan Lafley, who *BusinessWeek* calls "a catalyst and encourager of change," to explore Lafley's thoughts on doing these very things. The second front is in providing the management skill to cope with the ramifications of constant change. This means identifying and supplying the organization with operating managers prepared to provide operational leadership and vision as never before. Let's explore each of these five aspects to organizational leadership.

## Strategic Leadership: Embracing Change

The blending of telecommunications, computers, the Internet, and one global marketplace has increased the pace of change exponentially during the last 10 years. All business organizations are affected. Change has become an integral part of what leaders and managers deal with daily.

The leadership challenge is to galvanize commitment among people within an organization as well as stakeholders outside the organization to embrace change and implement strategies intended to position the organization to do so. Leaders galvanize commitment to embrace change through three interrelated activities: clarifying strategic intent, building an organization, and shaping organizational culture.

### Clarifying Strategic Intent

Leaders help stakeholders embrace change by setting forth a clear vision of where the business's strategy needs to take the organization. Traditionally, the concept of vision has been

---

[14] Anthony Bianco, "The New Leadership," *BusinessWeek,* August 28, 2000.
[15] John P. Kotter, "What Leaders Really Do," *Harvard Business Review,* May–June, 1990, p. 104.

**BusinessWeek** Chief Exec. A. G. Lafley says he shares his predecessor's zeal to revamp P&G. The difference is the approach. Since becoming Procter & Gamble's chief executive in June 2000, Alan G. "A.G." Lafley has led a turnaround that has defied expectations. In 2003 P&G posted a 13 percent increase in net income on 8 percent higher sales. That would bring P&G's annual compounded earnings growth rate under the three years of Lafley's leadership to 15 percent—a rate well above rivals. During that period, P&G's stock price has climbed by 58 percent, while the Standard & Poor's 500-stock index fell by 32 percent.

Less obvious than his turnaround success, however, is how Lafley is changing P&G. He's undertaking the company's most sweeping remake since it was founded in 1837. Nothing is sacred any longer at the Cincinnati-based maker of Tide, Pampers, and Crest.

Lafley has inverted the invent-it-here mentality by turning outwards for innovation. He's broadening P&G's definition of brands and how it prices goods. He's moving P&G deep into the beauty-care business with its two largest acquisitions ever, Clairol in 2001 and Wella in 2003. And he's redefining P&G's core business by outsourcing operations—like information technology and bar-soap manufacturing.

What's surprising is that at the start, Lafley was perceived as a tame pair of hands—far from a person who would conduct a radical makeover. He followed a forceful change agent, Durk Jager, who had tried to jump-start internal innovation, launching a host of new brands. Jager also criticized P&G's insular culture, which he sought to shake up. In the end, though, he overreached, as P&G missed earnings forecasts and employees bucked under his leadership.

Lafley answered some questions recently about his views on leading **change** at P&G:

**Q:** When you started, you weren't perceived as a forceful change agent like your predecessor. Yet you're making more dramatic changes. Can you discuss that?

**A:** Durk and I had believed very strongly that the company had to change and make fundamental changes in a lot of the same directions. There are two simple differences: One is I'm very externally focused. I expressed the change in the context of how we're going to serve consumers better, how we're going to win with the retailer, and how we're going to defeat the competitor in the marketplace.

The most important thing—I didn't attack. I avoided saying P&G people are bad. I thought that was a big mistake [on Jager's part]. The difference is, I preserved the core of the culture and pulled people where I wanted to go. I enrolled them in change. I didn't tell them.

**Q:** Why did you both see a need for change?

**A:** We were looking at slow growth. An inability to move quickly, to commercialize on innovation and get full advantage out of it. We were looking at new technologies that were changing competition in our industry, retailers, and the supply base. We were looking at a world that all of a sudden was going to go 24/7, and we weren't ready for that kind of world.

**Q:** Was the view on the need for change widely held within P&G?

**A:** It depends on who you ask. Without a doubt, Durk and I and a few others were in the camp of "We need a much bigger change."

a description or picture of what the company could be that accommodates the needs of all its stakeholders. The intensely competitive, rapidly changing global marketplace has refined this to be targeting a very narrowly defined strategic intent—*an articulation of a simple criterion or characterization of what the company must become to establish and sustain global leadership.* Former IBM CEO Lou Gerstner is a good example of a leader in the middle of trying to shape strategic intent. "One of the great things about this industry is that every decade or so, you get a chance to redefine the playing field," said Gerstner. "We're in that phase of redefinition right now, and winners or losers are going to emerge from it. We've got to become *the leader in 'network-centric computing.'*" It's an opportunity brought about by telecommunications-based change that will change IBM more than semiconductors did in the last decade. Said Gerstner, "I sensed there were too many people inside IBM who wanted to fight the war we lost," referring to PCs and PC software, so he aggressively instilled network-centric computing as the strategic intent for IBM in the next decade.

**Q:** Jager says he tried to change P&G too fast. What do you think about that?

**A:** I think he's right.

**Q:** Are you concerned about the same thing?

**A:** I'm worried that I will ask the organization to change ahead of its understanding, capability, and commitment, because that's a problem. I have been a catalyst of change and encourager of change and a coach of change management. And I've tried not to drive change for a sake of change.

**Q:** How do you pace change?

**A:** I have tremendous trust in my management team. I let them be the brake. I am the accelerator. I help with direction and let them make the business strategic choices.

**Q:** Did the fact that P&G was in crisis when you came in help you implement change?

**A:** It was easier. I was lucky. When you have a mess, you have a chance to make more changes.

**Q:** Jager tried to drive innovation from within. You would like P&G to ultimately get 50 percent of its ideas from outside. Why?

**A:** Durk and I both wanted more innovation. We both felt we absolutely, positively had to get more innovation. We had to get more innovation commercialized and more innovation globalized. So we were totally together.

He tried to drive it all internally. He tried to rev the R&D organization, supercharge them, and hoped that enough would come out of there that we would achieve the goals of commercializing more of it and globalizing more of it.

We got in trouble cause we pulled stuff out that was half-baked or that was never going to be successful. We hadn't developed it far enough.

The difference is that my hypothesis is that innovation and discovery are likely to come from anywhere. What P&G is really good at is developing innovations and commercializing them. So what I said is, "We need an open marketplace."

We're probably as good as the next guy at inventing. But we are not absolutely and positively better than everybody else at inventing. There are a lot of good inventors out there.

**Q:** How hard will it be to shift P&G's R&D focus outwards, given that it has historically focused inwards?

**A:** It will be a challenge, but I think we'll get there. It's like a flywheel. That first turn is really difficult. Then the second turn is a little bit easier. This has been like turning a flywheel. We will have failures. We will have to celebrate that failure.

**Q:** When you couple your outward focus on innovation with your moves toward outsourcing, it seems you're making P&G a less vertically integrated company.

**A:** I don't believe in vertical integration. I think it's a trap. I believe in horizontal networked organizations.

Our core capability is to develop and commercialize. Branding is a core capability. Customer business development is a core capability. We concluded in a lot of areas that manufacturing isn't. Therefore, I let the businesses go do more outsourcing. We concluded that running a back room wasn't a core capability. You do what you do best and can do world-class.

**Source:** "P&G: New & Improved," *BusinessWeek*, July 7, 2003.

---

Clarifying strategic intent can come in many different forms. Coca-Cola's legendary former CEO and Chairman Roberto Goizueta said, "Our company is a global business system for which we raise capital to make concentrate and sell it at an operating profit. Then we pay the cost of that capital. Shareholders pocket the difference." Coke averaged 27 percent annual return on stockholder equity for 18 years under his leadership.

Exhibit 10–10 shows how CEO Alan Lafley articulates a radically different strategic intent for the *new* P&G that involves P&G's legendary R&D focusing outward, instead of inward, and outsourcing noncore activities in a historically vertically integrated firm. While Coke and P&G are very different situations, their leaders were both very effective in shaping and clarifying strategic intent in a way that helped stakeholders understand what needed to be done.

### Building an Organization

The previous section examined alternative structures to use in designing the organization necessary to implement strategy. Leaders spend considerable time shaping and refining their organizational structure and making it function effectively to accomplish strategic intent. Since leaders are attempting to embrace change, they are often rebuilding or remaking their organization to align it with the ever-changing environment and needs of the strategy. And since embracing change often involves overcoming resistance to change, leaders find themselves addressing problems like the following as they attempt to build or rebuild their organization:

- Ensuring a common understanding about organizational priorities.

- Clarifying responsibilities among managers and organizational units.

- Empowering newer managers and pushing authority lower in the organization.

- Uncovering and remedying problems in coordination and communication across the organization.

- Gaining the personal commitment to a shared vision from managers throughout the organization.

- Keeping closely connected with "what's going on in the organization and with its customers."

Leaders do this in many ways. Larry Bossidy, Chairman of Honeywell and co-author of the best seller, *Execution*, spends 50 percent of his time each year flying to Allied Signal's various operations around the world meeting with managers and discussing decisions, results, and progress. Bill Gates at Microsoft reportedly spent two hours each day reading and sending E-mail to any of Microsoft's 36,000 employees that want to contact him. All managers adapt structures, create teams, implement systems, and otherwise generate ways to coordinate, integrate, and share information about what their organization is doing and might do. Others create customer advisory groups, supplier partnerships, R&D joint ventures, and other adjustments to build an adaptable, learning organization that embraces the leader's vision and strategic intent and the change driving the future opportunities facing the business. These, in addition to the fundamental structural guidelines described in the previous section for restructuring to support strategically critical activities, are the issues leaders constantly address as they attempt to build a supportive organization.

### Shaping Organization Culture

Leaders know well that the values and beliefs shared throughout their organization will shape how the work of the organization is done. And when attempting to embrace accelerated change, reshaping their organization's culture is an activity that occupies considerable time for most leaders. Listen to these observations by and about Ryanair CEO Michael O'Leary about competing in the increasingly competitive European airline industry and arch-rival easyJet:

> It was vintage Michael O'Leary. On May 13, the 42-year-old CEO of Dublin-based discount airline Ryanair outfitted his staff in full combat gear, drove an old World War II tank to England's Luton airport, an hour north of London, then demanded access to the base of archrival easyJet Airline Co. With the theme to the old television series The A-Team blaring, O'Leary declared he was "liberating the public from easyJet's high fares." When security—surprise!—refused to let the Ryanair armor roll in, O'Leary led the troops in his own rendition of a platoon march song: "I've been told and it's no lie. EasyJet's fares are way too high!" So it is that there are new rivals for O'Leary to conquer. "When we were a much smaller company, we compared ourselves to British Airways. But they are such a mess, most people just feel sorry for them," O'Leary says. "Now we're turning the guns on easyJet."[16]

It appears that Ryanair CEO O'Leary wanted an organizational culture that was aggressive, competitive and somewhat free-wheeling in order to take advantage of change in the

---

[16] "Ryanair Rising," *BusinessWeek,* June 2, 2003.

**BusinessWeek**

## EXPERIENCE

- Multinational Corp.—Worked with top-notch mentors in an established company with global operations. Managed a talented and fickle staff and helped tap new markets.

- Foreign Operation LLC—A stint at a subsidiary of a U.S. company, or at a foreign operation in a local market. Exposure to different cultures, conditions, and ways of doing business.

- Startup Inc.—Helped to build a business from the ground up, assisting with everything from product development to market research. Honed entrepreneurial skills.

- Major Competitor Ltd.—Scooped up by the competition and exposed to more than one corporate culture.

## EDUCATION

- Liberal Arts University—Majored in economics, but took courses in psychology (how to motivate customers and employees), foreign language (the world is a lot bigger than the 50 states), and philosophy (to seek vision and meaning in your work).

- Graduate Studies—The subject almost doesn't matter, so long as you developed your thinking and analytical skills.

## EXTRACURRICULAR

- Debating (where you learned to market ideas and think on your feet).

- Sports (where you learned discipline and teamwork).

- Volunteer work (where you learned to step outside your own narrow world to help others).

- Travel (where you learned about different cultures).

**Source:** "A Résumé for the 21st Century," *BusinessWeek*, August 28, 2000.

---

European airline industry. He did this by example, by expectations felt by his managers, and in the way decision making is approached within Ryanair.

Leaders use reward systems, symbols, and structure among other means to shape the organization's culture. Travelers' Insurance Co.'s notable turnaround was accomplished in part by changing its "hidebound" culture through a change in its agent reward system. Employees previously on salary with occasional bonuses were given rewards that involved substantial cash bonuses and stock options. Observed a customer and risk management director at drugmaker Becton Dickinson, "They're hungrier now. They want to make deals. They're different than the old, hidebound Travelers' culture."

As leaders clarify strategic intent, build an organization, and shape their organization's culture, they look to one key element to help—their management team throughout their organization. As Honeywell's Chairman Larry Bossidy candidly observed when asked about how after 42 years at General Electric, Allied Signal and now Honeywell with seemingly drab businesses he could expect exciting growth: "There's no such thing as a mature market. What we need is mature executives who can find ways to grow." Leaders look to managers they need to execute strategy as another source of leadership to accept risk and cope with the complexity that change brings about. So assignment of key managers becomes a leadership tool.

## Recruiting and Developing Talented Operational Leadership

As we noted at the beginning of this section on Organizational Leadership, the accelerated pace and complexity of business will increase pressure on corporations to push authority down in their organizations ultimately meaning that every line manager will have to exercise leadership's prerogatives to an extent unthinkable a generation earlier. They will each be global managers, change agents, strategists, motivators, strategic decision-makers, innovators, and collaborators if the business is to survive and prosper. Exhibit 10–11, Strategy in

**EXHIBIT 10–12**
**What Competencies Should Managers Possess?**

**Source:** From Ruth L. Williams and Joseph P. Cothrel, "Building Tomorrow's Leaders Today," *Strategy and Leadership*, Vol. 26, October 1997, Reprinted with permission of Emerald Group Publishing Limited.

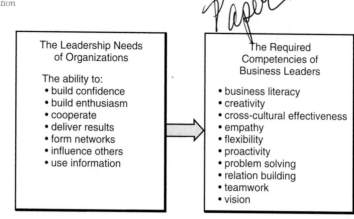

The Leadership Needs of Organizations

The ability to:
- build confidence
- build enthusiasm
- cooperate
- deliver results
- form networks
- influence others
- use information

The Required Competencies of Business Leaders

- business literacy
- creativity
- cross-cultural effectiveness
- empathy
- flexibility
- proactivity
- problem solving
- relation building
- teamwork
- vision

Action, provides an interesting perspective on this reality showing *BusinessWeek*'s version of a résumé for the typical twenty-first century operating manager every company will be looking for in today's fast-paced, global marketplace.

Today's need for fluid, learning organizations capable of rapid response, sharing, and cross-cultural synergy place incredible demands on young managers to bring important competencies to the organization. Exhibit 10–12 describes the needs organizations look to managers to meet, and then identifies the corresponding competencies managers would need to do so. Ruth Williams and Joseph Cothrel drew this conclusion in their research about competencies needed from managers in today's fast-changing business environment:[17]

> Today's competitive environment requires a different set of management competencies than we traditionally associate with the role. The balance has clearly shifted from attributes traditionally thought of as masculine (strong decision making, leading the troops, driving strategy, waging competitive battle) to more feminine qualities (listening, relationship-building, and nurturing). The model today is not so much "take it on your shoulders" as it is to "create the environment that will enable others to carry part of the burden." The focus is on unlocking the organization's human asset potential.

Researcher David Goleman addressed the question of what types of personality attributes generate the type of competencies described in Exhibit 10–12. His research suggested that a set of four characteristics commonly referred to as emotional intelligence play a key role in bringing the competencies needed from today's desirable manager:[18]

- *Self-awareness* in terms of the ability to read and understand one's emotions and assess one's strengths and weaknesses, underlain by the confidence that stems from positive self-worth.

- *Self-management* in terms of control, integrity, conscientiousness, initiative, and achievement orientation.

- *Social awareness* in relation to sensing others' emotions (empathy), reading the organization (organizational awareness), and recognizing customers' needs (service orientation).

- *Social skills* in relation to influencing and inspiring others; communicating, collaborating, and building relationships with others; and managing change and conflict.

---

[17] Ruth Williams and Joseph Cothrel, "Building Tomorrow's Leaders Today," *Strategy and Leadership* 26 (September–October 1997), p. 21.
[18] D. Goleman, "What Makes a Leader?," *Harvard Business Review* (November–December 1998), pp. 93–102.

**EXHIBIT 10–13**

**Management Processes and Levels of Management**

**Source:** C. A. Bartlett and S. Ghoshal, "The Myth of the General Manager: New Personal Competencies for New Management Roles," *California Management Review* 40 (Fall 1997); R. M. Grant, *Contemporary Strategy Analysis* (Oxford: Blackwell, 2001), p. 529.

| | | |
|---|---|---|
| Attracting resources and capabilities and developing the business | **RENEWAL PROCESS** Developing operating managers and supporting their activities. Maintaining organizational trust | Providing institutional leadership through shaping and embedding corporate purpose and challenging embedded assumptions |
| Managing operational interdependencies and personal networks | **INTEGRATION PROCESS** Linking skills, knowledge, and resources across units. Reconciling short-term performance and long-term ambition | Creating corporate direction. Developing and nurturing organizational values |
| Creating and pursuing opportunities. Managing continuous performance improvement | **ENTREPRENEURIAL PROCESS** Reviewing, developing, and supporting initiatives | Establishing performance standards |

| Front-Line Management | Middle Management | Top Management |
|---|---|---|

One additional perspective on the role of organizational leadership and management selection is found in the work of Bartlett and Ghoshal. Their study of several of the most successful global companies in the last decade suggests that combining flexible responsiveness with integration and innovation requires rethinking the management role and the distribution of management roles within a twenty-first century company. They see three critical management roles: the *entrepreneurial process* (decisions about opportunities to pursue and resource deployment), the *integration process* (building and deploying organizational capabilities), and the *renewal process* (shaping organizational purpose and enabling change). Traditionally viewed as the domain of top management, their research suggests that these functions need to be shared and distributed across three management levels as suggested in Exhibit 10–13.[19]

# ORGANIZATIONAL CULTURE

*Organizational culture is the set of important assumptions (often unstated) that members of an organization share in common.* Every organization has its own culture. An organization's culture is similar to an individual's personality—an intangible yet ever-present theme that provides meaning, direction, and the basis for action. In much the same way as personality influences the behavior of an individual, the shared assumptions (beliefs and values) among a firm's members influence opinions and actions within that firm.

A member of an organization can simply be aware of the organization's beliefs and values without sharing them in a personally significant way. Those beliefs and values have more personal meaning if the member views them as a guide to appropriate behavior in the organization and, therefore, complies with them. The member becomes fundamentally committed to the beliefs and values when he or she internalizes them; that is, comes to

---

[19]C. A. Barlett and S. Ghoshal, "The Myth of the General Manager: New Personal Competencies for New Management Roles," *California Management Review* 40 (Fall 1997), pp. 92–116; and "Beyond Structure to Process," *Harvard Business Review* (January–February 1995).

hold them as personal beliefs and values. In this case, the corresponding behavior is *intrinsically rewarding* for the member—the member derives personal satisfaction from his or her actions in the organization because those actions are congruent with corresponding personal beliefs and values. *Assumptions become shared assumptions through internalization among an organization's individual members.* And those shared, internalized beliefs and values shape the content and account for the strength of an organization's culture.

Leaders typically attempt to manage and create distinct cultures through a variety of ways. Some of the most common ways are as follows:

***Emphasize Key Themes or Dominant Values*** Businesses build strategies around distinct competitive advantages they possess or seek. Quality, differentiation, cost advantages, and speed are four key sources of competitive advantage. So insightful leaders nurture key themes or dominant values within their organization that reinforce competitive advantages they seek to maintain or build. Key themes or dominant values may center around wording in an advertisement. They are often found in internal company communications. They are most often found as a new vocabulary used by company personnel to explain "who we are." At Xerox, the key themes include respect for the individual and services to the customer. At Procter & Gamble (P&G), the overarching value is product quality; McDonald's uncompromising emphasis on QSCV—quality, service, cleanliness, and value—through meticulous attention to detail is legendary; Delta Airlines is driven by the "family feeling" theme, which builds a team spirit and nurtures each employee's cooperative attitude toward others, cheerful outlook toward life, and pride in a job well done. Du Pont's safety orientation—a report of every accident must be on the chairman's desk within 24 hours—has resulted in a safety record that was 17 times better than the chemical industry average and 68 times better than the all-manufacturing average.

***Encourage Dissemination of Stories and Legends about Core Values*** Companies with strong cultures are enthusiastic collectors and tellers of stories, anecdotes, and legends in support of basic beliefs. Frito-Lay's zealous emphasis on customer service is reflected in frequent stories about potato chip route salespeople who have slogged through sleet, mud, hail, snow, and rain to uphold the 99.5 percent service level to customers in which the entire company takes great pride. Milliken (a textile leader) holds "sharing" rallies once every quarter at which teams from all over the company swap success stories and ideas. Typically, more than 100 teams make five-minute presentations over a two-day period. Every rally is designed around a major theme, such as quality, cost reduction, or customer service. No criticisms are allowed, and awards are given to reinforce this institutionalized approach to storytelling. L. L. Bean tells customer service stories; 3M tells innovation stories; P&G, Johnson & Johnson, IBM, and Maytag tell quality stories. These stories are very important in developing an organizational culture, because organization members identify strongly with them and come to share the beliefs and values they support.

***Institutionalize Practices That Systematically Reinforce Desired Beliefs and Values*** Companies with strong cultures are clear on what their beliefs and values need to be and take the process of shaping those beliefs and values very seriously. Most important, the values these companies espouse undergird the strategies they employ. For example, McDonald's has a yearly contest to determine the best hamburger cooker in its chain. First, there is a competition to determine the best hamburger cooker in each store; next, the store winners compete in regional championships; finally, the regional winners compete in the "All-American" contest. The winners, who are widely publicized throughout the company, get trophies and All-American patches to wear on their McDonald's uniforms.

***Adapt Some Very Common Themes in Their Own Unique Ways*** The most typical beliefs that shape organizational culture include (1) a belief in being the best (or, as at GE, "better than the best"); (2) a belief in superior quality and service; (3) a belief in the importance of people as individuals and a faith in their ability to make a strong contribution; (4) a belief in the importance of the details of execution, the nuts and bolts of doing the job well; (5) a belief that customers should reign supreme; (6) a belief in inspiring people to do their best, whatever their ability; (7) a belief in the importance of informal communication; and (8) a belief that growth and profits are essential to a company's well-being. Every company implements these beliefs differently (to fit its particular situation), and every company's values are the handiwork of one or two legendary figures in leadership positions. Accordingly, every company has a distinct culture that it believes no other company can copy successfully. And in companies with strong cultures, managers and workers either accept the norms of the culture or opt out from the culture and leave the company.

The stronger a company's culture and the more that culture is directed toward customers and markets, the less the company uses policy manuals, organization charts, and detailed rules and procedures to enforce discipline and norms. The reason is that the guiding values inherent in the culture convey in crystal-clear fashion what everybody is supposed to do in most situations. Poorly performing companies often have strong cultures. However, their cultures are dysfunctional, being focused on internal politics or operating by the numbers as opposed to emphasizing customers and the people who make and sell the product.

### Managing Organizational Culture in a Global Organization[20]

The reality of today's global organizations is that organizational culture must recognize cultural diversity. *Social norms* create differences across national boundaries that influence how people interact, read personal cues, and otherwise interrelate socially. *Values* and *attitudes* about similar circumstances also vary from country to country. Where individualism is central to a North American's value structure, the needs of the group dominate the value structure of their Japanese counterparts. *Religion* is yet another source of cultural differences. Holidays, practices, and belief structures differ in very fundamental ways that must be taken into account as one attempts to shape organizational culture in a global setting. Finally, *education,* or ways people are accustomed to learning, differ across national borders. Formal classroom learning in the United States may teach things that are only learned via apprenticeship in other cultures. Since the process of shaping an organizational culture often involves considerable "education," leaders should be sensitive to global differences in approaches to education to make sure their cultural education efforts are effective. The discussion case on Procter & Gamble at the end of this chapter provides some relevant examples of how CEO Alan Lafley is trying to radically alter P&G's organization's culture.

### Managing the Strategy-Culture Relationship

Managers find it difficult to think through the relationship between a firm's culture and the critical factors on which strategy depends. They quickly recognize, however, that key components of the firm—structure, staff, systems, people, style—influence the ways in which key managerial tasks are executed and how critical management relationships are formed. And implementation of a new strategy is largely concerned with adjustments in these components to accommodate the perceived needs of the strategy. Consequently,

---

[20] Differing backgrounds, often referred to as *cultural diversity,* is something that most managers will certainly see more of, both because of the growing cultural diversity domestically and the obvious diversification of cultural backgrounds that result from global acquisitions and mergers. For example, Harold Epps, manager of DEC's computer keyboard plant in Boston, manages 350 employees representing 44 countries of origin and 19 languages.

**EXHIBIT 10–14**
**Managing the Strategy-Culture Relationship**

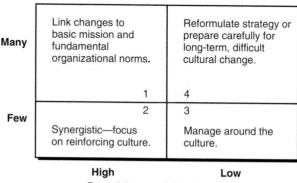

Changes in key organizational factors that are necessary to implement the new strategy

**Many**

| | |
|---|---|
| Link changes to basic mission and fundamental organizational norms.<br><br>1 | Reformulate strategy or prepare carefully for long-term, difficult cultural change.<br><br>4 |
| 2<br><br>Synergistic—focus on reinforcing culture. | 3<br><br>Manage around the culture. |

**Few**

**High**          **Low**

Potential compatibility of changes with existing culture

managing the strategy-culture relationship requires sensitivity to the interaction between the changes necessary to implement the new strategy and the compatibility or "fit" between those changes and the firm's culture. Exhibit 10–14 provides a simple framework for managing the strategy-culture relationship by identifying four basic situations a firm might face.

### Link to Mission

A firm in cell 1 is faced with a situation in which implementing a new strategy requires several changes in structure, systems, managerial assignments, operating procedures, or other fundamental aspects of the firm. However, most of the changes are potentially compatible with the existing organizational culture. Firms in this situation usually have a tradition of effective performance and are either seeking to take advantage of a major opportunity or are attempting to redirect major product-market operations consistent with proven core capabilities. Such firms are in a very promising position: They can pursue a strategy requiring major changes but still benefit from the power of cultural reinforcement.

Four basic considerations should be emphasized by firms seeking to manage a strategy-culture relationship in this context. First, *key changes should be visibly linked to the basic company mission.* Since the company mission provides a broad official foundation for the organizational culture, top executives should use all available internal and external forums to reinforce the message that the changes are inextricably linked to it. Second, *emphasis should be placed on the use of existing personnel* where possible to fill positions created to implement the new strategy. Existing personnel embody the shared values and norms that help ensure cultural compatibility as major changes are implemented. Third, *care should be taken if adjustments in the reward system are needed.* These adjustments should be consistent with the current reward system. If, for example, a new product-market thrust requires significant changes in the way sales are made, and, therefore, in incentive compensation, common themes (e.g., incentive oriented) should be emphasized. In this way, current and future reward approaches are related and the changes in the reward system are justified (encourage development of less familiar markets). Fourth, *key attention should be paid to the changes that are least compatible with the current culture,* so current norms are not disrupted. For example, a firm may choose to subcontract an important step in a production process because that step would be incompatible with the current culture.

IBM's strategy in entering the Internet-based market is an illustration. Serving this radically different market required numerous organizational changes. To maintain maximum compatibility with its existing culture while doing so, IBM went to considerable public and internal effort to link its new Internet focus with its long-standing mission. Numerous messages relating the network-centric computing to IBM's tradition of top-quality service appeared on television and in magazines, and every IBM manager was encouraged to go online. Where feasible, IBM personnel were used to fill the new positions created to implement the strategy. But because the software requirements were not compatible with IBM's current operations, virtually all of its initial efforts were linked to newly acquired Lotus Notes Software.

### Maximize Synergy

A firm in cell 2 needs only a few organizational changes to implement its new strategy, and those changes are potentially quite compatible with its current culture. A firm in this situation should emphasize two broad themes: (1) *take advantage of the situation to reinforce and solidify the current culture* and (2) *use this time of relative stability to remove organizational roadblocks to the desired culture.* Holiday Inns' move into casino gambling required a few major organizational changes. Holiday Inns saw casinos as resort locations requiring lodging, dining, and gambling/entertainment services. It only had to incorporate gambling/entertainment expertise into its management team, which was already capable of managing the lodging and dining requirements of casino (or any other) resort locations. It successfully inculcated this single major change by selling the change internally as completely compatible with its mission of providing high-quality accommodations for business and leisure travelers. The resignation of Roy Clymer, its CEO, removed an organizational roadblock, legitimizing a culture that placed its highest priority on quality service to the middle-to-upper-income business traveler, rather than a culture that placed its highest priority on family-oriented service. The latter priority was fast disappearing from Holiday Inns' culture, with the encouragement of most of the firm's top management, but its disappearance had not yet been fully sanctioned because of Clymer's personal beliefs. His voluntary departure helped solidify the new values that top management wanted.

### Manage around the Culture

A firm in cell 3 must make a few major organizational changes to implement its new strategy, but these changes are potentially inconsistent with the firm's current organizational culture. The critical question for a firm in this situation is whether it can make the changes with a reasonable chance of success.

A firm can manage around the culture in various ways: create a separate firm or division; use task forces, teams, or program coordinators; subcontract; bring in an outsider; or sell out. These are a few of the available options, but the key idea is to create a method of achieving the change desired that avoids confronting the incompatible cultural norms. As cultural resistance diminishes, the change may be absorbed into the firm.

In the Southeast, Rich's was a highly successful, quality-oriented department store chain that served higher income customers in several southeastern locations. With Wal-Mart and Kmart experiencing rapid growth in the sale of mid- to low-priced merchandise, Rich's decided to serve this market as well. Finding such merchandise inconsistent with the successful values and norms of its traditional business, it created a separate business called Richway to tap this growth area in retailing. Through a new store network, it was able to *manage around its culture.* Both Rich's and Richway experienced solid regional success, though their cultures are radically different in some respects.

### Reformulate the Strategy or Culture

A firm in cell 4 faces the most difficult challenge in managing the strategy-culture relationship. To implement its new strategy, such a firm must make organizational changes

# Strategy in Action
To Fix a Business, Change the Culture

## Exhibit 10–15

*Thomas Charlton, president and CEO of software outfit TIDAL, fits the latter category. As he tells it, the company was going nowhere when he stepped up from his former job as vice-president for sales to helm the entire business, which is based in Mountain View, Calif., and produces job-scheduling software that manages business processes in large corporate data systems. BusinessWeek Online invited Charlton to explain the challenges he faced, the steps he took to meet them, and the end result: the fastest-growing independent software vendor in the job-scheduling market.*

The date was May 15, 2000. I was the 33-year-old vice-president of sales for a privately held software company in Silicon Valley. The company had received an initial round of funding and I'd been hired to substantially increase revenues after 17 years of flat growth, and expand the sales organization from a staff of four tele-salespeople. Within 18 months of overhauling sales, our team had grown to almost two-dozen presales and account executives, and five regional offices. Revenues for the company more than doubled.

While my task had been accomplished I saw significant challenges ahead for TIDAL Software. The marketing department erroneously positioned the core product for a niche market, eliminating a huge source of prospects. The vice-president of development was reluctant to make simple changes to the product, even though it would result in winning large competitive deals. The CEO was not providing direction, and TIDAL's board of directors had lost confidence in the management team. And, although revenues had doubled, the infrastructure was growing faster than product sales. TIDAL was losing approximately $800,000 per quarter. We were in desperate need of cash to survive.

### STAY OR GO?

Moreover, the dot-com explosion was in full swing and sales-executive positions were plentiful. I was left with a few options: resign, grab one of the dot-com "dangling carrots" and retire in six months—or remain at TIDAL and watch a sinking ship.

The third choice was to make a radical proposal to the board that, if they turned control of the company over to me, we would grow revenues in record time. My recommendation came with one proviso: jettison the executive staff.

By my observation, TIDAL employees had a tremendous commitment to see the company succeed: Our flagship product could easily compete among the larger vendors. Our developers were capable of programming new features in record time and expanding the product line. The intrepid sales reps were unwilling to take "no" for an answer. Senior management, however, wasn't providing the proper mentoring to train and mobilize their teams and sustain the company's growth.

The problem was overwhelmingly a cultural one.

### HEADS ROLL

So, on that Monday in May, after receiving board support for taking operational control of the company and initiating a growth plan, the management team was removed . . . all managers in every department, with the exception of sales.

That afternoon, I faced the 40 remaining employees, who had invested a lot of time and energy in the company. I told them that it was up to us as a group of individuals to pull together as a team if we wanted to enjoy some of the Silicon Valley dream. I asked for their commitment over the next 12 months, with the option of evaluating my performance every 30 days. Except for one unplanned turnover no one left the entire year.

Once the foundation was laid, I chose an employee from each department to represent the company and meet with me to create and execute a turn-around plan. Together we engendered a renewed sense of pride for TIDAL. As the new president and CEO, I established the following rules of engagement for fostering a new culture and growing the company:

- Build trust upon reorganizing the company.

- Enlist the support and alignment of remaining employees, and prove my ability to lead.

- Establish a new performance-based culture.

- Instill in each employee that their value to the company is measured by their individual contribution to the organization. Personal relationships are secondary to the needs of the team's objective.

- Get employees very busy with projects that focus on the future and don't give them time to bemoan the past.

---

that are incompatible with its current, usually entrenched, values and norms. A firm in this situation faces the complex, expensive, and often long-term challenge of changing its culture; it is a challenge that borders on impossible. Exhibit 10–15, Strategy in Action, describes how 33-year-old Thomas Charlton transformed a 17-year-old Silicon Valley software vendor into the fastest-growing job-scheduling software vendor by radically changing its culture.

- Pick team leaders from each department and get them engaged with their teams in the success and growth of TIDAL.

- Have each employee set individual goals and objectives for his or her department that contributes to the overall revenue goals.

- Make sure each and every employee knows what the quarterly revenue goals are and knows what his or her specific role is in achieving those goals.

- Instill the belief that the entire company closes the sale—in other words, deals get done because every employee contributes his or her specific, measurable value to the sales process. Even tech-support personnel bring in sales leads.

- Learn more from direct interactions, rather than through hearsay, by inviting people to communicate openly and honestly with their managers and the executive team.

- Get employees to focus on the big picture by creating a safe structure where they have permission to communicate grievances, suggestions, etc. to their managers, with impunity.

- Encourage employees to take risks.

- Be a student and a teacher. Accept the wisdom of others, including frontline staff.

- Treat every employee as a solid contributor and encourage feedback, knowing they can see what the CEO can't always see. They may know what the CEO doesn't.

- Challenge employees and give them the opportunity to show conviction and commitment to the company's success. Test their mettle and turn employees into warriors who fight for the company.

- Understand how management style affects the bottom line.

- Put managers through rigorous training with quarterly training updates and evaluations.

- As employees helped TIDAL grow and become successful, they developed and grew themselves.

- By establishing a culture where people are encouraged to take risks in support of the company's success they experience their own personal growth and development.

- Find out why you're struggling. Don't just look to your own brain for the answer.

- Speak to Board members, employees and managers, and read the words of successful business leaders, don't just rely on your own intuition.

As the new culture supplanted the old, we set and achieved our business goals and were able to generate a second round of funding. Some of the results below include:

- TIDAL went from losing $800,000 per quarter to breaking even in three quarters. Instead of raising capital at a low valuation, the company sold its way out of debt.

- Revenues grew from $9.6 million to $14.7 million in the year following the restructuring, an increase of 67 percent.

- Overall, TIDAL revenues have increased 400 percent over the last three years.

- TIDAL raised $12 million in second-round funding from JP Morgan Partners.

- TIDAL moved from ranking one of 29 vendors to being a "Visionary" in [tech research outfit] Gartner's Magic Quadrant. It was also ranked the fastest-growing independent software vendor, and fourth by Gartner behind industry behemoths IBM, Computer Associates, and BMC.

- TIDAL is one of the only vendors to innovate in this space, with a whole-product strategy built around a new automation paradigm—event-driven scheduling.

These results were made possible by the 100 employees at TIDAL who embraced the new vision, direction, and culture, which they brought forth as a team. As CEO, I set the stage for them to perform.

**Source:** "To Fix a Business, Change the Culture," *BusinessWeek Online*, June 18, 2002.

When a strategy requires massive organizational change and engenders cultural resistance, a firm should determine whether reformulation of the strategy is appropriate. Are all of the organizational changes really necessary? Is there any real expectation that the changes will be acceptable and successful? If these answers are yes, then massive changes in management personnel are often necessary. AT&T offered early retirement to over 20,000 managers as part of a massive recreation of its culture to go along with major strategic changes in recent years. If the answer to these questions is no, the firm might reformulate its strategic plan so as to make it more consistent with established organizational norms and practices.

Merrill Lynch faced the challenge of strategy-culture incompatibility in the last decade. Seeking to remain number one in the newly deregulated financial services industry, it chose to pursue a product development strategy in its brokerage business. Under this strategy, Merrill Lynch would sell a broader range of investment products to a more diverse customer base and would integrate other financial services, such as real estate sales, into the Merrill Lynch organization. The new strategy could succeed only if Merrill Lynch's traditionally service-oriented brokerage network became sales and marketing oriented. Initial efforts to implement the strategy generated substantial resistance from Merrill Lynch's highly successful brokerage network. The strategy was fundamentally inconsistent with long-standing cultural norms at Merrill Lynch that emphasized personalized service and very close broker-client relationships. Merrill Lynch ultimately divested its real estate operation, reintroduced specialists that supported broker/retailers, and refocused its brokers more narrowly on basic client investment needs.

## Summary

This chapter examined the idea that a key aspect of implementing a strategy is the *institutionalization* of the strategy so it permeates daily decisions and actions in a manner consistent with long-term strategic success. The "recipe" that binds strategy and organization involves three key ingredients: *organizational structure, leadership,* and *culture.*

Five fundamental organizational structures were examined, and the advantages and disadvantages of each were identified. Institutionalizing a strategy requires a good strategy-structure fit. This chapter dealt with how this requirement often is overlooked until performance becomes inadequate and then indicated the conditions under which the various structures would be appropriate.

Organizational leadership is essential to effective strategy implementation. The CEO plays a critical role in this regard. Assignment of key managers, particularly within the top-management team, is an important aspect of organizational leadership. Deciding whether to promote insiders or hire outsiders is often a central leadership issue in strategy implementation. This chapter showed how this decision could be made in a manner that would best institutionalize the new strategy.

Organizational culture has been recognized as a pervasive influence on organizational life. Organizational culture, which is the shared beliefs and values of an organization's members, may be a major help or hindrance to strategy implementation. This chapter discussed an approach to managing the strategy-culture fit. It identified four fundamentally different strategy-culture situations and provided recommendations for managing the strategy-culture fit in each of these situations.

The chapter concluded with an examination of structure, leadership, and culture for twenty-first century companies. Networked organizations, with intense customer focus, and alliances are keys to success. Talent-focused acquisitions, success sharing, and leaders as coaches round out the future success scenario.

## Questions for Discussion

1. What key structural considerations must be incorporated into strategy implementation? Why does structural change often lag behind a change in strategy?

2. Which organizational structure is most appropriate for successful strategy implementation? Explain how state of development affects your answer.

3. Why is leadership an important element in strategy implementation? Find an example in a major business periodical of the CEO's key role in strategy implementation.

4. Under what conditions would it be more appropriate to fill a key management position with someone from outside the firm when a qualified insider is available?

5. What is organizational culture? Why is it important? Explain two different situations a firm might face in managing the strategy-culture relationship.

## Chapter 10 Discussion Case

# P&G: New and Improved

*How A. G. Lafley Is Revolutionizing a Bastion of Corporate Conservatism*

1  It's Mother's Day, and Alan G. "A.G." Lafley, chief executive of Procter & Gamble Co., is meeting with the person he shares time with every Sunday evening—Richard L. Antoine, the company's head of human resources. Lafley doesn't invite the chief financial officer of the $43 billion business, nor does he ask the executive in charge of marketing at the world's largest consumer-products company. He doesn't invite friends over to watch *The Sopranos,* either. No, on most Sunday nights it's just Lafley, Antoine, and stacks of reports on the performance of the company's 200 most senior executives. This is the boss's signature gesture. It shows his determination to nurture talent and serves notice that little escapes his attention. If you worked for P&G, you would have to be both impressed and slightly intimidated by that kind of diligence.

2  On this May evening, the two executives sit at the dining-room table in Antoine's Cincinnati home hashing over the work of a manager who distinguished himself on one major assignment but hasn't quite lived up to that since. "We need to get him in a position where we can stretch him," Lafley says. Then he rises from his chair and stands next to Antoine to peer more closely at a spreadsheet detailing P&G's seven management layers. Lafley points to one group while tapping an empty water bottle against his leg. "It's not being felt strongly enough in the middle of the company," he says in his slightly high-pitched voice. "They don't feel the hot breath of the consumer."

3  If they don't feel it yet, they will. Lafley, who took over when Durk I. Jager was pressured to resign in June, 2000, is in the midst of engineering a remarkable turnaround. The first thing Lafley told his managers when he took the job was just what they wanted to hear: Focus on what you do well—selling the company's major brands such as Tide, Pampers, and Crest—instead of trying to develop the next big thing.

4  Now, those old reliable products have gained so much market share that they are again the envy of the industry. So is the company's stock price, which has climbed 58 percent, to $92 a share, since Lafley started, while the Standard & Poor's 500-stock index has declined 32 percent. Banc of America analyst William H. Steele forecasts that P&G's profits for its current fiscal year, which ended June 30, will rise by 13 percent, to $5.57 billion, on an 8 percent increase in sales, to $43.23 billion. That exceeds most rivals. Volume growth has averaged 7 percent over the past six quarters, excluding acquisitions, well above Lafley's goal and the industry average.

5  The conventional thinking is that the soft-spoken Lafley was exactly the antidote P&G needed after Jager. After all, Jager had charged into office determined to rip apart P&G's insular culture and remake it from the bottom up. Instead of pushing P&G to excel, however, the torrent of proclamations and initiatives during Jager's 17-month reign nearly brought the venerable company to a grinding halt.

6  Enter Lafley. A 23-year P&G veteran, he wasn't supposed to bring fundamental change; he was asked simply to restore the company's equilibrium. In fact, he came in warning that Jager had tried to implement too many changes too quickly (which Jager readily admits now). Since then, the mild-mannered 56-year-old chief executive has worked to revive both urgency and hope: urgency because, in the previous 15 years, P&G had developed exactly one successful new brand, the Swiffer dust mop; and hope because, after Jager, employees needed reassurance that the old ways still had value. Clearly, Lafley has undone the damage at P&G.

7  What's less obvious is that, in his quiet way, Lafley has proved to be even more of a revolutionary than the flamboyant Jager. Lafley is leading the most sweeping transformation of the company since it was founded by William Procter and James Gamble in 1837 as a maker of soap and candles. Long before he became CEO, Lafley had been pondering how to make P&G relevant in the twenty-first century, when speed and agility would matter more than heft. As president of North American operations, he even spoke with Jager about the need to remake the company.

8  So how has Lafley succeeded where Jager so spectacularly failed? In a word, style. Where Jager was gruff, Lafley is soothing. Where Jager bullied, Lafley persuades. He listens more than he talks. He is living proof that the messenger is just as important as the message. As he says, "I'm not a screamer, not a yeller. But don't get confused by my style. I am very

decisive." Or as Robert A. McDonald, president of P&G's global fabric and home-care division, says, "people want to follow him. I frankly love him like my brother."

9  Indeed, Lafley's charm offensive has so disarmed most P&Gers that he has been able to change the company profoundly. He is responsible for P&G's largest acquisitions ever, buying Clairol in 2001 for $5 billion and agreeing to purchase Germany's Wella in March for a price that now reaches $7 billion. He has replaced more than half of the company's top 30 officers, more than any P&G boss in memory, and cut 9,600 jobs. And he has moved more women into senior positions. Lafley skipped over 78 general managers with more seniority to name 42-year-old Deborah A. Henretta to head P&G's then-troubled North American baby-care division. "The speed at which A. G. has gotten results is five years ahead of the time I expected," says Scott Cook, founder of software maker Intuit (INTU) Inc., who joined P&G's board shortly after Lafley's appointment.

10  Still, the Lafley revolution is far from over. Precisely because of his achievements, Lafley is now under enormous pressure to return P&G to what it considers its rightful place in Corporate America: a company that is admired, imitated, and uncommonly profitable. Nowhere are those expectations more apparent than on the second floor of headquarters, where three former chief executives still keep offices. John Pepper, a popular former boss who returned briefly as chairman when Jager left but gave up the post to Lafley last year, leans forward in his chair as he says: "It's now clear to me that A. G. is going to be one of the great CEOs in this company's history."

---

**OUTSOURCING** If it's not a core function, the new P&G won't do it. Info tech and bar-soap manufacturing have already been contracted out. Other jobs will follow.

**ACQUISITIONS** Not everything has to be invented in company labs. Lafley wants half of all new-product ideas to come from the outside.

**BUILDING STAFF** Managers are under much closer scrutiny, as Lafley scans the ranks for the best and the brightest and singles them out for development.

**BRAND EXPANSION** The Crest line now includes an electric toothbrush and tooth-whitening products along with toothpaste. Lafley is making similar moves elsewhere.

**PRICING** P&G isn't just the premium-priced brand. It will go to the lower end if that's where opportunity lies.

---

11  But here's the rub: What Lafley envisions may be far more radical than what Pepper has in mind. Consider a confidential memo that circulated among P&G's top brass in late 2001 and angered Pepper for its audacity. It argued that P&G could be cut to 25,000 employees, a quarter of its current size. Acknowledging the memo, Lafley admits: "It terrified our organization."

12  Lafley didn't write the infamous memo, but he may as well have. It reflects the central tenet of his vision—that P&G should do only what it does best, nothing more. Lafley wants a more outwardly focused, flexible company. That has implications for every facet of the business, from manufacturing to innovation. For example, in April he turned over all bar-soap manufacturing, including Ivory, P&G's oldest surviving brand, to a Canadian contractor. In May, he outsourced P&G's information-technology operation to Hewlett-Packard Co.

13  No bastion has been more challenged than P&G's research and development operations. Lafley has confronted head-on the stubbornly held notion that everything must be invented within P&G, asserting that half of its new products should come from the outside. (P&G now gets about 20 percent of its ideas externally—up from about 10 percent when he took over.) "He's absolutely breaking many well-set molds at P&G," says eBay (EBAY) Inc.'s CEO, Margaret C. "Meg" Whitman, whom Lafley appointed to the board.

14  Lafley's quest to remake P&G could still come to grief. As any scientist will attest, buying innovation is tricky. Picking the winners from other labs is notoriously difficult and often expensive. And P&G will remain uncomfortably reliant on Wal-Mart (WMT) Stores Inc., which accounts for nearly a fifth of its sales. Lafley is looking to pharmaceuticals and beauty care for growth, where the margins are high but where P&G has considerably less experience than rivals.

15  The biggest risk, though, is that Lafley will lose the P&Gers themselves. Theirs is a culture famously resistant to new ideas. To call the company insular may not do it justice. Employees aren't kidding when they say they're a family. They often start out there and grow up together at P&G, which only promotes from within. Cincinnati itself is a small town: Employees live near one another, they go to the same health clubs and restaurants. They are today's company men and women—and proud of it.

16  Lafley is well aware of his predicament. On a June evening, as he sits on the patio behind his home, he

muses about just that. The house, which resembles a Tuscan villa and overlooks the Ohio River and downtown Cincinnati, is infused with P&G history. Lafley bought it from former CEO John G. Smale three years before he was named chief executive. A black-and-gold stray cat the family feeds sits a few feet away and watches Lafley as he sips a Beck's beer. The clouds threaten rain. "I am worried that I will ask the organization to change ahead of its understanding, capability, and commitment," Lafley admits.

17    For most of its 166 years, P&G was one of America's preeminent companies. Its brands are icons: It launched Tide in 1946 and Pampers, the first disposable diaper, in 1961. Its marketing was innovative: In the 1880s, P&G was one of the first companies to advertise nationally. Fifty years later, P&G invented the soap opera by sponsoring the *Ma Perkins* radio show and, later, *Guiding Light.*

**P&G Famous Firsts**

**1931**

Promotion department manager and future CEO Neil McElroy creates modern theory of **brand management.**

**1960**

P&G wins **American Dental Assn.** approval of Crest as an effective cavity fighter.

**1961**

The company launches Pampers, **the first disposable diaper.**

**1986**

Pert Plus, **the first shampoo conditioner combination**, is unveiled.

18    Its management techniques, meanwhile, became the gold standard: In the 1930s, P&G developed the idea of brand management—setting up marketing teams for each brand and urging them to compete against each other. P&G has long been the business world's finest training ground. General Electric (GE) Co.'s Jeffrey R. Immelt and 3M (MMM) W. James McNerney Jr. both started out on Ivory. Meg Whitman and Steven M. Case were in toilet goods, while Steven A. Ballmer was an assistant product manager for Duncan Hines cake mix, among other goods. They, of course, went on to lead eBay, AOL Time Warner (AOL), and Microsoft.

19    But by the 1990s, P&G was in danger of becoming another Eastman Kodak (EK) Co. or Xerox (XRX) Corp., a once-great company that had lost its way. Sales on most of its 18 top brands were slowing; the company was being outhustled by more focused rivals such as Kimberly-Clark (KMB) Corp. and Colgate-Palmolive (CL) Co. The only way P&G kept profits growing was by cutting costs, hardly a strategy for the long term. At the same time, the dynamics of the industry were changing as power shifted from manufacturers to massive retailers. Through all of this, much of senior management was in denial. "Nobody wanted to talk about it," Lafley says. "Without a doubt, Durk and I and a few others were in the camp of 'We need a much bigger change.'"

20    When Jager took over in January, 1999, he was hell-bent on providing just that—with disastrous results. He introduced expensive new products that never caught on while letting existing brands drift. He wanted to buy two huge pharmaceutical companies, a plan that threatened P&G's identity but never was carried out. And he put in place a companywide reorganization that left many employees perplexed and preoccupied. Soaring commodity prices, unfavorable currency trends, and a tech-crazed stock market didn't help either. At a company prized for consistent earnings, Jager missed forecasts twice in six months. In his first and last full fiscal year, earnings per share rose by just 3.5 percent instead of an estimated 13 percent. And during that time, the share price slid 52 percent, cutting P&G's total market capitalization by $85 billion. Employees and retirees hold about 20 percent of the stock. The family began to turn against its leader.

21    But Jager's greatest failing was his scorn for the family. Jager, a Dutchman who had joined P&G overseas and worked his way to corporate headquarters, pitted himself against the P&G culture, contending that it was burdensome and insufferable, says Susan E. Arnold, president of P&G's beauty and feminine care division. Some go-ahead employees even wore buttons that read "Old World/New World" to express disdain for P&G's past. "I never wore one," Arnold sneers. " 'The old Procter is bad, and the new world is good.' That didn't work."

22    On June 6, 2000, his thirtieth wedding anniversary, Lafley was in San Francisco when he received a call from Pepper, then a board member: Would he become CEO? Back in Cincinnati, a boardroom coup unprecedented in P&G's history had taken place.

23    As Lafley steps into the small study in his house three years later, a Japanese drawing on the wall

reminds him of what it was like to become CEO. The room, with its painting of a samurai warrior and red elephant-motif wallpaper, alludes to his stint running P&G's Asian operations. Bookshelves hold leather-bound volumes of Joseph Conrad and Mark Twain. A simple wooden desk faces the window. Lafley focuses on the drawing, which depicts a man caught in a spider's web; it was given to him by the elder of his two sons, Patrick. "In the first few days, you are just trying to figure out what kind of web it is," he says.

24   In a sense, Lafley had been preparing for this job his entire adult life. He never hid the fact that he wanted to run P&G one day. Or if not the company, then a company. That itself is unusual since, like almost all P&Gers, Lafley has never worked anywhere else. After graduating from Hamilton College in 1969, Lafley decided to pursue a doctorate in medieval and Renaissance history at the University of Virginia. But he dropped out in his first year to join the Navy (and avoid being drafted into the Army). He served in Japan, where he got his first experience as a merchandiser, supplying Navy retail stores. When his tour of duty ended in 1975, he enrolled in the MBA program at Harvard Business School. And from there, he went directly to Cincinnati.

25   When he was hired as a brand assistant for Joy dish detergent in 1977 at age 29; he was older than most of his colleagues and he worried that his late start might hinder his rise at P&G. Twice within a year in the early 1980s, Lafley quit. "Each time, I talked him back in only after drinking vast amounts of Drambuie," says Thomas A. Moore, his boss at the time, who now runs biotech company Biopure (BPUR) Corp. On the second occasion, then-CEO John Smale met with Lafley, who had accepted a job as a consultant in Connecticut (NIPNY). Without making any promises, Smale says he told Lafley that "we thought there was no limit on where he was going to go."

26   Sure enough, Lafley climbed quickly to head P&G's soap and detergent business, where he introduced Liquid Tide in 1984. A decade later, he was promoted to head the Asian division. Lafley returned from Kobe, Japan, to Cincinnati in 1998 to run the company's entire North American operations. To ease the transition home, he and his younger son, Alex, who was then 12, studied guitar together. Two years later, Lafley was named CEO.

27   Along the way, he developed a reputation as a boss who stepped back to give his staff plenty of responsi-

bility and helped shape decisions by asking a series of keen questions—a process he calls "peeling the onion." And he retained a certain humility. He still collects baseball cards, comic books, and rock 'n' roll 45s. Whereas some executives might have a garage full of antique cars or Harley-Davidsons (HDI); Lafley keeps two Vespa motor scooters. "People wanted him to succeed," says Virginia Lee, a former P&Ger who worked for Lafley at headquarters and overseas.

28   As CEO, Lafley hasn't made grand pronouncements on the future of P&G. Instead, he has spent an inordinate amount of time patiently communicating how he wants P&G to change. In a company famed for requiring employees to describe every new course of action in a one-page memo, Lafley's preferred approach is the slogan. For example, he felt that P&G was letting technology rather than consumer needs dictate new products. Ergo: "The consumer is boss." P&G wasn't working closely enough with retailers, the place where consumers first see the product on the shelf: "The first moment of truth." P&G wasn't concerned enough with the consumer's experience at home: "The second moment of truth."

29   Lafley uses these phrases constantly, and they are echoed throughout the organization. At the end of a three-day leadership seminar, 30 young marketing managers from around the world present what they have learned to Lafley. First on the list: "We are the voice of the consumer within P&G, and they are the heart of all we do." Lafley, dressed in a suit, sits on a stool in front of the group and beams. "I love the first one," he laughs as the room erupts in applause.

30   When he talks about his choice of words later, Lafley is a tad self-conscious. "It's *Sesame Street* language—I admit that," he says. "A lot of what we have done is make things simple because the difficulty is making sure everybody knows what the goal is and how to get there."

31   Lafley has also mastered the art of the symbolic gesture. The eleventh floor at corporate headquarters had been the redoubt of senior executives since the 1950s. Lafley did away with it, moving all five division presidents to the same floors as their staff. Then he turned some of the space into a leadership training center. On the rest of the floor, he knocked down the walls so that the remaining executives, including himself, share open offices. Lafley sits next to the two people he talks to the most, which, in true P&G style, was officially established by a flow study: HR head Antoine and Vice-Chairman Bruce Byrnes. As

if the Sunday night meetings with Antoine weren't proof enough of Lafley's determination to make sure the best people rise to the top. And Byrnes, whom Lafley refers to as "Yoda"—the sage-like *Star Wars* character—gets a lot of face time because of his marketing expertise. As Lafley says, "the assets at P&G are what? Our people and our brands."

32 Just as emblematic of the Lafley era is the floor's new conference room, where he and P&G's 12 other top executives meet every Monday at 8 A.M. to review results, plan strategy, and set the drumbeat for the week. The table used to be rectangular; now it's round. The execs used to sit where they were told; now they sit where they like. At one of those meetings, an outsider might have trouble distinguishing the CEO: He occasionally joins in the discussion, but most of the time the executives talk as much to each other as to Lafley. "I am more like a coach," Lafley says afterward. "I am always looking for different combinations that will get better results." Jeff Immelt, who asked Lafley to join GE's board in 2002, describes him as "an excellent listener. He's a sponge."

33 And now, Lafley is carefully using this information to reshape the company's approach to just about everything it does. When Lafley describes the P&G of the future, he says: "We're in the business of creating and building brands." Notice, as P&Gers certainly have, that he makes no mention of manufacturing. While Lafley shies away from saying just how much of the company's factory and back-office operations he may hand over to someone else, he does admit that facing up to the realities of the marketplace "won't always be fun." Of P&G's 102,000 employees, nearly one-half work in its plants. So far, "Lafley has deftly handled the outsourcing deals, which has lessened fear within P&G," says Roger Martin, a close adviser of Lafley's who is dean of the University of Toronto's Joseph L. Rotman School of Management. All 2,000 of the information-technology workers were moved over to HP. At the bar-soap operations, based entirely in Cincinnati, 200 of the 250 employees went to work for the Canadian contractor.

34 Lafley's approach to selling P&G products is unprecedented at the company, too: He argues that P&G doesn't have to produce just premium-priced goods. So now there's a cheaper formulation for Crest in China. The Clairol deal gave P&G bargain shampoos such as Daily Defense. And with Lafley's encouragement, managers have looked at their most expensive products to make sure they aren't too costly. In many cases, they've actually lowered the prices.

35 And Lafley is pushing P&G to approach its brands more creatively. Crest, for example, isn't just about toothpaste anymore: There's also an electric toothbrush, SpinBrush, which P&G acquired in January, 2001. P&G is also willing to license its own technologies to get them to the marketplace faster. It joined with Clorox Co., maker of Glad Bags, last October to share a food-wrap technology it had developed. It was unprecedented for P&G to work with a competitor, says licensing head Jeffrey Weedman. The overall effect is undeniable. "Lafley has made P&G far more flexible," says Banc of America's Steele.

36 But Lafley still faces daunting challenges. Keeping up the earnings growth, for example, will get tougher as competitors fight back and as P&G winds down a large restructuring program—started under Jager but accelerated under Lafley. Furthermore, some of the gains in profit have resulted from cuts in capital and R&D spending, which Lafley has pared back to the levels of the company's rivals. And already, P&G has missed a big opportunity: It passed up the chance to buy water-soluble strips that contain mouthwash. Now, Listerine is making a bundle on the product.

37 Nor are all investors comfortable with growth through acquisitions. The deals make it harder for investors to decipher earnings growth from existing operations. Then there's the risk of fumbling the integration, notes Arthur B. Cecil, an analyst at T. Rowe Price Group (TROW) Inc., which holds 1.74 million P&G shares. "I would prefer they not make acquisitions," he says. Already, Clairol hair color, the most important product in P&G's recent purchase, has lost five points of market share to L'Oréal in the United States, according to ACNeilsen Corp.

38 Making deals, however, could be the only way to balance P&G's growing reliance on Wal-Mart. Former and current P&G employees say the discounter could account for one-third of P&G's global sales by the end of the decade. Meanwhile, the pressure from consumers and competitors to keep prices low will only increase. "P&G has improved its ability to take on those challenges, but those challenges are still there," says Lehman analyst Ann Gillin.

39 Still, Lafley may be uniquely suited to creating a new and improved P&G. Even Jager agrees that

**P&G Turning the Tide**

| | Sales | Operating Profit Margin | Outlook |
|---|---|---|---|
| **Baby and Family Care** | 23% | 17% | GOOD |

P&G now vies with Kimberly-Clark to dominate the disposable-diaper market. But competition has pushed prices down, which is why this division has the slowest profit-margin growth.

| | | | |
|---|---|---|---|
| **Fabric and Home Care** | 29% | 25% | VERY GOOD |

Lafley has aggressively cut costs in the company's largest division. But Tide in particular faces intense competition from lower-priced rivals. To compensate, Lafley is introducing high-margin products, such as the Swiffer Duster.

| | | | |
|---|---|---|---|
| **Beauty Care** | 28% | 23% | GOOD |

Lafley has quickly expanded this business by acquiring Clairol and Wella. But the company has less expertise here and still has to prove it can grow internally.

| | | | |
|---|---|---|---|
| **Health Care** | 13% | 18% | MIXED |

With its SpinBrush and tooth-whitening products, P&G has regained the lead in oral care from Colgate. The division will get a lift from distributing heart-burn drug Prilosec over the counter. But the pharmaceutical business depends on one big seller, Actonel for osteoporosis.

| | | | |
|---|---|---|---|
| **Snacks and Beverages** | 7% | 15% | WEAK |

Because the division generates the company's lowest profit margins, many expect Lafley to continue to extricate P&G from these businesses. He has already sold Crisco and Jiff to J. M. Smuckers.

*Share of total sales. Estimates for fiscal year ending June 30, 2003

Data: Banc America Securities

Lafley was just what the company needed. "He has calmed down the confusion that happened while I was there," says the former CEO. Jager left a letter on Lafley's desk the day he resigned telling his successor not to feel responsible for his fall. "You earned it," he recalls writing. "Don't start out with guilt."

**40** Lafley says he learned from Jager's biggest mistake. "I avoided saying P&G people were bad," he says. "I enrolled them in change." Lafley, a company man through and through, just can't resist trying out a new slogan.

**Source:** "P&G: New and Improved," *BusinessWeek,* July 7, 2003.

## Appendix **10**

# Primary Organizational Structures and Their Strategy-Related Pros and Cons

Matching the structure to the strategy is a fundamental task of company strategists. To understand how that task is handled, we first must review the five basic primary structures. We will then turn to guidelines for matching structure to strategy.

The five basic primary structures are: (1) functional, (2) geographic, (3) divisional, or strategic business unit, (4) matrix, and (5) product team. Each structure has advantages and disadvantages that strategists must consider when choosing an organization form.

## FUNCTIONAL ORGANIZATIONAL STRUCTURE

Functional structures predominate in firms with a single or narrow product focus. Such firms require well-defined skills and areas of specialization to build competitive advantages in providing their products or services. Dividing tasks into functional specialties enables the personnel of these firms to concentrate on only one aspect of the necessary work. This allows use of the latest technical skills and develops a high level of efficiency.

Product, customer, or technology considerations determine the identity of the parts in a functional structure. A hotel business might be organized around housekeeping (maids), the front desk, maintenance, restaurant operations, reservations and sales, accounting, and personnel. An equipment manufacturer might be organized around production, engineering/quality control, purchasing, marketing, personnel, and finance/accounting. Two examples of functional organizations are illustrated in Exhibit 10–A.

The strategic challenge presented by the functional structure is effective coordination of the functional units. The narrow technical expertise achieved through specialization can lead to limited perspectives and to differences in the priorities of the functional units. Specialists may see the firm's strategic issues primarily as "marketing" problems or "production" problems. The potential conflict among functional units makes the coordinating role of the chief executive critical. Integrating devices (such as project teams or planning committees) are frequently used in functionally organized firms to enhance coordination and to facilitate understanding across functional areas.

## GEOGRAPHIC ORGANIZATIONAL STRUCTURE

Firms often grow by expanding the sale of their products or services to new geographic areas. In these areas, they frequently encounter differences that necessitate different approaches in producing, providing, or selling their products or services. Structuring by geographic areas is usually required to accommodate these differences. Thus, Holiday Inns is organized by regions of the world because of differences among nations in the laws, customs, and economies affecting the lodging industry. And even within its U.S. organization, Holiday Inns is organized geographically because of regional differences in traveling requirements, lodging regulations, and customer mix.

**EXHIBIT 10–A**
**Functional Organization Structures**

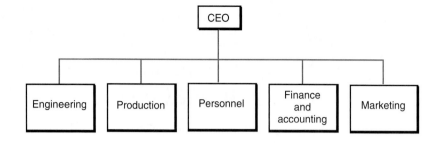

A process-oriented functional structure (an electronics distributor):

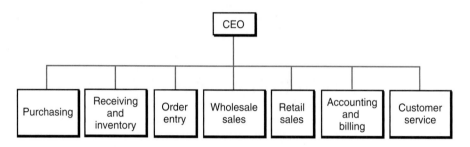

| **Strategic Advantages** | **Strategic Disadvantages** |
|---|---|
| 1. Achieves efficiency through specialization. | 1. Promotes narrow specialization and functional rivalry or conflict. |
| 2. Develops functional expertise. | 2. Creates difficulties in functional coordination and interfunctional decision making. |
| 3. Differentiates and delegates day-to-day operating decisions. | 3. Limits development of general managers. |
| 4. Retains centralized control of strategic decisions. | 4. Has a strong potential for interfunctional conflict—priority placed on functional areas, not the entire business. |
| 5. Tightly links structure to strategy by designating key activities as separate units. | |

   The key strategic advantage of geographic organizational structures is responsiveness to local market conditions. Exhibit 10–B illustrates a typical geographic organizational structure and itemizes the strategic advantages and disadvantages of such structures.

## DIVISIONAL OR STRATEGIC BUSINESS UNIT STRUCTURE

When a firm diversifies its product/service lines, utilizes unrelated market channels, or begins to serve heterogeneous customer groups, a functional structure rapidly becomes inadequate. If a functional structure is retained under these circumstances, production managers may have to oversee the production of numerous and varied products or services, marketing managers may have to create sales programs for vastly different products or sell through vastly different distribution channels, and top management may be confronted with excessive coordination

**EXHIBIT 10–B**
**A Geographic Organizational Structure**

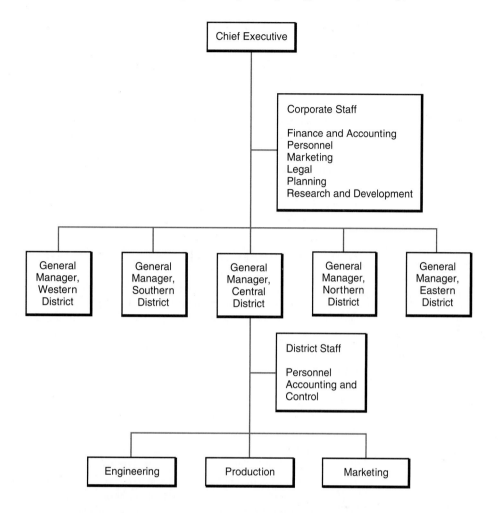

| **Strategic Advantages** | **Strategic Disadvantages** |
|---|---|
| 1. Allows tailoring of strategy to needs of each geographic market. | 1. Poses problem of deciding whether headquarters should impose geographic uniformity or geographic diversity should be allowed. |
| 2. Delegates profit/loss responsibility to lowest strategic level. | 2. Makes it more difficult to maintain consistent company image/reputation from area to area. |
| 3. Improves functional coordination within the target market. | 3. Adds layer of management to run the geographic units. |
| 4. Takes advantage of economies of local operations. | 4. Can result in duplication of staff services at headquarters and district levels. |
| 5. Provides excellent training grounds for higher level general managers. | |

demands. A new organizational structure is often necessary to meet the increased coordination and decision-making requirements that result from increased diversity and size, and the divisional or strategic business unit (SBU) organizational structure is the form often chosen.

For many years, Ford and General Motors have used divisional/SBU structures organized by product groups. Manufacturers often organize sales into divisions based on differences in distribution channels.

A divisional/SBU structure allows corporate management to delegate authority for the strategic management of distinct business entities—the division/SBU. This expedites decision making in response to varied competitive environments and enables corporate management to concentrate on corporate-level strategic decisions. The division/SBU usually is given profit responsibility, which facilitates accurate assessment of profit and loss.

Exhibit 10–C illustrates a divisional/SBU organizational structure and specifies the strategic advantages and disadvantages of such structures.

## MATRIX ORGANIZATIONAL STRUCTURE

In large companies, increased diversity leads to numerous product and project efforts of major strategic significance. The result is a need for an organizational form that provides skills and resources where and when they are most vital. For example, a product development project needs a market research specialist for two months and a financial analyst one day per week. A customer site application needs a software engineer for one month and a customer service trainer one day per month for six weeks. Each of these situations is an example of a matrix organization that has been used to temporarily put people and resources where they are most needed. Among the firms that now use some form of matrix organization are Citicorp, Matsushita, DaimlerChrysler, Microsoft, Dow Chemical, and Texas Instruments.

The matrix organization provides dual channels of authority, performance responsibility, evaluation, and control, as shown in Exhibit 10–D. Essentially, subordinates are assigned both to a basic functional area and to a project or product manager. The matrix form is intended to make the best use of talented people within a firm by combining the advantages of functional specialization and product-project specialization.

The matrix structure also increases the number of middle managers who exercise general management responsibilities (through the project manager role) and, thus, broaden their exposure to organizationwide strategic concerns. In this way, the matrix structure overcomes a key deficiency of functional organizations while retaining the advantages of functional specialization.

Although the matrix structure is easy to design, it is difficult to implement. Dual chains of command challenge fundamental organizational orientations. Negotiating shared responsibilities, the use of resources, and priorities can create misunderstanding or confusion among subordinates. These problems are heightened in an international context with the complications introduced by distance, language, time, and culture.

To avoid the deficiencies that might arise from a permanent matrix structure, some firms are accomplishing particular strategic tasks, by means of a "temporary" or "flexible" *overlay structure.* This approach, used recently by such firms as NEC, Matsushita, Philips, and Unilever, is meant to take *temporary* advantage of a matrix-type team while preserving an underlying divisional structure. Thus, the basic idea of the matrix structure—*to simplify and amplify the focus of resources on a narrow but strategically important product, project, or market*—appears to be an important structural alternative for large, diverse organizations.

**EXHIBIT 10–C**
**Divisional or Strategic Business Unit Structure**

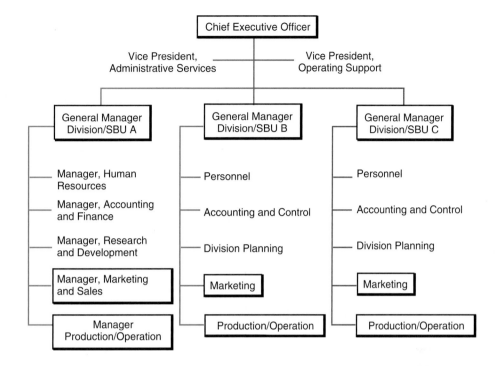

**Strategic Advantages**

1. Forces coordination and necessary authority down to the appropriate level for rapid response.
2. Places strategy development and implementation in closer proximity to the unique environments of the divisions/SBUs.
3. Frees chief executive officer for broader strategic decision making.
4. Sharply focuses accountability for performance.
5. Retains functional specialization within each division/SBU.
6. Provides good training grounds for strategic managers.
7. Increases focus on products, markets, and quick response to change.

**Strategic Disadvantages**

1. Fosters potentially dysfunctional competition for corporate-level resources.
2. Presents the problem of determining how much authority should be given to division/SBU managers.
3. Creates a potential for policy inconsistencies among divisions/SBUs.
4. Presents the problem of distributing corporate overhead costs in a way that's acceptable to division managers with profit responsibility.
5. Increases costs incurred through duplication of functions.
6. Creates difficulty maintaining overall corporate image.

**EXHIBIT 10–D**
**Matrix**
**Organizational**
**Structure**

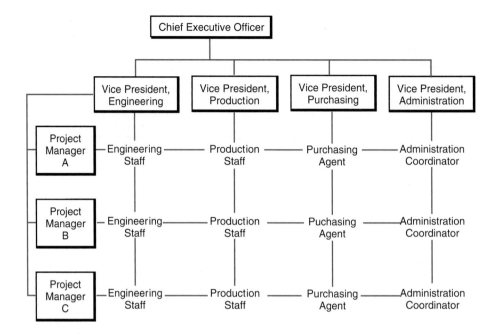

## Strategic Advantages

1. Accommodates a wide variety of project-oriented business activity.
2. Provides good training grounds for strategic managers.
3. Maximizes efficient use of functional managers.
4. Fosters creativity and multiple sources of diversity.
5. Gives middle management broader exposure to strategic issues.

## Strategic Disadvantages

1. May result in confusion and contradictory policies.
2. Necessitates tremendous horizontal and vertical coordination.
3. Can proliferate information logjams and excess reporting.
4. Can trigger turf battles and loss of accountability.

# Chapter **Eleven**

# Strategic Control and Continuous Improvement

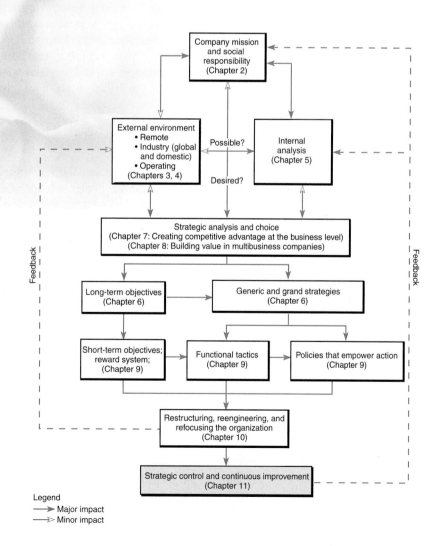

Company mission and social responsibility (Chapter 2)

External environment
• Remote
• Industry (global and domestic)
• Operating
(Chapters 3, 4)

Possible?

Internal analysis (Chapter 5)

Desired?

Strategic analysis and choice
(Chapter 7: Creating competitive advantage at the business level)
(Chapter 8: Building value in multibusiness companies)

Long-term objectives (Chapter 6)

Generic and grand strategies (Chapter 6)

Short-term objectives; reward system; (Chapter 9)

Functional tactics (Chapter 9)

Policies that empower action (Chapter 9)

Restructuring, reengineering, and refocusing the organization (Chapter 10)

Strategic control and continuous improvement (Chapter 11)

Feedback

Feedback

Legend
→ Major impact
⇢ Minor impact

Strategies are forward looking, designed to be accomplished several years into the future, and based on management assumptions about numerous events that have not yet occurred. How should managers control a strategy?

*Strategic control* is concerned with tracking a strategy as it is being implemented, detecting problems or changes in its underlying premises, and making necessary adjustments. In contrast to postaction control, strategic control is concerned with guiding action in behalf of the strategy as that action is taking place and when the end result is still several years off. Managers responsible for the success of a strategy typically are concerned with two sets of questions:

1. Are we moving in the proper direction? Are key things falling into place? Are our assumptions about major trends and changes correct? Are we doing the critical things that need to be done? Should we adjust or abort the strategy?

2. How are we performing? Are objectives and schedules being met? Are costs, revenues, and cash flows matching projections? Do we need to make operational changes?

The rapid, accelerating change of the global marketplace has made *continuous improvement* another aspect of strategic control in many business organizations. Synonymous with the total quality movement, continuous improvement provides a way for organizations to provide strategic control that allows an organization to respond more proactively and timely to rapid developments in hundreds of areas that influence a business's success. This chapter discusses traditional strategic controls and then explains ways that the *continuous improvement quality imperative* and the balanced scoreboard methodology can be key vehicles for strategic control.

## ESTABLISHING STRATEGIC CONTROLS

The control of strategy can be characterized as a form of "steering control." Ordinarily, a good deal of time elapses between the initial implementation of a strategy and achievement of its intended results. During that time, investments are made and numerous projects and actions are undertaken to implement the strategy. Also, during that time, changes are taking place in both the environmental situation and the firm's internal situation. Strategic controls are necessary to steer the firm through these events. They must provide the basis for adapting the firm's strategic actions and directions in response to these developments and changes.

The four basic types of strategic control are:

1. Premise control.

2. Special alert control.

3. Strategic surveillance.

4. Implementation control.

The nature of these four types is summarized in Exhibit 11–1.

### Premise Control

Every strategy is based on certain planning premises—assumptions or predictions. *Premise control is designed to check systematically and continuously whether the premises on which the strategy is based are still valid.* If a vital premise is no longer valid, the strategy may have to be changed. The sooner an invalid premise can be recognized and rejected, the bet-

**EXHIBIT 11–1   Four Types of Strategic Control**

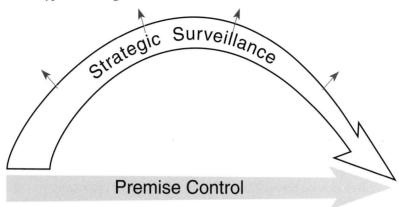

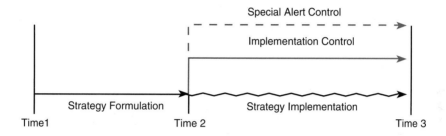

**Characteristics of the Four Types of Strategic Control**

| Basic Characteristics | Types of Strategic Control | | | |
| | Premise Control | Implementation Control | Strategic Surveillance | Special Alert Control |
|---|---|---|---|---|
| Objects of control | Planning premises and projections | Key strategic thrusts and milestones | Potential threats and opportunities related to the strategy | Occurrence of recognizable but unlikely events |
| Degree of focusing | High | High | Low | High |
| Data acquisition: | | | | |
|   Formalization | Medium | High | Low | High |
|   Centralization | Low | Medium | Low | High |
| Use with: | | | | |
|   Environmental factors | Yes | Seldom | Yes | Yes |
|   Industry factors | Yes | Seldom | Yes | Yes |
|   Strategy-specific factors | No | Yes | Seldom | Yes |
|   Company-specific factors | No | Yes | Seldom | Seldom |

Source: From Academy of Management Review by G. Schreyogg and H. Steinmann. Copyright © 1987 by Academy of Management. Reproduced with permission of Academy of Management via Copyright Clearance Center.

ter are the chances that an acceptable shift in the strategy can be devised. Planning premises are primarily concerned with environmental and industry factors.

### Environmental Factors

Although a firm has little or no control over environmental factors, these factors exercise considerable influence over the success of its strategy, and strategies usually are based on key premises about them. Inflation, technology, interest rates, regulation, and demographic/social changes are examples of such factors.

EPA regulations and federal laws concerning the handling, use, and disposal of toxic chemicals have a major effect on the strategy of Velsicol Chemical Company, a market leader in pesticide chemicals sold to farmers and exterminators. So Velsicol's management makes and constantly updates premises about future regulatory actions.

### Industry Factors

The performance of the firms in a given industry is affected by industry factors. These differ among industries, and a firm should be aware of the factors that influence success in its particular industry. Competitors, suppliers, product substitutes, and barriers to entry are a few of the industry factors about which strategic assumptions are made.

Rubbermaid has long been held up as a model of predictable growth, creative management, and rapid innovation in the plastic housewares and toy industry. Its premise going into the twenty-first century was that large retail chains would continue to prefer its products over competitors' because of this core competence. This premise included continued receptivity to regular price increases when necessitated by raw materials costs. Retailers, most notably Wal-Mart, recently balked at Rubbermaid's attempt to raise prices to offset the doubling of resin costs. Furthermore, traditionally overlooked competitors have begun to make inroads with computerized stocking services. Rubbermaid is moving aggressively to adjust its strategy because of the response of Wal-Mart and other key retailers.

Strategies are often based on numerous premises, some major and some minor, about environmental and industry variables. Tracking all of these premises is unnecessarily expensive and time consuming. Managers must select premises whose change (1) is likely and (2) would have a major impact on the firm and its strategy.

## Strategic Surveillance

By their nature, premise controls are focused controls; strategic surveillance, however, is unfocused. *Strategic surveillance is designed to monitor a broad range of events inside and outside the firm that are likely to affect the course of its strategy.*[1] The basic idea behind strategic surveillance is that important yet unanticipated information may be uncovered by a general monitoring of multiple information sources.

Strategic surveillance must be kept as unfocused as possible. It should be a loose "environmental scanning" activity. Trade magazines, *The Wall Street Journal,* trade conferences, conversations, and intended and unintended observations are all subjects of strategic surveillance. Despite its looseness, strategic surveillance provides an ongoing, broad-based vigilance in all daily operations that may uncover information relevant to the firm's strategy. Citicorp benefited significantly from a Brazilian manager's strategic surveillance of political speeches by Lula Da Silva, Brazil's new president, as discussed in Exhibit 11–2, Strategy in Action.

## Special Alert Control

Another type of strategic control, really a subset of the other three, is special alert control. *A special alert control is the thorough, and often rapid, reconsideration of the firm's strategy because of a sudden, unexpected event.* The tragic events of September 11, 2001, an outside firm's sudden acquisition of a leading competitor, an unexpected product difficulty, such as the poisoned Tylenol capsules—events of these kinds can drastically alter the firm's strategy.

---

[1] G. Schreyogg and H. Steinmann, "Strategic Control: A New Perspective," *Academy of Management Review* 12, no. 1 (1987), p. 101.

## IMPLEMENTATION CONTROL AT DAYS INN

When Days Inn pioneered the budget segment of the lodging industry, its strategy placed primary emphasis on company-owned facilities and it insisted on maintaining a roughly 3-to-1 company-owned/franchise ratio. This ratio ensured the parent company's total control over standards, rates, and so forth.

As other firms moved into the budget segment, Days Inn saw the need to expand rapidly throughout the United States and, therefore, reversed its conservative franchise posture. This reversal would rapidly accelerate its ability to open new locations. Longtime executives, concerned about potential loss of control over local standards, instituted *implementation controls* requiring both franchise evaluation and annual milestone reviews. Two years into the program, Days Inn executives were convinced that a high franchise-to-company ratio was manageable, and so they accelerated the growth of franchising by doubling the franchise sales department.

## STRATEGIC SURVEILLANCE AT CITICORP

Citicorp has been pursuing an aggressive product development strategy intended to achieve an annual earnings growth of 15 percent while it becomes an institution capable of supplying clients with any kind of financial service anywhere in the world. A major obstacle to the achievement of this earnings growth is Citicorp's exposure to default because of its extensive earlier loans to troubled developing countries. Citicorp is sensitive to the wide variety of predictions about impending defaults.

Citicorp's long-range plan assumes an annual 10 percent default on its developing economy loans over any five-year period.

Yet it maintains active *strategic surveillance control* by having each of its international branches monitor daily announcements from key governments and from inside contacts for signs of changes in a host country's financial environment. When that surveillance detects a potential problem, management attempts to adjust Citicorp's posture. For example, when Brazil's President-elect Lula Da Silva stated that his country may not pay interest on its debt as scheduled, Citicorp raised its annual default charge to 20 percent of its $2.5 billon Brazillian exposure.

## SPECIAL ALERT CONTROL AT UNITED AIRLINES

The sudden impact of an airline crash can be devastating to a major airline. United Airlines has made elaborate preparations to deal with this contingency. Its executive vice president, James M. Guyette, heads a crisis team that is permanently prepared to respond. Members of the team carry beepers and are always on call. When United's Chicago headquarters received word of the September 11th hijacking and crash, they were in a "war room" within an hour to direct the response. Beds are set up nearby so team members can catch a few winks; while they sleep, alternates take their places.

Members of the team have been carefully screened through simulated crisis drills. "The point is to weed out those who don't hold up well under stress," says Guyette. Although the team was established to handle flight disasters, it has since assumed an expanded role. The crisis team was activated when American Airlines launched a fare war. And according to Guyette, "We're brainstorming about how we would be affected by everything from a competitor who had a serious problem to a crisis involving a hijacking or taking a United employee hostage."

Such an event should trigger an immediate and intense reassessment of the firm's strategy and its current strategic situation. In many firms, crisis teams handle the firm's initial response to unforeseen events that may have an immediate effect on its strategy. Increasingly, firms have developed contingency plans along with crisis teams to respond to circumstances such as United Airlines did on September 11, 2001, as summarized in Strategy in Action 11–2.

## Implementation Control

Strategy implementation takes place as series of steps, programs, investments, and moves that occur over an extended time. Special programs are undertaken. Functional areas initiate strategy-related activities. Key people are added or reassigned. Resources are mobilized. In other words, managers implement strategy by converting broad plans into the concrete, incremental actions and results of specific units and individuals.

Implementation control is the type of strategic control that must be exercised as those events unfold. *Implementation control is designed to assess whether the overall strategy should be changed in light of the results associated with the incremental actions that implement the overall strategy.* The two basic types of implementation control are (1) monitoring strategic thrusts and (2) milestone reviews.

### Monitoring Strategic Thrusts or Projects

As a means of implementing broad strategies, narrow strategic projects often are undertaken—projects that represent part of what needs to be done if the overall strategy is to be accomplished. These strategic thrusts provide managers with information that helps them determine whether the overall strategy is progressing as planned or needs to be adjusted.

Although the utility of strategic thrusts seems readily apparent, it is not always easy to use them for control purposes. It may be difficult to interpret early experience or to evaluate the overall strategy in light of such experience. One approach is to agree early in the planning process on which thrusts or which phases of thrusts are critical factors in the success of the strategy. Managers responsible for these implementation controls will single them out from other activities and observe them frequently. Another approach is to use stop/go assessments that are linked to a series of meaningful thresholds (time, costs, research and development, success, and so forth) associated with particular thrusts. A program of regional development via company-owned inns in the Rocky Mountain area was a monitoring thrust that Days Inn used to test its strategy of becoming a nationwide motel chain. Problems in meeting time targets and unexpectedly large capital needs led Days Inn's executives to abandon the overall strategy and eventually sell the firm.

### Milestone Reviews

Managers often attempt to identify significant milestones that will be reached during strategy implementation. These milestones may be critical events, major resource allocations, or simply the passage of a certain amount of time. The milestone reviews that then take place usually involve a full-scale reassessment of the strategy and of the advisability of continuing or refocusing the firm's direction.

A useful example of implementation control based on milestone review is offered by Boeing's product-development strategy of entering the supersonic transport (SST) airplane market. Boeing had invested millions of dollars and years of scarce engineering talent during the first phase of its SST venture, and competition from the British/French Concorde effort was intense. Since the next phase represented a billion-dollar decision, Boeing's management established the initiation of the phase as a milestone. The milestone reviews greatly increased the estimates of production costs; predicted relatively few passengers and rising fuel costs, thus raising the estimated operating costs; and noted that the Concorde, unlike Boeing, had the benefit of massive government subsidies. These factors led Boeing's management to scrap its SST strategy in spite of high sunk costs, pride, and patriotism. Only an objective, full-scale strategy reassessment could have led to such a decision.

In this example, a milestone review occurred at a major resource allocation decision point. Milestone reviews may also occur concurrently when a major step in a strategy's implementation is being taken or when a key uncertainty is resolved. Managers even may set an arbitrary period, say two years, as a milestone review point. Whatever the basis for selecting that point, the critical purpose of a milestone review is to thoroughly scrutinize the firm's strategy so as to control the strategy's future.

Implementation control is also enabled through operational control systems like budgets, schedules and key success factors. While strategic controls attempt to steer the company over an extended period (usually five years of more), operational controls provide postaction evaluation and control over short periods—usually from one month to one year. To be effective, operational control systems must take four steps common to all postaction controls:

1. Set standards of performance.

2. Measure actual performance.

3. Identify deviations from standards set.

4. Initiate corrective action.

**EXHIBIT 11–3**   **Monitoring and Evaluating Performance Deviations**

| Key Success Factors | Objective, Assumption, or Budget | Forecast Performance at This Time | Current Performance | Current Deviation | Analysis |
|---|---|---|---|---|---|
| Cost control: Ratio of indirect overhead cost to direct field and labor costs | 10% | 15% | 12% | +3 (ahead) | Are we moving too fast, or is there more unnecessary overhead than was originally thought? |
| Gross profit | 39% | 40% | 40% | 0% | |
| Customer service: Installation cycle in days | 2.5 days | 3.2 days | 2.7 days | +0.5 (ahead) | Can this progress be maintained? |
| Ratio of service to sales personnel | 3.2 | 2.7 | 2.1 | −0.6 (behind) | Why are we behind here? How can we maintain the installation-cycle progress? |
| Product quality: Percentage of products returned | 1.0% | 2.0% | 2.1% | −0.1% (behind) | Why are we behind here? What are the ramifications for other operations? |
| Product performance versus specification | 100% | 92% | 80% | −12% (behind) | |
| Marketing: Monthly sales per employee | $12,500 | $11,500 | $12,100 | +$600 (ahead) | Good progress. Is it creating any problems to support? |
| Expansion of product line | 6 | 3 | 5 | +2 products (ahead) | Are the products ready? Are the perfect standards met? |
| Employee morale in service area: Absenteeism rate | 2.5% | 3.0% | 3.0% | (on target) | |
| Turnover rate | 5% | 10% | 15% | −8% (behind) | Looks like a problem! Why are we so far behind? |
| Competition: New product introductions (average number) | 6 | 3 | 6 | −3 (behind) | Did we underestimate timing? What are the implications for our basic assumptions? |

Exhibit 11–3 illustrates a typical operational control system. These indicators represent progress after two years of a five-year strategy intended to differentiate the firm as a customer-service–oriented provider of high-quality products. Management's concern is to compare *progress to date* with *expected progress*. The *current deviation* is of particular interest, because it provides a basis for examining *suggested actions* (usually suggested by subordinate managers) and for finalizing decisions on changes or adjustments in the firm's operations.

From Exhibit 11–3, it appears that the firm is maintaining control of its cost structure. Indeed, it is ahead of schedule on reducing overhead. The firm is well ahead of its delivery cycle target, while slightly below its target service-to-sales personnel ratio. Its product returns look OK, although product performance versus specification is below standard. Sales per employee and expansion of the product line are ahead of schedule. The absenteeism rate in the service area is on target, but the turnover rate is higher than that targeted. Competitors appear to be introducing products more rapidly than expected.

After deviations and their causes have been identified, the implications of the deviations for the ultimate success of the strategy must be considered. For example, the rapid product-line expansion indicated in Exhibit 11–3 may have been a response to the increased rate of competitors' product expansion. At the same time, product performance is still low; and, while the installation cycle is slightly above standard (improving customer service), the ratio of service to sales personnel is below the targeted ratio. Contributing to this substandard ratio (and perhaps reflecting a lack of organizational commitment to customer service) is the exceptionally high turnover in customer service personnel. The rapid reduction in indirect overhead costs might mean that administration integration of customer service and product development requirements has been cut back too quickly.

This information presents operations managers with several options. They may attribute the deviations primarily to internal discrepancies. In that case, they can scale priorities up or down. For example, they might place more emphasis on retaining customer service personnel and less emphasis on overhead reduction and new product development. On the other hand, they might decide to continue as planned in the face of increasing competition and to accept or gradually improve the customer service situation. Another possibility is reformulating the strategy or a component of the strategy in the face of rapidly increasing competition. For example, the firm might decide to emphasize more standardized or lower-priced products to overcome customer service problems and take advantage of an apparently ambitious sales force.

This is but one of many possible interpretations of Exhibit 11–3. The important point here is the critical need to monitor progress against standards and to give serious in-depth attention to both the causes of observed deviations and the most appropriate responses to them. After the deviations have been evaluated, slight adjustments may be made to keep progress, expenditure, or other factors in line with the strategy's programmed needs. In the unusual event of extreme deviations—generally because of unforeseen changes—management is alerted to the possible need for revising the budget, reconsidering certain functional plans related to budgeted expenditures, or examining the units concerned and the effectiveness of their managers.

Correcting deviations in performance brings the entire management task into focus. Managers can correct such deviations by changing measures or plans. They also can eliminate poor performance by changing how things are done, by hiring or retraining workers, by changing job assignments, and so on. Correcting deviations, therefore, can involve all of the functions, tasks, and responsibilities of operations managers. Managers in other cultures, most notably Japan, have for some time achieved operational control by seeking their unit's continuous improvement. Companies worldwide have adapted this point of view that operational control is best achieved through a pervasive commitment to quality, originally called *total quality management* (TQM), which is seen as essential to strategic success in the twenty-first century.

# THE QUALITY IMPERATIVE: CONTINUOUS IMPROVEMENT TO BUILD CUSTOMER VALUE

The initials TQM have become the most popular abbreviation in business management literature since MBO (management by objectives). TQM Stands for *total quality management,* an umbrella term for the quality programs that have been implemented in many businesses worldwide in the last two decades. TQM was first implemented in several large U.S. manufacturers in the face of the overwhelming success of Japanese and German competitors. Japanese manufacturers embraced the quality messages of Americans W. Edwards Deming and J. M. Juran following World War II, and by the 1970s Japanese products had acquired unquestioned reputations for superior high quality.

Growing numbers of U.S. manufacturers have attempted to change this imbalance with their own quality programs, and the practice has spread to large retail and service companies as well. Increasingly, smaller companies that supply big TQM companies have adopted quality programs, often because big companies have required small suppliers to adopt quality programs of their own. Exhibit 11–4, Strategy in Action, describes the aggressive quality imperative thrust on Detroit automakers today.

TQM is viewed as virtually a new organizational culture and way of thinking. It is built around an intense focus on customer satisfaction; on accurate measurement of every critical variable in a business's operation; on continuous improvement of products, services, and processes; and on work relationships based on trust and teamwork. One useful explanation of the quality imperative suggests 10 essential elements of implementing total quality management, as follows:

1. **Define *quality* and *customer value*.** Rather than be left to individual interpretation, company personnel should have a clear definition of what *quality* means in the job, department, and throughout the company. It should be developed from your customer's perspective and communicated as a written policy.

Thinking in terms of customer value broadens the definition of *quality* to include efficiency and responsiveness. Said another way, quality to your customer often means that the product performs well; that it is priced competitively (efficiency); and that you provide it quickly and adapt it when needed (responsiveness). Customer value is found in the combination of all three—quality, price, and speed.

2. **Develop a customer orientation.** Customer value is what the customer says it is. Don't rely on secondary information—talk to your customers directly. Also recognize your "internal" customers. Usually less than 20 percent of company employees come into contact with external customers, while the other 80 percent serve internal customers—other units with real performance expectations.

The value chain provides an important way to think about customer orientation, particularly to recognize *internal* as well as external (ultimate) customers. Operating personnel are *internal* customers of the accounting department for useful information and also the purchasing department for quality, timely supplies. When they are "served" with quality, efficiency, and responsiveness, value is added to their efforts, and is passed on to their internal customers and, eventually, external (ultimate) customers.

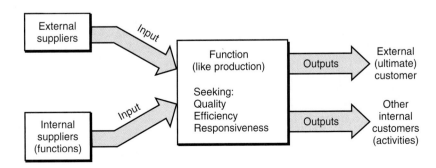

# Strategy in Action
Detroit's New-car Quality Is up, But What about the Long Term?

# Exhibit 11–4

**BusinessWeek** When J. D. Power & Associates Inc. released its all-important Initial Quality Study of new cars recently, domestic auto makers again crowed that they had narrowed the gap with Japanese vehicles and beat some of the pricey European makes. For four years, U.S. carmakers have been showing signs that they're getting quality right, and here, finally, was the proof. Domestic brands took three of the top six slots as once-moribund names such as Mercury and Buick—yes, Buick—jumped ahead of BMW and Toyota. General Motors Corp.'s resurgent Cadillac division trailed only Lexus.

But will Detroit be able to exploit its quality gains? Unfortunately, many consumers still have doubts, and for good reason. Scores for the entire GM, Ford Motor, and Daimler-Chrysler lineups are still below the industry average. Worse, Detroit has yet to make a convincing case that its cars hold up over time as well as Japanese models.

That's the acid test for most consumers. As it is, buyers still remember the bad old days, as recently as the early '90s, when U.S.-made vehicles were unreliable. Michael Austill, a Vestal (N.Y.) aerospace manager, suffered a 1980 Ford Fairmont, a clunky 1984 Pontiac 6000, and a 1995 Oldsmobile Aurora that was in the shop 18 times. He gave up on Detroit and has been happily driving Japanese and European cars since. "I have not [set] foot in a U.S. car showroom," says Austill.

The latest round of quality ratings probably won't convince buyers to abandon their skepticism. Although GM and Ford score well on initial quality—measured by problems per vehicle in the first three months of ownership—their cars still register as subpar over longer periods. In a recent issue of *Consumer Reports,* a survey of defects in three-year-old cars finds that all of the big-selling domestic names finished below the industry average. That will only change if Detroit is able to continue pushing tight controls that would allow better-built cars—such as Lincoln's Town Car, which gets high marks for reliability on the *Consumer Reports* survey—to work their way through the market. Says J. D. Power product research director Brian Walters: "It will take years of good performance for the domestic reputation to change."

The Big Three have worked hard over the past decade to adopt many of the quality initiatives of their Japanese rivals—and have come up with some of their own. All have tightened up inspections at their plants. They are working with suppliers to use proven reliable parts from existing vehicles in future models instead of engineering new parts from scratch. When launching some models, Ford keeps thousands of vehicles in holding yards for months of testing before shipping them to dealers.

To demonstrate confidence in its cars, Chrysler is offering extended warranties that can be transferred to subsequent owners. Says Chrysler marketing boss James C. Schroer: "We need to convince customers that the new vehicles being produced are reliable, and that when they go to trade them in, they'll get a good value." GM plans to launch an ad campaign in June called "Road to Redemption" that fesses up to years of inferior quality—and points to its Power ratings as evidence of a turnaround.

If only it were that simple. Detroit still has far to go. Imports have built a durable image for quality by focusing much more on the parts of a car that drivers actually feel. Japanese and European autos have plusher interiors and better knobs, switches, and gauges. Consumers have had such a dim view of domestic cars that they regard some foreign cars as better built even when they aren't. They believe European luxury cars made by Mercedes-Benz Audi, and Volkswagen are among the industry's best, says Power. But in actual studies measuring problems, none of them ranks near the top. All were topped in the Power survey by Cadillac, whose sales are up 17 percent thanks to its new CTS sedan.

There's only one way to change that perception: Keep improving. Power's Walters says strong results in initial quality eventually pay off in long-term studies. So while GM is eager to play up its gains, North America President Gary L. Cowger knows the company still has plenty of work to do. "We want to become the best in quality, bar none," he says. If the Big Three can pull that off, buyers may actually start to listen.

## A Discouraging Look Down the Pike
American buyers won't abandon their skepticism until the Big Three's cars perform better over time

| Initial Quality* | Long-Term Quality** |
|---|---|
| 1 Lexus | 1 Acura |
| 2 Cadillac ▲ | 2 Toyota |
| 3 Infiniti | 3 Lexus |
| 4 Acura | 4 Honda |
| 5 Buick | 5 Mazda |
| 6 Mercury | 6 Subaru |
| 7 Porsche | 7 Saab |
| 8 BMW | 8 Nissan |
| 9 Toyota | 9 Mitsubishi |
| 10 Jaguar | 10 Lincoln ▶ |

*Problems in the first 90 days of ownership.

**Problems after three years of ownership.

Data: J. D. Power & Associates 2003 Initial Quality

Survey: *Consumer Reports* 2003 Reliability Survey for long-term quality.

**Source:** "Way to Go, Detroit—Now Go a Lot Further," *Business-Week,* May 26, 2003.

3. **Focus on the company's business processes.** Break down every minute step in the process of providing the company's product or service and look at ways to improve it, rather than focusing simply on the finished product or service. Each process contributes value in some way, which can be improved or adapted to help other processes (internal customers) improve. Examples of ways customer value is enhanced across business processes in several functions are:

|  | **Quality** | **Efficiency** | **Responsiveness** |
|---|---|---|---|
| Marketing | Provides accurate assessment of customer's product preferences to R&D | Targets advertising campaign at customers, using cost-effective medium | Quickly uncovers and reacts to changing market trends |
| Operations | Consistently produces goods matching engineering design | Minimizes scrap and rework through high-production yield | Quickly adapts to latest demands with production flexibility |
| Research and development | Designs products that combine customer demand and production capabilities | Uses computers to test feasibility of idea before going to more expensive full-scale prototype | Carries out parallel product/process designs to speed up overall innovation |
| Accounting | Provides the information that managers in other functions need to make decisions | Simplifies and computerizes to decrease the cost of gathering information | Provides information in "real time" (as the events described are still happening) |
| Purchasing | Selects vendors for their ability to join in an effective "partnership" | Given the required vendor quality, negotiates prices to provide good value | Schedules inbound deliveries efficiently, avoiding both extensive inventories and stock-outs |
| Personnel | Trains workforce to perform required tasks | Minimizes employee turnover, reducing hiring and training expenses | In response to strong growth in sales, finds large numbers of employees and quickly teaches needed skills |

4. **Develop customer and supplier partnerships.** Organizations have a destructive tendency to view suppliers and even customers adversarily. It is better to understand the horizontal flow of a business—outside suppliers to internal suppliers/customers (a company's various departments) to external customers. This view suggests suppliers are partners in meeting customer needs, and customers are partners by providing input so the company and suppliers can meet and exceed those expectations.

Ford Motor Company's Dearborn, Michigan, plant is linked electronically with supplier Allied Signal's Kansas City, Missouri, plant. A Ford computer recently sent the design for a car's connecting rod to an Allied Signal factory computer, which transformed the design into instructions that it fed to a machine tool on the shop floor. The result: quality, efficiency, and responsiveness.

5. **Take a preventive approach.** Many organizations reward "fire fighters," not "fire preventers," and identify errors after the work is done. Management, instead, should be rewarded for being prevention oriented and seeking to eliminate nonvalue-added work.

6. **Adopt an error-free attitude.** Instill an attitude that "good enough" is not good enough anymore. "Error free" should become each individual's performance standard, with managers taking every opportunity to demonstrate and communicate the importance of this imperative.

7. **Get the facts first.** Continuous improvement–oriented companies make decisions based on facts, not on opinions. Accurate measurement, often using readily available statistical techniques, of every critical variable in a business's operation—and using those measurements to trace problems to their roots and eliminate their causes—is a better way.

8. **Encourage every manager and employee to participate.** Employee participation, empowerment, participative decision making, and extensive training in quality techniques, in statistical techniques, and in measurement tools are the ingredients continuous improvement companies employ to support and instill a commitment to customer value.

9. **Create an atmosphere of total involvement.** Quality management cannot be the job of a few managers or of one department. Maximum customer value cannot be achieved unless all areas of the organization apply quality concepts simultaneously.

10. **Strive for continuous improvement.** Stephen Yearout, director of Ernst & Young's Quality Management Center, recently observed that "Historically, meeting your customers' expectations would distinguish you from your competitors. The twenty-first century will require you to anticipate customer expectations and deliver quality service faster than the competition." Quality, efficiency, and responsiveness are not one-time programs of competitive response, for they create a new standard to measure up to. Organizations quickly find that continually improving quality, efficiency, and responsiveness in their processes, products, and services is not just good business; it's a necessity for long-term survival.

## Six-Sigma Approach to Continuous Improvement

Sometimes referred to as the "new TQM," Six-Sigma is a highly rigorous and analytical approach to quality and continuous improvement with an objective to improve profits through defect reduction, yield improvement, improved consumer satisfaction and best-in-class performance. Six-Sigma complements TQM philosophies such as management leadership, continuous education and customer focus while deploying a disciplined and structured approach of hard-nosed statistics. Critics of TQM see key success factors differentiating Six-Sigma from TQM.

- Acute understanding of customers and the product or service provided

- Emphasis on the science of statistics and measurement

- Meticulous and structured training development

- Strict and project-focused methodologies

- Reinforcement of the doctrine advocated by Juran such as top management support and continuous education

Companies such as Honeywell (1994), Motorola (1987), GE (1995), Polaroid (1998) and Texas Instruments (1988) have adopted the Six-Sigma discipline as a major business initiative. Many of these companies invested heavily in and pursued this model initially in order to create products and services that were of equal and higher quality than those of its competitors and to improve relationships with customers. Much like TQM, the technique implies a whole culture of strategies, tools, and statistical methodologies to improve the bottom line resulting in tremendous savings, subsequent improvement initiatives, and management action.

A Six-Sigma program at many organizations simply means a measure of quality that strives for near perfection in every facet of the business including every product, process, and transaction. The approach was introduced and established at Motorola in 1987, becoming the key factor in Motorola winning the 1988 Malcolm Baldrige Award for Quality, and has had impressive and undisputed results for many companies who have undertaken it. Allied Signal reported an estimated savings of $1.5 billion in its 1997 annual report while GE's savings in a 1998 annual letter to its shareholders reported benefits exceeding $750 million a year.

---

### How the Six-Sigma Statistical Concept Works

Six-Sigma means a failure rate of 3.4 parts per million or 99.9997%. At the six standard deviation from the mean under a normal distribution, 99.9996% of the population is under the curve with not more than 3.4 parts per million defective. The higher the sigma value, the less likely a process will produce defects as excellence is approached.

If you played 100 rounds of golf per year and played at:
**2 Sigma:** You'd miss 6 putts per round.
**3 Sigma:** You'd miss 1 putt per round.
**4 Sigma:** You'd miss 1 putt every 9 rounds.
**5 Sigma:** You'd miss 1 putt every 2.33 years.
**6 Sigma:** You'd miss 1 putt every 163 years!

---

Source: From John Petty, "When Near Enough is Not Good Enough," *Australian CPA*, May 2000, pp. 34–35. Reprinted with permission of CPA Australia.

Many frameworks, management philosophies, and specific statistical tools exist for implementing the Six-Sigma methodology and its objective to create a near perfect process or service. One such method for improving a system for existing processes falling below specification while looking for incremental improvement is the DMAIC process (define, measure, analyze, improve, control).

---

### Define

- Project Definition
- Project Charter
- Gathering Voice of the Customer
- Translating Customer Needs into Specific Requirements

### Measure

- Process Mapping (As-Is Process)
- Data Attributes (Continuous vs. Discrete)
- Measurement System Analysis
- Gage Repeatability and Reproducibility
- Measuring Process Capability
- Calculating Process Sigma Level
- Visually Displaying Baseline Performance

---

### Analyze

---

- Visually Displaying Data (Histogram, Run Chart, Pareto Chart, Scatter Diagram)
- Value-Added Analysis
- Cause and Effect Analysis (a.k.a. Fishbone, Ishikawa)
- Verification of Root Causes
- Determining Opportunity (Defects and Financial) for Improvement
- Project Charter Review and Revision

### Improve

---

- Brainstorming
- Quality Function Deployment (House of Quality)
- Failure Modes and Effects Analysis (FMEA)
- Piloting Your Solution
- Implementation Planning
- Culture Modification Planning for Your Organization

### Control

---

- Statistical Process Control (SPC) Overview
- Developing a Process Control Plan
- Documenting the Process

---

Six-Sigma programs promote an uncompromising orientation of all business processes toward the customer. The first step is always achieving an understanding of customer expectations so that suitable tools can be employed to improve both the internal and external processes. This program does not come fast and cheap; however, management commitment is crucial to the success, and employees must be trained in Six-Sigma methodologies. Exhibit 11–5, Strategy in Action, describes the use of Six-Sigma at Citibank.

## ISO 9004 and the Era of International Standards

The ISO 9004 quality management system standard, introduced in 1987, is international in both scope and impact. In early 2003 there were almost 400,000 firms registered in over 153 countries, almost 35,000 of those registered firms in the United States. The trend towards ISO 9004 registration and the creation of additional management system standards such as ISO 14004 (environmental), ISO 18004 (health and safety) and sector-specific standards such as QS-9004 (automotive) and AS-9004 (aerospace) has continued to grow and develop internationally. The standards are voluntary and apply to many kinds of businesses including manufacturers, distributors, services, software developers, public utilities, government agencies, and financial and educational institutions.

The *ISO 9004 standard* focuses on achieving customer satisfaction through continuous measurement, documentation, assessment, and adjustment. A diagram of the approach is provided below. The standard specifies requirements for a quality management system where an organization:

1. Needs to demonstrate its ability to consistently provide product and services that meet customer requirements, and

## THE BIG PICTURE

In 1997 Citibank set about to apply this technique to its nonmanufacturing environment by contracting with Motorola University Consulting and Training Services for extensive Six-Sigma training. The goal was to improve Citibank operations globally through defect reduction and process timeline improvement while increasing customer loyalty and satisfaction.

Citibank's mission focused on becoming the premier international financial company in the next millennium requiring excellence in every facet of the business and action on the part of every Citibank employee. This quality initiative began with training 650 senior managers by October 1997 and over 92,000 employees trained worldwide by early 1999.

## SIX-SIGMA TO THE RESCUE

The initial phase of the Six-Sigma process involved Motorola University training Citibank employees on both Cycle Time Reduction (CTR) and Cross Functional Process Mapping (CFPM). These methodologies essentially set the stage for Six-Sigma by mapping and eliminating wasteful and nonvalue-added processing steps from the business. In a nonmanufacturing company, 90 percent of activities may fall into this category. A sigma is a statistical term which measures to what degree a process varies from perfection. A rating of three sigma equals 66,807 defects per million opportunities; a rating of Six-Sigma equals 3.4 defects per million opportunities, or virtual perfection.

Six-Sigma is accomplished using simple tools, including the Pareto chart. The data on the chart identify which problems occur with the greatest frequency or incur the highest cost. It provides the direct evidence of what would be analyzed and corrected first. Typically 20 percent of the possible causes are responsible for 80 percent of any problem.

Citibank undertook the Six-Sigma process to investigate why it was not achieving complete customer satisfaction with a goal to have 10 times reduction in defects and cycle time by December 2000 and 10 times again every two years. Six-Sigma classifies a defect as anything that results in customer dissatisfaction and unhappiness. Indicators of less than optimal status are customer opinions such as:

- You're difficult to do business with;

- You don't fix my problems;

- You're not staying innovative and your systems are not state-of-the-art;

- You are slow and complicated.

## TEAM APPROACH

A team composed of bankers and operations people identified the entire funds transfer process, tabulating defects and analyzing them using Pareto charts. Highest on the list of defects for this process was the internal callback procedure, which required a staffer to phone back the requester to make sure that the instructions were correct, or had not been altered. "We cut monthly callbacks from 8,000 to 1,000 and we eliminated callbacks for 73 percent of the transactions coming in," says Cherylann Munoz, compliance director of Citibank's Private Bank in the United States and Western Hemisphere.

In Citibank's Global Cash and Trade Organization (GCTO), MU's Six-Sigma methodology helped track defects and documented the results by teaching team members to identify appropriate metrics, determine a baseline, establish appropriate standards, and monitor execution. The employees formed teams to solve any issues they discovered during this analysis.

To reduce the time for opening an account, Citibank formed a cross-functional global team of 80 people. The team first identified sponsors and formed a steering committee to champion the effort. Employees were invited to participate based on their subject matter know-how and ability to assist with the solution. The biggest hurdle for Citibank employees was allocating the time to participate while juggling their daily job responsibilities. Sue Andros, a global process owner in the GCTO responsible for the end-to-end customer experience says process mapping "lets people get to know one another."

"Team members worked well together, since achieving the objectives would make their professional responsibilities easier and would benefit their customers—a win/win situation for everyone," Andros says. "The focus on cycle time and deficiencies has made an impact on how we serve customers. It's not just a matter of doing things faster, it's doing things better. This means eliminating redundancy, minimizing hand-offs, and establishing metrics that reflect performance in the eyes of the customer."

Dipak Rastogi, executive vice president for Citibank's Eastern European/Central Asia and Africa region headquartered in London, agrees with those sentiments. "Introducing quality as a core strategy was viewed as a unique opportunity and differentiating feature not only with regard to our customers, but also our employees," says Rastogi. "When implemented correctly, quality increases customer satisfaction and leads to shorter reaction time and faster introduction of new products—providing a sustainable competitive advantage."

*(continued)*

## MANAGEMENT COMMITMENT

Teams involved in the Citibank quality initiative needed to have full autonomy to make decisions about changes to the established processes. Senior management sponsored these initiatives or served on steering committees to champion the work and there was an "open door" policy so that teams could gain access to them as needed. According to Peter Klimes, quality director for Citibank in the Czech Republic, the involvement of senior support is a continuous process all the way from setting critical business issues and objectives, to the final improvement implementation. "We have had a well-balanced split between projects initiated by senior management and those initiated by employees," Klimes says. "Our senior operations officer and our corporate bank head were our most active supporters of Six-Sigma projects. Their commitment helps balance back and front office aspects of projects."

**Source:** "Citibank Increases Loyalty with Defect-Free Processes," *The Journal for Quality & Participation,* Fall 2000, pp. 32–36.

2. Aims to enhance customer satisfaction through the effective application of the system, including processes for continual improvement of the system and the ensurance of conformity to customer requirements.

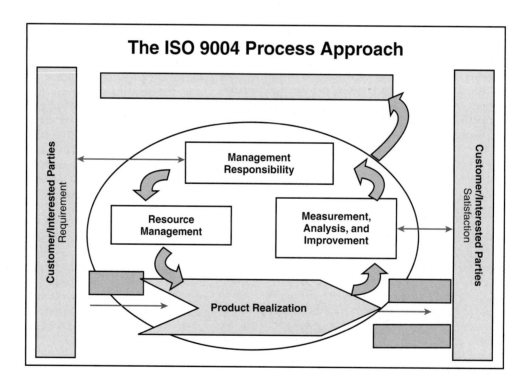

ISO 9004 has strong commonalities with other quality schemes such as Mil-Q, Deming's 14 points, TQM and the Malcolm Baldrige National Quality Award Criteria. The four focus areas of the ISO 9004 process approach are (1) management responsibility, (2) resource management, (3) product realization, and (4) measurement, analysis, and improvement. ISO 9004 differs from other quality approaches in that it involves formal certification by a sanctioned ISO certification source before a company can claim to meet the standard. Exhibit 11–6, Strategy in Action, describes how well-known golf club maker Ping chose to become ISO 9004 certified.

When John Solheim took the helm at golf equipment maker Ping in 1995, he had a legacy to protect and improve—that of his father, Karsten Solheim. When the employee handbook was written in 1993, Karsten wrote: "It is the customer who keeps us in business, and we must always be sure to give each one first-class treatment. The role of each employee is also very important because dedication to quality assures the success of the company."

The family business was founded over 42 years ago and is based in Phoenix. Today Ping is best known for its custom fit, custom-built golf clubs and competes in a highly innovative and competitive $4 billion golf equipment industry. John wasn't satisfied with the existing standard of quality and set about to find a way to measure the company business against an internationally accepted standard, ISO 9004. "By embarking on this journey, we hoped to measure ourselves against recognized criteria that would reassure us we were doing business appropriately," says Solheim. "We also believed such an accomplishment might help identify areas where we could advance." Both of Solheim's hopes were fulfilled.

## THE IMPLEMENTATION AND REGISTRATION PROCESS

After conducting some research, John Solheim decided to pursue registration to both ISO 9004 (quality management system standard) and ISO 14004 (environmental management system standard). This decision was based on several factors:

1. The ISO (International Organization for Standardization) standards are internationally recognized.

2. Attaining registration would provide Ping with a competitive advantage in the marketplace. Ping would be the first competitor in the golf industry to be registered to both ISO 9004 and ISO 14004 standards.

3. Ping wanted the benefits of implementing the management systems such as improved quality, increased environmental awareness, customer satisfaction, and continuous improvement.

Ping began the implementation process in November 1999. The first step was to develop documentation, identify and improve processes, and provide training to all personnel involved in the implementation. A preassessment audit acted as a dress rehearsal for employees and heightened their understanding of the requirements as well as identified opportunities for improvement in the existing system.

During this process Ping faced many challenges. First, its workforce consisted of over 1,000 employees who spoke at least six different languages. Additionally, company processes, documentation, and policies were very informal. Many hours were spent training and developing valuable manuals that are used as reference resources. "The registration process helped me see how everything in the company ties together and our processes really interrelate," said Solheim. "I thought I was fairly well-organized, but the registration audit taught me to dot my I's and cross my T's."

## BENEFITS

Ping's steering committee identified many benefits of the ISO 9004 and ISO 14004 registration.

1. Enhanced internal communication and increased focus on customer requirements throughout the organization.

2. The generation of useful information to allow more strategic decision making by all levels of management.

3. Better measurement of the processes that are responsible for quality and the ability to continually improve product quality.

4. Improved customer satisfaction and the continued reputation for quality, innovation, and service in the golf equipment market.

5. Development of a new customer service call system that improved customer response time.

6. Improved environmental performance resulting in reduced emissions.

7. Improved cycle times to meet our customers' demands.

Ping officially achieved registration on October 17, 2000. Ping is now in the process of implementing ISO 9004 and ISO 14004 in its sister company, Ping Europe Ltd., in Gainsborough, United Kingdom. This registration will include the Gainsborough Golf Club, a private 36-hole facility with a driving range and modern clubhouse. Ping believes this will be the first country club to ever be registered to international standards.

Now registered, the company is continuing to focus intensely on continuous improvement of the quality of its systems, operations, service, and products in a highly competitive worldwide market. "We continuously hone our ISO 9004 and 14004 systems, strengthening our quality and environmental objectives while looking for improvement opportunities. No one asked us to become ISO registered," Solheim says. "We raised our standards because golfers ultimately decide the fate of our products. Customer satisfaction will be the program's greatest benefit."

Upon introduction of the ISO 9004 series of standards, many American and multinational firms not only foresaw the competitive advantage possible by adopting ISO 9004, but also saw the value of quality management system implementation in achieving customer satisfaction. As a result, many of these larger firms subsequently imposed the requirements of ISO 9004 on suppliers as a condition to do business and as a way to reduce the supply base to only those suppliers committed to quality and service. It is believed by many that eventually ISO 9004 would reduce and possibly eliminate the need for customer-sponsored audits. In the ISO 9004 registration scheme, third-party auditors employed by registrars conduct ISO 9004 registration audits. National and international accreditation bodies accredit the registrars to certify and publish that the company has met the requirements of ISO 9004.

Customer mandates initially served as an incentive for suppliers desiring to retain existing levels of business with their customers to jump on the ISO 9004 bandwagon and pursue registration. In many cases registration to ISO 9004 gave these suppliers a clear competitive advantage in the marketplace. However, as many companies continue to pursue and maintain registration, ISO 9004 functions as a way of life for many companies and has become ingrained in daily processes, no longer thought of as a unique or identifiable program. Other companies, who were not pressured to implement ISO 9004, chose to put it into practice as a methodology by which to systematize their operations and to focus on and improve both daily operations and quality levels throughout their organizations.

Nevertheless, along with the establishment of ISO 9004 standards came many misperceptions. Here are just a few of the criticisms targeted at ISO 9004.

• *ISO 9004 is a European standard and cannot be applicable to American firms.* ISO 9004 has traceable American ancestry to military quality systems. The United States is a member of International Organization for Standardization (ISO) and participates in the formulation and continuing committee reviews of ISO 9004.

• *Implementing ISO 9004 is mandatory if you plan to do business in Europe.* This is true for a small number of firms manufacturing a relative handful of products—a list that may continue to grow in the coming years. But the doors to Europe did not slam shut on non-ISO 9004 registered companies in January 2003. Rather, ISO 9004 registration has increasingly become desired, expected and even required in certain markets and industries (i.e., Automotive QS-9004), but growth was driven primarily by customer requirements and competitive pressures.

• *ISO 9004 is all about paperwork.* Ironically, ISO 9004 had in most cases reduced the redundancy and massive manuals and shelves of procedures and books that already exist. Documentation is central to ISO 9004 requirements for the purposes of planning, controlling, training, and providing objective evidence of conformance. The goal is to make the documentation support the value-added activity clearly and concisely, eliminating redundancy while supporting usefulness. The standard does not prescribe specific solutions, tactics, strategies, or procedures which gives ISO 9004 enormous flexibility.

• *ISO 9004 is inspection-based as opposed to prevention-based.* ISO 9004 requires the quality management system monitor conformance to requirements. This is just one part of the measurement, analysis, and continuous improvement cycle at the heart of the standard. Implementation of the standard alone will not guarantee quality. Management commitment and employee involvement are instrumental in the implementation process.

Since its introduction, international participation in ISO 9004 continues to climb and offers organizations a framework for quality system management. It is no longer new or radical, yet it provides a common language for quality that is easily translatable and applicable across many countries, cultures, and businesses. The focus is not on products and services but rather on the organization's network of activities designed and operated to ensure that output meets the ultimate business objective: satisfying the customer.

## The Balanced Scorecard Methodology

A new approach to strategic control was developed in the last decade by Harvard Business School professors Robert Kaplan and David Norton. They named this system the *balanced scorecard.* Recognizing some of the weaknesses and vagueness of previous implementation and control approaches, the balanced scorecard approach was intended to provide a clear prescription as to what companies should measure in order to "balance" the financial perspective in implementation and control of strategic plans.[2]

The balanced scorecard was viewed as a *management system* (not only a measurement system) that enables companies to clarify their strategies, translate them into action, and provide meaningful feedback. It provides feedback around both the internal business processes and external outcomes in order to continuously improve strategic performance and results. When fully deployed, the balanced scorecard is intended to transform strategic planning from a separate top management exercise into the nerve center of an enterprise. Kaplan and Norton describe the innovation of the balanced scorecard as follows:

> The balanced scorecard retains traditional financial measures. But financial measures tell the story of past events, an adequate story for industrial age companies for which investments in long-term capabilities and customer relationships were not critical for success. These financial measures are inadequate, however, for guiding and evaluating the journey that information age companies must make to create future value through investment in customers, suppliers, employees, processes, technology, and innovation.[3]

The balanced scorecard methodology adapts the TQM ideas of customer-defined quality, continuous improvement, employee empowerment, and measurement-based management/ feedback into an expanded methodology that includes traditional financial data and results. The balanced scorecard incorporates feedback around internal business process *outputs,* as in TQM, but also adds a feedback loop around the *outcomes* of business strategies. This creates a "double-loop feedback" process in the balanced scorecard. In doing so, it links together two areas of concern in strategy execution—quality operations and financial outcomes—that are typically addressed separately yet are obviously critically intertwined as any company executes its strategy. A system that links shareholder interests in return on capital with a system of performance management that is linked to ongoing, operational activities and processes within the company is what the balanced scorecard attempts to achieve.

Exhibit 11–7 illustrates the balanced scorecard approach drawing on the traditional DuPont formula discussed in Chapter 5 and historically used to examine drivers of stockholder-related financial performance across different company activities. The balanced scorecard seeks to "balance" shareholder goals with customer goals and operational performance goals, and Exhibit 11–7 shows that they are interconnected—shareholder value creation is linked to divisional concerns for return on capital employed, which, in turn, is driven by functional outcomes in sales, inventory, capacity utilization, that, in turn, come

---

[2] This methodology is covered in great detail in a number of books and articles by R. S. Kaplan and D. P. Norton. It is also the subject of frequent special publications by the *Harvard Business Review* that provided updated treatment of uses and improvements in the balanced scorecard methodology. Some useful books include *Balanced Scorecard: Translating Strategies into Action* (Boston: Harvard Business School Press, 1996); *The Strategy-Focused Organization* (Boston: Harvard Business School Press, 2001). And, in HBR, "Using the Balanced Scorecard as a Strategic Management System," *Harvard Business Review* (January–February, 1996). Numerous useful websites also exist such as www.bscol.com.

[3] Another useful treatment of various aspects of the Balanced Scoreboard to include further learning opportunities you may wish to explore, especially with regard to the use of this approach with governmental organizations, may be found at www.balancedscorecard.org. Chapter 6 in this book describes how the Balanced Scorecard approach is used to help create measurable objectives linked directly to the company's strategy.

**EXHIBIT 11–7**
**Integrating Shareholder Value and Organizational Activities across Organizational Levels**

Source: R. M. Grant, *Contemporary Strategy Analysis* (Oxford, UK: Blackwell, 2002), p. 56).

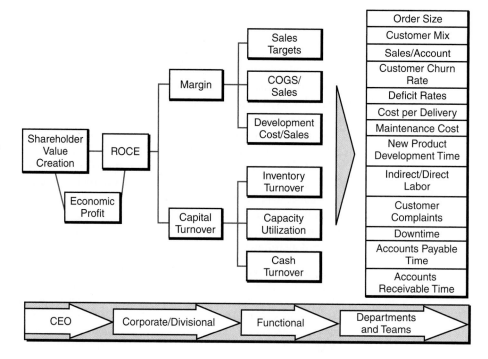

about through the results of departments and teams daily activities throughtout the company. The balanced scorecard suggests that we view the organization from *four* perspectives, and to develop metrics, collect data, and analyze it relative to each of these perspectives:

1. *The Learning and Growth Perspective: How well are we continuously improving and creating value?* The scorecard insists on measures related to innovation and organizational learning to gauge performance on this dimension—technological leadership, product development cycle times, operational process improvement, and so on.

2. *The Business Process Perspective: What are our core competencies and areas of operational excellence?* Internal business processes and their effective execution as measured by productivity, cycle time, quality measures, downtime, various cost measures among others provide scorecard input here.

3. *The Customer Perspective: How satisfied are our customers?* A customer satisfaction perspective typically adds measures related to defect levels, on-time delivery, warranty support, product development among others that come from direct customer input and are linked to specific company activities.

4. *The Financial Perspective: How are we doing for our shareholders?* A financial perspective typically using measures like cash flow, return on equity, sales and income growth.

Through the integration of goals from each of these four perspectives, the balanced scorecard approach enables the strategy of the business to be linked with shareholder value creation while providing several measurable short-term outcomes that guide and monitor strategy implementation. Kaplan and Norton provide this account of the use of the balanced scorecard at FMC:

> Strategists came up with 5- and 10-year plans, controllers with one-year budgets and near-term forecasts. Little interplay occurred between the two groups. But the [balanced] scorecard now bridges the two. The financial perspective builds on the traditional function

**EXHIBIT 11–8**
**Balanced Scorecard for Mobil Corporation's NAM&R**

| | | Strategic Objectives | Strategic Measures |
|---|---|---|---|
| Financially Strong | Financial | F1 Return on Capital Employed<br>F2 Cash Flow<br>F3 Profitability<br>F4 Lowest Cost<br>F5 Profitable Growth<br>F6 Manage Risk | • ROCE<br>• Cash Flow<br>• Net Margin<br>• Full cost per gallon delivered to customer<br>• Volume growth rate vs. industry<br>• Risk index |
| Delight the Consumer<br><br>Win–Win Relationship | Customer | C1 Continually delight the targeted consumer<br><br>C2 Improve dealer/distributor profitability | • Share of segment in key markets<br>• Mystery shopper rating<br><br>• Dealer/distributor margin on gasoline<br>• Dealer/distributor survey |
| Safe and Reliable<br><br><br><br><br><br>Competitive Supplier<br><br><br>Good Neighbor<br><br>On Spec On Time | Internal | I1 Marketing<br>  1. Innovative products and services<br>  2. Dealer/distributor quality<br><br>I2 Manufacturing<br>  1. Lower manufacturing costs<br>  2. Improve hardware and performance<br>I3 Supply, Trading, Logistics<br>  1. Reducing delivered cost<br>  2. Trading organization<br>  3. Inventory management<br><br>I4 Improve health, safety, and environmental performance<br>I5 Quality | • Non-gasoline revenue and margin per square foot<br>• Dealer/distributor acceptance rate of new programs<br>• Dealer/distributor quality ratings<br>• ROCE on refinery<br>• Total expenses (per gallon) vs. competition<br>• Profitability index<br>• Yield index<br>Delivered cost per gallon vs. competitors<br>• Trading margin<br>• Inventory level compared to plan and to output rate<br>• Number of incidents<br>• Days away from work<br>• Quality index |
| Motivated and Prepared | Learning and growth | L1 Organization involvement<br>L2 Core competencies and skills<br>L3 Access to strategic information | • Employee survey<br>• Strategic competitive availability<br>• Strategic information availabiilty |

performed by controllers. The other three perspectives make the division's long-term objectives measurable.[4]

Another example that helps you understand the integrating power of the balanced scorecard can be seen at Mobil Corporation's North American Marketing and Refining business (NAM&R). NAM&R's scorecard is shown in Exhibit 11–8. Assisted by Kaplan and Norton,

---

[4] R. Kaplan and D. Norton, "Putting the Balanced Scorecard to Work," *Harvard Business Review* (September–October, 1993), p. 147.

an unprofitable NAM&R adopted the scorecard methodology to better link its strategy with financial objectives and to translate these into operating performance targets tailored to outcomes in each business unit, functional departments, and operating processes within them. They included measures developed with key customers from their perspective. The result was an integrated system where scorecards provided measurable outcomes through which the performance of each department and operating unit, team or activity within NAM&R was monitored, adjusted, and used to determine performance-related pay bonuses.[5]

The balanced scorecard reflects continuous improvement in management thought about how to better manage organizations. Our coverage of the concept is brief, and you are encouraged to seek additional information and resources suggested in various footnotes or through your own current Web search. Strategic control, continuous improvement, specific measurable feedback and inclusion of everyone in some way responsible for customer satisfaction and organizational success are important developments in the art of strategic management and the science of its succesful application.

---

## Summary

Three fundamental perspectives—strategic control, continuous improvement, and the balanced scoreboard—provide the basis for designing strategy control systems. Strategic controls are intended to steer the company toward its long-term strategic goals. Premise controls, implementation controls, strategic surveillance, and special alert controls are types of strategic control. All four types are designed to meet top management's needs to track the strategy as it is being implemented, to detect underlying problems, and to make necessary adjustments. These strategic controls are linked to the environmental assumptions and the key operating requirements necessary for successful strategy implementation. Ever-present forces of change fuel the need for and focus of strategic control.

Operational control systems require systematic evaluation of performance against predetermined standards or targets. A critical concern here is identification and evaluation of performance deviations, with careful attention paid to determining the underlying reasons for and strategic implications of observed deviations before management reacts. Some firms use trigger points and contingency plans in this process.

The "quality imperative" of the last 20 years has redefined global competitiveness to include reshaping the way many businesses approach strategic and operational control. What has emerged is a commitment to continuous improvement in which personnel across all levels in an organization define customer value, identify ways every process within the business influences customer value, and seek continuously to enhance the quality, efficiency, and responsiveness with which the processes, products, and services are created and supplied. This includes attending to internal as well as external customers. The "balanced scorecard" is a control system that integrates strategic goals, operating outcomes, customer satisfaction, and continuous improvement into an ongoing strategic management system.

---

## Questions for Discussion

1. Distinguish strategic control from operating control. Give an example of each.

2. Select a business whose strategy is familiar to you. Identify what you think are the key premises of the strategy. Then select the key indicators that you would use to monitor each of these premises.

3. Explain the differences between implementation controls, strategic surveillance, and special alert controls. Give an example of each.

[5] "How Mobil Became a Strategy-Focused Organization," Chapter 2 in R. Kaplan and D. Norton, *The Strategy-Focused Organization* (Boston: Harvard Business School Press, 2001). For an online version of the Mobil NAM&R case study, see www.bscol.com.

4. Why are budgets, schedules, and key success factors essential to operations control and evaluation?

5. What are key considerations in monitoring deviations from performance standards?

6. What are five key elements of quality management? How are quality imperative and continuous improvement related to strategic and operational control?

7. How might customer value be linked to quality, efficiency, and responsiveness?

8. Is it realistic that a commitment to continuous improvement could actually replace operational controls? Strategic controls?

9. How is the balanced scorecard approach similar to continuous improvement? How is it different?

## Chapter 11 Discussion Case A

# Strategic Control at Xerox under Ann Mulcahy's Watch

BusinessWeek

1 Anne Mulcahy likes to tell the story of the business acquaintance who compared her to a farmer with a cow stuck in a ditch. The cow, of course, was copying and printing giant Xerox, of which Mulcahy became president in 2000 and CEO in August, 2001. It was no doubt the toughest assignment in her 27 years at the company: As she took charge, Xerox was experiencing its second consecutive year of steep losses amid rising rumors of bankruptcy. Mulcahy's job was to pull Xerox out of that ditch—and keep it out.

2 Mulcahy became the first woman CEO in Xerox's history, thanks in large part to her performance as its first female president and chief operating officer, a job she got after a succession of men had failed.

3 Mulcahy's turnaround strategy focused first on cash generation and cost reduction. Let's look at some of the basic controls that she used.

## IMPLEMENTATION CONTROL

4 Monitoring key strategic thrusts to raise cash along with setting short-term milestone reviews on cost-cutting measures were Mulcahy's main means of implementation control. She had a preference early-on for close person monitoring and involvement in these controls.

5 Early in her strategy, Mulcahy, president and CEO-in-waiting at the time, flew from headquarters in Stamford, Conn., to Rochester, N.Y., the home of Xerox's big operations, to deliver devastating news. The company was killing its entire line of desktop inkjet printers—a one-year-old business that employed 1,500 people worldwide and had been championed by Mulcahy herself. The division would not turn a profit for at least two years, though, and Xerox needed cash now. "In a year of tough decisions, this one was toughest," Mulcahy says.

6 Tough hardly does justice to that year. Xerox's directors suddenly promoted Mulcahy to president in May 2000, after ousting G. Richard Thoman, who lasted all of 13 months, and reinstalling Chairman Paul A. Allaire as CEO. The company was close to foundering after years of weak sales and high costs; employees were as disgruntled as customers.

7 Then, when Xerox's financial situation worsened later that year, the company was forced to take drastic action. With Allaire fixated on repairing the balance sheet, Mulcahy focused on operations, promising to slash $1 billion from Xerox's annual costs in two years. She set specific milestone targets as a roadmap to accomplishing those targets, including major decreases in personnel costs and manufacturing costs. 11,500 middle managers and factory workers later, and with a combination of significant outsourcing and manufacturing facility consolidation, she accomplished her objective in 18 months. Notably, her penchant for personal involvement was seen in this difficult task—she tried to make the announcements in person whenever jobs were cut or facilities shut down.

8 Her aggressive cost-cutting exceeded her original goal and helped generate a respectable $1.9 billion in operating cash flow and $91 million in net income on $15.8 billion in revenues by year-end, 2002. Worries over Xerox's ability to pay off $21.3 billion in liabilities—$9.2 billion of them long-term—have also been put to rest. At the end of 2003, it raised $3.6 billion with offerings of stock and bonds, and through bank financing, enough to earn itself a credit upgrade—from BB− to BB—from ratings agency Fitch.

9 The next milestone investors will want to examine and which are part of Mulcahy's implementation control involve steady improvements in earnings on a quarterly basis. In late 2003 as we write this book, Wall Street analysts expect $89 million, or 12 cents a share, on quarterly revenues of $3.9 billion. While that's a penny less than the first quarter's adjusted earnings, when it rang up $3.76 billion in sales, Xerox has proved that it can cut fat. The big challenge now will be whether it increase revenues. And it is the top line that Mulcahy's implementation control now turns toward.

10 Analyst Shannon Cross of equity research boutique Cross Research thinks overall sales will be down slightly in 2003, from $15.7 billion last year. To

meet analysts' 2004 expectations, Xerox would have to expand sales by about 7 percent next year—or further reduce expenses. The problem with the second option: Not much is left to cut.

## STRATEGIC ALERT CONTROL

11    As she sought to consolidate her operational control as the new president and COO of Xerox in early 2000, things went from bad to worse for Mulcahy. Not only did Xerox report its first quarterly loss in 16 years and see its debt load piling up, but three months into her new position the Securities & Exchange Commission began investigating whether Xerox used accounting tricks to boost income in the five previous years.

12    This startling announcement sent shock waves not only throughout Xerox and the investment community but, perhaps more critically, Xerox's customer base and their faith in Xerox's ability to survive. Bankruptcy rumors started.

13    Mulcahy had a management group set up a strategic alert control team to monitor every aspect of this issue—the SEC investigators, where the admonition from Mulcahy was full and complete cooperation; key customers; the business press—with the key concern being to try to quickly and responsively handle subsequent negative publicity combined with immediate efforts by herself and anyone needed to assure key customers and, most importantly, to get a settlement resolved quickly yet fairly so as to not jeopardize Xerox's fragile cash situation.

14    Finally, almost 20 months later, the Securities & Exchange Commission issued suspension orders against two former Xerox accounting officers, apparently closing the books on a scandal that last year forced the company to restate five years of sales revenues and pay a $10 million fine.

## PREMISE CONTROL

15    Mulcahy's second phase in turning around Xerox centers on revenue growth and product innovation. Expectations for their success in this regard are built on several premises which her management team will closely monitor.

16    Xerox's growth should approach 7 percent if some key premises hold out. Premise number one is that recent product price cuts and added focus on services should help Xerox grow faster than other printer-and-copier makers. Premise number two is that Xerox's strong presence overseas—which represents a big chunk of the 40 percent of its overseas revenue—will benefit from the weak dollar. Premise number three, Xerox sales are closely tied to the U.S. economy, which is recovering.

17    Premise number four is that price-cutting could grab it an additional 2 percent to 3 percent share of the printer market, where it now holds 18 percent, estimates Peter Grant, an analyst with market consultancy Gartner. In the past, Xerox sold its printers and copiers at a premium of 10 percent to 15 percent over rivals' products. Xerox introduced 21 new models in 2003 and cut prices to the most competitive levels in its history. As a result, Xerox wares now sell at or below the cost of competitors like Sharp, says Andy Slawetsky, a vice-president with imaging consultancy Industry Analysts. Independent tests already show that Xerox equipment makes copies faster than virtually all rivals, and customers consider its salesforce among the best-trained, adds Slawetsky. Also, Xerox software is considered an industry benchmark.

## STRATEGIC SURVEILLANCE CONTROL

18    Perhaps most critical to Mulcahy's strategy at Xerox are expectations or premises that a major trend is underway where companies are switching from black and white to color printers and copiers. So Mulcahy's long-term success is heavily dependent on this trend unfolding as a basis for major growth at Xerox. Xerox plans to capitalize on customers' transition from black-and-white copying and printing to color. Overall revenues from monochrome printers are declining, but the U.S. market for color printers will grow from $1.2 billion this year to $1.8 billion in three years according to some estimates. As corporations switch to color, revenues could grow dramatically, since Xerox receives about 9 cents per page on color copying, versus about 1.5 cents for black-and-white prints. Xerox also has increased its focus on services, already a $3 billion-plus part of its business. Strategic surveillance of developments in all industry sectors that use copiers and printers is a critical control priority at Xerox to maximize its chances to take advantage of the switch to color trend and the need for services in doing so.

**19** Also the subject of strategic surveillance are possible challenges: With Xerox dropping its prices, the competition will likely follow suit. In fact, Grant predicts that average selling prices for color printers will fall by more than 20 percent this year. That's less than last year's 25 percent decline, but Xerox would likely be obliged to respond with yet another cut. And its margins could drop from the current 42 percent to 40 percent, say analysts. In both products and services, Xerox will hit stiff competition. Hewlett-Packard (HPQ) is expected to come out with a new color printer-copier within the next 12 months. HP declined to comment on new-product introductions, but it's working to make its pricing easier to understand in the hope of appealing to small and midsize businesses, says Chris Morgan, vice-president for imaging and printing sales and marketing at HP. Both it and IBM (IBM) are pushing package deals for smaller companies, offerings that go beyond information-technology network services tied in with printers and copiers.

**20** Xerox insists it isn't worried. "We expect that [rivals] don't have a lot of room in which to cut prices," says a spokesperson. "At the same time, we're confident that Xerox has the right business model to drive profitable revenue from these products while remaining competitive in this aggressive industry." Again, this is a sure premise to be monitored and a candidate for strategic surveillance control.

**Source:** "That Heartbeat You Hear Is Xerox," *BusinessWeek*, July 16, 2003.

## Chapter 11 Discussion Case B

BusinessWeek

# The Web of Quality: Worldwide Links Mean Better Products

1  Just a decade ago, U.S. businesses were crowing about the promise of new quality-improvement programs. Since then, the U.S. quality movement has altered and improved business practices, and many American companies have matched Japan's vaunted quality benchmarks. Industrial offices buzzed with phrases such as "total quality management (TQM)" and "Six-Sigma accuracy." Such catchphrases are heard less frequently because they've been replaced by Internet jargon. And that raises a question: Where does quality stand in the Internet age?

2  Concerns about quality have by no means disappeared. Rather, at most successful companies, quality has become internalized, says quality consultant Joseph A. DeFeo, CEO of Juran Institute Inc. in Wilton, Conn. The special software and management practices associated with the movement are now in everyday use, he says, so quality has become less self-conscious. But it has reemerged as a critical issue because of the rapid development of Internet links among companies. Quality is no longer the concern of just a single factory but of whole supply chains. As companies outsource more of their work, they need to take increasing care to make sure their partners measure up on quality, says Michael J. Burkett, a senior analyst at Boston's AMR Research Inc., a manufacturing consultant.

3  This report explores the role of quality in today's increasingly networked world. The first section looks at how a unit of General Electric Co. is blazing new quality trails in a field it helped pioneer. The second lifts the lid on efforts by Mexico's manufacturers to meet the quality demands of customers in North America and overseas.

## GE: ZERO TO 60, NO SKID MARKS

4  Never before has General Electric Co. cranked out gas-powered turbines in such quantities. Given the growing preference for gas-powered generating plants over their much dirtier coal-burning cousins, demand is booming—with no sign of slowing. In May, GE's Power Systems unit installed five times the number of turbines it did a year earlier. Yet despite the problems of grappling with such a huge increase in production, GE has become progressively better at making good on delivery date promises. Indeed, the company has actually delivered many units ahead of schedule (see chart on p. 392). GE Power's success at managing its huge runup in output is a much-discussed success story among GE insiders—and a major reason they view Power Systems head Robert L. Nardelli as a top contender for GE's CEO job when Jack Welch retires.

5  While GE is hardly complaining about this upturn, executives realized that the runup would pose huge risks. In particular, they worried about maintaining their grip on quality, continuing to fill orders on time, and keeping customers happy. The last thing they wanted was to become another example of a company that lost control when it tried to goose production quickly after getting bombarded by orders. The production snafus at Boeing Co. in 1997 offered an ominous example of how things can go wrong in a big rampup. And when GE execs began taking notice in 1998 of industry numbers showing that electrical-power reserves in the United States were shrinking to alarming levels, Boeing's difficulties were painfully fresh.

6  OUTSIDE RISKS. To prepare for the projected hike in orders, GE Power Systems' managers visited companies that had lived through similar explosions in their businesses. They made a point of flying to Seattle to glean insights from Boeing officials. One thing became evident right away: The biggest risk to GE was outside the company. Suppliers that lacked GE's financial resources might not be able to expand production rapidly enough. At Boeing and other casualties of too-fast growth, most breakdowns occurred when suppliers overestimated their production capacity. Since more than 50 percent of a turbine's components are purchased from outside vendors, GE wasted no time shoring up its supply chain. In 1998, GE Power Systems launched an exhaustive study of the suppliers that provide key components for the gas turbines. After first screening 250 of its suppliers, it intensively audited 85 that posed the greatest risk. Teams consisting of specialists in supply sourcing, research and development, finance, and management spent up to two weeks at supplier facilities across the United States and around the world.

7  Since the last major rampup in production at Power Systems in the late 80s, GE had two new tools to help

it avoid supply-chain problems, says Victor R. Abate, general manager of fulfillment at Power Systems. One was the Internet. But more important was the company's vaunted Six-Sigma program, adopted in 1996. Six sigma is statistics-speak for 99.9999976 percent. Applied to manufacturing, it means a quality level of no more than 3.4 defects per million products. At GE, the Six-Sigma program also includes guidelines and tools for boosting productivity and wringing inefficiencies out of its manufacturing and service processes. Mark M. Little, a vice-president at GE Power Systems, says that with Six-Sigma's tools, GE no longer has to rely on bludgeoning suppliers to deliver. Instead, GE's auditors have the wherewithal to determine whether suppliers can hand over parts in time.

8    GE's vendor-checkers scrutinize myriad details right down to the individual machine tools that suppliers use to produce turbine parts. GE also evaluates the supplier's suppliers—their production capacity, shipping and delivery systems, and how rigorous their quality programs are. And the exam doesn't end there. Because a supplier might need to boost hiring, GE checks to see whether the company keeps a stack of résumés on hand. In the end, GE eliminated some suppliers and found backups for suppliers with obvious weaknesses. And they tagged some 350 potential problems that continued to be monitored until fixed by the suppliers.

9    INVALUABLE ASSET. Perhaps most important, the initial evaluation allowed GE to establish a framework for ensuring the quality of its supply chain as production rolled forward. Says analyst Nicholas P. Heymann of Prudential Securities Inc., who formerly worked as a GE auditor: "How many companies today have guys that can go into another company and fully assess where the flaws are—and not only that but also fix them? They've executed Six-Sigma all the way through the supplier chain."

10    That was an invaluable asset as orders flowed in and the stress on production systems mounted, both internally and among suppliers. With its new predictive tools, deep knowledge of its suppliers, and the ability to share information quickly via the Internet, GE could identify problems earlier and avoid potentially costly bottlenecks. "Whenever we see variation, we just attack it," Abate says.

11    Example: GE last year realized that a supplier of a core turbine component was poised to fall behind. Although the company was consistently delivering to GE on time, GE's Six-Sigma audit had found the supplier would be unable to keep up as GE went from producing 25 turbines to 45 per quarter in late 1999. GE sent a team to the company, and a settlement was

reached: The supplier would lease additional equipment to keep up with GE's production track. "With these very rigorous tools," says Little, "we now know what the leading indicators are, and we can act fast."

12    The Internet has made a big difference, too. When GE engineers are in the field, checking on deliveries at customers sites anywhere in the world, they can report on a problem on their laptops, and this information is available instantly throughout GE Power Systems. Before the Net, the field engineers would typically resolve each problem at the plant site—but GE managers would remain blissfully unaware of the solution, which would have to be engineered all over again the next time.

13    So what's the customer's view of how well GE is coping with its production surges? Duke Energy North America (DENA, a unit of Charlotte-based Duke Energy Corp.) is clearly satisfied. It placed a huge order with GE in the fall of 1998 to outfit nearly two dozen generating plants with gas turbines, four of which will be on line by month's end. Including service agreements, it was a $4 billion order. So far, everything has gone according to schedule or slightly ahead of it, says James M. Donnell, CEO of DENA. For Duke, there's a lot at stake. With summer already starting to stroke demand for electricity, each day that a gas-turbine plant isn't producing means a huge revenue loss. A 640-megawatt plant running at maximum capacity for 16 hours on a summer day, for example, translates into $1.75 million in gross revenues.

14    For GE the stakes are high, too. The company boasts that it has grabbed a 75 percent share of current turbine orders. With the power industry relying so heavily on one supplier, more eyes than ever will be watching to see if Power Systems can keep managing the boom.

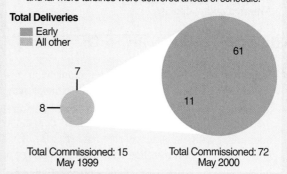

**Spinning Up Quality at GE**

Thanks to its six-sigma program, turbine production soared and far more turbines were delivered ahead of schedule.

**Total Deliveries**
- Early
- All other

7

8

61

11

Total Commissioned: 15
May 1999

Total Commissioned: 72
May 2000

**Source:** Petty, John, "When Near Enough is Not Good Enough," *Australian CPA*, May 2000, pp. 34–35.

# Guide to Strategic Management Case Analysis

## THE CASE METHOD

Case analysis is a proven educational method that is especially effective in a strategic management course. The case method complements and enhances the text material and your professor's lectures by focusing attention on what a firm has done or should do in an actual business situation. Use of the case method in a strategic management course offers you an opportunity to develop and refine analytical skills. It also can provide exciting experience by allowing you to assume the role of the key decision maker for the organizations you will study.

When assuming the role of the general manager of the organization being studied, you will need to consider all aspects of the business. In addition to drawing on your knowledge of marketing, finance, management, production, and economics, you will be applying the strategic management concepts taught in this course.

The cases in this book are accounts of real business situations involving a variety of firms in a variety of industries. To make these opportunities as realistic as possible, the cases include a variety of quantitative and qualitative information in both the presentation of the situation and the exhibits. As the key decision maker, you will need to determine which information is important, given the circumstances described in the case. Keep in mind that the results of analyzing one firm will not necessarily be appropriate for another since every firm is faced with a different set of circumstances.

## PREPARING FOR CASE DISCUSSION

The case method requires an approach to class preparation that differs from the typical lecture course. In the typical lecture course, you can still benefit from each class session even if you did not prepare, by listening carefully to the professor's lecture. This approach will not work in a course using the case method. For a case course, proper preparation is essential.

### Suggestions for Effective Preparation

1. *Allow adequate time in preparing a case.* Many of the cases in this text involve complex issues that are often not apparent without careful reading and purposeful reflection on the information in the cases.

2. *Read each case twice.* Because many of these cases involve complex decision making, you should read each case at least twice. Your first reading should give you an overview of the firm's unique circumstances and the issues confronting the firm. Your second reading allows you to concentrate on what you feel are the most critical issues and to understand what information in the case is most important. Make limited notes identifying key points during your first reading. During your second reading, you can add details to your original notes and revise them as necessary.

3. *Focus on the key strategic issue in each case.* Each time you read a case you should concentrate on identifying the key issue. In some cases, the key issue will be identified by the case writer in the introduction. In other cases, you might not grasp the key strategic issue until you have read the case several times. (Remember that not every piece of information in a case is equally important.)

4. *Do not overlook exhibits.* The exhibits in these cases should be considered an integral part of the information for the case. They are not just "window dressing." In fact, for many cases you will need to analyze financial statements, evaluate organizational charts, and understand the firm's products, all of which are presented in the form of exhibits.

5. *Adopt the appropriate time frame.* It is critical that you assume the appropriate time frame for each case you read. If the case ends in 2000, that year should become the present for you as you work on that case. Making a decision for a case that ends in 1999 by using data you could not have had until 2003 defeats the purpose of the case method. For the same reason, although it is recommended that you do outside reading on each firm and industry, you should not read material written after the case ended unless your professor instructs you to do so.

6. *Draw on all of your knowledge of business.* As the key decision maker for the organization being studied, you will need to consider all aspects of the business and industry. Do not confine yourself to strategic management concepts presented in this course. You will need to determine if the key strategic issue revolves around a theory you have learned in a functional area, such as marketing, production, finance, or economics, or in the strategic management course.

## USING THE INTERNET IN CASE RESEARCH

The proliferation of information available on the Internet has direct implications for business research. The Internet has become a viable source of company and industry data to assist those involved in case study analysis. Principal sources of useful data include company websites, U.S. government websites, search engines, investment research sites, and online data services. This section will describe the principal Internet sources of case study data and offer means of retrieving that data.

### Company Websites

Virtually every public and private firm has a website that any Internet user can visit. Accessing a firm's website is easy. Many firms advertise their web address through both TV and print advertisements. To access a site when the address is known, enter the address into the address line on any Internet service provider's homepage. When the address is not known, use of a search engine will be necessary. The use of a search engine will be described later. Often, but not always, a firm's web address is identical to its name, or is at least an abbreviated form of its name.

Company websites contain data that are helpful in case study analysis. A firm's website may contain descriptions of company products and services, recent company accomplishments and press releases, financial and stock performance highlights, and an overview of a firm's history and strategic objectives. A company's website may also contain links to relevant industry websites that contain industry statistics as well as current and future industry trends. The breadth of data available on a particular firm's website will vary but in general larger, global corporations tend to have more complete and sophisticated websites than do smaller, regional firms.

## U.S. Government Websites

The U.S. government allows the public to access virtually all of the information that it collects. Most of this information is available online to Internet users. The government collects a great range of data types, from firm-specific data the government mandates all publicly traded firms to supply, to highly regarded economic indicators. The usefulness of many U.S. government websites depends on the fit between the case you are studying and the data located on the website. For example, a study of an accounting firm may be supplemented with data supplied by the Internal Revenue Service website, but not the Environmental Protection Agency website. A sampling of prominent government websites and their addresses is shown below.

Environmental Protection Agency: www.epa.gov

General Printing Office: www.gpo.gov

Internal Revenue Service: www.irs.ustreas.gov

Libraries of Congress: www.loc.gov

National Aeronautics and Space Administration: www.hq.nasa.gov

SEC's Edgar Database: www.sec.gov/edgarhp.htm

Small Business Administration: www.sba.gov

STAT-USA: www.stat-usa.gov

U.S. Department of Commerce: www.doc.gov

U.S. Department of Treasury: www.ustreas.gov

One of the most useful sites for company case study analysis is the Securities and Exchange Commission's EDGAR database listed above. The EDGAR database contains the documents that the government mandates all publicly traded firms to file including 10-Ks and 8-Ks. A form 10-K is the annual report that provides a comprehensive overview of a firm's financials in addition to discussions regarding industry and product background. Form 8-K reports the occurrence of any material events or corporate changes that may be of importance to investors. Examples of reported occurrences include key management personnel changes, corporate restructures, and new debt or equity issuance. This site is very user friendly and requires the researcher to provide only the company name in order to produce a listing of all available reports.

## Search Engines

Search engines allow a researcher to locate information on a company or industry without prior knowledge of a specific Internet address. Generally, to execute a search the search engine requires the entering of a keyword, for example, a company name. However, each search engine differs slightly in its search capabilities. For example, to narrow a search on one search engine may be accomplished differently than narrowing a search on another.

The information retrieved by search engines typically includes articles and other information that contain the entered keyword or words. Because the search engine has retrieved data that contain keywords does not necessarily mean that the information is useful. Internet data are unfiltered, meaning they may not be checked for accuracy before the data are posted online. However, data copyrighted or published by a reputable source may greatly increase the chance that the data are indeed accurate. A list of popular Internet search engines is shown below:

Alta Vista: www.altavista.digital.com

DogPile: www.dogpile.com

Excite: www.excite.com

HotBot: www.hotbot.lycos.com

InfoSeek: www.infoseek.com

Lycos: www.lycos.com

Metacrawler: www.metacrawler.com

WebCrawler: www.webcrawler.com

Yahoo!: www.yahoo.com

Although Yahoo! appears in the above list, it is not a true search engine. Yahoo! actually catalogs websites for users. When keywords are entered into Yahoo!'s search mechanism, Yahoo! will return Internet addresses that contain the keywords. Therefore, Yahoo! is regarded as a very efficient means of locating a firm's website without prior knowledge of its exact web address.

## Investment Research Sites

Investment research sites provide company stock performance data including key financial ratios, competitor identification, industry data, and links to research reports and SEC filings. These sites provide support for the financial analysis portion of a case study, but only for publicly traded businesses. Most investment research sites also contain macro market data that may not be company specific, but may still affect many investors of equities.

Investment research sites usually contain a search mechanism if a desired stock's ticker symbol is not known. In this case, the company name is entered to enable the site to find the corresponding equity. Since these sites are geared toward traders who want recent stock prices and data, searching for data relevant to a case may require more elaborate investigations at multiple sites. The list below includes many popular investment research sites:

American Stock Exchange: www.amex.com

CBS Market Watch: cbsmarketwatch.com

CNN FinancialNews: money.cnn.com

DBC Online: www.esignal.com

Hoover's Online: www.hoovers.com

InvestorGuide: www.investorguide.com

Wall Street Research Net: www.wsrn.com

Market Guide: www.marketguide.com

Money Search: www.moneysearch.com

MSN Money: moneycentral.msn.com

NASDAQ: www.nasdaq.com

New York Stock Exchange: www.nyse.com

PC Financial Network: www.csfbdirect.com

Quote.Com: finance.lycos.com

Stock Smart: www.stocksmart.com

Wright Investors' Service on the World Wide Web: www.wisi.com

The Wall Street Journal Online: online.wsj.com/public/us

Zacks Investment Research: my.zacks.com

One site that conveniently contains firm, industry, and competitor data is Hoover's Online. Hoover's also provides financials, stock charts, current and archived news stories, and links to research reports and SEC filings. Some of these data, most notably the lengthy research reports produced by analysts, are fee-based and must be ordered.

## Online Data Sources

Online data sources provide wide access to a huge volume of business reference material. Information retrieved from these sites typically includes descriptive profiles, stock price performance, SEC filings, and newspaper, magazine, and journal articles related to a particular company, industry, or product. Online data services are popular with educational and financial institutions. While some services are free to all users, to utilize the entire array of these sites' services, a fee-based subscription is usually necessary.

Accessing these sites requires only the source's address, or the use of a search engine to find the address. The source's homepage will clearly indicate the nature of the information available and describe how to search for and access the data. Most sites have help screens to assist in locating the desired information.

One of the most useful online sources for business research is the Lexis-Nexis Universe. This source provides a wide array of news, business, legal, and reference information. The information is categorized into dozens of topics including general news, company and industry news, company financials that include SEC filings, government and political news, accounting auditing and tax data, and legal research. One particularly impressive service is a search mechanism that allows a user to locate a particular article when the specific citation is known. A list of several notable online data sources is shown below:

ABI/Inform (Proquest Direct): www.il.proquest.com/proquest

American Express: americanexpress.com

Bloomberg Financial News Services: www.bloomberg.com

*BusinessWeek* Online: businessweek.com

Dow Jones News Retrieval: http://bis.dowjones.com

EconLit: www.econlit.org

Lexis-Nexis Universe: www.lexis-nexis.com

# PARTICIPATING IN CLASS

Because the strategic management course uses the case method, the success and value of the course depend on class discussion. The success and value of the class discussion, in turn, rely on the roles both you and your professor perform. Following are aspects of your role and your professor's that, if kept in mind, will enhance the value and excitement of this course.

## Students as Active Learners

The case method requires your active participation. This means your role is no longer one of sitting and listening.

1. *Attend class regularly.* Not only is your grade likely to depend on your involvement in class discussions, but the benefit you derive from this course is directly related to your involvement in and understanding of the discussions.

2. *Be prepared for class.* The need for adequate preparation already has been discussed. You will benefit more from the discussions, will understand and participate in the exchange of ideas, and will avoid the embarrassment of being called on when not prepared. By all means, bring your book to class. Not only is there a good chance you will need to refer to a specific exhibit or passage from the case, you may need to refresh your memory of the case (particularly if you made notes in the margins while reading).

3. *Participate in the discussion.* Attending class and being prepared are not enough; you need to express your views in class. You can participate in a number of ways: by addressing a question asked by your professor, by disagreeing with your professor or your classmates (by all means, be tactful), by building on an idea expressed by a classmate, or by simply asking a relevant question.

4. *Participate wisely.* Although you do not want to be one of those students who never raises his or her hand, you also should be sensitive to the fact that others in your class will want to express themselves. You have probably already had experience with a student who attempts to dominate each class discussion. A student who invariably tries to dominate the class discussion breeds resentment.

5. *Keep a broad perspective.* By definition, the strategic management course deals with the issues facing general managers or business owners. As already mentioned, you need to consider all aspects of the business, not just one particular functional area.

6. *Pay attention to the topic being discussed.* Focus your attention on the topic being discussed. When a new topic is introduced, do not attempt to immediately introduce another topic for discussion. Do not feel you have to have something to say on every topic covered.

## Your Professor as Discussion Leader

Your professor is a discussion leader. As such, he or she will attempt to stimulate the class as a whole to share insights, observations, and thoughts about the case. Your professor will not necessarily respond to every comment you or your classmates make. Part of the value of the case method is to get you and your classmates to assume this role as the course progresses.

The professor in a strategic management case course performs several roles:

1. *Maintaining focus.* Because multiple complex issues need to be explored, your professor may want to maintain the focus of the class discussion on one issue at a time. He or she may ask you to hold your comment on another issue until a previous issue is exhausted. Do not interpret this response to mean your point is unimportant; your professor is simply indicating there will be a more appropriate time to pursue that particular comment.

2. *Getting students involved.* Do not be surprised if your professor asks for input from volunteers and nonvolunteers alike. The value of the class discussion increases as more people share their comments.

3. *Facilitating comprehension of strategic management concepts.* Some professors prefer to lecture on strategic management concepts on a "need-to-know" basis. In this scenario, a lecture on a particular topic will be followed by an assignment to work on a case that deals with that particular topic. Other professors will have the class work through a case or two before lecturing on a topic to give the class a feel for the value of the topic being covered and for the type of information needed to work on cases. Still other professors prefer to cover all of the theory in the beginning of the course, thereby allowing uninterrupted case discussion in the remaining weeks of the term. All three of these approaches are valued.

4. *Playing devil's advocate.* At times your professor may appear to be contradicting many of the comments or observations being made. At other times your professor may adopt a position that does not immediately make sense, given the circumstances of the case. At other times your professor may seem to be equivocating. These are all examples of how your professor might be playing devil's advocate. Sometimes the professor's goal is to expose alternative viewpoints. Sometimes he or she may be testing your resolve on a particular point. Be prepared to support your position with evidence from the case.

# ASSIGNMENTS

## Written Assignments

Written analyses are a critical part of most strategic management courses. Each professor has a preferred format for these written analyses, but a number of general guidelines will prove helpful to you in your written assignments.

1. *Analyze.* Avoid merely repeating the facts presented in the case. Analyze the issues involved in the case and build logically toward your recommendations.

2. *Use headings or labels.* Using headings or labels throughout your written analysis will help your reader follow your analysis and recommendations. For example, when you are analyzing the weaknesses of the firm in the case, include the heading Weaknesses. Note the headings in the cases that follow.

3. *Discuss alternatives.* Follow the proper strategic management sequence by (1) identifying alternatives, (2) evaluating each alternative, and (3) recommending the alternative you think is best.

4. *Use topic sentences.* You can help your reader more easily evaluate your analysis by putting the topic sentence first in each paragraph and following with statements directly supporting the topic sentence.

5. *Be specific in your recommendations.* Develop specific recommendations logically and be sure your recommendations are well defended by your analysis. Avoid using generalizations, clichés, and ambiguous statements. Remember that any number of answers are possible and so your professor is most concerned about how your reasoning led to your recommendations and how well you develop and support your ideas.

6. *Do not overlook implementation.* Many good analyses receive poor evaluations because they do not include a discussion of implementation. Your analysis will be much stronger when you discuss how your recommendation can be implemented. Include some of the specific actions needed to achieve the objectives you are proposing.

7. *Specifically state your assumptions.* Cases, like all real business situations, involve incomplete information. Therefore, it is important that you clearly state any assumptions you make in your analysis. Do not assume your professor will be able to fill in the missing points.

## Oral Presentations

Your professor is likely to ask you and your classmates to make oral presentations on a particular case. Oral presentations usually are done by groups of students. In these groups, each member will typically be responsible for one aspect of the overall case. Keep the following suggestions in mind when you are faced with an oral presentation:

1. *Use your own words.* Avoid memorizing a presentation. The best approach is to prepare an outline of the key points you want to cover. Do not be afraid to have the outline in front of you during your presentation, but do not just read the outline.

2. *Rehearse your presentation.* Do not assume you can simply read the outline you have prepared or that the right words will come to you when you are in front of the class making your presentation. Take the time to practice your speech, and be sure to rehearse the entire presentation with your group.

3. *Use visual aids.* The adage "a picture is worth a thousand words" contains quite a bit of truth. The people in your audience will more quickly and thoroughly understand your key points—and will retain them longer—if you use visual aids. Think of ways you and your team members can use the blackboard in the classroom; a graph, chart, or exhibit on a large posterboard; or, if you will have a number of these visual aids, a flip chart.

4. *Be prepared to handle questions.* You probably will be asked questions by your classmates. If questions are asked during your presentation, try to address those that require clarification. Tactfully postpone more elaborate questions until you have completed the formal phase of your presentation. During your rehearsal, try to anticipate the types of questions that you might be asked.

## Working as a Team Member

Many professors assign students to groups or teams for analyzing cases. This adds more realism to the course, since most strategic decisions in business are addressed by a group of key managers. If you are a member of a group assigned to analyze a case, keep in mind that your performance is tied to the performance of the other group members, and vice versa. The following are some suggestions to help you be an effective team member:

1. *Be sure the division of labor is equitable.* It is not always easy to decide how the workload can be divided equitably, since it is not always obvious how much work needs to be done. Try breaking down the case into the distinct parts that need to be analyzed to determine if having a different person assume responsibility for each part is equitable.

All team members should read and analyze the entire case, but different team members can be assigned primary responsibility for each major aspect of the analysis. Each team member with primary responsibility for a major aspect of the analysis also will be the logical choice to write that portion of the written analysis or to present it orally in class.

2. *Communicate with other team members.* This is particularly important if you encounter problems with your portion of the analysis. Since, by definition, the team members are dependent on each other, it is critical that you communicate openly and honestly with each other. Therefore, it is essential that your team members discuss problems, such as some members not doing their fair share of work or members insisting that their point of view dominate the team's report.

3. *Work as a team.* Since a group's output should reflect a combined effort, the whole group should be involved in each part of the analysis, even if different individuals assume primary responsibility for different parts of the analysis. Avoid having the marketing major do the marketing portion of the analysis, the production major handle the production issues, and so forth. This will both hamper the group's aggregate analysis and do all of the team members a disservice by not giving each member exposure to decision making involving the other functional areas. The strategic management course provides an opportunity to look at all aspects of the business situation, to develop the ability to see the big picture, and to integrate the various functional areas.

4. *Plan and structure team meetings.* When you are working with a group on case analysis, it is impossible to achieve the team's goals and objectives without meeting outside of class. As soon as the team is formed, establish mutually convenient times for regular meetings, and be sure to keep this time available each week. Be punctual in going to the meetings, and manage the meetings so they end at a predetermined time. Plan several shorter meetings, as opposed to one longer session right before the case is due. (This, by the way, is another way realism is introduced in the strategic management course. Planning and managing your time is essential in business, and working with others to achieve a common set of goals is a critical part of life in the business world.)

# SUMMARY

The strategic management course is your opportunity to assume the role of a key decision maker in a business organization. The case method is an excellent way to add excitement and realism to the course. To get the most out of the course and the case method, you need to be an active participant in the entire process.

The case method offers you the opportunity to develop your analytical skills and to understand the interrelationships of the various functional areas of business; it also enables you to develop valuable skills in time management, group problem solving, creativity, organization of thoughts and ideas, and human interaction.

# Cases

# Avon Calling—Lots of New Reps

1    It has been a cold spring on the East Coast, and one afternoon in late April, the temperature drops and the wind picks up. But that doesn't keep Luz Stella Bongiovi from buttoning up her black wool coat and walking three blocks from her office to Knickerbocker Avenue in Bushwick, a working-class section of Brooklyn. Standing in front of a jeans store on this bustling commercial strip, Bongiovi smiles warmly, offering passersby Avon catalogs in Spanish and English. The glossy pamphlets are crammed with cosmetics, but this ritual has become less about racking up sales of lipstick and face cream and more about a hunt for people, specifically future Avon sales representatives.

2    Bongiovi has a system that starts with the catalogs. Once someone takes one, she offers a free makeover, jots down her name and number, and soon schedules the beauty session. It's there that she has the time to pitch the benefits of selling Avon. Bongiovi has also run an ad in *el diario/La Prensa,* a New York Spanish-language newspaper. It generated 73 solid leads in six weeks. But no matter how she goes about drumming up interest, she saves the best for last. Bongiovi shows potential recruits photocopies of her own biweekly checks for recruiting and managing other reps. Each one is for about $2,000. And that's before the $5,000 she averages for her own sales. That usually clinches the deal.

3    Bongiovi is one of 25,000 U.S. reps of Avon Products (AVP) Inc. who are part of a multilevel sales force that Avon refers to as "Leadership." These independent contractors, who are paid a commission not only on their own sales but also on the sales of people they recruit and train, have been the driving force behind a four-year turnaround in Avon's U.S. business.

4    As Avon CEO Andrea Jung moves the program beyond the United States and further into the worldwide markets, which make up almost two-thirds of its business, she's joining a wave of mainline companies that are turning to multi-tiered marketing. Among the household names that have adopted the sales structure in some area of their business: Sara Lee (SLE), Virgin Group, AOL Time Warner (AOL) and Berkshire Hathaway (BRK). In 1990, only 20 percent of companies in the Direct Selling Assn. had multilevel pay packages, says President Neil H. Offen. Today, it's 80 percent. The need to keep up with other direct sellers is part of what drove Avon's multilevel effort.

5    Today's mainstream multilevel marketing is different from earlier, more controversial schemes at other companies that paid people to recruit others and often left the last taker holding expensive and unsellable goods. At legitimate companies, a leader's compensation is based on the group's total sales—not just the leader's skill at signing up recruits. So not only does Bongiovi make her own sales, but there is also an incentive for her to train her recruits to produce so that everyone prospers. And unlike earlier multilevel selling plans, if an Avon rep does drop out, she can recoup almost all her investment without question. Jung says the company hasn't suffered any taint from scandals elsewhere. "Multilevel done in a controlled way is a very powerful growth engine," she says.

6     For Avon, multilevel selling has helped reenergize a flagging U.S. sales force. During most of the 1990s, the number of new reps—who were brought in by company managers rather than Leadership reps—had stalled. While Avon was growing in Latin America, Eastern Europe, and Asia, by 1999 the number of Avon ladies in the United States had fallen by 1 percent from the year before.

7     That was the year Jung got the top job and set about reversing Avon's slide. She focused on reinvigorating the brand—which had an aging-grandmother feel to it—with new products, new packaging, and a new ad campaign. She also instituted beauty-advisory training for certain reps and pushed to expand Avon's online sales. The fourth leg of her strategy, however, was to make the rep job more attractive to ambitious women. To do that, she expanded the multilevel sales program. It had taken root, under a different name, in the early '90s, primarily in California, but Avon had put few resources into it.

8     The results have been stellar. The number of U.S. sales reps is climbing—up 3 percent in both 2001 and 2002—and sales, which last year totaled $6.2 billion globally, are growing by 4 percent a year. Profits climbed 20 percent, to $534 million last year. The stock, in turn, has spurted ahead 99 percent since Jung was appointed chief executive, to 58 a share. That compares with a 33 percent drop for the Standard & Poor's 500-stock index. Goldman, Sachs & Co. analyst Amy Low Chasen says the Leadership program is revolutionizing Avon's sales force. Chasen's long-term sales-growth estimates are 10 percent a year. "Leadership is a game-changer for Avon," says Jung.

9     The benefits for Avon go way beyond a rejuvenated sales force. The company has also begun to cut costs, reducing the number of district sales managers—the salaried people who had traditionally been solely responsible for recruitment and training—from 1,750 to 1,500. Women like Bongiovi have picked up a lot of their recruiting duties, so district managers can now oversee more salespeople. Michael Sanchez, Bongiovi's district sales manager, now manages 450 Avon reps, up from 300 five years ago. The change has contributed to U.S. profit growth of 11.2 percent a year for the past two years, almost twice the historical average, while operating margins climbed from 17.9 percent to 19.4 percent.

10     The big problem now is hanging on to new recruits. The turnover rate, always high in direct selling, is even higher in Avon's multilevel plan. In their first year, two out of three new sales reps leave. In Bongiovi's district, one rep got 44 recruits in two weeks, but lost 38. Bongiovi estimates she has a turnover of about 50 percent—lower than average. To lessen turnover, Avon is investing $20 million in programs, including nationwide training seminars to help leaders boost recruits' sales.

11     Jung has to listen to these big independent producers, the best of whom control millions of dollars of Avon's revenue. She and other top managers sit in full-day meetings with them, picking their brains and listening to their problems. That's how Bongiovi asked for—and got—Leadership pamphlets in Spanish and makeup shades that match olive skin better. "They treat us like managers," says Bongiovi, proudly. And she's got the paycheck to match.

Source: "Avon Calling—Lots of New Reps." Byrnes, Nanette. *BusinessWeek Online*, June 2, 2003.

Case 2                                                     **BusinessWeek**

# BMW

1    The lofty new modern art museum in Munich boasts a world-class collection of art, design, and architecture. But on May 19, the specially invited guests weren't there to gawk at the Picassos and Mirós. They were assembled to appraise the art Bavarians love best: The latest model from Bayerische Motoren Werke. More than 100 German car dealers crowded around the revamped 5 Series sedan, the heart of the BMW franchise. They gazed approvingly at the sleek surfaces and listened as engineers described the tight handling of the new steering and stability systems. Looming over the proceedings was a 10-meter high sculpture celebrating the beauty of auto design, created by none other than Christopher Bangle, the controversial American designer of BMW's new look, and godfather of the latest 5.

2    Super-theatrical? Well, sure. But to the auto world, the latest Bimmer to hit the road is always a subject worthy of high drama. The Internet chat rooms of the global car-buff community have been buzzing about the fifth-generation 5 Series for months now. And they have a lot more to talk about than the latest rendition of BMW's biggest moneymaker. The Munich company is rolling out a new or updated model nearly every three months through 2005 in a ramp-up more ambitious than anything the company has attempted before. "The [new] product initiative is critical to our future success," says BMW Chief Executive Helmut Panke. His goal: expand annual sales by 40 percent over the next five years, to 1.4 million cars, and beat out Mercedes-Benz (DCX) as the number one maker of premium cars in the world. "We won't give up, and we don't rest on our laurels," says the 56-year-old Panke. "We won't accept the position of number two."

3    Panke, a nuclear physicist by training who is passionate about cars, is pushing BMW into high gear. If the accelerated rollout works, BMW's new raft of models will power the carmaker to a new level of prominence and profitability in the global industry. But as factories ramp up production levels and juggle an increasingly complex variety of models, BMW will have to fight harder than ever to keep its margins and maintain the quality that underlies its success.

4    It all depends on how BMW's vaunted engineers and workers respond to the challenge. The expansion is well under way. In January, the company unveiled the new $377,760 Rolls-Royce Phantom, for which BMW is still building an exclusive dealer network. The $37,760 Z4 roadster, which arrived in the United States at the end of 2002, hits European showrooms this spring, together with a diesel version of the Mini, the old British subcompact that under BMW's ownership is fast becoming a cult car. Next comes the 5 Series sedan, which goes to market in July. In the fall, the X3, a downsized sport-utility vehicle, makes its debut. At yearend, a revival of the high-performance 6 Series coupe hits the road, featuring some of BMW's most powerful engines. "The year 2003 is very, very critical for BMW," says Christoph Stürmer, senior analyst at Global Insight Automotive in Frankfurt.

5    So is 2004. In the fall of that year, dealers will get their first deliveries of the new 1 Series subcompact that will go head-to-head with the Audi 3, the Mercedes A-Class, and the high-end versions of Volkswagen's Golf. Next year, BMW will introduce a 6 Series convertible and a station wagon version of the new 5 Series.

6    It's a high-speed shift from a carmaker that 10 years ago churned out just a handful of models—essentially the 3, 5, and 7 series. But remaking BMW became an imperative in the 1990s as the global auto market fragmented into hot new niches, and demand for luxury sedans—the company's core business—started to shrink as a percentage of total auto sales. "We can't make cars anymore that are three differently sized slices of the same sausage," says Panke.

7    What's more, Panke and his top officers are betting BMW's new-model momentum will propel it past rivals. The Bavarian giant has already overtaken Mercedes-Benz in the all-important U.S. market, with models appealing to a wide swath of X- and Y-generation managers, entrepreneurs, and professionals. "BMW is the brand people aspire to own. When people get to the point they can afford a luxury car, they buy a (BMW) 3 Series," says George Peterson, president of AutoPacific Inc. in Tustin, Calif. "Mercedes is much further down the list and slipping." BMW is also overtaking Toyota Motor Corp.'s luxury brand Lexus as the premium-car leader in the United States. While the two rivals ended 2002 neck and neck, BMW has outsold Lexus for the first four months of 2003—a quantum leap compared with the early 1990s, when the Japanese took the U.S. market by storm.

8    So far, BMW has steered its own redesign deftly. Despite a 53 percent increase in research and development and a 75 percent increase in capital expenditures over the past two years, BMW's net profit last year still rose 8.3 percent, to $2.36 billion, while revenues climbed 9.9 percent, to $49.5 billion. Operating margins, at 8 percent in 2002 and 8.7 percent in 2001—the heaviest years for investing—were again among the highest in the industry. Lehman Brothers Inc. auto analyst Christopher Will expects the new-model push will generate a 20 percent rise in revenues next year.

9    But can Panke keep his highly tuned company on track as it accelerates? "The core strength of BMW will be challenged," says Peter Soliman, vice-president at Booz Allen Hamilton Inc. in Düsseldorf. Management is being stretched to the limit, as BMW builds a new, $1.5 billion factory in Leipzig at breakneck pace. The Leipzig plant, slated for inauguration at the end of 2004, will employ 5,500 workers: the first 400 are already being trained in BMW's complex production methods.

10    Few expect a major product blunder from the company's highly esteemed Bavarian engineers. Even the top-of-the-line 7 Series sedan, which at first raised howls of criticism for a provocatively imposing trunk design and for its complicated electronic information system, has outsold its predecessor during its first full year on the market.

11    However, many are betting that BMW's vaunted profit margins will take a hit, at least in the short run. Although Panke vows earnings will be flat in 2003, analysts warn that they could slip by as much as 10 percent, as marketing costs peak this year on top of higher R&D spending. Panke's bet assumes turbocharged growth in the second half, prompted in part by the new 5 Series. The growing strength of the euro also poses a risk to BMW's dollar-denominated earnings. The company is hedged nearly 100 percent against its dollar risk this year and 60 percent for 2004—but only 30 percent for 2005.

12    The more pressing question: Can an ever-bigger BMW maintain the consistently high returns it once achieved with its exclusive portfolio? For starters, small cars such as the Mini, launched in 2001, and the 1 Series subcompact typically earn lower margins than do midsize sedans and luxury limousines. "Compared with volume producers, BMW's manufacturing costs are much higher, its product development process more costly, and its purchasing costs higher," warns Goldman, Sachs & Co. analyst Keith Hayes in a recent report. Reflecting these risks, BMW shares have slid 41 percent from a year ago, to $32. Chief Financial Officer Stefan Krause insists BMW will wring cost savings on the 1 Series to maintain its high margins. As for the Mini, he says profits are "way beyond our forecast," thanks to unexpectedly strong sales of loaded models. Buyers are snapping up options from navigation systems to sunroofs, ponying up as much as $35,000 for the cheeky little car.

13    But rivals are eager to point out other pitfalls. Robert A. Lutz, General Motors Corp. vice-chairman for product development, says Cadillac will not follow the path of German luxury brands in the march to obtain higher sales volumes: "After a couple of 1 Series, they'll have to bring in another brand on top to add prestige," he says. "The 1 Series will diminish the brand in the eyes of 7 Series buyers." Panke is adamant that future growth won't tarnish the BMW badge. "We are not competing with the mass market," he says.

14    BMW already may be showing some early signs of margin stress. Analysts warn the company has resorted to an aggressive leasing strategy to bolster sales in a weakening market in the U.S. and Europe, and to shore up aging models. That's standard industry practice, to be sure. But up to 75 percent of its luxury 7 Series sedans and 50 percent of the 5 Series are leased in the United States. The company makes its profit by selling the car at the end of the lease to the leaseholder, a BMW dealer, or others.

15    But there's a risk. If the sale price of the leased cars doesn't match BMW's high residual value estimate, then the company could suffer a lower return on those cars than it has traditionally achieved. And while BMW enjoys some of the highest residual values in the industry, often running over 60 percent for a three-year-old car, it's unclear what will happen to values if an increasing number of leased cars hit the market down the road. Deutsche Bank (DB) recently calculated an implied incentive of around $4,300 in the 7 Series lease rates. "The bottom line from our analysis shows clearly that in the United States, BMW is currently offering the most aggressive leasing terms," says Deutsche analyst Christian Breitsprecher in a recent report. Not so, says BMW's Krause—the leasing business is not being used to ratchet up subsidies on sales. For starters, he says, analysts' calculations use the original price for older models—models that don't apply to BMW's revamped lineup.

16    BMW is also redoubling efforts to keep costs down by sharing components across similar-sized cars, such as the 5 Series, the X5 and the 6 Series, as well as the 3 Series, the X3, and the 1 Series. The upcoming 1 Series will share about 60 percent of its components with the 3 Series. That will save costs, analysts agree, but if the cars are too similar, it could lead to a cannibalization of the sales of the higher-priced 3 Series. That's already happened at Volkswagen, which shares parts across a variety of brands.

17    As costs come under pressure, preserving quality will be critical. In the first quarter of 2003, BMW's Munich plant won the J. D. Power & Associates Inc. Gold Plant Quality Award. But in the premium car segment, blunders infuriate drivers more and get big headlines. BMW found out the hard way in 2001 when it introduced an innovative knob called the iDrive to control a slew of functions on the dashboard. Software problems with the iDrive left many owners fuming as their new, $69,000 sedans sat in the shop for weeks for software upgrades. First-time customers have had their frustrations, too. Peter Walker, a 33-year-old Woodland Hills (Calif.) information-technology consultant, plunked down $62,500 for a sporty BMW M3 last year. But an engine defect put the car out of commission at 14,500 kilometers. The repair, together with minor problems with the clutch and pedals, plagued Walker for most of a year. A BMW-certified tow truck even broke the rear suspension control arms. "It was just one nightmare to the next," Walker says, requiring endless phone calls and e-mail with the company. "Even then they gave me a rebuilt engine," fumes Walker, who thinks BMW's model push may well have overextended the automaker he grew up admiring.

18    The real risk lies in the new models soon to hit streets around the globe. To speed the upcoming X3 to market, BMW outsourced development and production to Austria's Magna Steyr, a unit of Canadian-based supplier and engineering services giant Magna International Inc. Magna Steyr is dedicating an entire factory in Graz to making up to 150,000 X3s a year. Auto experts say the move could be an innovative alternative to building new plants, but warn that the strategy leaves BMW with only limited control over the final product.

19    Despite the risks, many are betting the Bavarian champion can deliver. BMW's factories are considered the most flexible and most productive in Germany; its suppliers are the industry's best; and the workforce among the industry's most talented. BMW received more than 160,000 job applications last year for 3,500 openings. "Being able to attract and develop the best talent is BMW's hidden success factor," says Bernd Kreutzer, vice-president at consultants A.T. Kearney in Frankfurt. "It's hard to copy BMW because you can't copy culture."

20    Step inside BMW's factories and research centers, and the high-energy buzz is hard to miss. Everyone knows the story of the engineer who in the 1970s cut a hole in the roof of a 3 Series car in his garage and cobbled together BMW's first convertible to wow reluctant board members. Production engineers in the paint shop recently racked up an impressive first with a new powder-based technology to apply the final clear coat on a car, providing a more perfect finish and better scratch resistance, and completely eliminating toxic waste. "All the Japanese and American automakers have come to view it," says Walter Wimmer, head of the paint shop at the Dingolfing plant.

21    BMW's obsession with performance and brand image helped the German automaker close the yawning gap with Lexus in the United States in the 1990s. Munich headquarters read the message to improve quality and customer care loud and clear. BMW now offers a four-year warranty, including maintenance and service, in the price of the car, cutting out complaints that occasional technological glitches made the brand extremely expensive to maintain. "We took the pain out of owning a car," says Tom Purves, CEO of BMW North America.

22    Now BMW speeds customer feedback to headquarters faster than before. "[Quality] problems have to be solved in a matter of days, not months," says Norbert Reithofer, board member in charge of production. When the new 7 Series drew complaints for its befuddling iDrive, engineers went to work immediately on modifications now appearing in the new 5 Series, including a reduction in the number of control positions from eight to four and a handy reset button to return to the main menu. BMW also outfitted its dealers with kiosks and trained them to help customers master iDrive on dry ground. "We learned a lot from the 7 Series launch," says Purves.

23    Development teams that pore over everything from such market feedback to new innovations are encouraged to engage in "friendly fighting" to decide the vital characteristics of a new BMW. The development of the new 5 Series shows the concept in action. As the team convened in 1998, marketers demanded more leg room in the back seat and more trunk space: Buyers of the old model had complained it was too small to hold several golf bags. The members of the engineering staff protested. Their goal was a car that accelerated faster and handled even more smoothly. Added weight and length were taboo for the gearheads.

24    In the end, both sides won. The muscular-looking 5 Series is not only taller, longer, and lighter than its predecessor, it's packed with new technologies that boost engine power, torque, handling, safety, and fuel efficiency. Drive the 231-horsepower 530i 5 Series around a set of sharp curves and it grips the road more like a sports car than a sedan, with its smooth engine effortlessly delivering top acceleration and tight control. One technological coup: a system called "active front steering," which reduces the effort needed to turn at slow speeds and makes the steering more sensitive and agile at high speeds. The powerful front end was designed to appear deep and short to give it a "low, hunkered look," that matches the increased performance, says designer Bangle. A smoother integration of the trunk and angular rear lights gives the rear a racy attitude.

25    BMW's brand image is tied tightly to such innovation. "BMW really captured the performance space in the market for themselves. They own it," says AutoPacific's Peterson. Sportiness and style made a convert of Debra J. Rosman, senior director of marketing for the NBA's Miami Heat. Rosman traded in her Lexus RX300 SUV for a BMW X5 with leather seats, wood trim, and an on-board computer. "BMW is hipper and cooler," says Rosman, whose monthly lease payments are well above the $450 she paid for the Lexus. Even rivals get the point. "I have to give BMW credit for consistency in their message," says Mike Wells, vice-president for marketing at Toyota's Lexus Div. The engine and styling variations offered by BMW are "clearly an advantage," he adds.

26 Of course, Lexus is not about to concede. Neither is Mercedes, whose elegant E-Class still outsells BMW's 5 Series worldwide. Mercedes' Stuttgart designers gave the 2002 remake of the E-Class a sportier line, shooting for the more dynamic brand image that BMW has played to advantage. Then there's Audi, which aims to make its cars even more fun than Bimmers, and a whole new generation of models at Cadillac. It's going to be a helluva race.

Source: "BMW." Edmondson, Gail, Palmeri, Chris, Grow, Brian, and Tierney, Christine. *BusinessWeek Online*, June 9, 2003.

Case 3

BusinessWeek

# Can Dick Parsons Rescue AOL Time Warner?

1   Richard Dean Parsons' career to this point is a story of great promise fulfilled. He emerged from the mean streets of Bedford-Stuyvesant to post the highest score among all 3,600 law school grads who took the New York state bar exam in 1971. While still in his twenties, Parsons was an Afro-topped adviser to New York Governor Nelson Rockefeller and to President Gerald Ford. After a dozen years with an elite Manhattan law firm, the prodigy recast himself as a banker in time to save New York's largest savings banks from ruin. Next, he entered the media business, surviving years of fierce internecine warfare to become chief executive of AOL Time Warner Inc. (AOL) in 2002. Parsons, 55, will add the chairman's title at the annual meeting on May 16, capping his serpentine rise to the business world's pinnacle.

2   The quiet pride Parsons takes in his accomplishments is tempered by the enormous challenge he now confronts. He assumes sole command of a company born of the worst deal in the history of misbegotten megamergers. In January, 2000, at the peak of dot-com mania, patrician media giant Time Warner Inc. agreed to be acquired by Internet upstart America Online Inc. in a stock swap priced at $284 billion. Today, the stock market values AOL Time Warner at $61 billion. That's right: $223 billion in shareholder wealth, vanished. "They gave away their company for a mess of porridge, and they've got to live with that forever," says Rupert Murdoch, chairman of rival News Corp. (NEWS).

3   In Parsons' considered view, AOL Time Warner does not need radical surgery. The company's stock collapsed, but its business did not. To the contrary, operating cash flow generated by the likes of Warner Bros. (AOL), Time, and Turner Broadcasting System (AOL) rose to $7 billion in 2002 from $1.9 billion in 2000. Parsons is methodically trying to rebuild AOL Time Warner's shattered credibility on Wall Street by stressing incremental growth, cost control, debt reduction, and other lapsed fundamentals. Strategically, he has set a middle course. To pare down the company's $27 billion debt, the CEO has put "noncore" assets such as book publishing and CD manufacturing up for sale. Yet he resists calls to divest the flagging online division and excise the letters A-O-L from the corporate name.

4   "There's no magic in what we're doing. The days of magic are over," says Parsons, who also is grappling with investigations into America Online's premerger accounting by both the Securities & Exchange Commission and the Justice Dept. "But for the first time since the merger, this company is poised to surprise on the upside."

5   AOL Time Warner did modestly exceed expectations in its April 28 report of a 9 percent gain in first-quarter operating income, to $1.2 billion, on a 6 percent increase in revenue, to $10 billion. But a week later, one of the company's directors, Ted Turner, undercut Parsons' message of guarded optimism by reducing his holdings in AOL Time Warner by half, divesting some 60 million shares. The good news for Parsons is that AOL's stock proved remarkably resilient, barely budging on the news of Turner's massive sell-off. On the other hand, the company's stock is trading at about $13 a share, down from $20 when Parsons officially took charge last May. The immediate fate of America's most underachieving media giant now turns on this question: Does Dick Parsons have what it takes to salvage real value from Time Warner's train wreck of a merger?

6   Parsons inspires extravagant admiration among close colleagues past and present. If anyone can rescue AOL Time Warner, they say, Parsons can; just give him time. He is likely to get another year or two at a minimum, for he has impressed the people who count most: AOL Time Warner's board members and many of its largest shareholders. "Dick is the right guy to be running the company right now," says Gordon Crawford, senior vice-president at Capital Research & Management Co., AOL's largest shareholder, with a 7 percent stake.

**7**     But outside of the elite circles in which Parsons has moved ever since law school, he remains a largely unknown quantity. Despite his gilt-edged résumé—or perhaps because of it—he looks from a distance like an accidental media mogul. Skeptics say the genial chief executive is just a well-connected corporate diplomat, a schmoozy pol in pinstripes. Parsons is seen by some as a media-industry outsider who was just lucky to be the last man standing after the self-styled visionaries who made the merger—former Time Warner CEO Gerald M. Levin and former American Online CEO Stephen M. Case—self-destructed.

**8**     There was destruction aplenty, but this point of view gives Parsons too little credit. If he did not conspire to seize power, neither did he just sit back and let it fall into his lap. It might well turn out that reviving AOL Time Warner requires measures more drastic than Parsons is now taking. Dumping the online unit leaps to mind. But the unvarnished story of how he ended up in the corner office—told here for the first time in print—strongly suggests that if Parsons fails in his reclamation mission, it will not be for lack of grit or guile.

**9**     "Dick is a nice guy, but if that's all he was, he'd already be in the library under 'History,' " says John O. Utendahl, a Wall Street investment banker and a close friend. "Dick shows you what he wants you to see, and the part of him you don't often see is his assertive, unwavering killer instinct. People like to say that they play to win, but that's not the statement for Dick. I'd put it like this: There's nothing else on Dick's mind but winning."

**10**     It is generally thought that when Levin announced his resignation as CEO in late 2001, he was bowing to pressure from the board. There was pressure all right, but *BusinessWeek* has learned that it was applied by only one director—Chairman Steve Case—who irreparably damaged his own stature even as he hastened Levin's departure. Case mounted a one-man attempted coup, telephoning each director one by one to argue that Levin should be removed as CEO. Parsons, then co-chief operating officer, joined several outraged board members in standing up for Levin and making Case back down. "A number of us were absolutely opposed to the idea that the CEO could be fired on the telephone," says Stephen F. Bollenbach, chairman and CEO of Hilton Hotels (HLT) Corp. and a longtime Time Warner director. Case declined to comment on board matters.

**11**     Having dodged what another director termed "an assassination attempt," Levin, 62, decided to step down anyway in May, 2002, in favor of his chosen successor, Dick Parsons. The new CEO did not do to Case what Case had tried to do to Levin. But Parsons did firmly nudge the chairman toward the exit, with an assist from several shareholders who favored less gentle means. A second board battle was deftly avoided when Case announced in January that he was stepping down as chairman. "If it was just about tenacity," Case said, "I will assure you I would continue to fight on."

**12**     Parsons declines to comment about Case's showdown with Levin or his own private dealings with the ex-chairman. But AOL Time Warner's self-effacing new boss can't resist a little chest-thumping. "Surviving is winning, because if you are the last man standing, as they say, then you are the last man standing," Parsons says. "There is a certain amount of luck involved in anything in life. But I never had a doubt about how this would all work out."

**13**     It's a lovely sunny afternoon in April, and Parsons is sitting in his office talking bemusedly to his BlackBerry, trying to get it to behave. It's a one-sided conversation, to be sure, but Parsons persists. He talks to absolutely everyone, so why not try to reason with this inanimate lump of digital circuitry he holds in his massive hands?

**14**     When AOL Time Warner replaced Levin with Parsons, its leadership moved from one end of the personality spectrum to the other. The famously uptight Levin exuded an almost Nixonian aura of suspicion and social unease. When Levin appeared without a tie at the press conference announcing the big merger, the effect could not have been more disconcertingly incongruous had he forgotten his pants instead. But when Parsons removes his tie, he means business. Time Warner's movie and music divisions throw a lot of first-class parties, and Parsons goes to as many of them as he can. Last August, he flew all the way to

Barcelona for a big record industry bash. "Dick was still dancing when I left at 6:00 in the morning," recalls Roger Ames, chairman and CEO of Warner Music Group (AOL) "Yet he was there when the plane left at 7."

**15**    Parsons did paperwork much of the way back to New York, while Ames dozed next to him. Parsons, like Levin before him, puts in punishingly long hours. Yet he wears his diligence lightly. He is paid to be serious, but his default mode is loose and playful, with a touch of hipster diffidence. "This guy is a cool cat, and he's always been a cool cat," says Harry F. Albright Jr., a retired banker who has known Parsons since both worked for Nelson Rockefeller in the early 1970s. "He would just say what he thought, very calm and poised. There was no apple-polishing, no flattering the Governor. Nelson trusted Richard big time."

**16**    Parsons is a man of prodigious accomplishment and massive physical presence—he's a broad-shouldered, deep-voiced 6-foot-4—who nonetheless has been underestimated throughout his career. Is racism to blame? To a degree, no doubt, but it is also the result of his own effort. In the way that some folks labor to smooth their rough edges, Parsons has endeavored to shrink himself to better disarm foes and rivals. "Richard's ability to get people to underestimate him is a great skill," says Alberto Cribiore, a New York financier and a friend of Parsons since they were next-door neighbors in the mid-1970s. "If you are obvious, they know where to hit you. Who wins between the bull and the matador?"

**17**    Although Parsons is now the leader of one of the best-known companies in the land, he's still working the modesty thing pretty hard. "If someone stops me on the street or at a cocktail party or something like that and says: 'Well, what do you do?' I don't know what to say," Parsons says. "I always used to say: 'I'm a lawyer,' because that's what I was." Why doesn't he just identify himself as CEO of Time Warner? "I'm not yet fully comfortable with a new definition of who I am, professionally," replies Parsons, who has not practiced law since leaving Patterson, Belknap, Webb & Tyler in 1988.

**18**    Yet Parsons also says he never would have joined Time Warner in 1995 had he not believed that one day, he would be its CEO. Parsons, who was chairman and CEO of Dime Savings Bank of New York at the time, had been a Time Warner director since 1991. But no one, not even his colleagues on the board, saw him as Levin's eventual successor. Although Parsons started as Time Warner's president, Levin allowed his new number two no authority over the operating divisions and made no promises about the future. Succession was not discussed. Press reports theorized that Levin had chosen a weak president so as not to antagonize his cantankerous division chiefs. "I was a cajoler," Parsons recalls. "It was awkward until I established a basis for a personal relationship with the divisions."

**19**    Parsons gradually made himself indispensable to Time Warner by taking on tough assignments that the increasingly insular Levin could not or would not do himself. "Whenever we had a problem with one of the other units, Parsons was always the guy who would solve it," says Robert Daly, the longtime former co-chairman of Warner Bros. film studio. "And he would do it in a way that everyone would feel good about the outcome."

**20**    In filling the void left by Levin, Parsons aggrandized his own position even as he remained scrupulously loyal to the boss. "He never once overstepped his bounds as the number two," says Richard J. Bressler, a former Time Warner chief financial officer. Had Parsons shown less deference, might he have talked Levin out of making his worst mistake as CEO? Probably not. Combining with AOL was Levin's idea, but Parsons admits he was all for it. "I thought it would be good for both companies," he says. Even so, Parsons' disciplined subservience to Levin would later work to his advantage in limiting his personal culpability for the merger from hell.

**21**    For tax and accounting reasons, the $284 billion transaction was structured as an acquisition of Time Warner by AOL but was intended to be a merger of equals. The new company's 16-person board was evenly divided between former directors of AOL and of Time Warner, and responsibility for the operating divisions was split between co-Chief

Operating Officers—Parsons and Robert W. Pittman, 47, AOL's smooth but hard-driving president. The CEO job was not shared; it went solely to Levin. Case, 41, settled for chairman. "One of the catalysts of the merger from our end was that Steve wanted to back off from the business and not be a CEO any more," recalls a former AOL executive. "He wanted out, but with a little 'o.'" Case was not willing to be a figurehead. The merger agreement contained an unusually explicit description of Case's prerogatives as an "active chairman."

22      It quickly became apparent that, in practice, the notion of a merger of equals meant one thing to AOL's line managers and something quite different to Time Warner's. To the techno true believers who ran AOL, the content produced by Time Warner's cable TV, publishing, movie, and music groups was Old Media fodder for AOL's ever-widening Internet pipeline. But to the Time Warner crew, the Net was not a new universe but merely a new market that, if carefully exploited, could accelerate the growth of established media businesses. The conflicts inherent in these opposing world views were exacerbated by two forms of institutional arrogance: AOL's messianic pushiness and Time Warner's Establishment intractability. The result was a standoff. It wasn't so much that the company's pursuit of synergy between old and new media failed as that it never really began.

23      Despite the mounting strife in the ranks beneath them, Parsons and Pittman got along surprisingly well as co-COOs. Neither was inclined to meddle in the other's affairs, and when operational overlaps did cause conflicts, they sorted them out in private. "We did have substantive disagreements, but very few of them were ever visible to anybody else," Parsons says. "If we got a Thoroughbred in the AOL merger, it was Bob." Pittman declined to be quoted.

24      Nor was there overt conflict between Levin and Case, but that was only because they hardly interacted at all. Case worked mainly out of AOL's offices in Dulles, Va., rarely putting in an appearance at the New York City headquarters. "I knew that offering Jerry the CEO position would lessen my authority, but I thought it was the right thing to do . . . ," says Case. "In retrospect, perhaps it would have been better for me to have a larger role."

25      As 2001 wore on, it seemed to Case that Levin was so fixated on meeting the company's ambitious quarterly earnings projections that he had forgotten about the cross-company initiatives that were the reason for merging in the first place. By all accounts, the events of September 11 sent Levin into an emotional tailspin that caused him to withdraw even further into his self-imposed isolation. "After 9/11, Jerry basically just gave Steve the finger," says a former company executive. Levin did not respond to a request for an interview.

26      Case mounted his failed coup attempt in mid-November. Says one well-placed insider: "Steve made the mistake of thinking that silence on the other end of the telephone was approval, when it was just silence." At least two directors—Reuben Mark, the chairman and CEO of Colgate-Palmolive (CL) Co., and Francis T. "Fay" Vincent Jr., the former commissioner of Major League Baseball—went ballistic. "There was," Vincent acknowledges, "a hell of a fight."

27       Parsons  retreated to his apartment in Manhattan's Tribeca neighborhood on the weekend of Dec. 1 to ponder a course of action. Just a few weeks earlier, Levin had finally acknowledged Parsons as his heir apparent. Parsons had let it be known that he was seriously considering an offer from Philip Morris Cos., which was looking for a new CEO. Pittman, whom many outsiders considered AOL Time Warner's heir apparent, told Levin that he wasn't interested in the job and that losing Parsons would be a disaster—a message repeated by several key directors.

28      Sources close to Parsons say that he awoke on Sunday morning knowing what he had to do. Parsons called Case and said he would use whatever influence he had to oppose him in his bid to oust Levin. In conversations with friends and advisers, Parsons framed his decision in moral terms, as an assertion of loyalty and a belief in corporate due process. But it also was in his self-interest, since Levin's ouster could have given AOL the upper hand in

the company's civil war. Parsons still might have emerged as the next chief, but his head could just as easily be the next one on Case's chopping block.

**29** After Parsons was named CEO, he asked Pittman to stay on as sole COO. In April, 2002, a month before Levin's official departure, Parsons asked Pittman to go down to Dulles and figure out how to fix the online division, which by now was afflicted by plunging advertising and e-commerce revenues. Pittman reluctantly agreed to the special assignment but soon was so exhausted that he nearly had to be hospitalized. He resigned after the July 4 holiday. "Bob was completely burned out," says one confidante. "He just hit a wall."

**30** Much as he liked Pittman, Parsons was not unhappy to see him go, because he could now complete Time Warner's managerial takeover of America Online. In effect, he filled the co-COO posts that he and Pittman had recently vacated by promoting two of Time Warner's most respected division chiefs: Don Logan, 59, CEO of the Time Inc. magazine group; and Jeffrey L. Bewkes, 50, CEO of Home Box Office. Parsons describes these simultaneous appointments "as the most important move I have made as CEO."

**31** AOL was assigned to Logan, who purged the division of its most obstreperous champions of e-supremacy, including such notorious "Pittman panzers" as David M. Colburn, head of new business development, and Meyer Berlow, AOL's advertising chief. In August, Logan got Parsons' O.K. to bring in an outsider to head the division—Jonathan Miller, 45, a consumer marketer who had run USA Interactive's e-commerce group.

**32** But even as Parsons was consolidating his operational control in the latter half of 2002, his relations with Case were fraying. After Levin stepped down, Case took on added prominence as the co-head of a new strategy committee of the board. Even as AOL's accounting was coming under suspicion, he began an ill-timed campaign to raise his public profile, giving speeches in which he reaffirmed his faith in the Internet's golden promise.

**33** In September, 2002, AOL Time Warner issued a curious statement describing Case as Parsons' "primary thought partner and sounding board" but pointing out that "Dick ultimately is responsible for managing the company." Explains Parsons: "There was concern over the increasing drumbeat of 'who's in charge here?' Was Steve running the company? Is nobody running the company? What we were trying to move people toward was the realization that the CEO was running this company, like in most companies."

**34** Case had challenged Levin's authority but did not make the same mistake with his successor. "I thought it was best that I step down as chairman so people could move beyond finger-pointing about the past," says Case, who did not consult the CEO before he announced his resignation in January. Just two weeks later, Ted Turner announced plans to step down as vice-chairman. The board considered replacing Case with a nonexecutive chairman but unanimously decided to go with Parsons in the end. "To bring in another player at the top would have been awkward," one director says. "We'd had enough trouble already."

**35** Parsons might have been a media industry neophyte when he came to Time Warner, but at Dime Savings, he had already weathered a crisis more dire than most CEOs ever face. After taking over as chief in 1990, he rescued New York's largest savings bank from the brink of insolvency, keeping federal thrift regulators at bay as he overhauled the stodgy institution from top to bottom. "Looked at objectively, the chances of the Dime surviving were small," says Douglas E. Barzelay, its general counsel under Parsons.

**36** Parsons scoffs at the notion that he saved the Dime Savings Bank by pulling strings in Washington. "What was helpful was that having been effectively a bureaucrat myself, I could understand where the regulators were coming from and what we needed to do to get to where we needed to get," says Parsons, who spent three years in Washington as deputy counsel to Vice-President Rockefeller and as a domestic policy adviser to President Ford.

**37** Now, Parsons is struggling to apply this hard-won wisdom to his dealings with the SEC and federal prosecutors in Virginia. In June, 2002, the SEC alleged that AOL had inflated its premerger revenues through circular transactions with certain of its advertising and e-commerce clients—a practice known as "round-tripping." Parsons mistakenly proclaimed his company's innocence before Chief Financial Officer Wayne H. Pace had completed an internal investigation. In August, AOL Time Warner made the embarrassing disclosure that it had uncovered suspect transactions totaling $49 million. In October, Parsons disavowed an additional $190 million of revenue.

**38**    AOL Time Warner is in discussions with the SEC and with prosecutors, but a settlement does not appear imminent. For one thing, the SEC in March began pressuring the company to restate an additional $400 million in online advertising revenues tied to AOL Time Warner's $6.7 billion purchase of Bertelsmann's 50 percent interest in AOL Europe. As part of this deal, which was negotiated before the merger closed but was implemented when Levin was CEO, AOL agreed to pay Bertelsmann in cash if the Germans bought $400 million in online advertising. The SEC contends that AOL should have recorded the $400 million not as revenue but as a reduction in the purchase price. The company and its auditors, Ernst & Young, strongly disagree.

**39**    Dime Savings Bank's survival hinged on Parsons' dealings with the feds; AOL Time Warner's does not. Some shareholders worry that Parsons is indulging his lawyerly side by spending too much time battling over accounting arcana. "Why not say to Washington: 'What do you want? We'll give it to you,' " says Mario J. Gabelli of Gabelli Asset Management Co. "Why fight over something you inherited?"

**40**    The cloud over AOL's accounting has forced Parsons to delay an initial public offering of shares in Time Warner Cable (AOL) that had been scheduled for the second quarter. Expected to raise at least $2 billion, the IPO is the largest component of Parsons' plan to pay down total debt from the current $27 billion to $15.75 billion-to-$20 billion by the end of 2004.

**41**    Parsons has no choice but to get debt down, but this is hardly Dime Savings revisited. The company retains an investment-grade credit rating of BBB and throws off huge sums of cash. In 2002, every one of its divisions except AOL posted an increase in earnings before interest, taxes, depreciation, and amortization (EBITDA). At AOL, EBITDA plunged 44 percent last year and continued its swoon in the first quarter as the number of subscribers worldwide fell by 342,000, to 32.5 million. Under Logan and Miller, the AOL division is trying to reverse its decline by shifting emphasis from dial-up to broadband access and by trying to develop new "must have" proprietary programming. "If we are wrong about broadband, then we have to rethink it," Parsons says. "But given what we believe now, I think AOL fits."

**42**    There are shareholders who think Parsons is just postponing the inevitable funeral. "It doesn't take a team of McKinsey consultants to realize that AOL is a dying business," says a portfolio manager who has been selling Time Warner shares. Even if he is right, Parsons simply cannot afford to divest the online division as long as Time Warner remains in urgent debt-reduction mode. AOL may be a dwindling asset, but the division still generated $1.5 billion in EBITDA last year, and Merrill Lynch (MER) & Co. predicts only a slight decline, to $1.4 billion, for 2003.

**43**    While Parsons' down-the-middle approach has yet to significantly alter AOL Time Warner's income statement or its balance sheet, he already has brought a measure of order and harmony to a chronically divisive company. Parsons meets every Monday morning for a wide-ranging breakfast discussion with Logan, Bewkes, and Pace. "I am not Moses come down from the mountain with the stone tablets. It's a collaboration," Parsons says. "Getting your team together is the most important thing."

**44**    Even some of Parsons' admirers wonder whether he will be more than a transitional CEO. If Parsons succeeds in getting the company squared away over the next few years, they say, AOL Time Warner might be better off reverting to a visionary type of CEO to spur the growth of what is essentially a portfolio of mature businesses. "I'm not sure Dick's the guy to be running this company over the long run," says one investor. "But who knows? He may develop a vision as he goes on." He might, and he might also decide that life is too short to spend a whole lot more of it at AOL Time Warner. "I take this job seriously. It's important that I do it well, because a lot of people are counting on me," Parsons says. "But it's not my life. I exist apart from this job."

**45**     Since leaving Washington in 1977, Parsons has turned down job offers from several Republican Presidents, including the current one. He might just say yes the next time, or even run for high elective office in New York, as friends have been urging him to do for years. And then there is the winery that Parsons and his wife bought two years ago in Italy, near the Tuscan hill town of Montalcino. Parsons has decorated the label of his Il Palazzone wine with a mock Parsons' family crest and is thinking of adding this motto: "We drink all we can and we sell the rest." Parsons will drink his share of wine no matter what. But the events of the next year or two will go a long way in determining whether he is celebrating AOL's revival or drowning his sorrows.

Source: "Can Dick Parsons Rescue AOL Time Warner?" Bianco, Anthony, and Lowry, Tom. *BusinessWeek Online,* May 19, 2003.

# Case 4

BusinessWeek

# Can Ford Pull Out of Its Skid?

1   There's little doubt that 2003 was supposed to be a milestone for Ford Motor Co. (F) It marks not only the 100th anniversary of the company's founding by Henry Ford but also the year in which his great-grandson, Chief Executive William C. Ford Jr., 45, vowed to bring the automaker back into the black after it had lost $6.4 billion over the past two years. Based on a host of rosy assumptions, he told investors in January that the company would earn $1.3 billion. "When people look back on 2003," he said then, "I want them to remember it as a turning point."

2   But so far, nearly all the turns at Ford have been for the worse. The automaker's prospects are looking bleaker by the day as the industry girds for tougher times amid war and fears of a double-dip recession. Weak sales and rising inventories forced Ford to slash second-quarter production by 17 percent from last spring's levels. If rivals launch a brutal new round of incentives to revive flagging sales, Ford may be forced to match them as it struggles to hang on to its 21 percent market share. That would surely push auto operations into the red, triggering a ratings downgrade that would leave Ford's debt one step above junk status at best. In fact, by March 11, jittery investors had driven Ford stock down to an 11-year low of $6.60. Says Deutsche Bank Alex. Brown analyst Rod Lache: "Ford is facing insurmountable headwinds."

3   Even without the gloomy economic outlook, Bill Ford's turnaround seems to be stuck in neutral. He hasn't yet formed a cohesive and complete management team. The company's top brass has been forced to beat back rumors of infighting. Amid the turmoil, suppliers say Ford is delaying replacement of a raft of vehicles that account for one-quarter of its sales volume. And efforts to improve quality have stalled: The April issue of *Consumer Reports* ranks Ford dead last in reliability.

4   The most pressing concern is Ford's balance sheet, which is weighed down by enormous retiree obligations and $162 billion in debt, mostly belonging to Ford Credit. Unfunded retiree health-care liabilities topped $23 billion, Standard & Poor's estimates. The company expects to shell out $2.3 billion this year for U.S. retiree health benefits, up 21 percent from 2002. To shore up its U.S. pension funds, Ford will need to kick in $5 billion to $8 billion over the next five years, says UBS Warburg analyst Saul Rubin.

5   Ford dismisses market rumors of a Chapter 11 filing. It has $25 billion in cash, and little of Ford's $14 billion in auto-operations debt must be repaid soon: The average maturity is 27 years, and just $1 billion comes due in the next five years. When total debt is offset against cash, some $11 billion remains. In a true liquidity crunch, Ford could tap $7.8 billion in credit lines and sell assets, such as its Hertz Corp. car-rental unit. Meanwhile, Ford Credit's larger debt is backed by auto receivables. Says Warburg's Rubin: "Ultimately, we believe Ford has sufficient cash reserves to allow it to limp along."

6   But that cash cushion could run dangerously low if the industry keeps softening. U.S. auto sales in February fell 5 percent below the 16.5 million-unit annual pace that Ford is banking on. Deutsche Bank's Lache figures the company will burn through $5.7 billion in 2003. Auto operations alone could drain cash by $2 billion to $3 billion annually over the next several years, analysts say. Consider that during the downturn of the early 1990s, Ford ran through a total of $10 billion in cash.

7   Ford executives insist that they can weather a slump. "We believe we would be in the black at 15.5 million [vehicles]," Ford Chief Financial Officer Allan Gilmour said in January. But at that level, the car operations would surely sink into the red, with profits coming solely from

Ford Credit. Goldman, Sachs & Co. analyst Gary Lapidus thinks that Ford's auto unit will lose $850 million this year, leading by summer to an S&P downgrade of one-notch, to BBB−, just above junk level. When S&P reaffirmed Ford's BBB credit rating on March 7, it warned that it would reconsider that rating if auto results fell short of Ford's target.

8   The danger is that if cash from operations dries up, the car giant might have to delay new models in the pipeline and slow efforts to modernize factories. After a long dry spell, Ford is desperate for updated vehicles. It's in the process of upgrading three plants and plans to unveil a new generation of its best-selling F-150 trucks this fall. New Ford Freestar and Mercury Monterey minivans also arrive then. As in the past, Ford is counting on new models to provide a boost. Last year's redo of the Ford Expedition and Lincoln Navigator SUVs pumped up sales of those models 9 percent and 11 percent, respectively. But suppliers say that Ford already may have postponed the remakes of such mass-market cars as the Focus and the Crown Victoria. Ford denies that.

9   Just as critical would be any delay of Ford's plan to convert most of its North American plants to a flexible manufacturing system by 2010. Flexible factories allow a carmaker to switch from one model to another as needed and can pull off production changes without major disruptions. Ford trails General Motors Corp. and Japanese carmakers in adapting those systems.

10   Ford's older factories are one reason it has fallen so far behind on quality. Defects continue to plague new models, such as the Super Duty pickup trucks introduced late last year. A faulty valve sensor caused the engines of some Super Duties to cut out at highway speeds. Some trucks spent weeks in the shop before Ford replaced the sensors.

11   If those problems sound familiar, they should. Bill Ford put them on top of his priority list 17 months ago, when he ousted former CEO Jacques Nasser. But Ford's management fix still hasn't taken. The company was embarrassed by news leaks in mid-March that it had launched an internal investigation into whether Chief Operating Officer Nick Scheele had violated company policy with his order that all of Ford's ad business go to WPP Group Inc.— a firm run by a friend of Scheele's that also employs his son. Scheele rescinded the order, but more telling were the rumors within Ford that the probe was instigated by Scheele's rival, David Thursfield, who heads international operations. Scheele sent an e-mail calling those rumors "scurrilous."

12   Just as important are the posts Bill Ford hasn't filled. He is still searching for someone to replace Gilmour, 68, who is eager to hand off CFO duties and focus on his vice-chairman role. And Ford still needs a top "car guy," an executive with the passion and talent for new cars that Robert Lutz has shown at rival GM.

13   Those are pretty big holes to fill for a company that was supposed to be rounding the bend on its recovery. But with the auto industry headed for a bumpy ride, Ford isn't looking a whole lot better than when Bill Ford first jumped into the driver's seat.

Source: "Can Ford Pull Out of Its Skid?" Kerwin, Kathleen, *BusinessWeek Online,* March 31, 2003.

**Case 5**

BusinessWeek

# Can Mike Z Work More Magic at Motorola?

1     Mike S. Zafirovski had sobering news to deliver. Within 30 days of his appointment last July as chief operations officer of Motorola Inc. (MOT), Zafirovski, say current and former executives, met with managers and delivered a stinging message: Motorola is not as good as it thinks. Zafirovski candidly graded each of the businesses in areas ranging from market share and profitability to customer satisfaction—some B's and C's, and even some D's. But he expected straight A's.

2     Zafirovski had little time for niceties. On July 25, his predecessor, Edward D. Breen Jr., had bolted for the top job at troubled Tyco International Ltd., sowing distress at Motorola. Under Breen and CEO Christopher B. Galvin, Motorola was beginning to rebound from a dismal 2001, when it lost $5.8 billion. Breen, who declined to comment for this story, symbolized the sort of urgency and go-get-'em toughness that Motorola had lost over the years. He helped Galvin implement a cost-cutting program that shuttered United States manufacturing plants and will eventually shed more than a third of Motorola's 150,000 workers.

3     When Breen left, Galvin and the board promptly tapped Zafirovski, who had come to Motorola from General Electric Co. two years earlier. Known widely as Mike Z, he had hoisted Motorola's flagship cellular-phone business from the red in 2001 to a nearly 7 percent profit margin last summer. "Mike Z's leadership style is the best I've seen at energizing a broad-based organization while driving it to make the tough, but right, decisions," says Galvin.

4     Together they have steered Motorola toward recovery. Its balance sheet is strong. And after six quarters of losses, Motorola returned to profitability in the third quarter of 2002, ahead of rivals such as Lucent Technologies (LU) and Sweden's LM Ericsson (ERICY). And Zafirovski, with his lunch-bucket operating style, has complemented Galvin's big-picture focus.

5     It will take every last drop of turnaround magic, however, to bring once-dominant Motorola back to full strength. While the cell-phone unit has improved, its 17 percent market share leaves it a distant second to rival Nokia Corp.'s (NOK) 38 percent, according to Deutsche Bank Securities Inc. Moreover, Motorola has lost its lead in communications chips to Texas Instruments Inc., says Gartner Inc. And the wireless-networks business finished 2002 in the red and has gaping holes in its product portfolio. While Motorola's other units eke out profits, they account for less than a third of the company's $26.7 billion in revenues. "He has a big job," says Kevin Rendino, senior portfolio manager of the Merrill Lynch Basic Value Fund, which holds nearly 11 million Motorola shares. "This is a training ground to see if he's capable of running an entire business."

6     The good news for Mike Z? In the sputtering businesses in which Motorola competes, the company doesn't have to rocket to riches or blow by the likes of Nokia. Zafirovski and Galvin can succeed by achieving modest goals that appear within reach: 10 percent top-line growth and profits boosted by smoother operations. How to get there? "By gaining market share across the board, and [driving the] brand," Zafirovski told *BusinessWeek*.

7     That doesn't mean investors are thrilled. Many view Motorola as a conglomerate bogged down in slow-growth industries, and they're pushing for a divestiture of the struggling telecom-equipment business or a spin-off of the semiconductor division. Galvin shopped the equipment business last year and found no buyers. And he shows no sign of spinning off chips. With little prospect of a strategic fix, investors have driven down Motorola's stock

42 percent in the past year, to $8.35, keeping it in step with beleaguered telecom rivals. "They've made a lot of progress in cutting costs," says Tony Kim, an analyst at Credit Suisse Asset Management, which owns Motorola shares. "But it's not enough. They need to do more."

8    Zafirovski has plenty to keep him busy on the operations side. Borrowing from the playbook of Jack Welch, his old boss at GE, Zafirovski endorses Galvin's plan to weed out the lowest performing 10 percent of managers. He has pushed for employee bonuses based on profitability and cash flow. And he's "very focused on the customer," says Greg Santoro, vice-president of Web services at Nextel Communications (NXTL), one of Motorola's biggest customers. The company's first quarter results, due April 15, are likely to show net income of $70 million versus a $174 million net loss, excluding charges, the year before, according to Bear, Stearns & Co.

9    Zafirovski's driving ambition was apparent from a young age. When he was 16, his parents moved the family from the then-Yugoslavian region of Macedonia to the west side of Cleveland, where they found factory work. Despite knowing only a few English words when he started school a few days after arriving in the United States, Zafirovski spent three weeks mastering a 15-minute presentation to his American history class about his native country and received a standing ovation.

10    He shows the same dedication to fitness. At last year's Ironman competition in Lake Placid, N.Y., he finished ninth among men over 40, ending the grueling running, biking, and swimming race in 13 hours and 37 minutes. He then flew to Chicago late that night and reported to work hours later for Day One as COO.

11    Zafirovski earned plaudits at GE by turning around the lighting business in Europe—a job that called for shutting down several plants in Hungary. "He never missed," says Welch.

12    That experience came in handy when he moved to run Motorola's ailing cell-phone division in 2000. He promptly reduced Motorola's offering from 128 different phone types. Today fewer than 20 remain. He slashed operating expenses by 14 percent, to $3.1 billion, Deutsche Bank says. When managers told him that relations with customers were improving, Zafirovski demanded proof. Says a former manager of Mike Z's style: "Make the numbers or your ass is grass, and he's behind the mower."

13    Still, Motorola is miles behind Nokia. With a lead in multimedia phones, the Finnish company's margins in handsets reached 24.7 percent in the fourth quarter, far above Motorola's 9.1 percent. Zafirovski's goal is 15 percent margins, but first-quarter margins are expected to drop to 6 percent, according to Bear Stearns. "I don't know if the targets are realistic," says Bear Stearns analyst Wojtek Uzdelewicz.

14    If only Zafirovski's challenges stopped with wireless. Motorola's $5 billion semiconductor division faces an uphill slog. After reorganizing, closing several plants, and introducing new products, the unit is expected to boost revenue by 15 percent in 2003 to $5.5 billion and turn a $300 million profit, says Bear Stearns. But Motorola is in a tooth-and-nail fight with TI (TXN) and Qualcomm Inc. (QCOM) for the lead in the wireless chip market. And Intel Corp. (INTC) is now invading the wireless space with chips that even Motorola's phone unit is buying.

15    Hard-pressed to sell the networking unit, Motorola is investing in the business. It's pumping money into honing the software that serves as the brains for switching cell calls. It's developing Internet-based gear that it hopes will position the division for next-generation telecom systems. And the company is focusing on those few markets where it has thrived, such as China.

**16**     For the moment, Zafirovski's own report card is marked incomplete. The wireless-phone business is well on track toward recovery, but huge challenges remain in wireless infrastructure and semiconductors. Now it's up to Mike Z to pull off those straight A's.

## Corrections and Clarifications

"Can Mike Z. work more magic at Motorola?" (Information Technology, April 14) should have said that in last year's CEO Ironman Challenge in Lake Placid, N.Y., Motorola Inc. COO Mike S. Zafirovski finished ninth among men over 40. The CEO Challenge is a subset of the overall competition, in which he placed 78th out of 143 men in his age group (45–49).

Source: "Can Mike Z Work More Magic at Motorola?" Crocket, Roger O., and Reinhardt, Andy. *Business-Week Online,* April 14, 2003.

**Case 6**

BusinessWeek

# Can Siebel Stop Its Slide?

1 In the fall of 2001, business software pioneer Thomas M. Siebel was giddy as he looked ahead. Sure, the recession was hurting. But he claimed his company, Siebel Systems (SEBL) Inc.—the leader in software for managing sales forces and customer-service departments—would be more resilient than its competitors. "Everybody is going to be naked," Siebel said with relish. "We're going to find out who are the dilettantes. We're going to find out who are the scumbags, and who are the sleazeballs. Everybody is going to be exposed for who they are. It's going to be a remarkable time."

2 Two months later, he confidently predicted that the high-tech downturn was about to end. He could be certain, he said, because of the forecasting capabilities in his own software.

3 Well, both Tom Siebel and his software get failing grades for prognostication. The tech industry is still mired in slow growth, and Siebel Systems, software's highest flier in the go-go '90s, has tumbled farther than its "dilettante" rivals. Revenues last year tumbled 22 percent, to $1.6 billion, compared with a drop of only 2 percent for the overall corporate-applications-software industry. In the first quarter, Siebel's revenues dropped 30 percent, to $333 million. Siebel's stock price, at $8.50, is off a staggering 94 percent from its peak in 2000 of $119.

4 It wasn't just the economy that hobbled Siebel Systems. A 2001 product upgrade was so difficult to install that customers were reluctant to buy it. The company's reputation suffered from bad publicity about its customer-satisfaction record. And it lost ground to corporate-applications leader SAP (SAP) In 2002, Siebel Systems' share of the customer-management market it helped pioneer slipped from 29 percent to 23 percent, according to Gartner Dataquest (IT). Number two SAP gained three points, to 15 percent.

5 Has Tom Siebel learned enough from his struggles? Yes and no. He blames poor managers for weak sales last year, and has since shaken up the management ranks. Yet he denied there's anything wrong with the company that a strong economy can't fix. He believes that only 9 percent of the potential market for his software has been tapped and that his newest technologies will keep his company on top of its competition when demand returns. "If I were to take this company today and compare it to this company in 2000, there's no doubt in my mind I'd say this is a much better-positioned company," he says.

6 Analysts think he's overly optimistic. True, the customer-management software market is expected to start growing again next year, by 10 percent, to $3.3 billion. But analysts say Siebel Systems will no longer dominate. As the market leader, it gets most of the blame for a groundswell of dissatisfaction with this kind of software, which can cost upwards of $10 million and take a year or more to install. A recent Merrill Lynch (MER) & Co. survey found that only 45 percent of customers are fully satisfied with their purchases of this software. At the same time, Siebel Systems faces tougher competition than ever before, and Tom Siebel is "underestimating it," says analyst Joanie Rufo of AMR Research Inc. in Boston. The company's revenues are expected to drop 8 percent this year, to $1.5 billion, the lowest in four years, according to Banc of America Securities (BAC).

7 To turn the company around, the chief executive will have to overcome some daunting challenges. After gobbling up software at a frantic rate in the late 1990s, corporations are buying in smaller chunks. Increasingly, when they buy, they favor suppliers that offer broad suites of integrated products—including software for financial data, corporate planning, and human resources—while Siebel Systems focuses on one area. "Siebel will die. They're

the last of the nonsuite suppliers," predicts Oracle (ORCL) Corp. CEO Lawrence J. Ellison, a rival who offers a complete package. Once an Oracle exec, Siebel left to form his own company, and there has been bad blood between him and Ellison ever since.

8      While it's far-fetched that Siebel Systems will up and die, critics say the company has done precious little to improve its standing with customers. Last fall, its reputation took a hit after market researcher Nucleus Research Inc. contacted 23 companies Siebel had claimed as contented customers on its website—and discovered that 61 percent of them were displeased because they had not made back their investments after two years. In April, someone sent analysts negative information from one of Siebel's internal customer-service surveys—which prompted the company to complain to the FBI. Siebel also raised eyebrows when it revealed last year that it invested in SatMetrix Systems, the market research firm that conducts internal customer-satisfaction surveys that Siebel uses in its marketing.

9      Still, the company flatly denies it has a customer-satisfaction problem. It dismisses Nucleus' report, calling it "statistically insignificant," and claims there's nothing unethical about its investment in SatMetrix. To be fair, other application sellers, notably SAP in 1999, have had similar customer-satisfaction complaints, and they recovered. To improve success rates, last year Siebel Systems set up a team of 60 consultants who work with customers before they start on a project to ensure they have realistic expectations before they get started.

10     But that response seems unlikely to mollify purchasers. The company is so out of touch with the feelings of customers that it inadvertently referred *BusinessWeek* to an unhappy one—Deutsche Leasing in Frankfurt, Germany. Friedel Jonker, a tech project director, reports that two months ago, its salesforce-automation system went down for an entire day. To Jonker, it was a major gaffe. "We don't want this to happen again," he says. He plans to consider alternatives to Siebel Systems the next time he shops for software.

11     Tom Siebel does a better job when it comes to product integration issues. He's convinced that it does not make sense to offer a full suite of products. It's better, he says, to do one thing well. He acknowledges that his products need to meld with others without requiring customers to install hundreds of patches. So he just launched a new product line, called the Universal Application Network. Customer BMC Software (BMC) is using it to tie together software from Siebel, Oracle, and PeopleSoft (PSFT). "We found this is helping us take the duct tape out of the equation," says Jay Gardner, chief information officer at BMC.

12     That's only a partial fix, however. Ultimately, to be competitive, Siebel's software has to be upgraded to work better with so-called middleware technologies from Microsoft (MSFT) and IBM (IBM) that make applications from many companies interact well. In a radical move, Siebel has decided to build two separate versions of his applications. The strategy will cost about $550 million, though IBM and Microsoft will chip in. Plus, because it's building everything twice, Siebel likely won't have new products in the market until late 2004 or 2005. Other companies, such as SAP, are sticking with single versions of their products and adapting them to work well with the software from IBM and Microsoft. It's less costly, and they'll be quicker to market.

13     It's a big gamble for Tom Siebel, but his company has handled major tech overhauls before. "Siebel is a company that could pull this off," says Thomas Topolinski, an analyst at Gartner Dataquest.

14     Meanwhile, though, Siebel may have a growth problem. Corporations, aware that brand-new versions of its software are on the way, might wait for them instead of buying current releases. And all the while, SAP is gaining momentum. It's thriving by selling customer-management software to many of the 19,000 corporations that already own its other applications. Last year, its sales in this segment grew 66 percent, while Siebel's contracted by 20 percent, according to AMR. "Our goal is to be number one by the end of the year," says SAP CEO Henning Kagermann.

**15**     Tom Siebel scoffs at that claim. "It's not credible. They just give the software away," he says. But if he plans to stay ahead of SAP and regain his company's star status, he'll have to accept the fact that the software world has changed fundamentally—and that his company has to change with it.

Source: "Can Siebel Stop Its Slide?" Kerstetter, Jim. *BusinessWeek Online,* June 2, 2003.

Case 7                                                                    BusinessWeek

# Chipping Away at Qualcomm's Chips

**1**     Whenever Qualcomm Inc. CEO Irwin M. Jacobs goes to a party, he whips out his cell phone, uses it to videotape the other guests, and then plays the clips back for them on the phone's full-color screen. At this year's Super Bowl, held at Qualcomm Stadium in San Diego, he used the party trick to wow California Governor Gray Davis. Jacobs likes to boast that while Samsung Electronics Co. manufactures the phone, the Qualcomm chip inside is what makes the video and other wireless wizardry possible. "Whenever I show the phone off, everybody wants to know where they can buy one," Jacobs says.

**2**     The 69-year-old CEO has reason to gloat. Qualcomm has a near-monopoly on CDMA, a digital standard for handling mobile-phone calls that's surging in popularity around the world. Qualcomm sells 90 percent of the chips that power CDMA phones, and it earns royalties on every CDMA device sold. CDMA is expected to grow from 20 percent of the total wireless-phone market last year to 25 percent this year. That tailwind should help Qualcomm's sales to rise 30 percent this year, to $3.9 billion, while earnings jump 42 percent, to $1.1 billion, according to analysts' estimates.

**3**     Still, Jacobs won't be able to spend all his time partying with politicos. In recent months, two heavyweight rivals have unveiled plans to break Qualcomm's lock on the CDMA semiconductor market. Samsung, one of Qualcomm's biggest customers, recently said it will begin making its own CDMA chips to put into some of its mobile phones. And on May 15, Nokia, the world's largest manufacturer of cell phones, said it would team up with chipmakers Texas Instruments and STMicroelectronics to make CDMA chips for its newest phones.

**4**     The double-barreled assault is serious. Nokia and Samsung make nearly half of the 425 million cell phones sold in the world, so they have the muscle to affect market share and prices. On top of that, Texas Instruments plans to market modified versions of the CDMA chip it's developing with Nokia to other cell-phone makers, such as Motorola, LG Electronics, and Kyocera (KYO). "The market is crying out for some alternatives," says Tom Pollard, worldwide chipset marketing director for TI. "CDMA [phone] pricing is higher than other wireless standards. That comes with the territory when you have only one chip provider."

**5**     The cost of two giants looking to eat Qualcomm's lunch could be high. Analysts say Qualcomm's share of the CDMA chip market could fall from 90 percent to 80 percent in 2004. "It will be difficult for Qualcomm to grow at all in '04," says WR Hambrecht & Co. analyst Peter C. Friedland. The new competition likely will hit profits, too. Deutsche Bank (DB) analyst Brian T. Modoff expects the average $21 price tag for a Qualcomm chip to drop 15 percent over the next year. He is forecasting that Qualcomm's sales and earnings both will fall slightly in 2004, to $3.6 billion and $960 million, respectively.

**6**     Troubles in China and India, two of Qualcomm's most promising markets, could exacerbate the company's challenge. In China, the SARS scare has kept potential cell-phone buyers homebound. "That took a month's worth of selling out of the cell-phone market," says Jacobs. In India, the largest CDMA carrier, Reliance India Mobile, says they have attracted 1.1 million subscribers. But some analysts suspect the number is closer to 800,000, which could lead to lower sales and price cutting in the future. Because of excess inventory in both countries, Qualcomm warned analysts in April that chip shipments for this quarter would be on the low end of the 23-million-to-25-million range it had expected.

**7**     Jacobs vows that the company, often underestimated in the past, won't lose its edge. As part of his plan to keep Qualcomm on a hot streak, he is preaching the advantages of CDMA overseas in hopes of increasing the company's presence in such new markets as Indonesia and Thailand. On June 3, Qualcomm said it would invest $100 million in Chinese companies making CDMA phones and other products. And Qualcomm is pledging to keep its edge in technology. On May 22, it unveiled several new chip products designed to let manufacturers pack more multimedia features into phones at lower cost. And they're less power-hungry, which should help improve battery life on CDMA phones.

**8**    How will Qualcomm fare in this newly competitive environment? While market share and profits may take a hit, the company is likely to be a strong player in the years ahead. The key reason: The CDMA market is growing so fast that even if Qualcomm loses some share to rivals, its revenues likely will continue to head north after 2004. Research firm Herschel Shosteck Associates Ltd. estimates that CDMA phones will grow to 47 percent of the total market in 2007 from 25 percent this year. "The long-term picture is bright," says Rob Gensler, manager of T. Rowe Price Media & Telecom Fun (d PRMTX) which owns 5 million shares of Qualcomm.

**9**    To stay ahead of his competitors, Jacobs plans to increase the pace of innovation. The company is coming out with a host of new products that are likely to command premium prices. One of them would allow CDMA users to roam almost anywhere in the world, something that can't be done today because of conflicting wireless standards. "Qualcomm's chips have a level of integration that goes above and beyond what [competitors are] offering," says analyst Rich Valera of Needham & Co.

**10**    Qualcomm also is angling for a leading position in the world of next-generation phones. It has developed a technology called EV-DO, which lets CDMA carriers transmit data at blazing speeds. Forget about e-mail or stock quotes—with EV-DO, customers can watch streaming video on their mobile phones and laptop computers. "Our customers are thrilled with the speeds," says George Tronsrue, CEO of Monet Mobile Networks, which provides service in Minnesota, Wisconsin, and North Dakota. Verizon (VZ) Wireless, a big Qualcomm customer, will launch EV-DO systems in Washington and San Diego this summer.

**11**    Jacobs is even getting into the software business. In 2001, Qualcomm launched a product called Brew that lets software developers make games and other multimedia applications that CDMA subscribers can download to their phones. Qualcomm gets a cut of the fee carriers charge subscribers who use the programs. One of the newest Brew products is QChat, a technology that will enable CDMA phones to operate like walkie-talkies, much like the push-to-talk service that Nextel has marketed successfully to construction workers and other tradesmen. Jacobs' son, Paul, who manages the Brew unit for Qualcomm, says some wireless carriers plan to launch QChat next year, though he won't disclose which ones.

**12**    Brew does face stiff competition from other wireless data standards, notably Java software. Verizon, Alltel (AT), United States Cellular (USM), and five overseas carriers have adopted Brew. But the other large United States CDMA carrier, Sprint PCS Group, has yet to sign on. "They started down the Java path early, and it has been difficult for us to change that momentum," says Paul Jacobs. He concedes that Brew may not break even this year, as predicted, and he isn't sure when it will turn a profit.

**13**    The elder Jacobs isn't deterred by the challenges ahead. He believes that CDMA technology can double its worldwide presence over the next few years, and his company will lead the pack. If he wants to see a vision of the future, he just reaches into his pocket and pulls out his videophone with its Qualcomm engine.

Source: "Chipping Away at Qualcomm's Chips," Weintraub, Arlene, Kripalani, Manjeet, and Ihlwan, Moon. *BusinessWeek Online,* June 16, 2003.

**Case 8**

BusinessWeek

# Down for the Count at HVB

1   Dieter Rampl took on one of the toughest jobs in European finance on January 1. As the new chief executive of the giant German bank HVB Group, the 55-year-old Austrian must grapple with mounting losses, tumbling credit ratings, and a share price less than half what it was a year ago. What's more, he has to deal with a massive $460 billion loan portfolio riddled with bad debts. "I don't think I could sleep if I had [Rampl's] problems," says a managing board member of a rival bank. "The loan book alone would give me nightmares."

2   Rampl, a tall, slim man who laughs easily, says he sleeps fine, thank you, and is confident HVB can solve its problems. However, HVB's worried shareholders—especially reinsurance behemoth Munich Re Group, which owns 25 percent—will follow Rampl's progress keenly. What happens at HVB will reverberate far beyond its Munich base. The bank boasts more than $730 billion in assets, making it Germany's second-biggest after Deutsche Bank and tenth in the world. Its core holding is Bayerische Hypo-und Vereinsbank in Germany, but it also owns Bank Austria, the biggest in Austria, has the biggest presence of any bank in eastern Europe and is a major player in the Dutch property market. HVB has 8.5 million retail customers and is Europe's largest mortgage lender. It has a bigger loan book than any euro zone bank. And it is the leading lender to the *Mittelstand*—the small and midsize companies that form the backbone of the German economy.

3   Where did HVB go wrong? It goes back almost a decade. The group was formed by the merger of Bayerische Vereinsbank and Bayerische Hypothekenbank in 1998. In the early and mid-1990s, Hypothekenbank made real estate loans worth billions of dollars, especially in the former East Germany. But the eastern boom went bust, and property in the rest of Germany tanked along with the economy. HVB Group was left with a load of bad debt. Much of that has been paid off, but the rest still weighs on its balance sheet. On top of that, HVB made loans to a string of tottering and now-bankrupt German companies. First to fall were big corporations such as the construction outfit Phillip Holzmann, the Kirch media group, and engineering group Babcock Borsig. Then there was a spate of bankruptcies among the *Mittelstand* companies where HVB lends most of its money. "We all miscalculated a bit," says Rampl.

4   The result: The bank was forced to make new bad-debt provisions of $1.25 billion in the third quarter of 2002, more than double its operating profit of $545 million. Analysts now expect its loan losses to reach $3.75 billion for 2002, leading to a pretax loss of around $670 million. HVB says loan losses aren't likely to top $3.4 billion, but admits that's nothing to cheer about. Meanwhile, the group's paltry market capitalization—just $8.92 billion—could make it the victim of a takeover bid.

5   This year doesn't look any better, says Schroder Salomon Smith Barney analyst Kiri Vijayarajah. "Insolvencies are likely to continue rising in Germany, so the 2003 charge is likely to be heavier still." The painful losses mean the bank is being forced to use up capital that it ought to be investing in its businesses. The problem is aggravated by the erosion of the bank's own investment portfolio, which in the past helped underpin its share price. "The group could find itself locked in a vicious circle of continual attrition," says Marc Rubinstein, an analyst at Credit Suisse First Boston in London.

6   The circle is already looking pretty vicious. Standard & Poor's downgraded HVB from A to A- on December 9, due to its "deteriorated asset quality, weakening profitability levels, [and] modest capital strength," as well as "the reduced level of unrealized gains on the bank's investment portfolio," says analyst Stefan Best. That will make it more expensive for

the group to borrow money. "[It] represents a blow that cannot be overestimated," says Jörn Kissenkotter, an analyst who follows HVB for Hamburg private bank M.M. Warburg & Co.

7    Rampl and his predecessor, Albrecht Schmidt, who is now chairman of the supervisory board, say they are determined to put HVB right and win back investor trust. They have already unveiled a plan to save more than $500 million a year by shrinking the group's bloated 66,000-person workforce by 9,100 by the end of this year. They are also moving fast to reduce the size of the bank's loan book and free extra capital. On November 6, for example, HVB launched its largest-ever securitization deal, packaging and selling to other banks and investors $5.1 billion worth of residential mortgages. HVB also has sold its 48 percent stake in the Banco BBA-Creditanstalt in Brazil and is rumored to be seeking a buyer for Norisbank, a small Nuremberg-headquartered bank that specializes in consumer credit. On December 30, HVB announced the sale of Selftrade, its non-German online brokerage business. Its German online bank, DAB, may also end up on the block.

8    Rampl says one important restructuring move may come after HVB's annual shareholder meeting in May. He will bundle all of HVB's mortgage subsidiaries, which are now scattered around Europe, into a new real estate financing group. The company, with assets of almost $170 billion, "will be spun off from the group and operate independently," Rampl says. "[That means it] will be fully able to capitalize on its strength."

9    Admirers say Rampl, who joined the former Vereinsbank in 1968 as a trainee and has spent all but 11 years of his career at the group, has the skills and personality needed to push through far-reaching change. They cite his success at restructuring the corporate division over the past year. But even if he fixes all of HVB's structural problems, he still faces intense competition in HVB's core German market from both rival commercial banks and a plethora of state-backed banks that can undercut their publicly traded adversaries.

10    Some say part of the solution might be for HVB to buy Commerzbank, its smaller but equally troubled competitor in Germany. That would generate big economies of scale, and Munich Re likes the idea. But Rampl says it "isn't very sensible at this stage" because fixing two hard-pressed banks is a lot trickier than patching up one. Either way, it's unlikely to happen in the near term: The last thing HVB needs is the cultural and managerial problems that would come with a big merger.

11    Besides, a merger would do nothing to solve HVB's most vexing issue. As Schmidt put it in an interview with a German newspaper on December 16: "Our bank's problem is Germany." It's hard to imagine HVB climbing back into the black anytime soon, unless Rampl has a plan to fix Germany, too.

Source: "Down for the Court at HVB." Fairlamb, David, *BusinessWeek Online.* January 20, 2003.

Case 9

BusinessWeek

# Expedia: Changing Pilots in Mid-Climb

1   Richard N. Barton was leading a charmed life. At 35, he ran one of the most successful Web businesses on the planet, online travel agency Expedia Inc. (EXPE). He harbored soaring ambitions. He saw Expedia taking control of much of the travel business, dictating terms and prices to airlines and hotel chains alike. In the past year, he had outmaneuvered none other than consummate dealmaker Barry Diller, chairman of USA Interactive (USAI), a 62 percent owner of Expedia. When Diller tried to buy the rest of Expedia, Barton's board thwarted him. Barton wasn't yet the king of travel, but he sure was a powerful prince on the rise.

2   And yet, as Expedia prepared to announce record sales and earnings for a breakout 2002 on February 5, Barton did something shocking: He quit. The travel industry, which had come to view the hard-charging Barton as a rising force for years ahead, was left wondering what happened. Barton, who has joined the board of USA Interactive, isn't providing many clues. He says simply that he, his wife, and children will pursue a more peaceful life for the next year or two in Italy and France. "The world for me is not necessarily creating this business," he says.

3   But sources within both companies say friction between Diller and the young CEO grew as they battled for control last year. That tension didn't evaporate after Barton prevailed. Anything but. It was clear to people involved that Diller would eventually try again. When Barton quit, he insisted it was the appeal of free time in Europe that led to his resignation. And Diller angrily denies that any tension between them led to Barton's departure, saying: "We didn't push him out. Nothing close to it."

4   Barton leaves behind long-time lieutenant Erik C. Blachford as CEO. The genial, 36-year-old Canadian joined Expedia in 1995 and now serves as the company's president of Expedia North America. He says he will follow the strategy Barton mapped out, and the market seems undaunted. After dipping below $56 on February 4, Expedia's shares are trading at about $63 thanks to better-than-expected earnings: The company reported 2002 net income of $66 million on revenue of $591 million. Analysts project an 79 percent jump in earnings for 2003, to $113 million.

5   Yet Blachford takes over at a time of nerve-jangling uncertainty. Looming war in the Middle East could knock whatever stuffing is left out of the beleaguered travel industry. And online copycats are nipping at Expedia's heels. What's more, as Blachford plows into the corporate market, he'll face richer and brawnier rivals than the mom-and-pop travel agencies Barton whipped in the consumer realm. "I think they're in for a rude awakening," says Pamela M. Arway, American Express Co.'s executive vice-president for business travel.

6   And it's not clear what role Chairman Diller will play. Already, he has rankled Expedia employees by forcing them to accept restricted stock and fewer stock options, which are potentially more lucrative. Will Blachford be able to stand up to Diller? To date, he has played the diplomat, smoothing over flaps with airlines and hotel chains while Barton pushed for industry domination. Blachford insists that "day to day, I call the shots," though he'll consult with USAI and collaborate with sister companies.

7   Fortunately for Blachford, he's taking over just as Expedia is hitting its stride. The company has been thriving even in the midst of a wake-me-when-it's-over travel slump. Gross sales grew some 75 percent last year, to $5 billion. Expedia zoomed past Sabre Holdings' Travelocity.com (TSG) to become number one in Web travel. And it's expanding rapidly into Europe, which now accounts for 10 percent of its business. "Expedia is going to be the biggest travel-distribution brand on the planet," predicts Philip C. Wolf, president of leading travel consulting firm PhoCusWright Inc. in Sherman, Conn.

**8**     Indeed, the six-year-old company is scaring the daylights out of the rest of the $550 billion travel industry. It is viewed as a fearsome mini-Microsoft Corp. Like Microsoft (MSFT), where it was created and which spun it off three years ago, Expedia is throwing its weight around, demanding better terms from airlines and hoteliers. "Expedia, which is another word for Microsoft, wants domination," says Samuel L. Katz, CEO of the travel-distribution unit of Cendant (CD), parent of Ramada Franchise Systems, an Expedia partner. "This is not a culture that divides the world up. It asks: 'How do we kill everyone else?'"

**9**     While Blachford projects a softer image than Barton, he insists Expedia will stay aggressive. The next target? Corporate travel, worth $70 billion a year in the United States—and the stomping ground of American Express (AXP). Expedia entered the business in November, capitalizing on easy-to-use, low-cost technology to undercut traditional corporate travel-services fees by over 75 percent. Analysts believe Expedia could be a solid number two in the corporate realm in as little as five years.

**10**     Such bullish predictions for Web merchants were common in the go-go '90s. The idea was that old-line industries would be "Amazoned"—elbowed aside by Net companies. While it hasn't happened in most industries, online forces, led by Expedia, are wreaking havoc in travel. The United States online consumer travel market jumped 37 percent, to $28 billion, last year, or 15 percent of the total market, and is on the way to double its share by 2005, according to PhoCusWright.

**11**     Early on, Expedia faced formidable foes. Travelocity Inc. and Preview Travel Inc. both launched earlier in 1996 and held the early lead. And while all three services grew fast, it looked at first as if the airlines would be able to hold them in check. In 1997, carriers sliced base commissions to online agencies from 10 percent to 8 percent—and later cut them to 5 percent and then zero. Then they launched their own competing website, Orbitz.com.

**12**     It wasn't until Barton broadened Expedia's offerings beyond airfares to include hotel rooms that he positioned the company to dominate online travel. Instead of angling for commissions of 10 percent, he bought hotel rooms at wholesale prices, marked them up an average of 26 percent, and resold them to consumers at attractive prices—the so-called merchant business.

**13**     Getting into hotels helped Expedia trump the airlines. As its audience grew, lured by hotel deals, Expedia was able to command the lowest airfares, which analysts had expected to go exclusively to Orbitz. And Expedia has been racing ahead ever since. Travelocity waited until last year before trying to match Expedia's hotel strategy, and Orbitz, late to the market, has been playing catch-up. "We haven't been very effective at neutralizing our biggest competitor," concedes Orbitz CEO Jeffrey G. Katz.

**14**     Expedia's big leap came just when it looked as if it was heading for deep trouble—after September 11. Sales had fallen by 65 percent just after the attacks. Yet rather than slice spending, as everybody else did, Barton boosted marketing by 56 percent and tech research and development by 35 percent for 2002. Now, just a year later, Expedia is doing 55 percent more business than Travelocity, and Expedia's share of the online travel market has risen to 19 percent, up from 12 percent two years ago.

**15**     Expedia's earnings are richer than those of its rivals, too: Operating profit margins are forecast to hit 26 percent this year. The company's main online competitors, Orbitz and Travelocity, don't break out financials, but Priceline.com (PCLN), a much smaller rival, reported a 1 percent operating profit margin last quarter. Expedia's fat profits allow it to undercut online rivals, outspend them for product development, and drive hard bargains with struggling suppliers.

**16**     Expedia aims to gain a similar edge in corporate travel. The initial goal: to win market share by using technology to lower transaction costs and make travel planning and expense accounting easier. The first service, aimed at smaller businesses, charges $5 per Web reservation plus a $100-per-year membership fee. A second service, expected to be launched by midyear, targets midsize-to-larger corporations with an array of online and telephone-agent services that are expected to include most of what companies can get from the large agencies. Pricing hasn't been set yet.

17    This is leading AmEx to take a page from Barton's book. Its new strategy is to offer a range of products at different levels of service. At the bottom, it now books 20 percent of its corporate travel electronically, and its most basic online service is now even cheaper than Expedia's, at a flat $149 per year. At the high end, AmEx provides clients with meeting-planning and international travel pieces that Expedia won't match with its upcoming service. Jim Lee, corporate travel manager for Honeywell Inc. (HON), says he'll stick with AmEx for its handholding. "I'm looking for the lifeline that says, 'I've always got somebody I can call,'" he says.

18    Still, analysts expect Expedia's corporate business to become as big as its consumer business is now. It won't offer the soup-to-nuts service American Express does, but basic point-to-point travel arrangements—at which it excels—account for up to 85 percent of major corporate accounts. Even Danny B. Hood, president of WorldTravel BTI, a top corporate agency and rival, believes Expedia will gain market share at a gallop—initially at the expense of small regional corporate travel agents. "They'll be one of the big players. No doubt about it," he says.

19    If Blachford can establish traction in the corporate business, he could gain the upper hand over the airlines when it comes to pricing. Bolstered by a large number of corporate accounts, Expedia would be able to steer more and more business to preferred airlines and hotel chains. With that clout, Blachford hopes to be able to force the airlines to sell more seats at wholesale. One early sign that the plan might work: JetBlue Airways Corp. (JBLU), which isn't hurting and usually avoids agents, is talking to Expedia about selling corporate tickets. "We need to make sure we gain access" to Expedia's customers, says Tim Claydon, JetBlue's vice-president for sales.

20    Expedia's suppliers are trying belatedly to blunt its power. This spring, a group of major hotel chains will relaunch Travelweb.com. But analysts say the site will have to build a huge audience before it has any clout. What's more, sites controlled by suppliers, such as Orbitz, have trouble promoting one brand over another. This dulls their marketing. "Suppliers had better get their act together or they're going to be slaves. They'll need Expedia like an addict needs a fix," says Henry Harteveldt, an analyst at Forrester Research Inc.

21    For now, the economy seems to be cooperating with Expedia. Trade groups say demand for trips and hotel rooms won't pick up much until 2004 at the earliest. Meanwhile, hotel construction continues apace. That means loads of discounted rooms—and plenty of leverage for Expedia. If it keeps growing fast over the next year, analysts say, its customer base could give it lasting clout.

22    Expedia isn't likely to become the Microsoft of travel. Not quite. Yet even with its top brass in turmoil, Expedia is in the pilot's seat—and no one else in the travel business will be comfortable for a long time to come.

Source: "Expedia: Changing Pilots in Mid-Climb," Mullaney, Timothy J., and Greene, Jay. *BusinessWeek Online*, February 24, 2003.

## Case 10

# FedEx and Brown Are Going Green

**1**  Practically every day, more than 70,000 boxy brown UPS delivery trucks rumble to life across the country. They travel more than 1.3 billion miles annually to deliver some 4.7 billion packages, combusting tens of millions of gallons of diesel fuel along the way. No wonder United Parcel Service (UPS) Inc. will try just about anything to save a few pennies for each of those miles. The Atlanta-based shipper once developed a motor that could burn cheap corn oil.

**2**  The engine never made it out of the lab. But that hasn't kept UPS from hunting for cheaper, cleaner replacements for the old, smoke-belching diesels that power most of its trucks. "We're driven to cut costs in finding cleaner fuels," says Thomas H. Weidemeyer, UPS's COO and president of its air unit. Today, UPS's green fleet includes around 2,000 vans running on everything from compressed natural gas to electricity. Compared with standard diesel engines, the CNG vans shave 15 percent in fuel costs and emit 35 percent less pollution.

**3**  That's just a fraction of what's to come. UPS and its big rival FedEx (FDX) Corp. are beginning to swap out the old diesels from their combined armada of 100,000-plus delivery vehicles. In their place, they're testing a variety of cleaner technologies, including diesel-electric hybrids and hydrogen fuel cells. In part, they're doing this to satisfy Washington's push to cut emissions, given that trucks produce more than 30 percent of urban smog.

**4**  The biggest motivation is cost savings, though. The delivery giants are finding that green machines, while pricey to buy, are cheaper to maintain and operate. Hybrid electric vehicles, for example, can cut fuel costs by half, while lowering emissions by 90 percent. Of course, such big cuts in pollution also make great PR for a historically dirty industry. Still, "the driving motivation here is the bottom line," says Donald Broughton, a transportation analyst at A. G. Edwards (AGE) & Sons Inc. "[These CEOs] haven't suddenly joined Greenpeace."

**5**  Where FedEx and UPS lead, the rest of the nation's 5-million strong delivery fleet will follow. Over the coming decade, the price of hybrid trucks will likely fall as a result of FedEx' 30,000-unit order for hybrid electric vans. If so, others are ready to make a commitment. The U.S. Postal Service plans to mix hybrids into its fleet of 142,300 trucks once the price is right. "These technologies provide a huge potential for the transportation sector as a whole," says Margo T. Oge, director of the office of transportation and air quality at the Environmental Protection Agency.

**6**  This movement started with small steps. In the late '80s, UPS invested heavily in CNG-powered trucks. Even after Washington reversed its backing—and funding—for CNG a few years into the trial, UPS continued to build the necessary infrastructure. Since 1998, it has been testing a hybrid electric van. And UPS is also expanding its fleet of ultralow-emission diesel trucks to 5,000 from 3,200. Next year, UPS will work with the EPA and DaimlerChrysler (DCX) to test the first hydrogen-powered fuel-cell delivery truck in the United States.

**7**  FedEx is tinkering with its fleet, too. In May, the Memphis-based company announced it had bought 20 hybrid delivery trucks, the vanguard in a program that will eventually replace its entire fleet of 30,000 express delivery vans. "FedEx really raised everybody's eyebrows," says Fred Silver, director of business initiatives at WestStart, a nonprofit transportation technologies think tank in Pasadena, Calif.

**8**  Hybrids are nothing new, to be sure. Toyota (TM) Motor Corp. and Honda (HMC) Motor Co. sell passenger cars powered by mixed gas-electric motors. But FedEx is the first in this country to try to adapt the technology for diesel delivery vehicles on such a large scale.

Mitchell Jackson, FedEx's managing director of corporate and international environmental programs, boasts: "We've got the most innovative project on the ground in the industry today. This is not a demo. It's a commercial vehicle."

9    Indeed, most experts—even those at UPS—believe hybrids offer the best near-term promise. Hybrids combine a high-efficiency diesel or gas engine with an electric motor. A computer orchestrates how to channel energy around the engine, the electric motor, and the wheels most efficiently. Hybrids require less maintenance because they run cleaner. Plus, the braking systems last longer because the motor itself helps slow the vehicle down—in a process that recaptures much of the energy used in decelerating. Between fuel savings and lower maintenance costs, FedEx claims it will break even on the hybrid vans in about a decade.

10    The scale of FedEx's commitment is likely to transform the economics of hybrid commercial vehicles. What are now exotic custom-builds could soon become mass-produced and less expensive. Smaller players could then consider hybrid trucks. "FedEx is taking a big gamble," says Andrew J. Hoffman, a Boston University professor who specializes in corporate environmental strategies. "But it's a gamble that should jump-start the commercialization of this technology."

11    Cleveland-based Eaton (ETN) Corp., which makes the key electro-mechanical power systems for FedEx's hybrids, says it expects to sell up to 30,000 such units within the next five years—and not just to FedEx. "This should be a substantial new business for us," says Tim J. Morscheck, Eaton's vice-president of technology in the trucking division. Morscheck believes the hybrids will get cheaper as sales volume grows.

12    The numbers are beginning to add up. In a recent report, consumer consultant J. D. Power & Associates Inc. estimated there will be more than 500,000 hybrid vehicles on the road by 2008—40 percent of them trucks. After years of experimentation, UPS and FedEx are now ready to deploy green vans in a big way—possibly heralding the end of the smoke-belching delivery van.

Source: "FedEx and Brown Are Going Green." Haddad, Charles and Tierney, Christine, *BusinessWeek Online*. August 11, 2003.

## Case 11

BusinessWeek

# GE: Little Engines That Could

**1** Representatives from four of the world's top jet-engine makers did their best last October as they made their final presentations to Chinese officials at Shanghai's Portman Ritz-Carlton Hotel. The leaders of the most populous nation had said that despite past failures, China would once again try to build a fleet of 500 regional jets in time for the 2008 Beijing Olympics. And each plane, of course, would need engines.

**2** So executives from Rolls-Royce (RYCEY), Pratt & Whitney (UTX), Snecma—a French-government-owned engine shop—and General Electric (GE) waited nervously to see who would win the prize. Months of preparation had led up to that day. "I don't think there was a night that I didn't go to bed with heartburn," says David L. Joyce, GE's vice-president for commercial-engine operations. Now, Joyce can throw away the Tums: GE won the $3 billion contract.

**3** Chalk up another victory for GE Aircraft Engines (GEAE), based in Evendale, Ohio, near Cincinnati. GE already controls 64 percent of the world market for commercial-jet engines, largely on the strength of its popular CFM56, which is used on narrow-body planes such as the Airbus A320 or Boeing Co.'s 737, and the GE-90, which carries Boeing's (BA) big 777 aloft. Yet GEAE executives believe the explosive growth in regional jets—those with up to 100 seats and ranges of up to 1,500 miles—will be the division's future.

**4** Why? Mainly because air carriers appreciate their lower operating costs. Bankrupt airlines such as US Airways Group Inc. (U) and United Airlines Inc. (UAL) will probably end up replacing many big jets with the smaller, cheaper ones. And on short hops, consumers prefer them to propeller planes. The number of regional jets in service has swelled to 1,300 from 85 in 1993. And with airlines mothballing big planes in the desert, that number is expected to grow.

**5** The story behind the successful gamble on regional-jet engines illustrates one of the big strengths of a diverse company such as GE—and one of its typical strategies. With both short-cycle businesses, which pay off quickly, and long-cycle ones, whose payoffs are years down the road, GE can invest heavily in new technologies it believes in, even when the payoff is not imminent. In the '90s, GE could afford to invest in new jet-engine technologies because of the strong performance by some of its shorter-cycle businesses—primarily NBC (GE) and GE Plastics. "When we had tough times, we didn't cut back on R&D or on product support," says Brian H. Rowe, retired CEO of GEAE.

**6** True, the current airline slump has slowed total revenues from GE's jet-engine unit to $10.6 billion in 2002, a drop of 7 percent from the previous year—although operating profits remained constant at $2.1 billion, thanks in part to $500 million in cost-cutting. And GE regional-jet engines totaled only $660 million in sales in 2002, along with $200 million in service fees—only about 10 percent of GEAE's revenues. That represents deliveries of 584 regional-jet engines this year.

**7** But that's just the start. GE already has orders and options over the next decade for nearly 5,600 CF34 engines—those that power 50- and 90-seat jets—not including any orders from the $3 billion China contract. David L. Calhoun, the current chief executive of GEAE, believes that an additional 5,000 regional jets could be sold over the next decade. With just one competitor in the 50-seat market, for instance—Britain's Rolls-Royce PLC—GEAE has a virtual lock on one of the few growing segments in commercial aviation. This year, in fact, GE will ship 69 percent of all regional-jet engines. Says Teal Group Corp. aerospace analyst Richard L. Aboulafia: "That market is not only growing but could be crucial to the survival and recovery of the airline industry."

**8**     GE's stock price is down 40 percent in the past 12 months, to about $25. So GE Chairman and CEO Jeffrey R. Immelt clearly appreciates that the payoff for GE's long-ago investment is beginning to kick in. "In 20 years," he says, "we have gone from being a follower to being an extraordinarily strong number one." But perhaps the best is still to come. Because GEAE will sell spare parts and service contracts for its engines, Immelt believes that the rapid growth of the regional-jet market creates "an aggressive services play that will contribute significant income for decades." Service revenue just for regional-jet engines is expected to hit $1.4 billion by 2010 and climb much higher after that.

**9**     Few in the industry paid attention to the regional-jet market in the early 1990s. Bombardier Inc. conceived and put on the market its 50-passenger regional jet, powered exclusively by GE's CF34—originally intended to feed airline hubs from small airports. With GE rolling the dice by investing more than $1 billion in new engine technology, it took early adopters Lufthansa (DLAKY) and Comair, a large regional carrier now owned by Delta Air Lines (DAL), to get the market going. Then, in the late '90s, Bombardier and Brazilian rival Embraer expanded to 70- and 90-seat jetliners. Two lessons became clear: Passengers preferred small jets to turboprops, and operating costs for regional jets were lower.

**10**     That has become especially true with the decline in air travel following the September 11 terrorist attacks. A recent study by Raymond James & Associates Inc. (RJF) found that a 50-seat regional jet carrying 43 passengers could generate a 16 percent profit margin, compared with a 27 percent loss for a 120-seat 737 carrying 76 passengers. "Full-service carriers will continue to shrink, and [regional jets] and low-fare products will continue to grow," says Fred Buttrell, CEO of Delta Connection Inc., the largest regional-jet operator.

**11**     GE's plans for higher regional-jet-engine profits could unravel, however. Its business model is based on the assumption that air travel will overcome the downturn and start growing again at 5 percent annually. Yet analysts expect the major airlines to lose $4 billion in 2003, with no recovery until 2005 or 2006. A longer slump or a Chapter 7 bankruptcy filing by a major carrier would continue to depress results.

**12**     Another worry: GE could lose more of its lucrative service business in the regional-jet market to cheaper competitors. Delta Connection, for one, already buys engine maintenance from among the handful of GE's small, privately held rivals. GE cannot afford to ignore that: Its most lucrative service contracts are in markets such as regional jets, where it faces the least competition. It is a hallmark of GE to profit not only from the sale of goods but also from the sale of services. So Calhoun says he will aggressively fight to keep GEAE's 95 percent market share for regional-jet-engine maintenance intact.

**13**     China is another question mark, say analysts. The Chinese have failed three times in the past decade to develop a 100-seat regional jet. The country lacked the industrial infrastructure to build top-quality modern jets, and it was difficult to make a deal without being in the World Trade Organization.

**14**     But this time, the bidding was straightforward, without the complicated negotiations that hobbled prior attempts. "China was a huge win for us," says Immelt, "and illustrative of our overall strategy there." He adds that the win sets a successful pattern for all of GE's businesses in China. GEAE is slated to be a big part of GE's presence in China in the future. But the nicest part for the engine maker: If the Chinese deal should fall apart, the division should be able to do fine without it.

Source: "GE Little Engines that Could." Holmes, Stanley. *BusinessWeek Online,* January 20, 2003.

Case 12                                                                 **BusinessWeek**

# Mitsubishi Moves into High Gear

**1**   To launch its latest model in Japan—the Colt subcompact—Mitsubishi Motors Corp. invited hundreds of loyal customers to enjoy free food and drinks in a Tokyo hotel ballroom festooned with silver and blue balloons. Anyone who signed up for a new car got a gift box with a baseball cap, a teddy bear, and an electric blue scarf—and the chance to pose for a photo with Rolf Eckrodt, president of Mitsubishi Motors.

**2**   As a scoreboard tallied up the number of cars sold—by the end of the day it read 1,302—Eckrodt pumped his fist in the air and told the crowd: "This will have a very strong impact on the 65,000 people working for Mitsubishi Motors." Then, ever the salesman, he added: "Don't forget to sign the contract, by the way."

**3**   Eckrodt's hard sell signals the Colt's crucial role in turning Mitsubishi around. Japan's fourth-largest carmaker has been a headache for DaimlerChrysler since it bought a controlling stake three years ago and installed Mercedes-Benz veteran Eckrodt as troubleshooter-in-chief. Just after DaimlerChrysler took over, Mitsubishi admitted hiding defects that led to the recall of 2 million vehicles. In the past two years it has rolled out only three new models, and has seen its Japanese market share collapse to 5.8 percent last year from 11.4 percent in 1995. In 2000 and 2001, Mitsubishi racked up a total of $2.5 billion in losses.

**4**   But Eckrodt has spent the past two years shifting the company into higher gear. He has dismembered Mitsubishi's *keiretsu*—or corporate family—of cosseted parts makers and now encourages bids from outsiders. He cut 12,000 jobs—15 percent of Mitsubishi's staff. And he started piggybacking on DaimlerChrysler's marketing and manufacturing strengths. The new Colt shares 65 percent of its parts with the next-generation DaimlerChrysler Smart Car and costs about 30 percent less to make than the model it replaced, Eckrodt says.

**5**   Now, the Japanese company is no longer a drag on DaimlerChrysler's results. Mitsubishi expects to report profits of $316.7 million on sales of $28.3 billion for the year ending in March, versus earnings of $93.8 million on $26.7 billion in revenues last year. The bottom line improvement has helped Mitsubishi's share price climb 15 percent in the past three months, to a recent $2.27. But that's still 33 percent below the carmaker's 12-month high last May, due to investor concerns that strong U.S. sales may sputter in the uncertain economy. So persuading Japanese consumers to pay $8,700–$12,500 for the Colt is crucial: Eckrodt wants a revival in Japanese sales to offset any softness in the United States.

**6**   To underscore the changes, Mitsubishi is playing up the car's "German-Japanese" roots in ads. And as part of his pitch, the 60-year-old Eckrodt sent out hundreds of letters with his signature asking longtime customers in Japan to check out the new Colt. His letters were part of an aggressive promotional effort that boosted the car's first-month sales to more than 15,000—double the company's target—despite tough competition from such top sellers as Honda Motor Co.'s Fit and Nissan Motor Co.'s March.

**7**   The pug-nosed, 1.5-liter Colt (an updated version of the Colt once exported to the United States as a Dodge) has earned high marks for styling from the Japanese auto press. Its aerodynamic body and smart, roomy layout—it has a bench seat in front, virtually unheard of in subcompacts—has lured straying customers back into the fold. "I like the interior—especially the bench seat," says Machiharu Shibayama, 27, as she sweeps her green-tinged bangs from her face. "Besides, my family has always bought Mitsubishi." She, too, signed on for one of the cars at the launch event.

**8**   Mitsubishi needs that kind of loyalty. Even if demand for the Colt holds firm in Japan, the automaker doesn't expect to break even there until 2005. And Mitsubishi is still haunted by a reputation for poor quality. Last year, nine models in Japan were recalled to fix faulty parts. That spotty record calls into question the effectiveness of the "quality gates" DaimlerChrysler added to Mitsubishi's plants. The gates—where supervisors run through a quality checklist at various stages of production—were one of the first changes ordered by the Germans. Eckrodt is well aware of ongoing "problems on the quality side," which he says are a top priority.

9    To win back customers, Mitsubishi is also betting on better design. By 2005, it hopes to have at least six new models in Japan, each with distinct styling aimed at wooing younger, urban drivers. The first will be the Grandis, a minivan due out in May. "We're trying to be serious but fun," says senior executive officer Olivier Boulay, Mitsubishi's design chief. To make sure the Grandis appeals to its target audience, Mitsubishi dispatched designers from its R&D center in rural Okazaki to Tokyo for several weeks. There they met with young people and soaked up big-city ambience before heading back to their workshops.

10    Mitsubishi has already captured the imagination of post-baby boomers in the United States Some 16.4 percent of its buyers are under age 25, the youngest of any automaker, according to J. D. Power & Associates research. That could give Mitsubishi a leg up on the competition if those buyers stay loyal. To keep them coming back for more, it's rolling out new products tailored to the U.S. market, including the Endeavor sport-utility vehicle due in February. "We appeal to those who want something a little more edgy than Honda and Toyota," says Pierre Gagnon, president and CEO of Mitsubishi Motors North America. The company expects to sell 600,000 cars in North America by 2007, 66 percent more than last year—and may even build a new U.S. factory.

11    Others, though, are targeting the same piece of the market. At a base price of $15,499, the 2.4-liter Hyundai Sonata sedan, for instance, represents a strong challenge to the comparable Mitsubishi Galant, listed at $17,767. At the same time, Honda and Toyota Motor Corp. are rolling out products with cutting-edge technologies such as gas-electric hybrid engines that cash-poor Mitsubishi can't afford. Worse, Mitsubishi's younger demographic makes it especially vulnerable in a softening economy since younger buyers are the first to hold off on big-ticket purchases when cash is tight.

12    DaimlerChrysler can breathe a sigh of relief after a rocky two years with Mitsubishi. But Eckrodt needs to keep the turnaround going. Don't be surprised to see him showing up in more Mitsubishi showrooms, with his salesman's hearty handshake and steady smile. Buy one of his cars and he might even drop you a thank-you note.

Source: "Mitsubishi Moves into High Gear." Dawson, Chester and Kerwin, Katie. *BusinessWeek Online,* February 10, 2003.

## Case 13

BusinessWeek

# Pumping Up BP

1   It's a major oil deal, a masterstroke for Vladimir Putin, a warning shot to OPEC, and a coup for John Browne, the restless chief of Anglo-American energy giant BP. The Feb. 11 announcement that BP PLC (BP) would pony up $7.1 billion in cash, stock, and assets for a 50 percent stake in what will be Russia's third-largest oil company could even shake up the industry as much as Browne's 1998 acquisition of Amoco, a deal that triggered huge consolidation.

2   The BP agreement with the owners of Tyumen Oil Co., a major Russian oil and gas producer, boosts the London company's oil reserves by a third. But the agreement has significance far beyond the oil patch. Energy is the most political of businesses, and this deal is clearly a bargain struck between Russia and Britain, America's closest ally. As such, it is a reward for British Prime Minister Tony Blair, who was quick to embrace Russian President Putin after the former KGB boss took power in 2000. Having such a marquee Western name as BP link its future to Russia is a boon to Putin, who considers Russian energy companies key levers of his foreign policy. Putin is signaling by the agreement that Russia is welding itself more firmly than ever to the West—and that other multinationals can safely seek investment in Russia. Putin also wants to harness BP's savvy and capital for Russia's purposes. BP's main Russian partner, Mikhail Fridman, says that before Putin blessed the deal, he insisted that the new joint venture focus on expanding westward into the old Soviet bloc and beyond.

3   With tensions increasing over Iraq, BP's move also fits well with the West's strategic goal of developing Russia as an alternative source of crude to OPEC and its Persian Gulf kingpins. BP's deal could open the way for a surge of badly needed Western capital to expand Russia's output and build export pipelines. If so, Russia would gain an edge in its jousting with Saudi Arabia for influence in the world markets. The Saudis and others have only themselves to blame for not gaining huge investment bucks themselves. For the past decade, BP has been trying hard to land deals in the kingdom as well as in Kuwait and Iran, with little success.

4   Of course, Russia hasn't exactly been a cakewalk for investors—indeed, BP itself has been badly burned in the past. But in a conversation in his spacious but spartan office in BP's new London headquarters, Browne expresses confidence that he made the right call. "If you look at the world today, there are very few places to go," he says, unwinding over coffee and a cigar after a three-hour marathon presentation to investors. "Russia is the world's largest oil and gas producer, there are sizable resources yet to be found, and it is uniquely accessible to us."

5   Browne and his aides are experimenting with a new model for investing in Russian oil. BP will contribute most of its existing Russian assets, valued at close to $900 million, and pay $6.75 billion in cash and stock, stretched over three years, for 50 percent of a company that mainly consists of TNK (Tyumen Oil), Russia's fifth-largest oil producer, and Sidanco, which ranks seventh. Together, the two companies produce about 1.2 million barrels per day. Three Russian investors—Fridman, 38, who controls 50 percent of TNK, as well as Len Blavatnik, 45, and Viktor Vekselberg, 45—will realize enormous hard-currency gains from the deal.

6   If the deal flies, it will give BP a Russian beachhead that Exxon Mobil Corp. (XOM) and Royal/Dutch Shell Group (RD) are going to find difficult to match. "This is an important breakthrough for BP," says J.J. Traynor, an analyst at Deutsche Bank in London. "It puts

pressure on all the other companies." BP is also counting on its politically well-connected partners to run interference for the new company as it seeks to expand on its already considerable Russian holdings. The new company may go after promising new fields in Eastern Siberia or gas deals for China, analysts say.

7    Ironically, Browne was nearly snookered out of Russia in the late 1990s by the same business barons whom he now embraces. Back in 1997, BP purchased a 10 percent share in Sidanco for $484 million. But in a hardball application of Russia's laws that outraged Browne and spooked other foreign investors, Tyumen's owners elbowed BP aside and gained control of one of Sidanco's prime oil fields. The nasty legal dispute wasn't settled until 2001, when Tyumen's owners returned the field to Sidanco. The Russian owners took a majority stake in Sidanco, while BP upped its share to 25 percent and won management control. Gradually—and surprisingly—the enemies turned into partners, even allies.

8    This "bloody nose" was a crucial learning experience, Browne now says. Browne praises the strides Russia has made in bettering its business climate. Fridman counters that the environment is not "dramatically different" from the robber baron days of a few years ago. What made the deal possible is "a kind of trust between the partners," he says.

9    Good feeling aside, BP is doing its best to protect its shareholders from what can be a rapacious environment. The key Russian partners will be unable to sell their shares in the new company until 2007, giving them an incentive to make the arrangement work. BP will provide the CEO, Robert Dudley, and the chief financial officer. The partners will split board members, but the company will be incorporated outside of Russia with the option of referring disputes to arbitration in Sweden.

10    There's always the possibility of a blow-up. But Browne says BP teams have been poring over TNK's books and examining the company's fields for a year, and that BP knows what it is buying. He's hoping to achieve significant gains by bringing better technology and management to existing fields and by standing at the head of the line for new opportunities. The Russian side is betting that an alliance with a name-brand Western player will make it easier for them to acquire marketing and refining assets in Central and Eastern Europe, where Russian-owned companies have been viewed with considerable suspicion.

11    The Russians have an excellent hand to play. BP needs to replace its fields in the North Sea and Alaska's Prudhoe Bay, mainstays since the 1970s. And while the company has spent the past decade trying to strengthen its comparatively weak position in the Persian Gulf, it has been unable to secure major assets in Kuwait, Iran, or Saudi Arabia. "The Middle East clearly has the right opportunities for someone," says Browne. "But it may not be a Western oil and gas company." In contrast, cold, perilous Russia seems welcoming indeed.

Source: "Pumping Up BP," Reed, Stanley, and Starobin, Paul. *BusinessWeek Online*, February 24, 2003.

**Case 14**

BusinessWeek

# Rick Wagoner's Game Plan

**1**   It's a chief executive's nightmare. The better you execute, the more improvements you make—the more your stock drops. That was the position G. Richard Wagoner Jr. found himself in last October. A day after General Motors Corp. (GM) announced that it had lifted operating earnings 30 percent in a stagnant car market, Standard & Poor's downgraded the automaker's debt with no warning. Surprised investors rushed to sell, and the stock dropped 8 percent. Credit analysts pointed to GM's $76 billion pension fund, which they estimated at the time to be underfunded by as much as $23 billion. GM will have to plow in billions of dollars for years to keep the fund flush, they said.

**2**   The earnings gain was no accounting fluke, either. GM finished the year just as strong, with an operating profit of $3.9 billion, nearly double what it earned in 2001, on 5 percent higher sales of $186.2 billion. GM clearly leads the rest of the U.S. Big Three car companies, reflecting real operational improvements that Wagoner, 49, helped make in the past decade, starting when he was chief financial officer and later as chief operating officer. After GM lost a staggering $30 billion during a single three-year stretch in the early '90s, Wagoner and Chairman John F. "Jack" Smith Jr. forced GM back to basics. They slashed costs, cut payroll, and overhauled aging plants. Once he took over the corner office in May, 2000, CEO Wagoner pulled the efficiency collar even tighter. Now, GM ranks close to Honda Motor Co. (HMC) and Toyota Motor Corp. (TM) in productivity and has made strides in quality. GM also recaptured leadership of the truck business from rival Ford Motor Co. (F), a coup that made the company billions. Last year, GM even nudged up its share of the U.S. market, to 28.3 percent from 28.1 percent.

**3**   But as good as those moves are, they pale next to the problems of GM's weak car brands and gargantuan pension payments. In essence, Rick Wagoner is battling 30 years of management mistakes that have left him with immense burdens and very little room to maneuver. Chief executives from Frederic Donner to Roger Smith built up a bloated bureaucracy that cranked out boring, low-quality cars. Turf battles at headquarters sapped resources and diverted attention from a rising threat out of Asia and Europe. Those competitors drove away with the U.S. car market. Now they're aiming to do the same in sport-utility vehicles and trucks—the last bastion of U.S. dominance. GM's most profitable segment is also under attack by environmentalists and safety regulators, and more and more buyers are flocking to smaller crossover SUVs.

**4**   Even worse for GM was the buildup of lavish health and retirement benefits for workers that it agreed to in fatter days as a way to buy peace with the United Auto Workers. The company says the gap between its pension funding and future liabilities is now $19.3 billion. That means GM will have to pump as much as $4 billion into the fund over this year and next. Providing health care to former and current workers will drain an additional $5 billion per year. The pension costs alone will cut projected 2003 net income from $4.2 billion to $2.8 billion. Providing for retirees saddles each car rolling off a GM assembly line with a $1,350 penalty versus a Japanese car built in a new, nonunion U.S. plant, says analyst Scott Hill of Sanford C. Bernstein & Co. That's a daunting handicap in an industry that struggles to make an average operating profit of $800 per vehicle.

**5**   Those huge legacy costs explain why Wagoner has kept the heat on his competition with the 0 percent financing deals he unleashed after September 11, 2001. Closing plants and accepting a smaller chunk of the U.S. market—the route his rival, Ford, has taken—would give GM fewer vehicles over which to spread those big pension and health-care costs. And thanks to an onerous deal it struck in 1990 with the UAW, GM has to pay furloughed workers about 70 percent of their salary for years after they're laid off. Says Wagoner: "We have a huge fixed-cost base. It's 30 years of downsizing and 30 years of increased health-care costs. It puts a premium on us running this business to generate cash. Our goal is to grow. We don't care who we take it from."

6    All that would make the outlook for GM pretty bleak, except for one thing: Eventually, those legacy costs start to diminish. Starting around 2008, the ranks of GM's elderly retirees will thin, relieving some of the burden. After that, more of the incremental gains Wagoner has been achieving will fall to the bottom line rather than to retirees. The results could be dramatic.

7    That makes Wagoner's imperative clear: He has to keep up cash flow to cover those costs until they start to shrink. At the same time, he must continue to rack up improvements in quality, efficiency, design, and brand appeal. If he can come anywhere close, he just might pull off an impressive turnaround. A stock market rebound would help immensely. GM's pension fund holds its own if it earns 9 percent a year on its investments. Each one-point rise above that is worth $700 million to the fund.

8    With much of the focus on GM's financial crunch, it's easy to lose sight of Wagoner's greatest achievement—and the best reason to believe that he might beat the legacy monster. Walk around GM's sprawling headquarters complex today and you soon realize that against all odds, Wagoner is making real progress in energizing GM's torpid culture. He broke with GM tradition by recruiting two respected outsiders for key positions—Robert A. Lutz as head of product development and John Devine as vice-chairman and chief financial officer. And he has given them extraordinary leeway to fix the company's problems.

9    To motivate his team, the self-effacing Wagoner leaves his ego at the door and lets his executives do their jobs. "Rick acts more like a coach than a boss," says David E. Cole, director of the Center for Automotive Research (CAR) in Ann Arbor, Mich. Thus it was Lutz who rolled out Cadillac's lavish Sixteen prototype luxury car at the Detroit auto show earlier this month as Wagoner sat in the background. Afterward, Wagoner chatted with a few reporters while Lutz held court beside the 16-cylinder vehicle, surrounded by a huge crowd, drinking a martini, and wearing someone's lipstick mark on his cheek.

10    That low-key style has helped Wagoner in tearing down GM's warring fiefdoms. Since giving the swaggering Lutz rule over product development, Wagoner has spiked the design-by-committee system and cut the time it takes to develop a new car to 20 months from nearly four years. GM used to have different studios for each division working on car designs that would get passed on to marketing, then engineering, then manufacturing. Lutz has one committee to cover the entire process. Every Thursday, he hashes out what vehicles should look like and which division will build them, along with a small group that includes Group Vice-President for Advanced Vehicle Development Mark T. Hogan, GM North America President Gary L. Cowger, Design Chief Wayne K. Cherry, and Chief Engineer James E. Queen.

11    But low-key doesn't mean hands-off. Lutz may make the day-to-day decisions on car design, but Wagoner reserves final say. He meets monthly with top execs, who see car designs much earlier in the process. The ones they think are promising move ahead fast. Says retired executive Richard C. Nerod, who ran GM's Latin America operations: "Rick cut out a lot of the infighting and the bull————."

12    Wagoner also exerts control by imposing tough performance standards. A legendary number-cruncher who rose up through GM's finance division, he holds top managers to strict measures. GM, like most big companies, always had performance goals. But they never went nearly as deep or into as much detail. Says Cowger: "Everything can be measured."

**13**   Everyone, too. Even Lutz, the larger-than-life product czar who flies his own fighter jet and sparked Chrysler's 1990s resurgence with cars such as the Dodge Viper and PT Cruiser, isn't exempt. Lutz was judged on 12 criteria last year, from how well he used existing parts to save money in new vehicles to how many engineering hours he cut from the development process.

**14**   Clearly, Wagoner's own ideas on how to fix GM have evolved. He seems to have learned from a brush with grand strategic vision back in the '90s, when, like now-deposed Ford CEO Jacques A. Nasser, he explored ways to grow outside of building cars. Wagoner was behind the decision to pump hundreds of millions into GM's OnStar Corp. telematics business and DirecTV satellite-TV service. Neither produced big revenues for GM. Now, with Devine applying a cold dose of realism to GM's finances, there's little illusion that such diversions can fix the cash crunch. "That was a dream a couple of years ago, but it's not reality," Devine says. "The math will tell you that the principal driver of revenue and profits is the car-and-truck business in North America and Europe."

**15**   If Wagoner has brought a new intensity to GM, he probably gets it from his mother, Martha, a onetime school teacher. Family members recall one Christmas several years ago when she doggedly kept baking cookies despite a broken arm. "My mom has a task orientation that you sometimes see in my brother," says Judy Pahren, a financial-services manager who is one of Wagoner's two sisters. Rick had a Norman Rockwell upbringing in Richmond, Va. He picked up a rabid devotion to Duke University basketball from his father, George, an accountant at Eskimo Pie Co. Wagoner got a chance to play for the Blue Devils as a walk-on. He demonstrated a deft shot but learned the limits of his athletic ability. "The knock on Rick was that you couldn't slide a phone book under his jump," says roommate Charles H. McCreary III. The devotion to alma mater remains, though: A few years ago, he ordered a custom "Duke blue" Suburban SUV.

**16**   After Duke, Wagoner got his MBA at Harvard Business School, surprising some upon graduation when he chose GM over potentially more lucrative jobs on Wall Street. Wagoner's knack for crunching numbers propelled him through stints at GM units in Canada, Europe, and Brazil. His big break came in 1992, when then-CEO Smith tapped him to be CFO after a boardroom coup. Even as CEO, Wagoner is known for a low-key lifestyle. He prides himself on juggling his work schedule to attend games and other activities of his three sons. And when entertaining, Wagoner is more likely to cook on his backyard grill than hire a caterer.

**17**   Wagoner's willingness to let others shine is a classic trait of leaders who have boosted their companies to exceptional performance, says Jim Collins, author of *Good to Great*. As a longtime GM insider, Wagoner has other advantages: He knows what brutal facts need to be confronted, and he can assess which veterans can handle key jobs. Says Collins: "Wagoner has the opportunity to take it back to great." But the odds are stiff—only 11 of 1,435 companies Collins studied made such a lasting transformation. And those that did required an average of seven years to get breakthrough results.

**18**   Still, competitors are impressed with the progress Wagoner has made. "I'm a big admirer of his management style," says crosstown rival William C. Ford Jr., chairman and CEO of Ford. He should be—GM's operating profit may not match the $4.6 billion number three Toyota made in just the six months through September. And GM's stock, trading around 37, is down 26 percent from a year ago. But that performance sure beats Ford's $872 million operating profit and 36 percent lower stock price.

**19**   It's a testament to Wagoner's ability to cut costs that GM managed nearly to double margins in North America last year, to 2.6 percent of sales. Thanks to efficiency gains, GM is now one of the leanest car builders, with variable costs—labor, parts, outsourced production, etc.—amounting to 62 percent of revenues, according to UBS Warburg. That puts it ahead of Ford and Chrysler (DCX) at 68 percent, and it isn't far behind leaders Toyota and Honda at 60 percent.

20    With lower costs than its domestic competition, GM is better able to withstand the price war it started with 0 percent financing. But Wagoner is betting that the cars he plans to launch in the next three years will be good enough to sell on merit, not price. A few "niche" vehicles, such as the hulking Hummer H2, are already out. But the assault begins in earnest later this year with the Chevy Malibu family sedan and Equinox car/SUV crossover, Cadillac SRX small SUV, and Pontiac Grand Prix sedan. "This is one major last-ditch effort to save themselves in the car market," says Joseph Phillippi, a former Wall Street analyst who consults for the industry.

21    Wagoner, who's not a classic Detroit "car guy," seems content to rely on Lutz and his team to fix the lineup. During one trip through the design studio last year, he spotted a sexy two-door version of the Cadillac CTS sports sedan. "I hope you guys figure out a way to build that," Wagoner said, but offered no solutions, recalls one senior designer. "Rick trusts my judgment implicitly," Lutz says, "but if I came up with some wacky product proposals, he'd pull me back."

22    The most dramatic gains won't come on a sketch pad anyway but in the way GM selects new car designs and then shepherds them through production. In the past, even if a bold design made it off a drawing board, it had little chance of surviving to the showroom. A concept would go from a designer to the marketing staff, which would try to tailor it to consumers. Then it would go to engineers, who would try to figure out how to build it, and so on. Separate teams worked with suppliers, factories, and parts suppliers on their individual slice of the process, with little interaction.

23    It was a recipe for mediocrity—and often disaster. The Aztek, which emerged in 2000 as a boxy, garish cross between an SUV and a minivan five years after designers first drew it up as a racy bid for younger drivers, is a prime example. Wagoner was determined to tear up that system by the roots. A few months after taking over, he ordered GM's product developers to ready the SSR concept vehicle for production. A combination of hot rod and pickup truck, it had been a big hit at the Detroit auto show. Wagoner thought its distinctive look, with chrome bars splitting the front grille and taillights, would be a great image builder. But the SSR still had to navigate the old GM system. Because it was announced before engineers had a precise blueprint to build it, the program quickly ran over budget. Today, its cost has ballooned way past the original $300 million projection, to almost $500 million. The $42,000 SSR will hit showrooms this summer, a quick turnaround for GM. But with only 5,000 sales projected per year, it makes for a very expensive showcase.

24    Since then, Wagoner and Lutz have smoothed things out a bit. Lutz, Cowger, Hogan, and the others decide what goes from the design studios into the funnel of cars that will be considered for funding by GM's Automotive Strategy Board, chaired monthly by Wagoner. Lutz says he and Wagoner have disagreed on some product decisions, but he hasn't been turned down yet. Now, 75 percent of the engineering work is finished when a program manager sits down to build a car.

25    That's how GM quickly green-lighted plans to resurrect the Pontiac GTO, its famous 1960s muscle car. For years, Pontiac and Chevrolet wanted a brawny car with rear-wheel drive, which is favored by driving enthusiasts. GM's Australian Holden Ltd. subsidiary had a promising candidate in its Monaro sports coupe, but the idea to bring it to the United States never made it out of committee. GM execs simply didn't want to spend what little money it would take to alter the Monaro to meet U.S. safety standards and American styling. Says Lutz: "I just asked, 'Why not?'" GM got the program together in less than 18 months. Later this year, Pontiac will roll out the GTO as a 340-horsepower Americanized Monaro.

26   Wagoner has also streamlined GM's factories. GM is now the most productive domestic automaker, having cut the time it takes to assemble a vehicle from an average of 32 hours in 1998 to 26 hours in 2001, according to Harbour & Associates. That compares with 27 for Ford, almost 31 at DaimlerChrysler, 22.5 at Toyota, and 17.9 at Nissan. A big factor was expanding parts shared across vehicles. The new Chevy Malibu, for instance, uses the same platform and many of the same parts as the Saab 9-3 sedan. GM's plants are also more flexible—each of seven full-size pickup and SUV plants can make any of the vehicles designed on that platform.

27   The cars rolling off GM's assembly lines today are undeniably better built than they used to be. Once ranked below the industry average, GM trails only Honda and Toyota in J. D. Power & Associates Inc.'s initial quality survey, which measures problems in the first 90 days of ownership. Some cars, such as the Chevrolet Impala, even beat the likes of the Toyota Camry. Last year, *Consumer Reports* recommended 13 GM vehicles—representing 41 percent of its sales volume—up from 5 last year. But one of GM's most stubborn woes is that many buyers still perceive the Chevy, Pontiac, and Buick brands as musty and secondrate. GM needs incentives averaging $3,800 a vehicle—more than twice what Toyota spends.

28   The biggest risk to GM's lineup is at the top. Its popular SUVs and pickups accounted for about 90 percent of profits last year but are under increasing assault from foreign competitors and safety regulators. Like his competitors, Wagoner is banking on crossover vehicles, which combine SUV-like space and looks with a carlike ride and better fuel economy, as a hedge against a big-truck backlash. Cadillac's luxury SRX hits the market this year as a viable rival to the Lexus RX 330 and Mercedes M-class, and Chevy will launch its Equinox as an all-wheel drive crossover. Next year, GM will start offering pickups and SUVs with hybrid gas/electric engines. New designs are also in the works. Lutz has tentatively approved a highly stylized 2007 replacement for the Chevy Silverado and GMC Sierra pickups, which hold a commanding 40 percent of the pickup market. It will be based on the slick Cheyenne concept truck that GM unveiled in January, which has improved driver and passenger room and doors on each side of the pickup bed to provide easier cargo access. But in small SUVs and gas mileage, GM is playing catch-up to the Japanese.

29   Wagoner and his team have little choice but to wait out their biggest mess—those massive health and pension costs. Wagoner is brutally realistic: "We'd be accused of a pipe dream if we said in 10 years these issues will go away." GM pays its UAW workers only slightly more per hour than Toyota, Honda, and Nissan (NSANY) pay their American factory workers. But the cost of pension and health-care benefits for current workers is huge—about $24 per hour at GM, versus $12 at the foreign factories. Pension obligations swelled after the 1990 contract, when then-Chairman Robert Stempel practically guaranteed almost no layoffs. Underestimating the speed of its decline, GM agreed to pay workers for years after a furlough. As losses mounted, GM resorted to early-retirement offers—avoiding billions in unemployment benefits but adding thousands of retirees. Since GM was shrinking faster than Ford, its pension rolls grew more quickly, to 2.5 retirees per worker today, versus Ford's 1-to-1 ratio. Last year, GM plowed almost $5 billion into the pension fund to shore it up as stock prices fell. But Carol Levenson, an analyst for bond research firm Gimme Credit, points out that GM had to take on $4.6 billion in debt to do it. Until the stock and bond markets spring back, it's three steps forward and two steps back.

30   That pressure should ease somewhat over the next decade. GM's average worker is 48 years old—five years older than those at Ford or Chrysler. GM's total number of retirees will drop below existing levels by 2010, says CAR's labor and manufacturing analyst, Sean McAlinden. Wagoner believes that even without another bull market to boost the pension fund, GM can handle the drain and maintain its $7 billion capital-spending

budget. Meanwhile, to pay down the pension shortfall, Devine is working to sell Hughes Electronics' DirecTV business, possibly to News Corp. (NWS)

**31**     Closing the gap on health-care costs will be tougher. This summer, GM and the UAW will start working on a new four-year labor agreement. GM is almost certain to ask for higher co-payments from its 138,000 UAW employees. The union is almost certain to balk. "We don't have an interest in cost-shifting," says Richard Shoemaker, head of the UAW's GM department. GM also is one of many companies pushing to have Medicare pick up a greater share of retiree drug costs. But even Wagoner admits: "I don't see that happening soon."

**32**     Can Wagoner return GM to dominance? He has made heroic gains. But he's taking nothing for granted. At a speech in Detroit last year, he told the story of William C. Durant, who pulled together such companies as Buick, Cadillac, and Olds to form GM in 1908. But Durant was more interested in cutting deals than managing, so he wound up running a bowling alley in Flint. "That fate has haunted GM chairmen for decades," Wagoner told his audience. He was joking, of course. But Wagoner will be the first to tell you that his own future is up in the air. It all depends on whether he can save GM from its past.

Source: "Rick Wagoner's Game Plan." Welch, David, and Kerwin, Kathleen. *BusinessWeek Onlilne,* February 10, 2003.

Case 15

# Southwest Is Holding Steady

**1** In the hours immediately after the terrorist attacks on September 11, 2001, the newly promoted executives at Southwest Airlines Co. (LUV) made a bold decision. Without even consulting the legendary co-founder and current chairman, Herbert D. Kelleher, Chief Executive James F. Parker and President Colleen C. Barrett swiftly agreed to grant refunds to all customers who asked for them, regardless of any ticket restrictions. Only later did Parker learn that the airline could have had to shell out several hundred million dollars, an unsettling prospect, given the uncertainty of the times and a $187 million profit-sharing payment that was coming due. "Fortunately, the potential flood of refund claims never came," says Parker, in his typically understated style. Quite the opposite: One devoted customer even sent $1,000 to support Southwest after the attacks.

**2** Now, the low-fare leader is watching its biggest competitors struggle mightily, in and out of bankruptcy court. So Southwest's gutsy leaders must be reveling in their rivals' misery, ready to press their advantage in the industry's worst-ever downturn, right?

**3** Not exactly. Steeped in Kelleher's disciplined operating philosophy, longtime lieutenants Parker, 56, and Barrett, 58, are throttling back on growth at the world's most admired and most profitable airline. While poised to swoop down if, say, United Airlines Inc. (UAL) or US Airways Group (U) has to drop a certain market, they won't try to push weakened rivals out. After all, this is a management team that, despite its fun-loving image, got where it is today by tempering opportunism with fiscal conservatism. Indeed, in choosing Parker and Barrett to succeed Kelleher in June, 2001, the board intended to signal "business as usual. . . . If it ain't broke, don't fix it," says director June M. Morris.

**4** And it sure ain't broke. Southwest is the only major carrier to remain profitable in every quarter since September 11. While its six biggest rivals have grounded 240 aircraft and laid off more than 70,000 workers, Southwest—which has never laid off a soul in its 31 years—has kept all of its 375 planes and 35,000 people flying. While others battled with unions to cut wages, Southwest quietly wrapped up five crucial agreements, ensuring labor peace with those groups until 2005. It is now in talks with flight attendants. Although its stock has dropped 25 percent since the attacks, Southwest is still worth more than all the other biggies combined. Its balance sheet is the best in the business, with a 43 percent debt-to-capital ratio. And luckily for Parker, it has $1.8 billion in cash, with an additional $575 million in untapped credit lines.

**5** Faced with such a strong competitor and with such a stormy economic climate, the big airlines are trying desperately to emulate Southwest's efficiencies. For some, including American Airlines (AMR) and United, comparable costs are as much as 170 percent of Southwest's. US Airways and United are both in bankruptcy, struggling to emerge as lower-cost contenders. Likewise, American and Delta Air Lines (DAL) are looking for ways to slash billions in costs without destroying the route networks and service that command prices higher than Southwest's. Meanwhile, younger low-cost carriers that offer more amenities, such as JetBlue Airways (JBLU) and AirTran Holdings (AAIR), are trying to grab a bigger chunk of the market.

**6** Not since the downturn of the early '90s has Southwest presented so clear a target for its rivals. "At some point, Southwest is going to be faced with much more aggressive and more cost-competitive rivals," predicts Robert L. Crandall, retired CEO at American.

**7** But Parker is determined that Southwest will continue to be, well, Southwest: a primarily short-haul airline that flies directly from city to city, with just one type of plane—the

Boeing 737—and the lowest costs. For all of its enviable numbers, the nation's fourth-largest airline still accounts for only 10 percent of domestic traffic. That's a dominant slice of the overall 16 percent share held by discount airlines, but it means Southwest still has plenty of opportunities to gain on its so-called hub-and-spoke rivals. Southwest aims to hike its capacity by at least 8 percent annually in the years ahead. "Obviously, we will not ignore any threat arising from our competitors' lowering their costs," says Parker. Nevertheless, he adds, "I don't see how they compete with the kind of point-to-point system we have at Southwest Airlines."

8    In some ways, the aftershocks of September 11 are making Southwest an even fiercer contender. Here's one way Parker and his crew have boosted loyalty and morale, long a key to Southwest's high productivity: When the federal government offered cash grants to prop up the industry, Parker included this money in the company's profit-sharing formula for employees, even though he wasn't required to. And although Southwest has never offered the industry's highest base salaries, Parker is now able to offer raises and stock options at a time when other airlines talk of sacrifice. "A whole new generation of Southwest employees hired in the last five or six years are now fundamentally understanding the advantages of the Southwest business model," says Brad Bartholomew, a Southwest pilot for 15 years. The pilots' new contract provides raises of at least 30 percent through 2006.

9    All things considered, the transition of power is proceeding smoothly, if slowly. Parker and Barrett admit they regularly seek Kelleher's counsel. And why not? The three go way back: Parker, a former Texas assistant attorney general, joined Kelleher's San Antonio law firm in 1979; Barrett was Kelleher's legal secretary. After fighting fierce battles to get Southwest aloft in 1971, Kelleher became permanent CEO in 1982. Parker joined him as general counsel four years later.

10    On the surface at least, the San Antonio–born Parker appears to be the polar opposite of Kelleher. His drawl and quiet diplomacy is a sharp contrast to Kelleher's manic energy and raucous laugh. "Because he looks like this pudgy, easygoing good ol' boy, he's very often underestimated," says a former exec. Parker's reserve belies a dry wit: At a graduation ceremony for new flight attendants last fall, Parker cracked that "when CEOs started going to jail, that's when Herb gave up the title." Style aside, the two have much in common: keen intelligence, a deep devotion to Southwest and its employees, and a taste for a good party. Colleagues even presented Parker with a beer keg for his new office; it is regularly replenished for after-hours parties.

11    The pony-tailed, chain-smoking Barrett, who was promoted to executive vice-president for customers in 1990, oversees most of the day-to-day operations. Although more officers report directly to her than before, her focus on service and the company culture hasn't changed. Besides keeping tabs on such basics as on-time performance (Southwest now ranks a lowly number six), she's the "sentimental slob" who collects letters from passengers praising the airline's often extraordinary service. A reluctant public speaker who doesn't know how to use e-mail, she lets Parker take the lead with Wall Street and the media.

12    And her former boss? Well, by all accounts, the flamboyant, irreverent Kelleher—once the star of the company's TV commercials—is staying out of day-to-day affairs. He no longer leads the executive planning committee, the airline's major policy-setting body, which meets every three weeks. In fact, he's so invisible that some employees send cards wishing him well in retirement, unaware that "he's working his ass off," says Barrett. In fact, the 71-year-old chairman is leading the airline's lobbying efforts in Washington, where airport security, terrorism insurance, and other matters have suddenly become vital to the industry's survival. At the same time, he maintains control of schedule planning and aircraft acquisitions, the backbone of Southwest's strategy.

13    The trio running Southwest may be cautious about the future, but they're not complacent. Southwest is poised to accelerate its modest growth plans if the right opportunities

come along. "A large, single-market opportunity has not fallen in their laps yet, but wait. They're certainly ready to exploit it," says analyst Samuel Buttrick of UBS Warburg. For instance, the company vastly expanded its presence at Chicago Midway Airport in 1991 when Midway Airlines Corp. ceased operations there, and it moved into Baltimore in 1993 and Raleigh-Durham in 1999 when US Airways and American scaled back in those cities. Now, it's the top operator at Chicago's Midway and in Baltimore.

14    Parker has his own worries. Despite Southwest's relatively good health, it is still suffering from a weak economy, fears of war and terrorism, and penny-pinching by business travelers. The company's net profit last year fell 52 percent, to $198 million, excluding special items, on flat revenues of $5.5 billion. Of course, that looks fabulous next to the combined losses of the major carriers—more than $13 billion in the past two years. Southwest's capacity grew by only 5.5 percent last year, its lowest rate since 1973. Traffic grew a weak 2 percent, hurt in part by airport security hassles. That compares with a 6.2 percent drop for United, and 4.2 percent at American. Parker predicts a "very gradual" recovery for his airline and the industry. As a result, the company says it will add only 4 percent to its capacity this year and no new cities to the 58 it already serves.

15    As for the competition, Parker and Kelleher, like many airline observers, believe the big carriers won't be able to reinvent themselves radically. There may be fewer of them, and they may operate with fewer hubs. Their costs will be lower, but not as low as Southwest's. And they'll continue to cater to higher-paying business passengers with broad networks, first-class service, and airport clubs. "They'll narrow the [cost] gap substantially, but not enough to keep Southwest from continuing to eat market share," agrees Michael Roach of Unisys R2A Transportation Management Consultants.

16    Of course, Parker also has to keep an eye on the low-cost upstarts. They are growing fast and are likely to target many of the same dense markets that Southwest would like for itself. JetBlue, in particular, is attracting loyal customers in droves, with such amenities as televisions in the seatbacks of its 37 airplanes and assigned seating, which Southwest's flights do not offer. But, so far, Parker isn't worried: "None of those 'Southwest-with-improvements' have shown they can produce an economically viable business model over a long time," he says. Only three years old, nonunion JetBlue enjoys unusually low maintenance, wage, and benefit costs, which are bound to rise in years ahead.

17    When pressed to describe his hopes for Southwest, Parker tells a story. Shortly after his promotion, he sat next to a lawyer from Amarillo on a Southwest flight. When the man found out who Parker was, he admonished him: "You've got a damn good airline here. Just don't f——— it up." So, says Parker, "that's kind of my goal."

Source: "Southwest Is Holding Steady." Zellner, Wendy, and Arndt, Michael. *BusinessWeek Online,* February 3, 2003.

# Staying on Top

1  Lots of executives at Johnson & Johnson have stories about William C. Weldon's powers of persuasion. The onetime drug salesman who now leads the health-care giant is famed for his ability to convince, cajole, or sometimes just sweet-talk colleagues into seeing things his way. A couple of years ago, Dr. Per A. Peterson, the chief of pharmaceutical research and development, was fed up with personnel headaches and told Weldon he was thinking of leaving the company. The next morning, Peterson, who lives minutes from Weldon in central New Jersey, got a call from the boss at 5:30, inviting him over for breakfast. As Weldon tended to the skillet, the two men discussed Peterson's concerns. And then they talked some more: Their conversation lasted well into the afternoon. Eventually, Peterson agreed to stay, and within a week Weldon had made the changes Peterson sought. "What else can you say to a guy who cooks you an omelette at six in the morning?" says Peterson with a laugh. "You say yes."

2  Weldon, 54, and one year into the job, will need those skills in spades as he guides J&J in the new century. The 117-year-old company is an astonishingly complex enterprise, made up of 204 different businesses organized into three divisions: drugs, medical devices and diagnostics, and consumer products. Much of the company's growth in recent years has come from pharmaceuticals; they accounted for almost half of J&J's sales and 61 percent of its operating profits last year. With revenue of $36 billion, J&J is one of the largest health-care companies in the United States. That allows it to take bigger risks: When a surgical device business lost some $500 million between 1992 and 1995, J&J hardly felt it.

3  Consumers know Johnson & Johnson for its Band-Aids and baby powder. But competitors know the company as a fierce rival that boasts a rare combination of scientific expertise and marketing savvy. It regularly develops or acquires innovative products and then sells them more aggressively than almost anyone around. Even if a hospital might prefer to purchase its surgical tools from one company and its sutures from another, it could likely end up buying both from J&J because J&J offers favorable prices to hospitals that buy the whole package. J&J can also trade on its "heritage," as Weldon calls it, when it comes to persuading doctors to try its new drugs and devices. Or when it comes to persuading consumers: When J&J launched anemia drug Procrit in 1991, few expected it to make much of a difference to the company's performance. Not only did J&J spend millions to educate physicians about the condition, it also ran a series of ads on television—an unusual move considering that the drug is marketed specifically to treat anemia in chemotherapy patients. But it worked: Procrit is now J&J's best-selling drug.

4  The company Weldon inherited from his predecessor, Ralph S. Larsen, has been one of the most consistent, most successful health-care companies for years. Others around it are suffering as patents for important drugs expire with little of real consequence to replace them. That's expected in an industry so dependent on the unpredictable pace of scientific innovation. But not at J&J. The company is famed for delivering at least 10 percent earnings growth year in and year out going back nearly two decades. In the first quarter, it reported a 13 percent rise. Its stock price, meanwhile, has increased from less than $3, split-adjusted, in the mid-1980s to almost 20 times that now. Over the past two years, as the Standard & Poor's 500-stock index has fallen 28.1 percent, J&J stock has increased 19.4 percent. And in 2002, J&J earned $6.8 billion (excluding special charges), compared with $5.9 billion the previous year.

5  Maintaining that record could be Weldon's biggest challenge: Just to keep up, he must in essence create a new $4 billion business every year. But J&J's crucial drug business is finally succumbing to the pressures slowing down the rest of the industry. Procrit sales were

nearly flat in the first quarter because of a new rival, news that sent the stock down 3 percent in one day. And like its peers, J&J doesn't have much coming out of its labs now. Meanwhile, its new drug-coated stent has been held up at the Food & Drug Administration. Approval still seems highly likely. But if the device does not get the O.K., it would be a huge blow to J&J.

6    What makes matters worse for Weldon is that the other component of J&J's growth—acquisitions—could become more problematic, too. Over the past decade, J&J has bought 52 businesses for $30 billion; 10 percent to 15 percent of its top-line growth each year comes from such investments. But to buy something that really affects overall performance is a different proposition for a $36 billion company than it is for a $10 billion company. "You get to a point where finding acquisitions that fit the mold and make a contribution becomes increasingly difficult," warns UBS Warburg analyst David Lothson. "This puts pressure on the sustainability of this strategy, and ultimately it could break down."

7    J&J's success has hinged on its unique culture and structure. But for the company to thrive in the future, that system has to change. Each of its far-flung units operates pretty much as an independent enterprise. Businesses set their own strategies; they have their own finance and human resources departments, for example. While this degree of decentralization makes for relatively high overhead costs, no chief executive, Weldon included, has thought that too high a price to pay. Johnson & Johnson has been able to turn itself into a powerhouse precisely because the businesses it buys, and the ones it starts, are given near-total autonomy. That independence fosters an entrepreneurial attitude that has kept J&J intensely competitive as others around it have faltered.

8    Now, though, the various enterprises at J&J can no longer operate in near isolation. Weldon believes, as do most others in the industry, that some of the most important breakthroughs in twenty-first century medicine will come from the ability to apply scientific advances in one discipline to another. The treatment of many diseases is becoming vastly more sophisticated: Sutures are coated with drugs to prevent infections; tests based on genomic research could determine who will respond to a certain cancer drug; defibrillators may be linked to computers that alert doctors when patients have abnormal heart rhythms.

9    The company should be perfectly positioned to profit from this shift toward combining drugs, devices, and diagnostics, claims Weldon, since few companies will be able to match its reach and strength in those three basic areas. "There is a convergence that will allow us to do things we haven't done before," he says. Indeed, J&J has top-notch products in each of those categories. It has been boosting its research and development budget by more than 10 percent annually for the past few years, which puts it among the top spenders, and now employs 9,300 scientists in 40 labs around the world.

10   But J&J can cash in only if its fiercely independent businesses can work together. In effect, Weldon wants J&J to be one of the few companies to make good on that often-promised, rarely delivered idea of synergy. To do so, he has to decide if he's willing to put J&J's famed autonomy at risk. For now, Weldon is creating new systems to foster better communication and more frequent collaboration among J&J's disparate operations.

11   Already J&J has been inching toward this more cohesive approach: Its new drug-coated stent, which could revolutionize the field of cardiology, grew out of a discussion in the mid-1990s between a drug researcher and one in J&J's stent business. Now Weldon has to promote this kind of cooperation throughout the company without quashing the entrepreneurial spirit that has made J&J what it is today. Cultivating those alliances "would be challenging in any organization, but particularly in an organization that has been so successful because of its decentralized culture," says Jerry Cacciotti, managing director at consulting firm Strategic Decisions Group. Weldon, like every other leader in

the company's history, worked his way up through the ranks. Among other things, it made him a true believer in the J&J system. Whatever he hopes to achieve, he doesn't expect to undermine that.

12    In many ways, Weldon personifies the Johnson & Johnson ethos. Though he was one of the first J&J executives to go casual in the 1990s and sometimes schedules business lunches at his favorite burger joint in Manhattan, Weldon is compulsively competitive. As he says, "it's no fun to be second." One of his first bosses recalls how Weldon badgered him to release sales figures early because Weldon was desperate to know if he had won a company competition. Weldon is such an intense athlete that he was just a sprint away from ruining his knee altogether when he finally gave up playing basketball. It's not easy for him to keep a respectable distance from his managers now. "It's like a barroom brawl [where] you are outside looking in when you want to be in the middle of it," he says.

13    Weldon became famous for setting near-impossible goals for his people and holding them to it. "There was rarely an empty suit around Bill," says one former J&Jer. "If you weren't pulling your weight, you were gone." In the 1990s, when Weldon ran a business that sold surgical tools, executives back at headquarters in New Brunswick, N.J., used to systematically upgrade the reviews he gave his employees.

14    With that in mind, consider what Weldon is willing to do so that his changes don't threaten J&J's ecosystem: restrain himself. Although he talks incessantly about synergy and convergence, the steps he's actually taking to make sure his units cross-fertilize are measured ones. He isn't pushing specific deals on his managers. For example, industry sources say J&J has held on-and-off talks with Guidant Corp., which makes implantable defibrillators. That field of cardiovascular medicine is a growing market that's perfectly suited for some of these emerging combination therapies. But Weldon isn't leading the way in those talks. And he's delegating crucial decisions about how to spend R&D dollars.

15    Weldon is subtly turning up the heat on cooperation between his different units, however. J&J experts in various diseases have been meeting quarterly for the past five years to share information. Weldon and James T. Lenehan, vice-chairman and president of J&J, are now setting up two groups, focused on two diseases (they won't say which), that will work together more formally. After six months, each group will report on potential strategies and projects.

16    To understand Weldon's vision for the new J&J, it's useful to look at how he reshaped the pharmaceutical operation when he took it over in 1998. At the time, J&J's drug business was posting solid growth thanks to popular products such as the anemia drug Procrit and the antipsychotic medication Risperdal. But the drug R&D operation was sputtering after several potential treatments had failed in late-stage testing. Weldon's solution was to create a new committee comprised of R&D executives and senior managers from the sales and marketing operations to decide which projects to green-light. Previously, those decisions were made largely by scientists in the company's two major R&D operations; there was no such thing as setting common priorities. Weldon also created a new post to oversee R&D and gave the job to Peterson. "Some people may have thought Bill curtailed their freedom," says Peterson. "But we've improved the decision-making to eliminate compounds that just won't make it."

17    Although most of the changes Weldon instituted in the pharmaceutical business won't yield real results for years, there is some evidence that this new collaboration is working. Shortly after taking charge of the drug unit, Weldon visited J&J's research facility in La Jolla, Calif., to learn about the company's genomic studies. Researchers were focused on building a massive database using gene patterns that correlate to a certain disease or to someone's likely response to a particular drug. When they told Weldon how useful the

database could be for J&J's diagnostic business, he in turn urged Lenehan, who oversees the unit, to send his people out. Now, Peterson says, the diagnostics team is developing a test that the drug R&D folks could use to predict which patients will benefit from an experimental cancer therapy. If the test works, it could significantly cut J&J's drug-development costs.

18    Even the company's fabled consumer brands are starting to take on a scientific edge. Its new liquid Band-Aid is based on a material used in a wound-closing product sold by one of J&J's hospital-supply businesses. And a few years ago, J&J turned its prescription antifungal treatment, Nizoral, into a dandruff shampoo. Indeed, these kinds of products are one reason operating margins for the consumer business have increased from 13.8 percent in 2000 to 18.7 percent in 2002.

19    But perhaps the most promising result of this approach is J&J's drug-coated stent, called Cypher. A few years after that first meeting between researchers, J&J created teams from the drug business and the device operation to collaborate on manufacturing the stent, which props open arteries after angioplasty. "If we didn't have all this [expertise]," Weldon says, "we'd probably still be negotiating with [outside] companies to put this together." And to show that he is letting managers mind their own businesses, Weldon says that he only gets briefed about the stent's progress every month (though he does invite Robert W. Croce, the division head, to dinner for more casual updates). "They are the experts who know the marketplace, know the hospitals, and know the cardiologists," Weldon says of the Cypher team. "I have the utmost confidence in them."

20    With that empowerment, though, comes the clear expectation that J&J's experts will go after their markets with the same tenacity Weldon displayed in his climb to the top. Before heading up the drug division, Weldon made his reputation at J&J in the early '90s as head of a new unit, Ethicon Endo-Surgery Inc. Ethicon Endo was supposed to establish itself in the emerging field of endoscopic surgery. J&J did what only a company of its resources can: It poured hundreds of millions into building a full line of tools for surgeons. And Weldon did what he does best: He went after the leading company, United States Surgical Corp., as if it were a mortal threat.

21    Weldon spent much of his time on the road, traveling the country from his base in Cincinnati to meet with surgeons and hospital executives. Once he canceled a flight home from San Diego after hearing that a potential customer was wavering. He went back the following morning to nail down the deal. Weldon often set more ambitious goals than headquarters did. Nick Valeriani, who was then vice-president of sales and marketing, recalls: "We'd have a great year and Bill would say, 'Nice job. Why couldn't it have been 25 percent higher?'" By 1996, J&J surpassed U.S. Surgical, which was later bought by Tyco International Ltd.

22    That's not to say that Weldon doesn't understand the power of positive reinforcement. Twice he wheedled higher bonuses for his managers out of New Brunswick. Another time at Ethicon Endo, he closed up shop for a day of rest after a particularly harried couple of months. He never told anyone at headquarters. And no one in New Brunswick ever said a word about it. "Hell, you are the goddamn boss," he says. "Sometimes it is better to beg forgiveness than to ask permission."

23    And for those executives who fell short, Weldon made it clear he didn't like to be disappointed. When a new J&J drug business, Centocor Inc., failed to meet the aggressive sales goals it set for 2000, Weldon was at the offices in Malvern, Pa., before the week was out. David P. Holveck, former company group chairman of Centocor who now runs J&J's venture-capital arm, says of Weldon: "He is a man of few words. But his body language was very clear: In this game there are two strikes. In 2001, we were expected to get it right." They did.

24      Not everybody appreciated Weldon's demands. None would speak for attribution, but several former executives at Ethicon Endo say Weldon alienated those he felt weren't part of the team. "He is an intimidator and a dominator," says one former executive who claims Weldon turned on him after he opposed an acquisition.

25      Weldon hasn't really ever taken much for granted. His father was a stagehand on Broadway for several years. While his mother, a seamstress, worked on costumes for the ballet and theater, Weldon would watch the shows from backstage. She handled Marilyn Monroe's wardrobe the night the actress sang *Happy Birthday* to President John F. Kennedy in 1962, and she retired last year at the age of 80. "My parents were very hardworking, union people," Weldon says. "It's a tough life."

26      When Weldon was in elementary school, the family moved to Ridgewood, N.J., which former classmates describe as a wealthy and somewhat socially competitive town. There, Weldon grew up in one of the less prosperous neighborhoods. He was an indifferent student but a determined athlete who played on both the basketball and football teams.

27      Weldon put himself through Quinnipiac University in Hamden, Conn., by working as a mover in Newark, N.J., on weekends and holidays. He says he got serious about his studies after he married his high school sweetheart, Barbara Dearborn, midway through college. Shortly after graduating with a major in biology, Weldon had his one and only interview at J&J. Howard Klick, who hired him as a sales rep at the McNeil Pharmaceutical unit, recalls asking him for a sales pitch on a pen. Weldon took the pen apart, then gave Klick the hard sell. "He was hungry," Klick says. "He had fire in the belly."

28      He'll need that drive if he's to maintain J&J's growth trajectory. At this point, most of J&J's important drugs are under assault from competitors. Growth of the company's biggest-selling product, the $4.3 billion Procrit franchise, has stalled in the face of Aranesp, a drug from archrival Amgen Inc. And side-effect problems have plagued the European version, called Eprex. As a result, Procrit, which grew at a 20 percent-plus rate over the past few years, may actually post a 2 percent decline in worldwide sales in 2003, according to J. P. Morgan Securities analyst Michael Weinstein. Meanwhile, J&J's $1.3 billion rheumatoid arthritis drug Remicade faces competing products from Amgen and Abbott Laboratories.

29      Weldon downplays the threat. He argues that Remicade has tremendous potential because it can be used to treat other conditions, including Crohn's disease, and that Procrit will continue to dominate the anemia market. And J&J does have 56 drugs in late-stage testing (though only eight are truly new).

30      With J&J's blockbusters slowing, Weldon may expect his successor at the drug unit to do something dramatic. That's what he did two years ago when he completed the company's biggest acquisition ever: buying drug-delivery player Alza Corp. for $13.2 billion to shore up the business. There are supposed synergies here too, he says. Alza's technology could help J&J devise safer and more effective formulations of existing drugs. Among them: a new sustained-release version of the epilepsy drug Topamax that could be used to treat obesity.

31      But buying growth is likely to be more of a challenge for J&J these days. For one thing, nearly every pharmaceutical operation around is looking to make deals. And there are relatively few companies with products that are far enough along and important enough to make a real difference to J&J.

32      Of course, the drug business' problems now fall to its new boss, Christine A. Poon, whom Weldon helped recruit from Bristol-Myers Squibb Co. But Weldon still jumps in every now and then. One weekend earlier this year, several senior executives were hammering out details on the $2.4 billion acquisition of Scios Inc., a biotech company that has a drug for congestive heart failure. They called Weldon at home to ask for his input on one

point. Weldon decided to go to the office to give his answer. And he stayed until well after midnight. Weldon says he wanted to make an appearance because it was Poon's first major acquisition. "I wanted to be there, if nothing else, to give her some moral support," he says.

**33**    But you know he got a thrill from being back in the thick of things. As Weldon leads the company into a new era, he'll have to be careful not to cross the line between supporting his executives and encroaching on their territory. Their autonomy has been central to Johnson & Johnson's success. To refine the J&J way, Weldon will have to be among the most disciplined and restrained of executives. Keeping a company on top can be just as hard as getting it there.

Source: "Staying on Top." Barrett, Amy. *BusinessWeek Online,* May 5, 2003.

Case 17

**BusinessWeek**

# The Linux Uprising

**1**   Meet Nicholas Walker, digital nomad. Like blues musicians who once wandered the South singing for their supper, this 18-year-old high school dropout lives out of a suitcase—sometimes trading his software programming skills for a place to crash or some spending money. His travels have taken him far and wide, from a programmers' confab in Istanbul to Massachusetts Institute of Technology's famed Artificial Intelligence Laboratory. Walker's fresh, earnest face tells all: He's an idealist. He believes in sharing his software innovations with others. "I'm not comfortable with selling the things I do and making money from them," Walker says during a stopover at his parents' home in New Hampshire.

**2**   Three hundred miles to the south, on the twelfth floor of a Manhattan office tower, Walker has an unlikely soul mate. Jeffrey M. Birnbaum, 37, is managing director for computing at brokerage giant Morgan Stanley's Institutional Securities Div. He's so buttoned-down that he wears a suit on Casual Friday. You would think this cog in the capitalist machine would have nothing in common with young Walker. But Birnbaum is betting Morgan Stanley's (MWD) technology future on the kinds of software projects, called "open source," that Walker participates in.

**3**   Birnbaum has fallen hard for Linux, a penny-pinching open-source alternative to computer operating systems such as Microsoft Corp.'s (MSFT) Windows and Sun Microsystems Inc.'s (SUNW) Solaris. He's busy replacing 4,000 high-powered servers running traditional software with much cheaper machines running Linux. Projected five-year savings: up to $100 million. Does it bother him that counterculture kids like Walker have a hand in Linux? Not a bit. "We see their work, and it's good," he says.

**4**   Just when it seemed the technology world had lost its fizz, a powerful movement is on the rise. A ragtag band of open-source programming volunteers scattered around the globe—and hooked up via the Internet—is revolutionizing the way software is made. At the heart of what they do is Linux, an operating system flexible enough to run everything from an IBM supercomputer to a Motorola (MOT) cell phone. Because it's open source, Linux can be downloaded off the Web for free—though it's typically bought by corporations as part of a package that includes service.

**5**   The computer realm may never be the same. Imagine the havoc in the energy business if some newcomer started giving away gasoline. Linux is bringing on a convulsion of that magnitude in tech. Practically every tech company is being forced to figure out how to take advantage of Linux—or to avoid being swept aside by it. And don't be fooled by Linux's harmless-looking penguin mascot, Tux: This stuff is shaking up the balance of power in the computer industry. It poses the biggest threat to Microsoft's hegemony since the Netscape browser in 1995.

**6**   Backed by technology titans such as Intel (INTC), IBM (IBM), Hewlett-Packard (HPQ), and Dell (DELL), Linux is just now going mainstream. From DaimlerChrysler (DCX) to Tommy Hilfiger (TOM)—not to mention just about every major brokerage on Wall Street—Linux is gaining ground. Coming from near zero three years ago, it has grabbed 13.7 percent of the $50.9 billion market for server computers. That figure is expected to jump to 25.2 percent in 2006, putting Linux in the Number Two position, according to market researcher IDC. And get this: Starting this year, Number one Microsoft's 59.9 percent share in the server market will reverse its long climb and slowly slide backwards, predicts IDC. Meanwhile, Linux is finding its way into countless consumer-electronics gizmos, including Sony PlayStation video-game consoles and TiVo TV-program recorders (TIVO). "Has

Linux come of age? The answer is absolutely, positively, unequivocally yes," says Steven A. Mills, group executive for IBM Software.

7    No one could have seen this one coming, not even Linus Torvalds, the young Finnish programmer who wrote Linux as a cut-down version of Unix for the PC in 1991. Torvalds figured it would be a free plaything for computer hobbyists who weren't satisfied by what big tech companies like Microsoft and IBM produced. "If someone had told me 12 years ago what would happen, I'd have been flabbergasted," says Torvalds.

8    How did Linux make the jump into the mainstream? A trio of powerful forces converged. First, credit the rotten economy. Corporations under intense pressure to reduce their computing bills began casting about for low-cost alternatives. Second, Intel Corp., the dominant maker of processors for PCs, loosened its tight links with Microsoft and started optimizing for Linux in addition to Windows. This made it possible for corporations to get all the computing power they wanted at a fraction of the price. The third ingredient was widespread resentment of Microsoft and fear that the company was on the verge of gaining a stranglehold on corporate customers. "I always want to have the right competitive dynamics. That's why we focus on Linux. Riding that wave will give us choices going forward," says John A. McKinley Jr., executive vice-president for global technology and services at Merrill Lynch & Co., which runs some key securities trading applications on Linux.

9    Microsoft takes the threat seriously. While it is holding on to its monopoly in desktop systems, Linux's march into servers threatens a key growth area—one that controls much of the Internet. Microsoft Chairman William H. Gates III and CEO Steven A. Ballmer decline to answer questions on the subject. But James Allchin, the group vice-president who runs the Windows business, calls Linux "the Number One competitor for this company," ahead of even IBM and Sun. Because it's free, Linux is undercutting Microsoft much the way Microsoft has gutted its rivals with lower prices for the past two decades. But Microsoft insists that Windows is more capable than Linux and argues that innovations—such as its Tablet PC technology—will keep coming from commercial software outfits.

10    Frustrations, though, run high. One Microsoft executive, chief strategist Craig Mundie, even calls Linux unhealthy for the technology industry. "It ultimately is a question about whether societies are going to value intellectual property or not," he says.

11    He has a point. The computer industry has been built on a simple premise: Companies invest to create software, sell it, and pour a good part of the proceeds into building more. Now, with the open-source philosophy, that stream of revenue is threatened. And it's not just because the Linux operating system is free. Before using open-source software, tech companies must sign a license in which they promise to give away innovations they build on top of it. "The business doesn't go away," says Eric von Hippel, a professor at MIT's Sloan School of Management. "But it changes forms. Instead of making money from the operating system, you are going to have to make it elsewhere."

12    For tech companies to thrive in this new world, they'll have to operate differently. This could mean building businesses around selling services, as IBM does, or creating software that runs on top of Linux, like Oracle Corp.'s database (ORCL). Dell Computer Corp. benefits from Linux and sidesteps its dangers by staying out of the software business altogether.

13    Longer term, the open-source movement threatens vast sectors of the software industry. True, since the volunteer programmers often lack specialized knowledge, complex business applications are probably beyond their range. But basic open-source databases and e-mail are already available. What happens if corporate customers begin gobbling them up? While no one knows how far open source will go, it could deflate profits.

14    Like all big shifts, the Linux phenomenon will produce winners and losers. Likely winners include IBM, which specializes in high-performance computing and is selling twice as many Linux servers as any other computer company. Processor maker Intel is riding Linux'

coattails into the world of high-powered computing. And Dell is pumping out low-priced Linux servers and selling them directly to companies via the Net.

15      While Microsoft stands to lose from Linux, the movement is inflicting far greater damage on Sun. Some of Sun's customers are migrating to Linux machines, which perform similar tasks at a fraction of the price. Online stock trading site E*Trade Group Inc. (ET), for example, replaced sixty $250,000 computers that run on Sun's Sparc chip with 80 Intel-based Linux machines costing just $4,000 a pop.

16      What could derail Linux? The biggest risks are intellectual-property issues. SCO Group, holder of the original patents for Unix software upon which Linux is based, has announced plans to form a licensing division and hire superlawyer David Boies to press its claims against sellers of Linux. Another potential problem: There are a handful of commercial versions of Linux. If they evolve into substantially different programs, software companies that sell applications might have to create a separate version for each type of Linux.

17      None of this, though, looks likely to halt Linux's advance any time soon. So far, the threat of patent claims is not deterring customers. And sellers of Linux vow to keep their versions compatible with one another. A recent survey by Goldman, Sachs & Co. shows that 39 percent of large corporations now use Linux. While many companies haven't tried it yet, analysts expect an improved version coming out this year to tempt a new wave of corporate tech buyers.

18      The Linux phenomenon spreads like water—finding its way into all sorts of surprising nooks and crannies. And that's by design. When Torvalds started writing the operating system on a $3,500 computer while a graduate student in Finland, he made it both compact and flexible, so it could be used in a host of ways. He also decided to share the technology freely with others. The idea: Take it, build something, share what you make. Within weeks of the now-auspicious Aug. 25, 1991, date, when Torvalds first posted the bare bones of his little program on the Internet, dozens, then hundreds, of people from Japan to New Zealand to the United States were responding with encouraging words, fixes, and new features. He had tapped into a vibrant underground community—true believers in the principles of open-source software—that would help him build Linux into a global phenomenon.

19      Torvalds, now 33, still orchestrates this digital quilting bee. He has final say on everything that goes into the updates of his operating system—and doesn't mind being called the "benevolent dictator" of Linuxland. These days, Torvalds' day job is programming for startup chipmaker Transmeta Corp. in Santa Clara, Calif. He speaks at Linux conferences from time to time. But for the most part he prefers to stay in the background, writing code, exchanging e-mails with his comrades-in-arms, and spending his free time with his wife, Tove, the six-time women's karate champion of Finland, and their two daughters.

20      Torvalds appears unspoiled by success. While he makes no money directly from Linux, he cashed in on the boom modestly by selling some stock he was given before the 1999 initial public offering of Linux seller Red Hat Inc. After that, he traded in his old Pontiac for a sporty BMW Z3. Mainly, he says, he just wants to have fun, which he considers a prerequisite for good programming. "People need to be able to goof off," he says.

21      The open-source movement's roots are decidedly more radical than Torvalds'. In this software revolution, Richard Stallman, a former programmer at MIT's Artificial Intelligence Lab, plays the role of Karl Marx. The 49-year-old Stallman, with his flower-child hair, has long believed in free software, uncontrolled by copyrights. Back in 1984, when he set out to build such a system, it seemed downright utopian. But Stallman persevered. With a small group of programmers, he started building free software programs. Stallman also created the licensing system on which Torvalds would eventually base Linux.

22      Open-source software programmers say they're different from Stallman in one major way: They don't have a problem with people making money off their work—or making

money themselves. Miguel de Icaza, the Mexican programmer who created GNOME, software that makes Linux easier to use, in 1999 co-founded Ximian Inc., a private Boston company that sells software for making Linux easier to install and update. Still, de Icaza says it's passion for the work and not the prospect of riches that drives him. "I can't tell if I have worked all my life or if I have never worked a single day of my life," he says.

23    But if Linux' surge continues, it will be due in large part to the Goliaths of the tech industry. Companies including IBM, Intel, Oracle, and Dell have thrown their weight behind it—and have given the technology credibility with corporate tech buyers. Intel, for instance, interested in expanding its role in the corporate server market, convened a meeting of Wall Street heavy hitters to consider Linux on Dec. 6, 2001, at the Michelangelo Hotel in midtown Manhattan. Gradually, Intel and the Wall Streeters persuaded software makers such as storage specialist VERITAS Software (VRTS) and financial-information suppliers such as Reuters Group (RTRSY) to up their commitment to Linux. "Intel's muscle on this was incredible," says Bridget E. O'Connor, chief technology officer at Lehman Brothers Inc. (LEH)

24    As it happens, Linux fits comfortably with the strategic imperatives of many of the industry's behemoths. Take IBM. For a change, it's on the cutting edge of a technology shift. That's because in late 1999, Samuel J. Palmisano, then head of IBM's server group and now the company's CEO, asked his staff what the next big trend would be in servers. Their answer: Linux. Within a matter of weeks, intensifying during what became known as the "Christmas meetings," IBM decided to make Linux a pillar of its strategy. During the next year, it earmarked $1 billion to retool its software and computers to run on Linux and devoted 250 engineers to working with the open-source community. With Linux, IBM was able to put tremendous resources behind the trend toward lower-cost Intel chips without becoming ever more dependent on Microsoft, its archrival in corporate computing.

25    Today, Linux and IBM are as inseparable as Las Vegas animal tamers Siegfried and Roy. Big Blue has more than 4,600 Linux customers. About 15 percent of the IBM mainframe capacity shipped in the first half of 2002 ran Linux. And in the fourth quarter, IBM sold $160 million worth of Linux servers, equal to the combined tally of its nearest competitors, Hewlett-Packard and Dell, according to market researcher Gartner Inc.

26    Get caught on the wrong side of Linux, though, and you take a pounding. Scott G. McNealy's Sun Microsystems, for example, is losing contracts to rivals who embraced Linux first. "Clearly, Linux poses the greatest threat, at least in the short term, to Sun," says Thomas P. Berquist, of Goldman Sachs.

27    McNealy is using a two-track strategy to grapple with Linux. For the top of the market, Sun is racing to keep its own Solaris software a step ahead of Linux. At the same time, it's selling basic machines running Linux for simple tasks such as serving up Web pages. "We have a very deliberate plan here. We're going to stay focused. We're not going to do what IBM or HP are doing—abandoning a 20-year investment in mission-critical Unix operating systems. They're marooning customers," he says.

28    While McNealy donned a penguin suit during an analyst's conference on Feb. 6, 2002, to show his love for the operating system, the penguin has yet to return the love. Sun just started selling Linux servers last fall. In the fourth quarter it racked up just $1.3 million in Linux server sales in the United States, compared with $675 million in sales of its Unix-based servers, according to Gartner.

29    Contrary to just about every other tech company and sage, Sun insists that the biggest impact from Linux will come on the desktop. It's tooling up to begin selling desktop computers loaded with Linux and its own Linux-based StarOffice suite of word processor, spreadsheet, and database programs. Yet analysts say Microsoft's Office software, with better than a 95 percent share of the market, is so entrenched that it will be hard to supplant.

Faced with the costly prospect of converting vast terabytes of Word and Excel documents, desktop users will likely stick with Microsoft, predicts analyst Al Gillen of IDC. "Microsoft won the desktop battle a long time ago," he says.

30    Still, large companies are jumping on the Linux bandwagon for servers. And with so many bruisers aboard, there's scant room for startups. Among them, only Red Hat is a bona fide success. Like a half dozen other upstarts, it sells packages including Linux software for desktop computers and servers. But because of the ban on selling Linux itself, Red Hat is essentially selling related software, ongoing technical support, and maintenance for corporations. Three years after going public, the company made its first-ever profit in its third quarter ended Nov. 30—a scant $305,000, on $24.3 million in revenues. It seems to have staying power, though, thanks to distribution deals with the likes of IBM, HP, and Dell. And it got certification on Feb. 11 to sell to the Defense Dept.

31    While a host of Linux-oriented startups were launched in the late 1990s, most of them were geared to selling to dot-coms—many of which have since gone out of business. A dozen Linux companies failed in the past two years, including Loki, a gaming company, and Eazel, which was making Linux easier to use. VA Software Corp. (LNUX), formerly VA Linux Systems, a maker of Linux-based computers, is just hanging on as a seller of software-development tools—this only three years after it broke all IPO records with a share price that soared 698 percent on the first day of trading.

32    A handful of industry giants can make the market grow faster than an army of startups ever could. That's especially true internationally, where the big companies can afford to operate sales forces in all the major countries and many minor ones. IBM, for instance, sold Linux computers to China's postal service for 3,200 post offices in a single province. Last June, Germany's Interior Ministry and IBM signed a contract to enable the public sector in Germany to buy Linux.

33    It's no surprise that industry giants such as IBM, Intel, HP, and Dell dominated the LinuxWorld conference at New York's Jacob K. Javits Convention Center in January. Their huge booths crowded out the more modest digs of Red Hat and Ximian on the show floor. During a ride down the escalator on the way out of the building, three Gen Y guys dressed in black and sporting multiple facial piercings seemed to represent a passing era. One of them, talking on a cell phone to a friend, called the gathering "boring." Down-escalator, a young woman dressed in a camouflage shirt and pants and a pink babushka heartily agreed. "It's all Big Business now. Linux has been taken over by the suits," she sneered.

34    Her name was oh-so avant-garde: Scirocco Six. Yet it turned out she was working for none other than Microsoft.

35    These days, even the titans of industry are hurrying to act like rebels. But as the Linux movement continues to push its freeware into the world, a delicate balance is forming. Its success hinges on keeping the peace between two extremes: the volunteer programmers like Nick Walker, who pull all-nighters writing code to change the world, and the commercial types like Morgan Stanley's Jeffrey Birnbaum, who use the software to save money. It's a weird twist on capitalism. But it just might work.

Source: "The Linux Uprising" Kerstetter, Jim, Hamm, Steve, Ante, Spencer E., and Greene, Jay. *BusinessWeek Online*, March 3, 2003.

**Case 18**

# The New Blue

1 The directors were just sitting down for the first IBM (IBM) board meeting of the year on Jan. 28 when CEO Samuel J. Palmisano dropped a bombshell. For years, the board had lavished wealth upon Louis V. Gerstner Jr., keeping his pay in line with other pinstriped superstars across Corporate America. But in a surprise break from the past, Palmisano asked the board to cut his 2003 bonus and set it aside as a pool of money to be shared by about 20 top executives based on their performance as a team. Palmisano doesn't want to say how much he's pitching in, but insiders say it's $3 million to $5 million—nearly half his bonus.

2 A crowd-pleasing gesture? It was just his latest salvo. Five days earlier, he took aim at a bastion of power and privilege at Big Blue, the 92-year-old executive management committee. For generations, this 12-person body presiding over IBM's strategy and initiatives represented the inner sanctum for every aspiring Big Blue executive. Palmisano himself was anointed back in 1997, a promotion that signaled the shimmering possibilities ahead. But on Jan. 23, the CEO hit the send button on an e-mail to 300 senior managers announcing that this venerable committee was finito, kaput. Palmisano instead would work directly with three teams he had put in place the year before—they comprised people from all over the company who could bring the best ideas to the table. The old committee, with its monthly meetings, just slowed things down.

3 All the while, Palmisano was piecing together an audacious program to catapult IBM back to the zenith of technology. It started at an Aug. 5 strategy meeting, when he asked his team to draw up a project as epochal as the mainframe computer—IBM's big bet from 40 years ago. Through the day, the team cobbled together a vision of systems that would alter the very nature of how technology is delivered. IBM would supply computing power as if it were water or electricity. But how to tackle a project this vast? No one knew where to begin. A frustrated Palmisano abruptly cut short the meeting and gave the team 90 days to assemble and launch the megaproject. Three months later, the CEO unveiled "e-business on demand." Standing in New York's American Museum of Natural History, not far from the hulking dinosaurs whose fate IBM narrowly skirted, Palmisano vowed to lead a new world of computing. "We have an opportunity to set the agenda in our industry," he says.

4 After one year on the job, Palmisano is putting his imprint on the company—and with a vengeance. Sure, IBM roared back to strength in the late '90s. But Palmisano is out to remake the company and hoist it back to greatness. Through much of the twentieth-century, under the leadership of Thomas J. Watson and his son, Thomas Jr., IBM not only ruled computing and defined the American multinational, it was the gold standard for corporations. From the days of tabulating machines all the way to the Space Age, when its mainframes helped chart the path to the moon, IBM was a paragon of power, prestige, and farsightedness. It was tops in technology, but also a leader in bringing women and minorities into a well-paid workforce and in creating a corporate culture that inspired lifelong loyalty. "We stood for something back then," Palmisano says.

5 To return IBM to greatness, the 51-year-old Palmisano is turning the company inside out. He's the first true-blue IBMer to take the reins since the company's fall from grace more than a decade ago. And while the new CEO never criticizes his predecessor, who rescued IBM and pushed many key technologies, Palmisano is quietly emerging as the antithesis of Gerstner. Where Gerstner raked in money, Palmisano makes a point of splitting the booty with his team. While Gerstner ruled IBM regally, Palmisano is egalitarian. The revolution he is leading spells the end of the imperial CEO at IBM. "Creativity in any large organization does

not come from one individual, the celebrity CEO," Palmisano says. "That stuff's B.S. Creativity in an organization starts where the action is—either in the laboratory, or in R&D sites, at a customer place, in manufacturing."

6    If that sounds like the IBM of old, that's exactly what Palmisano is hoping for. The flattening of the organization, the lowering of CEO pay, the emphasis on teams—it's all part of his broad campaign to return to IBM's roots. Palmisano believes that core values remain in what he calls the company's DNA, waiting to be awakened. And he thinks that this message, which might have elicited chortles during the tech boom, resonates in the wake of the market crash and corporate scandals. More important, he believes that only by returning to what made IBM great can the company rise again to assume its place of leadership in America and the world.

7    At the heart of Palmisano's plan is e-business on demand. The project, which is already gobbling up a third of IBM's $5 billion research and development budget, puts Big Blue in the vanguard of a massive computing shift. The company starts by helping customers standardize all of their computing needs. Then, in the course of the next 10 years, it will handle growing amounts of this work on its own massive computer grids. And this won't be just techie grunt work. The eventual goal is to imbue these systems with deep industrial expertise so that IBM is not only crunching numbers and dispatching e-mails but also delivering technology that helps companies solve thorny technical problems—from testing drugs to simulating car crashes. It's a soaring vision. But Palmisano has believers. "Sam is aiming to go where the market's going, not to where it's been," says Cisco Systems Inc. CEO John Chambers.

8    The obstacles he faces are immense. Start with the technology. The vision of on-demand computing is downright audacious. It proposes joining all of the thousands of computers and applications in enormous enterprises, and putting them to work seamlessly and in unison—not only in-house, but with partners and customers. Assembling the pieces will require every bit of IBM's vaunted smarts, and a scrap of luck as well. IBM officials say only 10 percent of the technology needed for this system is ready. And many of the necessary pieces, including futuristic software programs that will heal themselves, are at the basic test stage in IBM's labs. "There are huge, huge technical challenges," says A. Richard Newton, dean of the College of Engineering at the University of California at Berkeley.

9    Palmisano faces an equally imposing job at home. To make good on his vision, he must turn IBM itself into a user of on-demand computing and become a prototype for its customers. This entails recharting the path of every bit of information flowing inside the company. It means not just shifting the computer systems, but redefining nearly everyone's job. And if IBM meets resistance to these changes, it could stumble in producing the new technology. This could undermine IBM's $800 million marketing campaign for e-business on demand—and scare away customers in droves. Such a failure could punish IBM financially, forcing a retreat toward fiercely competitive markets such as servers and chips. "The two most important parts of their business—services and software—are tied to the [on-demand] strategy," says Gartner analyst Tom Bittman. "They need to succeed."

10    Is history on Palmisano's side? Try to think of a great technology company that took a life-threatening fall and then scratched and clawed all the way back to the very top. Westinghouse? Digital Equipment (DEC)? Xerox (XRX)? Some have survived. But if Palmisano leads IBM back to the summit, Big Blue will be the first full-fledged roundtripper.

11    To get there, he must win a brutal battle raging among the titans of tech. From Hewlett-Packard Co. (HPQ) to Microsoft Corp. (MSFT), the industry's bruisers are all pushing research into next-generation computing systems that will rival IBM's. Big Blue appears to be better positioned than its foes, thanks to a wider range of offerings. But, warns Irving Wladawsky-Berger, IBM's general manager for e-business on demand: "In

1996, we had the benefit of being considered irrelevant. [Microsoft's William H.] Gates and [Steven A.] Ballmer felt pity on us. Now they are all watching us. If we don't move fast, they will pass us."

12    The new initiative provides Palmisano with a prodigious tool to remake the company. Gerstner's reforms began the process, directing IBM toward software and services. But Palmisano's e-business on demand goes much further. It extends into nearly every nook of Big Blue, from its sales force and its army of systems consultants to the big brains cooking up the software code in the research and development labs. Management expert Jim Collins, author of *Good to Great,* says Palmisano's willingness to think and act boldly bodes well, and recalls earlier outsize bets in IBM's history, such as the development of the tabulating machine. "It reminds me of what Tom Watson Sr. did during the Depression," he says.

13    Palmisano already is banking on winning his share of the new business. Last year IBM saw revenue slip 2 percent, to $81.2 billion, with earnings tumbling 54 percent to $3.6 billion. But this year Palmisano is counting on e-business on demand to fuel the hottest sales growth at Big Blue since 1995. Analysts predict 9 percent revenue growth this year. And Palmisano expects 40 percent—nearly $3 billion—to come from new offerings in e-business on demand. These include servers running the free Linux operating system and grid software that pools the power of scores of networked computers into a virtual super-computer.

14    By pursuing this plan, Palmisano is fleeing the brutish world of hardware and seeking refuge in profitable software and services businesses. He bulked up for this drive last year by spending $3.5 billion for PricewaterhouseCoopers Consulting and another $2.1 billion for Rational Software Corp., a maker of software tools to write programs. And why not? According to IBM's internal research, 60 percent of the profits in the $1 trillion high-tech industry will come from software and services by 2005. That's up from 45 percent in 2002. "We're just going where the profit is," Palmisano says.

15    And he's leading Big Blue in a way it has never been led before. One year before Palmisano disbanded the Executive Management Committee, he had put in place his management teams for the future. He created three of them: strategy, operations, and technology. Instead of picking only high-level executives for each team, Palmisano selected managers and engineers most familiar with the issues. "Heads are spinning," says J. Bruce Harreld, senior vice-president for strategy. "He's reaching six levels down and asking questions."

16    Talk to Palmisano for an hour and he'll mention teamwork 20 times. His entire on-demand strategy hinges upon it. Why? For IBM to come up with a broad array of on-demand technologies in a hurry, the whole company has to work smoothly from one far-flung cubicle to another. That means bringing researchers in touch not only with product developers, but with consultants and even customers. Only by reaching across these old boundaries will IBM find out what customers are clamoring for—and produce it fast.

17    To head up this process, Palmisano has chosen Wladawsky-Berger, the renowned Cuban-born computer scientist who was IBM's e-biz guru in the 1990s. Today, Wladawsky-Berger's mission is to drive the strategy across the company. In the last two months, he has assembled 28 people working in every division of IBM into what he calls a "virtual team." These are Wladawsky-Berger's on-demand agents. They nose around their areas of expertise, looking for on-demand possibilities. New servers coming out later this year, for example, will be equipped to dispatch excess work to other machines on the network.

18    Still, it's no easy job coaxing separate divisions to dance in unison. Clashes are common, for example, when IBM's 160,000 Global Service workers descend into the research labs. Last year, researchers were hard at work on a program for supply chains in the electronics industry. Consultants ordered up a quick version of the same program for a carmaker. The two sides battled briefly until the researchers adapted a program for cars, and then went

back to work on electronics. The consultants' timeframe, says William Grey, manager of IBM's Finance Research, "is milliseconds. Ours is five years. There's a cultural gap that needs to be bridged."

19    The key is getting IBM itself to function as an e-business-on-demand enterprise. To drive this message through the company, Palmisano in January grabbed a star manager, Linda Sanford, and put her in charge of internal e-business on demand. Sanford, a senior vice-president, had revived IBM's storage business and was viewed as a bona fide up-and-comer at Big Blue. "I take a senior vice-president who has a great job, and say, 'O.K., you're going to make IBM on demand,'" Palmisano says. "Then, 320,000 people say, 'Holy . . . , this guy's serious.'"

20    Sanford faces an imposing job. First, she has to supervise the overhaul of IBM's massive supply chain. That means piling $44 billion of purchases into a single system. It's a slog. It means pushing IBM's engineers to switch to company-approved suppliers. Then a procurement rep is assigned to each development team, to make sure that they all use industry standard parts. It's intrusive. But like the rest of the on-demand program, it focuses the company onto a single effort. And it should pay dividends. Palmisano expects the entire initiative to yield 5 percent productivity gains, worth $2 billion to $3 billion a year, for the next five to 10 years.

21    Sanford also is working to create an online inventory of IBM's knowledge. She's turning the company's intranet into a giant collaboration portal. One feature is an "expertise locator" that helps an employee find, say, a software engineer with expertise in building databases in Linux. But at a meeting of the operations team at Armonk, N.Y. on a cold mid-February morning, a frustrated Sanford told key executives, including Palmisano, that the concept was a hard sell.

22    Palmisano, his face cupped in his hands, looked concerned. "There's a huge level of expectation on this portal," he said. "I just hope we can deliver." Sanford responded with a blunt message: If Palmisano wants the portal to succeed, he and his teams must lead by example, offering their own areas of expertise within a 30-day deadline. "We have to lead the way," she said.

23    For Palmisano, this means rallying the biggest brains and deepest thinkers in the company to the cause. In January he flew to Harvard University in Cambridge for a meeting with IBM's top computer scientists. His message was simple and straightforward: The dream of on-demand computing hinged upon their ability to produce technology breakthroughs.

24    While scientists are wrestling with future iterations of on-demand computing, IBM's sales team is rolling out the first products. New IBM servers include a feature called "hypervisors." These allow technicians to monitor as many as 100 servers at a time, shifting work from one machine to another. A new program from IBM's Tivoli group performs similar work, patrolling the network, constantly on the lookout for servers running short of memory. When it finds one, it automatically shifts the work to other computers. This is a key aspect of on-demand computing, and a potential money saver. Once systems can distribute work, companies will be able to run their servers at a high level, much closer to capacity. This reduces costs. And if work piles up, customers will ship excess tasks to IBM.

25    Many of them, IBM hopes, will eventually exit the computing business altogether and ship all their digital work to IBM. American Express likes the idea. A year ago, before Palmisano even came up with the new vision, AmEx signed a seven-year, $4 billion services contract with Big Blue. At first blush it looks like a standard outsourcing deal. The company has shifted its computers and 2,000 tech employees to IBM. But what makes it different is the economics. AmEx pays only for technology it uses every month. The advantages? AmEx is looking to save hundreds of millions of dollars over the course of the contract. And with IBM running the system, says Glen Salow, chief information officer at American Express, "they can upgrade technology five times faster."

26    Palmisano's vision for e-business on demand stretches beyond the technical challenges to the realm of human knowledge. In the services division, IBM has experts on industries ranging from banking to metals to autos. He wants to gather their knowhow—"deep process insights," he calls it—into the systems. Eventually, he sees IBM's on-demand offerings reinventing the company's corporate customers and shaking up entire industries.

27    IBM is developing 17 different industrial road maps for on demand. Pharmaceuticals is one. There, a computer grid will handle simulation and modeling to reduce the number of clinical trials needed. That, IBM says, could lead to improving the success rates of drugs, now from 5 percent to 10 percent, to 50 percent or better. IBM also believes it can help cut the time it takes to identify and launch a new drug to three to five years, down from 10 to 12, slicing the pre-launch cost of drug development to less than $200 million, from $800 million.

28    It's a splendid vision—and far too rich with opportunity for IBM alone. Microsoft has more cash than any tech company—$43 billion—and its .net Windows initiative is an effort to rule the next generation of computing every bit as ambitious as Palmisano's. But Microsoft trails Big Blue in the upper end of the corporate computing world. Sun Microsystems (SUNW), an early advocate of on-demand computing, is pushing its own effort to develop software, called N1, that will more efficiently manage Sun gear. Sun claims N1 will offer superior performance—at one-tenth the cost—because the software is designed only for Sun products. "Diversity is great in your workforce," says Sun Executive Vice President Jonathan Schwartz. "It sucks in your data center." IBM software head Steven A. Mills shoots back: "Nothing they have in N1 is unique."

29    A stronger contender is Hewlett-Packard, thanks to its array of hardware, software, and services. Analysts say HP leads IBM in a few important niches. HP, for example, has software called Utility Data Center, that shifts work across all of a company's computers, networks, and storage devices.

30    For now, IBM's wide-angle vision and broader range of technology gives it the overall lead. But to keep ahead, Palmisano maintains a routine of near-constant work. Even while on a Vermont ski vacation in early March, Palmisano spent a snowy Sunday afternoon reading briefing papers while his family hit the slopes. Rest assured, Palmisano won't be getting his weekends back anytime soon. He is remaking IBM, and that's a job that could last a full decade. If he pulls it off, though, a giant of technology will be reborn.

Source: "The New Blue." Ante, Spencer E. *BusinessWeek Online,* March 17, 2003.

Case 19

**BusinessWeek**

# The New Merrill Lynch

1   Merrill Lynch & Co. Chief Executive E. Stanley "Stan" O'Neal was always a cool hand in a crisis. He built his career on pulling the world's biggest brokerage out of tight fixes. Whether he was extracting its junk-bond group from the damage caused when the market imploded in 1990 or stanching Merrill's losses from the collapse of the hedge fund Long-Term Capital Management LP in 1998, he invariably came out looking good. His strength: O'Neal, 51, is utterly objective about what needs to be done, and he does it—however painful it might be.

2   Right now, that quality is at a premium. Wall Street is still under the cloud of scandal. It will cost Merrill $280 million to settle charges, which it neither admitted nor denied, that it misled investors and helped Enron Corp. cook its books. Federal courts ruled in January that fancy tax-avoidance schemes it sold to clients such as American Home Products, now called Wyeth Corp., were illegal. And it is facing investor suits that could cost it billions. Dealmaking is at a low ebb, and stock market investors are gun-shy in the worst bear market since the Great Depression.

3   So what's O'Neal doing in this crisis? In the five months that he has been CEO, he has dragged Merrill through more cultural change than it underwent in the previous five decades. O'Neal, a tightly wound 17-year veteran of the firm, openly sneers at the old, comfy "Mother Merrill" culture that tolerated bumbling performance by long-serving execs. In its place, he has established a Darwinian code that encourages managers to take risks and gives them six months to a year to show they can succeed—or get out. Profit makers get rewarded, not those who just pile up revenues.

4   O'Neal's management style is a painful break with the past, too. It's a lot more autocratic than that of retiring Chairman David H. Komansky and his predecessors. Already, O'Neal, who has been effectively in control for over a year, has sidelined the sprawling and ponderous executive management committee that once ruled the roost. The operating committee that replaced it is so shrouded in secrecy that even some senior managers don't know exactly who's on it. Insiders say it appears to be mainly a rubber stamp for the torrent of decisions that pours forth from a tightly knit Politburo consisting of O'Neal and three die-hard loyalists: Executive Vice-Chairman Thomas H. Patrick; Arshad R. Zakaria, president for global markets and investment banking; and CFO Ahmass L. Fakahany.

5   Now, as he steps into Komansky's shoes as chairman on April 28, O'Neal is putting the firm's future on the line with a huge and risky bet that propels it into head-to-head competition with even greater swaths of the financial industry. O'Neal declined to be interviewed by *BusinessWeek,* but he told investors in January that he aims to build "a new kind of financial-services firm" that redefines Wall Street by offering a far greater range of services, but with far fewer people and an unrelenting focus on profitability. He aims to capture most of his wealthy corporate and private clients' business. "We believe that it is no longer necessary for our clients to maintain a relationship with any other financial-services provider," O'Neal told investors. "Period."

6   Essentially, he wants to create a financial-services colossus that has both the breadth of a megabank such as Sandy Weill's Citigroup Inc. and the depth—and trading muscle—of an independent investment bank such as Goldman, Sachs & Co. It's not that he wants to compete with Citi across the waterfront in retail banking; he's just looking to grab a bigger share of his clients' wallets with services such as checking accounts and mortgages. Because Merrill has a worldwide network of 670 retail offices, most extra revenues from them

should drop straight to the bottom line. And he is courting super-rich investors, those with at least $10 million, more assiduously than ever. He's offering them white-glove services while banishing clients with less than $100,000 to two call centers.

7    What's more, armed with a war chest of $103 billion in capital—more than either Goldman or Morgan Stanley—Merrill can greatly ramp up trading of securities on its own account. That's a big change. Although Merrill underwrites lots of corporate and municipal debt, historically, it has left most of the gravy from trading it on the plate for others. Also, O'Neal is making substantial investments in commercial real estate while developing his own hedge-funds-of-funds. "Our business is becoming more capital-intensive," says Patrick.

8    That means, of course, O'Neal is charging into highly competitive areas. Most banks and brokers are eager to recruit rich individuals as customers. For instance, Charles Schwab & Co. bought New York's U.S. Trust Corp. in 2000 precisely with that goal in mind. But Merrill starts with a huge advantage: In 2002, over 60 percent of its clients' assets were in accounts of $1 million or more and 27 percent in those with $10 million-plus.

9    At least one part of O'Neal's vision—operating with a drastically slimmed-down roster—is largely realized. Since 2000, when O'Neal took over the retail business, Merrill has axed 22,000 people, or 31 percent of the payroll, many of them from its famed "thundering herd" of brokers. Some 6,600 are gone because they served customers with small portfolios who are now handled by 460 agents at the call centers.

10   The carnage had a huge cost in terms of lost business, but it worked wonders for the bottom line. In 2002, revenues slumped 28 percent, to $28 billion. Angry investors pulled a net $5 billion from their accounts in the first quarter this year, the first fall in five years. However, according to internal forecasts, Merrill was careening toward a $1.6 billion operating loss in what turned out to be the third year of the bear market. Instead, O'Neal delivered the firm's third-biggest operating profits, which translated into a fourfold jump in net profits, to $2.5 billion, as rivals such as Morgan Stanley and J. P. Morgan Chase saw their earnings wilt. He even managed to top archrival Goldman's $2.1 billion in net profits.

11   The cost-cutting elixir still seems to be working. In the first quarter, Merrill's earnings were up 27 percent from the final quarter of last year, coming in at 72 cents per share, 11 cents more than Wall Street analysts expected. Better yet, pretax profit margins perked up sharply, to 20.2 percent in 2002, from 6.3 percent the previous year, while return on equity nearly quadrupled, to 11.7 percent from 2.7 percent. The result: The stock has jumped 47 percent, to nearly 42 since hitting a 52-week low last October, nearly triple the 17 percent rise in the Standard & Poor's 500-stock index. And more analysts rate it a buy than any other investment bank besides Citigroup.

12   Still, critics contend O'Neal's strategy is flawed. They charge that Merrill's cutbacks are so severe that the firm will be left floundering once the market recovers. "O'Neal took the lead [in slashing staff] in the downturn," says James Mitchell, a Putnam Lovell NBF Securities Inc. financial analyst. "But when things turn around, that could be an issue."

13   Others say O'Neal is failing to deliver on some key promises he made to shareholders. The CEO said the firm would quit unprofitable lines. But it has remained the top underwriter of short-term debt, a low margin business. Rivals say the firm is chasing revenues to get to the top of the underwriters' rankings. Merrill insists they are no longer a concern.

14   His detractors shouldn't underestimate O'Neal. He has shown an uncanny knack for turning adversity to advantage ever since he picked cotton as a boy in dirt-poor Wedowee, Ala., in the days of segregated restaurants, theaters, and bathrooms. He put himself through college by working the 4 P.M.-to-midnight shift as a foreman of a General Motors assembly plant. GM paid for him to get an MBA from Harvard. By his late 20s he was working alongside GM's current CEO, G. Richard "Rick" Wagoner Jr., in the Treasurer's office, before leaving to join Merrill in 1986. "He's as smart as it gets," says Bennett Rosenthal, formerly

of Merrill's junk-bond group and now a partner at Ares Management in Los Angeles, an affiliate of Apollo Advisors.

15    Bright he may be, but according to others who've worked closely with him, O'Neal often comes across as insensitive in dealing with people. Stories about his high-handed treatment of colleagues abound. For example, when he became president (and CEO-in-waiting) in 2001, he was far from a gracious victor. One of the losers, Jeffrey M. Peek, then-head of asset management, found out that he didn't figure in O'Neal's future plans from a corporate flack. Last November, about two weeks before becoming CEO, he angered veterans when he, not Komansky, announced the promotion of his buddy Patrick.

16    Eventually, his lack of people smarts may come back to haunt him. O'Neal regularly offends his investment bankers by commenting both to them and to outsiders that the value of the merger and advisory business is debatable. Such treatment could make it harder for him to keep key staff if Wall Street's balmier days return. Already, 10 senior execs have exited since O'Neal officially became CEO in December, including Robert J. McCann, who retired at age 44 in January after working at Merrill for 21 years. That was just 15 months after O'Neal handpicked him to clean up Merrill's research mess as head of research.

17    A far bigger preoccupation for O'Neal seems to be that reforms in the wake of the Wall Street scandals have gone too far. "Today's business landscape is dominated by an atmosphere of cynicism and potential retribution; the message seems to be that risk is bad," he told the Greenlining Institute, a minority communities lobby group, in Los Angeles on April 10. "If we attempt to eliminate risk, the result will be, ultimately, economic stagnation or perhaps even economic failure."

18    So far, the risks O'Neal has taken have given Merrill positive momentum. To maintain it, he must build new high-margin franchises. That's what he's trying to do in Phase II of his top-to-bottom makeover. As he pushes into new businesses or bulks up to critical mass in existing ones, he's starting to hire on a selective basis. In the past 12 months, more than 400 bankers, salespeople, and traders have joined Merrill. The firm has doubled the staff that provides technological support and financing to hedge funds, a business dominated by Morgan Stanley and Bear, Stearns & Co. "Merrill has been aggressively repositioning its business to be in the top ranks," says Johann Wong, vice-chairman, CEO, and founder of hedge-fund watcher HedgeWorld.

19    In the retail business, O'Neal's battle plan requires remorseless segmentation of customers to ensure that serving them is profitable. That's why those with low account balances were diverted, much to their resentment, to impersonal call centers. Few clients with less than $100,000 in assets generate enough fees to cover the $1,500 that industry mavens say it costs Merrill to assign an investor a personal broker. The more affluent clients, especially if they use Merrill for other services in addition to brokerage, are moneymakers for the firm. Merrill estimates that this group has about $140 billion on deposit with other financial firms. It wants them to shift that cash—and roll over their 401(k) pension plans when they change jobs—into Merrill accounts.

20    The richest clients are the biggest prize of all. Not only do $10 million-plus accounts spin off substantial fees, they're also the natural market for high-margin investment products. Last year, Merrill clients invested $3.1 billion in its hedge-funds-of-funds and private-equity investments combined. O'Neal wants that to rise substantially, along with sales of sophisticated financial products such as futures and exchange-traded funds and fancy derivatives. He is determined to coddle the very rich as much as necessary to keep current clients loyal and win over new ones.

21    Before O'Neal can convince the rich that Merrill's fancy new funds are worth buying, he still may have to give its plain-vanilla mutual funds another shot in the arm. Since Merrill started to merge funds to bury the dogs, more than half are beating the average 3-year performance for their category. A key but hard-nosed group—outside financial advisers to

whom Merrill would like to sell its funds—are starting to take notice. On April 21, Jersey City (N.J.) clearinghouse Pershing LLC said it would give the 850 brokerages it serves access to Merrill's mutual funds.

22    Efforts to expand in investment banking are already paying off. First-quarter revenues shot up 37 percent, to $2.5 billion, thanks to nearly doubled debt-trading revenues. Operating profits from the sector rose 41 percent, to $785 million. The firm is also making inroads into so-called block trading to get closer to corporate customers and money managers. It buys large blocks of stocks from companies such as Bank of New York Co., as it did in January, and then sells them to investors. It can lose money if prices move against it while the stocks are still on its books. But it's worth the risk: Banks can make returns on equity of 20 percent or more, versus the typical single-digit returns from stock and bond underwriting.

23    Lending more to favored clients is on the rise as well. In 2002, Merrill granted loans totaling $35 billion, an 80 percent jump over the previous year, and made commitments to lend another $24 billion, a 60 percent increase. In this way, O'Neal is taking on power hitters such as Citigroup, Deutsche Bank, and Bank of America by extending credit to win more lucrative jobs from corporations.

24    Pension rollovers, complex derivatives plays, block trades: How does O'Neal hope to accomplish all this as well as keep his core franchises humming? He's drilling his mantra of discipline, discipline, discipline as far down the ranks as he can. He is also streamlining decision-making by combining divisions and dumping co-heads. On Dec. 3, the firm fused its international and domestic retail-brokerage operations.

25    Pressure to cut costs is still intense. O'Neal has created special SWAT teams in each business group to sniff out ways to use everything from people to computers and office space better. "[They're] coming up with ideas that involve consolidation or dismantling of processes that are redundant or don't add value," says CFO Fakahany.

26    Merrill is also pinching pennies by playing legal hardball against more customers who, upset with their losses in the post-bubble market, are suing the firm. Securities lawyers say Merrill is fighting more of the cases rather than settling. And they complain that the firm is also trying to drag out the process by stalling arbitration proceedings. Merrill declined to comment. However, it recently placed classified ads for lawyers to work as temps to help it fight off the barrage of complaints.

27    For now, O'Neal seems determined to tune out such problems and focus on producing the numbers he needs to declare victory. He outsmarted rivals by anticipating the seriousness of the downturn—and cutting costs—much earlier than they did. Now, the big question is whether he can outmaneuver them again when business on Wall Street finally picks up.

28    The diverse portfolio of businesses he has put in place is designed to enable Merrill both to weather a continuing bear market and benefit from an economic upswing. But that won't do him much good if he fails to win back investors' trust and gain the loyalty of his troops.

29    There are still people on Wall Street who think Merrill will end up as takeover bait for banks that want a bigger investment-banking presence when business picks up again. Possible suitors, senior merger advisers say, include Bank of America, Bank One, or British-based global bank HSBC. Those rumors will quickly fade if Stan O'Neal succeeds in realizing his vision at Merrill.

Source: "The New Merrill Lynch." Thornton, Emily. *BusinessWeek Online,* May 5, 2003.

Case 20

# The NFL Machine

1   In this era of bad-boy businessmen and the corporate perp walk, it's hard to imagine any CEO commanding a police escort—unless he's cuffed in the backseat of a patrol car. Still, that's what is waiting for Paul Tagliabue as his private jet touches down in Tampa in early December. Why the rock-star treatment? Simple. From September to February, this bookish 62-year-old with the button-down look of a corporate lawyer controls the passion of America—the 32 teams of the NFL. Besides, he can get Super Bowl tickets.

2   There are hours to go before the Tampa Bay Buccaneers face the Atlanta Falcons, but Tagliabue hops into a black Lincoln Town Car buffered by two police cruisers. As sirens blare and lights flash, the commissioner's car is guided through pregame traffic directly into the caverns beneath Raymond James Stadium. Fans treat him like a celebrity, too. "Hey commish, over here," shouts one Warren Sapp wannabe in a bright-red No. 99 jersey as he snaps a photo. The 6-foot, 5-inch Tagliabue signs autographs and chats with security guards before strolling out onto the lush field to watch warm-ups. He quickly notes that the socks of Falcons star quarterback Michael Vick are scrunched down around his ankles in violation of league rules. They are pulled up tightly by kickoff time.

3   Sometimes a quarterback finds himself in a sweet spot where everything works just right, week after week. Tagliabue in 2002, and now heading into the Super Bowl on Jan. 26 in San Diego, is in that kind of groove. Behind him is a thrilling, anyone-can-win season and a white-knuckle postseason. Ahead is a media empire in the making. The National Football League recently signed a $2 billion satellite-TV deal. There are three years left on an $18 billion network and cable contract. Twenty spanking-new football-only stadiums have been built or renovated in the past 10 years, thanks to the league's deft use of the bond market. Sponsors keep queuing up to get a piece of the NFL brand. Harmony reigns among players and owners. And heck, as John Madden might say, this is in the middle of an economic slump.

4   Maybe one reason for Tagliabue's championship season in the face of a stubborn downturn is that the NFL is not exactly a model of capitalism. The commissioner has made it his mission to distribute equally as much of the league's revenues as possible among the teams of the National Football Conference and the American Football Conference. "We're 32 fat-cat Republicans who vote socialist," Baltimore Ravens owner Art Modell quipped recently. It doesn't hurt that players have agreed to a hard cap on salaries and few guarantees. "I don't see this as us versus the owners, but instead it's us versus all the other entertainment choices out there: the movies, music, theater," says Gene Upshaw, the former Oakland Raider and Hall of Famer who represents 2,000 players as executive director of the NFL Players Assn.

5   To understand the success of the business that Tagliabue has built and runs with almost military precision, take a look at the season just past. It started in early September, when the commish and his marketing team were able to persuade New York City to shut down Times Square during rush hour on a workday for a kickoff concert featuring Jersey rockers Bon Jovi. Half a million people turned out.

6   By the final regular-season weekend at the end of December, 19 teams still had a shot at the playoffs and a record 24 games had been decided in overtime. Those photo finishes helped boost TV viewership by 5 percent over 2001, inching closer to the NFL's recent peak in 1999. An average of 15.8 million viewers this season tuned in to any one game on the networks, according to Nielsen Media Research. For a league that loves to boast about

competitive balance, it couldn't have been a more satisfying finale. "They wanted parity. They sure got parity," says Richard A. Bilotti, a media analyst at Morgan Stanley.

7      Life looks like a cakewalk for the 83-year-old NFL these days, but it's not as if the league hasn't had its issues. Grumbling that the game had gone flat led to the birth in 2001 of the testosterone-infused XFL—a smash-mouth spectacle featuring cheerleaders dressed like showgirls. But this production of World Wrestling Entertainment and NBC proved too staged, too self-parodying, and maybe even too violent to turn the curious into fans.

8      Not that violence isn't a good part of the NFL's appeal on-field—and a problem for the league off-field. The controversial 1998 book *Pros and Cons: The Criminals Who Play in the NFL* cited research showing that one in five players during the 1996–97 season had been charged with a serious crime at one time. "These guys are the gladiators of modern culture," says sports media consultant Neal Pilson. "And with that come pluses and minuses associated with players who are larger than life." It doesn't help that a string of crummy calls by refs in recent games have fans, owners, coaches, and players riled up. But most of the focus has been where it should be: between the chalk lines.

9      Beyond the compelling action on the turf, the NFL, already widely considered the most successful and opportunistic of the pro leagues, has struck half a dozen or so blockbuster business deals in the past year. The moves, from the new $2 billion, exclusive satellite television deal with DirecTV (triple the value of the previous pact) to a $300 million sponsorship by Coors, underscore how pro football has been able to leverage its mass following to double revenues in five years, to $4.8 billion in 2002. By comparison, the valuable cable networks at media giant Viacom, such as MTV and Nickelodeon, had revenues totaling $4.3 billion in 2001.

10     The NFL estimates that revenues will grow by an additional $1 billion over the next three years. "When [Tagliabue's predecessor] Pete Rozelle ran the league, it was a football business and a good one," says Paul J. Much, a senior managing director of investment firm Houlihan Lokey Howard & Zukin. "Now it's truly an entertainment business." Says Tagliabue: "In 1989, I inherited a great structural underpinning, the equal sharing of TV money. We've added three more pillars to that: branching into new media, including satellite TV; creating a narrow band between player salary cap and floor; and using our growing TV revenues to ensure that new stadiums could be financed."

11     As evidence of the faster march into showbiz and the push into distribution, *BusinessWeek* has learned that the NFL will hire Steve Bornstein, 50, one of the architects of ESPN and a former top executive at Walt Disney Co., to be in charge of TV and media. Bornstein will also be CEO of a 24-hour, NFL-owned, digital cable channel devoted to football—though the only games shown will be classics. The channel, which will include news and commentary, will launch later this year.

12     Also in the works are plans to sell the league's rich archives through a video-on-demand service that will allow fans to watch old game footage for a fee. In addition, Tagliabue is expected soon to announce a deal with Time Inc. to put out an NFL magazine. And ESPN is nearing a deal with the NFL Films unit to help develop two original movies.

13     Unlike other leagues with big corporate owners such as AOL Time Warner, News Corp., and Walt Disney, no company has ever owned an NFL club. The league maintains that individuals care more about winning and corporations care more about their shareholders—not that there's anything wrong with that. NFL ownership groups are restricted to 25 people, with the principal owner holding at least a 30 percent stake. And an owner can borrow only $125 million against the value of the team. By contrast, the free-spending lords of baseball were allowed to tap an MLB-backed loan pool almost at will—jacking up the teams' collective debt to $3.5 billion today from $593 million in 1993.

14     In the NFL, strict oversight ensures that the 32 teams equally divide about 63 percent of total revenues. That helps level the playing field when it comes to buying top talent. In fact,

the combined revenues of the top eight richest teams is just 28 percent more than the eight teams on the low end. The NFL closely guards revenue and earning numbers, but it is widely believed that almost every team turns an operating profit. In baseball, by contrast, revenue is largely dependent on how much teams derive from local broadcasting contracts, not national deals. In 2001, the local revenues generated by the richest team, the New York Yankees, were $218 million. The poorest team, the Montreal Expos, took in just $9.7 million.

15    Jerry Jones, 60, the hands-on owner of the Dallas Cowboys since 1989 and one of the most aggressive businessmen in the league, takes the view that sharing revenue is all well and good but that teams need to seize their own marketing opportunities. In fact, the NFL has sued Jones over his aggressive local sponsorship deals. Still, Jones doesn't seem bitter and likens owning a team to acquiring a piece of art. "You're not going to see an inordinate amount of annual return on your money," he says. "It's all in the potential appreciation."

16    On the other hand, revenue guarantees have been swiftly driving up the value of an NFL franchise. In 2000, advertising executive Daniel Snyder, 38, shelled out a record $800 million for the Washington Redskins and its stadium. Previous owner Jack Kent Cooke paid $300,000 for a 25 percent stake in the 'Skins in the early 1960s. The newest owner is Arthur M. Blank, 60, the retired co-founder of Home Depot. Last year, he spent $545 million for the Atlanta Falcons, which had the league's second-lowest attendance record—an average of 52,000 a game. Previous owner Rankin M. Smith Sr. paid $8.5 million in 1965.

17    H. Wayne Huizenga, 65, owner of the Miami Dolphins and ProPlayer Stadium, used to own MLB's Florida Marlins and the NHL's Florida Panthers. After losing more than $100 million collectively, he sold both. "[The NFL] is the only thing that makes sense in sports today," he says. Huizenga, who is chairman of several real estate companies and serves on the board of AutoNation Inc., says the disparity of local revenues in baseball and hockey makes it impossible to compete if you're not in the TV-rich market of New York City. "I keep hearing about the Yankees dynasty. It makes me sick. Put me in that local TV market, and I would have had a dynasty, too," says Huizenga. He won't disclose the Dolphins' financials but says: "We do make some money."

18    One of the most important changes in the economics of the league has been new stadiums. "It's been the biggest transformation in the balance sheet of the NFL since I've been commissioner," says Tagliabue. With criticism of public funding for stadiums growing louder, the owners in 1999 authorized the league to go to Wall Street to sell bonds, the proceeds from which would be used to lend money for construction at low interest rates. So far, $650 million in such loans has helped build or renovate eight stadiums, including Gillette Stadium in Foxboro, Mass., and Lincoln Financial Field in Philadelphia, which opens next season. Gone is the emptiness of yesteryear's cold concrete shells. The new stadiums—adult theme parks, really—create fresh revenue streams from sources such as luxury suites, club seats, high-tech signage, restaurants, and shops.

19    Still, the league faces sizable risks. More than 50 percent of revenues comes from the money television pays for the rights to show NFL games. The league is in year five of an eight-year, $18 billion package with ABC/ESPN, CBS, and Fox. But all three are part of media companies that have just endured one of the worst ad recessions in decades. When renegotiation time rolls around, it remains to be seen whether they will pony up as much as they have in the past. For example, News Corp., owner of Fox, in February announced a nearly $1 billion write-off from losses associated with its sports contracts.

20    Morgan Stanley last year estimated that media companies would lose a combined $2 billion on the NFL over the term of their deals. Still, as part of the current pact, the league has until Feb. 15 to renegotiate terms or extend the contract. Or it can just wait for it to expire in three years. "The networks are between a rock and a hard place because they are bleeding money, but they want to have the NFL as a platform to promote the rest of their schedules to that enormous audience," says Morgan Stanley analyst Bilotti. ESPN will be the only

one to make money on the current deal—an estimated $50 million profit, according to Morgan Stanley—in large part because it can get revenues from both advertising and hefty fee increases it charges cable and satellite operators.

21    NBC, a unit of General Electric Co., walked away from football in 1998, refusing to cough up for new rights after 34 years of broadcasting AFC (and earlier, AFL) games. CBS, which in 1994 lost the NFC to Fox, won the AFC contract by shelling out $4.1 billion over eight years. Executives at NBC, who also passed on an NBA contract last year, say privately that they have no regrets. They estimate that the net would have lost upwards of $1 billion if it had kept the NFL. "Look," says one network executive, "NBC was the Number One network in terms of ratings when they walked away, and they still are. In other words, if you don't have it, it doesn't kill you."

22    The fear in NFL offices is that other nets, pressured by parent companies, will take the NBC line in three years. "Will the next negotiation be a difficult one? Sure," says Howard Katz, president of ABC Sports, home of *Monday Night Football,* which has struggled with declining ratings, though viewership was up 4 percent this season over last.

23    So Tagliabue is already talking to the networks about flexible scheduling that would allow last-minute switches to more competitive games on Monday night. An additional prime-time game on Sunday is also under consideration. Such ideas aren't going over too well with Fox and CBS, which don't want to give up a daytime game to rival ABC/ESPN. The only certainty next time around, network execs say, is that there must be plans in place for a Los Angeles team.

24    More viewers, yes. But not all football, all the time. Talk about expanding the NFL's presence on TV fuels worries about consumers reaching a saturation point. "We're always concerned about commoditizing the NFL," says Chief Operating Officer Roger Goodell, 43, son of the late New York Senator Charles Goodell and thought to be the leading candidate to succeed Tagliabue. "But we still see extraordinary demand for what we offer. It's the best reality TV going."

25    At the same time that the TV contract expires, so does the league's labor agreement. The NFL is widely seen as having the most favorable player deal in pro sports, with average salaries at $1.2 million. True, the average NBA salary is $4.5 million. But don't cry too hard for the footballers, many of whom get fat signing bonuses not figured into that average salary. Philadelphia Eagles quarterback Donovan McNabb, the league's highest-paid player, for one, will make $21.7 million this year, almost all of it from his signing bonus. While the salary cap has been instrumental in bringing parity to the league, there is a downside: Teams sometimes must cut veteran players, alienating fans.

26    Overall, though, the league has a highly dedicated following. Despite some erosion of support in the face of so many other entertainment options, NFL fans remain the most loyal of any sport, followed by those of the NBA, then baseball and hockey, according to a newly released index from consultant Brand Keys Inc. One big reason so many are so hot for football is gambling. An estimated $560 million is wagered on NFL games each year in Nevada alone, the only state where sports betting is legal. Estimates of illegal betting, of course, go into the billions.

27    To understand the roots of the NFL's powerful and enduring brand, you have to go back to 1960 when new Commissioner Rozelle, then 33, persuaded Washington to pass the Sports Broadcasting Act. That allowed leagues to sell broadcast rights as a package and gave them much more clout in negotiating favorable contracts. The first NFL deal was reached a short time later with CBS, which agreed to pay $4.6 million, split among the teams.

28    Rozelle is credited with transforming modern sports by marrying games with TV, and needless to say, when he retired in 1989, his were big shoes to fill. The differences between

Case 21

BusinessWeek

# The Samsung Way

1  A black-suited Agent Smith sprints down a city street. As he is felled by an acrobatic kung fu kick from Trinity, the camera pulls back to show the action taking place inside a giant, floating Samsung TV. The screen rotates, revealing that the set is just three inches thick. "You cannot escape the Samsung 40-inch LCD flat-panel TV," intones the baritone voice of actor Laurence Fishburne. "Welcome to the new dimension."

2  The ad, now appearing in many U.S. theaters showing *The Matrix: Reloaded,* has an element of truth: Whether you're a consumer in America, Europe, or Asia, it's getting pretty darn hard to escape anything made by Samsung Electronics Co. Take the United States alone. Stroll the aisles of Best Buy (BBY) Co. electronics stores, and stylish Samsung high-definition TVs, phones, plasma displays, and digital music and video players are everywhere. Log on to the home pages of *USA Today* (GCI) CNN (AOL) and other heavily trafficked sites, and Samsung's ads are first to pop out. You see its blue elliptical logo emblazoned on Olympic scoreboards. And expect more Matrix tie-ins: Samsung is selling a wireless phone just like the one Keanu Reeves uses to transport himself in the movie. Samsung will be even more visible in this fall's sequel, *The Matrix: Revolutions.*

3  Samsung's Matrix moment is the latest step in its reincarnation as one of the world's coolest brands. Its success in a blizzard of digital gadgets and in chips has wowed consumers and scared rivals around the world. The achievement is all the more remarkable considering that just six years ago, Samsung was financially crippled, its brand associated with cheap, me-too TVs and microwaves.

4  Now the company seems to be entering a new dimension. Its feature-jammed gadgets are racking up design awards, and the company is rapidly muscling its way to the top of consumer-brand awareness surveys. Samsung thinks the moment is fast arriving when it can unseat Sony Corp. as the most valuable electronics brand and the most important shaper of digital trends. "We believe we can be Number One," says Samsung America Chief Executive Oh Dong Jin. Its rivals are taking the challenge seriously. "I ask for a report on what Samsung is doing every week," says Sony President Kunitake Ando.

5  A few measures of Samsung's progress: It has become the biggest maker of digital mobile phones using code division multiple access (CDMA) technology—and while it still lags Number Two Motorola (MOT) Inc. in handsets sold, it has just passed it in overall global revenues. A year ago, you'd have been hard pressed to find a Samsung high-definition TV in the United States. Now, Samsung is the best-selling brand in TVs priced at $3,000 and above—a mantle long held by Sony and Mitsubishi Corp. In the new market for digital music players, Samsung's three-year-old Yepp is behind only the Rio of Japan's D&M Holdings Inc. and Apple Computer (AAPL) Inc.'s iPod. Samsung has blown past Micron Technology (MU), Infineon Technologies (IFX), and Hynix Semiconductor in dynamic random-access memory (DRAM) chips—used in all PCs—and is gaining on Intel (INTC) in the market for flash memory, used in digital cameras, music players, and handsets. In 2002, with most of techdom reeling, Samsung earned $5.9 billion on sales of $33.8 billion.

6  Can the good times last? That's a serious question, since Samsung is challenging basic New Economy dogma. In high tech, the assumption is that developing proprietary software and content gives you higher margins and a long lead time over rivals. Yet Samsung defiantly refuses to enter the software business. It's wedded to hardware and betting it can thrive in a period of relentless deflation for the industry. Rather than outsource manufacturing, the company sinks billions into huge new factories. Instead of bearing down on a few "core

competencies," Samsung remains diversified and vertically integrated—Samsung chips and displays go into its own digital products. "If we get out of manufacturing," says CEO and Vice Chairman Yun Jong Yong, "we will lose."

7    Yet the industrial history of the past two decades suggests that this model does not work in the long run. The hazard—as many Japanese, U.S., and European companies learned in the 1980s and '90s—is that Samsung must keep investing heavily in R&D and new factories across numerous product lines. Samsung has sunk $19 billion over five years into new chip facilities. Rivals can buy similar technologies from other vendors without tying up capital or making long-term commitments. What's more, the life cycle of much hardware is brutally short and subject to relentless commoditization. The average price of a TV set has dropped 30 percent in five years; a DVD player goes for less than a quarter. The Chinese keep driving prices ever lower, leveraging supercheap wages and engineering talent. Meanwhile, the Japanese are building their own Chinese factories to lower costs. No wonder Samsung exited the low-margin market for TV sets 27 inches and under.

8    Faced with these perils, Samsung needs a constant stream of well-timed hits to stay on top. Even Sony has stumbled in this race: It now depends on PlayStation to support a consumer-electronics business whose glory days seem behind it. Other legendary hardware makers—Apple, Motorola, Ericsson (ERICY)—have learned the perils of the hardware way.

9    Investors got a sharp reminder of the risks Samsung is running when the company announced first-quarter results. In a tough environment, Samsung racked up the biggest market-share gain of any company in handsets, from 9.3 percent to 10.5 percent. Yet it had to lower prices to get there, and memory-chip prices also hit the bottom line. The result was a drop in first-quarter profits of 41 percent, to $942 million, on sales of $8 billion. Second-quarter profits could drop further, analysts say, hurt by lower sales in Korea's slumping economy—and in China and other Asian countries struck by the SARS epidemic. Controversy also flared in May when Samsung Electronics agreed to invest a further $93 million in a troubled credit-card affiliate. Many critics believe Samsung should divest the unit but that it is propping it up under orders of its parent, Samsung Group. Concern over corporate governance is the big reason Samsung continues to trade at a discount to its global peers. Even though it's regarded as one of the most transparent emerging-market companies anywhere, Korea's history of corporate scandals means many foreigners will always suspect its numbers.

10    If the earnings continue to soften, plenty of investors around the world will stand to lose. Samsung is the most widely held emerging-market stock, with $41 billion in market capitalization, and foreigners hold more than half its shares. Over the past five years, the shares have risen more than tenfold, to a recent $273. But concerns over 2003's earnings have driven the shares off their recent high this year.

11    The challenges are huge, but so are Samsung's strengths. It is used to big swings: Nearly half its profits come from memory chips, a notoriously cyclical business. Even in the weak first quarter, Samsung earned more than any U.S. tech company other than Microsoft, IBM, and Cisco. Meanwhile, Sony lost $940 million in this year's first three months and chip rivals Micron, Infineon, and Hynix lost a combined $1.88 billion. In cell phones, Samsung has kept its average selling price at $191, compared with $154 for Nokia (NOK) and $147 for Motorola, according to Technology Business Research. What's more, since 1997 its debt has shrunk from an unsustainable $10.8 billion to $1.4 billion, leaving Samsung in a healthy net cash position. And its net margins have risen from 0.4 percent to 12 percent.

12    Driving this success is CEO Yun, a career company man who took over in the dark days of 1997. Yun and his boss, Samsung Group Chairman Lee Kun Hee, grasped that the electronics industry's shift from analog to digital, making many technologies accessible, would leave industry leadership up for grabs. "In the analog era, it was difficult for a latecomer to

catch up," Yun says. But in the digital era, "if you are two months late, you're dead. So speed and intelligence are what matter, and the winners haven't yet been determined."

13    Samsung's strategy to win is pretty basic, but it's executing it with ferocious drive over a remarkably broad conglomerate. To streamline, Yun cut 24,000 workers and sold $2 billion in noncore businesses when he took over.

14    Samsung managers who have worked for big competitors say they go through far fewer layers of bureaucracy to win approval for new products, budgets, and marketing plans, speeding up their ability to seize opportunities. In a recent speech, Sony Chairman Nobuyuki Idei noted Samsung's "aggressive restructuring" and said: "To survive as a global player, we too have to change."

15    Second, Samsung often forces its own units to compete with outsiders to get the best solution. In the liquid-crystal-display business, Samsung buys half of its color filters from Sumitomo Chemical Co. of Japan and sources the other half internally, pitting the two teams against each other. "They really press these departments to compete," says Sumitomo President Hiromasa Yonekura.

16    The next step is to customize as much as possible. Even in memory chips, the ultimate commodity, Samsung commands prices that are 17 percent above the industry average. A key reason is that 60 percent of its memory devices are custom-made for products like Dell servers, Microsoft Xbox game consoles, and even Nokia's cell phones. "Samsung is one of a handful of companies you can count on to bridge the technical and consumer experiences and bring them successfully to market," says Will Poole, Senior Vice President at Microsoft's Windows Client Business, which works with the Koreans.

17    The final ingredient is speed. Samsung says it takes an average of five months to go from new product concept to rollout, compared to 14 months six years ago. After Samsung persuaded T-Mobile, the German-U.S. cell-phone carrier, to market a new camera-phone last April, for example, it quickly assembled 80 designers and engineers from its chip, telecom, display, computing, and manufacturing operations. In four months, they had a prototype for the V205, which has an innovative lens that swivels 270 degrees and transmits photos wirelessly. Then Samsung flew 30 engineers to Seattle to field-test the phone on T-Mobile's servers and networks. By November, the phones were rolling out of the Korean plant. Since then, Samsung has sold 300,000 V205s a month at $350 each. Park Sang Jin, executive vice-president for mobile communications, estimates the turnaround time is half what Japanese rivals would require. "Samsung has managed to get all its best companies globally to pull in the same direction, something Toshiba, Motorola, and Sony have faced big challenges in doing," says Allen Delattre, director of Accenture (ACN) Ltd. high-tech practice.

18    Samsung can also use South Korea as a test market. Some 70 percent of the country's homes are wired for broadband. Twenty percent of the population buys a new cell phone every seven months. Samsung already sells a phone in Korea that allows users to download and view up to 30 minutes of video and watch live TV for a fixed monthly fee. Samsung is selling 100,000 video-on-demand phones a month in Korea at $583 each. Verizon plans to introduce them in three U.S. cities this fall.

19    This year alone, Samsung will launch 95 new products in the United States, including 42 new TVs. Motorola plans to introduce a dozen new cell-phone models, says Technology Business Research Inc. analyst Chris Foster. Samsung will launch 20. Nokia also is a whiz at snapping out new models. But most are based on two or three platforms, or basic designs. The 130 models Samsung will introduce globally this year are based on 78 platforms. Whereas Motorola completely changes its product line every 12 to 18 months, Foster says, Samsung refreshes its lineup every nine months. Samsung has already introduced the first voice-activated phones, handsets with MP3 players, and digital camera phones that send photos over global system for mobile (GSM) communications networks.

20      Samsung has been just as fast in digital TVs. It became the first to market projection TVs using new chips from Texas Instruments (TXN) Inc. that employed digital-light processing (DLP). DLP chips contain 1.3 million micromirrors that flip at high speeds to create a sharper picture. TI had given Japanese companies the technology early in 1999, but they never figured out how to make the sets economically. Samsung entered the scene in late 2001, and already has seven DLP projection sets starting at $3,400 that have become the hottest-selling sets in their price range. "They'll get a product to market a lot faster than their counterparts," says George Danko, Best Buy's senior vice-president for consumer electronics.

21      Samsung hopes all this is just a warm-up for its bid to dominate the digital home. For years, Philips, Sony, and Apple have been developing home appliances, from handheld computers to intelligent refrigerators, that talk to each other and adapt to consumers' personal needs. Infrastructure bottlenecks and a lack of uniform standards got in the way.

22      Now, many analysts predict that digital appliances will take off within five years. By then, as many as 40 percent of U.S. households should be wired for high-speed Internet access, and digital TVs, home appliances, and networking devices will be much more affordable. Samsung is showing a version of its networked home in Seoul's Tower Palace apartment complex, where 2,400 families can operate appliances from washing machines to air conditioners by tapping on a wireless "Web pad" device, which doubles as a portable flat-screen TV.

23      It's a grandiose dream. But if the digital home becomes reality, Samsung has a chance. "They've got the products, a growing reputation as the innovator, and production lines to back that up," says In-Stat/MDR consumer-electronics analyst Cindy Wolf. With nearly $7 billion in cash, Samsung has plenty to spend on R&D, factories, and marketing.

24      Samsung Electronics' ascent is an unlikely tale. The company was left with huge debt following the 1997 Korean financial crisis, a crash in memory-chip prices, and a $700 million write-off after an ill-advised takeover of AST Technologies, a U.S. maker of PCs. Its subsidiaries paid little heed to profits and focused on breaking production and sales records—even if much of the output ended up unsold in warehouses.

25      A jovial toastmaster at company dinners but a tough-as-nails boss when he wants results, Yun shuttered Samsung's TV factories for two months until old inventory cleared. Yun also decreed Samsung would sell only high-end goods. Many cellular operators resisted. "Carriers didn't buy our story," says telecom exec Park. "They wanted lower prices all the time. At some point, we had to say no to them."

26      A top priority was straightening out the business in the United States, where "we were in a desperate position," recalls Samsung America chief Oh, appointed in early 2001. "We had a lot of gadgets. But they had nowhere to go." Samsung lured Peter Skaryznski from AT&T (T) to run handset sales, and Peter Weedfald, who worked at ViewSonic Corp. and *ComputerWorld* magazine, to head marketing.

27      Yun brought new blood to Seoul, too. One recruit was Eric B. Kim, 48, who moved to the United States from Korea at age 13 and worked at various tech companies. Kim was named executive vice-president of global marketing in 1999. With his Korean rusty, Kim made his first big presentation to 400 managers in English. Sensing Kim would be resented, Yun declared: "Some of you may want to put Mr. Kim on top of a tree and then shake him down. If anybody tries that, I will kill you!"

28      The first coup in the United States came in 1997 when Sprint PCS Group began selling Samsung handsets. Sprint's service was based on CDMA, and Samsung had an early lead in the standard due to an alliance in Korea with Qualcomm (QCOM) Inc. Samsung's SCH-3500, a silver, clamshell-shaped model priced at $149, was an instant hit. Soon, Samsung was world leader in CDMA phones. Under Weedfald, Samsung also pulled its appliances

off the shelves of Wal-Mart and Target and negotiated deals with higher-end chains like Best Buy and Circuit City.

29    Samsung's status in chips and displays, which can make up 90 percent of the cost of most digital devices, gives it an edge in handsets and other products. Besides dominating DRAM chips, Samsung leads in static random access memory and controls 55 percent of the $2 billion market for NAND flash memory, a technology mainly used in removable cards that store large music and color-image files. With portable digital appliances expected to sky-rocket, analysts predict NAND flash sales will soar to $7 billion by 2005, overtaking the more established market for NOR flash, which is embedded onto PCs, dominated by Intel and Advanced Micro Devices (AMD).

30    The company's breadth in displays gives it a similar advantage. It leads in thin-film LCDs, which are becoming the favored format for PCs, normal-size TVs, and all mobile devices. Samsung predicts a factory being built in Tangjung, Korea, that will produce LCD sheets as big as a queen-size mattress will help to halve prices of large-screen LCD TVs by 2005. Samsung also aims to be Number One in plasma and projection displays.

31    If Samsung has a major flaw, it may be its lack of software and content. Samsung has no plans to branch out into music, movies, and games, as Sony and Apple have done. Sony figures that subscription-to-content will provide a more lucrative source of revenue. Samsung's execs remain convinced they're better off collaborating with content and software providers. They say this strategy offers customers more choices than Nokia, which uses its own software.

32    Yun has heard tech gurus, publications, and even Samsung execs warn him to forsake the vertical model. His response: Samsung needs it all. "Everyone can get the same technology now," he says. "But that doesn't mean they can make an advanced product." Stay at the fore-front of core technologies and master the manufacturing, Yun believes, and you control your future. Many tech companies have tried that strategy and failed. Samsung is betting billions it can overcome the odds.

Source: "The Samsung Way." Edwards, Cliff, Ihlwan, Moon, and Engardio, Pete. *BusinessWeek Online*, June 16, 2003.

BusinessWeek

# Thinking Outside the Big Box

**1**  Two years ago, Staples (SPLS) Chairman Thomas G. Stemberg and then-President Ronald L. Sargent approached Microsoft Chairman William H. Gates III and CEO Steven A. Ballmer for some unusual career counseling. Stemberg, the visionary who founded Staples and built it into one of the most successful big-box retailers of the '90s, was itching to turn the CEO job over to longtime lieutenant Sargent and move on to other things in his life, much in the way Gates had passed the reins to Ballmer. The timing looked terrible, though. After years of blistering growth, Staples seemed to be hitting a wall—sales had stalled, while profits and the stock were cratering. After a long meeting at Microsoft headquarters, Ballmer—a classmate of Sargent's at Harvard University— urged them to go ahead anyway. He predicted, "You'll be fine," Stemberg recalls.

**2**  Ballmer was right about Sargent. Since the baton was passed in February, 2002, the low-key, notoriously frugal CEO has seamlessly taken command and outpaced the rest of the industry, allowing the more flamboyant Stemberg, 54, to assume the role of "entrepreneur in residence." But now Sargent, 47, faces a much tougher transition. The market for the office superstores that drove Staples' meteoric rise is maturing, as everyone from Wal-Mart Stores (WMT) Inc. to the local drugstore peddles cheap office supplies. To fuel a second burst of growth, Sargent is thinking far outside the big box. His audacious aim: to nearly double Staples' sales to $20 billion within the next five or six years, while boosting net income more than 20 percent a year on average.

**3**  To get there, Sargent envisions tearing up Staples' old image as just a purveyor of paper clips and PCs at its 1,300 North American superstores. He sees huge opportunities in the highly fragmented field of delivering office supplies from warehouses directly to businesses. Ultimately, he believes the delivery business could equal sales of the better-known stores. That would be a radical departure, since it means Staples would do much more business than it does now with large corporations. He's also charging into Europe. And he's counting heavily on selling services, including copying, UPS shipping, and such new initiatives as mobile technicians who fix computers and install networks.

**4**  Some outsiders question whether Sargent can pull off such an ambitious transformation. For one thing, with the $450 billion North American and European market for office supplies growing only about two percentage points faster than the economy, Staples will have to get most of its growth by wresting it away from competitors. And it will have to push stores into markets such as Chicago and Houston, now dominated by OfficeMax (OMX) Inc. and Office Depot (ODP) Inc.

**5**  In Europe, Staples is playing catch-up to Office Depot, which in June acquired a French delivery business that doubled its European sales. And in the delivery business, Staples trails both Office Depot and Boise Cascade (BCC) Corp., a leader in serving large companies. On July 14, Boise Cascade announced a deal to buy OfficeMax for $1.15 billion, thus broadening its reach into small business. Cautions Geoff Wissman, vice-president at consultants Retail Forward Inc.: "The market is fairly saturated, and the competitive intensity has increased."

**6**  Still, Sargent has made a career of confounding critics. His first big challenge came in 1990, when Stemberg asked him to take on Staples' then-$20 million delivery business. "We were like the bad guys inside Staples," recalls Sargent, "because the feeling was that if customers got products delivered, they wouldn't shop our stores." Today the $3.4 billion delivery business has Staples' highest operating-profit margins. As CEO, Sargent's sharp eye for cutting costs has helped him boost profitability, despite a tough economy. Sargent may have pulled down a salary and bonus of $1.9 million last year, but the son of a mechanic hasn't lost his blue-collar touch. He still keeps key financial data inside a five-year-old file folder that has been heavily taped to hold it together, and he drives an 11-year-old Toyota Camry.

7    Upon taking over as CEO, Sargent cut back on selling PCs and other low-margin items. He put the brakes on store expansion—Staples will open no more than 75 stores a year going forward, he says, down from 133 as recently as 2000. And he set up 45 task forces to find savings on everything from store leases to paper. The payoff? Operating-profit margins jumped to an industry-leading 5.9 percent of sales last year, from 4.5 percent in 2000. Net income surged to $446.1 million, from $265 million in 2001. And sales rose 8 percent, to $11.6 billion, last year, after barely budging in 2001. That has driven the stock to around $20, up from a low of $12 last fall.

8    Now the question is: Can Sargent work the same magic on the top line? Despite more than a decade of superstore growth, the business is still highly fragmented. In the delivery business, for instance, there are some 6,000 locally owned independent dealers, with average sales of just $3 million. Europe is even more ripe for consolidation.

9    But Staples faces daunting hurdles on the Continent. Far behind Office Depot in the delivery market, Staples last October bought the mail-order business of France's Guilbert for nearly $800 million. That boosted European delivery sales from $50 million to $450 million overnight. But partly because it still relies heavily on stores, Staples earned just $4 million on revenue of $1 billion in Europe last year, while Office Depot earned $212 million on sales of $1.6 billion. "They've struggled for the same reasons a lot of American retailers have had problems in Europe," including the high cost of land and restrictive rules in countries like Germany, says Office Depot CEO Bruce Nelson.

10    Investors seem willing to give Sargent the benefit of the doubt, as long as he's outperforming the competition. "They'll be a big beneficiary when the economy rebounds and small business expands," predicts Kevin Beatty, an analyst at MFS Investment Management, a major shareholder. Still, retailers have stumbled over far less ambitious expansion plans. Staples needs near-flawless execution if the handoff from Stemberg to Sargent is to go down in retailing circles as something akin to Gates-to-Ballmer.

Source: "Thinking Outside the Big Box." Symonds, William C. *BusinessWeek Online,* August 11, 2003.

## Case 23

# VW Needs a Jump

1   Volkswagen Chief Executive Bernd Pischetsrieder has laid low since taking the wheel of Europe's Number One automaker a year ago from autocratic Porsche scion Ferdinand Piëch. But that's true to character. As former CEO at BMW, Pischetsrieder had a penchant for planning strategy secretly and painstakingly with a small core of trusted cohorts and then springing decisions on his managers—including the surprise acquisition of Rover in 1994.

2   But investors feel they have waited long enough for the plotting Bavarian to make his bold move. After all, VW's problems were evident when Pischetsrieder took over—aging models, shrinking market share, too many brands of cars built on too few platforms. And as Pischetsrieder mulls his strategy, the situation is deteriorating. Market share in Europe continues to slip. Vehicle sales in the first quarter in the United States dropped almost 11 percent. The Peugeot 206 recently dethroned the VW Golf as the best-selling car in Europe. Golf sales are expected to fall 21 percent this year before the new version hits European showrooms in November. Especially disappointing were sales of VW's new luxury model, the $62,000 Phaeton. Group revenues stalled last year around $95 billion, and net profit dropped 11.2 percent, to $2.7 billion. Tough competition was one reason, but so was VW strategy: Its brands, from Seat to Skoda and VW to Audi, are all built on a handful of underlying platforms, blurring brand image and cannibalizing sales within the group.

3   Pischetsrieder has no time to lose. On April 24, the 54-year-old engineer warned that first-quarter profits will fall sharply. Analysts estimate the decline could be as much as 60 percent. Meanwhile, VW's stock is down more than 40 percent since Pischetsrieder took over. The VW chief insists that 20 new models will buoy unit sales in the second half of 2003, but a flush of younger cars alone will not fix VW's problems. The real challenge is rationalizing overlapping models across VW's four major brands. "Pischetsrieder is facing the mother of all marketing problems," says Stephen B. Cheetham, an analyst at Sanford C. Bernstein & Co. in London.

4   To speed change, Pischetsrieder needs to get his management team in place. "The time is now. These are the last months [for a new CEO] to channel energy in the right direction," says Christoph B. Stürmer, senior analyst at researcher Global Insight Automotive in Frankfurt. Pischetsrieder finally signaled a shakeup at the top on April 8, with the abrupt resignation of Robert Büchelhofer, the board member in charge of sales and marketing. Büchelhofer disagreed with a plan announced by Piëch and Pischetsrieder in 2002 to divide VW brands into two families: the sportier Audi group, including Seat and Lamborghini; and the VW group, made up of VW, Skoda, and Bentley. Under the new groupings, Audi will become a rival to BMW. Volkswagen—literally, "the people's car"—aims to shed its plebian image and offer more comfort and class.

5   But remaking brands and untangling overlapping models is no easy feat. Some models may have to be cut, riling employees and managers. Workers at Skoda in the Czech Republic already are angry about being relegated to making a "lesser VW" after years of strong growth, which fueled fund expansion upmarket into a pricier sedan. Uncertain where they are headed and what products they will make, Skoda workers staged a strike in October to express their discontent. "Skoda, the rising star at VW, now has its wings clipped," says one Frankfurt-based auto analyst.

6   Dealers meanwhile are livid about plans to increase the number of VW-owned dealerships and the failure to revitalize its best-sellers, the Golf and Passat. Faced with falling sales of aging models, recalls, and increasingly thin margins, some dealerships may go bankrupt this year, the Association of Volkswagen Dealers warned.

**7**     The bright spot is Audi, which Pischetsrieder wants to build into the leading premium brand in Europe. Audi spent billions over the past decade on engineering innovation and is several laps ahead of VW in sharpening its image. Powered by its four-wheel-drive models, including the A4 compact and A6 sedan, Audi outsells BMW in Western Europe, ranking second behind Mercedes-Benz among premium brands.

**8**     Yet Piëch's vision of an upmarket Volkswagen has put it on a collision course with Audi. Piëch funded VW's multibillion-dollar expansion into luxury models, such as the Phaeton and the $41,000-plus Touareg SUV, which many say should have belonged to the Audi family. While funding direct challengers to its own Audi unit, the effort siphoned resources from VW's core mass-market products. "VW and Audi share dealerships and showrooms. There is inevitably going to be cannibalization," says George Peterson, president of AutoPacific Group Inc. in Tustin, Calif.

**9**     Pischetsrieder also needs to grapple with VW's high cost base. The government of Volkswagen's home state, Lower Saxony, controls 20 percent of VW shares and traditionally resists layoffs or plant closures and supports the industry's most generous pay agreements. As a result, margins remain under pressure. In March, Pischetsrieder pledged to focus more on profitability and to save $1.1 billion this year, slashing capital spending by 10 percent in tandem with expected lower sales. Lowering capital spending? It works for a time, but it could put future model development at risk.

**10**     A lingering question is whether VW's corporate culture will be resistant to needed change. A brilliant engineer credited with the makeover of Audi, Piëch routinely bypassed middle management at VW—giving direct orders to engineers himself and terrorizing anyone who disagreed with him. Now, VW's traditional civil service-like bureaucracy is reestablishing its rule, setting up a plethora of councils and committees to oversee decision-making. What VW needs is a more market-savvy management that can leverage the company's exceptional strength in engineering. "The big danger is Pischetsrieder doesn't take the organization with him," says one analyst.

**11**     Pischetsrieder is starting to roll up his sleeves. Büchelhofer's departure is already the second boardroom reshuffle since the new CEO took the helm. In September, he appointed former BMW manager Hans Dieter Poetsch as chief financial officer to replace Bruno Adelt at the end of 2003. Adelt has been the focus of investor frustration over VW's opaque financial reporting. "VW is an enigma to analysts, its brands provoke questions in the minds of consumers, and its management earns the scorn of investors," says Jay N. Woodworth, president of consultancy Woodworth Holdings Ltd. in Summit, N.J. Not an enviable legacy. It's time for the Bavarian to act.

Source: "VW Needs a Jump." Edmondson, Gail. *BusinessWeek Online,* May 12, 2003.

**Case 24**

# Winning in China

1  It's a wild night at the old Exhibition Center in Shanghai. The Soviet-style palace, dating from the glory days of Moscow's friendship with the People's Republic, is the unlikely setting for a gala launch of new cellular phones from Motorola Inc. Outside the hall, white Motorola balloons flutter in the brisk winter air, while purple and red spotlights project the company's logo and Chinese slogan, Nih ao Moto (Hello Moto), on the building's pillared facade. Inside, hundreds of guests listen to popular tunes, watch movie trailers, and play games—all on shiny new Motorola phones. Then it's time for a banquet of Kung Pao chicken, shark fin soup, and other Chinese delicacies, while fashion models showing off Motorola handsets strut across the stage to a steady rock beat bouncing off the vast arched ceiling.

2  Quite a show—and a symbolic leap into the future for the American high-tech icon. The January event marked the first time Motorola has launched a new global product line in Asia. The choice of China should come as no surprise. As the world's largest cellular market, with 200 million subscribers, China is the marketing fixation of every company in the industry. And Motorola was a China pioneer. Current Chairman Christopher B. Galvin first visited Shanghai as a rising exec and met with Jiang Zemin—then a little-known local party functionary, now China's President—in 1986. The U.S. giant has been diligently nurturing the Chinese market ever since, investing $3.4 billion in manufacturing and research and development facilities there, more than any other Western company.

3  That commitment has paid off. Motorola sells more cell phones than anyone else in China: nearly 17 million in 2002, according to market researcher Adventis Corp. Last year, Motorola manufactured telecom and other equipment valued at some $5.7 billion in China, selling roughly $2 billion worth abroad—making it one of China's top exporters. Some 20 percent of the company's $26.2 billion 2002 revenue came from China, according to brokerage Bear, Stearns & Co., and Motorola executives confidently predict sales will continue to increase at double-digit rates.

4  Even more important, analysts say Motorola is profitable in China. And its China business is growing faster than that of any other region—big news for a company that has been languishing in the red and is expected to eke out just a small profit globally for 2002. "China has been great for Motorola," says Mike S. Zafirovski, the company's president and chief operating officer, who flew into Shanghai for the big bash. "It's very much a bright spot for our company."

5  But no number of sultry fashion models, flashing billboards, or plates of Kung Pao can hide the fact that the bright spot may soon start to dim. Archrival Nokia has poured $2.4 billion into China and has a giant complex making cell phones and components near Beijing. And Korea's Samsung Electronics is benefiting from looser regulations following China's 2001 entry into the World Trade Organization. Even more ominous for Motorola is new competition from local Chinese handset makers. They had less than 3 percent of the market as late as 1999 but today control some 26 percent, according to Adventis. Meanwhile, Motorola's market share fell to 28 percent last year, from 31 percent in 2000.

6  Motorola is in little immediate danger of losing its lead in China, but there's no denying its local rivals are coming on strong. Many Chinese companies plan to double or triple their capacity, flooding the market with millions more handsets and driving down prices on the low-end phones that have provided Motorola and its multinational rivals the bulk of their China sales. In the past year alone, the average price of a phone in China fell by 15 percent, to $170, according to Beijing-based Norson Telecom Consulting. "If the local guys get too

much market share, that could put huge pressure on Motorola," says Bear Stearns analyst Wojtek Uzdelewicz.

**7**     That's pressure the company can't afford. Outside China, key customers for Motorola's networking gear—wireless operators such as Europe's T-Mobile International and Verizon Communications in the United States—have slashed spending dramatically. Motorola's infrastructure business throws off so little profit that company executives have been open about wanting to sell it. Its semiconductor unit, although recently reorganized, isn't doing much better. And in the United States, Motorola's largest market for cellular phones, subscriber growth has begun to tail off, as nearly half of all Americans already carry phones. The bottom line: Investors have pushed Motorola shares down 60 percent, to $9.50 a share, over the past two years. No wonder China, the source of 30 percent of its handset sales, is a beacon for the company. "This is our most important market," says Scott A. Durchslag, Motorola's corporate vice-president for strategy and business development.

**8**     Yet Motorola has made some recent missteps in that critical market. The company made headlines with its promise to build a $1.5 billion semiconductor plant in Tianjin to make phone-handset chips, even though others in the semiconductor industry questioned whether the fab was needed. The facility was supposed to be one of the most advanced chipmaking factories in China. Today, the building is complete, but because of slack global demand for chips—and a glut of production capacity—the company has been slow to ramp up manufacturing. "We're in small production," says Joe Steinberg, Tianjin-based vice-president and general manager of Motorola's China chip division. "We're not adding capacity. It's prudent to wait until we have something tangible" in terms of demand.

**9**     The chip plant is crucial to Motorola's plans to deepen its roots in China. The company already employs some 1,300 Chinese engineers doing research for products such as mobile-phone handsets, semiconductors for PCs, and speech software. Motorola is also hiring more local designers, since China's millions of cellular subscribers are growing increasingly savvy and trend-conscious. "The Chinese have become very knowledgeable about phones," says Brian Holmes, Motorola's senior director for product marketing in China. "They do their homework."

**10**     So Motorola is putting more of an emphasis on models with flair. Consumers and analysts have criticized Motorola's Chinese phones as technology winners with ho-hum design, especially when compared with the gee-whiz models sold by local rivals. TCL International Holdings, a Hong Kong-listed manufacturer in Guangdong province, features a diamond-encrusted handset. Eastcom, a state-owned enterprise near Shanghai, sells a $425 phone that's covered in specially treated fish skin. To fight back, Motorola has introduced a faux-diamond-studded handset of its own. And it is hoping mainland consumers will fall for phones that can better handle Chinese-language text messages and can double as karaoke machines or e-books—features local rivals have a hard time matching. "In the past, Motorola's reputation was more for good quality. Now it's much more trendy," says Tim Chen, Beijing-based chairman of Motorola's China operations.

**11**     These days, Motorola is stressing the idea that its phones are fun. Of the 20-plus new models that Motorola will launch in China this year, at least a dozen will be phones that can send and receive photos, says Brian Lu, Beijing-based vice-president and general manager of Motorola's Greater China handset group. Lu vows that such products will tame the ambitions of Motorola's local rivals. "It will be difficult for [Chinese handset makers] in the long haul," he says. "They don't control the technology. They don't control the R&D. They own only a very small piece of the value chain."

**12**     Yet the Chinese may be stronger than Lu thinks. Take Ningbo Bird Co., a Chinese mobile-phone manufacturer that is currently ranked Number Six in China but is growing at a torrid pace. Ningbo Bird last year made more than 7 million phones and has just opened two new factories that boost its capacity to 20 million phones annually. Not bad for a company in only its third full year of mobile-phone production. "We want to be Number One in China," declares Ma Sitian, the company's deputy general manager. And even though Ningbo Bird initially relied on France's Sagem for its system designs, it now has technology partnerships with others, including LG of South Korea and BenQ of Taiwan.

**13**    The ability to buy technology off the shelf has helped Ningbo Bird to prosper even without a vertically integrated manufacturing and R&D operation like Motorola's. Furthermore, Ningbo Bird is boosting its own R&D capabilities and designed 15 percent of the phones it made last year—although none of them has the advanced features that Motorola claims will set it apart. Still, with all of its new capacity, Ningbo Bird will be looking to markets beyond China, starting in Southeast Asia. "The competition will be even more intense, so we have to export," says Ma.

**14**    That's what should scare Motorola the most. Virtually every product made in China—from sneakers to DVD players—quickly drops in price as manufacturers gain scale and low-paid workers churn out goods by the container-load. At the same time, even as demand for cell phones continues to climb in China, the rate of growth is slowing. So, like Ningbo Bird, other Chinese rivals will begin selling their phones abroad, potentially hurting Motorola's sales worldwide. With 1 billion mobile users today, most of the world's wealthiest people already have phones, says Ross O'Brien, Asia-Pacific director for telecommunications consultant Pyramid Research. Expanding the number of users will now require ever-more drastic price cuts. "You have to take the market down a notch," O'Brien says. "This is where China's vendors have the upper hand."

**15**    Team Motorola is determined to avoid that trap. To stay ahead of the game in China even as its handset business comes under increasing pressure, Motorola has hatched a strategy that executives dub "Two plus three plus three." The "two" refers to Motorola's primary operations in China, manufacturing and R&D. The first "three" refers to the businesses Motorola wants to expand there: semiconductor production, broadband equipment, and digital-trunking networks (the mobile-communications systems used by police, taxi drivers, and delivery fleets). The final "three" refers to targets Motorola has set for yearend 2006: $10 billion worth of production in China, purchases of $10 billion worth of components in the country, and $10 billion in direct or indirect investment by Motorola and its partners. In short, the company wants to cut costs via local sourcing and boost its strength in new areas where there are fewer worries about Chinese rivals flooding the market with me-too products.

**16**    A critical part of Motorola's strategy is to show Beijing its commitment to the Chinese economy. That's especially important given that local rivals are usually government-owned and have good *guanxi,* or connections, with local officials. Motorola, though, contends that it is as Chinese as any of its rivals, with more than 10,000 employees in the country—roughly the same number as Ningbo Bird. "We take pride in viewing ourselves as a very local company in China," says COO Zafirovski. And since Motorola isn't blind to Beijing's desire to boost China's science and technology prowess, it recently announced a $100 million expansion of an R&D center in the capital. Chinese officials appreciate the effort. "There is a lot of trust on the Chinese side because Motorola has put a lot of investment into the country," says Craig Watts, an analyst with Norson Telecom Consulting.

**17**    Motorola is even prepared to work with the companies that are eating away at its top position in handsets. The company has agreed to sell chips for cell phones to TCL and Eastcom. As a bonus, if Motorola can get local manufacturers on its customer list, the Tianjin chip fab might see enough business to get the production lines running full-bore. "The market will come back by the end of 2003," Chen says.

**18**    Motorola's Chinese adventure has been a great success so far, even as local rivals nip at its heels. Motorola "is well established," says Duncan Clark, an analyst with Beijing-based telecom consultant BDA China Ltd. "It will take some time to dislodge them." Given the threat to Motorola's market share in China, though, the company has to keep moving—especially in light of its history elsewhere. Bear Stearns estimates that since the mid-'90s, Motorola's market share in handsets has slipped from about 50 percent to 30 percent in the United States and from more than 30 percent to less than 10 percent in Europe. In the context of those setbacks, China is the gamble Motorola has to win.

Source: "Winning in China." Einhorn, Bruce, Roberts, Dexter, and Crockett, Roger O. *BusinessWeek Online,* January 27, 2003.

Case 25

# Yahoo! Act Two

**1**   When Terry S. Semel walked into the Sunnyvale (Calif.) headquarters of Yahoo! (YHOO) Inc. for his first day as chief executive on May 1, 2001, he faced an unenviable task. Ad sales at the Internet icon were plummeting, and the new CEO was replacing the well-liked Timothy Koogle, who had been pushed aside by the company's board. Worse, leery employees quickly saw that Semel, a retired Hollywood exec, didn't know Internet technology and looked stiffly out of place at Yahoo's playful, egalitarian headquarters. Would this guy tour the Valley in the purple Yahoo car, as Koogle did, or play a Yahoo kazoo? Fat chance. And instead of bunking in nearby Atherton or Palo Alto, like other Silicon Valley execs, he rode off every evening in a chauffeured SUV to a luxury suite at San Francisco's Four Seasons Hotel.

**2**   Two years after taking control as chairman and CEO, Semel has silenced the doubters. By imposing his buttoned-down management approach on Yahoo, the 60-year-old has engineered one of the most remarkable revivals of a beleaguered dot-com. Once paralyzed by management gridlock and written off as another overhyped has-been, Yahoo is roaring back. The company earned $43 million on revenues of $953 million in 2002, compared with a $93 million loss in 2001 on $717 million in sales. And Yahoo's momentum is growing. Net income hit $47 million in this year's first quarter as revenues powered ahead 47 percent. Analysts predict that this year's profits will quadruple, to more than $200 million, while sales climb 33 percent, to $1.3 billion. "What he has done is just phenomenal," says Hollywood pal Barry Diller, CEO of USA Interactive (USAI) Inc., a Yahoo competitor.

**3**   Semel has done nothing less than remake the culture of the quintessential Internet company. The new Yahoo is grounded by a host of Old Economy principles that Semel lugged up the coast from Los Angeles. The contrast with Yahoo's go-go days is stark. At Terry Semel's Yahoo, spontaneity is out. Order is in. New initiatives used to roll ahead following free-form brainstorming and a gut check. Now, they wind their way through a rugged gauntlet of tests and analysis. Only a few make the grade. It's a wrenching change. But Semel's self-effacing style, honed over years of navigating through the towering egos of Hollywood, helps soften the shock.

**4**   Yahoo's newfound success does, too. Semel has used the dealmaking skills that made him a legend in the movie business to land crucial acquisitions and partnerships that are producing rich new revenues for Yahoo. A deal with phone giant SBC Communications (SBC) Inc. launched Yahoo into the business of selling broadband access to millions of American homes—which should add $70 million in revenue this year. The buyout of HotJobs.com (YHOO) last year put Yahoo into the online job-hunting business, adding $80 million in revenue. Most important, a partnership with Overture Services (OVER) Inc. to carry ads on Yahoo's search-results pages is gushing some $230 million in revenue this year. The upshot? Semel's new businesses should make up half of Yahoo's top line in 2003. "We planted a lot of seeds a year and a half ago, and some are beginning to grow," he says.

**5**   Semel's strategy is gaining fans on Wall Street—and stoking new fears of a mini-Internet bubble. The company's shares have soared 200 percent in the past eight months, to $26. Sure, Yahoo's market capitalization is a mere 13 percent of its giddy all-time high of $127 billion in early 2000. But today's price-earnings ratio of 79 is triple that of heavyweight Microsoft (MSFT) Corp. and more than eBay (EBAY) Inc.'s 67, despite the online auctioneer's heftier revenues, profits, and growth projections. "Yahoo's valuation is a tough case to make," concedes Firsthand Funds Chief Investment Officer Kevin Landis, who nonetheless has bought 50,000 Yahoo shares in the past eight months based on the portal's turnaround and brighter industry trends.

6     Investors are betting on Semel to follow up his bold debut with a sizzling encore. Call it Act Two. For this next stage of growth, Semel envisions building Yahoo into a digital Disneyland, a souped-up theme park for the Internet Age. The idea is that Web surfers logging on to Yahoo's site, like customers squeezing through the turnstiles in Anaheim, will find themselves in a self-contained world full of irresistible offerings.

7     In the past, Yahoo attracted visitors with free services such as stock quotes and headlines and drew 90 percent of its revenue from online ads. Now, Semel is trying to charge for many services, coaxing Web surfers to spend hard cash on everything from digital music and online games to job listings and premium e-mail accounts with loads of extra storage. Already, he pulls in one-third of revenue from such offerings and hopes to drive it up to 50 percent by 2004. To do that, analysts say, he's likely to cut deals to add online travel and classified ads for cars.

8     But nothing is more key to Semel's strategy than his push into broadband. Lots of the services he's banking on, such as music and interactive games, are data hogs that appeal mostly to customers with high-speed links. Plus, broadband is always on, so many of Yahoo's customers will be lingering in Semel's theme park for hours on end, day after day. "The more time you spend on Yahoo, the more apt you are to sample both free and paid services," he says.

9     If Semel can pull it off, the new Yahoo could become one of the few enduring powerhouses on the Net. Customers who pay for its services could more than triple, to 10 million in 2005 from 2.9 million now, analysts predict. Profits could soar 75 percent over the next two years, to $350 million, and sales could surge 30 percent, to $1.7 billion, analysts say. "Yahoo has emerged as a durable digital franchise," says Alberto W. Vilar, president of Amerindo Investment Advisors Inc., which has an undisclosed stake. "If you take the long view, this stock could still double or triple."

10     But Semel doesn't have a monopoly on digital theme parks. AOL Time Warner (AOL) Inc. and Microsoft's MSN are pushing nearly identical agendas—and both boast advantages over Yahoo. AOL, despite its merger headaches, can tap into popular content from the world's largest media company, from CNN to Warner Music. MSN benefits from the software muscle and cash hoard of Microsoft, as well as broadband partnerships that cover 27 percent more lines into homes and businesses than Yahoo's SBC deal. It also may have an easier time getting Web surfers to pay for new offerings. "Yahoo's brand is built on free information services," says MSN Group Product Manager Lisa Gurry. She says coaxing Yahoo customers to pull out their wallets will be "very challenging."

11     An even greater challenge is coming from a newer competitor, Google Inc. In just four years, Google has turned into a global sensation and is now widely regarded as the preeminent search engine on earth. The risk to Yahoo is that the search king will give birth to a more potent business model. Instead of flocking to flashy theme parks such as Yahoo's, consumers are already starting to rely on Google's uncluttered search to find everything they need. Already, some online advertisers are moving their ad dollars to search engines. "We're shifting our emphasis away from portals [such as Yahoo, AOL, and MSN]," says Alan Rimm-Kaufman, vice-president for marketing at electronics retailer Crutchfield Corp. "The people stealing these ad dollars are [companies] like Google."

12     Hot competition in the search business could force Semel's next big move. His partnership with Overture, a company that delivers Internet advertising, is producing some 20 percent of Yahoo's revenues. Microsoft's MSN has a similar deal with Overture that also is paying off richly. Analysts say Semel could make an offer for Overture—if he thinks it's necessary to preempt a Microsoft acquisition. He is already sitting on $2.2 billion in cash, 50 percent more than the likely price tag for Overture. Still, Semel likely won't make a bid unless he's pushed into it because of the distractions of such a large merger. Yahoo and Overture declined comment on a possible deal.

**13**  Distraction is something Yahoo can ill afford as it adapts to the changes ahead. To date, Semel has honed the company's execution—cutting costs, filtering out iffy ideas, pursuing sure things, and making money. It's the perfect model for today's sickly market. But when the slump ends, new ideas will likely make a dramatic comeback. These could define the next generation of the Internet. The question is whether Yahoo, with its careful and laborious vetting process for new projects, risks losing out to Google or getting blindsided by a nimble newcomer.

**14**  Can Semel innovate, beat back the rising tide of competition, and live up to the latest round of great expectations for Yahoo? If he plays his cards right, yes. Despite the advantages of AOL and MSN, Yahoo has kept its position as the most popular site on the Web, according to Nielsen/Net Ratings. Yahoo claims 232 million monthly visitors. Semel is demonstrating the skills to turn this large chunk of humanity into paying customers, boosting the customer count eightfold, from 375,000 when he arrived two years ago. To combat Google, Semel is hurrying to beef up Yahoo's search capabilities. He closed a $290 million deal for search company Inktomi (YHOO) in March, and the marketing campaign to promote it blasted off in New York's Times Square on May 19. "Yahoo has reemerged as a potent force," says Derek Brown, an analyst at Pacific Growth Equities. "It's well-positioned to leverage its massive global user base and dominant brand."

**15**  The CEO's low-key approach has worked quiet magic through a 40-year career. When Brooklyn-born Semel arrived as a sales trainee at Warner Bros. in 1965, the 22-year-old accountant had little relevant experience but an understated confidence in himself. In an industry brimming with ego, Semel stayed offstage and worked to shine the light on others. It paid dividends. As he moved from Warner Bros. to Buena Vista and back again, Semel rose to the top on a vast network of friends and allies. He used these, along with his formidable negotiating skills, to create a giant. In a two-decade partnership as co-CEO with Bob Daly, Semel turned Warner Bros. from a $1 billion studio to an $11 billion behemoth, producing megahits such as *The Matrix*.

**16**  Through his retirement in 1999, Semel kept up the winning formula, making friends and minting millions. He says that in their two decades together, he and Daly never fought. If such a smooth track record is rare in high tech, it's even more uncommon in Hollywood. "When you're releasing 20 or 25 movies a year, you're navigating a minefield every weekend," says Barry M. Meyer, chairman and CEO of Warner Bros. Entertainment Inc. and a longtime Semel colleague. "His success at Yahoo does not surprise me at all."

**17**  It was Yahoo co-founder Jerry Yang who nudged Semel toward Yahoo in 2001. The two had met two years earlier at a media conference and had hit it off. By the spring of 2001, Yahoo was reeling from the falloff in Net advertising and needed a major overhaul. The question was whether the wealthy Semel, who was already dabbling in online entertainment companies, would dive into one of the biggest of them all at a time of crisis. Semel signed on with the proviso that Koogle step down as chairman.

**18**  When the new chief arrived, he ran into a few troubling surprises. Semel was shocked early on to learn that Yahoo did not have the technology in place to handle surging demand for services such as online personals, say two former executives. That spelled months of delay before Semel could push premium offerings.

**19**  Then there were the cultural challenges. Initially, Semel balked at the company's "cubicles only" policy, finally settling into a cube adjacent to a conference room so he could make phone calls in private. He stayed free of the Valley social scene, spending weeknights at the hotel in San Francisco and flying his private jet home to his swanky Los Angeles neighborhood of Bel Air on weekends.

**20**  Morale was also an issue. Compared with his predecessor, the relaxed and chatty Koogle, known by the troops as T. K., Semel came off at first as cold and rough. He chopped down the 44 business units he inherited to 5, stripping many execs of pet projects. Veteran Yahoo execs prodded Semel to mingle more with the rank and file and pushed him into grabbing lunch more often at the campus cafeteria. Still, such forays often fell flat. "T. K. was just one of the guys," says a former Yahoo manager. "When Semel talked to you, it felt like he was consciously making an effort to talk to employees."

21    Soon, Semel's strengths started to shine through. With his focus and dealmaking savvy, he appeared to have the tools to rescue Yahoo. Employees, with loads of underwater stock options, increasingly cheered him on. "People don't always agree with the direction they're getting, but they're happy the direction is there," says a current Yahoo manager who requested anonymity.

22    Walk through Yahoo's headquarters, past the purple cow in the lobby, the acres of cubicles, the workers in jeans, and you might think T. K. was still running the place. But sitting across from Semel, the change is evident. His voice quiet and steady, his language cordial yet deliberate, Semel seems incapable of the hype that once vaulted companies such as Yahoo into the stratosphere. This is the voice of the post-dot-com era. He steers attention to his colleagues. "I love [my managers] to do their homework," he says. "I love them to help make decisions, and they do. Somewhere in that process, I'll include myself—or they'll include me."

23    Semel's not kidding about the homework. In the old days, Yahoo execs would brainstorm for hours, often following hunches with new initiatives. Those days are long gone. Under Semel, managers must prepare exhaustively before bringing up a new idea if it's to have a chance to survive.

24    It's a Darwinian drama that takes place in near-weekly meetings of a group called the Product Council. Dreamed up by a couple of vice-presidents and championed by Semel and his chief operating officer, Daniel Rosensweig, a former president of CNET Networks (CNET) Inc., the group typically includes nine managers from all corners of the company. It's chaired by Geoff Ralston and often includes key lieutenants such as Jeff Weiner and Jim Brock, all senior vice-presidents. The group sizes up business plans to make sure all new projects bring benefits to Yahoo's existing businesses. "We need to work within a framework," says Semel. "If it's a free-for-all . . . we won't take advantage of the strengths of our company."

25    For years, managers built up their own niches around the main Yahoo site. No one, say former and current execs, appeared to be thinking about the portal as a whole, much less how the various bits and pieces could work together. "Managers would beg, borrow, and steal from the network to help their own properties," says Greg Coleman, Yahoo's executive vice-president for media and sales.

26    Semel wants to stitch it all together. He calls the concept "network optimization" and says it's a key goal for 2003. The idea is that every initiative should not only make money but also feed Yahoo's other businesses. It's the painstaking job of establishing these interconnections that eats up much of the time at council meetings. And the winnowing process is brutal. Of the 79 current ideas for premium services at some stage of planning inside Yahoo, only a few will launch in 2003, predicts Rosensweig.

27    Although some critics worry that innovative ideas may never see the light of day under Semel's tight control, he dismisses the prospect. Semel stresses instead the potential payoff: less clutter and a handful of high-performance services that feed each other. For a success story, he points to the company's recently relaunched search capabilities. Search for "pizza" and type in your area code, and Yahoo culls its Yellow Pages site to return addresses and driving maps to nearby pizza joints. Yahoo is the only heavyweight portal that integrates content this deeply with its search features.

28    Such smart execution was in dangerously short supply at Yahoo in the past. At the height of the Net bubble, Yahoo came off as arrogant. Its attitude, recalls Jeff Bell, a marketing vice-president at DaimlerChrysler (DCX) Corp., was "Buy our stuff, and shut up." Semel has turned that around, hiring traditional media sales veterans and introducing more flexibility. The payoff: As the online ad market has recovered, advertisers are flocking back to Yahoo. Daimler's Bell says his Yahoo ad budget has doubled over the past two years.

**29**    Entertainment companies are joining the rush to buy key Yahoo ad space. Some 42 movies advertised on Yahoo in the first quarter, up from zilch in the first quarter of 2001. "Getting a presence on Yahoo's home page is huge," says Sarah Beatty, a senior marketing vice-president at USA Network, which is running seven ad campaigns on Yahoo in 2003.

**30**    Semel has supplemented Yahoo's ad revenues with dealmaking in other businesses. Consider the SBC pact to market broadband Net access. SBC pays Yahoo about $5 out of the $40 to $60 customers pay each month for service. Revenues from the deal should jump from $70 million this year to $125 million in 2004.

**31**    Still, Yahoo remains vulnerable in broadband. MSN has cut similar deals with Verizon (VZ) Communications and Qwest Communications (Q) International Inc., which have 75 million lines to homes and businesses, versus SBC's 59 million. Semel's efforts to land other broadband deals have come up short. More worrisome is the fragile nature of these partnerships. If SBC concludes that the Yahoo brand isn't a big draw, it could cut Yahoo out and save itself millions. An SBC spokesman says it is "happy" with Yahoo.

**32**    Of all Semel's deals, none shines brighter than the partnership with Overture Services. The companies team up to sell ads near Yahoo's search results, a business known as "paid search." If a user searches for "cookware," for instance, advertisers from Macy's (FD) to Sur La Table can bid to showcase their links near the results. Overture delivers the advertisers and forks over roughly two-thirds of the revenue. While Yahoo had debated such a partnership for years under Koogle, Semel drove it through in a hurry.

**33**    Just in time for paid search to blossom into the latest Web sensation. The partnership notched Yahoo more than $130 million in revenues last year—14 percent of its business. Analysts expect revenues from the partnership to increase 75 percent in 2003, accounting for nearly 20 percent of Yahoo's revenues.

**34**    That assumes that Google won't spoil Yahoo's fun. The wildly popular search engine has emerged as the fourth-most-trafficked site on the Internet, with an estimated $700 million in 2003 revenues. And the world may be heading Google's way. Industry analysts say that as Web surfers gain expertise, they visit general-interest sites such as Yahoo less and instead cut to the chase by typing in keywords on a search engine. According to analytics firm WebSideStory, the percentage of website visitors arriving via search engines doubled in the past year, to 13 percent.

**35**    Google's strength puts Semel in a bind. He licenses Google's search engine, which is popular among Yahoo's users. Trouble is, by keeping Google on Yahoo, he publicly endorses a rival. His likely goal, say analysts, is to replace Google soon with Inktomi, the search engine he acquired in March. That would save $13 million a year in licensing and pull the plug on Yahoo's apparent backing of Google. The danger? If Yahoo's Google-loving customers balk at switching to Inktomi, they could ditch Yahoo and surf straight to the Google site.

**36**    His answer is a national marketing campaign to boost Yahoo as a search brand. It kicked off on May 19 in New York's Times Square with the unveiling of a huge computer-screen ad featuring live searches on the Yahoo site. At street level in New York, teams of Yahoo's costumed "searchers" paraded among the crowds waving five-foot-long search bars.

**37**    It's all part of the growing buzz at Yahoo. Using his mix of discipline, sales, and dealmaking, Terry Semel has pulled off a stunning revival. But can he pull off Act Two and build Yahoo into the digital theme park of his dreams? If he does, Semel will be one of the biggest winners: When he took the helm, he bought 1 million shares of Yahoo at $17 apiece. Those shares are up 60 percent. The fact that Yahoo shares are banging on the ceiling and not the floor is a vivid sign that Semel's turnaround may be just getting started.

Source: "Yahoo! Act Two" Elgin, Ben, and Grover, Ronald. *BusinessWeek Online*, June 2, 2003.

## Case 26  A Note on the Cuban Cigar Industry

### Akash Kapoor

1   The air was thick with anticipation. The tension was palpable. In 2002, Cuba was preparing to receive former U.S. President Jimmy Carter, the first U.S. president to visit Cuba following the embargo. Business leaders in the Northern Hemisphere were very attentive, as the possibility of a softening in U.S.–Cuban relations could lead to an easing of the embargo's restrictions, and the resumption of trade with the largest trading block in the Northern Hemisphere. John Hernandez, a recent MBA graduate from a prestigious institution in Canada and an avid cigar smoker, viewed this scenario and wondered what effect the visit could have on the current environment, and if there was potential to enter the Cuban cigar industry. With an inheritance of $1 million coming available in the next month, he thought back to his strategy sessions and looked to evaluate this industry.

## HISTORY

2   The history of Cuba and tobacco are interwoven. When Columbus arrived in Cuba, little did he know that the medicinal herb enjoyed by the natives would become the scourge of society to some and a multibillion-dollar industry worldwide. Although the origin of tobacco is still disputed, as is the derivation of the name tobacco, its introduction to Western civilization is well documented and accepted as owing to the expedition to the "New World" of Christopher Columbus.

3   Columbus sailed to the Americas in 1492. In his quest for the riches of the Orient, he came across a race of native people, called the Taino, who were smoking tobacco leaves roughly rolled into a shape which they called "cohiba." It is written by Batholomeu de las Casa of the first expedition into Cuba,

> These two Christians met many people on the road . . . men always with a firebrand in their hands, and certain herbs to take their smokes, which are some dried herbs put in a certain leaf . . . after the fashion of a musket . . . such as boys make at the feast of the Holy Ghost. These are lit at one end and the other end they chew or suck, and take it in with their breath the smoke. These were claimed to drive away all weariness, and were called Tobago.[1]

[1]Tabago, published by H. F. & Ph. F. Reemstra, Cigarette Makers, Germany, 1960.

**IVEY**

Richard Ivey School of Business
The University of Western Ontario

Akash Kapoor prepared this case under the supervision of Professor Paul W. Beamish solely to provide material for class discussion. The authors do not intend to illustrate either effective or ineffective handling of a managerial situation. The authors may have disguised certain names and other identifying information to protect confidentiality. Ivey Management Services prohibits any form of reproduction, storage or transmittal without its written permission. This material is not covered under authorization from CanCopy or any reproduction rights organization. To order copies or request permission to reproduce materials, contact Ivey Publishing, Ivey Management Services, c/o Richard Ivey School of Business, The University of Western Ontario, London, Ontario, Canada, N6A 3K7; phone (519) 661-3208; fax (519) 661-3882; e-mail cases@ivey.uwo.ca. Copyright © 2003, Ivey Management Services. Version: (A) 2003-02-04. One time permission granted by Ivey Management Services on July 8, 2003.

**4**    Tobacco was brought to the Western world after this expedition, and the Spaniards held a monopoly over the tobacco trade for many years. Cuba was considered to be Spain's lifeline between the Old and New Worlds. However, in 1762, Britain invaded and briefly dominated the island. During this brief period, Cuba was opened to worldwide trade and a new found prosperity. When Spain retook control one year later, trade restrictions were imposed; however, the seeds of prosperity had been planted in the community. In 1817, Spain removed trade restrictions and began a period of renewed prosperity. World demand for Cuban products was so high that in 1845, tobacco replaced coffee as the second most important agricultural product, and demand for Cuban tobacco continued to increase.[2] In the 1850s, paper bands were introduced in Cuba to distinguish the many prestigious brands of cigars. The powerful and wealthy members of high society soon wanted custom-designed bands as symbols of their importance and taste. Hence, the Cuban cigar established a reputation as an "accoutrement of wealth, power and prestige."[3]

**5**    In 1868, the first of two upheavals in the Cuban cigar industry took place. The Ten Years' War saw a number of growers flee the country for America, taking with them prized Cuban seed. Key West and Tampa were major beneficiaries of this migration.

**6**    The second upheaval came at the time of the revolution between 1959 and 1962. When Fidel Castro overthrew then-President Batista and nationalized approximately $1 billion of U.S.-owned property, the U.S. government subsequently imposed an economic blockade on Cuba. This action was a shock to the island's economy, as the United States was one of its largest trading partners. The revolution was a major and unexpected catalyst for worldwide competition, as Cuba saw a major departure of its key players in the industry. Not only did they bring seed, but they brought their knowledge, skill and expertise, keys to cigar making and production.

**7**    The first exodus gave the U.S. cigar industry a major boost, the ability to produce a cigar of similar quality sold at a much lower price. The revolution had a far greater impact on the Cuban cigar industry exodus of many key players and workers to other countries. This essentially opened the doors of the cigar industry to competition, as growers, manufacturers, rollers and actual Cuban seed and knowledge found their way to the United States, Dominican Republic and Honduras, to name but a few. In 1997, 250 million cigars were exported from the Dominican Republic, an example of the market which United States cigar consumers represent.

**8**    The Cuban revolution also brought with it a command economy, and the cigar industry in Cuba was not spared. The entire industry was placed under state control, and the celebrated brands of Cuban cigars were disbanded in favor of nameless cigars. However, after the disastrous response to these cigars and their horrendous quality, the state reinstituted the brands and allowed 'private farming' for tobacco plantations. It would take until the 1970s before they fully re-established the reputation that Cuban cigars had enjoyed for centuries.

**9**    In 1975, the World Court ruled that exiled Cuban cigar makers had the right to use their former brand names. Many great cigar families who had left their homeland, such as the Cifuentes family (Partagas) and the Menendez family (Montecristo), wished to continue production of their brand name cigars, and the ruling gave them the opportunity. This is why, in many cases, there are two versions of many Cuban brands: those produced with Cuban tobacco and those produced with non-Cuban tobacco. The families produced their own to-

---

[2]L. Glenn Westfall, *Don Vicente Martinez Ybor, The Man and His Empire: Development of the Clear Havana Industry in Cuba and Florida in the Nineteenth Century,* Garland Publishing, Inc., New York and London, c. 1987.

[3]Nathanial Lande and Andrew Lande, "The Havanas: Past, Present, and Future," *Smoke Magazine,* Summer 1998, Volume III, Issue 3.

bacco, and developed new packaging and cigar bands for their new versions of cigars. Partagas, Montecristo, Upmann, Hoyo de Monterrey, and Romeo y Julieta are some of the examples of Cuban brands that have dual versions.

10    Originally, Cuban tobacco leaves were shipped to Spain for rolling in the factories; however, when the shipments arrived and it was found that the fabricated cigars survived the journey in much better condition than the actual leaf, the cigar factories in Cuba were established. It is from these humble beginnings that the myth of the Havana cigar was born and continues to pervade today.

### The Product

11    The cigar has remained much the same over hundreds of years. There are three basic types of cigar produced in Cuba: handmade, hand-finished and machine-made. Structurally, the difference among the three is that handmade cigars use long filler and are bunched and rolled entirely by hand, whereas hand-finished cigars are bunched by machine and only the wrapper is put on by hand. Machine-made cigars are fully automated and generally use short filler and a composite binder. Long filler refers to a full tobacco leaf, short filler to cut up or leftover tobacco. The finished product, the cigar itself, comes in many different shapes and sizes. The distinction between brands comes from the blend used in the filler, the type of binder and the wrapper used to finish the product. These "recipes" are closely guarded secrets. The product itself however does not complete the package. It is at this point that the marketing and the mystique of the Havana cigar begins to take the product from the workers bench to the consumer. The bands, the boxes and the traditions were all elements of the Havana cigar.

### The Plants

12    The cigar is constructed from the leaves of two different tobacco plants. One plant yields the filler (tripa) and the binder (capote) of the cigar, and the other yields the wrapper (capa).

13    The Havana cigar contains leaves from two different types of tobacco plants, the criollo plant and the corojo plant. The criollo plant produces the tobacco to be blended and the binder that holds the tobacco together. The corojo plant produces the wrapper that finishes the cigar and dictates its final appearance. Recently, the Cubans have been experimenting with new strains of tobacco that are more resistant to the elements and pests, scourges of the tobacco industry. The criollo plant is grown in the sun; the corojo, or other strain for the wrapper, is grown under muslin cloth to protect it and to maintain a uniform leaf color and texture. This tending and careful harvesting of the wrapper leaves adds to the cost of the production.

14    Growing tobacco is a nine-month to 10-month process, beginning in the summer months with tilling and ground preparation, and ending with the harvesting of the leaves from January through March. Harvesting is a very large undertaking that takes time, patience and much labor. Therefore, the fields are planted a few weeks apart so harvesting is also staggered.

15    The various leaves on each tobacco plant are harvested on different days. A typical tobacco plant has 16 to 18 leaves. Pickers start from the bottom and work to the top, or coronas, because the leaves at the bottom of the plant ripen earlier. As such, harvesting occurs over a staggered period. The leaves at different levels are given different classifications, and their uses differ based on their characteristics. There are only five major categories; capa, capote, and those used for the filler, volado, seco and ligero. The picking of the leaves requires a great deal of judgment and experience on the part of the growers, as explained by one of Cuba's most revered tobacco growers, Don Alejandro Robaina.

Too early or too late, the cigar will not be good. You have to take the leaf at the precise moment.[4]

16 When the leaves are picked they are green. They are loaded into carts and taken to curing barns, or casas del tabaco. The drying process usually takes 50 days. Inside the barns, the leaves are strung with needles and threaded onto long poles. During the curing process, the leaves turn to a light brown. Once this occurs, they are removed from the barns and prepared for the first fermentation. This process allows the tobacco to undergo chemical changes, enhancing the flavor and aroma, while reducing the bitterness and the impurities within the tobacco. This first fermentation takes about 30 days. Depending upon the leaves, they are then classified and perhaps stripped of their stems. A second fermentation follows and lasts up to 60 days. The tobacco is then aired and packed in large square bales called tercios. These bales weigh about 150 pounds (68 kilograms) and are covered with royal palm leaves and burlap. The bales may be stored in the warehouse for up to two years before being shipped to the factories for cigar production.

### Putting the Cigar Together

17 The long-held legend of the Havana being rolled on the thighs of virgins is a fanciful myth. A journalist in the 1940s observed female workers sorting leaves and placing the piles in their laps, and the legend was born. The actual construction of the cigar is less fantastical, yet requires a great deal of skill and experience from the torcedores, or rollers. A cigar is put together by taking different leaves from the criollo plant and blending them according to the recipes that the master blender carefully guards and prepares. Many blends have been passed down from generation to generation, while others are newly conceived for new brands. Generally there will be up to three leaves in the blend, a combination of the ligero, seco and volado leaves. These leaves are placed on top of each other in the correct blend and formed carefully to ensure proper tightness and construction. The binder is then used to bunch the blended tobacco. After a process of shaping the bunches in pressed moulds, the wrapper is stretched over the bunched, formed leaves. The torcedores shape the wrapper to the correct size with a chaveta, or semi-circular knife. A piece is then taken from the excess wrapper to make the head of the cigar, which holds the cigar together. This is put on with an odorless, tasteless vegetable gum. The cigar is then inspected for girth and length and is then taken through a rigorous process of fumigation and aging, and then through to quality control for inspection, grading and presentation. The drying and aging of the cigars is necessary to remove excess moisture from the cigars, and to remove the harshness from the new cigar. A good roller in Cuba can produce 100 to 150 cigars a day. Machine-made cigars can be produced in quantity of 10,000 cigars a day. It is the premium cigars, however, that Cuba has been focused on to this point.

### Tobacco Growing Regions

18 The five main tobacco growing regions in Cuba are: Oriente (Eastern Provinces), Remedios (Villa Clara Province), Partidos (Eastern la Habano Province), Semi-Vuelta and the famed Vuelta Abajo (in Pinar del Rio Province) (see Exhibit 1). The average temperature is 25°C (75°F) and the average relative humidity is around 80 percent. The pinnacle of these regions is the Vuelta and Semi-Vuelta areas in the Pinar del Rio region. It is believed that this region is the cradle of the Havanas, producing the finest tobacco in the world. It is from this region that the tobacco and wrappers for the super premium cigars comes. Approximately 70 percent of all tobacco grown in Cuba is harvested here.[5] The distinction here is

[4]Jonathan Futrell and Lisa Linder, *Up in Smoke*, Conran Octopus Limited, London, c. 1998.
[5]"The Cigar Market." *Business Tips on Cuba*, July 1998, Printed in La Habana, Cuba.

**EXHIBIT 1** **Map of Cuba**

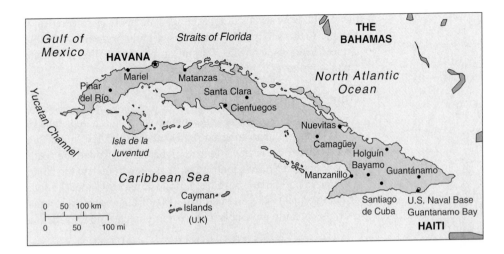

**Map of Tobacco Growing Regions in Cuba**

- VUELTA ABAJO
- SEMI-VUELTA
- REMEDIOS
- PARTIDO
- ORIENTE

the soil and the microclimate that keeps the humidity ideal for growing and cultivating tobacco. The private (run by families) farm system in Cuba also allows family traditions and secrets to remain and be passed on, in spite of the constant demand and pressure to increase yields. The Cuban government has been the only buyer of the output from these farms since the revolution. The other regions are not as famous as the Vuelta Abajo region, which is the only region that produces all the components used in the cigar; however, they do also produce some cigar quality tobacco. Generally speaking, the tobaccos from the other regions are used as follows: from the Partido region, the tobacco is used for wrappers; from the Semi-Vuelta, tobacco is used for filler and cigarettes; from the Oriente and Remedios regions, the tobacco is used for filler, cigarettes and for export to overseas markets. Thus, the very best tobacco of the Vuleta Abajo is in finite supply, and should the industry need to expand, these other regions may become a significant part of the future industry.

### Pests and Disasters

19    In all the regions, the farmers and growers are most concerned with the conditions of the plantations and the climate. A major crop can be decimated and yields can be affected within days should the climate become too extreme or disease become introduced into the crop. A major concern for growers is a disease called blue mould. It is a mildew that thrives in adverse climatic conditions and can destroy entire crops within days. It has affected all the major tobacco growing regions in the Caribbean at one time, and was more of a threat in Cuba when the economic crisis prevented the purchase of sufficient pesticides to combat

the mould. New strains of tobacco seed are being engineered and tested that may have a resistance to this scourge; however, this is always a significant variable which the industry examines every year, since without sufficient quality raw material, the system will be stretched to meet demand in the marketplace.

## Other Regions

**20**   As noted earlier, members of the tobacco labor force fled Cuba in great numbers and in two waves, taking Cuban tobacco seed with them. They found their way into many Central American and Carribean countries, where they planted the seeds and tried to replicate the Cuban tobacco. Other countries, such as Cameroon and the United States (Connecticut and Virginia in particular), have been producing quality tobacco for many years also. Whether or not the quality has attained that of the Cuban tobacco is a matter of great debate; however, the threat to the Cuban cigar is more intense now, as the market begins to slow down.

> Just as wine drinkers have adapted to new world blends, so the cigar lover is learning to embrace a different—and invariably cheaper—kind of smoke.[6]

**21**   See Exhibit 2 for more detailed information on the various tobacco growing regions and the characteristics of the tobacco in those regions.

## The Cuban Environment

**22**   The United States is one of the largest markets for cigars in the world. Thus a brief recount of the U.S. relationship with the Cuban environment is necessary.

**23**   Prior to the revolution, with then-President Batista in power, it was perceived that U.S. interests in Cuba moulded the direction of the country. Seventy percent of the land was controlled by less then 10 percent of landowners, with U.S.-owners controlling 25 percent of Cuban land. The sugar trade with the United States was enormous, fully accounting for one-third of U.S. sugar imports. The deterioration of relations between the two countries began with the revolution and culminated in the early 1960s with the Cuban missile crisis and imposition of the trade and financial embargo in 1962. The loss of U.S. trade and investment, particularly in the sugar industry, was devastating to the Cuban economy. It was at this point that the Russians stepped in and essentially subsidized the economy by picking up the sugar quotas the United States had cut off. Cuba's economy became heavily dependent on Soviet support, and it also adopted the command type of economy. Cuba's economy was heavily reliant on sugar, and thus became heavily dependent on the former USSR. Essentially, the Soviets bartered crude oil and refined products at below-market prices in exchange for Cuban sugar at relatively high price levels (51 cents per pound in 1986, compared with a world market price of six cents). The Russians thus counteracted most of the effects of the U.S. blockade and accounted for as much as one-fourth of Cuba's national income in some years.[7]

**24**   However, the effects of the embargo could still be felt. The Russian assistance hid the fact that Cuba was reliant on suppliers and markets as far away as Europe and Asia. Ships that traded with Cuba were unable to enter U.S. ports and thus incurred higher import costs as ships had to go to non-U.S. ports with empty ships. The higher transport are costs paid by the Cubans.

**25**   Between 1989 and 1991, the economies in Eastern Europe collapsed and the Soviet Union dissolved. This proved to be disastrous to the Cuban economy, as they lost their ma-

---

[6]Jonathan Futrell and Lisa Linder, *Up in Smoke*, c. 1998. Contran Octopus Limited, London.
[7]"Cuba's Agriculture: Collapse & Economic Reform," *Agricultural Outlook 1998*, Economic Research Service/USDA, pp. 26–31.

**EXHIBIT 2**
**Cigar Tobacco-growing Regions**

Source: Compiled from Altadis U.S.A. and *Cigar Aficionado* websites

**Dominican Republic (DR)**—The last 20 years have seen a surge in the quality and variety of cigar tobacco from the DR, and as such, it is now a major producer of top-quality tobacco. The primary growing region is the Cibao River Valley, near the city of Santiago in the northern half of the country. Most of the Dominican cigar makers are located close to this city. Most Dominican tobacco is derived from Cuban seed varieties. Although not as strong, it is quite full-flavored.

**United States**—North of Hartford, the Connecticut River Valley produces some of the finest wrapper leaf tobacco in the world—Connecticut Shade. The fine brown to brownish-yellow leaf has a high degree of elasticity, and it creates a mild- to medium-bodied smoke; it is widely used on premium cigars. Another variety, Connecticut Broadleaf, produces a dark, almost black leaf that is used on maduro-style cigars. It is heavier and veinier than shade-grown tobacco.

**Honduras/Nicaragua**—These Central American countries produce high-quality Cuban-seed and Connecticut-seed tobaccos, including shade-grown wrapper. Honduras has suffered from periodic blue mould infestations in recent years; Nicaragua's tobacco region is still recovering from a 10-year civil war. Both countries produce a full-bodied tobacco with strong, spicy flavors and heady aromas.

**Indonesia**—Sumatra-variety tobacco comes from this series of islands that make up Indonesia. The tobacco may be referred to as Java or Sumatra. Sumatra wrapper leaves are often dark brown and have neutral flavors. The majority of wrapper leaf grown there is used in the manufacture of small cigars.

**Ecuador**—Ecuador produces quantities of high-quality tobacco, both filler and wrapper, shade- and sun-grown. Growers there have been using both Connecticut- and Sumatra-seed varieties. In each case, the tobacco usually seems milder and less robust in strength and flavor than the originals.

**Mexico**—The San Andres Valley is world-famous for a sun-grown variant of Sumatra-seed tobacco. Mexican leaves are used widely as binder and filler in cigars. The variety also serves widely as a maduro wrapper because it can stand up to the cooking and sweating process that creates the darker leaf colors. Cigars manufactured in Mexico are usually made with 100 percent local tobacco.

**Cameroon/Central African Republic**—This area of West Africa is known for a high-quality wrapper leaf. In recent years, production has suffered from management changes and bad weather. The Cameroon leaf is prized for its neutral characteristics, which make it an ideal wrapper for full-flavored filler tobaccos.

jor source of foreign assistance, as well as their major markets. An ancillary event was the loss of Soviet subsidized oil, which plunged Cuba into an energy crisis. Cuban foreign trade fell 75 percent, and economic output fell 50 percent. By 1994, agricultural production had fallen 54 percent from 1989 levels.[8]

26  The response from the Cuban government was to implement an austerity program geared to steer through the crisis and begin rebuilding the Cuban economy. This "Special Period in Peacetime" program clamped down on rations, including food, fuel and electricity. Cuban leaders began to reform the economy by looking to the future of their country and studying activities that would develop and bring in hard currency. Industries such as tourism and biotechnology were encouraged, as was domestic food production.

[8]Ibid.

27    Another major initiative was the encouragement of foreign economic associations in areas such as mining, tourism and telecommunications, among others, as well as tobacco. The initiatives taken, including legalizing the use of American dollars, produced signs of economic recovery. While Cuba's economic recovery has started, there are still serious shortcomings and problems to be faced. For example, the Cuban trade deficit continues, foreign exchange problems persist and energy is still in short supply. Agricultural production has not completely returned to precrisis levels. Industry infrastructure remains in poor condition, and investment resources are still in short supply.

28    The situation amplifies the effect of the embargo on the Cuban economy. Denied access to the largest trading entity in the Northern Hemisphere makes the needs of the country more expensive. Measures taken in the 1990s have added to the pressure on Cuba to maintain its health and viability. The Helm-Burton Act, officially known as the Cuban Liberty and Democratic Solidarity Act of 1996, added to this burden in several ways. First, it limited the trade that subsidiaries of U.S. companies in other countries could conduct with Cuba. Second, it allowed the United States to impose sanctions on countries trading with Cuba. Third, it barred officials of corporations doing business in Cuba from entering the United States. Essentially, the United States is trying to extend its embargo to other trading partners of Cuba, in an effort to further alienate and pressure the Cuban regime. Exhibit 3 details the purposes of the Helms-Burton Act from the text of the agreement.

**EXHIBIT 3**
**Helms Burton Act**
**Excerpts H.R. 927**

Source: Thomas, Legislative Information on the Internet: http://thomas.loc.gov.

---

Cuban Liberty and Democratic Solidarity (LIBERTAD) Act of 1996 (Enrolled as Agreed to or Passed by Both House and Senate)

---

—H.R.927—

One Hundred Fourth Congress
of the United States of America
AT THE SECOND SESSION
Begun and held at the City of Washington on Wednesday, the third day of January, one thousand nine hundred and ninety-six
An Act
To seek international sanctions against the Castro government in Cuba, to plan for support of a transition government leading to a democratically elected government in Cuba, and for other purposes.

**SEC. 3. PURPOSES.**
The purposes of this Act are—
(1) to assist the Cuban people in regaining their freedom and prosperity, as well as in joining the community of democratic countries that are flourishing in the Western Hemisphere;
(2) to strengthen international sanctions against the Castro government;
(3) to provide for the continued national security of the United States in the face of continuing threats from the Castro government of terrorism, theft of property from United States nationals by the Castro government, and the political manipulation by the Castro government of the desire of Cubans to escape that results in mass migration to the United States;
(4) to encourage the holding of free and fair democratic elections in Cuba, conducted under the supervision of internationally recognized observers;
(5) to provide a policy framework for United States support to the Cuban people in response to the formation of a transition government or a democratically elected government in Cuba; and
(6) to protect United States nationals against confiscatory takings and the wrongful trafficking in property confiscated by the Castro regime.

## Present Day

**29**   Cuba has entered a pivotal point in its existence. With a population in 2002 of 11,224,321 and per capita gross national product (GNP) of only $1,700, Cuba was a poor country. In December 1999, the first commercial transaction took place between the United States and Cuba since the Kennedy administration imposed the embargo 40 years earlier. The restrictions of the embargo were eased slightly to allow foodstuffs to be bought, but only on a cash-and-carry basis. No credit could be granted to buy the goods. And despite the vehemence of the rhetoric against the Cuban government, Cuban Americans send home between US$600 to US$950 million every year. In every year in the past decade, the United Nations has overwhelmingly condemned the embargo. On November 27, 2001, the vote was a 167 to three renunciation of the embargo. As farm prices declined in the United States, pressure builds to open up a market 90 miles from U.S. shores. All this comes at a time when the Cuban-American population holds a great deal of political sway in the elections of Florida and in the United States. Some have even argued that George Bush owed his presidency to the State of Florida and its Hispanic voters.

> The Cuban national nightmare, the thing that keeps good revolutionaries awake at night in cold sweats, is the example of Puerto Rico—a Spanish Caribbean island whose independence and culture has been largely swallowed up by the giant to the north. There is an acute Cuban fear that American investment, American tourism, American cultural influence and an American political system (fueled, of course, by good old American campaign contributions) will someday swamp Cuban society and turn it into a cross between Cancun and Las Vegas.[9]

**30**   All of this was occurring at a time when there was increased investment and assistance into Cuba from countries other than the United States.

**31**   The debate on whether the embargo will be lifted or not is wide-ranging, with opinions and speculation across all spectrums of thought. Yet, whether or not the embargo will be lifted, the effect on the Cuban cigar industry is significant and affects the way the business operates. The industry has survived and even prospered without the U.S. market over the past 40 years. In today's marketplace, can Cuba sustain that?

## The Major Companies

**32**   The worldwide Cigar industry has two major corporations: Altadis and Swedish Match (see Exhibit 4). These two entities control, through ownership or interest in other companies, the distribution of Havana cigars and Cuban brand names worldwide. There are other smaller companies; however, we will focus on the major players that affect the Cuban cigar industry.

## Altadis S.A.

**33**   Altadis is the result of a 1999 merger, valued at US$3.3 billion, between two giants in the industry: Spanish Tabacalera S.A. and the French Seita S.A. (see Exhibits 5 and 6). In 2000, Altadis also completed a joint venture agreement with Habanos S.A., the company that holds the monopoly on Cuban cigar exports out of Cuba, and the company that owns all Cuban brands outside of the United States. Altadis purchased 50 percent of Habanos for US$477 million, giving it access to most of the major Cuban brands in all markets. As a result, Altadis is the largest cigar company in the world, selling 3.3 billion cigars in 2000. It had sales of over US$10 billion in 2001 and a market capitalization of US$7.2 billion.

**34**   When the two companies merged, the management of Tabacalera became responsible for the worldwide cigar and distribution businesses. Worldwide market share in the major mar-

[9]Walter Russell Mead, "End the Cuba Embargo Now," *Esquire,* New York, September 2001.

**EXHIBIT 4** **The Structure of Two Major Companies in Cigar Industry**

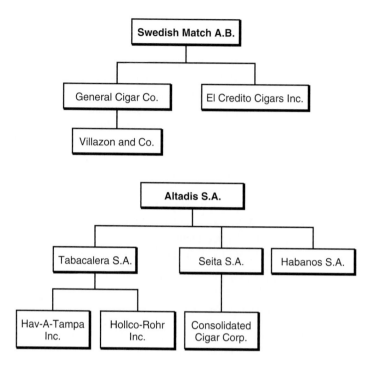

kets was as follows in the year 2000: United States 37 percent, Spain 42 percent, and France 33 percent.

**35**     The history of Tabacalera and Cuba is very strong and is in direct contrast to the relationship that competitors in the United States share with Cuba. Tabacalera, the Spanish catalyst behind the merger to form Altadis, was and is Cuba's biggest and most revered cigar partner. It is this former government-controlled entity that annually invests upwards of US$25 million into Cuba's industry, thereby serving the dual purpose of aiding the financially strapped industry and ensuring Tabacalera the largest access to Cuban tobacco and finished cigars. According to a cigar analyst, this relationship means that Altadis will have better and stronger relationships with the Cubans than any American company.

**36**     To give perspective on what the merger means, consider that prior to the merger:

1. Tabacalera and Seita were the largest purchasers of Cuban-produced cigars, accounting for almost 40 percent of the 1998 exports;

2. They were the two largest sources of financing for Cuban-produced tobacco at almost US$50 million for the 1998 tobacco harvest; and

3. They were the two largest purchasers of Cuban-produced tobacco leaf, accounting for almost all of the 13,000 tons exported in 1998.

These two companies that separately dominated the Cuban export market are now the largest cigar company in the world.

### Habanos S.A.

**37**     Habanos S.A. was formed in 1994 as the export, distribution and marketing arm of the state tobacco firm. They are the official owners of all of the Cuban brand names. As mentioned above, Habanos S.A. entered into a joint venture agreement with Altadis that has brought increased investment into the Cuban industry, as well as stability and increased production

**EXHIBIT 5**
History of Tabacalera S.A.

Source: http://www.altadis.com/en/quienes/nuestrahistoria.html#Spain.

| | |
|---|---|
| 1501 | Rodrigo de Jerez, a Spanish sailor who traveled with Columbus, is persecuted by the Inquisition for smoking in public, a deep-rooted custom among sailors, merchants and soldiers. |
| 1530 | The pipe begins to be used and, among the lower classes, the "roll of leaves," predecessor of the cigar, is popular. |
| 1571 | The Sevillian doctor Nicolas Monardes writes "De Hierba Panacea," the first book on tobacco, in which he disseminates the great virtues and medicinal effects of the plant. |
| 1620 | The first tobacco-processing plant was constructed in Seville. |
| 1758 | Inauguration of the Royal Factory of Seville, which was the world's largest tobacco processing factory until the middle of the twentieth century. |
| 1817 | The growing, processing and selling of tobacco was deregulated. |
| 1828 | The cigarette emerges as the new way of smoking. Cigarettes are sold in "rolls" and individually. |
| 1904 | The manufacture of "Elegantes" brand cigarettes begins in packs of 18 cigarettes. |
| 1933 | The "Ideales" brand of cigarettes is launched. Manufactured by a partially mechanized process using a mixture of select Cuban tobaccos, they become the most popular and most heavily consumed smoking items in Spain, and remain so until the 1960s. |
| 1941 | The Use and Consumption tax, a tobacco levy, is created. |
| 1945 | Incorporation of TABACALERA, S.A., the Spanish government tobacco monopoly. Commercial launch of "BUBI," the first brand of Virginia tobacco cigarettes manufactured by Tabacalera. |
| 1958 | Manufacture of filter cigarettes began in response to new market trends. |
| 1974 | In June, Tabacalera brought "Fortuna," a Virginia tobacco cigarette, onto the market. By the end of the year, this brand occupied the number-one slot in sales of Virginia tobacco cigarettes. |
| 1979 | The manufacture of cigarettes low in nicotine and tar began. |
| 1983 | It becomes obligatory to print the regulation health warning on packs of cigarettes. |
| 1986 | Spain enters the European Economic Community (EEC). The tax regulation affecting tobacco products changed with the advent of the VAT and a special levy on tobacco. |
| 1997 | The Tabacalera Cigars International (TCI) subsidiary is created as a vehicle for expansion into the USA, Central America and the Caribbean. TCI purchases Havatampa, the distributor Max Rohr, Tabacalera San Cristobal de Honduras and Tabacalera San Cristobal de Nicaragua. Tabacalera thus assumes world leadership in the cigar market. |
| 1999 | On February 1st, Logista began operating as an independent company. In December Tabacalera and Seita merge, creating ALTADIS. |

capacity. Also, the joint venture brought greater exposure for the Cuban cigars worldwide. In 2001, Habanos S.A. revenues were US$150 million, US$129 million of which was from exports and tourist sales of approximately 118 million cigars. The export of tobacco leaf brought in US$17 million. One of the major initiatives of the joint venture is to enter the machine-made cigar industry with Cuban-produced tobacco, gaining leverage from the country's existing reputation for tobacco. The machine-made cigar market is US$10 billion worldwide.

## EXHIBIT 6
### History of Sieta S.A.

Source: http://www.altadis.com/en/quienes/nuestrahistoria.html#France

| | |
|---|---|
| 1560 | Jean Nicot introduced tobacco into France. |
| 1674 | Under Louis XIV's reign, a tax farm was established for managing tobacco sales. |
| 1681 | Louis XIV's controller-general of finances, Jean-Baptiste Colbert, extended the farm's monopoly to include the manufacturing of tobacco products. A decree regulated a limited cultivation of tobacco. |
| 1791 | Abolition of the farm's monopoly. |
| 1810 | Napoleon Bonaparte reinstated the tobacco monopoly (cultivation, production and sale). A state agency was set up to operate the monopoly. |
| 1926 | French Prime Minister Raymond Poincaré created an organization responsible for reimbursing public debt, including a service to manage the tobacco monopoly called the Service d'Exploitation Industrielle des Tabacs (SEIT). |
| 1935 | Seit became Seita when it was given responsibility for managing production of matches (Allumettes). |
| 1959 | Seita became a French public industrial/commercial entity, an Etablissement Public à Caractère Industriel et Commercial (EPIC). |
| 1961 | Seita began direct distribution of tobacco products to tobacconists, taking over from the French tax authority. |
| 1962 | Seita's staff, comprised of civil servants or state employees, assumed an autonomous legal status. |
| 1970 | The EEC abolished customs barriers among member states. |
| 1980 | Under the law of July 2nd, Seita became a corporation, the capital of which could be partially divested by the French State. |
| 1984 | Gauloises Blondes were launched. Under the law of July 13th, the French State became Seita's sole shareholder. |
| 1993 | Jean-Dominique Comolli was appointed Seita's Chairman and Chief Executive Officer. |
| 1995 | Privatization of Seita. December 22nd: acquisition of Poland-based ZPT Radom. |
| 1998 | Strategic alliance between Seita and Tabacalera S.A. Acquisition of Reynolds in Finland. Creation of Seita Tupakka, renamed Altadis Finland. Acquisition of the leading American Cigar manufacturer, Consolidated Cigar Holdings Inc, renamed Altadis USA: The Seita Group becomes a world leader in cigars. |
| 1999 | Announcement of the merger of Tabacalera and Seita, giving rise to the creation of Altadis. |

### Altadis U.S.A. (formerly Hav-A-Tampa and Consolidated Cigar)

**38** In August 2000, Hav-A-Tampa and Consolidated Cigar were legally merged to form Altadis U.S.A. This created a powerful entity in the U.S. market as the new entity now controlled more than a third of the U.S. cigar market, including many of the non-Cuban-produced Cuban brands. Altadis sells close to two billion cigars per year, and through their equity position in the company, Cuban Cigar Brands, Altadis U.S.A. has sole ownership of their rights to these non-Cuban-produced Cuban brand names, including Montecristo and H. Upmann.

### Swedish Match and General Cigar

**39**   Swedish Match is the second largest cigar company in the world. With the acquisitions of El Credito Cigars Inc. and the machine-made cigar division of U.S. cigar company General Cigar Holdings Inc. in 1999, and the acquisition of 64 percent of General Cigar Holdings Inc.'s remaining business in 2000, Swedish Match purchased a significant role in the premium cigar market. General Cigar has the rights to market many of the non-Cuban-produced Cuban brand names in the United States, and has the best selling premium cigar in the United States, the Macunado (produced in Jamaica). Swedish Match is highly diversified in tobacco products and accessories, and through General Cigar has a well-established presence in the huge U.S. cigar market.

### Cigar Industry

**40**   Since the collapse of the Eastern European economies, Cuba's need for hard currency has been paramount to supply the country with the basic essentials. As such, the cigar industry in Cuba provided a much needed lift to the economy at a pivotal point.

**41**   The cigar industry is a study in Cuban history and in the Cuban people. It is a part of the culture and folklore. Domestically, 300 million cigars are smoked in Cuba annually; however, the domestic market is not often considered or focused on in analysis, as it is the foreign premium cigar exports that bring in the hard currency. The farms are small, and the communities lend help and support during harvest times. Communities work together and form traditions that have passed down for centuries. Notwithstanding, the workers in the cigar factories are paid per piece, often making more than the average salary. Farmers can buy tracks of land and they are responsible for that land, even though they must produce to meet the state quota. There is a sense of ownership once again, and this has lead directly to the resurgence of the industry after the post-revolution regime had nationalized the industry. Foreign ownership of land, however, is currently not permitted under the socialist regime.

**42**   The production in the premium cigar factories is under the direct control of Cuba's Union of Tobacco Enterprises and is completely separate from the Altadis-Habanos joint venture. However, the expertise of Altadis in various functions within the factories will surely be felt at some point, particularly in quality control. As the joint venture is responsible for the export and marketing of the products from these factories, Habanos has appointed exclusive dealers throughout the world to distribute the Havana cigars. Only these dealers have access to the cigar supply. Jurisdictions not covered by these dealers have sale and purchase agreements directly with Habanos S. A. From there, the dealers sell to wholesalers and retailers in their jurisdictions.

**43**   The production and export of cigars has undergone radical changes during and since the 1990s. The emergence of *Cigar Aficionado*, a magazine devoted to lovers of cigars and celebrity endorsement of cigar smoking, touched off a boom in the cigar market in the mid-1990s. The graphs in Exhibits 7 and 8 clearly show the increase in the 1990s of consumption in the U.S. market. Exhibit 9 shows the increased exports of Cuban cigars in this same period, none of which were to the United States. The boom in the industry touched off a period of growth and expansion, both worldwide and domestically. Tobacco acreage expanded, the number of farmers increased and factories were constructed. For example, in 1995, there were 25,000 small farmers in Cuba producing tobacco. This increased to 37,000 by 1998. During the same period, the number of factories increased to 33 from 17, and thousands of new rollers were being trained. The industry ramped up, expecting the surge in demand to continue through to the new millennium. Through the 1990s, Habanos S.A. consistently set its target production of cigars at 200 million by the year 2000.

**44**   New reforms broke up large, state-owned, cooperative plantations and allowed growers to buy land through governmental loans, and then pay in kind through tobacco harvests.

**EXHIBIT 7** U.S. Large Cigar Consumption (1920 to 2000)

Source: *Perelman's Pocket Cyclopedia of Cigars,* 2002 edition.

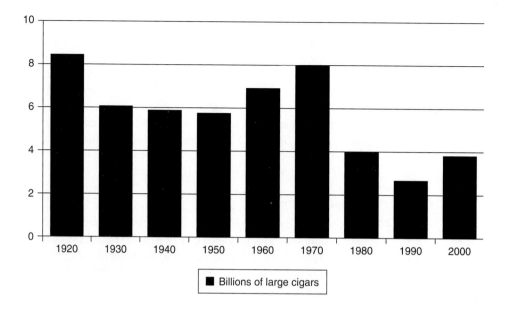

**EXHIBIT 8** The Premium Boom: Annual Imports of Premium Cigars into the United States (1990 to 2001)

Source: *Perelman's Pocket Cyclopedia of Cigars,* 2002 edition.

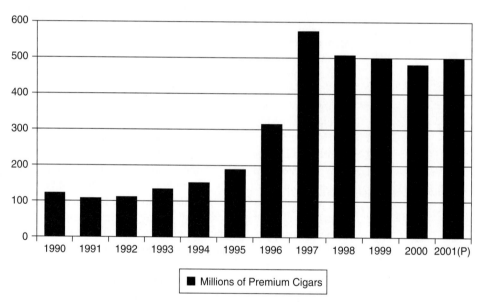

These same reforms helped to increase the quality and yields of tobacco, as an incentive was introduced in the form of ownership. In the early 1990s, yields of the precious wrapper tobacco were very low, sometimes below 10 percent. Initiatives such as this, as well as foreign investment in the industry, have gone a long way to improving quality and yields, although there is still room for major improvement. For example, yields of 25 percent to 30 percent for the wrapper tobacco are not uncommon in Cuba, although some in the premium regions have near-perfect yields. Contrast this with Connecticut, where it is common to average yields of 80 percent to 90 percent.

45    As tobacco firms increased production and worked on improving quality, the perception began to shift towards the thought that too much production would mean a decrease in quality, and cigar buyers worldwide began to question the astronomical production goals set by

**EXHIBIT 9**
**Cuba's Cigar Exports**

Source: Marvin R. Shanken, "Increased Production, Decreased Quality," *Weekly Wrapper,* posted March 21, 2001.

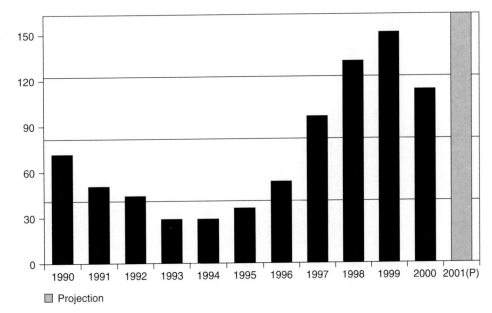

☐ Projection

Habanos. They questioned whether the quality of the Havana cigars could be maintained with new rollers, and ramped up production. After all, they had tripled production in a five-year time frame (see Exhibit 9).

46 The present day has seen those production goals scaled back since, as by all accounts, the boom of the 1990s has tapered off. The Cuban industry has experienced bouts with blue mould, tobacco theft and drought, all affecting the supply of tobacco necessary for production. In response, Habanos S.A. has changed its focus. Ana Lopez, the head of marketing for Habanos S.A. is clear on the direction of the Havana cigar: "We are not concerned with figures anymore . . . We are only interested in quality. Quality is the key for Cuban cigars at the moment."[10]

47 The shift in focus towards an emphasis on quality also affects the production numbers, as there will be more diligence in the entire process to ensure a superior product. In an industry often dominated by perception, the Cubans have recognized the importance of their product and their actions in bringing that product to the export market. The worldwide cigar companies have been consolidating through the late 1990s and early 2000, and as other producers in the world become more adept at the art of cigar making, the Cuban cigar will face serious challenges in the future. Yet, in the opinion of many, when the Havana is right, there is absolutely no substitute. The question is, Can they continue to get it right?

**Branding**

48 COHIBA, Montecristo, Romeo y Julieta. These names evoke reverence among cigar smokers. More than the actual cigar itself, the persona behind these brands extends throughout the world. It is this type of presence that gives the Havana cigar unparalleled acceptance the world over. The brands themselves differ in the size and the blend of the tobacco.[11] Given the importance of the brand to the Cuban mystique, the most serious threats to the Havana

[10]James Suckling, "The Rebirth of Habanos," *Cigar Aficionado,* posted on website July 1, 2002, www.cigaraficiando.com.
[11]For a list of popular vitolas, or sizes, visit the website:http://habanossa.com/galeras.asp.

cigars are brand pirating and forgeries. Fake cigars bearing the name of these famous brands have the potential effect of damaging the prestige of the brand name, as the cigar may have some of the attributes of the real thing, but the smoke itself would fail to satisfy the smoker. Products identifying themselves as Havana cigars, or using the name Havana or Cuba or even Vuelta Abajo in their title, have the effect of giving consumers the perception that the origin of the smoke is Cuban, when that may not be the case.

49    The most current example and case of brand infringement, as the Cubans would call it, is with the COHIBA brand. General Cigar registered the brand name COHIBA in 1978 and then put out a limited number of cigars in order to protect the copyright. COHIBA was created post revolution by the Cuban government, and is often considered the pinnacle of cigars. The General Cigar COHIBAs are manufactured in the Dominican Republic with non-Cuban materials. This is a point of great contention with the Cubans, as they contend that the COHIBA name is synonymous with Cuban cigars worldwide, and General Cigar is unrightfully using their brand name. The case was set to go to trial in late 2002.

50    However, this case exemplifies the importance of the brand and the image of the cigar. The General Cigar Company COHIBA is made from different materials in a different blend. It is, however, the name that consumers recognize and associate with the pinnacle of cigars. The Cubans do not want their flagship cigar to be diluted by another company using the name, and it is their stated ambition to protect their brand identities worldwide.

## The Future

51    The Cuban cigar industry is in a state of transformation. The demand for cigars has leveled off, and has even begun to drop somewhat in the worldwide market. The importance of the export business to the Cuban economy is inescapable. In order to move forward, the Cubans have begun to look closely at their industry and at the marketplace, and with the relationships and support they have built with foreign ventures, they are trying to improve. They are investigating new agricultural methods to improve yields and quality, and looking at methods and tobacco strains that will help stave off disease while maintaining the legendary appearance and flavor of the original plants. All these initiatives are geared towards bringing a better, more consistent product to the customer. The joint venture with Altadis has given them the avenue to pursue the US$10 billion machine-made cigar industry, with the introduction of miniversions of their popular brands. The distribution networks and experience that Altadis has in the machine-made market, combined with the branding of the Cuban product, has created considerable potential in this industry. However, it also poses many challenges.

## The Task

52    Armed with all this information, Hernandez must analyze the industry and the environment surrounding it in order to decide whether the potential of this industry is significant enough to warrant investment in it. He wondered if his studies in the MBA program had given him the tools to assess a possible start.

# Case 27   AllAdvantage.com: An Internet Infomediary

## Brent D. Beal

"You're bigger than life, just stay bigger than life"

*(Venture capital firm to Jim Jorgensen, founder and CEO of AllAdvantage.com,*
*February 2000)*

**1**   It was Monday, July 3, 2000 and Jim Jorgensen, founder and CEO of AllAdvantage.com, had a lot on his mind. AllAdvantage had just announced that its upcoming initial public offering (IPO), scheduled for mid July, would be delayed indefinitely due to "unfavorable market conditions."[1] Although withdrawing its bid to go public was a disappointment, Jorgensen believed it was only a temporary setback. The last 18 months had been exhilarating. AllAdvantage had gone from an idea to a 700-employee firm flush with more than $130 million in venture capital. Jorgensen believed the company was on the cusp of establishing itself as an internet infomediary—a trusted third party that would bring buyers and sellers together in cyberspace and profit from its role as matchmaker.

**2**   Despite its successes, the last six months has been difficult for the company. The Nasdaq stock index, which had peaked at 5048.62 on March 10, 2000, was now hovering around 3000 and there had been a decisive shift in investor expectations. Many new internet start-ups—companies from which AllAdvantage derived a significant portion of its revenue—were shutting down or being forced into bankruptcy. As a result, AllAdvantage was having difficulty selling its ad inventory. Jorgensen understood that the business climate in which the company had been founded, and in which it had prospered, had changed. AllAdvantage had pursued a "growth-at-any-cost" strategy in response to the demands of venture capitalists and the perceived expectations of the capital market. Now, Jorgensen realized, the only way for AllAdvantage to survive was to demonstrate that its business model created significant value—value that would soon lead to profitability. The rules of the game had changed, and unless AllAdvantage adapted it would face the same fate as other prominent dot-coms that had ceased to exist.

**3**   Jorgensen glanced up at the clock on the wall in his office—it was nearly noon. In less than 24 hours he would meet with AllAdvantage's top executives. Although the company had been gradually moving away from it's growth-at-any-cost strategy that had propelled it to prominence during the internet boom, there was a growing sense among the top management team that the pace of change would have to quicken. There were sharp differences of opinion, however, about what changes were needed and how the firm should go about moving towards profitability. Jorgensen knew that changing the firm's strategy would require coordinated and enthusiastic support from the company's leadership and that he, as founder and CEO, needed to present a coherent plan around which consensus could be built.

[1]This case is based on interviews, publicly available news releases and business-press commentary—the people and events described in the case are real. I thank Jim Jorgensen and Alex Gourevitch at AllAdvantage for their time and hospitality. I also thank Dennis Hallack for some valuable research assistance in the early stages of preparing the case.

He needed to decide what direction AllAdvantage would take—and time was running out. Jorgensen stood up abruptly and walked out of his office. "Maybe a walk around the parking lot will do me some good," he thought.

# THE COMPANY

4    AllAdvantage was founded by Jim Jorgensen and three Stanford graduate students (Carl Anderson, Johannes Pohle, and Oliver Brock) and launched from Jorgensen's garden shed on March 30, 1999. The idea for AllAdvantage emerged from a discussion about privacy on the internet.[2] It seemed to company founders that there needed to be a way for individuals to come together and sell their aggregated attention and demographic data to advertisers while maintaining their individual privacy. The "aha," according to Jorgensen, was the idea to develop a downloadable software program that members could install on their personal computers for viewing advertisements.[2] By the end of 1999 AllAdvantage had thrust itself front-and-center onto the internet scene. *The Wall Street Journal, The Washington Post, Fortune, BusinessWeek, Business 2.0* and other high-profile business publications were writing about the company, venture capital firms had injected more than $130 million into the venture, and a small army of experienced executives had joined the AllAdvantage management team.

5    AllAdvantage's wanted to be the leading internet infomediary. On one side of the infomediary equation were internet companies that desperately wanted to connect with customers interested in their products and services. On the other side of this equation were customers in search of products and services but wary of divulging personal information to potential advertisers out of both a desire to protect their privacy and to avoid being deluged by irrelevant (and annoying) sales pitches. AllAdvantage, with its proprietary ViewBar, promised to create value for both marketers and customers by playing matchmaker—marketers would be able to target their sales pitches to interested customers, and customers would be able to simultaneously protect their privacy and enjoy filtered advertising tailored to their personal preferences and tastes. In abstract, the infomediary business model was easy to understand. As explained in an article in the *Financial Times,*

> The company's business model is breathtakingly simple. It sells internet advertising, but instead of spending money on content to attract users to view a web page, it generates advertising inventory using an entirely different mechanism. Users download a piece of software called the ViewBar, which sits on their screen and pumps out a nonstop succession of advertisements[3]

6    Jorgensen realized early on that AllAdvantage would have to find a way to overcome the classic "chicken-and-egg" problem inherent in its business model: AllAdvantage couldn't sell advertising until it had an audience of potential customers for advertisers to target, but without advertising revenue, it would be impossible to attract an audience. The same dilemma is present in TV, radio, and print (i.e., magazines can't sell advertising without a

---

[2]In this context, spam is unsolicited commercial email—spamming is the act of sending such email.
[3]Banner advertising on the internet is usually discussed in terms of CPMs or cost per 1000 ad impressions. An ad impression occurs whenever a banner ad is served, which may occur, for example, every time a particular web page containing the banner ad is accessed. In AllAdvantage's case, AllAdvantage members were shown a constant stream of ads, and an impression represented approximately 20 seconds of display time on a user's computer screen.

subscription base, but can't build a subscription base without advertising dollars to pay for content with which to attract readers).

7    Jorgensen's unique solution to this problem is what distinguished AllAdvantage—unlike its infomediary counterparts in the physical world, AllAdvantage would not develop any content of its own. AllAdvantage would deliver advertising to subscribers via a small software program, the ViewBar, that would occupy a small one-inch strip at the bottom (or top) of a computer user's monitor. The ViewBar would piggyback on the internet itself—the internet would be the content. Unlike TV, radio, or print media, AllAdvantage wouldn't have to worry about content—it would just sell advertising. To motivate internet users to join the AllAdvantage community and download the ViewBar, AllAdvantage promised to pay $.50/hr for time spent surfing the internet with the ViewBar, up to 40 hours a month. Directly compensating individuals for viewing advertising, while impractical in the case of traditional media, was, Jorgensen believed, not only possible in cyberspace, it was an imperative. Consumers time was valuable and they had a right to be compensated for their attention. In addition to monetary compensation, Jorgensen believed that AllAdvantage members would value AllAdvantage's ability to deliver customized or targeted advertising tailored to members' specific tastes and predilections without requiring members to surrender personal information directly to individual companies and/or marketers.

8    To generate immediate interest and accelerate the growth of a community of AllAdvantage members, Jorgensen went one step further than simply compensating AllAdvantage members for surfing the internet with the ViewBar—AllAdvantage encouraged members to tout the company to friends, family and acquaintances by creating a multilevel compensation structure. In addition to the $.50/hr each member received for time spent surfing with the ViewBar displayed, each member also collected $.10/hr for the time each direct referral spent surfing and $.05/hr for referrals of referrals, down four levels. The multilevel marketing approach dramatically increased the earning potential for individuals willing to persuade their friends and acquaintances to join the AllAdvantage community—it created a viral marketing context in which "friends spammed[2] friends."[(4)]

9    Although AllAdvantage's practice of directly compensating internet users for viewing ads was criticized by some as fundamentally unsound,[(5)] the business model was similar in many respects to the prize giveaways conducted by radio stations. The profit potential, contrary to the views of some observers,[(6, 7)] was substantial. Each member cost AllAdvantage a maximum of $.80/hr ($.50/hr to surfing member plus an additional $.30/hr to referrers). During an hour of surfing AllAdvantage could display approximately 200 banner ads or one-fifth of a CPM.[3] The going rates for CPMs were between $10 (for random or run-of-the-network ads) and $60 (for highly targeted ads).[(8)] Even at the low end of this range ($10/CPM), AllAdvantage would make 2½ times the cost of member payments in ad revenue.

10   AllAdvantage's viral marketing approach produced impressive results—over 250,000 individuals signed up in the first 10 days.[(3)] In September of 1999 AllAdvantage served more than 1 billion ad impressions to its rapidly expanding membership. In November, AllAdvantage served 4 billion ad impressions.[(9)] By the start of 2000 the company had grown to nearly 600 employees and had begun preparing for a lucrative initial public offering (IPO). By July 2000, just 16 months after signing up its first member, total membership surpassed 7 million. According to Jim Jorgensen, Asset Management/Alloy Ventures, the first venture capital firm to invest in AllAdvantage, kept telling them, " [you're] bigger than life, just stay bigger than life."[(10)] There was a period in early 2000 when there was such palpable enthusiasm and sense of manifest destiny on the part of employees that some observers compared it with a young Apple in the early 80s.[(10)]

# ACHIEVEMENTS

**11**   As Jorgensen walked he couldn't help but reflect on all the things the company had done right over the last 18 months. AllAdvantage was now the recognized leader in the emerging pay-to-surf industry. AllAdvantage had no serious competition, although more than 40 copycat firms had emerged in the wake of the company's success. AllAdvantage was the only pay-to-surf company that had received significant venture capital financing. They were the only company that had achieved sufficient scale to support their own global sales force. Jorgensen reflected on the different challenges the company had faced—everything from software development to problems with member spam to international expansion. Each of these challenges had shaped the company in important ways.

## Software

**12**   In March of 1999 when the AllAdvantage founders decided to launch their new venture, the technology they planned to utilize to execute their business plan existed only on paper.[9] They had not developed the communication software that AllAdvantage members would need to download and install on their personal computers—software that would allow AllAdvantage to broadcast a constant stream of ads to member desktops while simultaneously tracking member movements and online preferences. The initial pitch to potential AllAdvantage members was something to this effect: "Sign up now and in a few months we'll have the software ready for you to download and you can start earning money."

**13**   A beta version of the software was subsequently released in June 1999. In July 1999 the ViewBar was formally released to all AllAdvantage members. A Mac version of the ViewBar was introduced in beta in November 1999 and formally released to all members in April 2000. A new version of the PC ViewBar was released in Februrary 2000 and included several features designed to make the ViewBar more than just a mechanism for delivering advertising. For example, the new ViewBar released in February 2000 included quick links designed to allow AllAdvantage members to hop directly from the ViewBar to sponsors' websites. It also included direct access to search engines.[11]

**14**   Jorgensen believed that its ViewBar technology was one of the most important assets that AllAdvantage possessed. It allowed AllAdvantage to track member movement on the internet and to use that information to target its advertising. With typical internet banner advertising, the advertiser had no control over when, how long, or how frequently someone would see a particular ad. The ViewBar overcame these limitations. Jorgensen was convinced that this capability gave AllAdvantage a competitive edge over other online advertising intermediaries.

## Financing

**15**   AllAdvantage successfully raised an impressive sum of money from private investors. In April of 1999, just two months after opening its virtual doors, AllAdvantage announced first-round funding of $2 million from Alloy Ventures. In September of that same year, the company raised an additional $31 million from a group of investors led by Walden Media and Information Technology Fund, Times Mirror TMCT Ventures, Partech International, J&W Seligman's New Technology Funds and, again, Alloy Ventures. In early February 2000, the company announced that it had secured $100 million in additional equity financing from a group of investors led by SOFTBANK Capital Partners. SOFTBANK invested $70 million—other investors included Putnam Investments and T. Rowe Price.

### Executive Talent

**16**  AllAdvantage had no problem hiring experienced executives. For example, in August 1999, AllAdvantage announced that David Backman-Robertson, former CNN Interactive Vice President, would assume the title of Vice President of Sales at AllAdvantage.com.[12] In September 1999, AllAdvantage.com announced that Rich LeFurgy, co-founder and current chair of the Internet Advertising Bureau, would join its Board of Directors.[12] These and other appointments demonstrated that AllAdvantage could successfully attract experienced management.

### International Expansion

**17**  By the end of 1999 AllAdvantage membership had grown to nearly 4 million. A significant percentage of those members lived outside the United States, United Kingdom and Canada.[9, 16] In order to leverage its growing international membership, AllAdvantage had moved rapidly to expand its service to as many foreign countries as possible. AllAdvantage launched in the United Kingdom in August of 1999 and by October had signed up more than 50,000 U.K. members.[17] In March of 2000 AllAdvantage announced that it had released localized versions of its software, the ViewBar, to members in France, Germany, Japan, the United Kingdom, and Australia/New Zealand. By the end of March AllAdvantage had local offices in the United States, London, Paris, Hamburg, Tokyo, and Sydney.[11] By July 2000, AllAdvantage offered paid web surfing in 20 countries.[18]

### Fighting Spam

**18**  It became apparent almost immediately that AllAdvantage's marketing strategy had an undesirable side-effect: it induced members to send unsolicited e-mail or spam. Although spam did not directly affect AllAdvantage operations, it was not a trivial issue. The multi-level marketing strategy employed by the company created significant incentive for members to build referral downlines. An AllAdvantage member, for example, could send out an e-mail to thousands of addresses gleaned from the internet or other sources with an eye-catching message like "Make Money Fast" and generate a significant number of referrals. Spam generated by AllAdvantage members had the potential to alienate key members of the internet community, including newsgroup moderators, network administrators, web-based e-mail providers and others. In the long run, the negative publicity and ill-will generated by AllAdvantage spam had the potential to undermine the company's legitimacy and hamper its ability to do business on the internet.

**19**  In August 1999, AllAdvantage hired Ray Everett-Church as Chief Privacy Officer and Vice President.[12] Church was the co-founder of Coalition Against Unsolicited Commercial Email or CAUCE. AllAdvantage also cancelled the accounts of members caught sending spam and routinely posted warnings against such activity on their internet site with lists of cancelled account numbers. These actions convinced the internet community that AllAdvantage was not just another "bulk e-mail pyramid scheme" and that its antispam stance was more than just self-serving posturing.[4] This was particularly important for AllAdvantage because its business depended on gaining the trust of its members—member that were asked to give AllAdvantage personal information with the understanding the AllAdvantage would not divulge that information to individual advertisers.

# PROBLEMS

**20**  Jim Jorgensen knew that the company's recent achievements didn't mean much now. What mattered was what the company did from here going forward. It seemed like just a few months ago AllAdvantage had seemed invincible. Where had things gone wrong? "Not all of this is our fault," Jim thought, "things happened that we couldn't have predicted."

21    AllAdvantage, like other dot-coms, was being advised by its venture capitalists, by its investment bankers and even by its own board members to burn cash like rocket fuel. What mattered was growth—what mattered was staying "larger than life." AllAdvantage was being advised that the equity markets would finance their losses if they stayed "larger than life." As Jorgensen explained,

> The bankers were a significant influence. When you're running a business, the business needs to be profitable in order to be sustainable. When you have bankers, venture capitalists, telling you, "just grab market share, just grab market share" it makes a difference. The bankers and venture capitalist suspended the profitability constraint—they were telling us we didn't need to be profitable until 2003.[10]

22    As long as equity markets were willing to finance the company's losses it made perfect sense to keep the throttle wide open. AllAdvantage was selling advertising to other dot-coms, other companies that needed to show growth, growth at almost any cost. In April of 2000, however, the situation changed dramatically. Equity markets, particularly the Nasdaq, experienced a significant correction and investor sentiment shifted dramatically. The market wasn't interested in just growth anymore—it wanted profits. Again, as explained by Jorgensen,

> We were out on the edge with dot-com money—and it was flyer money. Our clients were the first to get hurt when things turned. Things shuttered a little in April—advertising didn't drop but it didn't go up—that was when the Nasdaq went south. But in May advertising dropped and just got worse from there.[10]

23    Despite the shift in market sentiment, Jorgensen believed in the business model. He was certain that AllAdvantage had the potential to generate significant economic value because the cost of retaining the attention of its growing membership was significantly less than the advertising revenue that could be realized from selling access to its members (see Exhibit 1 for AllAdvantage ad rates). During the first quarter of 2000, however, AllAdvantage posted an operating loss of $66 million on revenues of just $9.1 million.[19] The company paid out $32.7 million directly to members during this same time period.[20] What had gone wrong? Why had projected profits failed to materialize? There were a number of reasons:

### Declining Advertising Rates

24    An opinion article in *InfoWorld* in 1999 began with this assertion: "ONLINE advertising is dead."[21] This was, of course, an overstatement designed to attract attention but nonetheless it served to highlight the fact that internet advertising, particularly banner advertising, was becoming increasingly difficult to defend as an effective advertising method. Click-through rates (the percentage of banner ads that viewers mouse click), which averaged more than 2 percent in 1997, have steadily declined to less than .5 percent. CPM rates (cost per thousand impressions) have been on a downward trend for the past several years[22] and a recent report from *AdRelevance* suggests that this trend might continue into the foreseeable future.[23] In July of 2000 rate card CPMs for full banner advertising (468 × 60 pixels) averaged approximately $30, down nearly 10 percent from an average of nearly $33 six months earlier.[23] The most common rate card price was $25. It was unusual for firms to sell advertising for full rate card price, however. The average discount during the first 6 months of 2000 was 33 percent.

25    AllAdvantage responded to falling CPM rates by shifting its advertising sales from intermediaries such as 24/7 and DoubleClick to direct sales. This had the immediate benefit of cutting out third party commission on ad sales, which often ran as high as one third of ad revenue, but forced AllAdvantage to increase its employee count to nearly 600, 220 of

**EXHIBIT 1**
**AllAdantage.com Ad Rates**

| Product | 468 H 60 Banner* | 120 H 60 Tile |
|---|---|---|
| Behavioral Targeting[†] | na | na |
| Web Page Targeting | $50 | $40 |
| Site Targeting | 50 | 40 |
| Keywords | 35 | 20 |
| Channel Targeting | | |
|   Retail/Auction | 30 | 15 |
|   Auto | 40 | 20 |
|   Careers | 40 | 20 |
|   Entertainment | 30 | 15 |
|   Finance | 40 | 20 |
|   Health and Beauty | 35 | 20 |
|   Higher Education | 35 | 20 |
|   News | 30 | 15 |
|   Sports | 25 | 12 |
|   Technology | 50 | 25 |
|   Travel | 60 | 30 |
|   Sub-channels | 60 | 30 |
|   Run-of-channels | 20 | 12 |
| Desktop Billboards[†] | na | na |
| Run-of-Web | $10 | $6 |
| Blitz | 150,000 | 100,000 |
| AllPlay! Sponsorship[†] | na | na |
| QuickLinks Sponsorship[†] | na | na |
| Filters | Add $5 per | Add $3 per |

*Prices are per CPM or thousand impressions, except for *Blitz,* which is per campaign.

†Rates negotiated on an individual basis between client and AllAdvantage.

which were involved in direct sales. It also required AllAdvantage to open local offices in London, Paris, Tokyo, and Sydney as well as throughout the United States.[19]

## Difficulty of Delivering Targeted Advertising

26    The rate card price for highly targeted banner advertising was substantially more than for run-of-site (or untargeted) ads. In July of 2000, highly targeted ad space was selling for as much as $100 per thousand impressions or four times the average CPM rate.

27    AllAdvantage had emphasized the potential of targeted advertising. Because the ViewBar was a two-way communication device and could access information displayed in members' browsers, AllAdvantage could track the sites that members visited and the keywords that members typed into search engines.[2] Information about member browsing habits, if exploited properly by AllAdvantage, would allow it to carefully target advertising to those members most likely to respond. AllAdvantage would then be able to charge a substantial premium for its advertising space.

28    Unfortunately, as of July 2000 AllAdvantage had not been very successful in exploiting the potential of targeted ads. Jorgensen explained:

> Not many companies sell it, so not many companies want it. It is a chicken and egg problem. Also, we have had a tough time with integration. DoubleClick's system (DART) serves ads, but it isn't set up to handle targeted ads. We had to build our ViewBar so that is acts like a web page so that it requests ads from DoubleClick. We have a lot of information about members in our computers, but we can't get that information into the stream—we can't get

that information into the communication that goes on between the ViewBar and DoubleClick. Only 2–3 percent of our ads are targeted. Most are just run of the web and we get a CPM of maybe $7 for that type of advertising.

### Poor Demographics

29    Some critics had honed in on the problem of self-selection, given the fact that AllAdvantage could only target members that had volunteered (by registering) to view the ads. As observed in an article in *InfoWorld Daily News*, "people who earn money surfing do so as a lark or are students or do not have much income, and so want the money rather than the personalized advertising . . . such surfers are not likely to spend money with online advertisers because they simply do not have the money to spare."[1] AllAdvantage tried to counter this assertion by releasing zip code membership information. The top three zip codes with the most AllAdvantage members were 90210 (Beverly Hills, CA), 24060 (Blacksburg, VA), and 94086 (Sunnyvale, CA—Silicon Valley). Despite this zip code information, the perception that AllAdvantage members may not represent an ideal demographic group may have had an adverse impact on its CPM rates.

30    Another factor may also have been the incentive structure created by the firm's multi-level marketing approach. The maximum amount that an individual member could earn for personal surfing was around $10, depending on the specific hour limit in place in the country in which the member resided and the month in which the member surfed. It is reasonable to suspect that this amount may represent inadequate compensation for surrendering a significant portion of one's desktop screen to a constant stream of advertising. The real money was in referrals. For example, Ron Streeter, a freelance graphic artist from Syracuse and AllAdvantage member, earned $2044 in November 1999, all but $12.50 was a result of indirect surfing or time his referrals and the referrals of his referrals spent online.

31    AllAdvantage only rewarded individuals for the time their referrals spent online up to the time they themselves spent online. In other words, if Ron Streeter had only surfed for 10 hours in November, he would have only received credit for the time his referrals surfed up to a maximum on 10 hours, and his check would have been reduced by about 60 percent. In other words, Mr. Streeter received around $80 an hour for surfing. This incentive structure locked people into surfing—they had to surf in order to benefit from the surfing time of referrals. Despite the best efforts of AllAdvantage to enhance the utility of the ViewBar or deliver personalized advertising to AllAdvantage members, for many members the primary benefit was purely financial. For these individuals, the constant stream of advertising was simply an inconvenience and they were unlikely to pay much attention to the ads. This suspicion is confirmed by members like Mike Jones, a freshman at the University of Virginia, who stated the following: "We do it just for the check . . . I've never heard of anyone who had bought anything from the ads."[8]

32    In contrast, the ideal AllAdvantage member would be an individual that valued the utility of the ViewBar and the opportunity to view targeted advertising that would allow the user to more efficiently locate needed items and/or services. Unfortunately, the incentive structure developed by AllAdvantage, although successful in turning the company into a marketing machine, probably did not attract the most desirable group of individuals from an advertiser's point of view. This may also have contributed to the company's inability to charge premium CPM rates.

### Fraud

33    Another factor contributing to AllAdvantage's losses may have been the fact that advertisers can't be sure that individuals are paying attention to their ads. Of course this same concern plagues almost every other advertising medium, from TV (viewers may opt to run to

the bathroom rather than view commercials), radio (listeners may switch channels), print (readers may simply ignore the ads), and so on. In AllAdvantage's case, some members simply blocked out the ad window with masking tape.[8]

**34**     Another concern was fraudulent surfing or "cheating." The ViewBar only records active surfing time—the software detects keyboard use and mouse movement and does not credit time spent connected to the internet but not actively viewing web content. Enterprising hackers, however, have written and popularized several programs that mimic active surfing. Many of these programs are available for free on the internet, including one called "FakeSurf." College dormitories are full of flashing monitors animated by fake surfing programs that allow students to literally make money while they sleep.[8] Phillip Greenspun, a researcher at MIT who teaches a class on advanced web programming, has asserted that any of his students could build a near-perfect surfing spoofer.[8] Officials at pay-to-surf companies have insisted that they can detect fake surfing.[24]

**35**     By far the most serious cases of fraudulent behavior by AllAdvantage members were attempts to artificially generate referrals and referral surfing time. For example, clever hackers attempted to write software that would directly interface with AllAdvantage's member database. They then attempted to register thousands of referrals and simulate surfing time for each of these referrals. AllAdvantage hired a Ph.D. from Cambridge to head a Community Protection Group—at its peak more than 20 full-time employees were part of this group. AllAdvantage also received some valuable tips from other AllAdvantage members. As Jim Jorgensen explained, "I'm sure we lost $100,000 or $200,000—I don't know how much. We got the problem solved but it was a distraction"[10]

**36**     AllAdvantage delayed member payments for May, June, and July of 2000, citing fraudulent surfing as the primary cause. Many members were advised that their checks would be substantially reduced once referral commissions from fraudulent surfing were subtracted.

### Difficulty of Keeping up with Membership Growth

**37**     Within 5 months of the firm's launch, AllAdvantage was signing up new members at a rate of 10,000 to 20,000 a day. More than 2 million members registered in the first 120 days.[13] Each new member that surfs 20 hours in a given month increases AllAdvantage's potential ad inventory by 4000 ad impressions. In September 1999 AllAdvantage served more than 1 billion ad impressions—in November the company served more than 4 billion impressions. "As far as our advertising inventory, we sold it all, but at what price? There is a limit to the number of advertisers that want to reach our members."[10]

# DECISIONS

**38**     Jorgensen knew that AllAdvantage must convince its backers that its business model created real economic value. Now that AllAdvantage had withdrawn its IPO bid, its investors would be particularly concerned about any future operating losses. Jorgensen was painfully aware that its balance sheet was a mess (see Exhibits 2 to 4).[25] Since its founding in March 1999, AllAdvantage had lost $102.7 million. From inception through March 31, 2000, AllAdvantage had paid out nearly $50 million in member payments, but only taken in slightly more that $14 million in advertising revenue.[26] If its investors were to be expected to back the company until it could go public, AllAdvantage would have to explain why these past operating results were not indicative of future financial performance. Jorgensen would have to chart a clear path to profitability and convince AllAdvantage investors that patience was in their best financial interest. Clearly AllAdvantage would have to embrace significant change.

# EXHIBIT 2
Consolidated Statement of Operations and Consolidated Balance Sheet*

| | Period from Inception (March 24, 1999) to September 30,1999 | Three Months Ended December 31, 1999 | Period from Inception (March 24, 1999) to December 31, 1999 | Three Months Ended March 31, 2000 |
|---|---|---|---|---|
| **Consolidated Statement of Operations Data:** | | | | |
| Revenues | 235 | 5,016 | 5,251 | 9,100 |
| Costs and expenses: | | | | |
| Direct member costs | 2,192 | 14,949 | 17,141 | 32,744 |
| Sales and marketing | 1,580 | 10,022 | 11,602 | 26,927 |
| General and administrative | 3,302 | 5,042 | 8,344 | 6,016 |
| Product development | 1,267 | 1,644 | 2,911 | 6,106 |
| Depreciation and amortization | 78 | 270 | 348 | 580 |
| Stock-based compensation | 244 | 1,303 | 1,547 | 2,788 |
| Total costs and expenses | 8,663 | 33,230 | 41,893 | 75,161 |
| Loss from operations | (8,428) | (28,214) | (36,642) | (66,061) |
| Interest expense | (570) | (257) | (827) | (536) |
| Interest income | 10 | 350 | 360 | 959 |
| Net loss | (8,988) | (28,121) | (37,109) | (65,638) |
| Net loss per share | (1.27) | (3.52) | (5.04) | (8.20) |
| **Consolidated Balance Sheet Data:** | | | | |
| Cash, cash equivalents and restricted cash | | | 30,019 | 87,345 |
| Total assets | | | 39,871 | 104,497 |

*Figures in thousands.

39    Despite the challenges that lay ahead Jorgensen was confident that the AllAdvantage business model had a great deal of potential. Although the company had its critics, its business model was similar in several respects to prize giveaways by radio stations or advertising firms that used drawings or raffles as incentive to encourage individuals to fill out information cards or listen to customized sales pitches. The basic idea of rewarding an audience for its time and attention was not new—it was a business model that had been proven effective in a number of different business settings. The only difference was that AllAdvantage had the capability to monitor individual behavior and offer rewards directly to each individual in the audience rather than give away prizes to a lucky few. When the costs and profit potential were broken down by member and hour, AllAdvantage's potential was obvious:

200 banner ads (one-fifth CPM)      $2.00 ($10 per CPM, one-fifth CPM)

1 hr. of surfing (by member)     −$.80 ($.50 to individual + $.30 to up line)

Total Profit (per member, per hour)     $1.20 (150% gross profit)

**EXHIBIT 3**

Balance Sheet*

| | December 31, 1999 | March 31, 2000 | Pro Forma Stockholders' Equity at March 31, 2000 |
|---|---|---|---|
| | | | (Unaudited) |
| **Assets** | | | |
| Current assets: | | | |
| Cash and cash equivalents | 20,019 | 85,345 | |
| Restricted cash | 10,000 | 2,000 | |
| Accounts receivable, net of allowance of $235 and $672 at December 31, 1999 and March 31, 2000, respectively | 4,523 | 7,641 | |
| Prepaid expenses and other assets | 624 | 1,470 | |
| Deferred offering costs | — | 675 | |
| Total current assets | 35,166 | 97,131 | |
| Property and equipment, net | 4,705 | 7,366 | |
| Total assets | 39,871 | 104,497 | |
| **Liabilities and stockholders' equity** | | | |
| Current liabilities: | | | |
| Accounts payable | 1,753 | 5,456 | |
| Accrued member payables | 12,239 | 30,759 | |
| Other accrued liabilities | 5,362 | 12,626 | |
| Customer advance | 19,830 | 19,601 | |
| Deferred revenue | 75 | 2,278 | |
| Current portion of capital lease obligations | 383 | 440 | |
| Total current liabilities | 39,642 | 71,160 | |
| Capital lease obligations, net of current portion | 254 | 212 | |
| Total stockholders' equity | (25) | 33,125 | 33,125 |
| Total liabilities and stockholders' equity | 39,871 | 104,497 | |

*Figures in thousands.

**40** AllAdvantage could display approximately 200 ads (one-fifth of a CPM) per hour to each member. At a CPM rate of $10 (substantially below the going rate for targeted banner ads), the firm would realize a gross profit of 150 percent. Even at a CPM rate of $5, AllAdvantage would enjoy a 25 percent gross margin. Jorgensen was confident that once the company worked through some of its growing pains (and the unusual or one-time expenses associated with such rapid growth), it would be in a position to earn a substantial return on investment. Jorgensen saw three broad approaches to the company's future:

**Tactical Responses**

**41** AllAdvantage had set out to be an internet infomediary—it's pay-to-surf program was a means to that end. The program had turned AllAdvantage into a marketing machine—it was signing up around 20,000 new member a day—and had propelled the company to prominence. Unfortunately, AllAdvantage's pay-to-surf approach had also produced a severe imbalance between member payments and advertising revenues. It contributed to this imbalance in at least two ways: (1) it obligated AllAdvantage to pay members regardless of

## EXHIBIT 4
**Cash Flow Statement***

| | Period from Inception (March 24, 1999) to December 31, 1999 | Three Months Ended March 31, 2000 |
|---|---|---|
| | (Unaudited) | |
| **Operating activities:** | | |
| Net loss | (37,109) | (65,638) |
| Selected changes in assets and liabilities: | | |
| Accounts receivable | (4,523) | (3,118) |
| Accounts payable and other accrued liabilities | 7,115 | 10,967 |
| Accrued member payables | 12,239 | 18,520 |
| Net cash used in operating activities | (9,914) | (26,844) |
| **Financing activities:** | | |
| Net cash provided by financing activities | 34,223 | 95,294 |
| Net increase in cash and cash equivalents | 20,019 | 65,326 |
| Cash and cash equivalents at beginning of period | | 20,019 |
| Cash and cash equivalents at end of period | 20,019 | 85,345 |

*Figures in thousands.

whether or not the company was able to sell its advertising inventory, and (2) it produced an incentive structure that attracted individuals that were unlikely to respond to advertisers' sales pitches, thereby making it difficult to AllAdvantage to demand high CPM rates.

42   Jorgensen knew that if he and his team of top executives intended to argue that the current imbalance between member payments and advertising revenue could be rectified, they would need to answer some difficult questions regarding the company's ability to sell its advertising inventory and the CPM rates that the company would likely be able to charge. The biggest uncertainly in this equation was AllAdvantage's ability to sell targeted rather than run-of-the-network advertising. Jorgensen understood that AllAdvantage's inability to sell targeted advertising, as it had initially planned, had resulted in realized CPM rates substantially below what the company had projected.

43   In addition to targeted advertising, AllAdvantage might also consider tying member payments to advertising revenues. Other pay-to-surf companies, like ValuePay.com, were offering to pay members a fixed percentage of advertising revenues and were therefore assured a positive gross margin—that is, if advertising revenue were less than expected, member payments would be reduced accordingly. Or AllAdvantage might elect to follow the lead of companies like IWon.com, FreeLotto.com, MyPoints.com or WebMillion.com and compensate viewers with something other than cash—perhaps points that could be redeemed for various prizes, entries in prize drawings, or coupons.

44   Jorgensen understood that AllAdvantage would have to take into account how its members might react to such changes. For example, in early June of 2000, AllAdvantage had "infuriated" its members by reducing the number of maximum hours it pays for watching ads.[27] AllAdvantage had consistently emphasized since its founding that it was working toward a maximum of 40 hours of paid monthly surfing for its members. When the ViewBar was initially released, the maximum was set at 15 hours, but was subsequently raised to 25. The announcement by AllAdvantage that maximum surfing hours would be reduced signaled to

members that the promise of 40 hours of surfing would probably never materialize. The lower surfing maximum translated into significant monthly earning reductions for members with substantial referral income—in many cases monthly earnings were reduced by 30 percent to 40 percent.

45    AllAdvantage downplayed the changes. In an email to members, CEO Jim Jorgensen characterized the changes as a "global rebalancing." AllAdvantage set the payout currency, the direct surfing compensation rate ($.53 in the United States), the primary, direct and indirect surfing compensation rates ($.53, $.10, and $.05, respectively, in the United States), the maximum payable hours per month (15 in the United States) and the minimum payout threshold ($30 in the United States) for members in all the international markets in which the company operated. The company pushed back its payment schedule from 30 days to 45.[26] The net result of these changes, according to AllAdvantage's legal filings, was to reduce "what would have been an average payment of $6.49 per user per month to $4.54—a reduction in expected member payments to members of just over 30 percent. Although these changes had raised the ire of some of its members, AllAdvantage did not expect member growth to slow considerably. Jorgensen understood, however, that there were limits to how much the company could reduce member payments and maintain its current growth rate. If AllAdvantage were to adopt a compensation policy that did not contain a multilevel component, for example, members would no longer have any incentive to sign up friends and acquaintances and member referrals would decline significantly.

46    How much emphasis should AllAdvantage place on growing its member base? How important was its member community to it long-range strategic objectives? Was it important that AllAdvantage keep paying its members? If so, how much? Should AllAdvantage continue paying cash? Should it continue paying members for the surfing time of referrals? Jorgenson was also aware that there were a growing number of AllAdvantage executives that felt that the pay-to-surf approach was now more of a liability than an advantage. As Alex Gourevitch, the company's PR Director, explained, "the lights were so powerful, the fragrance so strong, it was making our users lose sight of the usefulness of the ViewBar. It was making everyone miss what we were really about. We set out to be an infomediary."[28] Alex and other executives wanted to focus on the utility and convenience of the ViewBar rather than the company's pay-to-surf marketing approach. This certainly seemed reasonable, given the company's current situation. Jorgensen understood that these questions and issues would have to be addressed.

## Strategic Moves

47    AllAdvantage has actively set out to build a community of AllAdvantage members, but was this really essential to its stated objective of being an internet infomediary? Jorgensen thought about some of the new programs AllAdvantage had introduced in recent months. There was the AdVantage Network, for example. AllAdvantage intended to sell and deliver targeted advertising to internet users' persistent desktop objects (PDOs) on behalf of other companies that had built online communities centered around the delivery of advertising through software similar to the AllAdvantage ViewBar. In many cases these companies were more than happy to outsource the sale of advertising and content delivery to companies in a better position to perform these functions. As Jorgensen explained:

> We started the AdVantage Network, we started working with companies like Spinway, FreeI, Conducent, and Radiate, there are others, we started selling ads for them. At first we were just solving a reach problem. We were trying to serve the advertising community and we needed to be able to offer access to other communities, to more communities than just our own members.[10]

**48**    Jorgensen believed that the AllAdvantage AdVantage Network might result in some potentially profitable opportunities for the company. AllAdvantage was aware of these opportunities when they decided to launch the network. Again, as Jorgensen explained:

> We also thought that once we got our nose in the tent we could sell them our technology, we had the ViewBar and we had some experience handling permanent desktop objects. We had that capability and we thought that that might be something that we could do. We might be able to license them our technology or reach some other arrangement.[10]

**49**    The AdVantage network allowed AllAdvantage to access members of other ready-made communities. It gave AllAdvantage the chance to leverage its investment in its ViewBar technology and to more fully utilize its sales force and thereby realize some economies of scale. There were other opportunities in addition to the AdVantage network. For example, in March 2000 AllAdvantage announced that it had partnered with NetCreations, Inc., a leading provider of opt-in email marketing services.[29] NetCreations and AllAdvantage agreed to build email lists that would allow AllAdvantage members to receive ads and information tailored to their personal profiles. In May 2000 the firm announced that it had partnered with myCIO.com (a Network Associates, Inc. business) to provide antivirus software and software updates to AllAdvantage members.[30] In July, it signed an agreement with San-Francisco-based Providian Financial Corp., the nation's sixth largest card issuer, to promote Providian's Internet Aria Visa.[31] Also in July, AllAdvantage entered into an arrangement with RioPort Inc., a leading Internet music service provider, to offer its members a special discount on the popular RioPort Audio Manager jukebox software.[32] These arrangements weren't dependent on the capabilities of the ViewBar or, necessarily, on AllAdvantage maintaining its own community of members. Jorgensen wondered if AllAdvantage should put more effort into establishing similar types of marketing arrangements with other firms. Should it focus on licensing its technology to other firms with ready-made communities? Should it focus on providing services to these other firms.

### Exit Strategies

**50**    Although Jorgensen believed in AllAdvantage, he understood that unless he and his top managers could convince investors the AllAdvantage business model created economic value, the company would be forced to exit the industry. Although the company had nearly $85 million in the bank, its investors would not stand idly by while AllAdvantage burned through its cash. Unless its investors believed that money invested in AllAdvantage would generate a substantial return, they would not be willing to risk their capital.

**51**    Jorgensen thought about potential buyers for the firm. What exactly did AllAdvantage have to offer? What kinds of firms might be interested?

**52**    If the decision were made to exit the industry and a suitable buyer couldn't be found, then the firm would have to consider simply closing its doors, returning unused capital to its investors and selling off its assets. Jorgensen wondered what course of action would best serve the interests of the firm? Of employees? Of investors?

**53**    Jorgensen wondered if he should bring up the possibility of exit. Should they discuss it? Should selling the firm or shutting down be considered viable strategic options? Is ceasing operations an outcome that business managers should choose or is it something that creditors or investors force on a company? Jorgensen couldn't help but feel that it was inappropriate to raise the subject with his top executives—it might signal a lack of confidence on his part in their ability to run the company.

**54**    Jorgensen paused just outside the company's front door. He glanced at his watch—he'd been outside nearly an hour. Regardless of how things turned out, he thought, the last 18 months had been a wild ride. Jorgensen headed to his office to sketch out comments for tomorrow's board meeting. He'd probably be here all night.

# References

1. G. A. Chidi, Pay-to-Surf, *InfoWorld Daily News,* July 21, 2000.
2. Cash from Your Desktop Adverts, *Financial Times,* London, Edition 1, June 1, 1999, p. 15.
3. T. Jackson, Sweeping Costs Aside, *Financial Times,* London, London Edition 1, September 5, 2000, Inside Track: p. 15.
4. E. Foster, Viral Marketing Goes One Step Too Far—To a Place Where Friends Spam Friends, *InfoWorld,* February 7, 2000, p. 93.
5. M. Gimein, The Dumbest Dot-com, *Fortune.com,* June 19, 2000.
6. Dot-coms Lose Millions by Giving Money Away for Surfing the Internet, *The Plain Dealer,* August 7, 2000, p. C6.
7. M. Vickers, Dot-com Business Models from Mars, *BusinessWeek Online,* September 4, 2000.
8. A. E. Cha, and L. Walker, A Pyramid Marketing Ploy Clicks, *The Washington Post,* Final Edition, December 8, 1999, p. A1.
9. D. Batstone, Ad It Up, *Business 2.0,* February 1, 2000.
10. J. Jorgensen, Co-Founder and CEO of AllAdvantage.com, *Personal Interview,* December 12, 2000.
11. Alladvantage.com Unveils Multilingual Viewbar Communications Software, *Company Press Release,* April 25, 2000.
12. Alladvantage.com Appoints Distinguished Internet Privacy Advocate Ray Everett-Church Chief Privacy Officer, *Business Wire,* August 31, 1999.
13. Alladvantage.com Scores $31 Million and Strategic Allies with Plan to Bring Next-level Internet to Advertisers, *Business Wire,* September 8, 1999.
14. Alladvantage.com Appoints David Martin Vice President of Business Intelligence, *Company Press Release,* February 8, 2000.
15. Alladvantage.com Names Tobin Trevarthen Vice President, Business Development, *Business Wire,* May 23, 2000.
16. Advantages for the Advantaged, *Dow Jones News Service,* November 14, 1999.
17. D. Bonello, Alladvantage.com Rolls out First U.K. Surfer Payments to its Members, *New Media Age,* October 28, 1999, p. 9.
18. AllAdvantage.com Introduces Localized Payment Policy, *Company Press Release,* June 1, 2000.
19. T. Jackson, Boldness Bar None, *Financial Times,* London, London Edition 1, July 4, 2000, Inside Track: p. 14.
20. K. Balint, Surf for Cash, *The San Diego Union-Tribune,* August 27, 2000, p. H1.
21. D. Tweney, Online Advertising: A $3 Billion Industry Limping on its Last Legs, *InfoWorld,* October 4, 1999.
22. The Science (or Art?) of Online Media Planning, *AdRelevance (www.adrelevance. com),* 2000.
23. Online Advertising Rate Card Prices and Ad Dimensions, *AdRelevance (www.adrelevance.com),* 2000.
24. A. E. Cha, and L. Walker, Online Firms Pay Surfers to Click Away, *Newsbytes,* December 8, 1999.
25. C. Metinko, Hayward, California-Based Internet Habits Tracker Delays IPO Plan, *Contra Costa Times,* July 9, 2000.
26. C. Kirby, Pay-to-surf Not Paying Off for Web Sites, *The San Francisco Chronicle,* Final Edition, July 12, 2000, p. C1.
27. T. Bridis, Alladvantage.com Upsets its Paid Ad-Watchers, *Wall Street Journal,* June 5, 2000, p. B8.

28. A. Gourevitch, Director of Public Relations at AllAdvantage.com, *Personal Interview,* December 12, 2000.

29. Netcreations, Alladvantage.com Team up to Build 100% Opt-in Email Lists, *Business Wire,* March 13, 2000.

30. AllAdvantage.com Teams with MyCIO.com to Automatically Deploy Anti-virus Software Updates, *Company Press Release,* May 25, 2000.

31. Providian signs deal with infomediary, *Card Fax,* July 13, 2000, p. 2.

32. Infomediary at Work, *Business Wire,* July 28, 2000.

# Case 28   Avon Products, Inc.: The Personal Care Industry

## Gabriella Del Carro, Robert J. Mockler, Marc E. Gartenfeld

1   In the spring of 2000, Andrea Jung, president and CEO since November 1999 at Avon Products, Inc., faced the strategic decision of developing a growth strategy for a 115-year-old company. Avon Products Inc., the world's largest direct seller of beauty and related personal care products, sold to women in 137 countries via three million independent sales representatives who generated approximately $5.1 billion in annual revenues. Upon reviewing the financial statistics of Avon, Jung realized that not only had earnings risen in the low-single digits in the past few years, but also more disturbingly, the growth rate had shrunk during the same time. In light of this problem, Jung faced significant strategic decisions in growing the company in lieu of its stagnant sales, limited distribution capabilities, and shifts in personal care preferences and spending habits in the rapidly changing personal care industry.

2   For 115 years, Avon had enjoyed worldwide success mainly due to its unique direct selling distribution channel and worldwide brand name recognition. However, recent single digit growth indicated that the company needed to make significant improvements in its overall operations. In 1999, sales increased approximately 1 percent as gains in fashion, jewelry and accessories, and non-core categories offset declines in cosmetics, fragrances, toiletries, and apparel. The single digit growth rate had declined each year. Avon's direct selling model generated 95 percent of the company's revenues. In 2000, Jung was deciding whether or not to enter Avon into a nonexclusive partnership with JCPenney and Sears to supplement its sales representatives, expand its distribution capabilities, and attract new customers in order to incite sales and earnings.

3   Under careful consideration was the type of products to be sold in these stores. The company was leaning towards higher priced cosmetics, which would be sold exclusively in these department stores. By partnering with JCPenney and Sears, considered to be the weakest portion of the brand retail market, the company ran the risk of a possible further reduction of its brand name. Also, in marketing a higher-priced Avon line in those department stores, the company might be sending an unintentional message to consumers that the current Avon line was not of high enough quality to be sold in JCPenney and Sears. Avon had faced significant hard times in the past, and past efforts in diversifying products and distribution had put them at risk of debt and takeovers.

4   Avon was also spending $30 million to relaunch Avon.com, in order to enable consumers to buy products from sales representatives online or directly through the company. The company was intending to allow each sales representative to customize his or her own website which would be linked to the company's home page. However, personalized nonconsistent websites could further erode Avon's already weakened brand image.

5   The global personal care market, which included skin-care, hair-care, fragrance, color cosmetics, personal-hygiene, and other related beauty products, was valued at $171.39 billion in 1999, with overall growth of 2.8 percent from 1995 through 1999. The industry had to deal with significant changes, namely shifting distribution channels and market demands as well as new emerging consumer groups. Due to the low barriers to entry and aggressive competition in the industry, personal care product companies began to utilize the Internet as a distribution channel for their products. However, many of the well established retail and

Source: This case was prepared by Gabriella Del Carro, Marc E. Gartenfeld, and Professor Robert J. Mockler of St. John's University. Copyright © Robert J. Mockler.

direct selling companies had been overly cautious in developing extensive websites due to the fear of possible cannibalization. Younger companies, less established retailers, and niche operators, however, recognized the opportunities of the Internet and were increasingly eroding market share away from major players. Expanding target markets had also restructured personal care marketing and product plans. As a result of sustained marketing campaigns and greater product knowledge, consumers began to display more sophisticated buying behavior. This trend was attributed to the rising spending power of the younger generations and their corresponding demand for high quality beauty products. However, the young and affluent customer segment rarely shopped for personal care products via the direct selling channel. Other attractive customer segments in the industry included the Generation Y market, the ethnic market, and increasingly, the men's personal care market. Most of these customer bases were only presently being recognized.

6    In light of Avon's disappointing financial situation and new retail initiatives as well as changing market demands, Jung was considering the following strategic decisions. What type of product line extensions or divestitures should Avon undertake? How should the company establish a successful Internet presence? If the company ventured into retail outlets, which would best suit the company's current structure and future goals? How could the company create a consistent and strong brand image? These and other strategic decisions would have to be made, if Avon was to grow, prosper, and win against competitors in the near, intermediate, and longer term.

# INDUSTRY AND COMPETITIVE MARKET: THE PERSONAL CARE INDUSTRY

### Overall View of the Industry

7    The personal care industry, as shown in Exhibit 1, included all products intended to be applied to the body for cleansing, beautifying, promoting attractiveness, or altering the body's appearance. The products in the personal care industry were divided into skin care, makeup/color cosmetics, hair care, personal hygiene products, perfumes/fragrances, spa services, and other related items. The customers in the industry could be segmented according to their age (mature market, baby boomers, Generation X, Generation Y), by sex (male, female) and by ethnic origin (African-American, Asian-American, Latin-American). Products in the industry were distributed and sold via three methods, direct selling, retail selling, and online selling. The personal care industry was prominent in both the domestic and international markets and was regulated by the FDA, FTC, and DOT organizations. Competition stemmed mainly from Mary Kay Inc. and L'Oreal.

8    In 1999, the global market for personal care products was valued at $171.39 billion with overall growth of 2.8 percent from 1995 through 1999. Overall, the market for personal care products was expected to increase steadily in the future reaching $197.97 in 2003, as seen in Exhibit 2.

### Products/Services

9    The Food and Drug Administration (FDA) defined personal care products as articles intended to be applied to the human body for cleansing, beautifying, promoting attractiveness, or altering the appearance without affecting the body's structure or functions. Personal care products considered to be drugs or "cosmeceuticals" were articles intended to cleanse, beautify or promote attractiveness as well as treat or prevent disease or otherwise affecting the structure or any function of the human body.

**EXHIBIT 1**   **The Personal Care Industry**

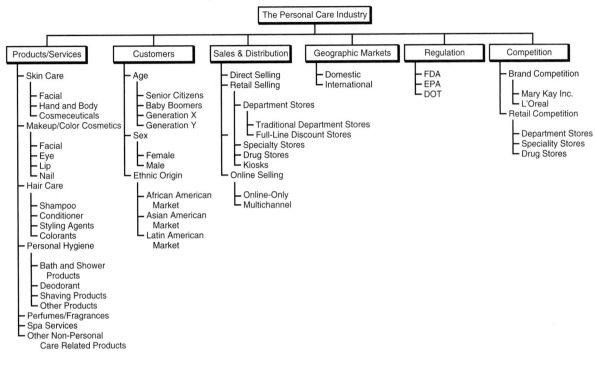

**EXHIBIT 2**
**Expected Sales in the Personal Care Market**

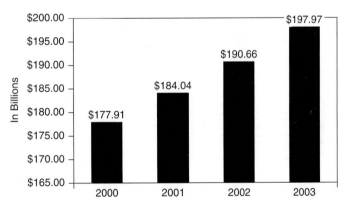

**10**   As shown in Exhibit 3, the products and services of the personal care industry consisted of skin care, makeup or color cosmetics, hair care, personal hygiene, perfumes/fragrances, spa services, and other related products.

### Skin Care

**11**   Skin care products, valued at $29.44 billion in 1999, were comprised of facial products, hand and body products, and cosmeceuticals.

**12**   Facial skin care products included cleansing creams and lotions. Cleansing creams did not contain surfactant and therefore were superior in avoiding irritation as soap commonly would. Facial cleansers worked by cleansing facial pores, either by removing makeup or excess dirt and oil. Facial lotions consisted of softening creams or moisturizers, which supplemented the water loss experienced when cleansing the facial area. Approximately 39

**EXHIBIT 3**   **Products/Services**

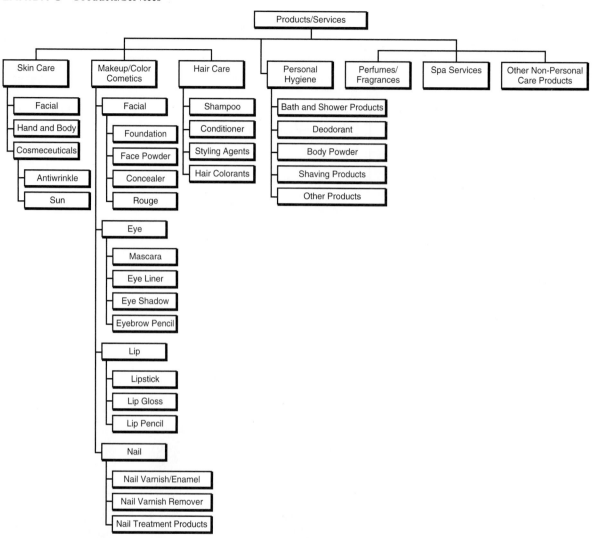

percent of households purchased facial cleansers and lotions at least once a year with expenditures averaging $14.41. Also, 22 percent of the purchases were attributed to perceived price savings.

13        Hand and body skin care consisted mainly of creams and lotions used to prevent or reduce dryness and roughness of skin due to prolonged exposure to household detergents and environmental factors such as wind, sun, and dry atmospheres. Similar to facial moisturizers, they replaced lost water and provided an oil fill to reduce subsequent moisture loss while the body's natural processes repaired the damage. Consumers tended to buy larger sizes and use larger quantities of hand and body lotion than in the facial segment. Due to this, consumers were becoming increasingly price sensitive to hand and body lotion products. At the same time, they demanded quality and effectiveness in the products they purchased. Approximately 73.7 percent of households bought skin and hand lotions with yearly

expenditures averaging $21.33. Consumers bought the products about four times a year with 21.3 percent purchasing the products due to perceived price savings or deals.

14   Skin cosmeceuticals comprised 25 percent of the total skin-care market in 1999 with sales of $1.5 billion. The growth was driven by the introduction of cosmeceutical ingredients in mass products—once the exclusive domain of high quality product manufacturers. It was projected that in the following years, the skin care market would be dominated by cosmeceuticals, especially in the more advanced economies. The entry of many mass companies into the market was likely to drive average prices up which in turn would increase revenue growth. The most common skin cosmeceuticals were antiwrinkle cosmeceuticals and sun cosmeceuticals.

15   Antiwrinkle cosmeceuticals contained ingredients such as Retinal (a vitamin A derivative) which served to maintain the skin's youthful appearance. These products reduced or prevented skin wrinkles, mainly in the facial area. Product claims of "anti-aging, wrinkle reduction, and improves fine lines" dominated the skin care segment, as consumers were eager to purchase products that delivered a glimpse of hope or promise for healthier looking skin and body.

16   The two types of sun cosmeceuticals were sunscreens and sun blocks. Sunscreens were creams, lotions, or oils that were SPF rated and reacted with chemicals in the skin to offer protection from the sun for a predetermined time period without risking sunburn. Sun blocks were opaque creams or pastes containing zinc oxide or titanium dioxide that prevented all ultraviolet radiation from reaching the skin and therefore, did not carry an SPF rating. Sunscreens with an SPF above 15 were sometimes referred to as sun blocks even though they still allowed some UV light to pass through. Sun cosmeceuticals mainly protected individuals from sun light–induced skin aging and melanoma, a form of skin cancer. Melanoma rates of mortality rose 191 percent in men and 84 percent in women between 1950 and the mid 1990s.

17   Keys to success with skin care products were products tailored to various needs and frequent new product introductions. In order to introduce successful new skin care products, strong company research and development was needed. Other keys to success were strong brand loyalty and strong brand image in order to make viable product claims.

### Makeup/Color Cosmetics

18   The makeup/color cosmetic segment, valued at $19.1 billion in 1999, was the highest revenue-generating segment in the personal care segment. As illustrated in Exhibit 4, the subsegments of the makeup/color cosmetic segment in order of sales volume were facial, eye, lip, and nail.

**EXHIBIT 4**
**1998 Sales in the Color Cosmetic Segment**

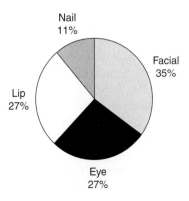

19    Facial makeup/color cosmetic products included foundation, face powder, concealer, and rouge. Facial cosmetics were the highest revenue-generating segment in the makeup/color cosmetic market.

20    Foundation was vanishing cream, comprised of an oil-in-water emulsion, providing the quality of sheen. Its main use was to create an even, adherent base for face powder, which when dusted on top of a foundation provided a peach-skin appearance. Foundation sales were $602.7 million in 1999, a 19.1 percent gain over 1998. Foundation experienced the most growth of any color cosmetic category, due in part to the use of sheer-skin effects.

21    Face powder was dusted on the face to create a finished look. It was comprised of talc for ease of spreading, chalk or kaolin for moisture-absorbing qualities, magnesium stearate for adherence, zinc oxide and titanium dioxide for thorough skin coverage, and pigments for added color.

22    Concealer, available in cream or stick form, was more opaque than foundation. It was applied to mask broken capillaries, blemishes, age spots, and especially dark eye circles.

23    Rouge provided heightened color to highlight the cheekbones. Blushers, the more modern version of rouge, were used to blend more color in the face and were available in powder, gel, or stick form. Small kits of compressed face powder and rouge or blushers were developed so that they could be conveniently carried by women in their handbags.

24    Eye makeup/color cosmetic products included mascara, eyeliner, eye shadow, and eyebrow pencil.

25    Mascara was a thick dark liquid available in a variety of shades that colored eyelashes and gave them the appearance of length and thickness.

26    Eyeliner was a kohl-based substance used to outline the eye area.

27    Eye shadow was a powdered or cream-based substance available in a variety of colors and tints applied to the eyelids in order to accentuate the area.

28    An eyebrow pencil was a kohl-based substance used to extend or darken the eyebrow.

29    Since eye cosmetics were used in a very sensitive area, product testing and safety were essential. Customers were increasingly demanding new products with an emphasis on all-in-one features such as new brow products that emphasized definition and contour, mascara products with gel-based consistency to promote thickness and shine, and monochromatic and metallic colors for eye shadows.

30    Lip makeup/color cosmetic products were comprised of lipstick, lip gloss, and lip pencil.

31    Lipstick, enclosed in a cyndrical base, was a small stick of waxy lip coloring available in a variety of shades and applied to the mouth area. The color was usually provided by pigment. Since lipsticks were placed on a sensitive surface and ultimately ingested, they were made according to the highest safety specifications.

32    Lip gloss was a gel-like formula which provided shine or luster when applied to the mouth area.

33    A lip pencil was a kohl-based substance used to outline the lip area for definition and accentuation.

34    The trend in lip products was moving towards all-in-one products which provided color, moisturizing capabilities, and also protected the lips from harmful UV-rays and included SPF, vitamins, botanicals, anti-oxidants, and exfoliators.

35    Nail makeup/color cosmetic products consisted of nail varnish or enamel, nail varnish remover, and nail treatment products.

36    Nail varnish was a clear or colored cosmetic lacquer applied to the fingernails or toenails.

37    Nail varnish remover was either an acetone or non-acetone based liquid substance which removed nail varnish or lacquer from fingernails and toenails.

**38**  Nail treatment products included all products used in the care of fingernails and toenails such as scissors, files, callous shavers, and cuticle oils.

**39**  Nail cosmetics experienced the lowest growth in the personal care industry due to fashion-related cycles and lack of new shades, colors, and product launches.

**40**  Growth in the overall makeup/color cosmetic segment was expected to remain strong in the future, especially as new products were expected to hit the market. Cosmetics were considered basic necessities and were purchased regardless of the health in the economy. Sales of cosmetics relied on disposable personal income, which was expected to increase 2.4 percent through 2003. However, the segment was heavily influenced by prevalent fashion trends as shown on beauty websites, in magazines, or at runway shows. Cosmetics were becoming more innovative and sophisticated as witnessed by the popularity of multifunctional all-in-one products, which performed more than one basic role. Consumers of makeup/color cosmetics were also seeking products tailored to their specific needs, which portrayed individualism and self-expression. Their increased product knowledge led to the demand for selection. Female consumers began to purchase cosmetics by the age of 12. By the age of thirteen, 90 percent of them regularly used cosmetic products.

**41**  Keys to success in regards to makeup/color cosmetics were developing products according to fashion trends, having a wide range of selection in each subcategory, and creating products according to needs. An additional key to success was to develop product awareness and recognition among young consumers. Also, since makeup/color cosmetics were at times used in very sensitive areas of the body, strong quality control was required.

### Hair Care

**42**  The hair care segment was comprised of shampoo, conditioner, styling agents, and colorants.

**43**  Shampoo, a soapless scented cleaning detergent used in washing hair, was the most popular hair care product. Due to consumer demand, special formulation shampoos were developed for particular hair types or for hair that had been subjected to a treatment such as coloring.

**44**  Conditioner was a cream-based formula applied to hair after the shampoo was rinsed off in order to repair damaged hair. Many new conditioning products offered a combination of benefits, such as protecting and strengthening the hair.

**45**  Styling agents included products that intended to give gloss, body, or holding power to the hair such as resin-based sprays, brilliantine, pomades, and alcohol-based lotions. It also included permanent wave and hair-straightening preparations that used chemicals to release hair from its natural set.

**46**  Hair colorants used permanent or semipermanent dyes to add color to hair, and hydrogen peroxide to alter natural hair color. Hair colorants were leading the hair care segment since it was being driven by increased purchases by women, men, baby boomers, and generation Y. It was reported that 50 percent of women colored their hair and 35 percent of them did it at home with a consistent growth rate projected for upcoming years. Those who began to color their hair in their mid-thirties were likely to color it for life.

**47**  Additionally, there was social pressure for baby boomers to appear young looking and to maintain this image. This vanity was increasing within the age group as more women entered the workplace to follow career paths. Hair colorants led to the introduction of styling products formulated for colored or UV damaged hair that could intensify color and longevity. The hair color category had grown 12 percent over the past year. The five most common hair problems among women were frizziness, dryness, damage, limpness, and scalp problems. All hair types universally experienced these problems to some degree. Hair structure and physical properties of hair care were important factors to consider in developing new hair care products. When formulating for the ethnic care marketplace, it was important to clearly understand the differences and address the specific care needed. Natural ingredients in hair products were expected to drive growth in the hair care segment for the next 10 years. This was due to consumers' recognition that herbs had fewer side effects, promoted health, and were perceived to be cleaner and simpler. In 1999, market saturation in the hair care segment was prevalent since there were two to three times more brands than in 1990. In order to succeed in this market, first value-added products needed to be introduced in order to distinguish between the numerous products, and second a complete line of hair-care products would need to be developed in order to increase profits.

48    Keys to success in regard to hair care products were products tailored to needs, use of natural ingredients, value-added products, and a complete line of products. Keys to success also included brand loyalty with existing consumers and brand awareness and recognition for new younger consumers by offering trendy coloring products.

### Personal Hygiene

49    The personal hygiene segment included bath and shower products, deodorant, shaving products, and other related products.

50    Bath and shower products included bubble bath, a foaming detergent added to a bath containing fragrances, for the purpose of creating lather in the water, and cleansing products such as bar soap and body wash which mildly cleansed the body, leaving the skin moist. Approximately 93 percent of the population used personal wash products with above average growth in shower gels and antibacterial products. However, bar soaps constituted two thirds of bath product sales.

51    Deodorant, either in solid, liquid, or spray form, was applied to the skin in order to mask unpleasant body odors.

52    Shaving products included razors, both electric and manual, and shaving creams utilized to smooth the skin and prevent nicks when removing hair from the face, underarms, and legs. Competition among electric razors was expected to increase due to technological innovations. Manual razors were considered commodities which were easily interchangeable. As a result, many companies reduced prices and sustained smaller profit margins in order to gain customer loyalty.

53    Other products in the personal hygiene segment included oral hygiene products which were comprised mainly of dentifrice used to cleanse teeth and feminine hygiene products.

54    In 1999, the total global market value of personal-hygiene was $22.4 billion. Personal-hygiene products did not always follow the same trends as other personal-care markets, since many personal-hygiene products were considered staples, as opposed to luxuries. Personal-hygiene products designed exclusively for men were valued at $1.7 billion in 1999. Manufacturers were increasingly targeting the "wellness" market, attempting to drive value from aromatherapeutic products designed to be a sanctuary from the stresses of modern life. These included essential oils, such as eucalyptus and menthol in bath additives, shower gels, and soaps. Many companies not primarily involved in personal care products often diversified themselves and produced personal hygiene products due to their non-cyclical need. Due to increased competition and number of products offered, a key to success was to develop all-in-one products and utilize aromatherapeutic ingredients. Most personal-hygiene products were distributed via retail outlets and oftentimes, the companies with the strongest brand name and highest profit margins would obtain premium shelf space. There were many generic brands available for the more price-conscious consumer.

55    Therefore, a key to success was to develop good relations with storeowners in order to obtain premium shelf space and increase sales. An additional key to success was strong brand loyalty.

## Perfumes/Fragrances

**56**   A perfume or fragrance was a liquid with a pleasant smell usually made from oils taken from flowers or spices, which was applied to the skin. The entire value of the global fragrance market, made up of male, female, unisex, and baby fragrances, was valued at $22.2 billion in 1999. Sales of men's prestige fragrances rose to $960 million in 1999, a 6 percent increase from the previous year. Women's fragrances decreased by 1 percent in the same year. Unisex fragrances were driving the market globally, growing from 6 percent of overall sales in 1995 to 8 percent in 1999. The fragrance market was highly sensitive to the marketing strategies of major fragrance houses. The association with clothing and sports was expected to drive the market in the future. During the 1990s, approximately 1,000 new perfumes were launched. Future trends included invisible scents which only reached the brain, microencapulation which would allow scents to remain on the skin for days, and natural "aromathermapeutic" scents which were mood stimulators, enhanced the senses, and reduced stress. Many companies offered single use sprays in order to increase brand awareness. Also companies were also offering refillable perfumes, which were 20–40 percent cheaper in order to ensure repeat sales. Overall, companies participating in the fragrance industry were subjected to rising price competition, price transparency, and limited future growth prospects. The fragrance market was heavily influenced by prevailing trends and further characterized by low-level brand loyalty. Consumers were becoming increasingly fashion-conscious with an emphasis on value. Recent product launches indicated that mental well-being was having an impact on innovation, encouraging consumers to purchase value-added products.

**57**   Keys to success in regards to fragrances were new product introductions with an emphasis on mental well-being, increased brand awareness through the increased distribution of samples, and strong brand loyalty.

**58**   Exhibit 5 indicates the expected future sales growth of personal care products from 1998 to 2005 segmented by type of product.

## Spa Services

**59**   Spas, also known as wellness centers, were locations where individuals received therapeutic and beautifying services such as massages, body wraps, manicures, pedicures, haircuts, color, and styling. Many spas sold a variety of prestigious premium priced personal care products. Spas were becoming more commonplace for both men and women. Most consumers received samples of the products, which were used in the service they received. As

### EXHIBIT 5
**Expected Future Sales Growth 1998–2005**

| Low Growth (<12%) | Premium women's fragrances, hand care, baby hair care, face masks, bath additives, styling agents, home perms, conditioners | High Growth (18–25%) | Shower products, eye makeup, post-shave products, salon hair care, body care, solid deodorants, talcum powder, premium unisex fragrances, cleansers, shampoo, spray deodorants |
|---|---|---|---|
| Medium Growth (12–18%) | Facial make-up, baby toiletries, mass women's fragrances, baby skin care, premium men's fragrances, 2-in-1 hair care products, mass unisex fragrances, suntan products, after-sun products, bar soaps, toners, mass men's fragrances | Exceptionally High Growth (>25%) | Baby sun care, hair colorants, lip products, self-tanning products, cream deodorants, facial moisturizers |

a result, many developed brand loyalty to products they perceived to be superior and unique for their needs.

**60** Keys to success with spa services were to offer samples of products used during the service, develop a strong brand image by developing and selling prestigious high priced products, and create products tailored to needs.

### Other Non-Personal Care Products

**61** A few personal care companies went beyond normal personal care product line extensions and offered non-personal care products such as jewelry, apparel, gift and decorative products, and home entertainment items.

**62** The key to success with other non-personal care products was to analyze each segment to see if it was profitable and fit the company's brand image.

# CUSTOMERS

**63** Customers in the personal care industry could be categorized according to age, sex, or ethnic origin.

### Age

**64** Customers could be segmented by age in four distinct markets, namely, the mature market, baby boomers, generation X, and generation Y. Exhibit 6 illustrates the age ranges and size of each age segment.

**65** The senior citizen segment was comprised of individuals aged 54 and over. The number of individuals in the United Stated aged 65 and older increased by over 3.7 million since 1990 reaching approximately 35 million people. The average household of senior citizens aged 65 to 74 spent nearly $30,000 a year on goods and services. However, as senior citizens aged, they tended to reduce their purchases of personal care products. In recent years, department stores, malls, and specialty stores showed the greatest net declines in attracting senior citizens' personal care purchases. The preferred channels of distribution were drugstores, mass merchandisers, and most importantly direct selling due to its convenience. Keys to success with senior citizens was a convenient channel of distribution, preferably direct selling.

**66** The baby boomer segment, estimated at 81 million people or 30 percent of the population, was comprised of individuals aged 35–53 years old and the largest demographic segment. Within this segment, households headed by 45- to 53-year-olds had the highest median income and a median net worth of $57,755, higher than any other prominent personal care product customer age group with increases expected to continue. Their disposable income was valued at $930 billion in 1998, an increase of 7 percent from 1996. The

### EXHIBIT 6
**Customers in the Personal Care Industry Segmented by Age**

| Senior Citizens | 54 and above years old<br>34.8 million people (over age 65) | Generation X | 23–34 years old<br>46 million people<br>17% of the population |
|---|---|---|---|
| Baby Boomers | 35–53 years old<br>81 million people<br>30% of the population | Generation Y | 5–22 years old<br>73 million people<br>28% of the population |

boomer's spending power was expected to grow 16 percent over the next five years, reaching $1,080 billion by 2003. This segment outspent all age groups in virtually every category including categories not targeted to them.

67    Due to the increasing age of this large demographic segment, they sought products which could reverse or halt the aging process and protect the skin from environment stresses, such as pollution, and ozone. Also, due to the aging of this segment, they increasingly purchased hair products that colored gray hair.

68    Exhibit 7 portrays the personal care items which were purchased regularly by baby boomers. The top five regular purchases in this segment were shampoo, deodorant, bath soap, hand and body lotion and conditioner. Exhibit 8 illustrates the products which baby boomers were most likely to buy in the future. As indicated, personal care products which were above expected levels and were expected to increase in popularity were hair colorants, feminine hygiene products, ethnic hair products, and various eye makeup products.

69    Both men and women baby boomers were value- and quality-conscious, but not necessarily price sensitive. Baby boomers were recreational shoppers and status brand purchasers. Therefore, keys to success included high quality and high value products. Since baby boomers shopped via numerous channels of distribution including high-end specialty stores, department stores, full-line discount stores, and direct selling, a key to success was selling products through numerous distribution channels. Due to their hectic lifestyles and subsequent time constraints, a key to success was to provide product information and education. Additional keys to success were creating products according to needs and strong brand loyalty.

**EXHIBIT 7**
**Personal Care Items Purchased Regularly by Baby Boomers**

| Product | Purchase Item Regularly (%) |
|---|---|
| Shampoo | 84 |
| Deodorant | 83 |
| Bath soap | 78 |
| Hand & body lotion | 53 |
| Conditioner | 46 |
| Hair styling products | 36 |
| Men's cologne | 33 |
| Lipstick | 32 |
| Facial moisturizer | 32 |
| Mascara | 32 |
| Facial cleanser | 31 |
| Eye makeup | 28 |
| Perfume—women's | 25 |
| Foundation | 24 |
| Nail polish | 23 |
| Hair colorant | 22 |
| Sunscreens | 21 |
| Blush | 20 |
| Face powder | 17 |
| **Overall** | **98%** |

**EXHIBIT 8**
**Personal Care Products Which Baby Boomers Were More Apt to Buy**

*Volume indices above 120 indicate that dollar sales among households headed by women ages 45–54 were notably above expected levels.*

| Category | Volume Index* |
|---|---|
| Feminine hygiene products | 230 |
| Pain remedies—back and leg | 164 |
| Hair colorants—women's | 158 |
| Ethnic hair products | 155 |
| Eyebrow and eyeliner cosmetics | 155 |
| Cream foundations | 152 |
| Dieting aids—appetite suppressants | 150 |
| Bath oil | 147 |
| Hand cream | 146 |
| Mascara | 145 |
| Perfume—women's | 143 |
| Skin Cream—all purpose | 141 |

**EXHIBIT 9**
**Personal Care Items Purchased Regularly by Generation X**

| Product | Purchase Item Regularly (%) |
|---|---|
| Shampoo | 83 |
| Deodorant | 79 |
| Bath soap | 77 |
| Conditioner | 52 |
| Hand & body lotion | 51 |
| Hair styling products | 40 |
| Men's cologne | 35 |
| Deodorant soap | 34 |
| Lipstick | 32 |
| Facial cleanser | 31 |
| Mascara | 29 |
| Facial moisturizer | 26 |
| Perfume—Women's | 26 |
| Eye makeup | 25 |
| Foundation | 22 |
| Nail polish | 21 |
| Face Powder | 19 |
| Blush | 17 |
| Sunscreens | 16 |
| Hair colorant | 14 |
| **Overall** | **97%** |

70    The generation X segment, averaging 46 million people, or 17 percent of the population, was comprised of individuals aged 23–34 who spent approximately $125 billion yearly. Exhibit 9 illustrates the most regularly purchased items by Generation X. As seen, the five most regular purchases by Generation X were shampoo, deodorant, bath soap, conditioner, and hand and body lotion. This age segment tended to purchase personal care products they perceived to be unique. This age segment was expected to have increasing disposable income to spend in the coming years on luxury goods. In the future, they were

expected to be loyal to the companies/brands from where they have made purchases in the past. Typically, the brand names were well known. They also tended to build loyalty to companies who demonstrated proactiveness to women's issues. Therefore, keys to success were a strong brand image, strong brand loyalty, offering unique products, and sponsorship of women's issues.

71    Generation Y were the 73-million 5–22 year old people who comprised 28 percent of the population. According to U.S. Census projections, Generation Y, nearly three times the size of twenty- and thirty-something Generation X, was expected to reach 33.6 million by 2005, making for the largest teen population in U.S. history. According to Teen Research Unlimited, Generation Y spent $150 billion in 1999 and influenced $450 billion in purchases. Spending in this segment centered mainly on food, clothing, entertainment, and personal care items. Generation Y purchased what they perceived to be quality yet affordable personal care products. They tended to prefer products created for them and addressing their needs. Most informed of all the populations, they were incredibly wired to the Internet, and used it for all of their needs, including product information and purchasing, chatting with friends, and education. Generation Y was heavily influenced by the fashion and music industries and were responsive to advertisements in these channels. However, they also developed brand loyalty to companies who subtly marketed to them. Since they tended to value self-expression and individualism, many experimented with hair coloring and were inclined to purchase nonpermanent hair colorants which would allow the color to wash out or fade in a short predetermined time period. Also, Generation Y was expected to increase sales in the skin care market. As their bodies began changing and developing, skin care issues, especially blemish concerns, were expected to proliferate.

72    Keys to success with Generation Y were quality products at affordable prices, products tailored to their specific needs, and trendy fashionable youth oriented products. In regards to marketing, keys to success were brand awareness and recognition, subtle marketing techniques, and promotions targeted specifically to them. The ability to distribute products through various distribution channels was an additional key to success.

### Sex

73    Customers in the personal care industry could be segmented according to sex, male and female. Females influenced an average of 90 percent of all household purchase decisions and were the main personal care product consumers. Approximately 72 percent of American women worked full time. The number of working wives with children under the age of six had risen by more than 400 percent since 1948, earning more than $1 trillion in 1994, a five-fold increase over 1975. Working women spent less time shopping and were more brand and store loyal than nonworking women. Working women were less likely to shop during evening hours and on the weekend, as well as less likely to buy through direct mail catalogs. The keys to success in targeting to women in general was utilizing various distribution channels.

74    The male consumer was increasingly purchasing personal care products, especially hair colorants and fragrances. Although hair colorants for men grew at a very slow pace from the 1950s to the 1990s, the last five years presented a 13.1 percent increase in this sector. A reason for this growth was twofold; first, the stereotype which disparaged men using products to enhance their appearance was virtually nonexistent in 1999; second, the baby boomer males, who were still in the workforce, were striving to maintain a youthful appearance in their work environment. The growth in the male fragrance market had been attributed in part to aggressive advertising in magazines targeted to males which were increasing in number. Men consumers were increasingly shopping for personal care products in retail locations due to their convenience. The most powerful driver for men was a brand name, since they were very loyal yet they were open to try new products. Nine out of

ten men who wore a fragrance chose it and purchased it by themselves, which was a significant change from a decade earlier, when men were influenced and reliant on women to make this decision. Men were increasingly purchasing hair styling aids in hairdressing salons. They were less price-sensitive than women and also more service-dependent. However, they demanded products created for them since they did not have an interest in purchasing female personal care products. The most powerful purchase driver for men was a brand name, since they were very loyal.

75    Keys to success with males were promotions targeted specifically to them, creating brand awareness through trials, utilizing masculine packaging for products, having a retail presence and providing services to influence decisions. Additional keys to success were a strong brand name and brand loyalty.

### Ethnic Origin

76    By the year 2050, nearly half of all Americans will be non-Caucasian. The three main segments in the personal care ethnic market were African Americans, Asians, and Latin Americans. African-American growth figures had been fairly constant with tremendous growth in the Asian and Latin American segments. Ethnic consumers spent more on personal-care products than any other consumer group, and subsequently demanded products tailored to their unique needs. Exhibit 10 illustrates the most demanded personal care products in the ethnic market. As seen, the ethnic market demanded hair care products over any other product segment in the personal care industry. Exhibit 11 shows the top selling items in the ethnic hair care market. As seen, hair chemical products and hair stylants were the most requested items.

77    The second largest segment in the ethnic market was color cosmetics. Most ethnic users were limited to using products tailored for Caucasian skin. There was also a need for specialized skin-care products.

78    The African-American consumers, comprised of approximately 34 million people, constituted the largest ethnic group in the United States and represented 12 percent of the pop-

**EXHIBIT 10**
**1999 Ethnic Market Expenditures in the Personal Care Industry**

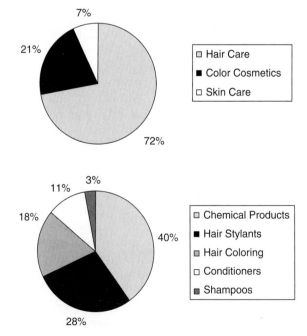

**EXHIBIT 11**
**1999 Ethnic Market Expenditures in the Hair Care Segment**

ulation. With a growth rate at 11 percent annually, the African-American segment was expected to grow to 45 million by 2020. Annual expenditures were expected to rise from $308 billion in 1990 to $532 billion in 1999, up 72.9 percent in nine years for a compound annual growth of 6.3 percent. About 50 percent of African-Americans were considered middle class, up from only 16 percent in 1990. Unlike other ethnic groups that were clustered in a few geographic or metropolitan areas, African-Americans drove the market in many U.S. cities.

79     African-American consumers tended to prefer popular or leading brands, were brand loyal, and were unlikely to purchase private-label and generic products. To satisfy the need in the marketplace, many personal care companies developed products targeted to African-American women, with an emphasis on hair care. It was noted that 64 percent of African-Americans versus 51 percent of Caucasians were willing to spend more for what they considered to be superior quality, which in turn led them to be 25 percent more likely to buy premium or brand names. African-American women spent three times more on hair-care products than the rest of the population. African-American women were influenced by their individual lifestyles and required hair designs that were versatile. Being that their hair was naturally fragile, to successfully target this market the industry needed to create products which were gentle, and rich in moisturizing and conditioning agents. The biggest need in this industry was for a relaxer that did not damage hair since 80 percent of African American women used chemicals on their hair, relaxers being most popular. Nearly 75 percent of African-American women had six perfumes on average. African-Americans demanded specialized skin products suited for their needs since dry skin was a common skin problem in this sector. In selling personal care products, it was determined that mass media did not communicate well in the African-American market. Many marketers supplemented their advertisements in magazines, newspapers, and media directed specifically to African-Americans. African-Americans were also more brand loyal to companies who sought to build relationships. Keys to success with the African-American segment were a premium brand name, products targeted to needs, specifically hair care and skin care products, specialized promotions, building relationships, and developing brand loyalty.

80     The Asian-American population, at approximately 7 million and encompassing 3 percent of the population, was the fastest-growing minority in the United States. Asian-Americans were considered to be better educated and more computer literate than the rest of the population. They spent more than $38 billion on consumer goods and services annually and they valued quality and were willing to pay for it. This ethnic segment tended to be very loyal consumers especially to retailers who made it known that they valued Asian-American patronage. They were more responsive to advertisements featuring models of their ethnicity. Asian-Americans sought products tailored specifically to their unique skin needs. In terms of irritation, Asian skin was more sensitive than Caucasian skin. As a result, many Asians who immigrated to the United States continued to use products from Asia to avoid irritation problems. Keys to success with Asian-Americans were products targeted to needs, high quality products, promotions targeted specifically to them, and developing brand awareness.

81     Latin-Americans represented about 9 percent of the United States population with a combined buying power of $205 billion. With a 53 percent population increase during the decade from 1980 to 1990 (and a 27 percent growth rate expected for the decade 1999 to 2010), Latin-Americans were projected to surpass African-Americans within 20 years as the largest American ethnic group. Latin-Americans preferred well-known or familiar brands and purchased those they perceived to be more prestigious. They generally enjoyed the act of shopping more than other ethnic groups, but tended not to be impulse buyers and were increasingly utilizing promotions and price reductions offered by companies when

buying. They also appeared to be engaged in the process of acculturation, whereby they were adopting the consumption patterns of the majority of United States consumers. Latin Americans also spent more time with mass media in the first language that they learned to speak. Latin Americans were beginning to be targeted by some larger cosmetic companies. Keys to success with Latin-Americans were brand recognition, price reductions/discounts, and foreign language advertisements.

# SALES AND DISTRIBUTION

**82**   Personal care products were sold and distributed via three main methods, specifically, direct selling, retail selling, and online selling.

### Direct Selling

**83**   Direct selling, which comprised face-to-face selling and remote selling, included both personal contact with consumers in their homes (and other nonstore locations such as offices) and telephone solicitations initiated by the retailer, emphasizing convenience and personalization.

**84**       As opposed to retail stores, consumers were often more relaxed in their homes and were more likely to be attentive since they are not exposed to competing brands as they were in stores. Senior citizens and those with children benefited from direct selling due to their limited mobility. For the company, direct selling presented lower overhead costs since store locations and fixtures were not necessary. Exhibit 12 illustrates the major product groups involved in direct selling. As seen, personal care items were the second most popular products sold via this channel. Exhibit 13 illustrates the popularity of face-to-face and remote selling.

**EXHIBIT 12**
**1999 Direct Selling—Percentage of Sales by Major Product Group**

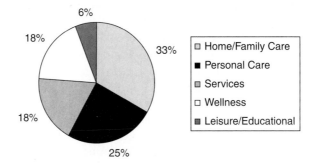

**EXHIBIT 13**
**Percentage of Sales by Type of Direct Selling Medium**

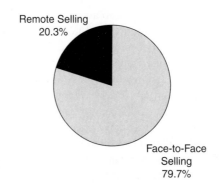

**EXHIBIT 14**
**Percentage of Sales**
**by Face-to-Face**
**Selling**

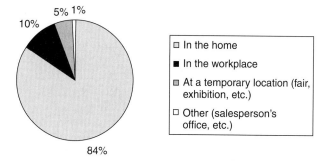

- ▢ In the home
- ■ In the workplace
- ▨ At a temporary location (fair, exhibition, etc.)
- ▢ Other (salesperson's office, etc.)

**EXHIBIT 15**
**Percentage of Sales**
**by Remote Selling**

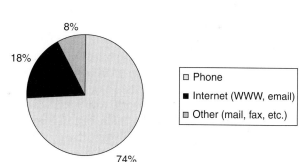

- ▢ Phone
- ■ Internet (WWW, email)
- ▨ Other (mail, fax, etc.)

85    Exhibits 14 and 15 indicate the percentage of sales attributed to the subsegments of face-to-face selling and remote selling. However, in recent times, sales from direct selling especially in the personal care industry were rising at a slow pace due to numerous reasons. More women were working and were not interested or available for in-home purchases. Improved job opportunities in other fields and the interest in full-time career-oriented positions reduced the number of people interested in direct selling jobs. Sales productivity was low because the average transaction was small and most consumers were unreceptive to this type of selling—many would not open their doors to salespeople or talk to telephone sales representatives.

86    Keys to success with direct selling were recruiting and maintaining quality and enthusiastic sales representatives. A key to success with current sales representatives was to offer incentives. Also, having strong internal relations was another important key to success.

### Retail Selling

87    Personal care products were mainly sold via four retail outlets, namely department stores, specialty stores, drug stores, and kiosks.

88    A department store was a large retail unit with an extensive assortment of goods and services that was organized into separate departments for purposes of buying, promotion, customer service, and control. It had the greatest selection of any general merchandise retailers, and often served as the anchor store in a shopping center or district, had strong credit-card penetration, and was usually part of a chain. There were two distinct types of department stores in which personal care products were sold; the traditional department store and the full-line discount store.

89    Traditional department stores, such as Macy's and Bloomingdale's, merchandised average to high quality products with moderate to above average pricing. Customer services ranged from medium to high levels of sales assistance, credit, and delivery. Macy's strategy was aimed at middle-class shoppers interested in a wide assortment and moderate prices,

while Bloomingdale's aimed at upscale consumers through more trendy merchandise and higher prices.

90      During the past decade, sales growth of traditional department stores was behind that of the full-line discount stores. There were several reasons for this decline. Traditional department stores no longer had brand exclusivity for the items they sold, since manufacturers' brands were available at specialty and discount outlets. Many stores were too large and had too much unproductive selling space and low-turnover personal care merchandise. Also, price-conscious consumers were becoming increasingly attracted to discount retailers. Department stores which represented approximately $80 billion in annual sales, cited a 1 percent decline in same-store sales from January 2000 to August 2000, despite a 7 percent increase in the overall retail industry. This was partly due to their high reliance on apparel, which comprised 75 percent of department stores' inventory, and their vulnerability to changes in consumer buying habits. Also, in the past, consumers shopped at department stores for their merchandise selection and service. However, they now purchased at mass merchants for the same reasons but also for convenience and price. Department stores, such as Macy's and Bloomingdale's, were trying to target Generation Y by offering more fashion-conscious products combined with a more exciting decor.

91      Keys to success with traditional department stores were offering medium to highly priced quality products managers having a wide assortment in the product mix, maintaining relationships with store managers for optimal displays and space, and hiring and maintaining qualified sales representatives for point of purchase assistance.

92      A full-line discount store was a high-volume, low-cost, fast-turnover outlet selling a broad range of merchandise for less than conventional prices. Its products were normally sold with minimal assistance in any single department and catalogs were normally not available. Durable goods accounted for approximately 60 percent of all sales. In 1993, Wal-Mart, Kmart, and Target, all three full-line discount stores, expanded operations to include almost 5,000 full-line discount stores that accounted for almost $70 billion in sales that year. The average outlet tended to be smaller than the traditional department store, which improved productivity. The growth in most of the personal care categories was stronger in full-line discount stores since they were able to attract some of the drug store customers. These locations were able to fuel growth by feeding off the heavy volume of customer traffic in their stores. Sales for facial cosmetics increased 15.7 percent in this outlet for 1999. Men's fragrances rose 12.5 percent and women's fragrances rose 6.7 percent. Full-line discount stores catered to middle to lower class consumer seeking average to good quality merchandise at competitive prices.

93      Keys to success with full-line discount stores were products which required minimal assistance and stressed convenience and variety, average to good quality products to attract more price sensitive middle class consumers, and creating strong relationships with store managers for optimal displays and space.

94      A specialty store concentrated on selling one general product type. Specialty stores carried a narrow but deep assortment of products in a chosen category and tailored their strategies to selective market segments. By doing this, the specialty store was able to maintain better selections, flexibility, and sales expertise than department stores. Specialty stores increased in popularity in the 1990s due to their strong consumer focus and image. For the first half of 2000, specialty stores experienced a 4 percent increase in sales. Specialty stores tended to target medium to highly affluent baby boomer and generation X consumers. An example of a personal care specialty store was Sephora, a company offering a hands-on shopping environment. Customers had the ability to browse through the various international unique and prestigious cosmetic selections that were organized alphabetically and by specific categories and had the choice to shop with no

sales assistance or detailed expert advice. The company was formed in 1993 and was currently the leading chain of perfume and cosmetics stores in France and the second in Europe, operating 143 international stores.

Keys to success in selling at specialty stores were unique and prestigious cosmetics and qualified sales representatives for point of purchase assistance.

**95**  A drug store was a location where medical prescriptions are filled and drugs and other articles were sold. Drug stores mainly sold mass-market personal care products that increased steadily in 2000 with strong growth expected in the near future. New brands, such as Olay and Neutrogena, as well as advanced product formulations from established mass-market brands, helped drug store chains gain loyalty from department store shoppers. Although space remained tight in chain drug store cosmetics departments, there was a growing trend to balance out the department with a product mix that was geared to a greater variety of consumers.

**96**  In addition to carrying traditional mainstream mass-market brands, chains were adding a broader assortment of products targeted toward professional, middle to high-income women. In addition, chains were looking at brands targeting less affluent women or women looking for a broad selection of fashion shades. Drug stores attributed their growth to strong marketing and merchandising initiatives, a marketing emphasis on cosmetics as a core department and partnerships with manufacturers resulting in customized promotions. Although full-line discount stores generated superior customer traffic, drug stores were able to drive growth through prominent window displays, aggressive and consistent advertising, offering competitive prices, providing in-store service, and being a leader in introducing new products. Manufacturers were able to capitalize on these opportunities by maintaining good relations with storeowners. As a result, drug stores managed their marketing mix effectively while providing high levels of consumer satisfaction. In 1999, chain drug stores experienced 9.6 percent gains in facial cosmetics. However, sales of nail cosmetics decreased 10.7 percent in the same year. Sales of men and women fragrances rose 5 percent and 2.2 percent, respectively. Other dollar personal care sales rose 3.9 percent to $1.42 billion, while unit volume fell 3.9 percent.

**97**  Keys to success with drug stores were maintaining good relations with store owners through a wide assortment of products in each category, products geared towards both affluent or nonaffluent customers, new product introductions, aggressive and consistent advertising, and offering competitive prices.

**98**  A kiosk was an attractive freestanding structure or self-contained unit located in malls, airports, and other high traffic areas which showcased a company's products and services and provided product information and in some cases, purchasing opportunities. Mall owners had increasingly utilized kiosks as a strategic tool to build up sales per square foot. Kiosks ranged in price from $4,000–$20,000 depending on the level of complexity and technology utilized in the design. The kiosk needed to be secure, well ventilated, and accessible to all types of people with different sizes, physical abilities and language skills. Currently, kiosks were becoming more computerized due to increased technology and offered video, audio, and interactivity, making the experience of using a kiosk more friendly and accessible. Although many personal care companies did not utilize kiosks in malls, those that did stressed the need for exciting, new products, enthusiastic and knowledgeable sales representatives, and samples and trials to distribute in order to increase brand awareness and product trial.

**99**  Keys to success with kiosks were exciting new products, enthusiastic and knowledgeable sales staff, increased product knowledge and education, strong brand image, samples and trials to increase brand awareness and trial, and prime location.

### Online Selling

**100**  With the emergence of the Internet as a shopping channel, many young personal care companies developed websites. This allowed them to utilize the Internet as a marketing tool by providing extensive company and product information, as well as presenting brand images and advertising. However, many older companies had been cautious in using the Internet as a shopping channel since they considered it beyond their core competencies. There was also concern that Internet sales might have undermined their retail position and cannibalized product sales. Less established companies were quicker and riskier in developing e-commerce sites, and as a result, enjoyed increasing market share and international sales. Retail sales on the Internet were growing rapidly. In 1998, online retailers in the United States generated $14.9 billion in revenues, with a 140 percent increase expected for 1999. This trend was expected to continue as more consumers experimented with online access and e-commerce shopping. Unlike some other industries, the personal care market online was not yet saturated. Therefore, personal care companies could still develop loyal customer bases which could allow for stronger market dominance. In 1998, there were two types of personal care retailers online, basically online-only retailers and multichannel retailers.

**101**  Online-only retailers did not have physical locations since they basically existed solely on the Internet. Their advertising and marketing budget was directed towards customer acquisition and retention and brand awareness.

**102**  Multichannel retailers had established brands and a physical presence and therefore did not need to spend as much to build their brand online than the online-only companies. Multichannel retailers were able to leverage existing marketing efforts by adding their Web address to promotions in order to encourage its customers to go online in an effort to capture an even larger share of their spending. Supplemental revenue accounted for less than half of one percent of their revenues as opposed to the 12 percent for online-only retailers.

**103**  Online selling posed a major problem for direct selling companies in general. Direct sellers' sales forces were usually compensated based on a percentage of sales. With the introduction of the online selling, sales representatives feared cannibalization of sales and loss of customers. As a result, many direct sellers were faced with strategic decisions on how to include the Internet as a channel of distribution while placating their sales representatives. At the end of 1999, more than 17 million households were shopping online, purchasing $20.2 billion over the Internet during the year. The number of online shoppers was expected to level off at about 50 million, but that trend was expected to be offset by a surge in average online spending per household, increasing from $1,167 in 1999 to $3,738 in 2004. At that point, online spending in the United States was expected to total $184 billion.

**104**  Exhibit 16 illustrates the behavior of consumers when purchasing personal care products via the Internet. In 1999, online personal care sales accounted for one percent of the personal care industry. Fragrance, makeup, and skin care accounted for 2 percent of all products sold online. A recent NPD report stated that 62 percent of polled consumers would

**EXHIBIT 16**
**Types of Online Personal Care Purchases**

**EXHIBIT 17**
**Why Shop for Beauty Products Online Instead of in Traditional Stores**

| | |
|---|---|
| Shop any time | 75% |
| Delivery of purchases | 54% |
| Ease of comparison shopping | 46% |
| Faster | 42% |
| Avoid sales tax | 38% |
| Find hard-to-find exclusive brands | 37% |
| Better prices | 31% |
| Avoid interacting with salespeople | 19% |
| Stores too far away | 13% |

consider purchasing personal care product online and cited convenience as the most influencing factor as seen in Exhibit 17.

**105**     Only 31 percent of those polled considered price to be an influencing factor to shop online versus in a retail store. In answer to this, many online companies did not offer discounted prices, rather they offered coupons and other incentives for shopping online. Another important factor influencing online purchasing decisions was brand names. Sixty-four percent of those polled stated that they would buy products that they had tried before. However, the type of products purchased influenced online purchasing behavior as well. For example, those purchasing fragrance, makeup, and skin products were brand loyal when purchasing online. On the other hand, consumers seeking bath and body products tended to try and find the lowest price for their preferred brand. Another trend in online beauty retailing was the diminishing distinction between prestige and mass market brands. Prestige beauty products traditionally sold only in department stores were featured next to mass beauty products on some sites.

**106**     The most successful and visited personal care websites were those that existed for a longer time and had a high level of advertising. Websites which featured health and beauty products were more visited than cosmetic-only websites. Health-related sites typically carried mass merchandise beauty brands. Cosmetic-only sites tended to carry only prestige or exclusive brands. Personal care websites were offering value-added incentives to enhance their positions. All of the companies provided quick, easy returns, many offer free shipping, and some sent free samples with orders. Increasingly, most sites were also providing a wealth of consumer information in the form of magazine-type articles, reviews, directories for purchasing and service, and makeup tips. However, almost two-thirds of consumers said they were unlikely or certain not to buy personal care products or services from the Internet since it was stated to be difficult to purchase cosmetics without a trial or sample. This was most prevalent with new product offerings.

**107**     In the future, the Internet was expected to become more popular and more acceptable among consumers as a shopping method. It was expected that conventional direct selling personal care companies would face exceptional competition in countries where computer use and penetration was high, such as in North America, Western Europe and parts of the Asia-Pacific region. By the year 2003, the Internet was expected to account for 8.2 percent of overall home-shopping sales.

**108**     Keys to success with the Internet were offering a convenient and easy way to navigate site, having online selling capabilities, providing coupons and price incentives to shop online, providing community and enhanced features on the website such as product information, articles, and so on, offering samples and trials, and advertising to get consumers to the website. Additional keys to success were a strong brand name to generate traffic and customer loyalty and developing an early, deep, and loyal customer base.

# GEOGRAPHIC MARKETS

**109** Personal care products were sold in both the domestic and international markets.

## Domestic

**110** The information provided in the preceding sections pertains to the domestic personal care market.

## International

**111** Overall, the largest continental market in the personal care industry was North and South America in 1999, with total sales of $43 billion. The increasing globalization of the world's economy presented significant opportunities for consumer goods manufacturers. Barriers to investment in emerging markets were dropping, and disposable income in these regions was gradually increasing, bringing with it demand for staple consumer products.

**112**     The global personal care industry was expected to experience continued growth in the future, as levels of consumption in undeveloped markets were still significantly inferior to those in Western Europe and North America. However, personal care companies in Western Europe were under increasing pressure to come up with new products to meet consumer demands for both wider choice and higher quality. In 1998, personal care and cosmetics companies experienced the impact of the downturn in Asia in both regional and global sales. To help minimize declining profits, firms restructured, focused on their core businesses and, in cases, expanded to gain a foothold in Asian countries in preparation for their inevitable recovery. Asia and Latin America were considered to have huge growth potential even though they were subject to economic downturns. The products with the greatest global growth potential were basic items such as deodorant, shampoo, and soap, especially in developing regions. For example, since 1994 deodorant experienced an 18.2 percent sales growth globally compared to only 11.6 percent growth for the personal care and cosmetics market overall. New or improved formulas emphasizing health and well-being and cosmeceuticals were common among products launched in 1999. European consumers wanted more variety, especially since they had a widening range of outlets from which to buy personal care products. Supermarket chains, which in some European countries now included pharmacies inside their stores, had been anxious to establish themselves as providers of quality cosmetics and toiletries. In the global market, market share of the top 20 players grew from 68 percent in 1996 to 72 percent in 1998, with the top 10 companies holding 54 percent. These top 10 companies were L'Oreal, Unilever, Procter & Gamble, Johnson & Johnson, Avon, Shiseido, Colgate-Palmolive, Revlon, Amway, and Bristol-Myers Squibb.

**113**     Keys to success in the international market were products tailored to needs, utilizing various distribution outlets, and having a presence in emerging countries.

# REGULATION

**114** The personal care industry was regulated by three main organizations, namely the Food and Drug Administration (FDA), the Environmental Protection Agency (EPA), and the Department of Transportation (DOT).

## Food and Drug Administration

**115** Cosmetics marketed in the United States needed to comply with the provisions of the Federal Food, Drug, and Cosmetic Act (FD&C Act) and the Fair Packaging and Labeling Act (FPLA). The Federal Food, Drug, and Cosmetic Act of 1938 was enacted by Congress to protect consumers from unsafe or deceptively labeled or packaged products by prohibiting the movement in interstate commerce of adulterated or misbranded food, drug devices, and cosmetics. The Fair Packaging and Labeling Act was passed by Congress to ensure that packages and their labels provided consumers with accurate information about the quantity of contents in order to facilitate value comparisons. The FD&C Act prohibited the distribution of cosmetics which were adulterated or misbranded. A cosmetic was considered adulterated if it contained a substance which might have made the product harmful to consumers under customary conditions of use; if it contained a filthy, putrid, or decomposed substance; if it was manufactured or held under unsanitary conditions whereby it may have become contaminated with filth, or may have become harmful to consumers; or if it was not a hair dye and it contained a nonpermitted color additive. A cosmetic was considered misbranded if its labeling was false or misleading, if it did not bear the required labeling information, or if the container was made or filled in a deceptive manner.

**116**  For enforcement of the law, the FDA conducted examinations and investigations of products, inspected establishments in which products were manufactured or held, and seized adulterated and misbranded products.

### Environmental Protection Agency (EPA)

**117**  The EPA regulated products so that they complied with the limitations on volatile organic compounds. Also, the EPA regulated the manufacturing process, such as wastewater and toxic emissions.

### Department of Transportation (DOT)

**118**  At the manufacturing level, the DOT controlled how raw materials were labeled and shipped. Keys to success in regards to FDA regulations were adherence to good manufacturing practices, effective self-inspections, and maintaining good relations with regulation authorities.

# COMPETITION

**119**  Competition in the personal care industry was mainly from brand competitors such as Mary Kay Inc. and L'Oreal and from retail competition.

### Mary Kay Inc.

**120**  Mary Kay Inc. was the United States number two direct seller of beauty products. It sold more than 200 products in eight product categories, namely facial skin care, cosmetics, fragrances, wellness products, sun protection, nail care, body care, and men's skin care with a fairly good brand name and loyalty. It sold quality products at affordable prices. In regards to its skin care line, the company tended to have weak research and development capabilities and therefore had limited new product introductions and a weak brand image. Its skin care and color cosmetic product lines included all-in-one features and products tailored to meet needs. However, the company has a limited selection within each product category.

**121**  The company's color cosmetic line had products tailored to needs and developed according to fashion trends. However, Mary Kay had a limited selection of color cosmetics. The company had a relatively weak personal hygiene segment and did not have either a spa line or a hair care line. Mary Kay had good brand awareness and loyalty with its fragrance line but was weak in regards to new product introductions with an emphasis on mental well-being or in distributing samples and trials.

**122**  Mary Kay had a limited women customer base mainly due to its lack of various distribution channels. Its most loyal customers were senior citizens due to the convenience of the company's direct selling channel. Mary Kay baby boomer customers were attracted to the company's high-quality product tailored to needs resulting in sufficient brand loyalty. However, boomers were not completely satisfied with shopping at Mary Kay since they desired product information and education and the existence of various channels of distribution.

123     The company did not target Generation X or Generation Y. Although ethnic models were used in advertising and promotions, the company did not have exclusive products for any ethnic segment. African-Americans valued a premium brand name, products targeted to needs, specialized promotions, and strong internal relations, areas in which Mary Kay was weak. Its quality products appealed to Asian-Americans but the company was weak in targeting the products to needs, targeting promotions in general, and developing brand awareness in this segment. Mary Kay did not have success with Latin-Americans since the company was weak in brand recognition, price reductions and discounts, and foreign language advertisements. Mary Kay was attempting to reach the male market in selling fragrances, personal hygiene, and skin products in masculine packaging. However, Mary Kay targeted promotions and advertising for male personal care products to women, resulting in a generally weak male customer base.

124     Mary Kay's products were distributed via 600,000 direct sales consultants in approximately 36 countries. Sales for the company reached $1 billion in 1999 and the company posted a 1-year sales growth of 0.0 percent and a 1-year employee growth of (7.1) percent. Although Mary Kay was experiencing virtually no growth with its direct selling model, the company decided not to expand into retail distribution in the near, intermediate, or long-term future in order to maintain strong internal relations. The company felt that doing so would demotivate their core sales representatives. The company successfully recruited and motivated their enthusiastic sales force through bonuses ranging from jewelry to the company trademark pink Cadillac. The company did have a convenient and easy to navigate website. It did not offer a community site linking consumers to articles and advice regarding gift ideas, business, health, diet, nutrition and fitness.

125     Mary Kay was a Food and Drug Administration (FDA) registered drug-manufacturing operation. It maintained adequate manufacturing practices, conducted self-inspections, and maintained relations with regulatory authorities.

126     The company did not advertise the website since it was not being utilized for online selling. Basically, consumers who reached the website were directed to a page which allowed them to locate a consultant in their area. Consumers had the ability to order from the Mary Kay consultant's website, allowing the company to develop a loyal customer base and a good brand name. Samples, trials, coupons, or price incentives were not readily available to customers either through the website or via direct selling.

## L'Oreal

127   L'Oreal was the world's largest beauty company, with products ranging from makeup, perfume, hair care, skin care, to apparel leading to a very strong brand image in the personal care market. L'Oreal was comprised of numerous brands including L'Oreal and Maybelline which were quality, unique, and affordable product lines; Lancôme, featuring more upscale premium priced products for more affluent customers; and Redken and Soft Sheen, which included hair line products.

128     L'Oreal's diverse product lines were sold in a variety of outlets including department stores, full-line discount stores, drug stores, specialty stores, and the Internet. The company did not use kiosks or direct selling. L'Oreal sold its average to good quality products to attract more price sensitive middle class consumers in full-line discount stores. These products required minimal assistance and stressed convenience and variety. The company was successful via this channel due to its strong relations with store managers for optimal displays and space. L'Oreal also distributed this type of product line via drug stores. The company enjoyed success due to its wide assortment of competitively priced products in each

category, products geared toward both affluent and nonaffluent consumers, frequent new product introductions, and aggressive and consistent advertising.

**129**     L'Oreal conducted cosmetology and dermatology research and had a 19.5 percent stake in a pharmaceutical company. Its diverse product mix enabled the company to enjoy worldwide success and obtain strong customer bases in every category loyal to its products. The company's research department employed approximately 2,100 scientists and filed for about 400 patents a year, 77 of them in 1999 with numerous product introductions each year. It devoted three percent of sales to cosmeceutical research, namely antiaging products and sunscreen products. It sold its products in 150 countries with products tailored according to regional needs and demands via various distribution channels. Interestingly, the company sold 56 percent of its products in Western Europe, 27 percent in North America, and 17.8 percent in the rest of the world.

**130**     Almost 90 percent of the company's sales were generated from ten brands, namely, Biotherm, Laboratoires GARNIER, Lancôme, L'Oreal, Maybelline, Redken, Helena Rubinstein, Vichy, and perfumes Giorgio Armani and Ralph Lauren. The Helena Rubinstein line were products emphasizing natural ingredients and wellness targeted to the baby boomer segment of the market. Lavin, a subsidiary of the Group L'Oreal, developed a wide range of ready-to-wear fashion for men and women, made-to-measure fashion for men, and accessories and perfumes.

**131**     Maybelline was a leader in quality, affordable, innovative, and trendy color cosmetics in a wide category sold both in the United States and internationally. Maybelline products were distributed in 40,000 retail outlets including drugstores, discount stores, supermarkets, and personal care specialty stores. They are also carried in more than 70 countries worldwide. Due to its well-known brand name and good relations with store employees, the company was able to obtain optimal shelf spacing. Maybelline products were available on the website and featured trendy fashionable products in order to develop product awareness and recognition with Generation Y customers. The Maybelline website offered content, community, price incentives, and purchasing options.

**132**     In July 1998, L'Oreal acquired Soft Sheen Products, a large manufacturer of ethnic hair care products. Soft Sheen, a major marketer in the United States, also has distribution in Africa. As a result, the company was considering distributing its numerous other brands into Africa. L'Oreal also owned Carson Inc., supposedly the largest marketer of ethnic hair- and skin-care products with global sales at $176 million. As a result African-Americans perceived the L'Oreal brands as having a premium brand name. They responded to the company's specialized promotions and efforts to build relationships. Asian-Americans responded to the company's quality products. Latin-Americans were also purchasers of L'Oreal products due to brand recognition, price reductions/discounts, and foreign language advertisements.

**133**     L'Oreal also successfully launched a complete hair care line both domestically and internationally. Its hair colorants, available in a variety of shades and including value-added features, targeted senior citizens, baby boomers, generation Y, and men. The company also had strong relations with male customers due to targeted promotions, creating brand awareness through trials, masculine packaging, having a retail presence, providing services to influence decisions, and having a strong brand name.

**134**     L'Oreal's convenient and easy to navigate main website gives customers extensive product and company information. Not all its brands are available for online purchasing. It currently was expanding its L'Oreal website internationally which in turn developed customized websites for each region, offering editorial content in the local language. At the time, only L'Oreal and Maybelline products could be purchased online. Through the samples and trials offered online as well as advertisements to get customers to the site, L'Oreal was able to build a strong brand name and loyal customer base.

**135**     The Lancôme line was mainly distributed in traditional department stores due to its superior quality, premium pricing, wide assortment in its product mix, relationships with store managers for optimal displays and space, and qualified sales representatives for point-of-purchase assistance. However, the product was available online and was highly successful. Approximately 52 percent of the visitors made a purchase and spent 30 percent more than consumers who bought via the traditional retail outlet. This line was popular with affluent senior citizens, baby boomers, and Generation X customers. Its Lancôme line, which was a unique and prestigious cosmetic collection, was also sold via specialty stores since they provided qualified sales representatives for point of purchase assistance.

136     The company utilized a quality control department to ensure that all products were developed, designed, and delivered according to the highest standards. It conducted its own self-examinations to see if the company was growing and continuing according to specifications. The company advertised its numerous brands in various magazines and television spots according to its target market. For example, the company often sponsored events in order to develop brand awareness in its younger customers. Also, the company often issued samples and rebate coupons to develop brand awareness and recognition.

### Retail Competition

137  Retail competition consisted of department stores, specialty stores, and drug stores. Traditional department stores offered a wide range of personal care products with an emphasis on skin care, color cosmetics, personal hygiene, and perfumes/fragrances such as Christian Dior, Elizabeth Arden, Hard Candy, Lorac, and L'Ancome. The brands sold via this channel were usually prestigious high-priced products geared toward medium to highly affluent consumers. They also appealed to affluent young senior citizens. In regards to baby boomers, department stores were strong in offering high-quality and high-value products. Traditional department stores within themselves also sold via the Internet and were therefore strong in providing boomers with numerous channels of distribution. The department stores generally featured personal care counters where consumers obtained personal assistance and product information via employees. Due to the higher price range of department store personal care products, they were highly tailored to baby boomer needs, thereby strengthening consumer loyalty. Traditional department store brands were also becoming increasingly popular with Generation X. Traditional department stores brands such as Polo Sport, Biotherm, Calvin Klein, and Nautica appealed to male customers since they contained masculine packaging, targeted promotions, provided services to influence decisions, and created brand awareness through trials.

138     Full-line discount stores sold personal care products in the skin care, color cosmetic, hair care, personal hygiene, and perfumes/fragrances categories. The brands sold via this channel included many private label product lines such as My Generation and Sonia Kashuk and affordable product lines including Vidal Sassoon, Pantene, Maybelline, Cover Girl, L'Oreal, and Revlon. The product lines were geared towards Generation X and Generation Y. The reason that full-line discount stores were so successful with Generation Y was due to its quality products at affordable prices, its trendy fashionable youth-oriented products tailored to needs, and strong brand awareness and recognition.

139     Specialty stores seemed to be in competition with traditional department stores since both channels carried high-quality high-priced personal care products. However, specialty stores such as Sephora tended to carry more obscure international brands such as Anna Sui, Benetton, Bvlgari, Nino Cerutti, and Poppy. As a result, specialty stores had high loyalty and recognition with both affluent baby boomers and Generation X.

140     Drug stores such as Genovese, CVS, and Rite Aid carried affordable mass merchandise personal care brands such as Oil of Olay, Neutrogena, Jane Cosmetics, Maybelline, and Revlon. Drug stores tended to compete with full-line discount stores in attracting Generation Y consumers with its quality products tailored to needs at affordable prices. However, drug stores also carried personal care product lines geared towards both nonaffluent and affluent male customers. Certain personal hygiene items, such as razors, toothpaste, and

shampoo and conditioner, were nonelastic generic products purchased by both affluent or nonaffluent men and women customers.

## OVERVIEW OF THE COMPANY

**141**    Avon Products, Inc. (Avon) was a manufacturer and marketer of personal care products, including skin-care, hair-care, color cosmetics, fragrances, personal hygiene, and a limited line of nonpersonal care products such as jewelry, apparel, decorative and home entertainment products and a provider of spa services. Avon commenced operations in 1886 and was incorporated on January 27, 1916. It provided one of the first opportunities for American women to be financially independent at a time when their place was traditionally at home. Avon distributed its products primarily through the direct selling channel. It was considered the world's largest direct seller of affordable quality beauty products. However the company also utilized kiosks and the Internet to increase its consumer base. The company marketed its products through its sales campaign brochures, sponsorship of women-related issues, and print and television advertisements.

**142**    Avon's main customers were women of all ethnic races with a concentration of those aged 35 and over. Avon had a prominent presence in the United States and 137 countries. The company had revenues of $5.3 billion in 1999 compared to $5.2 billion in 1998. In 1999, through their three million representatives, Avon handled over a billion customer transactions and sold over 2 billion units, making it the sixth largest global beauty company. Exhibit 18 gives a detailed overview of Avon Products, Inc. Avon's products and services, divided into major products, limited non-personal care products, and spa services, are detailed in Exhibit 19.

**EXHIBIT 18    Avon Products, Inc.**

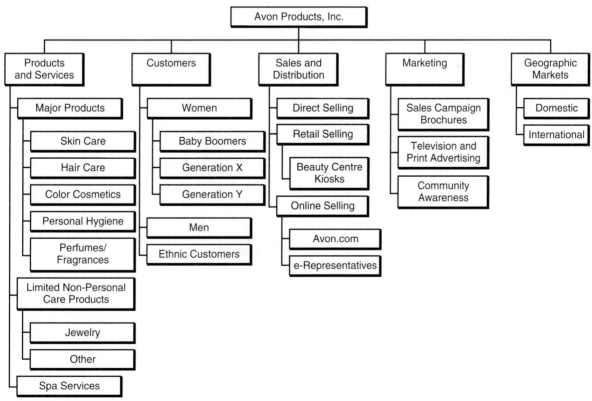

**EXHIBIT 19**
**Avon's Products and Services**

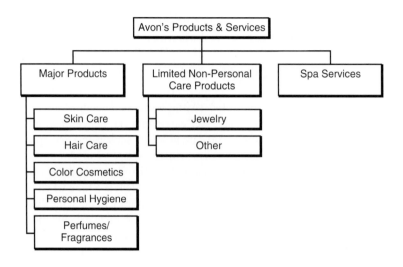

# PRODUCTS/SERVICES

143    In the past, Avon carried various product lines targeted to specific regional needs. However, in doing so, the company obtained a fragmented brand image. To rectify this problem, Avon developed universal global brands. Avon had distinguished itself as the supplier of high-quality beauty products at affordable prices. More beauty products carried the Avon brand name than any other in the world. Exhibit 20 illustrates Avon's product lines as a percentage of sales. It can be noted that skin-care, hair-care, color cosmetics, and fragrances were the largest grossing product lines. Exhibit 21 indicates the actual sales dollars generated by Avon's diverse product lines.

**EXHIBIT 20**
**Avon Product Lines as a Percentage of 1999 Sales**

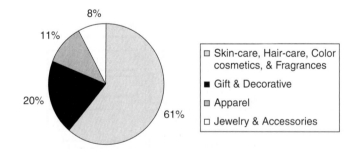

**EXHIBIT 21**
**Avon Product Lines: Actual Sales in 1999**

| Product | $ Millions |
| --- | --- |
| Skin-care, Hair-care, Color cosmetics & fragrances | 3,226 |
| Gift & decorative | 1,052 |
| Apparel | 556 |
| Jewelry & accessories | 455 |
| Total | 5,289 |

## Major Product Lines

**144**    Avon's major product lines included skin care, hair care, color cosmetics, personal hygiene, and perfumes and perfumes/fragrances. Avon was the creator of the first alpha-hydroxy skin-care products developed by a strong research and development department who was currently devising alternative skin care regimes and anticipating frequent new product introductions. Its skin-care products were tailored to needs being demanded by the market, specifically those of aging consumers and female consumers by offering high-quality and high-value products at affordable prices. By developing its ANEW product line, Avon was able to tap into the growing cosmeceutical market. It also fulfilled skin-care market opportunities by offering products, which included antiaging features, natural ingredients, environmental protection lotions for the face, and complete skin-care regimes. Due to this, Avon had a strong brand loyalty and brand image in the skin-care market.

**145**    Avon sold a strong performing line of value-added shampoos, conditioners, treatments, and styling products somewhat tailored to consumer needs. The company developed many types of shampoos and conditioners specifically focused on the five major types of hair problems, and color treated or graying hair. It also had a line of hair stylant products although they were designed for normal, not ethnic specific hair types. Avon also sold an Herbal Care line that utilized natural ingredients to achieve healthier-looking hair. The company did not have a hair coloring product line and therefore did not successfully build brand recognition and awareness among younger hair care consumers nor did it capitalize on the growing need of this product with the aging consumers. The company therefore was weak in owning a complete hair care line. Since Avon's customers needed to shop elsewhere for these products, the company had a weak brand image and loyalty with its hair-care products.

**146**    With the largest color palette in the world, Avon had superior quality and quantity of makeup. Its main cosmetic line, Avon Color, included a wide range of face, eye, lip, and nail cosmetics which were customized according to skin tones of various ethnic origins and prevailing fashion trends. The line was the company's largest global brand and the leading cosmetics brand in the world. Beyond Color was Avon's innovative antiaging line, which combined antiaging treatments with color cosmetics. Color Trend was Avon's global brand that embraced trendy cosmetics at affordable prices. Color Trend's full and minisized products were gradually gaining awareness. However, they were not yet being aggressively purchased by the desired target market, namely Generation Y. Currently, the line was only offered in Europe, Asia, and Latin America.

**147**    Avon sold a number of personal hygiene products, most of which fell into the bath and body category. It sold these products individually or as part of a gift set, which allowed consumers to enjoy price savings for purchasing more than one product. The bath and body products included aromatherapeutic ingredients and comprised all-in-one features. As a result, the company had strong brand loyalty in this segment. However, since the company was not yet established in the retail industry, it did not yet have strong relations with store managers, which was necessary for the long-term success of personal hygiene products. Skin-so-Soft, one of the company's best-known brands, was first introduced in 1961. Currently, the Skin-So-Soft brand encompassed a line of products that ranged from the original bath oil, to Bug Guard Plus with IR3535—a breakthrough technology that combined DEET-free bug repellent and PABA-free sunscreen. Naturals was a line of gentle and moisturizing cleansers and bubble bath products. The Aromatherapy line included candles, creams, lotions, bath products, and sprays that helped create a sense of well-being and revitalization.

**148**    Avon was the world's leader in perfume sales selling more units of fragrance than any other company in the world. It released one global fragrance brand per year, launched at the end of the year to coincide with the holiday season. Avon's first new fragrance of the millennium would be Incandessence, to be launched worldwide in October. Incandessence also would incorporate a unique perfume design. The company developed a special time-released construction that changed the scent as the day progressed. Each phase was composed of flowers, which reached their peak of fragrance release in the given time frame. The result was a prolonged experience and enjoyment of the fragrance. The company's global fragrances, Women of Earth and Perceive, were the best selling fragrance launches in the world. Its Perceive fragrance included mood-enhancing pheromone technology, which was intended to enhance feelings of confidence and well-being. The company had a number of fragrances for both male and female tastes. However, Avon did not issue samples throughout the years, which was imperative in the fragrance market. Despite this fact, Avon had good brand awareness and brand loyalty with its fragrance customers.

### Limited Nonpersonal Care Products

149   Avon's limited nonpersonal care products, which were considered to be part of the "Beyond Beauty" or "Beauty Plus" category, included jewelry and other products which consisted of home entertainment, gift and decorative items, and apparel.

150   Avon specialized in exclusively designed fashion jewelry including pierced and clip earrings, necklaces, bracelets, rings, and watches. Avon developed gold and silver-tone costume jewelry, and genuine sterling silver, featuring genuine and simulated stones and pearls. Jewelry designs were developed in small local markets before they were distributed globally, allowing the company to have the leading market share of costume jewelry worldwide.

151   While jewelry represented approximately 13 percent of Avon's domestic business, it accounted for a much smaller percentage of the company's international sales. Sales of fashion jewelry and accessories rose significantly in 1999 reflecting the success of sterling silver and bolder jewelry designs, the introduction of licensed luggage, and a strong performance in watches and handbags.

152   Home entertainment and gift and decorative items also posted strong growth due to the increased sales of inspirational and religious products. Avon's apparel line noted decreases in sales due to the underperformance of new product introductions. Not all the segments were profitable and some contributed to Avon's fragmented brand image. Therefore, Avon was weak in analyzing each business segment in order to gauge profitability and brand image development.

### Spa Services

153   Avon's spa services include hair care (cuts, style, and color), nail care (manicures and pedicures) personal hygiene (nutrition and lifestyle counseling, waxing) skin care (facials and body treatments) and cosmetics (makeup applications). New services include the opening of Eliza's Eyes at the Avon Centre, which was a boutique exclusively dedicated to the eyebrow. Also, in April 2000, the Avon Centre introduced Endermologie, a proven technique to reduce the appearance of cellulite and Dermabrasion, a technique known to treat hyperpigmentation, acne scars, and fine lines and wrinkles. Avon developed a complete line of spa products, which complemented the services at the Centre. These products were priced higher and were more value-driven than those featured in the brochure, resulting in an increase in more affluent consumers and brand image. These products, which were tailored to various customer needs, could be purchased either at the spa itself or on the company's website. The company did not offer samples of the products it used in the services, which was a common practice in the industry.

# CUSTOMERS

154    Avon's customers included women, comprised of senior citizens, baby boomers, Generation X and Generation Y, men, and consumers of ethnic origin.

## Women

155    Nearly half the women in the United States (48 million) relied on Avon and its personal care products. Approximately 50 percent of American women had purchased from Avon in 1999 and 90 percent had purchased from Avon in their lifetime. The company was hoping to tap into the 59 percent of women who said they would purchase Avon products if they were more accessible. Although some 70 percent of adult women in the United States said they would consider buying Avon through its direct selling channel, nearly half of them were not served by a representative, while a million more would buy Avon's products but preferred not to shop through a representative. With women in general, Avon was weak in providing various distribution channels.

156    Avon had a strong senior citizen customer base for two reasons. First, senior citizens had begun purchasing Avon products decades earlier and had developed strong loyalty to both the company and its product lines. Second, Avon's unique direct selling channel was a convenient channel of distribution for senior citizens due to their possible limited mobility.

157    Avon's customers included those of various ages and ethnic origins. Avon had fairly strong brand loyalty with older women consumers since they had grown accustomed to purchasing Avon's products through a sales representative who visited them at home. Women in the baby boomer segment were partial to Avon's high-quality high-value products, wellness products, and products tailored specifically to their needs and as a result had strong brand loyalty to the company. However, due to Avon's limited distribution channel and lack of extensive product information and education, the company did not provide an extremely satisfactory shopping experience to these customers.

158    Avon had good brand image and brand loyalty to Generation X due in part to its charitable sponsorships to women's issues and its unique products.

159    In regards to Generation Y, Avon had yet to establish brand recognition and awareness since the company had not targeted this demographic segment with specific products tailored to their needs or with trendy fashionable youth-oriented products. Those in this segment, who did shop with Avon, did so due to its quality products at affordable prices. Also, Avon was weak in advertising to this segment and in providing various distribution outlets in which to purchase products.

## Men

160    Avon had extremely few male customers since the company built its brand image as being a women's beauty and personal care company. For male consumers, Avon was weak in targeting promotions specifically to them as well as utilizing trials and samples in order to generate brand awareness and create a strong brand name and brand loyalty. The company did offer masculine packaging. Despite the fact that Avon was strong in providing services to influence decisions, it did not utilize the preferred male distribution outlet, namely retail stores.

## Ethnic Customers

161    Avon was increasingly gaining foothold in the African-American market. The company had just begun to develop color cosmetic products targeted towards darker skin tones. As a result, the company had good brand loyalty with this customer segment. The company featured African-American models in their sales brochures and found that to be an influencing

factor in gaining brand recognition. It was building good relationships with those of this ethnic origin through its direct selling model and sponsorships. Since it was one of the few personal care companies to begin to develop products geared specifically towards them, Avon was considered a premium brand name. Avon was not very focused on creating products specifically geared towards Latin-Americans and Asian-Americans, despite the fact that the company had developed some regional product modifications in Latin America and Asia in order to satisfy needs. The company did feature some Latin-Americans in their promotions with copy written in Spanish at times. However, they were just beginning to include Asian models in their advertisements. Although the company offered quality products, which Asians considered pertinent and price discounts which were of value to Latin-Americans, the company had not developed sufficient brand recognition and awareness with either of these consumer segments.

# SALES AND DISTRIBUTION

162   Avon's products were distributed via three methods; specifically direct selling, limited retail selling (kiosks), and online selling. To accelerate growth in the United States, Avon was seeking new channels to reach more customers and improve access to its products.

### Direct Selling

163   Three million representatives, approximately 500,000 of whom worked in the United States, sold Avon's products worldwide. Almost all the representatives were women who sold on a part-time basis. Representatives were independent contractors or independent dealers, and were not agents or employees of Avon. Representatives purchased products directly from Avon and sold them to their customers, both in the home and in the workplace. In the United States, the representative contacted customers, selling primarily through the use of brochures, which highlighted new products and specially priced items, while also utilizing product samples, demonstration products, and selling aids such as make-up color charts. Avon representatives built personal relationships with customers usually through phone calls or personal visits where samples and brochures were issued and recommendations were made. Purchasing through Avon representatives allowed consumers the convenience of purchasing items beyond normal business hours and avoiding lines and hassles normally associated with retail shopping. Avon had strong monetary and flexibility incentives for its sales representatives who generated 98 percent of the company's revenues. As an independent Avon sales representative, earnings were based on total sales, with total dollar amount increasing as the percentage increased. However, to encourage and motivate new representatives, Avon automatically guaranteed personal earnings of 40 percent on their first order, regardless of the dollar amount. Avon again guaranteed 40 percent personal earnings on the second, third, and fourth orders if the order was $50 or more. After the fifth order, earnings were based upon actual total dollar sales.

164       The company also built strong internal relations. In 1998, Avon launched its Leadership Representatives Program. Sales representatives were offered the opportunity to become Leadership Representatives, allowing them to receive significant cash bonuses for recruiting, training, and developing others in the field. Leadership Representatives were able to earn from 2 percent to 14 percent of the sales of the representatives they successfully recruited and motivated. The United States had more than 12,000 Leadership Representatives, an increase of 6,000 in 1998. Sales districts with the highest level of Leadership participation grew their sales in 1999 at more than double the rate of districts with the lowest participation. Also, since the representatives dedicated extensive time and energy into building their businesses, the company recognized individual achievements on all levels

through its President's Recognition Program, which allowed representatives to set their own sales goals and rewarded them based on these achievements. However, the company was weakening in its ability to recruit and retain quality employees since rumors of retail expansion proliferated throughout the company and the media.

### Retail Selling—Beauty Center Kiosks

**165** Avon Beauty Center Kiosks, freestanding minidisplay stores measuring approximately 10 feet by 14 feet and located in select urban malls across the United States, were designed to display an upscale beauty image, showcase the company's beauty brands, and encourage customer trial of product. The kiosks, first developed in 1998, were mainly created to attract the approximately 20 million to 30 million women who currently did not purchase Avon products. Each kiosk carried more than 350 Avon personal care products and offered makeovers and beauty product advice from Beauty Consultants as well as samples to increase brand awareness and trials thereby increasing Avon's brand image. Avon was currently evaluating the performance of its approximately 39 kiosk locations. Due to the infancy of the Beauty Center kiosks, Avon did not have accurate sales figures and projections to utilize in measuring their performance. At this point, the kiosks only sold Avon color cosmetics, fragrances and skin care products. They did not sell hair care products, personal hygiene products, jewelry, gifts or decorative products, or home entertainment items. On average, each carried only 400 products out of more than 5,000 that Avon had in total. The reasoning behind this was that by focusing on cosmetics, fragrances and skin care, Avon elevated its image as a beauty care brand. The Beauty Center personnel, who were enthusiastic and knowledgeable, were trained not to place too much pressure on consumers to make a purchase after a makeover or manicure. And, unlike department-store brands, the Avon makeovers emphasized not only a trial of the product but a learning experience on applying cosmetics, thereby successfully increasing product knowledge and education. Thus far, Avon had done an average of 230 manicures and 250 makeovers per location. About 95 percent of kiosk consumers were new to Avon, and approximately 70 percent made a purchase, requested a brochure and/or asked to be directed to a local Avon representative. The company planned to utilize the kiosks for new product launches in the future.

### Online Selling

**166** Avon's products were distributed online via two methods, namely the company's own website Avon.com and with the emerging e-representatives. Back in 1997, the company attempted to create a basic website and did so by offering only a small fraction of its products for sale. Management consciously downplayed the website's role to avoid problems with its representatives. However, as the importance of the Internet began to manifest itself in the industry, the company struggled with a strategy that would capitalize on the advantages of online selling while placating their core sales representatives. The internal struggle with an Internet strategy spanned three years and as a result, Avon lost its opportunity of being a market leader. Less established companies immediately took advantage of the explosive growth of the Internet and coveted approximately $1 billion online.

**167** Sales representatives protested when the company even attempted to print its web address on brochures and covered up the address with stickers thereby forcing the company to quickly remove it. They also voiced strong opinions in regards to the unfairness about Avon selling online while prohibiting its representatives to create their own sites. As a result, the company was planning to invest funds to develop the Avon e-representative initiative.

**168** Currently, the company offered online shopping in the United States, Brazil, Germany, Italy, and Japan. Domestically, since the company did not advertise the website to a great extent, it was weak in driving consumers to the site. The company was slowly building a loyal customer base since its global brand name attracted consumers to the site. The company was strong in offering a simple and easy to navigate website but was weak in offering samples or trials online. Another weakness of the website was its lack of community and content, which were further drivers to a website. The company did not offer price incentives or coupons to shopping online. Prices for items online were relatively comparable to those offered in the bimonthly sales brochure.

**169**     Avon planned to invest $60 million in the next three years to further develop its Internet presence. The company decided to allocate the money to develop customized Internet sites for its sales representatives, thereby creating "e-representatives." The e-representatives would extend to consumers the opportunity to order Avon products 24 hours a day, 7 days a week while still offering free delivery and personal service. Visitors would connect to Avon.com and locate e-representatives within their zip code.

**170**     The cost to become an e-representative was $15, with commissions ranging from 20 percent to 25 percent for orders shipped direct or 30 percent to 50 percent for ones they delivered. The program would significantly reduce organizational costs. Prior to the development of Avon.com, representatives completed a 40-page paper order form, which they submitted to the company via mail or fax. With the ability to complete online forms, the cost of processing the order would decrease from 90 cents per order to 30 cents per order. In total, e-representatives were expected to save the company $10 million by 2002 and were expected to add 1 percent to Avon's U.S. sales growth annually. The e-representative initiative program seemed to be successful in placating the irate sales representatives and integrating Avon's channels of distribution. However, top managers at Avon struggled with the possibility that this chosen Internet strategy may not have been the best solution for the company. If every sales representative participated in the program, then Avon would have approximately 500,000 websites. It was impossible to control the quality and content of each site thereby leaving the possibility of an inconsistent and misrepresentative Avon brand image. As a result, the company was pondering alternative Internet strategies.

# MARKETING

**171**     Avon marketed its products via three methods, namely sales campaign brochures, television and print advertising, and community awareness.

### Sales Campaign Brochures

**172**     Avon's products were marketed during 12 to 26 individual sales campaigns each year. Each campaign was conducted using a brochure offering a wide assortment of products, many of which changed from campaign to campaign based on changing fashion trends and consumer tastes. Each year, Avon printed over 600 million sales brochures in more than 12 languages. In the United States alone, the brochure was distributed to 14 million women every two weeks. Avon planned to allocate $20 million to upgrade the campaign sales brochure in order to project Avon's high-quality image to its varied customers.

### Television and Print Advertising

**173**     Avon decided to allocate approximately $40 million to create a more successful marketing plan for Avon in its domestic market. Some ideas were to target women over the age of 20 with an emphasis on cosmeceutical products. The company was also developing a global brand campaign featuring a new theme, "Let's Talk." Most of its advertising dollars were being planned for print ads in women's magazines such as *Ladies Home Journal*, *Glamour*, *O*, and *Cosmopolitan* and television advertising on networks (except ABC), syndicated programming and cable. Avon was debating to devote about 15 percent of its budget to Hispanic advertisement efforts.

### Community Awareness

174   Avon had sought to develop brand awareness through various charitable sponsorships devoted to women issues. Some activities included the Breast Cancer Awareness Crusade, the Avon Running—Global Women's Circuit (which promoted the importance of fitness in every woman's life), Women of Enterprise Program (which recognized five women entrepreneurs who had overcome incredible obstacles to reach their business successes) and the Avon Worldwide Fund for Women's Health. These programs raised millions of dollars for health-related problems of concern to women. Each of these initiatives had also been lucrative incentive for the company to expand its product line by correlating the event with a profitable item. For example, Avon created an attractive Avon Breast Cancer Crusade to which part of the proceeds went to research. Avon was the official cosmetics, fragrance and skin-care sponsor for the 1996 Summer Olympics Games and was the first major U.S. cosmetics company to announce a permanent end to animal testing.

# GEOGRAPHIC MARKETS

175   Avon was present in both the domestic and international personal-care markets.

### Domestic

176   The information provided in the previous sections pertains to the domestic personal care market.

### International

177   Avon's sales per geographic region are shown in Exhibit 22. The company currently had operations in 51 markets and sold its products in 137 countries. Latin America posted strong results in 2000 with revenues from Brazil, Venezuela, and Central America offsetting declines in Argentina, due to economic conditions there. The Asia/Pacific regions had strong growths in China, which helped compensate for the weakening Philippine peso. Sales in Europe were not as strong as in other markets due mainly to currency weaknesses. The company was aggressively pursuing new customers in emerging economies such as Taiwan, Malaysia, and Russia. Avon has a small retail presence in Asia and Latin America, mainly small boutiques sometimes run by its sales representatives. The success in the international sector could be partly attributed to Avon's ability to culturally adapt products according to regional needs. For example, Avon's Color Trend product line is featured mainly in Europe, Asia and Latin America. The line features trendy and fashionable color cosmetics at

**EXHIBIT 22**
**Avon's Sales by Geographic Region**

| Geographic Area | Millions ($) | Percentage of Total |
|---|---|---|
| North America | | |
| United States | 1,809 | 34 |
| Other Countries | 274 | 5 |
| Latin America | 1,608 | 30 |
| Europe | 878 | 17 |
| Asia/Pacific | 720 | 14 |
| **Total** | **5,289** | **100** |

affordable prices targeted specifically to younger personal care customers. Several of its global brands were not available in the United States since they were created exclusively with a particular international market in mind.

# MANAGEMENT

**178**  Andrea Jung was promoted from chief operating officer to chief executive officer in November 1999. She was the first female CEO in the company's 115-year history. Jung emphasized open communication with all levels and sought to create a CEO advisory council of the ten top performers from every level of the company and from all around the world. Sixteen senior operating and other key executives comprised the Avon Operating Council (AOC). The AOC, of which Andrea Jung was the leader, met bimonthly to review global operations and strategic initiatives in order to maximize shareholder wealth. The AOC's members represented an average of more than 20 years experience with the company. Avon had more women in management positions (89 percent) than any other Fortune 500 company. Of Avon's officers, 47 percent were women and five women sat on Avon's board of directors. The management of Avon was attempting to instill a sense of urgency around the need for decisive action and calculated risk-taking. As one manager stated, "Pride, speed, and performance have become the watchwords for all of our associates as we strive to foster a high-performance culture around the Avon world."

**179**  Avon's top managers were currently disputing strategic alternatives for growing the company. The most significant issues among management were Avon's slow earning growth, stagnant sales, limited distribution capabilities, and shifts in personal care preferences and spending habits. The Operating Council members' views differed on how to expand the company. Some individuals favored Avon's gradual involvement in retail with a focus on current customers. Others, however, preferred an aggressive retail growth strategy in order to obtain new and emerging personal care customers. The company would remain in a stagnant position until a consensus could be reached.

# REGULATORY

**180**  Avon maintained strong relations with government officials through its strong adequate manufacturing practices and internal quality controls and self-inspections.

# FINANCIAL

**181**  Exhibit 23 illustrates Avon's stock performance over the past five years.

**182**  The volatility was due in part to earnings growth falling short of targets, unprecedented stock market volatility and negative investor sentiment toward consumer products companies in general. In 1999, the stock price dropped sharply in the second half and finished the year down 25 percent. Avon's five-year net sales comparison is shown in Exhibit 24.

**183**  Although the company had positive net sales and earnings growth for the past five years, the increases were in the single digits and were declining each year. In fact, 1999's one-year revenue growth was a minute 1.5 percent. Most of Avon's product lines had single to double-digit growth except apparel, which fell in the single digits. As Allan Mottus, a consultant to beauty and retail companies stated in *BusinessWeek*, "We're in one of the greatest economies of all times, and Avon's still finding it hard to increase sales."

**EXHIBIT 23**
Avon's Stock Chart
1995–2000

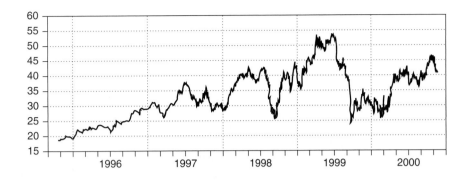

**EXHIBIT 24**
Avon's Five-Year Net
Sales Comparison (In
millions)

| | 1995 | 1996 | 1997 | 1998 | 1999 |
|---|---|---|---|---|---|
| Net Sales | $4,492 | $4,814 | $5,079 | $5,213 | $5,289 |

Source: Avon (1999), *Annual Report.*

## TOWARDS THE FUTURE

**184**    At the bimonthly meeting of the Avon Operating Council, Andrea Jung decided to present her retail objectives to the other sixteen members of the board. She felt this was imperative since although earnings were expected to remain positive for the future, the company's single digit growth, volatile stock, and seemingly archaic and limited distribution channel did not bode well for the company's intermediate and long-term future. Avon needed a new strategic plan, emphasizing where to sell its products, who would be its target market, and which product lines best fit its brand image.

**185**    As she stood in front of the members, Andrea Jung articulated her retail idea to broaden Avon's reach in the United States. Jung stated her main objectives, which were to partner with Sears and JC Penney department stores and create a store-within-a-store where it could introduce a new and more upscale exclusive product line. This retail initiative would be done in conjunction with direct selling. In implementing both strategies, Avon would benefit from increased profits, sales, and nationwide exposure allowing the company to continue attracting the baby boomer segment. The plan was financially appropriate since the company would only invest $15–20 million to launch the products in these locations and a bulk of the expenses, such as advertising, overhead, and employee salary, would be carried by the stated department stores.

**186**    Jung argued that such a strategy was feasible since retail selling was on the rise with an increase in customer traffic in virtually all traditional department stores. Baby boomers, whose spending power was expected to grow 16 percent in the next five years, were among Avon's main customers and were seeking alternative channels of distribution with personal care products, specifically traditional department stores. Direct selling was feasible since personal care products were the second most popular product group sold via this channel. Also, face-to-face selling comprised 79.7 percent of direct selling. Through the years, Avon was able to recruit and maintain quality and enthusiastic sales representatives by offering incentives to employees and maintaining strong internal relations. Also direct selling was the preferred shopping method for senior citizens, Avon's oldest and most loyal customers. The strategy was viable in light of the competition. Mary Kay Inc., Avon's direct selling competitor, was also strong in recruiting and maintaining quality and enthusiastic sales representatives through its unique incentive program and strong employee relations. However, Avon would win against Mary Kay by diversifying its distribution channels into retail traditional department stores, where Mary Kay was weak, thereby increasing its baby boomer customer base. The strategy would win against L'Oreal. L'Oreal had a strong market position in traditional department stores due to its medium to highly priced quality products, a wide assortment in its product mix, relationships with store managers for optimal displays and space, and qualified sales representatives for point of purchase assistance. However, traditional department stores were still seeking new products to add to their mix as well as high turnover personal care merchandise, namely the exact qualities of Avon's new traditional department store product line. The strategy would also win against leading traditional department stores' competing brands. Avon would match the competitive medium to highly priced products and have a competitive advantage of a globally recognized brand name and image.

**187**    After Jung finished the overview of her vision, the members of the board raised numerous objections. A senior member stated that in implementing such a plan, the company ran the risk of brand name erosion and sending mixed messages to consumers. If the retail products sold in stores were exclusive, consumers might deduce it to mean that the products sold in the brochure were of lesser quality. One of the newest inductees stated that Sears and JCPenney were recognized as the weakest portion of the mass retail market, tended to lack cosmetic consumers, and did not currently have the selling cosmetic infrastructure such as beauty advisors. He also warned Jung that upon hearing this plan of retail expansion, the sales representatives, who would fear job security, would be very irate.

**188**    To defend her strategy against the drawbacks presented, Jung stated that the company could allocate a portion of the following year's marketing budget to increase cosmetic traffic to JCPenney and Sears. Avon could promote its certified Beauty Advisors in order to build the traditional department stores' personal care infrastructure. Avon could also increase monetary incentives in order to placate irate sales representatives. Although Jung effectively defended her proposed strategy, the board, as a whole, advised Jung to obtain an outside opinion.

**189**    Jung decided to hire an outside consulting group to devise a strategic plan for Avon. Within two weeks, Jung was back in the same meeting room but listening to a different retail perspective. After carefully reviewing the industry and Avon's internal situation, the consultants advised Jung to take a three-step retail approach. First, the company would distribute its higher priced and superior quality spa products in specialty stores. Second, Avon should sell a more affordable line in full-line discount stores. And finally, the company should extend its unique kiosks in the domestic market. They informed Jung that the company would benefit from this strategy since it would attract diverse consumer groups, significantly increase sales and brand recognition across the nation, and placate both its irate shareholders and apprehensive sales representatives.

**190**    Specialty stores, which were increasing in customer popularity and were experiencing 4 percent annual growth which was expected to continue, sold superior quality and high-priced items to a selective market, namely medium to highly affluent baby boomers. Selling via this channel was feasible since Avon currently had a prestigious high-priced spa line with a strong brand image which attracted more affluent consumers such as baby boomers seeking products targeted to their needs. Therefore, synergy existed between the type of products typically sold in specialty stores and Avon's current product mix. Full-line discount stores had high customer traffic, were leaders in introducing new products, and attracted a less affluent personal care customer segment, namely Generation Y. As a result, Avon would be a good fit for full-line discount stores since it would create a new and more affordable product line sold in an alternative selling channel, which would appeal to younger personal care customers.

**191**    The consultants pointed out that although there was not yet enough information to evaluate the performance of kiosks, expanding the structures was viable since their current performance showed strengths in increasing product knowledge and education and introducing new products to the general public. The expansion of kiosks was realistic since the start up cost for a freestanding kiosk was reported to be approximately $6,000 and the selling concept was unique to the company, thereby giving Avon a competitive advantage. Also, since sales representatives would manage the kiosks, Avon would retain its enthusiastic and knowledgeable representatives as well as provide additional career expansion incentives. The consultants agreed with Jung that Avon would gain a competitive advantage over Mary Kay Inc. by expanding into retail distribution. Mary Kay did not have unique and prestigious cosmetic collections which could be sold via specialty stores, did not have a trendy and fashionable product line, which was imperative in full-line discount stores, and did not utilize kiosks as a channel of distribution. The proposal was a winning strategy against L'Oreal. Although Avon would compete parallel to L'Oreal in specialty stores and full-line discount stores, the company had a distinct competitive advantage in selling through its kiosks which would be useful in generating excitement and informing the public about Avon's new product lines. The strategy would also win against retail competition since Avon was a global brand name introducing new products backed by increased samples, trials, and product information.

**192**    As Jung listened she pointed out that there were three significant drawbacks to the solution. First, the plan was not currently financially feasible. The costs would be tremendous to expand in all three channels simultaneously. Second, Avon did not yet have strong relations in the retail market, which were necessary to gain placement in both the specialty stores and full-line discount stores. Thirdly, in regards to the expansion of the kiosks, there were 500,000 Avon sales representatives in the United States. Even if 75 percent decided to continue their direct selling method, there really would not be enough urban upscale retail space to accommodate that many kiosks. The consultants defended their points by stating that the proposed retail strategy could be done in stages beginning with the specialty stores and kiosks and followed by the full-line discount store expansion. The time between the stages could be determined based on the success and profitability of the first stage. Second, Avon would not have difficulty developing strong relations in the retail market. Managers were seeking high-quality products which carried a well-received brand name. Avon's personal care items were high margin products in a wide product category, thereby ensuring strong relations with retail managers. Third, in regards to the kiosk expansion problem, the consultants stated that as a longer-term strategy, the company could expand its kiosks into nonretail high customer traffic locations such as office buildings and airports. Jung thanked the consultants and left the boardroom.

**193**    Back in her office, Jung realized this was only the tip of the iceberg of the strategic decisions which needed to be made. There were still significant debates about which product lines should be expanded and divested and which consumer groups the company should focus on. Just the previous day, the marketing team presented a list of industry trends and opportunities, which indicated that Avon was operating in a rapidly changing industry. A major opportunity, which stood out in her mind, was the positive impact of the Internet on the personal care industry and she wondered which would be the best way for Avon to capitalize on its success. These and many other strategic issues plagued Jung as she debated over the best way to grow the 115-year-old company. However, if Avon was to stay abreast of the competition, immediate action needed to be taken and Jung did not have much time left to decide.

# Case 29  Castlerock Veterinary Clinic[1]

## Harold Z. Daniel, Hampton E. Griffin, Peter Tarasewich

1   The competitive environment of the veterinary health care and kennel business presented many challenges in rural Maine. Castlerock Corporation spent a great deal of time and money on a new kennel and hospital upgrade in an attempt to provide a complete set of services to its customer base. Corporation owner Dr. Robert C. McFarland tried to create a one-stop shopping experience with his investment. As a result, an assessment showed a favorable perception of the quality of services delivered by the clinic among its current customers, as well as among other pet owners.

2   Castlerock established an impressive competitive position in the market because of the quality of services it delivered, yet growth seemed stagnated despite continued upgrades and investments. McFarland sat at his desk and contemplated what the future of Castlerock would be, and how to continue his success,

> My situation has changed in the last 2 to 3 years. I'm lucky to be able to maintain 10 percent to 15 percent growth, versus the 20 percent to 30 percent or more that I had seen since the establishment of Castlerock. Opportunities are not as easy to find. There are more competitors than ever before, and expanding the business costs more than in the past. I thought that maybe new technology was the answer to cut costs and help me with marketing the clinic, so I invested in new computers and software. But the technology doesn't seem to be giving me the answers that I want or the flexibility I desire.

3   Robert McFarland realized that the strategies that worked well for him in the past were no longer going to meet his needs. While Castlerock seemed to have a good reputation among pet owners in the area that they served, new customers were not appearing at the frequency that they once had. The demand for services such as the kennel and grooming was also stagnant. McFarland desperately needed an answer to the question, "How do we grow the business now?"

## GROWTH OF CASTLEROCK

4   Castlerock Corporation was an umbrella organization composed of a veterinary hospital practice and a kennel. The veterinary hospital facility was completed in 1979, and housed examination rooms, operating rooms, and an in-house diagnostic lab. In 1985, a second structure was completed to house a separate kennel business for pet boarding and grooming, dog training, and retail sales.

5   McFarland was very proud of what he accomplished at Castlerock. He described his initial difficulties in starting a small business, but emphasized how his persistence and determination paid off.

[1]This case is based on field research. All individuals and events in the case are real, though names and data have been disguised. The authors wish to thank the anonymous reviewers as well as the current editor, David Rosenthal, and former editor Linda Swayne, for their helpful suggestions for improving the manuscript.

I've owned my own business for over 20 years. Helping pets feel better and comforting their owners always came naturally to me, business didn't. The first five years I was in business were spent really learning through trial and error about how to successfully operate a veterinary hospital and make a profit. Luckily I had a few good employees to help me through the early years. In year six, I had outgrown my original building and built my first addition. A few years later, I had enough demand to justify a separate kennel facility. When I saw an opportunity for expansion I took advantage of it.

6    McFarland was interested in animal healthcare and welfare from an early age. A bright but often impatient student, he excelled in both his undergraduate studies and in veterinary school. He graduated in the top of his class from Tufts University School of Veterinary Medicine in 1970, interned at a Boston animal medical center, and later became a well-respected staff veterinarian at a small clinic in Maine. He opened his own practice in 1975, and originally ran a mixed animal practice, providing healthcare to both companion animals and local livestock. In 1979, he began to limit his practice exclusively to companion animals, such as dogs, cats, birds, reptiles, rabbits, and other animals that are kept as household pets. Dr. McFarland himself specialized in surgery on dogs. McFarland also bought the land and building where his practice resided that same year.

7    Before opening his Castlerock facility, McFarland's business skills were limited to basic training in practice management, business law, and bookkeeping that was part of the curriculum at Tufts. His wife, a bookkeeper, was able to provide basic accounting functions for his clinic in the early days of his fledgling hospital facility. At year-end, she submitted its business records to a local accounting firm to prepare tax documents.

8    Seven employees (one veterinarian, two office staff, two veterinary technicians, and two assistants) staffed the original hospital facility. By 1998, the hospital facility stabilized at 25 employees (four veterinarians, five office staff, nine veterinary technicians, and seven assistants) and the kennel facility had grown to employ seven staff members (one manager, two trainers, and four assistants). Members of McFarland's veterinary staff specialized in such rare pets as arachnids, which includes large spiders like the tarantula, and reptiles, including lizards and turtles. The original hospital structure eventually could not accommodate the expansion in employees, equipment, and services. As a result, an additional structure was added to the hospital facility in 1985.

9    The day-to-day operations of the hospital were maintained by hospital manager and veterinary technician Lisa Snowe. Over the prior decade, the practice of veterinary medicine became more sophisticated and complex. Customers expected and were entitled to state-of-the-art veterinary care for their animals. To provide this type of service, a veterinarian uses the skills of trained and educated professionals known as veterinary technicians. Veterinary technicians were integral members of the veterinary health care team who were educated in the care and handling of animals, in the basic principles of normal and abnormal life processes, and in routine laboratory and clinical procedures. In general, a veterinary technician performed many of the same tasks for a veterinarian that nurses and other professionals performed for many physicians.

10    Lisa Snowe and Robert McFarland complemented each other well on a professional level. McFarland was at his personal best in the examination room, and Snowe, an extrovert, was a favorite with practically all visitors to Castlerock. Before coming to Castlerock, Snowe worked in retail sales and management, which helped her interact more successfully with customers at the clinic than most of her peers. Although very successful in her retail career, a lifelong love of animals inspired her to exit retail sales and pursue a career as a Veterinary Technician at a local technical college. Snowe proved to be a bright and talented student in the Veterinary Technology program, and interned at Castlerock as part of her clinical training. McFarland noted her talent with both pets and owners, and shrewdly recruited her for his practice before her graduation.

11    In addition to being a talented technician, Snowe possessed excellent human relations and personnel management skills and was liked by all of the employees. Besides training

the clinic staff for customer interaction, her responsibilities included scheduling and supervising employees. Snowe's combination of people skills and clinical training increased her value as an employee, helping McFarland better manage his clinic and administer better quality customer service. Eventually, Snowe became the hospital manager, devoting less and less time to duties as a veterinary technician.

12  Much of Castlerock's success can be attributed to the way in which Dr. McFarland recruited and hired new veterinarians and staff. McFarland took great pains to actively recruit students directly from veterinary schools to work in his practice as interns. This approach presented McFarland with a constant source of low-cost, highly qualified labor, and allowed him to put these young doctors through grueling rotations at his hospital. In return, the young doctors received the valuable experience of working with a well-respected, established veterinarian and surgeon, but with relatively low wages for their efforts.

13  As time passed, many of these young veterinarians became well known and easily identified within the small rural communities surrounding the clinic. Many of the young veterinarians, or "baby docs," left Castlerock to open clinics of their own in the surrounding area. McFarland, bearing no ill will toward what he considered his protégés, provided no barriers to their exodus. Many Castlerock customers followed the baby docs to their new practices. The new practices, however, often referred special or difficult cases back to McFarland because of his recognized expertise.

14  In fact, numerous veterinary practices from across the state referred their difficult or special cases to McFarland and the veterinarians at the Castlerock clinic for specific treatments. Likewise, he sought out other clinics to provide some limited services for cases in which he or his veterinarians lacked the specialized expertise (such as large farm animals) or for which his clinic lacked the appropriate specialized equipment for diagnosis or treatment. McFarland pointed out,

> Given the sparse and widely scattered expertise in some exotics (birds and other animals) or in some difficult and unusual surgical procedures, referrals are a common practice here in rural Maine. John over at the Bunyon clinic will refer some of his customers to us for specialized treatment that he cannot provide there, but which he knows that we can. We will reciprocate with difficult customers that he has the expertise to treat for us. This applies to equipment, too. Certain equipment, like a chemistry analyzer, can be very expensive. Why should Jerry up at the Howland clinic be burdened with debt to purchase a chemistry analyzer when we have a perfectly good one here? In these ways, we all expand our capabilities to serve the unique needs of our customers.

15  While McFarland readily identified referrals as an important part of the business, neither he nor his staff formally tracked the proportion of the total business represented by the delivery of services to customers referred by other veterinarians or clinics in the state. McFarland estimated that 90 percent of the clinic's typical monthly practice was comprised of members of his ongoing customer base, while 10 percent represented referrals from other veterinary practices in the state. He also guessed that, while 75 percent of the clinic's revenues resulted from the clinic's customer base, about 25 percent of the clinic's revenues were a result of referrals from other pet professionals or veterinarians. This was partly because these referrals, begun as professional courtesies, usually entailed more expensive procedures than the annual check ups featured in the services provided to the members of the clinic's ongoing customer base. These referrals represented a network of informal relationships among the different veterinary clinics in the state. Many of these veterinarians knew each other well, and McFarland was on a first-name basis with most of them,

> There is only so much that I can ask the staff to do. I don't know if tracking the sources of our customers would help me run this practice any better. Even if it did, I wouldn't know how to use that information. In most of these cases we are just trying to help someone out that may be in over their heads. We certainly like having someone to bail us out when we see a case that we aren't prepared for. We trust each other to help out. We have to.

**16**    Many times customers traveled upwards of 80 miles to bring their pet to a referred veterinarian. In rural areas, most small veterinary clinics tended to be staffed by general practitioners or general surgeons rather than veterinary specialists. When a special case arose, informal personal referral networks were available to find the most expert source of treatment within the region based on experience or reputation. Since most referrals were limited to a single visit or treatment for a single medical event, most customers maintained relationships with their primary veterinarians after receiving treatment at another clinic. As is often the case with the practice of human medicine, they saw the contact with the referral veterinarian as a temporary situation, precipitated by an unexpected medical event and the limitations of their primary veterinarian. McFarland said:

> I have a solid reputation in Maine, and I have benefited greatly from referrals from our satisfied customers. However, I would not take advantage of referrals from other veterinarians or clinics in the state by soliciting business from those clients and attempting to build our customer base that way. Once treated, clients that were referred by other veterinarians are returned to the originating veterinary practice for follow up and normal veterinary care. Additional direct communication with the client after our treatment would violate the trust of the referring practice or veterinarian and kill that business.

## HAPPY PET KENNELS

**17**    Happy Pet Kennels was designed for a maximum boarding capacity of 45 pets at the time of construction, and in 1988 was expanded to provide space for an indoor training arena. Over its first ten years of operation, the capacity of the kennel was increased to accommodate a maximum of 90 pets. Happy Pet Kennels offered many value-added services for pets. These services included "Doggy Daycare" (started in 1996), puppy, specialty, and advanced training classes conducted by two on-premise trainers, and on-site, on-demand grooming services. Heated kennel floors and retail product offerings were also implemented.

**18**    Originally, Happy Pet Kennels was developed as a separate business. At the time, the news media focused national attention on serious abuses in the kennel industry by a few kennel owners. McFarland had been concerned about the potential for the public perception of the kennel industry to negatively impact the perception of the kennel and, thereby, the veterinary clinic, which he considered to be the primary business of Castlerock Corporation. For this reason, the information systems for the two businesses were allowed to evolve separately.

**19**    Over time, McFarland saw the kennel as an important part of the overall business, enabling the company to offer a more complete range of services to its customers than other veterinary businesses in the area. These services included supporting the Castlerock clinic with accommodations for the extended recovery of veterinary patients. Similarly, the clinic helped support the kennel as the source of veterinary care for emergency cases that might suddenly arise in the kennel.

## THE COMPETING CLINICS

**20**    In 1999, Castlerock Veterinary Clinic was considered one of the premier facilities in Maine. Continually expanded and improved since 1979, the facility was well designed, modern, and spacious. The gross revenues of the hospital were about $850,000 per year, and the kennel typically brought in around $260,000 per year (of which $75,000 was from the sale of retail goods). The combined value of Castlerock's real estate and equipment was approximately $725,000. Customers spent, on the average, $38 per visit at the hospital and $10 per visit at the kennel.

**21**    Casterock's major competition consisted of three other clinics located within a 20-mile radius of its facility (See Exhibit 1). While the metropolitan area served by the Castlerock

**EXHIBIT 1**   **Locations of the Competing Veterinary Clinics.**

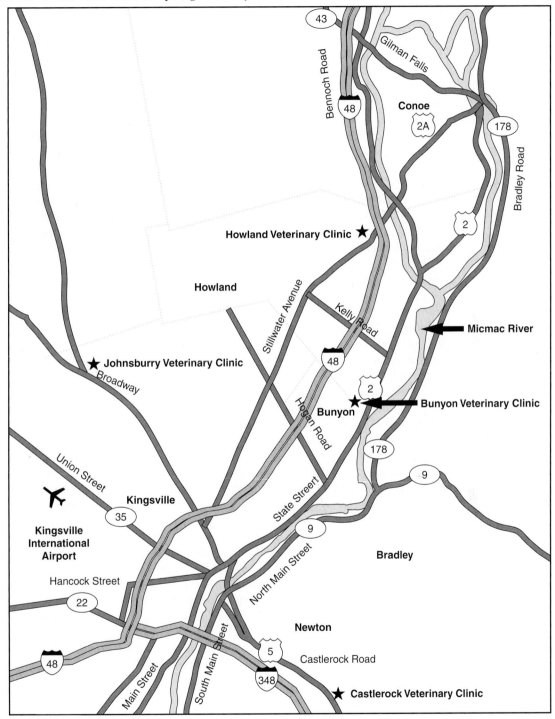

clinic had a substantial population of pet owners, most of that population was concentrated on the north side of the Micmac River that forms a natural boundary. The three major competitors, the Bunyon Veterinary Clinic, the Howland Veterinary Clinic, and the Johnsburry Clinic, possessed more convenient locations for most potential customers than the Castlerock clinic by virtue of being located closer to the center of population, (i.e., on the north side of the river). Castlerock, however, represented a more convenient location for the potential customers on the south side of the river and for potential customers residing in the nearby town of Newton, also located to the south of the river.

22      The Howland Clinic was known for its focus on holding down the cost of services. The management of the clinic refused to move to cleaner, more modern facilities. It featured two veterinarians and a small staff. Management focused on providing basic veterinary care, and there was no kennel facility associated with the clinic. Howland was a major competitor by virtue of its longevity in the market, having survived nearly as long as the Castlerock clinic. The Howland Clinic was managed by its founding veterinarian, who had a reputation for quality veterinary care with a blunt, somewhat less than inviting bedside manner. As a result, the clinic had a reputation for failures in building enduring relationships with some of its customers.

23      The Bunyon and Johnsburry Clinics were relative newcomers to the market, building bases of customers relatively quickly. John, one of McFarland's protégés, started the Bunyon Clinic. It featured 3 veterinarians and a staff of 15, including an office manager. Its business philosophy was similar to McFarland's, except that it chose to focus exclusively on the delivery of high-quality veterinary care, and regarded a kennel business as a distraction from that central mission. Among the clinic's veterinarians were a specialist in the unique needs of reptiles and another veterinarian that specialized in birds. McFarland referred customers with reptiles or birds to the vets at the Bunyon Clinic when those customers needed specialized care.

24      The Johnsburry Clinic grew into a relatively large business, with 5 veterinarians and a support staff of 30, including an office manager. Its philosophy was somewhat similar to that of the Castlerock clinic in that it maintained a kennel for boarding animals, whether for recovery from surgery or for more traditional long-term stays. Johnsburry had veterinarians specializing in the unique needs of cats. This clinic also had a location advantage in that it was positioned in the heart of the metropolitan area on the north side of the river.

25      McFarland and the veterinarians from the other clinics maintained relationships that went beyond purely professional. Many of the veterinarians were close friends with each other, and often their families would spend time socializing. Each year they held a barbeque on the fourth of July. Employees and veterinarians from the competing clinics also socialized at professional meetings such as conferences and conventions.

26      While none of the competing clinics openly promoted their business via advertising, Castlerock participated in local public affairs programming on one of the local television stations. John, at the Bunyon clinic, was also retained by one of the other television stations in the market for public affairs spots on the local news. Little attention was given to actively positioning the clinic with respect to its competition since direct competitive advertising was considered inappropriate within the veterinary community. Some newspaper advertising was done to support a few special events at the clinic. More recently, since people seemed willing to travel 80 miles or more to visit the clinic, special-events focused newspaper advertising was extended into areas further away from the clinic in order to attract potential customers from this broader market. Without the capability for evaluating these efforts, the effectiveness of its promotion strategy had never been determined with any confidence.

27      Consistent with the entrepreneurial, small market context of these businesses, specific information about the value of competing veterinary practices as well as their costs and rev-

enues was proprietary and a closely guarded secret. It was well accepted, however, that customers using the services of the Castlerock and Bunyon clinics tended to pay more for comparable services than customers of the Howland clinic.

# CURRENT MARKETING PERFORMANCE

**28**   Given that these were all private businesses, there was no means of measuring basic marketing performance like market-share. Therefore, Castlerock commissioned a telephone survey to gain a better understanding of its competitive position in the market. With over 21 veterinary practices listed in the local telephone book, it was not surprising that the research showed the market to be highly competitive and very sensitive to the quality of performance by doctors and staff. Quality performance clearly represented the "price" of entry into this market. All members of all market segments indicated that the quality of performance of the veterinary doctor and his/her staff was extremely important to customers. Doctor and staff performance did not differentiate among competing practices and all area clinics generated high doctor and staff ratings among their adopters.[2]

**29**   Based on knowledge of the competing clinics involved in the survey and their relative positions in the perceptual map of competing clinics[3] (Exhibit 2), the competing clinics were differentiated on the perceptions of (1) offering complete services, (2) the quality of the clinic environment, (3) convenience of the clinic's location, and (4) the degree to which the doctors are recognized as offering compassionate service. That is, as clinics are positioned further upward in Exhibit 2, they are more highly identified with having a pleasant environment. Similarly, as a clinic is positioned further to the right in Exhibit 2, they are identified as offering a more complete set of veterinary services.

**30**   Exhibit 2 was created using the perceptual ratings of the clinics provided by their core customers, that is, those customers who identified the respective clinics as their favorites. Since the Howland clinic occupies the lower left corner of Exhibit 2, its limitations were

**EXHIBIT 2**
**Perceptual Map of Competing Vet Clinics** *by Favorite Clinic.*

Source: Castlerock Veterinary Clinic Performance Survey

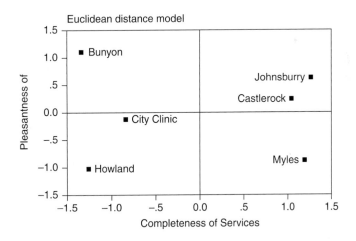

[2]By a clinic's adopters we mean those respondents claiming a respective veterinary clinic as their favorite, the clinic that they claimed to use most often.

[3]Note: The perceptual map in Exhibit 2 does not represent the perceptions of the general public. It instead represents the perceptions of the respondents' favorite veterinary clinics, the clinics that they claimed to use most often. With the exception of the Castlerock clinic, the attribute ratings necessary for this analysis were collected only for each respondent's favorite clinic. All respondents aware of the Castlerock clinic were asked to provide attribute ratings for that clinic. This reduced the data collection burden on both the interviewer and respondent, which can be very important in a telephone survey.

**EXHIBIT 3**
**Perceptual Map for**
**Castlerock Clinic** *by*
*Client-Relationship*
*Status.*

Source: Castlerock Veterinary
Clinic Performance Survey

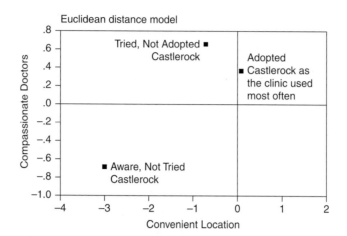

clearly perceived by the pet owning households included in the survey. Similarly, the location of the Bunyon clinic in the upper left corner showed its lack of a kennel was perceived, though this position by itself does not suggest that such a failure represents a liability for the business. The similarity of the Johnsburry and Castlerock businesses was also perceived as both clinics occupied a position in the upper right quadrant of the map, attesting to the perception of the clinics as having both a complete range of services and a pleasant environment.

31     Exhibit 3 provides a perceptual map featuring an analysis of the perceptions of the Castlerock clinic based on the nature of the customer relationship with the clinic. The points in the map represent the relative perception of the clinic by whether the respondent had only heard of the clinic, but never had direct contact with the clinic's veterinarians (Aware, Not Tried Castlerock), whether the respondent had direct experience with clinic veterinarians, but did not regard the clinic as their primary veterinary service provider (Tried, Not Adopted Castlerock) or whether the respondent regarded Castlerock as their primary veterinary service provider or favorite clinic (Adopted Castlerock as the clinic used most often).[4] Higher placement of a point on the map for a group of respondents would suggest that they perceived Castlerock veterinarians as more compassionate than other groups of respondents. Similarly, placement of a point to the right on the map for a group of respondents would suggest that they perceived the location of the Castlerock clinic as more convenient than other groups of respondents. Large distances between points on the map suggest that perceived deficiencies on these dimensions are responsible for the respondents' status with respect to the Castlerock clinic.

32     The perception of the Castlerock clinic's veterinarians as being compassionate as well as the perception of the clinic's location as being convenient discriminated between those pet-owning households with differing relationships with the clinic (Exhibit 3). Pet-owning households who were aware of the clinic, but failed to try its services, expected the clinic's doctors to be less compassionate and the location to be less convenient than did those who based their perceptions on having actually tried its services. This included both the households that failed to identify the clinic as their usual or favorite clinic and those who did not.

[4]Again, this analysis was only possible for the Castlerock clinic. The data for such an analysis of other competing clinics were not available.

**TABLE 1**

**Summary of Awareness, Trial, and Adoption for the Competing Veterinary Clinics by Market Segment**

Source: Castlerock Veterinary Clinic Performance Survey.

| | | Market Segments | | |
|---|---|---|---|---|
| | Total Sample | Bonded Households | Feline-Oriented Households | Doc in a Barn |
| Base: Total pet-owning households | (153) | (77) | (46) | (30) |
| Total aware of Castlerock | 63% | 60% | 60% | 77% |
| Total tried Castlerock | 27% | 27% | 30% | 23% |
| Adoption castlerock | 15% | 16% | 14% | 10% |
| **Conversion ratios Castlerock** | | | | |
| Awareness to trial | .43 | .45 | .50 | .30 |
| Trial to adoption | .56 | .59 | .47 | .43 |
| Total aware of Howland | 50% | 47% | 51% | 57% |
| Total tried Howland | 26% | 20% | 30% | 33% |
| Adoption Howland | 9% | 7% | 9% | 17% |
| **Conversion ratios Howland** | | | | |
| Awareness to trial | .52 | .43 | .59 | .58 |
| Trial to adoption | .35 | .35 | .30 | .51 |
| Total aware of Johnsburry | 67% | 69% | 60% | 73% |
| Total tried Johnsburry | 30% | 31% | 30% | 37% |
| Adoption Johnsburry | 8% | 11% | 21% | 7% |
| **Conversion ratios Johnsburry** | | | | |
| Awareness to trial | .44 | .45 | .50 | .51 |
| Trial to adoption | .27 | .35 | .70 | .19 |
| Total aware of Bunyon | 51% | 47% | 57% | 50% |
| Total tried Bunyon | 16% | 16% | 15% | 17% |
| Adoption Bunyon | 9% | 8% | 13% | 7% |
| **Conversion ratios Bunyon** | | | | |
| Awareness to trial | .31 | .34 | .26 | .34 |
| Trial to adoption | .56 | .50 | .87 | .41 |

33    The research confirmed that the Castlerock clinic was in many ways the market leader. In terms of awareness, trial, and adoption[5] the clinic led or matched its competitors (Table 1). Further, the survey showed that Castlerock led the market with respect to the perception of the quality of services provided, and led the market in terms of continued usage intent. The clinic also generated the highest *trial intent*[6] among all competing clinics. All four of the major competing clinics in the market, however, generated comparable levels of satisfaction among their core customers, (i.e., adopters).

34    The survey identified that the single location of the clinic represented the most important limitation on its continued growth. This resulted from the realization that lack of a convenient location represents a barrier to clinic trial and to adoption. The clinic was rated more highly for the convenience of its location by its adopters, as compared to those respondents

---

[5]Adoption is used as a measure of repeat usage, an indication of satisfaction with the delivery of veterinary services. In this case adoption is measured by the number of respondents claiming that the respective clinic attained the status of "the single clinic used most often" or favorite clinic.
[6]Trial intent refers to the usage intent among respondents aware of the clinic who had yet to use its services.

claiming trial but not adopting it or compared to the similar ratings among those respondents claiming awareness of the clinic but not trial. Further, aware non-triers more highly valued convenient location than did clinic triers. The survey also found that the vast majority of clinic adopters resided within 20 minutes drive of the clinic site.

35    Additionally, the research found that Castlerock attracted more of an important segment of the pet-owning population than its competition, this being the multiple pet household. These were high-volume customers, customers using more veterinary care services than their single pet counterparts. The down side was that this population was more sensitive to the pricing of services.

36    Finally, the survey identified three market segments, which are described below:

1. **Bonded Households** (50 percent): These households featured individuals who showed the greatest evidence of having bonded with their pets, indicating that the pet was regarded more like a child or best friend in the household. They evidenced a greater sensitivity to the pleasantness of the clinic environment than other segments, but also a high sensitivity to the convenience of the clinic's location. Further, they evidenced a greater desire for the convenience of having a complete set of veterinary services on site. Representing the best target market for the clinic, this was the market segment in which the Castlerock clinic led.

2. **Feline-Oriented Households** (30 percent): While these households exhibited the greatest number of multiple cats, they were least interested in "one-stop" shopping for veterinary services. That is, the members of this segment valued having a complete set of veterinary services less than the members of the other segments. This particular segment was dominated by the Johnsburry Clinic.

3. **"Doc in a Barn"** (20 percent): This group of pet-owning households almost exclusively highly valued the quality of veterinary care. They indicated relatively little value for offering complete services, pleasant clinic environment or convenient location. They also indicated a high sensitivity to the cost of services provided. Interestingly, this group of households showed the highest concentration of young children, suggesting that the pet was for the benefit of the child and perhaps not the adult in the household. The Howland Clinic, with its managerial focus on providing low-cost service, seemed to dominate this segment.

37    Table 1 shows the relative strength of the competing clinics across the three market segments identified in the research.

# PET OWNERSHIP AND VETERINARY CARE

38    Pet ownership was slowly increasing. According to an American Pet Products Manufacturers Association, Inc. (APPMA) pet owner's survey, nearly four-in-ten or 39,000,000 U.S. households owned at least one dog. This represented an increase of eight percent in the number of households owning a dog since a level of 36,000,000 two years earlier. Three-in-ten or 32,128,000 U.S. households owned at least one cat. This represented a two percent increase in ownership over the same two-year period.

39    On the average, owners took their dog(s) to the veterinarian once per year. Among all dog owners, 81 percent took their dogs to the veterinarian in the past 12 months. Almost three-in-ten dog owners took their dog to a groomer in the past six months. The average owner took their cat(s) to the veterinarian once per year. Among cat owners, seven-out-of-ten took their cats to the veterinarian in the past 12 months. Only two percent of cat owners took their cat to a groomer in the past six months.[7]

[7]American Pet Products Manufacturers Association *(1999). 1999/2000 APPMA National Pet Owners Survey.* Greenwich, CT: APPMA.

**TABLE 2**
**Basic Veterinary**
**Services at**
**Castlerock**

| Service | Typical Cost |
|---|---|
| Routine examination | $ 25 |
| Rabies vaccination | $ 10 |
| Spay/neuter | $ 40 |
| Teeth cleaning | $140 |

**40**     Dog owners changed veterinarians most often because of moving, followed by poor pet care by the veterinarian and poor attitude. Seven percent of total dog owners changed veterinarians in 12 months. The reasons cat owners gave for changing doctors included better hours/location, poor attitude of the previous veterinarian or facility, change of address, and a desire for lower fees. Only four percent of cat owners changed veterinarians in 12 months.

**41**     On the average, over a 12-month period, dog owners spent $138.00 on routine veterinary care and $245.00 on surgical veterinary care in 1998. Cat owners spent less than $200.00 in 12 months, spent on average $56.00 on routine veterinary care and $50.00 on surgical veterinary care. Owners spending more than $220.00 in 12 months spent on average $158.00 on routine veterinary care and $199.00 on surgical veterinary care. Table 2 shows some basic veterinary services, and what they would typically cost at Castlerock.

**42**     A large percentage of pet owners in almost all segments of the population have multiple pets. In 1998, over 30 percent of dog owners owned more than one dog, and almost 50 percent of cat owners owned more than one cat. However, according to recent demographic information, people living in the region of the country served by Castlerock spent less on average on their dogs and cats compared to other regions. The area surrounding Castlerock was experiencing a slight yearly decline in population, and also a shift towards more elderly residents on the whole.[8]

# INFORMATION SYSTEMS

**43**     Twelve months earlier, the Clinic's staff identified that one of their problems rested in the poor performance of their information management system. Clinic staff believed that their information system (IS) was no longer sufficient to maintain accurate, accessible, and timely records of Castlerock's customers and their pets. As Snowe explained,

> In the past, veterinary clinics primarily worried about curing a pet's disease or easing its pain. Now, veterinarians try to provide the pet owner with the best pet health care, convenience, and as many value-added services as possible. To continue to grow the practice within a highly competitive market, we have to exceed the expectations of our customers. We believe that we need as much information as possible about our customers and our market segment to better serve the customer and maintain and further develop our competitive edge. If we had this information, it would surely point us in the right direction for continued growth.

## Hospital

**44**     Castlerock's hospital facility utilized microcomputers and specialized software since opening in 1979. The latest hardware upgrade was performed in 1997, and utilized a local area network composed of a single server connected to five microcomputers. The microcomputers were installed with the Microsoft® Windows 95™ operating system and Office 97™

[8]Ibid.

software. A common dot matrix printer provided printing capabilities for the hospital, and a separate receipt printer was used for credit card transactions.

**45**     The hospital facility used the DOS-based Pet Office Professional industry-specific software package, which was designed to integrate customer medical records, billing, and routine updates for scheduled annual pet checkups. Although a recent upgrade was purchased in 1998, this specialized software changed very little in appearance and function since its introduction in 1988. Pet Office Professional could not be integrated with Microsoft® products, although Office 97™ was used for word processing and spreadsheet tasks within the hospital.

**46**     Approximately 50 appointments were scheduled each day at the hospital facility. Additionally, follow-up care, prescription transactions, and lab procedures accounted for another 100 to 125 transactions per day. Depending on the type of transaction, some billing was internal; the remainder billed to other local veterinary care providers. The Pet Office Professional software was designed to coordinate these activities and generate basic end of day, week, and month tallies by category at the request of the user.

### Kennel

**47**     Reflecting the original philosophy of keeping the kennel separate from the clinic, Happy Pet Kennels used two independent microcomputers linked to a common dot matrix printer and a separate receipt printer. The microcomputers were installed with the Microsoft® Windows 95™ operating system, and all kennel transactions were processed via the industry-specific DOS-based K-9 Boarding Buddy software package (which also could not be integrated with Office 97™).

**48**     Customers for the Happy Pet Kennel subsidiary generated about 60 to 100 transactions daily between the boarding, training, retail products, and grooming businesses. Lisa Snowe described a normal day at the kennel,

> Some pets come in for mornings only, while others may stay afternoons. Many pet owners are now choosing "Doggy Day Care" rather than leave their pets home alone. When the dogs are dropped off each day, we offer the owners a much better environment rather than letting their dogs stay at home all day. Our employees play with each dog, walk him or her or allow them limited interaction with other pets depending on the preferences of the owner. We also can groom the dogs, offer training classes, or set up appointments for pet health issues as needed since we also own a pet hospital. We are truly a one-stop shop.

### Limitations of Current IS

**49**     K-9 Boarding Buddy software was originally installed to aid in organizing and monitoring the growing kennel business per the recommendation of other veterinarians. Observed performance, however, did not match expectations or business requirements. Snowe admitted that the promises made by the company that produced their software did not seem to really fit their type of kennel business. "K-9 Boarding Buddy can't take multiple pet check-ins per kennel. Once you enter a pet in kennel number 3 for the day, we're stuck with that entry. If we change the information when another pet comes in, it's like we never had another pet in the same kennel, or even as a customer for that day!"

**50**     Identified shortcomings of the existing IS by staff members suggested a need to improve the competitive position of the hospital and kennel business with improved service to the existing customer base. McFarland noted one of the problems that was beginning to cause concerns about the future of the hospital and kennel customer relations,

> K-9 Boarding Buddy software can't track or update individual pet or pet owner files after the initial data entry. As a result, the K-9 Boarding Buddy program lets us enter new pets, but won't let us delete pets that are no longer with us. We make it a habit to mail our customers

notices on specials or to recognize the birthday of their pet. One poor man received a birthday notice for a dog that has been dead for over a year now. Thankfully he is a very good customer and has been very understanding, but what happens if more customers aren't as understanding?

51    The concerns of the clinic owner and facility manager were focused on the impact that the current information system would have on the level of customer retention and satisfaction. Snowe and McFarland both identified a need for more and better information about how the clinic and the kennel actually functioned. Snowe commented,

> What we need are statistics and averages. We need to track customers by the age of their pet, the number of years services have been provided, the amount of money spent per visit, total money spent by customer, and a running list of services each customer takes advantage of. We thought we could use our computers to tell us what percent of services are generating profits, which areas are breaking even, and what services are losing money. Our accountant tells us these things from a broad point of view each year in the audit, but we want details each week, not once each year. We need as much information as we can get our hands on. We thought the Pet Office Professional and K-9 Buddy software could tell us these things, but it just doesn't seem to work like we need it to.

52    McFarland and Snowe also knew that the now separate information systems of the hospital would have to be combined. As Snowe explained,

> The database information can't be sorted or shared between our personal computers' Windows software, Pet Office Professional software, the K-9 Boarding Buddy software, or between the two businesses. We can't electronically access or share the medical information from customers that use both our hospital and kennel. This inconvenience sometimes irritates our shared customers and our staff because two separate records are maintained. We need a better way to understand and monitor the daily operations of the hospital and kennel.

## GROWTH OPTIONS

53    Expanding Castlerock would require relatively large investments in new facilities and the purchase of additional equipment. Adding a new office to the existing practice (at a new physical location) would require an upfront investment of about $250,000, including land, a building, and basic medical equipment. Expansion would also require hiring an additional veterinarian, technicians, support staff, and another office manager at a cost of $120,000 per year plus debt service on the new mortgage on the new land and office building. McFarland could probably get a fifteen-year loan (at a 10 percent interest rate) to finance this effort. Based on the average performance of comparable practices, he expected annual revenues from such an office to be about $215,000.

54    An alternative requiring less initial investment that could lead to a more permanent expansion, such as that described above, involved opening a small scale "satellite" office using existing office space (an estimated rent of $800 per month). At least initially, it might be opened only two or three days a week. This would cost an additional $50,000 for equipment, and about $55,000 per year for personnel, and could probably be financed over seven years. Based on average statistics for comparable facilities, McFarland believed that this office would probably bring in about $50,000 per year in revenues.

55    Both of these options could appear to threaten his colleagues at the other clinics, raising the question of their potential competitive response to this move. Again, given the overlapping services offered, McFarland was also concerned about the amount of incremental sales volume represented by these revenue estimates. He was concerned that he might increase his expenses while failing to substantially increase his revenues, a result of switching much

of his customer base to new services or new service delivery locations without increasing the size of the customer base. This is a phenomenon called cannibalization.

56    McFarland considered introducing other services to the local market through the hospital and/or kennel. He read about how mobile pet clinics realized some success in other markets. This alternative was less expensive than opening another brick and mortar clinic, but he questioned the cost of launching such a service. By his best estimates, a mobile pet clinic required a minimum initial investment of $150,000 for a properly outfitted vehicle, the commitment of 2 to 3 staff at a cost of an additional $65,000 to $78,000 annually, plus the annual debt service (at 10 percent over 7 years) on the loan for the equipment investment. McFarland was unsure that he could generate the volume of business to warrant the initial expense. Based on the average performance of comparable operations in comparable markets, he estimated the potential volume of such an operation at about $180,000 per year. However, McFarland was not certain how much of that represented incremental volume for the total business. Depending on how far distant the mobile pet clinic might travel from his base clinic, McFarland believed that he might suffer no more than 25 percent cannibalization. He was also unsure how his colleagues at the competing clinics would regard his actions. Would they see this action as open competition for their customers? They might respond negatively to his innovation, withdrawing referrals, or maybe even reconsider their friendships with him.

57    Another possibility was caring for sick or injured pets at home while the owner was away at work or on vacation. This proved to be an attractive business in other markets. The service could be expanded further to provide attention and stimulation to pets that have no immediate veterinary medical needs. The delivery of such services required minimal investment in new facilities ($5,000), but required an investment in basic medical equipment ($30,000) and at least one vehicle ($25,000). The equipment could be financed over seven years at a rate of 10 percent, but the vehicle and improvements only over five years at 8 percent interest and 16 percent interest, respectively. Additional clinic staff would also be necessary at an additional cost of $35,000 per year plus debt service on the loan for the additional equipment. Based on statistics for comparable operations in other markets, McFarland believed that this service would produce $60,000 per year in additional revenues to the business. Since the services seemed unlikely to overlap with those provided by his base clinic, McFarland thought that almost all of this revenue represented incremental sales for the overall business, avoiding cannibalization. He was still concerned about how the veterinarians in the other clinics might react to his innovation. Would they regard this as openly competing for their customers?

## Future of Castlerock

58    Snowe and McFarland were concerned with the future of the clinic. Was it possible to achieve the growth rates of the past? How should management grow the business? What information systems and technology will be required to support the growth strategy? Intuition served the clinic well through most of its years in business. Now greater competitive forces were causing the clinic to ask questions that it could not answer.

59    When McFarland bought the new microcomputers and software, he thought he was going to save effort, gain efficiency, and identify areas for cost reduction and for growth potential. He purchased what he believed was the right equipment for his business only a year ago, but now he questions whether he has moved to a system that has actually hurt his business and limited its potential for growth. What worked for some of his associates in the industry just did not seem to fit his situation.

# Case 30 Citigroup in Post-WTO China[1]

## David W. Conklin

**1** When China entered the World Trade Organization (WTO), at the end of 2001, Citigroup was still at an early stage in its China strategy. In 1998, Citicorp and Travelers Group Inc. (Travelers) had merged to create the new entity Citigroup Inc. Travelers brought a vast array of financial services that added to Citigroup's existing portfolio of consumer and commercial lending. Travelers had developed a very extensive business in investment banking, asset management, life insurance and property casualty insurance, as well as consumer lending. Travelers' operating companies included: Salomon Smith Barney, Salomon Smith Barney Asset Management, Travelers Life & Annuity, Primerica Financial Services, Travelers Property Casualty Corp and Commercial Credit.

**2** Following the merger, John Reed and Sanford Weill became co-chairmen of the new Citigroup. After a brief period of turmoil, Sanford Weill became sole chairman and chief executive officer of the merged entity. Citigroup's 2001 Annual Report indicated remarkable success in the integration of Citigroup's many divisions. In his letter to shareholders, Weill emphasized that:

> In 2001, Citigroup solidified its position as one of the most successful financial services companies in the world, outperforming and leading the field in the most profitable and attractive growth areas. We registered double-digit increases across many lines of business, and a 20 percent return on equity. . . . Our achievements received important recognition when Citigroup, for the first time, was named one of America's 10 Most Admired Companies by *Fortune* magazine and ranked number one in our industry category.[2]

**3** In March 2002, Travelers' Property Casualty unit was spun off in the expectation that its activities would not be central to the financial services package being offered by Citigroup, and its rate of profit would likely be less than that of the other financial services.

**4** Citibank, part of Citigroup, was one of the first foreign firms that had obtained licences to conduct a limited range of commercial activities in China. By 2002, Citibank had become one of the strongest foreign banks operating in the People's Republic of China (PRC), but as a foreign bank it had only limited market access, even for its limited array of services. At headquarters, Citigroup wanted to determine the growth prospects for each of its divisions, and which of its vast array of financial services should be the focus for expansion in China.

[1]This case has been written on the basis of published sources only. Consequently, the interpretation and perspectives presented in this case are not necessarily those of Citigroup or any of its employees. This case is an update on Richard Ivey School of Business #9A97G016, "Citibank N.A. In China."
[2]*Citigroup Annual Report 2001, pp. 2–3.*

Could Citibank be a "model" for the other Citigroup divisions? One possibility, of course, would be to continue with Citibank's existing China services, and for Citigroup to "wait and see" the results of WTO membership.

# THE LIBERALIZATION DILEMMA

Optimism about the economic benefits of China's WTO membership may be premature. Realising them will require wrenching structural change that will produce losers as well as winners. The shocks could strain international trade relations for years to come—Guy de Jonquières, "Enter the dragon," *Financial Times,* December 10, 2001, p. 14.

Can the WTO's rules be implemented? If they are not, does the global trading club have sufficient regulatory clout to provide adequate redress for foreign interests? A cornerstone principle of the WTO is that member nations apply trade and investment rules in a transparent manner evenly across the country, and accord national treatment to foreign companies. In China's case, experience and discernable economic pressures suggest that the equal application of transparent laws enforced by an impartial legal system may remain a mere concept for many years to come—James Kynge, "Can Beijing make trade rules stick?" *Financial Times,* November 17, 1999, p. 6.

5    Prior to China's WTO membership, Citibank had been licensed only to provide corporate banking services, and only to foreign-invested enterprises. Furthermore, Citibank had been licensed to operate branches in only a few of the Chinese cities open to foreign banks. In order to grow beyond these cities and to expand from foreign corporate banking to the large and potentially lucrative domestic retail and corporate financial business, Citibank needed licences from the central bank.

6    The terms and conditions for WTO membership required China to open its financial system to foreign corporations. However, the pace for liberalization of regulatory restrictions was uncertain. Meanwhile, prior to WTO entry, overall results for foreign financial corporations had been poor:

The Asian financial crisis has taken its toll on foreign banks' gains in China. Figures collated from government documents indicate that foreign banks and financial institutions made an aggregate net profit of US$256 million in 1997 and US$215 million in 1998—and a loss of US$150 million in 1999. Most foreign banks do not break out their China operations in their annual reports and country CEOs decline to disclose how much their businesses are making—or losing. But *Asiamoney* believes that, apart from the 32 banks allowed to do renminbi business and those with capital market skills, many foreign institutions are still chasing the pot of gold at the end of the rainbow.[3]

7    On the one hand, the People's Bank of China (PBOC), China's regulatory agency, was under pressure in regard to China's WTO commitments. On the other hand, China's state banks were in appalling shape. Generally, they were run by bureaucrats, up to their knees in bad debts, still required to provide cheap funding to nearly bankrupt state enterprises and unable to set their own deposit and interest rate levels. It might take them years to become properly competitive. Meantime, it was up to the PBOC to see that strong foreign competitors like Citigroup had no chance to bulldoze them out of the market. Commentators presented frequent warnings about this dilemma:

China's accession to the World Trade Organization could cause a banking crisis unless radical reforms to its debt-ridden state banks are pushed through, the country's top government think-tank warned yesterday.[4]

[3]"What WTO Means for Chinese Banking," *Asiamoney,* July/August 2000, p. 23.
[4]James Kynge, "Fears for Banks over China Entry into WTO," *Financial Times,* November 17, 1999, p. 1.

Says a high-ranking central banker in Beijing: "We are happy for foreign banks to come in. But at the same time we are very concerned about the impact of WTO. Our banks lag behind the foreigners on almost every front: capitalization, overseas networks, services and modern management expertise."[5]

**8** In a 2002 *Financial Times* article, James Kynge attempted to estimate the extent of non-performing loans in China's banking system:

Nowhere is the cost of China's politically driven economy clearer than in the financial system. Lending directed by the state is largely responsible for the burden of nonperforming loans in the big four state banks. Official estimates put bad loans at about 30 percent of assets, but most analysts believe the figure to be nearer 50 percent. Bad loans elsewhere—such as at city commercial banks and rural credit cooperatives—take the total to more than 50 percent of the country's GDP in 2000, say several academics in state think-tanks.[6]

**9** The terms and conditions for WTO membership stipulated that all nongeographic restrictions with respect to type of customer were to be removed immediately for foreign currency business. This would permit foreign banks to conduct foreign currency business with Chinese-owned enterprises and Chinese persons, but only in specific cities provided for in a licence. Over the five-year period from 2002 to 2007, restrictions on renminbi business and remaining geographic restrictions were also to be removed.

**10** However, China's initial regulatory reforms in response to WTO membership included several provisions that would retard the promised expansion of foreign banks. In particular, to be eligible to participate in renminbi business, a foreign bank had to have been engaged in business operations in China for three years, and these operations had to have been profitable for two consecutive years prior to an application for a licence. Furthermore, each foreign bank branch would have to put in place very onerous funding requirements.

**11** Commentators believed that the PBOC would likely be imposing a wide range of additional restrictions, for example, in regard to: deposits, interest rates on loans, fees, reserve requirements, capital adequacy ratios, limits on the size of a single borrower's credit line, equity/asset ratios, ratios of renminbi capital to renminbi assets, and reserves against bad and doubtful loans. As of 2002, domestic foreign currency deposits could not exceed 70 percent of a bank's total foreign currency assets within China. Renminbi lending was limited to 50 percent of a foreign bank's total lending.

**12** As a result of mandatory waiting periods and high funding requirements for additional branches, banks were likely to find their expansion impeded. A 2002 *BusinessWeek* article summarized these restrictions in a rather pessimistic commentary:

There are new banking regulations, which foreign lenders say are aimed at protecting China's debt-laden banks. As of early February (2002), new branches are required to have a minimum of $72 million in operating capital, up from $15.7 million, in order to do local retail business. The requirement will likely make it too expensive for any but the largest foreign banks to set up mainland networks. Particularly galling to foreign bankers is the fact that the regulation was announced as part of a package intended to fulfill China's WTO commitments. Joachim Fuchs, general manager of the Shanghai branch of Commerzbank, says the requirement's real purpose "is to give the local banks breathing time."[7]

**13** As early as 1997, Chris Tibbs, the vice-president and head of corporate finance of Citibank's China operations, had been optimistic about regulatory change.

---

[5]"What WTO means for Chinese banking," *Asiamoney,* July/August 2000, 20.
[6]James Kynge, "China's burden," *Financial Times,* January 3, 2002, 10.
[7]"The wait for free trade with China just got a little longer: Beijing's new trade rules are slowing down imports," *BusinessWeek Online,* March 11, 2002.

The banking system in China is evolving faster than most other countries. Generally speaking, the bureaucrats who are responsible for the financial market reforms are quite intelligent people. They know very much where they want to go. They are more efficient than most of the countries I have worked in (Japan, North and South America, and Hong Kong). I am optimistic that things will work out. PBOC operates in a very cautious but intelligent manner. The PBOC will not hold off our expansion. Actually, it is encouraging us to expand: it wants to use Citibank as a tool to force Chinese banks to become more competitive as soon as possible.[8]

**14**    Though Citibank's senior China executives had worked hard to develop a good relationship with the PBOC and were clearly positive about that relationship, they may also have had reason to be concerned. Citibank was one of the most powerful foreign banks in China, and given Citigroup's deep pockets and obvious interest in emerging markets, Citigroup was the one that posed the most obvious competitive threat to China's struggling domestic banks. Should the PBOC feel that Citigroup was too large, too ambitious or too successful in China, it might respond by putting the brakes on Citigroup's China expansion plans and giving early licences to smaller, less threatening foreign financial institutions instead.

**15**    Early in 2002, Citibank became the first foreign bank to be given approval for foreign currency dealings with Chinese customers. While Chinese held 90 billion dollars in foreign denominations in mainland banks, the Citibank licence would give access only to Chinese in the city of Shanghai. Citibank hoped that other cities would soon be opened for this business. Meanwhile, other divisions of Citigroup would need to develop China strategies as well.

# IMPEDIMENTS TO ECONOMIC DEVELOPMENT

### The Need for Political Reforms

**16**    While the economy of China had experienced rapid growth, commentators pointed to a series of substantial challenges that confronted ongoing economic development. China's state-owned enterprises (SOEs) were poorly managed. SOEs still controlled more than 70 percent of all fixed assets and 80 percent of all working capital in manufacturing. The Chinese banks were unable to collect a major portion of the loans that they had made to the state-owned enterprises. The pension system was largely unfunded. Corruption was widespread.

**17**    WTO membership would exacerbate the financial difficulties of the SOEs, as they would now face better-quality imports and competition from the foreign-owned corporations that were now investing in China. China's leaders expressed the view that unprofitable SOEs should be allowed to go bankrupt if their debts exceeded assets. However, the process for bankruptcy was not clear. Furthermore, bankruptcies would throw tens of millions of Chinese workers out of their jobs. The threat of massive unemployment brought with it the risk of social unrest, and the prospect of authoritarian crackdowns as a political response.

**18**    Some commentators expressed the view that a successful economic transition would require political reform with a shift towards democracy, free speech and investigative journalism, and modern commercial laws with an independent judiciary:

All of these problems are structural in nature. They are all, to varying degrees, the products of an unreformed political system that has become a drag on development and a serious barrier to China's ambitions to become a global superpower.

[8]L. Li, A. Young, and D. Conklin, *Citibank N.A. in China,* Richard Ivey School of Business, Case# 9A97G016, 1997.

Nowhere in the WTO agreement, which took 15 years to negotiate, is it specified that Beijing must undertake political reform. But many Chinese academics and other experts believe that, without changes to government, China may be unable to deliver on its WTO promises.

It is still dangerous in China to advocate an end to the Communist party's monopoly on power. But an increasing number of academics, officials and ordinary people say in private that there is no alternative. Without checks and balances on Communist influence, China may be unable to provide the type of detached, impartial government that its increasingly sophisticated economy requires.[9]

## Human Resource Challenges

19    The qualifications necessary for successful corporate management in a free enterprise market economy are quite different from the qualifications required for management of SOEs under central planning. Somehow, the Chinese managers would have to learn a new set of skills and develop a new set of business procedures. Among the many business practices that would have to be developed were those related to accounting, cost control, finance and advertising. The concept of marketing and a concern for customer satisfaction had to be ingrained in managerial decision-making. Throughout the corporation, the necessary concern for quality and innovation might be slow to develop. A key issue was how quickly China's educational system could create business administration courses for university students and for part-time executive education.

20    Beyond the issue of skills and capability many observers pointed to traditional cultural impediments to income differentials, an essential aspect of motivation and reward in free enterprise economies. Government ownership focused on interpersonal harmony, and this fostered a distrust of performance appraisals. The hierarchical structure of SOEs meant that employees were not socialized to develop initiative. The absence of "consumerism" meant that there was little emphasis on the Western "work ethic."

21    One might look to expatriate managers to bridge the gap while the Chinese human resource portfolio was broadened and attitudes changed, but foreigners found it difficult to adapt culturally to life in China. For a corporation seeking to hire from the Chinese labor market, there was a difficulty in getting employees to leave the SOEs. A fluid labor market has not yet developed.

22    A separate but related set of human resource challenges had to do with the government bureaucrats, whose skill sets and practices also would have to be transformed if they were to regulate private sector corporations effectively and if they were to conduct macroeconomic policies appropriately. China faced the prospect of developing new systems for taxation, expenditure control, monetary policy and a host of sector-specific supervisory and regulatory programs, together with new commercial laws and procedures for their enforcement. For many decades, "Western" universities had offered programs in economics and public administration that could prepare students for careers in the civil service. In China, a revolution would be needed in traditional university curricula, which could require a very long time.

## E-commerce Limitations

23    In Western nations, the growth of e-commerce and the "new economy" had dramatically altered business practices and had brought ongoing productivity improvements. For China, participation in the new economy seemed a long distance away. The basic telecom infrastructure lacked broadband capacity except for a few cities, and so was limited in its ability

---

[9]James Kynge, "China's Burden," *Financial Times,* January 3, 2002, p. 10.

**EXHIBIT 1**
China—Major
Markets

| | Households (millions) | Annual Discretionary Income per Household (RMB) |
|---|---|---|
| Guangzhou (16% of IT investment) | 2.0 | 12,018 |
| Beijing (37% of IT investment) | 3.9 | 9,183 |
| Shanghai (25% of IT investment) | 4.7 | 8,773 |
| Wuhan | 2.1 | 6,262 |
| Xi'an | 1.8 | 5,999 |
| Chongqing | 9.2 | 5,896 |
| Shenyang | 2.1 | 5,364 |

to convey the files necessary for e-commerce. There was a possibility that foreign corporations could enter China and revolutionize the telecom infrastructure. WTO membership did require that foreign operators be permitted to enter China, but in 2002, they were restricted to ownership of less than 50 percent of each Chinese company. These ownership restrictions were likely to restrain the shift of necessary technologies and new plant and equipment investment from the advanced nations to China.

24    Apart from the weaknesses of the telecom infrastructure, there was an ongoing supervision on the part of the Chinese government in regard to Internet content. In recent years, for example, the rapid expansion of the Falun Gong movement had rested on Internet communications, and the government regarded Falun Gong as a political protest that should be quelled. Consequently, the government had imposed supervisory controls that could impede corporate Internet transactions. Various agencies played an active role in supervising the Internet, and the Ministry of Information Industry (MII) controlled the international Internet gateway.

### Regional Disparities

25    China's economic liberalization began in 1978 with the creation of "special economic zones" where foreign corporations could operate separate from the administrative structure of central planning. The success of this experiment meant that the coastal cities where these zones were located experienced economic progress that contrasted starkly with the ongoing rural stagnation of the rest of the country. In regard to prospects for e-commerce, Exhibit 1 indicates that over 75 percent of information technology investment in China was concentrated in just three cities: Guangzhou, Beijing and Shanghai. The enormous gap between the coastal cities on the one hand and the rest of the country on the other presented serious problems in regard to the economic development of the nation as a whole. Of course, the government of China clearly understood the difficulties that it faced in this regard, and was attempting to redress the balance, but it would likely take decades before the rest of China could become a part of the rapid growth paradigm.

## OPPORTUNITIES FOR FINANCING FOREIGN-OWNED CORPORATIONS

26    The prospect of China joining the WTO stimulated a huge increase in foreign direct investment (FDI), as Exhibit 2 indicates. China's current stock of FDI was already enormous in global terms. In 2001, it stood at $350 billion, with an annual increase of $40 billion to $45 billion. This placed China as number three in the world in terms of the stock of FDI, behind the United States at $1.1 trillion and Britain at $400 billion.

**EXHIBIT 2**

**China's Economy**

Source: *EIU Report—China 2002.*

| | 1998 | 1999 | 2000 | 2001* |
|---|---|---|---|---|
| GDP growth (%) | 7.8 | 7.1 | 8.0 | 7.3 |
| GDP per capita (US$) | 758 | 784 | 853 | 937 |
| Inflation, annual average (%) | −0.8 | −1.4 | 0.4 | 0.7 |
| Current account balance % of GDP | +3 | +2 | +1.9 | +1.8 |
| Foreign exchange rate (US$) | 8.3 | 8.3 | 8.3 | 8.3 |
| Debt as % of GDP | 16 | 16 | 13 | 12 |
| FDI inflows (US$ billion) | 45 | 40 | 40 | 45 |
| Internet users (millions) | | 16.9 | 26.5 | |

*Estimates

The mainland now accounts for about one-third of emerging markets' total stock of FDI, according to Nicholas Lardy of the Brookings Institution in Washington. Nearly four-fifths of all FDI going to Southeast and East Asia, not counting Japan, is sucked up by China—and to its neighbors' growing alarm.[10]

27    Citigroup could focus on providing foreign-owned corporations with certain of its services—but which services and how to organize them remained a question. Several economic realties would be important as Citigroup contemplated the future in China for its additional financial activities. Competition from other foreign banks had become intense. Japanese banks, in particular, seemed not so concerned with profit margins as with obtaining market share. Furthermore, it was not clear whether foreign capital inflows would be maintained at these levels.

28    While China's population—more than one billion, 200 million—and the economy's high growth rate were attractive to investors, nevertheless, the average per capita income for the nation as a whole was so low that decades of growth would be necessary before mass marketing of consumer goods and services could be effective. In fact, some pointed to the high growth rate of the economy as simply due to the very low level of production and consumption, and warned that growth was low in absolute dollar terms and would inevitably slow down as higher levels were reached. Perhaps investment would be focused principally on manufacturing for export, based on industrial wages as low as 20 to 30 cents per hour.

## OPPORTUNITIES FOR INVESTMENT BANKING SERVICES

29    With the privatization of SOEs, a huge opportunity would develop for Citigroup to participate actively in investment banking. Initial public offerings (IPOs) might include the sale of shares on either foreign or Chinese stock exchanges.

30    SOEs would need a great deal of advice in the IPO process, and the valuation of shares would be particularly difficult. Assets had been acquired at prices that had no relationship with free market prices. Future profit streams were perhaps impossible to predict. How to deal with debts to the state banks remained a common problem. Consequently, it was expected that the IPO process would generally involve a "bought deal" in which the investment bank would underwrite the entire issue, financing the deal with its own capital and then reselling to the public at a slightly higher price.

31    However, as of 2002, China's stock markets were fragmented, with restrictions on ownership of various types of shares, and they were at a very early stage of development.

[10]"China's Economic Power," *The Economist*, March 10, 2001, p. 23.

Foreigners tended to invest only in Chinese companies that had listed shares in the Hong Kong market, referred to as "H shares" or "red-chips." The legal system and regulatory standards in Hong Kong provided assurances that were not yet available in mainland China.

32    From a positive perspective, the privatization of SOEs would create an array of shareholders that would hopefully improve corporate governance and transparency and would provide an ongoing spur to competitiveness.

33    Perhaps investment banking, and provision of various services to privatized SOEs, might be a new and profitable strategy. Citigroup's 2001 annual report was extremely optimistic about the strength of its investment banking activities:

> By combining world-class investment banking services through SSB and world-class commercial banking through Citibank, we provide unique value propositions to our clients. . . . We became the leading global underwriter in combined equity and debt for the first time. . . . We became the leading global investment firm as measured by revenue. . . . We became the number one global fixed-income underwriter with record new-issue volume, earning *International Financing Review's* Global Bond House of the Year award.
>
> In 2001, CitiCapital, the commercial finance business of Citigroup, continued integrating acquisitions into its operations, most notably Associates Commercial Finance and the leasing businesses of the European American Bank. As the second-largest U.S.-based leasing company, CitiCapital serves equipment manufacturers, as well as dealers and buyers of transportation equipment, material handling and construction equipment, and business technology and medical equipment. It is also a leading provider of master leasing programs to large corporations.[11]

34    Citigroup Global Investments (CGI) undertook direct investments in the complete range of financial and real assets, utilizing the deposits and premiums of Citigroup's related divisions. These investments included fixed-income, equities, real estate, private equity, hedge funds and various structured investments. Through CitiStreet, Citigroup offered administrative and investment management services for pension, health and welfare plans. Should these activities be pursued in China?

# OPPORTUNITIES FOR INSURANCE, PENSIONS, AND ANNUITY PRODUCTS

35    China's insurance sector was expected to be one of the most lucrative and highly competitive over the next few decades. Insurance industry premiums in the Peoples Republic of China (PRC) had experienced a 20 percent increase year-over-year for the past several years. Despite such rapid growth, gross insurance receipts accounted for less than one percent of China's GDP, much below that of other developing countries and significantly below the worldwide premium average of five percent.

36    Lured by such staggering opportunity, over 90 foreign insurance companies had set up over 100 rep offices in China even prior to WTO entry. As these offices were restricted from signing legally binding contracts, they could not conduct business. However, they were in place to develop crucial relationships with key Chinese officials and industry contacts, as well as to conduct regional market research.

37    China's acceptance into the World Trade Organization (WTO) was contingent upon foreign access to its insurance markets. However, China's terms and conditions for WTO membership permitted China to restrict foreign ownership to 50 percent or less. This requirement to accept a joint venture partner—in practice, some government agency or SOE—could

---

[11]*Citigroup Annual Report*, 2001.

prove to be a major stumbling block for foreign insurance corporations. Despite the presence of so many rep offices and pressure from the United States, European Union (EU) and others to allow greater foreign access to its insurance market, the general consensus was that China would be slow in the gradual opening of its insurance market.

38   Beijing had awarded the first licence for a foreign company to operate in China on a trial basis in 1992, when the American International Group (AIG) received a licence to operate in Shanghai. By 1995, AIG was a successful operation, generating annual premiums of US$50 million, accounting for 88 percent of the market share for life insurance in Shanghai (800,000 individual policies). The success of AIG's operations in Shanghai had taken even their own executives by surprise, who consequently suspended their projections in light of performance that was "way beyond" their expectations. AIG's commanding market leadership position in the Shanghai market, gained at the expense of China's national insurers, and the speed at which they took over the market frightened many Chinese insurance firms, who were devastated by AIG and fearful that if Beijing did not respond quickly, China would be handing over their market to foreign insurers "on a silver platter."

39   In response, to protect China's infant domestic insurers, the People's Bank of China (PBOC) acted on several fronts. First, it applied pressure to domestic insurers to improve their marketing, products and service. It also increased licensing quotas to domestic insurers. Most seriously, however, was the PBOC's decree in 1995 that joint ventures (JVs) would be the only mode of entry available to foreign insurance firms. In 1996, Manulife launched the first Sino-foreign joint venture insurance company. However, many foreign corporations such as Citigroup might refuse to enter a joint venture, and even if they did, their rate of expansion could be limited by the financial strength of the joint venture partner.

40   Citigroup, through its Travelers Life and Annuity division (TL&A), achieved record operating earnings in 2001, placing it in the top three U.S. companies that provided individual life and annuity products. Over the period 1998 to 2002, TL&A moved from number 38 to number 18 in life insurance sales. It focused on high-net-worth customers, and it had record annuity sales in the pension close-out and structured settlement segments. With China's shift away from the government and SOE "safety net" to individual responsibility for personal financial planning, Citigroup faced perhaps unlimited growth potential for TL&A's services.

# OPPORTUNITIES FOR PERSONAL BANKING, CREDIT CARDS, E-BANKING, MORTGAGES, AND WEALTH MANAGEMENT

41   The domestic savings rate in China had been exceptionally high at about 40 percent of GDP. Liberalization of the financial services market could allow foreign banks to tap into these savings, which had previously been deposited in the state banking system.

42   While credit cards were an important and lucrative part of the Citibank consumer banking lineup elsewhere in Asia, many were pessimistic about the credit card business in China in the near term. Why? The Chinese government and the PBOC had great sensitivity toward inflation. The government believed, analysts said, that along with corruption, one of the contributing factors to the 1989 Tiananmen problem was out-of-control inflation. Thus, from the point of view of the government, inflation constraint was a very important goal. The prevailing view, furthermore, was that if China was to maintain its exemplary rate of economic expansion, the national savings rate would have to be maintained. Encouraging borrowing—via credit cards, for example—would increase inflation and discourage saving. Thus, analysts suggested, it would not be in the best long-term interest of either the country or its financial institutions to encourage hasty development of a retail credit card market. In any case, there were important economies of scale at the industry level, dependent

on the overall development of credit agencies, automatic banking machines and merchant enrollment. In determining its strategy, Citibank would have to project the growth rate of the credit card industry as a whole.

43      Citigroup was making rapid advances in offering its wide range of products on the Internet. It had established alliances with AOL Time Warner and Microsoft, and its online consumer accounts reached 15 million in 2001. In addition to providing Internet services to its customers, Citigroup achieved ongoing efficiencies within its organization as a result of Internet usage.

44      The shift from communism to free enterprise would bring with it the practice of personal home ownership. Conceivably, even rental apartment buildings might be privatized through the sale to corporations or through a transfer to the condominium concept. All of these actions would require mortgage financing of some type. One of Citigroup's divisions was the Citigroup Private Bank which acted as a gateway for the wealthy to the full resources of Citigroup, offering affluent families the complete range of portfolio management and investment advisory services. This gave clients of the Citigroup Private Bank multiple touch points with the various other divisions globally. Another division, Citigroup Asset Management (CAM) had over $400 billion in assets under management as it entered the year 2002, offering institutional, high-net-worth and retail clients a broad array of products and services. CAM was a market leader in U.S.-managed retail accounts, with a variety of mid-size mutual funds. CAM included a global research organization which contributed to Citigroup's institutional and retail asset management business. How long would it be before China might have a substantial number of high-net-worth families that could support these divisions?

# CITIGROUP WORLDWIDE

45      Citigroup was significantly more international in scope than its international competitors: it operated in more than 100 countries, had 268,000 employees, and in 2001, it derived more than $2.8 billion in core income from emerging markets (see Exhibit 3). Within Citigroup, Citibank had a particularly long history of emerging market expertise.

46      Citibank had not always been a world-class success story, however. The bank suffered through a very difficult period in the late 1980s and early 1990s as a result of its decentralized decision-making structure and what *Euromoney* called a "near fatal brush with commercial real estate lending"[12] in the United States. Thus, chairman and chief executive officer (CEO) John Reed spent much of the early 1990s engineering the bank's recovery—a brutal but apparently successful process. One of his most well-known reengineering efforts was the G-15. In 1993, at the height of the bank's real-estate lending crisis, he created a committee of the bank's top 15 business managers, who all reported directly to him. He required them all to fly to New York once a month for meetings that lasted an entire day and sometimes two, and were frequently highly confrontational, punishing all the managers involved, but analysts said it worked. By centralizing the decision-making in New York and forcing his managers to fight him on every major strategic decision, Reed managed to repair the bank's balance sheet, rebuild its tier-one capital and restore its credit ratings by 1996.[13] Although the G-15 structure was modified later, decision-making was still much more centralized at the time of the 1998 merger than it had been in the 1980s. For Citigroup, this issue of centralization and decentralization of decision-making would continue to be important, particularly in the unique market of China.

---

[12]Peter Lee, "Reed Reshuffles the Pack," *Euromoney,* April 1996, pp. 34–39.
[13]Ibid.

**EXHIBIT 3**
Citigroup Financial
Highlights, 2001 (in
millions of dollars)

Source: *Citigroup Annual
Report* 2001.

| Adjusted Revenue | $83,625 |
|---|---|
| | **Segment Income** |
| **Global Consumer** | |
| Banking/Lending | $ 4,217 |
| Insurance | 720 |
| Western Europe | 483 |
| Japan | 928 |
| Emerging markets | 1,166 |
| e-Consumer/Consumer Other | −148 |
| Total Global Consumer | 7,366 |
| **Global Corporate** | |
| Corporate & Investment Bank | 3,509 |
| Emerging Markets Corporate Banking and Global Transaction Services | 1,644 |
| Commerical Lines Insurance | 691 |
| Total Global Corporate | 5,844 |
| **Global Investment Management & Private Banking** | |
| Travelers Life & Annuity | 821 |
| The Citigroup Private Bank | 378 |
| Citigroup Asset Management | 336 |
| Total Global Investment Management & Private Banking | 1,535 |
| **Investment Activities (A)** | 530 |
| **Corporate/Other** | −706 |
| **Core Income** | 14,569 |
| Restructuring and Merger-Related Items—After Tax | −285 |
| Income before Cumulative Effect of Accounting Changes | 14,284 |
| Cumulative Effect of Accounting Changes (B) | −158 |
| **Net Income** | $14,126 |
| **Return on Common Equity (Core Income)** | 20.4% |

47    Reed had believed that Citibank's strategic advantage was in its international operations: global reach, local ties. Again, for Citigroup, whether to strive for a global presence would be an important issue in regard to each of its divisions and activities, as would the question of whether a major presence in China was necessary as a component of a global presence.

# CITIBANK'S COMPETITIVE ADVANTAGES

48    Citibank had created a unique and enormously successful set of competitive advantages in emerging market banking, and these competitive advantages would greatly help its China expansion. Whether these attributes could be extended to create synergies with Citigroup's other divisions remained a key question.

### The Global Network

When a multinational company wants to enter an emerging market it calls its lawyers, its accountants, the embassy and Citibank.—Shaukat Aziz, head of Asia/Pacific global finance operations.[14]

[14]Lehman Brothers Inc., *Citicorp Company Report,* December 12, 1996.

**49**     Citibank executives, as well as most banking analysts, would probably agree that Citibank's only true and sustainable advantage was its sprawling global network which was important in serving its powerful list of corporate banking clients but crucial too in developing its consumer franchise in lucrative offshore markets.

**50**     This network, moreover, was extraordinarily strong in the emerging markets which were most attractive to Citibank's key corporate banking clients and to its own consumer finance division. How had Citibank developed its emerging markets advantage?

### Time and Experience

**51**     Citibank had been in some of these markets for nearly 100 years. In the case of China, Citibank had originally entered the market in 1902 and so the year 2002 marked its centenary. By the 1930s, Citibank was one of the country's major foreign banks, operating 14 branches in nine cities. However, with the communist takeover, all of Citibank's branches were closed. In 1984, Citibank at last opened a new office in China in the city of Shenzhen and began the slow process of applying for licences to expand its operations.

**52**     Reed had clearly believed in the value of first-mover advantage and had worked to ensure that Citibank was usually among the first foreign banks to get its foot in any emerging market door. The bank's relative experience in these volatile markets created a level of operational expertise that, in times of turbulence, other banks found difficult to match. This was a particularly valuable asset in attracting and keeping important multinational accounts. Could other Citigroup divisions build on this Citibank expertise and reputation?

### Localization and Commitment

**53**     Citibank worked hard to develop close ties with the community and with the local central bank. Over 95 percent of Citibank's jobs held outside the United States were held by locally hired staff. The bank had a well-established reputation for commitment too, which made Citibank popular with governments: Unlike some other banks which moved into countries on the expectation of brisk profits and then moved out again when they were slow to materialize, Citibank moved in early with intent to stay. Executives routinely emphasized the bank's ability and eagerness to help the local financial services industry grow. Employees were seconded to central banks. Technology was transferred. Locals were trained.

**54**     Citibank was not above currying political favor either. In Taiwan, for example, the bank "wowed Taipei" by bringing former U.S. President George Bush and former British Prime Minister Margaret Thatcher to visit in the 1990s. This seemed to have worked particularly well. Rival bankers said, after that, Citibank got "just about anything they wanted from the central bank."[15] Someone, somewhere inside Citigroup was almost certainly wondering how this model could be made to work for the other divisions if they adopted a China expansion strategy.

### Technological Superiority

**55**     According to a Lehman analyst, Citibank was "ahead of the curve" with respect to technology and financial innovation.[16] Judging from the number of awards the bank won, this was not an uncommon view. Citibank was broadly perceived to be very strong in corporate banking services ranging from foreign exchange to cash management, debt capital markets to derivatives. And if this was the case in the United States, it was even more obvious in emerging market nations where competition was less well developed, financial systems less

---

[15]James Peng, "U.S. Giant Shakes up Taiwan Banking, Eyes China," *BC Cycle*, July 17, 1996.
[16]Lehman Brothers Inc., *Citicorp—Company Report*, December 12, 1996.

evolved. This was also the reason Citibank won numerous awards as best bank overall: best emerging markets bank, best Asian bank, best foreign bank in China, best foreign bank in a number of other emerging markets.[17] In other words, Citibank could usually provide better corporate banking service than local banks in many of its markets, and competitive service in more markets than any of its "foreign bank" competitors.

## Human Resources Practices

56 According to Chris Tibbs, human resources development had been one of the bank's most pressing issues in China in the 1990s. "The most challenging thing for us today is the human resource side of our business. Normally, a person needs to have about seven years of experience before becoming a capable manager. We started branch banking activity in China in the 1990s, and so we have trained local people to be successful managers for less than a decade." Despite this, the bank's human resources practices were broadly perceived as a powerful competitive advantage, in China and throughout Asia. Analysts in China said that Citibank people were frequently poached by other banks. Tibbs confirmed this, noting that the bank's counter-strategy (salary, environment and opportunity) was helpful in holding staff and even in bringing them back. "As a matter of fact," said Tibbs, "our people who went to work for ABN-Amro want to return to Citibank. We are the college of banking and the best bank in the world."

## Accounting Practices

57 The bank also had an advantage in Asia in its audit and accounting practice. This was particularly true in China, where Citibank was the bank the PBOC chose to work with to improve internal auditing within the domestic banking system. As of 1997, the PBOC was actually using Citibank's internal auditing standards as a guide for its own, and extending that standard to other Chinese banks. According to Tibbs, in fact, the PBOC was so pleased with Citibank's recommended internal control system that they used it to audit the bank's new Beijing branch only six months after opening.

> After our branch in Beijing had been open for about six months, we received a message from PBOC that it was going to audit us; it seemed strange that we had just been working for six months and it wanted to audit us. It turned out that it was because PBOC wanted to test its team of auditors, who were trained by us. This was the first time that Citibank was tested by its own students. After the team of auditors went through the auditing, Citibank suggested to them where they could possibly improve.

Analysts wondered if, in China, this advantage was a sustainable one.

58 In 1995, Reed had defined a clear strategy: Build on what the bank was already good at and on what was already profitable. Under the Citigroup umbrella, this focus on excellence continued in Citibank. As the 2001 *Annual Report* noted:

> Importantly, every business within the Consumer Group is either the leader or near the top of its class. In the primary areas of cards, consumer finance and banking, the businesses maintain distinct competitive advantages:
>
> • Low-cost producers with superior credit management,
> • Exportable business models with superior acquisition capabilities, and
> • A strong brand.[18]

---

[17] Titles awarded by *Euromoney, Corporate Finance, Institutional Investor.*
[18] *Citigroup Annual Report,* 2001.

### Global Relationship Banking (GRB)

**59**    In focusing on the top multinationals—most of them pursuing aggressive overseas growth strategies—Citibank was "serving global companies globally,"[19] an area where it had a distinct competitive advantage over both domestic and "foreign" banks in virtually all of the most attractive emerging markets.

**60**    In China prior to the WTO entry, Citibank also had a strategy for targeting strong SOEs.

> Our strategy is to identify 10 industries which would develop the fastest in a country, and target profitable companies within those industries. We are different from other banks in that we choose companies not only based on their numbers on the financial statements, but also the industrial sectors they are in and the qualities of the management team.[20]

**61**    In order to serve these customers seamlessly, each major Citibank GRB client had a "team" of its own. Bankers were encouraged to think of themselves as, for example, "on the Motorola team" instead of "in foreign exchange" or "from the Hong Kong office."

**62**    In the "Asian model" that Citibank executives would apply in thinking about their China strategy, the GRB franchise usually represented an important platform, allowing Citibank to embed itself in new economies, hiring locally, developing a relationship with domestic regulators and (this was an emerging idea at Citibank) beginning to serve ambitious local companies as well as Western multinationals. With licences and regulatory relationships in place, the consumer bankers could then move in,[21] offering whatever range of financial products was appropriate, marketing *Citibanking* ® as the country's new premium banking product.

### Global Consumer Finance

**63**    What Citibank aimed to provide worldwide was a one-stop shop for consumer financial services. This would mean uniform service wherever consumers chose to bank, and with the convenience and reliability that emerging markets clients probably associated more closely with their local McDonald's than with the kind of banking services they were receiving from their domestic banks. Citibank charged a premium price for these services but expected that, usually, the internationally minded and newly wealthy business elite in these nations would be willing to pay more for first-rate banking services.[22] Income statement figures suggest that they were.

### Marketing the Experience: Citibanking®

**64**    In emerging market countries like China, Citibank had the capacity to develop what marketers like to call "strong brand equity." It had cachet as an overseas bank. It had or could develop a reputation as a bank that provided superior service to those with money. And those who had money (who were increasing in number in these countries) were generally pleased to pay a premium for the level of reliable service and convenience—and the level of prestige—that they could get only from banking with Citibank. Citibank marketed its package of consumer banking services as an experience: "*Citibanking®*." This branding strategy was not yet an advantage in China as Citibank was not allowed to provide retail banking services there. Brand equity was perceived to be a great asset elsewhere in Asia, where Citibank's consumer banking business was growing at a very healthy clip. The

[19] Lehman Brothers Inc., *Citicorp Company Report,* December 12, 1996.
[20] L. Li, A. Young, and D. Conklin, *Citibank N.A. in China,* Richard Ivey School of Business, Case# 9A97G016, 1997.
[21] Kenneth Klee, "Brand Builders," *Institutional Investor,* March 1997, p. 89.
[22] Ibid.

importance of brand image to Citibank's financial franchise should not be underrated, therefore, and would certainly be a factor in any discussion of joint ventures or strategic acquisitions.

### Citibank's Joint Venture Strategy

**65** Citibank had been strongly averse to joint venture relationships, entering into such agreements only when forced by central bank authorities.[23] Citibank operated in China, as in most countries, as branches of the parent, not subsidiaries. In August 1997, Tibbs agreed with this negative attitude towards joint ventures (JVs).

> We recognize that most JVs do not last very long; JVs give an institution a short-term advantage, but not long-term benefit. A JV in China would be an expensive practice. We do not think that we need to do a JV in China. Up to three years ago, many institutions favored JVs. Now they realize that the environment in China is such that it is unnecessary for them to do JVs in order to get business. Today, foreign institutions are looking for majority shares of the partnership, or even 100-percent ownership. The expansion of Citibank in China may be possibly through merger and acquisitions instead of joint ventures.

**66** The door had not, however, been closed to the concept of growth through acquisition. In 1996, John Reed had suggested[24] that he was more comfortable with the concept of strategic acquisition than he had been in the past, as long as such an acquisition would build up one of the bank's key lines of business. The idea of an acquisition in China offered, at the very least, an opportunity to make another positive impression on China's central bank, the People's Bank of China. It might also reinforce Citibank's image as a committed foreign presence, deserving of access to the retail market. It would certainly, however, create branding issues. Thus, if Citibank's China staff were to propose an acquisition, they would do so with the expectation of significant concern from the Citigroup board.

**67** For Tibbs in the late 1990s, the acquisition of an existing Chinese financial institution was not a likely scenario, or even a desirable one:

> Acquiring a financial institution in China is not only not on our 'radar screen,' it is not something which I could see the government allowing anytime soon. Further, the time, resources and market momentum lost in repairing someone else's wrecked bank (portfolio) is so significant that this is not one's rational dream of how to get ahead quickly.[25]

## A UNIQUE STRATEGY FOR CHINA?

> We want to be totally global and totally local.—John Reed, Chairman and CEO, Citicorp(1993)[26]

**68** As Citigroup entered the twenty-first century, adaptation to local realities remained a central principle. The 2001 *Annual Report* emphasized what it referred to as its "embedded bank" strategy.

---

[23]The only joint venture banking relationships Citibank had been involved in during recent times was a joint venture branch with the Bank of Hungary (Citibank reacquired the last of the central bank's shares in 1995 and presently owned 100 percent of the branch) and the Saudi American Bank, a joint venture bank with the Saudi central bank.

[24]At his December 1996 meeting with equity analysts, quoted in many analyst reports on Citicorp, including the Merrill Lynch report of January 24, 1997.

[25]L. Li, A. Young, and D. Conklin, "Citibank N.A. in China," Richard Ivey School of Business, Case# 9A97G016, 1997.

[26] Bryan Batson, "Thinking Globally, Acting Locally," *China Business Review*, vol. 20, no. 3. (May/June 1993): pp. 23–25.

Our goal is to grow our market share over the next five years through our embedded bank strategy. By 'embedded bank' we mean a bank that has roots in the country as deep as any local indigenous bank, building a broad customer base, offering diverse products, actively participating in the community and recruiting staff and senior management from the local population. Our long history in these regions positions us as a genuinely local bank.[27]

Citigroup participates in a broad range of community building initiatives that foster healthy economies: microlending, affordable housing and special-needs facilities, small-business development and savings incentive programs. Our involvement includes offering customized products and services and access to technical assistance, along with the volunteer efforts of our employees.[28]

**69** As China entered the WTO, Citigroup faced many strategic issues, including:

- How could executives ensure that Citibank would maintain its first-mover advantage in China? How could China executives ensure that Citibank would be among the first foreign banks to capture the domestic retail market? Was the most obvious option a PBOC-sanctioned joint venture with a local bank?

- What additional financial activities should be the focus of Citigroup's China strategy? Could credit cards and e-banking play a significant role? Should substantial amounts of capital be put at risk in investment banking and "bought deals"? If not, would Citigroup be missing a chance of a lifetime to capture an exploding market of SOE privatizations? Would SOE privatizations and the new emphasis on individual responsibility bring with them a mushrooming demand for insurance and pension products?

- To what degree, and in what ways, could the other Citigroup divisions benefit from Citibank's experience in China in order to build a market there?

**70** Citigroup's senior management recognized the need to be proactive in a wide range of strategic issues. Could the China strategy be a model and learning platform for Citigroup as it extended its umbrella of activities in other emerging markets? As emphasized by Robert Rubin, member, board of directors and office of the chairman:

In the years ahead, globalization, the spread of market-based economics and new technologies will continue to present great opportunities in the developed and emerging markets. But the challenges will also be great, both to policymakers and to each of us as participants in the global economy.[29]

---

[27]*Citigroup Annual Report* 2001, p. 18.
[28]*Citigroup Annual Report* 2001, p. 26.
[29]*Citigroup Annual Report* 2001, p. 7.

# Case 31 Conoco's Decision: The First Annual President's Award for Business Ethics

## J. Brooke Hamilton III, Mark Smith, Steve L. Scheck

1   On a December Friday in 1999, Steve L. Scheck, General Auditor for Conoco Inc., directed the other members of the award selection team toward lunch in the corporate dining room. They had spent the morning reviewing all the nominees for Conoco's first annual President's Award in Business Ethics. The heavy lifting would take place that afternoon. The team was charged with deciding who should receive the award and how the process should be improved for next year.

2   As they walked through the corridors of the headquarters campus in Houston, Steve reflected on the events which had brought this group together. He recalled the meeting with Archie Dunham, Conoco's President, Chairman, and CEO, when the idea first surfaced. In their discussion, Dunham had indicated that he wanted to initiate a "President's Award for Business Ethics." "We have a President's award for the other core values of safety and health, environmental stewardship, and valuing all people," he stated. "Why don't we have an award for business ethics?" Steve had agreed to get started on the project right away. Now a year later and after a great deal of planning, the process was coming to fruition. The award recipient or recipients would be presented with a trophy at the company's honors banquet and featured in an awards video circulated internally and externally. All the nominees would receive a note of congratulations from the President, Chairman and CEO that certainly would provide some carryover in their annual performance evaluations. After the discussion of the candidates that morning, Steve had his own preliminary judgments on who should be selected. He was curious to see what the other members of the selection team thought.

## BACKGROUND AND HISTORY OF THE COMPANY

3   In 1999 Conoco was a large integrated oil company. The firm traced its origins back to the Continental Oil and Transportation Company first incorporated in Utah in 1875. At the time of the case it was a global firm operating in more than 40 countries in the oil exploration, transportation, refining and marketing sectors of the industry. The company had approximately 16,700 employees plus contractors and joint venture partners.

4   The firm's history has not been without difficulties. During the oil shocks of the early eighties, the company lost its independence. In 1981, DuPont acquired Conoco in order to insure adequate feed stocks for DuPont's chemical business. In 1992, the international oil analyst Schroder and Co. rated Conoco last in overall exploration results among the 14 firms it surveyed.

5   As the oil crisis abated, the need to secure feed stocks seemed less important to DuPont. Wall Street was pressuring the company to improve its performance. DuPont's response was

to streamline its operations. In the early 90s, Conoco's new president, Archie Dunham, began a program of rationalizing Conoco's assets and developing new sources of supply. The company was successfully spun off from DuPont in a complex public offering and stock swap in 1999. In 1999 the Schroder survey ranked the firm number one in exploration efficiency among the major oil companies.

6    The newly independent company had the task of reintroducing itself to the stock market and establishing its own identity. While retaining its decades old retailing identity as "The Hottest Brand Going!" Conoco's new corporate identity campaign centered on Domino, the fast cat, emphasizing that in the new global energy environment speed and agility matter more than size. Internally, the company emphasized a culture based on Conoco's core values of safety, environmental stewardship, valuing all people, and business ethics. The company developed compensation plans that closely align employees' interests with those of their shareholders. Under these plans, a portion of an employee's pay was tied to the total shareholder return, as well as other performance objectives, including upholding Conoco's core values. Conoco maintained that upholding these core values provided a powerful advantage for a company intent on global growth and that they were one of the reasons Conoco was welcomed around the world by customers, partners, governments and communities.

7    The management believed this values focus was particularly important for a global oil producer. The nature of the product, business, and technology required that the company have a big footprint. The firm must go where the oil is, move it, refine it and sell it where it is needed. Conoco employees are natives of many countries and expatriates in many countries. They deal with governments, suppliers, joint venture partners, contractors, workers and civilian populations in many places in the world All of this means dealing with the environmental and moral hazards of the world community. The oil industry has a bad press, some of it, possibly, well deserved. However, the world economy depends on the flow of oil and the industry is not going away any time soon.

8    Conoco was proud to have avoided major disasters, such as the Exxon *Valdez* oil spill. In 1998, it was the first of the major oil companies to have converted completely to double hulled tankers, a full 17 years before the U.S. government's deadline in 2015. It promoted this and other safety and environmental accomplishments prominently in its annual report. One of the ways it did this is by having awards and contests in these areas. The winners received a letter from the president, and their accomplishments and pictures were published in the annual report.

## DEVELOPMENT OF THE AWARD

9    Conoco had formal programs throughout the company to insure that employees understand and put into practice the company's core values of safety and occupational health, care for the environment, valuing all people, and business ethics (See *1999 Annual Report*, pp. 22–24, Exhibit 1). The ethics program included a formal ethics policy, procedures for insuring integrity and compliance with laws and ethics, and a 24-hour ethics action line for employees to seek guidance and report possible violations. In developing the Business Ethics award to complement this program, Steve had decided to work with a team of managers who were interested in the ethics process and who represented areas in which ethics questions would be a part of daily business. Debbie Tellez, Assistant General Counsel, Business Development; L. Cathy Wining, General Manager, Materials and Services; and Barbara Govan, Human Resources Generalist formed the core team which was completed by several key persons around the world to insure inclusion of global perspectives. The team met over a period of several months, with a number of drafts circulated and revised, to design a process for soliciting and judging nominees for the award (see Award Guidelines, Exhibit 2).

**EXHIBIT 1**

**Think Big, Move Fast: Delivering on Our Promises** (*Conoco 1999 Annual Report*, pp. 22–24)

**Our vision is to be recognized around the world as a truly great, integrated, international energy company that gets to the future first.** Conoco operates in more than 40 countries worldwide and at year-end 1999 had approximately 16,700 employees. Conoco is active in both the upstream and downstream segments of the global petroleum industry.

**Distinctive Corporate Culture Defines Conoco—Past, Present, and Future**

**Core Values—An Unwavering Commitment**

**Safety and Health:** Conoco is dedicated to protecting the safety and health of our employees, who maintained an outstanding safety performance in 1999. The total recordable injury rate of 0.36 per 100 full-time employees was just slightly above the previous year's record low. During the past five years, employee safety performance has improved more than 60 percent. Conoco has achieved these outstanding results through the company's efforts to continuously improve safety systems and processes, and because employees take personal responsibility for their safety and the safety of their co-workers. This sense of shared concern was reflected in the safety performance of the thousands of contractors who work at Conoco facilities. Contractor safety performance improved 17 percent in 1999, and 64 percent during the last five years. . . .

**Environmental Stewardship:** Conoco is working to minimize the impact of the company's activities on the environment. The number of significant environmental incidents was reduced to zero in 1998, with one occurring in 1999. "Significant" incidents are major releases or spills with the potential to affect our neighbors. Over the past five years, emissions of volatile organic compounds (which contribute to smog) have been reduced by an estimated one-third, while Conoco's global refining operations have continued to reduce flaring and sulfur emissions. Ernst & Young, a global accounting and auditing firm, is conducting an independent evaluation of Conoco's worldwide reporting processes for future data on safety, health, and environmental performance. This audit will help us better measure the company's progress in these areas. In the communities where Conoco operates major facilities, we maintain a flow of information to local residents through Citizens Advisory Councils, which bring together community representatives and Conoco managers. . . .

**Valuing All People:** Conoco operates in more than 40 countries and has a diverse global workforce. We draw on the different perspectives and cultures of our employees, along with their combined experience, knowledge, and creativity, to gain a powerful business advantage around the world. Throughout the company, we strive to create an inclusive work environment that treats all people with dignity and respect. In such an environment, employees are recognized and valued for their experience, intellect, and leadership.

**Business Ethics:** Conducting business with the highest ethical standards is critical to Conoco's continuing success. As Conoco becomes more global, the company is subject to an ever-widening variety of laws, customs, and regulations. This requires us to be flexible and innovative in our business dealings, while at the same time resolute about doing what's right, both legally and ethically. Adherence to the highest ethical standards is a condition of employment at Conoco. The company has a formal ethics policy and procedures for conducting business with integrity and in compliance with all applicable laws. Employees are required to review the policies and procedures regularly and complete an annual certificate of compliance. A 24-hour telephone hot line also provides employees a way to seek guidance or report possible conflicts.

**EXHIBIT 2**
Guidelines:
President's Award
for Business Ethics
(Conoco Inc., 1999)

*Purpose*

The **President's Award for Business Ethics** was created to support and recognize this as one of Conoco's four core values. This award recognizes individuals or groups that make significant and sustainable contributions to this core value.

The award is designed to inspire others by recognizing extraordinary examples of individual and/or group leadership that demonstrates on an ongoing basis, sustainable excellence in personal and business conduct. The people recognized are role models whose behavior embodies what Conoco stands for both internally and externally.

*Definition/Judging Criteria*

Living up to Conoco's core values in everything we do, individually and as a company, is fundamental to Conoco's success. Conoco must conduct its business with the highest ethical standards. As our activities grow and extend into new areas of the world, we are subject to an ever-widening variety of laws, customs, and regulations. We need to be flexible and innovative, and at the same time absolutely unwavering in doing what is right, ethically and legally, so that we may enhance our corporate image, and still gain competitive advantage and increase shareholder value.

Conoco's business conduct guide, *Doing the Right Thing,* provides a summary of the company's policies and standards, and of significant laws relating to our business. Every employee is personally responsible for compliance with those laws and standards. However, this award is designed to recognize those individuals who go beyond simply complying with company policies or the applicable laws.

It is designed to recognize those individuals who seek to change the actions, attitudes, or opinions of others with regard to what constitutes ethical behavior, both internally and externally. This may be done through the role modeling of a significantly higher standard of ethical conduct; through the implementation of policies and practices that drive our actions, or the actions of others externally, beyond the minimally acceptable standard or customary behavior; or through decision making that demonstrates that "doing the right thing" from an ethical perspective increases shareholder value.

Nominations should represent extraordinary behavior and will be judged according to specific criteria described below.

1. The significance of the achievement, effort, or behavior. Significant improvement above the minimum required standard for ethical conduct; linkage to business objectives and implementation of policy and standards; and/or successful performance in spite of difficult and challenging circumstances such as location, language, culture and/or alignment with and cooperation between Conoco and an external party.

2. The degree of innovation/creativity displayed. Proactive assessment of and response to a need; implementation of new approaches to address ethical business conduct.

3. The degree of extent of employee involvement or support with respect to the higher standard or expectation role modeled or implemented. A work environment exists that encourages employees to conduct themselves ethically at all levels; employees recognize the value of strong ethical behavior and are accountable for their conduct; employees are actively involved in the administration of company standards and training others; and/or rewards and recognition programs reinforce the desired behavior at all levels across the company.

4. The leadership qualities exhibited in challenging norms or customary practices. Persistence in implementing improvement programs or new approaches that lead to outstanding ethical performance.

5. The impact on the company's image/value; internally (with employees) and/or externally (with stakeholders such as partners, governments, suppliers, customers, and communities) in a way that creates shareholder value over time.

**EXHIBIT 2**
*(continued)*

### Eligibility

Nominees for this award may be an individual employee (regular or temporary), a team, an entire work unit or retiree of Conoco, for leadership or conduct while in Conoco service in the year of nomination. Contractors may be included in team or work unit awards. There may be multiple recipients each year, dependent upon the number and quality of nominations received. An organization's size or a person's position within the company is not a deciding factor.

### The Award

The President's Award for Business Ethics will be presented annually to award recipients or their representatives at a special recognition ceremony. This award will reflect a unique and globally symbolic representation of ethics and will be consistent in stature with that of other President's Awards. The award will remain with the group or individual. Any additional forms of recognition will be left to the discretion of the business units.

### Selection Team

Conoco Leadership Center—Legal and Finance are jointly responsible for coordinating the selection process to determine award recipients. Input on selection team membership will be solicited from multiple sources, with final selection of the team made by the president and CEO. The Selection Team will be vested with the power to select a winner(s) and other finalists. The team's decision will be reviewed and endorsed by the President and CEO.

The Selection Team will consist of employees who are recognized as credible role models and able to provide an objective assessment. Team makeup will reflect a broad and global cross-section of the organization. Diversity of thinking styles, beliefs, cultures, and backgrounds will be represented, as well as different salary grade, gender, ethnic and business perspectives.

To insure new perspective while maintaining continuity, we expect about one-third of the team's membership to transition in any given year. About one-third of the team will be comprised of former recipients of the award.

In addition to employees, global external resources will be invited to participate on the team to provide additional perspectives.

### Nomination

Each year Conoco's President and CEO will send a communication to all employees inviting nominations. The communications will be combined with nomination requests for the other three Conoco core values.

Nominations shall be submitted using **this on-line form,** or follow the format described below:

- The name, address, phone number and e-mail of the person submitting the nomination and responsible for providing any additional information if necessary.
- The name of the individual(s) being nominated. Indicate the name of the nominated team or work group if applicable.
- **REASON/RESULTS**—briefly describe **WHAT** was accomplished. Include details of any measures or impact of the behavior or activity involved to the extent possible, the drivers and the significance of the accomplishment.
- **STRATEGY AND TACTICS**—briefly describe **HOW** the results were achieved. What obstacles had to be overcome? What new or innovative tools or processes were used?
- **PEOPLE**—describe **WHO** was involved in this achievement and why they made a difference. Describe the leadership criteria exhibited and the degree of teamwork and networking that was necessary.

Nominations should consist of no more than three pages, including a brief introductory summary. Clear and concise nominations are encouraged. The Selection Team will make judgments based upon "substance" of the achievement, not form or length of the nomination.

# AWARD GUIDELINES

**10**    The purpose of the award was to "support and recognize ethics as one of Conoco's four core values," to recognize "extraordinary examples" of "leadership" that demonstrate "excellence" in "conduct" and to provide "role models whose behavior embodies what Conoco stands for" (Exhibit 2). Rather than simply stating that the award was to be given for ethical conduct, the guidelines made a number of distinctions. The award was to reward individuals or groups for good conduct and to inspire it in the actions, attitudes, and opinions of others. It sought to reward both individuals and groups, to recognize both significant and sustainable activities, to include both business and personal conduct, to be concerned with both ethics and law, and to represent Conoco's values both internally and externally. Conoco's business conduct guide, *Doing the Right Thing,* set the standards with which every employee was expected to comply. The Ethics award was to recognize individuals who had gone beyond compliance.

**11**    Instead of simply assuming that good conduct is worthwhile, the award guidelines spelled out why this and the other core values were important to Conoco:

> Living up to Conoco's core values in everything we do, individually and as a company, is fundamental to Conoco's continuing success. Conoco must conduct its business with the highest ethical standards. As our activities grow and extend into new areas of the world, we are subject to an ever-widening variety of laws, customs, and regulations. We need to be flexible and innovative, and at the same time absolutely unwavering in doing what is right, ethically and legally, so that we may enhance our corporate image, and still gain competitive advantage and increase shareholder value (Exhibit 2).

**12**    According to the Guidelines, the specific criteria for judging the Award candidates were:

1. Significance of the achievement

2. Degree of innovation/creativity

3. Degree of employee involvement

4. Leadership qualities exhibited

5. Impact on Conoco's image/value

**13**    The form on which all employees were invited to submit nominations asked for a description of:

1. The reason for the nomination, in terms of the results which were accomplished;

2. Strategy and tactics, describing how the results were achieved, including obstacles and innovations; and

3. People involved and why they made a difference, including aspects of leadership and teamwork.

**14**    Those eligible for the award included individual employees (regular or temporary), a team, an entire work unit, or retiree of Conoco, for leadership or conduct while in Conoco service in the year of the nomination. Contractors could be included in work units. Multiple recipients were possible. The award winner(s) were to be decided by a selection team representing diverse constituencies, and confirmed by Archie Dunham, the President, CEO, and Chairman. Persons outside the company (global external resources) were asked to participate in order to provide additional perspectives. For new perspective and continuity, one-third of the team was expected to change each year and about one-third was to be made up of former recipients of the award (Exhibit 2).

# THE SELECTION PROCESS

**15** The Selection Team met at Conoco's corporate campus in Houston in December 1999. The team had been chosen by the President, after input from a variety of sources. After introductions, the team members heard comments on the importance of the process by one of the champions of the Ethics Award and a member of the president's top management team, Bob Goldman, Sr. Vice President for Finance and CFO. The meeting facilitator then presented the ground rules for the deliberations and the discussion began. A Conoco employee selector, called a validator, had been assigned by the team chair to do a work up of each nominee before the meeting. Each validator gave a ten minute summary of this background information on his/her nominee to the group. The validator then placed that nominee into one of three categories: outstanding, good, or weak. The "outstanding" nominees were to constitute an initial short list of potential award winners, though other candidates could be added to this list by the committee. After each validator's presentation the selectors asked questions and discussed the nominee, but no comparative rankings were made by the committee at this phase of the discussion.

# PRESENTATION OF THE NOMINEES BY THE VALIDATORS

**16** Twelve nomination forms had been submitted by employees, with one nominee receiving two separate nominations. After each nominee was described to the committee by a validator, committee members were allowed to ask for clarifications regarding the facts presented or to add facts that had not been mentioned. Then the validator was asked to rank the nomination as "outstanding," "average," or "weak," in order to develop a short list for discussion of the relative strengths of the nominees.

### (1) Patrick R. Defoe, Asset Manager, Grand Isle, Louisiana

**17** The first nomination presented was Patrick R. Defoe, Asset Manager, Grand Isle, Gulf Coast & Mid-Continent Business Unit, Lafayette, La. "Patrick Defoe is an example of ethical leadership in a very unexciting business unit," his validator began. "The Grand Isle asset (50+ platforms and associated pipelines situated in the Gulf of Mexico) was a mature field, destined to be sold off within several years. The reservoir was depleting, making the property no longer internally competitive for development funding. That information gets around, and the tendency is for everyone involved, from the bottom to the top, to get lax on dotting the i's and crossing the t's. Everyone is worried about his/her own future with the company. Especially toward the end, as people begin transferring out or retiring, it's difficult to uphold the value of the asset for sale. Patrick would not let that happen. He let people know that there was work to be done and that it would be done according to Conoco standards. His persistent and sustained leadership approach over a six-year period turned around the performance of Grand Isle in every respect. He introduced new programs in vendor convergence, alliance contracting, and a proactive maintenance, and began to actively manage the unit's relationships with regulatory bodies such as the Minerals Management Service."

**18** "He would not tolerate ethical or other core value lapses from employees or from contractors. When computer equipment on some of the platforms was missing, phones were stolen, and employees cars were vandalized, he followed up with a thorough investigation rather than looking the other way. These could have been considered minor incidents since the monetary value was small and the unit would soon be sold. Patrick felt business ethics involved the small things as well as the big things. When there were allegations of environmental misconduct and unethical behavior involving documents, he called in Legal/Security and gave them a free hand to investigate no matter who was involved. As it turned out, both allegations were essentially unfounded but he implemented the minor changes recommended by the investigators."

19    "Pat Defoe motivated his people to deliver and they did in terms of costs per barrel, safety and environmental stewardship. As the description on the nomination form indicates, platform fires decreased from 17 in 1996 to none in 1999 and incidents of regulatory noncompliance dropped from 42 to 2 in the last year. The continuous improvement in the asset's performance was crucial to the successful sale which realized some $47M for the company's bottom line."

20    "How did he keep his employees motivated when they knew the property was up for sale?" one selector asked. "Usually employees just want to retire or get transferred out and leave the problems to someone else."

21    "He took it upon himself to actively network for other employment opportunities throughout Conoco," replied the validator. "While getting rid of an asset of this size inevitably results in some layoffs, he found places throughout Conoco, in Downstream, Natural Gas and Gas Pipelines, in Venezuela, Dubai, Indonesia and the United States. Upstream for high-performing individuals, while at the same time maintaining the quality of work at Grand Isle. He carved out several "win-win" solutions for Conoco. I can close by saying that this is a strong nomination. Because of his good work, Pat has been put in charge of assimilating an acquisition in Canada."

22    "A good example of the fact that no good deed goes unpunished!" one of the outside selectors noted.

### (2) Georgian LPG Terminal Project Team, Georgia and Russia

23    The next nomination presented was the Georgian LPG Terminal Project Team. The team members included David Huber, Lead, Conoco Energy Ventures, Istanbul & Batumi; Roy Mills, Finance, London & Batumi; Harry Crofton, Development Engineering, London; Mikhail Gordin, Supply Logistics, Moscow; Asuman Yazici, Marketing Manager, Istanbul; Fiona Braid, Legal, London; and Pat Cook, Human Resources, London. "This nomination represents ethical conduct in very difficult circumstances by employees, some of whom were fairly new in their positions with Conoco," the validator began. "It is an Indiana Jones story. You arrive at the airport in an exotic regional capital with a briefcase full of $100 dollar bills and you have to open a bank account, find a hotel room, and start doing business there."

24    "Conoco saw an opportunity to become the first Western oil company to establish offices and a hydrocarbon operation in Batumi by refurbishing a liquefied petroleum gas terminal there for transshipment and sale of LPG gas in Turkey and the eastern Mediterranean. The idea was to buy the product in Russia and ship it by rail to the terminal. This was Conoco's first venture into the area so it was critical that the team set the proper ethical tone for future business and that all employees, expatriot and native, uphold the Conoco values. The target was to have the first train load of gas arrive at the terminal just as the repairs were completed. They were financing the remedial work on the terminal, purchasing the LPG, arranging for transportation through customs in Russia, Azerbaijan, and Georgia, making terminal arrangements in Adjaria and reselling the product in Turkey. Roy Mills was overseeing the transfer of funds that had to be coordinated with the rebuilding of the terminal by a Turkish contractor based on engineering work monitored by Harry Crofton. Mikhail Gordin, who at that time was based in Moscow, was scouring the country to secure a supply of natural gas and negotiating a transportation agreement with both a freight forwarder and the local refinery management. There were many setbacks at both ends, frequently created by pressure to

sweeten deals and alter scheduled work plans. Though bribes and kickbacks are illegal in these areas, many companies who operate there accept them as distasteful necessities because the legal infrastructure is often insufficient to stop such practices. There was a lot of pressure on the team members to go along with these types of payments in order to keep the project on schedule. By their refusal to make any "extraordinary" payments and their constant reminder to local employees, suppliers, and local customs and tax officials that business would have to be done according to Conoco standards or not at all, the project now operates successfully without constant harassment for such payments."

25    "David Huber, the team lead, used his persistence and experience of working in Russia to convince the local government of Adjaria that LPG terminalling and transportation via Batumi would be an attractive business opportunity. The nominator points out that through his vision setting and understanding of the cultural differences and language barriers, David was able to assemble a multinational, multilingual team capable of working across all of the countries involved: Mikhail who was responsible for finding the gas and transporting it through customs in Russia, Azerbaijan and Georgia; David and Harry who made the terminal arrangements workable in Adjaria; and resale of the product in Turkey by Asuman. It is also important to mention the financial, legal, and human resources services provided by Roy, Fiona, and Pat."

26    "There was one other positive aspect of this story. In order for governments and businesses to understand the Conoco way of doing business, it was crucial to hire local employees who would adhere to Conoco values that ran contrary to some local practices. In an area where personal references are practically worthless, Human Resources, through Pat Cook, checked all references and used a special interview process to vet all new hires. Integrity was a prime concern and a killer factor in hiring. Team members reinforced this concern through advice regarding expected behavior, auditing, and recognition. In addition, in order to assure that good conduct was rewarded by salary schedules appropriate to the region, the team sought salary advice from the United Nations Development Program, a first for an energy company. The UNDP praised the company's treatment of employees in the region. Overall, I think this is a strong nomination."

27    "What worries me about this situation is that we would be rewarding employees for doing what was expected of them," objected a selector. "The company policy is clear about not paying bribes. These guys did what they were supposed to do."

28    "Were there any extra pressures from within the company," asked one of the outside selectors, "other than the usual concern to meet targets with a profitable project? That might make their behavior extraordinary. Remember, the guidelines talk about 'overcoming obstacles.'" (See Exhibit 3.)

29    "Well, these employees were relatively new in these particular jobs and new to that area, so even a failure caused by a conflict of Conoco's ethical practices with local practices could have been perceived as more serious than for a more experienced person. In a company like ours that really stands behind its values, failure on those grounds would have been accepted as the right way to do business, but the perception of danger might still be there for newer employees. From a business standpoint, however, there were no more than the usual pressures to succeed."

30    "There was no pressure directing them to violate the company's ethical standards, but there was extra pressure," another selector said. "Remember that our primary project in the region had already gone under, so the LPG terminal was our only active effort. We needed the terminal to succeed in order to have a platform from which to launch other projects. The team members knew that if they failed, Conoco would likely pull out of the region entirely."

**EXHIBIT 3**
**Organizational Structures that Block Ethical Action** (This exhibit is not a Conoco document but is included by the authors to facilitate case discussion.)

### ARE ILLEGAL AND UNETHICAL ACTIVITIES COMMON IN THE WORKPLACE?

The 2000 National Business Ethics Survey (hereafter NBES'00) conducted by the Ethics Resource Center, showed that in comparison to their 1994 survey data, companies are doing more in terms of their ethics programs—more have written standards, ethics training programs and means for employees to get ethics advice. Many ethics indicators have improved and a majority of employees are positive about ethics in their organizations. Many employees believe that their supervisors and organizational leaders talk about and model ethical behavior at work. Interestingly, there are relatively few differences in the ethics perceptions of employees in the government, for-profit, and non-profit sectors.

In a 1997 survey (hereafter "EOAS'97") conducted by the Ethics Officer Association and the American Society of Chartered Life Underwriters and Chartered Financial Consultants, **48 percent** of American workers admitted to illegal or unethical actions in the past year.

The NBES'00 reported that **33 percent** of American workers observed behaviors that violated either their organization's ethics standards or the law. [This report was based on a nationally representative telephone survey of 1,500 U.S. employees conducted between November 1999 and February 2000.]

A 1999 survey (hereafter KPMGS'99) conducted by KPMG LLP, a professional services firm, indicated that greater than **75 percent** of U.S. workers surveyed had observed violations of the law or company standards in the previous 12 months. Nearly **50 percent** said their company "would significantly lose public trust" if the observed infraction had been reported by the news media. [This report is based on questionnaires sent to the homes of 3,075 randomly selected U.S. working adults in October and November, 1999. 2,390 completed questionnaires were returned for a response rate of 78 percent.]

### WHAT ARE THE MOST COMMON ILLEGAL AND UNETHICAL ACTIVITIES?

The top five types of unethical/illegal activities in the EOAS'97 were:

1. Cutting corners on quality control
2. Covering up incidents
3. Abusing or lying about sick days
4. Deceiving or lying to customers
5. Putting inappropriate pressure on others

Others mentioned included cheating on an expense account, discriminating against co-workers, paying or accepting kickbacks, secretly forging signatures, trading sex for sales, and ignoring violations of environmental laws.

The five types of misconduct observed most frequently according to the NBES'00 were:

1. Lying
2. Withholding needed information
3. Abusive or intimidating behavior toward employees
4. Misreporting actual time or hours worked, and
5. Discrimination

Common infractions cited in the KPMGS'99 were sexual harassment and employment discrimination while other offenses mentioned included deceptive sales practices, unsafe working conditions, and environmental breaches.

### WHAT ARE THE FACTORS THAT LEAD TO ILLEGAL AND UNETHICAL ACTIVITIES IN THE WORKPLACE?

The top ten factors that workers reported in EOAS'97 as triggering their unethical activities are: balancing work and family, poor internal communications, poor leadership, work hours and workload, lack of management support, need to meet sales, budget, or profit goals, little or no recognition of achievements, company politics, personal financial worries, and insufficient resources.

*(Continued)*

**EXHIBIT 3**
*(continued)*

Midlevel managers most often reported a high level of pressure to act unethically or illegally (20 percent). Employees of large companies cited such pressure more often than those at small businesses (21 percent versus 14 percent). High levels of pressure were reported more often by high school graduates than by college graduates (21 percent versus 13 percent).

The NBES'00 indicated that one in eight employees feel pressure to compromise their organizations' ethics standards. Almost two-thirds who feel this pressure attribute it to internal sources—supervisor, top management, and coworkers. Employees with longer tenure in their organizations feel more pressure to compromise their organizations' ethics standards. Employees who feel this pressure to compromise observe more misconduct in the workplace.

The KPMGS'99 reported that nearly three-fourths of the respondents blamed cynicism and low morale as the reason for employee misconduct. 55 percent of respondents said their CEO was unapproachable if an employee needed to deliver bad news. 61 percent thought their company would not discipline individuals guilty of an ethical infraction.

### AN ORGANIZATIONAL FOCUS IS AS IMPORTANT FOR UNDERSTANDING ETHICAL BEHAVIOR AS AN INDIVIDUAL FOCUS

Since many of the causes cited as triggering unethical behavior are organizational factors, an organizational focus is as important as an individual focus for understanding the obstacles to ethical behavior. By focusing on structure, it is possible to identify certain common features of business organizations that act as organizational blocks to ethical behavior. These ways of organizing business activity can make it difficult for individuals to act in an ethical way, even if the corporation's ethics code requires ethical behavior. James A. Waters ("Catch 22; Corporate Morality as an Organizational Phenomenon," *Organizational Dynamics*, Spring 1978. Reprinted in Donaldson & Werhane, *Ethical Issues in Business*, 3rd Edition, 1988) identifies seven such blocks to ethical action.

(a.) Strong role models who follow unethical practices make it difficult for new employees trained by them to imagine how the assigned tasks could be done without unethical practices. Corporations must pay careful attention to the messages which new employees get during their training about the importance of following the firm's ethics code.

(b.) The strict line of command followed in many organizations makes it difficult for individuals down the chain to resist an immediate supervisor's order to do something unethical. The employee must assume that the order has come from higher up the chain and represents company policy. If there are no channels of communication for questioning the ethics of an action without going to the higher ups who presumably originated the order, the employee is unlikely to risk retribution by going above his/her supervisor's head. Thus, compliance in unethical activities can often be enforced by lower level supervisors without the higher company officials ever knowing about it.

(c.) The separation of policy decisions from implementation can be a strong block to ethical action. In most organizations, policy is set by upper management without discussion with lower level employees. Lower level employees may then be forced to resort to unethical activities in order to carry out unreasonable policies or goals set by the top management or risk losing their jobs.

(d.) The division of work necessary to accomplish the goals of large organizations also makes reporting unethical activities difficult. Employees in one channel do not see it as their responsibility to report wrongdoing in other channels nor do they usually have enough information about what is going on throughout the organization to be certain that the activities are unethical.

(e.) Task group cohesiveness can frustrate even well-structured internal reporting procedures. Members of a work group who are engaged in unethical activities will exert strong pressure on every member to be loyal to the group rather than report the activities to the company.

*(Continued)*

**EXHIBIT 3**
*(continued)*

(f.) Loyalty to the company can lead to protection from outside intervention by the law or adverse public opinion. Employees can avoid investigating reported unethical activities for fear that word will get out that wrongdoing has occurred.

(g.) Another organizational block is constituted by ambiguity about priorities. Corporate ethics codes may not make it clear to employees how conflicts between performance criteria and ethical criteria should be resolved. Companies may reward employees only on the basis of the "hard" measurable criteria of meeting sales goals or profit projections with no consideration given to the means used to achieve these ends.

Two further blocks which Waters does not mention are time pressure and inadequate resources. Time pressure may make unethical shortcuts seem like the most expedient solution to a workload which cannot be completed in the time permitted. Inadequate resources to complete the job with ethical means may also pressure employees into unethical shortcuts. Overcoming these organizational blocks in meeting the expected standards of behavior would qualify as "extraordinary" and worthy of recognition.

### (3) Eric Johnson, Excel Paralubes, Lake Charles, Louisiana

31    "This may not be as dramatic a story," began the validator, "but it represents behavior that deserves recognition just as well. It involves day-to-day ethical leadership that set the tone for the employees of one of our joint ventures. EXCEL Paralubes is an effort to leverage technology and personnel from Conoco and Pennzoil in the creation of a product and profits that neither organization could realize alone. Conoco is the managing partner in the venture, which is sited next to the Conoco facility in Lake Charles."

32    "The nomination came from a Conoco manager working as the Organizational Development Coordinator for Petrozuata Upgrader, another joint venture in Venezuela. The nominator had been part of the EXCEL startup and knew that EXCEL had developed innovative work processes that had contributed to the success of EXCEL and would be readily adaptable to help with organizational development in Petrozuata. He asked Eric to share them with Petrozuata. Eric responded that he would be happy to help but that certain of these processes represented a competitive advantage to the EXCEL joint venture. Though these processes would certainly add to the bottom line at Conoco through its Venezuela venture, they could not be given out in fairness to the joint venture partner, Pennzoil. This response from a loyal Conoco employee who was conscious of his ethical and legal obligations to his joint venture so impressed the nominator that he submitted Eric for the award. The nominator also stated that, following Eric Johnson's leadership in this area, he has conveyed this standard of conduct to his peers at Petrozuata so that they are aware of their obligation to protect not only Conoco's interests but those of their joint venture partners as well."

33    "As I looked into Eric's activities at EXCEL, I was more and more impressed that this was not an isolated incident and that Eric was modeling ethical conduct crucial to the success of Conoco joint ventures. If we are the managing partner in the venture, the other partner needs to be confident that the Conoco employees in charge will not show any favoritism to Conoco in cost sharing. And to hear tell from the EXCEL and Conoco people on the site, Eric is fair to a fault. The EXCEL operation is right next to the Conoco plant in Lake Charles, Louisiana, and the two plants jointly use some of the facility. Eric has gotten flak from his counterparts at the Conoco plant for not cutting them any slack on sharing costs for these joint facilities. They would rather not have these costs show up in their budgets but he reminds them that he is wearing his EXCEL hat and needs to look out for the interests of EXCEL. On one occasion for example, he made Conoco pay for its share of grading the road which borders both plant sites. While that may seem unimportant, it sets a tone for all of the Conoco employees lent to the venture and has given Pennzoil such confidence in the

fairness of the operation that they are planning additional ventures with Conoco. I think this nomination is another strong one."

34     "But again, isn't this conduct that we expect of all employees? Does it arise to an award level?" asked a selector.

35     "Well you need to realize that his long-term career is with Conoco and that most managers after several years with the joint venture return to work with their parent company. By upholding these standards he is risking burning some bridges with managers at Conoco that he might be working for or with in the future," replied the validator.

36     "We also have to consider that joint ventures of this kind are important to a company the size of Conoco and we haven't been doing them for that long. We need models for how to make those ventures work and an award might help to get the message out as to our company's expectations," another selector added.

### (4) Terry Beene, Retail Marketing, Houston, Texas

37     "When Conoco, for competitive reasons, elected to include convenience stores in our retail stations," the validator began, "the company found itself with a whole new kind of employee. Instead of the salaried engineers, managers, and support staff who make up most of the work force, we were responsible for recruiting, training, motivating, and monitoring a group of not very highly paid hourly workers who were our retail face to the public. In addition, these not very highly paid workers were surrounded by all kinds temptations in the form of merchandise and cash, in a situation where direct supervision was too costly. Looking at this problem, Terry decided that there were two main options. One was to assume that a small percentage of employees were going to steal and concentrate on catching and punishing them. The other was to assume that the great majority of employees were honest and that a program that spent time and money recognizing their honesty in the face of temptation would motivate them to continue their good conduct. Such a program could convert or drive out the bad actors as well."

38     "Terry decided to emphasize 'keeping honest people honest.' The program was designed to "catch people being honest and reward them for it." The first step was a strong training program for new employees that began with a unit that explained all the ways that employees can steal from a convenience store. Employees who expect to steal were thereby warned that the company knew all of their methods and most of the dropouts occurred in this early phase of the training. Honest employees understood what the temptations were and were taught how to avoid them. They understood that the company uses extensive control measures and that one of the purposes of these was to 'catch them doing something right.' Once on the job, the employees were continually motivated to be honest with visits by mystery shoppers who rewarded them on the spot for good behavior and reported on store procedures to management."

39     "A second phase of the program involved systemized operational practices designed to decrease the opportunity for theft to occur. There are extensive control measures to manage inventory and track sales through scanning technology and regular and surprise audits. Security cameras have been installed in virtually all stores within the last two years. Honest employees were encouraged to be honest by knowing that dishonest behavior would be caught and punished. But the emphasis even in the audits was to reward people whose inventory and cash are all properly accounted for rather than focusing on the threat which controls pose to those who do wrong. The desire to accurately measure inventory and control losses was the catalyst in the decision to employ new and innovative scanning technology. The data resulting from this Loss Control Program has also proved valuable in the development of trend reports and standardized operations reports that can highlight loss control problems before they become critical."

**40**     "The results of this approach to managing retail sales have been significant. While the standard rate of losses in the industry is 2 percent to 4 percent of gross revenue per year, Conoco's loss percentage has averaged 1.13 percent over the past three years. This difference translates into additional revenues of $1.5MM and $2.5MM per annum over the past two years. The turnover rate for employees is also significantly lower than the industry average, which contributes to lower recruitment and training costs."

**41**     "In his position as Director of Security in Retail Operations, Terry was the sole employee in the retail sector assigned to Loss Control. His work designing and selling this program throughout the sector resulted in a function-wide commitment to the Retail Loss Control Program at all levels. Because of his efforts, loss control focused not on fixing problems by firing dishonest employees but on training personnel to recognize the importance of honesty and on implementing sustainable processes to prevent problems from occurring. All in all I think this nomination warrants serious consideration."

### (5) Raymond S. Marchand, Upstream Aame, Damascus, Syria

**42**     "Raymond Marchand is a unique individual. Born a French-Algerian, Raymond has translated his dual nationality into a unique understanding of how to preserve Conoco values in some of the most complex and challenging business cultures in the world. As a young man he fought the Algerians as a member French foreign legion's "Blackfoot" brigade, a group that planned to parachute into Paris to assassinate French President DeGaul for granting Algerian independence. After his military service, Raymond began working for Conoco as a laborer in the 1960s and quickly advanced into management responsibility. He has been in charge of the company's operations in Chad, Egypt, The Congo, Somalia, Angola, and Nigeria, and is now heading operations in Syria. His leadership in doing business the Conoco way or not doing business at all involved relationships both outside and inside the company. By his own example he established a clear policy of integrity in all dealings with government officials and contractors, and taught both native and expatriot employees that requests for 'exceptional' payments could be refused continually without insulting the person making the request."

**43**     "Raymond is most masterful in difficult business environments. In Somalia the U.S. government employed his experience in negotiating in a corrupt environment without compromising his standards. As the situation there deteriorated, Raymond was forced to leave the country to the sound of gunfire. In Nigeria his high ethical standards and personal negotiating style changed the paradigm of what was acceptable business conduct for Conoco's Nigerian employees, our Nigerian indigenous partners, and our Nigerian government contacts. His approach took the risk of losing business opportunities. The respect he garnered for his way of operating, however, gained opportunities for Conoco, especially as a new government under President Obasanjo made the ideal of integrity fashionable in that country."

**44**     "Nigeria was a particularly challenging environment because 95 percent of the Conoco workforce was native born and had grown up in an atmosphere in which companies bought their way into whatever situation they wanted to be in. Marchand taught the whole organization from top to bottom that business could be conducted without such payments. His alternative to bribes was establishing relationships based on trust and dependability, an approach that requires spending the time to build personal relationships. Actions speak louder than words in establishing trust and as his nominator put it, 'You can see his heart behind everything he says and does.' With the company's indigenous partners he was successful in resolving contractual problems and educating them about Conoco's core values, especially ethical behavior. In doing so he earned not only their respect but a wider recognition within the business community and the government that Conoco's integrity is second to none in Nigeria."

45    "Because of his leadership, many of our operating costs have been lowered by newly empowered, bright young native Nigerian employees. Throughout Nigeria, I am told, all the Conoco employees respond to requests for 'extraordinary' payments with Marchand's characteristic smile, two raised and waving hands, and the phrase "No can do!" delivered in a loud friendly voice. This behavior has become so standard that most people do not even request payments from Conoco employees."

46    "Inside the company, Marchand has shown an equally high level of integrity. Whenever accusations have surfaced about irregularities in his operations, he has immediately requested a full company investigation of the matter and has insured the full cooperation of all employees in his shop. When notified that he was being posted to Syria, he requested a meeting with a management committee from Auditing and Legal Affairs to map out strategies for dealing with the business environment in that country. I think his career achievements set a standard against which future award nominations can be measured."

47    "That mention of career achievement raises some interesting points regarding the award criteria," observed an outside selector. "Should the President's Ethics Award recognize only heroic ethical conduct which goes beyond the standard expected of every employee or should employees be rewarded for meeting the expected standards? And if employees are recognized for meeting the expected standard, should this be only for consistent behavior over time (a lifetime of ethical action), or for behavior in difficult circumstances (pressures to meet other performance criteria)? Or would the company's objectives be furthered in giving awards sometimes for behavior which shows how the standards can be followed in ordinary circumstances (a good example, or "Charlie Brown" award)?"

48    "It seems that we have examples of all of these possibilities in this group of nominees," another selector said. "In giving this first award, the company will be setting some kind of a standard for future nominations, though an evolution of the standards is certainly possible. But I think it is important to keep in mind that our decision may encourage some and discourage other types of nominations from being submitted in the future."

49    "We might want to consider giving more than one award this first year, since we are reviewing conduct from several prior years rather than one prior year," one selector said.

50    "It is interesting," another selector noted, "that we have some real diversity among the nominees. We have overseas and domestic. We have upstream (exploration and production), midstream (transportation and refining) and downstream (retailing). We have career nominations and specific project nominations, and we have individuals and a team. The only kind of nomination missing is for a single action which was unique enough, had such important consequences, or was done under such difficult circumstances that it was significant enough for a nomination."

## MAKING THE DECISION

51    The morning passed quickly as the nominees were presented. "These five nominees have made the short list based on the validators' evaluations," the facilitator said as she stood up to indicate that the descriptive phase of the work was concluded. "But any of the others can be considered as we begin to make judgments this afternoon. Archie (President Dunham) considers this award to be important for Conoco. We have a real task ahead of us. Steve has promised us an excellent lunch before we decide who to recommend for the first President's Award for Business Ethics."

# Case 32   Corcoran.com and the Manhattan Real Estate Business*

## Alan B. Eisner, Richard Robinson, John A. Pearce II

1   1999 turned out to be a very profitable but trying year for Barbara Corcoran. The Corcoran Group generated $2 billion in sales with $200 million coming from Corcoran.com. The agency handles on average 800 to 1100 listings at one time. The average sales price in 1999 for all Corcoran Group business was $585,000. The average studio sale price was $145,000, the average 1-bedroom sale price was $261,000, the average 2-bedroom sale price was $611,000, the average 3-bedroom sale price was $1,583,000, and the average 4+ bedroom sale price was $3,920,000. The average sales price for a web-generated sale was $484,000.

2   Corcoran's main focus for 1999 was on developing its web-based business, www.corcoran.com. She was very confident that the web is revolutionizing the industry; 23 percent of all potential homebuyers use the web in their search for a home and 57 percent of real estate firms have a presence on the World Wide Web. According to www.onerealtorplace.com, seven out of ten real estate firms stated that they receive at least one percent of their business from the Internet.

3   Barbara believed that the web would prove to be very profitable for her firm in the future. In fact, in the real estate industry, commissions were generally 6 percent with 3 percent going to the listing broker and the other 3 percent going to the buyer's broker. However, a majority of the web deals have been full commission, meaning that the Corcoran Group was entitled to the full 6 percent.

4   The website had also been making the buying process more cost-efficient. A customer referred by the Corcoran website generally saw only 4 to 5 properties before buying, while a customer referred by another source saw on average 14 properties. This was because the customer is already primed and has done much of the legwork him or herself. Also, the web-based business is easier for her to track. Although all of the offices operate as separate entities, Barbara was able to have more control over and analyze the web-based more efficiently. She had to rely on her salespeople for analysis of her physical locations.

5   However, as confident as Barbara was about the future of her web-based business, she was very unsure about what to do with her current situation.

### Barbara Corcoran History

6   Barbara Corcoran was born in Edgewater, New Jersey, to a printing press salesman and full-time housewife. The Corcoran household was run very much like a business, since it was comprised of nine siblings. Consequently, this upbringing had a very strong influence on Barbara and her future endeavors. Barbara was the first in her family to attend college. She attended St. Thomas Aquinas College in Rockland County, New York, and graduated with a degree in teaching.

*Thank you to Barbara Corcoran, Randy Myer, and Nicole Belmont for their time and assistance in the research and data collection for this case.

Source: This case was prepared by Alan B. Eisner of Pace University, Richard Robinson of the University of South Carolina, and John A. Pearce II of Villanova University. It is intended to be used as a basis for class discussion rather than to illustrate either effective or ineffective handling of an administrative situation. All rights reserved to the authors. Copyright © 2002 Alan B. Eisner.

**EXHIBIT 1** Online
Property Listings

Source: Corcoran.com, visited
on January 17, 2000

| address | location | beds | baths | price |
|---------|----------|------|-------|-------|
| 211 Central Park West | Upper West Side | 4 | 3 | $8,250,000 |
| 888 PARK | Upper East Side | 3 | 3 | $7,150,000 |
| 166 DUANE | Tribeca | 4 | 3.5 | $3,500,000 |
| 1220 PARK | Upper East Side | 2 | 0 | $3,050,000 |
| 57 East 73rd Street | Upper East Side | 3 | 3 | $1,500,000 |
| 101 Central Park West | Upper West Side | 0 | 2 | $1,200,000 |
| 57 East 73rd Street | Upper East Side | 2 | 2 | $1,100,000 |
| 91 Central Park West | Upper West Side | 2 | 2 | $999,000 |
| 35 Sutton Place | Sutton Place | 2 | 2.5 | $975,000 |
| 565 PARK | Upper East Side | 3 | 2 | $945,000 |
| 565 PARK | Upper East Side | 2 | 2 | $925,000 |
| 40-50 East 10th Street | Greenwich Village | 1 | 2 | $925,000 |
| 55 WHITE | Tribeca | 2 | 2 | $925,000 |
| 54 West 74th Street | Upper West Side | 2 | 2 | $850,000 |
| 126 West 22nd Street | Chelsea | 0 | 2 | $785,000 |
| 23 East 10th Street | Greenwich Village | 0 | 0 | $750,000 |
| 20 Sutton Place South | Sutton Place | 2 | 2.5 | $749,000 |
| 530 East 72nd Street | Upper East Side | 1 | 1.5 | $595,000 |
| 123 East 75th Street | Upper East Side | 0 | 1 | $500,000 |
| Henry Street | Brooklyn Heights | 1 | 1 | $500,000 |
| 54 West 16th Street | Chelsea | 2 | 2 | $485,000 |

7   After college she was very confused about what she wanted to do for a living, so she moved into New York City and started a flower business. This lasted for only a year and a half because Barbara had a very hard time collecting money from her clients. Barbara then got a job as a secretary for the Giffuni brothers, a large building company. During this time, she began moonlighting as a real estate and rental agent to make extra money. Barbara discovered that she loved real estate and that this was the career path that she wanted to follow. Within a year, Barbara started Corcoran Simone Inc. with a $1,000 loan from her then boyfriend Ray Simone, a homebuilder.

### Barbara Corcoran's Entry into New York Real Estate

8   In 1973, Corcoran-Simone began operating out of Barbara's apartment. The focus of the business was rentals in the Upper East Side of New York City, primarily between 57th and 86th streets. At the time, New York City was clearly a rental town. There were few condominiums and only about 70 buildings were co-op. The New York City real estate market relied heavily on people moving in and out of the state and corporate transfers.

9   Meanwhile, New York City had been facing a fiscal crisis. Ford was president and New York City was going bankrupt. Consequently, New York City hit rock bottom and many people were moving out. Barbara, however, was optimistic for the real estate market and believed that things would just get better.

10   Things did get much better for Barbara; she formed a very lucrative relationship with Tycor Relocation in which she was responsible for finding rental apartments for transferees. This was a wonderful audience for Barbara to be selling to. It provided her with a constant stream of income, as well as, an eager client base. Slowly, she began shifting the focus of her business to the higher end of the market and she moved out of her apartment and into an office on East 61st Street.

11   In 1975, the economy began to improve and suddenly everyone wanted to live in New York City. Also, suddenly, everything in the city was becoming co-op. A buyer's market was created and everyone wanted to invest in New York City. Barbara was reluctant to enter the co-op market, however, due to the fact that she didn't have any experience in it and furthermore, she felt that it was a much different type of sale than a rental was. Nevertheless, she entered the market accidentally through a client who was referred from Tycor and wished to buy rather than rent.

**12** 1978 brought many changes for Barbara's office had moved to 58th Street and it housed twelve brokers. She ended her relationship with Ray Simone both personally and professionally. Also, Barbara hired her first part-time manager, Esther Kaplan.

Furthermore, Barbara stopped developing the rental end of her business and began focusing on selling co-ops. She hired more and more co-op brokers. The business began to split up into two distinct departments: rental and co-op. The brokers working for the departments were very different. Rental brokers were young brokers who paid their rent and bought their food on their rental income. They often viewed real estate as a temporary career, while co-op brokers tended to be well-off married women looking for extra income. Eventually, Barbara phased out the rental division completely because she wanted to cater solely to the high end of the market and to project a prestigious image for her company. She wasn't satisfied with the caliber of people she had working for her doing rentals, since she felt that they did not fit the image that she wanted for the Corcoran Group.

**13** In 1987, Barbara borrowed $250,000 to expand her business and buy into technology and a fancy office. This was a very important move for her. The office housed 35 brokers and had room for 35 more. She organized the office into teams. Each team had a part-time manager, who was also a salesperson, and they competed against each other to see which team produced the most sales. Managers' compensation was based on a percentage of the team's sales plus commissions from their own sales efforts.

**14** 1987 also brought about the stock market crash. This was bad timing for Corcoran since it had recently borrowed a large sum of money, moved and reorganized. The Corcoran Group's sales volume dropped to about a third of what it had been and stayed there for a couple of years.

**15** As a result, in the coming years, Barbara began hiring and recruiting aggressively. She felt that she needed to have two to three brokers doing the production of one because she had no money for advertising. Barbara was able to hire most co-op brokers on a commission-only basis, so she felt that the best way to increase sales would be to increase the number of brokers she had working for her. Also, at this time, she hired Esther to manage the office full-time and offered her stock options. The office also began to dabble in the west side of Manhattan real estate market. Additionally, the team structure was eliminated.

**16** In the early 1980s the real estate market became strong and Barbara opened her second office in Soho. However, she entered the downtown market too early. Few people were interested in living there yet. Furthermore, the real estate market began to change significantly. In the early 70s, the large real estate firms had 35 brokers and most property information was kept on index cards. By 1980, large firms employed 200 brokers and the quantity of properties quadrupled.

**17** This excess information resulted in Corcoran's first thrust at developing technology. Barbara wanted to develop a more efficient way of handling this data than index cards. So, in 1980 she had one of her employees develop a revolutionary punch card system. This system then evolved into a system, in which, employees cut and pasted their listings into a book. Employees again became very frustrated and Barbara had her first computer system installed, which turned out to be horrible.

**18** By 1995, Barbara had opened six more offices in Manhattan. She employed 150 brokers and primarily sold co-ops and condos. However, she re-entered the rental market at the insistence of her brokers. The brokers felt that there were so many high-end deals out there that they wanted to be a part of them. So, Barbara acquired a small rental firm with 15 brokers. The year 1995 was also very important because it was the year that Corcoran.com was launched.

### Corcoran.com

**19**   In 1994, Barbara had started a gallery in the front of one of her sales offices. Potential customers could come into the gallery and pick up a video filled with listings and view it at home. Corcoran spent a lot of money developing this idea, but it didn't go over very well. Customers weren't very receptive and salespeople didn't understand it. Most brokers felt that it was competition and resisted handing out the tapes.

**20**   Barbara realized that this concept wasn't going to work, so she converted the gallery into a regular sales office. However, she wanted to save face and find a way to make good use of the tapes. Barbara felt that she had always been ahead of technology and had read about the dot-com trend, so she decided to put the tapes on the computer.

**21**   Barbara hired Alvin, the computer-savvy manager of the gallery, to become head of IT. His role was to develop a user-friendly website on which users could pick, sort, and view listings (see Exhibit 1). He was very creative and developed a functional website for Barbara. In 1995 the website revolutionized the New York City real estate market and Corcoran had the "hottest website" in the industry. At the time, users could view approximately 40 of the Corcoran Group's 500 listings. She had her first sale within a week. In 1995, eight sales resulted from the website.

**22**   Later that year, Barbara's assistant, Scott, brought a temp named Shani to her attention. Scott thought Shani would be a very good fit for the IT department and a good complement to Alvin. Shani had reorganized the relocation department's paper system into a computer-based system and appeared to be a "computer genius." Barbara hired him to work under Alvin.

**23**   Shortly thereafter, Barbara realized that Shani would be better at managing the IT department than Alvin and slowly reversed their roles. Within nine months, Barbara had Alvin reporting to Shani. By 1997, Shani had complete control over the IT department and Alvin left the firm to work for Corcoran's competitor, Douglas Ellman Real Estate. Shani's main roles were to be in charge of developing a new internal software program as well as the website (see Exhibit 2).

**24**   Barbara was very dedicated to building her presence on the Internet. She believed that it was the way the industry was going and that it had endless possibilities. Barbara felt that her website would become very profitable for her, as well as, save time for her brokers. She wanted to give her customers access to information that in the past had only been

**EXHIBIT 2**   **The Corcoran website**

Source: Corcoran.com, visited on January 17, 2000

available to brokers through a multiple listing services (MLS). MLS systems are vehicles for information exchange between licensed real estate brokers. However, New York City is one of the last areas of the country where exclusive listings prevail and an MLS does not rule the market. Therefore, Barbara gave a lot of control over the website to Shani, since she felt that he knew the most about the Internet and what would be needed to grow it and how it operated.

25    Shani was very aggressive in his management style. He didn't want to report to Barbara and wished to handle matters on his own. Although Shani was overly aggressive, he was also very charismatic with enormous talent in motivating people. Barbara often thought of him as politician-like because he always got everyone to like her and support her initiatives. However, Shani was not a seasoned information technology professional and the scope of the projects was becoming increasingly larger in terms of strategic value to the firm. Shani's IT department consisted of 30 talented employees. Shani was successful at hiring talented employees; however, he was often disorganized and fell very short of deadlines or promised work. It was becoming increasingly apparent that Shani was working beyond his depth in terms of both technical and managerial content.

### Affiliates Program

26    Barbara's goal for her website was for it to house the largest listing of properties worldwide. In order to do this, her plan was to recruit a large network of real estate agencies worldwide to be affiliated with her website. She affiliates firms by linking them to her website. For instance, when a potential homebuyer enters her site and is looking for a home in another county, all they have to do is click on the location and they are automatically transferred to the properties offered by a reputable agency in that area (see Exhibit 3).

27    Once a firm was linked they have exclusivity for their area. Corcoran was compensated for this link by charging affiliates a 25 percent (of their commission) referral fee for any sale that is a result of the link. Barbara was able to track these sales by tracing the e-mails that were sent to affiliates from her site. She, however, wasn't able to track contacts that were made by means other than e-mail. In order to receive commission in these situations, Corcoran relied on brokers notifying her, which was questionable in some cases. So far, no significant income had been generated through international affiliates, however, although she wasn't sure exactly how, she planned on developing and cultivating this area.

**EXHIBIT 3**   The Global Team

Source: Corcoran.com, visited on January 17, 2000

**28**    In order to recruit desirable affiliates, Barbara hired Ondine, a beautiful and cultured young woman. Her job was to entice companies to join the Corcoran network. Although she had little prior experience, she was a great salesperson and was able to charm many firms into joining the network.

**29**    One tactic that Ondine and Barbara developed was to have a New York–based Corcoran International Conference. For the new affiliates, they invited top agencies from around the world to this conference as members of the Corcoran Affiliate Network. Ondine was able to sign up 33 overseas affiliates. During the conference, many of the international firms were interested in knowing which domestic firms would be joining the network. However, The Corcoran Group hadn't been actively pursuing the idea of domestic affiliates. Instead, it had chosen to focus almost exclusively on the international market in the first stage of development.

**30**    There are a couple of reasons that Barbara wasn't considering domestic affiliates. First of all, she wasn't sure which firms she wanted to be associated with. Secondly and most importantly, she didn't know what type of commission structure to use. She figured that there were three options available. Her first option was to charge a 20 percent referral fee (as she does with international affiliates) plus an annual affiliate fee. Her second option was to charge a per-salesperson annual fee of $250 per salesperson and her third option was to franchise. For franchising, she would receive 6 percent gross of the affiliate's revenue. The franchising option would double the revenue, but wasn't a very desirable option for Barbara. She felt that franchising only attracts those firms without an identity—not the good firms. She only wanted to associate with winners.

**Problems facing Corcoran**

**31**    The most serious dilemma facing Barbara was whether or not to spin-off www.corcoran.com from The Corcoran Group to make it a completely separate entity. This option was a result of several different circumstances surrounding the organization. The most important ones being that it would provide financing options needed for the growth and expansion of the website and it would provide Barbara with the ability to make decisions regarding the Internet business without directly affecting her traditional business, The Corcoran Group. Although this seemed like a solution to all her problems, this option appeared very challenging.

**32**    The first challenge facing Barbara was how to finance this new business. She had different options for financing that included going public, a private placement, or a debt offering. Each option had its strengths and weaknesses, though an initial public offering (IPO) seemed like the most logical choice. However, Barbara was indecisive over who should participate in the IPO. Should she include the brokers employed by the Corcoran Group in the stock offering or only employees of the Internet company? Additionally, if the broker weren't included, she wondered how many brokers might defect to another firm or go out on their own—*especially the more successful brokers.*

**33**    The second challenge facing Corcoran was regarding the organizational structure of the Internet company if Barbara decided to spin-off Corcoran.com. First, she had not decided who would manage the company. She wanted to find someone to run the new Internet business whom she both trusted and whom had the right skill set for the job. She thought of running both firms, but was feeling overwhelmed by the time commitment that running two companies might demand. Secondly, she could not decide how to share staff between the two companies or if she should dedicate employees to one company or the other.

**34**    Corcoran's IT department was undergoing a tremendous strain. As Shani was both developing the new in-house software system and the website software, the IT department was disorganized about priorities and roles for the projects. Shani had promised her much, yet delivered very little since taking over as head of IT. The website had not been updated in months and the in-house software system hadn't been developed. Many managers in the company, although they liked him, had begun to lose faith in Shani since he hadn't delivered on many of his promises. Barbara had relied on him to handle all of the IT functions, as she did not feel comfortable with her own technical abilities. However, now she was also starting to question Shani's technical and managerial abilities.

35  At the same time as the IT issues and possible Corcoran.com spin-off were unfolding, Barbara was expanding the Corcoran Affiliates Program and facing stiff domestic competition. Barbara needed to hire a sophisticated sales force to solicit and choose the target of 120 new domestic and international affiliates for the upcoming Corcoran World Conference in New York in the spring of 2000. The software needed to put the affiliate's listings on the Corcoran website still needed to be developed. The proper affiliation and referral fees for the domestic affiliates still had to be decided. Another situation that Barbara was concerned with was that her archrival, Douglas Ellman, recently launched a fabulous new website. It did not have better navigation, but it had a few gimmicks more than the Corcoran site. In fact, it contained many of the features that Barbara was still waiting for Shani to deliver. Corcoran's website had 150 percent more traffic than her rival's but she feared losing her large lead.

36  Further down the list, but also pressing was the issue of how to pay her brokers commission on website-generated deals. Normally, her brokers would get their proper percentage of the 3 percent buyer's broker commission. However, since the customers were already primed by their website visits, these sales were much easier for brokers. Barbara was thinking of charging her agents a 20 percent referral fee on the commissions resulting from the website. However, her agents had initially felt threatened by the web and were accustomed to getting the extra business without cost to them. It was hard enough to get her brokers to accept the Internet age, she worried that new fees and the question of broker participation in a spin-off might just be enough to alienate her otherwise generally loyal brokers.

37  In early 2001, Barbara Corcoran engaged a professor at a well-known New York area university and her team of MBAs to assess the Corcoran.com strategic situation and options. Three months later, in late April, Ms. Corcoran was in a taxi traveling to the university campus to hear the conclusions reached by this professor and her MBA consulting team. Weighing on her mind was the need to make a decision soon, mixed with excitement and anticipation about the objective assessment she so looked forward to hearing.

## Case 33 Dippin' Dots Ice Cream

### Brian R. Callahan, Alan B. Eisner, Richard B. Robinson, John A. Pearce II

## BASIC STORY OF DIPPIN' DOTS

### Background

1   Dippin' Dots is a 15-year-old company with over $45 million in annual sales employing 160 people, and headquartered in Paducah, Kentucky. The company's chief operation is the sale of Dippin' Dots ice cream to franchisees and national accounts throughout the world. Mr. Curt Jones is the founder and CEO of Dippin' Dots. So who is Curt Jones and what is Dippin' Dots?

2   Dippin' Dots is the marriage between old fashioned handmade ice cream and space-age technology. Dippin' Dots are tiny round beads of ice cream that are made at super-cold temperatures and served at subzero temperatures in a soufflé cup with a spoon. The super-cold freezing ($-365°F$) of Dippin' Dots ice cream done by liquid nitrogen cryogenically locks in both flavor and freshness in a way that no other manufactured ice cream can offer. Not only had Curt discovered a new way of making ice cream, but many feel his product proved to be much more flavorful and richer than regular ice cream. According to Curt, "I created a way . . . [to] get a quicker freeze so the ice cream wouldn't get large ice crystals. . . About six months later, I decided to quit my job and go into business."

3   Mr. Jones is a microbiologist by trade and one of Curt's areas of expertise is cryogenics. Curt's first job was researching and engineering as a microbiologist for the Lexington, Kentucky–based bioengineering company, ALLtech, Inc. During his days at ALLtech, Curt worked with different types of bacteria to try to find new ways of preserving them so they could be transported throughout the world. He applied a method of freezing using super-cold temperatures with substances like liquid $CO_2$ and liquid nitrogen; the same method is used to create Dippin' Dots.

4   One method Curt developed was to "microencapsulate" the bacteria by freezing their medium using liquid nitrogen. Other scientists thought he was crazy to think that he could do this because nothing like that had ever been done before. However, Curt was convinced his idea would work. He spent months trying to perfect this method, and continued to make progress in making his idea materialize.

5   While Curt was working over 80 hours a week in ALLtech's labs to perfect the microencapsulating process, he made the most influential decision of his life when he opted to take a weekend off to attend a family barbeque at his parents' house. It just so happened that the day of the barbeque his mother was making ice cream with his family. Curt began to reminisce about homemade ice cream prepared the slow, old-fashioned way. It was then that Curt began to wonder . . . could ice cream be flash frozen? Instead of bacteria medium, can I microencapsulate ice cream?

Source: This case was prepared by Brian R. Callahan of Pace University, Alan B. Eisner of Pace University, Richard Robinson of the University of South Carolina, and John A. Pearce II of Villanova University. It is intended to be used as a basis for class discussion rather than to illustrate either effective or ineffective handling of an administrative situation. All rights reserved to the authors.

**6**    The answer was yes to both questions he posed to himself. After virtually reinventing a frozen dessert that had been around since the second century B.C.,[1] Curt patented his idea to flash freeze liquid cream and eventually opened the first Dippin' Dots store. Today, the "Ice Cream of the Future" can be found at thousands of shopping malls, amusement parks, water parks, fairs, and festivals worldwide.

**7**    Dippin' Dots are transported coast-to-coast and around the world by truck, train, plane, and ship. In addition to specially designed cryogenic transport containers, Dippin' Dots are transported in refrigerated boxes known as Pallet Reefers. Both types of containers ensure the fastest and most efficient method of delivery of premium products to dealers around the globe. The product is served in 4 oz., 5 oz. and 8 oz. cups, and 5 oz. vending prepacks.

# PRODUCT SPECIFICS

**8**    Dippin' Dots are flash frozen beads of ice cream typically served in a 5 oz. cup or vending package. Dippin' Dots averages 190 calories per serving, depending upon flavor, and has 9 grams of fat. The ice cream is produced by a patented process that introduces flavored liquid cream into a vat with liquid nitrogen. The liquid cream is flash frozen in the 325-degrees-below-zero vat to produce the bead or dot shape. Once frozen, the dots are collected and either mixed with other flavors or packaged separately for delivery to retail locations. The product must be stored in subzero temperatures to maintain the dot consistency. Subzero storage temperatures are achieved by utilizing special equipment and freezers, and through supplementation with dry ice. To maintain product integrity and consistency, the ice cream must be served at 10 to 20 degrees below zero. A retail location must have special storage and serving freezers. Because the product must be stored and served at such low temperatures, it is unavailable in regular frozen food cases and cannot be stored in a typical household freezer. Therefore, it can only be consumed at or near a retail location, unless it is stored with dry ice to maintain the necessary storage temperature.

### Industry Overview

**9**    According to the International Ice Cream Association's 2002 edition of "The Latest Scoop" report, the production of ice cream and frozen desserts rebounded slightly in 2001, following two consecutive years of decline. According to data from ACNielsen, ice cream[2] and related frozen desserts are consumed by more than 90 percent of households in the United States.

**10**    Only a short while ago, the frozen dairy industry was occupied by family-owned businesses like Dippin' Dots, full-line dairies, and a couple of big international companies that focused on only one sales region. The past year has been marked by a slight increase in the production and sale of ice cream, as volume in traditional varieties remained flat and new types of ice cream forms emerged. Despite higher ingredient costs, manufacturers are con-

---

[1]Ice cream's origins are known to reach back as far as the second century B.C., although no specific date of origin nor inventor has been undisputably credited with its discovery. We know that Alexander the Great enjoyed snow and ice flavored with honey and nectar. Biblical references also show that King Solomon was fond of iced drinks during harvesting. During the Roman Empire, Nero Claudius Caesar (A.D. 54–86) frequently sent runners into the mountains for snow, which was then flavored with fruits and juices. Ice Cream Media Kit, International Dairy Foods Association.

[2]Ice cream consists of a mixture of dairy ingredients such as milk and nonfat milk, and ingredients for sweetening and flavoring, such as fruits, nuts and chocolate chips. Functional ingredients, such as stabilizers and emulsifiers, are often included in the product to promote proper texture and enhance the eating experience. By federal law, ice cream must contain at least 10 percent milkfat, before the addition of bulky ingredients, and must weigh a minimum of 4.5 pounds to the gallon.

tinually churning up, and out, new products ranging from super-premium selections to good-for-you varieties to co-branded packages and novelties. Most novelties can be found grouped together in a supermarket freezer case, small freezers in convenient stores, and in carts/kiosks/trucks at popular summertime events. Ice cream makers have been touched by consolidation trends affecting the overall food and beverage industry that extend beyond their products, as even the big names are being folded into global conglomerates. And, all of these trends are occurring as the country continues to struggle with a waning economic outlook.

11    In 2003, the ice cream segment looks to become a battleground for two huge international consumer products companies looking to corner the market of the ice cream business. Those two industry giants are Nestlé S.A. of Switzerland, the world's largest food outfit with more than $46 billion in annual sales, and Unilever PLC, of London and Rotterdam, with over $26 billion in annual receipts. Both have been buying into the United States for quite awhile, but Nestlé, who already owns the Haagen-Dazs product line, is looking to up the ante in a planned purchase of Dreyer's Grand/Edy's Ice Cream Inc., of Oakland, California. However, this multimillion dollar deal is in doubt as the Federal Trade Commission (FTC) announced that it would seek an injunction against any proposed deal. The FTC is concerned that the merger would stifle competition and create higher ice cream prices. This announcement came despite the latest industry happenings that Dreyer's and Nestlé had agreed to sell some assets to Integrated Brands, a unit of CoolBrands International Inc., Markham, Ontario. Deals like these may or may not happen, but one way or another, the two giants are likely to continue to compete for market share.

| 2002 Top Ten Ice Cream Brands (excludes Wal-Mart) | | |
|---|---|---|
| **Brand** | **Sales (millions)** | **Change (%) vs. last yr.** |
| Private label | $1,038.2 | 5.0% |
| Breyers | 616.3 | 3.0 |
| Dreyers/Edy's Grand | 294.6 | 1.4 |
| Blue Bell | 252.8 | 1.2 |
| Haagen-Dazs | 196.2 | 0.95 |
| Ben & Jerry's | 185.0 | 0.89 |
| Well's Blue Bunny | 134.0 | 0.64 |
| Turkey Hill | 108.4 | 0.52 |
| Healthy Choice | 105.6 | 0.51 |

Source: Dairyfield, Stagnito Communications, Inc.

12    The reason why fierce competition has developed in the frozen dairy industry is the market's potential. A look at the most recent product and sales trends of ice cream shows a category with surprising growth and innovation. According to Jay Brigham, executive vice president with a candy and inclusions company in Dallas, "Ice cream has a lot of potential." "I think if you look at what milk has done with single serve in the convenient store market, ice cream still has the potential to do something like that. It's a very innovative category, and there's a lot of opportunity to do things like color-changing ingredients, or to try poprocks or to develop sugar-free products for instance," Brigham says. Ice cream by its very nature is a source of imaginative flavors and forms as Curt Jones can explain.

13    Total frozen dessert output rose 0.5 percent to 1.616 billion gallons last year, translating to about 23 quarts per person. The estimated total value of the frozen dessert industry grew

**Ice Cream Dollar and
Volume Share by
Price 2002**

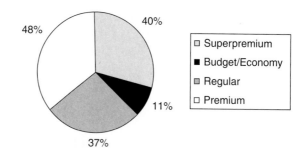

3 percent last year to $20.7 billion, attributable in part to higher prices driving consumers to spend more for ice cream. Of the total, $7.1 billion was spent on products for at-home consumption, while almost twice that, $12.9 billion went toward away-from-home purchases. Supermarket sales of both frozen desserts and novelties increased in sales value in 2002. Sherbet, sorbet, and gelato increased in volume, and regular ice cream sales rose in dollar value, while low-fat ice creams declined in total dollar value. Novelties meanwhile, grew in both volume and value in 2002, rising 7.1 percent and 2 percent, respectively.

14      Other figures compiled by Information Resources Inc. (IRI) of Chicago also reflect a dynamic industry. For a 52-week period ending November 3, 2002, IRI tallied total sales in supermarkets, drug stores and mass merchandisers (excluding Wal-Mart) at $4.51 billion, compared with the entire calendar year of 2002 at $4.34 billion, and 2000 at $4.15 billion. The figures translate to a 5.1 percent increase in dollar sales over the previous time period and a 2.2 percent increase in unit sales. According to IRI, ice cream sales increased 6.5 percent in dollars and 0.1 percent in units during the 52-week period ending May 19, 2002. Sales of frozen novelties shot up 8.3 percent and 2.3 percent, while ice pop novelties rose 5.6 percent and 0.7 percent, respectively.

15      As far as variety goes, based on supermarket statistics in 2002, ice cream volume sales by quality segment included super-premium at 3.5 percent, premium at 51.5 percent, and regular at 45 percent, according to IRI. Data published by International Ice Cream Association (IICA), shows that hard ice cream remains the segment leader in terms of total retail value at $4.8 billion, followed by frozen novelties at $2.3 billion, and hard frozen yogurt at $2 million. Away from home, soft ice cream sales notched $5.3 billion in sales, while soft frozen yogurt reached $1 billion.

16      For a 52-week period ending November 3, 2002, private label ice cream led the pack at $1.03 billion. The leading name brands include Breyers Ice Cream at $616.2 million, Dreyer's/Edy's Grand Ice Cream at $294.6 million, Haagen-Dazs at $196.1 million, Well's Blue Bunny Ice Cream at $133.8 million, Turkey Hill Ice Cream at $108.3 million, and ConAgra's Healthy Choice Ice Cream at $105.6 million.

17      The proposed Nestlé buyout of Dreyer's has caused concern on Wall Street, not only because of its impact on the race between Unilever and Nestlé, but also because of its effect on the ice cream industry. Analysts looking at the deal were focused on the distribution of Ben & Jerry's products. Before the announcement of the Nestlé deal, Ben & Jerry's was distributed in much of the country through a partnership with Dreyer's which operates a direct-store-distribution network. But with Nestlé hoping to take a larger interest in Dreyer's, (Nestlé currently owns 23 percent) it appeared Ben & Jerry's might be off the truck and scrambling to find alternative distribution solutions. Dreyer's stock, which had been selling for around $40 a share, immediately jumped to about $70 per share and kept inching up until the FTC's announcement which sent it back below $60. Dreyer's recently announced that its consolidated net sales for 2002 increased 11 percent to $1.35 billion. As of April 4, 2003,

the FTC is rumored to be putting together a draft consent decree on the $2.9 billion acquisition of Dreyer's Grand Ice Cream Inc. by Nestlé SA. Some may think that it is too early for the story to be true, but it underscores that the investor market thinks the process is moving forward and the deal will eventually clear.

**18**   Unilever has also made a number of strategic moves in the past year; whether or not they are related to the competition with Nestlé is hard to say. In October of 2002, it was announced that Good Humor-Breyers Ice Cream of Green Bay, Wisconsin, and Ben & Jerry's of Vermont had formed a unified out-of-home sales division named Unilever Ice Cream. The new organization brought together both companies and represented the five Unilever North American Ice Cream brands, which include Ben & Jerry's, Breyers, Good Humor, Popsicle and Klondike. Good Humor-Breyers has created several new co-branded novelties specifically for convenience store and vending locations. The company has also set out to expand the availability of single-serve novelties by placing freezers of product in Blockbuster Video Stores and Breyers-branded kiosks in thirty Chicago-area Loew's Theaters. In addition to prepackaged products, freshly scooped ice cream is served at the kiosks. The new sales team will focus exclusively on the out-of-home ice cream business and, therefore, exclude grocery channels.

| 2002 Top Ten Novelties Brands (excludes Wal-Mart) | | |
|---|---|---|
| Brand | Sales (millions) | Market (%) |
| Private label | $346.8 | 15.3% |
| Klondike | 177.3 | 7.6 |
| Nestle Drumstick | 120.0 | 5.2 |
| Silhouette | 102.0 | 4.4 |
| Popsicle | 97.6 | 4.2 |
| Weight Watchers Smart Ones | 62.4 | 2.7 |
| Well's Blue Bunny | 56.9 | 2.5 |
| Haagen-Dazs | 51.0 | 2.2 |
| Blue Bell | 46.5 | 2.0 |
| Dole Fruit & Juice | 44.8 | 1.9 |

Source: Information Resources, Inc.

### Industry Segmentation

**19**   Frozen desserts come in many forms. Each of the following foods has its own definition, and many are standardized by federal regulations:[3]

> *Ice Cream* consists of a mixture of dairy ingredients, such as milk and nonfat milk, and ingredients for sweetening and flavoring, such as fruits, nuts and chocolate chips. Functional ingredients, such as stabilizers and emulsifiers, are often included in the product to promote proper texture and enhance the eating experience. By federal law, ice cream must contain at least 10 percent milkfat, before the addition of bulky ingredients, and must weigh a minimum of 4.5 pounds to the gallon.

> *Novelties* are separately packaged single servings of a frozen dessert, such as ice cream sandwiches, fudge sticks, and juice bars, which may or may not contain dairy ingredients.

[3]All definitions taken from the IDFA website http://www.idfa.org/facts/icmonth/page4.cfm.

*Frozen Custard* or *French Ice Cream* must also contain a minimum of 10 percent milkfat, as well as at least 1.4 percent egg yolk solids.

*Sherbets* have a milkfat content of between 1 percent and 2 percent, and a slightly higher sweetener content than ice cream. Sherbet weighs a minimum of 6 pounds to the gallon and is flavored either with fruit or other characterizing ingredients.

*Gelato* is characterized by an intense flavor and is served in a semifrozen state. Gelato contains sweeteners, milk, cream, egg yolks, and flavoring.

*Sorbet* and *Water Ices* are similar to sherbets, but contain no dairy ingredients.

A *Quiescently Frozen Confection* is a frozen novelty such as a water ice novelty on a stick.

*Frozen Yogurt* consists of a mixture of dairy ingredients, such as milk and nonfat milk, which have been cultured, as well as ingredients for sweetening and flavoring.

# GROWTH STAGES

### Initiation

20    Dippin' Dots Inc.'s growth has been recognized in the United States and the world by industry watchdogs such as *Inc. Magazine.* Inc. ranked Dippin' Dots as one of the top 500 fastest growing companies two years in a row in 1996 and 1997. Most recently, Dippin' Dots Franchising, Inc. ranked number four on *Entrepreneur Magazine*'s 2001 list of the Top 50 New Franchise Companies and achieved the 144th spot on *Entrepreneur Magazine*'s "Franchise 500" for 2003.

21    However, Curt's and Dippin' Dots' success has not been without many obstacles. Once Curt perfected his idea, he needed to start a company for his new process of flash-freezing ice cream. Like many penniless entrepreneurs, Curt enlisted the help of his family to support him in his endeavor. He knew that it was essential to start selling his product, but he had nothing to protect his idea from competitors.

22    The first obstacle Curt had to face was finding funding to accomplish his goals. He needed money to apply for and process the patent to protect his intellectual property. He also needed seed money to start manufacturing his ice cream once the patent was granted. Coincidentally, at the same time he was trying to perfect flash freezing his ice cream, Curt was also working on a small business association (SBA) loan to convert the family farm into one that would manufacture ethanol. Instead of using the farm to produce the alternative fuel source of ethanol, Curt's parents took out a mortgage, and then a second mortgage, to help fund Curt's endeavor. Curt initiated his entire venture by self-funding his company with personal and family assets.

23    However, the money from his parents was only enough to pay for the patent and some of the crudest of manufacturing facilities (liquid nitrogen tanks in his parent's garage). Curt always knew that his ice cream would sell, but once his idea was patented he felt reassured by the protection from any competitors he could foresee. He now had to open a store to validate his beliefs that consumers would buy his product. Opening the store required more money—money that Curt and his family did not have. They were unable to get an SBA loan because they did not have a proven product that would sell. It was novel and looked promising, but it did not have a track record. So, Curt and his newly appointed CFO (his sister) went to an "alternative lender" whom lent them cash at an exorbitant interest rate which was "tacked on" to the principle weekly if unpaid.

24    With the seed money they needed, Curt Jones and family opened their first store. Soon after the store opened, around summertime, there was a buzz among the community and the

store was mobbed every night. Dippin' Dots was finally legitimized by public demand. Through the influx of cash, Curt was able to move his manufacturing operation into a vacant warehouse that he found through a friend of a friend. He set up shop and personally made flash-frozen ice cream for twelve hours every day to supply the store.

## Development

25  Once the store had been operating for a few months the Jones's were able to secure small business loans from local banks to cover the expenses of a modest manufacturing plant and office. At that same time, Curt's sister was making calls to any fair or event that she could to see if anyone would allow them to sell their product there. Luckily for the Joneses, the amusement park at Opryland in Nashville, Tennessee, was willing to have them as a vendor. Unfortunately, the first Dippin' Dots stand was placed in front of a roller coaster and people do not generally want ice cream before they go on a ride. After a few unsuccessful weeks, their stand was moved and business picked up considerably. Eventually, they were able to move to an inline location, which was similar to a store where they had their own personnel and sitting area to serve their customers.

26  Just by word of mouth, the buzz about Curt and Dippin' Dots got around and soon other entrepreneurs were contacting Curt to open up stores to sell Dippin' Dots. In 1991 a dealership network was developed to sell ice cream to authorized vendors and provide support with equipment and marketing. Over the course of nine years, Dippin' Dots grew into a multimillion dollar company with authorized dealers operating in all fifty states and internationally. During that time, Curt enlisted the employment of friends to assume corporate jobs. One of the major outlets for employees was the local penitentiary. Curt hired the ex-assistant warden to head up the administration, and in turn filled the ranks with ex-prison employees who were already familiar with a hierarchy of working for the warden.

## Plateau Busting

27  By the end of the 1990s Curt was happy with his company, but felt as if they had hit a plateau and needed to get to the "next level" to continue to prosper. He began working with his friend, and now controller and director of franchising, Chad Wilson, to develop the franchise system. By January of 2000, all existing Dippin' Dots dealers were required to sign a franchise agreement and pay the associated franchise fees for any "franchised" location they operated or planned to operate. A franchised location is any mall, fair, "national account" or large family entertainment center. The result was a huge influx of cash into Curt's spin-off company, Dippin' Dots Franchising.

## Milestones

1988: Dippin' Dots established as a company in Grand Chain, Illinois.

1989: First amusement park account debuts at Opryland USA in Nashville

1990: Production facility moves to Paducah, Kentucky

1991: Dealer network established for fair, festival, and commercial retail locations

1994: First International Licensee (Japan)

1995: New 32,000 sq. ft. production facility opens in Paducah

1997: Production facility expands by 20,000 square feet; earns spot on Inc. 500 list of USA's fastest-growing private companies

2000: Dippin' Dots Franchising, Inc. established and first franchise offered; initiation of litigation against competitors to protect patent

2001: Dippin' Dots enlists 30 new franchisees

2001: *Franchise Times* magazine listed Dippin' Dots third nationally behind Baskin Robbins and Dairy Queen in number of franchises

2002: Dippin' Dots Franchising, Inc. achieved 112th spot on *Entrepreneur Magazine* "Franchise 500" list

2002: Dippin' Dots Franchising, Inc. is ranked *Entrepreneur Magazine* 69th "Fastest Growing" franchise company

2002: Dippin' Dots Franchising, Inc.: Ranked the number one "New Franchise Company" by *Entrepreneur Magazine*

2002: Dippin' Dots became a regular menu offering for McDonald's restaurants in the San Francisco Bay area

2002: Dippin' Dots product and plant featured as one of the world's most unique frozen desserts on the Food Network's new show "Unwrapped"

2002: The Paducah plant finished a new freezer to hold 50,000 gallons of product at an average temperature of 55 degrees below zero (Dippin' Dots started with a 19,000-gallon freezer, and added a 45,000-gallon freezer in 1997)

2003: Dippin' Dots Franchising, Inc. achieved 144th spot on the *Entrepreneur Magazine* "Franchise 500"

2003: Dippin' Dots Franchising, Inc. was ranked number four on *Entrepreneur Magazine*'s list of the Top 50 New Franchise Companies

2003: Dippin' Dots Franchising, Inc. conducts first nationwide sweepstakes

2003: Dippin' Dots Korea Ansong manufacturing plant, a 20,000 sq. ft. facility located 80 miles south of Seoul in South Korea

### Future Growth

28  Dippin' Dots is counting on youthful exuberance to expand growth above the $33 million mark of last year. "Our core demographic is pretty much 8- to 18-year-olds," said Terry Reeves, corporate communications director. "On top of that, we're starting to see a generation of parents who grew up on Dippin' Dots and are starting to introduce the products to their kids."

29  First-quarter sales were well above last year and the heavy-revenue summer season does not start until theme parks open on Memorial Day, Reeves said. The company expects to hit $40 million this year, aided by several measures aimed at younger customers. First, McDonald's spent $1.2 million on advertising last year to roll out Dippin' Dots in about 250 San Francisco area restaurants. Because the response was good, McDonald's intends to expand into the Reno, Nevada, and Sacramento, California areas, believing it would do well. Jones called the deal "open-ended" if it works favorably for both firms. "I think both companies are proceeding with the impression that nothing is going to be overcommitted," he said. "We're growing at a 10 to 15 percent annual rate and we're excited about the potential of McDonald's, but it's too early to tell."

30  Second, Dippin' Dots ads have been running in issues of *Seventeen* and *Nickelodeon* magazines, marking the first time the company has purchased national consumer advertis-

ing. Reeves said the company has been "inundated with e-mails" since the June 2002 issue of *Seventeen* hit the newsstands. Additionally, Dippin' Dots has hired a Hollywood firm to place its ice cream in the background of television and movie scenes. On July 29 of 2002, the Food Network's "Summer Foods: Unwrapped" showcased Dippin' Dots as being one of the most unique and coolest ice cream treats. 'N Sync member Joey Fatone ordered a Dippin' Dots freezer for his home after seeing a Dots vending machine at a theater the band rented in Orlando. On April 25 of last year, Jones, Reeves, and other company officials served their products before an 'N Sync show in Memphis. Franchisees must contribute a half-percent of their gross incomes to an advertising fund, which Jones says has greatly enhanced marketing.

### Challenges

31  Dippin' Dots has been in business for 15 years now and has had much success. However, the company has met increased competition in the once scarce out-of-home ice cream market. The major threats to Dippin' Dots are Nestlé and Unilever, the industry giants that are now focusing on the out-of-home ice cream market. In addition, a very similar type of flash frozen ice cream called Frosty Bites was introduced in the Spring of 2000 by disenfranchised former dealers of Dippin' Dots who refused to sign the franchise agreement. Curt thought that franchising in 2000 would bring Dippin' Dots to the next level of success and put them on the map along with other franchises like Dunkin' Donuts, Baskin Robbins, Haagen Dazs and Good Humor. Unfortunately, such success was not instantly achieved. Instead of making an investment into the once dealer network to bolster retail sales, the company just began drawing profits from new franchise fees.

32  When Dippin' Dots became franchised many dealers had to come up with cash to pay for franchise rights per location they intended to develop. That was a considerable one-time investment without any immediate return. Dippin' Dots used that money, along with the incoming franchise fees for royalties of sales, for their own corporate means. This financially hurt existing dealers who were now new franchisees. Instead of a dealer growing their retail business, it limited their ability to expand, while most did not receive any benefit from the franchise system.

33  The belief of a franchise system is that it will create equity in each "franchised" location from the franchisor's goodwill. However, this is true when permanent leases of space and occupancy in a particular location is guaranteed. In the case of shopping malls, which are the most popular and most profitable venues for a franchisee, most lease agreements are based upon a temporary basis. Unlike permanent leases that guarantee space and occupancy for a specific amount of time, the temporary lease provides for a 30-day exception where upon notice from the landlord, the lessee has 30 days to leave the location. The benefit of a temporary lease is a much lower cost of rent, usually 25 to 30 percent below that of permanent lease rates. Temporary leases are crucial to Dippin' Dots franchisees because one could not even break even selling Dippin' Dots if they were paying 25 to 30 percent more in rent.

34  The 2003 franchise fee per location was $12,500. This is a considerable fee which includes only the right to operate in a retail location in a mall, fair or festival, regardless of the permanency of the lease. Furthermore, the franchise agreement protects a Dippin' Dots franchised location only for a radius of 30 feet from other franchisees. Therefore, it is possible that another franchisee could be sold a franchise to sell Dippin' Dots at the same venue only 30 feet away.

35  To start up a franchised location, one would need to make several costly purchases. The first expense would be a 10'×10' Dippin' Dots kiosk. Additionally, because Dippin' Dots must be served at subzero temperatures and stored at even colder temperatures, special freezers must be used. The cost of a 10'×10' franchisee conforming kiosk is $25,000.

Larger inline stores can exceed $100,000, depending upon building and labor costs. The cost of one serving freezer and two storage freezers is $5,500. According to the Franchise Agreement, each Dippin' Dots location must have at least 100 gallons of storage. Rents per mall vary, but most average between $3,000 and $5,000 a month. Labor costs of one employee at a mall location that operates 11 hours a day average $2,250 monthly. Typically, a franchisee will net around $2.00 per 5 oz. serving sold at $3.00. Therefore, total overhead costs are $6,250 ($2,250 in labor plus $4,000 in rent). Thus, a franchisee must sell at least 3,120 servings a month to break even.

36    As 2003 drew to a close, Jones, Reeves, and a few key managers decided they needed to assess their company's current situation and then identify and choose among the best strategic options for Dippin' Dots over the remainder of this decade and beyond.

# Case 34   Eli Lilly & Company: The Global Pharmaceutical Industry

## Elizabeth Petrovski, Robert J. Mockler, Marc E. Gartenfeld

1   The company under study was Eli Lilly & Company, a major pharmaceutical company within the health care industry. Eli Lilly, which had previously suffered from a sloppy, unfocused strategy and had recovered strongly in the mid-1990s due its highly successful antidepressant Prozac, was facing another bout of corporate depression in 1998–99. Eli Lilly was fighting to keep patent protection on Prozac which was to expire in the year 2003, and was involved in legal battles to stop the encroachment of generic drug companies into the antidepressant market. Prozac sales were almost $3 billion or 30 percent of Lilly's total revenues and a loss of the patent would seriously hurt company earnings. In February 1999, management at Eli Lilly had to design a strategy in order to protect future earnings in the case of losing the Prozac patent.

2   Eli Lilly was a research-based, global pharmaceutical firm that concentrated its efforts on the areas of drug research, development, and marketing in the following areas: neuroscience, endocrinology, oncology, cardiovascular disease, infectious diseases, and women's health. In addition to the Prozac patent woes, the company entered into an agreement with Sepracor Inc. to allow it to acquire exclusive rights to market a new form of Prozac. This would allow Lilly to keep the drug patented and thus a monopoly on the antidepressant market for another 15 years. For this they were under investigation by the Federal Trade Commission (FTC) for alleged antitrust activity. Future Prozac sales were also being challenged by new antidepressant compounds entering the market. Lastly, sales for Evista, a postmenopausal osteoporosis drug rolled out in early 1998, had been disappointing. These more or less represented Lilly's major issues at home.

3   Prozac was not alone in its pending expirations; in the U.S. industry, there were a number of blockbuster drugs nearing expiration around the year 2000 that would create an assault on earnings not easily overcome. On the upside, the U.S. market itself was still offering great growth potential and the late 1990s trends of globalization, an aging worldwide population, longer life expectancy, opening of new markets, and increased demand from third world nations experiencing rising standards of living, offered pharmaceutical firms worldwide continued sales growth.

4   Research and development had been said to be the lifeblood of the pharmaceutical industry. Those firms able to innovate and bring new drugs to the market were those that prospered. In an arena of rapidly increasing research and development costs, pharmaceutical firms that wished to remain competitive had been finding merger partners throughout the 1990s in order to spread these costs over a broader base of sales. U.S. pharmaceutical firms concerned about future growth in the United States increased their sales of drugs in foreign markets fourfold between 1980 and 1998. European-based companies attracted by the high growth of U.S. pharmaceuticals wanted a piece of the pie and thus were seeking U.S. merger partners.

5   In the midst of globalization across all industries where firms looked to capture new geographic markets to remain competitive—and specifically in the pharmaceutical industry where there was talk of global launch being a bi-product of industry consolidation—Eli Lilly's percent of revenues derived from sales abroad decreased dramatically from 44 percent in 1995 to 36 percent in 1998. The company's United States sales remained strong after

Source: This case was prepared by Elizabeth Petrovski, Marc E. Gartenfeld, and Professor Robert J. Mockler of St. John's University. © Robert J. Mockler.

*Threats*

a revamped strategy in the early 1990s; however, the U.S. market's future was uncertain in light of the dominance of managed care companies and an ever-expanding generics market.

6    With 30 percent of their revenues at stake, Eli Lilly's short-term future partially lay in the hands of the U.S. court system and simultaneously in the company's ability to bring new products to the market. Did Lilly have enough research and development and marketing muscle to go it alone in an industry in the midst of a consolidation trend? Should Lilly have considered the option of purchasing or teaming up with a generic subsidiary to fend off the encroachment of an expanding generic market? Would the addition of over-the-counter medicines be an appropriate hedge against patent losses? What kind of product mix in terms of therapeutic class, the area of disease for which a drug was created, was optimal? In light of pressures at home from generic drug companies and specifically Lilly's being threatened with the loss of Prozac's patent or at least its approaching expiration, could the company afford to allow foreign sales as a percent of total revenues to continue to decrease? The main question to be resolved was how to differentiate Eli Lilly & Company from its competition and so achieve a winning edge over competitors in intensely competitive, rapidly changing immediate, intermediate and long-term time frames.

## INDUSTRY AND COMPETITIVE MARKET

7    The health care industry, as shown in Exhibit 1, consisted primarily of the following entities: not-for-profit and for-profit health benefit providers, governments, research institutions, biotechnology companies, and foreign markets. For-profit health care benefit providers were broken down into service organizations, which provide hospital management, health care plans, or long-term care; and product organizations such as drug companies (drugmakers) and medical products and supplies companies. Drugmakers collaborate

**EXHIBIT 1**   **Health Care Industry**

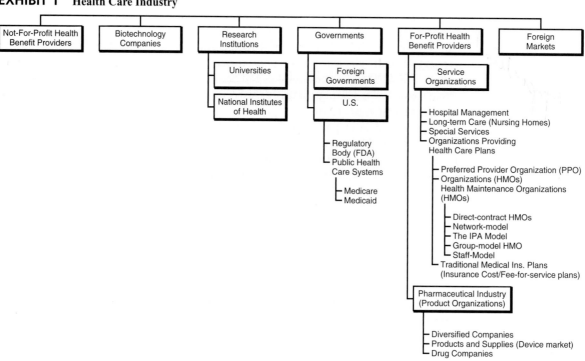

with research institutes including universities, national agencies, and biotechnology companies to develop therapeutic medicines. They were also one of the most regulated industries on the globe and had to answer to government regulatory bodies with regard to drug approval as well as industry practices. The amount of government interference depended on the country's political system and tended to vary around the globe.

8    The dynamics surrounding the industry in the United States had changed in the 1990s. Previously, pharmaceutical companies sunk massive funds into research and development of new drugs and heavily emphasized the sales to physicians. The companies and their one-sided pricing strategy were protected by patents and the public's general indifference to pricing due to reimbursement from health insurance programs. Managed care's emergence changed all this since they provided service to entire companies for fixed fees and thus were highly sensitive to pricing. Also entering the picture were pharmacy benefits-management companies (PBMs), that processed prescription drug claims for managed-care companies and large employers. In this way, buyers of drugs were able to decide which drug purchases to reimburse based on volume discounts provided by drug companies, putting pressure on prices which pharmaceutical companies charge.

# THE PHARMACEUTICAL INDUSTRY

9    The pharmaceutical industry, as shown in Exhibit 2, consisted then of the product organizations, such as drug companies (drugmakers), product, and supplies organizations. Also included in this group were diversified companies, those that combined different aspects of the production end of health care benefit providers.

10    Industry growth rates had been gargantuan since the end of World War II due to an ever-increasing demand for pharmaceuticals worldwide with the world per capita consumption of drugs increasing 70 percent between 1975 and 1990. The industry had actually grown

**EXHIBIT 2**   **Pharmaceutical Industry**

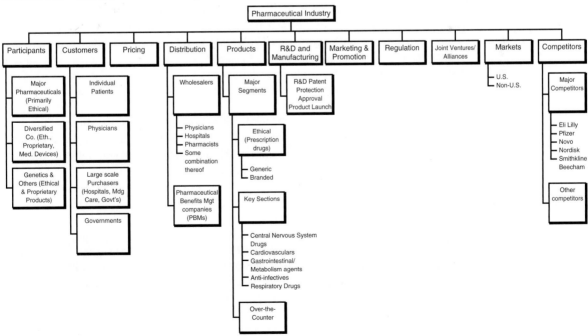

**EXHIBIT 3**
Projected World
Pharmaceutical
Market by Region
by 2002

| Market/Region | Projected Market Size (U.S.$ billion) |
|---|---|
| North America | 169.9 |
| Europe | 100.8 |
| Japan | 45.8 |
| Latin America & Caribbean | 30.5 |
| Southeast Asia & China | 20.1 |
| Middle East | 10.6 |
| Eastern Europe | 7.4 |
| India Subcontinent | 7.3 |
| Australasia | 5.4 |
| Africa | 5.3 |
| CIS | 3.2 |

dramatically during the time of the war in response to demand for penicillin and antiinfectives. Impressive growth rates at the end of the 1990s were tied to several factors both external and internal. External factors included increased demand due to the aging population and a large untreated population; a highly distinct internal factor was the tendency for firms to use cooperation (joint ventures and alliances) as a business strategy, which often resulted in increased margins. The most pervasive industry trend at the end of the 1990s, however, was the tendency for companies to combine forces. Mostly the merging craze was said to be the result of quickly escalating research and development costs, and in an industry whose major preoccupation was bringing new drugs to market, this was seen as a means to beef up research capabilities and seize economies of scale, thereby protecting future profits. Thus at this point in time, size was often considered to be a key to success.

11    The size of the global industry was $250 billion in 1999 and 6–7 percent annual worldwide sales growth was predicted for the years 1999–2003, shown in Exhibit 3. In addition, discoveries in rational drug design and molecular biology were also cited as contributing to industry growth. Rational drug design involves the use of computer technology to study cellular targets in order to modify them in the treatment of disease. In the United States toward the end of the 1990s, the Food and Drug Administration (FDA) adopted practices which allowed for the swifter passage of new drugs to market while the European Union established its own FDA counterpart.

12    The pharmaceutical industry in general was not subject to the fluctuations of the business cycle from which other companies' sales suffered. Related was the fact that the price of pharmaceuticals was relatively inelastic, that is, individuals would not decrease consumption of a particular drug due to an increase in price.

# PARTICIPANTS

13    The participants consisted of producers and marketers of ethical, proprietary, and generic types of drugs. Ethical drugs were those which were sold to patients only through a prescription while proprietary were those which were sold over-the-counter without the consultation of a physician. Ethical drugs fell into either the branded or generic categories. The major pharmaceutical companies primarily produced ethical products and this end of the producing groups was fairly concentrated at the end of the 1990s, that is, the top ten companies accounted for almost 40 percent of world retail sales as shown in Exhibit 4. Another

**EXHIBIT 4**
Leading Companies
in 1998 Global
Pharmaceutical
Sales*

| Companies | Sales (billions U.S.$) | World Market Share | Growth (from previous year) |
|---|---|---|---|
| Novartis | $10.6 | 4.2% | 5.0% |
| Merck & Co. | $10.6 | 4.2 | 8.0 |
| Glaxo Wellcome | $10.5 | 4.2 | 1.0 |
| Pfizer | $9.9 | 3.9 | 21.0 |
| Bristol-Myers Squibb | $9.8 | 3.9 | 11.0 |
| Johnson & Johnson | $9.0 | 3.6 | 8.0 |
| American Home Products | $7.8 | 3.1 | 1.0 |
| Roche | $7.6 | 3.0 | 6.0 |
| Lilly | $7.4 | 2.9 | 17.0 |
| SmithKline Beecham | $7.3 | 2.9 | 6.0 |
| *Leading 10 Corporations* | *$90.7* | *36.1* | *8.0* |

*Proposed mergers not included.

trend during this period was drug companies making headway into the lifestyle drug segment actually creating new markets with new drug discoveries, such as Merck's Proscar treatment for enlarged prostrate glands and Pharmacia & Upjohn's Rogaine hair growth stimulant. A key to success then was the ability to direct research toward not only therapeutic treatment for disease, but toward lifestyle improvement drugs.

### Major Pharmaceuticals

14   Major pharmaceuticals or research-based firms included those companies whose most distinguishing characteristic was their ability to devote a significant portion of their earnings to research and development. Most of the largest firms were spending between 14–18 percent of their earnings on R&D in the late 1990s as opposed to the average U.S. manufacturing firm, which spent less than 4 percent of its revenues on R&D. These firms concentrated primarily on the research, development, manufacture, and marketing of ethical/prescription products. Thus a key to success in this sector was the ability to devote a significant portion of earnings to R&D.

### Diversified Companies

15   Other pharmaceutical companies produced combinations of ethical and proprietary drugs and still some others also manufactured medical devices. In this latter case, company revenues were normally equally divided between ethical and proprietary pharmaceuticals and medical devices. Proprietary or over-the-counter drugs were consumer-oriented in that they tended to be mass-marketed and thus carried much lower margins than the ethical category. Most over-the-counter medications had their start as prescription drugs and came into being as the result of the expiration of the patent. Thus R&D was no longer the most crucial aspect in this sector, but the ability of the firm to support large schemes of advertising and promotion and thus, a key to success.

### Generic Companies

16   Lastly, other companies produced primarily generic products, and thus, in the interest of competition, provided the customer with added choices of medications. Generic drugs were compounds, which contained the same active ingredient as the branded counterpart. More-

over, they acted as the motivating force for innovation by the ethical producers as once a product patent expired, its profit potential was all but finished. The modern generic industry evolved in the United States by 1984 legislation which gave any generic company challenging a branded drug the right to sell their version for six months before other generics were allowed to compete. Thus a key to success for ethical producers was the ability of a company to defend patents against encroachment of generic substitutes.

17    Glaxo Wellcome's Zantac was a shining example of how a company's profits could be eroded upon the entrance of a generic substitute. When the patent on this drug expired in July of 1997, generic rivals entered the market at prices 80 percent less than the original. This brought the company's sales from $3 billion in 1996 to 2.1 billion in 1997. Thus in order to stay profitable, the ethical producers had to continue to bring innovation to the market. Some ethical producers owned a generic-producing subsidiary as a means of protecting their earnings from patent losses.

18    The top ten world generic markets were valued at $14.3 billion in 1997 with growth rates almost double that of the total retail sector. Between 1997 and 2002, 120 patented molecules representing $15 billion were scheduled to expire including top-sellers Prozac, Losec, and Renitec. Some loss of market share was imminent in all cases of patent expiration; however, the exact loss would depend on specific conditions in the market. The United States, United Kingdom, and Germany were all considered to have relatively sophisticated generics markets at the end of the 1990s, attested to by high volume and low prices.

# CUSTOMERS

19    With an industry such as this, customers ranged from individuals who purchased pharmaceutical products over-the-counter to those hospital patients who were administered medications where choice might not have played a role in the decision. The importance of these varied by geographical market in the late 1990s with countries in the midst of altering public health care systems, and thus the dynamics in certain markets were going through a process of change. For example, in countries where DTC (direct-to-consumer) advertising was gaining in acceptance and practice, such as in the United States, individual customers were being increasingly targeted. In other markets where governments heavily subsidized pharmaceutical care, governments were the customer and in 1999 were still strongly influencing the practices of drug manufacturers.

### Individual Patients

20    Individual patients purchased ethical pharmaceuticals through the recommendation of a physician whose counsel they sought or received through treatment of a debilitating illness. Through the growing use of DTC advertising, buyers of ethical products were becoming more informed, and therefore were playing a larger role in the drug purchase decision process. The decision being only on the part of a physician was occurring less often. Individuals selected over-the-counter drugs, sometimes termed self-medications, and thus personal decision and marketing constituted a much larger role in this sector.

21    Growth in the pharmaceutical industry beyond 1999 took into account a lengthening of life expectancy in Western cultures and an aging of the world population (the over-65 population was expected to rise from 380 million in 1997 to 800 million by the year 2025), translating into greater demand for pharmaceuticals. Long life expectancy would not necessarily translate, however, to healthier geriatric-age individuals. Pharmaceutical companies which would be able to target conditions such as heart disease, stroke, arthritis, cancer, depression, impotence, osteoporosis, and Alzheimer's disease would experience the strongest growth. In addition, The World Health Organization was predicting a doubling of

cancer cases in many countries during the period 2000–2025, with a 33 percent increase in lung cancer in women and 40 percent increase in prostate cancer for men in Europe by the year 2005. A key to success therefore was the ability of companies to identify and develop treatments for future widespread maladies.

### Physicians

22   In the United States, physicians were typically the target of pharmaceutical marketing practices prior to the 1990s and thus carried much influence in treatment decisions affecting the final customer, the patient. In the United States, the emergence and dominance of managed care in the health care industry was reducing the influence of the physician in the purchase decision.

### Large-Scale Purchasers

23   Large-scale buyers such as hospitals and managed care health providers received discounted pricing due to the size of their purchases. In the United States during the 1990s, the dominance of managed care in the health care provider industry was changing the way pharmaceutical firms reaped profits. Sixty-five percent of all prescriptions by mid-1998 were for persons covered by managed care organizations, an increase from 30 percent at the beginning of the 1990s. This percentage was expected to reach 75 in the year 2000. Due to increased large-scale purchases by managed care companies, pharmaceutical companies had to provide discounting while increasing their volumes to stay profitable. This would support size as being another key to success.

### Governments

24   Governments also acted as customers when they purchased for different government agencies and public health care systems. In the United States, Medicare and Medicaid, the two major government health care programs, were expected to account for almost one-fifth of drug sales. In countries with public health care systems, governments were the customers and therefore had much more control over industry practices, contracts, and most importantly, pricing. In Europe, government interference in the industry in the form of price controls were the norm in order to keep national drug budgets under control. Attempts at deregulation by the European Union were unsuccessful in 1998.

## PRICING

25   Pricing of pharmaceutical products varies by geographical market, but mainly followed two paths: pricing set by the market (in the United States and the United Kingdom) and prices set by governments (most others). Other governments were taking part in efforts to reduce regulation including that of pricing; however, prices set by the market were still mainly prevalent in the United States and United Kingdom. In the United States market specifically, prices were being put under pressure in the 1990s by large purchasers who could command volume discounts; however, volume sales were still providing strong revenue growth. This obviously was expected to have a profound effect on geographical choices of marketing by drug manufacturers. In countries with a national health plan that covered pharmaceutical care, pharmaceutical companies had practically no influence over product decisions by governments. In terms of pricing then, access to the United States market was a key to success. However, having acute awareness of deregulation in other markets around the globe in order to make wise market-entry decisions was also considered a key to success.

# DISTRIBUTION

26 Distribution of pharmaceutical products was accomplished through wholesalers, physicians, hospitals, and retailers (pharmacists). In the United States, approximately 70 percent of prescription pharmaceuticals were distributed through wholesalers to hospitals, health maintenance organizations (HMOs), and retail pharmacies. The remaining were sold by manufacturers to physicians, hospitals, retailers, and others.

27 In the United States, wholesalers could potentially wield much power, as they were able to influence the breadth of a product's distribution through exclusive agreements with drug manufacturers to distribute specific drugs in specific regions.

28 Pharmaceutical firms worldwide counted on salespeople to market their products through relationship building with doctors and pharmacists and dissemination of literature. This practice was taking on a more multidimensional twist in the United States, and as the industry went through transformation, marketing was also directed toward managed care organizations including HMOs and directly to patients. At the end of 1998, several companies were greatly increasing their sales forces, otherwise known as "detail people" within the industry in order to handle the introduction of new products. Thus a key to success involved a company's possession of a sizeable sales force.

### Pharmaceutical Benefits Management companies (PBMs)

29 PBMs acted as intermediaries between pharmaceutical manufacturers and large drug purchasers by means of aiding large drug purchasers in managing pharmaceutical costs. They sold pharmaceuticals to large employers, HMOs, hospitals, and other large health benefit providers, thus carrying immense purchasing clout and were able to pass on savings to large customers. Specifically, their principal aim was to process prescription-drug claims for managed-care companies and large employers. In this way, drug buyers could choose which prescriptions they wanted to reimburse based on volume discounts. They emerged in the United States as an offshoot of managed care and thus were partly responsible for the altering of pharmaceutical distribution in the 1990s. As a result of their intermediary role, they were able to wrestle away some of the drugmakers' profits. In order to counteract this profit-squeezing phenomenon, some pharmaceutical manufacturers responded by acquiring PBMs as part of their business portfolios, which was met with mixed success.

*strategy* {

30 Due to major differences in health care systems around the globe, the role of PBMs outside of the United States was limited. However, as early as 1997, U.S. PBM companies were seeking out ways to enter pharmaceutical markets abroad. At this point in time, it appeared that their role would be slightly different in a place such as Europe. PBMs had more of a role of medical care information coordinator in order to provide European patients with more informed decision-making capability in terms of choosing medicines. It was also apparent in the late 1990s that the European system of health care was on the verge of being changed since countries could not afford to continue the systems they had enjoyed. Some European firms were involved in ventures with U.S. companies in the interest of introducing a type of managed care to Europe.

# PRODUCTS

31 Products in the industry could be classified by their therapeutic benefit—the class of disease they treated. They could also be classified by how they were prescribed: through a doctor's prescription only or over-the-counter sales. Further, prescription drugs could be either branded, products which were the direct result of lengthy and costly research and develop-

ment trials, or of the generic type, those which mimic their branded counterpart in terms of therapeutic benefit and thus emerged when patents expired.

### Ethical (Prescription) Drugs: Branded and Generic + Key Sectors

**32**   At the end of the 1990s, prescription drugs fell into these five main therapeutic sectors: central nervous system, cardiovascular, gastrointestinal/metabolism agents, antiinfective, and respiratory drugs. Most major pharmaceutical producers concentrated their efforts in selected areas due to the high cost of research and development. For example, Merck & Co. traditionally had specialized in antihypertensive and cholesterol-lowering products while Glaxo-Wellcome had dominated the respiratory drug category. With managed care service providers dominating the U.S. market there was speculation that offering wider spectrums of products would increasingly become a key to success.

**33**   These therapeutic sectors could be further classified into therapeutic classes, that is, by the specific maladies that they treated. For example, the central nervous system sector included the classes of sedatives, antidepressants, drugs for Alzheimer's Disease, Parkinson's disease, and ALS (Lou Gehrig's disease). The top ten therapeutic classes accounted for 30 percent of total revenues worldwide in 1998 and three of these leading ten were experiencing 20 percent sales growth per year and more as shown in Exhibit 5.

**34**   An industry trend gaining momentum in the late 1990s, in response to the higher R&D cost, was the tendency for drug companies to seek second and third therapeutic benefits from a previously marketed drug. This practice helped to bring down a company's R&D expenditure. There were several success stories including Glaxo-Wellcome's discovery that their antidepressant drug marketed under the name Zyban, had been found to be an effective smoking cessation treatment while Viagra, Pfizer's blockbuster impotence drug, had been originally tested to treat angina (heart drug).

**35**   In general, when assessing the strength of a pharmaceutical company, the product portfolio was one of the main focuses in addition to research and development capabilities. One must appraise not only the sales potential of current products, but future potential of those products including pending patent registrations, and finally, products in the company's pipeline. What new drugs would they be bringing to market in the future? These were all keys to success in the 1990s.

**36**   Related to this then was the actual business portfolio which companies had to design from a strategic point of view quite carefully. The merger and acquisition situation reflected a need to increase company size; however, attention had to be paid to the types of business

**EXHIBIT 5**
**Leading Therapy Classes in 1998 Global Pharmaceutical Sales**

| Class | Sales (U.S.$ billions) | Percentage of Market | 1998 Growth |
|---|---|---|---|
| 1. Antiulcerants | $12.9 | 5.1 | 3.0% |
| 2. Cholesterol and triglyceride reducers | 9.6 | 3.8 | 20.0 |
| 3. Antidepressants | 9.4 | 3.7 | 21.0 |
| 4. Calcium antagonists plain | 8.7 | 3.4 | 1.0 |
| 5. Cephalosporins and combinations | 6.8 | 2.7 | −1.0 |
| 6. ACE Inhibitors plain (antihypertensive) | 6.5 | 2.6 | 4.0 |
| 7. Non-narcotic analgesics | 6.2 | 2.5 | −4.0 |
| 8. Antirheumatic | 6.0 | 2.4 | 4.0 |
| 9. Antipsychotics | 3.9 | 1.6 | 30.0 |
| 10. Broad-spectrum penicillins | 3.8 | 1.5 | 4.0 |

in which a company participated. At the end of the 1990s, among the firms who had experienced success, there existed varying types of business portfolio strategies which included areas of ethical drugs, OTC drugs, animal products, pharmacy benefit management, and medical devices, all related businesses. Within pharmaceutical units, companies had to choose among therapeutic areas. A company's business unit portfolio depended on their known strengths and management's preferences. One common denominator was a firm's having a clear and defined focus. That is, the choice of areas in which to concentrate was not necessarily vital, but recognizing where they could succeed and then moving in that direction was. Firms whose focus was unclear, such as SmithKline Beecham, ended up having to defend weak earnings reports and make excuses to shareholders. Thus a key to success was the ability to select and effectively manage the combination of business units in operation under any one firm's control.

### Generic Drugs

37    Also relevant in this sector of producers was the participation of generic drug companies. In the United States growth in generics had been spurred by a growth in the service sector of managed care and the number of branded drugs that were to lose patents around the year 2000. The former situation was a response to a larger trend of cost control within the health care industry in general. The philosophy behind managed care was preventative maintenance to keep costs down, that is, treating patients before any serious type of malady occurred. Generic drugs, which were chemical equivalents to branded drugs, entered the market at a time when a patent on a branded drug expired. Generic drugmakers avoided costs of research and development, FDA approval, and advertising, necessary investments by their counterpart brand producers. They were able to pass these cost savings (50–90 percent) on to customers, and thus generics were highly appropriate for the cost-conscious managed care service sector. This obviously did not bode well for the brand producer who had lost the patent.

### Over-the-Counter

38    Over-the-counter drugs came into existence when the patent on a prescription drug expired. In fact, in the United States most of the OTC products on the market started out as ethical products. After the expiration of an ethical drug's patent, a company might have applied to the FDA for over-the-counter status which could be a very lucrative road to take. Over-the-counter drugs faced a very different market than the ethical sector since they more or less responded to the forces of supply and demand. They could actually be considered part of the consumer products industry, where heavy spending on marketing was essential to build brand recognition and customer loyalty to retain market share. Companies had often used line extensions then to increase sales in other segments, such as children's versions of adult medicines. Further, like consumer products, they had low margins—all these characteristics were dissimilar to the ethical sector. Over-the-counter drugs did not have the heavy FDA reporting requirements characteristic of the ethical sector. A key to success in this sector was therefore the company's portfolio of recognizable brands.

# RESEARCH AND DEVELOPMENT/MANUFACTURING

39    There were three main stages in the life cycle of a prescription drug: research and development, patent protection, and FDA approval/product launch.

### Research and Development

40    Development of new drugs, requiring years of laborious research, started either in an academic or industrial laboratory and might have been an accidental discovery but most often

the result of work completed with a specific objective in sight. Raw materials used in the production of drugs included plant substances, animal substances, or inorganic compounds. The work involved the screening of multitudinous combinations of compounds, most of which in the end were discarded. Compounds which looked to be successful began the long process of animal tests for useful properties, potency, and toxicity. If the compound was proven to be effective with animals, it began the process of human trials which could take from one to five years.

41    The FDA identified three phases through which a new drug had to pass before it was brought to market.

- Phase I        Drug was given to a small number of healthy people to test its safety.

- Phase II       Drug was administered to people with the disease for which it was intended to treat.

- Phase III      Rigorous tests were performed involving larger groups of ill patients.

42    Out of 20 drugs passing through these three stages, one or two actually gained approval for marketing. More staggering perhaps was the fact that only one in 5,000 compounds discovered ever reached the pharmacy shelf, and fewer than one-third of companies recouped their R&D investment.

43    A new drug was given three designations: (1) a chemical name based on the structure of the compound; (2) a generic name, simpler than the chemical name; and (3) a brand name used to identify it to the public as well as registering for trademarks.

44    Above all, R&D—specifically a company's product portfolio and pipeline—was said to indicate the health of a company, not to mention direct its strategic objectives, as shown in Exhibit 6.

45    R&D in the industry in the late 1990s was attracting major attention since companies were under continuous pressure to innovate. R&D expenditures more than doubled between 1991 and 1998 while the industry was expected to grow approximately 7 percent beyond 1998. This translated to a requirement of 24 to 36 new products launched by 2005, earning over $1 billion each in order to support this growth. Thus, the pressures on companies with regard to R&D investment were tremendous approaching the year 2000.

**EXHIBIT 6**
**Pipeline Importance**

| | Company A | Company B | Company C |
|---|---|---|---|
| | Multinational | Global | Regional/Transnational |
| Organizational | Decentralized | Centralized | Integrated teams |
| Strategy | Locally driven and implemented | Established globally Implemented locally | Established globally Refined regionally Implemented locally |
| Communication | Bottom up | Top down | Team-based |
| Product portfolio | Aging; me too | Narrow & innovative | Broad & innovative |
| Pipeline (5-year horizon) | Limited potential for innovation | High potential for innovation | High to moderate potential for innovation |

The quality of a company's product portfolio and its R & D pipeline affect its global marketing strategy and organizational structure.

### Patent Protection

46  Patent protection usually began after the compound had been discovered and had a duration of 20 years. This was stipulated under the rules of the World Trade Organization's (WTO) protection of intellectual property. As the process of clinical development and human trials was taking up to 10 years in the 1990s, the shelf life of a drug would normally be 10 or 12 years. Some industry analysts put it another way—companies would have to create five new drugs per year in order to keep up with industry growth rates.

47  By the end of the 1990s, companies were facing a changing environment in the area of intellectual property protection due to intended global streamlining of patent protection from country to country, especially under the efforts of the WTO. In many cases, patent protection outside the United States, however, was still much weaker than that of the United States, and companies had to guard their intellectual property well.

48  In the late 1990s, an industry trend involved not only protecting patented drugs from generics entering the market, but also trying to extend a patent in some form or another to protect the earnings captured by a particular drug, especially for those which had so-called blockbuster status. One way for companies to do this was to change the drug product ever so slightly, just enough to require a new patent, for example changing a drug from injectable to tableted form. In the United States, this was a major complaint by generic companies. Upon the entrance of a generic drug, it was more important then for ethical producers to turn to marketing for product differentiation. When a drug arrived on the market, its therapeutic benefit was its selling point; however, with the arrival of generic challengers, it now became more important to distinguish the branded drug from competitors; therefore, marketing and product differentiation was the new goal. Thus a key to success was the ability for companies to protect patents, find creative ways to extend patent protection, and lastly, in the event of competitors entering the market, creatively differentiate a drug from those of competitors.

### Approval/Product Launch

49  In the United States a drug had to be approved by the FDA before it could be brought to market, which involved the company filing complete information about the new compound including its material composition, formulation materials, manufacturing methods, controls, packaging, and proposed text for the label. It also had to be proven to be effective for the treatment for which it was intended. Outside the United States, a regulatory body within the country where the drug would be marketed must give approval. At the end of the 1990s, the FDA was still considered the world's drug approval organization since many drugs were being developed in the United States where pharmaceutical firms were strongest and R&D was successful. Many drugs started their existences in the United States and would be marketed overseas after a successful U.S. launch.

50  In general, when assessing the value of a drug company, the number of drugs in the research and development pipeline was critical. Furthermore, much attention was given to the phase (I, II, or III) or development cycle drugs had achieved, this being an indication of a company's success in terms of future profit growth potential.

## MARKETING AND PROMOTION

51  Marketing and promotion (termed direct-to-consumer or DTC) played a significant role in the over-the-counter sector of the pharmaceutical industry, whereas within the ethical sector, research and development had traditionally been the lifeblood of the sector for survival. This distinguishing factor between the two sectors started to become somewhat blurred in the 1990s in the United States. Within the ethical sector, total advertising ex-

penditures between 1993 and 1997 went from $183 million to $875 million. Underlying factors included a loosening of advertising regulations in the ethical sector by the FDA, customers' desire to be informed about health care and medications, as well as the widespread use of the Internet.

52    With the growth in DTC marketing, the dynamics of industry distribution were somewhat altered. In the past, doctors were alone in being able to prescribe drugs with pharmacists the only ones to distribute them. With the increase in DTC advertising, patients began to request name brands from their physicians. Ethical producers found DTC advertising to be extremely effective since it served not only as a selling device but also as a means of keeping the medical profession abreast about specific drugs. The use of DTC advertising could also create a stronger association between ethical product brand names and company names in the eyes of consumers and now more than ever, patients themselves. This would make a company's image even more critical as a part of marketing and promotion.

53    The trend toward DTC advertising in the ethical sector, however, had not yet arrived in Europe where health care was still mostly not privatized. It was clear, however, that DTC practices were beginning to spread outside the United States. In the United Kingdom, DTC advertising was still illegal; however, to overcome this DTC advertising had taken the form of centering ads around a disease with only a mention of a drug company for the cure. The International Federation of Pharmaceutical Manufacturers Association (IFPMA), an agency which promoted cooperation between countries in terms of health care and pharmaceutical practices and whose members were regional and national associations representing research-based pharmaceutical companies, required all members and those they represented to accept the association's provisions in the *IFPMA Code of Pharmaceutical Marketing Practices.*

54    Publicity, as with other industries, especially adverse publicity, could influence markets more powerfully than any form of paid advertising or promotion and this industry was very sensitive to any negative publicity due to the nature of the products. Negative publicity in the past had usually been the result of ineffective drugs or worst case scenario, drugs which had a strong debilitating effect on patients. Thus a key to success was efficacy and safety of products.

# REGULATION

55    The FDA had always been considered the world's "Gold Standard" in terms of safely approving drugs for marketing. With the a newly unified Europe the European Medicines Evaluations Agency (EMEA) was created by the European Council in 1995, intending to streamline practices among countries within the EU, which then seriously challenged the stand-alone authority of the FDA. In the United States in the early 1990s there was a move by the FDA to bring drugs to market more swiftly with approval times having been shortened from 35 months in 1992 to 22 months in 1997.

56    Further steps were being taken to deregulate the European licensing system in the mid-1990s. Greatly affecting the European market were regulations on pricing within the industry. Price controls enforced by European governments, who were usually footing the health care bills, ensured that prices did not get out of control, and put increased pressure on European companies' profits. As late as December 1998, the European Council was still not willing to pass deregulation laws and was more concerned with cost containment. With center-left governments dominating the environment in Europe, not much hope for deregulation in the late 1990s was in sight.

57    Regulation streamlining at the end of the 1990s was one of the dynamics changing the global industry as well. Worldwide, the goal of regulation existed to accomplish two main

objectives: allow the entrance of pharmaceutical products into markets while also protecting the health of the public. Regulation and compliance in different markets had always lead to difficulty for drug marketers seeking to expand outside of their home markets. Specifically, regulation systems in the United States, Europe, and Japan varied greatly and profoundly affected means for achieving profitability by outsiders in those markets.

58  Japan's Ministry of Health and Welfare (the Koseisho), responsible for operation of Japan's Health Care System including the surveillance and regulation of drugs, traditionally did not allow companies to submit foreign clinical studies on drug treatments, but only those studies carried out on Japanese patients.

59  The International Conference on Harmonization (ICH) was founded in 1991, and since its inception had concentrated its efforts on streamlining and bringing uniformity to drug approval processes across the three geographical markets which happened to be the three largest pharmaceutical markets at the end of the 1990s, the United States, Japan, and Europe. The implications of this effort would have a profound effect on marketing practices within the global pharmaceutical industry. This was due to the fact that approval times between these three countries varied considerably with the guaranteed completion of an application being shortest by the EMEA. In addition, the application and market maintenance fee structures for drugs varied across these markets with that of the European Union being the least costly. Based on this, it appeared then that testing, manufacturing, and marketing a new drug in Europe had its advantages over other markets. Therefore, a key to success was that companies had a presence in Europe in order to benefit from these advantages as well as participate in a region comprising 30 percent of the global pharmaceutical market. In addition, firms had to be in an optimal position to participate in these three geographical markets in time for harmonization of drug approval laws which were expected to have a profound effect on the industry.

# JOINT VENTURES/STRATEGIC ALLIANCES TO MERGERS AND ACQUISITIONS

60  Combining forces ranging from joint ventures, or strategic alliances, to the most extreme form of union, mergers and acquisitions had been a common strategy in the industry since the 1980s, in order to put more muscle behind costly research, development, and scientific breakthrough. The marketing arm of the business also became a factor in firms joining forces in order to have a more extensive sales force.

## Joint Ventures and Strategic Alliances

61  Joint ventures and alliances had long been a common strategy as pharmaceutical firms did well to create alliances with smaller biotechnology or biopharmaceutical companies who were possibly developing new drugs. Conversely, smaller pharmaceutical firms might have sought alliances with larger firms who had more marketing muscle in order to bring a new discovery to the market. In addition, companies often had relationships with university scientists and in the United States, the National Institute of Health, which had the power to forward products still in the research chain of development to drug companies. As with joint venture strategy in many industries, the advantages of having a foreign partner when entering foreign markets lie in the foreign partner's familiarity with business practices in a particular country. Lastly, alliances between foreign companies allowed drugmakers to license drugs discovered in foreign countries in the home market. In the late 1990s, United States drugmakers were increasingly collaborating with biotechnology firms in order to develop therapeutic compounds through genomics (genetics) research. Thus, a key to success was a company's ability to create joint ventures and strategic alliances.

## Mergers and Acquisitions

62   Mergers and acquisitions, the most extreme form of joint ventures, had been increasingly evident in the business environment of the pharmaceutical industry since the beginning of the 1990s. One study states that in the first six months of 1990 alone, 151 mergers in this industry were announced. Some of the more famous mergers had been Beecham with Smithkline; Merrell Dow with Marion, Bristol-Myers with Squibb, and Upjohn with Pharmacia.

63   There existed a new wave toward consolidation during the late 1990s with the way of mergers and acquisitions. This trend had as its basis the same catalyst seen in joint ventures, but incorporated other factors into the equation. In general, the new European single market and the recent entrance of the Euro ushered in a flood of mergers and acquisitions in Europe. Specifically the pharmaceutical industry just had been ripe for these kinds of unions due to the steep costs of R&D said to be the lifeblood of any pharmaceutical company. In 1999, the cost of bringing a new drug to market was estimated to be $350–$500 million and generally took 15 years. Therefore, there were many who supported the argument that size mattered when it came to pharmaceuticals. The industry's global revenues of $250 billion in 1999 were expected to reach $400 billion by the year 2003, yet no one company had been able to boast more than 5 percent of total market share.

64   Prior to 1980, pharmaceutical companies had as their strengths innovation, patent protection of drugs, as well as pricing flexibility. While United States pharmaceutical firms had been able to boast strong growth over the years, as reflected in high equity drug stock prices, this growth (once in double-digit figures) was expected to slow in 1999 to a level of 9 percent. Conversely, European firms' growth rates were at a level of approximately 6 percent and were expected to remain flat along with those of Japan. U.S. growth was boosted by the increase in managed care facilities while in Europe national governments were mainly responsible for health care systems which included the use of price controls. No movement toward privatization was necessarily in sight. In the United States managed care represented 50 percent of the medical products market and was expected to reach 90 percent by the end of the year 2000. Thus, European players were seeking U.S. partners to gain exposure in the strong U.S. market, not to mention the realization of economies of scale.

65   Initially, the move toward consolidation was due to weakness in comparison to U.S. companies. Specifically, this indicated that companies might not have had enough projects in the research and development arena in order to protect future earnings. With the surge in M&As, average company size was on the increase, and thus optimum company size for this industry likely had to be redefined. This was exemplified by the fact that the largest pharmaceutical firm in 1997, Glaxo Wellcome, boasted $11.6 billion in sales and with the group of proposed mergers, if realized, would have put the top company, AHP-SmithKline Beecham at $27.0 billion in sales, as Exhibit 7 indicates.

**EXHIBIT 7**
**Proposed Mergers**

Source: CWResearch

| Drug Deals (combined pro forma sales in billions of dollars) | |
|---|---|
| **Proposed Mergers** | |
| AHP-SmithKline Beecham (canceled) | $27.0 billion |
| AHP-Monsanto (canceled) | 23.0 billion |
| Glaxo Wellcome-SmithKline Beecham (canceled) | 19.0 billion |
| Zeneca-Astra | 15.9 billion |
| Hoechst-RP | 13.0 billion |
| Sanofi-Synthelabo | 6.1 billion |

66    All mergers were not necessarily successful. Three large mergers in 1998 did not happen as intended, and although the real issues were not disclosed, there appeared to be unwillingness on the part of management in all three cases to give up the reigns. Moreover, despite the presence of the single European market, there were still many practices which varied from country to country, including tax, accounting and auditing standards, pension provisions, corporate and shareholding structures, culture and language, industry structure, and regulatory requirements. At one point it appeared that these failures would put a damper on future unions, but in late 1998, Hoechst and Rhone-Poulenc, Sanofi SA and Synthelabo, Zeneca and Astra all announced their intention to join forces. European companies were said to be looking for American partners to seize a part of the massive U.S. market; however, lofty equity prices in early 1999 kept them at bay.

67    In general, global consolidation in this industry could protect future earnings through cost-cutting which in turn gave companies more time for development of new drugs enhancing a company's portfolio. It also insured against earnings risk when patents expired. Lastly, it enhanced a company's research and development prospects and expanded its global market reach. However, the benefits of M&A even during the consolidation trend of the late 1990s were in continuous debate. It had been noted that size had not always contributed to strength while it could certainly contribute to logistical headaches. Observation of past success stories exemplified the fact that smaller entities could be just as valid. An example was the European division of Pfizer, which was responsible for three quarters of the company's output with a mere one-third of the R&D resources. Alas, in the late 1990s, it appeared that on mergers the jury was still out.

# MARKETS

68    In that many U.S. pharmaceutical companies made a distinction between domestic activity and activity abroad when speaking about financials and so on, the discussion of markets would be focused in this way. Typically, one of the main difficulties in marketing pharmaceuticals abroad was considered to be the differing regulatory environments which appeared to be moving in a direction of convergence at the end of the 1990s.

## North America (U.S.)

69    The North American market boasted 40 percent of world market share as of early 1999 as well as the highest growth rates among all the regions worldwide, supported by product innovation and volume sales to managed care facilities. It was the market which European companies had their eyes on for expansion and partially responsible for the great industry consolidation in progress in 1998. European and smaller firms looked for merger partners to compete with stronger U.S. players or actually sought U.S merger partners in order to capture part of the U.S. market. In various research studies performed on the U.S. pharmaceutical industry in the 1980s, results were varied on predicting the future competitiveness of American companies. One study sighted the fact that FDA regulations and longer regulatory review periods would hamper the U.S.' future competitiveness, but by 1999, this issue had already been addressed and perhaps rectified by a new FDA regulation passed in 1998, which shortened the average review period for new drugs. Essentially, the U.S market was extremely attractive and healthy pharmaceutical firms derived significant portions of their earnings from the U.S. market, thus strong operations and sales in this market were keys to success.

**EXHIBIT 8**

Five-Year Forecast
of the Global
Pharmaceutical
Markets (1998–2002)

| Regions | CAGR % 1998–2002 | Regions | CAGR % 1998–2002 |
|---|---|---|---|
| North America | 9.8% | Eastern Europe | 8.6% |
| Europe | 5.8 | Middle East | 10.6 |
| Japan | 4.9 | Africa | 3.3 |
| Latin America & Caribbean | 8.4 | Indian Sub-Continent | 8.6 |
| Southeast Asia/China | 11.0 | Australasia | 9.8 |
| Eastern Europe | 8.6 | CIS | 6.7 |
| **Total World Market** | | | **8.0%** |

## Foreign Markets (Non-U.S.)

70   Between 1999 and 2004, in addition to North America, the fastest growing markets in the industry were predicted to be the Middle East, Australasia, and Southeast Asia, including China, shown in Exhibit 8. Europe was expected to continue to be plagued by price controls. Southeast Asia, which was experiencing rapid growth before the Asian crisis, was expected to return to that phase by 2001–2002.

71   The most distinguishing characteristics between the United States and foreign markets were the ways in which drugs were brought to market; regulatory procedures varied greatly from country to country, as well as the ways in which market forces worked. Outside the United States, even though it was less difficult and costly to move a drug through the phases of development, actual sales practices of the drug company to the customer, usually the government, involved more relationships building, covert pacts, and price controls. Thus market forces took a backseat position.

72   At the same time that the American market was experiencing strong growth at the end of the 1990s, Europe's growth was expected to be approximately 7 percent. The European market was considered to be lagging at the end of the 1990s and not necessarily the place to be for pharmaceutical players. The fault lay partially with the European socialized health care system which in maintaining price controls and other government intervention tools, squeezed drug company budgets. The hope in Europe was for deregulation to take hold, which would unleash price controls and increase volume. European companies in the midst of this situation speculated that they would not be sought out for merger partners, but for take-over candidates.

73   As with other industries in China, the pharmaceutical industry faced large prospects for growth due to current small per capita consumption, an already rapidly growing industry, and the tendency for Chinese consumers to switch to Western style medicines in lieu of traditional Chinese medicines (homeopathic). A major drawback of marketing in China lay in the fact that although China had laws protecting intellectual property, they did not cover pharmaceuticals; the law specifically permitted copying of patented medicines. Companies for whom this had been an issue in the past had registered complaints with Chinese authorities without necessarily achieving success. Even with this major impediment, China's market was considered to be too great to overlook. In 1999 this market was expected to grow by 14 percent; however, due to the continuing Asian financial crisis, products planned for export were to be offered in the domestic market, adding to severe competition pressures. Profits earned in the industry in China were expected to decrease by 250 million yuan in the same year. A key to success therefore in this market was to establish a presence, with the expectation that rewards would not necessarily be near-term.

74    Japan boasted the highest per capita prescription drug market outside the United States in 1998, and thus was the second largest market in the world behind the United States. However, at that time Japan's government still exercised stiff control over drug prices including required across-the-board price cuts on drugs every few years. In the mid-1990s, Japan was seen as an ideal geographic location to facilitate expansion into Asia, specifically into South Korea and China.

# COMPETITORS

75    Due to the business structure of the pharmaceutical industry, the structure of competition was also unique. One could witness a strategy dichotomy. On one hand, the high cost of research and development bore witness that size was important, and specialization of R&D in certain therapeutic areas would help to keep costs down, thus focus was essential. On the other hand, for distribution's sake, being able to offer various types of products allowed companies to offer one-stop shopping to customers, drug wholesalers, and hospitals. The competition appeared to be more focused on the former situation and thus concentrated in certain therapeutic areas. Geographies were also an important consideration, as not only did therapeutic area dictate competitive strength, but breadth of sales and marketing—strength in specific geographical areas—would also indicate more or less the type of competition, direct or nondirect.

76    Another important consideration was the fact that drug companies as in other industries could decide how to design their business portfolios, that is, some companies concentrated solely on ethical products, often including some participation in the animal health care market. This was seen as being a business providing synergies with human health care. Some firms included OTC product manufacture in their portfolios, thus they were participating also in the consumer products industry where emphasis was on marketing—brand recognition and consumer loyalty. Even though the emphasis in this sector was different, it was a way to protect earnings when patents for strong-selling products expired.

77    Due to the nature and structure of the pharmaceutical industry at the end of the 1990s, competition in a particular therapeutic area could emerge from any corner of the industry. Companies could seek out alliances for product development and marketing and thus competition could emerge from companies which previously might not have had a strength in a particular area. Once a product entered the market, other even nongeneric companies could try to mimic the product by studying its patent application.

## Major Competitors

78    Thus, through the means of classifying competition according to therapeutic strengths, the following competitors could be discussed: Novo Nordisk A/S, Pfizer, Inc., and SmithKline Beecham plc.

79    The Danish company Novo Nordisk A/S was still the world's leading producer of insulin and industrial enzymes. Health care products comprised 75 percent of the company's sales in 1997. The company also produced insulin injection and monitoring systems, treatments for osteoporosis and menopause, growth hormones, antidepressants, and epilepsy treatments. More than half of the company's sales were within Europe at the end of the 1990s.

80    The company's most prevalent strengths were its health products for diabetes which, until 1998, were mainly marketed in Europe. In 1998, the company signed an agreement with Schering-Plough in order to make inroads into the U.S. market with their diabetes drugs. This move proved to be successful as the company experienced a 20 percent increase in insulin sales in the United States in 1998. Other prevalent products included Seroxat intro-

duced in 1992 for depression, Gabitril for epilepsy, and NovoSeven for hemophilia, both introduced in 1995.

81  The company portfolio's inclusion of industrial enzymes represented another way pharmaceutical firms diversified in order to take advantage of manufacturing synergies. In early 1999, however, the company embarked on a major strategy shift when they revealed that the two businesses would be split in separate legal entities. This decision was a result, in part, of the industry's merger mania creating powerful rivals with which Nordisk felt they could not compete with their then-current business portfolio. The company was also following an industry trend of companies sharpening their focus around core strengths. It also cast massive speculation that the pharmaceutical entity would then be seeking a merging partner.

82  The merger speculation about Novo Nordisk was also born out of the fact that the company had a relatively small size in terms of annual sales ($2.5 billion in 1997) and smaller firms like Norkisk, seeking out R&D and marketing muscle, were ripe to merge with other firms. Novo Nordisk had been strong in terms of R&D expenditure as a percent of sales—in 1997, the company spent 16.3 percent of earnings on R&D.

83  Pfizer was one of the leaders in production of ethical drugs (number one in the United States); it was a producer of animal health treatments and consumer health products sold over-the-counter. Pfizer was the creator of the anti-impotence drug Viagra, launched in 1998. Prescription drugs produced included treatment for cardiovascular disease, antidepressants, antibiotics, and cholesterol lowering drugs. Health care products accounted for 85 percent of the company's revenues. Pfizer's strength lay in its research and development capabilities, and the company had 170 drugs in its research pipeline in 1999. It also had a strong presence in the consumer products market with such known brands as BenGay muscle rub, Visine eyedrops, and Bain de Soleil sunscreens.

84  Pfizer was an example of a company that had ethical and OTC products in their business portfolio. It was considered one of the powerhouses in the industry with a formidable R&D team that consistently devoted 15 percent of the company's revenues to R&D. Their drug pipeline was the envy of the industry with 60 new drugs in the early stages of development and an approximate total of 170 drugs in the pipeline in 1998. Pfizer had overcome hard times during the 1980s when it experienced gaps in the product pipeline. After suffering through years of weak earnings due to strong investment in R&D and a vast sales force, the company came back with a vengeance and during the early 1990s had moved from number 13 in terms of worldwide prescription drug sales to number 4. Pfizer's sales force reached 14,500 in 1998. The company had a few top-selling drugs in its portfolio at the end of the 1990s including Viagra, Norvasc, a hypertension drug which had sales of $2.2 billion in 1997, and Zoloft, an antidepressant which was a strong competitor to Prozac.

85  Smithkline Beecham, based in the United Kingdom, produced both prescription and over-the-counter treatments. Prescription drugs included antidepressants and vaccines for illnesses such as diphtheria, tetanus, and hepatitis. It was also a leader in workplace drug testing. Planned mergers with Glaxo Wellcome and American Home Products failed; however, the company was still actively seeking a merger partner in 1998–99.

86  The company's total revenues in 1998 were over $13 billion, 60 percent of which were derived from pharmaceutical sales and 30 percent from consumer products. The antidepressant Paxil/Seroxat was the company's second-best-selling drug in that year behind the antibiotic Augmentin. In 1998, SmithKline found itself continuing on a path of strategic missteps. Previously, the CEO Mr. Jan Leschly had tried to lead the company toward more broadened strategic goals that included the purchase of a pharmacy-benefit management business. A mere increase of 4 percent in sales in 1998 was proof that this approach had failed. Other players in the industry had been doing just the opposite at the end of the 1990s—streamlining businesses and focusing their strategies. Other signs of difficulty

included the closing of excess manufacturing plants and layoffs of approximately 3,000 people. SmithKline's R&D expenditure dropped to 10 percent in 1998 from 17 percent in the previous year, also demonstrating signs of trouble.

### Other Competitors

87    Other competitors produced ethical drugs for humans and animals, OTC drugs, and generic drugs. They included Schering-Plough Corporation, Merck & Co., Inc. (tied for the number one selling company by worldwide sales with Novratis AG), Scheim Pharmaceutical, Inc., a producer of generic drugs, Bristol-Myers Squibb Co., Glaxo Wellcome plc, and Novartis AG.

88    In general, competition dynamics were unique within this industry in the sense that in any given period, companies could be direct competitors because of the products they were developing or marketing at a particular time. Other companies would be considered indirect competitors, since their business portfolios could contain drug treatments for different therapeutic areas and therefore they would not be in direct competition. Competition pressures could change instantly, since even drugs in the late stages of development did not necessarily "make it" into the market and thus completely change a company's therapeutic strengths. Given the consolidation trend in the 1990s, the composition of the industry was changing, which consequently changed the dynamics of competition.

# THE COMPANY

89    Colonel Eli Lilly, pharmacist and Union officer in the Civil War, founded Eli Lilly & Company in 1876, and the company remained family-owned until 1953. Eli Lilly expanded into the world market in the 1950s and 1960s and over the years had experimented with different business portfolio strategies, including diversifying into the cosmetics industry with the purchase of Elizabeth Arden in 1971 (it was sold in 1987) and IVAC (a medical instruments manufacturer) in 1977. Lilly's launch of Humulin (synthetic insulin) in 1982 made it the first pharmaceutical firm to market a genetically engineered drug.

90    Prior to the 1990s, drug makers used a common strategy in the eternal struggle for profit growth. Heavy emphasis was placed on research and development in the interest of developing new drugs while the nurturing of strong sales forces enabled them to move products through selling to physicians. Drugs, protected by patents, were not vulnerable to price competition. Further, patients covered by traditional health insurance plans were unaffected by price in general.

91    In the 1990s, sanctioned by the Clinton Administration, managed care became the approach to low-cost health care and changed the dynamics of the American industry. Pharmacy benefits-management (PBMs) firms emerged to help large companies control the costs of pharmacy benefits programs. They emphasized use of alternatives to branded pharmaceuticals carrying lofty prices and thus put earnings pressure on pharmaceutical firms. In the early 1990s, weakened equity prices of pharmaceutical firms reflected this pressure. Lilly lost $11 billion in market capitalization in 18 months.

92    Some U.S. firms responded by beating the PBMs at their own game—they purchased them. In 1994, Lilly purchased PCS Health Systems for $4 billion. However, the distinct strategic advantage that Lilly anticipated, funneling its own products through PCS, did not happen. Partially responsible were perceived conflicts of interest by drug customers as well as the U.S. Federal Trade Commission (FTC). Lilly sold off PCS Health Systems in 1997, resulting in a substantial write-off. As PBMs had proven to be profitable entities, other pharmaceutical companies such as Merck were willing to retain them as part of their business portfolios.

93    Selling PCS was to be part of a general transformational strategy which Randall Tobias, the then CEO of Lilly, implemented in the mid-1990s. After an evaluation of the business portfolio of the company, Mr. Tobias realized that Lilly's strength was in its core business: pharmaceuticals. As a result he divested some of the noncore entities including medical device businesses, cosmetics, agricultural products, and a hard gelatin capsule business. In addition, acquisitions were made and relationships fostered in order to strengthen the core business, including a strategic alliance to develop and market a blood substitute product, ownership of Sphinx Pharmaceuticals, primarily a research and development division, as well as a stake in a biotechnology firm to have access to the testing of cutting-edge chemical substances.

94    It appeared that some of these efforts had paid off by the end of the 1990s. Lilly's earnings per share had boasted growth of 21 percent versus 20 percent for Merck and 13 percent for Pfizer in 1997.

# PRODUCTS

95    In the mid to late 1990s, Lilly's structure was revamped around the five core therapeutic areas in which they had already carried a strong presence by that time: infectious diseases, cancer, cardiovascular products, endocrinology, and neuroscience.

96    Between 1995 and 1998, new Lilly products accounted for 78 percent of the company's sales growth. Some of the major drugs are shown in Exhibit 9.

### Prozac

97    Prozac accounted for almost 30 percent of company sales and was used for treatment of depression and bulimia. Prozac was part of the company's group of neuroscience products, their largest-selling product group. The pending expiration on the patent for this product in the year 2003 was making company executives nervous and sent them scrambling for ways to hang on to its success, including an agreement with Sepracor to develop a new version of Prozac minus the side effects. Prozac's success was challenged in some geographic markets, such as in Australia and Canada, where generic competition had made some inroads and in France where competition had put pressure on sales.

98    Lilly's impressive results at the end of 1998 were due mostly to the blockbuster Prozac, whose sales grew 8 percent worldwide, mostly supported by United States sales which grew by 10 percent. International sales of Prozac remained essentially flat due to competition in

**EXHIBIT 9**
Eli Lilly and Co.
Net Sales in 1998
($ Millions; percentages represent changes from 1997)

| Class | Sales | Percent Change from 1997 | Percent of TOTAL |
|---|---|---|---|
| Prozac | $2,811.5 | 10% | 30 |
| Zyprexa | 1,442.7 | 98 | 16 |
| Anti-infectives | 1,160.9 | (9) | 13 |
| Insulins | 1,154.9 | 8 | 13 |
| Animal health | 614.4 | 4 | 7 |
| Axid | 418.0 | (20) | 4 |
| ReoPro | 365.4 | 44 | 4 |
| Gemzar | 306.8 | 76 | 3 |
| Humatrope | 268.0 | 3 | 3 |
| Evista | 144.1 | N/M | 1 |

foreign markets. Prozac had been the company's savior, responsible for Lilly's turnaround in the mid-1990s. However in early 1999, Wall Street analysts were a bit skeptical about the company's future due to the impending patent expiration. In April of 1999, Lilly had reported first quarter Prozac sales down 4 percent from the previous year with U.S. sales down 6 percent and a 2 percent rise in world sales.

99    Another way Lilly tried to protect its patent on Prozac was to market the drug in other forms, such as a once-a-week pill. This new form of Prozac had been submitted to the FDA for approval in early 1999.

100    Even if Lilly was able to retain patent protection on Prozac until 1993, there were competitors producing other antidepressants that were showing promise, for example, Celexa, marketed by Warner-Lambert and Forest Laboratories, Inc. In addition, even though Prozac had shown strong sales growth overseas, and sales had increased 10 percent in the United States in 1998, some experts were not necessarily optimistic about its future with Lilly. Lilly stock suffered a blow in March, 1999, dropping over 5 percent after one securities analyst lowered estimates for Prozac sales in 1999.

101    During February 1999, Lilly and Barr Laboratories Inc. reached a partial settlement with regard to Barr's patent-rights lawsuit, which was a victory for Lilly in that it barred Barr from manufacturing generic versions of Prozac (fluoxetine). However, the case was not completely resolved due to appeals filed by Barr.

102    Prozac was threatened not only by patent infringement, but also by the increasing sales growth of other similar products. Two of Lilly's major competitors were in the process of marketing antidepressants; Pfizer's Zoloft and SmithKline Beecham's Paxil were second and third, respectively, in terms of sales in the antidepressant market.

### Anti-infectives (Antibiotics)

103    Fifteen percent of company sales in 1997, Lilly's sales of anti-infectives decreased 13 percent. This was one therapeutic area where strong competition from generics in the United States and overseas led to the sales decline. Sales outside the United States accounted for approximately 75 percent of anti-infective sales.

### Insulins

104    Insulins included Humulin and Humalog. Lilly was also strong in the production of insulins constituting 13 percent of the company's sales in 1998.

### Other

105    The following, newer products (launched in 1996) accounted for 13 percent of company sales in 1997:

*Zyprexa.* This product was an antischizophrenic—a treatment for schizophrenia and related psychoses. Zyprexa boasted sales of $1.4 billion, 16 percent of the company's sales, in its first year of existence on the world market. Whether it would become another Prozac remained to be seen.

*Gemzar.* This was a product treating cancer.

*ReoPro.* This was a cardiovascular agent product.

*Evista.* An estrogen-like compound which prevented osteoporosis and perhaps breast cancer, representing Lilly's late 1990s effort toward moving into women's health care, had disappointing sales in the first year of only $144 million or 1 percent of the company's sales in 1998. The British drug company, Zeneca Inc., sued Lilly in February, 1999, for its making claims about Evista as a treatment for breast cancer as

**EXHIBIT 10**
Eli Lilly & Company
Patent Expirations
for Major Thera-
peutic Products

| Product | Year | Product | Year |
|---------|------|---------|------|
| Prozac | 2001, 2003 | ReoPro | 2015 |
| Axid | 2002 | Gemzar | 2006 |
| Zyprexa | 2011 | Evista | 2012 |
| Humalog | 2013 | | |

research in this area had not been completed. Lilly executives responded by saying that this had been identified as part of the company's long-term strategy for Evista, but as of yet, they said such claims had not been made by Lilly.

**106**   All other products in addition to the ones discussed above comprised 13 percent of company sales. Lilly also had devoted a portion of their efforts in the animal health sector, which comprised 7 percent of the company's sales in 1998.

**107**   Patent protection of a company's products was a good indicator of strength of future profits since it was important in operation of the company at the end of the 1990s, especially in the realm of high R&D costs. Lilly's product patent expiration scenario at the end of the 1990s was centered around Prozac, whose patent in the United States was due to expire in 2001 while the patent for how it functioned was to expire in 2003, as shown in Exhibit 10.

# DISTRIBUTION

**108**   Within the United States, Lilly used 200 independent wholesale distributing outlets to distribute its pharmaceutical products. The company's primary objective in distribution was ensuring that customers—physicians, pharmacies, hospitals, and health care professionals—had immediate access to their products. In 1998, four primary wholesale distributors were responsible for 55 percent of the company's consolidated net sales, the remaining distributed by smaller wholesalers, none of which accounted for more than 7 percent of consolidated net sales.

**109**   Distribution outside the United States was accomplished through salaried sales representatives. Neuroscience products made up the largest therapeutic class of drugs marketed outside the United States. In the late 1990s, Lilly stepped up marketing efforts in certain emerging markets, such as Central and Eastern Europe, Latin America, Asia, and Africa. However, sales outside the United States remained at 37 percent of company sales, down from 44 percent in 1995.

# ALLIANCES

**110**   Consistent with the strategic business model industrywide, Lilly was heavily involved in alliances to perform research. At the end of 1997, the company was involved in 50 significant research alliances, 30 of which were signed in 1997.

**111**   Other alliances and agreements involved crucial aspects of drug marketing and served to lengthen Lilly's so-called monopoly on patented drugs. In late 1998, Lilly signed an agreement with Sepracor, a company that specialized in removing side effects from drugs currently on the market and licensing the rights to market the new product back to the original company. In this case, Sepracor was researching a new form of Prozac, which if successful, would allow Lilly to continue with their exclusive rights to Prozac, the blockbuster drug that in 1998 was responsible for 30 percent of Lilly's revenues. It was not without opposition from other industry participants that Lilly was proceeding with this agreement. The U.S.' FTC was

**EXHIBIT 11**

Eli Lilly & Company Overseas Sales (in $U.S. millions)

| Year | Amount | Year | Amount |
|------|--------|------|--------|
| 1989 | 1,335.7 | 1994 | 2,430.2 |
| 1990 | 1,636.9 | 1995 | 2,950.9 |
| 1991 | 1,807.0 | 1996 | 3,081.0 |
| 1992 | 1,996.2 | 1997 | 3,105.9 |
| 1993 | 2,097.5 | 1998 | 3,400.6 |

**EXHIBIT 12**

Eli Lilly & Company Sales 1998 by Geographic Breakdown

| Region | U.S.$ Million | Percent of Total |
|--------|---------------|------------------|
| United States | 5,837 | 63 |
| Western Europe | 1,692 | 18 |
| Other regions | 1,708 | 18 |
| Total | 9,237 | 100% |

investigating the agreement in early 1999 due to a lawsuit against Lilly by Barr Laboratories, a generic drugmaker, which stood to lose the marketing of a generic form of Prozac and thus the entry of competition, if the Lilly-Sepracor deal was allowed to proceed. Other research collaborations included collaboration with Takeda Chemical Industries, Ltd., a Japanese pharmaceutical company to comarket the company's oral diabetes treatment, which was still under regulatory approval in 1999. In 1998, Lilly made an agreement with ICOS Corporation to make an eventual joint venture for the study of treatments for sexual dysfunction.

## OVERSEAS MARKETS

112    In the late 1990s, Lilly was selling in 159 countries worldwide. The company had research and development facilities in nine countries, including North America, Europe, and Japan. They had manufacturing facilities in 20 countries, including locations in Australia, South America, China, the Middle East, Europe, and the United States.

113    In 1997, while the company's overall sales increased 16 percent, sales in the United States increased 28 percent and outside the United States sales increased by merely 1 percent. The weakness in overseas sales was in part due to unfavorable exchange rates and price decreases. However in 1998, overseas sales experienced a turnaround due to the successes of some of the new drugs, but foreign sales as a percentage of total sales still remained at approximately 36 percent of total revenues in 1998, as shown in Exhibits 11 and 12.

## RESEARCH AND DEVELOPMENT

114    Lilly Research Laboratories (LRL) was the division of the company responsible for R&D for pharmaceutical products and animal health products. In 1997, Lilly's expenditure for R&D was $1.3 billion or 16 percent of sales. This was in line with major competitors where the percent spent on R&D ranged from 14 to 18 percent. In 1998, research and development costs increased by 27 percent, which the company stated was due to greater R&D efforts as well as the development of external R&D collaborations. One of the industry benchmarks was comparing the rate of sales growth versus the rate of R&D expenditure growth. When R&D growth was higher, pressure was put on earnings. In Lilly's case, although sales growth had been strong, R&D expenditures were increasing at a faster rate. This might have been the result of Prozac earnings being directed toward new research and development.

# TOWARD THE FUTURE

**115**     The most prevalent industry factor at work at the end of the 1990s was the quickly escalating R&D costs, which necessitated wisely choosing core businesses in order to enjoy higher margins. The tendency for companies to join forces in order to confront this phenomenon was beginning to change the average size of pharmaceutical manufacturing organizations. Lilly had already experienced some success with reorganizing their business around their core competencies, five specific therapeutic categories in the mid-1990s after the entrance of a new CEO, Randall Tobias, in 1993. It was through this reorganization that the blockbuster product Prozac emerged, boosting the company's sales and making Lilly a top-ten contender within the industry. Lilly realized that Prozac had boosted them into this prestigious group of players; however, they had to design a new strategy post-Prozac to continue their strong growth in light of market and internal conditions.

**116**     The U.S. market, which had usually boasted strong growth rates throughout the second half of the century had once again been booming due to product innovation and strong volume sales. Smaller pharmaceutical firms, especially those outside the United States, wanting to get a piece of the action looked for merger partners with whom they could join either to increase their R&D muscle or to have immediate access to the American market. Even with a U.S. market offering strong growth rates, this could not be counted on due to the dominance of managed care, which was changing the dynamics of the industry and putting downward pressure on prices. The industry had to focus also on global launch, even though markets outside the United States appeared to be less attractive with socialist governments and price controls.

**117**     Another prevailing external factor was the aging of the world population and the lengthening of life expectancy. Experts had cited several conditions from which the oldest age groups would suffer that would be prevalent in this environment and a key to success in the future would be the ability to address these particular areas with treatment.

**118**     Lilly realized that they were in a middle-of-the-road position in the sense that in the current environment of rising R&D costs, their pipeline of drugs contained some decent candidates to forge strong future sales growth. However, it remained to be seen whether the company could manage the loss of Prozac and still provide excellent growth and shareholder value. Wall Street analysts were on the fence about Lilly and some recommendations were: yes, buy pharmaceuticals, but hold off on Lilly. Internally, Lilly was going through some of its own transitions. Randall Tobias who led the company through the mid-1990s reorganization and had guided the Prozac success story decided to retire in 1998. The new CEO, Sidney Taurel, had to decide a strategic direction to carry the company forward into the new millennium in light of industry and company conditions.

**119**     At a meeting of the board of directors in the Spring of 1999, Mr. Taurel was evaluating possible alternatives provided by various directors. Mr. Charles E. Golden, executive vice president and chief financial officer, realized that Lilly had already tightened their therapeutic focus into five basic areas that would help them capture and take advantage of an aging world population—they already had a presence here. Mr. Golden recognized the fact that Lilly like many other pharmaceutical firms were at the mercy of their drug pipeline—at the time they were approaching a possible loss of Prozac. There were some promising drugs in their pipeline, specifically, Zyprexa which had blossomed in its second year of sales to a $1.4 billion selling drug. The other promising candidates were ReoPro and Gemzar, but neither of these looked to have the strength of Prozac. Thus, the company had to devise a way to maintain its main contender status within the industry by continuing the growth rates they had achieved with Prozac. They did not want this success story to be a one-time deal.

**120**     Mr. Golden felt that they had to expand the company by locating a merger partner in order to enter a compatible sector that would provide earnings with a type of insurance when the drug pipeline had possible gaps. In this way, Lilly could continue to pursue pharmaceuticals and use their strength in R&D, as they had done previously, but would have the added protection of consumer products which focused more on marketing and sales, an area which Lilly had been strong. While both consumer product and pharmaceutical demand was considered to be relatively insensitive to swings in the business cycle, a consumer goods unit would equal revenues minus the pipeline problem. He sited Pfizer, the powerhouse company whose drug pipeline had been formidable against the competition, but at the same time the company had been able to focus on building strong brand recognition with consumer products. The fact was that strength in one sector had not deterred them from performing well in the other. In other words, the businesses were compatible and this addition could be strategically beneficial. In addition, since most OTC medicines had their beginnings as ethical products, Lilly would be able to make this transition on its own upon expiration of patents. It seemed a logical move on the part of Mr. Golden.

121    Mr. Taurel listened carefully to these arguments. The idea of making strides toward becoming a powerhouse like Pfizer had always attracted him, and the theory behind Mr. Golden's presentation were certainly logical. Pfizer was living proof that this type of strategy with varying business units could work; however, he felt rather uneasy about such a radical strategy change. After all, his predecessor had refocused Lilly's strategy around the company's core competencies and had sold off other business units making strong focus one of the company's strengths. He felt that although the loss of Prozac might have serious consequences for earnings, Lilly's pipeline was still promising and had been effective against competition in similar therapeutic areas. He added that the company should perhaps be keeping their eggs in this strategic basket and not be so quick to reverse the internal company trend of the mid-1990s. He was willing to listen to other proposals.

122    Another officer at Lilly, Mr. Gerhard N. Mayr, President, Intercontinental Operations, although not opposed to finding a merger partner, had a different idea. He noted that Lilly had excellent success in the United States, a market which had provided strong growth potential, the most attractive market in the industry. However, he recognized that other competitors were experiencing higher sales percentages overseas as a percent of total sales and that Lilly, if it wanted to retain its status in the industry, could not necessarily rely only on the U.S. market for future growth. Secondly, the company size in terms of sales was changing due to the trend of mergers and acquisitions and at least near-term, they were loosing their position as a top-contender in terms of sales.

123    Lilly's success story with Prozac had become in 1998 mostly a U.S. phenomenon. That is, Prozac sales overseas had been basically flat due to competition from European firms. Even though Lilly was already operating in some 150 countries, sales outside the United States did not well represent the company's investment in these markets. Had they had better representation in those markets, perhaps in the form of a European partner with compatible therapeutic competencies, they would be able to accomplish a three-fold objective: further strengthen their R&D capabilities since R&D in Europe was highly respected; pick up synergies with a foreign partner while increasing their capital base in an environment of mergers and acquisitions, quickly expanding the average size of firms in the industry; and increase their presence in Europe, allowing them to participate in more opening markets in the future. In this way, the company could also remain focused on its core competencies, an industry key to success in the late 1990s. He noticed that companies like SmithKline Beecham were experiencing problems because of too broadly designed strategies, thus Lilly had to stick with its therapeutic competencies, however, with a partner.

124    Mr. Taurel had listened to both of these arguments intently, but was not necessarily intent on making an immediate decision. Both his board members had put forth ideas that had strategic sense; however, he felt that the situation merited deeper thought and analysis.

# Case 35 FreshDirect

## Keeley Townsend, Alan B. Eisner, Richard B. Robinson, John A. Pearce II

# COMPANY PROFILE

1   Operating out of its production center in Long Island, Queens, FreshDirect offered online grocery shopping and delivery service to Manhattan's East Side and Battery Park City. When it was launched in July 2001 by Joe Fedele and Jason Ackerman, FreshDirect pronounced to the New York area that it was "the new way to shop for food." This was a bold statement given that the last decade had been witness to the demise of numerous other online grocery ventures. However, the creators of FreshDirect were confident in the success of their business because their entire operation had been designed to deliver one simple promise to grocery shoppers, "higher quality at lower prices."

2   While this promise was an extremely common tagline used within and outside of the grocery business, FreshDirect had integrated numerous components into their system to give real meaning to these words. In order to offer the highest quality products to its customers, FreshDirect had created a state-of-the-art production center and staffed it with top-notch personnel. The 300,000 square foot production facility, located in Long Island, Queens, was composed of 12 separate temperature zones, ensuring that each piece of food was kept at its optimal temperature for ripening or preservation. Each department of the facility, including the coffee roaster, butcher, and bakery, was staffed by carefully selected experts, enabling FreshDirect to offer premium fresh coffees, pastries, breads, meats, and seafood. Further quality management was achieved by the SAP manufacturing-software system that controls every detail of the facilities operations. All of the thermometers, scales, and conveyor belts within the facility were connected to a central command center. Each specific setting was programmed into the system by an expert from the corresponding department, including everything from the ideal temperature for ripening a cantaloupe to the amount of flour that goes into French bread. The system was also equipped with a monitoring alarm that alerts staff of any skew from the programmed settings.

3   Another quality control element that had been made an integral part of the FreshDirect facility was an extremely high standard for cleanliness, health and safety. The facility itself was kept immaculately clean and all food-preparation areas and equipment were bathed in antiseptic foam at the end of each day. Incoming and outgoing food was tested in FreshDirect's in-house laboratory, which was managed by a 32-year veteran U.S. Department of Agriculture inspection supervisor, who ensures the facility adheres to USDA guidelines and the HACCP food safety system, and that all food passing through FreshDirect meets the company's high safety standards.

4   System efficiency had been the key to FreshDirect's ability to offer its high-quality products at such low prices. FreshDirect's biggest operational design component for reducing costs had been the complete elimination of the middleman. Instead of going through an intermediary, both fresh and dry products were ordered from individual growers and producers, and shipped directly to FreshDirect's production center, where FreshDirect's expert

Source: This case was prepared by Alan B. Eisner of Pace University, Keeley Townsend of Pace University, Richard Robinson of the University of South Carolina, and John A. Pearce II of Villanova University. It is intended to be used as a basis for class discussion rather than to illustrate either effective or ineffective handling of an administrative situation. All rights reserved to the authors.

staff prepare them for selling. In addition, FreshDirect does not accept any slotting allowances. This unique relationship with growers and producers had allowed FreshDirect to enjoy reduced purchase prices from its suppliers, enabling them to pass even greater savings on to their customers.

5      The proximity of FreshDirect's processing facility to its Manhattan customer base had also been a critical factor in their cost-effective operational design. The processing center's location in Long Island City, Queens, puts approximately 4 million people within a 10-mile radius of the FreshDirect facility, allowing FreshDirect to deliver a large number of orders in a short amount of time. Further cost controls have been implemented through FreshDirect's order and delivery protocols. Orders must be for a minimum of $40 and the delivery charge was $3.95 per order, with a rule that prohibits tipping the delivery person. Delivery was made via one of FreshDirect's 23 trucks and was only available during a prearranged 2-hour window on weeknights after 4:30 and all day on the weekends, which keeps delivery trucks out of the heaviest New York City traffic and thus reduces FreshDirect's delivery-related costs.

## FOUNDING PARTNERS

6      FreshDirect was launched in July of 2001 by Joe Fedele and Jason Ackerman. CEO Fedele was able to bring a wealth of New York City food industry experience to FreshDirect. In 1993 he cofounded Fairway Uptown, a 35,000 foot supermarket located on West 133rd Street in Harlem. Many critics originally scoffed at the idea of a successful store in that location, but Fairway's low prices and quality selection of produce and meats made it a hit with neighborhood residents, as well as many downtown and suburban commuters.

7      Jason Ackerman gained grocery industry exposure as an investment banker with Donaldson Lufkin & Jenrette, where he specialized in supermarket mergers and acquisitions.

8      Fedele and Ackerman first explored the idea of starting a chain of fresh-food stores, but realized maintaining a high degree of quality would be impossible with a large enterprise. As an alternative they elected to pursue a business that incorporated online shopping with central distribution.

9      FreshDirect acquired the bulk of its $100 million investment from several private sources, with a small contribution coming from the State of New York. By locating FreshDirect's distribution center within the New York State border, and promising to create at least 300 new permanent, full-time private sector jobs in the state, FreshDirect became eligible for a $500,000 training grant from the Empire State Development Jobs Now Program. As its name implies, the purpose of the Jobs Now program was to create new, immediate job opportunities for New Yorkers.

## BUSINESS PLAN

10     While business started out relatively slow, Fedele had hoped to capture around 5 percent of the New York grocery market and projected revenues of about $100 million in the first year and $225 million by 2004. As of February 2003, FreshDirect had reached the 2,000 orders-a-day milestone and was attracting around 3,000 new customers a day, for a total customer base of around 40,000.[1] FreshDirect service was originally slated for availability citywide by the end of 2002. However, in order to maintain its superior service and product quality,

---

[1]"Five Months in Manhattan and FreshDirect Passes the 2,000-Order-a-Day Mark and had Over 40,000 Customers." *Business Wire*, February 12, 2003.

FreshDirect had chosen to slowly expand its service area. Service was now expected to cover New York City and parts of Suffolk and Nassau County by the end of 2003, and possibly start up in several other metropolitan regions nationwide by 2005.

11    The company had employed a relatively low-cost marketing approach, which, until recently, consisted mainly of billboards, public relations and word-of-mouth to promote their products and services. Recently FreshDirect hired Trumpet, an ad agency that had been promoting FreshDirect as a better way to shop by emphasizing the problems associated with traditional grocery shopping. For example, one commercial stresses the unsanitary conditions in a supermarket by showing a grocery shopper bending over a barrel of olives as she sneezes, getting an olive stuck in her nose, and then blowing it back into the barrel. The ad ends with the question "Where's your food been?" Another ad shows a checkout clerk morph into an armed robber, demanding money from the customer, and then morphing back into a friendly checkout clerk once the money was received. The ad urges viewers to "Stop getting robbed at the grocery store."

12    Another innovative marketing approach that had been quite successful was the offer of free food. FreshDirect offers $50 worth of free groceries to any first-time service users, believing that once people see the quality of the food and the convenience of the service they will return as paying customers.

## OPERATING STRATEGY

13    FreshDirect's operating strategy had employed a make-to-order philosophy, eliminating the middleman in order to create an efficient supply chain. By focusing their energy on providing produce, meat, seafood, baked goods and coffees that were made to the customer's specific order, FreshDirect offers its customers an alternative to the standardized cuts and choices available at most brick-and-mortar grocery stores (see Exhibits 1 and 2). This strategy had created a business model that was unique within the grocery business community.

14    A typical grocery store carries about 25,000 packaged goods, which account for around 50 percent of its sales, and about 2,200 perishable products, which account for the other 50 percent of sales. In contrast, FreshDirect offers around 5,000 perishable products, accounting for about 75 percent of its sales, but only around 3,000 packaged goods, which comprise the remaining 25 percent of sales. While this stocking pattern does enable a greater array of fresh foods, it severely limits the number of brands and available sizes of packaged goods, such as cereal, crackers and laundry detergent. However, FreshDirect believes customers will accept a more limited packaged good selection in order to get lower prices, as evidenced in the success of wholesale grocery stores which offer bulk sales of limited items. In fact, Jason Ackerman identified the ideal FreshDirect customer as someone who buys their bulk staples from Costco on a monthly basis, and buys everything else from FreshDirect on a weekly basis.

## FRESHDIRECT'S WEBSITE

15    FreshDirect's website not only offers an abundance of products to choose from, it also provides a broad spectrum of information on the food that was sold and the manner in which it was sold. Web surfers can take a pictorial tour of the FreshDirect facility, get background information on the experts that manage each department, get nutritional information for food items, compare produce or cheeses based on taste, price and usage, specify the thickness of meat orders and opt for one of several marinades or rubs, search for the right kind of coffee based on taste preferences, and read ingredient and nutritional information for a

**EXHIBIT 1**

**Example of FreshDirect meat selection options**

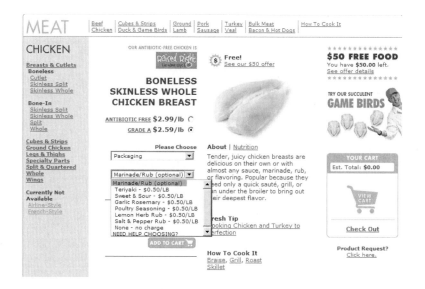

**EXHIBIT 2**

**Home Page at FreshDirect.com**

variety of fully prepared meals. For example, if you want to purchase chicken, you were first asked to choose from Breasts & Cutlets, Cubes & Strips, Ground, Legs & Thighs, Specialty Parts, Split & Quartered, Whole, or Wings. Once your selection was made, lets say you choose Breasts & Cutlets, you were given further options based on your preference for skin, bone and thickness. The final selection step offers you a choice of rubs and marinades, including Teriyaki, Sweet & Sour, Garlic Rosemary, Poultry Seasoning, Lemon Herb Rub, and Salt & Pepper Rub. All along the way the pages offer nutritional profiles of each cut of meat as well as tips for preparation and proper storage.

16      FreshDirect employs two different delivery models, one for its urban customers and another for those in the suburbs. Customers within the city were attracted to the FreshDirect service because it eliminates the need to carry groceries, for what could be a substantial distance, from the closest grocery store, or to deal with trying to park a car near their apartment in order to unload their purchases. Orders made by customers within the city were delivered directly to their homes via FreshDirect truck during a prearranged two-hour delivery window (see Exhibit 3).

**EXHIBIT 3**
**FreshDirect delivery options**

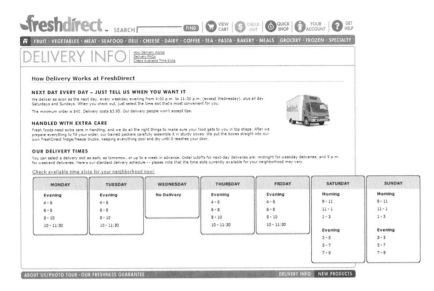

**17** Suburban customers were serviced in a slightly different manner. Most suburban residents have the convenience of automobile access and easy parking, but were looking for a time-saving device. The widespread congregation of these residents in train station parking lots or office parks make these areas perfect central delivery stations. FreshDirect sends a refrigerated truck, large enough to hold 500 orders, to these key spots during designated periods of time. Suburbanites can then return to their cars, swing by the FreshDirect truck, pick up their order, and head home.

## THE RETAIL GROCERY INDUSTRY

**18** In 2001, the U.S. retail grocery industry was a $517 billion business, with almost $400 billion of sales made by supermarkets.[2] The top ten supermarket chains in the United States commanded over 44 percent of the market share for the grocery industry.

| Supermarket Chain | Market Share (%) (2001) |
|---|---|
| Wal Mart Super Centers | 9.6 |
| Kroger | 7.3 |
| Albertson's | 5.6 |
| Safeway | 5.0 |
| Koninklijke Ahold | 3.4 |
| Supervalue | 3.1 |
| Costco Wholesale Corp. | 3.0 |
| Sam's Club | 2.7 |
| Fleming | 2.3 |
| Publix Super Markets | 2.2 |
| *Total Market Share* | *44.2* |

Source: *Advertising Age*, http://www.adage.com/

[2]Food Market Institute, *Supermarket Facts: Industry Overview 2001*,
www.fmi.org/facts_figs/superfact.htm

**19**     In 2001, no single supermarket chain had an industry market share above 10 percent. The typical supermarket store carried an average of 32,000 items, was an average of 44,000 square feet in size, and averaged $19 million in sales annually.

**20**     The supermarket business had traditionally been a low-margin business, with net profits of only 1 to 2 percent of revenues. Store profits depended heavily on creating a high volume of customer traffic and rapid inventory turnover, especially for perishables such as produce and fresh meat. Competitors had to operate efficiently to make money, and tight control of labor costs and product spoilage was essential. Because capital investment costs were modest, involving mainly the construction of distribution centers and stores, it was not unusual for supermarket chains to realize 15 to 20 percent returns on invested capital.

# THE ONLINE GROCERY SEGMENT

**21**     The online-grocery shopping business was still in the early stages of development in 2001. Analysts believed that the online grocery segment accounted for less that 1 percent in sales in 2001, with total sales at around $1 billion, but expect sales to reach US$11 billion by 2006.[3] So far, online grocery shopping had been slow to catch on, and industry newcomers had encountered high start-up and operating costs. Sales volumes and profit margins have remained too small to cover the high costs. The problem, according to industry analysts, was that consumers had been largely disappointed in the service, selection, and prices that they had so far gotten from industry members.

**22**     However, some analysts expected online grocery sales to grow at a rapid pace as companies improved their service and selection, PC penetration of households rose, and consumers became more accustomed to making purchases online. An article in *Computer Bits* examined the customer base for online grocers, looking specifically at the types of consumers that would be likely to shop online and the kinds of home computer systems that were required for online shopping. An Anderson Consulting report, cited in the *Computer Bits* article, identified six major types of online shoppers (see Exhibit 4) and estimated that by 2007, 15 to 20 million households would order their groceries online. A MARC Group study concluded "consumers who buy groceries online were likely to be more loyal to their electronic supermarkets, spend more per store visit, and take greater advantage of coupons and premiums than traditional customers."

**EXHIBIT 4**

**Types of Online Shoppers and Their Propensity to be Attracted to Online Grocery Shopping**

| Types of Online Shoppers | Comments |
|---|---|
| Traditionals | Might be an older technology-avoider, or simply a shopper who lives to sniff-test their own produce and eyeball the meat selection. |
| Responsibles | Feed off the satisfaction of accomplishing this persistent to-do item |
| Time-Starved | Find the extra costs associated with delivery fees or other markups a small price to pay for saving them time. |
| New Technologists | Use the latest technology for any and every activity they can, because they can. |
| Necessity Users | People with physical or circumstantial challenges that make grocery shopping difficult. Likely to be the most loyal group of shoppers. |
| Avoiders | Dislike the grocery shopping experience for a variety of reasons. |

Source: A study by Anderson Consulting cited in Sherry Anderson, "Is Online Grocery Shopping for You," *Computer Bits,* vol. 11, April 2000.

[3]Keith Regan, "Jupiter Halves Forecast for Online Grocer Revenue," *E-Commerce Times,* May 21, 2001.

**23**    One of the problems with online grocery shopping was that consumers were extremely price sensitive when it came to buying groceries. The prices of many online grocers were above the prices at supermarkets and shoppers, in many cases, were unwilling to pay online grocers extra for the convenience of home delivery. Consumer price sensitivity meant that online grocers had to achieve a cost structure that would allow them to (1) price competitively, (2) cover the costs of picking and delivering individual grocery orders, and (3) have sufficient margins to earn attractive profits and returns on investment. Some analysts estimated that online grocers had to do ten times the volume of a traditional grocer in order to be successful.

### Supermarket Chains as Potential Competitors in the Online Grocery Segment.

**24**    Many established brick-and-mortar grocers have now begun offering online grocery shopping in an attempt to maintain and expand their customer base. Two basic models have been used for online order fulfillment; one was to pick items from the shelves of existing stores within the grocer's chain, and the other was to build special warehouses dedicated to online orders. The demand for home delivery of groceries had been increasing, but in many market areas the demand had not yet reached a level that would justify the high cost of warehouses dedicated to the fulfillment of online orders.

**25**    Safeway began an ambitions online grocery venture by establishing GroceryWorks, an online shopping system that included a series of warehouses dedicated to filling the online orders. Unfavorable returns forced Safeway to reevaluate their system, and they eventually chose to form a partnership with Tesco, a U.K.-based grocer. Tesco fills its online orders from the shelves of local stores in close proximity to the customer's home. Safeway and Tesco were now working together on GroceryWorks in Portland, Oregon, where they have received a positive initial response from customers.

### Gomez Advisor's Ratings of Online Grocers

**26**    Gomez Advisors provided user-oriented ratings of numerous types of online companies, ranging from banks to auction sites to travel agents to sellers of sporting goods. Many online shoppers were using the Gomez ratings to help them select which Internet providers to do business with. Gomez evaluated online grocers on five aspects (see Exhibit 5):

- Ease of use—whether the website had well-integrated features that minimized order time and that gave shoppers product comparison capabilities.

- Onsite resources—the breadth of product selection and the quality of information resources provided to users.

- Relationship services—whether the grocer provided such "extras" as in-home visits with first-time customers, account representatives to answer questions, and willingness to fill unique orders.

- Overall cost—this criterion included product costs (based on nonpromoted prices of a market basket of commonly purchased items), delivery charges, length and frequency of price promotions, and membership fees (including whether there were free trial periods for new members).

- Customer confidence—financial stability, reliability of customer service, and guarantees for what was sold.

**EXHIBIT 5**
**Gomez Ratings of the Top Ten Online Grocers, Fall 1999**

| Company | Ease of Use | Overall Cost | Customer Confidence | Onsite Resources | Relation-ship Services | Overall Score | Comments |
|---|---|---|---|---|---|---|---|
| Peapod | 9.07 | 7.96 | 5.41 | 7.90 | 3.75 | 6.97 | Rated third (score of 6.17) for time-short shoppers looking for the best deal with the least hassle. |
| HomeGrocer | 7.33 | 7.41 | 4.82 | 7.74 | 5.00 | 6.67 | Rated second best (score of 7.02) for selective shoppers wanting THE best quality products and delivery service; also rated second best (score of 6.80) for shoppers looking for specific meal solutions (recipes, seasonal foods, and prepared foods). |
| Webvan | 8.22 | 7.16 | 2.63 | 7.32 | 5.00 | 6.36 | Rated best (score of 7.23) for selective shoppers and best (score of 7.14) for shoppers looking for specific meal solutions. |
| Streamline | 4.62 | 5.93 | 5.16 | 7.47 | 7.50 | 6.31 | Rated best (score of 6.92) for time-short shoppers. |
| ShopLink | 6.36 | 6.98 | 5.33 | 5.93 | 6.25 | 6.26 | Rated second best for time-short shoppers (score of 6.70). |
| HomeRuns | 5.56 | 8.75 | 4.97 | 3.41 | 2.50 | 5.18 | Ranked best (score of 8.68) for bargain shoppers who love to browse and the thrill of shopping for the best deal. |
| NetGrocer | 8.22 | 3.33 | 2.97 | 5.49 | 3.75 | 4.70 | |
| Albertson's | 4.67 | 8.16 | 3.99 | 0.90 | 2.50 | 4.13 | Ranked second (score of 7.54) for bargain shoppers. |
| Grocer Online | 5.42 | 3.46 | 6.64 | 0.36 | 2.50 | 3.73 | |
| YourGrocer | 4.53 | 3.84 | 5.91 | 2.70 | 5.00 | 3.68 | |

Source: www.gomez.com, February 6, 2000.

# YOURGROCER.COM

27    FreshDirect's most geographically significant competitor in the online grocery industry was YourGrocer.com. YourGrocer was launched in New York City in 1998 with plans on being the lead online grocery service for the New York metropolitan area. However by November of 2001 the company ran out of money and was forced to shut down. In the spring of 2002 new capital resources were found and the company reopened for business. However, the second time around their approach was a little different.

28    YourGrocer was created with a bulk-buying strategy, believing that customers would order large, economical quantities of goods from the website and the company would use their trucks to make home deliveries. During YourGrocer's first life, the ambitious business plan covered a large service area, and included the acquisition of another online grocery company, NYCGrocery.com. But in its second life, which began in April of 2002, the business plan looked a little different. The company cut down the size of its staff, got rid of warehouses, decided to rent its delivery vans instead of owning them, and scaled down its delivery routes.

## EXHIBIT 6
**Profiles of Selected Online Grocers**

| Name | Area Covered | Min Order | Delivery Charge | Delivery Method | Specialization |
|---|---|---|---|---|---|
| FreshDirect | Manhattan's Eastside, Battery Park City | $40 | $3.95 No tipping. | Trucks; avail. weeknights after 4:30 and all day on weekends | Mostly perishables: fresh produce, meats, baked goods Low prices because there was no middleman |
| YourGrocer | Manhattan, Bronx, Westchester, Greenwich | $75 | $9.95 | Rented vans; avail. on select days & times, depending on location | Bulk orders of packaged goods |
| Peapod | Chicago, Boston, DC, Southern Connecticut, Long Island | $50 | $4.95 for order > $75 $9.95 for order < $75 Tipping optional | Truck; avail 7AM–1PM & 4PM–10PM weekdays, 7AM–1PM weekends | Partner with Giant Foods and Stop & Shop; items picked off of local store shelves near customer's home |
| NetGrocer | 48 Continental states and DC | none | $3.99–$599.99 Depends on order size and destination | FedEx; will receive order within 1–4 business days | Only non-perishables; no fresh produce |

Source: Company Websites

## EXHIBIT 7
**Comparison of Prices for Selected Online Grocers, February 2003**

| Grocery Item | FreshDirect's Price | YourGrocer's Price | PeaPod's Price | NetGrocer's Price |
|---|---|---|---|---|
| Tide Laundry Detergent | $7.99/100 oz | $21.99/300 oz (~$7.33/100 oz) | $8.79/100 oz | $9.99/100 oz |
| Wish-Bone Italian Dressing | $1.49/8 oz | $4.69/36 oz (~$1.04/8 oz) | $1.69/8 oz | $1.79/8 oz |
| Cheerios | $3.69/15 oz | $7.49/35 oz (~ $3.21/15 oz) | $3.89/15 oz | $4.29/15 oz |
| Ragu Spaghetti Sauce | $1.99/26 oz | $7.99/135 oz (~$1.54/26 oz) | $1.99/26 oz | $2.49/26 oz |
| Granny Smith Apples | $1.29/lb | $5.99/5 lb bag (~$1.20/lb) | $2.99/3 lb bag (~$1.00/lb) | Fresh produce not available |

Source: Company websites.

**EXHIBIT 8**
YourGrocer.com
Website

**EXHIBIT 9**
**YourGrocer's Service**
**Focus**

New YourGrocer will focus on providing the three benefits that families in the area most value:

1. Easy ordering over the Internet or on the phone, which saves hours of thankless shopping time.

2. Delivery right to the home or office, which eliminates the burden of lifting and transporting heavy and bulky items each month.

3. Meaningful savings everyday, which reduces the prices paid for stock-up groceries and supplies by 20 to 30 percent on average, below local supermarkets.

Queens, Nassau County, and New Jersey were eliminated from the service area, which now only includes Manhattan, the Bronx, Westchester County and Fairfield County.

**29**    YourGrocer offers a limited selection of items that can only be purchased in bulk. Deliveries were made in time slots that vary, depending on what part of the New York area you live in. There was a $75 minimum order and the delivery charge was $9.95. Exhibits 6-10 profile YourGrocer and other key online grocery competitors of FreshDirect.

# PEAPOD

**30**    Founded in 1989 by brothers, Andrew and Thomas Parkinson, Peapod (see Exhibits 11-12) was an early pioneer in e-commerce, inventing an online home-shopping service for grocery items years ahead of the commercial emergence of the Internet. With its tagline "Smart Shopping for Busy People," the company began providing consumers with a home shopping experience in the early 1990s, going so far as to install modems in their homes to provide an online connection. From its founding in 1989 until 1998, the company's business model involved filling customer orders by forming alliances with traditional grocery retailers. The company chose a retail partner in each geographic area where it operated and used the partner's local network of retail stores to pick and pack orders for delivery to customers. Peapod personnel would cruise the aisles of a partner's stores, selecting the items each customer ordered, pack and load them into Peapod vehicles, and then deliver them to customers at times chosen by customers. Peapod charged customers a fee for its service and it also collected fees from its retail supply partners for using their products in its on-

**EXHIBIT 10**
YourGrocer's
Delivery Service
and Product List

## DELIVERY SCHEDULE

Orders must be in by 5 PM the night prior to delivery for Monday to Friday orders. **NOTE:** Drivers were responsible to deliver to doorstep only.

| Shipping Times | Current Status |
|---|---|
| **Bronx** | |
| Bronx Monday 7–10 PM | *Same day delivery n/a* |
| Bronx Wednesday 5–9 PM | Open with **2** slots left |
| Bronx Friday 5–9 PM | Open with **2** slots left |
| **Brooklyn** | |
| Brooklyn Monday 6–9 PM | *Same day delivery n/a* |
| Brooklyn Wednesday 6–9 PM | Open with **3** slots left |
| Brooklyn Friday 3–7 PM | Open with **5** slots left |
| **Connecticut** | |
| Connecticut Monday 6–9 PM | *Same day delivery n/a* |
| Connecticut Wednesday 5 PM–9 PM | Booked |
| Connecticut Friday 12–3 PM | Open with **4** slots left |
| **Manhattan** | |
| Manhattan Monday 8 AM–12 PM | *Same day n/a* |
| Manhattan Monday 1–5 PM | *Same day delivery n/a* |
| Manhattan Monday 5–9 PM | *Same day delivery n/a* |
| Manhattan Tuesday 8 AM–12 PM | Booked |
| Manhattan Tuesday 1 PM–5 PM | Available |
| Manhattan Tuesday 5–9 PM | Available |
| Manhattan Wednesday 1 PM–5 PM | Available |
| Manhattan Wednesday 8 AM–12 PM | Available |
| Manhattan Wednesday 5–9 PM | Available |
| Manhattan Thursday 9 AM–1 PM | Available |
| Manhattan Thursday 12 Noon–5 PM | Available |
| Manhattan Thursday 5–9 PM | Open with **5** slots left |
| Manhattan Friday 8 AM–12 PM | Available |
| Manhattan Friday 12 Noon–5 PM | Available |
| Manhattan Friday 5 PM–9 PM | Open with **5** slots left |
| Manhattan Saturday 8–12 Noon | Available |
| Manhattan Saturday 11–2 PM | Available |
| **Westchester** | |
| Westchester Monday 1–5 PM | *Same day delivery n/a* |
| Westchester Monday 6–9 PM | *Same day n/a not* |
| Westchester Wednesday 1 PM–5 PM | Open with **5** |
| Westchester Wednesday 6–9 PM | Open with **4** |
| Westchester Thursday 10 AM–3 PM | Available |
| Westchester Friday 2 PM–5 PM | Available |
| Westchester Friday 6–9 PM | Open with **3** slots left |

*YourGrocer charges $9.95 for each delivery.*

## PRODUCT LIST

**Bakery Products**
Bread, Rolls & Croissants
Muffins & Baked Desserts
**Beverages**
Soda & Water
Iced Tea & Juice/ Juice Drinks
Coffee, Tea, Cocoa & Milk
Mixes
**Breakfast Products**
Other Breakfast Items
Cereal
**Canned Foods & Dried Fruits**
Fruit
Vegetables
Canned Meats & Seafood
**Condiments & Ingredients**
Cooking Ingredients
Jams, Peanut Butter, Mayo,
Mustard, Sauces
Baking Ingredients
Salad Dressings &
Condiments
**Candy & Gum**
Chocolate Candy
Gum, Mints, and Hard Candy
All Other Candy
**Dairy Products**
Cheese
Juice & Yogurt
Milk, Butter & Eggs
**Deli**
Cheese
Cold Cuts
Specialty Foods
Fresh Pasta and Italian
Dishes
**Fresh Produce**
Fresh Vegetables
Fresh Fruit
**Frozen & Cooler Products**
Asian Dishes
Vegetables
Pastry & Breakfast Items
Poultry
Appetizers
Italian & Mexican Dishes
Seafood & Shrimp
Meat
**Pasta, Soup & Rice**
Pasta & Rice
Soup

**Snack Foods**
Nuts & Trail Mix
Chips & Crackers
Granola & Health Bars
Cookies
**Baby Products**
Diapers, Formula & Food
**Cleaning Supplies**
Cleaning Products
Laundry Products
**Drugstore Products**
Personal Care Products
Hair Care Products
Medications
Dental Care Products
Vitamins, Diet Supplements
**Household Items**
Batteries, Bulbs, Tapes, etc.
Appliances
**Office Products**
Office Products
**Paper & Plastic Products**
Paper Towels, Tissue & Toilet Paper
Plates, Cups, Napkins, Food Wrap
**Pet Food & Supplies**
Pet Food & Supplies
**Gift Certificates**
Gift Certificates
**Dieting**
Foods & Beverages
Diet Shakes, Bars
Other
**Lunchbox & Snack Packs**
Lunchbox Selections
**Seasonal Aisle**
Season Needs
Valentines Day
**Company Kitchen**
Company Kitchen Selections
**Care Givers Section**
Ensure, Beverages, Food
Incontinence Products
Medications, Personal Care
**Our New Products**
New Products
**Party Makers**
Party food, Appetizers
Plates, cups, etc

line service. Over the next several years, Peapod built delivery capabilities in eight market areas: Chicago, IL; Columbus, OH; Boston, MA; San Francisco/San Jose, CA; Houston, TX; Dallas, TX; Austin, TX; and Long Island, NY.

31   In 1997, faced with mounting losses despite growing revenues, Peapod management opted to shift to a new order fulfillment business model utilizing a local company–owned and operated central distribution warehouse to store, pick, and pack customer orders for delivery. By mid-1999 the company had opened new distribution centers in 3 of the 8 markets it served—Chicago, Long Island, and Boston; a fourth distribution center was under construction in San Francisco.

32   In 1999, Peapod formed a strategic partnership with the McLane Group L.P., advertised as a leader in distribution-logistics services and technology for food companies. Peapod's goal was to utilize McLane's state-of-the-art distribution management systems in order to improve Peapod's centralized distribution and warehouse operations.

33   In the late spring of 2000, Peapod created a partnership with Royal Ahold, a Netherlands-based, international food provider. At the time, Ahold operated five supermarket companies

**EXHIBIT 11**
**Peapod Website**

**EXHIBIT 12**
**Peapod Product Selection**

in the United States: Stop & Shop, Tops Market, Giant-Landover, Giant-Carlisle and BI-LO. In September of 2000, Peapod acquired Streamline.com, Inc.'s operations in Chicago and Washington, D.C. markets, and announced that it planned to exit from the its market in Columbus, Ohio, as well as its markets in Houston, Dallas, and Austin, Texas. All of these moves were made as a part of Peapod's strategic plan for growth and future profitability.

**34** Under Peapod's initial partnership agreement with Ahold, Peapod was to continue on as a stand-alone company, with Ahold supplying Peapod's goods, services, and fast pick fulfillment centers. However, in July of 2001, Ahold acquired all outstanding shares of Peapod and created a merger of Peapod with one of Ahold's subsidiaries.

**35** Peapod provided online shopping and delivery service in five metropolitan areas: Chicago, Boston, Southern Connecticut, Long Island and Washington, D.C. in 2003. Peapod employs a centralized distribution model in every market: in large markets, orders were picked, packed, loaded and delivered from a free-standing centralized fulfillment center; in smaller markets, Peapod establishes "fast-pick" centralized fulfillment centers adjacent to the facilities of our retail partners. Peapod's proprietary transportation routing system ensures on-time delivery and efficient truck and driver utilization.

# NETGROCER

**36**  NetGrocer.com was founded in 1996 and advertises itself as the first online grocer to sell nonperishable items nationwide (see Exhibits 13 and 14). NetGrocer services all 48 continental U.S. states and the District of Columbia. All customer orders were filled in its single, 120,000 square foot warehouse in North Brunswick, New Jersey. Orders were shipped via Federal Express and were guaranteed to reach any part of NetGrocer's service area within 2 to 4 days.

**EXHIBIT 13**
**Netgrocer.com**
**website**

**EXHIBIT 14**
**NetGrocer Shipping**
**Charges**

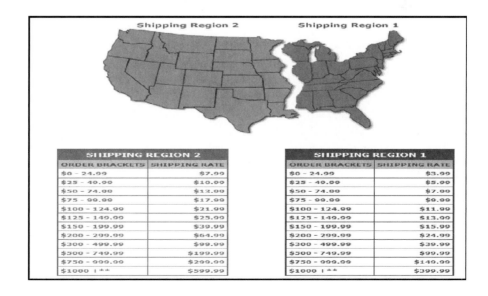

| SHIPPING REGION 2 | | SHIPPING REGION 1 | |
|---|---|---|---|
| ORDER BRACKETS | SHIPPING RATE | ORDER BRACKETS | SHIPPING RATE |
| $0 – 24.99 | $7.99 | $0 – 24.99 | $3.99 |
| $25 – 49.99 | $10.99 | $25 – 49.99 | $5.99 |
| $50 – 74.99 | $13.99 | $50 – 74.99 | $7.99 |
| $75 – 99.99 | $17.99 | $75 – 99.99 | $9.99 |
| $100 – 124.99 | $21.99 | $100 – 124.99 | $11.99 |
| $125 – 149.99 | $25.99 | $125 – 149.99 | $13.99 |
| $150 – 199.99 | $39.99 | $150 – 199.99 | $15.99 |
| $200 – 299.99 | $64.99 | $200 – 299.99 | $24.99 |
| $300 – 499.99 | $99.99 | $300 – 499.99 | $39.99 |
| $500 – 749.99 | $199.99 | $500 – 749.99 | $99.99 |
| $750 – 999.99 | $299.99 | $750 – 999.99 | $149.99 |
| $1000 +** | $599.99 | $1000 +** | $399.99 |

**37**     NetGrocer offered its customers a large selection of brand name and specialty nonperishable items that were difficult to find in a local supermarket. The key customer segment for NetGrocer's services were busy families, urban dwellers, special food needs groups (e.g. dieters, diabetics), and senior citizens. Customers purportedly enjoyed the benefits of convenient online shopping from home, 24 hours a day, access to thousands of products, and order delivery right to their home. Manufacturers also benefitted from NetGrocer, as they were able to distribute their products nationwide, rapidly and easily.

**38**     In 2002, NetGrocer became a part of a larger grocery enterprise. A new entity named NeXpansion was created which included the existing NetGrocer service, but also included a new service called Endless Aisle. Rather than competing with local grocery stores, Endless Aisle offered local grocers a way to greatly expand their product assortment. The way the program worked was through the installation of Endless Aisle kiosks into participating brick-and-mortar supermarkets. Shoppers could visit the kiosk to shop online for products that were not available in their grocery store, such as specialty products, regional hard-to-find items, and product categories that were not traditionally carried by grocery stores. The products offered through Endless Aisles were designed to complement, not compete, with the local grocery store's product selection. Consumers enjoy one-stop shopping for all of their grocery needs and local retailers benefitted from the Endless Aisles service because they were able to offer their customers easy access to a much wider range of products, without having to use valuable shelf space for products that had a lower sales velocity.

# Case 36 Honda Insight—Personal Hybrid

## James Johng, Yong-Joo Kang, Melissa A. Schilling, Jane Sul, Masayuki Takanashi

**1**   In 1997, Honda introduced a two-door gas/electric hybrid vehicle called the "Insight" to Japan. The Insight's fuel efficiency was rated at 61 miles per gallon in the city, and 68 miles per gallon on the highway, and its battery did not need to be plugged in for recharging. By 1999, Honda was selling the Insight in the United States, and winning accolades from environmental groups. In 2000 the Sierra Club gave Honda its "Award for Excellence in Environmental Engineering," and in 2002 the Environmental Protection Agency rated the Insight the most fuel-efficient vehicle sold in the United States for the 2003 model year.

**2**   Developing environmentally friendly automobiles was not a new strategy for Honda. In fact, Honda's work on developing cleaner transportation alternatives had begun decades earlier (see Exhibit 1, Honda's Environment and Technology Timeline). Gaining mass market acceptance of such alternatives, however, had proven somewhat more challenging.

## HISTORY OF HONDA

**3**   Honda was founded by Mr. Soichiro Honda (1906–1991) in 1946 as the Honda Technical Research Institute. The company began as a developer of engines for bicycles, but by 1949 it had produced its first motorcycle, called the "Dream." In 1959, Honda entered the U.S. market by opening the American Honda Motor Company. A few years later, in 1963, Honda released its first sports car, the S500, in Japan. Honda Motor Co. Inc. grew rapidly to become one of the largest automobile companies in the world. Its "Glocalization" strategy of building factories around the world that would meet the need of local customers had resulted in a total worldwide presence of more than 100 factories in 33 countries. Furthermore, while other auto manufacturers engaged in a frenzy of merger and acquisition activities in the late 1990s, Honda steadfastly maintained its independence. In 2002, it was Japan's third-largest auto manufacturer (after Toyota and Nissan), and the world's largest motorcycle manufacturer, with sales of more than $55 billion (see Exhibit 2 for geographic and product breakdown of sales). In 2002, it was ranked number 41 in Fortune's Global Most Admired Companies.

### Honda's Environmental Orientation

At Honda, being an environmental leader means never uttering the words, "It can't be done." That's why for more than two decades Honda has led the way in balancing what consumers want with what the environment needs. Technologies change over time—but our commitment to the environment never will.

*Honda Corporate*

Source: James Johng, Yong-Joo Kang, Melissa A. Schilling, Jane Sul and Masayuki Takanashi prepared this case as the basis for class discussion rather than to illustrate either effective or ineffective handling of an administrative situation. The authors wish to gratefully acknowledge the help and support of our classmates for their input and comments. All rights reserved to the authors. Copyright© 2003 Melissa A. Schilling.

**EXHIBIT 1**
Honda's Environment and Technology Timeline

**1970**

**Efficient Start:**
The lightweight and fuel-efficient N600 is the first Honda car sold in America.

**The World's First:**
CVCC (Compound Vortex Controlled Combustion) technology is announced by Honda, which in 1975 led to the world's first engine to comply with the 1970 Clean Air Act emission requirement without a catalytic converter.

**1971**

**1973**

**Marine Engines:**
Since 1973, Honda has manufactured only four-stroke outboard motors, which are about 90% cleaner, 50% more fuel-efficient and 50% quieter than typical two-stroke outboard motors that release oil directly into the water. In 1998, Honda became the first company with an entire line of high-performance outboard motors to meet the Environmental Protection Agency's (EPA) year 2006 emission standard.

**Fuel-Efficiency Leadership:**
The Honda Civic CVCC is ranked first in fuel efficiency in the EPA's first-ever list of the Top 10 fuel-efficient cars.

**1977**

**1986**

**50-Plus:**
The Civic CRX-HF is the first mass-produced four-cylinder car to break the 50 miles per gallon fuel-economy mark.

**Redefining the Possible:**
The foundation technology for Honda's achievements in high performance, low emissions, and high fuel efficiency is announced: the VTEC™ (variable valve timing and lift electronic control) automobile engine.

**1988**

**1989**

**Solvent-Free:**
Honda becomes the first automaker in America to use solvent-free waterborne paint in mass production.

**Continued Leadership:**
Fuel-economy leadership puts four Honda models on the EPA's list of the Top 10 fuel-efficient cars.

**1995**

**The First Lev:**
The 1996 Honda Civic is the first gasoline-powered car to meet California's Low-Emission Vehicle (LEV) standards, reducing smog-related hydrocarbon pollutants by 70% below federal standards.

**Solar Power:**
Honda's two-passenger solar car, the Dream, breaks World Solar Challenge records.

**1996**

**The One and Only:**
The only automatic transmission vehicle to make the EPA's Top 10 fuel-efficient cars: the Honda Civic HX Coupe with CVT (continuously variable transmission).

**Getting to Zero:**
Honda announces a virtually pollution-free, gasoline-powered internal-combustion engine, the ZLEV (Zero-Level-Emission Vehicle).

**1997**

**Clean and Quiet Trimmers:**
Honda enters the handheld power-equipment market with an incredibly quiet, fuel-efficient and virtually smoke-free trimmer/brushcutter powered by the world's first 360-degree inclinable, four-stroke miniengine.

# EXHIBIT 1
*(continued)*

**Nationwide Rollout:**
Honda is the first manufacturer to voluntarily make its Low-Emission Vehicles available in all 50 states. By 1999, two-thirds of all Honda cars sold in the United States are voluntarily equipped with advanced low-emission technology.

**EV Plus:**
With an EPA-rated city driving range of 125 miles, Honda begins leasing the first four-passenger electric vehicle with advanced battery technology to consumers.

**Cleanest in the World:**
Production begins on the 1998 Honda *Civic GX* natural-gas vehicle. Manufactured with a sealed evaporative-fuel system, the GX is recognized by the EPA as being the cleanest internal-combustion engine in the world.

**HYPER:**
Honda introduces the HYPER VTEC four-stroke engine in the CB400 motorcycle in Japan, lowering emissions and increasing fuel efficiency, while also improving performance. Honda has committed to to producing motorcycles and scooters with only four-stroke engines for on-road use by the year 2002.

**SULEV Accord:**
The *2000 Accord* is the first gasoline vehicle to meet CARB's Super-Ultra-Low-Emission standard.

**Civic Hybrid:**
The Honda *Civic Hybrid* ushers in a new era of hybrid technology, and Honda becomes the first to mass produce the hybrid powertrain to the consumer market.

**"Green" Facility:**
*Honda opens* a a 212,888-square-foot warehouse, designed, constructed, and now operating using environmentally friendly products and practices. Honda's new "green" facility will supply parts to nine Western states and act as a training center and zone office in Gresham, Oregon.

**Ultra-Low:**
The first gasoline-powered car in America to meet the California Air Resources Board's Ultra-Low-Emission-Vehicle (ULEV) standard—the toughest in the country—the 1998 Accord ULEV with an automatic transmission goes on sale.

**1998**  **Low-Emission Minivan:**
Available with less than half the smog-producing emissions than federal requirements for minivans, the 1999-model-year *Odyssey* minivan is an environmental leader

**1999**  **Honda's Hybrid Technology:**
Honda develops a fuel-efficient low-emission *hybrid* engine that achieves 61 mpg city/70 mpg highway (EPA fuel-economy estimates), with a gasoline engine and an electric motor.

**2000**  **Responsible Fun:**
The high-performance Honda *S2000* roadster meets the strict LEV standard with a high-revving, 240-horsepower engine.

**2001**  **Fuel Efficiency:**
For the third straight year, the Honda *Insight* is named the "Most Fuel-Efficient Car in America" by the EPA.

**2002**  **Fuel Cell Certification:**
The *FCX* from Honda becomes the first fuel-cell vehicle in the world to receive government certification. Honda once again proves its commitment to a cleaner environment by paving the way for the commercial use of fuel-cell vehicles.

**EXHIBIT 2**
Honda's 2002 Sales:
Geographic and
Product Breakdowns

Source: Hoovers.com

| | 2002 Sales | | | 2002 Product Breakdown | |
|---|---|---|---|---|---|
| | $ millions | Percent of total | | $ millions | Percent of total |
| North America | 32,330 | 46 | Automobiles | 44,501 | 80 |
| Japan | 28,600 | 41 | Motorcycles | 7,114 | 13 |
| Europe | 4,529 | 7 | Financial services | 1,571 | 3 |
| Other regions | 4,164 | 6 | Other | 2,205 | 4 |
| Adjustments | (14,370) | — | Adjustments | (138) | — |
| Total | 55,253 | 100 | Total | 55,253 | 100 |

**EXHIBIT 3**
Honda's U.S. Auto
Production and Total
Factory Emissions

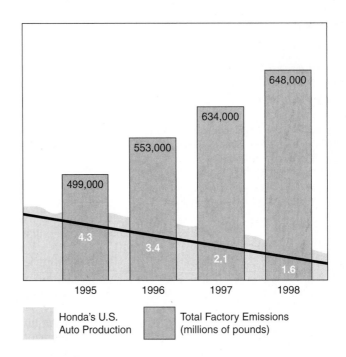

4    In 1972, Honda introduced the Civic, which became an immediate success, ranking first in U.S. fuel-economy tests for four consecutive years starting in 1974. Through the 1980s and 1990s, Honda made a number of advancements in environmentally friendly transportation. In 1986, it developed the first mass-produced four-cylinder car that could break the 50 miles per gallon barrier, the Civic CRX-HF. In 1989, it became the first auto manufacturer in the United States to use solvent-free paint in its mass production facilities. In 1996, Honda introduced a record-breaking solar powered car, and in 1998 it introduced a completely electric vehicle. Though the electric car was not a commercial success, developing the electric vehicle built a foundation of expertise that Honda would later employ in its development of fuel cell technology. Fuel cells were considered to offer great potential for the eventual replacement of combustion engines.

5    Honda's environmental strategies also extend into its factory design and alternative transportation initiatives. Honda's Green Factory program has driven down its chemical emissions by more than 65 percent per car produced (see Exhibit 3).

6    Honda also worked with the Bay Area Rapid Transit, CalTrans, University of California Davis, and University of California, Riverside to develop innovative car-sharing programs

called "CarLink" and "Intellishare." Both programs encouraged individuals to share the use of fuel-efficient Honda models for commuting and personal errands. These projects were developed with the intention of developing a greater understanding of whether such programs would be effective, and what the obstacles would be to their implementation.

# HYBRID ELECTRIC VEHICLES (HEVS)

**7**  By the 1980s and 1990s, under growing pressure from organizations such as the Environmental Protection Agency (EPA), a few automobile manufacturers had introduced electric vehicles (EVs) (see Exhibit 4 for an interesting history of the electric vehicle). None of these vehicles, however, had achieved widespread acceptance or commercial success. The electric vehicle's limited range and its need to be plugged in for recharging were obstacles to mass market adoption. However, by the late 1990s, automobile manufacturers were tinkering with hybrid vehicles that offered a compromise between the combustion engine's environmental impact and the electric vehicle's awkwardness. Both Honda and Toyota introduced hybrids (the Insight and Prius, respectively) in Japan in 1997. After some initial commercial success, both companies brought their hybrid models to the United States in 1999.

**8**  HEVs are electric vehicles that use another source of energy besides the battery used by EVs. In most cases, the alternative power source is the internal combustion engine. In such cases, the HEV combines the internal combustion engine with the battery and electric motor, creating a vehicle that is able to provide at least two times the fuel economy of a gasoline-only vehicle. Basically, the HEV is able to utilize the benefits of both power systems, by providing the fuel economy and environmental friendliness of an EV with the torque and range of a gasoline vehicle. This results in a "best of both worlds" vehicle. While some industry experts argued that HEVs were a temporary solution that would give way to vehicles with better battery technology in the future, others believed that it would be a significant amount of time before other clean cars would provide real competition to the hybrids.[1]

## Advantages of HEVs

**9**  HEVs have several advantages over gasoline vehicles, such as regenerative braking capability, reduced engine weight, lowered overall vehicle weight, and increased fuel efficiency, and decreased emissions. First, the regenerative braking capability of HEVs helps to minimize energy loss and recover the energy used to slow down or stop a vehicle. Given this fact, engines can also be sized to accommodate average loads instead of peak loads, significantly reducing the engine weight of HEVs. Additionally, the special lightweight materials that are used for the manufacture of HEVs further reduce the overall vehicle weight of the vehicle. Finally, both the lowered vehicle weight and the dual power system greatly increase the HEV's fuel efficiency and reduce its emissions.

**10**  In developing HEVs, automobile manufacturers kept in mind that consumers were most concerned with four specific attributes (performance, reliability, safety, and fun) when purchasing cars.[2] Since the performance of the HEVs were in most cases on par with or better than the conventional vehicles, consumers were presented with a very competitive substitute for their conventional vehicles. In addition, since the feel and drive of the HEVs were designed to be similar in every way to the gasoline vehicles, HEVs required almost no education of the consumer. As stated by Thomas G. Elliot, executive vice-president of North American Honda, "Hybrids are the kind of car that most consumers can live with.

---

[1] "Hybrid Cars Try Merging Into the Mainstream," *Reuters News Service,* May 30, 2002.
[2] "An 'Insight'ful First Year," *American Honda Motor Co, Ltd.,* February 6, 2001.

**EXHIBIT 4**
**History of Electric Vehicles (Evs)**

Electric vehicles (EVs) are vehicles that are powered by an electric motor instead of an internal combustion engine. This means that unlike the conventional gasoline vehicles, the motor is driven by power stored in batteries. Counter to popular belief, EVs have a very long history. In fact, EVs were seen soon after Joseph Henry first introduced the DC powered motor in 1830.

### The Early Years (1890 to 1930)

One of the first EVs, the 1902 Wood's Electric Phaeton, was simply a horseless carriage powered by electricity. Costing about $2000, the Phaeton had a range of approximately 18 miles and reached a maximum speed of only 14 mph. Woods would go on to develop a hybrid car that incorporated both an internal combustion engine and an electric motor in 1916.

Electric cars outsold both steam and gasoline powered cars in 1899 and 1900. This success was attributed to the many advantages offered by the EVs, such as its lack of vibration, smell, and noise that was normally associated with gasoline cars, and faster start-up times compared to the steam cars. Also, the EV's limited range did not pose a serious constraint since most travel during this time period was for local commuting.

But this success was not long-lived due to some major developments that took place in the early 1900s. The development of better road systems increased the demand for longer-range vehicles. The discovery of crude oil in Texas made gasoline affordable for the average consumer. Furthermore, Henry Ford's mass production of internal combustion engine vehicles brought their prices down to the $500 to $1000 range, making them considerably less expensive than a typical electric vehicle.

### The Middle Years (1930 to 1990)

By about 1935, EVs had all but vanished. It was not until the 1960s that EVs reemerged, driven by a growing need for more environmentally friendly cars. At this time research and development of the EVs started up once again. During the 1960s and 1970s, companies such as Battronic, Sebring-Vanguard, and the Elcar Corporation developed a number of EVs. These EVs had an average top speed of about 40 to 45 mph, a range of approximately 50 to 60 miles, and their batteries required recharging. Some were adopted for use as passenger busses or delivery vehicles (e.g., in 1975, the U.S. Postal Service bought 350 electric jeeps from the American Motor Company to be used in a test program), but the vehicles failed to penetrate the mass market.

### Recent Years (1990 to present)

The 1990s brought about a resurgence in EVs due to several legislative and regulatory events that occurred in the United States, such as the 1990 Clean Air Act Amendment, the U.S. 1992 Energy Policy Act, and regulations issued by the California Air Resources Board (CARB). With the government taking a strong stance on air pollution control, many states passed laws that required reductions in gasoline use and vehicle emissions. In fact, certain states even issued Zero Emission Vehicle requirements.

Given this pressure from the government, the "Big Three" U.S. automobile manufacturers (General Motors, Ford, and DaimlerChrysler), together with the U.S. Department of Energy, and several other companies became actively involved in EV development through the Partnership for a New Generation of Vehicles (PNGV). Through this collaboration, several EVs were developed, including the Solectria Geo Metro, which was powered by an alternating current motor and lead-acid battery, and the Ford Ecostar utility van, which was powered by an alternating current motor and sodium sulfur battery.

By the late 1990s, automobile manufacturers such as GM, Honda, Toyota, Nissan, and Ford had released a variety of EVs, but the EV did not catch on with the consumers. The EVs were not only very expensive (between $30,000 and $40,000 on average), but also required their owners to plug the vehicles into an electrical outlet for recharging. This added inconvenience made consumers shy away from the EVs.

Then in 1997, Toyota and Honda released the world's first hybrid electric vehicles (HEV), Toyota's Prius, and Honda's Insight. These hybrids not only had much lower emissions than solely gasoline-powered vehicles, but also did not require the owners to plug the vehicles in to an outlet like the EVs did. Unlike purely electric vehicles, hybrid electric vehicles gradually began to penetrate mainstream consumer markets.

The technology is almost transparent to them,"[3] Thus, for the driver, the HEV offered similar or superior performance compared to a conventional vehicle and, and at the same time, provided a practical way for consumers to help save the environment and still take advantage of the added benefit of fuel cost savings and government tax incentives.

11    The only downside to the HEV was its price. As of mid-2002, HEVs in the United States cost around $4,000 more than equivalent standard models. Many believed that the lackluster growth in sales of HEVs would soon change once the cost issues were resolved. In fact, as Mr. Ted Miller, a senior official of the U.S. advanced battery consortium (USABC) put it, "If you can deliver a hybrid vehicle to a customer for nearly the same price as a typical (nonhybrid) vehicle, demand can be fairly significant."[4]

### Types of Hybrid Systems

12    There are basically two types of hybrid configurations: the parallel hybrid and the series hybrid system (see Exhibit 5). Series hybrids use the internal combustion engine in connec-

**EXHIBIT 5**
**Parallel and Series Configured Hybrids**

Source: DOE HEV Website (http://www.ott.doe.gov/hev/).

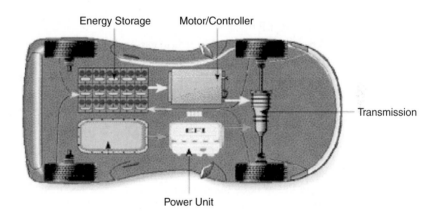

**Parallel Configuration**

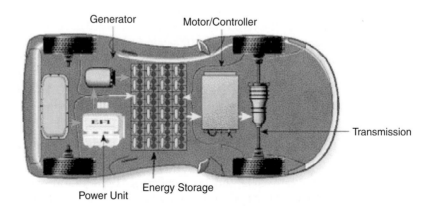

**Series Configuration**

[3]"Q&A with Thomas Elliot," *BusinessWeek Online,* August 14, 2000.
[4]"Low Growth Seen for HEVs," *Reuters News Service,* September 11, 2002.

tion with a generator to supply electricity for the battery and the electric motor. Since the series HEVs have no direct mechanical connection between the hybrid power unit and the wheels, all motive power is transferred electrically to a motor that drives the wheels. Some benefits of a series configuration over a parallel configuration are: (1) the engine never idles, which reduces vehicle emissions; (2) the combustion engine helps to run the generator at optimum levels; and (3) it provides greater choice of vehicle components.

13    On the other hand, the parallel hybrid, or power-assist vehicle, has a direct mechanical connection between the hybrid power unit and the wheels, and at the same time, it has an electric motor driving the wheels. This means that a hybrid configuration will allow a vehicle to use the power from the internal combustion engine for highway driving and then switch to the power from the electric motor for accelerating. Some benefits of a parallel configuration over the series configuration are: (1) the vehicle has more power, since it is supplied simultaneously with power from both the engine and the batteries; (2) it does not need a generator like the series configuration as the motor regenerates the batteries; and (3) it is more efficient.

### The Honda Insight

14    The Insight is a two-door hybrid gasoline-electric car that has been known to run up to seventy miles on a single gallon of gasoline on the highway and sixty-one miles in the city. The Insight's fuel efficiency was achieved in two primary ways. First, the car's electric motor produced its power from a nickel metal hydride battery pack that was continuously charged by regenerative braking. Regenerative braking permits energy that would be wasted by braking to be recaptured for future usage. Second, the Insight's body was light and aerodynamic. The frame and body were constructed mostly of aluminum, shaving almost 40 percent off a car's typical weight. Aluminum is both lighter and more rigid than traditional steel (Honda had acquired extensive expertise in the design of aluminum car bodies with its pioneering work on the Acura NSX sports car). The Insight's fenders were made of recyclable plastic. It also employed aluminum alloy wheels, a magnesium oil pan, and plastic front head cover, which allowed the Insight to tip the scales at only 1,850 lbs. All this helped to improve the Insight's energy efficiency while also increasing its rigidity. The teardrop shaped body, enclosed rear wheel wells, and an under-car cover of the car resulted in a coefficient of drag (Cd) of only 0.25, the lowest Cd of any production car.

15    The Insight used a simplified parallel hybrid powertrain whereby an electric motor was coupled to the gasoline motor at the spot where the flywheel usually goes. Called the Integrated Motor Assist (IMA) system, it consisted of Honda's VTEC-E gasoline engine and a permanent magnet electric motor in either a 5-speed manual transmission or a continuously variable transmission (CVT). In the Insight's parallel hybrid arrangement, the electric motor added power to the engine's efforts under hard acceleration, which produced less mechanical loss. But this came at a cost. Since both motors were on the same shaft, the electric motor could not be used exclusively during acceleration.

## COMPETITION IN THE HYBRID ELECTRIC VEHICLE INDUSTRY

16    As of early 2002, only two companies, Honda and Toyota, had successfully penetrated the hybrid market. Compared to their Japanese rivals, the "Big Three" U.S. automakers were basically playing catch-up. Although all of them had schedules to release their own HEVs in the near future, Honda and Toyota were quickly positioning themselves as the carmakers of the future (see Exhibit 6 for pictures of the hybrid competitors). Honda, in particular, was perceived to be a leader in technology by many such as Daniel Becker, director of global

**EXHIBIT 6** **Hybrid Competitors**

## Toyota Prius

## GM Precept Concept Car

## Ford Prodigy Concept Car        ## Ford Escape

## DaimlerChrysler

## 2002 Jeep Liberty
## Limited Edition

warming policy for the Sierra Club, who said the Honda "started the race for hybrids" and "put on vehicles fuel-saving technologies that Detroit only keeps on the shelves."[5]

**17**     Though these two companies were unlikely to be without competition for very much longer, they were "gaining valuable experience in the production of sleek, affordable, and environmentally friendly cars."[6] In fact, both companies had stepped up schedules to release more HEVs in an effort to maintain their position. For example, in mid-2002, Honda released a hybrid version of its very popular Civic.

### Toyota

**18**     While the Toyota Prius and the Insight had a lot in common, there were some interesting differences between the two cars in terms of format, features, technologies employed, and performance. Though the two cars could be seen as rivals within the same market, the Insight and the Prius were in many ways not direct competitors, but rather two different offerings. The differences between the two cars might not have seemed significant to some consumers but they were different enough to appeal to different market segments. This was partly a result of the strategic direction the two companies decided to adopt when they entered the market, in order to differentiate themselves, and partly a result of moves made early on in the development of the two vehicles and the technologies available to them.

**19**     Like the Honda Insight, the Toyota Prius utilized advanced engineering to combine a gas engine with an electric motor to create an environmentally conscious, fuel-efficient, hybrid sedan that gets about 52-mpg city and 45-mpg highway. While the Insight achieved better efficiency than the Prius in both city and highway driving, the Prius was unique in that its city efficiency was better than its highway efficiency. In addition, unlike the Insight, the Prius was a four-door mid-sized sedan with back seats for extra passengers, something that the two-door Honda Insight lacked. Thus, the Prius made more sense for people who regularly traveled with more than two people and could serve as the one and only car for a family.

**20**     The Prius utilized a planetary gear arrangement between the gasoline and electric powertrains, which made the Prius much more than a car with an electric motor tacked on to the existing drivetrain. Gearing the two motors appropriately during acceleration for the Prius was done by an onboard computer, which Toyota called the Toyota Hybrid System (THS). This system constantly scanned the usage of the electric motor to make it either deliver power to the wheels or to generate electricity from excess engine power, achieved by varying clutches that decided how much engine or motor power entered the planetary gears and got delivered to the wheels. This made the gearing on the Prius unlike any conventional automatic or standard transmission and enabled the Prius to have ample power.

### Other Competitors

**21**     Together with the U.S. Department of Energy, the "Big Three" U.S. automobile manufacturers formed a partnership to develop and produce HEVs. Through this program, the three automobile manufacturers had each developed possible future competitors to the Honda Insight.

**22**     General Motors (GM) developed the Gen2 Stirling HEV in 1998 and was planning on further enhancing the Gen2's designs in order to release another concept car called the GM Precept. Though GM did not have a hybrid car commercially available as of 2002, it was doing a lot of research in this area and was slated to release an electric version of its Chevy

[5]"Honda Takes Up Case in U.S. for Green Energy," *New York Times,* June 13, 2002.
[6]*Paul Raeburn,* "Commentary: The Japanese Are Making the Right Bet on Hybrids," *BusinessWeek Online,* August 14, 2002.

Silverado in 2004. Ford had also developed several prototypes, such as the Ford P2000 and the Ford Prodigy through the partnership program, but was a little further along in releasing a HEV vehicle than GM was. The Ford Escape, a sports-utility HEV vehicle, was slated to be released in 2003 and would try to capitalize on both the movement towards cleaner cars and the popularity of sports utility vehicles at the same time. Though the Ford Escape would not likely compete directly with the Insight, it illustrated the fact that other competitors were well on their way to releasing viable commercial HEV vehicles. Similar to Ford, DaimlerChrysler was another automaker that had been able to release a commercially viable HEV vehicle. Through its development of the ESX2 and ESX3, DaimlerChrysler had developed and showcased a hybrid version of its popular sport utility vehicle, the Jeep® Liberty, with its patented Through-the-Road (TTR) hybrid system. The Liberty HEV achieved a 30 percent improvement in fuel efficiency compared with a conventional six-cylinder Liberty, without sacrificing the vehicle's utility, comfort, or performance. In addition, DaimlerChrysler was slated to release an electric version of its Dodge Durango sometime in the near future.

23    In addition to these three automakers, several other companies, such as Volvo and Mazda, had also expressed intentions of entering the HEV market so that they would not be left out of the environmentally friendly automobile market. Flexible fuel automobiles from Volkswagen and alternative-fuel cars from Mitsubishi were also ready to be introduced. French carmaker Renault was also working together with Chrysler to release HEVs as well.

24    Finally, HEVs would also see potential competition from other alternative fuel cars. Vehicles that utilized fuel cells, ethanol, methanol, natural gas, LPG, biofuels, hydrogen, and reformulated gasoline were all potential competitors in the clean-car market.

# OTHER STAKEHOLDERS IN THE HEV MARKET

25    HEVs were subject to pressures from other key players such as the government and environmental organizations. Governmental pressures on automobile manufacturers to develop cleaner vehicles came in the form of regulations, partnerships, and tax incentives, while environmental organizations exerted pressure through the media and use of lobbies. Each player was significant in its own right in driving the development of HEVs.

### The Department of Energy

26    The Department of Energy began the Hybrid Electric Vehicle (HEV) Program in 1993. The HEV program was developed as a five-year cost-shared program that was a partnership between the U.S. department of Energy and the three largest American auto manufacturers: General Motors, Ford, and DaimlerChrysler. The plan called for the automakers to produce production-feasible HEV engines by 1998, first generation prototypes by 2000, and market-ready HEVs by 2003. The goal of the program was to produce vehicles that achieved at least double the fuel efficiency of today's cars. Ideally, the goal was to develop an automobile that traveled 80 mpg and had comparable performance, safety, and costs. As the program progressed, the goals began to merge with the goals of the Partnership for a New Generation of Vehicles (PNGV).

### Partnership for a New Generation of Vehicles (PNGV)

27    PNGV was a partnership between the U.S. government and the "Big Three" automakers that aimed to strengthen America's competitiveness by developing technologies for a new generation of vehicles. The goals of the PNGV were to significantly improve national competitiveness in manufacturing, to implement commercially viable innovations from ongoing research in conventional vehicles, and to develop vehicles that could achieve up to three

times the fuel efficiency of comparable 1994 family sedans. But despite the bold goals of the PNGV, the "Big Three" had been "slow to bring alternative technologies to the market."[7]

### California State

28  California was the only state that was allowed under the Clean Air Act in 1967, to set its own tougher regulations for emissions, a loophole that existed because of the previously extreme levels of smog around Los Angeles. Despite fierce opposition from the car and oil industry, in July 2002, California became the first state in the nation to regulate emissions of the greenhouse gas carbon dioxide from motor vehicles through the passing of the California Climate Bill. The law granted the California Air Resources Board (CARB) power to set economically feasible maximums on emissions standards for gases such as carbon dioxide. Those standards would be set by 2005 and were required in automobiles sold by 2009. Because the Clean Air Act allowed any state to adopt California's strict emissions standards in place of weaker federal rules, a number of states, including New York, Massachusetts, Maine, and Vermont followed in California's footsteps. It was believed that the law would ultimately force automakers to focus more on fuel-efficient vehicles, including HEVs.

### Internal Revenue Service

29  In August 2002, the U.S. Internal Revenue Service made the Prius the first hybrid car for which drivers could claim a $2,000 clean-burning fuel federal income tax deduction. Honda also applied for certification and attained approval from the IRS in September of 2002, which made the Insight and the hybrid version of its Civic model eligible for the same tax break. Such tax incentives are expected to be available to almost all future HEVs in the market in an effort to popularize the HEVs and make HEVs more affordable.

### The Sierra Club

30  The Sierra Club was extremely active in the push for more environmentally safe vehicles. They praised the efforts of Honda and Toyota by honoring both companies with awards for excellence in environmental engineering, making it the first time in The Sierra Club's 108-year history that an automobile manufacturer had been honored (see Exhibit 7). Viewing the hybrid cars as the "wave of the present,"[8] The Sierra Club was focused on trying to push the "Big Three" into releasing their HEVs. In fact, in June 2002, The Sierra Club announced the launch of a three-year campaign to urge the "Big Three" automakers to improve the fuel economy of their vehicles.

31  Besides pressuring the automakers directly, The Sierra Club also used public opinion polls to indirectly pressure the automakers. One such public opinion research poll showed that consumers wanted automakers to offer cars and trucks with better fuel economy. This research highlighted that Americans wished to reduce America's dependence on foreign oil, save money at the gas pump, and cut pollution. The Sierra Club hoped that campaigns such as this would urge consumers to ask auto dealers for a "Freedom Option Package," a set of fuel-saving components which could be added to most standard models. If this proved to be successful, the fleets of the "Big Three" would be improved to gas mileages of 40 miles per gallon or more. In addition, this campaign would also mobilize the club's 700,000 members across the country to hold events at local auto dealers, highlighting public demand for these fuel-saving technologies. Such pressures would only bring about further development of

---

[7]Beth Belton, "The Man Behind Toyota's Green Machine," *BusinessWeek Online,* November 13, 2000.
[8]Paul Raeburn, "Commentary: The Japanese Are Making the Right Bet on Hybrids," *BusinessWeek Online,* August 14, 2002.

**EXHIBIT 7**
Honda Insight
Accolades

Source: "Honda Insight Tops
Rankings in 2001 ACEEE
Green Book," *PR Newswire,
February 23, 2001*

| Agency | Award |
| --- | --- |
| *Popular Mechanics* | Design & Engineering Award |
| *Automobile* Magazine | 2000 Technology of the Year |
| *Popular Science* | Best of What's New Award |
| American Woman Motorscene | Most Likely to Change the World |
| Clean Car Coalition | Clean Car Salute |
| Edmunds.com | Most Significant New Vehicle |
| The Sierra Club | Environmental Engineering Award |
| American Council for an Energy Efficient Economy (ACEEE) | Number 1 gasoline-powered performer for 2000 |
| U.S. DOE and Environmental Protection Agency | Number 1 fuel-efficient vehicle sold in America |

environmentally friendly vehicles, such as the HEVs, and spur the automobile industry into adopting stricter standards for vehicle emissions.

### Other Players

**32**　Besides those mentioned above, agencies such as the Environmental Protection Agency (EPA) were also fighting for tougher emissions standards that would force automakers to produce clean-cars such as the HEV. Oil companies, like ExxonMobil, were also key players in the future of environmentally friendly automobiles such as the fuel cell cars. In fact, the oil companies were participating in many clean-car initiatives and collaborative research, which would significantly affect the future of HEVs.

## HONDA'S STRATEGIES FOR THE INSIGHT

### New Product Development Process

**33**　Honda's new product development process for the Insight was characterized by three distinct stages: the concept stage, the preproduction stage, and the production stage (see Exhibit 8 for pictures and specifications of each stage).

### Concept Stage: The "J-VX"

**34**　At the 1997 Tokyo Motor Show, Honda showed its ambition for a hybrid gas-electric car in the form of the J-VX concept car. The J-VX was presented as a superefficient sports car. Much of the focus was on J-VX's sporty side with special emphasis on the light materials as giving it the "quick, agile handling only available in lightweight sports cars." Nonetheless, J-VX was designed to achieve a new level of efficiency and low emissions with a fuel efficiency of 30 km/liter.

**35**　　The J-VX had a stereotypical concept car radical design with its primary color design, and air belts (seatbelts that would inflate much like airbags). In addition, the entire roof of the J-VX concept car was tinted glass. J-VX's IMA powertrain utilized an ultracapacitor rather than batteries for energy storage. Rather than storing electrical energy chemically, capacitors stored a charge in the form of electrons. A capacitor has the advantage of a virtually unlimited lifetime, and the ability to deliver its power very quickly. However, this ability to release the energy very quickly would prove to be very dangerous, particularly in an accident.

## EXHIBIT 8
**New Product Development Process for the Insight**

Source: Insight Central Website (http://www.insightcentral.net)

**Honda J-VX (1997)**
**Classification:** Concept car
**Propulsion:** Gasoline-electric hybrid
**Gas engine:** 1.0 liter, 3 cylinder VTEC
**Electrical Storage:** Ultra-capacitor

**Honda VV (Early 1999)**
**Classification:** Pre-production prototype
**Propulsion:** Gasoline-electric hybrid
**Gas engine:** 1.0 liter, 3 cylinder VTEC
**Electrical Storage:** NiMH battery

**Honda Insight (Late 1999)**
**Classification:** Production car
**Propulsion:** Gasoline-electric hybrid
**Gas engine:** 1.0 liter, 3 cylinder VTEC
**Electrical Storage:** NiMH battery

### Pre-production Stage: The "VV"

36    While Honda's production car was based on the J-VX with the same 30 km/liter (70 mpg) fuel efficiency level, changes had to be made to the J-VX concept to ensure the creation of a more practical product that consumers would want to buy. Kazuhiko Tsunoda, chief engineer of the Insight project, stated that the Insight had to be "a real-world product for the global market." Honda had made previous advances, such as the Natural Gas Civic GX, but did not receive favorable reviews by the customers. Thus, Honda set the following goals: (1) to create the world's most efficient production car, and to achieve extremely low emissions; (2) to make the car fun to drive; (3) to achieve the levels of safety and comfort that consumers expect; and (4) to be able to sell at reasonable prices.

37    On January 4, 1999, Honda unveiled its preproduction prototype hybrid at the North American International Auto Show in Detroit. The VV coupe shown at this time was very similar to the final production car. The car was to achieve 70 mpg, weigh less than 2,000 pounds, and to meet ULEV emissions levels. Although the hybrid propulsion system re-

mained much the same, rather than a capacitor, a battery was used for energy storage. The internal combustion engine underwent much development to further reduce weight and friction while improving emissions.

**38** With further investment in body technologies, the VV coupe enjoyed even better aerodynamics. Although a hybrid gas-electric powerplant was an integral part of the final production car, Honda viewed that the body technology was just as important in ensuring energy efficiency. The aerodynamics and lightweight aluminum construction of the body were to play a big role in reducing its energy requirements.

**39** Rear seats were eliminated for more cargo area, better aerodynamics, and further weight savings. The glass roof also disappeared, as it would have added to both the weight and expense of the car. With the elimination of the rear seats and glass roof, the Insight began to take on more similarity to the last generation Honda. The car was no longer classified as a sports car. More emphasis was put on efficiency and low emissions. However, the fun-to-drive sporty nature was still important.

### Production Stage: The Insight

**40** The production car, the Honda Insight, was almost identical to the VV coupe in technology and engineering. Honda had made a few minor cosmetic and functional developments to ensure a product ready for full production. The headlight shape was refined, the aluminum wheels lost their plastic covers, a rear wiper was added, and the interior appearance was modified slightly. In addition, the entire engine bay's plastic cover was removed to make room for additional sound insulation on the hood.

### Market Entry

**41** Toyota Motor Corp.'s Prius had been the world's first hybrid car when it was released in 1997. However Toyota made the strategic choice to release the Prius only in Japan. Honda responded by quickly introducing its Insight, and being first to bring the hybrid to North America. Honda made a considerable commitment to get this title of "first to the (American) market" and as stated by an engineer involved in the development of the Insight, "we (Honda) were particular about becoming first."[9] This strategic move helped Honda reinstate its prominence in the development of environmentally friendly vehicles.

**42** Since its release, sales of the Honda Insight had been better than expected, leading many industry analysts to question whether Honda's timing was more a result of "serendipity, not strategy" (see Exhibits 9, 10 and 11).[10] The Insight, as well as the Prius, hit the U.S. market at a time when gas prices in the United States were rising, averaging around $1.65 a gallon nationwide and over $2.00 in the Midwest. The debate regarding the Insight's timing had been argued both ways by the different camps. But whether the success of the product was due to planning or luck, Honda's moves paid off. The success of the Insight in penetrating the U.S. market was particularly notable given that the hybrid technology was new for most consumers and small cars were usually the industry's slowest sellers.

### Marketing

**43** Comparisons between the Honda Insight and the Toyota Prius were inevitable. Technologically the two cars were some of the most advanced cars ever offered to consumers, and were both marketed as "green" cars. In order to differentiate the cars, Honda and Toyota used

[9]"Toyota, Honda Forge Ahead in Hybrid Vehicle Development," *AP Newswire,* March 13, 2002.
[10]David Welch and Larry Armstrong, "A Fast (and Lucky) Start for Japan's Hybrid Cars," *Business Week Online,* July 6, 2000.

**EXHIBIT 9**
Honda Insight Sales
Statistics

Source: American Honda
Motor Co.

| Insight Sales Statistics: United States | | | | |
|---|---|---|---|---|
| **Monthly Sales** | **1999** | **2000** | **2001** | **2002** |
| January | — | 51 | 294 | 237 |
| February | — | 159 | 340 | 221 |
| March | — | 187 | 424 | — |
| April | — | 357 | 573 | — |
| May | — | 380 | 903 | — |
| June | — | 412 | 439 | — |
| July | — | 354 | 323 | — |
| August | — | 490 | 305 | — |
| September | — | 446 | 300 | — |
| October | — | 375 | 506 | — |
| November | — | 291 | 242 | — |
| December | 17 | 286 | 319 | — |
| **Annual Sales** | **17** | **3,788** | **4,968** | **458** |
| **Total to date** | **9,231** | *(as of March 1, 2002)* | | |

| Comparison of Worldwide Sales with Other Models | |
|---|---|
| **As of May 2002** | |
|  | **Units Sold** |
| Accord | 37,954 |
| Civic | 32,365 |
| Odessey | 11,632 |
| CR-V | 10,640 |
| TL | 5,606 |
| MDX | 3,806 |
| Integra | 2,408 |
| CL | 1,691 |
| Passport | 1,314 |
| S2000 | 1,312 |
| RL | 1,056 |
| **Insight** | **903** |
| Prelude | 833 |
| NSX | 17 |

very different marketing strategies. Toyota decided to build interest in its car through a demo program for its U.S. introduction. Basically, a Prius was given to several families in each of the larger metropolitan areas and the families were allowed to drive it around free for four weeks. This program not only improved consumer awareness of the Prius but it also gave the Prius visibility and credibility among the consumers. Even Toyota President Fujio Cho personally volunteered to promote the sale of the Prius by switching his luxury, black-coated company car to a white Prius.[11]

---

[11]"Toyota, Honda Forge Ahead in Hybrid Vehicle Development," *AP Newswire,* March 13, 2002.

**EXHIBIT 10**
**Honda Financial and**
**Operating Highlights**

Source: Honda Motor Co., Ltd.
*2002 Annual Report.*

| Financial Highlights | | | |
|---|---|---|---|
| **Honda Motor Co., Ltd. And Subsidiaries** | **Yen** *(millions except per share amounts)* | | **U.S. Dollars** *(millions except per share amounts)* |
| **Years ended or at March 31** | **2001** | **2002** | **2002** |
| Net sales and other operating revenue | 6,463,830 | 7,362,438 | 55,253 |
| Operating income | 406,960 | 639,296 | 4,798 |
| Income before income taxes and equity in income of affiliates | 384,976 | 551,342 | 4,138 |
| Net income | 232,241 | 362,707 | 2,722 |
| Per common share (Basic) | 238.34 | 372.23 | 2.79 |
| Per American share (Basic) | 119.17 | 186.11 | 1.40 |
| Cash dividends paid during the period | 22,412 | 24,360 | 183 |
| Per common share | 23 | 25 | 0.19 |
| Per American share* | 11.5 | 12.50 | 0.09 |
| Stockholders' equity | 2,230,291 | 2,573,941 | 19,317 |
| Per common share | 2,288.87 | 2,641.55 | 19.32 |
| Per American share* | 1,144.43 | 1,320.77 | 9.91 |
| Total assets | 5,667,409 | 6,940,795 | 52,089 |
| Depreciation | 170,342 | 194,944 | 1,463 |
| Capital expenditures | 285,687 | 303,424 | 2,277 |

*Honda's common stock-to-ADR echange ratio was changed from two shares of common stock to one ADR, to one share of common stock to two ADRs, effective January 10, 2002. Per American share information has been restated for all periods presented to reflect this four-for-one ADR split.*

| Operating Highlights | | | |
|---|---|---|---|
| **Years ended March 31** | **Automobiles** | | **Percent Change** |
| **Unit Sales Breakdown (thousands)** | **2001** | **2002** | **(2002/2001)** |
| Japan | 776 | 878 | 13.14 |
| North America | 1,346 | 1,368 | 1.63 |
| Europe | 191 | 176 | (7.85) |
| Other Regions | 267 | 244 | (8.61) |
| Total | 2,580 | 2,666 | 3.33 |
| **Years ended March 31** | **Automobile Business** | | **Percent Change** |
| **Net Sales Breakdown (millions of yen)** | **2001** | **2002** | **(2002/2001)** |
| Japan | 1,529,428 | 1,654,238 | 8.16 |
| North America | 2,999,478 | 3,529,560 | 17.67 |
| Europe | 311,295 | 336,844 | 8.21 |
| Other Regions | 391,125 | 409,100 | 4.60 |
| Total | 5,231,326 | 5,929,742 | 13.35 |

## EXHIBIT 11

**Honda's North American Operations**

Source: Honda Motor Co., Ltd.
*2002 Annual Report.*

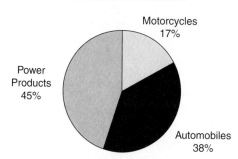

**Unit Sales Breakdown**

Motorcycles 17%

Power Products 45%

Automobiles 38%

### Fiscal 2002 Topics

1. New plant in Alabama opened and commenced production of the Odyssey minivan and its V-6 engines.
2. Accord became the best-selling car of 2001 in the United States.
3. AquaTrax F-12 and AquaTrax F-12X personal watercraft launched.

### Outlook

1. Fiscal 2003 unit sales forecast for motorcycles: up 6.8%, to 630,000; automobiles: an increase of 8.9%, to 1,490,000.
2. Introduction of new Pilot SUV and all-new Element light truck.
3. Launch of Metropolitan scooter.

### Principal Automobile Manufacturing Facilities

| Location | Start of Operations | Number of Employees |
| --- | --- | --- |
| Marysville, Ohio | Sept. 1979 | 7,515 |
| Anna, Ohio | July 1985 | 2,740 |
| East Liberty, Ohio | Dec. 1989 | 2,788 |
| Lincoln, Alabama | Nov. 2001 | 2,019 |
| Swepsonville, North Carolina | Aug. 1984 | 370 |
| Timmonsville, South Carolina | July 1998 | 1,496 |

44    Honda, on the other hand, decided to rely solely on its existing brand image as a forward-thinking automaker and its "first-mover" status in its advertising for the Insight. Honda felt that the main marketing task that Honda had was to educate the consumer and address some of the misconceptions associated with hybrid vehicles. Hence, the television commercials and the advertisements used by Honda highlighted the "Insight's industry-leading fuel economy and that the car's battery did not need to be 'plugged-in' for recharging."[12]

45    Realizing that the typical buyer of a hybrid vehicle was an environmentalist and technophile who yearned for the latest in automotive gadgetry, Honda targeted "techies" for the Insight.[13] In fact, Robert Bienenfeld, Insight marketing manager, said "the typical Insight buyer is a male engineer in his mid-40s who's interested in technology."[14] Given this

[12](http://www.autointell.com,) "Hybrid Car Sales Surge Along with Gas Prices: New Honda Insight Ad Hits Airwaves," *Automotive Intelligence News* June 13, 2001.
[13]Lillie Guyer, "The Little Engines that Could, now go Whirrr," *Advertising Age,* April 9, 2001.
[14]David Welch and Larry Armstrong, "A Fast (and Lucky) Start for Japan's Hybrid Cars," *BusinessWeek Online,* July 6, 2000.

fact, Honda used a small budget for its national TV and Internet advertising, since most of the Insight buyers were thought to search out information about the Insight independently. Most of Honda's budget was actually used to develop "materials for dealers to use in talking with local media in their own cities."[15] Art Garner, a spokesman for American Honda, explained that prepping "dealers to talk about the Insight with the local media was the best way to take advantage of the interest generated by rising gas prices without spending more on a national effort."[16]

**46**   Also, in keeping with Honda's philosophy of making environmental technology accessible to consumers, Honda priced the Insight at less than $20,000, with a full complement of standard comfort and convenience features added in. Although Honda was actually making a loss on each Insight that it sold, it felt that hybrid technology could become profitable in the long-term. Honda felt that the real-world experience that it would build up by working with hybrid technology and the continuance of its "green" car company image were strong enough motivations to sell the Insight at a loss for the first few years.

### Manufacturing and Distribution

**47**   The Honda Insight was produced in Japan at the Takanazawa plant, which is about 80 km north of Tokyo. The Takanazawa plant was the same plant that was used for the production of other low volume, unique technology vehicles such as the Acura NSX. On a daily basis, only about 20 to 30 Insights were manufactured, much lower than the numbers for the Civic or the Accord. Honda adopted a limited production volume strategy for the Insight initially, as it was unsure of the market demand for hybrid vehicles. But given the "overwhelming" demand for the Insight in the United States, Honda increased its sales target for the United States from 4,000 to 6,500 vehicles for 2002.

### Foregoing Partnerships

**48**   Automakers all over the world witnessed a global realignment of the auto industry during the 1990s. This led to partnerships and acquisitions such as Nissan Motor Co.'s partnership with Renault SA and Mitsubishi Motor Corp.'s tie-in with DaimlerChrysler AG, all in an effort seek foreign investment in order to survive. Even amongst all this realignment, Honda and Toyota decided to keep their independence. In fact, Honda President Hiroyuki Yoshino ruled out the possibility of his company forging a partnership with a foreign automaker, saying, "It's better for a person to decide about his own life rather than having it decided by others."[17] Hence, Honda decided on solo development of the hybrid vehicle.

**49**   With its stable financial condition and its core products, the Civic and the Accord, still maintaining their leadership in the global markets, Honda had the funds and technology to develop the hybrid vehicle alone. However, even Honda's strongest competitor, Toyota, was considering cooperative development by 2002. Toyota President Cho said that although Toyota is "not thinking of a capital tie-up with foreign carmakers," it was considering "the possibility of establishing cooperation with a wide spectrum of makers in the areas of technology and production."[18]

[15]Margaret Kittman, "Hybrid engine cars do better with hybrid marketing tactics," *Advertising Age News,* September 25, 2000.
[16]Ibid.
[17]"Toyota, Honda Forge Ahead in Hybrid Vehicle Development," *AP Newswire,* March 13, 2002.
[18]Ibid.

## EXHIBIT 12
**R&D Expenses Comparison**

| R&D Expenses Comparison (Percent of Total Revenues) | | | | | | | | |
|---|---|---|---|---|---|---|---|---|
| | 1993 | 1994 | 1995 | 1996 | 1997 | 1998 | 1999 | 2000 | 2001 |
| Honda | 4.82% | 4.89% | 5.12% | 5.19% | 4.74% | 4.76% | 5.00% | 5.48% | 5.46% |
| Toyota | | | | | | | | 3.52 | 3.58 |
| Ford | 4.63 | 4.06 | 4.83 | 4.64 | 4.10 | 4.36 | 3.73 | 4.00 | 4.56 |
| General Motors | 4.51 | 4.67 | 5.28 | 5.63 | 4.93 | 5.34 | 4.06 | 3.57 | 3.50 |
| DaimlerChrysler | | | | | 3.76 | 3.77 | 3.83 | 3.90 | 3.88 |

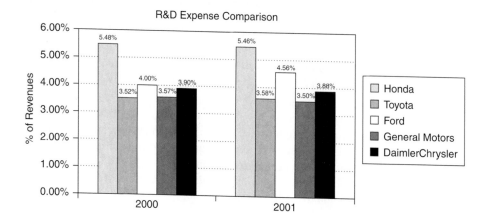

### Standing Firm on Environmental Issues

50   By June 2002, Honda was the only major auto manufacturer that had not joined the Alliance of Automobile Manufacturers, the industry trade group that led the fight against tougher fuel and emissions standards. As voiced by Tom Elliot, "We (Honda) cannot agree with the alliance on several issues."[19] By holding itself to a higher standard, Honda stood to carve itself a position as the technological leader in environmentally friendly automobiles. Compared to other automakers, Honda devoted the highest percentage of its revenues into research and development of improving technologies (see Exhibit 12). Honda's effort to position itself as the environmental leader in auto manufacturing appeared to be paying off, as evidenced in a statement by Daniel Decker, director of the global warming policy for the Sierra Club: "The only hope I see for a future with cleaner cars is Honda."[20]

## THE FUTURE OF HEVS

51   In 2003, HEVs were widely believed to have the potential to allow continued growth in the automotive sector, while also reducing critical resource consumption, dependence on foreign oil, air pollution, and traffic congestion. However, the success of hybrids was far from assured. While the technology's capabilities held great promise, the widespread penetration of hybrids hinged on the economics of producing a complex hybrid power system. The hybrid's complexity, and the fact that some of the necessary complementary technologies

[19]"Honda Takes Up Case in U.S. for Green Energy," *New York Times*, June 13, 2002.
[20]Ibid.

(such as storage and conversion systems) still had room for improvement, caused opinions to be mixed on the hybrids' ultimate impact in the marketplace.

**52**    Complicating matters was the fact that many in the industry had their sights set on a different environmentally friendly technology: fuel cells. Fuel cells offered much greater energy efficiency when converting fuel to electricity than the combination of an internal-combustion engine with a battery. By converting chemical energy directly into electrical energy, fuel cells had been known to achieve a conversion efficiency of better than 50 percent. In July 2002, Honda succeeded in manufacturing the first fuel cell vehicle to receive certification by the U.S. Environmental Protection Agency (EPA) and the California Air Resources Board (CARB) by meeting all applicable standards. This new fuel cell vehicle, called the FCX, was certified as a Zero Emission Vehicle and by the EPA as a Tier-2 Bin 1 National Low Emission Vehicle (NLEV), the lowest national emission rating. But fuel cell cars were still considered to be dangerous due to the storage of hydrogen, a highly combustible substance, within the car. Though there appeared to be an industrywide move towards creating environmentally friendly automobiles, *which* environmentally friendly technology would become dominant was still highly uncertain.

# Case 37 Huxley Maquiladora

1   On Monday, June 24, 2002, Steve Phillips, head of the Huxley Maquila project team, had to make a recommendation about moving production to Mexico. The final report of the team, outlining the results of six months of investigation, was on his desk. The task now was to recommend at Thursday's board of directors meeting whether to establish a manufacturing plant, and if so, where and how.

## COMPANY BACKGROUND

2   Huxley Manufacturing Co. was part of the materials technology division of a holding company based in the eastern United States, which had interests in chemicals, aluminum, packaging and aerospace. Huxley employed 1,800 people in three defense-related businesses and recorded $472 million in annual sales in 2001. Huxley headquarters were located in San Antonio, Texas, a city that had a strong Mexican influence; over 50 percent of its population was Hispanic. A U.S. military base and hospital were also located in the area.

3   Huxley took pride in its cutting-edge engineering technologies in raw material processing and part assembling. It had demonstrated superiority in the use of aluminum hybrids, ceramics and composite metals to increase the survivability of military equipment. These materials met tough performance standards for weight, size, and durability, all of which were critical characteristics for military applications. Only two or three of Huxley's competitors whose manufacturing facilities were confined to the United States were capable of designing, processing, and assembling to the same standards.

4   Huxley's three businesses had historically been managed separately, with little information sharing and communication among the units. This corporate need for separation had resulted from the secrecy that had been required in Huxley's work for the defense industry.

5   During the 1990s, Huxley faced several factors that converged to profoundly reshape the U.S. defense industry. The first factor was the increasing "knowledge intensity" of defense products, resulting in higher development costs. These rising costs could be attributed primarily to the increasing technological complexity of almost all types of military systems, and to the rapid pace of technological innovation. Higher costs of research and development (R&D) for each generation of weapons caused absolute costs to rise, and the increasingly knowledge-intensive nature of weapon production had the effect of rendering even the largest multidivisional firms incapable of funding R&D independently.

**Richard Ivey School of Business**
The University of Western Ontario

Jaechul Jung and Joyce Miller prepared this case under the supervision of Professor Paul Beamish solely to provide material for class discussion. The authors do not intend to illustrate either effective or ineffective handling of a managerial situation. The authors may have disguised certain names and other identifying information to protect confidentiality. Ivey Management Services prohibits any form of reproduction, storage or transmittal without its written permission. This material is not covered under authorization from CanCopy or any reproduction rights organization. To order copies or request permission to reproduce materials, contact Ivey Publishing, Ivey Management Services, c/o Richard Ivey School of Business, The University of Western Ontario, London, Ontario, Canada, N6A 3K7; phone (519) 661-3208; fax (519) 661-3882; e-mail cases@ivey.uwo.ca. One time Permission to reproduce granted by Ivey Management Services on July 28, 2003. Copyright © 2002, Ivey Management Services. Version: (A) 2002-10-10.

6    Furthermore, the forecast was uncertain for the political environment in which defense firms in the United States were operating. With the end of Cold War, high funding levels for equipment in the American defense budget fell. There were declining numbers of military personnel and a debate on the most appropriate force structure and roles for the American armed forces in the new era. In such a political environment, the U.S. economic decline of recent years only exacerbated the situation facing U.S. firms in the defense industry. As well, the September 11, 2001 attacks had highlighted the need for greater intelligence gathering, not necessarily more hardware. These factors combined to reduce U.S. government spending on defense to 2.4 percent of the gross domestic product (GDP) in 2000, compared with the 6.4 percent under the Reagan administration.

7    In order to deal with this adverse environment, the U.S. government had moved away from the use of sole vendors to more competitive bidding for contracts to supply military equipment. As a result, price had become a more important selection criterion. U.S.-based firms were still the major suppliers, but some foreign-produced goods were also purchased by the U.S. armed forces.

# THE GROUND TRANSPORTATION BUSINESS

8    Under such transforming environmental pressure, Huxley began searching for feasible solutions to reduce its production costs in its ground transportation unit (GTU). Technological developments in composite materials, hybrid electric power systems, integrated vehicle survivability and other features positioned Huxley's GTU at the forefront among competitors.

9    The GTU had operations near San Diego, California, and Dallas, Texas, and was negotiating to acquire a $30 million sales company in Denver, Colorado, which would function similarly to the plant in San Diego. The GTU manufactured steering column components (SCCs) at its California site. The production of SCCs for combat vehicles generated annual revenues of about $130 million. There had been continual demands for replacement SCCs, in addition to new purchases during the annual procurement wave.

10    Although the production of SCCs required heavy capital investment, labor-intensive processes made up the major portion of production costs. Examples included the processes of lamination and filing: by adhesively bonding thin, composite metal layers and filing them to fit specifications, the finished assembly combined strength and lightness, which were critical characteristics for successful maneuvering. Machines were currently available to complete these vital processes, but manual processing still turned out a superior product.

11    Filing by hand required enormous patience and precision and had been done by females who worked 42 hours a week and received an average wage of $12.30 per hour. The GTU provided a 30-hour job training program before a newcomer began in SCC production. Even after training, some of the new workers found they could not master the required job skills and quit during the three-month probationary period. The rejection rate had been around 10 percent monthly. Aside from being required to meet specified performance standards in precision, working with metals, requiring physical strength and patience, made this job unattractive. As a result, in spite of the comparatively high wages for women, the turnover rate in this position had always been relatively high—up to 11 percent monthly. Robert Chan, the chief executive officer (CEO) of Huxley, once stated, "Such labor-intensive tasks are excellent candidates for us to attempt offshore production." Many U.S. companies had gained their competitive advantages by running their labor-intensive operations in developing countries, which provided well-educated labor forces at low wage costs.

12    Along with the worsening external environment, Chan's participation in a business conference in Mexico in 2001 triggered him to seriously consider Mexico as a strong candidate

to transplant Huxley's SCC manufacturing plants. After evaluating the manufacturing processes in the GTU, Huxley's management then identified several labor-intensive activities in the large San Diego plant related to SCC manufacturing, and agreed provisionally to move the plant. As a subsequent step, Chan launched the Huxley Maquila project team, composed of five members chosen from various backgrounds and led by Phillips. During the six months prior to the June 2002 report, Phillips sent three team members to Mexico to gather local information.

# THE MAQUILADORA PROGRAM

**13**   The term *maquiladora* came from the Spanish term *maquila* (to perform a task for another; to assemble). During the Mexican colonial period, the miller kept a certain amount of a farmer's corn after he ground it for him. The payment was known as the *maquila*. The current use of the term *maquiladora* referred to any Mexican company that assembled imported, duty-free components and then re-exported them as finished products.

**14**   In May 1965, the *maquiladora* industry began, with a border industrialization program. The new policy allowed machinery, equipment, material and component parts to be imported duty free on an "in-bond" basis. The posting of a bond with the Mexican Customs Bureau guaranteed that assembled or manufactured products were exported to the country from which they had first been exported or to a third country. *Maquiladoras* had grown during the years to become the industrial backbone of the country's northern border, with more than 3,500 plants now employing 1.2 million people. Most of the plants were concentrated in Ciudad Juarez, Chihuahua, across from El Paso, Texas, and Tijuana, Baja California, across from San Diego, California (see Exhibit 1).

**15**   *Maquiladoras* handled a variety of tasks from textile, automobile, and electronics production to the assembly of toys and sporting goods. In the 1960s and '70s, many U.S. firms

**EXHIBIT 1**
**Mexico's Network of Maquiladoras in November 2001**

| State | Number of Maquiladoras |
|---|---|
| 1. Baja California | 1,226 |
| 2. Baja California Sur | 7 |
| 3. Sonora | 246 |
| 4. Chihuahua | 432 |
| 5. Sinaloa | 10 |
| 6. Durango | 73 |
| 7. Coahuila | 267 |
| 8. Nuevo Leon | 169 |
| 9. Tamaulipas | 401 |
| 10. Zacatecas | 20 |
| 11. San Luis Potosi | 15 |
| 12. Aguascalientes | 72 |
| 13. Jalisco | 131 |
| 14. Puebla | 116 |
| 15. Distrito Federal | 29 |
| 16. Edo. Mexico | 47 |
| 17. Yucatan | 121 |
| 18. Guanajuato | 68 |
| 19. The rest of the country | 77 |
| Total | 3,527 |

Source: INEGI.

transferred the labor-intensive and assembly portions of their manufacturing activity to these companies. The most prominent advantage to setting up a *maquiladora* was access to cheap Mexican labor. From the 1960s to the '70s, Mexican manufacturing wages were about 15 percent to 25 percent of those in the United States. Yet Mexican wages were higher than those in many Asian countries like Singapore and South Korea. However, in the 1980s, subsequent currency devaluations decreased Mexican hourly wages to well below those of Hong Kong, South Korea, Singapore and other low-wage competitor countries. Mexican wages dropped to about 10 percent of U.S. wages at that time.

**16**     Currently, there were still countries like China providing lower wage labor forces than Mexico. Wages for Mexican garment workers were approximately double those in China, but the benefits of faster delivery and lower shipping costs often outweighed this difference. Mexican products could reach the U.S. market within two or three days, compared with the three to four weeks required for shipment from China. Combined with access to the U.S. market, the wage levels of the 1980s established *maquiladora* manufacturing as one of the most competitive manufacturing platforms in the world. Finally, the regions became a portal for Asian and European firms to enter the North American market (see Exhibit 2).

**EXHIBIT 2**
**Foreign Direct Investment in Mexico by Country and Sector Between 1994 and September 2001 (%)**

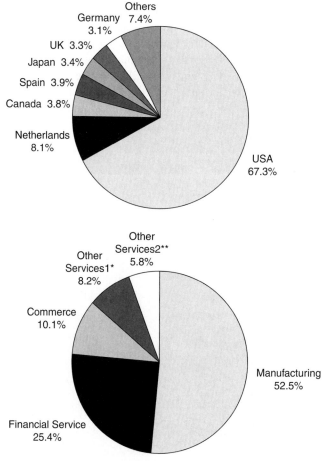

*Other Service1     Agricultural, mining, constructing, electricity, transportation and communication, and water.
**Other Service2     Social and communal service: hotels and restaurants, professional, technical and personal.
Source: Ministry of Economy, Mexico.

# NAFTA (THE NORTH AMERICA FREE TRADE AGREEMENT)

**17**   The North America Free Trade Agreement (NAFTA) was launched in 1994 by Mexico, Canada, and the United States. NAFTA participants planned to phase out all tariffs among the three countries over a 15-year period. Since its implementation, tariffs had been eliminated on 84.5 percent of all nonoil and nonagricultural Mexican exports to the United States and on 79 percent of exports to Canada. In order to receive preferential NAFTA tariffs, a minimum of 50 percent of product content had to come from one of the three countries for most products. For autos and light trucks, the requirement level was stricter, at 62 percent.

**18**   The content requirements and tariff reductions, coupled with the already existing *maquiladora* laws in Mexico, made *maquiladora* manufacturing much more competitive under NAFTA. By 2001, Mexico had received $108.7 billion in foreign direct investment (FDI). Among the FDI, U.S. and Canadian firms made up 71 percent, with most from the United States (see Exhibit 2). NAFTA, as well, had nurtured a rapid increase in Mexican exports. The export total of $60 billion in 1993 had soared to $182 billion by 2000 (see Exhibit 3). Between 1993 and 2000, Mexico's annual average exports to the United States increased 19 percent, while those of the rest of the world grew only eight percent. In 2000, trade between Mexico and the United States totalled $263 billion, three times that of 1993.

**19**   Currently, Mexico had free trade agreements (FTAs) with 32 countries. In particular, trade with Latin American partners was rapidly growing. In fact, Mexican exports to Costa Rica and Venezuela in 2000 had grown by 259 percent and 303 percent, respectively, since 1994.

## Mexico

**20**   Mexico was a country of approximately 100 million people and 1,958,000 square kilometers, sharing a 3,200-km border with the United States. Prior to the Mexican-American War in the mid-nineteenth century, Mexico governed what was now the southwestern United States. Even after annexation of half Mexico's territory by the United States, Mexicans continued to live in the area and their number had substantially increased through emigration. Mexico's current relationship with the United States was largely economic, stimulated by

**EXHIBIT 3**
**Mexico's Export**
**Increase**

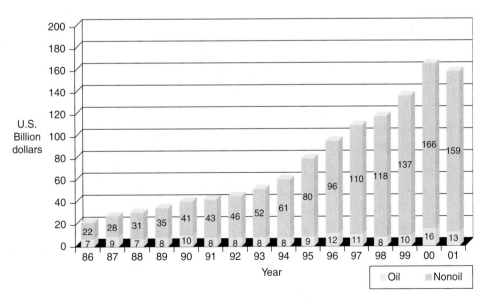

Source: Ministry of Economy, Mexico; BANXICO.

NAFTA. Although the Mexican economy was currently experiencing recession triggered by U.S. economic decline, it had grown steadily since its economic crisis in 1994.

21     On the political side, the Mexican Revolution in the early twentieth century had shaped Mexico's economic, political and social life since that time. The Institutional Revolutionary Party (PRI) continued its dominance as a governing party up to recent years, providing political stability. Based on its stable political leadership, Mexico showed rapid economic growth and became one of the most industrialized countries in Latin America. However, as in other Latin American countries, Mexico was now undergoing rapid transformations in economic and political spheres. The changes in the economic environment and the economic crisis of the 1980s resulted in a rejection of old economic models and an acceptance of new economic policies. The new model was based on opening Mexico's economy to foreign trade and investment, reducing government intervention in the economy. Participation in NAFTA was one manifestation of this change. Economic changes had, in turn, brought about a process of democratization that finally reached a major milestone in July 2000 as Vicente Fox of the National Action Party (PAN) was elected the country's president, ending the 71-year hegemony of the PRI.

22     On the other hand, the temporarily duty-free import programs of NAFTA were eliminated as of January 1, 2001, on trade between Mexico, the United States, and Canada (Article 303 of the NAFTA). Hence, *maquiladoras* could not continue to benefit from access to duty-free import materials and they had to change their sourcing strategies. Responding to this change, the Mexican government introduced the Sectorial Promotion Program (PROSEC), which allowed low import taxes (zero percent to five percent) on parts or materials intended for assembly and export to the United States or Canada.

# THE HUXLEY MAQUILA PROJECT REPORT

23     The Huxley Maquila project team focused on the tasks of creating feasibility studies for operating in Mexico, location and site selection, and appraisal of various entry modes. The three team members stationed in Mexico played major roles in sourcing necessary data. The project report was submitted to Phillips, director of the project team, on June 19, 2002. Regarding transferring the SCC manufacturing process of the GTU, the report predicted that the 57 workers directly affected would be absorbed in other Huxley operations or terminated with a severance package. The report suggested that a 25,000-square-foot plant would be adequate and could still accommodate a possible worker increase of at least 50 percent in the future. Much equipment would be required, including benches, steel tables, holding fixtures and so on. The report noted:

> The SCCs assembly processes are labor intensive and had documented description of the method, sequence and dimensions for initial training, and would qualify for favorable PROSEC treatment. The San Diego plant had a significant problem with high turnover rate because working with metals was a dirty job. With appropriate training, young Mexican women would probably perform these tasks better than their counterparts in the U.S. since they are more patient. Even by taking a conservative figure like $2.10 as the fully fringed hourly pay, the direct labor savings would be considerable.

24     After investigating numerous sites, the Huxley Maquila project team gave its attention to Coahuila, Mexico's third largest state, lying to the south of Texas. Coahuila shared 512 kilometers of border with the state of Texas. Its geographical proximity made Coahuila the crossing point between the United States and the central and southern regions of Mexico. Prior to NAFTA's implementation, 156 *maquiladoras* were operating in the Coahuila state. As of November 2001, 267 *maquiladoras* were up and running (see Exhibit 1). The project report noted that Coahuila's geographical closeness to Huxley's headquarters in San Antonio, Texas, and the SCC plant in Dallas, Texas, was one of the merits of the location.

**25**     Among several attractive spots for a new plant, the project team members considered Ciudad Acuna, the best border site and Saltillo, the capital of Coahuila, as the best site in the interior. A border location minimized transportation costs, facilitated trouble-shooting by managers and engineers based in U.S. headquarters, and permitted factory managers to live in the United States and commute across the border. However, the influx of *maquiladora* operations had strained the infrastructure of many border cities. Public services could not cope with the population growth in Ciudad Acuna. The city's annual budget was insufficient to keep up the pace, resulting in a city with quite a large portion of its streets unpaved and water and sewage systems lacking in many of its makeshift neighborhoods. The most significant problem was the housing shortage, which stemmed from the flood of migrants from the interior of Mexico seeking *maquiladora* jobs. A team member of the project commented:

> People are lured from the interior by the promise of a job. They move in with relatives or friends, then quit when they can't find permanent accommodation. The Mexico government doesn't have enough resources to fund construction of sufficient low-cost housing. The current housing situation will not be improved soon.

**26**     The shortage of housing created a significant labor problem for *maquiladora* operators. Turnover rates ranged from seven to 13.5 percent per month along the border. While interior regions offered a more stable labor force and cheaper Mexican material, these advantages came with higher transportation costs and a lower quality of life for foreign managers. Infrastructure, including roads, housing, utilities and especially communications in the interior, would have to be carefully evaluated. Exhibit 4 details various factors that needed to be considered for location selection of the SCC plant.

**27**     The project report included three options for operating in Mexico as a *maquiladora*. These were subcontracting, shelter operation, and wholly owned subsidiary.

### Subcontracting

**28**     The easiest way to operate as a *maquiladora* was to subcontract the manufacturing services of a Mexican company. Under this arrangement, a Mexican service firm manufactured items according to the specifications of the foreign-based client. The client provided the raw materials, components, and specialized equipment, and the subcontractor was responsible for all the manufacturing and assembly work as well as the import-export process. The foreign client rarely supplied a plant manager.

**29**     The Mexican subcontractor was generally paid for each product based upon a per-piece price agreement. This subcontracting arrangement made sense for well-documented operations requiring a small number of employees. The client could enjoy a reduction or elimination of capital expenditures for facilities, equipment, and management. The Huxley Maquila project team report estimated that a Mexican firm could be subcontracted at a rate of about $5 per direct labor hour. To start contracting product assembly in Mexico took 30 to 45 days.

### Shelter Operation

**30**     A "shelter" was an intermediary option. Under such a program, the non-Mexican manufacturer was "sheltered" from most of the legal and financial exposure of operating in Mexico. Among the non-Mexican manufacturers operating in the *maquiladora* industry, about 10 percent were shelter operations. Under this arrangement, the Mexican service firm provided foreign manufacturers with customized administration. This allowed the client to maintain complete control over the Mexico production management while ensuring that all administrative requirements were being met by the offshore operation. The shelter service provider supported (1) administration: accounting and tax service, licences

**EXHIBIT 4**
**Location Profiles**
**Border Site (Ciudad**
**Acuna) Versus**
**Interior Site (Saltillo)**

| | | Border site:<br>Ciudad Acuna | Interior site:<br>Saltillo |
|---|---|---|---|
| Demographic<br>aspects | Total Population<br>Males<br>Females | 78,232<br>39,564<br>39,668 | 577,352<br>285,507<br>291,845 |
| Aviation<br>service | Nearest Airport | Piedras Negras<br>International Airport—<br>83 km away | Plan de Guadalupe<br>International Airport—<br>13.5 km away |
| | Flights | • Monterrey | • Mexico, D.F.<br>• Houston, TX.<br>• Dallas, TX. |
| | Frequency<br>Capacity<br>Cargo Service | Monday–Sunday<br>19 to 33 passengers<br>None | Monday–Sunday<br>51 to 101 passengers<br>Daily, 100 tons and up |
| Highways | Federal Highway | • Hwy. 2 reaches Nuevo<br>Laredo, Tamps through<br>Piedras Negras | • Hwy. 57 connects<br>with Piedras Negras,<br>Queretaro, Qro. and<br>Mexico City.<br>• Hwy. 40 connects<br>Torreon, Coah. with<br>Reynosa, Tamps. and<br>Mazatlan, Sin.<br>through Saltillo |
| Railroads | | The Northern railroad<br>connects Ciudad Acuna,<br>and Zaragoza. | The railroad connects<br>Parras, General Cepeda,<br>Saltillo and Ramos<br>Arizpe. |
| Industrial<br>park | | Three industrial parks | Five industrial parks |
| Primary<br>industry | | Automobile, aluminum<br>blinds, material<br>lamination, and<br>electrical harnesses | Automobile harnesses,<br>plastic lids, aircraft<br>harnesses, electronic<br>cards, agro-chemical,<br>and appliances |
| Labor cost<br>(hourly wage<br>for general<br>laborer) | Manufacturing<br>Assembly | $0.94<br>$0.65 | $1.38<br>$1.06 |
| Water | Water ($/m$^3$)<br>Drainage | $0.97<br>$0.24 | $1.30<br>$0.32 |
| Electricity | Less than 25KW<br>More than<br>25KW | $2.54<br><br>$11.52 | Same<br><br>Same |

**EXHIBIT 4**
*(Continued)*

| | | Border site:<br>Ciudad Acuna | Interior site: Saltillo |
|---|---|---|---|
| Telephone | Local | Base rate: $0.16<br>Day rate: $0.16<br>Evening rate: $0.16 | Same |
| | National<br>long distance | Base rate: $0.27<br>Day rate: $0.24<br>Evening rate: $0.12 | Same |
| | Long distance<br>to U.S.A. | Base rate: $1.00<br>Day rate: $0.88<br>Evening rate: $0.59 | Same |
| Education | Professional<br>Technical School<br>in the near<br>region | 13 | 36 |
| | Universities in<br>the near region | 10 | 19 |
| Commerce<br>and services | Hotels | 10 | 20 |
| | Shopping<br>centers | 3 | 10 |
| | Banks | 8 | 63 |
| | Hospitals | 11 | 12 |

Source: Secretariat of Planning and Development Government of the State of Coahuila.

and permits, and performance monitoring; (2) human resource management: Mexican personnel administration and payroll services; and (3) import and export service: customs services related to Mexican and U.S. government requirements. The foreign company controlled the production process and provided equipment, raw materials, components, and plant managers.

31    Billing of operation was directly related to the number of hours provided by the service firm. The fully burdened hourly rate for a shelter operation was around $3.50. Depending on the complexity of the setup, it generally took 45 to 120 days from receipt of authorization to production startup. The shelter operation was attractive for several reasons. First, it allowed fast, easy startup with little capital investment. At the same time, it provided complete control over the quality of the work. In addition, if the client wished, the shelter operation could be converted to a "full-blown presence" in Mexico as the company grew, or control could be turned over to the shelter partner to form a contract operation.

# WHOLLY-OWNED SUBSIDIARY

32    Known as a "stand-alone," a wholly-owned subsidiary offered potentially the lowest operating costs, as long as overheads were strictly controlled. Such an operation was often the best alternative when significant engineering and/or product development support was required. This approach was the most complex of the three options. To set up a wholly owned *maquiladora,* foreign firms had to (1) search, select, and negotiate to get a plant site; (2) staff and recruit employees; (3) implement systems, controls, and procedures; and (4) get government permits and licences. The foreign firm needed to establish relationships at local, state, and federal government levels and had to understand and manage the details of doing

**EXHIBIT 5**
**Mexican Minimum Wage for Unskilled Workers in 2000 (in U.S. dollars)**

| | Minimum Wage |
|---|---|
| 1. Regional minimum hourly wage* | $0.51 |
| 2. Annual salary (365 days)** | $1,117.92 |
| 3. Christmas bonus (Aguinaldo-15 days) and vacations (5 days) | $64.21 |
| 4. Employer's payroll taxes and state taxes | $44.71 |
| 5. Average fringe benefits | $254.69 |
| 6. **Total Annual Cost (=2+3+4+5)** | **$1,481.53** |
| 7. **Fully Fringed Hourly Cost*** | **$0.68** |

Note: The minimum wage (salario minimo) is the income level determined by the federal government to be adequate to meet the basic needs of a typical family.

*Including social security contributions, the INFONAVIT worker's housing fund and the retirement savings plan.

**Considering weekly working hours (44) and annual working days. (300 = 365 – Sundays (52) – legal holidays (8) – vacations (5)).

***Fully Fringed Hourly Cost = Total Annual Cost/Annual Working Hours (2,192).

Source: International Labor Organization; BANCOMEXT.

business in Mexico, which could be particularly burdensome in the areas of hiring, compensating, and terminating labor. Before starting operations as a *maquiladora,* the company had to ensure that it had in place all the required licences and permits. The Secretary of Commerce agency in Mexico (SECO) permitted firms to operate under the *maquiladora* program. It generally took anywhere from six months to one year to set up a wholly owned *maquiladora.* Some typical costs for operating a wholly owned subsidiary in Mexico were:

| | |
|---|---|
| Feasibility consulting fee | $18,000 |
| Mexican legal fee | $7,000 to $10,000 |
| Construction for shell building including land with improvement | $14 to 25 per square foot |
| Annual leasing of factory space | $3.68 to $5.47 per square foot |
| Developed land price, in case of purchasing land | $1.05 to $2.30 per square foot |
| Average hourly wage for unskilled labor (including fringes) | $1.80 to $2.20 per hour |
| Average plant manager wage (including fringes) | $84,000 per year |

33    In addition to these costs, the report included transportation and a few more cost factors, which were applied commonly to the three operation options. Most maquiladora machinery, raw materials, and semifinished products entered and left Mexico by truck. The average round-trip rate from Ciudad Acuna to the U.S. border was around $150. In the case of Saltillo, the cost rose to $1,000. American and Mexico broker fees accounted for an additional $625 per round-trip shipment. Each day a round-trip truckload shipment was expected from Monday to Friday, except on the eight national holidays throughout the year. The report estimated that miscellaneous costs and Mexican corporate tax would be annually $43,050 and $12,500 in the case of shelter operation and wholly owned subsidiary. The one-time operation startup in Mexico would cost approximately $97,000, which contained training a manager, visits from California staff, and a facility upgrade.

## REMAINING ISSUES

34    In its final section, the project report added several concerns regarding operating in Mexico as a *maquiladora.* The report pointed out that fulfilling the financial, legal, and logistic requirements would merely enable a *maquiladora* to operate. Managing the human relations aspects would determine its success or failure. The report stated:

Managing a maquiladora is not at all the same as managing a plant in the United States. The maquiladora management has to become acquainted with the cultural values and customs of its workers, and this understanding has to be carried over to home office.

35    Despite benefits enjoyed by government and industry, the situation for the low-wage *maquiladora* workers themselves was not bright. Since the late 1990s, labor groups had protested the low wages, unsafe working conditions, and sexual and other forms of harassment that took place. For instance, in 1997 the Han Young de Mexico plant in Tijuana was enveloped in a strike that attracted international attention. Protesters claimed that there were many companies along the borders that treat their employees "like trash." These conflicts appeared to originate from an excessive exploitation of Mexican employees and a misunderstanding of Mexican cultural values.

36    These mistreatments by foreign-owned *maquiladora* put those firms at risk and added to the housing shortage, employee recruitment, and training problems. To attract new employees and lessen the expressed anger of existing workers, some of the *maquiladoras* had come up with their own solutions, like supporting the local government in housing initiatives, running commuter buses, and introducing high-cost training programs.

## PHILLIPS' RECOMMENDATION

37    Based on the report's comments, Phillips concluded that entry-into-Mexico decision should be implemented carefully if Huxley wanted to take full advantage of low-cost production. A successful launch and management of the plant would require special attention. The plant would need to be run not only to the standards of its own headquarters, but also considering Mexican cultural values and practices. Launching and managing a plant in a foreign country would be a different experience for Huxley's managers, who were accustomed to U.S. management practices.

38    On Thursday, June 27, a board of directors meeting would be held regarding the transfer of the San Diego plant. Phillips was scheduled to present a briefing on the *maquiladora* project report and to provide his recommendations on this plant transfer decision. He fully understood the eagerness for "testing offshore waters" and, at the same time, the complexity of launching and managing a plant in a neighboring foreign country. He had only three more days to reach his final conclusion and prepare for the coming briefing.

# Case 38   IBM Global Services: The Professional Computer Services Industry

## Robert J. Mockler, Vincent Pawlowski, Dorothy G. Dologite, Marc E. Gartenfeld

1   In early 2001, Mr. John Joyce, Chief Financial Officer of International Business Machines (IBM), in presenting the company's fourth quarter and full year 2000 results to industry securities analysts at the Investors Relations meeting, January 17, 2001, commented that although IBM Global Services (IGS) had posted growth, quarter to quarter and year to year, results for 2000 were not what they wanted (IBM, 2001A). IBM Global Services had not met the company's objectives for the full year or last quarter in either revenue or pretax income (PTI), and its direct expense grew faster than its revenue. This certainly raised some concerns considering IGS' position as IBM's growth engine and second largest contributor to the company's bottom line. Mr. Joyce was also very careful to remind analysts that a slowing economy and its potential impact on Information Technology spending was still a wild card for future growth. The main question to be resolved was to create an enterprisewide strategy that would differentiate IBM Global Services from its competition.

2   Since December 1996 when IBM established IBM Global Services (IGS), IGS had achieved outstanding business results. IGS had grown its business faster than the industry, and IBM Global Services was then widely recognized as the largest computer services company in the world, surpassing EDS. Prior to this period, Integrated Systems Solution Corporation (ISSC), an IBM subsidiary and the predecessor of IGS, had similar results. It was accepted that the success of IBM's services business was a major contributor to IBM's overall business recovery and that the future of IBM was dependent upon the future success of IBM Global Services. Exhibit 1 identifies the segments of IBM (Hardware, Global Services, Software, Global Financing, Enterprise Investments/other) and the company's percentage of revenue by segment.

3   The Computer Services Industry, which includes three broad main categories of services, Processing Services (data entry, credit card authorization, billing payroll processing), Network Services (electronic data interchange services, electronic mail delivery, file transfer, and electronic funds transfer), and Professional Computer Services (technology consulting, custom programming, systems integration and outsourcing) had experienced a prolonged period of strong growth. This growth was expected to continue into 2001 and beyond primarily due to the service demands associated with the use of the Internet in business. This rapid growth was stimulating increased competition as well as high acquisition and alliance activity. However, a major impediment to sustained growth was the shortage of computer professionals, including programmers and system designers. This shortage was also significantly increasing the labor costs within this industry.

4   Louis V. Gerstner, Jr., Chairman and CEO of IBM, had driven IBM to follow an overall strategic focus to maintain a superior standing in the computer industry (Hardware, Software, Services and Financing). However, as IBM entered the twenty-first century a smaller percentage of its customers were expected to buy an item with "IBM" stamped on it. Mr. Gerstner made this clear in a statement made in late 1999.

Source: This case was prepared by Vincent Pawlowski, Marc E. Gartenfeld, Dororthy Dologite, and Professor Robert J. Mockler of St. John's University. © Robert J. Mockler.

**EXHIBIT 1**
IBM Company's
Percentage of
Revenue by Segment

| | 2000 | 1999 | 1998 |
|---|---|---|---|
| Hardware | 42.7 | 43.3 | 44.2 |
| Global Services | 37.5 | 36.7 | 35.4 |
| Software | 14.3 | 14.5 | 14.5 |
| Global Financing | 3.9 | 3.6 | 3.5 |
| Enterprise Invest./other | 1.6 | 1.9 | 2.4 |
| Total | 100 | 100 | 100 |

Sometime within the next five years, more than half of our revenues and workforce will come from services. This will mean that, very soon, revered IBM brand attributes like quality, reliability and innovation will primarily be descriptors of IBM people—their knowledge, ideas and behavior—just as today they describe IBM ThinkPads, servers and software."

*Louis V. Gerstner, Jr. Chairman and CEO, IBM*

5    The future of IBM was expected to be determined by its effectiveness in competing in the rapidly growing and highly competitive Computer Services Industry, specifically in the Professional Computer Services segment.

6    In light of IGS' declining financials and its overall importance to the future success of the IBM Corporation, Mr. Gerstner was asking his IGS executive management team to consider changing the way IGS was doing business. IGS' immediate task was to make several strategic decisions in the areas of target customers, services to be offered, geographic market expansion, and changes to its management system to take advantage of the industry trends, and to attract and retain skilled resources. These and other specific strategic questions needed answering if IBM Global Services was to differentiate itself from its competition and so achieve a winning edge over competitors within intensively competitive, rapidly changing immediate, intermediate, and long-term time frames.

# INDUSTRY AND COMPETITIVE MARKETS

7    The overall Computer Services Industry is a segment of the Computer Industry. The Computer Industry is comprised primarily of hardware, software, and services, as shown in Exhibit 2.

### Computer Services Industry

8    The segment of focus, Computer Services, can be divided into three main categories: Processing Services, Network Services, and Professional Computer Services, as shown in Exhibit 3.

9    Computer Services firms typically enter long-term relationships with their customers. This is true of all three segments (Professional Computer, Processing, and Network Services). These firms do so by signing contracts that specify the amount of time the designated services are to be provided and the monetary value of the services. Revenues derived from multiyear contracts can be accurately predicted by the computer services vendor and by financial analysts. Some computer services firms do business through annual or other short-term contracts that are renewed at expiration with great predictability. Computer services vendors undertake efforts to increase their "retention rates," or percentage of contract renewals, which usually run well over 90 percent.

**EXHIBIT 2**   The
**Computer Industry**

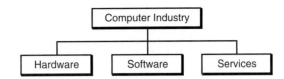

**EXHIBIT 3**   The Computer Services Industry

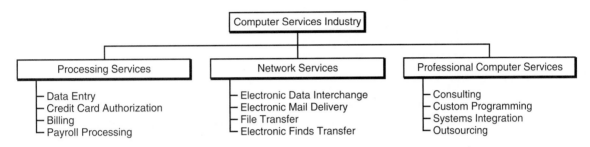

10    With a solid knowledge of revenues under multiyear contracts and past retention rates for contracts coming up for renewal, computer services firms can predict with a high degree of confidence the amount of revenues that they'll earn in a set time period. Based on these accurate revenue assessments, computer services companies can set and manage expenses at the levels necessary to earn the required return in each period. Rarely do computer services vendors post results that are materially different from those expected by the company or stock analysts.

11    According to Standard and Poor's Industry Survey, the computer services industry had experienced a prolonged period of strong growth, which was expected to continue into 2001 and beyond. Spending on computer services was forecasted to rise about 11 percent in 2001 to an estimated $429.9 billion. This was on top of the 11 percent growth in 2000, when sales reached an estimated $387.5 billion.

12    A large percentage of 2000's growth came in the second half of the year. This concentration reflected the year's having gotten off to a slow start, due to the lack of any Year 2000 (Y2K) impact, and a corresponding shortfall in spending, as well as a delay in spending by IT managers. In 1999, the sector total of $349 billion represented 13 percent growth over 1998.

13    According to Standard and Poor's Industry Survey, the global computer services industry would continue growing at a compound annual rate of 11 percent through 2004. The United States accounted for about 46 percent of the worldwide market for computer services in 1999, a percentage that was expected to remain steady over the next several years. The overall computer services business is a broad-based industry and is highly fragmented, with the 10 largest firms accounting for about 33 percent of total worldwide services revenues.

14    According to the U.S. Department of Labor, 1.96 million people were employed in the computer and data processing services industry at the end of October 2000, a rise of 6.5 percent from the 1.84 million employed at the end of 1999. The figure in 1999 represented growth of 8.2 percent from the 1.7 million employed at the end of 1998. However, while industry employment has been growing significantly faster than the U.S. economy, a major impediment is a shortage in skilled technology labor.

15    The United States is the world's largest producer and consumer of computer products and services. As presented in the U.S. Department of Commerce's Industry Outlook '99,

**EXHIBIT 4**
Top 10 Global
Service and Support
Suppliers, 1996
(millions of dollars)

| Company | Country | Revenues |
|---|---|---|
| IBM | U.S. | $22,785 |
| Electronic Data Systems | U.S. | 14,441 |
| Hewlett-Packard | U.S. | 9,462 |
| Digital Equipment | U.S. | 5,988 |
| Computer Science | U.S. | 5,400 |
| Accenture (Anderson Consulting) | U.S. | 4,877 |
| Fujitsu | Japan | 4,160 |
| Cap Gemini Sogeti | France | 4,104 |
| Unisys | U.S. | 3,949 |
| Automatic Data Processing | U.S. | 3,567 |

Services and support includes outsourcing, facilities management, systems integration, IT consulting, contract programming, and disaster recovery.

where it referenced a Datamation magazine's 1996 survey of computer companies worldwide, this survey indicated that 8 of the top 10 companies are U.S. companies. The survey results are shown in Exhibit 4. Within each specific product or service sector, the U.S. portion of leading companies is equally high. Additionally, most of the innovative and fastest growing computer services companies are in the United States. Because of the world dominance of U.S. companies, global trends and issues tend to be the same as those which affect the domestic industry.

16    One of the most significant trends in the computer services industry was convergence within the overall computer industry. Companies in diverse areas, computer hardware, software, information services, data communications, telecommunications, were rapidly forming alliances with each other through joint ventures, mergers, and acquisitions. These alliances allowed companies to integrate computer technology products with computer services so that they can offer a greater selection of products and services (services within all three segments). A key objective of these alliances was to remain viable in an increasingly competitive national and international marketplace by increasing the company's pool of resources with minimal training expense, increasing revenue growth and increasing the breadth of service offerings.

17    In the past alliances and acquisitions were common among hardware and software companies and hardware and communications equipment companies. In 2001 they were springing up among firms in much more diverse areas: hardware and software, data communications, Internet applications and World Wide Web development, graphic development, networking, and information publishing. Not only were large, well-known companies forming alliances among themselves, they were also forming them with smaller, more obscure companies. Small companies were forming alliances to keep a firm grip on their markets.

18    These alliances were designed to ensure the participating firm's competitiveness in the marketplace by offering business and residential consumers a broader range of high-quality products and services. Alliances and acquisitions also offered the ability to increase a company's skilled resources without the need for extensive training of existing or newly hired resources. This strategy also offered the opportunity to increase revenues by acquiring the other company's markets and service offerings.

19    All this was causing a blurring of traditional industry categories in computer information technology and communications. In the past distinctions among hardware manufacturers, software developers, communication equipment producers, service providers, and telecommunications companies were relatively clear. However, computer companies were

diversifying operations to enter the more lucrative computer services industry. Hewlett-Packard is an example of this with its introduction of e-services. Companies were branching out into a wide variety of activities through alliances with or acquisitions of other companies and diversification of their own internally developed services mixes.

20    Another factor in this increased spending was the trend towards client server architectures and away from traditional mainframe architectures. These factors were providing great opportunities for computer services providers offering services such as systems integration, consulting, maintenance, outsourcing, and disaster recovery.

21    As previously stated, the Computer Services segment can be divided into three main categories: Processing Services, Network Services, and Professional Computer Services.

## The Processing Services Segment

22    This segment comprises vendors that process customers' transactions and data using the vendor-owned computer systems (often with proprietary software). IDC estimates that the sector's revenues were $65.3 billion in 1999, with forecast growth of 6.6 percent in 2000, to $69.6 billion, and 6.5 percent in 2001, to $74.1 billion. IDC expects the sector to grow at about a 6 percent compound annual rate through 2004. The largest independent computer services processing vendor is Automatic Data Processing Inc. (ADP), a major supplier of employer, brokerage, dealer, and claims services, with revenues of $6.3 billion in fiscal 2000 (September).

23    The outlook was very good for data processing services. Traditional data processing services had strong growth opportunities. These services include data entry, credit card authorization, billing, and payroll processing. They are commonly referred to as back-office functions because they are routine, high-volume, easily automated functions. Many service providers in this area are small companies that target local businesses as clients. The demand for traditional data processing services is directly related to the strength of the local and national economies.

## The Network Services Segment

24    The network services companies provide a broad range of value-added network services, including electronic interchange services, electronic mail delivery, file transfer, and electronic funds transfer. These firms are increasingly providing more sophisticated forms of electronic commerce, including services that facilitate sales and customized research over the Internet.

25    The dominant factor in the growth of network services is the acceptance of the Internet as a business tool. In addition, the growth of the Internet as a means of electronic communications in residential markets will have a positive effect on certain network services companies. The third segment of this industry is Professional Computer Services, the focus of this paper.

## The Professional Computer Services Segment

26    The broad professional services segment, which is the industry's largest, includes Services, supported Technology Platforms, targeted Customers, methods of Sales and Distribution, targeted Markets, the Competition and the supportive Management System as shown in Exhibit 5.

27    The professional computer services segment was expected to experience strong growth, except in certain areas, such as custom programming. Growth in this area could level off as a result of the wide selection of sophisticated off-the-shelf hardware and software solutions. Other factors, such as greater hardware compatibility, the efficiencies offered by

**EXHIBIT 5**   **The Professional Computer Services Industry**

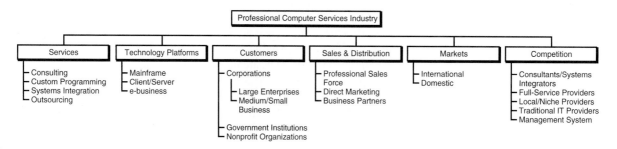

28   Numerous factors stimulated growth in this segment overall. Foremost among them are businesses' continued preference for client server architectures, the increased complexity of new information technology products, and the need to integrate them successfully into business operations. Additional factors contributing to the growth of this segment were the many information technology vendors, the convergence of information technology and communications technology products, and the need to integrate these products efficiently and effectively into business operations.

29   An additional trend in the global professional computer services sector was the record levels at which foreign businesses have been purchasing computers, software, and data communication equipment. This buying rush had been stimulated in part by reduced tariffs on information technology products in many countries. This expansion of the information technology infrastructure internationally benefits the companies offering professional computer services by providing greater opportunities for related services.

30   Another important trend in this segment industry was the growing proportion of spending on professional services relative to spending in the information technology markets overall, both at the national and international level. Expenditures on software and computer services have increased continuously compared with those of hardware, particularly in countries whose information technology and telecommunications infrastructure are relatively strong and developed. On average, one-fifth of information technology expenditures go to support services such as outsourcing, systems integration, consulting, customer programming, and disaster recovery. That share of spending was becoming the single largest segment of Computer Information Technology spending.

31   In a related trend, firms that traditionally specialized in computer products are developing new services and generating a higher proportion of revenues from them. This has occurred as prices for computer components have fallen in a fiercely competitive environment. According to Standard and Poor's, the IBM Corporation earned about $18.4 billion, about 24 percent of its revenues, in the 12 months ending 1997, from computer related services. And this has been steadily increasing each year since. Digital Equipment Corporation derived about 42 percent of its revenues from computer services, an amount totaling $6.2 billion in that same period (1997). The database market leader Oracle Corporation has expanded its consulting business; in this same period, computer services accounted for $3 billion (51 percent) of the company's revenues. Its closest competitor, Sybase Inc., derived about 46 percent of its revenue from consulting, education, and other computer services associated with sales of its core software products.

32   This increase in spending was due to advances in technology and the growing complexity of computer information technology, communication, and telecommunications systems.

**EXHIBIT 6**
**Top Information Technology Issues Worldwide (Based on a Nov. 1999 survey of information services executives)**

1. Organizing and utilizing data.
2. Aligning IS and corporate goals.
3. Connecting electronically to customers, suppliers, and/or partners.
4. Integrating systems.
5. Developing an electronic business strategy.
6. Capitalizing on advances in IT.
7. Instituting cross-functional information systems.
8. Cutting IS costs.
9. Using IT for competitive breakthroughs.
10. Improving IS human resources.

In addition, maintaining, supporting, and integrating information technology, computer services, and telecommunications in a multivendor environment generates a greater demand for computer services, such as consulting or outsourcing. This was illustrated by an industry survey performed by Computer Science Corporation in which they surveyed information services executives from several countries. Exhibit 6 presents these top ten issues, many of which offer opportunities for professional computer services; for example, issues 2 and 3 can be addressed through consulting services, issue 4 through systems integration services, issues 6 and 8 through outsourcing services.

33   Another significant trend was the prevalence of acquisitions, as companies scrambled to increase their technical skills, increase their service offerings, enter new markets, or establish themselves in new geographic areas.

34   Perhaps the most important factor in the growth of Professional Computer Services was the Internet. Businesses were attempting to take advantage of the Internet's potential while maintaining security and control over critical business data and information. This had created great demand for systems integration and computer consulting to resolve these sometimes-divergent goals.

35   A troublesome trend in the industry, which would slow future growth, was the shortage of skilled professionals. This shortage was impacting the availability of programmers and system designers. This shortage was also significantly increasing the labor costs within this industry. All service providers faced the challenge of attracting and retaining these highly sought after skills. However, there were some studies that suggested that this shortage was not as serious as it was being portrayed. These studies suggested that there was no shortage and that the industry created its own problems by using overly specific criteria for employment and by failing to make good use of older workers.

## Services

36   The services offered in the Professional Computer Services segment are consulting, custom programming, systems integration, and outsourcing. These services are applied across multiple technology platforms, which are discussed later. The greatest opportunities were available in consulting, systems integration, and outsourcing. They had enjoyed the most significant growth and, as previously stated, this trend would continue because of the continued complexity of information technology.

37   Computer consulting firms work with corporations to create and implement strategies to cope with the most complex business problems. These consultants combine their industry-specific experience with technology expertise to help clients improve overall performance and competitiveness. These firms address a client's issues by assessing and defining long-term information technology (IT) systems management strategy; designing administrative processes and selecting tools to manage systems; and creating an organizational structure that supports ongoing evaluation of system performance against dynamic business needs.

**EXHIBIT 7**
Worldwide
Consulting Services
(millions of dollars)

| | 1998 | 1999 | 2000 | F2003 | Annual Percent Growth 1998–2003 |
|---|---|---|---|---|---|
| Business Consulting | 6,674 | 8,118 | 9,856 | 17,850 | 21.7 |
| IT Consulting | 22,763 | 26,551 | 30,887 | 49,675 | 16.9 |
| Total | 29,437 | 34,669 | 40,743 | 67,525 | 18.1 |

F-Forecast

38      Many of the same factors driving demand for other technology services are driving demand for consulting services. In the private sector, companies are struggling to deal with continual changes in the regulatory environment, increased global competitions, post-merger integration issues, industry consolidation, the new digital economy, and growth strategies. This expected growth is presented in Exhibit 7.

39      In the public sector, pressure from taxpayers constantly requires governments to do more with less. The same pressures exist in the private sector as well. In order to compete more effectively, companies need to look for ways to expand revenues, cut costs, operate more efficiently, manage risk more effectively, and improve customer service. Consulting organizations help clients get a handle on these major issues. These services are also crucial for a government agency or company seeking to pursue an Internet strategy.

40      The keys to success in the area of consulting are offering a wide range of consulting services including both business and information technology services, requiring both business and technical expertise. This is because customers were taking a new look at how business and IT service would help them achieve success; these two areas (business and technology) were now tightly integrated. It is equally important to have highly skilled consulting resources. These resources need to have strong consulting skills, technology and industry knowledge, and expertise.

41      Professional services firms involved in custom programming provide clients with programmers on a temporary, per diem basis. Such firms are known as "body shops." Fees typically correlate with the technical skill required for the project. Customers of professional services firms include organizations whose current personnel lack the needed expertise, as well as firms undertaking projects that require additional staff but not permanent new hires. Demand for professional computer services, such as custom programming, had been aided by a long-standing shortage of computer professionals, including programmers and systems designers, available to work in business and government.

42      The general demand for software applications had grown substantially faster than the productivity of computer programmers. Although such an environment should be positive for the computer services industry, revenue growth in the custom programming business was actually slowing. The proliferation of prepackaged software and new software application development tools had decreased the demand for custom programming services. In addition, customer attitudes were changing. They were now looking for total, integrated solutions from its service providers. They no longer wanted to purchase the hardware, software, and communications equipment, and then have to manage the integration themselves through customer programming.

43      The keys to success in custom programming are computer programming expertise and a wide range of programming knowledge. Through this expertise a firm would develop a reputation for quality code. Effective maintenance of the application is another key to success; this is related to the overall quality of the code. This will ensure the profitability of the engagement and continue to enhance the reputation of the custom programming provider.

44    The systems integrator's role is to produce a unique computer system that meets a client's specific needs. The process is generally executed in various phases of a system's life cycle: planning, design, construction, implementation, and operation. A rapidly growing sector, systems integration owes its popularity to quickly advancing technology, a shortage of technical personnel, and the complexity of automating front office processes. Its two major markets are government and the commercial market.

45    The outlook for the commercial systems integration market was bright; it was expected to expand significantly faster than the government market. With such attractive prospects, integration firms that traditionally served government agencies have entered the commercial arena. Hardware vendors and the major accounting firms, as well as dedicated systems integrators, all hoped to ride the wave of growth in commercial systems integration. This growth is illustrated in Exhibit 8.

46    Keys to success in the area of systems integration are the ability to ascertain a client's requirements and translate them into a total, end-to-end solution. Success requires a thorough knowledge and ability to execute a system's life cycle: planning, design, construction, implementation, and operation. A clear demonstration of these skills leads to another key to success, a reputation as a quality systems integrator.

47    In the computer services industry, outsourcing involves a client organization hiring a computer services firm (or "outsourcing vendor") to perform a portion of its data processing and data management tasks. As part of the contract (which is often many years in length), the outsourcing vendor typically agrees to purchase the client's computer center facilities in order to execute the contract. This includes hiring the customer's data processing employees.

48    Outsourcing helps relieve companies from the task of managing computing resources, allowing them to focus on their core business. It furnishes the flexibility needed to expand the customer's data processing capabilities on a seasonal or ongoing basis, adopt new technologies, migrate key applications to new platforms and quickly develop, test, and deploy new applications. It also provides the technical skill and support to supplement the customer's in-house staff as needed. It matches computing resources to changing business requirements, and helps minimize the customer's technology investment by leveraging the vendor's expertise. Outsourcing can also provide flexibility to adopt and deploy new technology.

49    The outsourcing market is growing as a viable alternative to in-house information systems management. Major players include Andersen Consulting, Computer Sciences, Electronic Data Systems, and IBM. The widespread success of outsourcing is confirmed by the numerous "megacontracts" that large corporations from a variety of industries have awarded in recent years. Valued at hundreds of millions, or billions, of dollars over several years, these mega contracts involve varied types of services. Growth in this segment is presented in Exhibit 9.

**EXHIBIT 8**
**Worldwide Systems Integration Services (millions of dollars)**

| | 1998 | 1999 | 2000 | F2003 | Annual Percent Growth 1998–2003 |
|---|---|---|---|---|---|
| Application | | | | | |
| Development | 57,028 | 67,063 | 78,009 | 128,595 | 17.7 |
| Integration | 32,815 | 39,737 | 48,329 | 88,863 | 22.0 |
| Deployment | 21,527 | 25,320 | 29,718 | 45,919 | 16.4 |
| Total | 11,370 | 132,120 | 156,056 | 263,377 | 18.8 |

F-Forecast

**EXHIBIT 9**
Worldwide
Outsourcing Services
(millions of dollars)

| | 1998 | 1999 | 2000 | F2003 | Annual Percent Growth 1998–2003 |
|---|---|---|---|---|---|
| Operational Services | 44,521 | 51,532 | 59,779 | 92,929 | 15.9 |
| Application Management | 7,858 | 9,412 | 11,246 | 18,929 | 19.2 |
| Help Desk | 4,178 | 4,873 | 5,696 | 8,926 | 16.4 |
| Business Continuation | 6,197 | 7,264 | 8,595 | 14,666 | 18.8 |
| Asset Management | 2,637 | 3,198 | 3,919 | 7,144 | 22.1 |
| Transaction Processing | 17,874 | 19,340 | 21,221 | 30,544 | 11.3 |
| Total | 83,265 | 95,619 | 110,456 | 173,138 | 15.8 |

F-Forecast

50      Outsourcing services can include facilities management (in which the outsourcing vendor operates the client's data center on-site); remote computing (in which processing is done off-site); and communications network management, contract software programming, and software maintenance. Because no company can depend on a single customer, vendors generally manage more than one megacontract at a time.

51      The key to success in this area is to quickly assume the IT support requirements of the client without disrupting their operations. This requires significant investment in data centers strategically placed within the chosen geographic markets, the ability to provide the required resources, and/or absorb the resources (both hardware and human resources) transferred from the client to the vendor's operation.

52      The overall key to success in the area of services is to achieve market presence and share by providing a wide range of service offerings, with the ability to customize the service to meet the needs of specific industries or businesses. A provider also has to have the ability to offer a continuous flow of new services as IT trends evolve; this is accomplished through strong research and development. Another key to success is to achieve brand identification through wide advertising. These services must be based on the current technology platforms being utilized by their clients.

### Supported Technology Platforms

53      These services cover all technology platforms: mainframe (enterprise systems), client/server, and e-business. Each of these platforms presented opportunity to Professional Computer Services providers.

54      The mainframe is the largest computer, a powerhouse with extensive memory and extremely rapid processing power. It is used for very large business, scientific, or military applications where a computer must handle massive amounts of data or many complicated processes. The death of the mainframe was prematurely announced in the later 1980s and early 1990s.

55      This technology made a resurgence due to its relatively cheaper support costs, as compared to client/server technology; its ability to manage huge amounts of data and databases; and its scalability. IBM, the traditional leader in mainframe technology, led this effort by repositioning the mainframe as an enterprise server. This resurgence in the use of mainframes as enterprise servers offered continued opportunity for this technology.

56     The client/server platform is a model for computing that splits processing between "clients" and "servers" on a network, assigning functions to the machine most able to perform the function. The client is the user's point of entry for the required function and is normally a desktop computer, a workstation, or a laptop computer. The server provides the client with services or application access. The server can be a mainframe or a smaller specialized computer. Even though the relative support cost of client/server technology is high, its flexibility and cost of initial hardware investment is an advantage.

57     The high total cost of ownership, including initial purchase costs, the cost of hardware and software upgrades, maintenance, technical support and training, is still relatively high for client/server technology. The advent of network computers is helping to address this issue, and is a key component of the emerging "network economy."

58     Network computing utilizes a simplified desktop device that does not store software programs or permanent data. Users download whatever software or data they need from a central computer over the Internet or an organization's own internal network. The high total cost of ownership for client/server technology makes outsourcing of these services very attractive, and offers Professional Computer Service providers a clear opportunity. The emergence of network computing, driving the new network economy, offers significant opportunities for the Computer Industry overall, but especially the Professional Computer Services segment. Companies will be looking at computer servers as just another utility, with vast networks delivering applications, data, and computing capabilities to an estimated one trillion network-connected devices by the year 2005. Companies will be relying on Computer Services firms to provide all their IT needs. The network economy was expected to bring into question how companies acquire and manage information technology since the IT infrastructure will be moved out of the corporate data center, and onto a global network. Companies will be renting it as a service with the expectation that it will vastly increase a company's access to computing power, expertise, and innovation.

59     E-business is a suite of products (hardware, software, and services) that enables an organization to use the Internet and other digital mediums for communication and coordination, and the management of the firm. It is an enabler that extends the reach of existing management. It includes, but is not limited to, e-commerce, the process of buying and selling goods and services electronically involving transactions using the Internet, networks, and other digital technologies.

60     This technology was emerging as the primary technology platform for the new economy. It was revolutionizing the way business operated and was managed. This was providing Professional Computer Service Providers significant opportunity in the areas of outsourcing of web content hosting (a company hosting its website on a vendor's infrastructure and having the vendor provide total management); consulting (providing a client advice and direction as it stakes its claim in the e-business marketplace safely, quickly, and profitably); and custom programming (providing application development services which understand, use, and expand a client's intranet, extranet, and messaging potential through complex web application development).

61     This technology offered great opportunity for Professional Computer Service companies since it was estimated that over 50 percent of large companies and 75 percent small and medium businesses were still in the early stages of web adoption as of 2000. Early adoption is defined as only having a web presence, that these companies were still not leveraging the full power of the Internet for transaction processing and delivery services. Therefore these companies would be looking for various services to enable them to conduct business over the web.

62     The key to success in the technology area is to have excessive knowledge across all technology platforms. Although e-business was clearly the industry focus at this time, many

companies had significant investment in large mainframes, and client/server was still the predominant architecture used throughout the industry. The ability to build new solutions based on current and future technology was also crucial. This required a strong research and development capability.

### The Growth and Impact of The Internet

63    Originally, the Internet was an inexpensive and helpful communication device for academics and defense industry engineers. In the mid-1980s it began to be used for a broader purpose after the invention of the World Wide Web. The development in the early 1980s of graphic viewers to interface with the Web was the breakthrough that enabled a larger portion of the computer-using population to embrace the Internet. As the Internet grew into the mid-1990s, the Web and on-line transactions remained in their infancy. However, as the year 2000 approached, the ability to buy and sell electronically matured, and a fundamental transformation occurred in the United States and the global market place.

64    Internet use became oriented more toward business needs: advertising, marketing, communication, and to an extent sales. The corporate world's use of the Internet has outpaced its earlier uses such as file access and file transfer. Internet technology is having a profound effect on global trade of software products, and technical, financial, professional, and many other services, but especially computer services.

### Customers

65    The customer base for the Computer Services Industry includes a wide range of organizations. It primarily offers services to corporations, including large enterprises and medium and small businesses, as well as government institutions and private institutions.

66    Large corporate enterprises with more than 1,000 employees offered the Professional Computer Services segment an opportunity to provide its broad range of services to the company's management. The large enterprises had several motivations in seeking Professional Computer Services. These companies clearly saw Information Technology (IT) as critical to competitive advantage. IT executives were involved in business strategy and the business executives were involved in IT decisions. These companies are typically not IT innovators, but are fast followers, and are uncomfortable with the Internet, but planned significant use of the Internet. They preferred all-in-one solutions, which were often customized solutions, which bundle computer products and Professional Computer Services. They usually prefer long-term relationships with one or two services providers.

67    Keys to success to attract and retain large corporations included the ability of the service provider to provide a customizable, all-in-one solution. The service provider needed to have a proven track record in providing services to meet the specific needs of the company's industry. Therefore, a broad range of service offerings, skilled resources with the ability to customize these offerings, and the knowledge of the customer's industry were crucial. Having these keys to success would enable a service provider to attract and retain large corporate customers by meeting their specific requirements.

68    Medium and small corporations with fewer than 1,000 employees offer the Professional Computer Services segment a significant opportunity because they are one of the untapped growth areas. However, they are very difficult to market to and support. Therefore, a company that can effectively market to and efficiently support medium and small corporations can have a strategic advantage over their competition.

69    These companies are comfortable with Internet technology and have widely deployed it. They prefer long-term, trusted advisors, and they very often purchase services, but are highly price sensitive. They typically cannot, do not, meet IT requirements internally (especially small businesses) and do not want customized solutions. It is estimated that

almost half (45 percent of future opportunities in Professional Computer Services will come from small and medium businesses. This market, for instance, was growing faster than either large enterprise or consumer markets. In the United States alone there were 22 million small businesses. They typically have simpler business and IT processes and while they are highly diverse and costly to reach, many, but not all, understand that the Web can enable them to compete with much larger firms on equal footing since everyone is just a click away on the Web.

70      Keys to success to attract and retain medium and small corporations and businesses is the ability to provide standardized solutions at a competitive price. In addition, due to the challenge of effectively marketing and supporting this type of customer, a strong direct marketing capability was also crucial.

71      Government institutions are as large, if not larger than, large enterprise corporations and require high maintenance. Many government operations such as NASA and NATO are highly technology oriented and therefore present an opportunity for Professional Computer Services Providers. For example, the largest user of system integration services is the U.S. government. However, ongoing pressure to reduce government spending in general and to cut defense budgets in particular had produced uncertainties in this segment. This trend is truly global. But, it may also have a reverse effect for some government institutions that seek to reduce their cost through efficiencies brought about by computer innovations. This could lead to an increased demand for Professional Computer Services.

72      The keys to success with government institutions is to have knowledge of and ability to leverage the bureaucracy found in such organizations.

73      Nonprofit organizations may be large or small. They include education providers, community organizations, and religious organizations to name a few. They do offer an opportunity since they require computer service solutions just like any other customer; however, they are typically very price sensitive. Like medium and small corporations, the key to success for nonprofit organizations is the ability to provide standardized solutions at the lowest cost possible.

74      Overall keys to success in attracting and retaining customers include knowing how to service customers through knowledge of their specific industry or business, and by targeting the customer segments with the greatest growth potential.

### Sales/Distribution

75      The sales and distribution strategies within the Professional Computer Services Industry utilize professional sales forces, direct marketing, and/or working through business partners.

76      Typically Professional Computer Service providers employ trained professionals to sell their services. These resources are usually trained to support a specific industry sector (for example, the manufacturing, financial, or entertainment sectors). Industry knowledge is crucial in this services segment. Customers want and expect that their providers know their industry-specific requirements and can translate these requirements into meaningful solutions. They may also have skills for a specific technology or offering.

77      These highly skilled and expensive resources are usually applied to the firm's largest customers. These customers require this personalized, face-to-face support, and their contract values can support the cost of the sales force. The key to success for a professional sales force is the ability to market the company's services in the context of the client's industry or business. This requires in-depth industry and technology knowledge.

78      The underlying logic of direct marketing is making direct contact with customers through alternate media (for example telephone, telemarketing, mail, or the Internet). Many Professional Computer Services companies employ telemarketing and the Internet to sell to customers, especially small to medium-sized customers.

79      The key to success with Direct Marketing as a channel is to ensure customers have ready access to these sales resources. The ability to reach a person, with limited delay, is a must. Many telemarketing functions offer 24/7 coverage, and many firms are incorporating a "call me" facility from their websites, which allow a customer to receive a call back within a specified period of time.

80      Business Partners are independent distributors who enter into agreements with Professional Computer Service providers to market and distribute all or part of the provider's solutions. Business Partners develop, market, influence, sell, deliver and/or support solutions with components (hardware, software, and services) from the service company it has partnered with.

81      The key to success with Business Partners is to develop strong relationships with this alternate channel by providing quality services for them to market, and offering incentives to ensure your services are reaching the customers.

82      An overall key to success in the area of Sales and Distribution is to control cost by applying appropriate sales channels to the customer segment.

## Domestic and International Markets

83      Global demand for Professional Computer Services was growing tremendously. The United States accounted for about 46 percent of the worldwide market for Professional Computer Services in 1999. Significant growth was expected for the United States as well as in Europe and Asia, especially in the areas of system integration and outsourcing. Many leading Professional Computer Services firms generate up to one-third of their revenue abroad, so their performance can be affected by growth trends in the real Gross Domestic Product (GDP) of foreign economies. IT spending as a percent of GDP was growing in every country, led by English-speaking countries. France and Germany were projected to join these leaders as well. Asia represented another growth area, including China, even though it was behind the worldwide average for IT spending.

84      The size and growth opportunities available in international markets would continue to attract Professional Computer Services companies. With a significant percentage of revenues tied to foreign markets, many firms are subject to foreign currency risk. For U.S.-based firms overseas sales are translated from local currencies into dollars; a strong dollar hurts reported earnings, while a weak dollar helps.

85      The European and Asian markets represented significant opportunity for Professional Computer Service providers. This was especially true for outsourcing opportunities across all technology platforms, but especially true for e-business.

86      The key to success in this area is to maintain and grow market share by servicing a diverse set of markets (geographic and industry-specific). This is accomplished from a geographic perspective by having a presence in each of the major markets. A service provider would have to have data centers strategically located in the geographies in order to effectively provide outsourcing services.

## Management System

87      The sustained growth of Computer Services, and in particular, Professional Computer Services, had triggered a serious shortage of skilled IT professionals, and this had ignited a war for talent among IT service providers. By 2001, an estimated 800,000 IT positions in the United States and Europe were unfilled for lack of qualified candidates, and fewer college graduates were choosing computer sciences. Professional Computer Service providers faced the challenge of attracting and retaining these required resources.

88      In an industry where skilled resources are the most important resource, Professional Computer Services providers must have a management system which attracts and retains their employees by enabling them to realize their business and professional growth potential.

# COMPETITION

89    Each of the various computer services market segments is dominated by several large vendors that use size, reputation, expertise, and marketing prowess to secure the largest contracts awarded by the largest organizations. These are the companies that are likely to bid successfully on the largest contracts in this industry.

90    Computer services firms are entrusted to install, manage, or otherwise refine an organization's computer networks or perform crucial processing tasks. Therefore, it's rare for a small, unknown computer services firm with limited operating experience to win business with a Fortune 1000 company or other large organization. Opportunities do exist, however, for smaller vendors to service the computing needs of small office, home office, and personal computing markets, where the jobs are less complex.

91    Customer demand is attracting increasing competition from traditional services competitors and spawning new competition as services providers seek leadership positions across the full spectrum or in elements of the services value chain. The four prevalent types of competitors are:

- Consultants/Systems Integrators (like Accenture, formally Andersen Consulting)

- Full Services Providers (such as EDS and CSC)

- Local/Niche Providers (for example, NTT or ADP)

- Traditional IT Providers (like HP or Oracle, Sybase)

92    In its most recent quarterly report, 4Q 2000, Computer Sciences (CSC) continued showing revenue growth in the 12 percent range. It signed $4.4 billion worth of new contracts in the quarter, with new deals up 45 percent in the first half of its fiscal year. Electronic Data Systems had been harder hit by the Y2K slump, but reported 8 percent growth in its most recent quarter. EDS is starting work on a $6.9 billion deal with the U.S. Navy, signed in the previous quarter. The other services industry news was no news at all: the planned takeover of PriceWaterhouse Coopers' consulting business by HP was called off due in large part to HP's inability to pay for the expensive deal with its slumping stock. The following competitive analysis is based on the leader within each of the four types of competitors.

# CONSULTANTS/SYSTEMS INTEGRATORS (ACCENTURE)

93    Accenture, formally Andersen Consulting, a unit of Andersen Worldwide, is a global management and technology consulting organization generating $8.9B in FY99-ending December 31, 1999. This represents an 8 percent increase over 1998 results and a 10 percent increase after removing the impact of international exchange rates. The company's mission was to help its clients create the client's future. Accenture was repositioning itself by moving beyond consulting to become a network of businesses that will be a market maker of the new e-business economy. To execute this mission, Accenture integrated its various industry specializations with its competencies in strategic services, change management, processes, and technologies to provide a total solution for its customers. To serve its strategic deliverables, the company offers its customers a variety of services addressing supply chain management, electronic commerce, customer relationship management, enterprise business solutions, and knowledge management. The partnership also provides outsourcing of business operations through its Business Process Management operation, along with custom programming and system integration services. Accenture lacked the broad service offerings provided by a Full-Service Provider such as IBM Global Services.

94     After a prolonged two-and-a-half year struggle, on August 7, 2000, an international arbitrator ruled that the links between accountancy firm Arthur Andersen and Andersen Consulting be severed immediately. Under the ruling, the consulting arm will lose the right to the Andersen name at the end of the 2000 calendar year, an outcome seen as a victory for the consulting group. Arthur Andersen had claimed that Andersen Consulting should pay a termination fee of $14.5B to leave the umbrella organization, a claim that was denied. However, Arthur Andersen retained rights to jointly developed software and gained $1B in undistributed funds. The split freed Andersen Consulting from an SEC ruling on conflict of interest between audit and consulting that now limits the kinds of consulting work permitted to Big Five accounting firms. Beginning January 1, 2001, Andersen Consulting began operating under its new brand name Accenture, described as a combination of "accent" and "future" that means to accelerate, to amplify, and to exceed expectations. This name change triggered a massive advertising campaign to achieve brand identification as a worldwide Professional Computer Services provider.

95     Accenture announced record global revenue for the fiscal year ending August 31, 2000, a 15.4 percent increase over the previous year. The firm had achieved double-digit growth for the past 7 consecutive years and 11 of the past 12 years. The company was known for the following strengths.

### Global Presence

96     Accenture had grown significantly from its formation in 1989 with $1.6B in revenue and 21,400 employees to become a leading management and technology consulting firm, generating $8.9B in revenue in 1999, and employing approximately 65,000 people in 48 countries. The company claimed 85 percent of the Fortune 100 global companies as customers, which they market to via dedicated sales/consulting resources known for their skills and industry knowledge; an Internet presence which was limited to presenting information only, no transactions; and good relationships with business partners. They had effectively marketed and serviced large, small, and medium businesses by providing all-in-one solutions, and to a limited extent, competitively priced standardized solutions. In the e-commerce area, Accenture claimed their clients include more than half of both the Fortune Global 500 and The Industry Standard 100, representing the most important companies of the Internet economy.

### Broad Industry Coverage

97     Accenture targeted 16 industry segments, grouped into five global market units: Financial Services, Products, Communications and High Tech, Resources, and Government. The firm's Government and Communications industries led all its industry sectors with 35 percent and 29 percent growth, respectively. The firm estimated its electronic commerce revenue to be $1.5B in 1999, triple the firm's $500M e-commerce revenue in 1998. Its Consumer and Pharmaceutical Products, Electronics/High Tech, and Insurance industries also showed double-digit growth again in 1999. Financial Services that represented the fastest growing global market in 1998 at 33 percent exhibited 0 percent growth in 1999 resulting from an 18 percent decline in Health Services, offsetting an 11 percent gain in Insurance. While the Communications and High Tech global market also showed significant growth in 1999 at 29 percent, overall it slowed from a 25 percent increase in 1998, reflecting a drop in Media and Entertainment revenue growth from 31 percent to 4 percent. Professionals in the company's industry practices form teams with representatives from the firm's competencies in technology, strategy, change management, and process.

### Strong Research and Development Effort

**98**   Through R&D activities, Accenture would assess the business impact of new technologies and apply emerging technologies to create innovative business solutions. The company operated the Center for Strategic Technology Research (CSTaR) conducting leading-edge research on technologies. Specifically, CSTaR continually investigates how the convergence of computing, communication, and content technologies would change how we work and live in the next three to five years. Despite these strengths, Accenture exhibited some weaknesses and faced some risks.

### Change in Top Management

**99**   In September 1999, Andersen Consulting Managing Partner and CEO George Shaheen resigned his position to join an Internet grocer, Webvan Group, with a compensation package estimated at more than $100M. Mr. Shaheen had served as Chief Executive since the firm's formation in 1989, overseeing the firm's increase in revenue from $1.3B in 1989 to $8.3B in 1998. Several industry analysts questioned Accenture's continued success with the departure of Shaheen. In November 1999, the partners appointed a longtime Andersen Consulting partner, Joe W. Forehand, as the new CEO and Managing Partner. Mr. Forehand, who had held leadership positions in 11 of the 16 industries served by Andersen Consulting, planned to focus on taking Andersen Consulting to its "next level of marketplace leadership." Forehand faced the challenges of the transformation of Accenture into a profitable e-business consultancy, the branding challenge of a name change, and industrywide alteration of the long-standing billing per-hour formula to a fixed-fee market.

### Competitive Market

**100**   Accenture faced an increasingly competitive market as management consultants, systems integrators, and systems vendors continued to expand their operations into related technology consulting and outsourcing operations. In addition, the Big Five accounting firms now also relied on the profitable consulting within the Professional Computer Services area. Smaller niche firms had also arisen to provide more focused competition in localized markets. The company faced increased competition in the e-business area with many consulting firms establishing e-business strategies. In addition, the company competed with smaller firms, which were perceived as providing leading-edge knowledge while being nimble and flexible, and were increasingly attracting large corporate clients as well as experienced consultants. However, Accenture had strong market intelligence due to its worldwide network of consultants and the relationships it had developed as being a part of the Andersen Worldwide team.

### Employee Turnover

**101**   Due to industry growth, Accenture faced a tight market for recruiting and retaining employees. While the company had improved its employee turnover rate somewhat, it still saw top employees in the IT field leaving to join Internet startups that offer large compensation packages typically with significant stock options. IPO slowdowns were expected to temper this trend in 2001, but burnout from long hours and travel did remain issues. This was a sign that Accenture did not have an effective management system to attract and retain skilled resources.

### Limited Service Offerings

**102**   Accenture had a distinct weakness since it was limited in the services provided, focusing solely on consulting and systems integration. They did not provide outsourcing services, an area that presented significant opportunity. This was especially true because businesses were implemented e-business solutions, and with the emergence of network computing, both led to the growth of outsourcing services.

# FULL SERVICES PROVIDERS (EDS)

103 EDS, which takes credit for pioneering the concept of outsourcing nearly four decades ago, was among a handful of large outsourcers offering an end-to-end services portfolio, including management consulting, e-business solutions, business process management, and information solutions.

104 Since entering the arena, EDS claimed to have become a global leader in providing e-business and information technology services to 9,000 business (large and small providing all-in-one and standardized solutions) and government clients in approximately 55 countries around the world. EDS markets through a worldwide network of direct sales force with an industry orientation, a limited Internet presence (no transaction capability), and good business partner relationships. The company posted revenues of $18.53 billion in 1999 and signed new contracts in 1999 valued at more than $24.9 billion. The company was known for the following strengths.

### Global Presence and Broad Industry Coverage

105 The company has more than 121,000 employees worldwide and brings deep industry practice knowledge to solve challenges in a wide variety of industries, including communications, energy, financial, government, health care, manufacturing and retailing, and transportation. Business alliances with industry-leading organizations, including relationships with companies such as WebMethods, SeeBeyond, and SAP America, have been key to EDS efforts to extend its clients' reach in the marketplace with new services.

### Operational Efficiency

106 The company has recently set in motion changes designed to streamline its operations, including reducing its workforce and rearranging its offerings, to make it a leaner, more efficient competitor and to update its image as a lumbering, stodgy behemoth. EDS increased its investment in research and development to enable a continuous flow of new services supporting current and future technologies. The company was known for the following weaknesses.

### Aggressive Buying of Market Share

107 Several industry analysts were questioning EDS' strategy for competing against outsourcing leader IBM Global Services. EDS was sacrificing profit margin by aggressively buying market share. The concern was that EDS was paying too much to win outsourcing contracts. EDS was paying several times what would normally be a competitive rate, an example of which was the 2001 contract to assume management of the Sabre's air-travel infrastructure.

# LOCAL/NICHE PROVIDERS (ADP)

108 ADP, with nearly 500,000 clients across multiple industries, was one of the largest companies in the world dedicated to providing computerized transaction processing, data communications, and information services for specific niche markets. However, ADP's services were very narrowly focused, allowing them to focus on the customer segments with the greatest growth potential for ADP's service offerings. The company's services included employer services such as payroll, payroll tax, and human resource management; brokerage services such as securities transaction processing, and investor communication services; in-

dustry specific computing and consulting services for auto and truck dealers; dealer services, such as computerized auto repair estimating; and auto parts availability services. All of ADP's computing services enabled clients to process and/or distribute data (its own, ADP's, or that of third parties) and/or to interactively access and utilize ADP and third-party databases and information, utilizing ADP's batch, interactive, and client site systems. These services are marketed through a network of highly skilled direct sales force resources. ADP focused on providing custom and standardized solutions at a competitive price. The core services were supported by consulting services, custom programming, and systems integration. ADP's consultancy was very strong due to its narrow focus allowing for strong industry and technical expertise in the areas they serviced.

109     Employer Services, Brokerage Services, Dealer Services, and Claims Services were the company's four largest businesses. Together, they represent over 95 percent of ADP's revenue and are the key strategic elements of the company's future growth. The company was very strong financially with approximately $6.3 billion in annual revenues, over $4.5 billion in shareholders' equity, over 12 percent growth in revenue and earnings, about 20 percent return on equity, 156 consecutive quarters of record revenues and earnings per share, and 39 consecutive years of double-digit increases in EPS.

110     For fiscal 2000, which ended 30 June 2000, revenues grew 13 percent to about US$6.3 billion. Prior to nonrecurring charges in 1999, pretax earnings increased 21 percent, and diluted earnings per share increased 16 percent of $1.31. During fiscal 1999 the company sold several businesses and decided to exit several other businesses and contracts. It also recorded transaction costs and other adjustments related to Employer Services' acquisition of Vincam. The combination of these transactions resulted in nonrecurring charges of $0.03 in fiscal 1999. Fiscal 2000 was ADP's thirty-ninth consecutive year of double-digit earnings per share growth since becoming a public company in 1961. The company was known for the following strengths.

## Strengths

111     ADP continued to operate from a position of solid financial results and liquidity. Standard & Poor's includes ADP among only 10 companies to which it gives its highest AAA rating. The company remained very strong financially with more than $6.3 billion in annual revenues, over $4.5 billion in shareholders' equity, over 12 percent growth in revenue and earnings, about 20 percent return on equity, 156 consecutive quarters of record revenues and earnings per share, and 39 consecutive years of double-digit increases in EPS. The market potential for the company was still excellent. Employer Services (ES) was its oldest business and was the leading provider of outsourced payroll and Human Resource Management services. However, very good potential remained in every ES market segment as the outsourcing trend continued to gain momentum. For instance, ADP's business that provided payroll and other services to small and medium businesses in North America had over 370,000 clients, yet this represented only a fraction of the 11 million companies plus 24 million home-based businesses in the U.S. market that could potentially use the company's services. About 60 percent of middle-market companies still had not yet chosen to outsource payroll and Human Resource Management. Also, although the company's National Accounts business in North America had grown to over $800 million annually, the market potential among ADP's existing large-employer clients was over $11 billion. ADP did not fully leverage these relationships as a distribution channel. The company was known for the following weaknesses.

## Weaknesses

112     ADP had grown essentially through an ongoing strategic program of acquisitions, rather than through internal growth. Some industry analysts believed that continued growth through acquisition for the company will become increasingly difficult over time, and may

ultimately lead to the need for costly restructuring. Further, with the continued growth of other competitive organizations, and the advances made in the various technologies required to support customers in the markets in which ADP served, there was an expected increase in competition for the company to deal with in the future. Factors such as those indicated above may, at some point, cause the company to be unable to report the same high levels of continuing growth as it had in the past. For example, increased competitive pressures may ultimately prevent ADP from maintaining its string of 156 consecutive quarters of double-digit earnings per share (EPS) growth. In addition, due to its narrow focus, and targeting local and niche customers, it was weak in addressing the needs of large corporate customers, and did not have nor need a large Internet presence.

## TRADITIONAL IT PROVIDERS (HEWLETT-PACKARD)

113   Much of Chairman, President, and CEO Carly Fiorina's tenure at Hewlett-Packard (HP) had been focused on the reorganization of a company plagued by high overhead costs and the inability to respond to market conditions. Through a combination of layoffs, product line reorganizations, and a refocusing on the computer services sector, Ms. Fiorina transformed HP into a focused competitor. The company's financial results indicated that Hewlett-Packard had some success in this area. After posting weak quarter-over-quarter results during much of 1998 and into 1999, results for the quarter ending June 2000 showed a 16 percent revenue increase.

114   However, during fiscal 1Q01, revenue grew only 2 percent to $11.9 billion, from $11.6 billion the pervious year. Consequently, HP missed the forecast of $12.4 billion on its top line by 4 percent. HP's EPS for the first quarter 2001 were $0.16, compared with $0.40 the previous year. HP's officials blamed a slowdown in the U.S. economy, execution issues, pricing pressure on the PC and printing businesses, and adverse currency effects when explaining why the company missed its forecast. The disparity between the contributions of earnings for each business unit was increasingly steady. Its Image and Printing segment was of increased importance to HP. The Computing System segment's top line increased 2 percent, representing 40 percent of the total revenue. The third major business division, Computer Services, posted the highest year-over-year growth rate of 13 percent, and represents 15.5 percent of revenue. However, Computer Services' operational results declined 19 percent from $125 million to $101 million when comparing first quarter 2000 to first quarter 2001. HP should have been concerned with the fact that they were growing faster in this area with diminishing profitability.

115   HP credited part of its revenue growth to its e-services strategy, designed to highlight the way HP technology supports the growth of electronic services over the Internet. In general, the company's product strategy essentially utilizes all of the company's products ranging from inkjet printers and consumer appliances to PCs, workstations, and high-end Unix servers. This had given Hewlett-Packard a focused message that appeared to be winning over some customers. Previously, Hewlett-Packard seemed to be outmaneuvered by rivals such as Sun Microsystems and IBM. HP had also implemented an industry orientation to its market strategy, but it was still fundamentally a hardware company. But as a hardware company, it had a good ability to build new solutions based on current and future technologies due to its research and development capabilities.

116   HP, as with all of the competitors within the traditional IT provider category, was limited in the range of services it provided. Typically these companies focused on their original core product and wrapped services around that competency. In the case of HP it was equipment, and for Oracle and Sybase it was software, specifically database management software and services. All were seeking to provide e-business support and services, but did not have the full range of services as some of the other categories of competitors.

They were weak in the areas of consulting, custom programming, systems integration and outsourcing.

## THE COMPANY

**117** Since December 1996 when IBM established IBM Global Services (IGS), IGS had achieved outstanding business results. IBM Global Services had grown its business faster than the industry, and IGS was widely recognized as the largest services company in the world, surpassing EDS as shown in Exhibit 10. Previously, ISSC, an IBM subsidiary, had similar results. It was accepted that the success of IBM's services business was a major contributor to IBM's overall business recovery.

**118** IBM Global Services' results in 2000 were not what the company's executives wanted. IGS didn't meet its objectives for the full year or last quarter in either revenue or pretax income (PTI), and its direct expense grew faster than its revenue. IGS' investment in Web Hosting was showing promise with revenue growth of more than 200 percent last year. Web Hosting, part of e-business services, was a new business and had required significant investment and has not as yet contributed to gross profit.

**119** IGS in the year 2000 did grow 5 percent (12 percent at constant currency rate) in the fourth quarter to $9.2 billion, reflecting revenue growth across all services categories. E-business services revenues grew more than 70 percent year over year. Revenue comparisons for IBM Global Services were adversely affected by a year-over-year decline in the Y2K services business and the sale of the IBM Global Network to AT&T in 1999, ending IGS' direct involvement in the Network Services segment. After adjusting for these factors, IBM Global Services revenues (excluding maintenance) increased 10 percent (17 percent at constant currency rate).

**120** IGS had been very successful in increasing its revenue, broadening its range of service offerings, and building its pool of resources through acquisitions and alliances. In the first quarter of 2001, they had acquired Mainspring Corporation, an e-business consulting firm for $80 million; Informix, a database application and consulting company for $1 billion; and entered into strategic alliances with Ariba, a provider of business-to-business (B2B) applications and services; and i2, a supply chain management and e-business consulting firm.

**121** In light of the significant opportunities the Computer Services Industry presents and IBM's desire to transform itself more into a Service Company (both IT and Business services) through its IGS business unit, IGS will need to consider changing the way they conduct business. This services orientation will require them to answer the question of how to convert the e-business mind share that they have developed to true market share. (IBM coined the term e-business.) How will IGS expand its outsourcing service to include the other geographies, such as Europe and Asia? How can IGS take advantage of the services opportunities in the small and medium business market segment, and be profitable while doing so? And what management systems investments are necessary to

**EXHIBIT 10**
**Top Five Service Providers in 1999**

| Company | Type of Services | Revenue (US$ Billions) | Market Share (%) |
|---|---|---|---|
| IBM Global Services | Multisegment | $34.6 | 8.2% |
| EDS | Multisegment | 18.6 | 4.4 |
| Accenture | Consultancy | 10.3 | 2.5 |
| Computer Sciences Corp | Multisegment | 8.9 | 2.1 |
| Hewlett-Packard | Multisegment | 7.9 | 1.9 |

Multisegment = full-service provider (consulting, custom programming, system integration, outsourcing).

support this business transformation? These and other strategic decisions will have to be made if IBM Global Services is to succeed and win against the competition.

# SERVICES

**122** IBM Global Services offers consulting services, custom programming, systems integration, and outsourcings services through three lines of businesses (LOB). Each line of business is segmented along industry lines so they have an in-depth understanding of the customer's specific challenges and requirements.

## Consulting and Custom Programming

**123** Consulting and custom programming services are offered through IGS' Business Innovation Services (BIS) line of business. Business Innovation Services provides business and industry consulting and custom programming. By combining industry expertise with leading-edge technologies, BIS develops innovative solutions to help its customers solve complex challenges associated with business, such as growing revenue and profit, attracting and retaining customers, reducing costs and time to market in inventory, and enabling new business designs and processes.

**124** Business Innovation Services had a network of worldwide consultancy practices staffed with highly trained consultants. These practices had an industry orientation, focusing on five main industry sectors: communications, distribution, financial services, industrial, and public. The revenue from the consultant practices was steadily increasing while the revenue from the custom programming services offered by BIS remained flat year to year.

## System Integration

**125** This service is provided through IGS' Integrated Technology Services (ITS) line of business. ITS understands that improving the effectiveness and efficiency of computer systems is vital to business growth. It helps companies gain greater productivity and optimizes return on the companies' computer investments. ITS builds the technical infrastructures that enables new business initiatives and helps customers keep pace with rapidly changing technology. ITS can help assure the continued performance and value of a customer's systems and networks. They assess the customer's systems environment, define and prioritize initiatives for improvement, and provide support and training to the customer's IT department and end users.

**126** IBM Global Services Integrated Technology Services had a proven track record of helping customers pull all their information technology systems together. ITS ensures the reliability of systems and networks, maximizes IT efficiency and flexibility, secures Internet transactions, provides support and training, and maintains server hardware, software, and networks. ITS experts helped companies worldwide to address the total IT picture, from architecture and proof of concept to network consulting and integration. ITS was very strong in providing true end-to-end solutions.

## Outsourcing

**127** This service is provided through IGS' Strategic Outsourcing (SO) line of business. SO understands that gaining a competitive advantage through outsourcing involves evaluating the customer's business strategy and differentiating core from noncore operations. SO provided its customers a flexible management strategy, immediate technological improvements through world-class skills, infrastructure and management processes, as well as ongoing, reliable, and secure management of business operations. SO will take over all aspects of running a customer's data center or companywide computer infrastructure.

128    IGS' Strategic Outsourcing was the world's largest and most experienced outsourcing provider, with over 73,000 servers and mainframes under its management in 133 global data centers. Fifteen of these centers were focused exclusively on e-business, hosting a customer's Internet and/or Intranet sites. Although IGS SO had this extensive global reach, they did not have a significant outsourcing market share in Europe and parts of Asia. When putting together an outsourcing deal, IGS' believes it is imperative that they protect the interests of both IGS and the customer. They seek to maintain an acceptable level of profitability while guarding the customer's investment by ensuring IGS' ability to deliver a full range of quality services throughout the life of the contract.

## SUPPORTED TECHNOLOGY PLATFORMS

129    IGS, as well as IBM overall, offers solutions across all technology platforms: mainframe, client/server, and e-business. IGS had been the industry leader and innovator in all three areas. IBM demonstrated this commitment to technology leadership and the rapid delivery of customer solutions incorporating this technology innovation through its extensive investment in research and development.

130    IBM had led all companies in the number of patents issued by the U.S. government patent office during the eight years leading up to 2000. IBM led all companies again in 2000 U.S. patents with 2,886 issued patents. As of 2000, IBM held nearly 34,000 patents worldwide, including about 19,000 in the United Sates. In addition, the company is one of the largest non-European patent holders in Europe and one of the largest non-Japanese patent holders in Japan. IBM's expenses in research and development were $5,151 million in 2000, $5,273 million in 1999, and $5,046 million in 1998. Although all of its major competitors had good R&D capabilities, no one matched IBM's investment or success, as illustrated by the number of patents held worldwide.

131    IBM was the leading manufacturer of mainframes and has successfully repositioned this technology, once thought to be a "dinosaur" and a dead-end technology, as an enterprise server and a mass storage access device. E-business spans many of IGS' offerings and contributed significantly to its 2000 performance. The company's total discrete e-business revenue grew more than 70 percent to approximately $5 billion in 2000. This increase was driven by e-business consulting, e-business systems integration, and e-business hosting services (a form of outsourcing).

132    IBM had been focusing on the Internet, e-business, and the network economy enabling technology for several years. The network economy was defined as the expected shift of computing to the network. This represented the next major opportunity for IGS, the emerging model of delivering technology and services on an as-needed, pay-as-you-go basis. This was the basis for what was being called the future "network economy" or "e-utility." This was expected to drive a new emerging world economy, calling attention to the distinct economic behaviors that result from global interconnection of information systems.

133    Although IGS had sold off IBM Global Network Services to AT&T, this was just the network infrastructure, the circuits and switching equipment. That business was very competitive and required constant capital improvements and investment. IGS retained the centralized computing capability that would be the true driver of this next generation of computing.

## CUSTOMERS

134    IBM Global Services understands that customers are looking to Professional Computer Service providers to guide them in transforming their businesses through the integration of business and Information Technology strategies. The customers expect to receive value for

the dollars spent on information technology. IGS provides that value by helping them enhance the customer's global reach, strategy execution, competitive advantage, supplier relationship, and customer loyalty. IGS was achieving this once again through its industry orientation, segmenting its customers not only by size but also by the customer's industry (i.e., retail, manufacturing, transportation, financial).

135     IGS' broad range of service offerings, industry orientation, extensive research and development capabilities, and strong market intelligence enables them to provide both customizable, all-in-one solutions for large customers and competitively priced standardized solutions for small and medium business customers.

136     IGS serviced both large companies and small and medium businesses. However, IGS' services, known for their quality and innovation, were more in line with the needs of large companies, due to cost and complexity. Therefore they were not targeting a customer segment with significant revenue potential. However, there was a renewed emphasis on attracting medium/small businesses by including a small and medium sector to IGS' industry alignment.

# SALES / DISTRIBUTION

137     IBM, including IGS, was world renowned for its superior sales force. For many years, IBM was symbolized by its highly trained and aggressive sales force known for their skills and trademark blue suits, white shirts, and wingtip shoes. Although by the mid-1990s the company's image had softened, and there was a more casual approach to sales to match the changing corporate environment, IBM was still praised for its superior sales force.

138     IGS had the ability to call on a wide network of industry-specific sales force experts. These resources were also highly trained to market services across industry sectors. This dedicated sales force was skilled and knowledgeable in specific technologies and offerings. IGS ensured the effectiveness of its sales force by requiring them to be certified in specific technology and industry knowledge. The certification was a combination of internal and external education requirements, and the successful certification from outside boards (i.e., Microsoft certifications, CISCO certifications, and The Project Management Institute's certifications).

139     IBM had a worldwide network of Telemarketing centers. These centers were established to market specifically to medium-size customers, offering a limited product line (midrange and personal systems). This strategy had proven successful in North America so it was being expanded to all the major geographies (Latin America, Europe, and Asia).

140     IBM, including IGS, was also in the process of re-inventing itself as an e-business, practicing what it was preaching. It was using the Internet to market, sell, and deliver certain products. IBM had successfully launched a business-to-consumer site, a business-to-business website, and an on-line technical support site. However, these channels were focusing on particular products (midrange and personal systems, and software that could be delivered electronically). Services were not being aggressively marketed or delivered through the Internet.

141     IBM had established a strong business partner program. As of 2001, there were approximately 45,000 business partners comprising 90,000 program and contractual relationships across IBM technologies, products, services, and solutions. IGS understood that these relationships were invaluable in the ongoing creation and delivery of solutions that efficiently address customer requirements and market opportunities such as e-business. In 2000, revenue growth through business partners was up 11 percent year-to-year. Business Partners generated nearly 35 percent of IBM's revenue in 2000, compared with 20 percent four years ago. A significant portion of this was in the services area. In 1998, Business Partners were

responsible for more than 60 percent of the revenue derived from the medium and small business market, which many agreed, was a rich services opportunity.

142    A major strength of IGS was its resources' skills and expertise. This is of paramount importance in a services business where a company's skills and expertise become its product. These skills include specific technology knowledge, but even more importantly, specific industry knowledge.

# MARKETS

143    IGS' strengths were its global reach, providing a customer with services locally and internationally. IGS could provide services consistently across many countries and available in multiple locations under a single contract. IGS is the industry's number one worldwide provider of Professional Computer Services with more than 136,000 employees worldwide, in 160 countries. IGS markets all its services across these global markets. However, it had not fully leveraged its outsourcing capabilities to foreign markets. This was especially true in the geographies of Europe and Asia.

144    A major weakness of IGS, which can also be a strength, was its size. It was often slow to bring new services to market due to the size and complexity of the company and its management system. An example of this slow responsiveness was its introduction of e-business co-location facilities. Co-location facilities offered Internet startups with a low-cost hosting facility where they would manage their own application, providing them the required flexibility, but they did not have to be concerned with the management of the network, infrastructure, and security. IGS introduced this offering at the end of the "dot-com" boom, thereby losing out on the explosive growth in this area and then being stuck with expensive data center floor space.

# MANAGEMENT SYSTEM

145    For many years, prospective employees saw employment at IBM as a great opportunity. Several surveys had identified IBM as one of the best companies, from an employee benefits perspective. This distinction had eroded over the years since the 1980s. This was due in part to the company's financial difficulties in the mid-1980s through early 1990s. Part of the company's recovery plans included mass layoffs and reduction in benefits.

146    Although these were harsh measures, they were effective. By the mid to late 1990s, IBM, and in particular IGS, was once again an industry leader. Another change in the corporate culture, due to the hard times of early 1990, was a flattening of the management structure and the elimination of corporate bureaucracy, which had previously paralyzed the company, making it slow to make decisions. This new, more casual management style was more attractive to the resources the company was then trying to attract.

147    However, IGS still had not embraced many of the strategies other consulting and services firms were utilizing for some time. These strategies included aggressive stock option programs covering more than just the company's executive ranks, and attractive signing bonuses. A stock option program is an opportunity for employees to share in the company's success over the long term, by establishing a financial link to the shareholder value they work to produce. Stock option and signing bonus programs can deliver a competitive edge in employee recruitment, retention, and motivation. In an industry where knowledge represents a key asset, IGS had to continue to successfully recruit and hold onto top employees. This was a weakness across the industry due to the shortage of IT professionals.

# LOOKING TOWARDS THE FUTURE

148    IBM Global Services is well positioned in the Professional Computer Services Industry; however, the company was worried that this position would erode if it did not take advantage of the existing industry trends when making key strategic decisions. The recent financial performance was disappointing, although continued to show growth in this important segment for the IBM Corporation.

149    Mr. Gerstner, IBM's CEO, stated that the future of IBM would depend on the performance and growth of services, especially in the area of e-business, and in the future, the emerging "network economy" or "e-utility" model. This would be accomplished by focusing its resources on expanding services across the entire spectrum of e-business solutions, targeting nontraditional customer segments and markets/geographies.

150    Key IGS executives were proposing one alternative which was to concentrate solely on e-business service offerings. This would limit its expansion in traditional offerings such as client server and enterprise systems (mainframe). IGS' priority would be to capture a wide set of service opportunities and secure e-business leadership in the marketplace. They would achieve this by aggressively ramping up its e-business service offerings, including e-business consulting, e-business integration services, and e-business outsourcing services, while maintaining traditional services.

151    This strategy was feasible since the Internet and e-business services were viewed as the growth engine for this segment and IBM already had significant brand recognition in this area. They had coined the term e-business. IGS could turn this e-business mind share into true market share by offering all the necessary services a company needs to be successful in the web-based economy. This targeted focus would not dilute IGS resources across multiple service lines, especially custom application development which this alternative would abandon. This was supported by the fact that e-business revenue grew more than 70 percent to approximately $5 billion in 2000, with expected strong growth in subsequent years.

152    This alternative could win against the competition because of IGS' existing reputation as a world leader in professional computer services. In addition, the shift of resources to focus on e-business service offerings would assist in addressing the shortage of skilled resources, offering further advantage over its competition (consultants/system integrators, full-service providers, local/niche providers, and traditional IT providers). IGS would be positioned as the leader of e-business services, the most rapidly growing segment of services. IGS was better than the competition in several areas; for example, although all the competition had embraced e-business, Accenture in the area of consulting services, EDS in the area of outsourcing, and HP in the area of hardware, none had the capability to provide IGS' broad range of e-business services. Plus, by focusing its vast resources solely on e-business, IGS could more rapidly bring solutions to market. This strategy also has the potential of laying the foundation to exploit the emerging network economy or e-utility model. This is the reshaping of the IT infrastructure from one that is largely internally built and managed by a company to one built and managed by external service providers for on-demand usage by a company. This could truly differentiate IGS from its competition. IGS' ability to market using all three challenges of a dedicated professional sales force, direct marketing, and business partners was another advantage.

153    A major drawback with this shift away from being a full professional service provider to one focusing solely on e-business offerings, was that IGS would be losing potential future revenue from traditional professional computer services sources. In addition, often customers contracted for other services contract their existing service provider as they migrate to e-business. Ways around these drawbacks would be ensuring IGS is truly positioned as the world leader in e-business, accomplished through a worldwide promotion strategy.

**154**    Other IGS executives were proposing another alternative which was to expand the service offerings to provide a full range of professional services, but with an emphasis on e-business, network computing, and the future "network economy." IGS would offer consulting, systems integration, and outsourcing to accommodate a client's needs, once again abandoning a significant focus on custom application development.

**155**    This strategy was feasible since the Internet and e-business services was viewed as the growth engine for this segment and IBM already had significant brand recognition in this area. However, this strategy would not limit the targeted services. IGS would provide a full range of services from the traditional of client/server and enterprise systems (mainframes), to the emerging e-business, and the future network computing. This strategy is feasible because it would continue to attract clients with a broad range of requirements, many of which have not embraced e-business or are at various stages of their migration to e-business and still require other services. It is also feasible due to IBM's extensive investment in research and development, ensuring the continuous flow of services needs to support this type of strategy.

**156**    This alternative could win against the competition because of IGS' existing reputation as a world leader in professional computer services. IGS' brand recognition and global reach provided them advantages in pursuing these opportunities. IGS' competition (consultants/system integrators, full-service providers, local/niche providers, and traditional IT providers) did not have the same name recognition with e-business as IGS enjoyed; they all faced the increased demands of their customers to provide all-in-one solutions for large customers and at the same time provide standardized solutions at a competitive price, an area that IGS held an advantage. IGS was better than the competition in several areas, but especially in the ability to provide a continuous flow of new products and services. This was due to extensive investment in research and development (over $5 billion per year) as compared to competitors such as EDS and HP.

**157**    A drawback to this strategy is the overextension of the company's resources to attempt to be all things to all clients. The size of the company has been a weakness before; offering too broad a range of services could impact negatively IGS' speed in bringing new services to market. Another drawback of offering such a broad range of services is the cost required to build and maintain the required skills, central delivery centers, facilities, and equipment. Ways around these drawbacks is IBM's continued investment in research and development and a continued evolution of the company's management structure, allowing for a large company to have the speed of a smaller firm.

**158**    Based on these arguments, it was difficult to decide which alternative to choose or whether or not to consider a third alternative. In general, Lou Gerstner, and the IGS executive team, needed to decide which strategic decisions to implement in many different areas. There were many significant decisions to be made relative to which customers, which services, and which geographic markets to focus on, to name just a few. IBM Global Services can provide a broad range of service choices for companies of all sizes, in many different geographies. The challenge facing them is to decide which combination of alternatives will take advantage of the industry trends, differentiate them from the competition, and secure the continued growth and success of IBM Global Services.

## Case 39 I'm From the Government—And I'm Here to Help You

## Karl Borden and James C. Cooper

1    Jay Carlos had been thinking that everything was going just a tad too well to last. For the first time in a long time, there were no fires to put out. After five business start-ups and 20 years as an entrepreneur, he knew that crisis management is the rule rather than the exception in small business. His premonition was realized when the phone rang and the program services director, Kris, for his chain of homes for the mentally retarded said, "An OSHA[1] inspector named Olive Stone just walked in the door and wants to review our blood-borne pathogen policy and employee hepatitis vaccination procedure. What should I do?"

## INDUSTRY AND COMPANY BACKGROUND

2    It was in the mid-1970s that the national attitude toward the mentally retarded started changing. Prior to that time, most mentally retarded adults were cared for either in their parents' or another relative's home, or were placed in large state hospitals along with the mentally ill. As parents aged or relatives were unavailable, most retarded people eventually wound up residing in the large state institutions. Treatment consisted largely of chemical restraints (drugs) to inhibit aggression, and confinement to protect the public from their occasionally erratic and antisocial behavior.

3    Gradually, however, a more enlightened attitude toward the mentally retarded developed. Social service professionals recognized that the mentally retarded were capable of living fuller lives, that most of their socially maladaptive behaviors derived from emotional immaturity and arrested developmental processes, and that a more normalized living environment not based on a medical model could be a less expensive alternative to hospital care.

4    An industry was created as the market responded to state governments' calls to contract with nonprofit or profit-making private institutions willing to provide specialized behavioral treatment in a more normalized home environment for the retarded. As with most industries, market niches and specializations developed. Some homes specialized in the profoundly retarded, those with the lowest level of mental abilities and in need of the greatest degree of physical care. Others specialized in the severely, moderately, or only mildly retarded. Some homes were owned and operated by large, nationwide corporations, usually chains of nursing homes that had decided to enter the new market; others were developed by church-affiliated or philanthropic nonprofit foundations, and still others were small

Source: Reprinted by permission from the *Case Research Journal,* Volume 22, Issue 3. Copyright 2002 by Karl Borden and James C. Cooper and the North American Case Research Association. All Rights Reserved.

[1]OSHA (the Occupational Safety and Health Administration) was created as a Federal agency by the Occupational Safety and Health Act of 1970 (Public Law 91-596). The ambitious goals of the agency are "To assure safe and healthful working conditions for working men and women; by authorizing enforcement of the standards developed under the Act; by assisting and encouraging the States in their efforts to assure safe and healthful working conditions; by providing for research, information, education, and training in the field of occupational safety and health; and for other purposes." To these ends, the Agency has broad authority to institute, interpret, and enforce occupational health and safety regulations, including substantial power to levy and collect fines. The agency (as of 2001) employs over 2,100 inspectors, working out of over 200 local offices spread throughout the country, and conducts surprise visits to job sites (the OSHA Act provides for a $1,000 fine for anyone revealing that an OSHA inspection is about to occur).

businesses developed by psychologists or other entrepreneurs who saw an opportunity for profitable investment.

5   East Hampshire Homes was one of the latter. Jay Carlos and his wife Leigh were a businessman/entrepreneur and registered nurse, respectively, in Concord, New Hampshire, when a local delegation of parents and relatives of institutionalized mentally retarded adults approached them. It was they (the relatives) who proposed to the Carloses that they build a home for the mentally retarded as a business venture, with the hope that the result would be a facility available to their institutionalized sons and daughters.

6   Jay and Leigh Carlos knew little about the mentally retarded, but were always interested in investment opportunities. After six months of study, they decided the potential return was worth the risk. Two years, $250,000 in investment capital, and numerous regulatory and legal hurdles later, they opened their first home. Fifteen years later, they were operating a small two-home chain with a total of 23 beds, over 100 employees, and an adult day-care program for their residents. In addition, the site was already acquired for the next eight-bed home, and ground would soon be broken on an expanded day-care center.

# BLOOD-BORNE PATHOGENS AND HEPATITIS B[2]

7   Leigh Carlos, RN, MSN, FNP,[3] as head of East Hampshire's medical services, was responsible for company compliance with federal, state, and local health and safety regulations. As such, she had carefully considered the risks associated with blood-borne pathogens in general and with hepatitis B in particular.

8   East Hampshire's homes were not "skilled nursing" facilities. That is, while they employed nurses (mostly licensed practical nurses) and oversaw the medical and physical well-being of their residents, they did not provide round-the-clock, skilled nursing care. Unlike a hospital or nursing home, injections were unusual and staff contact with blood or other bodily fluids was rare.

9   Risk of exposure to blood-borne pathogens such as hepatitis B was, Leigh felt, far less than in an acute-care or nursing facility. It was, however, higher than in other work environments. East Hampshire Homes had developed, over the years, into an organization that specialized in mild-to-moderate mentally retarded residents with severe behavioral dysfunctions. Many of its residents exhibited violent behavior patterns, which were controlled with a combination of medications and behavioral programming directed by company psychologists. When residents did become physically aggressive they had to be physically restrained, and in some instances staff were in danger of resident biting or scratching behavior that could result in exposure to the hepatitis pathogen.

10   Leigh took the risk of such exposure seriously. As the organization's population of residents with such behavioral disorders grew, she addressed the question of staff risk in a businesslike manner. First, she carefully investigated Federal occupational safety regulations to determine what the company's obligations were. Then, within the scope of those regulations, she developed what she thought was a cost-effective compliance policy to provide for an adequately safe environment for her employees.

11   The OSHA regulations appeared to provide her with a significant amount of discretion. From 29 CFR 1910.1030(a):

---

[2]Health professionals may be aware that since this case occurred the Federal government has moved to require widespread hepatitis B vaccination for both employers and students in public schools and universities. As of the incident recounted in this case, however, such was not the case.
[3]MSN=Masters of Science in Nursing; FNP=Family Nurse Practitioner.

> For Ambulatory Residential Facilities: It is the employer's responsibility to determine which job classifications involve occupational exposure. The employer is only required to make the vaccine available and provide the other protections . . . to those employees having occupational exposure. Occupational exposure is defined as reasonably anticipating exposure to blood or other potentially infectious materials as the result of performing one's job duties.

Leigh believed that her employees were significantly less at risk than those of acute care facilities. In addition to the lack of skilled nursing services, the East Hampshire client population was a relatively stable one. Of the 23 beds, only one or two typically turned over to a new resident each year. Staff turnover rates, on the other hand, were typical of the industry at 35 to 40 percent per year. Leigh therefore reasoned that the way to control exposure to the pathogen was by immunizing all of the residents and requiring that all potential new residents be tested for hepatitis B before being admitted to any East Hampshire facility. A positive test result would preclude admission. If no residents brought the pathogen with them, there would be no possibility of staff exposure from that source.

12    Of course, some risk of exposure from other staff members still existed, but Leigh reasoned that this risk was no greater than that faced in the normal course of employment in our society. The risk was the same as for an employee at the grocery store, the bank, or any other place of work. This normal risk, she felt, did not call for any special action by East Hampshire beyond the vaccination of residents.

# JAY'S STORY

13    "Kris, I'm not sure what we should do here. We don't have an employee vaccination program, and our understanding has been that we don't need one. I think we need some quick legal advice. You say the OSHA inspector named Olive Stone is in the office now? OK. Keep her waiting there . . . tell her the home office is consulting on our response and we'll be right back to you. I'm calling our attorney right now. Offer her coffee and be polite."

14    Jay immediately called his attorney, Fred Fleagle. Fred had been the Carlos' business attorney for four years, since leaving office as the state Attorney General and running a losing race as the Republican candidate for U.S. Senator. He was very politically connected in the state and had excellent contacts with his former colleagues in the state bureaucracy, an important consideration, the Carloses felt, in an industry as heavily regulated by state and Federal agencies as theirs.

15    Fred's response to the situation was immediate: "Don't let her inspect without a search warrant," he said. "Understand that you're not trying to be difficult or contrary, but without a search warrant you have no ability to limit the scope of her inspection and you have no idea what she is looking for. Politely ask her to return another day with a search warrant so that we have a legal trail to follow if we object to her findings and want to appeal."

16    Jay said he would do that, and Fred emphasized remaining polite and cooperative but firm about the need for a warrant. Jay then suggested that he might himself call the person in the state department office who oversaw financial and contractual relationships between the state Department of Health and Welfare and homes for the mentally retarded. "After all, they may have some guidance for us here. If OSHA is going to require hepatitis vaccinations for all employees of homes like ours, that will cost the state millions of dollars. Their own legal department might want to become involved." Fred thought that was a good idea.

17    Jay called Kris, the program director, back and gave him instructions for the OSHA inspector. He emphasized being polite but firm. Then he called the head of the state agency overseeing group homes for the mentally retarded, Mr. B. Yuri Kratt. Jay had known Yuri and worked with him for over 10 years now, ever since Yuri had been promoted into the job, and their relationship was a good one as Jay had worked hard to develop positive working

relationships with key state department representatives. Yuri listened to Jay's story and immediately agreed that the implications of OSHA requiring employee hepatitis vaccinations were substantial for the state's budget, as such a cost would form part of the underlying cost structure of the industry which, eventually, the taxpayers of New Hampshire paid for. He said he would call their own legal department and see if they had any advice and would like to intervene in East Hampshire's defense.

# ONE HOUR LATER

**18**　Jay felt he had now done what he could do for the short term and that the situation, while not a pleasant one, was at least under control. He had never before had any contact with OSHA inspectors, but his general impression from media reports and business colleagues was not a positive one.[4] He had heard many horror stories about the agency overstepping its authority. But he had no personal experience with such actions, and was inclined to believe that, since East Hampshire had carefully followed the regulations and procedures required on this matter, they would be okay. He did take the time to pull a file folder with his notes from several years earlier when he and Leigh had considered the matter and implemented the screening policy. What he found reassured him that they were in compliance. His attorney's advice had been followed, and his contacts in the state department were thinking of providing assistance.

**19**　The phone rang. "Jay, Yuri here. I have some bad news for you. I want you to listen carefully to what I'm saying. And then I want you to make another phone call. First, our legal department will not help you. They say flatly that they will not under any circumstances tangle with OSHA. We're staying out of it. Period. And that's from the top—legal made a quick call to the director and he says the same. Don't touch OSHA."

**20**　"Second, I want you to call Warren Belle at New Horizon Homes over in Manchester. You know Warren. He has a story to tell you. I can't tell it—but he can. Just call him."

# WARREN'S STORY

**21**　Jay put the phone down with some concern. Yuri hadn't sounded the same during the second phone call. He was clearly speaking between the lines, and what he seemed to be saying was that the state bureaucrats themselves were afraid of OSHA. Warren Belle at New Horizon Homes was an East Hampshire competitor, but competition in this industry was often on friendly terms. Jay had known Warren for several years. He made the call.

**22**　Warren was in the office and took the call, listening to Jay recount the morning's events. When he heard the word OSHA he stopped him. "Jay—I've got only one thing to say, and I suggest you listen to it. Do whatever they ask you to do. Do it now. Do it exactly the way they ask you to do it. Do it no matter what it costs. Don't fight. And don't listen to your lawyer."

**23**　"Jay," said Warren, "OSHA came by here two months ago. We had exactly the same policy in effect that you do now. We did exactly what you have done and called our attorney,

---

[4]Jay's impressions are not uncommon. OSHA itself recognizes its public image problem. The OSHA website (see http://www.osha.gov) states frankly (as of October, 2001) "in the public's view, OSHA has been driven too often by numbers and rules, not by smart enforcement and results. Business complains about overzealous enforcement and burdensome rules. Many people see OSHA as an agency so enmeshed in its own red tape that it has lost sight of its own mission. And too often, a "one-size-fits-all" regulatory approach has treated conscientious employers no differently from those who put workers needlessly at risk.

and he gave the exact same advice to require a warrant. The OSHA inspector came back the next day with a warrant and six of his buddies. They started at one end of our building and went to the other, and within a few hours we had accumulated $13,500 in fines. One of the fines was for $2,500 because we had not posted a detailed list of the chemical ingredients in the Dawn Dishwashing Soap in the kitchen. Then the inspector said 'Are you ready to do what we want, or do we have to come back tomorrow to accumulate another $13,000 in fines?' We wound up doing what they wanted, which was to implement a vaccination program, and we still had to pay the $13,500 in fines."

24    "But Warren," said Jay, "the regulations are clear. We're an exception and don't have to have the vaccination program if our people aren't at risk. You know that a hepatitis B vaccination series costs $180 per person. Taking into account staff turnover, such a program would cost us almost $30,000 per year."

25    "Jay, do you know how OSHA gets its budget?" asked Warren. "Were you aware that they have almost no budget other than what they collect from fines?[5] Do you know they get to retain the fines they collect to finance their own operations? Do you know that there is no statutory limit to the amount of the fine they can levy for even the smallest offense?[6] Do you know that there is no appeal outside the agency other than a full-blown and expensive court case?[7] Do what they say. Do it now. Don't mess around with these guys. They're like a goon squad. You don't fight—you just hand over your wallet and hope they don't beat you up." Jay hung up the phone with a different perspective.

## FRED'S ADVICE

26    Jay knew he had another call to make immediately. He picked up the phone and dialed Fred Fleagle's number again. Fred took the call right away, and Jay told him Warren's story.

27    "Well, Jay," said Fred, "I have to admit that I've heard some nasty stories about OSHA. But after you called this morning I rechecked the regulations on this thing just to refresh my memory and to make sure your policy fits. It couldn't possibly be clearer. Your policy is directly in line with the regulations. Admittedly there is room for some interpretation of what constitutes an "at risk" employee, but the regulation leaves that interpretation in the hands of the employer. I think you're absolutely in the right here and should stand up for your

---

[5]This comment by Warren is not strictly true. OSHA does have its own budget. Fines, however, are retained by the agency and add to their operational resources.

[6]Warren's statement is not quite correct. The Occupational Safety and Health Act of 1970 (Public Law 91–596, 91st Congress, S.2193, December 29, 1970 states: "Any employer who willfully or repeatedly violates the requirements of section 5 of this Act, any standard, rule, or order promulgated pursuant to section 6 of this Act, or regulations prescribed pursuant to this Act, may be assessed a civil penalty of not more than $70,000 for each violation, but not less than $5,000 for each willful violation." On November 5, 1990, Pub. L. 101–508 amended the Act by increasing the penalties for willful or repeated violations of the Act in section 17(a) from $10,000 for each violation to "$70,000 for each violation, but not less than $5,000 for each willful violation," and increased the limitation on penalties in sections (b), (c), (d), and (i) from $1000 to $7000 for serious and other-than-serious violations, failure to correct violative conditions, and violations of the Act's posting requirements. For all practical purposes, however, short of a full-blown civil case against the government, the Agency determines what constitutes either a "serious" or a "willful" violation, and also determines what constitutes "each" violation (every day a condition exists could potentially be a new violation with additional maximum penalties).

[7]The Occupational Safety and Health Act of 1970 states "Any person adversely affected or aggrieved by an order of the Commission issued under subsection (c) of section 10 may obtain a review of such order in any United States court of appeals for the circuit in which the violation is alleged to have occurred or where the employer has its principal office, or in the Court of Appeals for the District of Columbia Circuit, by filing in such court within sixty days following the issuance of such order a written petition praying that the order be modified or set aside."

rights. If they come back with a warrant, let them in. If they wind up fining you or demanding that you implement a vaccination program, we'll just take them to Federal court. And we'll win."

28    "Yes. And tell me, Fred, how long will that take, and at $150 per hour what will it cost me to win?"

29    "Well, Jay, it could take some years to come to an absolute conclusion. And I won't say it would be cheap. The government has access to plenty of staff lawyers of course and you can't get your costs back even when you prevail."

30    "That doesn't sound encouraging, Fred."

31    "Yeah, Jay, but damn it, this is the sort of thing that someone has to stand up to. It's the kind of big government bullying that I ran for the Senate to try to put an end to. You know, that's another option for us. I'm pretty politically connected in this state. We have a Republican Governor, one Republican Senator, and a Republican Statehouse. I could make a few phone calls—see if we can't get these OSHA guys to call off the dogs. Whattya want me to do?"

# Case 40   JP Morgan Chase & Co.: The Credit Card Segment of the Financial Services Industry

## Robert J. Mockler, Steven Preziosi, and Damon Swaner

1   In January 2001, Chase Cardmember Services (CCS) executive Richard Srednicki was faced with the task of turning around the industry's fifth largest credit card issuer. CCS was at a stage in which its success over the next two years would determine its fate. While the U.S. credit card market had been saturated for several years, other firms had still managed to grow by introducing new products or finding profitable niches. CCS had done neither. Because the recent JP Morgan–Chase Manhattan merger involved the use of the pooling of interests method, the newly created financial services giant was unable to sell-off its credit card business for two years. This gave CCS 24 months to develop, implement, and begin to reap the benefits of a new long-term enterprisewide winning strategy.

2   All of the players in this industry faced the same problem, how to acquire and retain profitable customers. This made for a competitive, mostly zero-sum game. As a result, there had been rapid consolidation in the industry with the largest firms controlling an increasing percentage of the total market.

3   CCS was in a unique position in the market. It had grown into a large player primarily as the result of the combinations of other portfolios as part of several large bank mergers during the 1990s. Now it needed to find a way to grow its business internally. A new management team installed in early 2000 had reenergized the business and worked diligently to build momentum and focus the employees on growth and profitability. However, the desired result of changing CCS into a long-term winner in the market was still far off.

4   In order to determine how it would position itself in the industry and how it would convince customers that CCS could service them better than the other card issuers in the market, CCS management had to resolve a number of strategic questions. A strong customer service focus was an absolute necessity in order to retain customer loyalty. A focus on new products, underserved segments, new technologies, and value-added services was also required. Finally, a strong financial discipline and high return on investment was needed in order to continue to secure capital from its parent company. These and other strategic questions needed to be answered if CCS was to differentiate itself and so win against the competition in the near, intermediate, and long-term time frames.

# INDUSTRY AND COMPETITIVE MARKET—
# THE FINANCIAL SERVICES INDUSTRY

5   The financial services industry consists of investment banks, insurance companies, broker/ dealers, asset managers, venture capital firms, and commercial banks, as shown in Exhibit 1. Investment banks provide services including underwriting of public and private offerings, research, trading advisory services for mergers and acquisitions, and financial engineering. Insurance companies provide means of decreasing one's exposure to risk through policies that pay on the occurrence of some event. Broker/dealers perform two different functions,

**EXHIBIT 1**   Structure of the Financial Services Industry

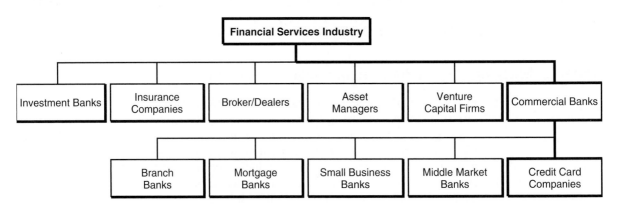

acting as agents bringing buyers and sellers of securities together, and also acting as market makers standing ready to buy and sell securities by presenting a bid ask spread at all times. Asset managers provide pension and mutual fund management services. Venture capital firms provide funding to startup companies and firms looking to expand. Commercial banks include the traditional branch banking functions of deposit taking and lending. This sector also includes mortgage banking, small business and middle market banking activities, and credit card issuance.

### Investment Banks

**6**   One of the many important roles of the investment bank is to assist companies in raising capital through its function as underwriter. Investment banks buy securities from a company and then sell them in secondary markets. Types of underwriting activities include initial public offerings, sale of bonds, commercial paper, and private debt and equity offerings. Investment banks also play an important role in the creation of value for companies through mergers and acquisitions. In this capacity investment banks bring companies together with the end result of either combining the firms or facilitating the exchange of assets. Finally, one of the most important functions of the investment bank is to provide research and assessments of individual companies and sectors as a basis for its own investment or for sale to other investors.

### Insurance Companies

**7**   Insurance companies provide a means of dealing with risk. Insurance companies will pay out an agreed upon sum contingent on the occurrence of some event. Typical insurance policies include life insurance, auto insurance, medical insurance, and various types of disaster insurance. The insurance company is compensated for absorbing this risk by a premium that is paid periodically, usually monthly, by the insured.

### Broker/Dealers

**8**   The broker/dealers, although usually the same firm, provide two different types of services. As a broker, the firm acts as an agent bringing buyers and sellers of securities together and executing transactions on their behalf in the over-the-counter markets and at the exchanges. Brokers are not participants in the transaction and do not take on any risk but rather are compensated exclusively through commissions. As a dealer, the firm is party to the transactions in which it participates. Dealers must stand ready to buy and sell at any time and must provide a bid price, which is what the dealer is willing to pay for a certain security, and an ask price, which is the price at which the dealer is willing to sell. Dealers are compensated by the spread between the price paid for the security and the price at which it is sold.

### Asset Managers

9  Asset management includes various large investors like pension funds, mutual funds, hedge funds, and 401(k)s. All of these types of funds fall under the rubric of institutional investors. Institutional investors increasingly play a larger role in the secondary market by allowing small investors to diversify their portfolios into investments that they would not normally be able to afford. By pooling the assets of many investors, large funds are able to participate in IPOs, commercial paper markets, and bond markets, all of which are normally beyond the reach of the smaller investor.

### Venture Capital Firms

10  Venture capital firms provide funding to startup companies, expanding companies, and companies that are restructuring. Generally venture capitalists take on great risk in their investments. However, the venture capitalists ask much in return for their investment. They may take a large share in ownership of the company along with a seat on the board of directors. Investments are made by venture capital firms with one of three types of exit strategies in mind: taking the company public, selling to a larger company, or bankruptcy. Although a large number of all investments fail, the remaining investments made generally yield venture capital firms a very high return on their money.

### Commercial Banks

11  Commercial banks perform a variety of services such as cash management, usually through a branch banking network, and lending. Commercial bank lending encompasses several different types of credit including mortgages and credit cards, and also provides banking services to small businesses and middle market companies.

12  Commercial banks traditionally made money on the spread between the interest rate paid on deposits and the rate at which it lent. However, due to the competitive pressures brought on by globalization and the Financial Services Modernization Act of 1999, the face of banking in the United States had dramatically changed. Under the old law (Glass-Steagall) the businesses of investment banking, commercial banking, and insurance were either not allowed to mix with each other or were only allowed in a very limited way. The passage of the Financial Services Modernization Act allowed these three businesses to operate under a new type of holding company and had paved the way for much of the consolidation that was occurring in the financial services industry. In addition to legislative initiatives, the financial services industry, commercial banking especially, had been forced to change due to the arrival of the Internet. Every aspect of commercial banking operations had been modified in some way in order to accommodate Internet use. This study focuses on the credit card segment of the commercial banking sector of the financial services industry.

## CREDIT CARD SEGMENT

### History and Trends

13  The credit card industry in the United States can trace its roots to just prior to World War I. In 1914, Western Union began to provide a deferred-payment service to its most creditworthy customers. Over the next several decades, department stores and other retailers began

to provide revolving credit accounts to many of their customers as well. In the 1950s, the popularity of revolving credit accounts grew and the retailers began using imprinted cards to help streamline the transaction process and identify customers. As customers made purchases using their cards, the charges were posted directly to the cardholders' accounts at the store, with bills being sent out monthly.

14    The biggest advances began to occur when the banks realized the potential of this new payment method. The large U.S. banks discovered that credit cards fit nicely into their current business, which was lending money and then collecting from borrowers over time with interest. While the retailers were beginning to earn substantial revenue on the interest from their credit accounts, the firms also recognized the potential for even larger profits from increased sales that standardized, universally accepted credit cards could provide.

15    By the late 1960s, many banks began issuing cards to their customers and merchants began accepting them as payment. These early cards required payment in full within a short period of time, usually less than 90 days. However, banks quickly recognized the revenue potential of simply extending the repayment time while continuing to charge interest. Soon after, banks, led by Bank of America, created associations to act as clearinghouses for credit card transactions. Some of these associations included BankAmericard, BankMark, and MasterCharge and were the forerunners of the current two associations, Visa and MasterCard.

16    Also in the late 1960s, another use for credit cards began to develop, the travel and entertainment (T&E) market. Cards issued by American Express, Diner's Club, and Carte Blanche, called charge cards as opposed to credit cards, became popular with travelling businessmen. The difference between charge cards and the bank-issued credit cards was that these cards did not involve the charging of interest, which was the banks' primary motivation for entering the industry. These cards were paid in full by the cardholder at the end of each billing cycle, which was usually one month. These firms derived revenue from charging the customers higher annual fees and the merchants higher transaction fees for accepting the cards.

17    By the late 1970s, card usage was commonplace. The bank-issued cards, T&E cards, and the original retailer-issued cards were all flourishing. Technological advances had helped ensure accuracy in the process and most large merchants were participating in accepting the cards.

18    In the 1980s Sears, the largest retail issuer of cards, introduced its DiscoverCard that included a unique value proposition, an annual rebate on the cardholder's total card purchases. Competition among credit card issuers began to accelerate rapidly. Citibank led the way with the development of the AAdvantage card, which offered American Airlines frequent flyer miles with each purchase. The use of direct mail campaigns increased dramatically as banks searched to expand their customer base beyond the reach of their traditional branch-banking network. During the 1980s the volume of credit card debt outstanding grew from $71 billion in 1980 to $242 billion by 1990.

19    The increase in credit card usage was even more dramatic in the 1990s, driven by a strong economy, aggressive marketing by credit card issuers, and changes in consumer spending preferences. During the 1990s, credit card debt outstanding grew to $675 billion by the end of the decade.

20    By 2000, the industry had begun to consolidate. The smaller banks did not have the scale to compete with the few remaining large issuers. Competition in the market for creditworthy customers had grown fierce, forcing banks to look for new niches. MBNA established a niche in an area ignored by large banks, affinity marketing. It focused on partnering with as many local partners as possible, including universities, organizations, and athletic teams. This allowed it to capitalize on the brand loyalty customers had not to MBNA, but to its affinity partners. CapOne found a niche with the lower-credit-quality customers offering higher priced, or secured, lines of credit. Also with competition began to come substitute

**EXHIBIT 2**   Structure of the Credit Card Segment of the Commercial Banking Sector

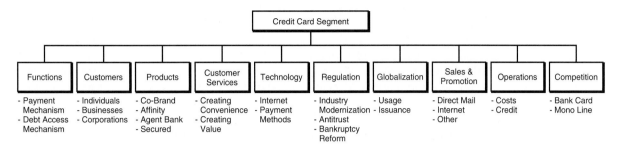

products, most notably debit cards, which provided the same payment features as credit cards but drew funds from the cardholder's deposit or checking account, as opposed to drawing on a line of credit.

21   The growth in credit card usage was expected to continue. Established as the dominant payment method for Internet commerce, credit card usage would grow as web purchasing grew. Also, as consumers' reliance on using cash for purchases continued to decrease, credit cards had additional opportunity for growth. The trend toward consolidation in the industry was likely to continue, as was the impact of technological advancement on credit cards. The credit card segment of the financial services industry is broken down further in Exhibit 2.

### Functions of the Credit Card Segment

22   The credit card segment served two major functions for its customers (called cardholders). First, it was a payment mechanism providing a means for cardholders to complete transactions for goods and services. Second, it was a debt-access mechanism, allowing cardholders to borrow the funds used in completing transactions.

### Payment Mechanism

23   In this role, the credit card issuers provided cardholders a means of paying for goods and services. The advantage over other forms of payments (cash, personal checks) were that customers could make purchases without having to physically interact with a merchant (i.e., telephone, Internet). It also allowed cardholders to keep track of all of their purchases with one monthly statement. In this arena, credit cards faced major competition from debit cards, which allowed cardholder's the purchasing advantages provided by credit cards, but linked the payments to the cardholder's deposit accounts.

24   Trends in the technology area, such as greater Internet use and the change in lifestyle and buying habits that it had created, increased the average American's credit card use during the 1990s. This created a great opportunity for payment method providers to increase market share. One major key to success in the payment mechanism role was to become customer's first-choice payment mechanism by maintaining universal acceptance of card and through aggressive sales and advertising. Other keys to success were to increase card usage with value-added services like purchase protection or rebates, to develop cardholder loyalty by deepening relationships through affinity or cross-selling other products, and to develop aggressive advertising campaigns to attract new customers. Also important was leveraging the issuer's other business lines, particularly commercial bank segments as a means of acquiring new customers.

### Debt Access Mechanism

**25**   In this role, cards allowed customers to pay for items with borrowed funds. This allowed cardholders to detach their purchasing from their income. With over $600 billion in credit card debt outstanding, credit card purchasing helped drive the U.S. economy. This volume of debt outstanding tripled during the 1990s and was 11 times the 1980 level by the end of the decade. The unique advantage of credit cards was the combination of these two functions in allowing cardholders to make all of their purchases when needed, and make payments when available (provided they make their nominal monthly minimum payments).

**26**   Credit card issuers earned revenue primarily from interest charged on debt outstanding. Customers that maintain outstanding debt on their credit card are called "revolvers," short for revolving credit users. Customers that use their credit cards primarily for transactions and do not maintain a debt balance are called "transactors." Transactors were much less profitable and were becoming a larger percentage of cardholders. In 1992, 29 percent of all cardholders were transactors; by 1998 the share was 42 percent. This trend was forcing issuers to look for ways to increase customer profitability. One way to increase revenue from transactors was to charge an annual fee. However, given the multitude of choices available, annual fees were unattractive to customers unless they were associated with a value-added service for which customers were willing to pay (i.e., Citibank's AAdvantage card).

**27**   Opportunities had been created for credit cards as a debt-access mechanism by the increase in credit card usage as a payment mechanism. For example, in 1990 credit cards accounted for only 10.3 percent of total consumer payments, a number that is expected to increase to 23 percent by 2003. Credit card dollar volume was also expected to exceed $2.0 trillion by 2003. The keys to success in this area were to attract and maintain debt by offering competitive rates to develop cardholder loyalty through affinity or depth of relationship to attract new customers through aggressive advertising and to limit loan losses through strong credit and collections policies.

### Customers

**28**   The credit card industry can be broken down into the three main types of customers served: individuals, businesses, and corporations.

**29**   In the individual consumer market, the largest of the three, credit cards allowed cardholders to manage their finances. This market was fiercely competitive with constant advertising and direct mail campaigns needed to sustain market share. Cardholders with outstanding debt could transfer balances to lower interest rate cards with increasing ease. Value-added services, including loyalty programs, rebates, and rewards were required for customer retention as they increased cardholder attachment to the card and lessened the likelihood they would switch to a competing card.

**30**   Customers were segmented by creditworthiness. Customers that were considered creditworthy were called the "prime" market. Issuers usually determined a customer's creditworthiness by reviewing their credit bureau report, which contained a credit bureau score (FICO score). The higher the score, the more creditworthy the customer. Customers that had derogatory credit bureau marks, usually caused by missed payments or loan defaults, were considered the "low prime" market. Customers that were the worst credit quality, including customers that had previously filed bankruptcy, were considered "subprime." The low and subprime markets had historically been underserved compared to the prime market in the United States.

**31**   The prime customer market had been the most competitive as the average U.S. household already had 2.4 credit cards by the end of 2000. All issuers were competing to be the card of choice for these customers since they were the most likely to have the means to pay back the borrowed funds. Loan losses were a concern in the credit card industry and failure to control their level would have a large impact on an issuer's profitability. Opportunities in this area stemmed from trends in increased usage of credit cards. Additionally, opportunities had been created by the increase in the number of people shopping on the Internet. It was estimated that 17 million U.S. households would be shopping online by the end of 2001 and that by 2004, 49 million households would be spending as much as $184 billion online. The keys to success in the prime market were to increase customer card usage by offering value-added services like purchase protection or frequent flyer programs, and to attract new customers through aggressive advertising. Also important was to develop cardholder loyalty through affinity or depth of relationship, which made it less likely that cardholders would switch to a new card.

**32**   The low prime and subprime markets had been less saturated than the prime markets, but by 2001 were becoming increasingly more competitive as issuers sought out new customers. The trends that affected the prime market, including increased card usage and Internet purchasing, also affected this market. However, previously issuers were hesitant to enter this market for fear of high loan loss rates. Opportunities in this area, however, did exist as issuers like Cap One and Providian had proved that credit card issuing to this segment could be done profitably. Despite higher loan losses, these customers were more likely to revolve than prime customers were, thus incurring higher finance charges. The keys to success in this market were limiting loan losses by maintaining strong credit policies, attracting new customers through aggressive advertising, limiting losses by maintaining a strong collections department, and increasing profitability by selling charged-off accounts.

**33**   The loan loss rate, also called the charge-off rate, is shown for various credit card issuers in Exhibit 3. Issuers charge-off accounts after they reach 180-days past due. The charge-off rate is calculated by dividing total charge-offs by total average receivables. Companies that continually add new accounts, like Cap One and MBNA, tend to have lower charge-off rates. Firms with more mature portfolios and fewer new accounts have higher loss rates. Acquiring new accounts in the prime market in particular was the focus for most issuers.

**34**   Credit cards served both functions, payments and debt access, for small businesses/merchants and organizations. This market was less competitive and smaller than the individual consumer market. Account acquisitions in this market were more heavily dependent on the businesses banking relationship with the parent company. Thus firms with a strong commercial bank presence had an advantage. Opportunities in this area stemmed from trends in the Internet's growth as a purchasing tool for consumers and a marketing tool for businesses. For example, 44 percent of U.S. companies were selling online in 2000 and 36 percent more said they would do so by the end of 2001. Additionally, small businesses that used the Internet had grown 46 percent faster than those that did not. In terms of dollars and cents, Internet advertising generated $1.92 billion in 1998, which was double the 1997 figure, and small and home offices spent over $51 billion on high-tech goods in 1998.

**EXHIBIT 3**
**Loan Loss Rates 1999**

| Cap One | 3.85% |
|---|---|
| MBNA | 4.33 |
| Citigroup | 4.56 |
| Amex | 5.00 |
| Bank One | 5.23 |
| Discover | 5.42 |
| Bank of America | 5.57 |
| JP Morgan Chase | 5.66 |
| Household | 6.65 |
| Fleet | 6.78 |

**35**     The keys to success in the business market were to maintain customer loyalty by offering programs and promotions that rewarded businesses for using the card such as rebates on purchases, and leveraging banking relationships that businesses had with the issuer's parent company to attract new business cardholders. Also important were attracting and maintaining debt by offering competitive rates and creating convenience for businesses through flexible payment arrangements.

**36**     In the corporate card market, the focus was solely on the payment function of credit cards. Employees of major corporations carried credit cards for travel and entertainment purchases. At the end of each month, the employee submitted their expenses and their corporation paid the credit card bill. American Express had historically been the dominant player in this market. This market was less reliant on the traditional form of account acquisition in the credit card segment, direct mail, and instead relied on a sales force that sought out new corporate clients.

**37**     Opportunities in this market stemmed from the development of Internet technologies that allowed networking. One key to success was creating convenience for corporate cardholders through the creation of Intranet-type platforms that allowed online billing, reconciliation, and approval of charges within the corporate structure. Other keys to success were to leverage the parent company's investment bank by using relationships other firms had with the parent as a basis for winning these companies' corporate card business, and to maintain an aggressive sales force that would also seek out new corporate customers.

### Products

**38**     The major products of the credit card segment were Visa and MasterCard-associated credit cards. However, these cards could also be co-branded cards, affinity cards, agent bank cards, or secured cards, among other types.

**39**     With over 77 percent of the market, Visa and MasterCard controlled most of the credit card market. Most bank card issuers and monolines issued both Visa and MasterCard-associated cards. Visa and MasterCard were associations on whose networks most credit card transactions were cleared. American Express and Discover each had its own networks and did not issue Visa or MasterCard-associated cards. Members of the Visa and MasterCard associations were prohibited from issuing American Express or Discover cards but were allowed to issue both MasterCard and Visa cards.

**40**     A recent trend in the industry had been issuers choosing either Visa or MasterCard as a primary partner. Citibank and Chase had both chosen MasterCard while NationsBank and Providian had chosen Visa. In doing so, the issuers were working out more favorable fee arrangements with their primary association. Opportunities in this area stemmed from the association with either Visa or MasterCard in order to extend geographically the areas of acceptance of the issuing bank's cards. The key to success in this area was to create convenience for the cardholder by using the association with Visa or MasterCard to create wider acceptance of the issuing bank's card.

**41**     Cards partnered with large corporations had become an important part of the credit card industry. Partners included airlines, hotel chains, long-distance telephone companies, retailers, and gasoline companies. These cards generally offered cardholders some type of rebate or reward each time the card was used. For example, the Shell Oil card from JP Morgan Chase offered cardholders a 1 percent rebate for every dollar charged to the card, plus a 5 percent rebate on any Shell gasoline charged to the card. These rebates could then be used to offset future Shell gasoline purchases. However, the rewards paid to customers reduced the profitability of the relationship for card issuers. As a result, co-branded cards needed to strike a balance between offering attractive rewards to entice customers, and remaining profitable. Cards with particularly rich rewards or with high levels of transactors, such as airline co-branded cards, generally charged annual fees.

**42**    Opportunities in this area stemmed from the issuers' ability to leverage cardholder's brand loyalty to the co-brand partner and to provide customers with value while remaining profitable. The keys to success were to create brand loyalty by offering discounts and promotions on products and services, to increase card usage by sending cardholders targeted offers or coupons for use with the co-brand partner, and to create value for co-brand partners by providing cardholders rebates when purchasing from the partner, thus increasing the likelihood that these customers would choose to purchase from the partner over the partner's competitors. Also important were partnering with large, well-known national brands to gain market share and attract new customers, and to attract profitable customers through lucrative rewards programs that added significant value to the degree that customers would pay an annual fee for the card.

**43**    Affinity cards were partnered with a company or organization, but the nature of the relationship was different from co-branded cards. Affinity cards did not offer cardholders rewards. Instead, they were marketed to potential customers that were or wanted to be identified as being affiliated with the card's partner. Most universities, athletic teams, and professional organizations were currently in affinity partner relationships with card issuers. Since the target market for any affinity card was generally smaller than with co-branded cards, issuers needed to have numerous affinity partners to be successful in this market. The opportunity to create lasting brand loyalty existed in this market by partnering with various organizations that cardholders were closely associated with.

**44**    One of the leading affinity card marketers was MBNA. MBNA had created affinity cards with various causes such as the United Negro College Fund, developed affinity cards for over 500 colleges and universities, and developed affinity cards with military and law enforcement agencies such as the U.S. Marine Corps and the National Association of Chiefs of Police. These kinds of affinity partnerships created greater loyalty among cardholders. MBNA lost only 2 percent of its profitable customers annually as compared to the industry average of 15 percent.

**45**    A major key to success in this arena was having flexible systems and processes that allow for the issuer to manage thousands of affinity partners. Also important were maintaining an effective sales force that actively sought out new partners and a strong marketing team that was able to identify new segments.

**46**    The trend in the financial services industry towards consolidation had affected the credit card segment. Many smaller credit card issuers were finding they did not have the scale to manage a credit card portfolio profitably and were exiting the business. However, the small and mid-size banks still wanted to be able to issue credit cards to their customers. In an agent banking relationship, a bank was able to provide its customers with a credit card without having to manage a credit card portfolio. An example of an agent banking transaction would be MBNA's purchase of the credit card portfolio of First Tennessee Bank.

**47**    In an agent bank relationship, the smaller bank's customers were issued a card in the name of their bank, but the cards were owned and serviced by a larger card issuer. The advantage for the smaller company was it could continue to meet the needs of its clientele. The advantage for the issuing company was the additional loans. The relationship was similar to that of a co-branded or affinity card, but in this case the partner was another financial institution. Since customers tended to be loyal to the bank where they had their accounts, the issuing firm was able to obtain loans from a population to which it would otherwise not have had access. Also, customers were less likely to default on loans to banks in which they had their other accounts. Thus agent banking cards generally had lower loan loss rates.

**48**     As the segment continued to consolidate, more portfolios were likely to come up for sale. For the issuers that had the capital to compete for these acquisitions, and the ability to integrate new portfolios into its current business, this trend provided a substantial opportunity. Another key to success was to develop effective partnerships with the agent bank partners to ensure the banks continued to solicit new customers for the agent bank card. Also, it was important to maintain an experienced agent bank team to service the portfolio and manage the relationship with the agent bank.

**49**     With 78 percent of the $675 billion in outstanding credit card debt controlled by the top ten issuers, the remaining 22 percent represented a lucrative cache of potential loyal customers. This 22 percent, or approximately $150 billion, was more than double the portfolio of any one issuer other than Citibank at the end of 2000.

**50**     Secured cards were offered to customers with poor credit quality. They required customers to keep cash on deposit with the card issuer. In return they were given a card with a credit limit equal to the amount of their deposit. This allowed customers to whom issuers were not willing to grant credit to take advantage of the payment function of credit cards. Cap One had successfully entered this market and as a cardholder demonstrated his or her ability to use credit, Cap One would then convert them to a regular credit card. The key to success with secured cards was to aggressively advertise to targeted customers or regions with lower credit quality in order to attract new cardholders.

### Customer Services

**51**     Important to success in the credit card segment was maintaining customer loyalty. With all the brands of credit cards as well as other payment methods available, the one thing that a credit card issuer could do to distinguish itself from the competition was to provide greater convenience and value for its customers. The opportunities to create convenience and value stemmed from several different factors. Innovations in payment methods and the demand for a greater variety of payment methods had forced many payment method providers to create new ways to pay for goods and services. Additionally, technological advances, such as the Internet, had created new methods of buying goods and services and created demand for new and more secure ways to pay for those goods and services.

**52**     Letting the customer choose the way they wished to pay was an important part of creating convenience for customers and ultimately led to the kind of brand loyalty that was desired. One way to provide convenience and choice was to make a number of different payment systems available to the customer. Examples of these included credit cards, debit cards, which allowed customers to make payments that were directly withdrawn from the checking account, and stored value cards, which allowed customers to place a fixed amount of money on the card to make purchases. The stored value cards protected the customer in case the card was lost or stolen, as only the amount of money that has been placed electronically on the card would be lost. Another payment method, which was a product of the Internet age, was the smart card. The smart card contained an electronic chip that held a great deal of customer information and allowed for greater protection for purchases made over the Internet. Creating cards that combined the functionality of any or all of these types of cards presented a potential opportunity for issuers.

**53**     Value for customers came in many forms. Examples included services or rewards programs such as frequent flyer programs for individual customers, or ease of settlement and usage for business and corporate customers. For all customers a key to success was the development and creation of value-intensifying services in conjunction with payment methods. Examples were adding services to each type of card like extending warranties for goods bought with the card, offering cash back or insurance for goods bought with the card, and co-branding cards with retailers, restaurants, or airlines so cardholder's could get discounts or rebates from those partners.

54    Offering electronic bill payments would create value to both corporate and individual customers. The bills would be sent to individuals online and paid for online. This would reduce the time and cost of bill collecting for many corporate customers while providing a convenient way to pay bills for individual customers. Additionally, electronic bill payments would increase traffic on the payment method provider's website and from there a whole array of value-creating services could be provided. For example, purchasing platforms, which are electronic exchanges that connect buyers and sellers, could be linked to the payment provider's website. These purchasing platforms would be commercial hubs for both business-to-business (B2B) and business-to-consumer (B2C) type business. These platforms create value for businesses and convenience for their customers while extending the market share of the payment method.

### Technology

55    Technological advances dramatically affected the credit card segment. The Internet and new payment methods like smart cards were providing new opportunities for growth for card issuers.

56    The growth of purchasing on the Internet had been exponential, as shown in Exhibit 4. Credit cards were involved in 90 percent to 95 percent of Internet sales transactions. Because of the Internet's increasing popularity, businesses of all kinds had grown and gained access to new customer bases as consumers were increasingly shopping online.

57    Although there had been tremendous growth in e-commerce and the Internet industry, many people who browsed online were still hesitant to shop online for fear of a security breach when placing personal information over the Internet. New security systems were in development, but had not yet reached the majority of online consumers. The credit card had a substantial opportunity in this area.

58    The keys to success were to partner with highly trafficked websites to attract potential customers, to create value-added services like online purchase protection or rebates for online purchases, and to maintain aggressive customer advertising targeted to online shoppers. Also important were to create a secure Internet environment through development of high security systems for credit card use over Internet and to create value and convenience for cardholders and merchants through the development of B2C websites featuring merchants that accepted an issuer's cards and offered discounts to cardholders.

**EXHIBIT 4**
**Growth of Internet Purchasing**

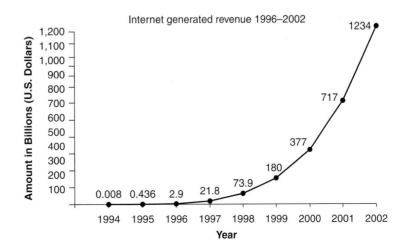

Internet generated revenue 1996–2002

59    The technological advances that had changed banking and the credit card industry had affected payment methods. The creation and increasing popularity of various payment systems had created greater value and convenience for consumers. One innovation in electronic payments was the smart card. The smart card contained a computer chip that activated a digital wallet when making purchases online. The chip contains a digital ID number, which authenticated the cardholder and then launched the digital form-filling wallet when one was required to fill out forms to make purchases online.

60    The smart card gained rapid adoption in Europe and Asia, but growth in the United States had been slow. In 2000, the total world market for smart cards was approximately $2.6 billion, but only $100 million was in the United States. The United States had a well-developed infrastructure to accept magnetic-strip (traditional) credit cards and had been slow to make the investment to convert to smart cards. However, the potential increases in online purchasing suggested an opportunity for issuers was to develop cards that contained both a magnetic strip and a smart chip like Amex's Blue card. These cards could still be used within the current infrastructure, but also offer the Internet-purchasing benefits of a smart card.

61    The keys to success for issuers in this area were to continuously develop technology, maintain strong advertising to make consumers aware of the technology, and maintain an aggressive sales force that will bring new payment systems to consumers and merchants. Also critical was to make the transition from regular credit cards to new payment methods as cost-efficient as possible for merchants and to create convenience and choice for cardholders by offering various products, including dual cards.

### Regulation

62    New laws and stricter application of regulations had had an effect on the financial services industry, and on commercial banking in particular. In 1999, the Financial Services Modernization Act was passed, ushering in sweeping changes in the banking industry. This legislation, along with the application of antitrust laws and the bankruptcy reform act had potential effects on the credit card segment.

63    The Financial Services Modernization Act of 1999 repealed the Glass-Steagall Act that prohibited cross-sector affiliation between the banking and securities industries. It also repealed the 1956 Bank Holding Company Act, which prohibited unions between the banking and insurance industries. The legislation established a new entity called a Financial Holding Company. In order for a bank holding company to qualify as a Financial Holding Company, all of its depository institution subsidiaries must be well managed and well capitalized and must have a satisfactory Community Reinvestment Act (CRA) rating. A financial institution seeking to become a multipurpose financial institution could structure itself in two ways. It could become a Financial Holding Company and set up affiliates. This provided the most flexibility and greatest possibility for one-stop shopping. Alternatively, it could create subsidiaries. While the federal government had issued an interim rule that stated those banks and their subsidiaries were allowed to operate many financial services, insurance underwriting, merchant banking, and real estate development were not allowed.

64    This legislation had spurred a flood of mergers and acquisitions among financial institutions. One of the largest mergers in U.S. history resulted, the Travelers–Citigroup merger. This created a financial powerhouse that had operations in investment banking through its Solomon Smith Barney arm, insurance through Travelers, and commercial banking through Citibank.

65    The antitrust laws have also affected the credit card industry. In October of 1998 the Department of Justice (DOJ) brought an antitrust suit against Visa and MasterCard. The allegations were that Visa and MasterCard were not really competitors. The DOJ claimed that the two associations operated under a "duality" whereby member banks were allowed to is-

sue both Visa and MasterCard-branded plastic. According to the DOJ this duality meant that these brands were in effect one business and that this one business held a dominant market position. This enabled them to stifle competition from rivals by forbidding banks from issuing rival cards like American Express or Discover.

**66**     The DOJ recommended that major card-issuing banks commit their credit and debit cards exclusively to either Visa or MasterCard. The implications of antitrust charges and subsequent recommendations by the DOJ had caused a shift in the allegiance of many major banks. Since the lawsuit was initiated many banks had chosen to focus their business with one brand or the other. For example, Citigroup and Chase chose to predominately use MasterCard, and Bank One and Bank of America chose to predominately use Visa. The result of this shift to either Visa or MasterCard meant another layer of competition between card issuers.

**67**     The Bankruptcy Reform Act could also have an impact on the industry. The new law would require all cardholders meet certain income guidelines and seek out credit counseling before being allowed to file for bankruptcy. This could have long-term positive results for issuers, but may also result in a short-term dramatic increase in loan losses as cardholders attempt to file before the new law takes effect. Issuers had benefited in 1999 and 2000 from a declining bankruptcy trend as shown in Exhibit 5, but a dramatic increase, even short-term, would negatively affect issuers' profitability.

## Globalization

**68**     The effect of the globalization of the financial services industry has also had an impact on the credit card sector. Globalization led to increased worldwide acceptance of credit cards and also led U.S. issuers to begin issuing cards to customers outside the United States.

**69**     Visa and MasterCard had expanded their networks globally, allowing U.S. customers to use their cards around the world. American Express and Discover built proprietary networks to also allow cardholders worldwide usage. Issuers without a proprietary network could take advantage of the Visa and MasterCard networks and allow their cardholders to use the cards around the world. This allowed credit cards to act as a universal payment mechanism, with the issuer handling the foreign exchange portion of the transactions. As a result, credit cards brought added convenience for customers travelling abroad.

**70**     Some U.S. issuers had also built international credit card portfolios. Citibank and American Express were two of the largest U.S. issuers in the global market. American Express operated in the major markets in Europe and Japan, where it had over 1 million cards issued. Citibank had been able to expand based on its international consumer banking operations and looked to continue to grow this business. International name recognition was

**EXHIBIT 5**
U.S. Bankruptcy
Filings

| Year | Totals Filings | Business Filings | Consumer Filings |
|------|----------------|------------------|------------------|
| 1991 | 943,987 | 71,549 | 872,438 |
| 1992 | 971,517 | 70,643 | 900,874 |
| 1993 | 875,202 | 62,304 | 812,898 |
| 1994 | 832,829 | 52,374 | 780,455 |
| 1995 | 926,601 | 51,959 | 874,642 |
| 1996 | 1,178,555 | 53,549 | 1,125,006 |
| 1997 | 1,404,145 | 54,027 | 1,350,118 |
| 1998 | 1,442,549 | 44,367 | 1,398,182 |
| 1999 | 1,319,465 | 44,367 | 1,281,581 |
| 2000 | 1,253,444 | 35,472 | 1,217,972 |

required to be a successful international issuer, thus firms with a worldwide commercial banking presence had the advantage. Also required was an international operational and legal infrastructure enabling issuers to lend to customers in other countries.

71    However, U.S. firms without an international consumer banking presence had found it difficult to issue cards in foreign markets partially due to the lack of name recognition but also due to cultural differences.

### Sales and Promotion

72    The primary account acquisition method during the 1990s was direct mail. However, a new acquisition channel developed in the Internet and issuers continued to look for other ways to attract customers.

73    Direct mail acquisitions helped fuel the growth in credit card issuance during the 1990s. However, by 2001 mailboxes were being stuffed with more credit-card solicitations than ever, with the typical U.S. household receiving more than three card offers a month. In 2000, card issuers mailed a record 3.54 billion solicitations, up from 2.87 billion in 1999.

74    With this increase in solicitations also came a record-low response rate of 0.6 percent in 2000, compared with 1.0 percent in 1999. To be successful, issuers needed to develop creative campaigns to attract customers and to use technology to segment and target the base of potential customers. Also, issuers needed to seek out other means of acquiring customers.

75    The use of the Internet as an acquisition channel increased dramatically with many issuers offering on-line applications and instant approval decisions. Partnering with or advertising on highly trafficked websites was important to success. Also important was instant decisioning, which allowed new cardholders to immediately begin using their new credit card number to make purchases on the web. However, as this grew, the potential for fraudulent applications also grew.

76    Other methods of account and customer acquisition included in-branch invitations and cross-selling customers from other businesses within the bank. In-branch invitation acquisitions stemmed from customers applying for credit through a firm's commercial banking branch network. Bank card issuers had an advantage over monolines in this area.

77    Cross-selling also provided an acquisition channel. For firms that operated in other segments beyond credit cards, customers of these other products provided acquisition targets. For example, banks that issued mortgages or auto loans could also issue credit cards to these customers.

### Operations

78    Credit card issuers needed to manage their operations effectively in order to remain profitable. One important area were the costs of doing business, including personnel costs. Another important operation was credit, which determined the firm's lending criteria.

79    Beyond the costs of acquiring customers, credit card issuers had other costs that needed to be managed effectively. The personnel cost of customer service and collections comprised a considerable portion of the issuer's expenses. The cost of printing and delivering monthly statements to customers was also substantial. The Internet had provided an opportunity to reduce this particular cost. As issuers migrated customers to electronic statements, there could be reductions in paper, printing, and postage costs.

80    Another important operational area was credit underwriting. This involved determining who should be offered credit and how much they should be offered. Issuers usually developed risk criteria using individual's credit bureau scores (otherwise called FICO scores). This score took into account the individual's past credit and payment history. Cardholders with missed payments or loan defaults would have lower FICO scores. Issuers offering

**EXHIBIT 6**

**Top Ten Credit Card Issuers (as of 12/31/00)**

| Rank/Issuer | 4Q/00 | 4Q/99 | Change |
|---|---|---|---|
| 1. Citigroup | $87.7b | $72.4b | +21% |
| 2. MBNA America | 70.4b | 58.8b | +20 |
| 3. Bank One/FUSA | 67.0b | 69.4b | −18 |
| 4. Discover | 47.1b | 38.0b | +24 |
| 5. Chase Manhattan | 36.2b | 33.6b | + 8 |
| 6. American Express | 28.7b | 23.4b | +23 |
| 7. Providian | 26.7b | 18.7b | +43 |
| 8. Bank of America | 24.3b | 20.9b | +16 |
| 9. Capital One | 22.7b | 15.7b | +45 |
| 10. Household | 15.2b | 13.3b | +14 |

credit to these low or subprime customers usually charged higher rates or fees to account for the increased risk of nonpayment.

## Competition

81     The credit card industry consolidation was resulting in the largest issuers controlling an increasing percentage of the market. At the end of 2000, the top ten issuers controlled 78 percent of the total market. Competition among the leaders had been fierce, with most of the country saturated with cards from the several large firms, and offers from all of the large firms on a regular basis. The growth of the top ten issuers is shown in Exhibit 6.

82     Low introductory interest rates had become common, with issuers content to issue loans below their own cost of funds for a time in hopes that the cardholders would stay long enough to become profitable customers.

83     Value propositions had become increasingly important as issuers vied to become the card of choice, and retaining current cardholders had become as important as acquiring new customers.

84     Banks historically made up the largest segment of the credit card industry. However, throughout the 1990s, companies whose sole business was credit cards began to take in increased share of the market. These firms, called monolines, used creative advertising and searched out new niches to win customers from the bank card issuers.

85     Citibank had historically been the largest player in the credit card market. Much of the innovation in the industry (co-branded cards, aggressive direct mail campaigns) began with Citibank. Many of the executives across the credit card industry began their careers with Citibank, including the CCS executive Richard Srednicki. In 1998, Citibank purchased the AT&T Universal Card portfolio, which allowed it to regain the leadership position that was briefly lost to Bank One after the latter's purchase of First USA. In 2000, Citibank purchased the Associates portfolio, signaling to the industry that it would continue to be an aggressive acquirer and would use acquisitions to continue to fuel its growth.

86     Citibank's greatest advantages were that it had the worldwide presence that made it attractive to business travelers and vacationers and it had the scale to operate efficiently. Citibank had credit card operations in 48 countries worldwide.

87     Citibank had the top airline co-brand credit card with its partnership with American Airlines. It also had the top telecommunications co-brand as a result of the acquisition of the AT&T portfolio. Also, its over 100 million cardholders provided a substantial base from which to cross-sell other products in an attempt to deepen cardholders' relationships with the company and so make it less likely they would switch to another issuer's card.

88     Citibank attempted to limit its loan losses by maintaining strong collection departments and policies. It had also proven the ability to effectively integrate acquired portfolios,

including agent banking portfolios. However, in 2001 it increased its focus on acquiring international credit card portfolios, which may have signaled a strategic decision to focus less on domestic portfolio acquisitions. Finally, Citibank had not made an effort to compete in the corporate card business and as a result had not developed the technological platform that would allow it to enter this market in the near term.

89    Other Bank Card Issuers included most of the U.S. large and mid-size banks. However, many of these banks did not have the scale to operate a credit card business efficiently and as a result the trend had been towards exiting this business. Even large banks, like the Bank of New York and First Union, had sold off its credit card portfolios.

90    Bank One became a large credit card issuer with its acquisition of the monoline First USA, which grew dramatically during the 1990s with aggressive direct mail campaigns and very low introductory rates. It had an extensive co-brand network and an affinity relationship network of over 2000 partners.

91    However, despite its size, Bank One ran into considerable financial trouble. In 2000, it was forced to take large write-offs associated with the credit quality of its credit card portfolio and then continued to struggle to remain profitable with large amounts of customers accruing interest rates below the bank's cost of funds. Bank One had the scale to compete effectively, but needed to work on strengthening its profitability, as well as its credit and collections policies.

92    Other bank card issuers faced similar problems. Due to size limitations, most did not have the international name recognition to compete in the international card issuance market, the capital to compete for portfolio acquisitions, or the technology to compete in the corporate card market.

93    Monoline issuers had unique advantages and disadvantages over the bank card issuers. One disadvantage was that monolines did not have the same access to capital that the larger banks had. However, the credit card segments within the large banks had to compete for that capital with other, possibly more profitable, businesses within the bank. Monolines did not have this dilemma and as a result may be more flexible in their choices of investment projects.

94    MBNA had one of the most unique situations in the industry. In slightly over a decade, it built its company from a small Maryland bank into one of the largest credit card issuers in the United States. It held a competitive advantage in the sector of affinity marketing, an offshoot of co-branding, with over 4,000 affinity relationship partners.

95    MBNA had built partnerships with thousands of small groups across the United States, from athletic teams to universities to professional groups. It also had used its affinity relationship strategy to become a successful issuer in the United Kingdom, Ireland, and Canada.

96    MBNA's advantage was that it was able to use the affinity that individuals had for any one of its partners as a method for issuing them a credit card. Also, since people were less likely to default on a card that was associated with an organization that they were a part of or had affinity towards, the loan loss rates on MBNA's portfolio had continued to be lower than the industry averages. Another advantage was its relentless focus on effective credit underwriting and customer service. Customer service was part of the MBNA culture and was imbued in each function, from account acquisitions through collections. MBNA had not opted to compete in the corporate card market and did not have the investment banking presence to win corporate card business.

97    American Express (Amex) was the leader in the corporate card market as well as the charge card (nonrevolving credit) market. However, it had also become an aggressive marketer of revolving credit cards, first with its Optima card and most recently with Blue. It also had worldwide name recognition partially due to the historical popularity of its travelers check product. However, its worldwide card position is skewed more towards the charge card business as opposed to the credit card business.

**98**     Amex had several advantages over other competitors. One advantage was that it owned a global processing platform and thus did not use the MasterCard or Visa networks. This allowed it to build its brand name while other issuers' names often got lost behind the MasterCard or Visa brands. Amex also had a loyal customer base that paid their bills. As a result, Amex had a lower percentage of delinquent accounts (measured as accounts 90 or more days past due) than any of its competitors. Amex had also focused on customer service and had maintained a strong collections group that also helped to limit its loan losses. This base of loyal customers also provided a receptive audience for Amex to cross-sell other products. For example, in 1999 Amex cardholders accounted for 30 percent of all new customers with American Express Financial Advisors. This helped build the depth of relationship needed to retain customers. Amex's strong brand name also provided a base from which to launch new products, like the Blue card.

**99**     The Blue card was unique in that it contained a "smart" chip as well as a magnetic strip as the means of identification. Amex had marketed it as the card for the new economy and had seen rapid growth in this portfolio. The Blue card was able to be marketed as the card for the new economy since the smart chip would allow for secure Internet transactions using a reader hooked up to the users' computer. However, as of early 2001, fewer than 1 percent of Blue cardholders were using the smart chip capability to make Internet purchases. This suggested that the success of the Blue launch was related more to a creative marketing campaign than a fundamental change in the industry.

**100**     In the corporate card market, Amex was the recognized leader. However, smaller competitors had built more flexible technology platforms for servicing corporate clients and had begun winning business away from Amex. In 2000, CCS purchased Paymentech, the largest of these competitors.

**101**     Historically, Amex had been an occasional acquirer of portfolios. However, by 2001 it had become a potential target for acquisition by larger financial services organizations like Citigroup and Morgan Stanley Dean Witter. It had run into some financial difficulty, making it less likely that it would be competing for agent bank acquisitions in the near term.

**102**     Other Monoline Issuers will have an impact on the future of the credit card industry. Discover had rebounded after years of stagnation with a strong marketing campaign and its cash-back approach, which allowed cardholders to obtain a rebate in cash each year on a percentage of their purchases. Several other companies including CCS had attempted a similar card without Discover's success.

**103**     Cap One had become an aggressive marketer of credit cards during the latter part of the 1990s. It focused on lending to all levels across the credit spectrum, from "superprime," the most creditworthy customers within the prime market, to subprime, the least creditworthy customers. It had a very profitable secured card with which it served the subprime market. For a fee, and a required up-front cash deposit, a high-credit-risk customer could obtain a low-credit-limit card with which to build or rebuild their credit. Once they had done so, Cap One would then offer them a more flexible credit arrangement.

**104**     Cap One had continued to grow rapidly using technology to segment the market of potential customers and target offers specifically to their needs and preferences. During the fourth quarter of 2000, Cap One added three times as many new customers as any other issuer.

**105**     Providian Financial had also grown through marketing to the subprime segment. It was also a buyer of distressed credit card assets, which were loans that other banks had charged off. However, Providian's loan loss rates had been double those of Cap One.

**106**     Beyond Amex, and to a lesser degree MBNA, the monolines did not have the international name recognition required to issue internationally. Nor did these firms have the commercial or investment banking presence to leverage for their individual and corporate customer businesses. Also, while many of these companies were growing rapidly, they did not have the access to capital to be strong competitors for portfolio acquisitions.

**EXHIBIT 7**
**JP Morgan Chase**
**Commercial Bank**

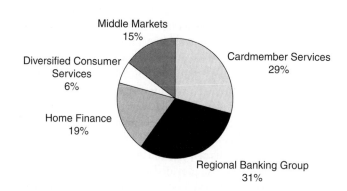

## THE COMPANY OVERVIEW

**107** Chase Cardmember Services (CCS) made up 29 percent of the cash operating earnings of JP Morgan Chase's commercial banking sector as shown in Exhibit 7, but just over 7 percent of the earnings of the entire JP Morgan Chase company. CCS had benefit from the trend toward consolidation in the financial services industry during the 1990s. It had become one of the few remaining large issuers in the credit card segment as a result of two large bank mergers; Chemical Bank with Manufacturer's Hanover and this combined Chemical Bank with Chase Manhattan. The combination of these companies and the resultant combinations of the credit card portfolios helped CCS grow to a degree that none of the individual firms had been able to do through internal growth or customer acquisitions.

**108** CCS had also benefited from the consolidation trend specifically in the credit card segment, with numerous commercial banks exiting this segment. This was evidenced by its purchase of the entire credit card portfolio of the Bank of New York. While opportunity for CCS abounded as the number of portfolios up for sale increased, including mid-size and large portfolios, CCS had still not proven it could grow its business via means other than portfolio acquisitions.

## PRODUCTS

**109** CCS offered Visa and MasterCard products including co-branded cards, agent bank cards, and a very minor secured card product, but did not offer affinity cards. CCS also had a small but growing business and corporate card presence.

### Co-Branded Cards

**110** Co-branded credit cards were one area that CCS had competed in strongly, with offerings in various industries, including gasoline, airlines, and retailing.

**111** The Shell Oil Card was the largest co-branded card that was part of the CCS portfolio. The CCS partnership with Shell began with Chemical Bank and had been maintained through several mergers. This was the one CCS credit card that advertised regularly on television. Advertisements could also be found at Shell gas stations around the United States. The card offered a 5 percent rebate on gas purchases made at Shell gas stations and a 1 percent rebate on all other purchases. These rebates could only be used at Shell gas stations to offset the cost of future gas purchases. The card was similar to cards offered by other oil companies.

112    The Shell card was the leading gasoline co-branded card. Gasoline co-branded cards developed as an offshoot to the gasoline cards that most oil companies had issued. The advantages for customers were that the co-branded card carried either a MasterCard or Visa logo and could be used for purchases other than gas and allow them to earn rebates on their purchases. The advantage for Shell was the additional business by customers that would only want to buy gas from them, so they could earn the rebates offered by the card. The advantages for CCS bank were the additional loans and becoming the card of choice for customers loyal to Shell.

113    The Shell card, like other co-branded cards offering rewards or rebates, tended to attract customers that charged frequently, but also paid off their balance each month (called "transactors"). In general, CCS made most of its profits from customers that did not pay their balance each month, thus accruing finance charges (called "revolving"). Many cards that attracted "transactors" attached an annual fee to the card, but the Shell card remained attractive to customers since it did not have an annual fee.

114    The Wal-Mart Card was CCS' second largest co-branded card. This card was launched with the nation's largest retailer in 1996. The card did not offer any value enhancement but carried a low fixed interest rate.

115    This strategy was consistent with Wal-Mart's philosophy of everyday low prices. No value enhancement was added to the card because Wal-Mart did not want any customer to receive benefits not available to all of its customers.

116    This approach worked successfully for several years and the portfolio grew steadily. However, competition in the industry had reduced interest rates across the board. In order to acquire new customers, most card issuers were offering very low introductory interest rates. Because of the nature of the relationship with Wal-Mart, CCS was prohibited from making similar offers. Thus, the portfolio growth had slowed considerably as customers had become used to receiving low introductory offers.

117    The Continental Airlines Card was CCS' airline co-branded card. Prior to 1997, CCS had been the issuer of the British Airways co-branded credit card. This card had a limited appeal outside of East coast–based business travelers and wealthy individuals. At the same time, Marine Midland was struggling to maintain its credit card business and was looking for a buyer for the Continental Airlines portfolio. CCS decided to sell the British Airways portfolio and purchase the Continental Airlines portfolio from Marine Midland. This card had a much broader appeal nationwide as a result of Continental's large U.S. presence.

118    The Continental Airlines card allowed cardholders to earn Continental frequent flyer miles for each dollar charged to the card. The card had a high annual fee compared with other CCS offerings, but also offered bonus miles for opening the account, helping to overcome cardholders' aversion to annual fees.

119    The card was primarily marketed through direct mail, but was also advertised on Continental Airlines flights and in airports at Continental terminals. The appeal was to business travelers, families looking to earn miles towards vacations, and anyone who flew often on Continental. The card was similar to offers by other airlines, particularly the Citibank AAdvantage card, which was partnered with American Airlines.

120    The Toys R Us Card was a small portfolio that was obtained when CCS purchased the credit card business of the Bank of New York in 1998. The card appealed primarily to parents with young children. The card was relaunched in 1999 and allowed cardholders to earn rebate points that could be redeemed at Toys R Us and Toys R Us.com. The portfolio remained small and was marketed primarily at Toys R Us locations and on the Toys R Us.com website.

121    The Verizon Card was the descendant of the Bell Atlantic co-branded card prior to the phone company's merger with GTE and its subsequent name change to Verizon. In 2001, CCS chose to terminate its relationship with the telecommunications company.

122     Like the Shell card and co-branded cards from other issuers, the Verizon card tended to appeal to "transactors," or customers who charged frequently, thus earning significant rebates, but did not carry a balance monthly and did not accrue interest charges. CCS ending this relationship was possibly a signal that the industry was moving away from "transactor" cards that were unprofitable.

### Agent Bank Cards

123     CCS had agent banking relationships with two banks. The first was the Bank of New York. This was a small portfolio of individuals and businesses that had Bank of New York credit cards that were issued and serviced by CCS. The other, larger relationship was with Huntington Bank. CCS purchased this portfolio in 1999, and it was the first all-agent bank portfolio that CCS had purchased.

124     CCS continued to look to be a portfolio acquirer and recognized that many of the portfolio sales in the future would involve agent banking relationships. It had experience in integrating and managing two agent banking relationships and was looking to build on this experience. Other large firms, like Citibank and MBNA, had also been acquiring agent banking relationships, as evidenced by MBNA's purchase of the First Tennessee Bank portfolio. Agent banking relationships could also be sought out and developed without having to purchase portfolios, but this was less common.

125     This area represented an opportunity for growth for CCS as it gained experience from its two agent bank relationships, had the capital to fund agent bank portfolio acquisitions, and portfolios continued to come up for sale.

### Business and Corporate Cards

126     A growing and profitable segment of the CCS portfolio was the business and corporate card sector. The business card market involved cards issued to small businesses, many of them already having a banking relationship with Chase (or the Bank of New York and Huntington Bank, in the case of agent bank business cards.)

127     However, a larger area for growth appeared to be the corporate card market. This involved issuing and servicing the credit cards issued to employees within large corporations. This sector was dominated by American Express. However, CCS had recently acquired the corporate card business of Paymentech. As part of this purchase, CCS acquired Paymentech's industry-leading platform for acquiring and servicing corporate cards and CCS President Richard Srednicki had stated that this was a strategic growth area for the business.

128     The corporate card business was less dependent on interest charges, as most corporations paid incurred expenses on a monthly basis. Also, since the corporation guaranteed payment on charges made by its employees, loan losses were no concern. The revenue was derived mainly from fee income. This reduced CCS' reliance on interest rate sensitive revenue. Also, JP Morgan Chase had a strong investment bank that CCS could leverage to acquire additional corporate clients.

## TECHNOLOGY

129     CCS had made several attempts to incorporate new technology into its business. It had worked to incorporate the Internet and was also working to begin incorporating smart card technology.

### Internet

**130**   In 1999, CCS launched a co-branded card with the Internet retailer Shopnow.com. The card offered reward points for merchandise purchased at the site. However, in 2000 Shopnow.com realized that the value proposition for general purpose online retailers was limited and decided to change its name to Network Commerce and its business focus to B-to-B commerce. As a result, the Shopnow.com card never became the CCS entry into the new economy that it had hoped.

**131**   It was, however, a good example of how CCS might fit into the core business of JP Morgan Chase going forward. The Shopnow.com card was developed after the Chase venture capital business funded Shopnow.com. This card was designed not only to help CCS, but also to help Shopnow.com, which would in turn increase the value of Chases' investment in the company. Although it was unsuccessful, it set a precedent for potential future synergies within JP Morgan Chase.

**132**   CCS had also developed an Internet presence as part of the www.chase.com site. The site allowed cardholders to check their current and previous statements online and, if they had a Chase checking account, pay their bill online.

### Payment Methods

**133**   By the start of 2001, CCS had not issued a card that incorporated smart card technology. However, it was developing a smart card and was also looking into the possibility of combining smart card technology with its co-branded cards. The Continental Airlines card, which had a more affluent customer base compared to its other co-branded cards, was one possible alternative.

# REGULATION

**134**   The regulatory environment provided several opportunities and threats for CCS.

### Financial Services Modernization

**135**   This legislation had spurred a flood of mergers and acquisitions among financial institutions; among them was the merger of J. P. Morgan and Chase Manhattan. The resulting company, JP Morgan Chase, was a large multifaceted financial services company or one-stop shopping facility for financial services.

**136**   The creation of this large financial services conglomerate had presented a challenge for CCS. CCS had now become a much smaller part of a larger company and there was the possibility that it would be deemed not part of the core business of the new firm. The situation also presented an opportunity for CCS. CCS could present itself as an integral part of a financial services team that could provide a true one-stop-shopping financial services experience for customers. For example, for any business that did its investment banking, middle market, or branch network banking with JP Morgan Chase, CCS could add value by providing various payment methods for these customers. The key to success was to demonstrate to JP Morgan Chase that CCS could provide valuable services to existing clients by helping to create a true one-stop-shopping financial services experience for clients.

### Antitrust

**137**   The pending antitrust suit involving MasterCard and Visa was not likely to have a dramatic impact on CCS. Even if the government forced the Associations to drop the prohibition on member banks from issuing American Express or other non-Visa or non-MasterCard cards, CCS would likely opt not to issue American Express cards as it was seen as an independent competitor. By 2000, CCS had already agreed to become primarily a MasterCard issuer.

# GLOBLIZATION

**138**   Since CCS cards were affiliated with Visa or MasterCard, its cardholders could use their cards worldwide. However, CCS had opted to exit the international card issuance business.

**139**   Until mid-2000, CCS had a profitable and growing credit card business in Hong Kong, where it was the third-largest credit card issuer. The Manhattan Card, as it was called, was considered the premier elite credit card in Hong Kong. This card portfolio was the largest part of JP Morgan Chase's international consumer banking operations, which also included branch banking networks in Hong Kong, Panama, and the Virgin Islands.

**140**   However, in 2000 the corporation made the strategic decision to exit the international commercial banking business. As a result, the Hong Kong credit card business was sold to Standard Chartered Bank for $1.32 billion and CCS became a domestic-only card issuer. After the merger with JP Morgan, CCS did have an internationally recognized brand name that it could leverage if it decided to reenter the international card issuance business. It also had the capital needed if it wanted to expand internationally via acquisition of foreign credit card businesses.

# FINANCE

**141**   CCS had been a profitable and important segment of Chase Manhattan prior to the JP Morgan merger. However, as a result of the JP Morgan–Chase Manhattan merger, CCS' parent became primarily an investment bank. This could make it difficult for CCS to obtain capital from the corporation to fund portfolio acquisitions and other growth-oriented activities. CCS needed to focus on maintaining a high return on investment, as it has to compete for capital with profitable investment banking and venture capital projects in other parts of the corporation.

**142**   CCS made money primarily on interest charged to customers who borrowed money (revolved). It also made money on late fees charged to customers not making timely payments and over-limit fees charged to customers exceeding their credit limit. Another source of profit was insurance premiums charged to customers enrolling in payment insurance, which helped customers maintain their credit rating in the event they became unemployed.

**143**   Other CCS revenues included interchange income, which was a transaction-processing fee charged to merchants accepting credit cards as payment, cash advance fees, and annual fees. However, as more customers became transactors, CCS profitability was likely to become challenged as interest income decreased.

**144**   Another threat to CCS was the economy, as loan losses also affected its profitability. Bankruptcies had been on the decline during 1999 and 2000 as the economy had been strong. This had helped CCS to reduce its overall loan losses. However, if this trend turned around, the credit card industry as a whole would be significantly affected. The Bankruptcy Reform Act currently before Congress could help offset some of this risk by making it difficult for some individuals to file bankruptcy. However, if the economy worsened, the volume of bankruptcies was still likely to increase dramatically.

**EXHIBIT 8**
**CCS Charge-off Rates**

| CCS Charge-off Rates (losses as a % of total loans) | | | | | | | 1999 | 1998 | 1997 |
|---|---|---|---|---|---|---|---|---|---|
| 3Q00 | 2Q00 | 1Q00 | 4Q99 | 3Q99 | 2Q99 | 1Q99 | Full Year | Full Year | Full Year |
| 4.97% | 5.09% | 5.39% | 5.25% | 5.57% | 5.85% | 6.18% | 5.66% | 6.02% | 5.58% |

**EXHIBIT 9**
**CCS Revenue**

| Year Ended December 31, (in millions) | 1999 | 1998 |
|---|---|---|
| Reported Credit Card Revenue | $1,698 | $1,474 |
| Less Impact of Credit Card Securitizations | (318) | (299) |
| Operating Credit Card Revenue | $1,380 | $1,175 |

145    Periodically, Chase securitized a portion of its credit card portfolio by selling a pool of credit card receivables to a trust, which issued securities to investors. The receivables underlying the securities that were sold to investors were not included in Chase's consolidated results. Securitization changed CCS' status from that of a lender to that of a servicer. When credit card receivables were securitized, CCS ceased to derive interest income on those receivables and instead received fees for continuing to service them. As a result, securitization did not significantly affect Chase's reported and operating net income. Exhibit 9 shows CCS revenue for 1998–1999. Operating revenue is the revenue CCS derives from its business activities. Reported revenue includes the additional income CCS derives from its securitization activities.

# MANAGEMENT

146    Richard Srednicki began his career at Citibank and contributed to its growth into the leading U.S. credit card issuer during the 1980s. One of his more recent assignments was as an executive at AT&T in charge of the AT&T Universal Card. During his tenure, the AT&T card business was sold to Citibank as AT&T decided to exit the credit card business. CCS faced a similar situation in which it was possible its parent could possibly someday also want to exit the business.

147    David Coulter, the former CEO of Bank of America, was now running the JP Morgan Chase commercial bank, of which CCS was a major part. The success of CCS would likely be critical to Mr. Coulter's success as head of the commercial bank and he had said that CCS was not for sale and would continue to look to be a portfolio acquirer.

148    However, the decision of whether JP Morgan Chase would remain in the credit card segment probably rested with the CEO William Harrison and the board of directors. Mr. Harrison's experience had been more on the investment side of the banking industry, and the JP Morgan merger solidified that portion of the business without having a dramatic impact on the commercial banking operations. Analysts had suggested that the slower-growth commercial banking business might not be a good fit with the expanding investment banking business.

# LOOKING TOWARD THE FUTURE

149    Given the trends of consolidation and technological advance in the credit card segment, CCS management was exploring a number of strategic alternatives. The pressure was on to begin clarifying its strategic direction to both the investment community as well as the JP Morgan Chase board of directors. One decision that had to be made was the geographic scope CCS would take in expanding its business. Mr. Srednicki was considering two alternatives that were proposed.

150    The first alternative for CCS was one centered on growth both domestically and internationally. In this alternative, CCS would build a global credit card franchise allowing it to diversify its current business by expanding into other countries, particularly those countries where the JP Morgan and Chase names had substantial name recognition.

**151**     This alternative was feasible since although JP Morgan Chase no longer had an international commercial banking presence, it did have a strong international presence in the investment banking sector. CCS could leverage this brand-name recognition in countries like Canada, the United Kingdom, and Japan to expand to international consumers. CCS has the capital required to purchase portfolios anywhere in the world, which also made international expansion feasible. Finally, CCS could compete for international corporations' business for its corporate card business as well.

**152**     This alternative could win against the competition because among its competitors, only Citibank and Amex had greater name recognition worldwide and Amex was more focused on the charge card market. With the trend toward consolidation affecting the international financial services industry along with the domestic industry, the credit card segment worldwide was likely to consolidate faster than one firm alone can absorb. CCS has the capital required to acquire international portfolios as they came up for sale and as a result, CCS was in a position to win against all of the other competitors except Citibank. If it participated during this consolidation, along with Citibank, it would allow it to build an international presence that could be leveraged in the future. If it did not participate in this consolidation in the near term, it would limit its ability to ever compete in this market. It could also win against all competition in the international corporate card business. It has the industry-leading technology platform that can be applied to corporate card portfolios domestically and internationally and the worldwide investment banking presence to leverage for acquiring new business.

**153**     The main drawbacks to this strategy were CCS' lack of an international commercial banking presence to leverage for acquiring new customers, an international infrastructure for servicing these customers, and Citibank's more dominant position in this area.

**154**     However, CCS could find ways around these problems. While Citibank did have a dominate position in this area, the industry was consolidating faster than Citibank alone could absorb. If CCS were to begin competing for and winning portfolios, it could participate with Citibank in absorbing this consolidation. Also, it could develop the required international infrastructure through acquisition as well. Where Citibank might be more inclined just to purchase the portfolio of an international card issuer, CCS could look to also purchase the issuer's infrastructure.

**155**     A second alternative was one centered solely on domestic expansion. Mr. Srednicki had inherited a business that had already determined it would exit the international card business. In doing so it recognized that there was more opportunity domestically that it wished to focus on. This alternative would keep CCS on that path and allow it to focus its resources entirely on the opportunities in the domestic market like corporate cards and agent banking cards.

**156**     This alternative was feasible as CCS had the access to capital required to be an acquirer of domestic portfolios and could do so more frequently without having to also acquire the infrastructure that international expansion would require. Also, domestically CCS had a strong commercial banking presence that was very helpful in acquiring loyal customers.

**157**     This alternative would allow CCS to win against the competition, as many competitors did not have the capital needed to be an aggressive acquirer. With this access to capital, and with Citibank focused on building its international business, CCS had a competitive advantage for domestic portfolio acquisitions. Also, most large U.S. corporations already had some relationship with JP Morgan Chase. As a result, CCS was in position to leverage these relationships, along with its industry-leading technology platform for servicing corporate clients to win against the competition in the corporate card business. Internationally, CCS would have to compete for business with foreign banks whose relationship with foreign corporations might limit CCS' success in the corporate card market.

**158**     The major drawback to this alternative was the possibility that Citibank would change its focus from international expansion back to domestic expansion. Citibank's scale made it a difficult head-on competitor that could limit CCS' success in the domestic market.

**159**     However, CCS could find ways around this problem. As in the international market, the domestic credit card market was consolidating faster than one company could absorb. As a result, CCS could still succeed by participating along with Citibank in the segment's consolidation. It does have the advantage over Citibank in the corporate card segment, and could use this advantage to become the dominant acquirer of corporate card portfolios.

**160**     Mr. Srednicki needed to decide which strategic decision to implement. While CCS had a strong domestic presence and no international presence, the trend toward consolidation internationally made this a good time to build an international business. If he chose not to take advantage of this opportunity now, it was likely that CCS would not be able to enter this market successfully in the future. However, in both domestic and international markets, Citibank had advantages over CCS. With Citibank focusing internationally, this was a good time for CCS to focus on domestic opportunity. Mr. Srednicki's decision would determine what direction CCS would take in order to win against increasing competition in the near, intermediate, and long term.

# Case 41 mGAMES

## Scott Hill

**1**   Jeffrey Lopez hung up the phone, leaned forward and buried his face in his hands. It seemed a challenge at this particular moment to try to remember why he had been so excited about his appointment as president and chief executive officer (CEO) of mGAMES (a developer of gaming software for mobile devices) just eight months ago. Lopez stood up from his large mahogany desk, walked to the window and looked out over the horizon toward Boston. It was 9:15 A.M. on Monday, July 22, 2002, and Lopez had just finished taking two telephone calls. The first had come from Benson Marks, principal shareholder and chairman of the board of mGAMES. In their call, Marks had told Lopez that he had just gotten off the phone with an old friend at Credit Suisse First Boston in New York. Specifics could not be provided, but rumors were circulating throughout the bank that a large and well-respected personal digital assistant (PDA) manufacturer was in the process of arranging financing to make a play for mGAMES. During the conversation, Marks reminded Lopez that he did not believe a takeover could be achieved without his consent—since he held 44.5 percent of mGAMES shares—but he also acknowledged that over the past year he had become increasingly concerned with the performance of mGAMES. "Now Jeff . . . you know I'm 100 percent behind you. But we've got to do something here. I need you to put a plan together and I'd like to see something within the next week."

**2**   The second call had come from Bjorger Pedersson, senior vice-president of product development with a large Scandinavian telecommunications company (sales of US$23 billion). Lopez had not spoken to Pedersson since first meeting him six months earlier at an industry conference in Las Vegas, but he remembered clearly how the two of them had seemed to really click. Pedersson was clearly excited and got right to the point:

> Jeffrey, our people have been looking at your organization now for the past five months. We've been trying to identify potential strategic partners for game development, and mGAMES is number one on our list. We want to work with you. In fact, we are thinking about an exclusive agreement that would essentially take up all of your capacity. We've got $70 million set aside for this to help set you up . . . and we've also already allocated some space for you in our new research facility in Menlo Park, California.
>
> We'd like you to fly here as soon as possible to begin discussions. This could be very big. Our projections show that mobile gaming will be a $6 billion market in five years. As our exclusive partner, the upside in this deal for you guys is enormous.
>
> I know we are jumping the gun a little. But our board wants us to move as quickly as possible, and I am looking for a partner who understands the importance of speed. I've got strict orders to have an agreement in place—with someone—within 45 days.

Scott Hill prepared this case under the supervision of Professor Allen Morrison solely to provide material for class discussion. The authors do not intend to illustrate either effective or ineffective handling of a managerial situation. The authors may have disguised certain names and other identifying information to protect confidentiality. Ivey Management Services prohibits any form of reproduction, storage or transmittal without its written permission. This material is not covered under authorization from CanCopy or any reproduction rights organization. To order copies or request permission to reproduce materials, contact Ivey Publishing, Ivey Management Services, c/o Richard Ivey School of Business, The University of Western Ontario, London, Ontario, Canada, N6A 3K7; phone (519) 661-3208; fax (519) 661-3882; e-mail casesivey.uwo.ca. Copyright © 2002, Ivey Management Services. Version: (A) 2002-08-12. One Time Permission to Reproduce granted by Ivey Management Services on July 28, 2003.

Richard Ivey School of Business
The University of Western Ontario

3      When the conversation with Pedersson ended, Lopez was clearly excited. However, as he looked again out the window, his ears resonated with the final words he had heard during the earlier conversation with Benson Marks: "mGAMES needs a plan that it can win with! Not only now, but for years to come."

# PDAS, MOBILE PHONES, AND HANDHELD GAMING DEVICES

4      Beginning in the mid-1990s, handheld devices—PDAs and mobile phones—had become the largest new consumer-based technology craze worldwide. By the end of 2001, it was estimated that over seven million mobile phones were manufactured and shipped worldwide every week. PDAs were also growing in popularity, and though at the end of 2001 only 28 million total units had been cumulatively sold, projections were that another 10 million units would be shipped during 2002.

5      There were some geographic differences in the adoption of various handheld units. Most Asian, European, and Middle Eastern consumers had been early to adopt mobile phones and seemed reluctant to buy into the concept of the PDAs. By 2001, mobile phones had become an essential part of their lifestyle, even to the extent that the quality of any given individual's mobile phone was often recognized as a status symbol. The weak adoption of PDAs in these parts of the world was partially due to the fact that early PDAs offered software in English only.

6      In contrast, North Americans were PDA-crazy, being particularly attracted to the potential for the power of PC-type functionality in the palm of their hands. Compared to Asians and Europeans, North Americans had been relatively slow to adopt mobile phones. One reason for this was because of industry restructuring following the breakup of AT&T and the repositioning of the Baby Bells. The result was not only consumer uncertainty but also a range of often confusing and expensive calling plans. Another reason for the comparatively slow adoption of cell phone technologies was the bulkiness of early mobile phones. However, by 2002, the market in North America had become essentially saturated with many wireless plans offering even lower long-distance rates than wired alternatives.

7      With North American cellular markets maturing and growth of PDAs accelerating, there was great uncertainty as to who would win out in the future of the handheld device business. Some observers predicted that rather than one format conquering the other, they would all add features and begin to look and perform similarly. Indeed, convergence between mobile phone and PDA technologies was occurring on all fronts. According to Phil Redman of the Gartner Group, "the handset (mobile phone) manufacturers are gunning to take on the PDAs and vice versa. Handsets are simply becoming wireless PDAs."[1]

8      By 2002, an increasing number of new mobile phones offered built-in personal planning software packages, and a greater number of new PDAs offered short message service (SMS), voice and/or e-mail communication capabilities. In an exciting yet ambiguous market environment, the only certainty was that consumers were getting tired of carrying multiple devices around.

9      Convergence in the industry was also occurring when gaming functionality was considered. Nintendo's portable Gameboy system had long since offered personal planning and task list cartridges, and rumors were now circulating that the new Gameboy Advance system—to be released in the fall of 2002—would also offer wireless communication capability. Telecom manufacturers like Ericsson and Nokia were also reportedly engaged in the development of handheld gaming devices that had advanced gaming controls, wireless

---

[1]*Infoworld,* November 26, 2001, p. 1.

**Convergence in the
Handheld Industry**

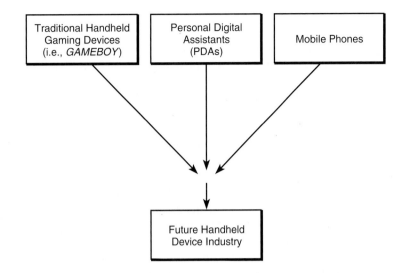

communication capability and PDA functionality. Handspring's new model had a slot to accept cartridges for playing games and running applications, and Palm had also added card slots to its latest models. David Grasior, president of wireless platform provider Synovial, asserted that "the handheld device of the future will do the things that keep you entertained when you're away from your PC and productive when you don't have a PC handy."[2]

**10**     The ongoing convergence of gaming devices, PDAs, and mobile phones is shown in the diagram above.

**11**     Competition in the emerging "handheld device industry" was fierce. Essentially, every established PC manufacturer, every telecom manufacturer, most electronics manufacturers and many others sought to become players in this multibillion-dollar segment. New technologies and new models were constantly being released. Color capability, communication capabilities, screen size, processor speed, RAM capacity, overall size of the unit and total functionality were all key criteria in the consumer's purchase decision.

**12**     Like many others, Alex Green, vice-president of business development for Motorola, believed that gaming functionality would become increasingly important in the market for handheld devices. He summarized where he saw this industry heading:

> [The future will bring us] cell phones with the power of an Xbox, PDAs on which you could play multiplayer Half-Life, with users all over the world, in real time, with real-time taunting over the microphone.[3]

# MOBILE GAMING

**13**     Handheld gaming devices of one variety or another had been around for several decades. Electronic gaming devices were a big hit when they first arrived on the market in the mid-1970s and were fashioned so that each device was its own game. It did not take long for the major electronics manufacturers to realize the market potential for these electronic games, and soon thereafter, handheld electronic gaming became a multimillion-dollar industry. As technology evolved, more competitors entered the market. To compete, game manufacturers rolled out ever-more complex games, leading industry sales to skyrocket. Things looked

[2]*Computer Games Magazine,* December 6, 2001, p. 2.
[3]"Gaming Gifts on the Go," *Computer Games Magazine,* June 12, 2001, p. 2.

very promising for these manufacturers—until Nintendo revolutionized the market for handheld gaming devices with the launch of the cartridge-based Gameboy system in the early 1990s. The Gameboy system captivated young consumers, providing them with the new-found ability to play multiple games with advanced graphics on a single handheld gaming device. By 1995, Nintendo possessed over 85 percent share of the handheld gaming device market.

**14** However, like console-based gaming, the market for handheld games on the Gameboy device was somewhat fickle. Consumers constantly demanded more advanced technology including improved performance controls, greater processor speeds and better graphics. While new and exciting games were absolutely critical to the success of any handheld gaming device, the pattern was consistent: after a couple strong years with any particular hardware product, sales would flatten until something bigger and better was released.

**15** In the late 1990s, the first wave of what some called "the gaming-generation" arrived in the workplace, in conjunction with technology advances and the increasing popularity of mobile phones and PDAs. Game designers and manufacturers soon began to realize the huge upside potential of wireless gaming on handheld devices. In fact, many believed that with the continuous influx of the gaming-generation into the working world, it would actually be wireless gaming functionality that would become the most important driver in the success of any handheld device. In 2001, Datamonitor Research projected that wireless gaming would become a $6-billion market worldwide by 2005, with four out of every five handheld device users playing wireless games.[4]

**16** Despite the longer-term promise, in 2002, games designed for mobile phones and PDAs were a far cry from the action-packed games available on Gameboy or other hand-held gaming devices. Game developers were still restricted by network and device limitations. As a result, there was some uncertainty as to which market segment would be the first to adopt the concept of wireless (interactive) gaming. When speaking about this market, the president of one mobile game development company argued:

> [The hand-held segment] is not—nor will it ever be—the 'gamer' market for people who play Quake, Ultima, Everquest and Doom. It's about games that everybody already knows how to play. People think it takes complex games to get people hooked. It doesn't. People also get hooked on very fun, simple games. Our research shows that 80 percent of people play these familiar games.[5]

**17** Other industry insiders disagreed. They believed technology improvements within the handheld device industry would captivate even the most hard-core gamers. The president of a major wireless airtime provider commented:

> Those guys still have to get up and go to the bathroom, and they have to get more Cheetos. You don't want to lose track of the game while you're getting a Coke and a 14-pound bag of M&M's. If you play Diablo, and someone would let you do it wirelessly from a PDA, would you pay $9.95 to do it? You better believe it![6]

**18** In short, while there were too many variables to allow an accurate assessment of how the market for wireless gaming would play itself out, those closest to the industry considered the $6-billion projection by 2005 to be conservative. Perhaps Greg Costikyan, chief design officer for unplugged Games—the individual regarded as the pre-eminent authority in the wireless gaming industry—summed things up best: "Someone's going to make a lot of money here."

---

[4]Betsy Harter, *Wireless Review;* Overland Park, February 1, 2001; p. 1.
[5]Ibid. p. 2.
[6]Ibid. p. 3.

# MGAMES

**19** The mGAMES company developed, manufactured, and distributed gaming software for various handheld and mobile devices. In 2001, net company sales reached $60.04 million and operating profits were $8.87 million. (See Exhibits 1, 2, and 3 for a review of mGAMES' financial performance.) In July 2002, mGAMES had 92 employees divided among software development, operations, marketing, sales and service. With the exception of five regional sales managers, all employees were based at company headquarters. Just over 70 percent of company revenue came from sales in the United States and Canada, 20 percent came from Europe, and 10 percent came from Japan.

**20** The company began operating independently in 1995 as a wholly owned affiliate of BHM Inc. BHM was a video game development company that started up in 1984 in Hastings, Massachusetts, by Benson H. Marks, using inheritance money he had received from the sale of his grandfather's extensive collection of classic cars. Marks, who in 1984 was 42 years old, held a master's degree in computer engineering from the University of Waterloo in Canada and an MBA degree from the Massachusetts Institute of Technology in Boston.

**21** With a personal interest in video games and first-hand knowledge of the spectacular financial success realized by companies such as Commodore and Atari, Marks visualized an incredible future for the video game industry. He anticipated software would absorb the bulk of industry profits and that the greatest profits would come to firms that developed niche and game-based software. In May 1984, Marks launched BHM by hiring four graduates from MIT's combined computer science/computer engineering program. Noal Fisher, a 29-year-old computer engineer, was appointed general manager of software operations with a mandate to lead the charge in the development of video games that would, in Marks' words, "give kids something to really talk about."

**EXHIBIT 1**   Income Statement (in millions of dollars)

|  | 1995 | 1996 | 1997 | 1998 | 1999 | 2000 | 2001 |
|---|---|---|---|---|---|---|---|
| **Net sales** | 16.81 | 22.65 | 33.13 | 41.09 | 45.81 | 55.89 | 60.04 |
| **Cost of goods sold** | 6.40 | 9.33 | 16.84 | 19.74 | 22.96 | 27.50 | 30.12 |
| **Gross profit** | **10.41** | **13.32** | **16.29** | **21.35** | **22.85** | **28.39** | **29.92** |
| **Selling & admin expenses** | 2.31 | 3.11 | 5.22 | 7.94 | 8.23 | 11.07 | 12.26 |
| **R&D Expenses** | 1.26 | 1.97 | 2.86 | 3.91 | 4.53 | 6.64 | 7.67 |
| **Depreciation and amortization** | 0.35 | 0.51 | 0.61 | 0.72 | 0.80 | 1.07 | 1.12 |
| **Operating profit** | **6.49** | **7.73** | **7.60** | **8.78** | **9.29** | **9.61** | **8.87** |
| **Total interest** | 0.12 | 0.29 | 0.38 | 0.43 | 0.48 | 0.70 | 0.76 |
| **Non-op income/Expenses** | 0.21 | 0.46 | 0.89 | 1.13 | 1.27 | 1.43 | 1.50 |
| **Pretax income** | 6.16 | 6.98 | 6.33 | 7.22 | 7.54 | 7.48 | 6.61 |
| **After tax income** | **3.92** | **5.61** | **5.06** | **6.35** | **6.40** | **6.02** | **5.44** |

**EXHIBIT 2**   Unit and Dollar Sales

|  | 1995 | 1996 | 1997 | 1998 | 1999 | 2000 | 2001 |
|---|---|---|---|---|---|---|---|
| **Unit sales** (in millions of units) | 1.42 | 2.12 | 2.79 | 3.55 | 4.2 | 4.16 | 3.89 |
| **Sales** (in $ millions) | 17.26 | 23.45 | 33.28 | 41.32 | 48.66 | 58.13 | 63.01 |

**EXHIBIT 3**
2001 Balance Sheet
(in millions of
dollars)

| Assets | | Liabilities | |
|---|---|---|---|
| Cash and equivalents | 0.70 | Notes payable | 1.20 |
| Accounts receivable | 4.52 | Accounts payable | 4.96 |
| Inventories | 6.12 | Accrued expenses | 3.96 |
| Other current assets | 9.56 | Taxes payable | 1.81 |
| | | Other current liabilities | 1.21 |
| **Total Current Assets** | **20.90** | **Total Current Liabilities** | **13.14** |
| Gross plant | 6.74 | Deferred taxes | 0.90 |
| Accumulated depreciation | −1.75 | Long-term debt | 8.20 |
| Net plant | 4.99 | Other long-term liabilities | 0.62 |
| Deferred charges | 0.46 | **Total Liabilities** | **22.86** |
| Intangible leases | 31.50 | | |
| Other long-term assets | 0.32 | | |
| **Total Assets** | **63.16** | | |
| | | **Equity** | |
| | | Preferred stock | 27.00 |
| | | Common stock | 7.00 |
| | | Retained earnings | 5.70 |
| | | Other liabilities | 0.60 |
| | | **Total Equity** | **40.30** |
| | | **Total Liabilities and Equity** | **63.16** |

22    From 1984 to 1994, BHM's software division experienced several ups and downs in its quest to develop hit video games. All BHM games that were deemed to have potential to become hits were sold or licensed to companies including the likes of Nintendo and Sega. These companies would then rebrand or relabel the games for distribution under their own name. In total, BHM saw 34 of its games brought to market and sold over 4.7 million copies worldwide in this nine-year period of time. Beginning in 1994, the company also began to market games under its own BHM brand. The advantage of self-marketing was that it allowed software companies to sell successful games (with some modifications) on multiple hardware platforms. Over time, the major hardware manufacturers also developed their own in-house software divisions to compete against the independent vendors. What emerged was a complex system whereby companies like Nintendo and Sega developed some proprietary games and contracted for the development of other games. In addition, independent companies like BHM developed and sold their own branded games and essentially worked as contractors to balance out their business portfolio.

23    Despite the early growth of BHM, Marks constantly wondered about the future of his business, specifically, the potential for new gaming applications. BHM's game development costs were rising year after year in the face of increased competition and more complex technologies. Along with increased development costs came bigger gambles on the next "great game." Failure could be devastating: successful games would gush cash for the company, particularly given the low variable costs of production (less than five percent).

24    In early 1994, Marks received a call from Ichiro Hasegawa, senior vice-president with a major Japanese entertainment hardware and software company. Hasegawa expressed the organization's interest to enter into an arrangement with BHM to modify a number of its games for distribution in Japan. In addition, Hasegawa indicated his company's interest in starting a mobile gaming unit that would design and manufacture hand-held gaming de-

vices. Marks handpicked five of his top software developers and announced the beginning of a new mobile gaming division and the acquisition of additional space for a small-cartridge manufacturing facility. Noal Fisher was assigned to be the division's director. From 1993 to 1994, the division modified and manufactured 26 game cartridges from the BHM library for the Japanese company, generating average annual sales of $12.1 million and pre-tax profits of $4.3 million.

25    With this success, in 1995, the mobile gaming division was spun off into mGAMES, a wholly owned affiliate of BHM. Fisher was appointed president and CEO and Marks became chairman of the board. By this time, the software engineering staff had increased five-fold to 26 people. Twelve individuals were employed in manufacturing and shipping, and six more served as full-time sales and customer service representatives.

26    Over time, additional customers were added to mGAMES' roster. In 1997, Marks took mGAMES public, selling some 55.5 percent of his shares in the process. At the time, net sales were $33.1 million, and operating profits were $7.6 million. In looking back at the events surrounding the public offering, Marks commented:

> We decided to take it public because the mobile gaming industry had such a promising future. The projections I'd seen suggested that new mobile products and associated gaming applications would cause the market to grow to the billion-dollar level in the next five years. At the time of the initial offering, the stock was trading at 40 times its earnings. My other businesses weren't coming even close to doing that well. This was a hot industry and the P/E multiple was outstanding. I also thought that with publicly traded shares, it would be easier to secure financing for our long-term growth.
>
> In retrospect, the timing of the IPO might have been a mistake. Back then, Palm had sales of a couple million. Well look at them today! Also, no one thought games would ever be played on cell phones like they are today.

27    In taking mGAMES public, Marks was able to maintain effective control because no other single shareholder held more than three percent of the stock.

28    Not long after the IPO, however, mGAMES' sales began to waver. Demand for its games tapered off toward the end of 1998, and management was finding it increasingly difficult to deal with customers like Nintendo and Sega. As a result, analysts had downgraded the stock to a sell rating, and Benson Marks found himself again on a quest for new gaming applications.

29    It was during a fall fishing trip in the Florida Keys in 1998 that Marks had the fortune of meeting Nathan Dorward, a senior executive with a major PDA manufacturer. Dorward talked about his company's forays into the development of "full-fledged computers that would rest in the palm of your hand." Dorward was also familiar with recent developments in wireless communications, and he raved to Marks about the potential for these handheld computers to "talk to one another wirelessly through the air." Soon thereafter, Marks returned to Hastings, excited about the associated potential for new gaming applications.

30    In early 1998, mGAMES introduced four new PDA-based games, all downloadable over the Internet. Three of the games were designed to be used on machines that used Palm-based operating systems; the fourth game was designed for a new PDA operating system being developed by Microsoft. The games generated $4.9 million in new sales and, by the end of 1999, the stock was back on track. In the year 2000, mGAMES signed development contracts with a total of five global companies interested in tapping into the PDA gaming market.

## Changes in Top Management

31    In October of 2001, Noal Fisher announced that he would be stepping down as president of mGAMES to assume a senior executive position with a major California-based technology

company. The move was a surprise to his staff who believed that Fisher had seemed happier than he had been in some time. When queried at his going-away party, his response was "the time just seems right. We are coming off some important successes and I am ready for my next big challenge. Besides, I have always wanted to get closer to 'the valley.' " Benson Marks' public statements reflected his appreciation for all that Fisher had achieved, and he offered Fisher his best wishes in his new position.

32    One month later, Marks appointed 39-year-old Jeffrey Lopez to the vacated position of president and CEO of mGAMES. Lopez, who was at the time serving as the vice-president of sales and marketing at mGAMES, assumed his new duties on November 5, 2001.

33    Lopez was born in Boston and graduated from the University of Massachusetts with an undergraduate degree in computer science. After graduating, he entered the MBA program at New York University and graduated in the top 10 percent of his 1991 class. Interested in working in the computer industry, Lopez moved to Seattle to join Microsoft. Over the next several years, Lopez took on increasingly senior positions at Microsoft, including management positions in marketing, sales, and business development. Lopez was described by his friends as "very smart," "a workaholic," "driven," and "at times hot-headed."

34    Lopez first became acquainted with Benson Marks at a trade show in Orlando in 1993. The men kept in touch over the next three years and, in 1997, Marks asked whether Lopez would ever be interested in working for mGAMES. "He had the track record and experience to lead the company into the future of the mobile game development industry. He was my first choice for the job." One month later, Lopez joined the company in the newly created position of vice-president of sales and marketing. Lopez explained his reason for joining mGAMES:

> I guess part of what intrigued me was wanting to be a big fish in a much smaller pond. I was looking for a company where I had a lot more autonomy and could have a bigger impact. I also could see that mGAMES was in a fantastic industry segment. Another reason I took the job—on top of the $150,000 signing bonus—was that I missed living in the East. My parents were in the Boston area and were getting older. I wanted to be closer to them.

35    The majority of mGAMES' employees were extremely pleased with the appointment. David Salt, mGAMES' chief financial officer (CFO) reported:

> I think Marks made the right decision in picking Lopez. The president needs to be someone who will move mGAMES towards the future of the mobile gaming industry. Jeff has the experience and credibility. I think he will be the guy to initiate change and listen to the ideas, not only of customers—but employees as well.

## Emerging Challenges

36    In assuming his new position, Lopez was aware of several challenges facing the company. One problem was the escalating costs of developing new games. The company's best selling game, Messenger of the Deep, accounted for nearly 17 percent of mGAMES' 2001 sales, representing approximately 883,000 units at $11.40 each. (More complex variations of Messenger of the Deep were also manufactured by sister company BHM for the Sony PlayStation and Nintendo 64, with an average retail price of $45.95.) While Messenger was a solid performer, it was by no means a blockbuster. True blockbuster games generated sales of over three million cartridges and provided enormous cash flow.

## New Game Development

37    Cash flow was essential for funding new games. In 2001, development costs in the industry averaged over $600,000 for each new mobile game, up almost 300 percent since the mid-1990s. While mGAMES was able to piggyback on the full versions of some BHM games de-

veloped for Sony's Playstation or the new Nintendo Game Cube, portable games had to be much simpler, and the crossover potential was minimal. Also, as separate companies, mGAMES had to pay market-based fees to BHM to license its games. And even though mGAMES had an inside track on accessing BHM's "hits," by the time they were identified as hits and then converted to run-on mobile devices, they were usually on the downward side of customer interest. To complicate matters, hardware advances pioneered by Sony, Nintendo and more recently by Microsoft had significantly raised customer demands for faster and ever more elaborate mobile games. As the complexity of the development process increased, so too did development costs. Of mGAMES' library of 117 games, only seven had been introduced to the market in 2001, and by mid-2002, only three new games had come out.

## Internal Issues

38    The company was having internal problems with production and inventory control. All sales of video games were subject to extensive performance parameters, and rejected cartridges became the sole financial burden of mGAMES. In 2001, mGAMES' rejection rates were nearly twice the industry average. Some blamed cartridge labeling and packaging problems for high rejection rates. Others blamed software glitches that caused almost 30 percent of PDA customers to have their systems lock up in downloading games from the Internet. While the Internet downloading problem had been rectified, the cartridge labelling problems continued.

39    In addition to quality control problems, the sales staff frequently blamed software developers for producing inferior games with weak "look and feel." Software developers, in turn, blamed the sales and marketing staff for ineffective research and for weak customer contacts. The production department was often blamed either for overproducing or for not having the right products available when needed. When Lopez met individually with managers to discuss possible solutions, he was disappointed with their responses. Shelley Coutu, vice-president of product development commented:

> Pressure from the sales staff to have new products developed or to increase production is unrealistic. I don't think they understand what goes into developing the product. This isn't like the old days when we were developing Pong-like games. These games are incredibly complex and the worse thing that could happen once the project ships is to find a software glitch.

40    Mike Colbert, vice-president of production, argued:

> My life would be a lot simpler if sales could just give us accurate forecasts. It is impossible to plan without knowing what the customer wants. I've lost 20 percent of my staff over the past eight months because they are tired of putting in unplanned 16-hour days. A lot of my people are getting demoralized.

41    In June 2002, tensions had risen to a boiling point. The monthly meeting of the executive council (Lopez, plus the CFO and all six vice-presidents) had ended badly when Coutu and Peter Ames, vice-president of sales, got into a shouting match. For the past nine months, sales of games for Sony's Playstation had not kept up with the growth in hardware sales. When pressed for a reason, Ames and Coutu pointed the finger of blame at each other, and things quickly went from bad to worse. After the meeting, David Salt huddled with Lopez to share his observations:

> These kinds of conflicts have to end. I don't know why Noal Fisher ever promoted Colbert to the job. Quite frankly he needs to be replaced. His outburst was out of line and he really adds nothing to the team.

42    Lopez, who was relatively new to the company, was still trying to sort out the people and personalities. Since taking over, he and Salt had become good friends and he welcomed the

private chats they seemed to have on an increasingly frequent basis. While he agreed that Colbert's reactions were inappropriate, he thought that Coutu could have been more helpful as well, and he was puzzled as to why Salt had such a one-sided interpretation of events.

**43**     Despite these problems, there was some excitement within the organization around the current ramp-up project the company had undertaken in preparation for the launch of Nintendo's new Gameboy Advance system. Preliminary reviews of that system had been spectacular. Sega was also developing a competitive system and had made it clear that it would also like mGAMES to continue to be involved in its business. Industry analysts were projecting revitalization in the market for handheld gaming devices, and market analysts projected a promising future for mGAMES. Early estimates around the market size for games developed for the new Nintendo system alone were in the $1-billion range over the next two years.

**44**     Before July 22, 2002, Lopez had intended to focus his short-term efforts on addressing the mounting internal problems facing mGAMES and by focusing on the handheld gaming device segment. However, after taking the two telephone calls he'd received that morning, this priority now seemed to fade.

## Other Considerations

**45**   As part of the Gameboy Advance ramp-up project, Lopez recognized that mGAMES would require additional office and research and development space in order to support the major new initiative into wireless gaming applications anticipated for the new Nintendo system. Lopez and Salt had done some preliminary budgeting; they were projecting the need to spend $1.2 million more on research and development during the remainder of 2002 and $3.1 million in 2003. Together with increased investment in sales and manufacturing, plus factoring in added overhead costs, Lopez figured that a net new investment of about $5.6 million would be required over the next 18 months to move the company to the forefront of wireless mobile gaming. These numbers were very preliminary and were to be the focus of the next planned executive committee meeting in early August.

**46**     Related to the expansion, Lopez had just learned that the tenant in the top two floors (18,000 square feet) of the mGAMES office building had just gone bankrupt. Lopez had received confirmation from the building manager that a significant discount on mGAMES' overall price per square foot was theirs for the taking if they agreed to take both floors. Lopez figured they would only need one-half of the additional square footage (9,000 square feet) now but that the additional space might be desirable in another six months. The building manager was pushing mGAMES for a three-year commitment and indicated that if he did not have a contract signed before July 30, 2002, he would turn it over to another company that had already expressed an interest in taking over both floors.

## Weighing Options

**47**   Lopez was a believer in the future of wireless gaming. He believed in the growth projected for the industry in the next five-year period and was eager for mGAMES to become a major player in that growth. Like everyone else who worked around the industry, he was unsure how the whole technology convergence would play out. However, with the number of mobile phones that were being shipped every week, he suspected the telecom manufacturers might have the advantage in the long run. In the nearer term, however, most observers predicted that the action would most likely be focused on the new generation of gaming devices just hitting the market. Here, the market would include new cartridge-based games plus downloadable and wireless games. Several other members of the mGAMES' management team, as well as two prominent members of the company's board of directors, also extremely excited about the company's forays into wireless gaming—particularly the recent development agreements that had been signed with the PDA manufacturers.

48  However, Jane Parkes, mGAMES' vice-president of marketing, was far less optimistic. She was concerned about the validity of the projections for the future of wireless gaming, particularly the feasibility of wireless gaming on mobile phones. Small screen size and Internet access fees were viewed as major obstacles to mobile phone–based gaming. Lopez was aware, however, that Parkes was extremely excited about the new Gameboy Advance system and the associated new opportunities that mGAMES would expect to enjoy upon its launch. Parkes had clearly expressed her belief that mGAMES' hopes to improve upon its 7.3 percent market share in this segment would rest on the success of this launch. Any investment in new wireless technology would not only be expensive and technically risky, but would detract from the company's current focus on cartridge and downloadable games.

49  As Lopez stared out the window, he reflected on the road that mGAMES had traveled. He knew that the calls he had received that morning meant that mGAMES could no longer continue to cater to all the handheld device manufacturers. It was time to make some choices. He clearly understood that the organization had Nintendo and Sega to thank for its previous success, and he tried to predict the ripple effect of breaking ties with these Japanese manufacturers. While no one could be certain what the future would hold for mobile gaming, most everyone in the industry believed that the future was bright, and Lopez wanted mGAMES to play a big part in it.

# Case 42 Microsoft's Xbox[1]

## Stephen Karl, Joshua J. Kittner, and Melissa A. Schilling

**1**    In the Fall of 1999, Microsoft announced to the world that it would enter the videogame console business with its own technologically advanced game console, the Xbox. The Xbox was targeted at the 18- to 34-year-old male, making it positioned directly against Sony's Playstation2. By the time the Xbox hit the market, Playstation2 (PS2) would already have a significant lead in installed base and availability of games (there were more than 300 PS2 game titles available at the end of 2001), but Microsoft was counting on the technological advantages offered by the Xbox to tip consumer preferences. The Xbox operating system ran on a 733 MHz microprocessor from Intel, which was more than twice as fast as the processors used in any other game console on the market—including the Toshiba 300 MHz microprocessor supplied in the Playstation2. The Xbox had 64 megabytes of memory and a data rate of 400 megabits per second per pin with 6.4 GB per second bandwidth, enabling more information to be processed faster. The Xbox memory chip would give game developers nearly twice the memory offered in other game consoles. The Xbox also offered a 10 gigabyte hard drive, enabling gamers to save a virtually unlimited number of games. Customers also did not have to trade off technological advantages against price: the Xbox launched at a retail price of $299, significantly less than its production costs (it was estimated that Microsoft lost between $100 and $125 per unit).

**2**    Both the Xbox and Nintendo's GameCube were launched in November of 2001 (in time for the extremely important Christmas season) and sold briskly. By the year's end, it was estimated that 1.3 million GameCube units had been sold, and 1.5 million Xbox units had been sold.[2] However, both of the new consoles were outrun by PS2, which sold approximately 2 million units in the month of December 2001 alone. By the end of 2001, PS2 had a worldwide installed base of over 20 million units (see Exhibit 1 for comparative specifications for PS2 and Xbox). While some analysts considered this evidence that Microsoft stood a poor chance of overtaking Sony's position in the gaming market, others were wary of discounting Microsoft too soon. It was, after all, the company that had defined many of the rules of competition in high-technology industries where complementary goods (such as software or games) were important. Would Microsoft be able to capture and dominate the videogame industry as it had done in personal computer operating systems and several software applications markets? Unlike Sony, Microsoft had almost no experience in designing and manufacturing hardware. Microsoft also did not have the consumer electronics brand equity of Sony. Many industry observers wondered why Microsoft, which had come to rely almost wholly on OEM agreements and licensing for its revenue, would choose to enter such a completely different market. Did Microsoft consider the videogame console to be a threat to its PC operating system business? Or was Microsoft just looking for a new and exciting market in which to extend its reach?

## MICROSOFT'S HISTORY

**3**    Childhood friends Bill Gates and Paul Allen shared a fascination for computers throughout their early lives. As teens, Gates and Allen worked together for several years helping local Seattle businesses, such as Information Sciences Inc., develop programs and locate bugs in

[1]This case was prepared by Stephen Karl, Joshua J. Kittner, and Melissa A. Schilling as the basis for class discussion rather than to illustrate either effective or ineffective handling of an administrative situation. All rights reserved to the authors. Copyright © 2002 Melissa A. Schilling.
[2]D. Frankel, "Videogame Business Boffo on Big Launches," *Video Business,* December 31 2001, p. 38.

## EXHIBIT 1
Comparison of Xbox to Playstation 2

| | Xbox | PlayStation 2 |
|---|---|---|
| CPU | 733 MHz Intel | 300 MHz |
| Graphics Processor | 300 MHz custom-designed X-Chip, developed by Microsoft and nVidia | 150 MHz Sony GS |
| Total Memory | 64 MB | 38 MB |
| Memory Bandwidth | 6.4 GB/sec | 3.2 GB/sec |
| Polygon Performance | 300 M/sec | 66 M/sec |
| Sustained Polygon Performance (full features) | 100 + M/sec | 20 M/sec |
| Micropolygons/particles per second | 300 M/sec | Not supported |
| Particle Performance | 300 M/sec | 150 M/sec |
| Simultaneous Textures | 4 | 1 |
| Pixel Fill Rate—No Texture | 4.8 G/Sec (anti-aliased) | 2.4 G/sec |
| Pixel Fill Rate—1 Texture | 4.8 G/Sec (anti-aliased) | 1.2 G/Sec |
| Compressed Textures | Yes (8:1) | No |
| Full Scene Anti-Alias | Yes | No |
| Micro Polygon Support | Yes | No |
| Storage Medium | 4× DVD, 8 GB hard disk, 8 MB memory card | 2× DVD, 8 MB memory card |
| I/O | 4× DVD | 2× DVD |
| | 8GB hard disk | 8MB memory card |
| | 8MB memory card | |
| Audio Channels | 64 | 48 |
| 3D Audio Support | Yes | No |
| MIDI DLS2 Support | Yes | No |
| AC3 Encoded game audio | Yes | No |
| Broadband Enabled | Yes | Future upgrade |
| Modem Enabled | Future upgrade | Yes |
| DVD Movie Playback | Built in | Utility required to be on memory card |
| Game pad included | No | Yes |
| Maximum resolution | 1920 × 1080 | 1280 × 1024 |
| Maximum resolution (2 × 32bpp frame buffers + Z) | 1920 × 1080 | 540 × 480 |
| HDTV Support | Yes | Limited |
| Launch Date | Fall 2001 | Fall 2000 |

Source: http://www.webdesk.com.

existing computer systems. Along the way, Gates and Allen would develop valuable programming knowledge. In 1973 Gates left Seattle to begin studies at Harvard University. However, following MIPS' 1974 introduction of the Altair, arguably the first personal computer,[3] Allen convinced Gates to drop out of school and develop a software program for the Altair. The program enabled basic operating directions to be read into the machine using paper tape. With this Microsoft was born.

---

[3]The Altair was a kit that included an Intel microprocessor and enough hardware to assemble a box with toggle switches and lights, but no terminal, keyboard, or software. It was essentially useless, but it inspired the imaginations of thousands of young computer hobbyists who could, for the first time, own their own computer.

**4**    Microsoft's big break came when it licensed an operating system program, MS-DOS (a clone of CP/M, the dominant operating system software for the proliferation of personal computers based on Intel microprocessors) to IBM in 1980. Following a fallout with IBM, Microsoft began work on a graphical user interface, called Windows, to make MS-DOS more user friendly. Notably, the Windows program (introduced in 1984) was remarkably similar in appearance and function to Apple's graphical Macintosh operating system introduced in 1983. Microsoft developed several updated versions of Windows, and by 1993, a million copies of Windows were being sold per month. By 1995 the company held roughly 80 percent of the personal computer operating system market. The company eventually branched out into other areas of consumer and business software, and by anchoring all of its applications to the dominance of Windows, it gained tremendous market share in several computer software categories, including word processing, spreadsheet applications, database applications, presentation software, utility software (such as disk compression and memory management), and eventually web server software and browsers.[4]

**5**    In the Fall of 1999, Microsoft announced its intention to enter the videogame console industry. Microsoft had neither the arcade experience possessed by Nintendo and Sega, nor the extensive consumer electronics experience of Sony. However, Microsoft did have some experience and brand image in the computer gaming industry. Microsoft had been successful developing games, such as Flight Simulator and the Age of Empires series. Microsoft had also been successful in offering online gaming. The Microsoft Gaming Zone, which allows for multiplayer gaming, had over 12 million registered members as of 2001, and was considered by many to be the precursor for multiplayer gaming on the Xbox.

# THE VIDEOGAME INDUSTRY—SEVEN GENERATIONS

### Generation One

**6**    The birth of the videogame industry can be traced to Ralph Baer and Sanders Associates, a military electronics consulting firm. The Pentagon came to Sanders in 1965 with a need for computer simulations to help increase a soldier's ability to think strategically and improve reflexes.[5] It was also desired that the system be able to be used on inexpensive equipment, such as a television monitor. In the past, games such as "Spacewars" could only be played on $40,000 terminals.

**7**    Baer and a team of engineers, including Bill Harrison and Bill Rusch, worked over the course of the year to produce a working prototype of a videogame console. In 1966, the team displayed their work to a Pentagon review board. The Pentagon was unimpressed with the system, but allowed research to continue. At this meeting, Baer gave his opinion that videogames could be a profitable form of personal entertainment. Baer's superiors, however, believed that the military would benefit from gaming technology more than civilians, and kept the project top secret.[6]

**8**    Eventually, the Pentagon became disenfranchised with the videogame idea, and Baer was granted the right to commercially produce his product. Baer signed on with Magnavox, and the Odyssey was born in 1972, becoming the first home videogame system. In its first

---

[4]Microsoft leveraged its control in the operating system market into the applications markets in a number of ways, including bundling arrangements (whereby a copy of a particular application was included in the Windows purchase), and by giving its internal applications developers priority access to the Windows code, making it possible for them to develop programs sooner, and that worked better with Windows, than applications developed by competitors such as Lotus.

[5]S. Hart, "Guns, Games, and Glory: the Birth of Home Videogames," *www.geekcomix.com/vgh*, 2000.

[6]S. Hart, "A Brief History of Videogames," *www.geekcomix.com/vgh*, 2000.

year the Odyssey sold 100,000 units at a price of $100. However, the Odyssey would soon come to an end.

9    In 1971, Nolan Busnell and Al Alcorn had created the arcade game Pong. The team decided to transform the arcade hit into a home version, entitled Atari Pong. The home version of Pong was a single unit with built in paddles and speakers. Though the Atari could only play Pong (unlike the Odyssey, which could play twelve games), most customers were unwilling to pay more for the Odyssey because the multiple game system only had a few desirable games. Pong, and over 60 similar knock-offs, would soon flood the market because of the creation of LSI (large-scale integrated) circuits, which allowed the systems to be priced low. Pong dominated the market until 1977 and the introduction of the Atari VCS/2600, the leader of the second generation of videogames.[7]

### Generation Two

10    The second generation of systems saw the implementation of a microprocessor, first in the Fairchild Channel F system, then in other systems. The microprocessor allowed for better graphics and sound, as well as more complex games. Atari was still the leader in the industry, but the advancements of other companies, such as Fairchild, led Bushnell to press for the development of a new system using the microprocessor and allowing for multiple games. This system was called the VCS/2600, and sold for $200, with games selling for between $20 and $40. Atari sold over $5 billion worth of 2600 systems and products over a five-year period. The height of this generation saw yearly sales of $3 billion in the United States alone.[8]

### Generation Three

11    The third generation of videogame systems, 1981–1984, was a brief and dark episode in the history of videogames. Though this generation saw the introduction of several new systems, including the Atari 5200 and 7800, and Coleco's ColecoVision, it ended in a crash that many observers thought the industry would not survive. In 1985, worldwide sales of videogame systems amounted to only $100 million worldwide, and analysts were proclaiming the videogame industry dead. Speculation about the reasons for the crash included a noticeable difference between the quality of arcade games and home games, and oversaturation of the market by lackluster game titles. Game titles for the Atari system had been rapidly produced both by Atari's licensees and by unlicensed developers, resulting in a proliferation of dubious-quality games. Distributors and retailers that had stocked the titles ended up with large amounts of worthless inventory.

### Generation Four

12    The fourth generation, 1985 to 1989, saw the rebirth of the home videogame industry. The reduction in cost of Dynamic RAM chips, which allowed for greater memory storage and faster access of data, coupled with the introduction of higher-powered eight-bit processors, allowed home gaming systems to compete with arcade games. Companies that dominated previous generations, such as Atari and Magnavox, released updated versions of their older systems. However, two new companies from Japan, Sega and Nintendo, who also produced arcade games, achieved the greatest success.[9]

13    In 1984, Sega was the first of the Japanese companies to introduce a new console, called the Master System, to the market. The strong initial sales of the Master System were an indicator that the videogame market was growing again. Realizing this, Nintendo's Hiroshi

[7]S. Cohen, *Zap! The Rise and Fall of ATARI* (New York: McGraw Hill, 1984), p. 46.
[8]E. Provenzo, *Video Kids: Making Sense of Nintendo,* (Cambridge, Massachusetts: Harvard University Press, 1991), p. 10.
[9]www.videotopia.com.

Yamamuchi pressed his engineers to design their own home console. The Nintendo Entertainment System was released only six months after Sega's product.

**14**    The Master System seemingly was poised to be the leader of the market, with a technologically superior product. The Master System had two cartridge ports, one for playing normal cartridges and the other smaller port for playing games that required less memory. Sega also used this smaller port to develop 3D technology. 3D glasses with small LCD displays could be plugged into this port, and images would flash on the LCD screens in conjunction with the primary image on the television to produce a 3D effect.

**15**    Nintendo's early deliveries of its system were filled with defects, angering retailers and consumers. However, Nintendo's executives used almost all of the company's financial resources for advertising. Nintendo also focused on the establishment of quality games and characters, and was able to produce more games than those available for the Master System. The Master System went on to sell two million units and at times held an 11 percent market share. The NES sold 19 million units by 1990, and could be found in more than a third of the households in America and Japan.[10] Nintendo's "Super Mario Brothers 3" grossed over $500 million in America in 1989, selling seven million copies in the United States and four million in Japan. By 1990 Nintendo passed Toyota as Japan's most successful company.

**16**    Sega, however, was able to stay afloat based on the success of its arcade games and was working to transform its arcade architecture for home system use. Nintendo was not concerned. Bill White, a Nintendo executive, said "(our players) are extremely happy with the existing system . . . we haven't maxed out our eight-bit system yet."[11]

### Generation Five

**17**    In 1989 Sega released the Genesis, a 16-bit system with a 7.6 MHz processor. NEC, another large Japanese gaming company, had released its 16-bit system, the TurboGraphix 16, six months earlier. However, Sega had a large catalog of arcade games for the new system while NEC's system did not. Nintendo tried to form an alliance with NEC to use the TurboGraphix 16 as its new system, but this union ultimately fell through. The summer of 1990 saw the Genesis take more than 55 percent of new system sales and 20 percent of the gaming market from Nintendo. Many of the third-party game developers dropped their Nintendo accounts to begin working with Sega.

**18**    In response, Nintendo engineers began working on a new 16-bit system. Released in 1991 it was called the Super Nintendo Entertainment System (SNES), and had a better graphics processor, could produce more screen colors, and had better audio output than the Genesis. The SNES, however, only had a 3.58 MHz processor and Sega highlighted this fact. Both companies would continue to upgrade their systems, but neither would achieve true market dominance. In 1992, Nintendo had controlled 80 percent of the videogame market based on combined 8-bit and 16-bit sales, but in 1994 and 1995, Sega was the market leader.[12]

### Generation Six

**19**    The sixth generation of videogames began with a dispute between Sony and Nintendo concerning a CD peripheral that the companies were jointly developing. The basis of the disagreement was that Sony's legal staff had skillfully written an agreement that would give Sony publishing profits from SNES CD-based games. Nintendo, however, wanted to keep

---

[10]D. Sheff, *Game Over: How Nintendo Zapped an American Industry, Captured Your Dollars and Enslaved Your Children,* (New York: Random House, 1993), preface.

[11]"Nintendo's Show of Strength," *Dealerscope Merchandising,* February 1991, p. 15.

[12]A. Brandenberger, "Power Play (B): Sega in 16-bit video games." *Harvard Business School Case,* #9-795-103, 1995.

these royalties. Thus Nintendo went to Phillips to create a CD-Rom that would work with the CD-interactive, Phillips new gaming/home entertainment product. Sony, which had a prototype finished, began to work on a CD only (as opposed to game cartridge-based) 32-bit machine, which came to be known as the PlayStation.

20 Atari also made a startling reentry to the videogame industry, by introducing its 64-bit Jaguar (actually two 32-bit chips working in tandem). It had a 13.3 MHz clock speed and was technically equivalent to a 32-bit system. However, game developers had lost confidence in Atari, and the resulting lack of game support led to the failure of the system. Sega had also begun to work on a 32-bit system named the Saturn.

21 Sega and Sony released their new entrants into the market in 1995. Sega announced that it would release the Saturn on September 2; however, it ended up releasing it in early May at $400. Sales were low and few titles were initially available because game developers were caught off guard by the early release. By contrast, Sony launched the PlayStation at $300, $100 less than expected, with a large catalog of games and rave reviews.

22 Nintendo did not respond to the moves of its competitors until 1996 (after more than two years of preannouncements), when it introduced the Nintendo 64, a cartridge-based system.[13] Nintendo sold over 1.7 million units in three months, despite the fact that there were only two software titles available at the console's release (one being Super Mario). Nintendo claimed that it could have sold 2.5 million units during the holiday season if it could have produced that many.

23 In April of 1997, Sony announced that it had sold 11 million PlayStations in Japan, the United States, and Europe.[14] Four months later this number had almost doubled at 20 million. Later in the year Sega began to develop a new 128-bit system, named the DreamCast, that was based on Microsoft's Windows CE operating system. Shortly after this, Sony began working on the successor to the PlayStation. In 1999, Nintendo announced it was planning on releasing a new system called the GameCube[15] using an IBM processor, and later that year Microsoft announced that it would be entering the videogame industry with the release of the Xbox.[16] The seventh generation had arrived.[17]

# THE VIDEOGAME INDUSTRY—COMPETITIVE ENVIRONMENT

### Market and Demographics

24 In 1999, sales of videogame hardware, software, and other accessories exceeded $7 billion, with software sales alone of $3.3 billion.[18] Ninety-three million players bought software for their Sony PlayStation, Nintendo 64, or PC.[19] Children's leisure software for the PC topped $17.5 billion with 77 million units sold in 1999. The Yankee Group predicted that by the end of 2003, 43.5 million homes in the United States would have a videogame console, up from 35.9 million in 1998. The seventh generation consoles, such as the PS2, GameCube, Xbox, and DreamCast, would account for 85 percent of this installed base.

25 Many homes also had multiple consoles; in 2001, 23 percent of console households had two or more systems, and 20 percent had three or more systems. Furthermore, the demo-

---

[13]www.nintendo.com.
[14]www.sony.com.
[15]Yuri, Kageyama, "Nintendo Unveils New Videogame Console," *Associated Press,* August 24, 2000.
[16]www.microsoft.com.
[17]www.videogames.com.
[18]www.pcdata.com.
[19]www.tdctrade.com.

graphics of videogames appeared to be changing. Whereas the arcade games on which videogames had initially been based primarily targeted adolescents, in 2001 over 40 percent of videogame players were over 18 in console households, and 41 percent were over 18 in PC-based households.[20] Female players were also becoming a growing constituency, accounting for 15 percent of the videogame market by Spring of 2000.[21]

26    With the exception of the GameCube, the seventh generation had moved toward becoming home entertainment systems, rather than just dedicated gaming systems.[22] The systems incorporated functions such as the ability to play DVDs and CDs, e-mail, and Web surfing. The impact these systems would have on other platforms, such as the PC, was uncertain. However, 23 percent of home PC users said the primary function of the PC was for playing games, while 21 percent said game playing was the second most frequent activity on the computer.[23]

### Suppliers

27    Microsoft developed the operating system for the Xbox in-house. Microsoft gained experience in this area when it developed the operating platform for Sega's Dreamcast. George T. Chronis, executive editor of the videogame trade magazine *Games Business,* pointed to that angle: "Microsoft has learned a lot helping Sega create a competitive console . . . They've taken that and they're going to apply it to their own piece of hardware."[24] The operating system would use a simple, stripped down version of Windows. The development costs of the operating system were minimal due to Microsoft's previous experience and expertise in operating system design.

28    The Xbox operating system would run on a 733 MHz microprocessor that would be supplied by Intel. The estimated price for the microprocessor was $425, which was more than the targeted retail price of the whole console at $300.[25] This processor would be more than twice as fast as any current game console processor on the market, including Toshiba's 300 MHz processor in the Sony PS2. Originally Microsoft was going to be supplied by Advanced Micro Devices (AMD) but later chose Intel based on its past relations with the company.

29    Another major component was the memory system. Microsoft signed Micron to a six-year contract to supply the majority of the SDRAM chips. The Xbox would have 64 megabytes of memory and a data rate of 400 megabits per second per pin with 6.4 GB per second bandwidth. This means that more information, in larger chunks, could be processed faster. The Xbox memory chip gave game developers nearly twice the memory offered in other game consoles. Robert Bach, Chief Xbox Officer, described the benefit of working with Micron, "Working with Micron to pack this amount of memory into Xbox will liberate game developers to produce more exhilarating, imaginative, and immersive game play for gamers."[26]

30    Microsoft would incorporate its DirectX interface technology that it used in its PC systems through the nVidia graphic chip and Wolfson Microelectronics audio chip. This technology allowed it to improve graphics, audio, and multimedia integration in games. The 300 MHz 3-D nVidia graphic chip processes more than 1 trillion operations per second, which allows sharper images for high resolution graphics because colors and shapes are changing

[20]www8.techmall.com.
[21]http://www.gametrends.com.
[22]*DVD for Games Machines,* (U.K., Miller Freeman LTD, 2000.)
[23]http://www.gametrends.com.
[24]T. Ham, and J. Gaudiosi, "Microsoft and Sony Prepare for Mortal Combat," *Washington Post,* March 10, 2000, p. E11.
[25]N'Gai Croal, 2000 "How to Be A Player," *Newsweek* 135 (12) 2000, p. 62.
[26]Microsoft press release, June 12, 2000.

at a faster rate. The system can support 1920 X 1080 pixels. This means that images, such as a character's face, would be able to be seen in more detail, due to a larger amount of pixels being used. The Wolfson chip had the ability to send 6-speaker Dolby encoding through 256 channels to stereo speakers, allowing the games to be heard in surround sound. NVidia would also provide the 10/100 Mbps for DSL or cable connection for online game playing. Other suppliers included Seagate who would provide the hard drive, Integrated Circuit Systems who would provide the connections, wiring, and timing between the hardware components, and Applied Microsystems who would supply the technology for the DVD aspect.

31      Despite all the advanced technology, many consumers worried about the reliability of the game console, noting the propensity of Microsoft-based systems to crash. To reassure customers of the game system's reliability, Microsoft pointed out that the Xbox would operate its games from a DVD to avoid hard drive failures. In addition, Microsoft noted that the Xbox had only one function to perform while PC systems crash due to the large number of applications vying for operating system resources.[27]

32      Microsoft outsourced assembly of the Xbox to Flextronics. Flextronics was one of the world's largest contract electronics manufacturers, and Microsoft believed that using Flextronics would help ensure quality assembly and a smooth launch. Additionally, in 2001, Flextronics was already acting as the OEM for all of Microsoft's other hardware products. Flextronics' nine worldwide production centers allowed for quick market reaction and the capacity to meet demand on the launch date (problems with meeting launch and demand targets had plagued Sony on the release of its PS2 in October, 2000, causing many customers to opt for different consoles). Flextronics' main North American productions would be staged in Mexico. Microsoft would also be the only producer to set up locations in Europe with its Hungary location. The Hungarian facilities had cost $110 million and would employ 10,000 workers. Microsoft predicted that its $3 billion contract would result in 6 to 7 percent of GDP for the Hungarian nation, and be the ninth largest employer.[28]

33      Microsoft has had tense relationships with suppliers in the past. Suppliers often questioned Microsoft's dedication to projects and many times it was the suppliers who took the financial brunt of unsuccessful projects. For example, Microsoft entered the handheld computer market with its Windows-based PDA in the early 1990s. Unfortunately, Microsoft did not meet its sales forecast. While Microsoft's development costs had been minimized by building the handheld's system based on Windows and its other applications, other suppliers were left with large amounts of inventory, sunk development costs, and binding contracts.[29]

## Competitors

34      The gaming industry is led by a consolidated group of competitors, including Sony, Sega, and Nintendo. The industry practice of subsidizing console production with game royalties has made it difficult for smaller competitors to enter. A company must be able to bear substantial early losses to accumulate a sufficient installed base to reap the benefits of game licensing. Only then can the company hope to recoup its high production and R&D costs.

## Sega

35      Founded in 1951 by David Rosen, Sega began as an art export company that moved into photograph booths. In the 1960s Sega (*Se*rvice *Ga*mes) began making coin-operated games.

---

[27]Dean Takahashi, 2000. "Microsoft Goes Gaming," *Electronic Business* 26 (5) 2000, p. 44.
[28]MTI Econews.
[29]Nicholas Weaver, "Why the Xbox Could Easily Fail and Why Microsoft So Greatly Desires a Success," www.cs.Berkley.edu.

**EXHIBIT 2**
Sega Financials

Source: Hoovers.

| Income Statement | Mar 01 | Mar 00 | Mar 99 |
|---|---|---|---|
| All amounts in millions of U.S. dollars except per share amounts. | | | |
| Revenue | 1,922.9 | 3,213.6 | 2,234.9 |
| Cost of goods sold | 1,727.5 | 2,753.3 | 1,694.4 |
| Gross profit | 195.4 | 460.3 | 540.5 |
| Gross profit margin | 10.2% | 14.3% | 24.2% |
| SG&A expense | 607.1 | 842.8 | 522.9 |
| Depreciation and amortization | — | — | — |
| Operating income | (411.8) | (382.5) | 17.5 |
| Operating margin | — | — | 0.8% |
| Total net income | (409.5) | (406.4) | (360.0) |
| Net profit margin | — | — | — |
| Diluted EPS ($) | — | — | — |

| Balance Sheet | Mar 01 | Mar 00 | Mar 99 |
|---|---|---|---|
| Cash | 297.9 | 890.1 | 845.5 |
| Net receivables | 164.9 | 356.8 | 358.4 |
| Inventories | 131.6 | 403.7 | 517.0 |
| Total current assets | 766.7 | 2,003.4 | 2,148.2 |
| Total assets | 2,251.8 | 3,557.5 | 3,573.3 |
| Short-term debt | 716.7 | 199.1 | 390.7 |
| Total current liabilities | 1,227.8 | 1,863.2 | 1,046.2 |
| Long-term debt | 234.2 | 310.6 | 1,802.3 |
| Total liabilities | 1,519.8 | 2,792.3 | 2,895.0 |
| Total equity | 732.1 | 765.1 | 678.3 |
| Shares outstanding (mil.) | — | — | — |

Some figures may not add up due to rounding.

In 2001, this division remained along with its Amusement Park Division (which only operated in Japan), and the Home Entertainment Division.

36    Sega has had a history of technologically sound but poorly received systems, including the Master System in the mid-80s and Saturn in 1995. However, its Genesis system in 1989 was a success and a leading competitor of the Nintendo system. Sega's seventh generation system, the Dreamcast, was released in early 2000. Prior to the Dreamcast's release, Sega was suffering from its lowest market share in years at 12 percent. Fortunately, Sega was able to beat competition to the market with the Dreamcast (the Dreamcast was the first 128-bit system to market) and was able to climb to 25 percent market share by the Fall of 2000. Sega's success turned out to be short lived when Sony released the much-anticipated PlayStation2. Despite 25 percent price cuts, the Dreamcast was crushed in the holiday sales season.

37    In year end 2000, Sega issued a press release that changed its previous estimates from a $14 million profit to a $200 million loss, giving it a fourth straight losing quarter (See Exhibit 2 for full financials). Sega also released its future business plan.[30] Sega decided to license out its Dreamcast platform and exit console production. These announcements caused Sega's stock price to plummet and made Sega a possible takeover candidate. In early January, 2001, the *New York Times* reported that Nintendo was interested in purchasing Sega for $2 billion for its game development expertise. However, on March 30, 2001, Sega announced it had different plans: it

[30]Timna Tanners, "Game Developers see Sega as Both Boon and Threat," *Reuters News,* February 7, 2001.

**EXHIBIT 3**
Nintendo Financials

Source: Hoovers.

| Income Statement | Mar 01 | Mar 00 | Mar 99 |
|---|---|---|---|
| All amounts in millions of U.S. dollars except per share amounts. | | | |
| Revenue | 3,661.2 | 5,279.4 | 4,806.0 |
| Cost of goods sold | 2,204.3 | 2,745.2 | 2,609.6 |
| Gross profit | 1,456.9 | 2,534.2 | 2,196.3 |
| Gross profit margin | 39.8% | 48.0% | 45.7% |
| SG&A expense | 786.4 | 1,557.3 | 927.9 |
| Depreciation and amortization | — | — | — |
| Operating income | 670.5 | 976.9 | 1,268.4 |
| Operating margin | 18.3% | 18.5% | 26.4% |
| Total net income | 764.7 | 531.3 | 720.5 |
| Net profit margin | 20.9% | 10.1% | 15.0% |
| Diluted EPS ($) | 5.40 | 3.75 | — |

| Balance Sheet | Mar 01 | Mar 00 | Mar 99 |
|---|---|---|---|
| Cash | 6,530.2 | 5,630.5 | 5,361.3 |
| Net receivables | 433.1 | 680.6 | 523.4 |
| Inventories | 178.6 | 287.5 | 269.8 |
| Total current assets | 7,585.5 | 7,675.5 | 6,794.6 |
| Total assets | 8,458.8 | 8,846.5 | 7,500.4 |
| Short-term debt | 0.0 | 0.0 | 0.0 |
| Total current liabilities | 1,779.1 | 1,603.8 | 1,586.2 |
| Long-term debt | 0.0 | 0.0 | 0.0 |
| Total liabilities | 1,826.8 | 1,667.4 | 1,621.0 |
| Total equity | 6,632.0 | 7,179.1 | 5,879.4 |
| Shares outstanding (mil.) | — | — | — |

Some figures may not add up due to rounding.

would be signing a long-term alliance with Microsoft. The companies would kick off the relationship by releasing 11 of Sega's upcoming games on the Xbox platform.

### Nintendo

38   Originally founded in 1889 as a producer of playing cards, Nintendo blossomed into a multibillion dollar company. It was the leader in the 1980s with the Nintendo Entertainment System (NES) and was a major contender in the late 1990s with the Nintendo 64. Nintendo was also one of the first handheld game producers. In handheld games, it controlled 90 percent of the Japanese market and 99 percent of the North American and European markets.[31] Its dominance in this industry had allowed Nintendo's business to remain profitable despite stiff competition in console gaming systems (see Exhibit 3 for full Financial Reports).

39   Of the competitors vying for the market in 2001, Nintendo would be the last company to come out with a seventh generation console that could compete with the PlayStation2, Dreamcast, or Xbox. The arrival of the GameCube was delayed because of Nintendo's tardiness in sending development kits that were essential to developers to produce games. Analysts saw Nintendo's late arrival as costly to market share.

40   Despite this weakness, one of Nintendo's greatest strengths was its game development. It produced 80 percent of its games in-house and continually had three to five games on the

[31]B. Fulford, "Super Hiroshi-san," *Forbes,* May 1, 2000, p. 90.

Top 10 Sellers List year after year. In addition, the majority of other top sellers were also available on the Nintendo system as well. It had been especially strong in marketing to younger users with Mario Brothers, Donkey Kong, and Pokemon. In 2000, Zachary Liggett, an analyst with WestLB Panmure in Tokyo noted, "They still have a huge hold on the little kiddie market."[32] Nintendo hoped that its success with children's games would enable it to be successful with the GameCube.

### Sony

**41**  The Sony company began in a bombed out building in Tokyo in 1946 after World War II. Masaru Ibuka, an engineer, and Akio Morita, a physicist, invested the equivalent of $1,500 to start a company with 20 employees repairing electrical equipment and attempting to build its own products. Focusing on innovation, Sony would grow into a company that would ultimately invent the Trinitron TV, the Walkman, floppy disk, the CD, and PlayStation.

**42**  Sony first entered the game console market when Nintendo asked it to develop a new platform in 1992. Sony hoped to leverage its new SuperDisc audio disk that it had developed with Philips in the gaming platform. After several contract disputes with Nintendo and Philips, it ceased the relationship with Nintendo and commenced development of its own console. It was well publicized that Sony had spent over $500 million in developing the PlayStation. From the time it launched the product in 1995 to 1998 it sold nearly 40 million consoles worldwide. As of 2001, Sony Computer Entertainment, led by CEO Ken Kutaragi, was providing 40 percent of parent Sony Corporation's profit (see Exhibit 4 for full Financial Reports).

**43**  By the end of 1999, the PlayStation controlled about 75 percent of the game console market, and it planned to defend against competition from Nintendo's Nintendo 64 and Sega's Saturn by introducing an even more advanced console, the Playstation2. PS2 was launched in early November of 2000, but shipments were slowed by a shortage of supply and faulty systems, creating obstacles for the crucial holiday retailing season. There was speculation that Sony intentionally short supplied the market to create hype and increase demand. This speculation was at its height when several news sources reported that Saddam Hussein had smuggled 4000 Playstation2 units into Iraq with the presumed intention of using them for military purposes. Some experts estimated that an integrated bundle of 12 to 15 Playstation2s could provide enough computer power to control Iraqi unmanned aerial vehicle (the United Nations forbids computer hardware from being sold or transferred to Iraq).[33]

**44**  In the 2000 holiday season, sales of the original PlayStation (with redesigned looks under the name PSOne) were twice those of the new PlayStation2. Sony came under Wall Street criticism for releasing the revamped PSOne so close to the release of the PS2. The slowing in the economy made the PSOne, priced at $100, seem more attractive than the $300 priced PS2. One game analyst noted, "I think some parents thought they could get the PS2 for their kids. Now they see they can't, and the PSOne looks like a pretty good deal."[34] The PS2 accounted for only 6 percent of console sales during the holiday while Sony's PSOne accounted for 61 percent, surpassing Sega's 17 percent with the Dreamcast and Nintendo 64's 15 percent. Sony was able to regain its lost market share but was unable to establish PlayStation2 as the dominant game console.

**45**  Some analysts speculated that Microsoft would be unable to compete against Sony in the videogame console market. For example, Motoharu Sone, an analyst at Universal Securities, noted, "Its [Sony's] hardware specifications are second to none, and it is perhaps hard

[32]Yuri Kageyama, "Nintendo Unveils New Videogame Console," *Associated Press,* August 24, 2000.
[33]N. McDowell, 2000. "Saddam at It Again," www.sonyweb.com/news, December 19, 2000.
[34]www.yahoo.cnet.com.

**EXHIBIT 4**
**Sony Financials**

| IncomeStatement | Mar 01 | Mar 00 | Mar 99 |
|---|---|---|---|
| All amounts in millions of U.S. dollars except per share amounts. | | | |
| Revenue | 58,518.0 | 63,082.0 | 57,109.0 |
| Cost of goods sold | 38,901.0 | 43,849.0 | 39,066.0 |
| Gross profit | 19,617.0 | 19,233.0 | 18,043.0 |
| Gross profit margin | 33.5% | 30.5% | 31.6% |
| SG&A expense | 13,071.0 | 14,071.0 | 12,615.0 |
| Depreciation and amortization | 4,743.0 | 2,892.0 | 2,582.0 |
| Operating income | 1,803.0 | 2,270.0 | 2,846.0 |
| Operating margin | 3.1% | 3.6% | 5.0% |
| Total net income | 134.0 | 1,149.0 | 1,505.0 |
| Net profit margin | 0.2% | 1.8% | 2.6% |
| Diluted EPS ($) | 0.15 | 1.24 | 1.65 |

| Balance Sheet | Mar 01 | Mar 00 | Mar 99 |
|---|---|---|---|
| Cash | 4,858.0 | 5,906.0 | 4,978.0 |
| Net receivables | 10,362.0 | 9,957.0 | 8,519.0 |
| Inventories | 7,543.0 | 8,106.0 | 7,379.0 |
| Total current assets | 27,820.0 | 29,572.0 | 25,798.0 |
| Total assets | 62,624.0 | 64,219.0 | 52,944.0 |
| Short-term debt | 10,251.0 | 9,679.0 | 7,156.0 |
| Total current liabilities | 21,174.0 | 20,381.0 | 16,327.0 |
| Long-term debt | 6,749.0 | 7,678.0 | 8,720.0 |
| Total liabilities | 44,100.0 | 43,626.0 | 37,617.0 |
| Total equity | 18,524.0 | 20,593.0 | 15,328.0 |
| Shares outstanding (mil.) | 919.6 | 907.3 | 819.9 |

Some figures may not add up due to rounding.

to catch up, particularly in terms of graphics. It already has 70 million original PS users, and many of them would shift to buy PS2 because games are compatible. These two factors will likely keep Sony from losing dominance."[35]

### Videogame Developers

46  The success of a game console relied heavily on the availability of popular games for the system. The more popular games available for a system, the more attractive it became to potential customers. In turn, the more customers adopted a particular system, the more attractive that system came to potential game developers. Thus a self-reinforcing cycle could propel a particular system to an extremely powerful position if that system could attain an advantage in either the availability of complementary goods, or the size of its installed base, or both. This cycle, known as a "network externalities" effect, was common in industries in which standards, compatibility, and complementary goods (such as games) were important.[36] By 2001, Microsoft was well established as a leader in developing PC games (see Exhibit 5). It would try to leverage those strengths in developing console games. However, there were fairly significant differences in game development between the platforms. As noted by Don Coyner, director of marketing at Microsoft's Games division, "Each has a

---

[35]T. Ham, and J. Gaudiosi, "Microsoft and Sony Prepare for Mortal Combat," *Washington Post,* March 10, 2000, p. E11.
[36]Network externalities are *positive consumption externalities* that occur when the user of a good derives more benefit from that good the more other users there are of the same (or similar) good.

**EXHIBIT 5**
**Top-Selling PC Titles (as of May 2000)**

Source: PC Data.

| Title | Developer | Category | Price |
|---|---|---|---|
| 1. Who Wants to Be a Millionaire | Disney | Family Ent. | $19 |
| 2. The Sims | Electronic Arts | Strategy | $42 |
| 3. Roller Coaster Tycoon | Hasbro | Strategy | $27 |
| 4. Age of Empire II | Microsoft | Strategy | $44 |
| 5. Roller Coaster Tycoon Expansion | Hasbro | Strategy | $19 |
| 6. Sim City 3000 | Electronic Arts | Strategy | $39 |
| 7. Unreal Tournament | Infogrames | Action | $43 |
| 8. Half-Life | Havas | Action | $32 |
| 9. Rainbow Six Gold | Red Storm | Strategy | $28 |
| 10. Who Wants to Be a Millionaire, 2nd | Disney | Family Ent. | $18 |

**EXHIBIT 6**
**Top-Selling Game Console Titles (as of May 2000)**

Source: PC Data.

| Title | Developer | Platform | Category | Price |
|---|---|---|---|---|
| 1. Pokemon Stadium | Nintendo | Nintendo 64 | Action | $60 |
| 2. Pokemon Yellow | Nintendo | Game Boy | Adventure | $26 |
| 3. WWF | THQ Inc. | Playstation | Sports | $41 |
| 4. Gran Turismo 2 | Sony | Playstation | Simulation | $40 |
| 5. Pokemon Trading Card | Nintendo | Game Boy | Action | $25 |
| 6. Syphon Filter 2 | 989 Studio | Playstation | Action | $41 |
| 7. Pokemon Blue | Nintendo | Game Boy | Adventure | $25 |
| 8. Pokemon Red | Nintendo | Game Boy | Adventure | $26 |
| 9. Crazy Taxi | Sega | Dreamcast | Simulation | $50 |
| 10. Mario Party 2 | Nintendo | Nintendo 64 | Family Ent. | $50 |

**EXHIBIT 7**
**Comparison of Profitability by Category (as of May 2000)**

Source: PC Data.

| | Console Profit | PC Profit |
|---|---|---|
| Action | 35.4% | 12.6% |
| Adventure | 19.7 | 12.3 |
| Arcade | 2.7 | 2.6 |
| Children | 3.3 | 6.9 |
| Family entertainment | 1.6 | 14.8 |
| Simulation | 13.6 | 11.6 |
| Sports | 19.1 | 8.8 |
| Strategy | 4.0 | 28.5 |
| Other | 0.5 | 1.9 |

very distinct audience . . . PC games are more cerebral, while console games are more visceral. If you look at the top 10 games lists for these two platforms, you'll see that they don't really match up"[37] (See Exhibits 5, 6, and 7). Microsoft would now be making a whole new style of game. In order to make this transition, Microsoft acquired a few small-name developers such as Bungie. In addition, it would only produce 30 percent to 40 percent of the games in-house, while relying on third-party developers to produce the majority of games, similar to Sony's strategy (see Exhibit 8).

[37] "Xbox to Deliver Ultimate Console Gaming Experience," www.game-revolution.com, *Microsoft Press Release*, 2000.

## EXHIBIT 8
**Titles Scheduled for Release on Launch Date**

| Title | Developer | Genre | Title | Developer | Genre |
|---|---|---|---|---|---|
| 1906: Arctic Odyssey | DarkWorks | Other | Nightcaster | VR-1 Entertainment | RPG |
| Amped: Snowboarding | Microsoft | Racing | Munch's Oddysee | Oddworld Inhabitants | Other |
| Arctic Thunder | Midway Home Ent. | Racing | Project K-X | Dream Factory | Other |
| Azurik: Rise of Perathia | Adrenium Games | Action | Psychotixic | NuClearVision Ent. | Shooters |
| Battlefield 1942 | Digital Illusions | Action | Mechwarrior X | Microsoft | Shooters |
| Black and White | Lionhead Studios | Action | Medal of Honor | 2015 | Strategy |
| Bounty Hunter | Warthog PLC | Action | Metal Dungeon | Panther Software | RPG |
| Breed | Brat Designs | Action | Metal Gear Solid X | Konami Corp | Shooters |
| Brute Force | Acclaim | Other | New Legends | THQ | Action |
| Call of the Dragonfly | Lost Boys Interactive | Other | NFL Fever 2002 | Microsoft | Sports |
| Codename: Gotham | Bizarre Creations | Racing | Nightcaster | VR-1 Ent. | RPG |
| Crash Bandicoot X | Konami Corporation | Action | Munch's Oddysee | Oddworld I | Other |
| Crimson Skies | Microsoft | Sims | Project K-X | Dream Factory | Other |
| Dead or Alive 3 | Tecmo, LTD. | Action | Psychotixic | NuClearVision Ent. | Shooters |
| Defender of the Crown | Cinemaware Inc. | Other | Republic | Eidos interactive | Other |
| Divine Divinity | Larian Studios | RPG | Salt Lake City | Attention to Detail | Sims |
| Dragon's Lair 3D | Blue Byte Software | Action | Seraphim | Valkyrie Studios | Action |
| Dreadnoughts | Xenopi | Action | Urban Warfare | Zombie VR Studios | Shooters |
| Druid King | Sidhe Interactive | RPG | Silent Hill X | Konami Corp | Other |
| Earth and Beyond | Westwood Studios | Action | Silent Space | Crytek Studios | Strategy |
| Engalus | Crytek Studios | Other | Ski-Doo X Racing | Daydream Software | Racing |
| eRacer | Rage | Racing | Soldier of Fortune | Majesco Inc. | Shooters |
| F1 World Grand Prix 3 | Hasbro Interactive | Racing | SRC | Criterion Software | Other |
| Fuzion Frenzy | Blitz Games Ltd | Other | SSX Snowboarding | Electronic Arts | Sports |
| Giants | Interplay Ent. | Strategy | Stunt Driver | Climax Ltd. Co. | Sports |
| Halo | Bungie | Shooters | Tetris World | THQ | Other |
| Harry Potter | Electronic Arts | Other | The Sims | Electronic Arts | Sims |
| Heaven and Hell | MadCat Interactive | RPG | The Thing | Konami Corp | Other |
| Internal Affairs | Attention to Detail | Other | Title Defense | Climax Ltd. Co. | Sports |
| Jurassic Park X | Konami Corporation | Other | Tony Hawk 2 | Activision, Inc. | Sports |
| Knockout Kings | Electronic Arts | Sports | Tour De France | Konami Corp | Other |
| Madden NFL 2002 | Electronic Arts | Sports | V.I.P. | Ubi Soft Ent | Other |
| Malice | Argonaut Games | Other | Virtual Velocity | Ubi Soft Ent | Other |
| Max Payne | Remedy Ent. | Shooters | Warcaster | Tremor Ent. | Other |
| Mechwarrior X | Microsoft | Shooters | Warzone Online | Paradox Ent. | Other |
| Medal of Honor | 2015 | Strategy | Wiggles | Innonics | Strategy |
| Metal Dungeon | Panther Software | RPG | WWF Raw Is War | THQ | Other |
| Metal Gear Solid X | Konami Corporation | Shooters | X-Isle | Crytek Studios | Other |
| New Legends | THQ | Action | Yager | Yager Development | Action |

**47**  To attract third-party developers, a company needed to be able to convince the market that its console would be successful, and supply effective development kits that facilitated programming for the operating system of the console. Microsoft's brand name enabled the company to enlist most of the major third-party game developers to produce games for the Xbox (see Exhibit 9). Microsoft also got rave reviews from the developers for the simplicity of the programming games for the Xbox. Because Microsoft leveraged its user-friendly DirectX technology, PC game developers were already familiar with the technology, enabling an easy transition from PC to console. Furthermore, since DirectX was a commonly used tool among amateur game developers, Microsoft allowed online Xbox applications development for a small fee.

**EXHIBIT 9**
**Game Developers for the Xbox**

| | | | | |
|---|---|---|---|---|
| Acclaim | Digital Illusions | Koei Co. Ltd. | Reflections Interactive | Volition, Inc. |
| Activision, Inc. | Digital Rim | Konami Corporation | Remedy Entertainment | VR-1 Ent. |
| Adrenium Games | DigitalWare Inc. | Kool Kizz | Revolution Software | Warthog PLC |
| Aki Corp. | Dma Design Ltd. | Kuju Entertainment | Ripcord Games | Westwood Studios |
| Alfa System Co. Ltd. | Dream Factory | Larian Studios | Riverhillsoft Inc | XeNN inc. |
| ALTAR Interactive | DreamCatcher | Legend Ent. | Rockstar Games | Xenopi |
| Anchor Inc. | DreamForge | LightWeight Co. Ltd. | Saffire Corporation | Yager |
| Angel Studios Inc. | Dwango Co., Ltd. | Lionhead Studios | SCi Entertainment Group | Yuki Enterprise |
| Arc System Works | Dynamix | Lost Boys Interactive | Shoeisha Co., Ltd. | Zombie VR |
| Argonaut Games | Edge of Reality | MadCat Interactive | Sidhe Interactive | Zono, Inc. |
| Arika Co. Ltd. | Eidos interactive | Majesco Inc. | Sierra | |
| Artdink Corp | Electronic Arts | Mass Media Inc. | Silicon Dreams Studio Ltd. | |
| Artoon Co. Ltd. | Empire Interactive | Max-International Inc. | Simon & Schuster Interactive | |
| Ask Co. Ltd. | Eon Digital Ent. | MGM Interactive | Sky.Co., Ltd. | |
| Atlus Co. Ltd. | Epic Games | Microids | SouthPeak Interactive | |
| Attention to Detail | Escape Factory | Microsoft | Spike Co., Ltd. | |
| Awesome Dev. | Fox Interactive | Midas Interactive | Starbreeze Studios | |
| bam! Entertainment | From Software | Midway Home | Stormfront Studios | |
| Bandai Co. Ltd. | Funcom | Monolith Productions | T&E Soft, Inc. | |
| Barking Dog Studios | Gameplay | Monster Games Inc. | Taito Corporation | |
| Bethesda Softworks | Gathering | Mythos Games Ltd | Takara Co., LTD. | |
| BioWare Corp. | Genki Co. Ltd. | Nagi Corporation | Take-Two Interactive | |
| Bizarre Creations | Global A Ent. | Namco Limited | Takuyo Kougyo Co., Ltd. | |
| Blitz Games Ltd | h.a.n.d. inc. | Nest Corporation | TDK Mediactive, Inc. | |
| Blue Byte Software | H.I.C. Co. Ltd. | Neversoft Ent. | Tecmo, LTD. | |
| Blue Shift, Inc. | Hasbro Interactive | Nihilistic Software Inc. | Telenet Japan Co., LTD. | |
| Brat Designs | Havas Interactive | Nihon Create Inc. | Terminal Reality | |
| Bungie | Headlock Inc. | NovaLogic Inc | The Codemasters | |
| Bunkasha Publishing | Heavy Iron Studios | NuClearVision | The Collective, Inc. | |
| Capcom Co. Ltd. | Housemarque | Oddworld Inhabitants | The LEGO Company | |
| Charybdis Limited | Hudson Soft | Over Works Inc. | The Pitbull Syndicate | |
| Cinemaware Inc. | Humongous Ent. | Pacific Coast P&L | The Whole Experience | |
| Climax Ltd. Co. | id Software, Inc. | Panther Software | THQ | |
| Conspiracy Ent. | I-Imagine Interactive | Panther Software Inc. | Titus | |
| Core Design Ltd. | Image Corporation | Papyrus | TopWare Interactive | |
| Crave Entertainment | Imagineer Co. Ltd. | Paradigm Studios | Totally Games | |
| Criterion Software | Incredible Tech. | Paradox Entertainment | Treasure, Inc. | |
| Cryo | Infogrames | Pipe Dream Interactive | Tremor Entertainment | |
| Crystal Dynamics | Innonics | Qube | Ubi Soft Entertainment | |
| Crytek Studios | Interplay Ent. | R A C | Valkyrie Studios | |
| DarkWorks | Jaleco Ltd. | Radical | Valve, LLC | |
| Datam Polystar | Kaboom Studios | Rage | Victor Interactive | |
| Daydream Software | Kalisto Ent. | Rainbow Studios | Video System Co., Ltd. | |
| Deep Red Games | Kemco/Kotobuki | Raven Software | Virgin Interactive | |
| Digital Anvil | Kodiak Interactive | Red Storm | VIS entertainment PLC | |

**48**   Microsoft's major disadvantage in the videogame industry was its inexperience in developing characters to attract the younger portion of the market. Characters such as Sonic the Hedgehog, Mario, Solid Snake, and Pokemon had proved crucial in the success of Nintendo and Sega. To combat this, Microsoft announced that it would team up with the Danish company Legos to build brand image among the younger generation. Corey Wade, an analyst at

Alexander & Associates, which studies home entertainment trends, criticized Microsoft: "I don't think they have a clue now how to come up with a Nintendo-style game aimed at a 12-year-old."[38] In 2001, Nintendo had approximately a 15 percent market share and that was expected to grow with its release of the GameCube. Microsoft appeared better positioned to battle Sony for the remaining market share—that of the teen and twenties male.

# MICROSOFT'S STRATEGY

49  Though producing consumer electronics hardware did not seem an obvious fit with Microsoft's product portfolio, many industry observers speculated that Microsoft had begun to see the videogame console industry as a threat to its dominance in PC operating systems. Sony, Nintendo, and Sega were all producing consoles that would enable gamers to access the Internet. This idea had been pioneered by Nintendo in 1989, when it formed a joint venture with AT&T to network NES households and allow downloading of games and videogame chat lines. This venture never fully materialized and the idea was scrapped, however the DreamCast and PS2 resurrected the idea and provided modems for on-line access. Rumors also circulated that Sony planned to incorporate a Linux (an alternative PC-operating system) port on the Sony Playstation2—a move that would understandably raise some concerns at Microsoft. Should the gaming console prove to become a primary portal to the Internet, it posed a real threat to the PC industry.

### Organizational Structure

50  To manage the development and deployment of the new game console, Microsoft established a new division that would be led by CXO (Chief Xbox Officer) Robert Bach, who would report directly to Bill Gates. The Xbox division would be highly autonomous, with its own branches for marketing, operations, and technical development. In general Microsoft was known to utilize very flexible structures and frequent reorganization. Some analysts saw this as an indication of instability and evidence of poor management. There were also high reorganization costs involved in the constant change. A Microsoft spokesperson played down such criticisms, noting that Microsoft "continually makes adjustments to the organization to meet the changing nature of needs."[39]

### Marketing

51  Microsoft planned a marketing budget for the Xbox of $500 million to be spent over a span of 18 months, the biggest launch in the company's history[40] (see Exhibit 10 for company financials). The budget would include funding for in-store merchandising, promotion, retailer incentives, events, sponsorships, and traditional advertising. Promotional partners in the fast-food, beverage, and sports industries were expected to share the expenses. Microsoft planned on using broad consumer media (television, radio, the Internet, and business publications) and trade publications. In addition, Microsoft reimbursed qualified resellers and original equipment manufacturers (OEMs) for certain advertising expenditures.

52    McCannErickson Worldwide, an advertising agency based in New York, would handle the $150 million Xbox advertising account. The focus of the advertising campaign was expected to be a sense of passion and exhilaration. Microsoft would also continue to tout the

---

[38]T. Ham, and J. Gaudiosi, "Microsoft and Sony Prepare for Mortal Combat," *Washington Post,* March 10, 2000, p. E11.
[39]James Niccolai, and Clare Haney, www.thestandard.com, March 12, 1999.
[40]T. Elkin, 2000. "Gearing Up for Xbox Launch," *Advertising Age,* 71(48), 2000, p. 16.

**EXHIBIT 10**
**Microsoft Financials**

Source: Hoovers.

| Income Statement | Jun 01 | Jun 00 | Jun 99 |
|---|---|---|---|
| All amounts in millions of U.S. dollars except per share amounts. | | | |
| Revenue | 25,296.0 | 22,956.0 | 19,747.0 |
| Cost of goods sold | 1,919.0 | 2,254.0 | 1,804.0 |
| Gross profit | 23,377.0 | 20,702.0 | 17,943.0 |
| Gross profit margin | 92.4% | 90.2% | 90.9% |
| SG&A expense | 10,121.0 | 8,925.0 | 6,890.0 |
| Depreciation and amortization | 1,536.0 | 748.0 | 1,010.0 |
| Operating income | 11,720.0 | 11,029.0 | 10,043.0 |
| Operating margin | 46.3% | 48.0% | 50.9% |
| Total net income | 7,346.0 | 9,421.0 | 7,785.0 |
| Net profit margin | 29.0% | 41.0% | 39.4% |
| Diluted EPS ($) | 1.32 | 1.70 | 1.42 |

| Balance Sheet | Jun 01 | Jun 00 | Jun 99 |
|---|---|---|---|
| Cash | 3,922.0 | 4,846.0 | 4,975.0 |
| Net receivables | 3,671.0 | 3,250.0 | 2,245.0 |
| Inventories | 0.0 | 0.0 | 0.0 |
| Total current assets | 39,637.0 | 30,308.0 | 20,233.0 |
| Total assets | 59,257.0 | 52,150.0 | 37,156.0 |
| Short-term debt | 0.0 | 0.0 | 0.0 |
| Total current liabilities | 11,132.0 | 9,755.0 | 8,718.0 |
| Long-term debt | 0.0 | 0.0 | 0.0 |
| Total liabilities | 11,968.0 | 10,782.0 | 8,718.0 |
| Total equity | 47,289.0 | 41,368.0 | 28,438.0 |
| Shares outstanding (mil.) | 5,383.0 | 5,283.0 | 5,109.0 |

Some figures may not add up due to rounding.

technological superiority of the Xbox in comparison to the Playstation2 and GameCube. The gaming division's marketing department had the goal of making the Xbox one of the top five consumer brands worldwide. To help accomplish this, John O'Rourke, vice president of marketing for the Xbox, employed an experienced staff that included (among others) Don Coyner (Director of Marketing, Games Division), who had spent seven years at Nintendo, and Jennifer Booth (Marketing Director, Research), who had launched Sony's original PlayStation in 1995.[41]

### Research and Development

53 In 1991, Microsoft established its own computer science research organization, Microsoft Research, after it saw a need to support long-range research that would be the foundation for future products. Microsoft spends $250 million a year on its four research labs, part of a $4 billion research and development budget, which is, among large technology companies, one of the highest ratios of investment to revenue.

54 Microsoft Research has committed time and money to research in graphics, such as animation, multiresolution geometry and layered depth images, audio, and artificial intelligence. All of these areas have been vital in the development of the Xbox and games

[41]www.gamingmaxx.com.

produced by Microsoft.[42] While in general Microsoft's corporate research labs focus on goals extending five to ten years beyond current product cycles, their close interaction with the rest of the company allowed for short-term results with the various product development groups. For example, some CD-ROM game titles use technology or tools created by Microsoft Research.

# THE NEXT BOX?

**55** Microsoft was a very large, well-known company with tremendous capital to access and unsurpassed brand recognition. Microsoft had also demonstrated repeatedly its mastery of strategically developing and deploying technology in industries characterized by network externalities, in which standards and complementary goods played crucial roles. Such industries had a tendency to select one (or a few) winners, and exclude all other would-be competitors. Microsoft's reputation for dominance in such industries likely played a significant role in its ability to attract game developers, and in industry analysts' perceptions of the firm's likelihood of success.

**56** However, it was also impossible to overlook the fact that Microsoft's dominance had always been in software. The production of hardware—especially consumer electronics—posed very different requirements for inventory, manufacturing, and distribution. Furthermore, Microsoft's success in many of its software categories could be traced to its dominance in PC operating systems; however, the market share of Windows would likely prove to be of little use in the game console market. Finally, Microsoft would be marketing to new types of customers, both in terms of distributors and end consumers. Though it would likely sell the Xbox through some of the same distributors with which it had relationships for selling software, it would now need much greater penetration into distributors such as Toys R Us, Babbages, and Circuit City. It would also need to cultivate a radically different brand image in the game console market than the one which it had achieved in the software market, and to make much greater use of marketing channels such as television advertising and gaming magazines.

**57** Overall, the videogame console market represented a fundamentally different kind of business for Microsoft, and it would be battling very large, well-established competitors. Not everyone was sure it was a battle it would win. Would the Xbox's technological advantages be able to attract gamers away from the game consoles of Nintendo and Sony? Though Microsoft had legions of third-party developers signed up for game licensing, such agreements often did not translate into actual game titles. After all, 3DO, a company that had launched a videogame system in 1993, had signed on 300 game developers at its launch, but those license arrangements only translated into five actual game titles by March of 1994. It seemed clear that PC game developers would embrace the Xbox, but Microsoft's intention was not to simply attract current PC gamers to the platform—its intention was to battle for a share of Sony and Nintendo's market of console gamers (see Exhibit 11 for pictures of the competing game systems and Exhibit 12 for a competitive summary of 128-bit systems).

---

[42]www.research.microsoft.com.

**EXHIBIT 11  Pictures of Products**

*Source:* www.xbox.com, www.sega.com, www.nintendo.com, www.sony.com.

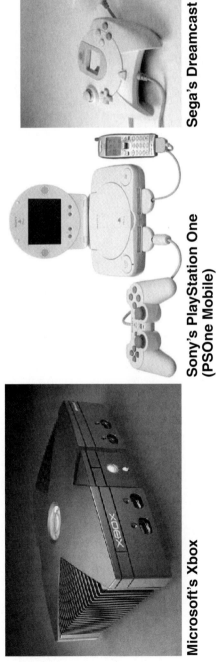

Sega's Dreamcast

Nintendo's GameCube

Sony's PlayStation One
(PSOne Mobile)

Sony's PlayStation2 (PS2)

Microsoft's Xbox

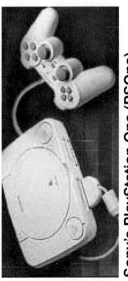

Sony's PlayStation One (PSOne)

**EXHIBIT 12**    Competitive Summary of the 128-bit U.S. Videogame Console Market

| Competitors | Sony Playstation2 | Microsoft Xbox | Nintendo GameCube |
|---|---|---|---|
| **Introduction** | March, 2000 | November, 2001 | November, 2001 |
| **Price** | $299 | $299 | $199 |
| **Technological functionality** | CD/DVD based<br>128 bit<br>300 MHz clock speed<br>MB RAM<br>Broadband compatible | CD/DVD based<br>128 bit<br>733 MHz clock speed<br>64 MB RAM<br>Broadband compatible | Mini-disc based<br>128 bit<br>485 MHz clock speed<br>40MB RAM |
| **Backward compatibility** | Yes | Not applicable | No |
| **Developers** | Internal and external;<br>40% of games produced<br>  in-house | Internal and external;<br>40% of games produced<br>  in-house | Internal and external;<br>80% of games produced<br>  in-house |
| **Game titles** | About 300 by December,<br>2001; 483 by March, 2002 | About 40 by December<br>2001; 205 in March, 2002 | About 20 by December,<br>2001; 117 in March, 2002 |

# Case 43 Valassis Communications

## Deborah R. Ettington

Valassis will be the leader in online promotions.

*Alan F. Schultz, Chairman, President, and CEO*

**1** In May 2000, Valassis Communications Incorporated (VCI) was an $800 million company headquartered in Livonia, Michigan, a suburb of Detroit. Its primary business was printing free-standing inserts (FSIs), a four-color booklet of coupons, and other promotions inserted in Sunday newspapers throughout the United States. However, with rapid growth of the Internet, Alan Schultz led the company into a number of new ventures to take advantage of opportunities in an online world.

**2** Schultz, 41, was elected CEO and President in June 1998, and appointed Chairman of the Board of Directors in December 1998. Previously he served as EVP and COO (1996–1998) and EVP Sales and Marketing (1992–1996.) He joined Valassis in 1984 when it merged with his previous employer, Inserts. Schultz replaced long-term CEO David Brandon, who left to become President and CEO of nearby Domino's Pizza.

**3** Schultz spent a total of $10.6 million cash on strategic acquisitions and equity investments in 1999 and had just announced another alliance in April 2000. These investments were intended to support a three-pronged E-commerce strategy:

1. Attract revenues from growing e-commerce media sales;

2. Build a significant web presence with an online coupon service, and eventually with other Internet products and services;

3. Capitalize on the growth of the online grocery business.

**4** To support this strategy, Schultz announced in June 1999 that Suzanne C. ("Suzie") Brown would fill the newly created position of Vice President, Internet and E-commerce Services. Brown was formerly vice president of Western Sales, where she had been leading the company's Internet efforts since January 1999. Prior to joining Valassis in 1984, Brown worked for Procter & Gamble, a leading consumer packaged goods manufacturer. In 1994 she left Valassis to work for Advo, a competitor, but returned in 1996. Brown described her perspective on the new position:

> Just as the marketing environment has evolved over the years, so has Valassis. It's amazing to have witnessed our company quickly changing from an FSI provider to a full-service solution provider, including technology and Internet-related products and services. There are tremendous opportunities awaiting Valassis in the realm of the Internet and I'm thrilled to be driving such forward-thinking initiatives.

**5** Schultz was optimistic when he announced 1999's financial results.

> With another record year behind us, our focus is on the future. The long-term outlook is exceptionally promising: the FSI industry is strong, our core businesses are meeting or beating annual expectations, and our new ventures are building momentum.

**EXHIBIT 1**   Stock Performance

| VCI High and Low Stock Prices During 1998 and 1999 | | |
|---|---|---|
| **Quarter Ended** | **High** | **Low** |
| 3/31/98 | $27 | $22 |
| 6/30/98 | 27 | 23 |
| 9/30/98 | 27 | 20 |
| 12/31/98 | 34 | 19 |
| 3/31/99 | 37 | 29 |
| 6/30/99 | 41 | 34 |
| 9/30/99 | 47 | 35 |
| 12/31/99 | 44 | 37 |

Source: 1999 10K report.

| VCI and S&P 500 Monthly Data July 1999 to May 2000 | | |
|---|---|---|
| **Date** | **VCI** | **S&P. 500** |
| 7.30.99 | 37.25 | 1328.72 |
| 8.31.99 | 43.75 | 1320.41 |
| 9.30.99 | 43.94 | 1282.71 |
| 10.29.99 | 43.00 | 1362.93 |
| 11.30.99 | 39.38 | 1388.91 |
| 12.31.99 | 42.25 | 1469.25 |
| 1.31.00 | 34.00 | 1394.46 |
| 2.28.00 | 26.50 | 1348.05 |
| 3.31.00 | 33.31 | 1498.58 |
| 4.28.00 | 34.06 | 1452.43 |
| 5.15.00 | 34.44 | 1452.36 |

Sources: www.valassis.com/Investor, www.spglobaldata.com.

| Stockholder Returns (Dividends Reinvested) | | | | | | |
|---|---|---|---|---|---|---|
| | **Base= 1994** | **1995** | **1996** | **1997** | **1998** | **1999** |
| VCI | 100 | 116.67 | 140.83 | 246.67 | 344.17 | 422.5 |
| S&P 500 | 100 | 137.58 | 169.17 | 225.6 | 290.08 | 351.12 |

Source: Proxy Statement 4/12/2000.

6   Yet, despite these initiatives, in May 2000 the company's stock was trading in the mid-30's, well below its high of 47 in the third quarter of 1999. (Exhibit 1 shows stock price history.) What would it take to convince investors of the promising future foreseen by management? Was the company moving fast enough to exploit the growth potential of the Internet? Or was it moving too fast and jeopardizing its strong position in the paper coupon industry?

# THE U.S. COUPON INDUSTRY

### The History of Couponing

7   The first discount coupon was attributed to Asa Candler, the druggist who bought the formula for Coca-Cola. In 1894, he gave out handwritten tickets for a free glass of his new drink. C. W. Post distributed the first grocery coupon worth one cent toward a purchase of Grape Nuts, in 1895. Coupons increased in popularity during the Depression as households struggled to save money on their grocery bills. By 1965, one-half of Americans were coupon users, increasing to 65 percent in 1975 and 81 percent in 1998.[1]

8   In the 1970s, about 70 percent of coupons were distributed on newspaper pages ("ROP," or run-of-press) with only about 7 percent running in FSIs. During the 1980s, packaged goods manufacturers shifted their ads to FSIs, so that by 1991, 80 percent of coupons ran in FSIs. Other distribution methods included handouts, attachment to the package, magazines, direct mail, and newspapers. (Exhibit 2 shows distribution by media type.) Coupon

[1]Coupon Council at www.couponmonth.com/pages/allabout.htm (accessed 5/21/00).

**EXHIBIT 2**
**Distribution of Coupons by Media Type—1997**

Source: *Brandmarketing,* April 1998, vol. V, no. 4, p. 12.

| Distribution Medium | Percent of Total |
|---|---|
| Free Standing Insert | 80.5 |
| Handout | 8.7 |
| In/On Package | 3.3 |
| Magazine | 3.2 |
| Direct Mail | 2.6 |
| Newspaper | 1.3 |
| Other (including Internet) | 0.4 |
| Total | 100.0 |

**EXHIBIT 3**
**Effective Redemption Rates for Coupons 1990–1996 (Base Year 1990)**

Source: NCH NuWorld Marketing, "Worldwide Coupon Distribution and Redemption Trends."

| Year | Distribution (Billions) | Redemption (Billions) | Redemption Rates (%) | Average Duration (months) |
|---|---|---|---|---|
| 1990 | 279.4 | 7.1 | 2.5 | 4.9 |
| 1991 | 292.0 | 7.5 | 2.6 | 4.4 |
| 1992 | 310.0 | 7.7 | 2.5 | 4.0 |
| 1993 | 298.5 | 6.8 | 2.3 | 3.1 |
| 1994 | 309.7 | 6.2 | 2.0 | 3.4 |
| 1995 | 291.9 | 5.8 | 2.0 | 3.3 |
| 1996 | 268.5 | 5.3 | 2.0 | 3.0 |
| 1997 | 250.2 | 4.9 | 2.0 | 3.1 |
| 1998 | 249.0 | 4.8 | 1.9 | 3.1 |
| 1999 | 256.0 | 4.7 | 1.8 | 3.2 |

distribution peaked in 1994 at over 300 billion coupons and declined or remained steady through 1998. Redemption rates also declined during this period. (Exhibit 3 contains coupon distribution and redemption rates.)

### Differing Views of the Value of Couponing

9    The coupon industry was often criticized for high costs and ineffectiveness. For example, one industry observer complained about the use of doubled coupons by retailers in *Discount Store News:*

> Sure, I know it helps build traffic in stores, spike sales, squeeze the competition and move merchandise through the pipeline. But in the final analysis, I believe excessive couponing hurts retailers, suppliers, and consumers and damages the spirit of partnership. It does not single-handedly improve profitability nor enhance image.
>
> It also annoys, alienates, and confuses consumers and does little to encourage store loyalty. It creates long lines that most retailers can't handle; it creates out-of-stocks, which force rain checks that in turn create other fulfillment issues. And it creates price wars that few retailers can win.[2]

10   One leading coupon distributor, Procter & Gamble, even experimented with dropping coupons completely in three New York markets in 1996. Angry consumers wrote letters to the editor, picketed, boycotted, and petitioned to get their coupons back. P&G restored the coupons. In October 1997, P&G, nine other consumer products firms, and Wegmans Food

[2]Lisanti, T. "The almighty coupon, redux," *Discount Store News* 37 (18) p. 13.

Market Inc., without admitting guilt, agreed to pay a total of $4.2 million to settle state antitrust charges that they had colluded to reduce the number of shopping coupons distributed in western New York.

**11**  Manufacturers also reduced the number of coupons by trying multibrand coupons, and by using more targeted promotions. One approach offered by Catalina Marketing's Checkout Coupons® used consumer purchases to trigger coupons distributed at the checkout register. The redemption rate for Checkout Coupons® in 1996 was 9 percent, compared to an average redemption rate of about 3 percent. David Diamond, executive vice president for marketing and new applications, explained Catalina Marketing's appeal:

> Fundamentally, it is both more effective and efficient to target. You are not chopping down trees and sending lots of FSIs for dog food to people who don't own dogs. And you can personalize communication based on the buying habits of the person.

**12**  However, the industry emphasized research indicating that consumers were still attracted by discount offerings. Some industry experts agreed, arguing that brand marketers and consumers actually liked coupons. For example, Joan Johnson, President of Punch Marketing, a marketing communications company located in Clemmons, North Carolina, was quoted in *Supermarket News:*

> It is amazing and somewhat laughable that a consumer promotion that has so much consumer loyalty is being vilified. It is largely coming because retailers have to bear the administrative logistics and they are tired of that. To think that a consumer is never going to be interested in saving money again is ridiculous. It is simply not human nature.[3]

**13**  When a customer purchased a product using a coupon, the retailer discounted the customer's bill, and transmitted the coupon to a clearinghouse. The clearinghouse sorted the coupons and billed the manufacturers, who reimbursed the retailers for the face value of the coupon, plus a handling fee.

**14**  The industry had cooperated to address high costs of redemption. In January 1998, the Grocery Manufacturers of America (GMA) and the Joint Industry Coupon Committee (JICC) released a report, "Coupons: A Complete Guide." The purpose of the report was to offer best practices for most efficient use of coupons, including use of more sophisticated bar codes, scanning devices, and elimination of unclear coupons that were hard to handle at the register.

### Couponing Rebounds

**15**  Coupon distribution was back up in 1999, increasing 3 percent over 1998, with 92 percent of coupons distributed by FSIs, down slightly from 1998. Consumer packaged goods manufacturers spent more than $6 billion on coupons. Exhibit 4 shows the breakdown of this spending. Electronic distribution methods grew by 20 to 30 percent but still accounted for less than half a share point of total coupon distribution. The average FSI redemption rate decreased slightly to 1.1 percent, while redemption rates for other methods increased. Early evidence of electronic coupon usage showed much higher redemption rates, ranging from 20 percent to as high as 50 percent for personalized coupon packages. Exhibit 5 shows demographics of coupon users.

**EXHIBIT 4**
**Breakdown of Coupon Spending—1999**

Source: NCH NuWorld Marketing.

| | |
|---|---|
| Total spending | $6.153 billion |
| Face value | $3.6 billion (59%) |
| Distribution | $2.0 billion (32%) |
| Processing, handling, and other | $0.5 billion (9%) |

[3]Turesik, R. "Sticking with coupons," *Supermarket News,* BrandMarketing supplement, April 1998, 5 (4) p. 12.

**EXHIBIT 5**
Demographics of
Coupon Users—1998

Source: NCH NuWorld
Marketing Limited, reprinted in
http://www.couponmonth.com.

| Age | Percent Using Coupons | Income | Percent Using Coupons |
|-----|-----------------------|--------|-----------------------|
| 18–24 | 74 | <$15,000 | 74 |
| 25–34 | 82 | $15–25,000 | 83 |
| 35–44 | 83 | $25–40,000 | 76 |
| 45–54 | 82 | $50,000+ | 83 |
| 55–64 | 81 | | |
| 65+ | 82 | | |

**16**    From the manufacturer's perspective, coupons remained an important marketing tool. Wally Marx, president of Wallace Marx & Associates, Edina, Minnesota., a marketing consulting firm, explained in a *Brandmarketing* interview:

> The bottom line is coupons are alive, well, and healthy—an essential part of the marketing mix. They are a very effective way to introduce new brands, gain trial, and encourage pantry loading, and are probably the lowest-cost sampling method. Marketers are learning to use coupons more efficiently and more effectively, better targeting markets, better valuing their coupons by using high values in markets with high potentials, and tightening purchase requirements and expiration dates.[4]

## INTERNET SHOPPING AND COUPON USE

**17**    NPD Group, a marketing research firm, reported in May 1999 that 49 percent of Web-surfing respondents were aware of Web-based coupons, and 87 percent of these intended to either begin using them or increase the frequency with which they used them. Online coupon users were typically between the ages of 25 and 44. A third of them had annual household incomes exceeding $75,000, versus 23 percent of the U.S. population in that income range.

**18**    Forrester Research, Inc., a leading technology research firm, predicted in May 2000 that the number of households shopping online would nearly double, to 38 million, in the next two years. A study by the Boston Consulting Group, a prominent management consultancy, indicated that the demographic profile of new Internet users was changing to look more like the general population. New Internet users over the past year were 53 percent female, versus 42 percent for those using the Internet for 3 years or more. Half of new users had household incomes below $50,000, versus 34 percent of experienced users. New users included 35 percent with a high school education or less, compared to 17 percent of experienced users. Another research firm, Jupiter Communications, estimated that 42 percent of the U.S. population would be online by the end of 2000, compared to 14 percent in 1996.

## COMPANY HISTORY

**19**    George F. Valassis incorporated Valassis Communications, Inc. in 1970 as a sales agent for printing companies. In 1972, it pioneered free-standing inserts (FSIs.) George Valassis sold the company to Australia-based Consolidated Press Holdings (CPH) in 1986 for $365 million. CPH sold half its interest for nearly $1 billion when VCI went public in 1992. The company used much of the proceeds from the IPO to pay CPH a large dividend, leaving the company with about $550 million debt and a shareholders' equity deficit of about $400 million. CPH sold the remainder of its interest in the company in a secondary offering completed in July 1997.

[4]Brumback, N. "Coupon comeback," *Brandmarketing*, October 1999, 6(9) p. 24.

**EXHIBIT 6**
Income Statements
($millions)
Years Ended
December 31,
1995–1999

Source: *Annual Reports* and
*10K Statements*.

| | 1999 | 1998 | 1997 | 1996 | 1995 |
|---|---|---|---|---|---|
| Revenue | | | | | |
| FSI | 586.7 | 567.7 | 521.3 | 504.1 | 480.7 |
| VIP | 118.1 | 103.1 | 89.2 | 89.4 | 76.8 |
| TMS | 69.0 | 48.4 | 41.0 | N/A | N/A |
| Other | 20.8 | 22.2 | 24.0 | N/A | N/A |
| Total Revenue | 794.6 | 741.4 | 675.5 | 659.1 | 613.8 |
| Cost of products sold | 491.6 | 485.1 | 436.2 | 473.1 | 466.1 |
| SG & A | 83.1 | 77.2 | 77.4 | 67.1 | 59.5 |
| Amortization | 5.2 | 8.1 | 8.6 | 8.2 | 9.6 |
| Restatement* | 0.0 | 0.0 | 0.0 | 3.1 | (3.1) |
| Operating earnings | 214.7 | 171.0 | 153.3 | 107.6 | 81.7 |
| Minority interests | 0.0 | 0.0 | 0.0 | 0.0 | (1.4) |
| Write downs/ sale of business | 0.0 | 0.0 | 0.0 | 0.0 | 16.9 |
| Interest expense | 26.0 | 34.5 | 38.3 | 39.6 | 40.5 |
| Income taxes | 67.5 | 52.2 | 45.1 | 28.2 | 13.0 |
| Income before extraordinary loss | 121.1 | 84.3 | 69.9 | 39.8 | 12.7 |
| Extraordinary loss (net of taxes)† | 6.9 | 13.6 | 0.0 | 0.0 | 0.0 |
| Net income | 114.2 | 70.7 | 69.9 | 39.8 | 12.7 |

*Restated in 1998 due to change from LIFO to FIFO inventory valuation.

†Results for the following years include: *1998,* A one-time charge of $3.7 million, net of tax, for expenses related to the early retirement and resulting amendment to the employment contract of the former CEO, as well as an extraordinary loss of $13.6 million, net of tax, due to the early extinguishment of debt; *1999,* An extraordinary loss of $6.9 million, net of tax, due to early extinguishment of debt, as well as a tax benefit, net of associated close-down costs related to Valassis of Canada, of $2.7 million.

20    After earning $82 million in 1993, Valassis experienced double trouble in 1994. A new competitor, Sullivan Graphics Inc., entered the FSI business, triggering a price war, followed soon by a paper price increase of 65 percent. Valassis lost $400,000 in 1994. Sullivan exited the business after less than a year, selling out to News America, the only other competitor in the FSI business. Valassis' financial performance improved steadily after 1995. By 1999 revenues were $795 million, with net income of $114 million. Exhibits 6 to 9 contain financial data.

# VCI PRODUCTS AND SERVICES

21    The company described its product portfolio in the *Annual Report* as follows:

> Valassis Communications, Inc. leads the marketing services industry by providing a wide range of strategic marketing solutions for manufacturers and retailers. The company's products and services meet a variety of marketing objectives by delivering the right communications to the right consumers at the right time through the right media. From mass to one-to-one marketing, Valassis' strategic solutions include newspaper-delivered co-op and specialty inserts, advertising, product sampling, direct mail, and e-commerce solutions, as well as consulting services.

22    Three business divisions (Free-Standing Inserts, Valassis Impact Promotions, Targeted Marketing Services) comprised most of Valassis' revenue. An equity investment in Customer Relationship Marketing Group represented a new business area. Exhibits 10 and 11 contain financial performance by segment.

**EXHIBIT 7**
Consolidated Balance
Sheets at December
31 ($ millions)
1995–1999

Source: *Annual Reports* and
*10K Statements.*

| | 1999 | 1998 | 1997 | 1996 | 1995 |
|---|---|---|---|---|---|
| **Assets** | | | | | |
| Current assets: | | | | | |
| Cash and equivalents | 11.1 | 6.9 | 35.4 | 60.2 | 34.4 |
| Accounts receivable | 94.1 | 95.4 | 81.7 | 92.8 | 84.4 |
| Raw material inventory | 11.7 | 11.8 | 11.0 | 6.1 | 13.8 |
| WIP inventory | 17.5 | 20.1 | 15.7 | 14.7 | 14.3 |
| Prepaid expenses and other | 6.0 | 5.8 | 4.5 | 1.9 | 3.7 |
| Deferred income taxes | 1.5 | 1.8 | 2.0 | 2.1 | 4.3 |
| Refundable income taxes | 0.4 | 1.2 | 0.8 | — | 0.1 |
| Total current assets | 142.3 | 143.1 | 151.1 | 177.8 | 155.0 |
| Net PP & E | 52.8 | 46.4 | 40.2 | 34.8 | 34.9 |
| Net intangible assets | 40.1 | 41.2 | 47.3 | 55.9 | 64.1 |
| Equity investments and advances to investees | 9.6 | — | — | — | — |
| Other assets | 2.4 | 1.4 | 2.3 | 5.2 | 4.9 |
| Total assets | 247.2 | 232.0 | 240.9 | 273.7 | 258.9 |
| **Liabilities and Stockholders' Deficit** | | | | | |
| Current liabilities: | | | | | |
| Accounts payable | 77.7 | 69.1 | 59.2 | 67.3 | 72.0 |
| Accrued interest | 3.6 | 4.5 | 5.1 | 6.1 | 6.4 |
| Accrued expenses | 30.5 | 26.3 | 25.9 | 22.4 | 21.2 |
| Progress billings | 57.7 | 58.6 | 58.2 | 57.2 | 49.2 |
| Current portion, LT debt | — | — | — | 7.3 | — |
| Income taxes payable | — | — | — | 1.1 | — |
| Total current liabilities | 169.6 | 158.6 | 148.4 | 161.4 | 148.8 |
| Long-term debt | 291.4 | 340.5 | 367.1 | 395.9 | 416.0 |
| Deferred income taxes | 1.9 | 1.5 | 2.3 | 2.6 | 3.0 |
| Total debt | 462.9 | 500.6 | 517.8 | 559.9 | 567.8 |
| Minority interests | — | — | — | 0.4 | 0.4 |
| Stockholders' deficit: | | | | | |
| Common stock | 0.6 | 0.6 | 0.4 | 0.4 | 0.4 |
| Additional paid-in capital | 76.9 | 69.4 | 72.4 | 41.3 | 39.6 |
| Accumulated deficit | (51.7) | (165.9) | (236.6) | (306.5) | (349.5) |
| Foreign currency translations | (0.5) | (0.3) | (0.1) | (0.3) | 0.2 |
| Treasury stock, at cost | (240.9) | (172.3) | (113.0) | (21.5) | — |
| Total stockholders' deficit | (215.6) | (268.5) | (276.9) | (286.6) | (309.3) |
| Total liabilities and stockholders' deficit | 247.2 | 232.0 | 240.9 | 273.7 | 258.9 |

### Free-Standing Inserts (FSIs)

23   Almost three-quarters of the company's revenue ($585 million) came from free-standing inserts (FSIs.) These FSIs were referred to as "co-op" promotions because the booklets contained promotions from a number of companies in different product categories (versus "solo" inserts that featured only one company's products.) Valassis' FSIs were delivered to over 58 million households across the United States (61 percent of total U.S. households)

**EXHIBIT 8**
Consolidated
Statements of Cash
Flow 1997–1999
Years Ended
December 31
($millions)

Source: *Annual Reports* and
*10K Statements.*

| | 1999 | 1998 | 1997 |
|---|---|---|---|
| CF from operating activities | | | |
| Net earnings | 114.2 | 70.7 | 69.9 |
| Adjustments: | | | |
| Depreciation | 7.7 | 7.6 | 6.8 |
| Amortization | 5.2 | 8.2 | 8.8 |
| Provision for losses on A/R | 1.9 | 0.9 | 0.9 |
| Stock-based compensation | 2.2 | 2.7 | 1.4 |
| (Gain)/loss on sale of PP&E | (0.1) | 0.0 | (0.2) |
| Deferred income taxes | 0.7 | (0.6) | (0.1) |
| Minority interest | 0.0 | 0.0 | (0.5) |
| Changes in assets and liabilities | | | |
| Total adjustments | 32.5 | 17.3 | 20.6 |
| Net cash provided by operations | 146.7 | 87.9 | 90.5 |
| | | | |
| CF from investments: | | | |
| Additions to PP&E | (14.3) | (13.4) | (13.0) |
| Proceeds from sale of PP&E | 0.2 | 0.1 | 1.0 |
| Investments and acquisitions | (10.7) | (0.5) | 0.0 |
| Other | (0.2) | (0.2) | 0.1 |
| Net cash used in investments | (24.9) | (13.9) | (11.9) |
| | | | |
| CF from financing: | | | |
| Issuance of common stock | 11.9 | 30.0 | 17.1 |
| Purchase of treasury shares | (80.5) | (105.7) | (91.5) |
| Repayment of long-term debt | (219.7) | (153.7) | (36.2) |
| Borrowings of long-term debt | 99.7 | 127.0 | 0.0 |
| Capital contribution | 0.0 | 0.0 | 7.3 |
| Revolving line of credit | 70.9 | 0.0 | 0.0 |
| Net cash used in financing | (117.7) | (102.5) | (103.3) |
| | | | |
| Net (decrease)/ increase in cash and equivalents | 4.2 | (28.5) | (24.7) |
| Cash and equivalents at beginning of year | 6.9 | 35.4 | 60.2 |
| Cash and equivalents at end of year | 11.1 | 6.9 | 35.4 |

**EXHIBIT 9**
Revenue by Location
1997–1999
($ millions)

Source: *10K Report.*

| | 1999 | 1998 | 1997 |
|---|---|---|---|
| United States | $774.0 | $721.1 | $657.2 |
| Canada | 20.6 | 20.3 | 18.3 |
| Total | $794.6 | $741.4 | $675.5 |

43 times a year through over 530 Sunday newspaper editions. Its FSI business held approximately 50 percent market share.

24     Valassis also offered an FSI program for smaller counties not efficiently covered by national FSI programs. This C&D County Supercenter Program was started in 1995 to meet the needs of customers interested in targeting Wal-Mart grocery shoppers and was distributed to over 5 million households. In Canada, Valassis published Shop & Save FSI, distributed to approximately 5 million households (45 percent of Canadian households.)

25     FSI promotions could be tailored to particular markets by varying coupon values, promotion copy, and terms of the offer. To increase the value of coupons for its customers, Valassis offered Horizons Coding. This bar coding on the FSI coupons allowed brand marketers to track redemption rates better by individual newspapers, and coupon style and format.

**EXHIBIT 10**
Revenue and Profit
by Business Segment
1997–1999
($ millions)

Source: *10K Report.*

| | 1999 | 1998 | 1997 |
|---|---|---|---|
| *Free-Standing Inserts (FSI)* | | | |
| Revenues from external customers | $585.4 | $567.7 | $521.3 |
| Intersegment revenue | 6.1 | 4.4 | 0.6 |
| Depreciation/ amortization | 11.0 | 13.2 | 12.6 |
| Segment profit | 161.8 | 121.5 | 99.8 |
| *Valassis Impact Promotions (VIP)* | | | |
| Revenues from external customers | $118.1 | $103.1 | $89.2 |
| Intersegment revenue | — | — | — |
| Depreciation/ amortization | 1.8 | 2.2 | 2.1 |
| Segment profit | 12.2 | 9.0 | 9.8 |
| *All Others* | | | |
| Revenues from external customers | $90.9 | $69.4 | $62.7 |
| Intersegment revenue | — | — | — |
| Depreciation/ amortization | 0.1 | 0.3 | 0.7 |
| Segment profit | 14.5 | 4.8 | 3.1 |

**EXHIBIT 11**
Valassis Operating
Divisions

Source: *Annual Report* and
10K.

| | 1999 Revenues ($ millions) | 2000 Growth forecast (%) |
|---|---|---|
| Free-Standing Inserts (FSI) | 585 | 4 to 6 |
| Valassis Impact Promotions (VIP) | 118 | 15 |
| Targeted Marketing Services (TMS) | 69 | N/A |
| Product Sampling and Advertising | N/A | 20 |
| Run-of-Press (ROP) | N/A | 0 |
| Promotion Watch | N/A | 0 |
| Customer Relationship Marketing | | |
| Group (CRMG) | 0 | N/A* |
| Other Revenue | 22 | N/A |

*CRMG was expected to begin reporting revenue in the second half

26    FSIs were particularly popular with consumer packaged goods manufacturers and franchise retailers. No single customer accounted for more than 10 percent of FSI sales.

### Valassis Impact Promotions (VIP)

27    Valassis Impact Promotions (VIP) offered specialty promotions in a variety of shapes, sizes, and formats such as inserts featuring a single customer ("solos,") die-cuts, door hangers, box toppers, posters, calendars, and magnets. Promotions could be delivered through newspapers and direct mail. VIP promotions could be run any day of the year in any U.S. newspaper, allowing orders to be placed on a national, regional, or local basis.

28    Traditional customers were food service franchises and retailers, while new customers were in such categories as telecommunications and computer hardware.

### Targeted Marketing Services (TMS)

29    Targeted Marketing Services (TMS) included sampling, on-page newspaper promotion ("ROP" or run-of-press) and advertising, and Promotion Watch, a security consulting business for implementing sweepstakes contests. TMS products included:

• Newspac®, a sample attached to a brochure inserted into the newspaper

- Newspouch®, a product sample inside a newspaper delivery bag
- Direct mail sampling
- Brand Bag ™ and Brand Bag+ ™, advertisements printed on newspaper delivery bags that could include an attached coupon
- Targeted FSIs for individual customers
- Targeted Solo Inserts promoted manufacturers' products in conjunction with specific retail locations.

**30**   Valassis also helped customers with different packaging options for samples. Customers could target their promotional programs based on demographics, geography, retail locations, or competitive users.

**31**   Promotion Watch provided promotion security consulting services, including execution of sweepstakes and contests. Valassis helped customers with the entire process, from preliminary planning, through the writing of official rules, overseeing the printing and placement of winning pieces, and conducting background investigations of winners.

Traditional customers were consumer packaged goods companies, with new customers in the categories of e-commerce, mass merchandisers, telecommunications, financial institutions, and automotive.

### Customer Relationship Marketing Group (CRMG)

**32**   In 1999, Valassis purchased a 30 percent equity stake in Relationship Marketing Group (RMG), a company that provided grocery retail frequent shopper data. RMG, founded in 1995, brought relationships with over 1,500 grocery retail outlets nationwide. The purpose of the new Customer Relationship Marketing Group (CRMG) was to build long-term relationships with retailers by helping them target promotions.

**33**   Suzanne E. Griffin, Vice President and General Manager of CRMG, explained the purpose of the program:

> It will allow retailers to reach the right consumers, with the right offer, at the right time, in the specific promotional medium that the individual consumer will respond to. This will be accomplished through a proprietary system which collects, integrates, analyzes, and applies customer data.

CRMG was expected to begin reporting revenue in the second half of 2000.

### Other Marketing Services

**34**   Valassis also offered services to assist customers in planning, executing, and evaluating the success of their promotions. Research Services obtained and provided industry research on coupon distribution and redemption trends and competitive activity. TACTest was a program allowing quick testing of multiple promotion options using split market runs in nine test markets. Media Services provided analysis of current market coverage and competitive activity, and identified high opportunity areas.

### Discontinued Operations

**35**   Effective January 2000, Valassis closed Carole Martin Gifts, an unprofitable Canadian mail order business, part of a 1995 acquisition. Previous divestitures included a discontinued joint venture, Valassis de Mexico in 1997, and Valassis France also in 1997.

# VALASSIS OPERATIONS

### Production and Procurement

**36**   Valassis printed its own FSIs at three facilities located in Livonia, Michigan (225,000 square feet); Wichita, Kansas (138,000 square feet); and Durham, North Carolina (110,000 square feet). The company believed that in-house printing provided an advantage in quality control. Pre-press operations (preparing customers' materials for printing) were located in Plymouth, Michigan, near the Livonia facility.

**37**   Valassis claimed to be the low-cost producer in the industry, due to its efforts to lower the three largest components of cost of goods sold:

- Paper (41%)
- Media (fees paid to newspapers to insert coupons) (36%)
- Printing (23%.)

**38**   Valassis purchased primarily one type of paper (coated groundwood No. 5 sheet) from three primary suppliers. During 1999, Valassis negotiated multiple-year contracts for 75 percent of paper requirements, preventing prices from varying more than 6 to 10 percent in a 12-month period. Remaining paper requirements were purchased on 3 to 6 month contracts. On average, the company maintained less than 30 days paper inventory.

**39**   In 1995 and 1996, paper prices fluctuated dramatically, increasing nearly 70 percent in 1995, before returning in early 1997 to 1994 levels. Prices increased less dramatically in 1997 and the first half of 1998, and decreased during the second half of 1998 and throughout 1999. Management expected flat paper prices in 2000 due to favorable supply conditions.

**40**   Media costs were driven by the size of FSI inserts and contract terms. The average size of FSI booklets increased in 1998 and 1999, reducing the cost per coupon due to distribution efficiencies. Valassis was the sixth largest buyer of newspaper space in the United States. This position helped to negotiate lower contract prices. FSIs were estimated to represent 5 to 8 percent of newspaper revenue, and were an important reason consumers subscribed to Sunday newspapers.[5]

**41**   Valassis had decreased printing costs annually for 11 years through investment in new technology that also improved customer service. For example, in October 1999 the company produced its first variable data printing job on a web printing press for T.G.I. Friday's® Restaurant System. The variable data using Valassis' proprietary Aztec Code included the customer's address, address of the closest restaurant, the customer's dining points, and a promotional offer. The company reported that very few U.S. printers used a web press system for this type of application. Ron Goolsby, Vice President, Livonia Printing Division, explained:

> Providing more valuable products and services to our clients is always one of our goals at Valassis. With this upgrade in printing technology, we have the capability to shorten the make ready and production time of a 750,000-piece job, from three weeks to just 24 hours.

**42**   The pre-press operation was in the process of converting to a full digital workflow, using state-of-the-art computer-to-plate technology. This technology enabled increased efficiency, sharper images, and reduced turnaround time. The company planned to spend approximately $15 million each year for the next 3 to 5 years to increase printing capacity and replace or rebuild equipment as required.

[5]Cohen, B. & Settles, R. "Free standing coupon inserts: walking or running to electronic channels?" http://www.digitaledge.org/monthly/2001_02/coupons/coupons101.html.

## Sales

**43**  Valassis operated 10 regional sales offices in Atlanta, Boston, Chicago, Dallas, Livonia, Los Angeles, Minneapolis, Montreal, Toronto, and Wilton, Connecticut. Account managers from various product lines served customers in teams, using a consultative selling approach, helping customers choose the right markets, media, and designs to meet their marketing objectives. A significant portion of revenue was from repeat business.

**44**  FSI customers were billed 75 percent of each order 8 weeks before publication and the balance immediately prior to publication. These progress billings were shown on the balance sheet as a current liability and recognized as revenue when published.

## Finance

**45**  Valassis did not pay cash dividends, but was actively repurchasing common stock. The firm had recently announced a third consecutive 5-million share common stock repurchase program, and planned to allocate at least half of future cash flow to share repurchases. Schultz explained the rationale for this program:

> Repurchasing our stock has been an excellent investment and has enhanced shareholder value. We continue to believe share repurchase is one of the most efficient uses of our substantial cash flow. The new authorization also demonstrates our strong confidence in the future.

**46**  The company also restructured long-term debt in 1999, lowering interest expense by approximately $8 million. Over the past four years, the firm expended a total of $426 million on share repurchase and debt reduction.

**47**  The company completed a 3-for-2 stock split effective May 13, 1999, in the form of a 50 percent stock dividend. Schultz explained the rationale for a stock split:

> The board of directors has determined that a desirable trading range for our stock is between $30 to $50 per share. Based on the consumer orientation of our products, we want our stock to be a reasonable purchase for individual investors.

**48**  On September 2, 1999, the company adopted a "Shareholder Rights Plan." The plan involved declaring a dividend of one Preferred Stock Purchase Right for each outstanding share of the Company's common stock. The Rights would be exercisable only if a person or group not approved by the Board of Directors acquired 15 percent or more of Valassis' common stock or announced a tender offer for 15 percent or more of the common stock. (Exhibit 12 contains board composition.) Schultz explained the purpose of the plan:

> The Rights are intended to enable all of our shareholders to realize the long-term value of their investment in Valassis. The Rights do not prevent a proxy contest or a takeover, but should encourage anyone seeking to acquire Valassis to negotiate with the Board prior to attempting a takeover.

## Human Resource Management

**49**  Valassis employed over 1,600 employees across the United States and Canada. The majority of employees were involved in manufacturing (64 percent), with the rest in sales and marketing (23 percent), MIS, and administration (12 percent). None of the employees were represented by unions (unusual in Southeast Michigan.) In 1999, Valassis was named one of *Fortune* magazine's "100 Best Companies to Work for in America" for the fourth consecutive year, moving to the No. 26 position from No. 37 in 1998 (Exhibit 13). *Working Mother* magazine also named Valassis to its 1999 list of "100 Best Companies for Working Mothers," and *Crain's Detroit Business* identified Valassis as one of the "Best Places to Work in Southeast Michigan."

**EXHIBIT 12**
**Valassis' Board of Directors**

Source: *Proxy statement* 4/12/2000 and 1999 *Annual Report,*

| Director/Affiliation | Age | Date Appointed to Directorship |
|---|---|---|
| *Alan F. Schultz*<br>Chairman, President and CEO, Valassis Communications, Inc. | 41 | December 1995 |
| *Richard N. Anderson*<br>Executive Vice President, Manufacturing and Purchasing, Valassis Communications, Inc. | 54 | December 1998 |
| *Patrick F. Brennan*<br>Retired President and CEO, Consolidated Papers, Inc. (paper manufacturer) | 68 | August 1998 |
| *Seth Goldstein*<br>Entrepreneur-in-Residence and Principal, Flatiron Partners (an Internet venture capital firm) | 29 | March 1999 |
| *Brian J. Husselbee*<br>President and CEO, NCH NuWorld Marketing Limited (coupon clearinghouse) | 48 | August 1998 |
| *Joseph E. Laird, Jr.*<br>Co-founder, Chairman and CEO, Laird Squared, LLC (investment bank specializing in database information industry) | 54 | June 1999 |
| *Robert L. Recchia*<br>Executive Vice President and CFO, Valassis Communications, Inc. | 43 | October 1991 |
| *Marcella A. Sampson*<br>Retired Dean of Students and Director of Career Services, Central State University, Ohio | 69 | August 1998 |
| *Ambassador Faith Whittlesey*<br>Chairman and President, American Swiss Foundation; President, Maybrook Associates, Inc.; Former U.S. Ambassador to Switzerland and member of Senior White House Staff | 61 | January 1992 |

**EXHIBIT 13**  *Fortune*'s "100 Best Companies To Work For"

| Year Ranked | Position in Ranking | Number of Employees (U.S./Outside U.S.) | Percent Women | Percent Minorities | Job growth | Voluntary Turnover (previous year) | Average Training hrs./year/ employee |
|---|---|---|---|---|---|---|---|
| 1999 | 26 | 1357 /69 | 51% | 11% | 15% | 5% | 58 |
| 1998 | 37 | 1274/ 221 | 49 | 9 | 4 | 8 | 58 |
| 1997 | 67 | 1182/ 56 | 47 | 8 | (8) | 10 | 53 |

Source: *Fortune,* 1/10/00, 1/11/99, 1/12/98.

**50**      Valassis offered a number of programs to help employees balance home and work. Some of the more unusual programs included paid paternity leave, back-up child care, Gourmet to Go (meals ordered by 10 A.M., delivered by 4 P.M.), Wheels on Loan when personal vehicles were being repaired, employee discounts for household cleaning services, and dry cleaning and hair salon on site. Marcia Hyde, Vice President of Human Resources, empha-sized the value of the company's focus on work/life balance issues.

> Our employee work/life balance program is a win-win situation. Employees are at their most innovative and productive when they aren't feeling pulled from their families due to the pressures of everyday life. We go the extra mile to make their lives simpler, and the pay-off is happier employees who stay with Valassis for long, full careers.

51    Another area where Valassis continued to invest was employee education. The Valassis Learning Network included training programs for new employee orientation, understand-ing the business, personal productivity, leadership development, and life management de-velopment. Family members could also take courses ranging from baby-sitting skills to interviewing techniques and public speaking. Employee children received high school graduation gifts from the company.

52    In the area of health and wellness programs, the company provided on-site fitness facil-ities, an on-site doctor, "Doctor On-Line" to answer medical questions, and a resource and referral service.

53    Compensation included profit sharing and team achievement bonus plans covering all salaried and hourly employees.

# COMPETITORS

54    Valassis shared the FSI market evenly with one direct competitor, News America Market-ing. Other competitors included companies that distributed coupons in other ways, for ex-ample by direct mail (Val-Pak Direct Marketing Systems), in-store at checkout, or at the shelf (Catalina Marketing), and over the Internet. Exhibit 14 contains information about major competitors. Valassis also competed with all other media for the advertising and pro-motion budgets of manufacturers and retailers. Exhibit 15 shows 1999 advertising expen-ditures by media.

### News America

55    News America was the U.S. operating division of The News Corporation Ltd., Rupert Mur-doch's huge media and entertainment conglomerate. News Corp.'s empire encompassed

**EXHIBIT 14**
**Valassis Competitors (U.S. $ millions)**

*Sources:* www.sec.gov (EDGAR online); www.newscorp.com; www.coxenterprises.com; *Printing News* (6/19/00), printingnews.com/pages/issues/2000; www.datatrak.com/BGFDatat.pdf; forbes.com (Forbes 500 Largest Private Companies- 1998, 1999); www.transnationale.org; www.hoovers.com; www.sunflowergroup.com; Cohen, M., Durchslag, S. & Goldstein, L. "Valassis, Sunflower in Discovery" *Promo*, August 1999, The Law, ISSN: 1047–1707.

| Company | Ownership | Year Founded | 1999 Revenue | 1999 Net Income | 1998 Revenue | 1998 Net Income |
|---|---|---|---|---|---|---|
| News Corp. Ltd.* | public | 1997* | $13,585 | $678 | $12,641 | $1,140 |
| Cox Enterprises Inc. | family | 1898 | 3,378 | N/A | 3,130 | N/A |
| International Data | private/public | 1964 | 2,560 | N/A | 2,060 | N/A |
| Big Flower Holdings | private† | 1992†† | 1,800 | N/A | 1,740 | 38 |
| ADVO, Inc. | public | 1929 | 1,040 | 39 | 1,047 | 36 |
| Valassis | public | 1970 | 795 | 114 | 741 | 71 |
| Catalina Mktg Corp. | public | 1983 | 265 | 37 | 217 | 33 |
| Sunflower Group | private | 1964 | 80e | N/A | 67e | N/A |

*Parent of News America. News America Marketing was created in 1997 by combining News Corp's existing FSI business with ACTMEDIA. Magazines/Inserts business was 10% of News Corp. revenue in 1999.

†BFG was acquired by Vertis, Inc., a private investor group in 2000.

††BFG was founded in 1992/93 to acquire Treasure Chest Advertising, founded in 1967.

**EXHIBIT 15**
U.S. Advertising
By Medium–1999
($ Millions)

Source: *Advertising Age,*
September 25, 2000, p. S4.

| Medium | Expenditures |
|---|---|
| Magazine | $15,529.9 |
| Sunday magazine | 1,111.4 |
| Newspaper | 17,844.1 |
| National newspaper | 3,332.2 |
| Outdoor | 1,993.8 |
| Network TV | 18,003.1 |
| Spot TV | 15,387.0 |
| Syndicated TV | 2,996.2 |
| Cable TV | 8,754.6 |
| Network radio | 463.5 |
| Spot radio | 2,373.2 |
| Internet | 1,940.0 |
| Yellow Pages | 12,652.0 |
| Total Measured | $102,381.0 |
| Total Unmeasured* | $112,920.1 |
| Total Advertising | $215,301.1 |

*Unmeasured media include direct mail, promotion, co-op, couponing, catalogs, business and farm publications, special events, and other.

newspapers, magazines, book publishers, paper manufacturing, television broadcasting, movie production, TV and cable stations, and the Los Angeles Dodgers. News America's portfolio of products sharing the SmartSource™ brand included FSIs, in-store advertising, at-shelf couponing, sampling, and demonstration events. News America had recently announced minority investments in Planet U (expert in Internet electronic couponing,) and SoftCard Systems (provider of incentive programs aimed at frequent shoppers).

56    Sullivan Marketing, Inc. had attempted unsuccessfully to enter the FSI market in November 1993. Sullivan claimed that Valassis and News America violated antitrust laws by operating as a duopoly from 1988 until 1992. In February 1994, Sullivan exited the market by transferring its contracts and sales agreements to News America.

### Cox Enterprises

57    Cox Enterprises, Inc. was another media conglomerate containing businesses that competed with Valassis. These included Carol Wright, Val Pak Direct Marketing Systems (direct mail coupons), and Cox Sampling (solo direct mail sampling). Val-Pak launched its own online website in 1999, using its database of over 30,000 coupons. Coupons for selected areas could be printed off the website, or shoppers could register for email delivery of coupons in selected categories. Val-Pak had announced an alliance with Catalina Marketing's Supermarkets Online to provide co-branded web pages. This alliance promised consumers easy access to local and national coupon offers. Cox Enterprises also comprised newspapers, book publishing, telecommunications, television and radio, and auctions, among other businesses.

### Catalina Marketing

58    Catalina Marketing Services, a unit of Catalina Marketing Corporation marketed Checkout Coupon® and other electronic marketing programs to supermarkets and mass-merchandisers. Its scanner coupons cost about $90 per thousand people reached (versus $6 to 7 per thousand for FSI coupons), but prompted redemption rates of 9 percent (versus 3 percent for FSI.)[6] In 2000, Catalina had over 13,500 U.S. stores in its network, plus over 2,000 in Europe and almost 400 through a Japanese joint venture.

[6]Thomas, P. (*Wall Street Journal*) "Web trade-off: personal profile for market savings; coupons tailored to family shopper," reported in *The Arizona Republic*, 6/23/98, Business, p. E4.

59    Due to its extensive store network, Catalina's Supermarkets Online was the leader in Internet couponing. ValuePage® was accepted in over 11,500 supermarkets within the Catalina Marketing Network. Coupons were provided by email, based on consumer buying preferences, and manufacturers were charged only for redeemed coupons, at a lower price than Catalina's scanner coupons. However, Supermarkets Online was not yet profitable.

60    Catalina was pursuing other alliances besides the one with Val-Pak. It entered a joint venture with ACNielsen to combine Catalina's frequent shopper data and Nielsen's consumer data to provide information to manufacturers and retailers. In March 2000, it announced an alliance with MyPoints.com, a provider of Internet direct marketing services to jointly market online direct marketing and loyalty solutions. PCData Online ranked MyPoints a top-ten Internet shopping site in January 2000.

### Other Competitors

61    Valassis competed with numerous other companies in specific segments of its business. ADVO, Inc. provided direct mail services such as ShopWise™ and the Missing Child card program. Sunflower Group specialized in sampling. Big Flower Holdings included Treasure Chest Advertising, the nation's largest printer of advertising circulars and inserts, plus TV listings and Sunday comics. International Data provided consumer promotions management services including promotion analysis, coupon processing and redemption, direct mail, and sampling. Its online database, BrandData™, offered information about the success rates of coupons and competitors' coupons.

62    Valassis was also witnessing new market entry through forward and backward integration. For example, in January 2000, Kraft Foods announced an alliance with Meredith Corporation, a large magazine publisher, and News America Corp. The alliance would produce "Food & Family," a custom-published insert to replace Kraft's spending on co-op FSIs. The publication was planned to appear monthly, through newspaper distribution, and include articles and recipes in addition to coupons for Kraft brands. Another example was NCH NuWorld Marketing Ltd., primarily a provider of coupon processing and marketing information services. However, in August 1999, NCH announced a license agreement with Evolve Products, Inc., a producer of hand-held display remote controls, to develop in-home coupon distribution through cable television. Newspapers were also getting into the online coupon business. For example, Nando Media, a division of McClatchy Newspapers, had allied with NetValue Inc. to offer major retailers online coupons.

## VALASSIS' E-COMMERCE STRATEGY

63    Valassis responded to the growth of Internet usage and increased competition in the coupon industry by developing a three-pronged E-commerce strategy:

• Selling traditional media products to Internet companies
• Delivering coupons online
• Investing in the online grocery business.

### Selling to Internet Companies

64    The first part of the e-commerce strategy was to sell its traditional offline media (e.g., FSIs and sampling) to online companies. The company's research indicated that 56 percent of FSI readers used the Internet and 63 percent of "wired" FSI readers had visited a website that they had seen listed in print advertising such as a magazine or newspaper. One example of this approach was "Surf and Save," a special FSI section featuring E-commerce companies. Suzie Brown explained the potential for this segment:

These rapidly emerging companies are looking for effective tools to increase web traffic. Our products, such as the FSI, and our targeted marketing services provide effective and efficient new ways for e-commerce marketers to get in front of millions of consumers every week. With the introduction of so many e-commerce sites, it's incredibly important for them to differentiate themselves and gain critical mass in their respective categories. Even the most fabulous on-line shopping experience can't be successful if nobody knows where to find it.

**65**  In October 1999, Valassis added to its own "Surf and Save" product by acquiring The Net's Best (TNB), LLC for $3.9 million, net of cash acquired, plus future payments contingent on performance. The Net's Best, started a year earlier with a $1 million venture capital investment, maintained a website designed for Internet shoppers and produced a newspaper-delivered FSI sold to companies doing business on the Internet. Valassis intended to maintain the name, The Net's Best, while merging the acquired company's six employees with Valassis' FSI operations. In 2000 Valassis planned to publish 12 co-op e-commerce inserts and 12 targeted solo e-commerce inserts, reaching 29 million households. Suzie Brown explained the objective of the acquisition:

> This acquisition will allow us to expedite our growth plans. Valassis will compliment the TNB FSI with our co-op FSI, polybag advertising, direct mail, and other media capabilities. Our goal is to be the premier provider of marketing services to the Internet and e-commerce industries, and this acquisition brings us that much closer to the goal.

### Delivering Coupons Online

**66**  The second part of Valassis' E-commerce strategy was to expand into online coupons. It implemented this strategy through strategic investments and alliances. The first move in 1999 was to purchase 51 percent of Merge, LLC, renamed Save.com, an online coupon and promotion network.

**67**  Save.com was a network approach to online couponing, where coupons could be delivered to consumers at their favorite websites as well as on the Save.com site. The software would also permit delivery through CD ROMs, and installation on original computer equipment. A proprietary scanner code (Aztec code) provided security and maintained consumer profile data.

**68**  After a successful pilot test in September 1999, Valassis planned a national roll out in the second quarter of 2000. The test ran in two markets on seven participating websites, featuring over 130 national brands. Of all coupons viewed, 30 percent were selected (the "click" rate) compared to an industry average rate for banner advertisements of only 0.4 percent. Of those coupons clicked, 69 percent were printed. Suzie Brown was pleased with the results and optimistic about the future of online coupons:

> The high level of registration and downloads attests, once again, to consumers' insatiable appetite for value, particularly when it's this easy to do. As more and more families become wired, Save.com will become a daily tradition, just as Sunday free-standing inserts have been a weekly American tradition for decades.

**69**  In May 2000, Save.com purchased two websites, MyCoupons.com and DirectCoupons.com, from DirectStuff.com for an undisclosed amount of cash and a 2-year marketing alliance. Valassis estimated the value of the total deal at $23 million. As part of the marketing alliance, DirectStuff.com would continue to manage both sites, as well as Save.com's website. MyCoupons.com was a consumer site that provided coupons, and DirectCoupons.com was a weekly email publication with 450,000 subscribers. DirectStuff.com was started in 1994, and offered its first coupon website in 1995. By 2000, the company had 22 employees and three divisions, Advertising Network (online advertising), Publications Network (email publications for coupons and recipes) and Gift Certificate Network.

**70**     In addition to the Save.com equity investment, in April 2000, Valassis announced a strategic alliance with Coupons.com, a privately held company that delivered coupons directly to consumers over the Internet.

### Investing in Online Groceries

**71**     The third part of Valassis' E-commerce strategy was to participate in the growth of the online grocery business. It implemented this strategy through a strategic investment by acquiring 54 percent of Independent Delivery Services (IDS), a subsidiary of Dawick Enterprises, in 1999. IDS provided the technology for existing supermarkets to enter the online grocery business. Alan Schultz, Valassis' President, discussed the rationale for this investment:

> The potential for this service is huge. We believe that the traditional grocery store, who already has a relationship with the consumer, will ultimately win the battle for online grocery shoppers. The IDS service is what traditional grocery chains need to successfully migrate into Internet selling and compete with start-up e-commerce grocery companies. It is our intention to provide grocery retailers with a variety of products and services to build customer loyalty. The investment in IDS helps put Valassis in direct contact with retailers, who play a critical role in one-to-one relationship marketing. Not only does this investment move forward our Internet initiatives, it is also another step toward a comprehensive customer attainment and retention system.

**72**     One example of an enhanced service was a recent partnership between IDS and BeeLine Shopper.com to help consumers with special diet or nutritional needs develop their shopping lists. Dawn Dawick, President and CEO of IDS, was also enthusiastic about the partnership:

> IDS's market leadership and retail relationships, combined with Valassis' marketing expertise and relationships with major consumer package goods companies, will allow us to create the WIN-WIN-WIN all the way down the channel.

**73**     Valassis also sought synergies across its online and offline businesses. For example, it had recently announced the intention to use the small "white space" at the top of each page of FSIs to deliver banner messages promoting the company's online products and services. The Independent Delivery Services (IDS) investment was expected to enhance the retailer relationships being developed by the Customer Relationship Marketing Group (CRMG.)

**74**     Valassis reported $4.4 million in e-sales during the first quarter of 2000 and predicted a total for the year of $20 million. Schultz and Brown were pleased with their results so far. But had they gone far enough to compete in an online world and meet the expectations of their customers and investors? Or were they moving too quickly, investing in areas with unknown profit potential? What challenges did their e-commerce strategy pose for their bread-and-butter FSI business? Was the organization equipped to handle the revolution underway?

# Case 44  Pacific Cataract and Laser Institute: Competing in the LASIK Eye Surgery Market

## John J. Lawrence, and Linda J. Morris

**1**   Dr. Mark Everett, clinic coordinator and Optometric Physician (OP) of the Pacific Cataract and Laser Institute (PCLI) office in Spokane, Washington, looked at the ad that Vancouver, Canada–based Lexington Laser Vision (LLV) had been running in the Spokane papers and shook his head. This was not the first ad nor the only clinic advertising low-priced LASIK eye surgeries. Dr. Everett just could not believe that doctors would advertise and sell laser eye surgery based on low price as if it were a stereo or a used car. The fact that they were advertising based on price was bad enough, but the price they were promoting—$900 for both eyes—was ridiculous. PCLI and its cooperating optometric physicians would not even cover their variable cost if they performed the surgery at that price. A typical PCLI customer paid between $1750 and $2000 per eye for corrective laser surgery. While Dr. Everett knew that firms in Canada had several inherent cost advantages, including a favorable exchange rate and regulatory environment, he could not understand how they could undercut PCLI's price so much without compromising service quality.

**2**   PCLI was a privately held company that operated a total of 11 clinics throughout the northwestern United States and provided a range of medical and surgical eye treatments including laser vision correction. Responding to the challenge of the Canadian competitors was one of the points that would be discussed when Dr. Everett and the other clinic coordinators and surgeons who ran PCLI met next month to discuss policies and strategy. Dr. Everett strongly believed that the organization's success was based on surgical excellence and compassioned concern for its patients and the doctors who referred them. PCLI strived to provide the ultimate in patient care and consideration. Dr. Everett had joined PCLI in 1993 in large part because of how impressed he had been at how PCLI treated its patients, and he remained committed to this patient-focused value.

**3**   He was concerned, however, about his organization's ability to attract laser vision correction patients. He knew that many prospective PCLI customers would be swayed by the low prices and would travel to Canada to have the procedure performed, especially since most medical insurance programs covered only a small portion of the cost of this procedure. Dr. Everett believed strongly that PCLI achieved better results and provided a higher quality service experience than the clinics in Canada offering low-priced LASIK procedures. He also felt PCLI did a much better job of helping potential customers determine which of several procedures, if any, best met the customers' long-term vision needs. Dr. Everett wondered what PCLI should do to win over these potential customers—both for the good of the customers and for the good of PCLI.

Source: This case was prepared by the authors for the sole purpose of providing material for class discussion. It is not intended to illustrate either effective or ineffective handling of a managerial situation. The authors thank Dr. Mark Everett for his cooperation and assistance with this project. Reprinted by permission from the *Case Research Journal*, volume 22, issue 3. Copyright © 2002 by the *Case Research Journal*, John J. Lawrence, and Linda J. Morris. All rights reserved.

# PACIFIC CATARACT AND LASER INSTITUTE

**4**    Pacific Cataract and Laser Institute (PCLI) was founded in 1985 by Dr. Robert Ford and specialized in medical and surgical eye treatment. The company was headquartered in Chehalis, Washington, and operated clinics in Washington, Oregon, Idaho, and Alaska (see Exhibit 1 for a map of PCLI locations). In addition to laser vision correction, PCLI provided cataract surgery, glaucoma consultation and surgery, corneal transplants, retinal care and surgery, and eyelid surgery. Dr. Ford founded PCLI on the principle that doctors must go beyond science and technology to practice the art of healing through the Christian principles of love, kindness, and compassion. The organization had defined eight core values that were based on these principles. These core values, shown in Exhibit 2, guided PCLI's decision making as it attempted to fulfill its stated mission of providing the best possible "co-managed" services to the profession of optometry.

**EXHIBIT 1**    **Map Showing PCLI Clinic Locations (Clinics designated by a ◆; Anchorage, AK clinic not shown)**

**EXHIBIT 2**
**Pacific Cataract and Laser Institute's Core Values**

- We believe patients' families and friends provide important support and we encourage them to be as involved as possible in our care of their loved ones.
- We believe patients and their families have a right to honest and forthright medical information presented in a manner they can understand.
- We believe that a calm, caring, and cheerful environment minimizes patient stress and the need for artificial sedation.
- We believe that all our actions should be guided by integrity, honesty, and courage.
- We believe that true success comes from doing the right things for the right reasons.
- We believe that efficient, quality eye care is provided best by professionals practicing at the highest level of their expertise.
- We believe that communicating openly and sharing knowledge with our optometric colleagues is crucial to providing outstanding patient care.
- We believe that the ultimate measure of our success is the complete satisfaction of the doctors who entrust us with the care of their patients.

5   Co-management involved PCLI working closely with a patient's optometrists, or OD (for Doctor of Optometry). In co-managed eye care, family ODs were the primary care eye doctors who diagnosed, treated, and managed certain diseases of the eye that did not require surgery. When surgery was needed, the family OD referred patients to ophthalmologists (e.g., PCLI's eye surgeons) for specialized treatment and surgery. Successful co-management, according to PCLI, depended on a relationship of mutual trust and respect built through shared learning, constant communication, and commitment to providing quality patient care. PCLI's co-management arrangements did not restrict ODs to working with just PCLI, although PCLI sought out ODs who would use PCLI as their primary surgery partner and who shared PCLI's values. Many ODs did work exclusively with PCLI unless a specific patient requested otherwise. PCLI-Spokane had developed a network of 150 family ODs in its region.

6   PCLI operated its 11 clinics in a very coordinated manner. It had seven surgeons that specialized in the various forms of eye surgery. These surgeons, each accompanied by several surgical assistants, traveled from center to center to perform specific surgeries. The company owned two aircraft that were used to fly the surgical teams between the centers. Each clinic had a resident optometric physician who served as that clinic's coordinator and essentially managed the day-to-day operations of the clinic. Each clinic also employed its own office support staff. PCLI's main office in Chehalis, Washington, also employed patient counselors who worked with the referring family ODs for scheduling the patient's surgery and a finance team to help patients with medical insurance claims and any financing arrangements (which were made through third-party sources). Dr. Everett was the Spokane clinic's resident optometric physician and managed the day-to-day activities at that clinic. Actual surgeries were performed in the Spokane clinic only one or two days a week, depending on demand and the surgeons' availability.

## LASER EYE SURGERY AND LASIK

7   Laser eye surgery was performed on the eye to create better focus and lessen the patient's dependence on glasses and contact lenses. Excimer lasers were the main means of performing this type of surgery. Although research on the excimer laser began in 1973, it was not until 1985 that excimer lasers were introduced to the ophthalmology community in the United States. The FDA approved the use of excimer lasers for photorefractive keratectomy (PRK) in October, 1995, for the purpose of correcting nearsightedness. PRK entailed using computer-controlled beams of laser light to permanently resculpt the curvature of the eye

by selectively removing a small portion on the outer top surface of the cornea (called epithelium). The epithelium naturally regenerated itself, although eye medication was required for 3 to 4 months after the procedure.

8    In the late 1990s, laser in-situ keratomileusis, or LASIK, replaced PRK as the preferred method to correct or reduce moderate to high levels of nearsightedness (i.e., myopia). The procedure required the surgeon to create a flap in the cornea using a surgical instrument called a microkeratome. This instrument used vacuum suction to hold and position the cornea and a motorized cutting blade to make the necessary incision. The surgeon then used an excimer laser to remove a micro-thin layer of tissue from the exposed, interior corneal surface (as opposed to removing a thin layer of tissue on the outer surface of the cornea as was the case with PRK). The excimer laser released a precisely focused beam of low-temperature, invisible light. Each laser pulse removed less than one hundred-thousandth of an inch. After the cornea had been reshaped, the flap was replaced. The actual surgical procedure took only about 5 minutes per eye. LASIK surgery allowed a patient to eliminate the regular use of glasses or contact lenses although many patients still required reading glasses.

9    While LASIK used the same excimer laser that had been approved for other eye surgeries in the United States by the Ophthalmic Devices Panel of the FDA, it was not an approved procedure in the United States, but was under study. LASIK was offered by clinics in the United States, but was considered an "off-label" use of the laser. "Off label" was a phrase given to medical services and supplies which had not been thoroughly tested by the FDA, but which the FDA permitted to be performed and provided by a licensed medical professional. Prescribing aspirin as a blood thinner to reduce the risk of stroke was another example of an off-label use of a medical product—the prescribing of aspirin for this purpose did not have formal FDA approval but was permitted by the FDA.

10    The LASIK procedure was not without some risks. Complications arose in about 5 percent of all cases, although experienced surgeons had complication rates of less than 2 percent. According to the American Academy of Ophthalmology, complications and side effects included: irregular astigmatism, resulting in a decrease in best corrected vision; glare; corneal haze; over-correction; under-correction; inability to wear contact lenses; loss of the corneal cap, requiring a corneal graft; corneal scarring and infection; and in an extremely rare number of cases, loss of vision. If lasering were not perfect, a patient might develop haze in the cornea. This could make it impossible to achieve 20/20 vision, even with glasses. The flap could also heal improperly, causing fuzzy vision. Infections were also occasionally an issue.

11    While PRK and LASIK were the main types of eye surgery currently performed to reduce a patient's dependence on glasses or contact lenses, there were new surgical procedures and technologies that were in the test stage that could receive approval in the United States within the next three to ten years. These included intraocular lenses that were implanted behind a patient's cornea, laser thermokeratoplasty (LTK) and conductive keratoplasty (CK) that used heat to reshape the cornea, and "custom" LASIK technologies that could better measure and correct the total optics of the eye. These newer methods had the potential to improve vision even more than LASIK and some of these new processes also might allow additional corrections to be made to the eye as the patient aged. Intraocular lenses were already widely available in Europe.

## LASIK MARKET POTENTIAL

12    The market potential for LASIK procedures was very significant and the market was just beginning to take off. According to officials of the American Academy of Ophthalmology, over 150 million people wore glasses or contact lenses in the United States. About 12 mil-

lion of these people were candidates for current forms of refractive surgery. As procedures were refined to cover a wider range of vision conditions, and as the FDA approved new procedures, the number of people who could have their vision improved surgically was expected to grow to over 60 million. As many as 1.7 million people in the United States were expected to have some form of laser eye surgery during 2000, compared to 500,000 in 1999 and 250,000 in 1998. Laser eye repair was the most frequently performed surgery in all of medicine.

13    Referrals were increasingly playing a key role in the industry's growth. Surgeons estimated that the typical patient referred five friends, and that as many as 75 percent of new patients had been referred by a friend. A few employers were also beginning to offer laser eye surgery benefits through managed care vision plans. These plans offered discounts from list prices of participating surgeons and clinics to employees. Vision Service Plan's (VSP) partners, for example, gave such discounts and guaranteed a maximum price of $1,800 per eye for VSP members. The number of people eligible for such benefits was expected to grow significantly in the coming years. PCLI did not participate in these plans and did not offer such discounts.

### LASIK at PCLI

14    The process of providing LASIK surgery to patients at PCLI began with the partnering OD. The OD provided the patient with information about LASIK and PCLI, reviewed the treatment options available, and answered any questions the patient might have concerning LASIK or PCLI. If a patient was interested in having the surgery performed, the OD performed a pre-exam to make sure the patient was a suitable candidate for the surgery. Assuming the patient was able to have the surgery, the OD made an appointment for the patient with PCLI and forwarded the results of the pre-exam to Dr. Everett. PCLI had a standard surgical fee of $1400 per eye for LASIK. Each family OD added on additional fees for pre- and post-operative exams depending on the number of visits per patient and the OD's costs. Most of the ODs charged $700 to $1,200, making the total price of laser surgery to the patient between $3,500 to $4,000. This total price was presented to the patient rather than two separate service fees.

15    Once a patient arrived at PCLI, an ophthalmic assistant measured the patient's range of vision and took a topographical reading of the eyes. Dr. Everett would then explain the entire process to the patient and discuss the possible risks and have the patient read and sign an informed consent form. The patient would then meet the surgeon and have any final questions answered. The meeting with the surgeon was also intended to reduce any anxiety that the patient might have regarding the procedure. The surgical procedure itself took less than 15 minutes to perform. After the surgery was completed, the patient was told to rest his/her eyes for a few hours and was given dark glasses and eye drops. The patient was required to either return to PCLI or to his or her family OD 24 hours after their surgery for a follow-up exam. Additional follow-up exams were required at one week, one month, three months, six months, and one year to make sure the eyes healed properly and to ensure that any problems were caught quickly. The patient's family OD performed all of these follow-up exams.

16    Three of PCLI's seven surgeons specialized in LASIK and related procedures. The company's founder, Dr. Robert Ford, had performed over 16,000 LASIK procedures during his career, more than any other surgeon in the Northwest. His early training was as a physicist, and he was very interested in and knowledgeable about the laser technology used to perform LASIK procedures. Because of this interest and understanding, Dr. Ford was an industry innovator and had developed a number of procedural enhancements that were unique to PCLI. Dr. Ford had developed an enhanced software calibration system for PCLI's lasers that was better than the system provided by the laser manufacturers.

17    More significantly, Dr. Ford had also developed a system to track eye movements. Using superimposed live and saved computer images of the eye, PCLI surgeons could achieve improved eye alignment to provide more accurate laser resculpting of the eye. Dr. Ford was working with Laser Sight, a laser equipment manufacturer developing what PCLI and many others viewed as the next big technological step in corrective eye surgery—custom LASIK. Custom LASIK involved developing more detailed corneal maps and then using special software to convert these maps into a program that would run a spot laser to achieve theoretically perfect corrections of the cornea. This technology was currently in clinical trials in an effort to gain FDA approval of the technology, and Dr. Ford and PCLI were participating in these trials. Although Dr. Ford was on the leading edge of technology and had vast LASIK surgical experience, very few of PCLI's patients were aware of his achievements.

**Competition**

18    PCLI in Spokane faced stiff competition from clinics in both the United States and Canada. There were basically three types of competitors. There were general ophthalmology practices that also provided LASIK surgeries, surgery centers like PCLI that provided a range of eye surgeries, and specialized LASIK clinics that focused solely on LASIK surgeries.

19    General ophthalmology practices provided a range of services covering a patient's basic eye care needs. They performed general eye exams, monitored the health of patients' eyes, and wrote prescriptions for glasses and contact lenses. Most general ophthalmology practices did not perform LASIK surgeries (or any other types of surgeries) because of the high cost of the equipment and the special training needed to perform the surgery, but a few did. These clinics were able to offer patients a continuity of care that surgery centers and centers specializing solely in LASIK surgeries could not. Customers could have all pre- and post-operative exams performed at the same location by the same doctor. In the Spokane market, a clinic called Eye Consultants was the most aggressive competitor of this type. This organization advertised heavily in the local newspaper, promoting a price of $1,195 per eye (see Exhibit 3). The current newspaper promotion invited potential customers to a free LASIK seminar put on by the clinic's staff, and seminar attendees who chose to have the procedure qualified for the $1,195 per eye price, which was a $300 per eye discount from the clinic's regular price.

20    Surgery centers did not provide for patient's basic eye care needs, but rather specialized in performing eye surgeries. These centers provided a variety of eye surgeries, including such procedures as cataract surgeries and LASIK surgeries in addition to other specialty eye surgeries. PCLI was this type of a clinic. The other surgery center of this type in the Spokane area was Empire Eye. PCLI viewed Empire Eye as its most formidable competitor in the immediate geographic area. Empire Eye operated in a similar way as PCLI. It relied heavily on referrals from independent optometric physicians, did not advertise aggressively, and did not attempt to win customers with low prices. It did employ a locally based surgeon who performed its LASIK procedures, although this surgeon was not nearly as experienced as Dr. Ford at PCLI.

21    LASIK clinics provided only LASIK or LASIK and PRK procedures. They did not provide for general eye care needs nor did they provide a range of eye surgeries like surgery centers. These clinics generally had much higher volumes of LASIK patients than general ophthalmology or surgery centers, allowing them to achieve much higher utilization of the expensive capital equipment required to perform the surgeries. The capital cost of the equipment to perform the LASIK procedure was about U.S.$500,000.

22    The largest of these firms specializing in LASIK surgeries was TLC Laser Eye Centers, Inc. TLC was based in Mississauga, Ontario, and had 56 clinics in the United States and seven in Canada. During the first quarter of 2000, TLC generated revenues of U.S.$49.3 million by performing 33,000 surgeries. This compared with first quarter of 1999 when the

**EXHIBIT 3** **Eye Consultant's Advertisement**

**Special Offer**

# LASIK

# $1195 PER EYE *

**INCLUDING** pre- and post operative care!

**WHEN: Thursday**
**June 1**
**6:00 p.m.**
**WHERE: Clear Vision**
**Laser Center**
**Quail Run Office Park**
**2200 E. 29th Avenue**
**Suite 110**
**CALL TODAY**
**Seating is Limited**

**See LASIK Live!**

Come to this free LIVE LASIK seminar
to receive this special offer.

*ONLY for seminar attendees who
schedule a procedure within 90 days!

Compare our Quality ~ Compare our Price
**Save $600 on Both Eyes!**

**EYE CONSULTANTS**

The Doctors You Trust
For Excellence
In Local Eye Care

**CALL XXX-XXXX**

company had revenues of U.S. $41.4 million on 25,600 procedures. TLC was the largest LASIK eye surgery company in North America and performed more LASIK surgeries in the United States than any other company. The closest TLC centers to Spokane were in Seattle, Washington, and Vancouver, British Columbia. The second largest provider of LASIK surgeries in the United States was Laser Vision Centers (LVC), based in St. Louis, Missouri. Its closest center to Spokane was also in Seattle.

23    Almost all of the Canadian competitors that had been successful at attracting United States customers were clinics that specialized solely in LASIK surgeries. The largest Canadian competitor was Lasik Vision Corporation (LVC), based in Vancouver, British Columbia. LVC operated 15 clinics in Canada and 14 in the United States, and was growing rapidly. LVC had plans to add another 21 clinics by the end of 2000. During the first quarter of 2000, LVC generated revenues of U.S.$20.1 million by performing 26,673 procedures. This compared to first quarter of 1999, when the company had revenues of only U.S.$4.3 million on 6,300 procedures.

24    In total, there were 13 companies specializing in providing LASIK surgeries in British Columbia, mostly in the Vancouver area. One of the British Columbia firms that advertised most aggressively in the Spokane area was Lexington Laser Vision (LLV). LLV operated a single clinic staffed by nine surgeons and equipped with four lasers. The clinic scheduled surgeries 6 days a week and typically had a 2-month wait for an appointment.

25    The service design process at LLV was designed to accommodate many patients and differed significantly from PCLI's service process. To begin the process, a patient simply called a toll-free number for LLV to schedule a time to have the surgery performed. Once the patient arrived at the LLV clinic he/she received a preoperative examination to assess the patient's current vision and to scan the topography of the patient's eyes. The next day the patient returned to the clinic for the scheduled surgery. The typical sequence was to first meet with a patient counselor who reviewed with the patient all pages of a LASIK information booklet that was sent to the patient following the scheduled surgery date. The patient counselor answered any questions the patient had regarding the information in the booklet, and ensured that the patient signed all necessary surgical consent forms. Following this step, a medical assistant surgically prepped the patient and explained the post-care treatment of the eyes. After this preparation, the surgeon greeted the patient, reviewed the topographical eye charts with the patient, explained the recommended eye adjustments for the patient, and reiterated the surgical procedure once again. The patient would then be transferred to the surgery room where two surgical assistants were available to help the doctor with the five- to ten-minute operation. Once the surgery was completed, a surgical assistant led the patient to a dark, unlit room so that the patient's eyes could adjust. After a 15-minute waiting period, the surgical assistant checked the patient for any discomfort and repeated the instructions for post-care treatment. Barring no problems or discomfort, the surgical assistant would hand the patient a pair of dark, wrap-around sunglasses with instructions to avoid bright lights for the next 24 hours. At the scheduled postoperative exam the next day, a medical technician measured the patient's corrected vision and scheduled any additional postoperative exams. If desired, the patient could return to the clinic for the one-week, one-month, and three-month postoperative exams at either the LLV clinic or one of the U.S.-based partner clinics of LLV. In some cases, the patient opted to have these postoperative exams performed by his/her family OD.

26    U.S. patients traveling to LLV or the other clinics in British Columbia to have the surgery performed needed to allow for three days and two nights for the surgery. A pre-exam to ensure the patient was a suitable candidate for the surgery was performed the first day, the surgery itself was performed the second day, and the 24-hour postexam was performed on the third day. Two nights in a hotel near LLV cost approximately $100U.S. and airfare to Vancouver, British Columbia, Canada cost approximately $150U.S. from Spokane, Washington. Lexington Laser Vision had a sister clinic in the Seattle area where patients could go for postoperative exams. LLV requested patients undergo follow-up exams at one week, one month and three months. These exams were included in the price as long as the patient came to either the Seattle or Vancouver clinics. Some patients outside of the Seattle/Vancouver area arranged with their family ODs to perform these follow-ups at their own expense to avoid the time and cost of traveling to Seattle or Vancouver, British Columbia.

**EXHIBIT 4***    LASIK-related Revenue and Cost Estimates for PCLI's Competitors (all figures are in U.S.$)

| Competitor | Eye Consultants | Empire Eye | TLC Clinic | Lexington Laser Vision† |
|---|---|---|---|---|
| Type of operation | General Ophthalmology Practice | Eye Surgery Center | Specialized LASIK Clinic | Specialized LASIK Clinic |
| Location of operation | Spokane, WA | Spokane, WA | Seattle, WA | Vancouver, B.C. |
| Number of procedures/year | 600 | 1000 | 4000 | 10,000 |
| Price to customer, per eye | $1,195 | $1,900 | $1,600 | $500 |
| Estimated revenues | 717,000 | $1,900,000 | $6,400,000 | $5,000,000 |
| **Estimated expenses** | | | | |
| Payments for pre- and postoperative care†† | 120,000 | 450,000 | 1,400,000 | 1,500,000 |
| Royalties | 150,000 | 250,000 | 1,000,000 | 0 |
| Surgeon's fees/salary | 120,000 | 300,000 | 1,200,000 | 1,500,000 |
| Medical supplies | 30,000 | 50,000 | 200,000 | 500,000 |
| Laser service | 100,000 | 100,000 | 200,000 | 400,000 |
| Depreciation | 125,000 | 125,000 | 250,000 | 500,000 |
| Marketing | 75,000 | 75,000 | 400,000 | 500,000 |
| Overhead | 200,000 | 350,000 | 500,000 | 600,000 |
| Total annual expenses | $925,000 | $1,700,000 | $5,150,000 | $5,500,000 |

*This table was developed based on a variety of public sources on both the LASIK industry in general and on individual competitors. In a number of cases, the figures represent aggregated 'estimates' of data from several sources. Estimated expenses are based largely, but not entirely, on discussion of the LASIK industry cost structure provided in "Eyeing the bottom line: Just who profits from your laser eye surgery may surprise you." by James Pethokoukis, *U.S. News and World Report,* March 30, 1998, pp. 80–82.

†This cost structure was thought to be typical of all of the specialized LASIK clinics located in British Columbia, Canada that competed with PCLI.

††In some cases, these costs are paid directly by the patient to the postoperative care provider, they have been included here because they represent a part of the total price paid by the customer.

27    A breakdown of the estimated cost structure for each of these different competitors is shown in Exhibit 4. Dr. Everett believed that both Eye Consultants and LLV were probably incurring losses. Both were believed to be offering below-cost pricing in response to the significant price competition going on in the industry. Eye Consultants was also believed to be offering below-cost pricing in order to build volume and gain surgeon experience. PCLI's own cost structure was fairly similar to Empire Eye's cost structure, as both operated in a similar fashion.

# THE CANADIAN ADVANTAGE

28    LASIK clinics operating in Canada had a number of advantages that allowed them to charge significantly less than competitors in the United States. First, the Canadian dollar had been relatively weak compared to the U.S. dollar for some time, fluctuating between C$1.45 per U.S. dollar and C$1.50 per U.S. dollar. This exchange rate compared to rates in the early 1990s that fluctuated between C$1.15 per U.S. dollar and C$1.20 per U.S. dollar. On top of this, the inflation rate in Canada averaged only 1.5 percent during the 1990s compared to 2.5 percent in the United States. This dual effect of a weakened Canadian dollar combined with somewhat higher inflation in the United States meant that Canadian providers had, over time, acquired a significant exchange rate cost advantage.

29    Second, laser surgery equipment manufacturers charged a $250 patent royalty fee for each surgery (i.e., each eye) performed in the United States. The legal system in Canada prevented equipment manufacturers from charging such a royalty every time a surgery was performed, amounting to a $500 cost savings per patient for Canadian clinics. Competitive pressure

among surgery equipment manufacturers had caused this fee to drop in recent months to as low as $100 for certain procedures performed on some older equipment in the United States, giving U.S. clinics some hope that this cost disadvantage might decrease over time.

30    Third, clinics in the United States generally paid higher salaries and/or fees to surgeons and support staff than did their Canadian rivals. The nationalized health system in Canada tended to limit what doctors in Canada could earn compared to their peers in the United States. LASIK clinics themselves were not part of the Canadian national health system because they represented elective surgeries. However, Canadian LASIK clinics could pay their surgeons a large premium over what they could make in the nationalized system, but this was still significantly less than a comparable surgeon's earnings in the United States. This cost differential extended to the referring optometrists who provided pre- and postoperative exams and whose fees were typically included in the price quoted to customers. Many Canadian clinics relied more heavily on advertising and word-of-mouth customer referral rather than referrals from optometrists and deemphasized pre- and postoperative exams.

31    Fourth, there was some speculation among U.S. clinics that some low-priced Canadian clinics were making a variety of care-compromising quality trade-offs, such as not performing equipment calibration and maintenance as frequently as recommended by the equipment manufacturers and reusing the microkeratome blades used to make the initial incision in the cornea. Canadian clinics denied that the choices that they made compromised the quality of care received by the patient. Finally, it seemed clear to Dr. Everett that Canadian providers were in the midst of a price war and that at least some of the clinics were not generating any profit at the prices they were charging.

32    Canadian providers also had significant noncost advantages. Because of differences in the approval process of medical equipment and procedures, laser eye surgery technologies were often available in Canada before they became readily available in the United States. Approval of new medical technologies in Canada was often based on evidence from other countries that the technology was safe, whereas approval of new medical technologies in the United States required equipment manufacturers to start from scratch with a series of studies. As a result of this, and combined with the volume that the Canadian clinics' low prices generated, many Canadian clinics had more experience with laser eye surgery than comparable clinics in the United States. Experience was a critical factor in a clinic or specific surgeon having low rates of complications. Further, the differences in the approval processes between the countries allowed Canadian providers the ability to offer advanced equipment not yet available in the United States. For example, the FDA approved the first generation of excimer laser for use in the United States in October of 1995. No centers in Canada, however, had purchased this particular laser since 1995 because more advanced versions of the technology had become available for use in Canada. While some of these equipment advances have had minimal impact on the results for the average patient, they have, at the very least, provided Canadian clinics a marketing advantage.

### U.S. Competitors' Responses to the Canadian Challenge

33    The surgeons and staff at PCLI knew from reading a variety of sources and from following changes in the industry that most U.S.–based clinics were experiencing some loss of customers to Canadian competitors. These companies were responding in a variety of ways in an attempt to keep more patients in the United States. One company in the industry, LCA, had created a low-priced subsidiary, LasikPlus, as a way to compete with lower priced competitors in Canada. LasikPlus had facilities in Maryland and California and charged $2,995 compared to the $5,000 price charged by the parent company's LCA Vision Centers. One way that the LasikPlus subsidiary had cut cost was by employing its own surgeons. Regular LCA Vision Centers provided only the facilities and equipment, and contracted out with independent surgeons to perform the procedures.

**34**     Another strategy that U.S. firms were using to compete was to partner with managed care vision benefits firms, HMOs, and large businesses. TLC Laser Eye Centers had been the most aggressive at using this strategy. It had partnered with Vision Service Plan (VSP) to provide the surgery to VSP members at a $600 discount, and had partnered with HMO Kaiser Permanente to provide Kaiser members a $200 discount. TLC was also attempting to get employers to cover part of the cost for their employees, and was letting participating companies offer a $200 discount on the procedure to their employees. Over 40 businesses had signed up by late 1999, including Southern California Edison, Ernst and Young, and Office Depot. TLC was not the only provider pursuing this strategy. LCA Vision centers had partnered with Cole Managed Vision to provide the surgery to Cole members at a 15 percent discount.

**35**     One of the significant advantages that U.S. providers had over their Canadian competitors was convenience, since patients did not have to travel to Canada to have the procedure performed. Most facilities providing the surgery in the United States, however, were located in major metropolitan areas, which may not be seen as being all that much more convenient for potential patients living in smaller communities and rural areas. One competitor had taken this convenience a step further. Laser Vision Centers was using mobile lasers to bring greater convenience to patients living in these smaller communities. It used a patented cart to transport the laser to ophthalmologists' offices, where it could be used for a day or two by local surgeons. LVC could also provide a surgery team in locations where no surgeons were qualified to perform the procedure. The company was serving patients in over 100 locations in this manner and was expanding its efforts.

**36**     Technological or procedural advances offered clinics another basis on which to compete. For example, during the summer of 1999, Dr. Barrie Soloway's clinic was the first in the United States to get an Autonomous laser. This laser was designed to overcome a major problem in eye surgery, the tendency for the eye to move while the procedure was being performed. In an interview with *Fortune* magazine, Autonomous's founder, Randy Frey, described the advantages of this new technology.

> At present, doctors stabilize the eye merely by asking the patient to stare at a blinking red light. But, says Frey, aiming a laser at the eye is "a very precise thing. I couldn't imagine that you could make optics for the human eye while the eye was moving." The eye, he explains, makes barely perceptible, involuntary movements about five times a second. This "saccadic" motion can make it difficult to get a perfectly smooth correction. "The doctor can compensate for the big, noticeable movements," Frey says, "but not the little ones."

> Frey's machine uses radar to check the position of the eye 4,000 times a second. He's coupled this with an excimer laser whose beam is less than one millimeter in diameter, versus six millimeters for the standard beam. Guided by the tracker, this laser ablates the cornea in a pattern of small overlapping dots (Murray, 1999).

**37**     There were a number of technological advances under development like the autonomous laser system that could have a significant impact on this industry. With approvals for new procedures generally coming quicker in Canada than the United States, however, it was unclear whether technological advances could help U.S. providers differentiate themselves from their Canadian competitors.

### The Upcoming Strategy and Policy Meeting

**38**     Every time Dr. Everett saw an exuberant patient after surgery, or read a letter of gratitude from a patient, he knew in his heart that they were doing something special. He was energized by the fact that the laser vision corrections they were performing were changing peoples' lives. He was also proud of the fact that they continued to treat all of their customers as special guests. But he knew that for every LASIK patient they saw at PCLI, there was another potential PCLI patient who went to Canada to have the surgery performed. PCLI had the capacity to do more laser vision correction surgeries in Spokane than they were presently doing, and he wanted to make use of that capacity. He felt both PCLI and prospective patients from Spokane and the surrounding communities would be better off if more of these patients chose PCLI for laser vision correction surgeries.

39    But Dr. Everett was not sure what, if anything, should change at PCLI to attract these potential customers. PCLI had already begun to advertise. Advertising, in general, was not a commonly used practice in the U.S. medical community, and some in the medical profession considered much of the existing advertising in the industry to be ethically questionable. While Dr. Everett was comfortable with the advertisements they had started running three months ago (see Exhibit 5), he was still unsure whether PCLI should be advertising at all. More importantly, he felt that advertising represented only a partial solution, at best. What was needed was a clear strategic focus for the organization that would help it respond to the Canadian challenge.

40    One obvious answer was to also compete on price. But he simply could not conceive of PCLI treating eye surgery like a commodity and competing solely on price. Such a strategy seemed inconsistent with PCLI's core values, unwise from a business standpoint since PCLI's operating costs were much higher than its Canadian competitors, and simply wrong from an ethical standpoint. The problem was, he was not sure what strategic focus PCLI should pursue in order to retain its strong position in the Pacific Northwest LASIK market. What he did know was that whatever this strategy was to be, it needed to emerge from next month's meeting, and he wanted to be prepared to help make that happen. He wanted to have a clear plan to bring to the table at this meeting to share with his colleagues, even if it was simply a reaffirmation to continue doing what they were presently doing.

**EXHIBIT 5**    **Pacific Cataract and Laser Institute Advertisement**

# Case 45   Perdue Farms Inc.: Responding to Twenty-first Century Challenges*

## George C. Rubenson and Frank Shipper

# BACKGROUND/COMPANY HISTORY

> I have a theory that you can tell the difference between those who have inherited a fortune
> and those who have made a fortune. Those who have made their own fortune forget not
> where they came from and are less likely to lose touch with the common man. (Bill Sterling,
> "Just Browsin" column in *Eastern Shore News,* March 2, 1988)

1   The history of Perdue Farms Inc. is dominated by seven themes: quality, growth, geographic expansion, vertical integration, innovation, branding, and service. Arthur W. Perdue, a Railway Express Agent and descendent of a French Huguenot family named Perdeaux, founded the company in 1920 when he left his job with Railway Express and entered the egg business full-time near the small town of Salisbury, Maryland. Salisbury is located in a region immortalized in James Michener's *Chesapeake* that is alternately known as "the Eastern Shore" or "Delmarva Peninsula." It includes parts of *DEL*aware, *MAR*yland and *Virgini*A. Arthur Perdue's only child, Franklin Parsons Perdue, was also born in 1920.

2   A quick look at Perdue Farms' mission statement (Exhibit 1) reveals the emphasis the company has always put on quality. In the 1920s, "Mr. Arthur," as he was called, bought leghorn breeding stock from Texas to improve the quality of his flock. He soon expanded his egg market and began shipments to New York. Practicing small economies such as mixing his own chicken feed and using leather from his old shoes to make hinges for his chicken coops, he stayed out of debt and prospered. He tried to add a new chicken coop every year.

3   By 1940, Perdue Farms was already known for quality products and fair dealing in a tough, highly competitive market. The company began offering chickens for sale when Mr. Arthur realized that the future lay in selling chickens, not eggs. In 1944, Mr. Arthur made his son Frank a full partner in A. W. Perdue and Son, Inc.

4   In 1950, Frank took over leadership of the company that employed 40 people. By 1952, revenues were $6,000,000 from the sale of 2,600,000 broilers. During this period, the company began to vertically integrate, operating its own hatchery, starting to mix its own feed formulations and operating its own feed mill. Also, in the 1950s, Perdue Farms began to contract with others to grow chickens for them. By furnishing the growers with peeps (baby chickens) and the feed, the company was better able to control quality.

5   In the 1960s, Perdue Farms continued to vertically integrate by building its first grain receiving and storage facilities and Maryland's first soybean processing plant. By 1967, annual sales had increased to about $35,000,000. However, it became clear to Frank that profits lay in processing chickens. Frank recalled in an interview for *BusinessWeek* (September 15, 1972) "processors were paying us 10¢ a live pound for what cost us 14¢ to produce. Suddenly, processors were making as much as 7¢ a pound."

*George C. Rubenson and Frank Shipper, Department of Management and Marketing, Franklin P. Perdue School of Business, Salisbury University. Copyright 2001 by the authors. Acknowledgements: The authors are indebted to Frank Perdue, Jim Perdue, and the numerous associates at Perdue Farms, Inc., who generously shared their time and information about the company. In addition, the authors would like to thank the anonymous librarians at Blackwell Library, Salisbury State University, who routinely review area newspapers and file articles about the poultry industry—the most important industry on the *Delmarva* Peninsula. Without their assistance, this case would not be possible.

**EXHIBIT 1**

# PERDUE
# MISSION 2000

## Stand on Tradition

*Perdue was built upon a foundation of quality, a tradition described in our Quality Policy . . .*

# Our Quality Policy

**"We shall produce products and provide services
at all times which meet or exceed the expectations of our customers."**

**"We shall not be content to be of
equal quality to our competitors."**

**"Our commitment is to be increasingly superior."**

**"Contribution to quality is a responsibility
shared by everyone in the Perdue organization."**

## Focus on Today

*Our mission reminds us of the purpose we serve . . .*

# Our Mission

**"Enhance the quality of life with great food and agricultural products."**

*While striving to fulfill our mission, we use our values to guide our decisions . . .*

**EXHIBIT 1**  *(Continued)*

# Our Values

- **Quality:** We value the needs of our customers. Our high standards require us to work safely, make safe food and uphold the Perdue name.

- **Integrity:** We do the right thing and live up to our commitments. We do not cut corners or make false promises.

- **Trust:** We trust each other and treat each others with mutual respect. Each individual's skill and talent are appreciated.

- **Teamwork**: We value a strong work ethic and ability to make each other successful. We care what others think and encourage their involvement, creating a sense of pride, loyalty, ownership and family.

# Look to the Future

*Our vision describes what we will become and the qualities that will enable us to succeed . . .*

# Our Vision

*"To be the leading quality food company with $20 billion in sales in 2020.*

Perdue in the Year 2020

- **To our customers**: We will provide food solutions and indispensable services to meet anticipated customer needs.

- **To our consumers**: A portfolio of trusted food and agricultural products will be supported by multiple brands throughout the world.

- **To our associates**: Worldwide, our people and our workplace will reflect our quality reputation, placing Perdue among the best places to work.

- **To our communities**: We will be known in the community as a strong corporate citizen, trusted business partner and favorite employer.

- **To our shareholders**: Driven by innovation, our market leadership and our creative spirit will yield industry-leading profits.

**6**   A cautious, conservative planner, Arthur Perdue had not been eager for expansion and Frank Perdue himself was reluctant to enter poultry processing. But, economics forced his hand and, in 1968, the company bought its first processing plant, a Swift and Company operation in Salisbury.

**7**   From the first batch of chickens that it processed, Perdue's standards were higher than those of the federal government were. The state grader on the first batch has often told the story of how he was worried that he had rejected too many chickens as not Grade A. As he finished his inspections for that first day, he saw Frank Perdue headed his way and he could tell that Frank was not happy. Frank started inspecting the birds and never argued over one that was rejected. Next, he saw Frank start to go through the ones that the state grader had passed and began to toss some of them over with the rejected birds. Finally, realizing that few met his standards, Frank put all of the birds in the reject pile. Soon, however, the facility was able to process 14,000 broilers per hour.

**8**   From the beginning, Frank Perdue refused to permit his broilers to be frozen for shipping, arguing that it resulted in unappetizing black bones and loss of flavor and moistness when cooked. Instead, Perdue chickens were (and some still are) shipped to market packed in ice, justifying the company's advertisements at that time that it sold only "fresh, young broilers." However, this policy also limited the company's market to those locations that could be serviced overnight from the Eastern Shore of Maryland. Thus, Perdue chose for its primary markets the densely populated towns and cities of the East Coast, particularly New York City, which consumes more Perdue chicken than all other brands combined.

**9**   Frank Perdue's drive for quality became legendary both inside and outside the poultry industry. In 1985, Frank and Perdue Farms, Inc. were featured in the book, *A Passion for Excellence,* by Tom Peters and Nancy Austin.

**10**   In 1970, Perdue established its primary breeding and genetic research programs. Through selective breeding, Perdue developed a chicken with more white breast meat than the typical chicken. Selective breeding has been so successful that Perdue Farms chickens are desired by other processors. Rumors have even suggested that Perdue chickens have been stolen on occasion in an attempt to improve competitor flocks.

**11**   In 1971, Perdue Farms began an extensive marketing campaign featuring Frank Perdue. In his early advertisements, he became famous for saying things like "If you want to eat as good as my chickens, you'll just have to eat my chickens." He is often credited with being the first to brand what had been a commodity product. During the 1970s, Perdue Farms also expanded geographically to areas north of New York City such as Massachusetts, Rhode Island and Connecticut.

**12**   In 1977, "Mr. Arthur" died at the age of 91, leaving behind a company with annual sales of nearly $200,000,000, an average annual growth rate of 17 percent compared to an industry average of 1 percent a year, the potential for processing 78,000 broilers per hour, and annual production of nearly 350,000,000 pounds of poultry per year. Frank Perdue said of his father simply, "I learned everything from him."

**13**   In 1981, Frank Perdue was in Boston for his induction into the Babson College Academy of Distinguished Entrepreneurs, an award established in 1978 to recognize the spirit of free enterprise and business leadership. Babson College President Ralph Z. Sorenson inducted Perdue into the academy which, at that time, numbered 18 men and women from four continents. Perdue had the following to say to the college students:

> There are none, nor will there ever be, easy steps for the entrepreneur. Nothing, absolutely nothing, replaces the willingness to work earnestly, intelligently towards a goal. You have to be willing to pay the price. You have to have an insatiable appetite for detail, have to be willing to accept constructive criticism, to ask questions, to be fiscally responsible, to surround yourself with good people and, most of all, to listen. (Frank Perdue, speech at Babson College, April 28, 1981)

**PHOTO OF MR. ARTHUR, FRANK AND JIM**

14    The early 1980s saw Perdue Farms expand southward into Virginia, North Carolina and Georgia. It also began to buy out other producers such as Carroll's Foods, Purvis Farms, Shenandoah Valley Poultry Company and Shenandoah Farms. The latter two acquisitions diversified the company's markets to include turkey. New Products included value-added items such as "Perdue Done It!," a line of fully cooked fresh chicken products.

15    James A. (Jim) Perdue, Frank's only son, joined the company as a management trainee in 1983 and became a plant manager. The latter 1980s tested the mettle of the firm. Following a period of considerable expansion and product diversification, a consulting firm recommended that the company form several strategic business units, responsible for their own operations. In other words, the firm should decentralize. Soon after, the chicken market leveled off and then declined for a period. In 1988, the firm experienced its first year in the red. Unfortunately, the decentralization had created duplication and enormous administrative costs. The firm's rapid plunge into turkeys and other food processing, where it had little experience, contributed to the losses. Characteristically, the company refocused, concentrating on efficiency of operations, improving communications throughout the company, and paying close attention to detail.

16    On June 2, 1989, Frank celebrated 50 years with Perdue Farms, Inc. At a morning reception in downtown Salisbury, the Governor of Maryland proclaimed it "Frank Perdue Day." The Governors of Delaware and Virginia did the same. In 1991, Frank was named Chairman of the Executive Committee and Jim Perdue became Chairman of the Board. Quieter, gentler and more formally educated, Jim Perdue focuses on operations, infusing the company with an even stronger devotion to quality control and a bigger commitment to strategic planning. Frank Perdue continued to do advertising and public relations. As Jim

Perdue matured as the company leader, he took over the role of company spokesperson and began to appear in advertisements.

17    Under Jim Perdue's leadership, the 1990s were dominated by market expansion into Florida and west to Michigan and Missouri. In 1992, the international business segment was formalized serving customers in Puerto Rico, South America, Europe, Japan and China. By fiscal year 1998, international sales were $180 million per year. International markets are beneficial for the firm because U.S. customers prefer white meat while customers in most other countries prefer dark meat.

18    Food service sales to commercial consumers has also become a major market. New retail product lines focus on value-added items, individually quick frozen items, home meal replacement items and products for the delicatessen. The "Fit 'n Easy" label continues as part of a nutrition campaign using skinless, boneless chicken and turkey products.

19    The 1990s also saw the increased use of technology and the building of distribution centers to better serve the customer. For example, all over-the-road trucks were equipped with satellite two-way communications and geographic positioning, allowing real-time tracking, rerouting if needed, and accurately informing customers when to expect product arrival. Currently, nearly 20,000 associates have increased revenues to more than $2.5 billion.

# MANAGEMENT AND ORGANIZATION

20    From 1950 until 1991, Frank Perdue was the primary force behind Perdue Farms' growth and success. During Frank's years as the company leader, the industry entered its high-growth period. Industry executives had typically developed professionally during the industry's infancy. Many had little formal education and started their careers in the barnyard, building chicken coops and cleaning them out. They often spent their entire careers with one company, progressing from supervisor of grow-out facilities to management of processing plants to corporate executive positions. Perdue Farms was not unusual in that respect. An entrepreneur through and through, Frank lived up to his marketing image of "it takes a tough man to make a tender chicken." He mostly used a centralized management style that kept decision-making authority in his own hands or those of a few trusted, senior executives whom he had known for a lifetime. Workers were expected to do their jobs.

21    In later years, Frank increasingly emphasized employee (or "associates" as they are currently referred to) involvement in quality issues and operational decisions. This later emphasis on employee participation undoubtedly eased the transfer of power in 1991 to his son, Jim, which appears to have been unusually smooth. Although Jim grew up in the family business, he spent almost 15 years earning an undergraduate degree in biology from Wake Forest University, a master's degree in marine biology from the University of Massachusetts at Dartmouth, and a doctorate in fisheries from the University of Washington in Seattle. Returning to Perdue Farms in 1983, he earned an EMBA from Salisbury State University and was assigned positions as plant manager, divisional quality control manager, and vice president of Quality Improvement Process (QIP) prior to becoming Chairman.

22    Jim has a people-first management style. Company goals center on the three P's: People, Products, and Profitability. He believes that business success rests on satisfying customer needs with quality products. It is important to put associates first because "If [associates] come first, they will strive to assure superior product quality—and satisfied customers." This view has had a profound impact on the company culture which is based on Tom Peters view that "Nobody knows a person's 20 square feet better than the person who works there." The idea is to gather ideas and information from everyone in the organization and maximize productivity by transmitting these ideas throughout the organization.

23      Key to accomplishing this "employees first" policy is workforce stability, a difficult task in an industry that employs a growing number of associates working in physically demanding and sometimes stressful conditions. A significant number of associates are Hispanic immigrants who may have a poor command of the English language, are sometimes undereducated and often lack basic health care. In order to increase these associates' opportunity for advancement, Perdue Farms focuses on helping them overcome these disadvantages.

24      For example, the firm provides English-language classes to help non-English speaking employees assimilate. Ultimately employees can earn the equivalent of a high-school diploma. To deal with physical stress, the company has an ergonomics committee in each plant that studies job requirements and seeks ways to redesign those jobs that put workers at the greatest risk. The company also has an impressive wellness program that currently includes clinics at 10 plants. The clinics are staffed by professional medical people working for medical practice groups under contract to Perdue Farms. Employees can visit a doctor for anything from a muscle strain to prenatal care to screening tests for a variety of diseases and have universal access to all Perdue operated clinics. Dependent care is available. While benefits to the employees are obvious, the company also benefits through a reduction in lost time for medical office visits, lower turnover and a happier, healthier, more productive and stable work force.

## EXHIBIT 2

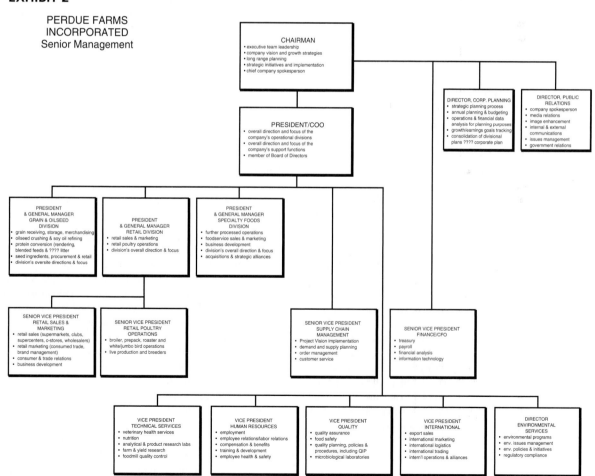

PERDUE FARMS INCORPORATED
Senior Management

# MARKETING

25    In the early days, chicken was sold to butcher shops and neighborhood groceries as a commodity, that is, producers sold it in bulk and butchers cut and wrapped it. The customer had no idea what firm grew or processed the chicken. Frank Perdue was convinced that higher profits could be made if the firm's products could be sold at a premium price. But, the only reason a product can command a premium price is if customers ask for it by name—and that means the product must be differentiated and "branded." Hence, the emphasis over the years on superior quality, broader breasted chickens, and a healthy golden color (actually the result of adding marigold petals in the feed to enhance the natural yellow color that corn provided).

26    In 1968, Frank Perdue spent $50,000 on radio advertising. In 1969, he added $80,000 in TV advertising to his radio budget—against the advice of his advertising agency. Although his early TV ads increased sales, he decided the agency he was dealing with didn't match one of the basic Perdue tenets: "The people you deal with should be as good at what they do as you are at what you do." That decision set off a storm of activity on Frank's part. In order to select an ad agency that met his standards, Frank learned more about advertising than any poultry man before him and, in the process, catapulted Perdue Farms into the ranks of the top poultry producers in the country.

27    He began a ten-week immersion on the theory and practice of advertising. He read books and papers on advertising. He talked to sales managers of every newspaper, radio, and television station in the New York area, consulted experts, and interviewed 48 ad agencies. During April, 1971, he selected Scali, McCabe, Sloves as his new advertising agency. As the agency tried to figure out how to successfully "brand" a chicken—something that had never been done—they realized that Frank Perdue was their greatest ally. "He looked a little like a chicken himself, and he sounded a little like one, and he squawked a lot!"

28    McCabe decided that Perdue should be the firm's spokesman. Initially Frank resisted. But, in the end, he accepted the role and the campaign based on "It takes a tough man to make a tender chicken" was born. The firm's very first television commercial showed Frank on a picnic in the Salisbury City Park saying:

> "A chicken is what it eats . . . And my chickens eat better than people do. . . I store my own grain and mix my own feed . . . And give my Perdue chickens nothing but pure well water to drink . . . That's why my chickens always have that healthy golden yellow color . . . If you want to eat as good as my chickens, you'll just have to eat my chickens."

29    Additional ads, touting high quality and the broader breasted chicken read as follows:

> Government standards would allow me to call this a Grade A chicken . . . but my standards wouldn't. This chicken is skinny . . . It has scrapes and hairs . . . The fact is, my graders reject 30 percent of the chickens government inspectors accept as Grade A . . . That's why it pays to insist on a chicken with my name on it . . . If you're not completely satisfied, write me and I'll give you your money back . . . Who do you write in Washington? . . . What do they know about chickens?
>
> The Perdue Roaster is the master race of chickens.
>
> Never go into a store and just ask for a pound of chicken breasts . . . Because you could be cheating yourself out of some meat . . . Here's an ordinary one-pound chicken breast, and here's a one-pound breast of mine . . . They weigh the same. But as you can see, mine has more meat, and theirs has more bone. I breed the broadest breasted, meatiest chicken you can buy . . . So don't buy a chicken breast by the pound . . . Buy them by the name . . . and get an extra bite in every breast.

30    The ads paid off. In 1968, Perdue held about three percent of the New York market. By 1972, one out of every six chickens eaten in New York was a Perdue chicken. 51 percent of New Yorkers recognized the label. Scali, McCabe, Sloves credited Perdue's "believability" for the success of the program. "This was advertising in which Perdue had a personality that

## Purdue's First Television Commercial

SCALI, McCABE, SLOVES INC.

CLIENT: PERDUE FOODS INC.

PRODUCT: PERDUE CHICKENS

TITLE: "MY CHICKENS EAT BETTER THAN PEOPLE"

LENGTH: 30 SECONDS

COMMERCIAL NO.: TV-PD-30-2C

1. FRANK PERDUE: A chicken is what it eats. And my chickens eat better than . . .

2. people do. I store my own grain and mix my own feed.

3. And give my Perdue chickens nothing but pure well water to drink.

4. That's why my chickens always have that healthy golden-yellow color.

5. If you want to eat as good as my chickens, you'll just have to eat my chickens.

6. That's really good.

lent credibility to the product. If Frank Perdue didn't look and sound like a chicken, he wouldn't be in the commercials."

31    Frank had his own view. As he told a Rotary audience in Charlotte, North Carolina, in March, 1989, "the product met the promise of the advertising and was far superior to the competition. Two great sayings tell it all: 'nothing will destroy a poor product as quickly as good advertising,' and 'a gifted product is mightier than a gifted pen!'

32    Today, branded chicken is ubiquitous. The new task for Perdue Farms is to create a unified theme to market a wide variety of products (e.g., fresh meat to fully prepared and frozen products) to a wide variety of customers (e.g., retail, food service, and international). Industry experts believe that the market for fresh poultry has peaked while sales of value-added and frozen products continue to grow at a healthy rate. Although domestic retail sales accounts for about 60 percent of Perdue Farms revenues in FY2000, food service sales now account for 20 percent, international sales account for 5 percent and grain and oilseed contribute the remaining 15 percent. The company expects food service, international, and grain and oilseed sales to continue to grow as a percentage of total revenues.

### Domestic Retail

33    Today's retail grocery customer is increasingly looking for ease and speed of preparation, that is, value-added products. The move toward value-added products has significantly changed the meat department in the modern grocery. There are now five distinct meat outlets for poultry:

1.  The fresh meat counter—traditional, fresh meat; includes whole chicken and parts

2. The delicatessen—processed turkey, rotisserie chicken

3. The frozen counter—individually quick frozen items such as frozen whole chickens, turkeys, and Cornish hens.

4. Home meal replacement—fully prepared entrees such as Perdue brand "Short Cuts" and Deluca brand entrees (the Deluca brand was acquired and is sold under its own name) that are sold along with salads and desserts so that you can assemble your own dinner

5. Shelf stable—canned products

**34**     Because Perdue Farms has always used the phrase "fresh young chicken" as the centerpiece of its marketing, value-added products and the retail frozen counter create a possible conflict with past marketing themes. Are these products compatible with the company's marketing image and, if so, how does the company express the notion of quality in this broader product environment? To answer that question, Perdue Farms has been studying what the term "fresh young chicken" means to customers who consistently demand quicker and easier preparation and who admit that they freeze most of their fresh meat purchases once they get home. One view is that the importance of the term "fresh young chicken" comes from the customer's perception that "quality" and "freshness" are closely associated. Thus, the real issue may be "trust," (i.e., the customer must believe that the product, whether fresh or frozen, is the freshest, highest quality possible and future marketing themes must develop that concept).

### Food Service

**35**     The food service business consists of a wide variety of public and private customers including restaurant chains, governments, hospitals, schools, prisons, transportation facilities and the institutional contractors who supply meals to them. Historically, these customers have not been brand conscious, requiring the supplier to meet strict specifications at the lowest price, thus making this category a less than ideal fit for Perdue Farms. However, as Americans continue to eat a larger percentage of their meals away from home, traditional grocery sales have flattened while the food service sector has shown strong growth. Across the domestic poultry industry, food service accounts for approximately 50 percent of total poultry sales while approximately 20 percent of Perdue Farms revenues come from this category. Clearly, Perdue Farms is playing catchup in this critical market.

**36**     Because Perdue Farms has neither strength nor expertise in the food service market, management believes that acquiring companies that already have food service expertise is the best strategy. An acquisition already completed is the purchase in September 1998 of Gol-Pak Corporation based in Monterey, Tenn. A further processor of products for the food service industry, Gol-Pak had about 1600 employees and revenues of about $200 million per year.

### International

**37**     International markets have generally been a happy surprise. In the early 1990s, Perdue Farms began exporting specialty products such as chicken feet (known as "paws") to customers in China. Although not approved for sale for human consumption in the United States, paws are considered a delicacy in China. By 1992, international sales, consisting principally of paws, had become a small, but profitable, business of about 30 million pounds per year. Building on this small "toehold," by 1998 Perdue Farms had quickly built an international business of more than 500 million pounds per year (see Exhibit 3) with an-

**EXHIBIT 3**
**International Volume**

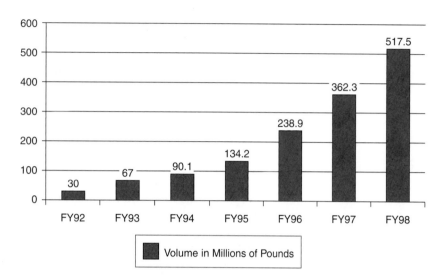

Volume in Millions of Pounds

nual revenues of more than $140 million, selling a wide variety of products to China, Japan, Russia, and the Ukraine.

**38**    In some ways, Japan is an excellent fit for Perdue Farms products because customers demand high quality. However, all Asian markets prefer dark meat, a serendipitous fit with the U.S. preference for white breast meat because it means that excess (to America) dark meat can be sold in Asia at a premium price. On the downside, Perdue Farms gains much of its competitive advantage from branding (e.g., trademarks, processes, and technological and biological know-how) which has little value internationally because most of Asia has not yet embraced the concept of branded chicken.

**39**    To better serve export markets, Perdue Farms has developed a portside freezing facility in Newport News, Virginia. This permits poultry to be shipped directly to the port, reducing processing costs and helping to balance ocean shipping costs to Asia which are in the range of 2/3 cents per pound (contracting an entire ship equal to 300 to 500 truckloads).

**40**    Shipping poultry to Asia is not without problems. For example, in China, delivery trucks are seldom refrigerated. Thus, the poultry can begin to thaw as it is being delivered, limiting the distance it can be transported prior to sale. One shipload of Perdue Farms chicken bound for Russia actually vanished. It had been inappropriately impounded using forged documents. Although most of its dollar value was eventually recovered, it is important for firms to be aware of the possible difficulties of ocean shipping and the use of foreign ports.

**41**    Initial demand for product in Russia, Poland, and Eastern Europe was huge. By FY 1998, a significant portion of international volume was being purchased by Russia. Unfortunately, the crumbling of Russia's economy has had a devastating effect on imports and sales are currently off significantly. Such instability of demand, coupled with rampant corruption, makes risking significant capital unacceptable.

**42**    Import duties and taxes are also a barrier. In China, according to the USDA, import duty rates for poultry are a whopping 45 percent for favored countries and 70 percent for unfavored countries. And, there is a 17 percent value-added tax for all countries. Import duties and taxes in Russia have been similarly high. Hence, profits can be expected to be slim.

**43**    Perdue Farms has created a joint partnership with Jiang Nan Feng (JNF) brand in order to develop a small processing plant in Shanghai. Brand recognition is being built through normal marketing tools. The products use the first "tray pack" wrapping available in Shanghai supermarkets. This new business shows promise because the sale in China of homegrown, fresh dark meat is a significant competitive advantage. Additionally, although government regulations do not presently permit importation to the U.S. of foreign-grown poultry, the future possibility of importing excess white meat from Shanghai to the United States is attractive since Asian markets, which prefer dark meat, will have difficulty absorbing all of the white breast meat from locally grown poultry. Perdue Farms' management believes that investments in processing facilities in Asia require the company to partner with a local company. Attempting to go it alone is simply too risky due to the significiant cultural differences.

# OPERATIONS

44  Two words sum up the Perdue approach to operations—quality and efficiency—with emphasis on the first over the latter. Perdue more than most companies represents the Total Quality Management (TQM) slogan, "Quality, a journey without end." Some of the key events are listed in Exhibit 4.

45  Both quality and efficiency are improved through the management of details. Exhibit 5 depicts the structure and product flow of a generic, vertically integrated broiler company. A broiler company can choose which steps in the process it wants to accomplish in-house and which it wants suppliers to provide. For example, the broiler company could purchase all grain, oilseed, meal, and other feed products. Or, it could contract with hatcheries to supply primary breeders and hatchery supply flocks.

46  Perdue Farms chose maximum vertical integration in order to control every detail. It breeds and hatches its own eggs (19 hatcheries), selects its contract growers, builds Perdue-engineered chicken houses, formulates and manufactures its own feed (12 poultry feedmills, one specialty feedmill, two ingredient-blending operations), oversees the care and

**EXHIBIT 4**
**Milestones in the Quality-Improvement Process at Perdue Farms**

|  |  |
|------|-------|
| 1924 | Arthur Perdue buys leghorn roosters for $25 |
| 1950 | Adopts the company logo of a chick under a magnifying glass |
| 1984 | Frank Perdue attends Philip Crosby's Quality College |
| 1985 | Perdue recognized for its pursuit of quality in *A Passion for Excellence* |
|      | 200 Perdue Managers attend Quality College |
|      | Adopted the Quality Improvement Process (QIP) |
| 1986 | Established Corrective Action Teams (CATs) |
| 1987 | Established Quality Training for all associates |
|      | Implemented Error Cause Removal Process (ECR) |
| 1988 | Steering Committee formed |
| 1989 | First Annual Quality Conference held |
|      | Implemented Team Management |
| 1990 | Second Annual Quality Conference held |
|      | Codified Values and Corporate Mission |
| 1991 | Third Annual Quality Conference held |
|      | Customer Satisfaction defined |
| 1992 | Fourth Annual Quality Conference held |
|      | How to implement Customer Satisfaction explained to team leaders and Quality Improvement Teams (QIT) |
|      | Created Quality Index |
|      | Created Customer Satisfaction Index (CSI) |
|      | Created "Farm to Fork" quality program |
| 1999 | Launched Raw Material Quality Index |
| 2000 | Initiated High-Performance Team Process |

**EXHIBIT 5**

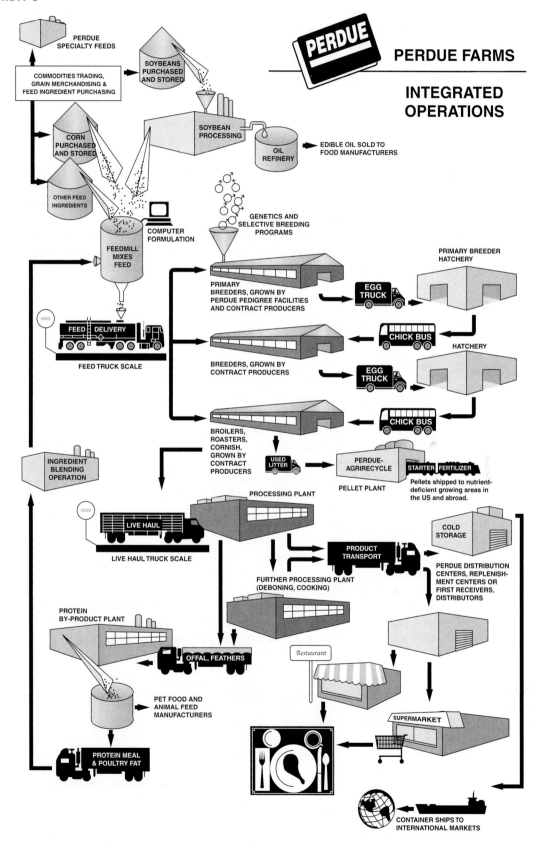

PERDUE SPECIALTY FEEDS

COMMODITIES TRADING, GRAIN MERCHANDISING & FEED INGREDIENT PURCHASING

SOYBEANS PURCHASED AND STORED

**PERDUE**

## PERDUE FARMS

### INTEGRATED OPERATIONS

CORN PURCHASED AND STORED

OTHER FEED INGREDIENTS

SOYBEAN PROCESSING

OIL REFINERY

EDIBLE OIL SOLD TO FOOD MANUFACTURERS

COMPUTER FORMULATION

GENETICS AND SELECTIVE BREEDING PROGRAMS

FEEDMILL MIXES FEED

PRIMARY BREEDER HATCHERY

PRIMARY BREEDERS, GROWN BY PERDUE PEDIGREE FACILITIES AND CONTRACT PRODUCERS

EGG TRUCK

FEED DELIVERY

CHICK BUS

HATCHERY

FEED TRUCK SCALE

BREEDERS, GROWN BY CONTRACT PRODUCERS

EGG TRUCK

CHICK BUS

INGREDIENT BLENDING OPERATION

BROILERS, ROASTERS, CORNISH, GROWN BY CONTRACT PRODUCERS

USED LITTER

PERDUE-AGRIRECYCLE PELLET PLANT

STARTER FERTILIZER

Pellets shipped to nutrient-deficient growing areas in the US and abroad.

PROCESSING PLANT

LIVE HAUL

PRODUCT TRANSPORT

COLD STORAGE

LIVE HAUL TRUCK SCALE

FURTHER PROCESSING PLANT (DEBONING, COOKING)

PERDUE DISTRIBUTION CENTERS, REPLENISH-MENT CENTERS OR FIRST RECEIVERS, DISTRIBUTORS

PROTEIN BY-PRODUCT PLANT

OFFAL, FEATHERS

*Restaurant*

PET FOOD AND ANIMAL FEED MANUFACTURERS

SUPERMARKET

PROTEIN MEAL & POULTRY FAT

CONTAINER SHIPS TO INTERNATIONAL MARKETS

feeding of the chicks, operates its own processing plants (21 processing/further processing plants), distributes via its own trucking fleet, and markets the products—see Exhibit 5). Total process control formed the basis for Frank Perdue's early claims that Perdue Farms poultry is, indeed, higher quality than other poultry. When he stated in his early ads that "A chicken is what it eats. . . . I store my own grain and mix my own feed. . . . and give my Perdue chickens nothing but well water to drink. . . . ," he knew that his claim was honest and he could back it up.

47    Total process control also enables Perdue Farms to ensure that nothing goes to waste. Eight measurable items—hatchability, turnover, feed conversion, livability, yield, birds per man-hour, utilization, and grade—are tracked routinely.

48    Perdue Farms continues to ensure that nothing artificial is fed to or injected into the birds. No shortcuts are taken. A chemical-free and steroid-free diet is fed to the chickens. Young chickens are vaccinated against disease. Selective breeding is used to improve the quality of the chickens stock. Chickens are bred to yield more white breast meat because that is what the consumer wants.

49    To ensure that Perdue Farms poultry continues to lead the industry in quality, the company buys and analyzes competitors' products regularly. Inspection associates grade these products and share the information with the highest levels of management. In addition, the company's Quality Policy is displayed at all locations and taught to all associates in quality training ( Exhibit 6).

# RESEARCH AND DEVELOPMENT

50    Perdue is an acknowledged industry leader in the use of research and technology to provide quality products and service to its customers. The company spends more on research as a percent of revenues than any other poultry processor. This practice goes back to Frank Perdue's focus on finding ways to differentiate his products based on quality and value. It was research into selective breeding that resulted in the broader breast, an attribute of Perdue Farms chicken that was the basis of his early advertising. Although other processors have also improved their stock, Perdue Farms believes that it still leads the industry. A list of some of Perdue Farms technological accomplishments is given in  Exhibit 7.

51    As with every other aspect of the business, Perdue Farms tries to leave nothing to chance. The company employs specialists in avian science, microbiology, genetics, nutrition, and veterinary science. Because of its research and development capabilities, Perdue Farms is often involved in USDA field tests with pharmaceutical suppliers. Knowledge and experience gained from these tests can lead to a competitive advantage. For example, Perdue has the most extensive and expensive vaccination program in the industry. Currently, the company is working with and studying the practices of several European producers who use completely different methods. The company has used research to significantly increase productivity. For example, in the 1950s, it took 14 weeks to grow a 3-pound chicken. Today, it takes only seven weeks to grow a 5-pound chicken. This gain in efficiency is due princi-

**EXHIBIT 6**
**Quality Policy**

- WE SHALL produce products and provide services at all times that meet or exceed the expectations of our customers.
- WE SHALL not be content to be of equal quality to our competitors.
- OUR COMMITMENT is to be increasingly superior.
- CONTRIBUTION TO QUALITY is a responsibility shared by everyone in the Perdue organization.

**EXHIBIT 7**
**Perdue Farms Inc.
Technological
Accomplishments**

- Conducts more research than all competitors combined
- Breeds chickens with consistently more breast meat than any other bird in the industry
- First to use digital scales to guarantee weights to customers
- First to package fully-cooked chicken products in microwaveable trays
- First to have a box lab to define quality of boxes from different suppliers
- First to test both its chickens and competitors' chickens on 52 quality factors every week
- Improved on-time deliveries 20 percent between 1987 and 1993
- Built state-of-the-art analytical and microbiological laboratories for feed and end-product analysis
- First to develop best management practices for food safety across all areas of the company
- First to develop commercially viable pelletized poultry litter

pally to improvements in the conversion rate of feed to chicken. The current rate of conversion is about two pounds of feed to produce one pound of chicken. Feed represents about 65 percent of the cost of growing a chicken. Thus, if additional research can further improve the conversion rate of feed to chicken by just 1 percent, it would represent estimated additional income of $2.5 to $3 million per week or $130 to $156 million per year.

# FINANCE

52    Perdue Farms, Inc., is privately held and considers financial information to be proprietary. Hence, available data is limited. Stock is primarily held by the family with a limited amount held by Perdue Management. Common numbers used by the media and the poultry industry peg Perdue Farm's revenues for FY2000 at about $2.5 billion and the number of associates at nearly 20,000. *Forbes* magazine has estimated FY2000 operating profits at about $160 million and net profits at about 22 million.

53    The firm's compound sales growth rate has been slowly decreasing during the past 20 years, mirroring the industry which has been experiencing market saturation and overproduction. However, Perdue has compensated by using manpower more efficiently through improvements such as automation. For example, 20 years ago, a 1 percent increase in associates resulted in a 1.6 percent increase in revenue. Currently, a 1 percent increase in associates results in an 8.5 percent increase in revenues (see Exhibit 8).

54    Poultry operations can be divided into four segments: retail chicken (growth rate 5 percent), food-service chicken and turkey (growth rate 12 percent), international sales (growth rate 64 percent over past six years) and grain and oilseed (growth rate 10 percent). The bulk of Perdue Farms sales continues to come from retail chicken—the sector with the slowest growth rate. The greatest opportunity appears to lie in food-service sales, where the company is admittedly behind, and international sales where political and economic instability in target countries make the risk to capital significant.

55    Perdue Farms has been profitable every year since its founding with the exception of 1988 and 1996. Company officials believe the loss in 1988 was caused by overproduction by the industry and higher administrative costs resulting from a decentralization effort begun during the mid-eighties. At that time, there was a concerted effort to push decisions down through the corporate ranks to provide more autonomy. When the new strategy resulted in significantly higher administrative costs due to duplication of effort, the company responded quickly by returning to the basics, reconsolidating and downsizing. The loss in 1996 was due to the impact of high corn prices. Currently, the goal is to constantly streamline in order to provide cost-effective business solutions.

**EXHIBIT 8**
Annual Compound
Growth Rate through
FY2000

|  | Revenue | Associates | Sales/Associate |
|---|---|---|---|
| Past 20 years | 10.60% | 6.48% | 3.87% |
| Past 15 years | 8.45 | 4.48 | 4.48 |
| Past 10 years | 7.39 | 4.75 | 2.52 |
| Past 5 years | 8.39 | 0.99 | 7.33 |

56    Perdue Farms approaches financial management conservatively, using retained earnings and cash flow to finance most asset replacement projects and normal growth. When planning expansion projects or acquisitions, long-term debt is used. The target debt limit is 55 percent of equity. Such debt is normally provided by domestic and international bank and insurance companies. The debt strategy is to match asset lives with liability maturities, and have a mix of fixed rate and variable rate debt. Growth plans require about two dollars in projected incremental sales growth for each dollar in invested capital.

# ENVIRONMENT

57    Environmental issues present a constant challenge to all poultry processors. Growing, slaughtering and processing poultry is a difficult and tedious process that demands absolute efficiency in order to keep operating costs at an acceptable level. Inevitably, detractors argue that the process is dangerous to workers, inhumane to the poultry, hard on the environment and results in food that may not be safe. Thus media headlines such as "Human Cost of Poultry Business Bared," "Animal Rights Advocates Protest Chicken Coop Conditions," "Processing Plants Leave a Toxic Trail," or "EPA mandates Poultry Regulations" are routine.

58    Perdue Farms tries to be proactive in managing environmental issues. In April 1993, the company created an Environmental Steering Committee. Its mission is "to provide all Perdue Farms work sites with vision, direction, and leadership so that they can be good corporate citizens from an environmental perspective today and in the future." The committee is responsible for overseeing how the company is doing in such environmentally sensitive areas as waste water, storm water, hazardous waste, solid waste, recycling, bio-solids, and human health and safety.

59    For example, disposing of dead birds has long been an industry problem. Perdue Farms developed small composters for use on each farm. Using this approach, carcasses are reduced to an end-product that resembles soil in a matter of a few days. The disposal of hatchery waste is another environmental challenge. Historically, manure and un-hatched eggs were shipped to a landfill. However, Perdue Farms developed a way to reduce the waste by 50 percent by selling the liquid fraction to a pet food processor that cooks it for protein. The other 50 percent is recycled through a rendering process. In 1990, Perdue Farms spent $4.2 million to upgrade its existing treatment facility with a state-of-the-art system at its Accomac, Virginia, and Showell, Maryland, plants. These facilities use forced hot air heated to 120 degrees to cause the microbes to digest all traces of ammonia, even during the cold winter months.

60    More than 10 years ago, North Carolina's Occupational Safety and Health Administration cited Perdue Farms for an unacceptable level of repetitive stress injuries at its Lewiston and Robersonville, North Carolina, processing plants. This sparked a major research program in which Perdue Farms worked with Health and Hygiene Inc. of Greensboro, North Carolina, to learn more about ergonomics, the repetitive movements required to accomplish specific jobs. Results have been dramatic. Launched in 1991 after two years of development, the program videotapes employees at all of Perdue Farm's plants as they work in order to describe and place stress values on the various tasks. Although the cost to Perdue Farms has been sig-

nificant, results have been dramatic with workers' compensation claims down 44 percent, lost-time recordables just 7.7 percent of the industry average, an 80 percent decrease in serious repetitive stress cases and a 50 percent reduction in lost time or surgery back injuries (Shelley Reese, "Helping Employees get a Grip, *Business and Health,* Aug. 1998).

61    Despite these advances, serious problems continue to develop. In 1997, the organism *Pfiesteria* burst into media headlines when massive numbers of dead fish with lesions turned up along the Chesapeake Bay in Maryland. Initial findings pointed to manure runoff from the poultry industry. Political constituencies quickly called for increased regulation to insure proper manure storage and fertilizer use. The company readily admits that "the poultry process is a closed system. There is lots of nitrogen and phosphorus in the grain, it passes through the chicken and is returned to the environment as manure. Obviously, if you bring additional grain into a closed area such as the Delmarva Peninsula, you increase the amount of nitrogen and phosphorus in the soil unless you find a way to get rid of it." Nitrogen and phosphorus from manure normally make excellent fertilizer that moves slowly in the soil. However, scientists speculate that erosion speeds up runoff, threatening the health of nearby streams, rivers, and larger bodies of water such as the Chesapeake Bay. The problem for the industry is that proposals to control the runoff are sometimes driven more by politics and emotion than research, which is not yet complete.

62    Although it is not clear what role poultry-related nitrogen and phosphorus runoff played in the *Pfiesteria* outbreak, regulators believe the microorganism feasts on the algae that grows when too much of these nutrients is present in the water. Thus, the EPA and various states are considering new regulations. Currently, contract growers are responsible for either using or disposing of the manure from their chicken houses. But, some regulators and environmentalists believe that (1) it is too complicated to police the utilization and disposal practices of thousands of individual farmers and (2) only the big poultry companies have the financial resources to properly dispose of the waste. Thus, they want to make poultry companies responsible for all waste disposal, a move that the industry strongly opposes.

63    Some experts have called for conservation measures that might limit the density of chicken houses in a given area or even require a percentage of existing chicken houses to be taken out of production periodically. Obviously this would be very hard on the farm families who own existing chicken houses and could result in fewer acres devoted to agriculture. Working with AgriRecycle Inc. of Springfield, Missouri, Perdue Farms has developed a possible solution. The plan envisions the poultry companies processing excess manure into pellets for use as fertilizer. This would permit sale outside the poultry growing region, better balancing the input of grain. Spokesmen estimate that as much as 120,000 tons, nearly one-third of the surplus nutrient from manure produced each year on the Delmarva Peninsula, could be sold to corn growers in other parts of the country. Prices would be market driven but could be $25 to $30 per ton, suggesting a potential, small profit. Still, almost any attempt to control the problem potentially raises the cost of growing chickens, forcing poultry processors to look elsewhere for locations where the chicken population is less dense.

64    In general, solving industry environmental problems presents at least five major challenges to the poultry processor:

• How to maintain the trust of the poultry consumer,

• How to ensure that the poultry remain healthy,

• How to protect the safety of the employees and the process,

• How to satisfy legislators who need to show their constituents that they are taking firm action when environmental problems occur, and

• How to keep costs at an acceptable level.

**EXHIBIT 9**
**Perdue Farms**
**Environmental Policy**
**Statement**

Perdue Farms is committed to environmental stewardship and shares that commitment with its farm family partners. We're proud of the leadership we're providing our industry in addressing the full range of environmental challenges related to animal agriculture and food processing. We've invested—and continue to invest—millions of dollars in research, new technology, equipment upgrades, and awareness and education as part of our ongoing commitment to protecting the environment.

- Perdue Farms was among the first poultry companies with a dedicated Environmental Services department. Our team of environmental managers is responsible for ensuring that every Perdue facility operates within *100 percent compliance of all applicable environmental regulations and permits.*
- Through our joint venture, Perdue AgriRecycle, Perdue Farms is investing $12 million to build in Delaware a first-of-its-kind pellet plant that will convert surplus poultry litter into a starter fertilizer that will be marketed internationally to nutrient deficient regions. The facility, which will serve the entire Delmarva region, is scheduled to begin operation in April, 2001.
- We continue to explore new technologies that will reduce water usage in our processing plants without compromising food safety or quality.
- We invested thousands of man-hours in producer education to assist our family farm partners in managing their independent poultry operations in the most environmentally responsible manner possible. In addition, all our poultry producers are required to have nutrient management plans and dead-bird composters.
- Perdue Farms was one of four poultry companies operating in Delaware to sign an agreement with Delaware officials outlining our companies' voluntary commitment to help independent poultry producers dispose of surplus chicken litter.
- Our Technical Services department is conducting ongoing research into feed technology as a means of reducing the nutrients in poultry manure. We've already achieved phosphorous reductions that far exceed the industry average.
- We recognize that the environmental impact of animal agriculture is more pronounced in areas where development is decreasing the amount of farmland available to produce grain for feed and to accept nutrients. That is why we view independent grain *and* poultry producers as vital business partners and strive to preserve the economic viability of the family farm.

At Perdue Farms, we believe that it is possible to preserve the family farm; provide a safe, abundant and affordable food supply; and protect the environment. However, we believe that can best happen when there is cooperation and trust between the poultry industry, agriculture, environmental groups and state officials. We hope Delaware's effort will become a model for other states to follow.

65    Jim Perdue sums up Perdue Farms' position as follows: "we must not only comply with environmental laws as they exist today, but look to the future to make sure we don't have any surprises. We must make sure our environmental policy statement (see Exhibit 9) is real, that there's something behind it and that we do what we say we're going to do."

# LOGISTICS AND INFORMATION SYSTEMS

66    The explosion of poultry products and increasing number of customers during recent years placed a severe strain on the existing logistic system which was developed at a time when there were far fewer products, fewer delivery points and lower volume. Hence, the company had limited ability to improve service levels, could not support further growth, and could not introduce innovative services that might provide a competitive advantage.

**67**     In the poultry industry, companies are faced with two significant problems—time and forecasting. Fresh poultry has a limited shelf life—measured in days. Thus forecasts must be extremely accurate and deliveries timely. On one hand, estimating requirements too conservatively results in product shortages. Mega-customers such as WalMart will not tolerate product shortages that lead to empty shelves and lost sales. On the other hand, if estimates are overstated, the result is outdated products that cannot be sold and losses for Perdue Farms. A common expression in the poultry industry is "you either sell it or smell it."

**68**     Forecasting has always been extremely difficult in the poultry industry because the processor needs to know approximately 18 months in advance how many broilers will be needed in order to size hatchery supply flocks and contract with growers to provide live broilers. Most customers (e.g., grocers, food service buyers) have a much shorter planning window. Additionally, there is no way for Perdue Farms to know when rival poultry processors will put a particular product on special, reducing Perdue Farms sales, or when bad weather and other uncontrollable problems may reduce demand.

**69**     Historically, poultry companies have relied principally on extrapolation of past demand, industry networks and other contacts to make their estimates. Although product complexity has exacerbated the problem, the steady movement away from fresh product to frozen product (which has a longer shelf life) offers some relief.

**70**     In the short run, Information Technology (IT) has helped by shortening the distance between the customer and Perdue Farms. As far back as 1987, PCs were placed directly on each customer service associate's desk, allowing them to enter customer orders directly. Next, a system was developed to put dispatchers in direct contact with every truck in the system so that they would have accurate information about product inventory and truck location at all times. Now, IT is moving to further shorten the distance between the customer and the Perdue Farms service representative by putting a PC on the customer's desk. All of these steps improve communication and shorten the time from order to delivery.

**71**     In the longer run, these steps are not enough due to the rapidly expanding complexity of the industry. For example, today, poultry products fall into four unique channels of distribution:

1. Bulk fresh—*Timeliness and frequency of delivery are critical to ensure freshness.* Distribution requirements are high volume and low-cost delivery.

2. Domestic frozen and further processed products—*Temperature integrity is critical,* distribution requirements are frequency and timeliness of delivery. This channel lends itself to dual temperature trailer systems and load consolidation.

3. Export—*Temperature integrity, high volume, and low-cost are critical.* This channel lends itself to inventory consolidation and custom loading of vessels.

4. Consumer packaged goods (packaged fresh, prepared and deli products)—*Differentiate via innovative products and services.* Distribution requirements are reduced lead time and low cost.

**72**     Thus, forecasting now requires the development of a sophisticated supply chain management system that can efficiently integrate all facets of operations including grain and oilseed activities, hatcheries and growing facilities, processing plants (which now produce more than 400 products at more than 20 locations), distribution facilities and, finally, the distributors, supermarkets, food service customers and export markets (see Exhibit 5). Perdue Farms underlined the importance of the successful implementation of supply chain management by creating a new executive position, Senior Vice President for Supply Chain Management.

**73** A key step in overhauling the distribution infrastructure is the building of replenishment centers that will, in effect, be buffers between the processing plants and the customers. The portside facility in Norfolk, Virginia, which serves the international market, is being expanded and a new domestic freezer facility added.

**74** Conceptually, products are directed from the processing plants to the replenishment and freezer centers based on customer forecasts that have been converted to an optimized production schedule. Perdue Farms' trucks deliver these bulk products to the centers in finished or semifinished form. At the centers, further finishing and packaging is accomplished. Finally, specific customer orders are custom palletized and loaded on trucks (either Perdue-owned or contracted) for delivery to individual customers. All shipments are made up from replenishment center inventory. Thus, the need for accurate demand forecasting by the distribution centers is key.

**75** In order to control the entire supply chain management process, Perdue Farms purchased a multimillion dollar information technology system that represents the biggest nontangible asset expense in the company's history. This integrated, state-of-the-art information system required total process reengineering, a project that took 18 months and required training 1,200 associates. Major goals of the system were to (1) make it easier and more desirable for the customer to do business with Perdue Farms, (2) make it easier for Perdue Farms associates to get the job done, and (3) take as much cost out of the process as possible.

## INDUSTRY TRENDS

**76** The poultry industry is affected by consumer, industry, and governmental regulatory trends. Currently, chicken is the number one meat consumed in the United States with 40 percent market share (Exhibits 10 and 11). Typical Americans consume about 81 pounds of chicken, 69 pounds of beef, and 52 pounds of pork annually (USDA data). Additionally, chicken is becoming the most popular meat in the world. In 1997, poultry set an export record of $2.5 billion. Although exports fell 6 percent in 1998, the decrease was attributed to Russia's and Asia's financial crisis and food industry experts expect this to be only a temporary setback. Hence, the world market is clearly a growth opportunity for the future.

**77** The popularity and growth of poultry products is attributed to both nutritional and economic issues. Poultry products contain significantly less fat and cholesterol than other meat products. In the United States, the demand for boneless, skinless breast meat, the leanest

**EXHIBIT 10**

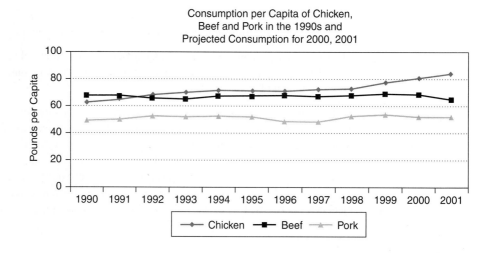

Consumption per Capita of Chicken, Beef and Pork in the 1990s and Projected Consumption for 2000, 2001

**EXHIBIT 11**

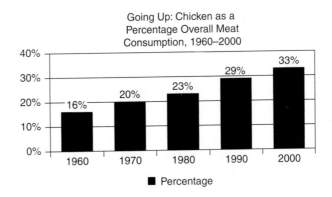

Going Up: Chicken as a Percentage Overall Meat Consumption, 1960–2000

meat on poultry, is so great that dark meat is often sold at a discount in the United States or shipped overseas where it is preferred over white meat.

78 Another trend is a decrease in demand for whole birds to be used as the base dish for home meals and an increase in demand for products that have been further processed for either home or restaurant consumption. For example, turkey or chicken hot dogs, fully-cooked sliced chicken or turkey and turkey pastrami—which neither looks nor tastes like turkey—can be found in most deli cases. Many supermarkets sell either whole or parts of hot rotisserie chicken. Almost all fast-food restaurants have at least one sandwich based on poultry products. Many up-scale restaurants feature poultry products that are shipped to them frozen and partially prepared in order to simplify restaurant preparation. All these products have been further processed, adding value and increasing the potential profit margin.

79 The industry is consolidating, that is, the larger companies in the industry are continuing to buy smaller firms. Currently there are about 35 major poultry firms in the United States but this number is expected to drop to 20 to 25 within the next 10 years. There are several reasons for this. Stagnant U.S. demand and general product oversupply create downward price pressure that makes it difficult for smaller firms to operate profitably. In addition, pressure for efficiency improvements requires huge capital outlays. Finally, mega-retailers such as Sam's Club and Royal Ahold (the Dutch owner of several U.S. supermarket chains) do not like to manage individual contracts with numerous smaller processors. Mega-retailers prefer to deal with mega-suppliers.

80 The industry is heavily regulated. The Food and Drug Administration (FDA) monitors product safety. The USDA inspects poultry as it arrives at the processing plant. After it is killed, each bird is again inspected by a USDA inspector for avian diseases, contamination of feces or other foreign material. All poultry that does not meet regulations is destroyed under USDA supervision. USDA inspectors also examine the plant, equipment, operating procedures and personnel for compliance with sanitary regulations. Congress has mandated that the USDA make this information available online. Additional intensive inspections of statistically selected samples of poultry products have been recommended by the National Academy of Sciences. Thus, additional FDA regulations for product quality are anticipated.

81 Although poultry produces less waste per pound of product than cattle or hogs, all meat industries are experiencing increased scrutiny by the Environmental Protection Agency (EPA) regarding the disposal of waste. In general, waste generated at processing plants is well controlled by regulation, monitoring, and fines. When an EPA violation occurs, the company that operates the plant can receive a substantial fine, potentially millions of dollars.

82 Still, the most difficult problems to deal with are those that occur as a cumulative result of numerous processors producing in a relatively limited area. For example, increasing poultry production in a given area intensifies the problem of disposal of manure. In

manmade fertilizer, phosphorous and nitrogen exist in approximately a 1 to 8 ratio whereas in poultry manure the ratio can be 1 to 1. Thus, too much poultry manure can result in serious phosphorous run-off into streams and rivers, potentially resulting in aquatic disease and degradation of water quality. In 1997, an outbreak of *Pfiesteria,* a toxic microbe, occurred in the tributaries of the Chesapeake Bay. Although the poultry industry insisted that there were many possible reasons for the problem, the media and most regulatory spokespersons attributed it primarily to phosphorous run-off from chicken manure. After much negative publicity and extensive investigation by both poultry processors and state regulatory agencies, the State of Maryland passed the Water Quality Act of 1998, which required nutrient management plans. However, many environmentalists continue to believe that the EPA must create additional, stricter federal environmental regulations. Recent regulatory activity has continued to focus on Eastern Shore agriculture, especially the poultry industry. However, new studies from the U.S. Geological Survey suggest that the vast majority of nutrients affecting the Chesapeake Bay come from rivers that do not flow through the poultry-producing regions of the Eastern Shore. The studies also found that improved agricultural management practices have reduced nutrient runoff from farmlands. Jim Perdue says "While the poultry industry must accept responsibility for its share of nutrients, public policy should view the watershed as a whole and address all the factors that influence water quality."

83    Other government agencies whose regulations impact the industry include the Occupational Safety and Health Administration (OSHA) for employee safety and the Immigration and Naturalization Service (INS) for undocumented workers. OSHA enforces its regulations via periodic inspections, and levies fines when noncompliance is found. For example, a Hudson Foods poultry plant was fined more than a million dollars for alleged willful violations causing ergonomic injury to workers. The INS also uses periodic inspections to find undocumented workers. It estimates that undocumented aliens working in the industry vary from 3 percent to 78 percent of the workforce at individual plants. Plants that are found to use undocumented workers, especially those that are repeat offenders, can be heavily fined.

# THE FUTURE

84    The marketplace for poultry in the twenty-first century will be very different from the past. Understanding the wants and needs of generation Xers and echo-boomers will be key to responding successfully to these differences.

85    Quality will continue to be essential. In the 1970s, quality was the cornerstone of Frank Perdue's successful marketing program to "brand" his poultry. However, in the twenty-first century, quality will not be enough. Today's customers expect—even demand—all products to be high quality. Thus, Perdue Farms plans to use customer service to further differentiate the company. The focus will be on learning how to become indispensable to the customer by taking cost out of the product and delivering it exactly the way the customer wants it, where and when the customer wants it. In short, as Jim Perdue says, "Perdue Farms wants to become so easy to do business with that the customer will have no reason to do business with anyone else."

86    In the poultry business, customer purchase decisions, as well as company profitability, hinge on mere pennies. Thus, the location of processing facilities is key. Historically, Perdue Farms has been an Eastern Shore company and has maintained major processing facilities on the Eastern Shore. However, it currently costs about 1½ cents more per pound to grow poultry on the Eastern Shore versus what poultry can be grown for in Arkansas. This

difference results from the cost of labor, compliance with federal and state environmental laws, resource costs (e.g., feed grain) and other variables. Clearly, selecting favorable sites for future growing and processing facilities is key. In the future, assuming regulations will permit the importation of foreign-grown poultry, producers could even use inexpensive international labor markets to further reduce costs. The opportunity for large growers to capture these savings puts increased pressure on small poultry companies. This suggests further consolidation of the industry.

87     Grocery companies are also consolidating in order to compete with huge food industry newcomers such as WalMart and Royal Ahold. These new competitors gain efficiency by minimizing the number of their suppliers and buying huge amounts from each at the lowest possible price. In effect, both mega-companies—the supplier and the buyer—become dependent on each other. Further, mega-companies expect their suppliers to do more for them. For example, Perdue Farms considers it possible that, using sophisticated distribution information programs, they will soon be able to manage the entire meat department requirements for several supermarket chains. Providing this service would support Perdue Farms' goal of becoming indispensable to their first line retail customer, the grocer.

88     The twenty-first century consumer will demand many options. Clearly, the demand for uncooked, whole chickens purchased at the meat counter has peaked. Demand is moving toward further processed poultry. To support this trend, Perdue Farms plans to open several additional cooking plants. In addition, a criterion for future acquisitions will be whether they support value-added processing. Products from these plants will fill food service requirements and grocery sales of prepared foods such as delicatessen, frozen, home meal replacement, and shelf-stable items. Additionally, the twenty-first century customer will be everywhere. Whether at work, at a sports event, in school, or traveling on the highway, customers expect to have convenient refreshment machines available with a wide selection of wholesome, ready-to-eat products.

89     Designing a distribution system that can handle all of these options is extremely difficult. For example, the system must be able to efficiently organize hundreds of customer orders that are chosen from more than 400 different products that are processed and further prepared at more than 20 facilities throughout the southeast for delivery by one truck—a massive distribution task. As executives note, the company survived up until now using distribution techniques created as many as 20 years ago when there were a handful of products and processing facilities. However, the system approached gridlock during the late 1990s. Thus, Perdue Farms invested in a state-of-the-art information processing system—a tough decision because "we could build two new processing plants for the price of this technology package."

90     International markets are a conundrum. On one hand, Perdue Farms' international revenue has grown from an insignificant side business in 1994 to about $140 million in 1999, approximately 5 percent of total revenues. Further, its contribution to profits is significant. Poultry is widely accepted around the world providing opportunities for further growth. But, trying to be global doesn't work. Different cultures value different parts of the chicken and demand different meat color, preparation, and seasoning. Thus, products must be customized. Parts that are not in demand in a particular country must be sold at severely reduced prices, used as feed, or shipped frozen to a different market where demand exists. While this can be done, it is a distribution problem that significantly complicates an already difficult forecasting model.

91     International markets can also be very unstable, exposing Perdue Farms to significant demand instability and potential losses. For example, in 1997, about 50 percent of Perdue Farms' international revenues came from Russia. However, political and economic

problems in Russia reduced 1999 revenues significantly. This high level of instability, coupled with corruption that thrives in a country experiencing severe political and economic turmoil, introduces significant risk to future investment.

**92**     Clearly, the future holds many opportunities. But, none of them comes without risk and Perdue Farms must carefully choose where it wants to direct its scarce resources.

# Case 46   Prime Time Can Be Anytime:[1] TiVo Pioneers the Personal Video Recorder

## Shawn Clark, Mickey Revenaugh, Melissa A. Schilling, and Antoine Thesset

1   Michael Ramsay was having a busy Fall 2002. TiVo, the company he co-founded and of which he now served as Chairman and CEO, had just raised $25 million from institutional investors and announced a deal with consumer electronics giant Toshiba that boosted the company's stock price by 21 percent. The media industry was abuzz over TiVo's role in broadcasting new "advertaiment" films by cutting-edge directors for BMW, and celebrities from Samuel L. Jackson to Rosie O'Donnell were crowing about TiVo's impact on their lives. Not bad for a brand new technology with an awkward acronym: the PVR, or personal video recorder.

2   Like a VCR without videocassettes, the PVR allows users to digitally record up to 60 hours of TV, pause and rewind for "instant replay" during live shows, and skip commercials altogether. A PVR also connects to a network outside the home to access TV schedule information via an electronic programming guide so it can seek out and record shows based on keywords (such as a favorite actor's name), viewing preferences, and the like.

3   Ramsay's TiVo was the first and best-known of a small handful of PVR innovators, rightly seen by many as the bellwether of a new industry and the company whose name was now largely synonymous with the PVR. Now in its fifth year of operation, though, and lagging far behind early predictions of consumer adoption and profits, TiVo was the subject of intense speculation. "It's nonsense that the pioneers are the ones who get the arrows in their backs," Ramsay told a reporter.[2] But what if the cliché held true?

## A NEW TECHNOLOGY IS BORN

4   The concept of TiVo emerged in 1997 from the desire of founders Michael Ramsay and James Barton to ease the process of recording TV programs, providing the asynchronous consumption of broadcasts. (See Exhibit 1 for company leadership and Exhibit 2 for complete timeline.) The partners quickly assembled a team of marketers and engineers to help bring their product to market. The TiVo PVR was unveiled in January 1999 at the National Consumer Electronics Show in Las Vegas, and hit retail outlets that April. Prior to the existence of the PVR, audiences relied on VCRs to tape their favorite shows and watch them at their leisure. Videotape collections, however, are bulky, unmanageable, and subject to quality erosion over time. TiVo managed to quickly carve a niche by offering an automated, all-digital recording service on a set-top box connected to the TV set, very much similar to a digital VCR.

---

[1] TiVo company capsule, Hoover's Online, retrieved 9/20/02 from www.hoovers.com/co/capsule/3/0,2163,59993,00.html.

[2] D. Pomerantz, "Do you TiVo?," *Forbes.com* (online preview of 11/25/02 issue), retrieved on 11/16/02 from www.forbes.com/forbes/2002/1125/054.html.

**EXHIBIT 1**
**TiVo at a Glance**

Source: TiVo, Inc.

**Financials**

Market cap: $172M. (share price ranging from $2.25 to $7.80 in 2001–02)
Revenues, FY2002: ~ $62 million.
Net Activations, FY 2002: ~50,000

**Executive Management**

**Michael Ramsay**
TiVo Co-Founder, Chairman and CEO

**Jim Barton**
TiVo Co-Founder, Senior Vice President
and CTO

**Morgan Guenther**
President

**David Courtney**
Executive VP, Worldwide Operations &
Administration, Chief Financial Officer

**Ta-Wei Chein**
Senior VP and General Manager Media,
TiVo Technology and Licensing Business

**Brodie Keast**
Senior VP & General Manager,
TiVo Service

**Susan Cashen**
VP, Corporate Communications

**Andrew Cresci**
VP, OEM Service Partners

**Luther Kitahata**
VP, Software Engineering

**Jeff Klugman**
VP, Licensing Group

**Howard Look**
VP, TiVo Studios

**Joe Miller**
VP, Sales and Marketing

**Mark Roberts**
VP, Operations and Chief Information Officer

**Laura Schulte**
VP, Human Resources

**Matthew Zinn**
VP, General Counsel & Chief Privacy Officer

**Board of Directors**

**Michael Ramsay**
TiVo co-founder, Chairman and CEO

**Stewart Alsop**
General Partner, New Enterprise Associates

**Jim Barton**
TiVo Co-Founder, Senior Vice President
and CTO

**Larry Chapman**
President, DIRECTV Global Digital Media

**David Courtney**
Executive VP, Worldwide Operations &
Administration, Chief Financial Officer

**John S. Hendricks**
Chairman & CEO, Discovery
Communications, Inc.

**Michael J. Homer**
CEO, Kontiki

**Randy Komisar**
Virtual CEO

**Geoffrey Y. Yang**
Managing Director, Redpoint Partners

**David Zaslav**
President, NBC Cable

**5**     However, the power that the PVR gives consumers to view television on their own
timetables and skip the commercials represents a radically new programming consumption
pattern, threatening the structure and business model of the broadcasting industry. Furthermore, the development of a set-top box marked the entry of a new competitor for established
consumer electronics manufacturers. The impact of both of these can be seen in TiVo's list
of strategic partners/investors and in actions by the media industry to contain the PVR phenomenon, as described on page 46-3.

**EXHIBIT 2**

**TiVo History\***

| | |
|---|---|
| 02/20/2002 | DirecTV selects TiVo for next generation digital satellite receiver with DVR |
| 02/04/2002 | TiVo subscribers vote using their remotes: Britney Spears is Superbowl MVP |
| 01/08/2002 | TiVo and RealNetworks announce the integration of RealOne Player and RealOne Music into TiVo DVR |
| 01/08/2002 | TiVo introduces TiVo Series2 |
| 12/11/2001 | TiVo awarded two new patents covering core DVR functions and home networking capabilities |
| 12/07/2001 | TiVo and AT&T Broadband to introduce DVR to cable customers |
| 10/31/2001 | TiVo adds business unit to support licensing strategy |
| 10/18/2001 | TiVo signs licensing agreement with Sony |
| 10/17/2001 | TiVo wins prestigious Emmy Award for outstanding achievement |
| 09/2001 | TiVo introduces a new service for DirecTV subscribers: record two shows at the same time |
| 05/24/2001 | TiVo granted patent on PVR software and hardware design |
| 01/24/2001 | DirecTV receiver with TiVo wins Best of Show at CES |
| 09/18/2000 | TiVo first to deliver content-rich interactive advertising to subscribers |
| 07/25/2000 | TiVo and Comcast announce single market deployment of TiVo service |
| 06/28/2000 | Thomson Multimedia to deliver TiVo in the UK |
| 06/14/2000 | AOL and TiVo announce new strategic agreement and equity investment |
| 06/07/2000 | TiVo unveils TiVo Takes, a fully interactive video program |
| 02/29/2000 | TiVo and BSkyB alliance to introduce personal television in the UK |
| 09/30/1999 | Initial public offering |
| 09/08/1999 | TiVo and Sony form strategic partnership |
| 07/27/1999 | Major equity investments from CBS, Comcast Interactive Capital, Cox Communications, Discover Communications, The Walt Disney Company, Liberty Digital, Advance/Newhouse, and TV Guide Interactive |
| 06/09/1999 | NBC and TiVo form strategic equity partnership to develop enhanced content for TiVo service |
| 04/27/1999 | Significant equity investment from DirecTV |
| 03/31/1999 | TiVo and Philips Electronics form equity deal to support their partnership |
| Early 1998 | TiVo logo and name are born |
| Early 1997 | Michael Ramsey and James Barton formed the concept of TiVo |
| 1950 | First TV remote control "Lazy Bones" developed by Zenith |
| 1939 | Television introduced to the public at the World's Fair |

6    The early costs of product and services development led TiVo to partner with Philips Electronics through an equity deal in 1999. With the threats and opportunities of asynchronous consumption of TV programming rapidly gaining momentum, TiVo started focusing some of its efforts on enhanced content and features such as e-commerce, resulting in a 1999 strategic equity investment from NBC, one of the three largest broadcasters in the United States (with Disney's ABC and Viacom's CBS). This event represents a significant milestone for TiVo, highlighting its ability to deal with both electronics manufacturers and broadcasters. Other investors such as Cox Communications, Discover Communications, CBS, Comcast Interactive Capital, Disney, TV Guide Interactive, Liberty Digital, and Advance/Newhouse rapidly joined TiVo. Sony also became a strategic partner in September 1999, only a few weeks before TiVo raised capital on the market through its successful IPO of $88 million, with shares offered at $16 each and selling, at the high, for $40.

7    In June 2000, TiVo marked the launch of its interactive video program, soon after adding News Corp's BSkyB to its list of partners with the purpose to introduce TiVo's services on the British market. AOL also bought into this concept, agreeing to a strategic equity

purchase in June 2000. TiVo's services were to be released in the United States through partnerships with cable, multiple system operators (MSOs) and satellite operators, including Comcast, DirectTV, and AT&T Broadband. Further innovations and technology alliances led TiVo to release its second-generation set-top box in January 2002.

8    To sign on partners like these while avoiding risks of imitation, TiVo pressed hard to obtain patents on its PVR software and hardware design from the United States Patent and Trademark Office. TiVo managed to win several patents protecting its technology, and decided to further expand its mark on the market by creating a business unit in 2001 called TiVo Technologies (see Developing Other Revenue Sources, which follows), tasked exclusively with the licensing of its technology.

## Personal Video Recorder Market Dynamics

9    TiVo competes in the immense and highly competitive consumer electronics industry. Within this industry, it is in the interactive digital recording segment of the broader video recording category. The two largest technology platforms in the video recording category, VHS and DVD, are projected to have unit sales of 14.4 and 16 million for 2002, respectively.[3]

10    The new PVR industry has a few small key players and a wide array of larger indirect competitors (see Competitors Large and Small, which follows). In the quest for a dominant design, there are a number of hardware/software paradigms at play: direct to consumer as a separate set-top box; integrated with cable/satellite boxes; integrated with other home video equipment, and integrated with a personal computer.

11    Early projections of the growth of the PVR market indicate the excitement with which this new technology was perceived by industry-watchers: PVRs were expected to outstrip sales of DVDs and gain on the installed base of VCRs by 2005. The level of hype accompanying first-mover TiVo's launch surely reflected both the overheated nature of the times (it was the height of the Internet boom, when dramatic predictions of world-changing technologies went hand-in-hand with easy access to venture capital) and long-simmering interest in interactive television—on the part of the media industry, if not on the part of consumers. The buzz around TiVo, which made its name essentially synonymous with "PVR," attracted at least two direct fast followers (ReplayTV and Microsoft's Ultimate TV) as well as renewed interest in the technology on the part of indirect competitors such as the cable industry.

12    Clearly still in its formative stages, the industry has not yet settled on the ideal product configuration. Microsoft seems to be betting on a PC-integrated dominant design since it shut down its UltimateTV offering in January 2002, citing an overlap with its eHome and Freestyle extension efforts within the Windows XP operating system.[4] On the other hand, some industry analysts believe that PVRs are essentially a "feature" that will gradually be integrated into other consumer-electronic devices like DVD players.[5] One fact is certain: in the consumer electronics industry, having your design emerge as the dominant design can be very profitable, as Sony learned in the early days of the VCR industry when its Betamax standard was eclipsed by JVC's competing VHS standard. (As discussed below, Sony is a key TiVo manufacturing partner and licensor of the TiVo software.)

13    Further complicating any predictions is the fact that a PVR is both a physical product and a service. While the physical products will likely become a commodity, the service offerings (and fees for those offerings) are where these companies can earn consistent and

---

[3]"DVD players dominate in '02," *Entertainment Marketing Letter,* 15, no. 14 (Jul 15, 2002), p. 8.
[4]"Microsoft shutters UltimateTV," *Online Reporter,* no. 282, Jan 28, 2002.
[5]D. Hamilton, "VCRs: still standing," *Wall Street Journal,* Eastern ed. Mar 5, 2002, p. 8.

very scalable profits. At the beginning of 2003, there were two pricing models in the PVR industry: pay a lump sum up front for unlimited use of the equipment or buy the equipment and pay monthly usage fees. Prices for TiVo (whose price, including both box and service, was around $500 at the end of 2002) and its direct competitors have been experimenting with both of these models and associated price points as they try to hit the winning combination for greater market acceptance.

## COMPETITORS LARGE AND SMALL

14     The PVR industry has a handful of key technology owners: TiVo, SONICBlue (which owns ReplayTV), EchoStar (a dish TV purveyor), and until January 2002, Microsoft (which announced that it was phasing out its UltimateTV product in favor of other "eHome" initiatives). Entering into this mix prior to the emergence of a dominant design are major manufacturers like Matsushita—owner of Panasonic and JVC—Philips, and Sony, the last two of which are also investors in TiVo, as is DirecTV, another "co-opetitor."

15     TiVo has several direct competitors, one potential entrant of note, and a class of indirect competitors which may represent a future evolution of the technology that could leave TiVo behind.

16     DirecTV is the brand of Hughes Electronic Corp.'s direct broadcast satellite (DBS) service. With a base of roughly 10 million subscribers it is the largest U.S. DBS service. Hughes is a unit of General Motors. GM had agreed to sell the company to EchoStar Communications, DirecTV's main rival; however, the FCC rejected the deal citing that it "cannot find the merger is in the public interest."[6] Further complicating this situation, DirecTV also owns a 10 percent stake in TiVo. Over the past few years, DirecTV customers have been one of the largest sources of new TiVo customers.

17     EchoStar Communications is the second largest U.S. DBS provider, operating the DISH Network with 7.1 million subscribers. EchoStar's subsidiaries develop DBS hardware and data services. These include a private-label PVR that is incorporated into the satellite set-top box and competes directly with TiVo. Vivendi Universal has acquired a 10 percent stake. As noted above, EchoStar unsuccessfully attempted to buy Hughes Electronics, DirecTV's parent.

18     SONICBlue is a small manufacturer of consumer-electronics. Its most notable products are the Rio digital audio players and ReplayTV PVRs, which it acquired in August 2001. In 2001, SONICBlue had revenues of $213 million and losses of approximately $65 million. In 2002, the company became embroiled in a lawsuit with the entertainment industry over copyright infringement of its ReplayTV 4000 product. In addition, SONICBlue and TiVo itself were feuding in court until early November 2002, when they agreed to drop patent infringement suits they had filed against each other the previous year.

19     Of the potential entrants, only Microsoft looms large. Having already been in the market with its UltimateTV offering, it has shut down those operations and integrated a new product into the Windows XP operating system, called Freestyle extensions. Given Microsoft's past practices it is likely to enter the market by bundling the functionality in for free. Other potential entrants have been kept at bay via licensing deals and intellectual property protection. Firms such as Philips, Sony, and Toshiba have all inked deals with TiVo to license their technology for use within other products.

[6]*Hoover's Company Capsules*, Oct 9, 2002, retrieved 10/11/02.

## EXHIBIT 3

Source: FBR/Public
Documents/ITVMarketer.

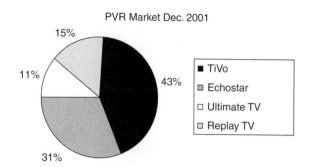

PVR Market Dec. 2001

- TiVo
- Echostar
- Ultimate TV
- Replay TV

**20**     TiVo's main indirect competitor is digital cable. In 2003 many digital cable subscribers could order fully featured video on demand through vendors such as Time Warner Cable. A service far more convenient than pay-per-view, video on demand allows the viewer to request a movie at any time, pause, rewind and fast-forward. TiVo and its competitors are an alternative to this service that enables customers to order any programming—not just movies. As bandwidth and technology advances, the cable and satellite services will likely provide these services as well—perhaps even using PVR-like technology. This acceleration of indirect competitors' entry in this market was highlighted by the 2002 offering from HBO named HBO On-Demand.

### A Massive Market's Reluctant Embrace

**21**     Although the market potential for TiVo and PVRs is 110 million households in the United States—all of those with television sets—sales of PVRs were forecast to reach over 15.3 million by 2006,[7] or 14 percent of U.S. homes that have a TV. (TiVo and its competitors have also established beachheads in Europe, particularly the United Kingdom.) Earlier forecasts had expected an installed PVR base of between 20 and 50 million units by 2005.[8] One survey reported that while 22 percent of consumers expected to buy a PVR within two years, another 71 percent said they probably never would.[9] Challenges cited for broader adoption by the market include the hassle of adding yet another set-top box to the TV set (for those buying the stand-alone service) to a basic lack of understanding about the product benefits.

**22**     Consumers that have adopted PVRs usually say they have done so to be able to pause, replay, or skip ahead when watching TV—or, according to almost two-thirds of them, to skip commercials.

**23**     The size and shape of the PVR market in the United States and the speed of adoption among consumers are topics of hot debate.

**24**     When TiVo was launched in the late 1990s, feverish projections put penetration of PVRs at 20 to 50 million units by 2005.[10] However, despite spending $50 million on an ad campaign in 2000, TiVo's revenues totaled a mere $3.7 million that year. Its customer acquisition costs were estimated to be over $1,000 per person. In 2002, the Yankee Group revised its forecasts to predict that 19.1 million U.S. homes would have PVRs by the end of 2006[11]; Screen Digest projected PVRs to reach 15.3 million installed units by 2006.[12] A Forrester

[7]The Personal Video Recorder: Market Assessments and Forecasts 2001–2006," *Screen Digest,* Aug. 2002.
[8]*NY Times.*
[9]Consumer Electronics Association survey, 2002.
[10]"PVR sales slower than first expected," *New York Times,* vol. CLI, no. 52,210; Aug 14, 2002, p. C6.
[11]Shim, R. "DVRs—are they hot or not?," *CNET News,* retrieved 10/12/02 from http://news.com.com/2100-1040-960554.html.
[12]"PVR sales slower than first expected," *New York Times,* vol. CLI, no. 52,210; Aug 14, 2002, p. C6.

**EXHIBIT 4**

Source: Forrester, Screen
Digest, and Yankee Group
forecasts.

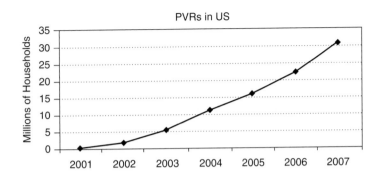

study projected that 39 million households would have digital video recording capability by 2007, but that only 12 million of these would use stand-alone units like the original TiVo box.[13] By comparison, in 2002 the installed base of DVDs was already 32 million units, while VCRs are in 96 million households.

25    As of Fall 2002, some 1.3 million Americans had PVRs, with that number estimated to hit 1.8 million U.S. homes by year's end.[14] As the market leader, TiVo alone claimed 500,000 subscribers by the end of 2002—an 18.4 percent increase since the beginning of the year. But as one media industry wag noted, "More U.S. homes have outhouses (671,000) than TiVos. . . ."[15]

26    Four factors have contributed to the slower-than-expected uptake of this new technology by consumers. The first hurdle is knowledge. As a new technology that replaces an older one (i.e., VCRs) but adds radically different capabilities, PVRs have not been well understood by consumers. As recently as Summer 2002, 70 percent of consumers surveyed by Forrester couldn't say what a PVR is or does.[16] Once they see the technology demonstrated, however, 79 percent of consumers with digital television service and 59 percent of those with analog service say they are very interested in PVR capabilities, according to the Cable & Telecommunications Association for Marketing.[17]

27    The second hurdle is price. To buy TiVo as a standalone product, consumers must purchase the set-top box (originally around $650, down to $400 from Sony in 2002) and the service (about $10 per month or $250 for lifetime). As an add-on service to DirecTV, the cost is approximately the same with the DirecTV subscription included. These price ranges are clearly much higher than simply purchasing a VCR (or even the projected price tags for DVD recorders), and far beyond the "magic threshold" of $300 for consumer electronics devices.

28    The third hurdle is ease of set-up and use. Adding yet another set-top box to the array in one's home entertainment center is disincentive enough for many consumers. In addition,

[13]Bernoff, J. (2002), "Some startling truths about on-demand TV," *TechStrategy,* Forrester Research, retrieved 10/13/02 from http://www.forrester.com/ER/Research/Brief/0,1317,15802,00.html.
Sorid, D. (2002), "Plugged in: cable connection weakest link on digital recorders," *Reuters,* retrieved 10/13/02 from www.reuters.com.
[14]Shim, R. (2002), "DVRs—are they hot or not?," *CNET News,* retrieved 10/12/02 from http://news.com.com/2100-1040-960554.html.
[15]Johnson, B. (2002), "More U.S. homes have outhouses than TiVos," *AdAge.com,* retrieved 11/16/02 from http://www.adage.com/news.cms?newsId=36471.
[16]Bernoff, J. (2002), "Some startling truths about on-demand TV," *TechStrategy,* Forrester Research, retrieved 10/13/02 from http://www.forrester.com/ER/Research/Brief/0,1317,15802,00.html.
[17]Everitt, D. (2002), "Scoop! Consumers do like iTV gizmos," *Media Life,* retrieved 10/12/02 from http://209.61.190.23/pages/templates/scripts/prfr.asp.

some users have reported difficulties setting up the service to work with a cable or satellite provider.

29    The fourth hurdle is a subtle one, in play with only the most technologically sophisticated consumers and less a stop sign than a flashing yellow: privacy. Because one's PVR is truly personal, keeping track of exact viewing habits and preferences, it can be used to gather and report vast amounts of very specific data that would be invaluable to marketers. For some in the media and advertising industry, this data is what TiVo and its counterparts can offer in exchange for letting viewers skip broadcast ads. Although TiVo and the others have stated privacy policies and opt-out provisions, they have all come under scrutiny from the Privacy Foundation for not making this capability transparent to consumers.

30    Once consumers take the PVR plunge, however, their devotion to the technology is palpable. In a recent study by NextResearch, 83 percent of PVR owners said they liked their new technology much better than their VCR, and 76 percent said it made TV "more fun." Nearly three out of four PVR owners (73 percent) actually found the technology easy to use—regardless of rumors to the contrary—and almost half (48 percent) declared its price "a bargain." Some 52 percent declared that they wanted a PVR for each of their television sets, and just over one in three (35 percent) already owned more than one device.[18]

31    Having a PVR can change a consumer's TV habits. Just under half the PVR owners in NextResearch's survey said they watched more television, sampled programs and channels they'd never used before (because of inconvenient or conflicting timing), and no longer "surfed" the channels while watching television. In another study, more than half of PVR owners reported that what they like best about the technology is the ability to pause TV programming and/or replay key scenes. Over a third enjoyed skipping through scenes of show like skipping ahead on a music CD. Perhaps most significantly, 61 percent cherished the ability to skip commercials[19] (although only 27 percent in the NextResearch study said they always actually did so). Satisfying this consumer desire places TiVo and its competitors at odds with their media partners, as seen below.

# PARTNERING FOR HARDWARE, SOFTWARE, AND CONNECTIVITY

32    Since it offers both a device and a service, TiVo has multiple suppliers, many of whom are actually partners with a vested interest in the company's success.

### Hardware Providers

33    The TiVo set-top box is essentially a simplified personal computer running a simple but highly stable operating system on a powerful fault-tolerant processor and a hard drive to record digital programs in compressed broadcast quality MPEG 2 MP/ML format. The processor is a PowerPC, running on Linux operating system. Hard drives are provided by the Consumer Electronic Business Unit (CEBU) of Quantum Corporation's Hard Drive Group, and are powered by Quantum QuickView audio/video.

---

[18]*The PVR Monitor* vol. 2, NextResearch, retrieved 10/13/02 from http://www.nextresearch.com/default.html.
[19]*Digital Video Recorder Interest and Awareness Survey*, Consumer Electronics Association, 2002.

### Set-top Box Manufacturers

**34**   TiVo established relationships with three of the largest consumer electronics manufacturers: Philips, Sony, and Thomson Multimedia. This approach was intended to establish TiVo as a new standard in home entertainment consumption and expand the reach of the distribution thanks to the vast global network of retailers and wholesalers available to Philips, Sony and Thomson Multimedia. Furthermore, the experience of these partners in industrial design expands the variety of devices offering similar functionalities, thus expanding the potential user base, and their brand equity as well as marketing strength will further assist establishing this new segment.

### Software Developers

**35**   Among the multiple pieces of software required to run the TiVo set-top box, Liberate Technologies is the dominant provider of the software platform. This acts as the underlying foundation for the functionalities offered on the TiVo box. Liberate also licenses its Liberate TV Navigator software to satellite and cable TV operators. Liberate develops multiple software programs enabling convergence between TV and PC functionalities—such as Liberate TV Mail, Liberate TV Chat—and developer's tools such as Liberate TV Producer Studio tools and Liberate TV Emulator tools.

**36**   Other major software providers include OpenTV Corp. for added functionalities on the platform required to offer interactive services for the content. OpenTV plays a critical role in enabling external providers and developers to author content using industry standards such as HTML and JavaScript, particularly considering its network of 1,300 content developers in its Partner Program. The Device Mosaic 5.0 version enables networks to display and manage HTML content on the screen, regardless of the source: TV network/cable head-end or Internet.

**37**   The operating system is Linux and TiVo follows industry standards established by bodies such as the Motion Picture Experts Group (MPEG) for the digital video signal recorded (MPEG 2). TiVo also uses open standards protocols established by leading software and hardware manufacturers such as Sun Microsystems for JavaScript to avoid risks of lock-in into a particular technology.

**38**   These supplier relationships are established through complex licensing deals in order to secure long-term agreements and establish the TiVo experience in the TV viewing market.

### Connectivity

**39**   The TiVo box requires an RJ-11 connection to a phone line in order to update the interactive program guide and download software updates. Therefore, TiVo relies on the availability and compatibility of operators in the user's area, which is not a truly limiting factor in the United States but may be overseas where phone jacks and telecommunications protocols may be different. Other connectivity suppliers include the various manufacturers of standard input: RF S-video, and RCA composite video.

# NOW PLAYING: THE CONTENT SIDE OF TiVo

**40**   While it may not seem obvious at first, consumers purchase TiVo boxes in order to desynchronize the TV viewing experience and digitally record their favorite shows to enjoy them at any time. Therefore, content providers play a critical role in the value chain supporting TiVo's market penetration. A lack of consistent quality programming available on TV would tend to shift entertainment consumption toward other alternatives such as video rentals,

**EXHIBIT 5**

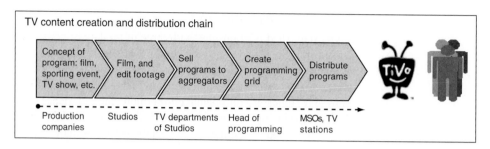

TV content creation and distribution chain

pay-per-view, Internet, gaming consoles and PCs, as well as entertainment outside of the home such as movie theaters, plays, live sports, art exhibitions, and so on. Therefore, all participants in the content creation chain play a distinct role as suppliers to TiVo:

- *Content owners:* film studios, professional sports teams, TV production companies, etc.

- *Content aggregators:* pay-per-view and video-on-demand, premium cable (HBO, Showtime, Cinemax, etc.), basic cable (Bravo IFC, USA, TBS, etc.), and broadcast TV channels (ABC, CBS, NBC, Fox, etc.).

- *Content distributors:* MSOs (Cablevision, Time Warner Cable, Adelphia, etc.), TV stations (KXYZs), syndication, DBS operators (EchoStar, DirecTV).

# PVRS AND THE ENTERTAINMENT INDUSTRY: LOVE, HATE, AND LITIGATION

**41**     A PVR would not be worth the hardware and software it was made of without content: the television programming, movies, and other entertainment fare that consumers want to capture for viewing at their convenience. This would suggest a symbiotic relationship between PVR innovators and the media industry with significant mutual benefits (much like the current relationship between entertainment companies and the VCR and DVD industries).

**42**     However, many in the entertainment industry view PVRs as a threat. First, PVRs more readily enable viewers to skip commercials altogether while watching TV. This further reduces the number of viewers who will see the commercial, a metric used for advertisement pricing— not welcome news in a market that has already seen revenues plummet. While TiVo's management argued that the personalized programming enabled by the PVR would actually enable advertisers to more closely target their desired markets, most advertisers were skeptical that this benefit would outweigh the exposure lost from consumers skipping commercials.

**43**     Second, the PVR technology has the potential for a Napster-like file-sharing system to emerge. Like Napster, this will likely be met with a fierce intellectual property response. There were already several lawsuits with the courts or pending that could dramatically change the landscape of this industry. A consortium of companies in the entertainment industry has successfully sued SONICBlue to report on its customers' usage patterns and report it back to the entertainment industry. This lawsuit stemmed from ReplayTV's latest feature allowing users to share videos over a high-speed internet connection. Some ReplayTV customers in turn are suing the entertainment industry over this as an invasion of privacy.

## To Build or Buy? TiVo's Product Development and R&D

**44**     As a new company deploying a very new technology in a time of rapid technological change, TiVo's earliest strategy was joining forces with content providers, consumer electronics manufacturers, and technology providers to focus on the development of interactive video services.

**45**    At the time of TiVo's inception in 1997, many start-up companies managed to secure venture capital but quickly ran out of time and money due to a penchant for embarking on large in-house technology projects to build every feature from scratch—even though these features and functions did not all constitute a source of competitive advantage. Rather than dedicating its scarce resources in developing proprietary software to support all aspects of the service and features, TiVo elected to use established standards and limit internal software development to the features that truly differentiated its service from others.

**46**    As an example, Open TV provides software that enables developers of interactive video services to create features appealing to consumers under an attractive revenue model for MSOs, satellite operators, and other premium TV access providers. TiVo elected to author and develop its key interactive features using Open TV software and to use Liberate Technologies for its Liberate TV Navigator software. The use of outsourced technology enabled TiVo to ramp up faster as the technologies served as a foundation from which to build TiVo's services. To protect its key proprietary features from imitation, TiVo filed patents with the United States Patent and Trademark Office.

**47**    Other key partners of TiVo's development include MSOs and satellite operators such as DirecTV, BSkyB, Comcast, AT&T Broadband, as well as some content producers such as NBC, Discovery and Disney (see Now Playing, above). Most of these partners seem to be silent strategic investors providing capital to secure an outpost to observe the evolution of the PVR market at a tactical level.

### Through the Factories and Into the Stores

**48**    To get its set-top boxes built and into the hands of consumers, TiVo has turned to partnerships with large consumer electronics manufacturers, including three industry giants: Sony, Philips and Thomson. Thomson manufactures TiVo-branded devices as well as set-top boxes for satellite service provider DirecTV. Under licensing agreements with large electronics manufacturers, TiVo provides its patented technology to OEMs such as Philips and Sony that include it in their own branded PVRs. For instance, Sony signed a 7-year licensing agreement with TiVo in 2001. Similarly, Toshiba announced the expansion of an agreement from June 2001 with its Toshiba America Electronics Components and Toshiba Semiconductors business units to supply the TiVo technology directly on chips, which can be included more easily into third-party electronic devices such as DVD players, set-top boxes, and so on.

**49**    Through these manufacturers TiVo has gained expertise and economies of scope and scale. Their unique industrial design skills, global distribution networks, and marketing strength have further aided TiVo's attempt to establish a new standard in TV watching. Without these consumer electronic partnerships, these resources would be out of TiVo's reach, due to the capital requirements that can only be met by companies with a scope of activity similar to these conglomerates. By partnering with these firms and licensing its key features to them, TiVo compensates for its limited scope and manages to leverage their resources as well

**EXHIBIT 6**
**TiVo Products in 2002**

| Model | Price | Recording Capacity | Program Source |
|---|---|---|---|
| TiVo Series2 DVR | $299* | 60 hours | All |
|  | $349* | 80 hours | All |
| Sony Digital Network Recorder | $399* | 80 hours | All |
| DIRECTV Receiver with TiVo | $199 | 35 hours | DirecTV |
| AT&T Broadband TiVo Series2 DVR | $199* | 40 hours | AT&T Broadband |

*After mail-in rebate.

as receiving indirect benefits of an "endorsement" of the technology by these consumer electronics firms. In addition, these partnerships provide TiVo with intangible benefits in the form of experience curve learning in design and consumer needs. These large manufacturers know how to design equipment for the mass market and will likely pass some of this knowledge on to TiVo.

## MARKETING AN INNOVATION: FIRST, CREATE A NEED

50   For an altogether new technology like the PVR, the marketing function includes both creating/developing a market and positioning oneself to meet a market need. TiVo has used several strategies to meet these marketing imperatives—none of which have come cheap.

51   Since its launch in 1997, TiVo spent a reported $178 million on sales and marketing—compared to $79 million it has invested in R&D. The marketing investment has included the "TiVo, TV Your Way" 2000 national advertising blitz, which featured the now-infamous ad in which a TV executive—blamed in the voiceover for "decid[ing] what we watch and when we watch it"—is thrown out a skyscraper office window by two beefy Everymen. Viacom Inc.'s CBS television network, a TiVo investor, declined to run at least one of those spots,[20] and the media industry in general has not forgotten.[21]

52   Meanwhile, TiVo has grappled with multiple challenges on the marketing front. The first has been the consumer's slowness to warm to the new technology, particularly at its initial steep price point and combination upfront/recurring cost structure. (TiVo responded by bringing the initial price down, with indeterminate results so far.) The Internet bust in 2000 and lagging economy since has tightened the flow of capital, while TiVo's own stock price has plummeted—leaving it with fewer resources with which to blitz the market into an understanding of PVRs and what they do. The exit of Microsoft from the direct PVR market in early 2002, which was certainly something of a competitive relief, also means that the task of developing consumer understanding of PVRs weighs heavily on TiVo, with backup only from a distracted ReplayTV (now owned by SONICBlue and embroiled in Napster-like legal wrangling with the media industry). Finally, the cable and satellite industries are once again lurching forward with deployment of digital television and video-on-demand technologies, which threaten to make the stand-alone PVR obsolete.

53   TiVo has attempted to combat these developments through a combination of consumer education (including demonstrations at home electronics retail emporia), more benefits-focused television advertising, and clever product placement on shows like *The Mind of a Married Man*. On the cable/satellite front, TiVo has also developed an extensive co-marketing partnership with DirecTV which offers consumers a set-top box that integrates both satellite TV and TiVo functions, lets viewers record two shows at once, and provides up to 35 hours of storage. The lifetime cost of the box and service is estimated to be about $600, not including DirecTV.[22] The DirecTV partnership arrangement reportedly brings in more new TiVo subscribers than TiVo has sold on its own in a comparable period. (Had DirecTV's bid to purchase EchoStar not been blocked in court, this partnership might have grown even larger.) For TiVo, the bundling arrangement makes its technologically advanced capabilities (such as the interactive program

[20]Kranhold, K., (2000) , "TiVo ad campaign's sly humour isn't a hit with CBS executives," *FinancialExpress.com*, retrieved 11/16/02 from http://www.financialexpress.com/fe/daily/20000706/fst06033.html.
[21]Goetzl, D. (2002), "As speakers fault TiVo marketing campaign," *AdAge.com*, retrieved 11/16/02 from http://www.adage.com/news.cms?newsId=34048.
[22]"PVR shoot-out," *Tech TV,* retrieved on 9/26/02 from www.techtv.com (see also Exhibit 13).

**EXHIBIT 7**

TiVo Income Statement: Tivo Inc., Consolidated Statements of Operations, (in thousands, except per share data)

| | Three Months Ended | | 12 Months Ended | |
|---|---|---|---|---|
| | 31-Jan-02 | 31-Jan-01 | 31-Jan-02 | 31-Jan-01 |
| **Revenue:** | | | | |
| Revenue | $6,753 | $2,166 | $19,297 | $4,636 |
| Revenue-related parties | — | — | 100 | — |
| Total revenue | 6,753 | 2,166 | 19,397 | 4,636 |
| **Costs and expenses:** | | | | |
| Cost of revenue | 4,830 | 5,661 | 19,888 | 19,099 |
| Cost of revenue-related parties | — | — | 61 | — |
| Research and development | 5,815 | 5,888 | 26,859 | 25,092 |
| Sales and marketing | 2,649 | 46,905 | 28,509 | 106,444 |
| Sales and marketing-related parties | 24,959 | 21,093 | 75,832 | 58,011 |
| General and administrative | 4,486 | 4,483 | 18,495 | 15,057 |
| Stock based compensation | 273 | 562 | 1,247 | 2,968 |
| Total operating expenses | 43,012 | 84,592 | 170,891 | 226,671 |
| Loss from operations | (36,259) | (82,426) | (151,494) | (222,035) |
| Other income and (expenses), net | (1,845) | 2,219 | (2,161) | 7,370 |
| **Net loss before taxes** | (38,104) | (80,207) | (153,655) | (214,665) |
| Provision for Income Taxes | — | — | (1,000) | — |
| **Net loss** | (38,104) | (80,207) | (154,655) | (214,665) |
| Series A preferred stock dividend | (428) | (1,272) | (3,018) | (1,937) |
| **Net loss attributable to common stock** | (38,532) | (81,479) | (157,673) | (216,602) |
| | | | | |
| Net loss per share—basic and diluted | (0.85) | (2.00) | (3.67) | (5.75) |
| Shares used in per share computation | 45,276 | 40,774 | 42,956 | 37,640 |
| **Other Data** | | | | |
| Net Activations | 100,000 | 70,000 | 226,000 | 131,000 |
| Cumulative Subscribers | 380,000 | 154,000 | 380,000 | 154,000 |
| Adjusted EBITDA*('000s) | (23,800) | (64,500) | (100,400) | (182,200) |

*Adjusted EBITDA is operating income plus depreciation, amortization, and other noncash charges plus the change in deferred revenue over the reporting period.

guide) more transparent and easier for consumers to use. At the same time, the need for the core PVR functions, such as seeking out and recording of shows, becomes much more obvious when there are literally hundreds of channels to choose from. A similar partnership with AT&T Broadband will likely be affected by that service's pending merger with Comcast.

54    Overall, since the heady days of tongue-in-cheek TV ads, TiVo's rate of direct marketing spending has slowed just more than a fourth of what it was at its peak ($102 million in 2000; see Exhibit 7 for financial reports). Some suspect that the big outlays have shifted from direct marketing spending by TiVo to a less obvious flow of cash to marketing partners such as DirecTV, since the company is reporting expenditures in 2001 of $76 million for "sales and marketing-related parties," an increase of more than 40 percent. "Add it up, and TiVo has spent $767 to win each of its 464,000 subscribers," one media analyst observed dryly.[23]

[23]Pomerantz, D., "Do you TiVo?," *Forbes.com* (online preview of 11/25/02 issue), accessed at http://www.forbes.com/forbes/2002/1125/054.html on 11/16/02.

**EXHIBIT 8**
TiVo Balance
Sheet: Tivo Inc.,
Consolidated Balance
Sheets, (in thousands)

| | 31-Jan-02 | 31-Jan-01 |
|---|---|---|
| **Assets** | | |
| Cash, cash equivalents and short-term investments | $ 52,327 | $ 124,474 |
| Restricted cash | 51,735 | 50,104 |
| Accounts receivable, net | 2,185 | 1,834 |
| Accounts receivable–related parties | 6,687 | 4,816 |
| Prepaid expenses and other | 13,146 | 6,693 |
| Prepaid expenses and other–related parties | 12,423 | 1,698 |
| Property and equipment, net | 18,146 | 21,924 |
| **Total assets** | **$ 156,649** | **$ 211,543** |
| | | |
| **Liabilities, Redeemable Convertible Preferred Stock & Stockholders' Equity (Deficit)** | | |
| Accounts payable and accrued liabilities | $ 28,377 | $ 45,155 |
| Accounts payable and accrued liabilities–related parties | 28,902 | 49,839 |
| Deferred revenue | 36,338 | 18,323 |
| Deferred revenue–related parties | 11,427 | — |
| Capital lease obligations | 538 | 1,334 |
| Convertible notes payable, long-term | 24,280 | — |
| Convertible notes payable–related parties, long-term | 12,453 | — |
| Redeemable convertible preferred stock | 46,555 | 46,555 |
| Total stockholders' equity (deficit) | (32,221) | 50,337 |
| **Liabilities, redeemable convertible preferred stock & stockholders' equity (deficit)** | **$ 156,649** | **$ 211,543** |

| TiVo Inc. 2002 Selected Balance Sheet Items (in thousands) | 31-Jul-02 | 31-Jan-02 |
|---|---|---|
| Cash, cash equivalents and short-term investments | 26,753 | 52,327 |
| Restricted cash | — | 51,735 |
| Accounts receivable, net | 6,333 | 2,185 |
| Accounts receivable–related parties | 4,286 | 6,687 |
| Inventories | 2,719 | — |
| Accounts payable and accrued liabilities | 32,798 | 28,377 |
| Accounts payable and accrued liabilities–related parties | 8,751 | 28,902 |
| Deferred revenue | 44,928 | 36,338 |
| Deferred revenue–related parties | 4,466 | 11,427 |

# DEVELOPING OTHER REVENUE SOURCES

55 Given its marketing and deployment challenges, it is not too surprising that TiVo has begun exploring new paths for its technology.

56 A significant evolution in TiVo's history was the inception of TiVo Technologies, headed by Ta-Wei Chein, Senior Vice-President and General Manager, in October 2001. While this business unit has not received as much publicity as its parent, its ambitions may be of a greater magnitude. TiVo's primary business is the development of hardware and software for the PVR market. However, TiVo Technologies acts as its licensing arm, providing these

**EXHIBIT 9**
**TiVo Financials**

**TiVo performance vs. Nasdaq and SonicBlue (SBLU)**

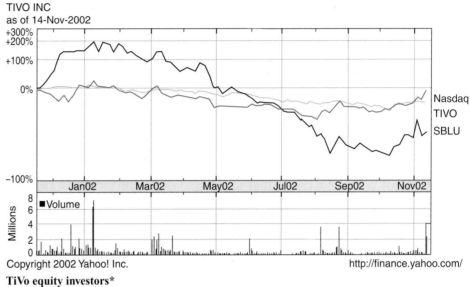

TIVO INC
as of 14-Nov-2002

Copyright 2002 Yahoo! Inc.                                    http://finance.yahoo.com/

**TiVo equity investors***

Advance/Newhouse

DIRECTV.

encore

Liberty Digital

PHILIPS

SHOWTIME

SONY

TV Guide Interactive

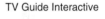

*Downloaded from *http://www.tivo.com/5.4.asp* on 11/16/02.

hardware and software solutions to clients willing to sell PVR devices or integrate its functionalities into cable and satellite set-top boxes.

57    Potentially even more controversial has been TiVo's promotion of "advertainment"—special-format commercials that TiVo downloads onto consumers' set-top boxes to help advertisers "establish . . . far deeper communications with consumers."[24] A "Digital Feng Shui" promotion with Best Buy, for example, provided Sheryl Crow and Vanessa Carleton music videos, movies like "Mr. Deeds," and other media goodies for TiVo customers whose boxes were digitally tagged for the retailer. In the United Kingdom, TiVo users were surprised in May 2002 to find an entire BBC sitcom downloaded (by arrangement between the

[24]TiVo Company Information, retrieved 11/1/02 from http://www.tivo.com.

network and the service) to their TiVo boxes while they slept. In late fall 2002, TiVo part-nered with BMW to push its minifilm series, "The Hire," out to TiVo users in the United States, who can now watch their choice of short, action-oriented films for the carmaker by directors from Ang Lee to Guy Ritchie. TiVo owners who purchased the box and service so they could skip commercials may be particularly puzzled by this new business effort, which one TiVo fan calls ironically "the latest installment in the long-running series 'Keep TiVo, Inc. Solvent'."[25]

## WILL THE TRAILBLAZER SURVIVE THE TRAIL?

58    Given all of the economic, competitive, and market arrows TiVo has taken in the five short years of its existence, Michael Ramsay's curt assessment of the pioneer's dilemma might be seen as either the ultimate in bravado or the sober view of a survivor. Can TiVo leverage its core assets to cash in on the interactive, asynchronous TV future it helped create? Or will TiVo and its PVR one day seem as anachronistic as an eight-track tape?

**EXHIBIT 10**
**TiVo Ratios (vs. competitors)**

Source: MultexInvestor
http://www.multexinvestor.com.

|  | TiVo | SONICBlue | Industry | Sector | S&P500 |
|---|---|---|---|---|---|
| **Price to Sales (TTM)** | 3.54 | 0.15 | 3.78 | 2.27 | 3.02 |
| **Sales Growth (MRQ) vs Qtr.** | | | | | |
|   **1 Yr. Ago** | 751.51 | 43.1 | 10.31 | 10.03 | 7 |
| **Sales Growth (TTM) vs TTM** | | | | | |
|   **1 Yr. Ago** | 460.67 | 22.03 | 8.73 | 8.97 | 2.71 |
| **Quick Ratio (MRQ)** | 0.64 | 0.97 | 1.18 | 0.81 | 1.11 |
| **Current Ratio (MRQ)** | 0.8 | 1.19 | 1.46 | 1.38 | 1.64 |
| **LT Debt to Equity (MRQ)** | NM | 2.13 | 0.64 | 0.83 | 0.74 |
| **Total Debt to Equity (MRQ)** | NM | 2.37 | 0.68 | 0.97 | 0.98 |
| **Interest Coverage (TTM)** | −43.17 | −8.05 | 3.86 | 6.53 | 10.29 |
| **Gross Margin (TTM)** | 36.64 | 18.11 | 43.92 | 40.22 | 47.47 |

TTM = Trailing Twelve Months; MRQ = Most Recent Quarter.

[25]Rywalt, C. (2002), "TiVo taken hostage," retrieved on 11/17/02 from www.teevee.org.

**EXHIBIT 11**
**Competing Products and Services**

Replay TV 5000

### Replay TV 5000 Features Highlight

- Tape-Free Recording—Easy one-touch recording with convenient on-screen channel guide, including a full 14 days of programming information.
- Live TV Control—Pause, rewind, instant replay, slo-mo or frame-advance.
- Commercial Advance®—Choose to playback recorded shows without commercials.
- Highest Recording Capacity—From 40 to 320* hours of recording space, depending on model.
- Progressive Scan—Supports high-quality picture playback on digital TVs.
- Advanced Capabilities—Home networking for room-to-room video streaming,* broadband Internet, wireless USB network connectivity* and digital photo capabilities.

*The ReplayTV 5320, software support for wireless USB (802.11 b) Network Devices and software support for video sharing and streaming between ReplayTV 5000 and ReplayTV 4000/4500 are estimated to be available Q1 2003.

**EXHIBIT 12**
**Comparison with Competitors**

| PVR Shoot-Out | | | | |
|---|---|---|---|---|
| **PVR Comparison Chart** | | | | |
| | **ReplayTV 4000 Series** | **TiVo** | **TiVo with DirecTV** | **UltimateTV** |
| **Price** | $700 | $400 | $350–$400 | $350–$400 |
| **Monthly service charges** | Free | $10/month or $250/lifetime | $10/month or $250/lifetime | $10/month |
| **Required services** | Ethernet connection | Phone line | Phone line, DirecTV service ($32/month) | DirecTV service ($32/month) |
| **Interface rating** | ★★★★★ | ★★★★★ | ★★★★★ | ★★★★★ |
| **Features rating** | ★★★★★ | ★★★★★ | ★★★★★ | ★★★★★ |
| **Requirements rating** | ★★★★★ | ★★★★★ | ★★★★★ | ★★★★★ |
| **Overall cost with lifetime service** | $700 | $650 | $600–$650 + DirecTV | $350–$400 + $10/month + DirecTV |

Note: All PVRs in this comparison featured approximately 40GB of hard disk storage space. This equates to about 40 hours of recording capability at the lowest quality.

## EXHIBIT 13 Competing Products and Services
**HBO OnDemand**

# Case 47  The Apollo Group, Inc. (University of Phoenix)[1]

## Richard B. Robinson, John A. Pearce II, and Alan B. Eisner

1   As an entrepreneur, John G. Sperling was a late bloomer. A Ph.D. who had spent most of his career teaching at San Jose State University, he didn't launch Apollo Group, Inc.—parent of the University of Phoenix, the nation's largest private university—until 1976, when he was 55. But what Sperling lacked in precociousness he more than made up for in ambition: His goal was nothing less than to turn conventional higher education on its head.

2   Rather than catering to 18- to 22-year-olds looking to find themselves, Sperling focused on the then-neglected market of working adults. And he recruited working professionals as teachers, rather than tenured professors. Although UOP and its online campus, University of Phoenix Online, have more than 9,000 faculty, only about 250 are full-time. Most radical of all, while nearly all other universities are nonprofits, Sperling ran his university to make money. Those ideas sparked overwhelming resistance from the education establishment, which branded UOP a "diploma mill." The result? "We faced failure every day for the first 10 years," says Chairman Sperling, who turned 83 in 2004.

3   By mid-2003 Apollo soared all the way to the number seven spot on *BusinessWeek*'s Hot Growth 100 Companies list. The Phoenix-based company, whose day-to-day operations are run by CEO Todd S. Nelson, 45, generated average annual revenue growth of 27 percent over the past three years, to $1.4 billion in 2003. Profits rose 41 percent per year, to $247 million. And with a price-earnings ratio of 56, Apollo had one of the richest price-earnings multiples on Wall Street.

4   Tuition at Apollo averages only $10,000 a year, 55 percent of what a typical private college charges. A key factor, says Sperling, is that universities for the young require student unions, sports teams, student societies, and so on. The average age of a UOP student is 35, so UOP doesn't have those expenses. It also saves by holding classes in leased office spaces around the country. And 75,000 of its 200,000 students study at University of Phoenix Online.

---

**APOLLO GROUP**

**WHAT'S HOT**  Online education for working adults. Last year, University of Phoenix Online's enrollment surged 70%.

**RANKING  #7**

**SALES  $1.34 billion**

**EARNINGS  $247 million**

**LOCATION  Phoenix**

---

[1]This case was developed by Richard B. Robinson of the University of South Carolina and John A. Pearce II of Villanova University and Alan B. Eisner, Pace University based on publicly available information from The Apollo Group, Inc., interviews with UOP students and professors, and selected *BusinessWeek* articles. All rights reserved to the authors.

5    Sperling is still frustating against the establishment. His latest target: textbooks. "AGI's goal is to move all of AGI's texts and materials into electronic format," he says. Some 30,000 Apollo students use digital materials. By early 2004 it should be everyone.

6    From 2001 to 2003, the University of Phoenix Online (UOPX) pulled off the rarest of feats: Its stock skyrocketed, hitting an all-time high of $47.17 on May 12, 2003, despite the worst tech-stock bear market in history. Apollo Group, which also owns the University of Phoenix, the nation's largest private university, first floated UOPX as a tracking stock in September, 2000—just months before the broader tech market cratered.

7    The aim, says Apollo CEO Todd Nelson, was to raise the money needed to help Phoenix Online keep up with blistering enrollment growth in its online degree programs. And that growth has scarcely faltered. Phoenix Online's shares have soared 557 percent, making it one of the best-performing tracking stocks ever and helping it reach the number 17 spot in *BusinessWeek*'s 2003 Info Tech 100 list.

8    Phoenix Online appears to be clearly the dominant player in a nascent market that still has lots of potential for growth. The bricks-and-mortar University of Phoenix was one of the first institutions to identify and serve the burgeoning market for educating working adults. In the late 1980s, long before the Web debuted, the school began to experiment with offering its classes online. It got off to a slow start, "and we lost money for a number of years," recalls Brian Mueller, Phoenix Online's CEO.

9    As a result of this head start, however, Phoenix Online was ready to capitalize on an online-education market that began exploding in the mid-1990s. Today, about 13 percent of the 500,000 or so U.S. students earning a degree via the Net are enrolled at Phoenix Online, figures Sean Gallagher, an analyst at Boston-based market researcher, Eduventures Inc.

10   Phoenix Online also garners an outsize share of the industry's revenues—about one-third of the total. That's because as the market leader, it can charge higher tuition than most rivals. Undergraduates pay a little more than $10,000 a year at Phoenix Online, while students seeking a masters degree pay nearly $12,500. "They're by far the giant in this industry," says Gallagher. Appendix A at the end of this case lists some of the other key players or "competitors."

11   Is the best yet to come? Both Phoenix Online and the broader industry are still in their infancy. "There are 70 million working adults in this country who don't have a college degree," says Cappelli. Increasingly, they realize that they need a degree to get ahead. But because they often have a family as well as a job, studying online is the most convenient solution.

12   Howard Block, an analyst at Banc of America Securities, predicts "dramatic enrollment growth" for Phoenix Online. He expects that half of the students in post-secondary education will one day make at least some use of the Internet to earn their degrees.

## GLOBAL OUTREACH

13   Another plus: Phoenix Online began to tap the international market only about six months ago. So far, "we're bringing in about 500 students a month," says Mueller. "But that's just the tip of the iceberg."

14   Though Phoenix Online now offers classes only in English, it plans to begin doing so in Spanish and possibly Mandarin as well. Ironically, one of the hottest tech stocks of recent years has done all this with plain-vanilla technology. While other companies charged into online education with dazzling digital content, Phoenix Online offers a text-heavy format that can easily be accessed with dial-up modems.

15   This might sound like a recipe for failure. But Phoenix Online realized that interaction with humans—the professor and other students in the class—was far more important to suc-

cess than interaction with the digital content. Thus, Phoenix Online keeps its classes small, averaging just 11 students. And to combat the Achilles heel of distance education—a high dropout rate—it offers its students plenty of hand-holding, including round-the-clock tech support. The result: 65 percent of its students go on to graduate.

**16**     Some see plain technology as a potential negative for the virtual college. "At some point, Phoenix Online will need to upgrade the sophistication of its platform," warns Trace Urdan, an anlayst with ThinkEquity Partners, a boutique investment bank. That will require more spending on research and development and information technology, he warns, which could crimp margins. Still, any extra spending could be easily offset if Phoenix Online bumped up its class size to 15 students, argues Block. Even with today's small classes, operating profit margins now top 30 percent.

# BLURRING LINES

**17**     The biggest concern over Phoenix Online centers on how long it will be listed. "UOP's intention is to fold it back in to Apollo eventually," says Apollo CEO Nelson. He explains that over time, a blurring of the line between Phoenix Online and students at traditional University of Phoenix campuses will occur as those campuses make growing use of digital technology. But Nelson promises that such a move isn't imminent—and certainly not over the next four quarters.

**18**     Probably, as Phoenix Online balloons in size, its growth rate will slow from the 80 percent revenue gain it posted in each of the last two years. In the first six months of its current fiscal year, revenues climbed at a slightly cooler pace of 67 percent.

### The Trend Toward Privatization In the Education Industry

**19**     The $800 billion education industry seemed poised for rapid growth in 2001, propelled by public pressure to fix failing schools. But the war on terrorism put school reform on the back burner, and the deepening recession forced many states to scale back school spending. Meanwhile, venture capitalists—who had pumped $5.5 billion into for-profit education companies in 2000—turned down the spigot, cutting new investments by 75 percent in 2001.

**20**     As a result, 2002 ushered in a mixed future for education. Public spending on schools and colleges—which accounts for the bulk of education revenues—were squeezed as the recession cuts into tax receipts. Prior to September 11, "the rate of spending increases on

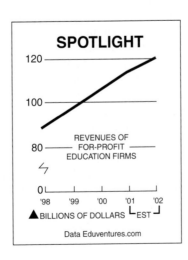

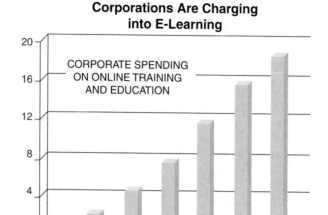

**Corporations Are Charging into E-Learning**

CORPORATE SPENDING ON ONLINE TRAINING AND EDUCATION

▶ BILLIONS OF DOLLARS    Data: International Data Corp.

education had already slowed sharply," says Ted Sanders, president of the Education Commission of the States, which monitors nationwide education trends. Higher education has been hit the hardest, he says, forcing a 16 percent hike in tuitions at public universities in the following two academic years, up from a 4.6 percent increase in 2001.

21    Even in this difficult environment, many companies in the for-profit education arena are succeeding. Eduventures, a Boston researcher, expects the $113 billion for-profit sector to grow 5 percent annually—far faster than education or the economy as a whole. Consider the companies that manage public schools for a profit. They continue to face intense opposition from teachers' unions and other critics. But H. Christopher Whittle, CEO of Edison Schools Inc. (EDSN), the largest for-profit schools operator, still expects revenues to soar 42 percent, to more than $500 million, in the fiscal year ending June 30. And on December 21, after an acrimonious debate, school privatization got its biggest boost yet when the state of Pennsylvania took over the deeply troubled Philadelphia school system. As part of the takeover, Edison expects to receive a contract to manage 45 of the city's schools.

22    A renewed federal focus on school reform may help the industry. Federal and state legislation is ensuring that alternatives such as charter schools, which are publicly funded, can be run by private companies. Meanwhile, legislated requirements that children be tested annually in grades 3 through 8 will create a bonanza for testing companies. Over the next five years, hundreds of millions of dollars will be spent "to help teachers and administrators prepare for these tests," says Jonathan Grayer, president of test-prep leader Kaplan Inc.

23    Equally strong tailwinds are behind companies such as Education Management Corp. (EDMC) and Apollo Group, Inc. (APOL), which provide post-secondary education to working adults. The recession helped boost enrollment at schools such as Apollo's University of Phoenix because more workers look to retool during downturns. Fred McCrae, an education analyst at Thomas Weisel Partners LLC, thinks post-secondary outfits "should grow earnings 20 percent to 25 percent."

24    In contrast, there won't be much growth in the $32 billion industry that provides corporate training, predicts Gregory M. Priest, CEO of SmartForce PLC (SMTF). This area will suffer as corporate America continues to cut costs. But companies that provide training over the Internet, such as SmartForce, will shine. E-learning spending by companies should grow 73 percent, to $7.3 billion, predicts International Data Corp. And once workers are ex-

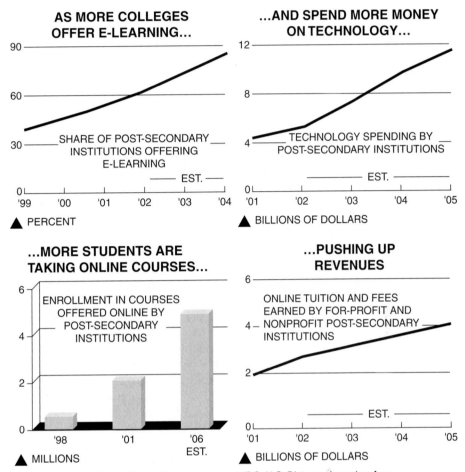

## The E-Learning Explosion

**AS MORE COLLEGES OFFER E-LEARNING...**

SHARE OF POST-SECONDARY INSTITUTIONS OFFERING E-LEARNING

— EST. —

▲ PERCENT

**...AND SPEND MORE MONEY ON TECHNOLOGY...**

TECHNOLOGY SPENDING BY POST-SECONDARY INSTITUTIONS

— EST. —

▲ BILLIONS OF DOLLARS

**...MORE STUDENTS ARE TAKING ONLINE COURSES...**

ENROLLMENT IN COURSES OFFERED ONLINE BY POST-SECONDARY INSTITUTIONS

▲ MILLIONS

**...PUSHING UP REVENUES**

ONLINE TUITION AND FEES EARNED BY FOR-PROFIT AND NONPROFIT POST-SECONDARY INSTITUTIONS

— EST. —

▲ BILLIONS OF DOLLARS

Data: International Data Corp., Eduventures.com, IDC, U.S. Distance Learning Assn.

posed to e-learning on the job, they're increasingly turning to institutions that allow them to earn college degrees online.

25   To be sure, the plunge in venture-capital funding triggered a brutal shakeout beginning in 2001. "Most of the companies built on bad ideas over the past three years are gone," says Peter Stokes, an executive vice-president at Eduventures. But for the survivors, the outlook is bright. "For-profit companies will play a larger and larger role in education," says Gregory W. Cappelli, an analyst at Credit Suisse First Boston. Looks like the handwriting is on the classroom wall.

### The Online Trend

26   The dot-com bubble may have burst in the world of commerce, but the promise of harnessing the Internet for paradigm-changing growth—and even profits—still thrives in the halls of academia. At the University of Maryland University College, enrollment in classes offered over the Net soared to 63,000 in the past academic year, up 50 percent from the year before. UMUC students can now earn some 70 degrees and certificates entirely online. The University of Phoenix Online, a subsidiary of the nation's largest for-profit university, saw

revenues jump some 76 percent in the fiscal year ended Aug. 31, to $181 million, while profits grew 82 percent, to $32 million.

27    Since the U.S. Army began rolling out an e-learning program in 2001, annually more than 10,400 soldiers are taking classes and earning degrees online from 24 participating colleges. Students at eArmyU, as it's known, receive a free laptop and printer and 100 percent of their tuition. No wonder the Army expects enrollment to hit 80,000 by 2005 as it takes the program Armywide.

28    Nearly two years after the dot-com fizzle began, e-learning has emerged from the wreckage as one of the Internet's most useful applications. Nearly half of the 4,000 major colleges and universities in the United States now offer classes over the Internet or use the Web to enhance campus classes, according to market researcher International Data Corp. About 2 million students take online classes from U.S. higher-ed institutions, and their ranks could swell to 5 million by 2006, estimates John G. Flores, head of the U.S. Distance Learning Assn., a nonprofit trade group outside Boston (charts). And it's not just a U.S. phenomenon: Students from developing countries are jumping online, too.

29    These classes are opening new horizons for the fastest-growing segment of higher education: working adults, who often find it difficult to juggle conventional classes with jobs and families. Adults over 25 now represent nearly half of higher-ed students; most are employed and want more education to advance their careers.

30    E-learning is an influence in the traditional college class as well. Online classes won't replace the college experience for most 18- to-24-year-olds. But from the Massachusetts Institute of Technology to Wake Forest University in North Carolina, colleges are using the Web in on-campus classes to augment textbooks and boost communication.

31    There are still plenty of hurdles to clear before the e-learning world can take off. For one thing, most of the success is with established universities, like UMUC, which can leverage their brand names to reach out to working adults. The for-profit startups, by contrast, have struggled with accreditation and poor name recognition. Many have fallen by the wayside, including BigWords.com (AMZN), an Amazon-like purveyor of textbooks, while only a handful make money, like Phoenix Online.

# MASS MARKET?

32    Quality is a problem, too, which is a key reason why many online students drop out. That will force a further shakeout, eliminating mediocre players. Many colleges also are still grappling with such issues as how much time their faculty should devote to e-teaching. And long-established rules make it difficult for online students to get financial aid. Even as these problems are resolved, "online learning will never be as good as face-to-face instruction," argues Andy DiPaolo, director of the Stanford Center for Professional Development, which offers online graduate classes to engineers.

33    Still, spending on higher-ed e-learning technology will more than double by 2005, says Eduventures.com, a Boston-based education market researcher. The current economic slump could even spur enrollments, economists say, since many workers look to retool during downturns. Within four or five years, online universities could be among the largest higher-ed providers, says Andrew Rosen, chief operating officer of test-prep king Kaplan Inc. (WPO), which has several online colleges, including Concord Law School, the largest virtual law program, with 800 students.

34    Ultimately, the greatest e-learning market may lie in the developing world, where the population of college-age students will explode in coming years. Just as cell phones leapfrogged land-based telephones in many developing countries, so may e-learning help to educate the masses in countries that lack the colleges to meet demand—and can't afford to build them.

# ROAD WORK

**35**     Looking way out, as far as midcentury, e-learning could "become the environment in which the majority of human beings are educated beyond the secondary level," asserts University of Melbourne President Alan Gilbert. His school, along with Canada's McGill University and more than a dozen other universities, is part of U21 Global, a virtual university being created through a joint venture with textbook giant Thomson Learning. It aims to enroll 100,000 students by the decade's end, mostly in Asia.

**36**     Meanwhile, e-learning demand in the United States is rising, driven by higher education's changing demographics. Take Dr. Michael Kaner, a 43-year-old dentist in suburban Philadelphia who's halfway through adding a law degree to his credentials. Attending a night program at an area law school wasn't practical, he says, since it would have required 12 hours of commuting a week. So in 1999, Kaner signed up for Kaplan's Concord law program. Although the classes require 25 to 30 hours a week, there's no commute and he studies when it suits him. "This is the only way I could pursue a law degree," says Kaner, who hopes to build a part-time legal practice specializing in dental issues.

**37**     Similarly, Judy Rowe, who dropped out of college in the 1960s after running out of money, was able to earn a bachelor's degree in psychology from UMUC last year while working as a flight attendant for American Airlines Inc. "I took my laptop with me and did my assignments on the road," says Rowe, who's now thinking about a second career in psychology.

# COST-EFFECTIVE

**38**     E-learning is also a good fit with the military, where frequent transfers make it hard to pursue a degree. Last year, the Army awarded PWC Consulting a $453 million, five-year contract to create an electronic university that allows soldiers to be anywhere and study at Kansas State University or any of the 24 colleges involved in the program.

**39**     eArmyU already has changed the perspective of soldiers like Sergeant Jeremy Dellinger, 22, who had been planning to leave the Army to go back to school when his basic enlistment ends. Then he enrolled in eArmyU to earn his bachelor's degree from Troy State University in Alabama. "Now I can get my degree and still do the work I love" as a supply sergeant, says the Fort Benning (Ga.)–based soldier. Like Dellinger, about 15 percent of those who have signed up so far have reenlisted or extended their tours. By cutting turnover, "eArmyU could almost pay for itself," says program director Lee Harvey, since it costs nearly $70,000 to train green recruits.

**40**     Corporations, too, see e-learning as a cost-effective way to get better-educated employees. Indeed, corporate spending on e-learning is expected to more than quadruple by 2005, to $18 billion, estimates IDC. At IBM (IBM), some 200,000 employees received education or training online last year, and 75 percent of the company's Basic Blue class for new managers is online. The move cut IBM's training bill by $350 million last year, because online classes don't require travel.

**41**     Even as online higher ed catches on, however, few private-sector providers are turning a profit. During the boom years, venture capitalists pumped some $5 billion into e-learning companies, says Adam Newman, a senior analyst at Eduventures.com. Roughly $1 billion went to companies that have already flamed out, he says. Beyond Phoenix, probably only half a dozen companies are making money now. Lack of name recognition is the biggest problem for companies like Capella, Jones International, and Cardean, UNext's virtual campus. And winning accreditation—crucial for attracting students—is tough going, too. It took Capella five years to make the grade; Jones waited four years. Concord's grads can sit for the California Bar Exam, but the American Bar Assn. still hasn't granted it accreditation.

# CAUTIOUS ELITES

**42** Even Phoenix Online, which has piggybacked on the fame of the bricks-and-mortar University of Phoenix, lost millions in its first six years, says Todd S. Nelson, CEO of parent Apollo Group. To hold students, Phoenix Online keeps classes small and insists on student involvement. "I had to sign on five of every seven nights," says Martin J. Boyle, the owner of a New Jersey-based security company who earned a Phoenix Online MBA last year.

**43** Phoenix Online aside, the big e-learning winners so far are the traditional nonprofit universities. They have captured nearly 95 percent of online enrollments, figures A. Frank Mayadas, head of e-learning grants at the Alfred P. Sloan Foundation. Most active are state and community colleges that started with strong brand names, a faculty, and accreditation, says Mayadas, as well as a tradition of extension programs.

**44** By contrast, many elite universities have been far more cautious about diluting the value of their name. Harvard Business School believes it would be impossible to replicate its classroom education online. "We will never offer a Harvard MBA online," vows professor W. Earl Sasser, chairman of HBS Interactive, which instead develops e-learning programs for companies. Similarly, last year the MIT faculty nixed teaching classes online, fearing "it would detract from the residential experience," says former faculty chair Steven Lerman.

**45** That didn't stop MIT from embracing the Internet in a different way. Over the next five years, MIT plans to post lecture notes and reading assignments for most of its 2,000 classes on the Web for free, calling the effort "OpenClassWare." Lerman says "it's a service to the world," but he says it's no substitute for actual teaching, so faculty aren't worried about a threat to classroom learning.

**46** A few other top schools see profitmaking opportunities. Since 1996, Duke University's Fuqua School of Business has been offering MBAs for working executives. In these blended programs, some 65 percent of the work is done online and just 35 percent in classes held during required residencies that consume 9 to 11 weeks over two years. Duke charges up to $90,000 for these programs—versus $60,000 for its traditional residential MBA. Yet they have been so popular that by next year, "we'll have more students in nontraditional programs than the daytime program," says Fuqua Dean Douglas T. Breeden. The extra revenues are helping Fuqua to double its faculty.

# "MORE ENGAGED"

**47** Even colleges not pursuing online classes are integrating the Internet into everyday campus life. Professors are using everything from digital reference works to Web-based tutors to augment textbooks. Colleges are rethinking classroom instruction, too. MIT has redesigned a semester of its mandatory undergrad physics class, replacing an impersonal lecture to more than 100 with lively sessions in which groups of three students with laptops solve problems posed by the professor. At Wake Forest, where all students receive laptops, Vice-President David G. Brown asks students in his freshman seminar to e-mail drafts of their papers to two fellow students, plus one of six alumni Brown has recruited to provide comments. Brown then e-mails papers, with his comments, to all students. "Students are more engaged," says Brown.

**48** Change comes slowly to higher education, but e-learning has revved up the pace. Even if it takes years to fully take hold, it has already achieved one oft-cited goal of the knowledge economy—getting more adults to study throughout their working lives.

## The Apollo Group, Inc.

**49**    The Apollo Group, Inc. (AGI) has been providing higher education to working adults for over 25 years through its four subsidiaries: The University of Phoenix, Inc., Institute for Professional Development, The College for Financial Planning Institutes Corporation, and Western International University, Inc. The consolidated enrollment in AGI's educational programs would make AGI's the largest private institution of higher education in the United States. AGI currently offers its programs and services at 71 campuses and 121 learning centers in 37 states, Puerto Rico, and Vancouver, British Columbia. AGI's combined degree enrollment increased to approximately 200,000 at August 31, 2003 from approximately 71,400 at August 31, 1998.

**50**    University of Phoenix had degree enrollments of approximately 200,100 adult students at August 31, 2003, is accredited by The Higher Learning Commission, and has been a member of the North Central Association of Colleges and Schools since 1978. University of Phoenix has successfully replicated its teaching/learning model while maintaining educational quality at 71 physical campuses and 121 learning centers in Arizona, California, Colorado, Florida, Georgia, Hawaii, Idaho, Illinois, Louisiana, Maryland, Massachusetts, Michigan, Missouri, Nevada, New Mexico, Ohio, Oklahoma, Oregon, Pennsylvania, Tennessee, Texas, Utah, Virginia, Washington, Wisconsin, Puerto Rico, and Vancouver, British Columbia. University of Phoenix also offers its educational programs worldwide through University of Phoenix Online, its computerized educational delivery system. University of Phoenix has customized computer programs for student tracking, marketing, faculty recruitment and training, and academic quality management. These computer programs are intended to provide uniformity among University of Phoenix's campuses and learning centers which enhances University of Phoenix's ability to expand into new markets while still maintaining academic quality. Currently, approximately 60 percent of University of Phoenix's students receive some level of tuition assistance from their employers.

## The Adult Education Market

**51**    The adult education market is a significant and growing component of the postsecondary education market, which is estimated by the U.S. Department of Education to be a more than $260 billion industry. According to the U.S. Department of Education, over 6 million, or 40 percent of all students enrolled in higher education programs are over the age of 24. This number is projected to reach 6.5 million in 2007 and 6.7 million in 2011. The market for adult education should continue to increase as working adults seek additional education and training to update and improve their skills, to enhance their earnings potential, and to keep pace with the rapidly expanding knowledge-based economy.

**52**    Many working adults are seeking accredited degree programs that provide flexibility to accommodate the fixed schedules and time commitments associated with their professional and personal obligations. AGI's format enables working adult students to attend classes and complete classwork on a more convenient schedule. Many universities and emerging technology-based education and training companies currently do not effectively address the unique requirements of working adult students due to the following specific constraints:

- Traditional universities and colleges were designed to fulfill the educational needs of conventional, full-time students aged 18 to 24, who remain the primary focus of these universities and colleges. This focus has resulted in a capital-intensive teaching/learning model that may be characterized by:

- A high percentage of full-time tenured faculty with doctoral degrees;

- Fully configured library facilities and related full-time staff;

- Dormitories, student unions, and other significant plant assets to support the needs of younger students; and

- An emphasis on research and the related staff and facilities.

53    The majority of accredited colleges and universities continue to provide the bulk of their educational programming from September to mid-December and from mid-January to May. As a result, most full-time faculty members only teach during that limited period of time. While this structure serves the needs of the full-time 18- to 24-year-old student, it limits the educational opportunity for working adults who must delay their education for up to five months during these spring, summer, and winter breaks.

54    Traditional universities and colleges are also limited in their ability to market to or provide the necessary customer service for working adult students because it requires the development of additional administrative and enrollment infrastructure. University of Phoenix maintains a single-minded focus on serving the needs of working adult students.

### Accredited Degree Programs

55    AGI currently offers 15 degree programs in business, education, information technology, and nursing that are accredited by The Higher Learning Commission or the regional accrediting associations of the Institute for Professional Development client institutions. This accreditation enables AGI to grant associates, bachelors, masters, and doctoral degrees, while also providing students with access to federal financial aid programs.

### Experienced Faculty Resources

56    While substantially all of AGI's faculty are working professionals, AGI requires each member of AGI's faculty to possess either a masters or doctoral degree and to have five years of recent professional experience in a field related to the subject they teach. AGI's classes are designed to be small, with an average of one instructor for every fifteen students. Faculty members are also required to be accessible to students by maintaining office hours.

### Current and Relevant Standardized Programs

57    AGI uses content experts selected from AGI's approximately 10,600 faculty to design AGI's curriculum. This enables AGI to offer current and relevant standardized programs to AGI's students.

### Benefits to Employers

58    The employers of AGI's students often provide input to faculty members in designing curriculum, and class projects are typically based on issues relevant to the companies that employ AGI's students. AGI's classes are taught by a practitioner faculty that emphasizes the skills desired by employers. In addition, the time flexibility provided by AGI's classes further benefits employers since it avoids conflict with their employees' work schedules. A recent survey by University of Phoenix showed that approximately 60 percent of its students receive some level of tuition assistance from their employers.

### The Apollo Group's Business Strategy

59    AGI's objective is to be the leading provider of accessible, high-quality education for working adults and a preferred provider of workplace training to their employers. AGI is managed as a for-profit corporation in a higher education industry served principally by not-for-profit providers. By design, AGI treats AGI's adult students as AGI's primary customers and the employers that provide tuition assistance to their employees through tuition reimbursement plans or direct bill arrangements as AGI's secondary customers.

*Establish New University of Phoenix Campuses and Learning Centers.* University of Phoenix plans to continue the addition of campuses and learning centers throughout the United States and Canada. New locations are selected based on an analysis of various factors, including the population of working adults in the area, the number of local employers and their educational reimbursement policies, and the availability of similar programs offered by other institutions.

*Expand Educational Programs.* AGI intends to respond to the changing educational needs of working adults and their employers by introducing new undergraduate and graduate degree programs as well as training programs. To its degree offerings, University of Phoenix has recently added the Master of Business Administration in Health Care Management and specializations in Marketing and Human Resource's Management to its Master of Business Administration, specializations in Elementary and Secondary Education and Adult Education and Distance Learning to its Master of Arts in Education, and a specialization in Educational Counseling to its Master of Counseling. To its certificate programs, University of Phoenix has recently added graduate certificates in e-Business, Technology Management, and Global Management, as well as a certificate in Operations and Supply Chain Management. AGI believes that expanding its program offerings will help AGI improve AGI's market position as a provider of higher education and training for working adults.

*Expand Access to Programs.* AGI plans to continue expanding AGI's distance education programs and services. Enrollments in distance education degree programs have increased to approximately 49,900 in 2002 from approximately 4,800 in 1998. University of Phoenix Online classes and programs are available via the Internet 24 hours a day, 7 days a week and can be accessed using basic technology, such as a Pentium-class personal computer, a 56.6K modem, and an Internet service provider, which enhances the accessibility of and the potential market for University of Phoenix Online programs.

*International Expansion.* AGI believes that the international market for AGI's services is a major growth opportunity. The United States is the most common destination for international students studying abroad. They believe that more working adult students would opt for a United States education that does not involve living in the United States because they could do so without leaving their employment and incurring the high travel and living costs and stringent visa requirements associated with studying abroad. AGI's belief is supported by the fact that University of Phoenix Online has students located in approximately 75 countries despite having used only limited advertising. In addition, many U.S. residents live and work in foreign countries and would benefit from the opportunity to continue their education while abroad. AGI plans to offer the University of Phoenix educational model at physical campuses in international markets.

*Degree Programs and Services–University of Phoenix Programs.* The following is a list of the degree programs and related areas of specialization that University of Phoenix offers:

- Associate of Arts in General Studies

- Bachelor of Science in Business

  Areas of Specialization

- Accounting

- Administration

- E-business

- Information Systems

- Management

- Marketing

- Bachelor of Science in Criminal Justice Administration

- Bachelor of Science in Human Services

- Bachelor of Science in Health Care Services

*Distance Education.* At August 31, 2002, there were approximately 49,900 degree-seeking students utilizing AGI's distance education delivery systems, approximately 99 percent of whom are enrolled at University of Phoenix Online.

**60** The following is a breakdown of AGI students by the level of program they are seeking, at August 31, 2002:

|  | Number of Students | Percentage of Students |
| --- | --- | --- |
| Bachelors | 101,700 | 64.5 |
| Masters | 48,000 | 30.4 |
| Associates | 7,700 | 4.9 |
| Doctoral | 400 | 0.2 |
| Total | 157,800 | 100.0 |

**61** We consider the employers that provide tuition assistance to their employees through tuition reimbursement plans or direct bill arrangements AGI's secondary customers.

**62** Based on student surveys of incoming students in the first half of 2002, the average age of University of Phoenix's students is in the mid-thirties, approximately 54 percent are women and 46 percent are men. Approximately 67 percent of University of Phoenix's students have been employed on a full-time basis for nine years or more.

**63** The approximate age percentage distribution of incoming University of Phoenix students is as follows:

| Age | Percentage of Students |
| --- | --- |
| 25 and under | 16.5 |
| 26 to 33 | 38.0 |
| 34 to 45 | 34.7 |
| 46 and over | 10.8 |
|  | 100.0 |

## Competition

**64** AGI's management offered the following brief competitive assessment: "The higher education market is highly fragmented and competitive with no private or public institution enjoying a significant market share. We compete primarily with four-year and two-year degree-granting public and private regionally accredited colleges and universities. Many of these colleges and universities enroll working adults in addition to the traditional 18- to 24-year-old students. We expect that these colleges and universities will continue to modify their existing programs to serve working adults more effectively. In addition, many colleges and universities have announced various distance education initiatives.

**65**    We believe that the competitive factors in the higher education market include the following:

- The ability to provide easy access to programs and classes

- Reliable and high-quality products and services

- Qualified and experienced faculty

- Cost of the program

- Reputation of programs, classes, and services; and

- The time necessary to earn a degree

**66**    In terms of nondegree programs offered by AGI, we compete with a variety of business and information-technology providers, primarily those in the for-profit training sector. Many of these competitors have significantly more market share and longer-term relationships with key vendors.

**67**    The Institute for Professional Development faces competition from other entities offering higher education curriculum development and management services for adult education programs. The majority of the Institute for Professional Development's current competitors provide short-term, prepackaged curriculum or turn-key programs.

# KEY MANAGEMENT PERSONNEL

**68**    John G. Sperling, Ph.D., is the founder and chairman of the board of directors of Apollo Group, Inc. Dr. Sperling was also president of Apollo Group, Inc. from its inception until February 1998 and chief executive officer of Apollo Group, Inc. until August 2001. Prior to his involvement with Apollo Group, Inc., from 1961 to 1973, Dr. Sperling was a professor of Humanities at San Jose State University where he was the director of the Right to Read Project and the director of the NSF Cooperative College–School Science Program in Economics. At various times from 1955 to 1961, Dr. Sperling was a member of the faculty at the University of Maryland, Ohio State University, and Northern Illinois University. Dr. Sperling received his Ph.D. from Cambridge University, an M.A. from the University of California at Berkeley, and a B.A. from Reed College. Dr. Sperling is the father of Peter V. Sperling.

**69**    Todd S. Nelson has been with Apollo Group, Inc. since 1987. Mr. Nelson has been the chief executive officer of Apollo Group, Inc. since August 2001 and the president of Apollo Group, Inc. since February 1998. Mr. Nelson was vice president of Apollo Group, Inc. from 1994 to February 1998 and the executive vice president of University of Phoenix from 1989 to February 1998. From 1987 to 1989, Mr. Nelson was the Director of University of Phoenix's Utah campus. From 1985 to 1987, Mr. Nelson was the general manager at Amembal and Isom, a management training company. From 1984 to 1985, Mr. Nelson was a general manager for Vickers & Company, a diversified holding company. From 1983 to 1984, Mr. Nelson was a marketing director at Summa Corporation, a recreational properties company. Mr. Nelson received an M.B.A. from the University of Nevada at Las Vegas and a B.S. from Brigham Young University. Mr. Nelson was a member of the faculty at University of Nevada at Las Vegas from 1983 to 1984.

**70**    Peter V. Sperling has been with Apollo Group, Inc. since 1983. Mr. Sperling has been a senior vice president since June 1998. Mr. Sperling was the vice president of administration from 1992 to June 1998 and has been the secretary and treasurer of Apollo Group, Inc. since 1988. From 1987 to 1992, Mr. Sperling was the director of operations at Apollo Education Corporation. From 1983 to 1987, Mr. Sperling was director of management information services of Apollo Group, Inc. Mr. Sperling received his M.B.A. from University of Phoenix and his B.A. from the University of California at Santa Barbara. Mr. Sperling is the son of John G. Sperling.

71    Laura Palmer Noone, J. D., Ph.D., has been with University of Phoenix since 1987. Dr. Palmer Noone has served as president of University of Phoenix since September 2000. From 1994 to 2000 she was the provost and senior vice president for Academic Affairs, and from 1991 to 1994, she was director of Academic Affairs at University of Phoenix, Phoenix campus. Prior to that, she was judge pro tem at the City of Chandler, and an attorney at law in general civil practice emphasizing business representation and civil litigation. She has also served as adjunct faculty at Grand Canyon University and Chandler-Gilbert Community College. Dr. Palmer Noone currently serves as a member of the Arizona State Board for Private Postsecondary Education and as a board of trustee member for the Florida Coastal School of Law. Dr. Palmer Noone also serves on the National Advisory Committee on Institutional Quality and Integrity. Dr. Palmer Noone received her Ph.D. from the Union Institute, her J.D. and her M.B.A. from the University of Iowa, and her B.B.A. from the University of Dubuque.

## FIVE YEAR PERFORMANCE

The following is in thousands, except per share amounts and operating statistics

| Year Ended August 31, | 2003 | 2002 | 2001 | 2000 | 1999 |
|---|---|---|---|---|---|
| **Income Statement Data:** | | | | | |
| Tuition and other revenues, net | 1,339,517 | $1,009,455 | $769,474 | $609,997 | $498,846 |
| Net income | 247,010 | $161,150 | $107,817 | $71,191 | $59,005 |
| Diluted net income per share* | 1.30 | $.87 | $.60 | $.41 | $.33 |
| Diluted weighted average shares outstanding* | 177,637 | 175,697 | 174,001 | 172,447 | 177,387 |
| **Balance Sheet Data** | | | | | |
| Total cash and marketable securities | 1,045,802 | $688,655 | $401,934 | $159,839 | $116,903 |
| Total assests | 1,378,204 | $979,642 | $680,343 | $404,790 | $348,342 |
| Current liablities | 335,223 | $264,314 | $182,200 | $131,089 | $108,787 |
| Long-term liabilities | 16,056 | $16,335 | $16,258 | $12,493 | $8,435 |
| Shareholders' equity | 1,026,925 | $698,993 | $481,885 | $261,208 | $231,120 |
| **Operating Statistics:** | | | | | |
| Degree enrollments at end of period | 200,100 | 157,800 | 124,800 | 100,900 | 86,800 |
| Locations at end of period: | | | | | |
| Campuses | 71 | 65 | 58 | 54 | 49 |
| Learning Centers | 121 | 111 | 102 | 96 | 80 |

*Adjusted for stock splits

## Appendix A:

# Guide to Online Universities

**As e-learning has exploded, hundreds of universities and for-profit start-ups have begun peddling classes over the Web. Here is a brief look at the range of providers.**

## UNIVERSITY OF MARYLAND UNIVERSITY COLLEGE

The largest state university provider of online classes, it moved online in the mid-90s, building on its long heritage of offering extension classes. Last year, enrollments in its online classes hit 63,000, up 50 percent in one year. Students can now earn 70 different degrees and certificates online. In addition to classes, UMUC provides a comprehensive array of online student services, from applications to academic advising and financial aid consulting.

### Cost

Same as for UMUC's traditional classroom classes. That means Maryland residents are charged just $197 per semester hour for undergrad classes, and $301 per semester for graduate classes. But out-of-state residents must pay over 50 percent more.

## UNIVERSITY OF PHOENIX ONLINE

The nation's largest for-profit virtual university, offering the same kind of business, education and technical classes for working adults that have made its bricks-and-mortar counterpart, the University of Phoenix, such a success. In business, students may earn everything from undergraduate degrees in accounting, management, and marketing to an MBA and even a Doctor of Management in Organizational Leadership. Phoenix Online provides lots of attention to its students. Classes are kept small, and instructors insist on participation.

### Cost

$400 to $500 per credit; an MBA degree costs about $23,000

## eARMYU (THE U.S. ARMY'S VIRTUAL UNIVERSITY)

Since January, eArmyU has allowed enlisted soldiers to take classes and earn degrees from 24 different institutions, ranging from Central Texas College to Utah State. So far, 10,400 soldiers have signed up on the three Army bases where it's offered. The plan is to offer it Armywide by 2003.

### Cost

Free to soldiers, who receive a laptop, printer, Internet connection and 100 percent of tuition. Civilians are not eligible for eArmyU.

## WESTERN GOVERNORS UNIVERSITY

Virtual university founded by 19 western states in 1997. A pioneer in "competency-based degrees," which require students to demonstrate mastery of a subject, rather than complete a certain number of credit hours. In practice, this means students are assessed when they enter a program. An individual class of study is then developed for each student to fill the gaps in their knowledge. The result is that the length of time needed to complete a degree varies widely, and is dependent on what the student knows. While it may sound radical, WGU is backed by some two-dozen corporate sponsors, including IBM, AOL, and Microsoft.

## Cost

WGU charges about $4,500 for the assessment and mentoring needed for a two-year degree. Students must pay separately for classes, which are offered by some 40 different institutions.

# CONCORD LAW SCHOOL

Launched by Kaplan Inc., a unit of the Washington Post Co., Concord has grown to become the nation's largest virtual law school, with 800 students at present. Kaplan argues that the law is ideally suited to online learning, because it facilitates communication (via e-mail) among students and professors. While the program is not yet accredited by the American Bar Association, students may sit for the California Bar Exam.

## Cost

$6,000 per year, or $24,000 for four-year law degree

# DUKE'S FUQUA SCHOOL OF BUSINESS

"Blended" MBA programs for working executives, in which 65 percent of the work is done over the Net, and 35 percent in classes that meet for 9 or 11 weeks during 20-month programs. There are two blended programs. The "Global Executive" program is designed for executives who manage a large international business unit or a global staff. The average global student has 14 years of professional experience. In contrast, the "Cross Continent" program is aimed at more junior managers—with an average of six years of experience—who have already demonstrated success at the department level.

## Cost

Up to $90,000 for "Global Executive" program, versus $60,000 for normal daytime MBA. The extra costs cover the residential program, which in the case of Global Executive is held in various spots around the world, including Europe, Asia, and the Duke campus.

# CARDEAN UNIVERSITY

The virtual university founded by UNext.com, one of the highest profile e-learning start-ups. UNext partnered with some of the world's best-known universities—including Stanford, the University of Chicago, and Columbia—to develop its cutting-edge Business curriculum. It is now offering classes to employees of General Motors and a number of other companies, and will shortly begin marketing its Business classes to consumers.

## Cost

About $25,000 for MBA.

# JONES INTERNATIONAL UNIVERSITY

The virtual university founded in 1993 by cable pioneer Glenn R. Jones, who earlier offered distance classes via cable TV through his Mind Extension University. Jones offers more than 40 executive and professional education programs. Students may earn a bachelor's degree in business, an MBA, as well as various masters degrees in education.

## Cost

Three-credit class runs $925; MBA costs about $12,000.

# CAPELLA UNIVERSITY

A for-profit virtual university that offers some 500 online classes every quarter. Students may choose from 15 different degree programs, and some 80 different specializations. Most of the 4,000 students study business, education, or information technology.

## Cost

Classes (which offer three to five credits) tend to cost from $1,150 to $1,600. A masters degree runs about $20,000, and a Ph.D. about $34,000.

# WALDEN UNIVERSITY

Originally founded in 1970 to offer graduate degrees, Walden moved online in the mid-1990s. Walden is 41 percent owned by Sylvan Learning Systems, which has other online education programs as well. Walden specializes in graduate programs in business, education, psychology, public health, and human services.

## Cost

An MBA runs about $20,000, while a Ph.D. can cost $47,000.

# THE ELECTRONIC CAMPUS OF THE SOUTHERN REGIONAL EDUCATION BOARD

A sweeping smorgasboard of online classes organized by the Southern Regional Education Board, an organization formed to promote education reform in 16 southern states. The electronic campus offers over 5,000 online classes from 325 different schools, ranging from Auburn University to West Virginia University.

## Cost

Tuition varies widely, since it is set by the college that actually offers a given class. As one example, a class on American History since 1865 offered by Oklahoma State costs $365.

# HARVARD EXTENSION SCHOOL

One's best chance to take an online class from Harvard, these classes are offered by Harvard's extension school. While the Harvard Extension School currently offers over 500 classes in the traditional classroom setting, only about three dozen are currently available online. However, the plan is to expand the number of online offerings. Most of the classes available this year are computer science classes, on topics like website development and algorithms.

### Cost

Same as for attending a class at the extension school. The cost ranges from $275 for a class on American Constitutional History taken without credit, to $1,750 for the class on website development.

## UT TELECAMPUS

An excellent example of the expanding e-learning programs offered by state university systems, the UT Telecampus was launched in 1998 by the University of Texas system. Students may earn an MBA, Masters in Computer Science, and various other online degrees from a school within the UT system. Students who wish to earn a degree must first apply and be admitted to one of the universities in the UT system. That campus will then serve as the student's "home" campus, and ultimately award the degree.

### Cost

Texas residents pay about $300 for a three-credit undergraduate class, and $500 for a three-credit graduate class. Nonresidents are charged roughly twice as much.

## STANFORD CENTER FOR PROFESSIONAL DEVELOPMENT

One of the most challenging and prestigious online programs. The Stanford Center offers both online degrees and nondegree classes from Stanford's School of Engineering and affiliated departments. The center now provides over 250 online credit classes in electrical engineering, mechanical engineering, computer science, etc. These are not watered down classes. They are taught by the Stanford faculty, and students must be admitted, just like on-campus students. The online classes are designed strictly for employed engineers and scientists. The attraction is that they may keep working, while furthering their education.

### Cost

About $3,000 for a credit class, or 40 percent more than it would cost to take a similar class on campus. Typically, the companies employing the students pick up the tab.

## FATHOM

One of the most noted sites launched to promote both lifelong learning, as well as professional development. Fathom was founded by Columbia University, and includes a number of other member institutions, from the American Film Institute to Britain's Victoria and Albert Museum. Students may enroll in everything from short seminars on the history of New York City to semester-length for-credit classes from various institutions.

### Cost

Ranges from under $50 for short seminars to around $450 for semester-length classes.

# Case 48 Treo: Handspring's Last Stand?[1]

## Chad Beaupierre, Scott Bevier, Roberto Ekesi, Vicken Librarikian and Melissa A. Schilling

**1**  It was December 2001 and the co-founders of Handspring, Donna Dubinsky and Jeff Hawkins, were sitting on a plane on the way to the CTIA Wireless IT and Internet convention in Las Vegas. Dubinsky and Hawkins were about to unveil their latest product, the Treo Communicator, at the most recognized trade show for wireless technologies. Unlike Handspring's previous Personal Digital Assistant offerings, this product was an integrated "smart phone" and represented Handspring's first attempt to enter the wireless communications market and a fundamental shift in corporate strategy.

**2**  Though Handspring was second only to Palm in worldwide handheld computer market share, Handspring had yet to turn a profit. PDA price wars and slumping sales had decimated margins in the PDA industry and left producers with large quantities of rapidly obsolescing inventory. Economic conditions had forced Handspring to mark down even its more advanced models. Facing increased economic pressures, a battered stock price, and increasing competition in the PDA market, Dubinsky and Hawkins were attempting to reinvent Handspring as a leader in the smart phone market (See Appendix 1 for an excerpt of a Handspring management discussion on repositioning the company). Smart phone shipments were expected to grow to almost five million units in 2002, amounting to $2.3 billion in sales.[2] Smart phones also had higher margins. However, entering the smart phone market also meant pitting the company against very large and established rivals such as Nokia, Samsung, and Ericsson. Could Handspring convince enterprises and individual consumers that it was the right company to deliver a competitive product in the wireless communications market? Would it be able to compete with competitors that had more experience and scale in the telecommunications market? If Handspring was able to successfully penetrate the smart phone market, would that be enough to turn the company's financial situation around?

## HANDSPRING'S HISTORY

**3**  Handspring was co-founded in July 1998 by Jeff Hawkins and Donna Dubinsky. Hawkins was the original founder of Palm Computing, a company that made handwriting recognition software for personal digital assistants (PDAs). US Robotics acquired Palm in 1995, bringing badly needed capital to fund development costs, and in 1996 the company introduced the first generation of Palm Pilot personal digital assistants (PDAs). However, after 3Com acquired US Robotics in 1997, Hawkins and Dubinsky decided to leave the company and start a new venture that would produce PDAs based on the Palm operating system: Handspring.[3] They completed their core management team with Ed Colligan, another former 3Com employee who had been responsible for marketing the Palm PDA devices (See Exhibit 1 for a full Management Team description). They positioned Handspring to

---

[1]Chad Beaupierre, Scott Bevier, Roberto Ekesi, Vicken Librarikian and Melissa A. Schilling prepared this case as the basis of class discussion rather than to illustrate either effective or ineffective handling of an administrative situation. All rights reserved to the authors. Copyright © 2003 Melissa A. Schilling.
[2]Salomon Smith Barney, "Smart handheld device market segments, worldwide, 1998–2004E," October 18, 2000.
[3]P. Tjhayadikarta, and M. A. Schilling, 2001. "Palm economy." *Boston University Teaching Case #2001–01.*

**EXHIBIT 1**
Handspring
Management Team

### Jeff Hawkins
#### Founder, Chairman, and Chief Product Officer

Jeff Hawkins co-founded Handspring with Donna Dubinsky in July of 1998 after their incredibly successful run together at Palm Computing. In 1994, Hawkins invented the original PalmPilot products and founded Palm Computing, now a 3Com company. He is often credited as the designer who reinvented the handheld market.

An industry veteran with nearly 20 years of technical expertise, Hawkins currently holds nine patents for various handheld devices and features. His vision for handheld computing dates back to the 1980s, when as Vice President of Research at GRiD Systems Corporation he served as principal architect and designer for the GRiDPad and GRiD Convertible. Prior to that, he held key technical positions with Intel Corporation. Hawkins earned his B.S. in electrical engineering from Cornell University.

### Donna Dubinsky
#### Founder, President and CEO

Donna Dubinsky co-founded Handspring with Jeff Hawkins in July 1998 to create a new breed of handheld computers for consumers. As president and CEO of Palm Computing, Dubinsky helped make the PalmPilot the best-selling handheld computer and the most rapidly adopted new computing product ever produced. When Dubinsky first joined Hawkins at Palm Computing in 1992, shortly after the company was founded, she brought with her more than 10 years of marketing and logistics experience from Apple and Claris. Dubinsky and Hawkins introduced the original PalmPilot in February 1996, a move that revitalized the handheld computing industry.

In addition to her position as CEO of Handspring, Dubinsky currently serves as a director of Intuit Corporation and is a Trustee of the Computer Museum History Center. She earned her B.A. from Yale University and her M.B.A. from the Harvard Graduate School of Business Administration.

### Ed Colligan
#### Founder, Chief Operating Officer

Ed Colligan joined Handspring to lead the development and marketing efforts for a new generation of handheld computers. As the Vice President of Marketing for Palm Computing, Ed Colligan worked with Jeff Hawkins and Donna Dubinsky to lead the product marketing and marketing communications efforts for Palm, including the successful positioning, launch, and marketing of the popular Palm product family.

Prior to Palm, Colligan was Vice President of Strategic and Product Marketing at Radius Corporation. During his eight years there, Colligan helped make Radius the brand leader in Macintosh graphics, graphic imaging, and hardware development.

Colligan's multiple successes have earned him several marketing industry accolades. *Marketing Computers Magazine* named him the 1997 Marketer of the Year, and *Advertising Age* named him one of the Top 100 Marketers of 1997, an award that spanned all product categories. He holds a B.A. from the University of Oregon.

### Bernard Whitney
#### Chief Financial Officer

Bernard Whitney joined Handspring as Chief Financial Officer in June 1999. He comes to Handspring from Sanmina, Inc., an electronics manufacturing company where he served as Executive Vice President and Chief Financial Officer. A primary focus at Sanmina was leading the systems technology and strategic development effort that included eight successful acquisitions.

Prior to Sanmina, Whitney served as Vice President of Finance for Network General Corporation, a network fault tolerance and performance management solutions company.

From 1987 to 1995, Whitney held a variety of positions in corporate finance for mass storage manufacturer Conner Peripherals. He has an M.B.A. from San Jose State University and B.S. in Business Administration from the California State University at Chico.

**EXHIBIT 2**
**Handspring**
**Historical Stock Price**

Source: *www.freerealtime.com*

2001 Handspring Stock Price

the public and investors as the same people doing the same thing, this time just better. The executive team's mantra was "Innovate, innovate, and innovate. Yet keep it small, simple, affordable, and connected."

4    Handspring entered the PDA market in mid-1999 with its Visor device. The Visor was priced lower than Palm's PDAs, and with its Springboard module, contained more functions than Palm's devices. The module allowed the PDA to be expanded by inserting a range of components, such as mobile phones, digital cameras, pagers, modems, or MP3 players, and additional software applications.[4] Handspring launched a global marketing program for its Visor and Springboard modules, selling through a variety of distribution channels that included the World Wide Web, value-added resellers, international distribution agencies, and retailers. Handspring's largest retailers were Best Buy, Staples, and CompUSA, which accounted for 14 percent, 13 percent, and 10 percent of sales, respectively. Competing primarily on design and price, the consumer segment was Handspring's primary target while the business segment received only a secondary focus.

5    Before long it became apparent that the Springboard modules, initially praised by consumers and feared by competitors, were not going to revolutionize the PDA market. The Springboard modules never achieved strong market acceptance because they were expensive and could only make the Visor devices imitate, and not replace, other devices. This lack of a compelling differentiating factor, combined with an increasingly competitive PDA market, had moved Handspring into a very vulnerable competitive position. Since the Fall of 2000, investors had seen Handspring's stock price drop from a high of $95 to as low as $1.20. By December 2001, Handspring's stock was trading at just over $6 a share (see Exhibit 2 for stock price history). Facing increasingly difficult economic conditions and a third straight year of increasing operating losses (see Exhibits 3, 4, and 5 for Handspring's financials), Handspring had to do something drastic. Though Handspring had already made one foray into merging cell phone and PDA capabilities with the VisorPhone (a Springboard module that acted as a cell phone), that product had received a lukewarm welcome. The module was expensive, and the combination of the module and the PDA was bulky and awkward. This time around the company decided to commit fully to the smart phone concept by introducing a product that would put phone capability and styling first, with PDA functionality second: the Treo.

[4]Stephanie Miles, "Is Palm ready for the handheld challenge?" *CNET News.com.*, September 13, 1999.

**EXHIBIT 3**

**Balance Sheet**

Source: Handspring 10K, June 30, 2001.

| Handspring, Inc. Consolidated Balance Sheets (in thousands, except share and per share amounts) | June 30, 2001 | July 1, 2000 |
|---|---|---|
| **Assets** | | |
| Current assets: | | |
| Cash and cash equivalents | $ 87,580 | $196,548 |
| Short-term investments | 33,943 | — |
| Accounts receivable, net of allowance for doubtful accounts of $2,239 and $50 as of June 30, 2001 and July 1, 2000, respectively | 12,850 | 20,484 |
| Prepaid expenses and other current assets | 19,473 | 1,776 |
| Inventories | 2,857 | 40 |
| Total current assets | 156,703 | 218,848 |
| Long-term investments | 80,237 | 2,664 |
| Property and equipment, net | 15,041 | 8,280 |
| Intangibles and other assets | 1,254 | 680 |
| Total assets | $253,235 | $230,472 |
| **Liabilities and Stockholders' Equity** | | |
| Current liabilities: | | |
| Accounts payable | $ 37,881 | $ 20,152 |
| Accrued liabilities | 70,152 | 16,034 |
| Total current liabilities | 108,033 | 36,186 |
| Long-term liabilities | — | 57 |
| Commitments and contingencies (Note 9) | | |
| Stockholders' equity: | | |
| Preferred stock, $0.001 per value per share, 10,000,000 shares authorized; nil shares issued and outstanding at June 30, 2001 and July 1, 2000 | — | — |
| Common stock, $0.001 per value per share, 1,000,000,000 shares authorized; 129,949,768 and 125,436,978 shares issued and outstanding at June 30, 2001 and July 1, 2000, respectively | 130 | 125 |
| Additional paid-in capital | 368,166 | 321,116 |
| Deferred stock compensation | (29,445) | (58,268) |
| Accumulated other comprehensive income (loss) | 994 | (64) |
| Accumulated deficit | (194,643) | (68,680) |
| Total stockholders' equity | 145,202 | 194,229 |
| Total liabilities and stockholders' equity | $253,235 | $230,472 |

6    The Treo is a single device that integrates the functionality of a cell phone, PDA, and pager with "always on" capability.[5] Unlike regular cell phones that have some organizer capabilities, smart phones such as the Treo had larger, sharper screens that could display regular web pages rather than the small subset of web pages designed to be readable on cell-phone displays.[6] At its launch, it was heralded as the smart phone with the tightest integration of these functions and capabilities. Handspring was betting that it could establish the Treo as the future in handheld communications.

[5]"Always on" refers to devices that are capable of remaining continuously connected to the internet.
[6]R. Pegoraro, "Even the best of the phone-PDA combos aren't good enough," *The Washington Post,* January 27, 2002, p. H7.

**EXHIBIT 4**
Statement of
Operations

Source: Handspring 10K, June
30, 2001.

| Handspring, Inc. Consolidated Statements of Operations (in thousands, except per share amounts) | | | |
|---|---|---|---|
| | Year Ended June 30, 2001 | Year Ended July 1, 2000 | Period From July 29, 1998 (date of inception) to June 30, 1999 |
| Revenue | $ 370,943 | $101,937 | $ — |
| Costs and operating expenses: | | | |
| Cost of revenue | 292,311 | 69,921 | — |
| Research and development | 23,603 | 10,281 | 2,738 |
| Selling, general and administrative | 145,132 | 42,424 | 2,451 |
| In-process research and development | 12,225 | — | — |
| Amortization of deferred stock compensation and intangibles(*) | 32,830 | 40,077 | 3,646 |
| Total costs and operating expenses | 506,101 | 162,703 | 8,835 |
| Loss from operations | (135,158) | (60,766) | (8,835) |
| Interest and other income, net | 12,195 | 675 | 446 |
| Loss before taxes | (122,963) | (60,091) | (8,389) |
| Income tax provision | 3,000 | 200 | — |
| Net loss | $(125,963) | $ (60,291) | $(8,389) |
| Basic and diluted net loss per share | $(1.21) | $(1.77) | $ (0.71) |
| Shares used in calculating basic and diluted net loss per share | 103,896 | 34,015 | 11,772 |
| (*) Amortization of deferred stock compensation and intangibles: | | | |
| Cost of revenue | $4,521 | $ 5,904 | $526 |
| Research and development | 6,926 | 8,059 | 1,217 |
| Selling, general and administrative | 21,383 | 26,114 | 1,903 |
| | $ 32,830 | $ 40,077 | $ 3,646 |

# TREO COMMUNICATOR

7    The Treo was designed to fit in the palm of one's hand and combined three existing products (cell phone, PDA, and pager) into one small package without compromising functionality or ease of use (see Exhibits 6 and 7 for Treo product overview and functionality). It was the first product to come close to realizing the product concept inspired by Gene Roddenberry's *Star Trek.* The Treo was equipped with a dual-band GSM world phone that would be upgradeable to GPRS (General Packet Radio Service) networks when they became more widely available. Handspring was also developing a version that would run on Sprint's third generation CDMA networks.

8        The Treo did not have the Springboard module, but it did feature a display (available in monochrome 16-shade gray scale or color) that was only slightly smaller than the standard Handspring Visor display, and that acted as a touch screen. Like the Motorola StarTac or Ericsson World Phone (or *Star Trek's* tricorders for that matter), the Treo had a flip cover protecting the display and keyboard area. The Treo also came with either a keyboard or writing

## Handspring, Inc. Consolidated Statements of Cash Flows (in thousands)

| | Year Ended June 30, 2001 | Year Ended July 1, 2000 | Period From July 29, 1998 (date of inception) to June 30, 1999 |
|---|---|---|---|
| Cash flows from operating activities: | | | |
| Net loss | $(125,963) | $ (60,291) | $(8,389) |
| Adjustments to reconcile net loss to net cash used in operating activities: | | | |
| Depreciation and amortization | 7,104 | 2,668 | 70 |
| Amortization of deferred stock compensation and intangibles | 32,830 | 40,077 | 3,646 |
| In-process research and development | 12,225 | — | — |
| Write-off of excess and obsolete inventories | 26,811 | — | — |
| Charitable contribution of common stock | — | 900 | — |
| Amortization of costs associated with financing agreement | — | 568 | 31 |
| Amortization of premium or discount on available-for-sale securities, net | (1,313) | (118) | (108) |
| Gain on sale of available-for-sale securities | (277) | — | — |
| Stock compensation to non-employees | — | 815 | 15 |
| Changes in assets and liabilities: | | | |
| Accounts receivable | 6,625 | (20,484) | — |
| Prepaid expenses and other current assets | (18,219) | (1,751) | (48) |
| Inventories | (10,011) | (40) | — |
| Intangibles and other assets | (40) | (616) | (64) |
| Accounts payable | 18,701 | 18,944 | 884 |
| Accrued liabilities | 34,584 | 15,941 | 67 |
| Net cash used in operating activities | (16,943) | (3,387) | (3,896) |
| Cash flows from investing activities: | | | |
| Purchases of available-for-sale securities | (244,972) | (4,474) | (10,965) |
| Sales and maturities of available-for-sale securities | 186,866 | 10,424 | 4,833 |
| Purchases of investments for collateral on operating leases | (51,287) | (2,106) | (150) |
| Purchases of property and equipment | (14,283) | (9,818) | (780) |
| Cash acquired from acquisition | 29 | — | — |
| Net cash used in investing activities | (123,647) | (5,974) | (7,062) |
| Cash flows from financing activities: | | | |
| Proceeds from borrowings | — | 6,000 | — |
| Principal payments on borrowings | (83) | (6,000) | — |
| Issuance of redeemable convertible preferred stock, net | — | 11,490 | 17,972 |
| Net proceeds from initial public offering and exercise of underwriters' over-allotment | 27,969 | 184,928 | — |
| Proceeds from issuance of common stock | 3,109 | 2,012 | 519 |
| Repurchase of common stock | (41) | — | — |
| Net cash provided by financing activities | 30,954 | 198,430 | 18,491 |
| Effect of exchange rate changes on cash | 668 | (54) | — |
| Net increase (decrease) in cash and cash equivalents | (108,968) | 189,015 | 7,533 |
| Cash and cash equivalents: | | | |
| Beginning of period | 196,548 | 7,533 | — |
| End of period | $ 87,580 | $196,548 | $ 7,533 |
| Supplemental disclosure of cash flow information: | | | |
| Cash paid for interest | $ 6 | $ 37 | $ 1 |
| Cash paid for taxes | $ 236 | $ 1 | $ 1 |

**EXHIBIT 6**
Treo Product
Overview

## Look

**The Treo communicator is one of the smallest Palm OS handhelds available.** But don't let the size deceive you. This stylish communicator has been jam-packed with features without compromising functionality or ease of use. And it comes in two models—with a built-in keyboard or with a Graffiti® writing area.

## Talk

**The Treo communicator does everything your mobile phone does. And more.** That's because this dual-band world phone has all the features you expect in a phone, like speed dial, three-way calling, and call history. Plus, it has extra features like full integration with the built-in PhoneBook so you can dial direct from your contact list, a personal speakerphone and free headset for handsfree operation, and so much more.

## Organize

**It's easy with this feature-rich Palm OS organizer.** With 16 MB of memory and a fast processor, the rechargeable Treo communicator has it all—Date Book Plus, PhoneBook (an improved Address Book), To Do List, Memo Pad, and more. Plus, you can install thousands of other cool Palm OS applications. Already have another Palm OS device? No worries. You can transfer your existing data to your new Treo communicator with ease.

## Send

**And receive. Email and short messages. And do it all wirelessly.** Now it's easy to read and send email from virtually anywhere. And, if your message is short, you can send an SMS text message to other mobile phone users in your network or even to an email address.

## Browse

**Now you can access the web from just about everywhere.** Every Treo communicator comes with Blazer™—the award-winning wireless web browser—so you can access virtually any website, not just those sites optimized for mobile access. Get directions, confirm your flight, check the weather—and see it all on the Treo communicator's organizer-sized screen.

## EXHIBIT 7
**TreoProduct Features**

**Full featured mobile phone**
- Dual-band world phone
- Integrated dialing from PhoneBook
- Instant Lookup—find any name in a few keystrokes
- Speed dialing
- 3-way calling
- Personal speakerphone
- Headset jack and included headset
- Call history
- Vibrating and system sound mute modes
- External ringer switch
- GPRS upgradeable upon availability

**Wireless messaging**
- Send and receive email messages from your POP3 email accounts with One-Touch Mail™
- Exchange SMS (Short Message Service) text messages with other SMS-enabled phones or any email address

**Simple input and navigation**
- Rocker switch with push select for one-handed navigation
- Choose between built-in keyboard model (Treo 180) or Graffiti® handwriting software model (Treo 180g):
  - QWERTY keyboard for fast and accurate data entry (Treo 180)
  - Graffiti handwriting recognition software for simple point and tap data entry (Treo 180g)

**Palm OS® organizer**
- One of the smallest Palm OS organizers yet
- Fastest Palm OS processor available
- Use organizer functions even when wireless mode is off
- 16 MB memory
- Fully compatible with Microsoft Outlook
- HotSync® cable for USB synchronization with computer
- Rechargeable Lithium Ion batteries
- Transfer existing Palm-Powered device data with one HotSync operation.
- Beam data and programs to other Palm OS handhelds
- Enhanced Handspring organizer applications (Date Book Plus, Advanced Calculator, PhoneBook, CityTime world clock)

**Wireless web**
- Includes award-winning Blazer™ browser
- View virtually any page on the Internet
- Customizable bookmarks
- Pages load up to four times faster than competing browsers
- Support for multiple markup languages, including HTML, WAP (WML/HDML), cHTML (I-Mode), and xHTML***
- 128-bit security enabling access to secure web sites (SSL)
- Full support for cookies
- Support for HTTP proxy servers

area (both models were offered to suit different customer preferences), built-in microphone, and infrared port. It measured 4.3″ × 2.7″ × 0.7″ and weighed only 5.2 ounces. Like other Handspring products, the backbone of the Treo was the Palm operating system. The Treo featured a 33MHz Motorola Dragonball processor, 16 Mega-bytes of memory, and a rechargeable Lithium Ion battery.

9    When the Treo model with the monochrome display was purchased with a one-year wireless service contract, the device sold for $399, but as a standalone product it was priced at $599 (prices were higher for color displays). To encourage existing Visor users to upgrade to the Treo, Handspring offered a $100 rebate to Treo customers who sent in the serial numbers from their Visors. Existing Visor users were a primary target for the Treo, as one of its key points of differentiation from other smart phones was the option to use the Graffiti handwriting recognition software used on Visor PDAs.

10    The communicator was fully integrated with the built-in Phone Book, allowing one to dial directly from the contact list. Moreover, the Treo had a speakerphone and was compatible with several external headset options. The Treo also possessed common PDA features such as Date Book Plus, Phone Book, To Do List, Memo Pad, and allowed its user to organize short-term and long-term schedules. The Treo's paging capabilities enabled users to send and receive e-mail and short SMS text messages from virtually any location. Importantly, the Treo provided web access to its users using Handspring's "Blazer" wireless web-browser. To go online a user had only to push a button and the Treo would connect automatically. It could bookmark up to 100 websites and run a wide range of applications,

such as one that provided maps of the New York City subway system or a program that translated between English, French, Spanish, German, and Italian. It could transfer data from various other Palm OS devices, and it could even run applications that were not developed to run on the Palm O/S.

**11**  Some analysts observed that Handspring's advantage might be that adding voice capabilities to a PDA would be simpler and more effective than adding PDA capabilities to a phone. John Troyer, Chief Strategy Officer at Neomar remarked, "I think it's a lot easier to put voice into a PDA than it is to jam a PDA into a phone." He said, "I think we're seeing the result of that." Critics were quick to point out, however, that the Treo's battery life was subpar with only 2.5 hours of talk time. Additionally, though the Blazer browser had earned accolades, surfing the web using GSM was "agonizingly slow," and thus web surfing functionality was unlikely to become a particularly valuable feature until GPRS network upgrades became available.[7] Furthermore, though the e-mail system shipped with the Treo at its launch was adequate for individual consumers, it lacked the security required by corporate users, thus third-party software was initially required for corporate customers. However, Handspring later joined forces with Visto, a leading provider of web-based e-mail and synchronization services, to develop a software program ("Treo Mail") which would bring wireless e-mail from any Microsoft Exchange or standard Internet account, thus fulfilling the needs of most mobile executives.

## REPOSITIONING HANDSPRING

> The theme for the company is Treo.
>
> *Ed Colligan, Chief Operating Officer, Handspring*

**12**  Treo represented more than just an additional product in Handspring's portfolio—Handpring was "betting the farm" on the success of the new device. As stated by CEO Donna Dubinsky, Handspring would be "transitioning out of the organizer business and into the communicator business."[8] Handspring would continue to support the Visor so long as there was demand, but would direct all of its development and promotion effort towards the communicator. Some analysts wondered why Handspring would abandon the Visor platform, risking alienating third-party developers for the platform and rendering all Springboard development and inventory obsolete.[9]

**13**  Treo also represented a shift in market focus for Handspring. Though individual consumers would still be targeted (see Exhibit 8 for customer segments), the Treo would be targeted primarily at the enterprise market. Management believed the integration of phone, PDA, and pager made the Treo an appealing corporate productivity tool and that the growth potential in the business-to-business (B2B) market was greater than that in the business-to-consumer (B2C) market. At a major corporate software convention in Las Vegas, Ed Colligan stated, "We believe that this is a really compelling enterprise device for wireless voice and data. I think as we build critical mass in the enterprise with the Treo, you'll see more applications. It takes a breakthrough device to get developers going."

**14**  To attract share in the enterprise market, the product would require great breadth in available software applications and supporting tools. To ensure that a wide range of applications for the device would be available, Handspring formed several co-marketing agreements with software companies that had already developed widely used applications for Visor and

---

[7]K. Shaw, "Handspring Treo: An end user review," *Network World,* Feburary 4, 2002, www.nwfusion.com.
[8]M. Moore, "Treo melds phone, wireless net, PDA in 'Star Trek' style." *Houston Chronicle,* January 24, 2002.
[9]J. Sullivan, "Handspring bets the farm on Treo—then postpones it," *Wireless Data News,* January 30, 2002, p. 1.

**EXHIBIT 8**
Treo 180 Consumer
Segments

**The mobile professional**

With all the hours you put in, you need to be connected to your desktop . . . not chained to it. The Treo communicator lets you take your office anywhere, providing access to email, the web, a mobile phone and a Palm OS® organizer in one compact device.

Add:

**Documents to Go.** Now you can view and edit Microsoft® Word, Excel, PowerPoint and other documents on your Treo communicator.

**SiPix Pocket Printer A6.** Print via IR with this portable printer . . . even when you're away from the office.

**The networker**

You know who you are. The person everyone turns to for the latest scoop. With your Treo communicator they can count on you to always be in touch via SMS, email or phone.

Add:

**Yahoo! Messenger.** Chat via instant message with all your online buddies.

**Treo Car Lighter Adapter.** Recharge your Treo communicator while you drive to your next meeting or power lunch.

**Action Names.** Never forget an important event or contact again.

**The world traveler**

Some people bar hop, you country hop. With the GSM world phone, web access to maps, and an included travel charger the Treo communicator is the perfect lightweight travel companion.

Add:

**Travel Charger Kit.** Be ready wherever your road takes you with this 100-240 volt North American travel charger with UK, EU and AU adapters.

**Small Talk.** Communicate in the local language with the world's first two-way real-time language translator.

**TravelTracker.** Track all your travel details including flights, hotels, dinner reservations, and transportation.

**The gamer**

You know that all work and no play makes for a dull life. Luckily, your Treo communicator is the perfect way to remedy that. Balance duty with diversion by getting a couple of games to help you unwind or just pass the time.

Add:

**PacMan.** Gobble up points when you're stuck in the airport or waiting in line.

**PocketChess™ Deluxe.** Challenge yourself—or a friend—to a game of chess.

**The city slicker**

You live for the city—the hottest restaurants, the chicest stores, the trendiest clubs. Your Treo communicator helps you find them all with instant web access and makes it easy to spread the word with SMS, email and mobile phone.

Add:

**Vindigo.** You know where you are and what you want. Shopping, food or fun—Vindigo gets you there.

**Zagat.** Eat your way through the best restaurants in 23 cities.

Palm PDAs and cell phones. These software companies produced applications for a myriad of purposes like personal use (e-mail, maps, browsers), business use (groupware, sales force automation, CRM, spreadsheets), and entertainment (games, pictures, personal rings).

**15**    Handspring marketed and distributed the Treo to both consumers and businesses through various channels including retail and on-line stores as well as B2B agreements. For example, Handspring formed sales and marketing relationships with Neomar and Infowave whereby the companies would jointly promote Handspring's Treo and later companies' wireless data access platforms. In addition to its own direct sales, Handspring appointed the major wholesaler Ingram Micro to focus on the enterprise market, and D&H Distributing to promote its products on college campuses.

**16**    Because the Treo was the company's first cell-phone-based product offering, GSM wireless service providers had become a new and significant retail channel. The company formed partnerships with Cingular Wireless and Voicestream to sell the Treo with wireless service plans. To unlock global markets, Handspring also established similar deals with foreign wireless networks in Europe and Asia. For example, Handspring formed a strategic distribution agreement with APE Telecom, one of Sweden's leading producers of mobile communication products, to cover the marketing and distribution of the Handspring Treo to the Swedish market.

### Internal Development

**17**    Handspring's products were designed by its internal engineering, marketing, and manufacturing organizations. Technologies required to support product development were either created internally or licensed from external providers. Its internal staff included engineers from many disciplines including software architects, electrical engineers, mechanical engineers, radio specialists, user interface design specialists, and others. Once a project was approved, a cross-functional team was assembled to design the product and transition it into manufacturing. To develop innovative products while minimizing time to market, the company used parallel development teams working on multiple projects. Before products were released into production, they had to pass a series of quality benchmarks and manufacturing guidelines.

**18**    Handspring's research and development expenditures in 2001 totaled $23.6 million, up from $10.3 million in 2000 and $2.7 million in 1999. As of August 31, 2001, it had 93 people engaged in research and development activities, and planned to focus its development efforts on wireless communicators.

### Supply-chain Management

**19**    Though design, marketing, and sales were conducted primarily in-house, Handspring was the quintessential outsourcer when it came to manufacturing and service. External parties handled manufacturing and assembly, customer and technical support, and repair services. All production of the Visor PDAs had been outsourced to Flextronics and Solectron. Visor phone had been built in partnership with Option International of Leuven, Belgium. Motorola provided microprocessors, Wavecom supplied the Treo with its integrated dual-band GSM radio module for wireless voice and data communications, and Acura Tech Ltd. supplied connector systems. Several components (such as the microprocessors) were available only from a single source.

**20**    Outsourcing components and manufacturing enabled Handspring to focus on its core competencies, and helped to minimize inventory levels. Handspring's supply chain management techniques backfired, however, when component shortages delayed the Treo's introduction in the United States and prompted the company to lower its production targets. Handspring consequently decided to route most of its early production to Europe where the GSM standard is more widespread and customers are considered to be more ready for smart phones.

**EXHIBIT 9**
**Worldwide Handheld Operating System Shares for 1998 and 1999, and Forecasts for 2000 to 2004**

Source: Salomon Smith Barney, October 18, 2000.

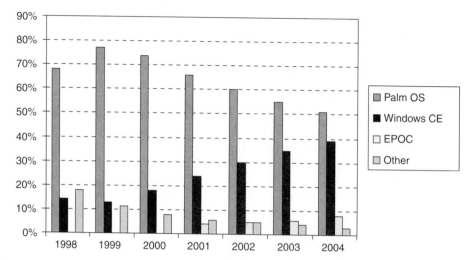

## Choosing Sides in Standards Battles

21     The developers of the Treo had to place bets on who would win in two separate standards battles: operating systems for handheld computers, and wireless telecommunication standards for mobile phones. The Palm operating system (OS) was an obvious choice given Handspring's history. The Palm operating system also held a commanding 77 percent worldwide market share at the end of 1999, and though estimates indicated that the share declined to 66 percent by the end of 2001, that still represented a significant lead over the next leading contender, Microsoft's Windows CE. However, forecasts for future trends in handheld operating systems were troubling—Microsoft's share was predicted to gain significantly—mostly at the expense of the Palm OS share. (see Exhibit 9 for worldwide handheld operating system shares).

22     In the wireless telecommunications standards battles, Treo had put its money on the Global System for Mobile Communications (GSM). The Treo utilized GSM technology on two bands—900/1900 MHz in North America, and 900/1800 MHz in Asia and Europe. Though GSM was the dominant standard globally, in the United States a wireless telecom standards battle was still unfolding. Following deregulation of the telecommunications industry in the United States in 1996, several national wireless networks had emerged (e.g., Cingular, Verizon, VoiceStream, Sprint PCS, and AT&T wireless) and industry players supported different digital voice wireless platforms. Of these platforms, the GSM served as the leading format for second generation wireless communications with the largest worldwide installed base by 2000 (for an explanation of the various generations of wireless telecommunications service, see Exhibit 10).

23     GSM was developed in the 1980s to set a common standard for digital wireless voice communication in Europe, as European markets began to unify. However, by March 1999, all three of the largest wireless handset makers—Ericsson, Motorola, and Nokia—were also manufacturing wireless phones based on Qualcomm's Code Division Multiple Access (CDMA) 2G wireless format.[10] 25 percent of worldwide wireless subscribers were forecasted to have adopted CDMA technology by the end of 2002, making it the second most widely used 2G format.[11] The third most prevalent wireless platform technology, TDMA, was developed by AT&T. It was used primarily in North America and accounted

[10]P. Henning, "Qualcomm, Ericsson Unite Over New Wireless Standard," *Red Herring,* www.redherring.com., 2000.
[11]Anonymous, *S&P Telecommunications Wireless Industry Survey,* (New York: McGraw-Hill, 2000) p. 5.

## EXHIBIT 10
**Three Generations of Wireless Telecommunications**

Original cellular networks (now referred to as first generation) supported only analog voice communication. However, in the 1990s, the second generation (2G) of wireless communication emerged that supported voice and text transmission over digital networks.

**2G Wireless.** In 2G wireless communications, calls were established using an exclusive circuit, so that the connection was lost as soon as such a call was ended. Networks were capable of handling only a certain number of such "circuit-switched" calls.

The 2G wireless industry underwent rapid change in the 1990s. The 1996 Telecommunications Act unleashed rapid increases in competition in the wireless industry, and several national wireless service providers emerged in the United States, including AT&T Wireless, Sprint PCS, Nextel Communications, Verizon Wireless, Cingular Wireless, and VoiceStream Wireless. On a global scale NTT DoCoMo, Vodafone, Telecom Italia, and France Telecom all emerged as leading wireless service providers. Additionally, many smaller carriers emerged in the industry to gain over 17 percent of the wireless market. With the increase in competition, pricing for voice wireless service fell to its most "attractive" prices ever, drawing more users to wireless phones. At the same time, revenue per subscriber had been declining in many countries, like the United States, due to the lingering effects of deregulation as the price of wireless services continued to fall. This shift toward marginal pricing as the wireless voice market matured drove wireless companies to continue differentiating their products through development of new technology. One of the primary areas targeted was the development of networks that would enable broadband Internet access. In the late 1990s, wireless service providers began planning to upgrade their existing networks and to build new wireless transmission systems to incorporate these new wireless technologies. To support the data needs of broadband wireless, networks needed to be updated to "packet-switching networks" that would allow a continuous connection for wireless users to send and receive data at any time.[*]

**2.5G Wireless: The Bridge to the Future.** Before entirely new 3G wireless systems were installed worldwide to support the needs of emerging wireless technology, many network providers planned to update existing networks to support packet-switching technology that would provide an "always on" continuous connection, but at slower speeds than would be possible with 3G networks. These "bridging technologies" were known as 2.5G systems because they relied on equipment from existing 2G networks. CDMA technology proved to be an initial leader in the move to 2.5G systems because the core CDMA technology was already based on an underlying packet-switching technology, requiring only a system upgrade. To upgrade GSM networks, General Packet Radio Service (GPRS) technology was planned to allow handsets an always-on connection by upgrading existing signals.

Most wireless companies saw 2.5G technologies only as a stepping stone to 3G, since 3G systems would ultimately be cheaper to operate and would offer data connection speeds up to ten times faster than 2.5G networks. However, as some industry researchers pointed out, 2.5G phones could "steal 3G's thunder" if users resist 3G technology in favor of lower usage costs of 2.5G systems, thereby forestalling 3G indefinitely.[**] One of the first operational 2.5G wireless packet transmission networks was NTT DoCoMo's i-mode network that became operational in February 1999. By March 2000, the network, which ran on TDMA technology, had already achieved close to 21 million subscribers.

**Planning for 3G Wireless.** By 2001 all major wireless manufacturers were active in the development of 3G wireless technologies and planning had begun for installation of 3G wireless networks across the globe. These new networks would be able to fully support the broadband data needs of emerging wireless technologies, while providing a continuous connection to the wireless Internet.

As 3G wireless systems, based on new frequencies from their 2G predecessors, became closer to a reality, multinational wireless companies worked to band together to ensure compatibility among different 3G systems. By 2001, 27 wireless service providers and vendors, including handset manufacturers Ericsson, Motorola, and Nokia, had joined together to form the 3G.IP group, focused on promoting a common IP based wireless system for 3G mobile communications technology while ensuring rapid standards development. 3G.IP focused on 3G development using WCDMA technology that has CDMA technology at its core, but that could easily be added to the existing global GSM core network. WCDMA appeared to be a leading platform among competing 3G wireless technologies, although no clear standard had yet emerged by early 2001.

[*]Anonymous, "Two Stumbling Steps Toward 3G," *The Economist Technology Quarterly,* December 9, 2002, www.economist.com.

[**]Matthew M. Nordan of Forrester Research, quoted in: A. Reinhardt, S. Baker, W. Echikson, K. Carlisle, and P. Schmidt, "Who Needs 3G Anyway?" *BusinessWeek: European Business,* March 26, 2001, p. 18.

for 9 percent of worldwide cellular subscribers in 2000. Most network system providers, like Ericsson, produced networks for all types of leading network technologies.

24    Globally, GSM was the dominant standard, and it was also better positioned for the transition to 2.5 and 3G GPRS service. However, in the United States in 2001, GSM only had an 11 percent market share; most U.S. wireless service providers adhered to the CDMA or TDMA standards. The Treo would thus function seamlessly in Europe and Asia, but coverage in the United States would be spotty.

### Building a Web of Alliances

25    To ensure that the Treo would have a wide range of high-quality applications available for it, Handspring built a web of alliances with third-party software developers. In addition to the relationship with Visto described previously, Handspring also teamed with several leading wireless solution providers (including Aether Systems, Infowave, Neomar, Synchrologic, Wireless Knowledge, and others) to ensure that e-mail delivery would be secure. Handspring forged a relationship with Avantgo for its Internet ability, and with Pumatech for desktop synchronization.

26    Handspring also established marketing agreements with several other key software developers. It teamed with Extended Systems Inc. to co-market the Treo and other Handspring products with the latter's Xtnd Connect Server, which enabled wireless synchronization between corporate servers and handheld devices. Handspring partnered with Synchrologic Inc. to market the Treo and other devices with Synchrologic's iMobile Suite software, which allowed wireless access to groupware, sales force automation, and customer relationship management data.

27    Handspring and Handango combined forces to build two online software stores. One store would be dedicated to individual consumers while the other store would be dedicated to businesses. The stores would sell products ranging from productivity-enhancing software to games. In addition, each company would actively market the other's products via their company websites, newsletters, and other media. Handspring also allied with Brightpoint, a large distributor of mobile phones, to distribute the Treo and provide integrated logistics services for the device.

28    One of Handspring's most important alliance relationships was with Palm. Handspring had entered into a nonexclusive licensing agreement with Palm to use the Palm operating system. This agreement did not expire until the end of 2009, but due to its nonexclusively clause, Handspring would be able to migrate the Treo to another operating system if market demand warranted this. Given the dynamic nature of the marketplace, keeping the Treo flexible was a priority.

## COMPETITION

29    Handspring would be facing an expanded set of competitors in the handheld communication devices market. Handspring would be competing in a head-to-head battle with established mobile phone manufacturers to obtain market share. In Spring of 2002, the global market share leaders in handheld communications devices were Nokia, Motorola, Ericsson, and Samsung (see Exhibit 11 for comparative market shares). Whereas the market for mobile phones was mature, the smart phone market was relatively new and growing, and was expected to attract the attention of most of the major mobile phone manufacturers. In fact, Nokia, Samsung, and Kyocera already had smart phones available on the market.

**EXHIBIT 11**
**Worldwide Wireless
Telecommunications
Market Share in 2001**

Source: www.cellular.co.za.

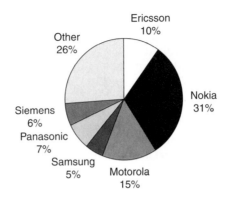

The three smart phones that offered the most direct competition for the Treo were the Kyocera QCP 6035 and the Samsung SPH-1300, and Nokia 9290 (see Exhibit 12 for product images and comparative specs). The functionality provided by each of these phones was nearly identical, offering few opportunities for differentiating the products to consumers. The major differences between the models were in size and weight with the Treo being the smallest and lightest. It was 11 percent smaller and lighter than Samsung's SPH-I300, 35 percent lighter and 60 percent smaller than the Kyocera QCP 6035, and 20 percent lighter and 35 percent smaller than the Nokia 9290. Handspring hoped that the compact design would prove to be a critical factor in mobile phone purchases. The various models also differed in the included accessories, protective covers, and input methods, where a clear winning approach was not yet evident.

31   Because it was being heavily marketed as an employee productivity tool for the enterprise, the Treo would also be in competition with PDAs. It would be in most direct competition with products such as the Palm Pilot i705 and the RIM Blackberry 5810 which provided wireless connectivity (see Exhibit 13 for product images and comparative specs). Though not nearly as large as the mobile phone competitors, Palm and RIM were both well-recognized and established competitors in the PDA market.

32   Both of these PDAs offered "always on" connectivity, though the Palm i705 did not offer voice capability and thus was not truly a mobile phone. RIM's Blackberry 5810's phone capability was available only through an integrated headset jack. The device was priced at $499, and was lighter (but larger) than the Treo, and like the Treo it used the GSM network but did not operate in Europe (a different model, the 5820 was required for use in Europe).

# THE FUTURE . . .

33   Handspring shipped 47,000 units of the Treo in the first quarter of 2002, and Wall Street had responded warmly, pushing Handspring's stock price up 34 percent. But both Dubinsky and Hawkins knew that the Treo would be a key inflection point in Handspring's history. Like many young startups, Handspring still had not achieved profitability, and the patience of the investing public was wearing thin. The company desperately wanted to avoid the recent fate of many other bankrupt technology companies. Would Handspring have the resources necessary to battle giants like Nokia and Samsung? Would Handspring be able to effectively penetrate the enterprise market, and would this market shift pay off? Would the higher margins of smart phones rescue the

**EXHIBIT 12**
Treo and Smart
Phone Competitors

**Treo 180**

**Price:** $399 with service activation from VoiceStream and Cingular, $599 without service.
**Weight:** 5.2 oz
**Memory:** 16 MB
**Size:** 4.3" × 2.7" × 0.7"
**Touch screen:** Yes
**Talk time:** 2.5 hours
**Standby time:** 60 hours
**Network:** Dual band GSM
**Short messaging:** Yes
**Email:** Yes
**Operating System:** Palm

**Samsung I300**

**Price:** $499 from Spring
**Weight:** 6.0 oz
**Memory:** 8 MB
**Size:** 4.9" × 2.28" × 0.8"
**Touch screen:** Yes
**Talk time:** 4 hours
**Standby time:** 100 hours
**Network:** Dual band CDMA and analog
**Short messaging:** Yes
**Email:** Yes
**Operating System:** Palm

**Kyocera Smartphone**

**Price:** $349 from Verizon
**Weight:** 7.3 oz
**Memory:** 8 MB
**Size:** 5.6" × 2.5" × 0.86"
**Touch screen:** Yes
**Talk time:** 5 hours
**Standby time:** 180 hours
**Network:** Tri-mode: CDMA digital PCS, CDMA digital and analog
**Short messaging:** Yes
**Email:** Yes
**Operating System:** Palm

**Nokia 9290 Communicator**

**Price:** Expected to launch at about $799
**Weight:** 8.7 oz
**Memory:** 8 MB
**Size:** 4.0" × 1.9" × 0.8"
**Touch screen:**
**Talk time:** Up to 10 hours
**Standby time:** Up to 230 hours
**Network:** 1900 MHz GSM
**Short messaging:** Yes
**Email:** Yes
**Operating System:** Symbian EPOC

**EXHIBIT 13**
PDA Competitors

**Palm i705**

**Price:** $499
**Weight:** 5.9 oz
**Memory:** 8 MB
**Size:** 4.65″ × 3.06″ × 0.61″
**Touch screen:** Yes
**Talk time:** NA
**Standby time:** 168 hours
**Network:** NA
**Short messaging:** NA
**Email:** Yes
**Operating System:** Palm

**Blackberry 5810**

**Price:** $499 plus service from VoiceStream and AT&T
**Weight:** 4.7 oz
**Memory:** 9 MB
**Size:** 4.6″ x 3.1″ x 0.7″
**Touch screen:** No
**Talk time:** 3.5 hours
**Standby time:** 144 hours
**Network:** 1900 MHz GSM/GPRS
**Short messaging:** Yes
**Email:** Yes
**Operating System:** Java 2 Micro Edition

company from its financial woes, or were smart phones destined for the same heavy price cutting that had afflicted PDAs? The company had made a serious gamble, and now all eyes were watching to see how the relatively new company would fare in the high stakes battle to secure the next dominant design in personal computing and communicating technology.

If we are unable to compete effectively with existing or new competitors, our resulting loss of competitive position could result in price reductions, fewer customer orders, reduced margins and loss of market share.

The market for handheld computing and wireless communication products is highly competitive and we expect competition to increase in the future. Some of our competitors or potential competitors have significantly greater financial, technical, and marketing resources than we do. These competitors may be able to respond more rapidly than we can to new or emerging technologies or changes in customer requirements. They may also devote greater resources to the development, promotion, and sale of their products than we do.

Our products compete with a variety of handheld devices, including keyboard-based devices, subnotebook computers, smart phones, and two-way pagers. Our principal competitors, and possible new competitors, include:

- Palm, from whom we license our operating system

- Licensees of the Microsoft's PocketPC operating system for handheld devices such as Casio, Compaq, and Hewlett-Packard

- Licensees of Symbian EPOCH operating systems for wireless communication devices such as Panasonic and Siemens

- Other Palm OS operating system licensees, including Acer, Handera, Sony, and Symbol

- Smart phone manufacturers such as Ericsson, Kyocera, Motorola, Nokia, and Samsung

- Research In Motion Limited, a leading provider of wireless e-mail, instant messaging, and Internet connectivity, and

- A variety of start-up companies looking to compete in our current and future markets

We expect our competitors to continue to improve the performance of their current products and to introduce new products, services, and technologies. Successful new product introductions or enhancements by our competitors could reduce the sales and market acceptance of our products, cause intense price competition, and result in reduced gross margins and loss of market share.

Our failure to compete successfully against current or future competitors could seriously harm our business. To be competitive, we must continue to invest significant resources in research and development, sales, and marketing. We cannot be sure that we will have sufficient resources to make these investments or that we will be able to make the technological advances necessary to be competitive.

## Case 49 Robin Hood

### Joseph Lampel

1   It was in the spring of the second year of his insurrection against the High Sheriff of Nottingham that Robin Hood took a walk in Sherwood Forest. As he walked he pondered the progress of the campaign, the disposition of his forces, the Sheriff's recent moves, and the options that confronted him.

2   The revolt against the Sheriff had begun as a personal crusade. It erupted out of Robin's conflict with the Sheriff and his administration. However, alone Robin Hood could do little. He therefore sought allies, men with grievances and a deep sense of justice. Later he welcomed all who came, asking few questions and demanding only a willingness to serve. Strength, he believed, lay in numbers.

3   He spent the first year forging the group into a disciplined band, united in enmity against the Sheriff and willing to live outside the law. The band's organization was simple. Robin ruled supreme, making all important decisions. He delegated specific tasks to his lieutenants. Will Scarlett was in charge of intelligence and scouting. His main job was to shadow the Sheriff and his men, always alert to their next move. He also collected information on the travel plans of rich merchants and tax collectors. Little John kept discipline among the men and saw to it that their archery was at the high peak that their profession demanded. Scarlock took care of the finances, converting loot to cash, paying shares of the take, and finding suitable hiding places for the surplus. Finally, Much the Miller's son had the difficult task of provisioning the ever-increasing band of Merrymen.

4   The increasing size of the band was a source of satisfaction for Robin, but also a source of concern. The fame of his Merrymen was spreading, and new recruits were pouring in from every corner of England. As the band grew larger, their small bivouac became a major encampment. Between raids the men milled about, talking and playing games. Vigilance was in decline, and discipline was becoming harder to enforce. "Why," Robin reflected, "I don't know half the men I run into these days."

5   The growing band was also beginning to exceed the food capacity of the forest. Game was becoming scarce, and supplies had to be obtained from outlying villages. The cost of buying food was beginning to drain the band's financial reserves at the very moment when revenues were in decline. Travelers, especially those with the most to lose, were now giving the forest a wide berth. This was costly and inconvenient to them, but it was preferable to having all their goods confiscated.

6   Robin believed that the time had come for the Merrymen to change their policy of outright confiscation of goods to one of a fixed transit tax. His lieutenants strongly resisted this idea. They were proud of the Merrymen's famous motto: "Rob the rich and give to the poor." "The farmers and the townspeople," they argued, "are our most important allies. How can we tax them, and still hope for their help in our fight against the Sheriff?"

7   Robin wondered how long the Merrymen could keep to the ways and methods of their early days. The Sheriff was growing stronger and becoming better organized. He now had the money and the men and was beginning to harass the band, probing for its weaknesses. The tide of events was beginning to turn against the Merrymen. Robin felt that the campaign must be decisively concluded before the Sheriff had a chance to deliver a mortal blow. "But how," he wondered, "could this be done?"

Source: Prepared by Joseph Lampel, New York University. Copyright © 2001, by Joseph Lampel.

**8**     Robin had often entertained the possibility of killing the Sheriff, but the chances for this seemed increasingly remote. Besides, killing the Sheriff might satisfy his personal thirst for revenge, but it would not improve the situation. Robin had hoped that the perpetual state of unrest, and the Sheriff's failure to collect taxes, would lead to his removal from office. Instead, the Sheriff used his political connections to obtain reinforcement. He had powerful friends at court and was well regarded by the regent, Prince John.

**9**     Prince John was vicious and volatile. He was consumed by his unpopularity among the people, who wanted the imprisoned King Richard back. He also lived in constant fear of the barons, who had first given him the regency but were now beginning to dispute his claim to the throne. Several of these barons had set out to collect the ransom that would release King Richard the Lionheart from his jail in Austria. Robin was invited to join the conspiracy in return for future amnesty. It was a dangerous proposition. Provincial banditry was one thing, court intrigue another. Prince John had spies everywhere, and he was known for his vindictiveness. If the conspirators' plan failed, the pursuit would be relentless, and retributions swift.

**10**    The sound of the supper horn startled Robin from his thoughts. There was the smell of roasting venison in the air. Nothing was resolved or settled. Robin headed for camp promising himself that he would give these problems his utmost attention after tomorrow's raid.

## Case 50  XM Radio: The Sky is the Limit
### XM Radio and Its Uncertain Future

## Joseph Jordan, Melissa A. Schilling, Matthew Shaffer, Jason Sullivan, and Nancy Wolfe

**1**  Hugh Panero paced his office and thought back to how much progress XM Radio had made in 2001. His company had launched two satellites and begun commercialization of the first commercial satellite radio service. So far, he thought, results had been mixed. Subscription rates had surpassed initial market expectations, but the company was burning cash at a rapid rate. The market was proving increasingly difficult to please. On March 19, 2002, as the XM Radio released its 2002 Annual Report, shares dropped 15 percent in one day, as doubts grew regarding its ability to survive in the face of mounting losses. In addition, its major rival, Sirius, was about to launch its competing nationwide service. As President and CEO of XM Radio, Panero had many difficult issues ahead of him in seeking to establish a solid foundation for his fledgling company. What were the best ways to increase adoption rate, subscriber base, and most importantly, company profitability? How would players in the traditional radio industry react to the new threat his company posed? Would the market support multiple standards or would only one prevail? Finally, how closely should XM align with Sirius to increase the likelihood of the satellite radio market's commercial success?

## THE LAUNCH OF XM RADIO

**2**  XM Satellite Radio Holdings Inc., based in Washington, D.C., was originally formed as American Mobile Radio Corporation in 1992. By 1997, the company had gained one of only two FCC licenses for a satellite radio service in the "S" band frequency in the United States, after spending more than $80 million in a two-day auction process. The technology behind satellite radio service essentially provided a third frequency band that promised better clarity (digital transmission technology) and deeper programming choices than the existing AM and FM formats. XM's broadcasts were targeted for reception in the home, in the car, or on portable radios, such as a Walkman. For this service, subscribers paid a monthly $9.99 fee.[1] Analysts likened XM's radio service to cable television service, as it provided a seamless national signal, rather than spotty local coverage, with improved crispness and variety of content.[2] A brief timeline of XM's operations is provided in Exhibit 1.

**3**  XM's business model called for two primary revenue sources. First came the $9.99 subscription fee. By the end of 2001, subscribers were estimated at approximately 30,000. Near-term subscription expectations from research analysts were impressive, calling for approximately 350,000 by the end of 2002 (Exhibit 2). The majority of these early subscribers were located in urban areas, with 75 percent paying in advance for the entire quarter.[3] In addition to subscription fees, XM attempted to sell advertising space in several of its programming channels. Management hoped that its service would appeal to radio advertisers

---

[1]XM Satellite Radio Holdings, Inc. *Annual Report,* March 2001.
[2]S. G. Cowen, December 26, 2001.
[3]Yukuri Iwatani, "XM Satellite Loss Widens, Sets '02 Subscriber Estimate," *Variety,* January 24, 2001.

**EXHIBIT 1**  XM
**Corporate Timeline**

Source: Company data.

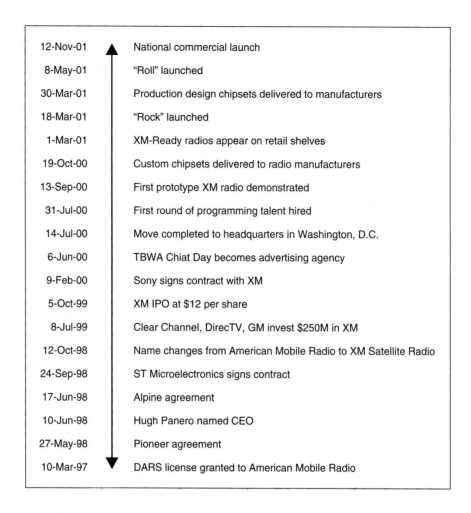

|  |  |
|---|---|
| 12-Nov-01 | National commercial launch |
| 8-May-01 | "Roll" launched |
| 30-Mar-01 | Production design chipsets delivered to manufacturers |
| 18-Mar-01 | "Rock" launched |
| 1-Mar-01 | XM-Ready radios appear on retail shelves |
| 19-Oct-00 | Custom chipsets delivered to radio manufacturers |
| 13-Sep-00 | First prototype XM radio demonstrated |
| 31-Jul-00 | First round of programming talent hired |
| 14-Jul-00 | Move completed to headquarters in Washington, D.C. |
| 6-Jun-00 | TBWA Chiat Day becomes advertising agency |
| 9-Feb-00 | Sony signs contract with XM |
| 5-Oct-99 | XM IPO at $12 per share |
| 8-Jul-99 | Clear Channel, DirecTV, GM invest $250M in XM |
| 12-Oct-98 | Name changes from American Mobile Radio to XM Satellite Radio |
| 24-Sep-98 | ST Microelectronics signs contract |
| 17-Jun-98 | Alpine agreement |
| 10-Jun-98 | Hugh Panero named CEO |
| 27-May-98 | Pioneer agreement |
| 10-Mar-97 | DARS license granted to American Mobile Radio |

**EXHIBIT 2**
**Early Subscription Estimates**

Source: Morgan StanleyEquity Research, January 25, 2002.

| XM 2002 Subscriber Estimates | Q4 2001 | Q1 2002 | Q2 2002 | Q4 2002 |
|---|---|---|---|---|
| Subscribers | 27,733 | 70,000 | 130,000 | 351,000 |

that previously needed to work with multiple spot or syndication buys to gain national reach.[4] Current financial data are included in Exhibits 3 through 8.

4  Programming was offered on 100 channels with a wide variety of programming choices designed to both offer broad appeal and target specific groups that XM believed likely to adopt the service. Programs included original talk shows and music produced in a state-of-the-art studio at XM headquarters (by the company's XM Originals unit), as well as branded programming supplied by well-known content providers. In-house talent included industry veterans and musicians, such as reggae legend Junior Marvin and Smithereeens' leader Pat DiNizio, and branded channels were developed by MTV, VH1, ESPN Radio, Radio Disney, CNN, CNBC, USA Today, Fox News, BET, E!, Radio One, Clear Channel, and Hispanic

[4]XM Satellite Radio Holdings, Inc. *Annual Report,* March 2002.

**EXHIBIT 3** **Select Financial Information, XM Satellite Radio Fundamentals**

Source: Yahoo.com, March 28, 2002.

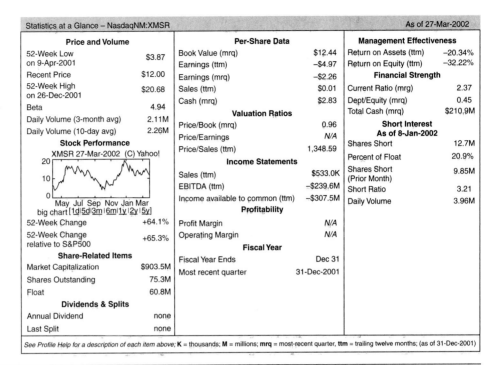

| Statistics at a Glance – NasdaqNM:XMSR | | As of 27-Mar-2002 |
|---|---|---|

**Price and Volume**

| | |
|---|---|
| 52-Week Low on 9-Apr-2001 | $3.87 |
| Recent Price | $12.00 |
| 52-Week High on 26-Dec-2001 | $20.68 |
| Beta | 4.94 |
| Daily Volume (3-month avg) | 2.11M |
| Daily Volume (10-day avg) | 2.26M |

**Stock Performance**

XMSR 27-Mar-2002 (C) Yahoo!

big chart [1d|5d|3m|6m|1y|2y|5y]

| | |
|---|---|
| 52-Week Change | +64.1% |
| 52-Week Change relative to S&P500 | +65.3% |

**Share-Related Items**

| | |
|---|---|
| Market Capitalization | $903.5M |
| Shares Outstanding | 75.3M |
| Float | 60.8M |

**Dividends & Splits**

| | |
|---|---|
| Annual Dividend | none |
| Last Split | none |

**Per-Share Data**

| | |
|---|---|
| Book Value (mrq) | $12.44 |
| Earnings (ttm) | –$4.97 |
| Earnings (mrq) | –$2.26 |
| Sales (ttm) | $0.01 |
| Cash (mrq) | $2.83 |

**Valuation Ratios**

| | |
|---|---|
| Price/Book (mrq) | 0.96 |
| Price/Earnings | N/A |
| Price/Sales (ttm) | 1,348.59 |

**Income Statements**

| | |
|---|---|
| Sales (ttm) | $533.0K |
| EBITDA (ttm) | –$239.6M |
| Income available to common (ttm) | –$307.5M |

**Profitability**

| | |
|---|---|
| Profit Margin | N/A |
| Operating Margin | N/A |

**Fiscal Year**

| | |
|---|---|
| Fiscal Year Ends | Dec 31 |
| Most recent quarter | 31-Dec-2001 |

**Management Effectiveness**

| | |
|---|---|
| Return on Assets (ttm) | –20.34% |
| Return on Equity (ttm) | –32.22% |

**Financial Strength**

| | |
|---|---|
| Current Ratio (mrq) | 2.37 |
| Dept/Equity (mrq) | 0.45 |
| Total Cash (mrq) | $210.9M |

**Short Interest As of 8-Jan-2002**

| | |
|---|---|
| Shares Short | 12.7M |
| Percent of Float | 20.9% |
| Shares Short (Prior Month) | 9.85M |
| Short Ratio | 3.21 |
| Daily Volume | 3.96M |

*See Profile Help for a description of each item above;* **K** = thousands; **M** = millions; **mrq** = most-recent quarter, **ttm** = trailing twelve months; (as of 31-Dec-2001)

## M Satellite Radio Bond Issues

| Moody | S&P | Qty | Coupon | Maturity | Yield | Price |
|---|---|---|---|---|---|---|
| Caa | CCC+ | 75 | 14.000 | 2010 | 21.767 | 71.188 |
| Caa | CCC+ | 100 | 14.000 | 2010 | 22.820 | 68.250 |

Source: BondPage.com, March 28, 2002.

**EXHIBIT 4** **Stock Price History**

Source: moneycentral.msn.com, March 28, 2002.

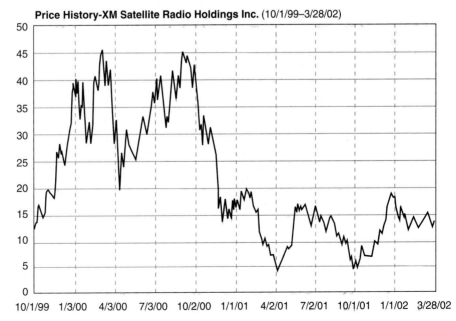

**Price History-XM Satellite Radio Holdings Inc.** (10/1/99–3/28/02)

**EXHIBIT 5**
**Market Factors**

### Bridge Corporate Spreads for Industrials

| Rating | 1yr | 5 yr | 10 yr | 30 yr |
|---|---|---|---|---|
| Aaa/AAA | 28 | 43 | 67 | 80 |
| Aa2/AA | 38 | 58 | 87 | 97 |
| A2/A | 63 | 100 | 136 | 154 |
| Baa2/BBB | 108 | 150 | 180 | 204 |
| Ba2/BB | 250 | 325 | 375 | 450 |
| B2/B | 450 | 550 | 600 | 800 |
| Caa/CCC | 800 | 1100 | 1300 | 1500 |

Source: BondsOnline.com, March 28, 2002.

### U.S. Treasury Bond Rates

| | |
|---|---|
| 3 month | 2.14 % |
| 10 year | 4.49 % |
| 30 year | 5.30 % |

Source: Money.CNN.com, March 28, 2002.

Broadcasting Corporation.[5] By early 2002, listeners could choose from ten rock channels, fifteen hit channels, seven urban channels, six country channels, six jazz channels, four dance channels, five Latin channels, six world-music channels, four classical channels and six oldies channels.[6] In addition, subscribers could continue to receive local sports, weather, and traffic as local AM/FM terrestrial radio was available through the receiver units.

5    XM's service initially launched in two pilot cities, San Diego and Dallas/Ft. Worth, in September of 2001. In mid-October service was expanded across the southern United States, and nationwide service became available in November 2001.[7]

**Satellite Radio 101**

[5]Chris Jordan, "For More and More Music Fans, Satellite Radio is Heaven Sent," *SonicNet,* February 7, 2002.
[6]Amanda Barnett, "Satellite Radio Lifting Off," CNN.com Sci/Tech, July 24, 2001.
[7]www.xmradio.com, XM home page.

**EXHIBIT 6**

**Income Statement**

|  | 31-Dec-2001 | 31-Dec-2000 | 31-Dec-1999 |
|---|---|---|---|
| Revenue: |  |  |  |
| Subscriber revenue | $ 246 |  |  |
| Ad sales revenue | $ 294 | $ 0 | $ 0 |
| Less: Agency commissions | ($ 43) | $ 0 | $ 0 |
| Other revenue | $ 36 | $ 0 | $ 0 |
| Total revenue | $ 533 | $ 0 | $ 0 |
| Operating expenses: |  |  |  |
| Broadcasting operations: |  |  |  |
| Content/programming | ($ 27,924) | ($ 6,878) | ($ 1,014) |
| System operations | ($ 67,571) | ($ 23,227) | ($ 2,877) |
| Customer care and billing operations | ($6,034) | ($ 856) | $ 0 |
| Sales and marketing | ($ 99,789) | ($ 16,078) | ($ 3,351) |
| General and administrative | ($ 24,595) | ($ 16,624) | ($14,496) |
| Research and development | ($ 14,255) | ($ 12,701) | ($ 7,440) |
| Depreciation and amortization | ($ 41,971) | ($ 3,115) | ($ 1,513) |
| Total operating expenses | ($282,139) | ($ 79,479) | ($30,691) |
| Operating loss | ($281,606) | ($ 79,479) | ($30,691) |
| Other income (expense): |  |  |  |
| Interest income | $ 15,198 | $ 27,606 | $ 2,916 |
| Interest expense | ($ 18,131) | $ 0 | ($ 9,121) |
| Other income, net | $160 | $ 0 | $ 0 |
| Net loss | ($284,379) | ($ 51,873) | ($36,896) |
| 8.25% Series B PS dividend requirement | ($3,766) | ($ 5,935) | $ 0 |
| 8.25% Series C PS dividend requirement | ($ 19,387) | ($ 9,277) | $ 0 |
| Series B PS deemed dividend | $0 | ($ 11,211) | $ 0 |
| Series C PS beneficial conversion feature | $0 | ($123,042) | $ 0 |
| Net loss attributable to common stockholders | ($307,532) | ($201,338) | ($36,896) |
| Net loss per share: |  |  |  |
| Basic and diluted | ($ 5.13) | ($ 4.15) | ($ 2.40) |
| Weighted average shares used in computing net loss per share-basic and diluted | 59,920,196 | 48,508,042 | 15,344,102 |

Source: XM Satellite Radio Holdings Inc 10-K405 2001-12-31: Income Statement.

# SATELLITE RADIO 101

**6**   Satellite radio provided significant advances over traditional radio signals. While most radio signals broke up about 30 to 40 miles away from their source, requiring listeners to scan for alternatives, satellite radio stations could broadcast a signal in excess of 22,000 miles with tremendous clarity.[8] XM's 100 channels achieved this performance and digital quality through two satellites in geostationary orbit that could cover the entire continental United States. "Rock" and "Roll" were model BSS 702 high-power satellites, built and launched by Boeing Satellite Systems, and were monitored and controlled for XM by Telestat Canada. One spare satellite remained grounded for future emergencies or system growth.

[8]Kevin Bonsor, "How Satellite Radio Works," www.howstuffworks.com.

## EXHIBIT 7
### Balance Sheet

| | 31-Dec-2001 | 31-Dec-2000 |
|---|---|---|
| | (in thousands except share data) | |
| **Assets** | | |
| Current assets: | | |
| Cash and cash equivalents | $ 182,497 | $ 224,903 |
| Short-term investments | $ 28,355 | $ 0 |
| Restricted investments | $ 44,861 | $ 45,585 |
| Accounts receivable, net of allowance for doubtful accounts of $10 and $0 | $ 478 | $ 0 |
| Prepaid and other current assets | $ 15,720 | $ 8,815 |
| Total current assets | $ 271,911 | $ 279,303 |
| Other assets: | 0 | 0 |
| Restricted investments, net of current portion | $ 27,898 | $ 115,581 |
| System under construction | $ 55,056 | $ 815,016 |
| PP&E net of accumulated depreciation and amortization of $43,384 and $2,337 | $1,066,191 | $ 50,052 |
| Goodwill and intangibles, net of accumulated amortization of $3,974 and $2,599 | $ 22,626 | $ 24,001 |
| Other assets, net of accumulated amortization of $2,167 and $672 | $ 12,521 | $ 9,265 |
| Total assets | $1,456,203 | $1,293,218 |
| **Liabilities and Stockholders' Equity** | | |
| Current liabilities: | | |
| Accounts payable | $ 36,559 | $ 31,793 |
| Accrued expenses | $ 26,098 | $ 6,039 |
| Accrued network optimization expenses (note 15) | $ 8,595 | $ 0 |
| Current portion of long-term debt | $ 1,910 | $ 556 |
| Due to related parties | $ 26,052 | $ 15,429 |
| Accrued interest | $ 15,664 | $ 13,397 |
| Total current liabilities | $ 114,878 | $ 67,214 |
| Long-term debt, net of current portion | $ 411,520 | $ 262,665 |
| Royalty payable, net of current portion | $ 1,800 | $ 2,600 |
| Other non-current liabilities | $ 1,354 | $ 4,787 |
| Total liabilities | $ 529,552 | $ 337,266 |
| Stockholders' equity: | | |
| Series A convertible preferred stock, par value $0.01 (liquidation preference of $102,688); 15,000,000 shares authorized, 10,786,504 shares issued and outstanding at December 31, 2000 and 2001 | $ 108 | $ 108 |
| Series B convertible redeemable preferred stock, par value $0.01 (liquidation preference of $43,364); 3,000,000 shares authorized, 867,289 shares issued and outstanding at December 31, 2000 and 2001 | $ 9 | $ 9 |
| Series C convertible redeemable preferred stock, par value $0.01 (liquidation preference of $244,277 and $263,664 at December 31, 2000 and 2001, respectively); 250,000 shares authorized, 235,000 shares issued and outstanding at December 31, 2000 and 2001 | $ 2 | $ 2 |
| Class A common stock, par value $0.01; 180,000,000 shares authorized, 34,073,994 and 74,482,168 shares issued and outstanding at December 31, 2000 and 2001, respectively | $ 745 | $ 341 |
| Class B common stock, par value $0.01; 30,000,000 shares authorized, 16,557,262 and no shares issued and outstanding at December 31, 2000 and 2001, respectively | $ 0 | $ 166 |
| Class C common stock, par value $0.01; 30,000,000 shares authorized, no shares issued and outstanding at December 31, 2000 and 2001 | $ 0 | $ 0 |
| Additional paid-in capital | $1,316,761 | $1,061,921 |
| Accumulated deficit | ($ 390,974) | ($ 106,595) |
| Total stockholders' equity | $ 926,651 | $ 955,952 |

## EXHIBIT 8
**Cash Flow Statement**

| | 31-Dec-2001 | 31-Dec-2000 | 31-Dec-1999 |
|---|---|---|---|
| | | (in thousands) | |
| Cash flows from operating activities: | | | |
| Net loss | ($284,379) | ($ 51,873) | ($ 36,896) |
| Adjustments to reconcile net loss to net cash used in operating activities: | | | |
| Bad debt expense | $10 | — | — |
| Depreciation and amortization | $ 42,422 | $ 3,369 | $ 1,478 |
| Loss on disposal computer equipment | $ 435 | — | — |
| Amortization of deferred financing fees | — | — | $ 509 |
| Non-cash stock-based compensation | $ 4,867 | $ 2,743 | $ 4,210 |
| Non-cash charge for beneficial conversion feature of note issued to investors | — | — | $ 5,520 |
| Changes in operating assets and liabilities: | | | |
| Increase in accounts receivable | ($ 488) | — | — |
| Increase in prepaid and other current assets | ($ 6,905) | ($ 7,738) | ($ 905) |
| Decrease in other assets | — | — | $ 43 |
| Increase in accounts payable and accrued expenses | $ 29,531 | $ 16,026 | $ 7,519 |
| Increase (decrease) in amounts due to related parties | $ 2,696 | $ 26 | ($ 1,316) |
| Increase in accrued interest | $ 8,763 | — | $ 3,053 |
| Net cash used in operating activities | ($203,048) | ($ 37,447) | ($ 16,785) |
| Cash flows from investing activities: | | | |
| Purchase of property and equipment | ($ 58,520) | ($ 41,925) | ($ 2,008) |
| Additions to system under construction | ($142,321) | ($424,342) | ($159,510) |
| Net purchase/maturity of short-term investments | ($ 28,355) | $ 69,472 | $ 69,472 |
| Net purchase/maturity of restricted investments | $ 40,317 | ($106,338) | — |
| Other investing activities | ($ 32,482) | ($ 56,268) | ($ 3,422) |
| Net cash used in investing activities | ($221,361) | ($559,401) | ($234,412) |
| Cash flows from financing activities: | | | |
| Proceeds from sale of common stock and capital contribution | $199,219 | $133,235 | $114,428 |
| Proceeds from issuance of Series B convertible redeemable PS | — | $ 96,472 | — |
| Proceeds from issuance of 14% senior secured notes and warrants | — | $322,889 | — |
| Proceeds from issuance of Series C convertible redeemable PS | — | $226,822 | — |
| Proceeds from issuance of sub'd convertible notes to related parties | — | — | $ 22,966 |
| Proceeds from issuance of 7.75% convertible subordinated notes | $125,000 | — | — |
| Proceeds from mortgage on corporate facility | $ 29,000 | — | — |
| Proceeds from loan payable | $ 35,000 | — | — |
| Proceeds from issuance of convertible notes | — | — | $250,000 |
| Repayment of loan payable to related party | — | — | ($ 75,000) |
| Payments for deferred financing costs | ($ 6,124) | ($ 8,365) | ($ 10,725) |
| Other net financing activities | ($ 92) | — | ($ 84) |
| Net cash provided by financing activities | $382,003 | $771,053 | $301,585 |
| Net increase (decrease) in cash and cash equivalents | ($ 42,406) | $174,205 | $ 50,388 |
| Cash and cash equivalents at beginning of period | $224,903 | $ 50,698 | $ 310 |
| Cash and cash equivalents at end of period | $182,497 | $224,903 | $ 50,698 |

Source: XM Satellite Radio Holdings Inc 10-K405 2001-12-31: Cash Flow.

**EXHIBIT 9** **Sample Product Offerings**

*Source: www.xmradio.com.*

The XM frequencies were 12.5 MHz of S-Band: 2332.5 to 2345.0 MHz. To support the satellite broadcast a network of terrestrial repeaters received and retransmitted the satellite signals.[9] In addition, to provide a memory buffer to overcome signal delays and gaps in the event a traveling listener passes through a tunnel, the "Rock" satellite broadcasted 4.7 seconds ahead of "Roll."[10] Programming was supported by the largest digital radio facility of its kind in the country with 82 end-to-end fiber-optic programming and broadcast studios at XM headquarters. The company had spent approximately $1.6 billion to date to get the broadcasts up and running.[11]

7    To receive XM broadcasts, consumers required a special receiver. Initially, these were available as part of a car radio, as an addition to an existing car radio (not requiring replacement of current hardware such as a CD player), or as a home audio component. Prices for car equipment ranged from around $150 for an add-on functionality for existing equipment to $1000 for a full-function stereo with XM and many other capabilities. Home receivers started at around $200. GM, through its OnStar division, anticipated offering XM satellite receivers in new models, beginning with several 2003 models in the fall of 2002.[12] Exhibit 9 shows samples of XM-ready equipment.

## THE SATELLITE RADIO MARKET

8    The digital satellite radio broadcasting system—digital audio broadcasting (DAB)—sought to address the shortcomings of terrestrial radio by providing a broad range of programming with consistent quality and coverage. DAB was seen as a new way to compete against the content and signal shortcomings of terrestrial radio and playback devices and was thought to enable subscription and/or advertising revenues unique to the radio market. To complete the required access to the spectrum, satellite coverage, and quality programming, XM faced only one significant competitor in the United States: Sirius Radio.

[9]XM Radio, March 2002.
[10]Paul Heltzel, "Tuning in to Satellite Radio," *Technology Review,* January 25, 2002.
[11]XM Radio, March 2001.
[12]XM Radio, March 2002.

**EXHIBIT 10**
**Market Information**

Source: Company data, NPD
Intellect, CEA CSFB estimates.

**Initial Consumer Demand Comparisons**

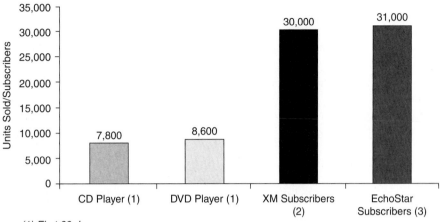

(1) First 60 days
(2) First 56 days
(3) First 70 days

9    The overall potential market consisted of over 200 million registered automobiles and 100 million households in the continental United States. Each year 26 million new car radios were added to the market (15 million new and 11 million after-market). Market research firms estimated the total size of the satellite radio market at 43 to 49 million subscribers.[13] Projected subscriptions for XM, and adoption rate comparison against other technologies are provided in Exhibit 10.

10   According to the Radio Advertising Bureau, 75 percent of all Americans age 12 and up listened to radio daily, and 95 percent weekly. Their choices of specialized contents were fairly limited. Huge segments of the music industry got little or no coverage by mainstream radio (71 percent of radio stations provided only the top 5 formats)—especially ethnic music formats such as African, Asian, Caribbean, and so on. With average listening times often in excess of three hours per day, especially in commuter situations, the demand for richer content appeared substantial. Also, more than 105 million listeners lived outside the 50 largest radio markets. These less densely populated areas represented great potential for interest in satellite radio.[14] The target market and opportunity breakdown are provided in Exhibit 11.

# SUPPLY CHAIN AND ALLIANCES

11   XM broke its suppliers down into two primary categories: equipment and content. Equipment suppliers included manufacturers of chipsets, satellite systems, radio receivers, and terrestrial repeaters. A list of equipment suppliers by category can be found in Exhibit 12. Independent content suppliers included original content providers, such as Bloomberg, Disney, ESPN, CNN, and MTV.[15]

[13]XM Radio, March 2002.
[14]XM Radio, March 2002.
[15]XM Radio, March 2002.

**EXHIBIT 11**
**Target Market and Opportunity Breakdown**

Source: Yankee Group, JD Power, U.S. Census, U.S. Department of Transportation, Company Reports, CSFB, Hadia Advertising Bureau, Digital Radio: A Survey of Consumer Expenditures, Veronis, Suhler & Associates Duncan's American Radio

| Target Market | Opportunity |
|---|---|
| General radio market | 95% of all Americans age 12 and up listen to radio weekly |
| | 75% of all Americans age 12 and up listen to radio daily |
| Car radio market | 75% of consumers choose radio most |
| | 11% of consumers choose CDs most |
| | 6% of consumers choose cassettes most |
| | 9% of consumers choose "other" most |
| Commuters | 115 million commuters |
| | 34 million travel over 45 minutes one-way |
| Niche music listeners | Classical, jazz, rap, gospel, soundtracks |
| | 21% of recorded music sales |
| | generally unavailable on radio |
| | of 30 music formats, over half are not available in NYC |
| Hispanic market | 2001E—33 million people in U.S. |
| | 2008E—39 million people in U.S. |
| Sports | Limited national coverage |
| | Classic sports market |
| Truck drivers | 3 million professional truck drivers |
| | 1.1 million long-distance haulers |
| Marine market | 7 million recreational boaters |
| Recreational vehicles | 9 million recreational vehicles |
| Sparse radio zones | 22 million people have access to < 5 radio stations |
| | 1.6 million people have access to 1 radio station |
| | 1 million people receive no radio stations |

**EXHIBIT 12**
**Equipment Suppliers by Category**

Source: XM Satellite Radio Holdings, Inc. 10K-405, March 19, 2002.

| Category | Company |
|---|---|
| Chipsets | STMicroelectronics |
| Radio units | Delphi-Delco Electronics |
| | Sony |
| | Pioneer |
| | Alpine |
| Satellite systems | Boeing Space Systems |
| Terrestrial repeaters | Hughes Electronics Corporation |
| | LCC International (*design*) |

**12**    In addition, XM built alliances and partnerships in many distribution channels to reach their target audience. These alliances included automobile manufacturers, electronics companies, and distributors/retailers. Some of the most notable partners included General Motors (which invested $50 million in XM), Freightliner, Sony, Pioneer, Delphi, Boeing, Best Buy, and Circuit City. By early 2002, XM devices were available at over 6,000 retail outlets in total. Key existing investors were both strategic and financial in nature. They included GM, Clear Channel, DirecTV, Telcom Ventures, Columbia Capital, and Madison Dearborn Partners.[16]

[16]XM Radio, March 2002.

# SIRIUS COMPETITION

**13** As mentioned, competition in digital audio broadcasting required both strength of signal through satellite coverage and programming depth. XM faced significant competition for subscription and advertising dollars from Sirius Radio as well as other radio players.

### Sirius Satellite Radio, Inc.

**14** Sirius Radio, formerly CD Radio, was the second company to be granted rights by the FCC in 1997 to broadcast over satellite. Only four companies had applied for a license to broadcast on that band. Both Sirius and XM Radio spent in excess of $80 million for their exclusive distribution rights to satellite radio and in excess of $1 billion each in undertaking their respective launches.[17]

**15** Sirius offered 100 channels (60 commercial free music and 40 news, sports, entertainment programming) similar to those of XM and, in addition, had exclusive relationships with National Public Radio (NPR), Hispanic Radio Network, and National Lampoon. On the automobile manufacturer front, Sirius enjoyed exclusive partnerships with Daimler-Chrysler, Ford and BMW—comprising significantly more of the auto industry than XM's alliances. However, the Sirius rollout was slightly behind that of XM, with nationwide coverage targeted for the third quarter of 2002. Sirius' service was available for a monthly subscription fee of $12.95. This rate was higher than XM's subscription fee of $9.99; however, Sirius planned for its music programming to be 100 percent commercial-free. Its talk programming would feature some on-air advertising.[18] Exhibit 13 provides data on Sirius Corporation, and Exhibit 14 provides comparison data for Sirius and XM.

### WorldSpace

**16** The global satellite radio leader in regions outside the United States was WorldSpace. WorldSpace had launched two satellites, AfriStar and AsiaStar, into geostationary orbit in October 1998 and March 2000, respectively. AmeriStar, covering Central and South America, was scheduled for launch in late 2001, but had run into delays. Each of the satellites emitted three signals and carried more than 40 channels of programming to overlapping areas of approximately 5.4 million square miles in the 1467–1492 MHz range of the L-Band spectrum. WorldSpace was an early investor in XM Radio and did not have FCC clearance to provide service in the United States.[19]

### Alternatives

**17** The market for traditional AM/FM radio service was well established and provided a subscription-free alternative to potential listeners, based on advertising revenues for which XM attempted to compete. In addition, XM listeners would still have to rely on these traditional providers for local content, such as sports, weather, and news. Other options for home listeners included not only traditional radio, but also Internet-based radio and direct satellite audio, which could be packaged as part of television feed from such providers as EchoStar Communications.[20]

---

[17]wireless.fcc.gov/auctions/15.
[18]Paul Heltzel, "Tuning in to Satellite Radio," *Technology Review,* January 25, 2002.
[19]Kevin Bonsor, "How Satellite Radio Works," Marshall Brain's HowStuffWorks, http://www.howstuffworks.com/satellite-radio.htm/.
[20]XM Radio, March 2001.

**EXHIBIT 13**
Sirius Satellite Radio
Corporate
Information

**Company Information:**
*Sirius Satellite Radio,* Inc. (formerly CD Radio) is headquartered in New York, N.Y., and is publicly traded on NASDAQ. Sirius is one of two FCC licensees to deliver satellite radio programming.

**Exchange/Symbol:** *Nasdaq/SIRI*

**Date of IPO:** September 13, 1994

**Date of Service Launch:** February 14, 2002

**Service Fee:** Monthly subscription fee, approximately $12.95 per month

**Broadcast Frequency:** 12.5 MHz of S-Band: 2320.0 to 2332.5 MHz

**Satellite Information:**
Three Space Systems/Loral 1300 satellites in a high-altitude elliptical orbit directly over the continental United States to ensure signal elevation angles of 60 to 90 degrees. Sirius Radio contends that this ensures that each satellite will spend about 16 hours a day over the United States, and that at least one satellite is over the country at all times. Sirius Radio also has a back-up satellite standing by just in case of problems.

**Radio Manufacturing Partners:**
Alpine, Clarion, Delphi Delco, Jensen, Kenwood, Panasonic, Pioneer, Sony, Visteon

**Automotive Partners:**
BMW, Chrysler, Mercedes-Benz, Jeep, Mazda, Dodge, Freightliner and Sterling Trucks, Ford, Lincoln, Jaguar, Volvo, Porsche

**Retail Partners:**
Best Buy, Circuit City, Good Guys, Sound Advice, Tweeter, Crutchfield, Al and Ed's Autosound, Car Toys, Ultimate, Sound Experience, Pana-Pacific, Mickey Shorr

**Ownership Information:**
Oppenheimer funds
Blackstone Alternative Asset Management LP
David Margolese
Prime 66 Partners LP
DaimlerChrysler Corporation
Ford Motor Company

Source: Sirius Satellite Radio, Inc., *Annual Report,* March 2001.

## POSITIONED FOR SUCCESS?

**18** XM's stated goal was "to become a premier nationwide provider of audio entertainment and information programming in the vehicle, home, and portable markets."[21] The company's early focus was threefold:

- To educate consumers about satellite radio

- To develop XM brand awareness/differentiation

- To develop a large customer base

**19** Once the ground and space infrastructure were established, the company targeted these three primary areas for spending. Management expected that the early campaign, when

[21]XM Radio, March 2001.

## EXHIBIT 14
**Selected Comparisons of Sirius and XM Radio**

| DARS Subscriber Projections (in thousands) | | | | | | | | |
|---|---|---|---|---|---|---|---|---|
| | 2000A | 2001A | 2002E | 2003E | 2004E | 2005E | 2006E | 2007E |
| XMSR | 0 | 28 | 351 | 1,100 | 2,176 | 4,392 | 7,195 | 10,110 |
| SIRI | 0 | 0 | 201 | 825 | 1,962 | 4,225 | 7,066 | 10,010 |

Source: Morgan Stanley Equity Research, January 25, 2002.

| Projected Market Share | | | | | |
|---|---|---|---|---|---|
| | 2001A | 2002E | 2003E | 2004E | 2005E |
| XMSR | 100.0% | 63.6% | 57.1% | 52.6% | 51.0% |
| SIRI | — | 36.4% | 42.9% | 47.4% | 49.0% |

Source: Morgan Stanley Equity Research, January 25, 2002.

| XM Annual Projections (in thousands of dollars) | | | | | |
|---|---|---|---|---|---|
| | 2001A | 2002E | 2003E | 2004E | 2005E |
| Total Revenue | 500 | 20,400 | 103,600 | 237,300 | 500,200 |
| Expenses | (239,500) | (274,700) | (280,300) | (362,000) | (498,700) |
| EBITDA | (239,000) | (254,300) | (176,800) | (124,600) | 1,500 |
| D&&A | (42,600) | (95,500) | (96,500) | (96,900) | (97,300) |
| Net Income | (284,400) | (415,900) | (347,400) | (307,200) | (189,300) |

Source: Morgan Stanley Equity Research, January 25, 2002.

combined with greater equipment availability, would help it in turn sign up more consumers. Acquisition costs were estimated at approximately $1,930 per subscriber in 2001 but were expected to decline to $100 by 2005. This situation would require deficit spending, and the company was projected to lose money at least through 2005.[22]

**20**   XM's marketing strategy could be broken down into four primary thrusts: product differentiation, promotion, distribution, and pricing:

*Product:* XM emphasized the following points of difference between its service and traditional radio (see Exhibit 15).

*Promotion:* A mass-market campaign was launched to coincide with the national roll-out in late 2001 under the tagline "Beyond AM, Beyond FM, XM." In addition, the company targeted selective events and independent brands for sponsorship, including NASCAR. Trade promotions were used to help spark subscriber growth and included $50 per subscriber dollar equipment subsidies and $75 per subscriber dealer incentives.[23] XM's advertising budget was targeted at $65 million for the year 2002, reduced from $100 million to conserve cash.

[22]XM Radio, March 2002.
[23]S.G. Cowen, December 26, 2001.

**EXHIBIT 15**

Source: XM Radio, March 2001.

| Feature | XM Radio | Traditional AM/FM Radio |
|---|---|---|
| **Convenience: go anywhere capability** | Virtually seamless signal coverage in the United States | Local area coverage |
| **Choice: wide variety/ number of stations** | Up to 100 channels with a wide variety of programming | Limited formats in many markets |
| **Improved audio quality** | Digital quality sound | Analog AM/FM quality sound |
| **Fewer commercials** | Average 6–7 minutes per hour; some channels commercial free | Average 13–17 minutes per hour |
| **More information about music** | Text display with title/name | No visual display of song/artist |

*Distribution:* Distribution was initially focused on consumer electronic retailers for home receivers and after-market automobile receivers. Later, XM planned to expand distribution to automobile manufacturers for original equipment automobile radios, beginning with General Motors' inclusion in 23 of its Year 2003 models available in the fall of 2002. In many cases, the company embraced dealer incentives, including both revenue shares of approximately 7 percent and flat annual payments (in the case of GM for approximately $35 million spread over the first four years of operations) to facilitate wider distribution.[24] Finally, various retailers expressed early interest in announcements to distribute and promote XM Radio products and services. The retailers included Circuit City, Best Buy, Radio Shack, Sears & Roebuck Co., Tweeter, Ultimate, Al and Ed's, CarToys, Sound Advice, Mobile-One, Crutchfield, Cowboy Maloney's Electronic City, and Magnolia Hi-Fi.[25]

*Pricing:* Subscriptions were priced at $9.99 per month, with an upfront $10 to $15 activation fee. XM based its pricing strategy essentially on that of cable television, as consumers had demonstrated a willingness to pay a monthly fee for a wider variety of content than was available for free "over the air." Initial surveys showed consumers did not desire to pay for something they were already getting for free. However, when shown that "free radio" often plays as much 22 minutes of advertising per hour plus repetitive programming, they acknowledged the value in XM's service.[26]

21    In addition, there were additional upfront equipment costs of approximately $500 to $900, based on unit quality and the nature of installation. As of early 2002, XM did not plan to share in any of the revenues generated by hardware sales. Management hoped that its initial subscription price would remain stable, while hardware prices might be driven down if enough consumers adopted the service. Historical analysis had demonstrated that prices might drop as much as 30 percent per year if XM Radio proved comparable to successful consumer electronics markets.[27]

---

[24]Robertson Stephens Media Research, *Company Update: XM Satellite Radio,* February 20, 2002.
[25]XM Satellite Radio Holdings, Inc. *Annual Report,* March 2001.
[26]Sanders Morris Harris Research, February 5, 2002.
[27]Sanders Morris Harris Research, *Company Update: XM Satellite Radi,* February 5, 2002.

## ESTABLISHING THE STANDARD

**22**   Aside from such initiatives as consumer education, hardware partnerships and content development, XM Radio was forced to deal with the issue of industry standards in a direct manner fairly quickly. XM and Sirius partnered with many of the same manufacturing partners including Alpine, Clarion, Delphi Delco, Panasonic Pioneer, Sony, and Visteon. The two companies had also teamed up with similar retailers (Best Buy, Circuit City, Good Guys) to help distribute satellite radio receivers, antennas, and other devices. Most notable, however, was XM's entrance in February 2000 into a joint development agreement with Sirius to cooperate in the design and development of a unified standard for satellite radios in order to enable consumers to purchase one radio capable of receiving either service. The agreement arose in response to discussions as part of a patent infringement lawsuit that Sirius Radio filed against XM Radio in January of 1999. The agreement called for the cross licensing of the non-core intellectual property of the two companies at commercial rates and the resolution of all disputes through arbitration. Also, future agreements with car and radio manufacturers would be driven to the universal standard, and distribution and content partnerships were to be on a nonexclusive basis.[28]

## RECEPTION REMAINS UNCLEAR FOR XM RADIO

**23**   Hugh Panero sat back in his chair and thought through his company's position. It had been first to market and initial demand seemed quite strong. However, the market was still young and the future remained uncertain. The alliance with Sirius reduced competition in the short run, but it was unclear how it would affect XM's growth and profitability in the long-term. XM had market leadership, but a dwindling cash position. Could it develop a large enough customer base and business network to lock out Sirius? And how would the established radio broadcasters (and their large, well-funded owners) fight back against the satellite-based upstarts?

[28]XM Radio, March 2002.

# Case Index

# Subject Index